T3-BRR-200

FAIRHOPE PUBLIC LIBRARY
041386

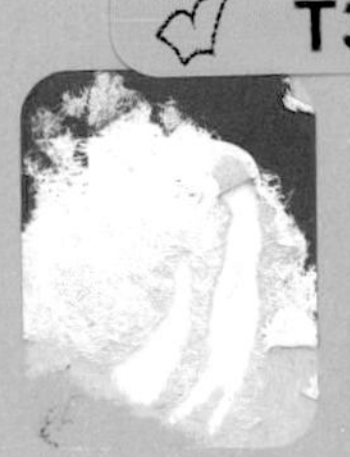

AZALEAS

AZALEAS

Revised and Enlarged Edition

FRED C. GALLE

TIMBER PRESS
Portland, Oregon

To Betty, Phil and Peggy who endured and spent many lonely hours while I was in pursuit of Azaleas and writing the book. Thanks also to Mrs. Cason J. Callaway and my Azalea friend Dr. Henry T. Skinner for sharing his knowledge and continual encouragement.

Library of Congress Cataloging-in-Publication Data

Galle, Fred C.
Azaleas / Fred C. Galle.
p. cm.
Bibliography: p.
Includes index.
ISBN 0-88192-091-6 : $65.00
1. Azalea. I. Title.
SB413.A9G34 1987
635.9'3362--dc19 87-24604
CIP

TIMBER PRESS
9999 SW Wilshire
Portland, Oregon 97225

ISBN 0-88192-091-6

Printed in Hong Kong for the Publisher

Color plate errata

1. "Spring Glory" with Dogwood and Crabapple,
   Sally Guy's Garden, Richmond, Virginia.
7. Marginal and surface hairs on *R.* ***nakaharai.***
9. *R. albrechtii* **Albrecht Azalea.**
   R. farrerae **Farres Azalea.**
11. *R. luteum* **Pontic** Azalea.
14. *R. vaseyi* **Pinkshell** Azalea.
    R. canadense **var.** *albiflorum* White Rhodora.
18. *R. reticulatum* Rose Azalea.
    R. reticulatum **var.** *albiflorum.*
19. ***R. simsii variegata*** **'Varigated' Sims Azalea.**
21. *R. weyrichii* **Weyrich Azalea.**
24. **'Koningin** Emma' syn. 'Queen Emma' Mollis Hybrid.
28. **'Rosata'** *R. viscosum* X 'Koster's Brilliant Red' Hybrid.
49. *R. kaempferi* **var.** ***albiflorum.***
50. *R. sataense* Sata Azalea.
    R. kiusianum Kyushu **Azalea.**
52. *R. scabrum* Luchu Azalea.
    'Linearifolium' (syn. ***R. linearifolium*****)** Spider Azalea.
53. *R.* ***serpyllifolium*** var. *albiflorum.*
54. *R. indicum* 'Macrantha Double'.
56. *R. rubropilosum* Red **Hair** Azalea.
    R. ***kanehirai*** Taibei Azalea.
57. *R. yedoense* **var.** *poukhanense* **Korean** Azalea.
59. 'Nuccio's Variegated Red Ruffles' **sport of 'Ruffled Giant'.**
62. 'Southern Charm Variegated' sport of **'Southern** Charm'.
74. 'Kimi no Hana'. **STEWART.**
87. 'Red Tip' **Robin Hill** Hybrid.
88. **'Margaret** Douglas' Back Acres Hybrid.
89. 'Red **Slippers'** Back Acres Hybrid.
92. 'Elaine' **Carla** Hybrid.
    'Greta' **Carla** Hybrid.
    'Pink Cloud' **Carla** Hybrid.
93. **'Germanique' Deckert** Hybrid.
96. **'Izumi** no Mai' Kuwana Hybrid.
100. **'Robin Hill Wendy'.**

CONTENTS

PREFACE

This book would never been completed without the advice and encouragement of many friends. It was not intended to be a revision of *The Azalea Book* by Fredric P. Lee. However I honored his friendship and knowledge along with other Azalea Historians such as B. Y. Morrison, Clement Bower, and our plant explorers such as Ernest Wilson, Prof. C. S. Sargent, Dr. John L. Creech, and many others for their endless information and plants they introduced.

Over four years ago I met with Drs. John L. Creech, Henry T. Skinner, and August E. Kehr for their guidance on an outline and their support of the project. Their review and comments on the manuscript, plus encouragement were most helpful. The letters and advice from Henry Skinner are treasured and his loss will be felt by all Azalea enthusiasts.

Complete acknowledgment of help received would be difficult for many friends reviewed sections of the book and answered my many questions. Their answers and support have added to my knowledge of Azaleas and to the contents of the book. A special group of people includes Robert Barry, Silver Spring, Md.; Ir. A. S. Bouma, Boskoop, The Netherlands; Christopher D. Brickell, Wisley, England; Dr. Terry Davis, Gainesville, Fla.; George W. Harding, Germantown, Md.; Arthur Headlam, Melbourne, Australia; Dr. and Mrs. Charles J. Hiers, Auburn, Ala.; T. C. C. Hutchinson, New Plymouth, New Zealand; Dr. Masaaki Kunishige, Mieken, Japan; Julius Nuccio, Altadena, Ca.; Neville McMinn, Victoria, Australia; Dr. W. Schmalscheidt, Oldenburg, Germany; Robert G. Shanklin, Pensacola, Fla.; Hideo Suzuki, Kumagaya, Japan; C. Gordon Tyrrell, Pine Mountain, Ga.; Dr. Sandra McDonald, Hampton, VA.; Dr. A. C. Leslie, R.H.S. Wisley, England; Richard Dunmire, Palo Alto, CA.; Kendon Stubbs, Charlottesville, VA.; Donald H. Voss, Vienna, VA.; Dr. Samuel B. Jones, Athens, GA.; Mrs. Jay Murray, Colts Neck, NJ.; and the many friends that sent in corrections and encouragement.

Special thanks to the following who wrote special chapters for the book, Dr.J. Heursel, Melle, Belgium; Dr. August Kehr, Hendersonville, N. C.; and Dr. Robert C. Lambe and his associates, Blacksburg, Va.

Thanks to the American Rhododendron Society and Azalea Society of America Chapters for supplying information on their Azaleas and their patience in reviewing the written descriptions. And finally special appreciation to my many old and new Azalea friends for their encouraging words and letters. They will never know how often their comments and letters came when I was having difficulty seeing the end of the project.

Descriptions of some Azalea cultivars are very brief. Numerous letters and phone calls in tracking down information ended with a blank wall. I can only encourage hybridizers to register their plants with the American Rhododendron Society or the International Rhododendron Register so the valuable information on the hybridizer, parentage and complete descriptions will be on record. Registration of the names will be of tremendous help in the future. One needs only to check the Index of Azalea Names to see the number of different plants with the same name. A book of this scope is never finished, and I apologize for the brief information on some plants and any omissions. I will welcome suggestions and information on Azaleas and criticism to help toward more detailed information and knowledge on Azaleas.

Fred C. Galle
1987

SECTION I

1. AZALEAS IN THE LANDSCAPE

The charm of variety, color and profusion of beautiful flowers belongs to the azaleas. Hardy azaleas for the garden can be selected for each climatic region in the eastern half of the country and also most of the Pacific Coast. These include both evergreen and deciduous plants from low dwarfs to large shrubs—ten or more feet in height. Azaleas come in a range of forms and adaptability offering endless possibilities in the landscape.

LANDSCAPE PLAN

Design, composition, scale, and texture are the essential elements in landscape planning. One cannot choose azaleas or any plants for a garden without establishing a basic plan or landscape design. The landscape planting should fit the site, the architecture, and the homeowner. While gardening is one of the major leisure forms of recreation, it must vie for time devoted to other recreational activities of the homeowner. The garden should not become a maintenance burden, but should fit into the budget of leisure time to prune, fertilize, control pests, and do general seasonal grooming. Azaleas, through the proper selection of varieties suitable to the location, are generally considered low maintenance plants.

A well-planned garden, like a beautiful painting, has its effects on the viewer as the result of careful design and composition. Throughout the garden there should be a sense of unity and orderly arrangement of landscape features and plants in relation to their architectural surroundings. Scale in the landscape relates to the unity of the planting, tree and shrub groups, the land form, and the architectural features. The plants, as well as the architectural features, should be in scale with one another. Throughout the garden there should be unity and harmony achieved with an understanding of the natural forms, and a repetition and dominance of plant textures. A garden does not need to be of large dimensions. It may be a small terrace, a part of a natural woodland, or it may flow into an open stretch of lawn. A garden should exist for the enjoyment of the owners and be a place for retreat from the perplexities of the day. A garden of charm has the appearance of being casually refined and well organized, but is not created without time and effort.

Texture is an important facet of the landscape and is often referred to as the subtle thread or theme running through a well conceived design. The architectural features such as buildings and walks add structural texture to the design and should complement the overall texture determined by the foliage of the trees and shrubs. The texture of the evergreen leaves of Kurume azaleas would be considered fine, while many of the deciduous azaleas and many evergreens such as the Glenn Dale azaleas would be considered as medium texture in contrast to the leaves of white oak or Southern magnolia, which are coarse textured. One should be able to sense the beauty of a garden at any season. Azalea gardens that are irresistible in the spring should display year-round beauty through a skillful blending of plants and other components of a varied texture. A beautiful landscape is a tasteful blending of the ever changing seasonal forms and textures of plants.

Each season produces texture and pattern changes. A deciduous azalea or Japanese maple is admired in the summer for the foliage and in the winter for the form of branches and twigs. In the spring as new life begins, the form of the landscape and textures again change, with the soft greens of new leaves adding a new dimension.

When azaleas are in full bloom, the texture and color composition of the garden may be very bold and should be studied and planned carefully. Azaleas can provide some daring color schemes, so it is best to keep one color or color tone dominant over a large area. If startling colors are used together they should be used in large color masses of three or more plants rather than as individual specimens.

While an azalea enthusiast might wish to use only azaleas in the landscape, most gardeners perfer to use azaleas as a dominant landscape plant in harmony with other plants.

Selecting azaleas to use in the landscape is challenging. Foremost is the selection of species and varieties adaptable to the area. Fortunately, with the large number of species and hybrids available, one can usually find an azalea to fit the needs and requirements of the site. It is doutful if any other group of woody plants is so versatile.

When selecting azaleas, think of the color and season of bloom, the ultimate natural size and form of the plant, the texture and type of foliage and whether evergreen or deciduous. The discussion on azalea species and hybrids, plus the list of recommended varieties for different areas of the country and climatic zones will serve as a guide and an aid in the selection of azaleas. Much of the pleasure and challenge of gardening is in searching for and trying out new and different plants to see if they are adaptable to one's garden and gardening skills.

Azaleas are best used in the naturalized or informal garden with some shade. However, heavy, constant shade or a location on the north side of a building may be too extreme. Filtered sunlight in a woodland garden under tall deciduous trees trimmed fifteen or twenty feet above the ground or a garden in an open glade is ideal. Azaleas grow best at the edge of woodland areas, in partial shade of a building or in front of tall plants where they have tempered, but no direct, sunlight all day. An open site, where direct sun reaches not more than three or four hours a day, is suitable. Avoid midday and afternoon sun on late flowering azaleas such as Satsukis and some of the deciduous species such as *R. prunifolium*. Azaleas also need good air drainage and a location free from frost pockets.

Azaleas can be used as border plants, as background for perennials, annuals and bulbs, or in combination with other woody plants. Both evergreen and deciduous azaleas are handsome as foundation plants around the home. Some dwarf or lowgrowing evergreen azaleas are used as low hedges or edgings, while others are dense and tall enough for tall hedges and screens.

Azaleas are often seen in the newly landscaped property as foundation plants around the home. While there is a need for foundation or base planting, many modern and contemporary homes today do not require a heavy mass of plants completely around the foundation. In fact, many homes are best viewed with a sparse foundation planting, with mass border plantings used around and in front of the house or in masses around trees. Carefully choose the azaleas for the foundation planting to avoid flower colors that clash with the color of the building. The compact twiggy evergreen azaleas are generally used. However, tall plants may be needed and even the very dwarf creeping forms can be used as facing plants in front of larger plants. The colorful deciduous azaleas should also be considered for the foundation planting and can be advantageously used around wood shingle, stone, and stained wood homes. The tracery and shadows of the bare branches in the winter add interest to the architectural features. Avoid using too many different colors in the foundation planting. Select one or two varieties or varieties of similar color and mass plants of the same color together.

In many gardens, azaleas are selected which provide only one major burst of color in the spring and with no color until the next season. However, with proper selection of species and varieties, one can have azaleas in bloom for over two months or provide foliage color in winter as do the *R. indicum* types.

Coordinate the selection of colorful azaleas as a painter would, developing pleasing color combinations to the eye which harmonize with the surroundings. Study the various types of azaleas and note the vast color range and season of bloom. Select varieties that will combine in harmonious color schemes at the time of bloom. White flowers are good agents for blending the more vivid hues. Separate brilliant colors, which may clash, with clouds of white azaleas or rich evergreen foliage. White and light colored azaleas can be used to soften and blend strong colors. This is very tactfully done by separating two strong colors with white or lighter colors. The warm reds and lavender to purples should be isolated from the hot oranges to orange-red shades. Striped azaleas at a distance tend to create a pale impression and can be combined with darker colors. Many striped Glenn Dale azaleas were bred for this purpose.

The strong vivid colored azaleas are often overused to the point of being monotonous and overpowering. This is particularly the case with some of the vivid red and violet-red azaleas. How much more pleasing colored azaleas are by themselves or in combination with white or light pink varieties!

It is also important to use azaleas in mass for their colorful flowering effect and plant form. Thus, combinations of three to five or more plants of one variety are more pleasing than five individual strong colors. Careful blending of the same color can be done by selecting azaleas with the same tone or hues.

Observe established plantings of azaleas in public and home gardens to help select varieties that will blend harmoniously by color and form. Contrasting colors can be used for special effects, like adding whipped cream on top of dessert. One or two white azaleas planted in a mass of pink or reds gives this effect. Or add a pink or red azalea like a cherry, in a mass of white flowering plants. Use care—this is easily overdone to the point of appearing polka-dotted and distracting.

Fortunately, azaleas are easy to transplant, so poor color combinations can be noted while the plants are in flower and moved. Pleasing color combinations can be developed by selecting and planting container grown azaleas while they are in flower, thus avoiding color clashes immediately.

Deciduous azaleas are especially desirable for naturalizing in a woodland landscape with indigenous plants. Deciduous azaleas can be used in combination with evergreen azaleas and with many other fine narrow and broad leaf evergreen shrubs. They add height and twiggy branch formations to the evergreen garden scene. Many of the native deciduous azaleas add a delightful fragrance and fall foliage coloration not found in evergreen plants.

Azaleas grow in a wide variety of plant forms. The evergreen azaleas range from prostrate creeping forms to medium dense twiggy shrubs, to large upright, to rounded large shrubs—eight to ten feet or more in height. Dedicuous azaleas, depending on species and variety, can be low shrubs, large, or even small trees fifteen to twenty feet in height. But, know what you are buying—it is not uncommon for nurseries to advertise dwarf azaleas, while still in a container, that are green giants just waiting to grow.

Informal free flowering massed plantings of azaleas around a tree or group of trees are very pleasing. This can be accomplished with different groups of azaleas, and the planting can combine medium to large plants with low and dwarf varieties as facing plants. Thus, low and slow growing varieties in the foreground backed with taller plants in varied graduation of heights will form a pleasing mass planting.

Azaleas adapt well to pruning and can be used in a formal garden as trimmed hedges or trimmed specimens. Trimmed azaleas are often grown for the patio. Azaleas are used in oriental gardens trimmed in cloud form, often with more emphasis on the shape and style of the plant than on its flowering effect. But remember sculptured plants become high maintenance plants.

Attractive hedges of any length and color are possible with azaleas. The hedges can be in a natural free form or closely clipped and trimmed. With proper selection, a low, compact hedge is possible, requiring minimum pruning. For a tall hedge the medium to large azaleas should be used. To keep a hedge uniform in shape, color and foliage, it is best to use only one variety of plant.

Arranging plants into a pleasing and beautiful garden is a continuing challenge. A well designed garden based on careful selection and placement of colorful azaleas combined with other plants will offer years of beauty.

For selecting plants to use with azaleas, please refer to the chapter on companion plants.

2. COMPANION PLANTS FOR THE AZALEA GARDEN

Azaleas must be used in an acid soil and preferably in a garden with some shade. Thus, companion plants selected for use with azaleas should be adapted to acid soils and shade. Selecting plants requires knowledge, ingenuity, and often experimentation. Selection must take into account the climatic zones to which the companion plants are adapted. A successful, shady acid soil garden, whether azaleas dominate or not, is a hallmark of a distinguished gardener.

Companion plants need to be selected for their foliage, texture, whether deciduous or evergreen, habit of growth, and other characteristics, such as flowers, fragrance, fruit, and fall foliage, that will enhance and blend with azaleas and help realize your garden design. Azalea gardens should have compelling interest. They should not be just spring flowering gardens, but year around gardens with interest at all seasons.

An azalea garden oriented to members of the Heath Family might include trees such as Sourwood (*Oxydendrum arboreum*) or Manzanita (*Arctostaphylos manzanita*). The beautiful evergreen rhododendrons and Mountain Laurel (*Kalmia latifolia*) might be used both for their floral display and attractive foliage. Other genera suitable for inclusion with azaleas are the evergreen and deciduous species of *Leucothoe* and *Vacciniums* and the deciduous *Elliottia, Enkianthus, Menziesia,* and *Zenobia*. For fine textured azaleas consider *Leiophyllum,* Sand Myrtle, and the Heaths and Heathers (*Erica* and *Calluna* spp.) for their tiny foliage and interesting small flowers. Trailing Arbutus along with some nonericaceous plants such as ferns and bulbs could complete the garden.

Flowering plants added to heighten the azalea floral season include Dogwoods, Redbuds, *Fothergilla, Pieris,* Crabapples, etc. Plants flowering before and after the general Azalea season include *Forsythia, Viburnum,* Mountain Laurel, *Stewartia, Camellia,* and numerous bulbs and herbaceous plants.

The fragrance of native azaleas is supplemented or contrasted with such fragrant plants as *Styrax, Osmanthus, Daphne, Viburnum,* etc.

Fruiting shrubs for the fall and winter seasons include Hollies, *Viburnum, Skimmia, Aucuba* and in the spring the blue fruit of *Mahonia.*

Both evergreen and deciduous shade-tolerant companion plants can be selected for their foliage alone. The foliage of narrow-leaved evergreens—such genera as Yews (*Taxus*), Hemlocks (*Tsuga*), Plum Yew (*Cephalotaxus, Podocarpus*), Chinese Fir (*Cunninghamia*), and *Cryptomeria*—adds interesting contrast.

The numerous attractive broad leaved evergreens including many species and cultivars of Holly, *Aucuba,* Boxwood, *Osmanthus, Mahonia, Danae, Camellia,* and Cherry Laurel, and of course, Mountain Laurel and evergreen Rhododendrons should certainly be considered. Many deciduous plants which add attractive fall foliage include Sourwood, *Euonymus; Fothergilla* and Japanese Maples deserve a representation in our ideal garden.

In every part of the temperate world there are beautiful wild flowers and ferns available which are marvelous additions to the Azalea garden. Shade tolerant perennials range from the large deciduous foliage of Hostas, to the leafy foliage of Iris (*I. cristata* and *I. tectorum*) and the grass-like foliage of *Liriope* or the evergreen foliage of Pachysandra and Gingers (*Asarum* or *Hexastylis*). Other perennials noted for their attractive foliage or flowers include Coral Bells (*Heuchera*), Strawberry Begonia or *Saxifraga, Primulas,* hardy Begonias, *Epimedium,* Lily of the Valley, and *Vinca minor.* All make splendid contributions to the garden dependent only on the taste and creativity of the gardener. Both *Galax* and *Shortia* are almost a must for every shady Azalea garden.

Bulbs blend well with Azaleas from the very early spring and fall flowering *Crocus* and encompassing the spring bulbs Daffodils (*Narcissus*), Squills (*Scilla*), Snowdrop and Snowflakes (*Galanthus* and *Leucojum*), Triteleias, Glory of the Snow (*Chionodoxa*) and *Alstroemeria* for the mediterranean climates. In the warm humid summer climates, there are both spring and late summer flowering *Zephyranthes* spp. or Rain Lilies. Lilies (*Lilium* spp. and cultivars) and late spring and early summer flowers; *Cardiocrinum, Crinum,* and *Spekelia* make significant contributions to the Azalea garden. The *Lycoris* spp. Spider Lilies and *Colchicum* spp., Autumn Crocus, bear flowers in late summer and early fall followed by fine foliage in late fall, winter, and early spring.

Numerous ground covers are available from the more vigorous genera such as ivies (*Hedera helix*), *Pachysandra,* Periwinkle (*Vinca minor*), and Lily of the Valley (*Convallaria majalis*). Slower growing ground covers include the small woody plants of *Sarcococca hookeriana* Cowberry, *Vaccinium vitis-idaea,* Bearberry, *Arctostaphylos uva-ursi* to the perennial Foam Flowers *Tiarella* spp., and *Epimedium.*

It is to be hoped that the Azalea enthusiast will accept the challenge to learn of suitable companion plants and select them with discrimination and restraint for his garden. Select plants adapted to your climatic area, for their intrinsic quality, and the role they will fill in the garden. Remember, the plants should be adaptable to acid soils and for most situations must be shade tolerant.

The following list will serve as a general guide to the diverse but excellent companion plant materials available.

SMALL TO MEDIUM TREES

	Hardiness Zones	Deciduous or Evergreen	Remarks
Acer palmatum Japanese Maple	6–9	D	10–20′, many cultivars available
Amelanchier laevis Serviceberry	4–9	D	30′, wht. fls. early spring, other species available
Arbutus unedo Strawberry tree	8–9	E	15–30′, fls. in fall, best in mediterranean climates
Arctostaphylos manzanita Manzanita	7–9	E	15–20′, wht. to pink fls., spring, best in mediterranean climates
Cercis canadensis Redbud	5–9	D	purplish pink to wht., spring fls.
Chionanthus virginicus Fringe tree	4–9	D	lacy wht. fls., mid-spring
Cornus florida Flowering Dogwood	4–9	D	25′, beautiful wht. & pink bracts, spring, good fall foliage, many cultivars available
Cornus Kousa Kousa Dogwood	4–9	D	25′, wht. pointed bracts mid-spring, good fall foliage
Cryptomeria japonica Cryptomeria	5–9	E	15–30′, small dark gr. needles, many cultivars available
Enkianthus campanulatus Red Vein Enkianthus	5–8b	D	15–30′, clustered wht. fls. spring, good fall foliage
Eriobotrya japonica Loquat	8a–10	E	20′, large leathery foliage, frag. fls.
Franklinia alatamaha Franklinia	5–8b	D	30′, large wht. fls. late summer, good fall foliage
Gordonia lasianthus Gordonia	8b–10	E	39′, large wht. fls. late summer
Halesia carolina Carolina Silverbell	5–9	D	40′, early bell-shaped wht. fls., *H. diptera* larger fls.
Ilex aquifolium English Holly	7–9	E	30′, glossy foliage, red to yellow fruit, many cultivars available
Ilex opaca American Holly	6–9	E	tall pyramidal tree 40′, red to yellow fruit, selected cultivars available
Ilex latifolia Lusterleaf Holly	6b–9	E	30–40′, large foliage, red fruit
Magnolia grandiflora Southern Magnolia	7–10	E	40–60′, lg. glossy foliage; large wht. fls. frag.
Magnolia virginiana Sweetbay Magnolia	6–10	Semi to E	40′, leaves white beneath, wht. frag. fls.
Oxydendrum arboreum Sourwood	5–9	D	30–40′, clusters wht. fls. late spring, excellent fall foliage
Prunus caroliniana Carolina Cherry Laurel	8–10	E	24′, creamy wht. fls.; withstands shearing
Prunus spp. Flowering cherries	5–8	D	various species and cultivars, best in sun or light shade
Pyrus calleryana 'Bradford' pear	5–8	D	25′, wht. fls. early spring; bronze-red fall foliage
Rhus spp. Sumac	6–9	D	several species, compound leaves, red fall foliage, red fruit
Stewartia pseudocamellia Japanese Stewardia	6–9a	D	25′, wht. fls. late spring, good fall foliage, other species available

Styrax japonica Japanese Snowbell	6–9a	D	25′, small bell-like wht. frag. fls., mid-spring
Taxodium distichum Bald Cypress	6–10	D	30–50′ deciduous conifer.
Tsuga canadensis Canada Hemlock	4–9a	E	excellent evergreen, many cultivars available

SHRUBS

	Hardiness Zones	Deciduous or Evergreen	Remarks
Abelia × grandiflora Glossy Abelia	6a–9	E	6′, small pinkish fls. summer, other cultivars available
Aucuba japonica Japanese Aucuba	7–10	E	6–8′, large glossy foliage, also variegated, dioecious, red fruit
Buxus microphylla Littleleaf Box	5–9	E	3–4′, hardy, cultivars available
Buxus sempervirens Common Box	6–10	E	6–15′, small dark green foliage, many cultivars, 'Vardar Valley', hardy
Camellia japonica Camellia	7–10	E	10–20′, select adaptable cultivars
Camellia reticulata	8b–10	E	Large flowers, less hardy
Camellia sasanqua Sasanqua Camellia	7b–10	E	10–20′, fall flowering, many cultivars
Cephalotaxus harringtonia Japanese Plum Yew	7–10	E	6–15′, similar to *Taxus*, needle foliage, purplish fruit
Clethra alnifolia Summersweet	4–9	D	6–8′, small frag. wht. flowers summer, 'Rosea' pink fls.
Clethra arborea Lily of the Valley Clethra	9–10	E	10–15′, for mediterranean climates, small wht., frag. fls.
Cleyera japonica Cleyera	7b–9	E	6–12′, glossy foliage, wht. flowers
Corylopsis sinensis Chinese Witch Hazel	6–8b	D	10–15′, yellow flowers late winter
Danae racemosa Alexandrian Laurel	7–10	E	3–4′, attractive glossy foliage, spreading habit, red fruit
Daphne × burkwoodii	5–8b	E	5′, pink in bud, frag. wht. fls. early spring, 'Somerset' green foliage 'Carol Mackie' variegated
Daphne cneorum Rose Daphne	4–7b	E	6–12″, frag. pink fls. early spring, small narrow leaves
Daphne odora Winter Daphne	7b–9	E	4–6′, frag. rose flowers, 'Marginata' variegated foliage
Elliottia racemosa Elliottia	7–9	D	10–15′, small wht. frag. fls. summer, rare
Euonymus alatus 'Compacta'	4–9	D	6–8′, vivid scarlet fall foliage, winged stems
Euonymus japonicus Japanese Euonymus	7b–10	E	2–3′, 'Microphyllus' small foliage, other cultivars available
Fothergilla gardenii Fothergilla	5–8b	D	wht. terminal fls. spring, fall foliage, *F. major & F. monticola* large

Gardenia jasminoides Gardenia	8–9b	E	6–8′, wht. frag. fls. 'Radicans' dwf. 3′
Hamamelis mollis Chinese Witch Hazel	6–8b	D	6–15′, frag. yellow flowers late winter
Hydrangea paniculata Panicle Hydrangea	4–9	D	10–15′, cluster of wht. fls. early summer, 'Tardiva' select cultivar
Hydrangea quercifolia Oakleaf Hydrangea	6–9	D	5–8′, wht. fls. late spring, reddish fall foliage, other species and cultivars available
Ilex cornuta 'Burfordi'	7–10	E	10–20′, glossy foliage, red fruit; 'Dwf. Burford' smaller, 'Rotunda' dwf. spiny foliage; 'Carissa' dwf. terminal spine
Ilex crenata 'Helleri'	7–9	E	3–6′, dwf. small foliage; numerous cultivars available
Ilex decidua Possumhaw Holly	6–9	D	8–15′, deciduous red fruit, gray stems
Ilex vomitoria Yaupon Holly	7–10	E	10–25′, red fruit, can be sheared, 'Nana' dwarf, sparse fruit
Kalmia latifolia Mountain Laurel	5–9a	E	8–20′, wht. to pink fls. late spring, cultivars available
Leucothoe axillaris	6–9	E	4–6′, excellent foliage, sml. wht. fls. *L. fontanesiana,* larger
Leucothoe populifolia	7–9	E	10–15′, excellent foliage
Mahonia aquifolium Oregon Holly-grape	5–8a	E	3–6′, compound leaves yellow fls., blue fruit
Mahonia fortunei	7–9	E	
Mahonia lomarifolia	8b–10		
Nandina domestica (Heavenly bamboo) or Nandina	7–10	E	6–8′, compound leaves, wht. fls., red fruit in clusters. 'Alba' yellow fruit 'Harbour Dwarf' 2′
Osmanthus fragrans Tea Olive	8–10	E	15–20′, fragrant small fls. in late fall and winter
Osmanthus × *fortunei* Fortune Osmanthus	7b 10	E	10 20′, fragrant small fls. in fall
Osmanthus heterophyllus Holly Osmanthus	7–10	E	10–15′, spiny leaves, fragrant fls. in fall, 'Variegatus' lv. margin white
Pieris japonica Japanese Pieris	6b–9	E	6–10′, drooping panicles of white to pink fls. in early spring, cultivars available
Pieris floribunda Fetterbush or Mt. Andromedia	4–8a	E	6–8′, erect panicles of small wht. fls. early spring
Pittosporum tobira Japanese Pittosporum	8b–10	E	8–10′, attractive foliage, frag. creamy wht. fls. early spring
Podocarpus nivalis Plum Yew	6b–9	E	6′, small needle-like foliage, other species available for warmer climates
Prunus laurocerasus 'Zabel' Cherry Laurel	6b–9	E	4–6′, dark green elliptical leaves, small wht. flowers in spring
Rhododendron spp.	4–9	E	numerous small and large evergreen species and cultivars, select adapted to your area

Sarcococca hookeriana Sarcococca	6–8a	E	2′, low shrub, frag. small flowers, other species and varieties available
Skimmia japonica Skimmia	7b–9	E	3–4′, dioecious, frag. wht. fls., red fruit
Skimmia reevesiana Reeves Skimmia	7b–9	E	2–3′, bisexual fls., red fruit
Taxus spp. Yews	5–7b	E	numerous species and cultivars available from spreading dwfs. to small trees
Vaccinium spp. Blueberry	Vary 6–10	E&D	numerous species and cultivars, select adapted to your area
Viburnum × *burkwoodii* Burkwood Viburnum	6–9	D to E	3–4′, early wht. fragrant flowers
Viburnum × *juddii*	5–9	D	3–4′, early wht. frag. fls., blackish fruit
Viburnum plicatum Japanese Viburnum	5–8	D	8–10′, wht. fls., red fruit, numerous cultivars available, other deciduous and evergreen species available

GROUND COVERS AND PERENNIALS

	Hardiness Zone	Height	Remarks
Ajuga reptans Carpet Bugle	3–9	6–9″	blue fls., spreads, various cultivars available
Arctostaphylos uva-ursi Bearberry	3–7b	6–12″	small evergreen leaves, red berries
Aquilegia canadensis Columbine	4–9	12–24″	scarlet fls., hybrids and species available
Asarum canadense Wild Ginger	3–8b	6″	deciduous, spreading, fls. inconspicuous
Asarum (Hexastylis) spp. Gingers	6–9	6″	numerous species available
Asperula odorata Sweet Woodruff	4–9	8″	wht. fls., spreads
Aspidistra elatior Cast Iron plant	8b–10	12–18″	tough evergreen foliage, shade
Astilbe × *arendsii* Hybrid Astilbe	6–8a	24″	fluffy spikes of fls. white, pink, purple
Calluna vulgaris Heather	4–7b	4–18″	tiny evergreen foliage, numerous cultivars
Convallaria majalis Lily of the Valley	3–8b	8″	white to pink fls. spring
Dicentra spectabilis Bleeding Heart	4–8b	12–14″	pink heart-shaped fls. spring
Epigaea repens Trailing Arbutus	3–8b	4–6″	trailing evergreen, frag. white to pink fls., difficult to transplant
Epimedium spp.	4–8b	6–12″	white, yellow or pink flowers early spring
Erica carnea Spring Heath	5–7b	6–12″	tiny evergreen foliage, small white to pink flowers
Euonymus fortunei 'Longwood' Euonymus	6–8b	6″	small, evergreen foilage, spreading
Ferns			numerous species available, evergreen or deciduous, select acid soil types
Galax urcecolata (G. aphylla) Galax	4–8b	6–12″	round evergreen foliage, bronze fall color, small white fls.

Hedera helix English Ivy	5–10		evergreen vines, select branching adapted cultivars
Helleborus niger Christmas Rose	4–7	12–18″	white flowers
Helleborus orientalis Lenten Rose	6–9	12 18″	evergreen, nodding fls., wht. to purple
Heuchera sanguinea Coral Bells	4–9	12–24″	basal rounded leaves, spikes of bell-like flowers, white to red
Hosta spp. Hosta or Plantain Lily	4–9	8–24″	numerous species and cultivars, exquisite foliage small to large, wht. to lav. fls.
Iberis sempervirens Candytuft	4–9	8–12″	evergreen, low, white flowers, many cultivars
Iris cristata Crested Iris	4–9	6″	spreading, blue to wht. fls. shade tolerant
Iris tectorum Roof Iris	6–9	12–18″	crested, blue to wht. fls., shade tolerant
Maianthemum canadense Wild Lily of the Valley	3–8	6″	low, spreading, tiny wht. fls., spring red berries, shade
Maianthemum kamtschaticum	6–9	6–8″	west coast U. S. A.
Mertensia virginica Virginia Bluebell	4–8a	18–24″	attractive pink flowers fading to blue
Pachysandra procumbens Alleghany Pachysandra	4–8	8–12″	gray-green foliage, deciduous in cold climate wht. fls. spring, shade *P. terminalis* dark green, vigorous. 'Variegata' available
Phlox divaricata Blue Phlox	4–9	6–12″	spreading, blue to white flowers
Phlox stolonifera Creeping Phlox	4–9	6–12″	low, creeping, violet to purple fls.
Polygonatum spp. Solomon's Seal	4–9	6–18″	several species, pendant, bell-like flowers
Potentilla tridentata Three-Toothed Cinquefoil	3–8a	6″	evergreen dark green compound leaves
Primula japonica Primrose	5–8a	12–18″	colorful fls. wht., yellow to red. Other spp. available
Pulmonaria spp. Lungwort	5–8	6–12″	spreading, some variegated leaves, blue fls., shade
Sanguinaria canadensis Strawberry Begonia	4–9a	4–6″	wht. veined leaves, low spreading, small wht. fls.
Sedum spp. Stonecrop	5–9	6″	low, spreading
Shortia galacifolia Oconee Bells	4–8b	6″	attractive evergreen foliage, bell-like wht. fls. early spring
Smilacina spp. False Solomon's Seal	4–9	24″	small wht. fls. in terminal clusters, fragrant
Tiarella cordifolia Foam Flower	4–9	6–12″	spreading, attractive spike of wht. flowers
Vinca minor Periwinkle	5–9	4–6″	evergreen groundcover, wht. to blue fls.
Viola spp. Violets	4–9	6–8″	numerous species, wht. yellow to blue fls.

BULBOUS PLANTS

	Hardiness Zone	Height	Remarks
Allium spp. Flowering Onions	4–10	12–36″	attractive sm. fls. spring, in round clusters, grass-like foliage

Alstroemeria spp.	8b–10	2–3′	yellow, red to purple flowers, mediterranean climates
Amaryllis belladona Amaryllis	8–10	2′	lg. fls., wht. pink to red spring
Anemone blanda Blue Anemone	6–9	6–8″	attractive blue flowers in spring
Arisaema spp. Jack in the Pulpit	4–8	12–24″	several species, spring flowering
Arum italicum Arum	7–9	12″	arrow-shape, mottled leaves in late fall and winter
Camassia spp. Camas	6–8	12–18″	Grass-like foliage, single blue to wht. fls. spring
Chionodoxa luciliae Glory of the Snow	4–8	24″	sml. bell-like fls. in clusters, white, pink or blue spring
Colchicum spp. Autumn Crocus	4–8b	4–6″	pink to lav.-blue fls. in fall
Crinum spp.	8–10	18–24″	large lily-like wht. to red fls. in summer
Crocus spp. Crocus	5–9	3–6″	numerous species and cultivars, wht., yellow blue to lavender early spring, some fall and winter
Cyclamen hederifolium (*C. neapolitanum*) Hardy Cyclamen	5–9	6″	attractive wht. to pink fls. fall; mottled winter lvs., other species available
Galanthus nivalis Snow Drop	4–9	12″	wht. flowers spring
Hyacinthus orientalis Hyacinths	6–9	12–15″	fragrant wht., pink to purple fls. in spring
Leucojum vernum Snowflakes	4–8	12″	drooping bell-like wht. fls. in spring, other species available
Liriope muscari Lilyturf	6b–10	12–18″	evergreen coarse grass-like foliage, white to blue fls. late summer
Lycoris radiata Spider Lily	7–10	18″	red flowers in late summer, fall to spring foliage
Lycoris squamigera Surprise Lily	5–9		pink flowers in late summer, other species for warmer climates
Muscari botryoides Grape Hyacinth	3–9	6″	wht. to pink to blue small fls. in early spring
Narcissus Spp. Daffodils	5–10	3–18″	popular garden bulb, many species and cultivars, fls. face sun (south) in spring
Rohdea japonica Nippon Lily	7a–10	12–18″	long leathery foliage, shade, fls., inconspicuous
Scilla sibirica Siberian Squill	4–10	6″	attractive blue fls. spring, other species and color forms available
Sprekelia formosissima Aztec Lily	8–10	18″	red lily-like fls. in early summer
Trillium spp. Trillium	6–9	12–18″	several species, attractive wild flower
Tulipa spp. Tulip	4–8a	12–18″	attractive flowering bulb in many colors, use pre-cooled bulbs in spring
Zephyranthes atamasco Rain Lily	7–9	15″	upright wht. single lily flowers
Zephyranthes candida Autumn Rain Lily	8–10	12″	wht. fls. late summer

SECTION II

3. RHODODENDRON OR AZALEA

TAXONOMY

Taxonomy or Systematic Botany is an important element in the understanding of plants. It deals with classification (relationships) and nomenclature (naming), which organizes and identifies the fascinating differences among the many species of plants. It is a complex, ever-changing science concerned with the arrangement of plants into phylogenic groupings and the naming of these groups. A plant name is the key, unlocking the door to its total biology.

The Greek philosopher, Theophrastus, (370–285 B.C.) is often called the "Father of Botany", while Carolus Linnaeus, the renowned botanist of the 18th century, is called the "Father of Taxonomy." The binomial system of nomenclature used today, of genus and species, was introduced by Linnaeus.

Plants are classified botanically by divisions, each in turn subdivided into classes, orders, families, genera, and species. Thus, the genus *Rhododendron,* which includes azaleas, is as follows:

Division: *Magnoliophyta* (Spermatophyta)
Class: *Magnoliopsida* (Dicotyledoneae)
Subclass: *Dilleniidae*
Order: *Ericales*
Family: *Ericaceae* or Heath Family
Genus: *Rhododendron*

The Rhododendrons and Azaleas belong to the *Ericaceae* (Heath family) which dates back to the late Cretaceous period, 70 million years ago. The Subclass *Dilleniidae* includes the Order *Ericales* and the Order *Theales*, and it is considered to be derived from the more ancient Subclass *Magnoliidae*. Within the Subclass *Dilleniidae* the Order *Ericales* is believed to have evolved from the Order *Theales* (which includes *Camellia* and *Stewartia*).

The *Ericaceae* comprise about 50 genera and approximately 1400 species generally of wide distribution, except for the deserts. In the tropics the plants are restricted to high and, therefore, cool elevations. Generally the plants in this family are found in acid soils and associated with endotropic mycorrhiza.

The larger genera of the Heath family are *Rhododendron* with 800 or more species; *Erica* with 500 species, *Vaccinium* to 400 species, including Blueberries, Cranberry, and Huckleberry; *Gaultheria*, 100 species; *Arctostaphylos*, 55 species; *Gaylussacia*, 40 species; and *Leucothoe*, 35.

Horticulturally the Heath family is important for its many evergreen and deciduous ornamental plants such as the many Rhododendrons and Azaleas, and the cultivated Blueberries and Cranberries, *Vaccinium* sp. A few of the genera are trees, such as Sourwood, *Oxydendrum arboreum* of the Southeast U.S. A few are ground covers or suffrutescent woody perennials such as Trailing Arbutus-*Epigaea repens*, Wintergreen-*Gaultheria procumbens*, and Bearberry-*Arctostaphylos Uva-ursi*. The majority vary from small to medium and large shrubs or small trees, including Sandmyrtle-*Leiophyllum*, Mountain Laurel-*Kalmia latifolia*, Tar Flower-*Befaria*, Heath and Heathers-*Erica* and *Calluna*, Labrador Tea-*Ledum*, Salal-*Gaultheria shallon*, *Pieris*, *Leucothoe*, and *Menziesia*.

The genus *Rhododendron* was first recognized by Linnaeus in *Species Plantarum* in 1753. Linnaeus created a separate genus *Azalea* containing six species.

In 1834, George Don in the third volume of his *A General System of Dichlamydeous Plants* subdivided *Rhododendron* into eight sections which are botanically retained today. *Azalea* was included under the genus *Rhododendron* by Don. In 1870, Dr. C.J. Maximowicz made a major contribution in the classification of *Rhododendron* and mainly oriental *Azalea* based on the position of leaf bud in relation to flower buds. More recent classifications reflect refinement rather than major changes. The eight sub-genera generally used today are those of Dr. Hermann Sleumer published in 1949 and 1980.

The question of splitting of *Azalea* into a separate genus came up as late as 1943, but it is hoped that this classification will never be accepted.

While the Sleumer classification was accepted by botanists, another classification of *Rhododendron* based on general similarities was introduced in the 1930's and generally accepted by horticulturists. This classification is called the Rhododendron Series or Balfourian System and presently divides the *Azalea* into six subseries.

NOMENCLATURE

Nomenclature is allied to taxonomy and deals with the correct name to be applied to a known taxon (a known plant).

A taxon (plural taxa) is a term applied to any taxonomic group at any rank such as species, genus, or family.

Once a specific plant has been identified and characterized, a correct name must be given. Naming is governed by rules developed and adopted by the International Botanical Congress which meets every 4–5 years. The rules adopted are formally presented in the edition of the International Code of Botanical Nomenclature (often referred to as the "Code") published following each Congress. The names so published are usually used by botanists and horticulturists thoughout the world.

Common names are not acceptable for use by botanists or horticulturists not only because such names are not universal but also because plants often have many common names. The name Wild Honeysuckle, for example, is often given to North America azaleas and also to species of the genus *Lonicera*. The common name is restricted to one language while a system of nomenclature must be international. Rhododendrons and azaleas have different vernacular or common names. In Japan, Rhododendrons are called "shakunage," and Azaleas "tsutsuji", while the common name for *R. japonicum* is "Renge tsutsuji". In Germany azaleas are called "azalee" or "azalie".

The genus name and the specific epithet (species name) form a binominal term (2 words) called the *species name*. The complete scientific name, in Latin form, must be followed by the authority of the name of the person or persons who first formally described the plant. The complete scientific name for the Alabama Azalea is *Rhododendron alabamense* Rehder. Thus the name of person or persons following the species name indicates the authority or author and is a source of historical information regarding the name of the plant. The authority may be abbreviated—for example, "L." for Linnaeus or Michx. for Andre Michaux. The abbreviations used for authors' names can be found in most botanical manuals and floras. Frequently a name will have two authorities with the first in parentheses, such as *R. indicum* (L.) Sweet, or *R. periclymenoides* (L.) Torrey (Michx.) Shinners. *R. indicum* was first described by Linnaeus as *Azalea Indicum* and later transferred to *Rhododendron* by Sweet.

The case of *R. periclymenoides* is more complex and is illustrative of a basic rule of nomenclature—that of historical priority of name—that is, the oldest name given a species must be retained if it is not incorrect. The relevant rule is as follows. "The nomenclature of a taxonomic group is based upon the priority of publication." This principle provides that the correct name is the earliest properly published name that conforms to the rules. Earliest published names take precedence over names of the same rank published later. Priority for plant nomenclature begins 1, May 1753, the date of publication of Linnaeus' *Species Plantarum.*

A. nudiflora given by Linnaeus in 1776, was an illegitimate (superfluous) renaming of *A. lutea* L. 1753, so it was changed to *R. nudiflorum* by Torrey in 1834. However, Michaux used and published the name *R. periclymenoides* in 1803. In 1962 Shinners rejected the name *R. nudiflorum* based on the priority of the earliest epithet so the species name is now *R. periclymenoides* (Michx.) Shinners.

For a more detailed review of taxonomy the following books are recommended:

Taxonomy of Vascular Plants. G.H.M. Lawrence. Macmillan 1951
Plant Systematics. S.B. Jones, Jr. McGraw Hill 1979
The Evolution and Classification of Flowering Plants. A Cronquist. Houghton Mifflin 1968
Manual of Cultivated Plants. A. Rehder. Macmillan Co. 1940

The reader will find several name changes in this book. In the discussion of species, where names which have changed, both the old and "new" names will be used followed by the authority.

The following name changes are some of the more noteworthy that the reader will encounter:

R. (nudiflorum) periclymenoides
R. (speciosum) flammeum
R. (roseum) prinophyllum
R. (eriocarpum) tamurae

Of major present concern in the horticultural world is the proposed name change *R. metternichii* Siebold and Zucc. to *R. japonicum* var. *japonicum* (Blume) C. K. Schneid, the deciduous azalea of Japan. According to the "Code" this must be accepted. However, at the 1982 International Botanical Congress in Australia, a decision was made that old established names can be approved and continued if sufficient evidence of utility is submitted. Such a case is being made for *R. metternichii.*

The name *R. japonicum* will remain for the deciduous Japanese azalea.

RHODODENDRON SERIES

The extensive collections of *Rhododendron* in the early 1900's from southern Asia made by Forrest, Rock, Kingdon-Ward, and others stimulated taxonomic work at Edinburgh Botanic Garden and Herbarium under the direction of Bayley Balfour. The horticulturally based classification consists of about 45 series. The artificial classification was intended as a temporary measure, but it became firmly entrenched following the publication of *The Species of Rhododendron* in 1930 by the Royal Horticultural Society. This system was designed to cope with the vast quantities of new plant material received from the Orient, North America, etc. Balfour intended to revise the temporary system but died before it could be accomplished.

The Series system does not attempt to classify species under their subgenera and section as proposed in the International Rules of Botanical Nomenclature. Further, it is based largely on cultivated plants rather than *Rhododendron* found in the wild.

This classification or effort to define the relationship between the species of *Rhododendron* was in need of revision. A more natural classification based on wild plants proposed by Sleumer was adopted by Cullen and Chamberlain, of the Edinburgh Botanical Garden, as the basis for a complete reassessment of the genus *Rhododendron*. This work is still in progress and depends heavily upon the cytology, anatomy, and phytochemistry of the genus. Results are published as they become available. The 1980 Royal Horticultural Society *Rhododendron Handbook* presented the old Balfourian system along with the new Cullen and Chamberlain revision, of the Edinburgh Botanical Garden, as the basis for a complete reassessment of the genus *Rhododendron* together with a third classification. The latter, proposed by C.D. Brickell, attempts to accommodate both points of view. Revision of the *Azalea* Series was incomplete and, therefore, not included. Professor W.R. Phillipson and Dr. M.N. Phillipson and others are working on the Azalea Series.

As stated earlier, taxonomy and classification are a complex everchanging science. Unfortunately at times the botanists' changes have become a wedge between botanist and horticulturist. The horticulturist, often with a limited knowledge of the International Botanical Code, is frequently reluctant to accept name and classification changes.

At present there is a proposal by Professor W.R. Phillipson to divide the azaleas botanically into seven sections. It is to be hoped that horticulturists will agree and accept seven series of *Azalea*. The proposal is to add a new section *Sciadorhodion* to include the following four species: *R. pentaphyllum, R. albrechtii, R. schlippenbachii,* and *R. quinquefolium*. The four species of this new section are characterized by the whorl of five obovate leaves at the end of the branches, seeds that are nonwinged, tomentum consisting of setae and the glandular hairs, and absence of the typical marginal hairs.

Thus the *Azalea* Sections and Subseries would be as follows:

I. Section *Pentanthera*—Subseries *Luteum;* includes all but two of the deciduous species of the United States, as *R. alabamense, arborescens, atlanticum, austrinum, bakeri, calendulaceum, canescens, periclymenoides (nudiflorum), oblongifolium, occidentale, prunifolium, prinophyllum (roseum), serrulatum, flammeum (speciosum),* and *viscosum,* and three azaleas, *japonicum, molle,* and *luteum,* from other regions.

II. Section *Rhodora*—Subseries *Canadense;* includes the deciduous species *R. canadense,* and *vaseyi* from the United States.

III. Section *Viscidula*—Subseries *Nipponicum;* is monotypic and includes only the deciduous species, *R. nipponicum,* from Japan.

IV. Section *Sciadorhodion*—Subseries *Schlippenbachii;* includes the four deciduous species, *R. pentaphyllum, albrechtii, schlippenbachii,* and *quinquefolium* from Japan and Korea.

Plate 1

Private Garden of George Harding, Maryland. HARDING

Hillside planting of azaleas, R. Stewart Garden, Virginia. R. STEWART

"Spring Glory" with Dogwood and Crabapple, Bickerstaff Garden, Richmond, Virginia. B. MILLER

Plate 2

Hillside planting of Glenn Dale Azaleas at National Arboretum. NATIONAL ARBORETUM

Kaempferi Azalea and Dogwood at Planting Fields, New York. PLANTING FIELDS

One azalea as a focal point in a garden. BROOKSIDE GARDENS

Valley Gardens, Windsor Great Park, England. GALLE

Azalea Bowl of Kurume Azaleas at Callaway Gardens, Georgia. GALLE

"A topping of strawberry ice cream" Kurume Azaleas should be used with restraint. GALLE

Plate 4

Exbury Azaleas on Battleston Hill at R.H.S. Garden at Wisley, England. GALLE

Knap Hill Azaleas on Battleston Hill at R.H.S. Garden at Wisley, England. GALLE

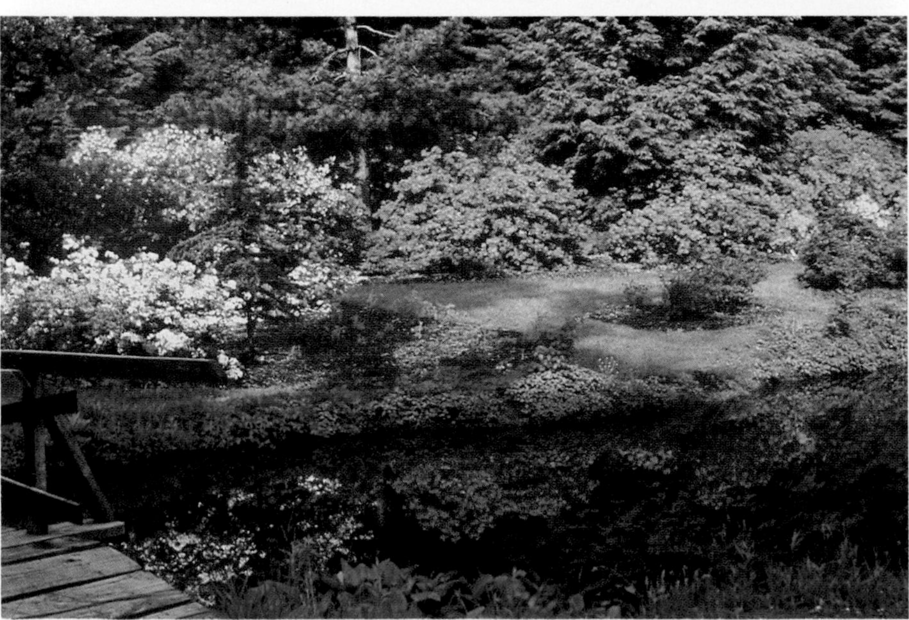

Exbury Azalea Planting at Holden Arboretum, Ohio. HOLDEN ARBORETUM

Lakeshore planting at Brookside Gardens, Maryland. BROOKSIDE GARDENS

Sheared Kurume Azaleas at the Emperor's Palace Garden, Tokyo. GALLE

'Fashion' and 'Glacier' Glenn Dale Azaleas in mass planting. GALLE

Plate 6

Restful planting of azaleas at the Ryoanji Temple Garden, Kyoto. GALLE

Sheared green mounds of azaleas in a private garden, Kyoto. GALLE

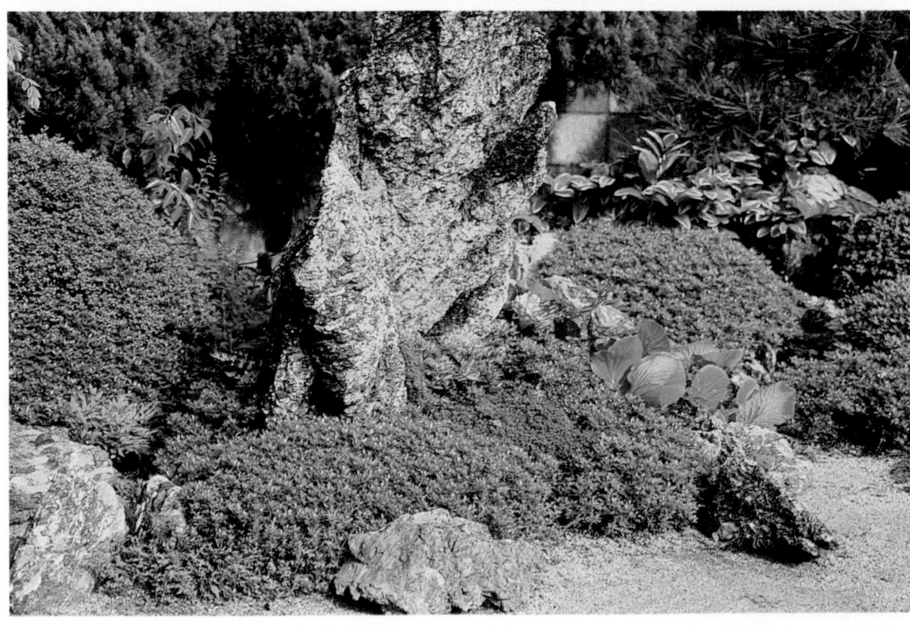

Sheared Satsuki Azaleas and stone in a private garden, Japan. GALLE

Plate 7

Marginal and surface hairs on *R. nakahari.* GALLE

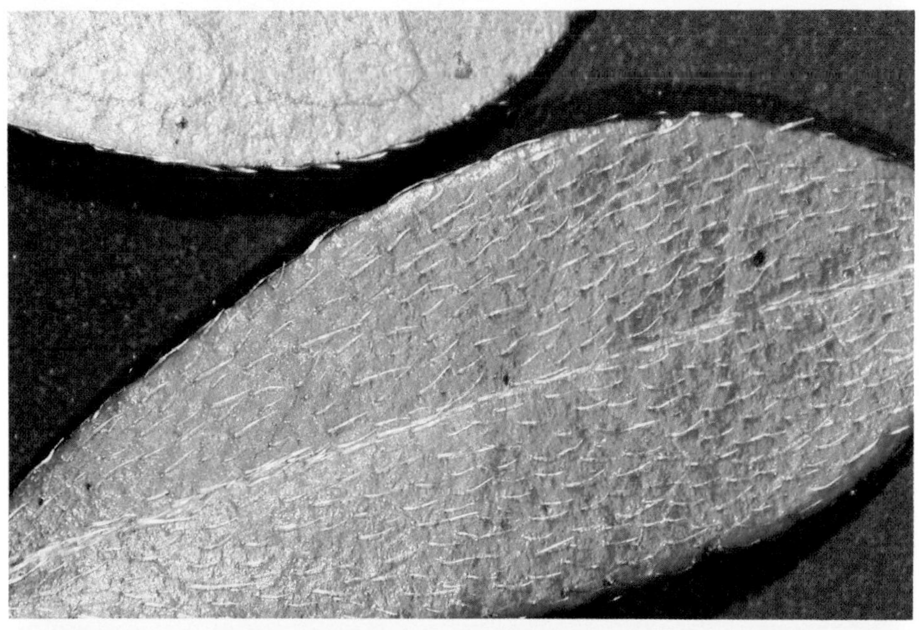

Marginal and surface hairs on *R. tashiroi.* GALLE

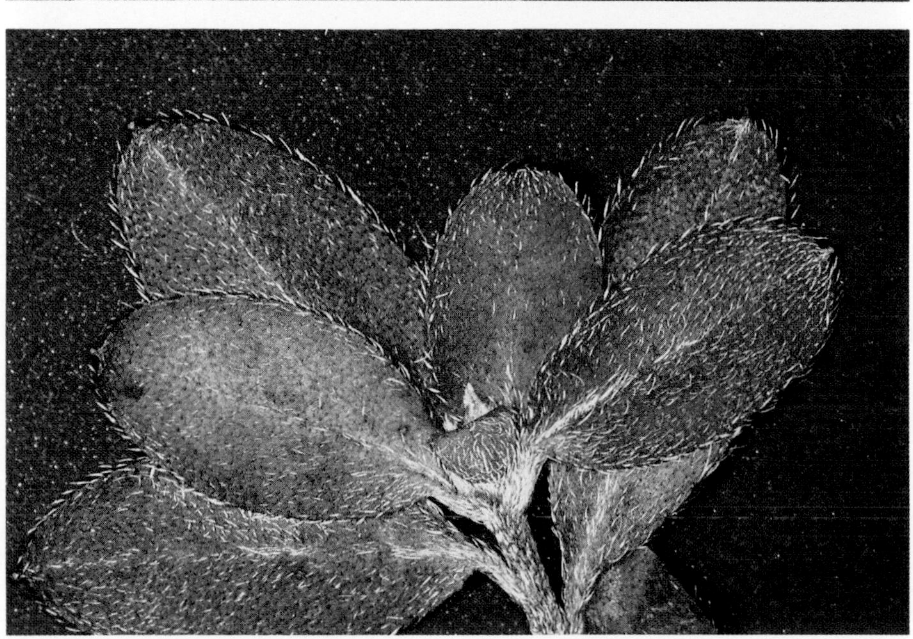

New leaves and prominent rusty hairs on *R. rubropilosum.* GALLE

Plate 8

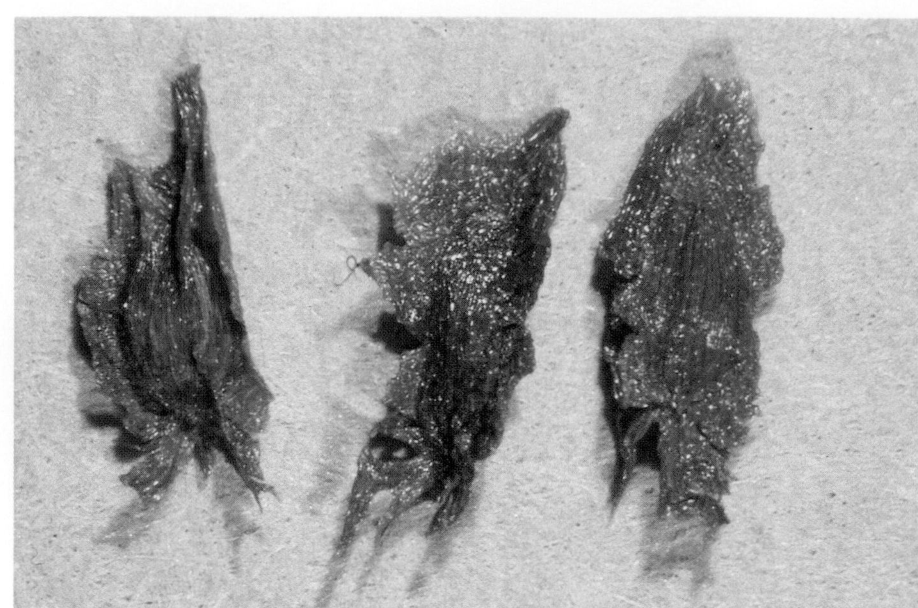

Winged seed of *R. bakeri.* GALLE

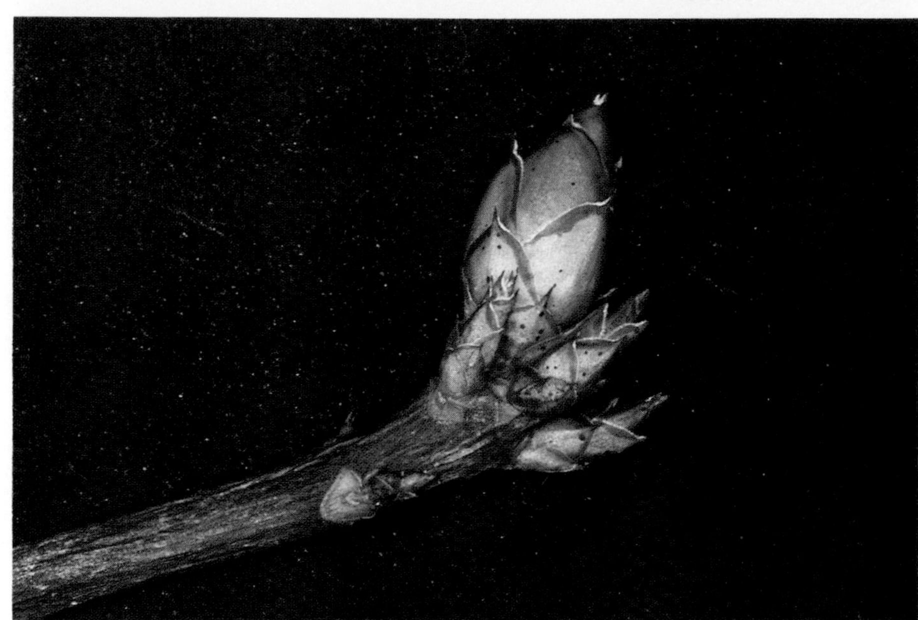

Glabrous buds and stems of *R. prunifolium.* GALLE

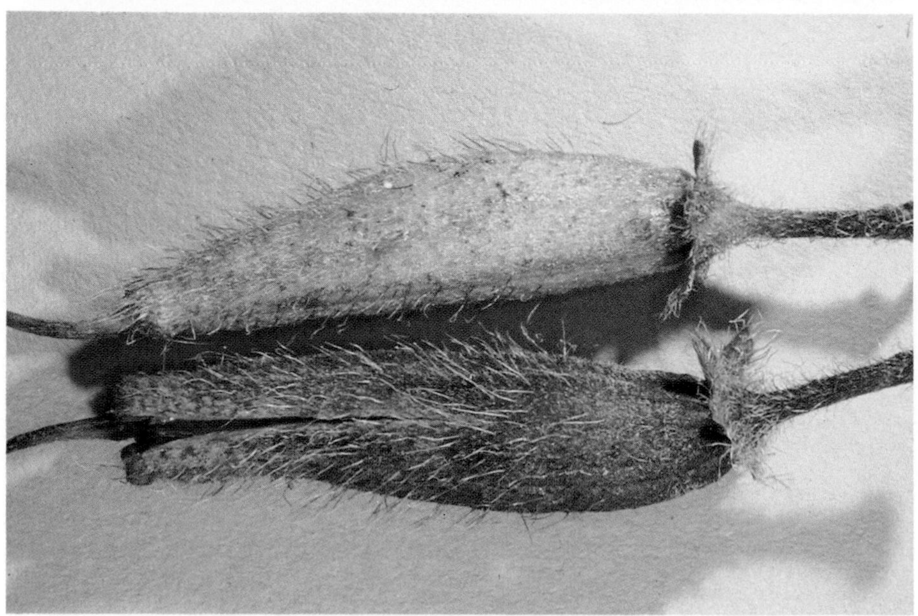

Seed capsules of *R. calendulaceum.* GALLE

V. Section *Tsutsutsi*—Subseries *Obtusum;* includes the evergreen or persistent leaved species of China, Japan, Korea, and Formosa, among those introduced being *R. indicum, kaempferi, kiusianum, komiyamae, macrosepalum, microphytum, nakaharai,* 'Obtusum', *oldhamii, yedoense, yedoense* var. *poukhanense, ripense* ('Mucronatum'), *rubropilosum, saisiuense, sataense, scabrum, serpyllifolium, simsii, tosaense, tschonoskii, tsusiophyllum,* and *otakumii (yakuinsulare).*

VI. Section *Tashiroi*—Subseries; is also monotypic and includes only the evergreen species *R. tashiroi,* from the Ryukyu Islands near southern Japan.

VII. Section *Brachycalyx*—Subseries *Farrerae;* includes the deciduous species from China, Korea, and Japan, *R. amagianum, farrerae, mariesii, nudipes, reticulatum, sanctum,* and *weyrichii.*

Each section and subseries represent *Azalea* species that are closely allied. Consequently, matters of cultivation, hybridization, propagation, flower-color range, and flower form, which differ between species of different groups, are generally more similar for species within the same group.

The subseries names are from one of the characteristic and usually well-known species in the subseries.

In addition to the familiar *Azalea* species there are foreign species being tested and others still to be introduced into cultivation. In the Subseries *Obtusum* for example there are *R. annamense* from Vietnam; *R. rivulare, lasiostylum,* and *sasaki* from Formosa; *R. subsessile* from Luzon in the Philippine Islands; *R. atrovirens* and *rufohirtum* from Yunnan Prov. China, *R. hainanense* from Hainan Prov., *R. mariae* from Kwangtung Prov., and *R. minutiflorum* from Kwangsi Prov.

Other rare species in the Section *Tsutsutsi* are *R. chuni kwangtungense, longiperulatum, macrogemmum, miyazawae, ovatosepalum, tamurae,* and *tsoi.*

CLASSIFICATION OF RHODODENDRON

Dr. Hermann O. Sleumer's classic paper *A System of the Genus Rhododendron L.* was originally published in 1949. Another paper on the classification was published in 1980, *Past and Present Taxonomic Systems of Rhododendron Based on Macromorphological Characters.* Both papers can be found in the *Contributions Toward a Classification of Rhododendron* published by the New York Botanical Garden.

Due to Dr. Sleumer's knowledge of and insight into the genus, his classification has withstood the test of time. Needless to say there are a few who disagree with his classification, but Systematic Botany is a complex ever-changing science.

Dr. Sleumer's classification divides the Azaleas into six sections with the Subgenus *Pentanthera* consisting of three sections: *Pentanthera, Rhodora,* and *Viscidula.* Professor W.R. Philipson's proposal for dividing the Azaleas into seven sections, with the addition of a new section *Sciadorhodion,* has been added.

Characteristics of the Eight Subgenera Rhododendron as developed by Dr. H.S. Sleumer with the addition of the new Azalea section *Sciadorhodion:*

I. Subgenus *Rhododendron:* leaves persistent, lepidote (scaly) beneath and sometimes above, flowers in terminal inflorescence
   1. Sect. *Rhododendron:* leaf scales with entire margin, 10 stamens projecting out of corolla. Type species: *R. ferrugineum.*
   2. Sect. *Pogonanthum:* leaf scales with lacerate margins, 5–10 stamens within the corolla. Type species: *R. anthopogon.*
   3. Sect. *Vireya:* leaf scales entire or lacerate margined. Seed with tail-like appendages at both ends. Lectotype species: *R. javanicum.*

II. Subgenus *Pseudoazalea*: leaves usually deciduous, lepidote, flowers in terminal inflorescence, appearing before the leaves in the spring. Type species: *R. trichocladum*.

III. Subgenus *Hymenanthes*: leaves persistent, elepidote (not lepidote), flowers in terminal buds, the new branches arising from leaf axils of previous year's growth. Type species: *R. metternichii*.

IV. Subgenus *Pentanthera*: leaves deciduous, not lepidote, flowers from terminal buds, corolla funnel-form, 5–10 stamens. Lectotype species: *R. nudiflorum*.

   1. Sect. *Pentanthera*: corolla funnel-shaped, stamens always 5. Type species: *R. luteum*.
   2. Sect. *Rhodora*: corolla rotate campanulate, lobed almost to the base, flowers appearing before or as leaves appear, stamens 7–10 and visible. Type species: *R. canadense*.
   3. Sect. *Viscidula:* corolla tubular campanulate, stamens short, flowers appearing with or after leaves, stamens 10. Type species: *R. nipponicum*.
   4. Sect. *Sciadorhodion*: leaves in whorls of 5 at the ends of the branches, stamens 10. Type species: *R. schlippenbachii**.

V. Subgenus *Tsutsutsi:* leaves deciduous or persistent, not lepidote, flowers from a terminal bud, new branches from axils of terminal whorled leaves, stamens 5–10. Lectotype species: *R. indicum*.

   5. Sect. *Tsutsutsi:* leaves persistent or deciduous, often dimorphic, leaves and branches with appressed setose hairs.
   6. Sect. *Tashiroi*: leaves persistent in whorls of 2–3 at end of branches, corolla campanulate. Type species: *R. tashiroi*.
   7. Sect. *Brachycalyx*: leaves deciduous in whorls of 2–3 at end of branches, corolla rotate-funnel-form. Type species: *R. farrerae*.

VI. Subgenus *Rhodorastrum:* leaves deciduous or semi-persistent, lepidote beneath, inflorescences lateral, the new branches arising from foliage beneath the inflorescence, flowers appearing before the new growth. Type species: *R. dauricum*.

VII. Subgenus *Azaleastrum:* leaves deciduous or persistent, not lepidote, inflorescences lateral, new branches from pseudo-terminal buds or axils of lower leaves. Lectotype species: *R. ovatum*.

VIII. Subgenus *Pseudorhodorastrum:* leaves persistent, lepidote (scaly), inflorescence lateral, new branches from pseudo-terminal buds or from axils of lower leaves. Type species: *R. virgatum*.

*names to be confirmed

AZALEA SERIES

The Key to azaleas within the Azalea Series is based on Dr. Sleumer's classifica tion of *Rhododendron* and encompasses the Subgenus *Pentanthera* and the Subgenus *Tsutsutsi*.

Subgenus *Pentanthera*
Lectotype species: *R. nudiflorum*

Section *Pentanthera*	=	Subseries *Luteum*
type species:		*R. luteum*
Section *Rhodora*	=	Subseries *Canadense*
type species:		*R. canadense*
Section *Viscidula*	=	Subseries *Nipponicum*
type species:		*R. nipponicum*
Section *Sciadorhodion*	=	Subseries *Schlippenbachii*
type species:		*R. schlippenbachii*

Subgenus *Tsutsutsi*
Lectotype species: *R. indicum*

Section *Tsutsutsi*	=	Subseries *Obtusum*
Section *Tashiroi*	=	Subseries *Tashiroi*
type species:		*R. tashiroi*
Section *Brachycalyx*	=	Subseries *Farrerae*
type species:		*R. farrerae*

Subseries names are subject to change.

Key to the Subgenera and Subseries

1. Flowers from terminal buds; new leaves and shoots from lateral buds, leaves deciduous
   Subgenus *Pentanthera*
   2. Leaves scattered along the branches
      3. Stamens always 5, corolla funnel-shaped
         Section *Pentanthera* = Subseries *Luteum*
         (Type species: *R. luteum*)

      3a. Stamens 8–10 (rarely 5–6, or 7)
         4. Corolla rotate campanulate, lobed almost to the base, stamens visible, flowers before or as the leaves unfold.
            Section *Rhodora* = Subseries *Canadense*
            (Type species *R. canadense*)

         4a. Corolla tubular—campanulate, stamens, included in the corolla. Flowers with or after the leaves.
            Section *Viscidula* = Subseries *Nipponicum*
            (Type species *R. nipponicum*)

2a. Leaves in whorls of 5 at the ends of the branches, stamens 10.
Section *Sciadorhodion* = Subseries *Schlippenbachii*
(Type species: *R. schlippenbachii*)

1a. Flowers and leaves from same terminal buds. Stamens 5–10.
Subgenus *Tsutsutsi*
(Lectotype species: *R. indicum*)

5. Leaves (persistent or deciduous) scattered along the branches.
Section *Tsutsutsi* = Subseries *Obtusum*

5a. Leaves in whorls of 2–3 at the ends of the branches.

6. Leaves persistent, corolla campanulate
Section *Tashiroi* = Subseries *Tashiroi*
Type species: *R. tashiroi*

6a. Leaves usually deciduous, some persistent, corolla funnel form.
Section *Brachycalyx* = Subseries *Farrerae*
(subseries *Schlippenbachii* in part)
Type species: *R. farrerae*

Keys to the species within each Section and Subseries follow:

SECTION *PENTANTHERA* – SUBSERIES *LUTEUM*

Deciduous shrubs, flowers from terminal buds; corolla funnel-form with 5 stamens. The subseries contains all but two of the deciduous species in North America and one each in eastern Europe, Japan, and China.

Key to the Species

1. Corolla wide funnel-form, with gradually expanding tube, nonglandular on the outside; yellowish blotch divided by light veining into small dots.

2. Leaves glabrous beneath, except on veins, winter floral buds glabrous, stamens shorter than the yellow to reddish orange corolla, 2–2½″ across; central and northern Japan.
R. japonicum Japanese Azalea

2a. Leaves soft pubescent beneath, winter floral buds pubescent, stamens as long as the yellow corolla, 2–2½″ across; eastern to central China.
R. molle Chinese Azalea

1a. Corolla funnel-form, with cylindrical tube, blotch if present not dissolved into dots.

3. Early flowering before or with the leaves (see 3a and 3b)

4. Flowers pale to deep pink occasionally white (see 4a & 4b)

5. Flowers variable in color, white to reddish with distinct yellow blotch, tube glandular, fragrant, 1½–2″ across or larger; floral winter buds glabrous or pubescent; North American native from southern Oregon to southern California, difficult to grow outside native habitat.
R. occidentale Western Azalea

5a. Flowers usually pink to deep pink, occasionally white without yellow blotch, fragrant.

6. Winter floral buds glabrous; leaves glabrous; glabrescent; corolla tube non-glandular; plants variably stoloniferous, North America, Carolinas to Tennessee, Ohio, and Massachusetts.
R. periclymenoides (nudiflorum) Pinxterbloom Azalea

6a. Winter floral buds pubescent, plants generally non-stoloniferous.

7. Corolla tube glandular, about as long as the lobes, lobes pointed; stamens about twice as long as the tube. Leaves with soft pubescence beneath, sometimes with glandular setae. The glandular leaf phase seems to be confined to the mountains of Virginia, U.S.A., North America range from Missouri, northern Indiana, Ohio to New England and southern Quebec.
R. prinophyllum (roseum) Roseshell Azalea

7a. Corolla tube glandular, distinctly longer than the lobes; stamens about thrice as long as the tube. Leaves usually felty pubescent beneath. Stoloniferous clones frequently occur. North America, South Carolina and Florida to eastern Texas and Tennessee.
R. canescens Piedmont Azalea

4a. Flowers white (occasionally pink in hybrid form), fragrant. See 4b.

8. Winter floral buds glabrous. Plants usually stoloniferous.

9. Corolla tube, broad with prominent rows of conspicuous long stipitate glands at the apex. Corolla, white or pink flushed, without yellow blotch, fragrant. Branches and underside of leaves usually glabrous. Often with glandular setae. Bushes low and very stoloniferous. North America, southeastern Pennsylvania, Delaware to coastal South Carolina and Georgia.
R. atlanticum Coastal Azalea

9a. Corolla tube narrow, glandular with prominent rows of stiputate glands at apex. Flowers lemon scented, usually with yellow blotch. Branches with glandular setae; crushed foliage with distinct spicy odor unlike other species. Bushes low stoloniferous. Hybrid forms taller, less stoloniferous and usually with pink blush. North America, north central Alabama and Georgia.
R. alabamense Alabama azalea

8a. Winter floral buds pubescent, plants somewhat stoloniferous.

10. Leaves variably pubescent 1½–4" long; corolla tube thin and sparingly pubescent; calyx-lobe, 1/32 to 1/8" long. North America, northern Arkansas to eastern Oklahoma and southeastern Texas.
R. oblongifolium Texas Azalea

10a. Leaves glabrous, except for abundant setae midrib, 1–2½" long; corolla tube soft (villous) pubescent, glandular, and thin; calyx lobes, short 1–32"; winter floral buds usually densely gray pubescent occasionally forms nearly glabrous. North America, Georgia and Alabama.
R. viscosum var. *aemulans* (See also 15a.)

4b. Flowers yellow to red; plants not stoloniferous.

11. Winter floral buds pubescent, flowers yellow and fragrant.

12. Leaves glabrescent beneath, glandular while young, corolla yellow, tube ½", lobes narrow and often reflexed, very fragrant; pedicels 1/2–4/5" long, glandular viscid. Eastern Europe to the Caucausus.
R. luteum Pontic Azalea

12a. Leaves densely pubescent beneath, corolla yellow to orange yellow, tube ¾" long, slightly fragrant, pedicels 1/5–3/5" long, pubescent, and glandular. North America, Northwestern Florida to southern Mississippi.

R. austrinum Florida Azalea

11a. Winter floral buds glabrous, flowers yellow to red, not fragrant.

13. Corolla tube usually pubescent with glandular setae, about as long or shorter than lobes. Flower width variable, but averaging 1¾–2" across wing petals; color clear yellow to orange and red. Branchlets and leaves variable pubescent. This is the large flower phase of the tetraploid Flame Azalea, which blooms in early May and occurs at lower elevations of the North American mountains from north Georgia to Virginia and perhaps to Pennsylvania and Ohio.

R. calendulaceum Flame Azalea (See also 16.)

13a. Corolla tube finely pubescent and eglandular; slender tube longer than the lobes. Flower width variable, but average about 1½" across wing petals; color orange-yellow to orange-red. Leaves glabrescent to glabrous. North America a relatively narrow band across central Georgia and down the Savannah River.

R. flammeum (speciosum) Oconee Azalea

3a. Mid-season flowering, with or after leaves, but before winter buds are formed. (See 3b.)

14. Flowers white to pink blush and fragrant.

15. Branchlets glabrous and smooth. Winter buds glabrous. Corolla tube sparingly glandular outside, usually pubescent inside. Style purplish red, usually glabrous. Leaves glabrous, occasionally eglandular setae. Bush non-stoloniferous. North America, New York and Pennsylvania to central Georgia and Alabama.

R. arborescens Sweet Azalea (See also 18a.)

15a. Branchlets and leaves pubescent with bristle-like setae. Winter buds glabrous to pubescent depending upon variety. Corolla tube thin and glandular. Style not colored and usually pubescent. Plant is variably stoloniferous; also variable as to habit, leaf size, flower size and time of bloom, which sometimes occurs well into July. Moisture-loving species, widespread in North America from Maine to South Carolina, Tennessee and Georgia.

R. viscosum Swamp Azalea (See also 10a.)

14a. Flowers yellow to red; non-fragrant.

16. Bushes non-stoloniferous, upright habit of growth. Corolla tube, usually pubescent with glandular setae, about as long or shorter than lobes. Winter buds glabrous. Flower width variable, but averaging about 1¾" across wing petals. The earlier description of *R. calendulaceum* applies in most respects, but the flowers are somewhat smaller and the blooming season later, from late May to mid-June. This is the high altitude, late phase Flame Azalea of North America in the southern Appalachians (Wayah Bald; Soco Gap, etc.) to Virginia.

R. calendulaceum Flame Azalea (See also 13.)

16a. Bushes variably stoloniferous, sometimes vigorously so. Plants low and twiggy. Similar to *R. calendulaceum* with respect to pubescence of vegetative and floral parts, flower color, etc., but corolla tubes are thinner and flowers somewhat smaller, averaging about 1¾" across wing petals. The diploid Cumberland Azalea flowers in June and early July in North America on the mountains of eastern Kentucky to Tennessee, western North Carolina, North Georgia and Alabama.

R. bakeri Cumberland Azalea (See also 19.)

3b. Late flowering, appearing after the winter buds are at least partly formed.

17. Flowers white, fragrant.

18. Branches densely strigose. Winter buds with more than 15 aristate mucronate scales, usually pale with conspicuous dark margin. Leaves often pubescent beneath, serrulate, ciliate margin. Corolla tube slenderly cylindric nearly to summit; about twice the length of lobes; tubes copiously glandular-pilose and sparingly villous outside. Style glabrous or minutely pubescent only at base and usually not colored. Bushes tall, infrequently similar to those of *R. viscosum,* including the variability of winter bud pubescence, but its leaves may be slightly larger than average for *R. viscosum* and individuals may flower in late October. North America, east central Georgia, Central Florida to Louisiana.

R. serrulatum Hammock-sweet Azalea

18a. Branches glabrous and smooth. Winter buds glabrous light brown. Corolla tube sparingly glandular outside, usually pubescent inside. Style purplish red, usually glabrous. Leaves glabrous, occasionally with eglandular setae. Late flowering phase of Sweet Azalea; North America, Georgia.

R. arborescens Sweet Azalea (See also 15.)

17a. Flowers yellow to red, non-fragrant, winter buds glabrous.

19. Branches with stiff bristles. Bushes variably stoloniferous, sometimes vigorously so, plants low and twiggy. See previous description. North America. Scattered individuals of southern Appalachians have been observed in flower in August and September.

R. bakeri Cumberland Azalea (See also 16a.)

19a. Branches glabrous and smooth. Bushes tall, round topped, non-stoloniferous. Winter buds glabrous. Leaves generally glabrous with eglandular setae on veins. Flowers generally orange-yellow to red with predominance of red-orange and red. The Plumleaf Azalea is restricted to the ravines of a small part of southwestern Georgia and adjacent Alabama, generally centering around Fort Gaines, Georgia in North America.

R. prunifolium Plumleaf (Prunifolia) Azalea

SECTION *RHODORA* – SUBSERIES *CANADENSE*

Two species from eastern North America. Upright shrubs, leaves deciduous, corolla rotate campanulate, lobes divided. Vegetative shoots from separate buds below the terminal flower buds.

Key to the Species

1. Stamens 10, corolla light reddish purple occasionally white, two lipped, two lower lobes divided to the base; leaves elliptic oblong, grayish tomentulose beneath, 1½–2½" long. Winter floral buds small. North America Labrador to Newfoundland, south through New England, central New York, to northeastern Pennsylvania and northern New Jersey.

R. canadense Rhodora

1a. Stamens 5–7, corolla with short tube, slightly two lipped, pink, or white, spotted reddish orange; leaves elliptic to elliptic oblong, glabrous green beneath, 2–4½' long. Winter floral buds broad ovoid ⅜–½". North America, western North Carolina.

R. vaseyi Pink Shell Azalea

SECTION *VISCIDULA* – SUBSERIES *NIPPONICUM*

This subseries contains only one species and is characterized by the nodding or pendulous, white, tubular campulate flowers, ¾″ long by ⅜″ broad, 6 to 15 in truss. The deciduous leaves are obovate oblong, 2½ to 7″ long. Central Japan.

R. nipponicum Nippon Azalea

SECTION *SCIADORHODION* – SUBSERIES *SCHLIPPENBACHII*

A new section or subseries characterized by the pseudo whorls of 5 large, usually obovate, deciduous leaves. The pubescence of the leaves consist of setae of stiff bristle and glandular hairs. Stamens 10.

Key to the Species

1. Flowers and vegetative shoots from the same terminal buds.
   2. Corolla white, 1½″, style glabrous; young branches glabrous leaves, broad elliptic to obovate 1⅛ to 2″ long. Japan.
      R. quinquefolium Cork Azalea
   2a. Corolla pink, occasionally white, 2⅜–3″, style pubescent; young branches glandular pubescent; leaves broad obovate 2–4″ long. Japan.
      R. schlippenbachii Royal Azalea

1a. Flowers from terminal buds, vegetative shoot from lateral buds.
   3. Leaves obovate to oblong lanceolate, pubescent beneath, 1½–4½″ long; corolla reddish purple, 2″; branches coarsely pilose. Korea.
      R. albrechtii Albrecht Azalea
   3a. Leaves elliptic to elliptic-lanceolate, glabrous beneath, with glandular hairs along the midrib, 1⅛–2⅜″ long; branches usually glabrous; corolla light to deep pink 1½–2″. Japan.
      R. pentaphyllum Five Leaf Azalea

SECTION *TSUTSUTSI* – SUBSERIES *OBTUSUM*

Low to medium shrubs, shoots usually covered with appressed flattened hairs. Leaves deciduous or persistent, usually dimorphic. Corolla 5-lobed, tubular campanlate to funnel-form. About 30–40 species in temperate regions of eastern Asia, from Korea and Japan to the Philippine Islands, Annam, and southwestern China.

Key to the Species

1. Corolla white, tubular campanulate, small spreading lobes. Branches strigose.
   2. Corolla, pubescent inside, shallow lobed ½″ across, ovary 3 locular; leaves elliptic to obovate ¼–⅜″ long, persistent. Japan.
      R. tsusiophyllum Tanakae Azalea
   2a. Corolla short, glabrous inside, ⅛–½″ across, ovary 4 to 5 locular; leaves ovate oblong ¼–¾″ long, persistent, Japan, Korea.
      R. tschonoskii Tschonoski Azalea

1a. Corolla usually colored, funnel-form, large ¾–2½″ across, branches strigose
   3. Bud scales not viscid, calyx and pedicels without glandular hairs.
      4. Stamens 5.

5. Leaves glabrous beneath, except on midrib 3/8–5/8″ long; corolla 1/2–3/4″ across. Japan.
   R. serpyllifolium Wild Thyme Azalea

5a. Leaves pilose beneath, corolla 3/4–2 1/2″ across.

6. Flowers before or with the leaves, in April, early May.

7. Leaves usually linear lanceolate, acute 1/2–1 1/8″ long; semi-evergreen; corolla reddish purple 3/4–1 1/8″ long; semi-evergreen; corolla reddish purple 3/4–1 1/8″ across. Japan.
   R. tosaense Tosa Azalea

7a. Leaves ovate, elliptic or obovate.

8. Corolla light purple to reddish purple occasionally white, 3/4″–1 1/8″; low spreading habit; leaves semi-evergreen to deciduous, obovate 1/2–3/4″ long. Kyushu Island, Japan.
   R. kiusianum Kyushu Azalea

8a. Corolla reddish orange, pink to purple and white, 1 1/2–2″; upright branching; leaves larger, 1–2″ long.

9. Plants tall open habit; leaves oblong to broadly ovate, 1–2″ long, evergreen. Japan.
   R. kaempferi Kaempfer Azalea

9a. Plants dense twiggy habit, resembles Kurume Hybrids; leaves elliptic-ovate, 3/4–1 1/2″; semi-glossy, evergreen; often flowers just before *R. kaempferi.* Kyushu Island, Japan.
   R. sataense Sata Azalea

6a. Flowers with or after the leaves, late May–June, leaves lanceolate, 3/4–1 1/2″ long, evergreen; corolla usually red 1 1/2–2 1/2″ across. Japan.
   R. indicum Indica Azalea

4a. Stamens 6–10.

10. Flowers before or with the leaves early to mid-May.

11. Style hairy at base; 1/2–1 3/4″.

12. Corolla light purple, 1″; Persistent leaves elliptic to lanceolate, 1/2–1 1/2″, covered with grayish hairs. Philippine Islands.
   R. subsessile

12a. Corolla pink, 3/4–1″, spotted darker; Persistent leaves oblong, lanceolate to elliptic lanceolate, 1/2–1 3/4″ with prominent reddish brown hairs. Formosa.
   R. rubropilosum Redhair Azalea

11a. Style glabrous

13. Persistent leaves, elliptic obovate 1/2–1 3/4″, prominent hairs; low prostrate shrub; corolla red, 1 1/4–1 1/2″, late April—early May before *R. tamurae.* Formosa
   R. nakaharai

13a. Leaves elliptic lanceolate, 3/4–2″ long; plants not prostrate.

14. Twiggy branched shrub; leaves persistent, elliptic to oblong-elliptic, 3/4–2″; corolla red 1 1/2–2″; China.
   R. simsii Sims Azalea

14a. Tall upright open shrub; leaves semi-persistent, lanceolate to ovate oblong, 3/4–1 1/2″; corolla reddish purple, 3/4–1 1/4″. Closely resembles *R. kaempferi,* but with 6–9 stamens. Japan.
   R. komiyamae

10a. Flowers with or after the leaves, late May–June, persistent leaves elliptic to obovate, 3/4–1 1/4″; corolla pink to purplish red,occasionally white, 1 1/2–2″; compact shrub. Similar to *R. nakaharai* but with larger leaves and flowers. Kyushu, Yakushima Islands, Japan.
   R. tamurae

3a. Bud scales viscid calyx and pedicel with appressed hairs, some glandular; stamens 5 to 10.

15. Stamens normally 5, calyx linear ¾–1¼″; leaves oblong to elliptic 1–1½″ long, with glandular hairs, semi-evergreen; corolla light purple to reddish purple; fragrant. Japan.

R. macrosepalum Big Sepal Azalea

15a. Stamens 6–10; calyx shorter.

16. Stem with appressed flattened eglandular hairs.

17. Corolla reddish orange to red, 2–2½″; calyx ¼–½″ long, pubescent and glandular; leaves 1¼–4″ long, subcrenulate, evergreen, Liukiu Islands.

R. scabrum Luchu Azalea (Kerama Tsutsuji)

17a. Corolla light to moderate purple, 2″; fragrant, calyx ¼–⅜″ with appressed eglandular hairs; leaves 1¼–3½″ long semi-evergreen to deciduous in colder areas. Korea.

R. yedoense var. *poukhanense* Korean Azalea
R. yedoense Yodogawa Azalea (double flowers)

16a. Stems with appressed, pilose and glandular hairs.

18. Stem and leaves with abundant reddish glandular hairs, leaves elliptic oblong to elliptic ovate, ¾–3½″ long, ¾–1½″ wide; persistent, corolla red 1½–2″. Late spring and summer. Formosa

R. oldhamii Oldham Azalea

18a. Stem and leaves with soft grayish to brownish hairs, some glandular, leaves lanceolate to ovate lanceolate, 1½–2½″ long 1″ wide, persistent. Corolla pale reddish purple to white, fragrant, 1½–2″, early midseason. Japan. "Mucronatum" white, is a cultivated form from Japan and China.

R. ripense Riverbank Azalea

SECTION *TASHIROI* – SUBSERIES *TASHIROI*

This subseries has only one species characterized by persistent leaves in whorls of 2–3, at end of branches; leaves oblong obovate to oblong elliptic 1¼–2½″ long with pubescent flattened hairs; corolla campanulate funnel-form, pale reddish purple spotted, 1–1½″. Closely allied to and serves as a link between subseries *Obtusum* and *Farrerae.* Ryukyu and Kawauaka Islands, South Japan.

R. tashiroi

SECTION *BRACHYCALYX* – SECTION *FARRERAE*

Medium to large shrubs characterized by the whorled 2–3 leaves at end of the stem; terminal buds produce flowers and leafy shoots. Leaves are deciduous or occasionally persistent, usually rhombic to obovate.

Key to the Species

1. Leaves broadest below the middle, ovate to ovate lanceolate.
   2. Leaves small 1¼–1½", long petioles tomentose; corolla light purple, dark spotting 1–2". China.
      R. farrerae Farrer Azalea
   2a. Leaves larger 1½–3" long, petioles glabrescent, corolla pink, darker spots, 1½–2". China.
      R. mariesii Maries Azalea

1a. Leaves rhombic, broadest about or above the middle.
   3. Flowers usually appear before the leaves, stamens unequal in length.
      4. Petioles glabrous, leaves broadly rhombic 1½–3", glabrous beneath except for midrib; corolla deep pink, darker spots. Japan.
         R. nudipes Nudipe Azalea
      4a. Petioles pubescent; leaves ovate rhombic, pubescent beneath, specially on midribs; corolla reddish purple spotted, Japan.
         R. reticulatum Rose Azalea
   3a. Flowers with or after the leaves, stamens nearly equal in length.
      5. Leaves glossy, petioles and pedicels wooly pubescent; flowers after the leaves.
         6. Corolla purplish pink to white, 1", May–June, pedicels 3/16–3/8" long; leaves broadly rhombic. Japan.
            R. sanctum Shrine Azalea
         6a. Corolla red, 2", July, pedicels ½–9/16" long, leaves ovate rhombic. Japan.
            R. amagianum Mt. Amagi Azalea
      5a. Leaves not glossy, petioles and pedicels with loose coarse hairs; corolla red, darker blotch, with the leaves, April–May; leaves in 2–3's ovate orbicular to rhombic. Japan, Korea.
         R. weyrichii Weyrich Azalea

4. AZALEAS—PLANTS, HABITS, FLOWERS, AND LEAVES

Azaleas are generally described as shrubs, although some of the deciduous species become small trees in the wild. It is not uncommon, for example, to find in established gardens in the southeastern U.S., such as Callaway Gardens, North American native azaleas 15 to 20 feet tall. Wild plants of the Piedmont area of Georgia, U.S.A., are often over 25 feet in height. Many of the deciduous azaleas of Japan have been observed as small trees. In the Nikko Chanokidaira Botanical Garden native plants of *R. quinquefolium* are small trees with trunks over 12 inches in diameter.

The evergreen azaleas include both upright and spreading shrubs, some less than two feet, others up to ten feet or more. The Kurume Azaleas generally have the reputation of being low growing and dwarf shrubs, but many cultivars today are eight to ten feet in height and still growing. Again, at Callaway Gardens, several Kurume Azaleas are 15 feet tall.

Evergreen azaleas are usually densely branched and twiggy, but the Kaempfer Azalea, *R. kaempferi,* tends to send up tall shoots which are filled out with age. At Planting Fields in New York, U.S.A., several Kaempfer Azaleas are at least 15 feet in height. Large massive Southern U.S. azaleas such as 'Formosa' are 12 to 15 feet across and equally as high.

Deciduous azaleas are usually more open or loosely branched, some having ascending and others, horizontal branches. The Royal Azalea *R. schlippenbachii* and the Pontic Azalea *R. luteum* are densely branched.

Among the azaleas one can select plants of nearly every habit or growth. The selections of *R. nakaharai* such as 'Mount Seven Star' and the North Tisbury hybrids are often only 12 to 18 inches in height after ten years and two to three times as wide. Weeping forms such as 'Flame Creeper' and 'Pink Cascade' are now available for hanging baskets and trailing over walls. Some azaleas like the Satsuki, Beltsville dwarfs and selections of the Greenwood hybrids, after 15 years, are less than 24 inches high and twice as wide. A 20 year old plant of

'Salmon Elf' at Callaway is approximately 30 inches tall and 50 inches wide. A 200-year-old plant of *R. scabrum* near Kurume, Japan, is over 15 ft. wide and 10 ft. high, with a trunk diameter of over 15 in.

A century-old plant of the Ghent hybrid 'Unique', at the Sunningdale Nursery in England, is over 16 ft. high and 30 ft. wide. The more spreading types such as 'Indica Alba' 'Mucronatum' will often be twice as broad as high. Old plants of this cultivar can be seen at Morris Arboretum in Philadelphia, U.S.A., over 25 ft. wide, possibly from repeated self-layering. Large wild colonies of individual plants of *R. atlanticum* in the sandy coastal regions of Virginia and New Jersey, U.S.A., may cover several thousand square feet. The size of an azalea after 10 years may vary considerably due to climatic regions. A Kurume Azalea in 10 years may be 4–5 ft. tall in the Southeastern states of North America, only 3–4 ft. in Washington, D.C., and smaller in areas north and the mid-West. In London, England, the plants are 3–4 ft.; in the colder regions of Europe they are even smaller. In contrast, they are taller in Australia and New Zealand.

Azaleas are not fast growers, and the very dwarf azaleas are really slow. Average growth of three to ten inches is common. However, by forcing with a regular fertilizer program, moisture and pinching, the rate of growth can be increased.

FLOWERS

The fascination of azaleas is a direct outgrowth of the wide variation in form, color, and size of the flowers. Understanding the structure of an azalea flower is a prerequisite to identifying the many species and cultivations.

Corolla. The typical azalea flower has five petals or lobes and is sympetalous or joined at the base from which the petals flare out. Collectively the petals form the funnel-shaped corolla, in the form of a tube, as lower portions fuse. The limbs or petals, the upper separate portion, may be overlapping, imbricated, or flaring.

The five petals are arranged in a symmetrical or butterfly fashion. Facing the flower, one petal, the standard or dorsal lobe is at the top. Two petals, the upper wings, are below the standard and on either side. Usually they constitute the greatest width of the flower. The two remaining petals, the lower wings, are lower and usually closer together, but can be spread out and are equal to or wider than the upper wings.

Calyx. The calyx surrounds the corolla at its base and is composed of five small green sepals that are partly fused at the base. The sepals are minute, ranging in length from 1/24 to 1/8 of an inch or longer. Occasionally, as in the Big Sepal Azalea *R. macrosepalum*, the sepals may be over an inch long and a prominent feature. On double and hose-in-hose flowers, the sepals become petaloid so are usually visible as a separate flower part.

Perianth. A collective term for the corolla and calyx.

Pedicel. A short, slender green stalk, called the pedicel, supports the flower and is attached to the branch. Depending on the species, the pedicel may be up to ¾ of an inch long, very short or sessile, meaning not stalked, or virtually absent. The flower is then sessile, meaning not stalked.

Pistil. The female portion of the flower or gynoecium is composed of the ovary, style, and stigma. The ovary is in the center and just above the base of the corolla. The ovary is the seed bearing part of the flower and consists of five cells or locules. The style is a hollow tube originating at the ovary and terminating in a small, rounded appendage called the stigma. The stigma when ripe is sticky on the surface to receive and retain the pollen.

Stamens. The stamens, or male organ of the flower, are composed of filaments supporting pollen-bearing anthers, and arise at the junction of the ovary and corolla. The stamens usually occur in multiples of five and are often of unequal length. In many of the deciduous azaleas, the stamens are exserted, extending beyond the corolla, and are a conspicuous, attractive part of the flower. The anthers, pollen-bearing parts of the stamens, are at the top of the filament and are divided into two sacs. The pollen grains are borne in tetrads and come out of apical pores at the end of the anthers. All the pollen comes out together in a stringy matrix. The shedding of pollen from apical pores by azaleas differs from most genera which discharge pollen by longitudinal splitting of the anthers.

Seed Production. The ovary after fertilization by pollen, develops into a five-parted seed capsule which may be only ¼ of an inch long in *R. serpyllifolium* or up to one and a half inches long in *R. japonicum*. The seeds are generally small and numerous and may be winged or nonwinged. The evergreen azaleas have nonwinged seed. The North American deciduous species all have winged seed except *R. arborescens* and *R. vaseyi*. The Asiatic deciduous species all have nonwinged seed except *R. japonicum, R. molle,* and *R. luteum*.

A beautiful study on the morphology of the capsules, seed, and calyx was done by Dr. Johannes Hedegaard titled, *Studies in the Genus Rhododendrons*.

FLOWER FORMS

Azalea flowers vary, often with one or more types on a single plant. The most common azalea flowers are single with five lobes. However, with increased petals through the metamorphosis of sepals, stamens, or both, various doubling effects occur that vary the flower's appearance. Even the shape of the petals will alter flower appearance. The indiscriminate use of terms such as semidouble, double, fully double, and others are often misused and misleading in describing flower form and appearance.

Unfortunately, the American Rhododendron Society has not promoted a classification of azalea flowers, but the following classification may be helpful.

I. Single types: The most common azalea flower form consists of a corolla of five or more petals or corolla lobes usually fused at the base. The calyx consists of five sepals and five calyx lobes usually fused at the base. Finally, there are five to ten stamens and a single pistil. The conspicuous stamens and pistil give this type its distinctive appearance. Examples: Kurumes, 'Hinodegiri', 'Debutante', 'Sherwood Red'; the species *R. kaempferi;* Glenn Dale hybrids, 'Treasure', 'Martha Hitchcock' and 'Ben Morrison'; Satsuki, 'Gumpo', 'Kobai', (five to seven petals).

II. Hose-in-hose: A non-botanical term and often used when the sepals are fully metamorphosed, enlarged and transformed into petals. Another description would be: Hose-in-hose, one corolla superimposed inside another or two cycles of petals one within the other. The petal-like calyces have been rotated with respect to the corolla and can be seen together with the petals. The calyx may or may not be present. In many early descriptions the presence of a calyx was not recorded. For the future, when known, the presence of a calyx should be recorded as Hose-in-hose, calyx present or green calyx present. If it is not stated, one can assume that the calyx is absent or not known. In irregular or partial hose-in-hose flowers, the calyx petals are only partially developed and cannot be seen from the front of the flower. A hose-in-hose configuration may also be found in semi and double flowers.

III. Semidouble types: Flowers with a true corolla but in which some of the stamens have been transformed into petals and with true or only partially transformed sepals. The transformed stamens are smaller than the true petals or contorted, or the anther or filament of the stamen remains evident. In addition, there may be a few normal stamens or a few stamens fully transformed into petals. Examples: Belgian hybrid, 'Crimson Glory', Southern Indian, 'William Bull' (may also be double).

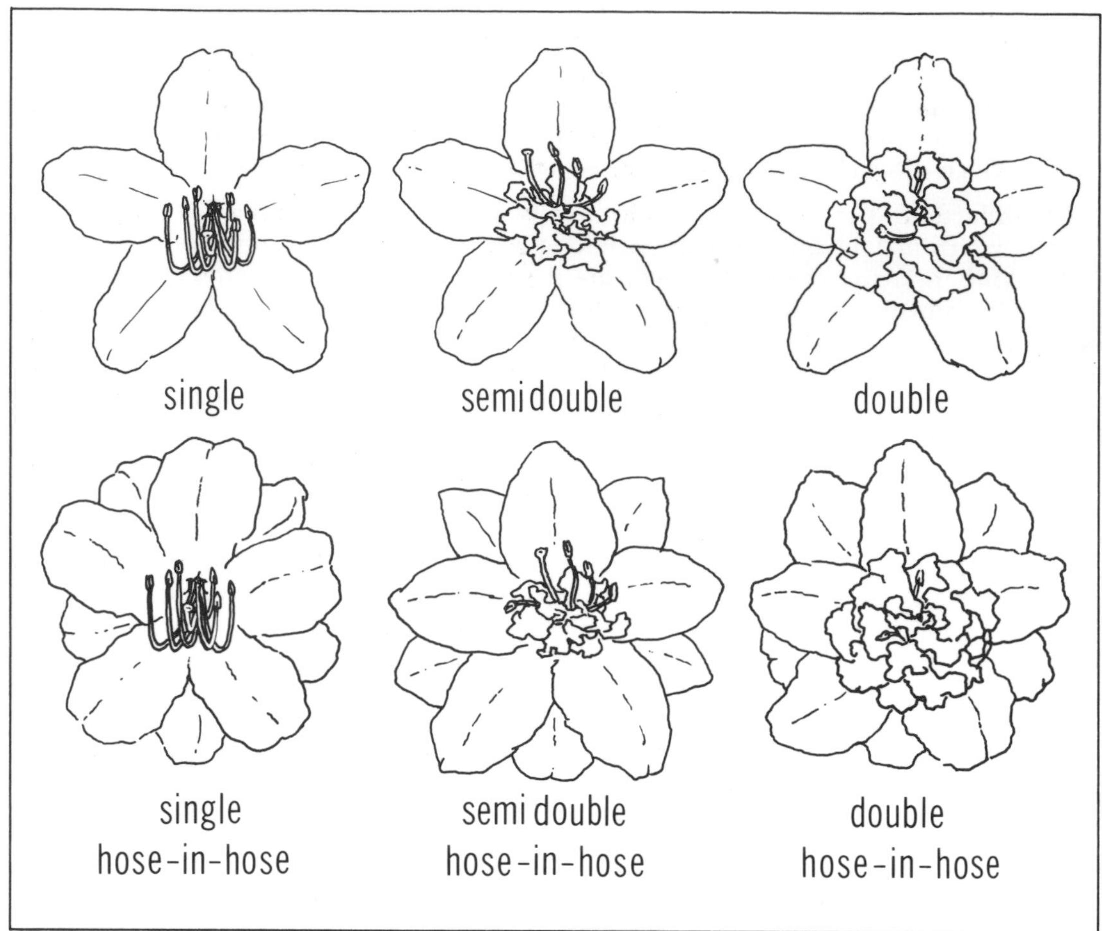

IV. Semidouble hose-in-hose types: Same as above with the calyx fully developed and visible and transformed to petals. The calyx and corolla look alike. Examples: Pericat hybrids 'Glory'; 'Rival' and 'Sweetheart Supreme'.

V. Double types: Flowers with true petals and complete or nearly complete transformation of stamens into petals. The green calyx or a small remnant is present. The pistil may be present or transformed. The petals may be up to thirty or more. Example: Gable hybrid, 'La Premier'; Satsuki, 'Beni-kirin', 'Balsaminaeflorum'.

VI. Double hose-in-hose type: similar to the double type but with hose-in-hose characteristics and the calyx not present. Example: 'Anna Kehr'. Many flowers described as double hose-in-hose have a remnant of a green calyx present and should be labeled as double hose-in-hose, calyx present.

VII. Spider type: The petals are not fused, forming a tube, but are separate, narrow, and strap-like. Typical examples are *R. macrosepalum linearifolium*, the cultivar 'Koromo-shikibu', and the Satsuki, 'Kinsai'. There is considerable variation, with often more than five narrow petals and examples where the stamens appear as narrow petals. While not common in deciduous azaleas, the cultivar, 'Chattahoochee' is a spider type, as is the triploid, *R. atlanticum f. tomolobum*.

FLOWER SHAPES

The variations in flower types and shapes as well as in size, color, and blooming period create differing esthetic effects and untiring charm. They should lead the perceptive and sensitive gardener to make a wide selection of cultivars.

Flower shapes vary and have often been described as types. Pointed petals produce a star effect. Other flower shapes include rounded petals and those whose margins are frilled, ruffled, or wavy. The flowers may be tubular, funnel-formed, or bell-shaped, while others have large, flat flowers without a prominent tube such as *R. schlippenbachii*. Combinations of the above produce interesting flowers as in 'Mayo's Magic Lily' which has a large tubular flower, with slightly pointed petals and partially petaloid sepals.

The form of the flower commonly varies among plants. This variation may be natural so that the flowers on two identical plants in the same area are different. Or flowers may differ from one area to another. A plant may be semidouble in one place and double in another. Spider types may have perfect flowers on the same plant.

FLOWER SIZE

The length of a flower is the distance from the base of the tube to the level of the top of the flaring petals. The width is the distance between the tips of the two upper wings or petals. The size of flowers vary from the tiny blossoms of the Tschonoski Azalea, *R. tschonoskii*, and Wild Thyme Leaf Azalea, *R. serpyllifolium*, to flowers of the new cultivars that often measure four to five inches across.

FLOWER CLUSTERS

Each flower bud may produce a single flower, a cluster, or an umbellate raceme, of up to 20 or more flowers. The number of flowers varies within each species. The more flowers to the cluster, the showier and more Rhododendron-like is the effect. Variations of season, environment, age, and health of the plant also affect the number of flowers to a cluster. Kurume, Back Acre, and other azaleas have only a few flowers to the cluster but, due to the denseness of branching, give a massive flower effect.

Some of the ball trusses or large flower clusters as noted on the Oconee Azalea, *R. flammeun (speciosum)*, and others may be genetic but still vary depending on the health and vigor of the plant.

The approximate numbers of flowers in a cluster for some species is as follows:

R. alabamense	6–30	*R. occidentiale*	10–30
R. arborescens	3–6	*R. phoenicum*	1–30
R. calendulaceum	5–25	*R. poukhanense*	1–3
R. flammeum	5–30	*R. prinophyllum*	5–9
R. indicum	1–2	*R. scabrum*	2–6
R. japonicum	5–12	*R. schlippenbachii*	3–6
R. luteum	7–12	*R. simsii*	2–6
'Mucronatum'	1–3	*R. vaseyi*	5–8
R. kaempferi	1–5		

The flower buds are at the tips of the branches, but a branch tip may have two or three flower buds, instead of a single bud, thereby increasing the cluster.

FLOWER COLORS

The beauty of azaleas resides in part in the marvelous range of color in the flowers. The colors are due to two main classes of chemical compounds or pigments. The fat-soluble carotenoids compounds are found in specialized protoplasmic bodies of the cell and provide yellow, orange, and red pigments. The anthocyanins belong to the water soluble flavonoid group of pigments and are responsible for the majority of pink, red-violet, and blue colors in flowers.

The complete function of pigments in flowers is not understood. The colors do attract pollinating agents. In general, bees prefer yellow and blue flowers; birds, red and orange; butterflies, bright colors, and moths, white or pale colors, in their search for nectar. Some pigments are invisible to humans but still guide insect pollinators that "see" by ultraviolet or infra-red perception.

The study of flavonoids in leaves and flowers of *Rhododendron* is ongoing among scientists in England, Germany, Japan, and the United States. The presence or absence of flavonoid compounds are potentially taxonomic markers. As more research and chemical data become known, flavonoids may provide additional tools for classification together with the morphological characters of plants.

Hybridizers will also find the information of value. For example, the violet colors in some azalaeas are generally due to the presence of malvindin 3, 5–diglucoside, the mauve pigment of many wild species. It has also been reported that an orange sport of "Red Wing" is due to the absence of a flavoid pigment as contrasted with its presence in the parental form.

Based on 58 flavonoid substances from the leaves of plants of the sub-genus *Pentanthera,* the species can be divided into five alliances. Also of interest, these same species lack the flavonoids gossypetin and coumarins common in most other *Rhododendron* species.

The chemical pigments determine the great variability of flower colors on the same plants as in the Satsuki and Glenn Dale cultivars where more than one color and different color designs are found on flowers of the same plant.

From biochemical studies in Japan, the Satsuki cultivars are divided into five groups based on their anthocyanin complement. Also 161 cultivars of Kurume Azaleas have been classified into seven groups. Some individual cultivars can be distinguished by their anthocyanin complement. However, for the complete identification of all azalea cultivars, more research on the flavonoids will be required.

Various terms are used to describe color patterns:

Self. All of one color.

Blotches. The attractiveness and color effect of many azalea flowers is accentuated by a blotch of a different color on the standard or top petal, which often extends to the two upper wings or petals. The blotch may be lighter or darker than the ground color.

Striped Flowers. Striped flowers have a peppermint stick appearance, a white flower striped, dotted, or flecked with another color such as pink, red, or magenta. There may be flowers of different colors on the same plant. This is common on Satsuki Azaleas. For example, the cultivar 'Ho-raku' often has flowers that are white with a chartreuse blotch, white with faint dots of purplish red, white flecked or striped purplish red, half purplish red and half white with dots, and purplish red selfs. Such variations in color among flowers on the same plant are characteristic of the Satsuki Azaleas, common among the Southern Indian Azaleas, and occasionally found among the Glenn Dales and Kurumes.

Bordered or Margined Flowers. Some white flowered azaleas have a colored margin or colored flowers with white margin. The effect is that of the throat differing in color from the rest of the flower. This very pleasing effect is found in Satsuki, Glenn Dale, Back Acre azaleas, and others. According to a Japanese authority, Satsuki cultivars ending in 'no tsuki' are only bordered flowers, but frequently in their books they show the same azalea with variations.

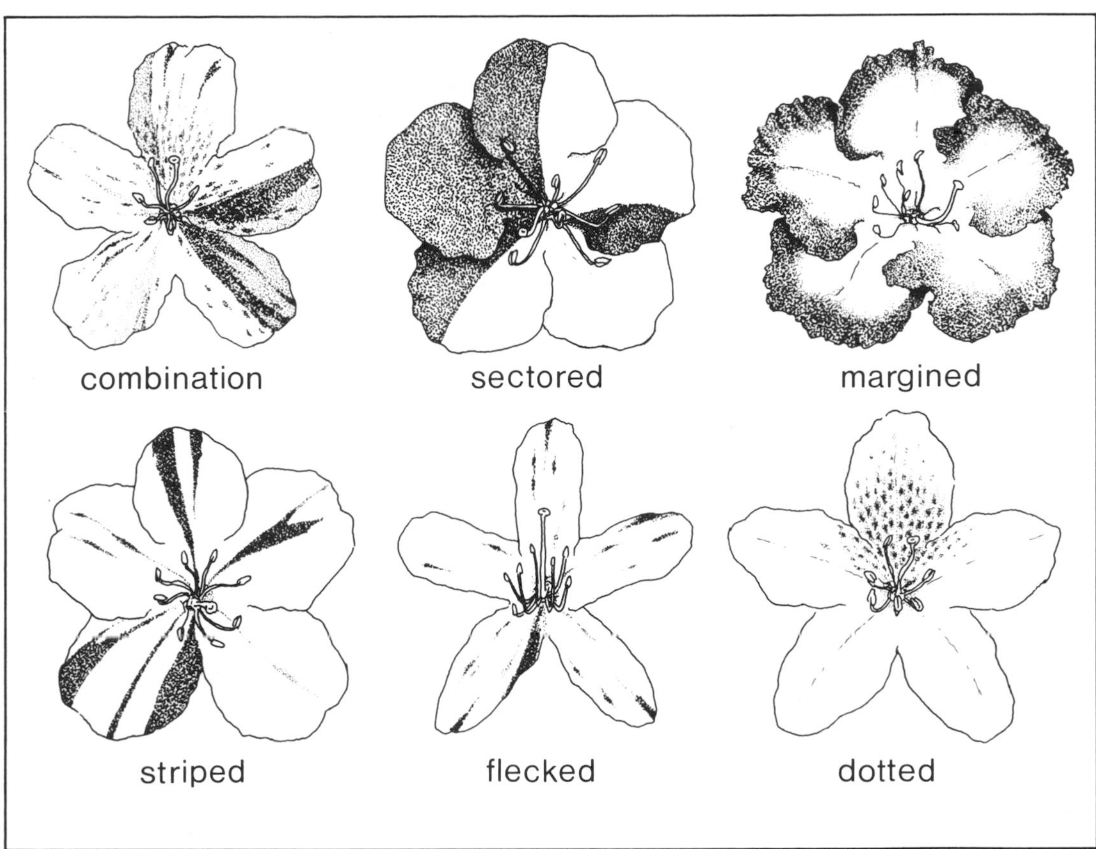

Sectorial Flowers. These color variations may at times arise from sectorial chimaeras or variegations, where an identical sector or wedge of a flower on a stem or on all stems of a plant has a different color from the rest of the flowers. Such chimaeras probably have a genetic basis. They are not graft chimaeras or graft hybrids resulting from development of a bud and branch at the point of union of a stock and scion. Where the dominant flowers are white, striped, dotted, flecked, or sectored in a particular color, the plant is likely to produce occasional branches with self colored flowers of that color. Branches with these self-colored flowers may be pruned out if a more uniform plant with the striped, dotted, flecked, or sectorial flowers is desired.

Azalea cultivars with these variations in flowers are admired by partisans and condemned by opponents. Often a flecked or dotted azalea appears as white from a distance, but when examined closely a different color combination is seen.

A plant with striped, dotted, flecked, bordered, or sectored flowers is not fixed except in the sense that it will continue to produce a known range of variants. These variants in order of common occurrence are:

1. Self-colored flowers of the color of the stripe.
2. Flowers characterized both by a white ground flushed with a hue derived from the color of the stripe, but usually lighter in tone, and by an irregular white margin.
3. Flowers with a white base and a margin of the color of the stripe.
4. Sectorial flowers with a wedge or half of the flower with the color of the stripe.
5. Least often, white flowers.

Cuttings taken from the branches showing any of these five variations tend to produce plants with the particular variation. Cuttings taken from the striped, (or dotted, flecked, bordered, or sectored) branches of the original plant produce plants that continue to throw the complete range of variants. This behavior has been observed in the Glenn Dales, Robin Hills, and Satsuki Azaleas and occasionally in the Belgian hybrid Azaleas.

Color. Clarity is important in describing plant and particularly flower colors, hues, tints, and shades. Comparison with a standard color chart and the use of commonly accepted color would be a marked improvement over today's practice. Unfortunately, color charts used for identifying and classifying flower color are no longer available. Those published in the past include the *Royal Horticultural Society Colour Chart,* (R.H.S.) published in 1966, the two volume *Horticultural Colour Chart,* (H.C.C.) published in 1944 by the Royal Horticultural Society, *Ridgeway's Color Standards,* (R), and the *Nickerson Color Fan* (N).

Color names are often misleading. To describe a red-headed woodpecker the color of red is relatively simple. However, in describing a flower color under various environmental conditions, the names used are often confusing and difficult to interpret by different users. The following names are often used to describe the same flower color: Amaranth-Pink, Pink, Phlox-Pink, Daphne-Pink, Rose, Neyron-Rose, Orchid-Rose, Cameo-Pink, and even Pink-Icing, Teenage-Pink, and Bridesmaid-Pink.

The color names used in this book are taken from the National Bureau of Standards (NBS) Special Publication 440, *Color Universal Language and Dictionary of Names.* The Inter Society Color Council (ISCC) and NBS have developed a method of designating colors related to the Color Names Dictionary.

All those color names in the list of the previous paragraph would use the Color Dictionary Names deep purplish pink or deep Pk (dark purplish pink is shown intact as d.p Pk). The ISCC-NBS Color Names follow a simple standardized formula which differentiates 267 blocks in the color spectrum, about the limit of different colors that one can remember.

The method in principle is simple. The terms *light, medium,* and *dark* designate degrees of value, and the adverb *very* is used to extend the range—thus "very light" and "very dark". These, and a series of hue names, used both as nouns and adjectives, are combined to form names for describing color in terms of its three perceptual attributes: hue, value, and chroma. For the colors of medium value or lightness, the adjectives "grayish", "moderate", "strong" and "vivid" designate increasing degrees of chroma. For colors of ligher value, the adjectives "pale" (or "light grayish"), "light", "brilliant" and "vivid" are used for the darker colors. Increasing chroma is reflected in the modifiers "dark grayish", "dark", "deep", and "vivid". The following pages contain all the hue names and abbreviations used in the ISCC-NBS system.

It is possible to convert many of these color numbers to the Royal Horticultural Society *Colour Chart.* Numbers and names correspond to the ISCC-NBS names such as 5YR8/7 light orange, 2.5R7/8 strong pink and others. Since the names used in the Nickerson fan are the NBS names, the numbers from old records and registrar lists will be eliminated.

The old Ridgeway Color names can be converted to ISCC-NBS names with the aid of the color dictionary, such as LaFrance pink=vivid pink, Rhodamine purple=vivid purplish red, Spinel pink=strong purplish red, Rose doree=deep yellowish pink, and others.

The ISCC-NBS names describe but do not pinpoint the true color. Thus, several adjacent colors from old color charts may have the same descriptive name, however, when possible the R.H.S. numbers will be included.

NATIONAL BUREAU OF COLOR NAMES WITH SYNONYMOUS NAMES

The source of synonymous names are from Ridgeway, R.H.S., and other sources. Please note that many common color names, such as orange, rose pink, lilac, violet, and others often refer to different NBS color names. The color salmon, depending on its color source, refers to over five different NBS centroid color chips.

Pale Pink 7

livid pink
almond
almond blossom

Light Pink 4

livid pink
venation pink
almond
rosy pink
pale vinaceous purplish
almond blossom
blush coral

Moderate Pink 5

livid pink
corinthian pink
light purplish vinaceous
pale vinaceous
almond blossom
hydrangea pink
lilac
chatenay pink
flesh color
pale vinaceous purplish
vinaceous
debutante pink
la france pink

Strong Pink 2

alizarine pink
vinaceous
camellia pink
light rose
salmon rose
hermosa pink
rose pink
camellia rose
carmine

Deep Pink 3

alizarine pink
geranium pink
vinaceous
light jasper red
empire rose
spinel rose
strawberry pink
coral
eosine pink
jasper pink
camellia rose
orange venaceous
porcelain rose
rose doree
watermelon
coral rose

Vivid Red 11

carmine
scarlet red
blood red
cherry
geranium lake
scarlet red
vermillion
rose red
spectrum red
carmine red
crimson
scarlet
turkey red
poppy red

Strong Red 12

nopal red
jasper red
bright red
cardinal
geranium red
scarlet
claret red
rose opal
cherry red
flame
geranium rose
light red

Deep Red 13

garnet brown
indian lake
ruby red
old red
ox blood red
pansy purple
garnet red

Light Yellowish Pink 28

flesh pink
shrimp pink
orient pink
salmon
light salmon
pearl pink
hydrangea pink
vinaceous buff
peach
shell pink
peach pink
pale pink

Moderate Yellowish Pink 29

buff pink
congo pink
fawn
hydrangea pink
pale cinnamon pink
pinkish buff
salmon color
vinaceous
yellow buff
chatenay pink
coral pink
flesh color
japan rose
peach
salmon
salmon rose
vinaceous cinnamon

Strong Yellowish Pink 26

congo pink
grenadine pink
orient pink
venetian pink
french rose
pink coral
salmon rose
coral pink
jasper pink
safrano pink
chinese coral
shrimp red
shrimp pink
salmon

Deep Yellowish Pink 27

begonia rose
jasper pink
azalea pink
coral pink
strawberry pink
geranium pink
rose doree
begonia
porcelain rose
salmon

Vivid Yellowish Pink 25

orange
azalea pink
melon pink
chinese orange

Moderate Reddish Orange 37

carrot red
light coral red
strawberry pink
light red
rose
orange red
coral red
peach red
burnt red
red
vermilion
salmon

Strong Reddish Orange 35

grenadine
burnt orange
orange red
vermilion
bright coral rose
scarlet
orange
red
bright coral red

Deep Reddish Orange 36

chinese red
vermilion
coral red
red

Vivid Reddish Orange 34

flame scarlet
capsicum red
fire red
scarlet
grenadine red
deep rose
orange
vermilion

Light Orange 52

orange pink
peach
orange
apricot
salmon color
salmon
buff

Strong Orange 50

cadmium orange
orange
marigold orange
pumpkin orange
cadmium yellow
carrot red
orange ochre

Pale Orange Yellow 73

light buff
pale salmon
sea shell pink
egg shell
olive yellow
pale pinkish salmon
salmon buff
blush yellow
peach cream
yellow buff

Light Orange Yellow 70

pale orange yellow
orange buff
indian yellow
orange

Brilliant Orange Yellow 67

bright yellow
maize yellow
reddish yellow
indian yellow
orange

Vivid Orange Yellow 66

bright yellow
bright reddish yellow
yellow
orange

Pale Yellow 89

ivory yellow
light ivory
amber white
yellow cream
light buff
egg shell
ivory white
yellow buff

Light Yellow 86

amber yellow
cream color
apricot yellow
orange buff
buff yellow
straw yellow
naples yellow
orange

Vivid Yellow 82

light cadmium
canary yellow
lemon yellow
sulphur yellow
yellow
buttercup yellow
chrome yellow
light yellow
bright gold

Brilliant Yellow 83

amber yellow
empire yellow
straw yellow
lemon
bright yellow
naples yellow
chinese yellow

Very Pale Purple 226

pale bluish lavender
pastel lavender
violet
pale mauve
pastel lilac
dull violet

Very Light Purple 221

pale hortense violet
lilac
light lilac
violet

Light Purple 222

dark lavender
pale hortense violet
pale lavender rose
phlox pink
violet
lilac
pale amparo purple
pale rose purple
rose purple

Moderate Purple 223

aconite violet
litho purple
mathews' purple
violet
purple
chinese violet
livid violet
viola
deep violet
lavender

Strong Purple 218

amparo purple
mathew's purple
royal purple
violet
pansy violet
litho purple
red violet
purple

Deep Purple 219

hyacinth violet
petunia violet
violet
purple
litho purple
spectrum violet
red violet

Pale Reddish Purple 244

deep vinaceous lavender
lilac
light vinaceous lilac
violet

Light Reddish Purple 240

eupatorium purple
liseran purple
reddish violet
violet
light vinaceous lilac
purple lilac
rose lilac
rose purple

Moderate Reddish Purple 241

bishop's purple
livid purple
dull dark purple
red violet
eupatorium purple
liseran purple
pansy violet
rose violet

Strong Reddish Purple 237

dull dark red
magenta
tourmaline pink
orchid
red violet
liseran purple
phlox purple
tyrean pink
lilac rose
reddish violet

Light Violet 210

deep lavender
light mauve
mauvette
lilac
light lavender violet
pale violet
violet

Pale Purplish Pink 252

pale lilac
lilac
baby pink
mauve pink
pale vinaceous
pastel mauve
light orchid pink

Light Purplish Pink 249

cameo pink
pale rhodonite pink
rose pink
rose
light pinkish lilac
pale vinaceous lilac
rosaline pink
lilac rose

Moderate Purplish Pink 250

pale laelia pink
pale persian lilac
fuchsia pink
light rose
light vinaceous lilac
light mauve
light orchid
rose pink

Strong Purplish Red 255

rosoline purple
spinel pink
magenta rose
rose madder
spinel red
china rose
madder pink
rose neyron

Deep Purplish Pink 248

amaranth pink
light mallow purple
mallow purple
pale rosoline purple
fuchine pink
phlox pink
bright rose
fuchsia pink
lilac rose
daphne pink
light rosoline purple
rose color
tourmaline pink
neyron rose
bluish pink
china pink
light orchid rose

Vivid Purplish Red 254

rhodamine purple
tyrian rose
dianthus purple
rose madder
tyrian purple
tyrian pink
rose
rose color
crimson
rose bengal
solferino purple
cobalt red
persian rose
rose carmine

FLOWER FRAGRANCE

The fragrance of flowers is difficult to describe and only a few pioneering efforts have been made to codify odors. Flower fragrance is best noted in the early morning or during damp weather and will vary among plants within a species.

Fragrance is common among the North American azaleas. The Sweet Azalea *R. arborescens,* Swamp Azalea *R. viscosum,* Coastal Azalea *R. atlanticum,* and Hammock-sweet Azalea *R. serrulatum* have a strong and at times heavy fragrance. To many, the Sweet Azalea smells like heliotope, the Swamp and Hammock-sweet Azalea like clover, and the Coastal Azalea like some rose cultivars. The Roseshell Azalea *R. prinophyllum* has a clove fragrance, while the Alabama Azalea *R. alabamense* has the pleasant and distantly spicy, lemony scent of jasmine. The Piedmont Azalea *R. canescens* and the Pinxterbloom Azalea *R. periclymeinoides* have a mild, sweet, musky fragrance of none at all. The Western Azalea *R. occidentale* and the Pontic Azalea *R. luteum* are strong and sweet.

Often *R. molle* and the Ghent azaleas have a musky (mild skunk) fragrance in the early morning. The persistent leaved azaleas, 'Indica alba' 'Mucronatum', *R. yedoense* var. *poukhanense* and the Big Sepal Azalea *R. macrosepalum* have a delicate scent, the last like red clover and most pronounced.

FLOWER BUD INITIATION

Long days and short nights promote azalea shoot or stem growth. When the growing period for an azalea stem is completed, vegetative buds form at the tip. These buds contain rudimentary stems and leaf primordia. In the *Obtusum* and *Schlippenbachii* Subseries, the terminal buds are also potentially flower buds, and with an appropriate combination of nutrition, moisture, and temperature will also contain rudimentary flowers. Azalea buds in these series are, therefore, "mixed" combining stem, leaves, and flower primordia. In the *Canadense* and *Luteum* Subseries, floral buds are separate.

Formation of the earliest stages of flower primordia within the buds is initiated from most species in late June or July, following spring growth, and is completed by the end of July or early August or slightly earlier in warm climates. Unlike many plant genera, relative length of day and night has little effect on the initiations of flower buds in azaleas. The buds form following a period of stem growth, provided temperatures are above 65°F. Once initiated, the buds will develop and grow at lower temperatures until dormancy occurs.

Soil moisture is important for bud initiation. The Royal Azalea, *R. schlippenbachii* for example, will not set or develop flower buds if the summer is dry and the moisture supply low. In the U.S., San Francisco, as contrasted to Berkeley across the bay, exemplifies an area that is generally too cool in summer to produce good stem growth and bud formation in most azaleas.

RECURRENT GROWTH

In many parts of the world particularly in the more southerly latitudes there may be two or more flushes of vegetative growth before flower bud initiation. This is not uncommon if plants receive adequate moisture and a good supply of nutrients. Hot dry temperatures with limited soil moisture restrict vegetative growth.

Often in midsummer, strong growth of long vegetative shoots will develop from or near the base of a plant. These are called "wild growth", "summer shoots", or "sucker growth". They should generally be pinched or cut back to induced lateral branching.

DORMANCY

The flower bud continues to develop in late summer and early fall before cold weather and dormancy occur. Most azaleas only require a cool period of four to eight weeks at temperatures around 45°F. Following this they can be forced into growth. (See Chapter on Special Cultures). Often plants exposed to hot, dry, summer temperatures, followed by cool weather and moisture, will have a spattering of flowers. While azaleas bloom in the tropics, they make a better display in temperate climates that have cooler temperatures part of the year.

TIME OF BLOOMING

In Colombia, latitude 6°N., Belgian Azaleas bloom the year around. They develop new shoots, form and develop buds and flowers continuously. There is no major flowering period or display for the bloom is spasmodic throughout the year.

In central Florida, 'Vittata Fortunei' *R. simsii* var. *vittatum* will start flowering in September and continue through the winter until April. Many of the Belgian hybrid Azaleas and Southern Indians such as 'Hexe de Saffelaere' and 'Duc de Rohan' will start blooming in November and December and continue into March with scattered bloom the rest of the year. Other Southern Indian Azaleas bloom from mid-February to mid-March. The Satsuki Azaleas bloom from late April well into the summer while some, such as 'Warai Jishi', produce a second bloom in the fall. Some plants of Hammock-sweet Azaleas, *R. serrulatum,* will flower in July or August, while others remain in almost continuous bloom from July to early November.

The San Francisco area has bloom from mid-September through May starting with some of the Belgian hybrids and Glenn Dales and ending with Kaempferi and Satsuki Azaleas.

In the far South, some of the Belgian hybrids and Glenn Dale Azaleas start blooming in late August and continue all winter except when there is frost. In Washington, D.C., and Seattle, Washington, the azalea blooming period extends from mid-April through most of June and early July including the late flowering deciduous azaleas such as the Western Azalea *R. occidentale* and the Swamp Azalea *R. viscosum*. The Plumleaf *R. prunifolium* and Hammock-sweet Azalea *R. serrulatum* will be later.

In general, the farther north, the shorter the blooming period for a plant, but the bloom is more concentrated and the display greater. The farther south, the longer the blooming period but with scattered bloom and less display at any one time.

FLOWERING CHART

In the flowering chart of certain species, cultivars, and hybrid groups and their blooming period at Callaway Gardens at Pine Mountain, Georgia, the main hybrid groups show not only the period over which one or more cultivars in that group are in bloom but also the extent of the bloom from that group as a whole. While the time of bloom will differ in other areas of the world, the chart is generally indicative of the order of bloom of the species, cultivars, and hybrid groups shown. Gardens in other areas can time flowering dates through the use of the following table.

Flowering dates for other areas based on the Callaway Gardens flowering chart.

Mobile Ala.	1–2 weeks earlier	Seattle Wa.	4–5 weeks later
Dallas Texas	2 weeks earlier	San Francisco Ca.	1–2 weeks earlier
Charleston S.C.	1–2 weeks earlier	Pasadena Ca.	2–4 weeks earlier
St. Louis Mo.	3–4 weeks later	London England	4 weeks later
Washington D.C.	2–3 weeks later	Boskoop Holland	4–5 weeks later
Chicago Ill.	4–5 weeks later	Brisbane Australia	Aug.–Sept.
Cleveland Oh.	4 weeks later	Sidney Australia	Sept.–Oct.
Hartford Conn.	4–5 weeks later	Kurume Japan	3–4 weeks later
Boston Mass.	5–6 weeks later	Tokyo Japan	4–5 weeks later
Portland Or.	4 weeks later		

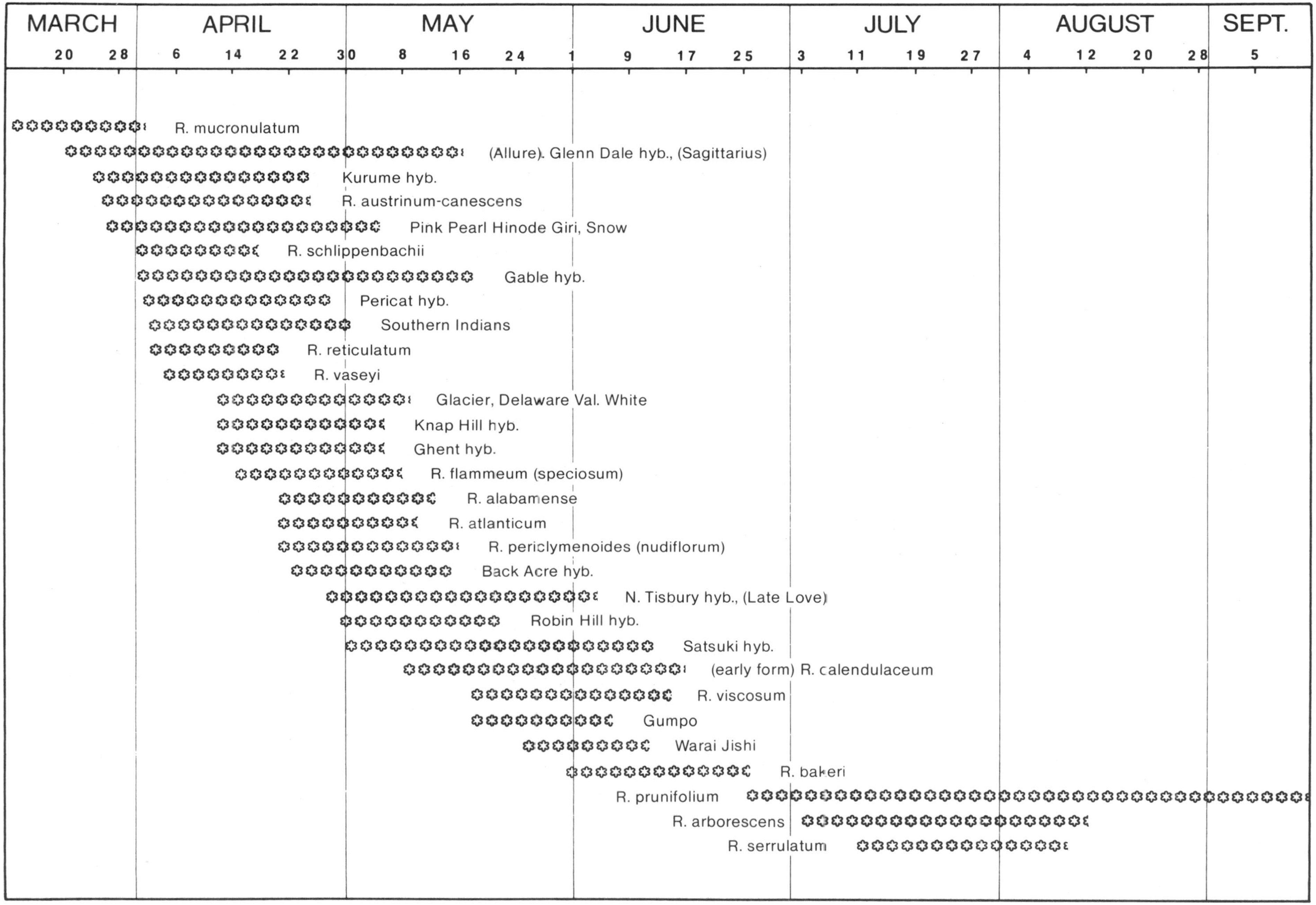

MARCH 20 28 | APRIL 6 14 22 30 | MAY 8 16 24 | JUNE 1 9 17 25 | JULY 3 11 19 27 | AUGUST 4 12 20 28 | SEPT. 5

R. mucronulatum
(Allure). Glenn Dale hyb., (Sagittarius)
Kurume hyb.
R. austrinum-canescens
Pink Pearl Hinode Giri, Snow
R. schlippenbachii
Gable hyb.
Pericat hyb.
Southern Indians
R. reticulatum
R. vaseyi
Glacier, Delaware Val. White
Knap Hill hyb.
Ghent hyb.
R. flammeum (speciosum)
R. alabamense
R. atlanticum
R. periclymenoides (nudiflorum)
Back Acre hyb.
N. Tisbury hyb., (Late Love)
Robin Hill hyb.
Satsuki hyb.
(early form) R. calendulaceum
R. viscosum
Gumpo
Warai Jishi
R. bakeri
R. prunifolium
R. arborescens
R. serrulatum

LEAVES

Azalea leaves possess esthetic features often overlooked. The obvious characteristic is an evergreen or deciduous species or cultivar. However, the size, shape, color, arrangement, and hairiness all add interest to a particular plant. The morphological characteristics of the leaves are a help in identifying species and assist in deriving the parentage of hybrids.

Leaf Size. The Wild Thyme Azalea *R. serpyllifolium* has elliptically shaped evergreen leaves 1/4 to 1/3 inches long. The 'Tschonoski Azalea' has narrow lanceolate, deciduous leaves 1/3 to one long, and 1/6 to a half inch wide.

At the opposite extreme, the uncommon Nippon Azalea *R. nipponicum* has deciduous leaves up to seven inches long and three inches wide. Both the Japanese Azalea *R. japonicum* and the Plumleaf azalea *R. prunifolium* have long leaves up to five and six inches long. More commonly, azalea leaves are one to two inches long in the evergreen species and three to four inches long with deciduous species.

Persistence of Leaves. The major division of azaleas is determined by persistence of leaf—deciduous azaleas lose their leaves in the winter while evergreen azaleas leaves are persistent. Most of the deciduous species are natives of the eastern United States; all the evergreen species come from eastern Asia. The designation of the two major groups of azaleas as deciduous or evergreen is, at best, only an approximation of the truth and may vary depending upon the climatic conditions.

Deciduous Azaleas: The deciduous azaleas do lose their leaves in the fall and put out new leaves in the spring, similar to many broadleaf flowering plants in colder regions.

Evergreen Azaleas: The group of persistent or evergreen azaleas often straddle the fence by being both deciduous and evergreen. They have dimorphic leaves, known as spring leaves and summer leaves. The spring leaves, unfolding at the time of flowering or immediately after, are thinner, lighter and generally larger than the summer leaves, and usually scattered along the branches. These leaves are short-lived, turning yellow and dropping off in the fall.

Leaf drop is hastened by summer drought. Novice gardeners often fear their evergreen azaleas are dying in the fall when the plants are merely shedding their spring leaves.

The summer leaves unfolding in early summer are smaller, darker, thicker, and more leathery than the spring leaves and are crowded at the tips of the branches. In most instances, the summer leaves are persistent and remain throughout the dormant period of winter until the following spring. In some cases the summer leaves of evergreen azaleas growing in warm climates may persist for several years.

The designations deciduous and evergreen are dependent on the climatic area and this accounts for the term persistent leaves. For example, the Hammock-sweet Azalea, *R. serrulatum,* is deciduous in warm temperature regions but will have persistent or nearly evergreen leaves in subtropical regions. Both the Korean Azalea, *R. poukhanense,* and Kaempfer Azalea *R. kaempferi,* are evergreen in warm temperature regions but usually deciduous in cool temperature regions. Thus, at best, evergreen azaleas are partially evergreen and partially deciduous.

LEAF SHAPES

The leaves of azaleas vary from obovate to ovate, to lanceolate, oblanceolate and some almost round or oblong. The Satsuki Azalea 'Kazan' (Rukizon) has small, broadly ovate leaves often described as heart-shaped, while the Spider Azalea, *R. macrosepalum linearifolium* has long, narrow leaves from one and a half inches to three inches long, but only 1/12 to 1/4 inches wide. Leaves, too, may be contorted or twisted as in the Satsuki cultivars, 'Rinpu', 'Saikan', 'Shungetsu', and others.

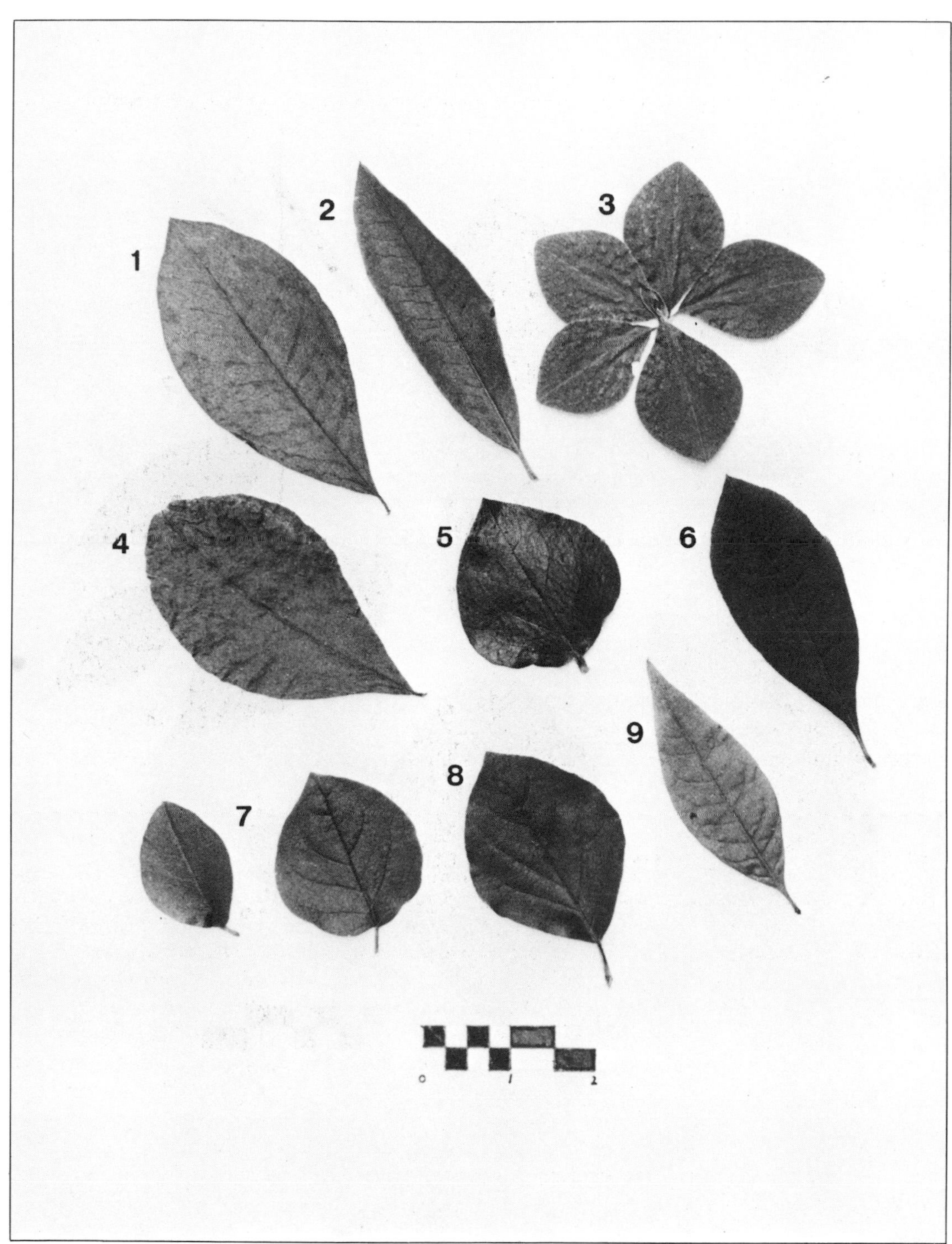

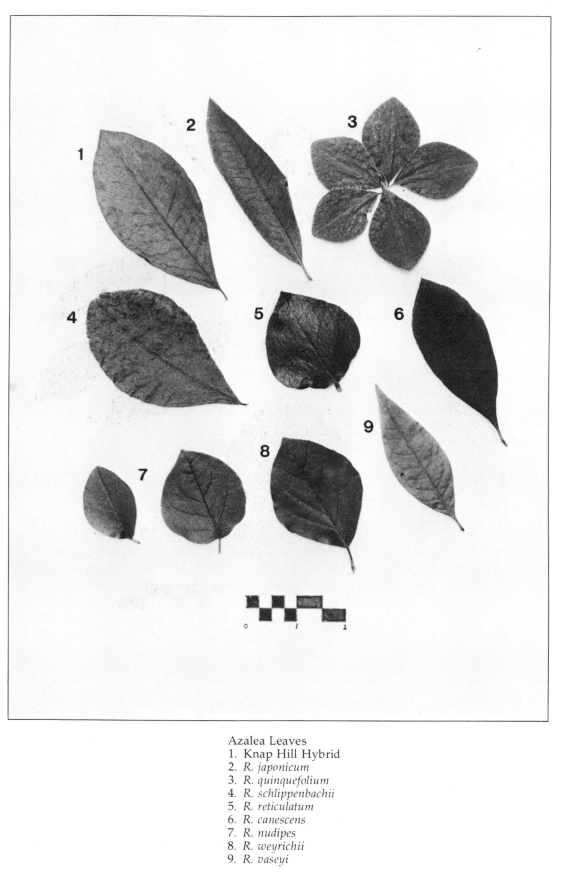

Azalea Leaves
1. Knap Hill Hybrid
2. *R. japonicum*
3. *R. quinquefolium*
4. *R. schlippenbachii*
5. *R. reticulatum*
6. *R. canescens*
7. *R. nudipes*
8. *R. weyrichii*
9. *R. vaseyi*

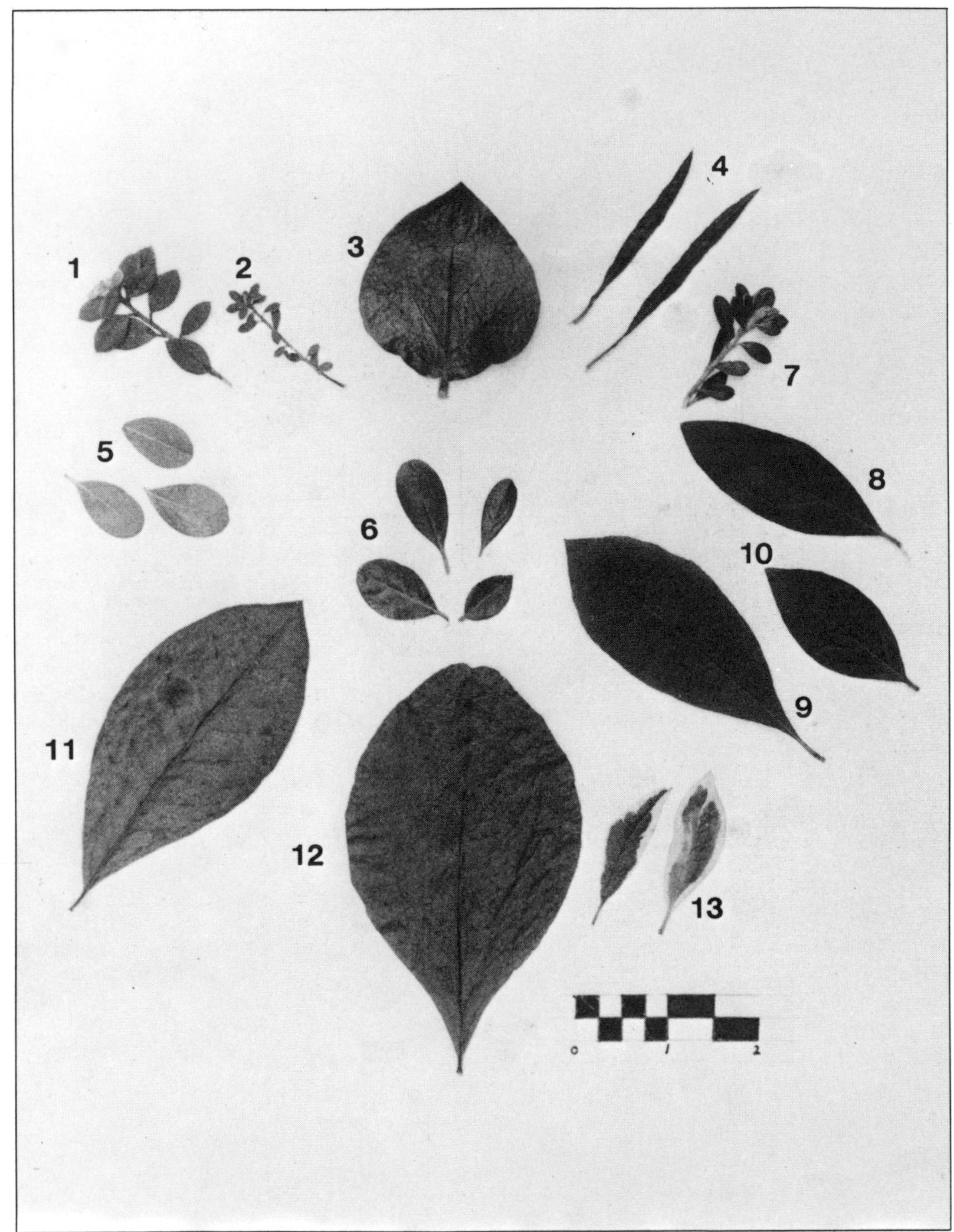

Azalea Leaves

1. *R. nakaharai*
2. *R. serphyllifolium*
3. *R. reticulatum*
4. *R. macrosepalum linearifolium*
5. *R. sataense*
6. Kurume Hybrids
7. *R. kiusianum*
8. *R. simsii*
9. *R. canescens*
10. *R. indicum*
11. Knap Hill Hybrid
12. *R. schlippenbachii*
13. Southern Belle (variegated)

LEAF COLOR

Leaves vary from the light green of the deciduous azaleas to the dark green of the summer leaves of many evergreen azaleas. White to light flowered azaleas usually have lighter green leaves and generally display less fall coloration and remain green, for example, 'Snow', 'Glacier', and 'Coral Bell'. Thus, from a planting of small seedlings, one can pick out those which will be light pink or white by the winter color of leaves.

The fall coloring of deciduous azaleas ranges from pure yellow through crimson to vinous-purple. The leaves of many evergreen azaleas through the fall and winter are green flecked with bronze or rust or carry red or dark red leaves. This is more common in the red to purple flowered cultivars. For example, the Glenn Dale Azaleas 'Campfire', 'Copperman', 'Fashion', 'Glamour', 'Kathleen', 'Phoebe', 'Refulgence', 'Rhapsody', 'Winner', and 'Zealot' display fall coloration in bronze or copper shades. Often the fall coloration occurs on both sides of the leaf with the under surface being lighter; in other cases the lower surface remains green.

A few years ago azaleas with variegated foliage were uncommon save for a few Satsuki cultivars such as 'Keisetsu' and 'Ukinishiki' with light yellow blotches scattered on the dark green foliage. A marginal variegated plant of *R. simsii* PI 391401, NA 36749, was first introduced to the University of California Botanical Garden in Berkeley from the U.S.D.A. and National Arboretum now believed to be sold as 'Purple Tabor' and other names. Two variegated Satsuki azaleas introduced from Japan are 'Shirafuji' and 'Murasakifuji'. In the 1980's four marginal variegated plants were introduced in the United States: 'Southern Bell', a sport of 'Pink Ruffles' and 'Red Ruffles Variegated'; 'Silver Streak', a Greenwood hybrid which is a sport of 'Deep Purple'; 'Girard's Variegated Gem', a sport of 'Border Gem'; and 'Silver Sword', a sport of 'Girard's Rose'. The latter turns a beautiful reddish tint in the fall while the others retain their greenness. A freckled leaf sport of 'Southern Charm' was introduced in the late 70's.

Variegated deciduous azaleas are very uncommon. A seedling was reported from Ohio but later died. The author has a two-year seedling of a North American azalea cross with both marginal and flecked variations of the foliage. A marginal variegated plant of *R. canescens* was collected in North Florida in 1981 by Bob McCartney of Aiken, S. C.

LEAF ARRANGEMENT

Azalea leaves are borne either alternately on the stem or in a spiral pattern. The spirals are often condensed, with the leaves crowded at the tip of the branches so they appear to be star-like whorls. In certain species, leaf arrangements become one of the main attractions. The following azaleas have whorls of five leaves at the end of the branches: Cork azalea *R. quinquefolium,* Five Leaf Azalea *R. pentaphyllum,* and Royal Azalea *R. schlippenbachii.* Many evergreen species, such as *R. kaempferi,* have leaves crowded at the ends of branches but without the appearance of whorls.

LEAF HAIRINESS

The function of leaf hairs is a matter of conjecture, and in fact may be a relic or subsidiary appendage making no special contribution to the well-being of the plant.

The pubescence or indumentum of azalea leaves is sparse compared with the leaves of many other species of *Rhododendron.* Some azalea leaves are glabrous, bald or not hairy, at maturity. Some have hairs only on the underside of the leaves along the veins. The pubescence of azalea leaves consists of hairs which may be straight or sometimes curly, but never branched, and usually closely adpressed to the surface of the leaf. The hairs are visible to the naked eye, and with a hand lens or low powered microscope one can see that they are flattened or laminated and not cylindrical. The hairs may be of uniform size, or as in the Piedmont Azalea *R. canescens,* may occur as a dense, felty pubescence of numerous, whitish and relatively short hairs, interspaced with occasional longer, thicker and more bristle-like hairs or setae which impart a strigose character to the leaf surface.

Bristle-like setae are usually sharp-pointed. But in some species such as the Coastal Azalea *R. atlanticum* and the Alabama Azalea *R. alabamense,* they are gland tipped (glandular setae), which cause the leaves to be sticky as they first unfold. Under the microscope these bulbous glands vary within plants of the same species from straw-yellow, through pink to deep red. Occasionally, small insects are trapped upon the sticky glands.

Hairs of azalea leaves may vary from yellow through bluish green to reddish. On young leaves, particularly of 'Indica Alba' and its allies and the Piedmont Azalea *R. canescens,* Roseshell Azalea *R. prinophyllum* and others, the hairs may be nearly white.

The Oldham Azalea *R. oldhamii* is one of the hairiest azalea species with conspicuous reddish brown hairs on both sides of the leaves and stems. The leaves of *R. rubropilosum* are also covered with numerous short hairs typically reddish brown in color. Some azaleas have hairs on both sides of the leaf such as 'Indica Alba', while others are hairy only on the underside such as the Big Sepal Azalea *R. macrosepalum.*

LEAF GLAUCESCENCE

Leaves of some species, such as *R. canadense,* have a gray waxy covering or bloom on the underside. Such leaves are said to be glaucous, like the skin of some plums. The bloom can be rubbed off. In some species as the Swamp Azalea *R. viscosum* and the Coastal Azalea *R. atlanticum,* some individuals have glaucous leaves while others do not. Plants with glaucous leaves occur haphazardly throughout the population so glaucescence is not a clear segregating characteristic. Unfortunately, it has been used by botanists as the basis for varietal status.

Without a hand lens, glaucescence and fine white hairs are easily confused, since both give the underside of a leaf a gray appearance. Like hairs, the function of glaucescence is not known.

LEAF ODOR

The leaves of many azaleas when opening in the spring have an unpleasant musky odor. This is usually noted in early morning or in the confined air of a warm place such as a greenhouse.

The Chinese and Japanese azaleas *R. molle* and *R. japonicum* and their hybrid offspring have foliage that is noticeably odoriferous in hot summer weather.

The leaves of some azaleas, as the Sweet Azalea *R. arborescens,* when dry have a persistent vanilla- or coumarin-like fragrance. Fresh leaves of *R. arborescens* have a spicy fragrance when crushed.

5. SPECIES, HYBRIDS, CULTIVARS, AND CLONES (AND THEIR NAMES)

The azaleas at a nursery or in a garden may be a species, hybrid, cultivar, or a clone selected from either a species or hybrid group. It is important to have an understanding of these categories when purchasing a particular azalea or reading about a new azalea in a catalog or in this book.

THE SPECIES

A species (the term is both singular and plural) is a group of individual plants, which are fundamentally alike, indicating a high level of genetic relationship. The species concept is often criticized and under continuing review by botanists as it cannot be defined in exact terms. In a study of a population of native plants, one must take into account, that no two plants are ever alike. The forces of nature and hereditary variances are important in the phenotype of a species.

A distinct population of native plants is given a collective name composed of the genus, and a species epithet, or name, both in a latinized form. Thus, the North American Western Azalea is named *Rhododendron occidentale* (Torr. & A. Gray) A. Gray. In this book it is abbreviated as *R. occidentale.* The various species within any one genus, such as *Rhododendron,* are in theory and fact separated from each other by different taxonomic combinations of reasonable distinct characteristics.

Unlike the generic name, the species epithets are lower case letters unless derived from personal names such as *R. Schlippenbachii,* the royal azalea. The International Code of Botanical Nomenclature *recommends,* however, that all specific names be lower case; thus, *R. schlippenbachii.* This recommendation is followed in this book.

SUBSPECIES, VARIETIES AND FORM

The natural variations found within a population of plants can be formally described as a subspecies, variety (varietas), and form (forma). These terms are often confusing to the gardener, and their usage varies, even among taxonomists.

A subspecies, while seldom used with azalea, is considered a major variation within the species, often a geographically distinct population such as *R. viscosum montanum* but also listed as *R. viscosum* var. *montanum*.

The term variety is applied to a lesser variation in the species. Thus the white glacous leaf forms of *R. canescens* are designated as a botanical variety *R. canescens* var. *candidum*.

Horticulturists often use the term indiscriminately to distinguish them from the pubescent leaf species form and incorrectly to describe horticultural varieties of cultivars instead of botanical varieties. Some botanists assign these important variations in morphological form and geographical distribution a varietial status (var.) while others use the term subspecies.

The classification forma (f.) is used to describe more local or sporadic variations of flower color on plant habit such as *R. canadense f. albiflorum* and *R. serpyllifolium f. albiflorum*.

CLONES AND CULTIVARS

A plant grown from seed or dug up in the wild, depending upon the variability of the particular species, variety or form, may not be identical to the parent plants or plants of the same species. To preserve a desirable feature of the plant, selected for its particular kind of flower, leaf or plant habit, it must be propagated vegetatively by cuttings, grafts, layers, divisions, or tissue culture. Such a plant is called a clone or horticulturally, a cultivar.

A clone is a genetically uniform plant propagated by asexual or vegetative means. A clone is a horticultural (man made) rather than a taxonomic (natural) distinction and should not be used for plants raised from seed.

The term cultivar, as described in the International Code of Nomenclature for Cultivated Plants, 1980, denotes an assemblage of cultivated plants which are distinguished by any character (morphological, cytological, or others) and which, when reproduced (sexually or asexually), retain their distinguishing characteristics.

Most horticulturists, unfortunately, do not distinguish between the terms cultivar, variety, and clone. *Hortus III* states—'A cultivar is a horticultural variety or race that has originated and persisted under cultivation not necessarily referable to a botanical species, and of botanical and horticultural importance, requiring a name'. The azalea 'Glacier', when propagated vegetatively by cuttings, can be called a clone or cultivar (or cultivated variety). This can be confusing, for an azalea clone is a cultivar but not all cultivar plants such as named pansy plants grown from seed are clones.

At present, we do not have a true breeding azalea, so all clonally propagated azaleas can be called cultivars or horticultural varieties. A cultivar and clonal name is clearly distinguished by the abbreviation cv. before the capitalized name, or preferably by enclosing it within single quotation marks, such as 'Glacier'.

It is not known whether a clone is permanently immortal or whether there is some overall limit to longevity to the line. Some clones have disappeared due to disease or by failure to propagate vegetatively. Some nurserymen are concerned that a clone can "run out". This could happen with a popular cultivar that is continually propagated from cutting-grown plants such as 'Christmas Cheer', 'Hinodegiri', and others that are propagated by the thousands. Cuttings for next year's crop are taken from liners or container grown plants established in the previous year, often without seeing the plants in flower. Maintaining stock blocks of original plants or comparing plants with an existing cultivar in an arboretum or botanical garden should be done periodically to prevent "running out" or clonal drift.

HYBRID GROUPS

The majority of today's showy garden azaleas are hybrids, resulting from crosses between parents of different species, varieties, or forms, or between parents of different hybrid groups. The individual plants grown from seed of any such cross are not identical in the way clonally propagated plants are. Repeating a hybrid cross such as 'Glacier' (*Malvatica* × *Yozakura*) or interbreeding of the individuals derived from it, usually makes for additional variation.

A *grex hybrida* (literally a hybrid group) is an English term seldom used in North America, but given to a total seedling population of a cross of species or hybrids. Such poly-hybrids (abbr.=polybred) can be given a hybrid group name referring to the total seedling variations and not to individual clones within the group. For example, grex names were given to the old hybrid groups such as Mortier hybrids × Mortieri (*R. calendulaceum* × *nudiflorum*) and Viscosepalum hybrids or × Viscosepala (*R. molle* × *R. viscosum*) now included in the Ghent hybrids or × Gandavense. Plants often listed as a hybrid group such as Ghent hybrids may only be seedling-grown plants. Desirable individuals of a hybrid group are selected out, propagated vegetatively, and given a clonal name—such as—Ghent hybrid-'Daviesi'.

The great variability inherent in azaleas makes clonally propagated plants of special importance. It behooves the azalea enthusiast to know whether he is buying a seedling of a clonal (vegetatively propagated) plant. A seedling grown plant may be listed only with the species name or hybrid group—for example, *R. calendulaceum,* Flame Azalea or Knaphill Azalea or Knaphill hybrid seedling. An asexually propagated plant is listed with the clone name such as *R. calendulaceum* 'Colossus', or Knaphill hybrid 'Gibraltar', or just 'Colossus' or 'Gibraltar'.

NAMING NEW PLANTS

To name a plant is a responsibility and should be done for markedly improved or quality plants. A good name can serve to promote or sell the plant, be easy to remember, and be an attractive euphonic name. It is important to avoid duplication of names and as an aid to so doing, the name should be registered. Following registration a complete description of the plant named should be published.

Information on specialized nomenclature problems relating to cultivated plants is available in the *International Code of Nomenclature for Cultivated Plants* (I. C. N. C. P.) (Brickell 1980). The I. C. N. C. P. is published under the auspices of the International Horticultural Congress which has the right to invite plant societies and institutions in one country or another to serve as International Registration Authorities. Currently Registration Authority for over 60 genera have been designated. To locate the Registrar for a particular genus, write the Arnold Arboretum, Jamaica Plain, Mass., USA, the National Arboretum in Washington, D.C., USA, or the Royal Horticultural Society in London, England. For example, the American Rose Society registers new rose names for rose breeders everywhere in the world. The American Hemerocallis Society and American Holly Society do the same for these genera.

The Royal Horticultural Society of Great Britain is the authority for international registration of *Rhododendron* and *Azalea.* Dr. Alan C. Leslie of Wisley Gardens in England is the registrar and is responsible for accepting new names and maintaining a permanent registration file of these names. The Society published in 1958 *The International Rhododendron Register* which lists names of both Rhododendron and Azalea that have been validly published up to September 1, 1958. A new *Register* is in process now and should be published by 1988. New Rhododendron and Azalea developed in the United States can be registered with the American Rhododendron Society, which in turn checks these names with the

Royal Horticultural Society. Information and registration cards (fee, $3.00) are available from Mrs. J. W. Murray, 21 Squire Terrace, Colts Neck, N.J. 07722 U.S.A. Names so registered and a description of the plant are published in the *Journal* of the American Rhododendron Society and the *Rhododendron and Camellia Yearbook* at the R. H. S.

This book contains, in the appendix, the names of all azaleas registered and also contains elsewhere (check Index of Azaleas by name) the names and descriptions of all azaleas that appear in *The International Rhododendron Register* and are believed to be still in existence and available. In addition, the names of nonregistered clones that do not appear in *The International Rhododendron Register* and its supplements are described in the Index of Azaleas.

Hopefully, the reasons for registration are evident. Frequent confusion has arisen in the past from use of the same clonal or common name for plants of different origins and produced by different breeders. Favorite names have often been used too frequently. For example, 'Favorite' has been used for Rhododendron clones as well as for a Ghent, a Mollis, an Indian, a Glenn Dale, and a Kaempferi Azalea. Other names such as 'Dawn', 'Gloria', 'Pink Beauty', 'Pink Lady', 'Rosebud', and many others have been used for two or more different azaleas. No gardener could order a plant of any of these names with assurance as to what cultivar will turn up, unless the group names is included. There are also names that are very similar such as 'Jeanne' and 'Jeannia', 'Bette' and 'Betty'. Very long names such as 'Mme. Caroline Legreele d'Hanis' and others are often misspelled or long names abbreviated and modified in different lists and catalogs until eventually we cannot be sure what a given plant name is. It is problems of this sort that international registration is meant to solve.

Breeders and introducers are not obligated to register their azaleas, and often the names of patented plants are not registered which only adds to the problem of the ultimate consumer—the gardener. Hopefully, the value of registration is now recognized so the confusion and mistakes of the past can be prevented in the future.

GUIDE TO REGISTRATION

The International Code of Nomenclature for Cultivated Plants (Brickell 1980) is available from the American Horticultural Society. It is an excellent reference in the naming of plants and should be in the hands of every breeder.

Some of the general rules governing clone and cultivar names are as follows:

1. New azaleas should be introduced only as clones and should be vegetatively propagated.
2. New clonal or cultivar names published after 1 January 1959 must be fancy names in any modern language and not in Latin form.
3. Clonal names, when following a botanical or common name, must be distinguished by the abbreviation cl. or enclosed in single quotes such as *R. austrinum* 'Millie Mac.' Two or more cultivars in the same genus are not permitted to have the same name.
4. Similar names which differ only slightly in spelling from existing names should be avoided.
5. New names should preferably consist of one or two words and must not consist of more than three words; an abbreviation or numeral is counted as a word.
6. Clonal names *cannot* be formed by combining parts of the Latin or species name. (such as *R. austatlantic*).

7. Avoid names, if possible, composed of abbreviations, numerals, or arbitrary sequence of letters.
8. Avoid proper names.
9. Spell out words instead of abbreviating except for the abbreviation 'Mrs.' (Example: 'Mountain Laurel' not Mtn. Laurel).
10. Avoid names exaggerating the merits of the cultivar which may become inaccurate through the introduction of new cultivars. (Example: Azalea 'Earliest Flower' or 'Largest Blossom.')
11. Avoid names that refer to some attribute likely to be common in other cultivars. (Example: Azalea 'Yellow Princess' not 'Yellow.')
12. Cultivar names in another language should be left unchanged. Translated names are regarded as the original name. (Example: 'Amagasa' and 'Gumpo' are Satsuki cultivars translated into romanized Japanese script.)

New azalea names are not recognized under the code unless they are officially registered and the name and description published. The parentage of new azaleas should be given when known, with the female parent listed first. In some countries the parentage often is listed in reverse or alphabetical order and the sex of each parent is indicated. (Example: 'Bright Star' ('Linda Jean' × 'Hahns Red') or 'Hahns Red'♂ × 'Linda Jean'♀). The description should include name of the originator and/or introducer, flower type, size, foliage characteristics, plant habit, and a season of bloom.

With a little imagination we should never run out of suitable names. For stimulation one only needs to look at other International Registers such as the list of roses, narcissus, and hemerocallis for ideas.

The important thing is to register new names to avoid the confusion and duplication of names so common in the past.

SECTION III

6. AZALEA LISTS

The Azalea lists are divided into two major groups, Deciduous Azaleas, Chapter 7 and Evergreen Azaleas, Chapter 8. The basic divisions and major groups are as follows:

DECIDUOUS

- Subgenus *Pentanthera*
- Subseries *Luteum*
  - Species
  - Hybrid Groups
    - Ghents
    - Mollis
    - Occidentale
    - Knap Hill (including Exbury, Ilam and others)
    - North American Clones and Hybrids
    - Inter-Group Hybrids

EVERGREEN

- Subgenus *Tsutsutsi*
- Subseries *Obtusum*
  - Species
  - Hybrid Groups
    - Belgian Indian
    - Southern Indian
    - Kurume
    - Kaempferi
    - Satsuki
      - Inter-Group Hybrids (Gable, Glenn Dale and others)

When seeking the description of a particular azalea, turn to the Index of Azaleas, Appendix I, for the page reference. Group names are also included in the Index.

DESCRIPTIONS

All available information will be found under the species or hybrid group heading. The descriptions include in summary form name of the clone, information on hybridizer and/or introducer, flower type, size, color, habit of growth, blooming period, and other major characteristics. Occasionally not all of this information is available so the description may give only a flower color.

Names of clones that have been lost to cultivation or were never generally distributed have been omitted. Old Azalea names may be found in the *International Rhododendron Register* published in 1958 and 1988 by the Royal Horticultural Society. A list of all registered azaleas will be found in Appendix H.

Flower Type, Size and Color

A special type of flower such as Hose-in-Hose, Semidouble, or Double will be noted; single flowers will not.

Size is expressed by width in inches; this characteristic as well as color may vary due to growing conditions and also from season to season.

Color names are taken whenever possible from the National Bureau of Standards (N.B.S.) Special Publication 440, *Color Universal Language and Dictionary.* The *Royal Horticultural Society Colour Chart* (R.H.S.) number and names will be given when available, for example, light yellow 14D, vivid red 45A, etc. Thus, many of the poetic and old non-descriptive color names will be changed to a N.B.S. color name. It is hoped that this practice will encourage a new standard for describing color. See Chapter 4.

The recorded color of an azalea flower is not absolute. The intensity of pigmentation in any clone will vary from year to year at the same site due to climatic or enviornmental factors. Altitude, temperature, light, soil chemistry, and abnormal growing conditions such as drought all have an effect on the flower color.

Plant Habit

The height for a mature plant in ten years, when known, will be given as low (up to 3 feet), medium (3 to 6 feet) and large (over 6 feet.) Other descriptive terms will be used, such as *upright* (erect-taller than broad), *spreading* (erect and broader than tall), and *compact* (dense and twiggy.) As plants mature, the habit of growth may also change. Many upright plants tend to fill out and spread, and many upright spreading plants tend to overarch. The same clone, on the West coast of North America, England, and Japan is generally lower growing than in the East or Australia. By the same token, a specific clone in colder climates is lower growing than in warmer climates. Plants grown in the shade are generally taller than those in the sun.

Hardiness Zones

The hardiness zones are given as guidelines to the adaptability of a plant; for more information see Chapter 9.

The Plant Name

In the list of botanical names a species is in italics or in capitals. The authority name will only be used in the description of species. In a list the name may appear either as:

R. calendulaceum Flame Azeala

or

CALENDULACEUM (Flame Azalea)

Synonyms, abbreviated syn., or alternate botanical or common names are placed in parentheses. Clonal names should properly be enclosed in single 'quotes.'

Some azaleas have been given one or more names; for example, Southern Indian hybrid 'Elegans Superba' (syn. 'Pride of Mobile') and 'Lawsal' (syn.'Pride of Summerville', 'Daphne Salmon' and 'Illuminator').

Substitute English names have also been given to many of the Kurume azaleas introduced from Japan. This is an unwise and confusing practice which only complicates nomenclature, for the Japanese name is a transliteration of the valid name and should be used. Consequently, the English substitute name is placed in parentheses—i.e. Kurume 'Hinode Giri' (syn. 'Red Hussar') and 'Kirin' (syn. 'Daybreak', 'Coral Bells', 'Pink Beauty'.) For some azaleas this has been difficult to accept so 'Coral Bells' will be used instead of 'Kirin', 'Pink Pearl' for 'Azuma Kagami' and many others. It is interesting to note that some azalea hybrids originating in the United States are given Oriental and Japanese names.

A "P.I." number after or in lieu of a name refers to a plant inventory number and indicates the plant was introduced by the United States Department of Agriculture. This is often abbreviated P.I. USDA or more simply P.I. The number identifies the plant in the Plant Inventory pamphlets and publications by the Department. 'P.I.' is an abbreviation for "Plant Inventory."

A "B.G." number refers to a plant introduced by Brookside Gardens in Maryland, U.S.A. (see Satsuki List)

The following explanatory examples will help the reader understand the structure of the lists.

DESCRIPTIVE LIST STRUCTURE

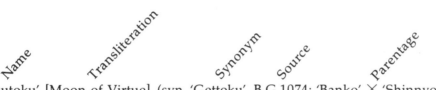

'Getsutoku' [Moon of Virtue] (syn. 'Gettoku', B.G.1074; 'Banko' × 'Shinnyono Tsuki'):

'Amagasa' [Umbrella] (syn. 'Tengasa'; seedling of 'Huzan'):

'Gumpo' [A group of Phoenixes] (syn. 'Gunpo', origin unknown, early 1900's):

'April Showers' (syn.'Apricot Falls'; 'Purple Weeper'× 'Trailing Queen'; Domoto):

'Clara Brown' ('Macrantha Orange' × 'Caldwellii'; D.Stewart '62):

'Anna Pavlova' (KH.; Kraus, intro. by Beneschoen '67)

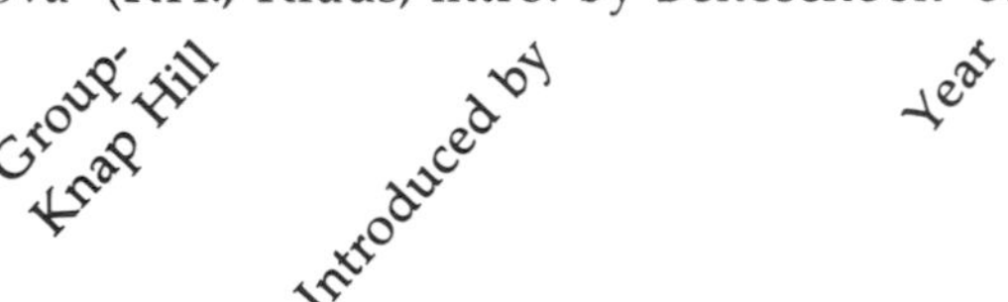

A NOTE ON HYBRIDIZING AND INTRODUCING NEW CULTIVARS

The hybridizing and selection of new azalea cultivars have taken great strides in the last twenty years. Literally hundreds of new azaleas have been named and introduced throughout the world. The largest number of introductions has come from hybridizers and nurseries located in Eastern and Southeastern U.S.A., Australia, and New Zealand, probably due to more nearly ideal climate, particularly for the use of evergreen azaleas in the landscape and azalea production by commercial growers. Europe, Western U.S.A. and the Orient are more restrained in introducing new azaleas. Hybridizers in the latter regions tend to test and evaluate their progeny for years before naming and registering. As the climate is often less ideal for evergreen azaleas, particularly in Europe and Northwestern U.S.A., selection, naming, and registering is done more carefully. In Japan many selections and sports of Satsuki, Kurume, and Hirado Azalea are still being named; but after all they have been growing and naming azaleas for over three hundred years. New and different cultivars are still desired—cold hardy evergreen azaleas are still challenges for the hybridizer.

Some countries or societies require testing at Research Stations and Gardens, and plants are evaluated for awards before introduction to the commercial world is permitted. It is being said by those using more rigorous standards of classification that some azalea hybridizers are on ego trips in naming all their seedlings. Whether this is true or not is to some degree in the eye of the beholder. Certainly more testing and evaluation of new introductions in different climatic zones would be of great value to the gardener in selecting plant for his garden. Registration of new cultivars is certainly a step in the right direction, not only to eliminate duplicate names but to have a record of parentage and a complete description of the plant. The lack of complete information is reflected in this book. Years of correspondence have proved no substitute for proper testing, description, and registration. On the other hand we have been the beneficiaries of years of devoted work by many conscientious hybridizers-nurserymen who have properly tested, evaluated, and registered new plants—again reflected in this book. We still have dedicated plantsmen often working in less than ideal climatic zones to develop more cold hardy and adaptable plants for their areas.

But economics is taking its toll. Many nurserymen cannot devote time and valuable land to the long term investment required in breeding and evaluating new cultivars. So unhappily they stay with the "bread and butter" items to meet the demands of the general gardening public seeking instant color. Consequently, dedicated amateur azalea enthusiasts are assuming a larger role in hybridizing. It is hoped that commercial growers will at least stay current with new plant introductions from research stations around the world, consult with local amateur azalea hybridizers, and stay in touch with the Azalea and Rhododendron Chapters in their area or climatic zones as to recommended azaleas and rhododendrons.

In a brief discussion with Joe Gable many years ago relative to the large number of azaleas being named and introduced he commented, "Some folks are really wasting good names." It is to be hoped that we will not waste good names but rather weed out the less than first-rate plants and only name and register our best.

7. DECIDUOUS AZALEAS

The first account of deciduous azalea goes back to fourth century (B.C.) Greece and relates the poisoning of 10,000 soldiers by honey of *R. luteum (Azalea pontica)*. The story is retold by both Pliny and Dioscorides. Joseph Pitton de Tournefort of Aix-en-Provence, France observed the plant in the Levant in 1700 but found no evidence that the legend was correct. He brought back a drawing but did not collect plants or seed.

Rhododendron poisoning has since been confirmed repeatedly. The poisonous compound is actylandromedal found in rhododendron nectar. It produces depression of blood pressure, shock, and finally death.

Peter Simon Pallas of Berlin in 1793 sent seed of the Pontic Azalea *R. luteum (Azalea pontic)* to nurserymen in England, but the plants were received with little interest, for the then formal style of gardening had focused on plants possessed of a formal habit.

R. viscosum was the first azalea grown in England in 1680 by Bishop Henry Compton from seed collected by John Bannister, a missionary in Virginia. In the same year *R. indicum (Azalea indica)* was introduced to Holland. The drawing by Bannister was labeled "Cistus virginiana flore et odore Periclymeni" which translated: "Virginia rock rose with flowers and odor of honeysuckle".

John Bartram, the first outstanding North American plantsman, collected plants for Peter Collinson of England in the early to mid-1700's. He is credited with introducing three azaleas to England; the two recorded were *R. viscosum* and *R. nudiflorum*, and it is presumed that the third was *R. calendulaceum*, William Bartram's 'Fiery Azalea', now commonly called the 'Flame Azalea'.

In 1823 a box of plants containing *R. molle (Azalea sinensis)*, the Chinese Azalea, arrived in England for a nurseyman of Hackney. In 1830 Dr. Phillip Fran von Siebold, a German doctor was forced to leave Japan and returned with several plants, including *R. japonicum*, known at that time as *Azalea mollis*, but incorrectly named by von Siebold as *Azalea sinensis (R. molle)*. Von Siebold was impressed with the similarity of these two plants and gave the plants of *R. japonicum (A. mollis)* the name *Azalea sinensis*. Unhappily the two species have been mixed and confused ever since.

The sources of von Siebold's plants are unknown; possibly they were derived from a garden but more likely were collected in the wild. The Japanese were more interested in the evergreen azaleas, and they thought *R. japonicum (mollis)* a plant of ill omen. It was mentioned as a garden plant in a Japanese book written in 1488 which indicated that it had been in cultivation 50 years before.

Azaleas when first introduced to Europe were grown as greenhouse plants, for they were thought to be unsuited for the formal gardens of the time. Later, as the fashion in landscapes moved to the natural and informal, azaleas began to find their place in gardens. The early Ghents, Mollis, and Knaphill hybrids were developed from greenhouse grown introductions.

In 1857 the Veitch Nursery flowered *R. occidentale* from seed collected by William Lobb in California, U.S.A.. This plant with its large, fragrant flowers in great trusses was the major contribution to the modern Knap Hill and Exbury azaleas.

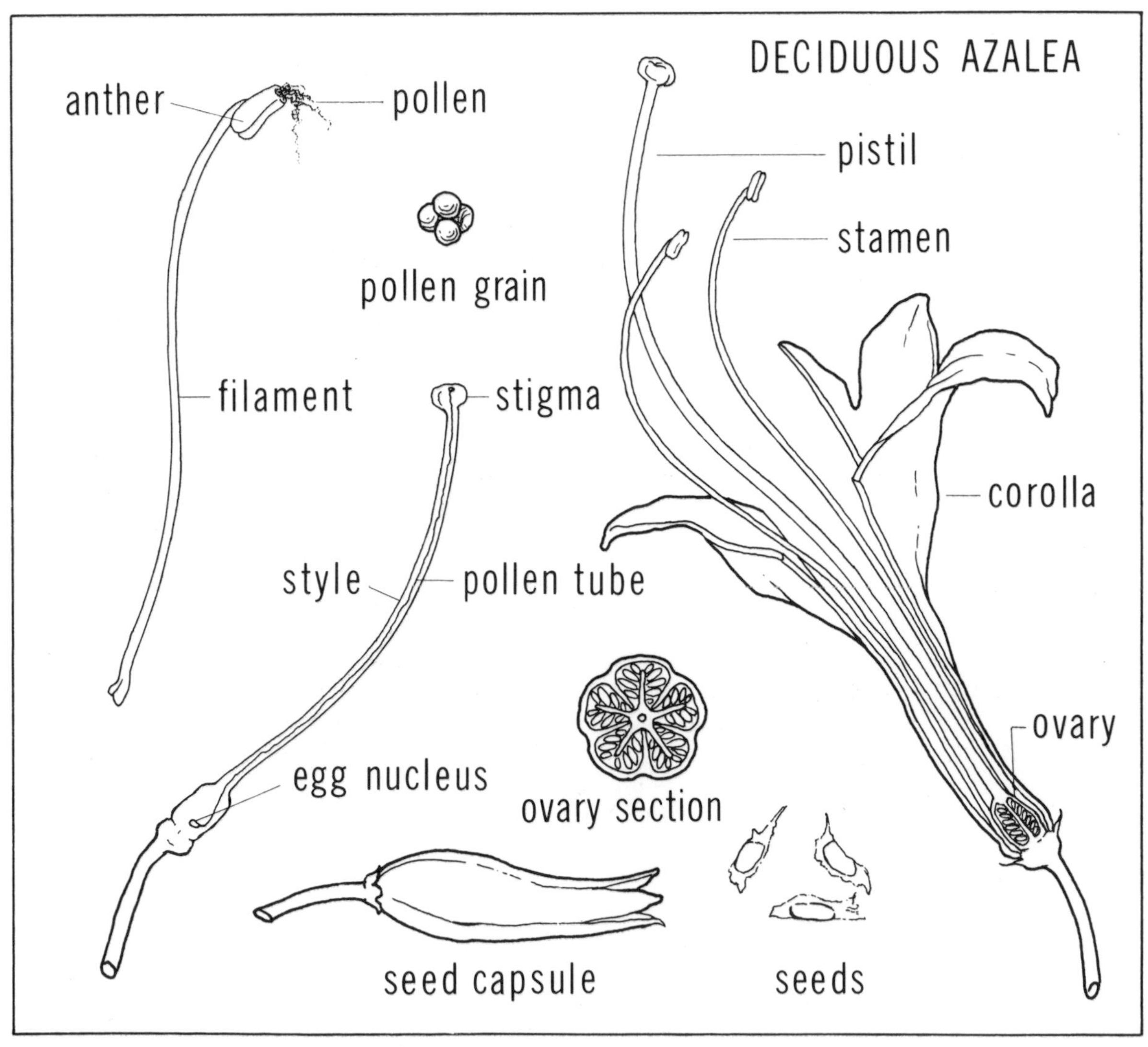

THE DECIDUOUS SPECIES OF AZALEA

The deciduous Azalea species are found in the following subseries: *Luteum, Canadense, Nipponicum, Schlippenbachii,* and *Farrerae.* The following description of deciduous *Azalea* species is organized by subseries.

LUTEUM SUBSERIES (Section *Pentanthera*)

The *Luteum* subseries includes three species—*R. japonicum, R. molle,* and *R. luteum* from outside North America and all the North American deciduous species except *R. canadense* and *R. vaseyi.* The type species for the subseries is *R. luteum* of southeastern Europe and western Asia.

The native North American species of deciduous azaleas have often been called the most beautiful of all indigenous plants. In North America they occupy two distinct geographical areas: 1. on the Atlantic coast extending from southern Quebec to central Florida and west to Vermont, eastern Ohio, southeastern Oklahoma, and eastern Texas; and 2. on the Pacific coast from southern Oregon to southern California.

The flowers are easily distinguished by the funnelform, subregular corolla of five petals, a distinct cylindrical tube, longer or shorter than the lobes, five exserted stamens, and a wide variation in flower color, ranging from white to yellow, orange, red, pink, and purplish pink. The deciduous leaves vary from nearly glabrous to finely pubescent. The branches in most species are usually pubescent and only glabrous in *R. arborescens* and *R. prunifolium.*

The relationship and hence identification of the eastern North American species has not been clear, and investigation is still in progress. The common alliances formulated by Skinner and Lee in *The Azalea Book* will be followed. Dr. Bruce King, in a study of the leaf flavonoids of the North American species, arranged the species into five groups based on biochemical data correlated with morphological features. For comparison of these two groupings see the following table.

The Grouping of Azalea in the *Luteum* Series by Alliances

SKINNER-LEE		KING*	
1. *Austrinum-Prunifolium* Alliance		Group I	
R. austrinum	*R. prunifolium*	*R. austrinum-R. occidentale*	
R. bakeri	*R. flammeum*	Group II	
R. calendulaceum	*R. luteum*	*R. bakeri*	*R. prunifolium*
2. *Alabamense-Atlanticum* Alliance		*R. calendulaceum*	*R. flammeum (speciosum)*
R. alabamense	*R. atlanticum*	Group III	
3. *Roseum-Nudiflorum* Alliance		*R. nudiflorum*	*R. prinophylum (roseum)*
R. canescens	*R. occidentale*	*R. canescens*	
R. periclymenoides (nudiflorum)	*R. prinophyllum (R. roseum)*	Group IV	
		R. arborescens	*R. alabamense*
4. *Arborescens-Serrulatum* Alliance		Group V	
R. arborescens	*R. serrulatum*	*R. atlanticum*	*R. serrulatum*
R. oblongifolium	*R. viscosum*	*R. oblongifolium*	*R. viscosum*
5. *Molle-Japonicum* Alliance		*(R. coryi)*	
R. molle	*R. japonicum*		

*Only the North American species—see bibliography appendix.

For a number of years prior to his death in 1947, C.D. Beadle, Superintendent of the Biltmore Estate at Asheville, N.C., with his assistant, Sylvester Owens, traveled widely throughout the southeastern states in search of unusual forms of the *Azalea* species. Many of his collected plants are still growing in the Biltmore Gardens and his remarkable assemblage of some 3,000 herbarium specimens resides in the National Arboretum Herbarium, together with water color paintings of many of these forms and species by Porcher Johnson. A manuscript describing many of these forms as new species was unfortunately destroyed by Beadle just before his death.

Commencing in 1951 Henry T. Skinner, at the time with the Morris Arboretum of Philadelphia and later Director of the United States National Arboretum, Washington, D.C., conducted field investigations of the azaleas native to the eastern United States. His journeys covered some 27,000 miles of continuous collecting during blooming periods and constitute one of the most intensive and inclusive field examinations to which any group of plants has been subjected. Observations of the large number of plants and specimens collected (about 8,800) have provided a far better understanding of these species.

A manuscript derived from the extensive data on the Azalea spp. native to the southern United States collected by the late Dr. Sigmond L. Solymosy, *A Treatise of Native Azaleas,* was published after his death by the Louisiana Society for Horticultural Research, Volume 4, No. 2, 1976.

The author also conducted a study on the southeastern species for a doctoral thesis while on the horticultural staff at the University of Tennessee. Unfortunately seven years of field and laboratory notes were lost to a bear on Gregory Bald in the Great Smoky Mountain National Park. A similar study of the Western Azalea *R. occidentale* was undertaken by the late Leonard F. Frisbie of Puyallup, Washington. He studied the distribution and ecology, and selected unusual forms for future cultivation. Dr. Frank Mossman and Britt Smith of Washington are continuing the study of *R. occidentale.*

Accounts of these studies may be found in "In Search of Native Azaleas" by Henry T. Skinner in Morris Arboretum Bulletin, January and April, 1955 (reprinted in condensed form in *Rhododendron and Camellia Yearbook* 1957, Royal Horticultural Society) and in "Classification of Native American Azaleas" by the same author in the *Proceedings of the International Rhododendron Conference,* American Rhododendron Society, 1961. Information on *R. occidentale* is reported in *"Rhododendron Occidentale Survey"* by Leonard F. Frisbie and Edward P. Breakey, in *Rhododendrons,* the Tacoma Rhododendron Society, July-August, 1954. Additional studies and reports by Dr. Mossman and Smith have been published in the American Rhododendron Society Bulletins. The results of Hui-Lin Li's chromosome investigations based upon the Skinner collections are set forth in "Chromosome Studies in the Azaleas of Eastern North America," *American Journal of Botany,* January 1957.

Dr. B. King's research "The Flavonoids of the Deciduous Rhododendrons of North America" is recorded in *American Journal of Botany,* March 1977 and also a report in *Contributions Toward Classification of Rhododendrons,* International Rhododendron Conference May 1978. "The Species of Rhododendron Native to North America" by Dr. Martha Roane was published in the *Virginia Journal of Science* Summer 1981 with an amended version in the *American Rhododendron Society Journal* July 1983.

The following descriptions of North American azaleas are based on these studies and personal observations.

The deciduous azaleas were among the first to be introduced to gardens of this country and Europe. Early interest was stronger in Europe than in the United States. Throughout the southern U.S.A. they were known as bush or wild honeysuckle and are still so called today. They were reportedly difficult to transplant so the traditional use was as collected flowering branches in the spring. It is interesting to note the value of the common name given to *R. nudiflorum.* The early Dutch settlers in America when New York was New Amsterdam named *R. nudiflorum* Pinxterbloom for Pinxter, an old American word for Whetsuntide.

Fortunately, interest in native plants has been rekindled. Seedling and cutting grown plants are again more widely available commercially, and North American azaleas have made a return to the garden.

Most North American azaleas display a great diversity of color, habit of growth, and other characteristics; and there are numerous natural hybrids where their habitats overlap. Fortunately, many of these superior and unusual forms are being preserved not only by asexual propagation but also by hybridizing within the species and with other deciduous groups.

The early English, Belgian, and Dutch hybridizers had only a few of the North American species available for their work. With the superior forms available today, new deciduous intraspecific and intragroup hybrids are becoming available. Continued work along these lines should produce new deciduous Azalea hybrids and hybrid groups superior in quality and better suited to various climatic regions.

The descriptions of the species of the native deciduous azaleas are arranged in alliances rather than alphabetically.

AUSTRINUM-PRUNIFOLIUM ALLIANCE

These are the North American azaleas of the yellow-orange-red color range. The parents of this alliance must have included a *R. austrinum-bakeri* type, early flowering, highly glandular, with yellow to orange flowers and a *R. prunifolium* type, later flowering diploid relatively non-glandular with red flowers. Both are diploids possessing the usual 2n=26 chromosomes.

From two such parental types all members of this alliance could readily have been derived, including one or more orange flowered complexes of similar plants that are polyploids with 2n=52 chromosomes. Such complexes are conspicuous in the mountain regions. *R. calendulaceum* as generally recognized includes a major segment of these polyploid complexes and is therefore regarded as an important derived member rather than a basic member of the alliance.

R. austrinum (Small) Rehder. Florida Azalea

First discovered by Dr. A. W. Chapman before 1865 and referred to in his *Flora* as *R. nudiflorum*. It was recognized as distinct and described as species *A. austrina* by Dr. John K. Small in 1913.

A medium to tall branched shrub to 15 feet, indigenous to woods and stream-sides of northern Florida and the Georgia-Alabama coastal plains to southeastern Mississippi, among the first of the North American species to bloom. The flowers, appearing before the leaves, are 1″ to 1½″ across, fragrant, in clusters of 8 to 15. Flower tubes pubescent and glandular, occasionally semidouble or petaloid. Twigs are reddish brown, pubescent and the winter flower buds are grayish with dense pubescence. The elliptic to oblong obovate leaves are pubescent on both sides.

The less common form, with pure yellow flowers and yellow tubes, is probably the original type. The reddish tubes and darker petaled forms of today's more typical *R. austrinum* have probably resulted from long term gene exchange with *R. canescens*. It is very similar to and difficult to distinguish from *R. canescens*, when not in flower.

It was first introduced into cultivation by the Arnold Arboretum in 1914. It is hardy in zones 6b–10a and easy to propagate by soft wood cuttings.

R. bakeri (W. P. Lemon & McKay) H. Hume. (syn. *R. cumberlandense*). Cumberland Azalea

First described as *A. bakeri* by Lemon and McKay in 1937 from plants collected in North Georgia and named for Dr. Wilford Baker of Emory University, Atlanta, Ga., U.S.A. Described as *R. cumberlandense* by E. Lucy Baun in 1941 from plants of the Cumberland Mountains of Kentucky. Generally considered by most authorities as one species but still regarded by a few as two *separate* species. An irregular-branched shrub ranging from less than two to eight feet, or more in open woods at high elevations of the Cumberland Plateau in Kentucky south across Tennessee to the mountains of northern Georgia, Alabama, and the higher elevations of western North Carolina. It is questionable in the Blue Ridge Mountains as often defined.

A diploid (2N=26), flowers smaller, flower tubes narrower, and blooms two to four weeks later that *R. calendulaceum,* but has the same color range from yellow, orange, reddish orange, to red. The small flowers 1½ to 1¾" appear after leaves are mature in late June and early July, corolla type, pubescent, ridged and sparingly glandular. Filaments twice as long as tube and sparsely pubescent for about ⅜" beyond the throat of corolla tube. Leaves nearly glabrous above and glabrous to moderately pubescent beneath. Hardy in zones 5b–8b, and moderate to difficult to propagate by soft wood cuttings according to specific clones.

Occasional hybrids with *R. arborescens* occur in clear yellow and pinks: the name *R. furbishi* has been applied to this group from North Georgia. In the mountainous areas of southwestern North Carolina and northern Georgia it is often difficult to distinguish between the diploid *R. bakeri* and the tetraploid *R. calendulaceum.* Natural hybrids are often reported between these two species. However, there is very little cytological proof that triploid hybrids exist, and there may be very few with non-disjunction of the diploid pollen. The hybrids are probably all tetraploids.

'Camp's Red Azalea' is the name of early usage for a group of plants on the summit of Big Black Mountain in Kentucky. The plants can basically be assigned to *R. bakeri.* The group was named in honor of Dr. Wendell H. Camp (red-haired and known to his friends as Red Camp) who was among the first to recognize the distinctiveness of this red azalea of the Cumberland Plateau before the species epithet *R. bakeri* was applied. His plant specimens collected in the 1930's from Big Black Mountain are in the herbarium of the New York Botanical Gardens. 'Camp's Red' is also a registered name for a single clone of the group introduced by H. T. Skinner. Reproducible by cuttings, the clone carries a strong red color when grown in the mountains and lighter color at lower elevations, as in Washington, D.C. The color of the flowers of 'Camp's Red' is the strongest red of any plant of the group observed by H. T. Skinner.

R. calendulaceum (Michaux) Torrey. Flame Azalea

The 'Flame Azalea' of southern New York was first mentioned by Cadwallader Colden in 1799. Michaux collected it in the Blue Ridge Mountains of North Carolina in 1795 and called it *A. lutea.* The first introduction and cultivation is not certain. There is a firm report that John Lyon brought plants to England in 1806, but it may have been introduced before 1800. It is presumed that John Bartram sent plants of *R. calendulaceum* to Peter Collinson in the mid-1700's along with *R. viscosum* and *R. nudiflorum.* The Flame Azalea played an important role in the early development of the Ghent Hybrids.

William Bartram, the son of John, in his book *Travels,* published in 1791, called it the Fiery Azalea, the Sky Paint Flower of the Cherokee Indians. "The epithet fiery I annex to this most celebrated species of azalea, as being expressive of the appearance of its flowers which are in general of the colour of the finest red lead, orange, and bright gold, as well as yellow and cream colour; these various splendid colours are not only in separate plants, but frequently all the varieties and shades are seen in separate branches on the same plants; and the clusters of the blossoms cover the shrub in such incredible profusion on the hillsides, that suddenly opening to view from dark shades, we were alarmed with apprehension of the hill being set on fire." Bartram sums up: "This is certainly the most gay and brilliant flowering shrub yet known."

R. calendulaceum is a tall shrub up to 12 feet or more on open, woody hillsides of the Appalachian Mountains from southern New York, Pennsylvania, and Ohio as northern limits, south to northern Georgia and to the Piedmont region above the fall line. The Flame Azalea is a tetraploid (2n=52), with flowers larger than other species 1½"to 2½" across, a wide range of colors from clear yellow to yellowish orange, orange, reddish orange to vivid red; orange blotch on upper lobe; opening with or after the leaves; non-fragrant, tube pubescent and glandular. The orange-red to red forms of this species are usually from higher elevations and later flowering. Plants are generally non-stoloniferous with densely pubescent stems and glabrous winter flower buds. Hardy in zones 5b–8b, and moderate to difficult to propagate from soft wood cuttings.

R. luteum Sweet *(R. flavum, A. pontica)*. Pontic Azalea

Native to eastern Europe in the Caucasus-region and northeast to Lithuania and Poland. It was introduced into England in 1793 and to the Arnold Arboretum in 1892. It is closely allied to *R. austrinum* but may not be as heat tolerant; hardy in zones 6b–8a; densely branched shrub 10 to 12′, stems and flower buds pubescent. The fragrant, tubular flowers are yellow with a darker blotch, 1½″ and numerous in a truss. The stamens extend beyond the corolla. The species is not commonly grown in North America, but it has become naturalized in parts of the British Isles and was important in the development of the Ghent hybrids. The Pontic Azalea is usually moderate to difficult to propagate by soft wood cuttings.

R. flammeum (Michaux) Sargent [syn. *R. speciosum* (Willd.) Sweet]. Oconee Azalea.

The exact date of discovery and introduction of this species is not known. It was first described by Aiton in England in 1789 as *A. nudiflora* var. *coccinea.* Plants were possibly sent to England by William Bartram before 1789. It was collected by A. Michaux above Savannah, Georgia and referred to in his Flora as *A. calendulacea* var. *flammea.* In 1811 the plant was described by Willdenow as *A. speciosa* from cultivated plants growing in the Berlin Botanic Garden.

A low to tall shrub of open woods and slopes in a broad band of the lower Piedmont region across central Georgia to South Carolina. Flowers open with the leaves, after *R. austrinum* and before *R. calendulaceum;* non-fragrant, 1¼ to 1¾″ across, range from yellowish orange, orange to red, large orange blotch on upper lobe, slender tubes, pubescent and usually eglandular (without glands). Winter flower buds are glabrous, varying from one terminal bud to a cluster of flora buds on pubescent stems. Hardy in zones 6b–9a, and moderate to difficult to propagate by soft wood cuttings.

Colorful hybrids from *R. flammeum* × *R. canescens* and possibly other species are found where these species overlap, ranging from pale yellow to bicolors, yellowish pinks to deep pinks and generally all fragrant. The hybrid floral buds are often glabrous at the top but with pubescent scales at the base. Low stoloniferous forms are often found in the wild. This characteristic is often maintained in some plants while others outgrow it after being transplanted to other sites.

The Oconee Azalea is a plant of low elevation, heat tolerant, and should be important to plant breeders. The red form of this species remains good under cultivation, unlike the color forms of *R. bakeri* from high elevations.

Plants described as *R. fastigifolium* are probably hybrids of *R. flammeum* × *canescens* so the name should not be retained as a species and should instead be called *R.* ×*fastigifolium.*

R. prunifolium (Small) Millais. Plumleaf Azalea

This species was first collected by R. M. Harper near Cuthbert, Georgia in 1913, described by Small in 1913 as *A. prunifolia,* and introduced into cultivation in 1918 by the Arnold Arboretum.

A medium to large shrub to 15 feet or more, along shady ravines and stream-banks in southwestern Georgia and eastern Alabama. Blooms after the leaves are fully developed in July-September; non-fragrant, 1½ to 1¾″ across, usually reddish orange to vivid red, occasionally light orange; tubes sparingly hirsute and usually glandular. Winter flower buds, greenish to light brown and glabrous, are similar to *R. arborescens* which has lighter colored stems and winter flower buds.

Should be used in partial shade for the late flowers. Hardy in zones 7a-9b, and moderate to easy to propagate by soft wood cuttings.

ALABAMENSE-ATLANTICUM ALLIANCE

Plants in this alliance are usually white, fragrant, and tend to be stoloniferous.

R. alabamense Rehder. Alabama Azalea

First described by Dr. C. Mohr in 1883, as having a snowy white flower and identified as *A. nudiflora alba.*

A low to medium stoloniferous shrub of dry, steep, rocky hillsides usually in deciduous or mixed forest to north central Alabama and west central Georgia. Specimens have been collected in Calhoun County, South Carolina, south of Columbia, S. C. Tall plants, over six feet, have been collected in the coastal plains of Marion and Miller Counties in south Georgia in flat sandy areas. The fragrant flowers, borne with the leaves in late midseason two to three weeks after *R. canescens,* 7/8" to 1½" across; white with prominent yellow blotch, pure white forms rare; tubes glandular, with distinct lemony-spice fragrance, occasionally with petaloid stamens. Leaves often glaucous or pale green beneath; winter flower buds glabrous. Hardy in zones 6b-9a. Moderate to easy to propagate by soft wood cuttings.

The low dwarf habit of plants found in the wild may be due to habitat. Low mature plants 18 to 24" high from poor, rocky scrub oak hilltops, developed into plants six feet or more in height when transplanted to more favorable sites. Hybrids with *R. canescens* produce attractive light to medium pink fragrant intergrades, taller growing up to 12 feet or more; winter flower buds pubescent or slightly so.

R. atlanticum (Ashe) Rehder. Coastal or Dwarf Azalea

First noted by Gransoius from a specimen in the British Museum collected by John Clayton in 1743; unfortunately, this specimen was overlooked by Linnaeus in *Species Plantarum.* It was rediscovered in 1916 and published as *A. atlanticum* by W. W. Ashe. As with many plants it was appreciated more in England than in its native land.

A low, stoloniferous understory plant of pines and forest margins, one to two feet tall, on the coastal plains from southern Pennsylvania and Delaware south to South Carolina and Georgia. Fragrant flowers before or with the leaves, usually white, but often flushed pink or purplish on the outside; some with yellow blotch; tube with numerous short glandular hairs. Leaves bright to bluish green, glabrous and glandular beneath. Hardy in zones 6a-9a.

The Coastal Azalea in light sandy soils develops into large extensive colonies often an acre or more, spreading by horizontal underground stems. Readily propagated by division, root and stem cuttings. Ease of propagation by cuttings is carried over to hybrid progeny.

Transplanting to heavier soils restricts its spread, but plants develop numerous multiple stems. Intergrades with *R. canescens* in the southern part of its range and *R. periclymenoides (nudiflorum)* farther north, resulting in taller plants, with less glandular, pale to purplish pink flowers, as in the Choptank Hybrids.

R. atlanticum* f. *tomolobum Fernald: a form with lobes dissected to the base into linear spatulate segments. Originally reported from Nansemond County, Virginia. Collected by H. Skinner in nearby Warwick County. Hui Lin Li reported the plant as triploid (2n=39).

ROSEUM-NUDIFLORUM ALLIANCE

The numerous pinks in subseries *Luteum* appear to have been derived from a combination between the reds of the *Alabamense-Atlanticum* alliance.

R. canescens (Michaux). Sweet, Piedmont or Florida Pinxter Azalea

First discovered by Mark Catesby about 1730 and published with a fairly good figure of it in 1731. It was collected in South Carolina between 1784 and 1796 by A. Michaux who first recognized it as a distinct species and described it as *A. canescens.* It was probably introduced into cultivation about the middle of the 18th century.

A medium to tall shrub to 15 feet or more in moist woodlands and along streamsides, sometimes stoloniferous; in the Coastal Plains from North Carolina to Florida west to Oklahoma and southeastern Texas. In the Piedmont from North Carolina, Georgia, Tennessee, Alabama, and Arkansas. The plants reported as *R. canescens* from Virginia are usually *R. roseum-nudiflorum-atlanticum* hybrids which often look similar to *R. canescens.*

Fragrant flowers before or with the leaves, 1" to 1½" across; white to medium and dark pink; usually with no blotch; tubes white to dark pink, hirsute and glandular. Attractive with stamens twice as long as tube, occasional petaloid to double forms. Yellow blotch may indicate intergrades with *R. austrinum* or *R. alabamense.* Leaves generally pubescent but considerable variation from grayish white to nearly glabrous. Hardy in zones 6b-10a, and moderate to easy to propagate by soft wood cuttings.

R. canescens var. ***candidum*** Rehder.

This variety differs from the typical form, in having a whitish glaucous and pubescent underside to the leaves and densely pubescent branches. It was first observed and described by Dr. Small from a restricted area of southern Georgia and northern Florida. He gave it specific rank under the name *R. candida.* However, later observations have shown that the characteristic glaucous leaves and variable branch pubescence occurs sporadically throughout the range of *R. canescens,* so that at best it should be regarded as a variety or form of the species.

R. periclymenoides (Michaux) Shinners [syn. *R. nudiflorum* (L.) Torrey]. Pinxterbloom Azalea

First discovered by the Rev. John Bannister, it was introduced into England around 1734 along with *R. viscosum,* also collected by John Bartram and sent to Peter Collinson. The nomenclature for this species has presented difficulties.

Linnaeus named this species *A. lutea,* but later changed to *A. nudiflora.* This, too, has now been dropped through adopting the name given by Michaux, *A. periclymenoides.*

A low to medium tall stoloniferous shrub, three to six or eight feet, of moist to dry open woods, in the Appalachian Mountains below 3,800 feet to the Piedmont and Coastal Plains; Massachusetts south to North Carolina; west to cental New York, Pennsylvania, Ohio, eastern Kentucky, and Tennessee to north Georgia and northern Alabama.

Flowers usually with the leaves, light fragrance, white to pale to deep pink to purplish pink occasionally petaloid to semi-double; 1 to 1½" across; tubes short, pubescent and nonglandular except in intergrades with *R. atlanticum* and *R. prinophyllum;* darker than petals. Stamens about three times as long as tube. Twigs pubescent, winter floral buds usually glabrous. Very hardy, zones 4b-9a and moderate to easy to propagate from cuttings.

R. prinophyllum (Small) Millais [syn. *R. roseum* Rehder]. Roseshell Azalea

This species was first mentioned in 1787 as a variety of *A. nudiflora* with broad rough leaves from New York. It is believed to have been in cultivation in Europe before 1812 as *A. rosea.* It was described as a distinct species *A. prinophylla* by Small in 1914 when he unfortunately overlooked the name *A. rosea* which had not been mentioned in any systematic work since 1812.

A medium to tall shrub to 15 feet, rarely stoloniferous, on hillsides, in open woods, and along stream banks from southwestern Quebec, through New England and northern Ohio and Indiana, west to Tennessee, central Arkansas, southeast Missouri and eastern Oklahoma; south at high elevations in the Appalachians to Virginia.

Flowers usually with leaves, pink to purplish pink, rarely white, clove-scented, petal distinctly pointed, tubes short, glandular; stamens twice the tube's length. Leaves are green to bluish green, pubescent beneath. Winter floral buds pubescent in contrast to *R. periclymenoides.* Very hardy, zones 4b-9a, and moderate to difficult to propagate from cuttings. Pure forms not commonly available. Forms less contaminated by hybridization

R. prinophyllum (roseum) Roseshell Azalea

are restricted to local areas on the Virginia Blue Ridge and other isolated areas. The distinct characteristics of this species may well make it the most primitive of this alliance.

R. occidentale (Torrey & Gray) A. Gray. Western Azalea

The only Azalea west of the Rocky Mountains, discovered by the expedition of Capt. Beechy in 1827. It was first referred to as *A. calendulacea* but recognized as a distinct species *A. californica* in 1855 and a year later as *A. occidentale.* William Lobb of England sent seed from California to the Veitch Nursery around 1850 and plants from this source soon played an important part in the decidous hybrids of Europe.

A medium to large shrub up to 15 feet. Found on the coast of Carmel, California to elevations up to 5,000 feet or more in southern Oregon, and in southern California. Isolated populations reported beyond this range. Generally associated with high humidity and cool temperatures. Often roots in running streams where moisture is available.

A very variable, attractive species typically diploid (2n=26); however, hexaploids (2n=78) are reported. Flowers with or after the leaves, mid-April to mid-August, gradual flaring tube. ½" to 4" across, white, yellow, orange pink to red, or various combinations in stripes and dots; usually strong yellow to orange blotch; margins entire to frilled or notched, occasionally petaloid, fragrant in clusters five to 50.

Leaves usually pubescent on both surfaces. Winter flower buds finely pubescent to glabrous, green to purplish red.

Hardy to lows of −12 degrees F in its habitat, zones 7a-9b. Generally unsuccessful in regions with warmer and more humid summers. Heat tolerant form reported from San

Jacinto Mountains near Idyllwild, California. The author has one seedling, surviving after five years in Georgia, whitish with faint yellow blotch typical of plants from this area. Propagation by soft wood cuttings is easy to moderate depending upon clonal material.

Crosses with other deciduous species have long been valuable in Europe and the West Coast of North America; and best as seed parent. Hybrids of *R. prunifolium* × *occidentale* seven years old in Georgia, are heat tolerant, but slow to flower.

It is of interest to note that D. King has grouped *R. occidentale, R. austrinum,* and *R. luteum* in the same alliance based on flavonal studies.

ARBORESCENS-SERRULATUM ALLIANCE

The "late whites" in subseries *Luteum* appear to have been derived from ancestral material of the *Alabamense-Atlanticum* alliance plus strong infiltration from the red end of the *Austrinum-Prunifolium* alliance. In this alliance late blooming and white flowers seem to have segregated, but often with strong residual suffusion of pink or red in the flower parts.

R. arborescens (Pursh) Torrey. Sweet or Smooth Azlaea

Described by John Bartram and listed in his catalog as *A. arborea* in 1814; it is believed that he sent plants to England before this as *A. verticillata.* Michaux observed the plant in 1795 on the Blue Ridge of North Carolina. It was described as a new species by Pursh from plants on the Blue Mountain of Pennsylvania and in John Bartram's garden.

A medium to large shrub 15 feet or more, along streams and on most mountain tops from New York and Pennsylvania, south to Georgia and Alabama; west to Kentucky and Tennessee. Flowers after leaves are mature, long tubed, white often with pink or reddish blush and yellow blotch, 1½ to 2" across style and stamens are characteristically reddish and prominent, strong heliotrope fragrance; tube pubescent and glandular on outside. Twigs are yellowish and glabrous, winter floral buds, yellowish and glabrous, often more than three in terminal. Leaves lustrous, more so than other species, and usually glabrous or only sparingly pubescent. Seed are unwinged in contrast to other species. Hardy in zones 5a-9a, and easy to propagate by soft wood cuttings.

A variable species important for its late fragrant flowers. A late flowering form is found in west central Georgia, and often called *Azalea Georgiana..*

R. arborescens var. *richardsonii:* Earlier described as a dwarf high elevation form, but its distinctness is open to question. It does not remain dwarf at Callaway Gardens.

R. viscosum (L.) Torrey. Swamp Azalea

The first North American Azalea grown in England in 1680 by Bishop Henry Compton from seed collected by John Bannister, an English missionary. It was later collected by John Bartram around 1734 and sent to Peter Collinson in England. It played an important role in the parentage of the earlier hybrid deciduous azaleas.

A variable low to medium tall shrub three to 15 feet, usually stoloniferous, in low marshy areas and along stream banks; to high mixed forest mountains, from Maine to Florida, west to Ohio, mountains of North Carolina and Tennessee, Arkansas, Louisiana, and southeast Texas.

Flowers appear after leaves are fully developed in May and June, long slender tube, glandular and viscid, white to pinkish tinge, glaucescent, spicy fragrance, 1" to 1½" across. Leaves usually glabrous, and occasionally glaucescent beneath. Twigs pubescent, winter flower buds of the low elevation forms are usually glabrous but may be finely pubescent. Very hardy, zones 4b-9a and easily propagated by cuttings or divisions.

Natural hybrids with *R. arborescens* are often found with pale pink to purplish pink flowered intermediates that are difficult to identify. Hybrids with *R. calendulaceum* vary from pale pink to yellowish pink with yellow blotches.

Several varietal forms have been named based on color of flower, leaves, and habit. Most of them are within limits of the species and do not deserve varietal status. The possible exceptions are *R. viscosum* var. *aemulans,* slow growing form from south central Georgia and Alabama, characterized by its densely pubescent winter buds and early flowering in late April to early May; and *R. viscosum* var. *montanum*, the equally low growing and highly stoloniferous form on the mountain tops of the North Carolina Blue Ridge. Its winter buds have comparatively few scales but these are highly pubescent.

R. oblongifolium (Small) Millais. Texas Azalea

Closely related to *R. viscosum* and *R. serrulatum.* First collected by A. Fender in Arkansas in 1850; and by C. Wright in Texas about the same time. Dr. Small described it as *A. oblongifolia* from a specimen collected in Texas by F. Tweedy and introduced by the Arnold Arboretum in 1917.

A medium shrub to six feet or more, occasionally stoloniferous, in sandy soils, along streams, open woods and sand bogs in Arkansas, Oklahoma, Louisiana and Texas.

Flowers with or after leaves mature in mid to late May, long slender tube, glandular, usually white, occasionally pale to light pink, lemony-spice fragrance, ¾ to 1⅛" across. Twigs pubescent, winter flower buds usually pubescent. Tolerant of deep shade. Hardy zones 7a-9a, and easy to propagate by soft wood cuttings.

Very similar to *R. viscosum* and might be best included as an earlier flowering form. It is heat tolerant and interesting but has little ornamental value. Dr. H. Skinner reports that hybrids with *R. bakeri* remain small flowered, and often small leaved and dwarf.

R. serrulatum (Small) Millais. Hammock Sweet Azalea

This species was first collected by T. Drummond about 1830 near New Orleans and also in Florida and listed as a form of *R. viscosum.* It was described as *A. serrulata* by Small in 1903; and introduced into cultivation by the Arnold Arboretum in 1919.

A large shrub to 15 feet or more in wooded swamps and hummocks of the Coastal Plains of Georgia, Florida, and west to Mississippi and southeast Louisiana. The plants often reported from Virginia and the Carolinas are variable forms of *R. viscosum.*

Flowers after the leaves are fully developed in July and August; in south central Florida flowering often occurs in November. Long slender tube, glandular viscid, white, occasionally pale pink, clove fragrance, ¾" to 1½" across. Twigs brownish, pubescent; winter flower buds glabrous or rarely pubescent, scales with darker margin. Hardy zones 7a-10a, and generally easy to propagate from soft wood cuttings. Often confused with *R. viscosum* in the lower South, but generally flowers later and is not stoloniferous, and generally with glabrous winter buds.

(***R. coryi*** Shinners)

First described by Dr. L. Shinners after its collector V. L. Cory who discovered the first specimen in Tyler County, Texas in 1950. It has since been found in adjacent Hardin and Newton Counties. It was described as low stoloniferous plant with fragrant white flowers and small leaves.

The late Dr. S. Solymosy of Louisiana concluded, and most botanists agree, that *R. coryi* does not deserve a specific rank but should be a variety of the highly variable *R. viscosum.*

MOLLE-JAPONICUM ALLIANCE

This alliance includes the only two Asiatic members of subseries *Luteum.* Flowers of these species are broader and more open and the tubes shorter than those of the North American species. They bloom before the leaves come out. Yellow to reddish orange colors bring this alliance most nearly akin to the *Austrinum-Prunifolium* alliance. However, in flower shapes, lack of glandular hairs, and other characteristics these Asiatics are at best grouped separately. They do hybridize, however, with other species in this subseries.

R. japonicum (A. Gray) Suringar. Japanese Azalea (Renge tsutsuji)

R. japonicum was first named *R. molle* which was also called *A. sinensis.* Thus, it was common to find *R. japonicum* called either *R. molle* or *A. sinensis* and there has been confusion ever since. In 1978 at the International Rhododendron Conference the name *R. japonicum* (Blume) Schneider was presented as the correct name for *R. metternichi,* and the name *R. glabrius* Nakai be used for the deciduous azalea *R. japonicum.* There was debate and question concerning this change and, generally confirmed, the name *R. japonicum* will be retained for the deciduous Azalea. *R. japonicum* occurs on Honshu, the main island of Japan, and also on Kyushu and Shikoku Islands. On Kyushu, *R. japonicum* is found in hot, sunny, low, rocky open hillsides and pastures; on Honshu it is found on the perimeter of moist sphagnum bogs up to 3,000 feet and occasionally in lightly wooded, coastal areas.

R. japonicum is a sturdy plant with vigorous upright stems usually 4 to 6′ and occasionally stoloniferous. The flower color ranges from yellow and orange-yellow in Kyushu to reddish orange and red and occasionally with pinkish cast, 2½–3″ across, broadly funnel-shaped, in clusters of 6 to 12. Very hardy plants from the northern range of Honshu are red-flowered, flowering before the leaves appear, and in the wild from April to late June, depending upon habitat. The five stamens do not exceed the corolla. The oblanceolate leaves are 2 to 4″ long and glabrous beneath; reddish fall color. The terminal flower buds are glabrous. It is hardy in zones 5a-8b and generally preferred over *R. molle* from China for its hardiness and in hybridizing. Plants introduced by the USDA encompass the range of habitats and flower color. It is usually moderate to difficult to propagate by cutting depending on clonal material.

R. molle G. Don (syn. *R. sinensis*). Chinese Azalea (Sheep Azalea)

Commonly distributed on hilly areas of eastern and central China, throughout the Chang Jiang Valley provinces, south to Guangdong and Fujian. A coarsely erect shrub 4 to 6′, stem pubescent and often setose or bristly. Flower buds are pubescent. The flowers, broadly funnel-shaped in trusses up to 20, open before or with the leaves in varying shades of yellow, 2–2½″ across, green spotting in the throat. The oblanceolate leaves up to 6″ have a soft nearly white pubescence beneath. The plant differs from *R. japonicum* in the pubescent leaves, and flower buds and typically smaller, yellow flowers. It is less cold hardy, zones 6b-8a, and generally difficult to propagate by soft wood cuttings. It is not commonly grown and is best known in the hybrid form with *R. japonicum* in the Mollis hybrids.

CANADENSE SUBSERIES (Subgenus *Pentanthera* Section *Rhodora*)

This subseries comprises two species from eastern North America. Flowers are bell-shaped, deeply lobed. The two lower petals are separate and wider than the other petals and are two lipped; stamens are 7–10. The type species is *R. canadense.*

R. canadense (L.) Torrey. Rhodora

First described from a cultivated plant in the Botanic Gardens at Paris in 1756, collected from Canada a few years earlier.

Described by Linnaeus as *Rhodora canadense* in 1762, introduced to England by Joseph Banks in 1767, and later included in the genus *Rhododendron.*

A low stoloniferous shrub three to four feet or less, along stream banks, swamps and in moist woods. The most northerly azalea species, in North America extending from Labrador, Newfoundland, Quebec south through New England, central New York to northeastern Pennsylvania and northern New Jersey.

Flowers appear before the leaves in April and May. Two-lipped. The lower lip divided nearly to the base into two distinct narrow lobes. The upper lip with three short lobes; 10 unequal stamens, purplish pink, rarely white, non-fragrant. Leaves are a dull bluish green; flora buds are very small, like leaf buds. Very hardy, zones 3b-7a. Prefers soils of low pH, 4.5

to 5.5, and does well in a cold, moist climate. Moderate to easy to propagate by soft wood cuttings.

Rhodora is a tetraploid (2n=52), does not cross readily with other species. 'Fraseri' (syn. *R.* × *fraseri; (R. canadense* × *R. japonicum)* was accomplished in 1912, with 1½" purplish pink flowers and might still be available in Holland and Canada.

R. canadense var. *albiflorum* has white flowers.

R. vaseyi A. Gray. Pinkshell Azalea

Discovered by George Vasey in 1878 in North Carolina and introduced into cultivation by the Arnold Arboretum soon after 1880. Dr. Small placed it in a separate genus *Biltia vaseyi.*

An upright medium to tall shrub to 15 feet, found at elevations of 3,000 to 5,500 feet in four mountainous counties of western North Carolina.

Flowers appear before the leaves, very short tube or bell-shaped base. Attractive flowers with five distinct wing-like petals, pale pink to purplish pink, greenish throat and reddish orange dots at base, 1½" to 2¼" across. Usually seven unequal stamens, sometimes five to six. Leaves are linear-oval, tapered at both ends. Twigs only slightly pubescent when young. Winter flower buds appear stalked from the shedding of lower scales, very broad ovate appearing rounded, dark green, finely pubescent.

Hardy zones 5a-9a. Plants are reported naturalizing in Massachussetts and adapting in lower elevations in the Southeast.

R. vaseyi var. *album* 'White Find' is a white flowered form and there are several colorful clonal forms available.

R. vaseyi is not known to cross with other species.

NIPPONICUM SUBSERIES (Section *Viscidula*)

This subseries is monotypic and includes only one species *R. nipponicum* from Japan.

R. nipponicum Matsumura. Nippon Azalea (Oba-tsutsuji)

A rare species from northern Honshu, Japan. A shrub to 6' with reddish brown peeling bark exposing lustrous brown stems. The small, unique, white bell-shaped, nodding flowers ½" with 10 stamens, are not conspicuous, being hidden by the large leaves two to six inches long. The leaves resemble *R. schlippenbachii* and turn orange to red in the fall. Introduced in 1914 by Arnold Arboretum from seed collected by E. H. Wilson and reintroduced by the USDA in 1953 and 1954. Hardy zones 6a-8b.

SCHLIPPENBACHII SUBSERIES (Section *Sciadorhodion*)

The four species of this new subseries and section are characterized by the whorl of five obovate leaves at the end of the branches, seeds that are non-winged and leaves lacking the typical marginal hairs; the tomentum consists of setae or bristles and glandular hairs. All have 10 stamens.

R. schlippenbachii Maximowicz. Royal Azalea (Kurofune Tsutsuji)

A common understory plant native to Korea and northeast Manchuria. Discovered by a Russian naval officer, Baron A. Von Schlippenbach, in 1854. It was described in *Kinshu Makura* (1692) and cultivated earlier in Japanese gardens. The name Kurofune Tsutsuji means "foreign ship" in deference to its introduction to Japan. A large shrub to 15' with glandular stems. The large 3–5" obovate to rhombic leaves are in whorls of 5 with good reddish fall color. The fragrant flowers vary; from light purplish pink to strong pink and occasionally white, with reddish brown dotted throat, funnel shaped 2–4" across in clusters of 3 to 6. The flowers open as the leaves are expanding and there is considerable variation in flower color and size from seed. It is one of the finest azaleas when grown well but often reported eccentric and unhealthy ("slipping backward"). Suggest planting in soils only slightly acid pH 6.5, plus extra calcium. The Japanese have selected compact dwarfs and color forms. Plant hardy in zones 5b-9a and roots easily from basal sucker shoots.

R. albrechtii Maximowicz. Albrecht's Azalea (Miyama Tsutsuji)

Discovered in Japan by Dr. M. Albrecht, of the Russian consulate, in 1860. Seed introduced in 1892 by Prof. Sargent and in 1914 by E. H. Wilson to the Arnold Arboretum. A shrub 6 to 8′ of scattered distribution in woody areas of northern Honshu and southern Hokkaido. The obovate to oblanceolate leaves 3–4½″ across are in whorls of 5. The vivid purplish red, 57B, flowers appear with the leaves, 2″ in clusters of 3–5. Plant hardy in zones 6b-8a.

R. pentaphyllum Maximowicz. Five-leaf Azalea (Akebono Tsutsuji)

First introduced into Europe and America by Yokohama Nursery Company as *A. quinquefolia* pink. A large shrub to small tree of southern Honshu and the islands of Shikoku and Kyushu. The flowers are a strong pink, 2″ across and open before the leaves. Young plants are slow to come into bloom. The leaves are in whorls of five and often confused when not in flower with *R. quinquefolium,* but the bark is smooth. A white flowered form is available. Plants hardy in zones 6b-8b.

R. quinquefolium Bisset & S. Moore. Cork Azalea (Goyo Tsutsuji)

Discovered by Mr. Bisset in 1876 and introduced to England by Lord Redesdale in 1896, but appears in *Kinshu Makura* in 1692. A large shrub or small tree characterized by its soft, corky, brown bark. Indigenous to the islands of Shikoku and Honshu, on rocky hillsides in the Nikko region, with trunks 12″ in diameter. The white flowers 1¾″ with a greenish blotch, appear as the leaves develop. The young 5-whorled leaves often have an attractive reddish margin. Hardy in zones 6a-8b.

FARRERAE SUBSERIES (Section *Brachycalyx*)

This series is characterized by a terminal, pseudo-whorl of three rhomboid deciduous leaves, although some species with leathery persistent leaves occur. This series includes species from China, Korea, and Japan.

R. farrerae Tate. Farrer Azalea, Lilac Azalea

Introduced into England by Capt. Farrer, East India Co. in 1829, and reintroduced by Robert Fortune in 1844 to the Horticultural Society of London. Seed introduced by P.I. in 1961. A bushy shrub to 6′, native to the mountainous regions of Kwangtung province in China and Hong Kong. Flowers before the leaves are purplish red with a darker blotch, 2″ across; stamens 8–10, shorter than the corolla. Characterized by the small ovate leaves, ½–¾″; often semipersistent, and large capsule ½–¾″. Not common. Hardy in zones 7b-9a.

R. amagianum Makina. Mt. Amagi Azalea (Amagi Tsutsuji)

A tall upright shrub or small tree in southern Honshu. Flowers strong yellowish pink, 40D, with deep purplish pink blotch, 1¾–2″ across; 10 stamens; bloom after the leaves. Leaves lustrous in 3′s, 2–3¼″, rhomboid or broadly ovate. Closely related to *R. sanctum* and *weyrichii.* Not common. Seed introduced in 1960 and 1963. Hardy zones 7a-8a.

R. mariesii Hemsley and Wilson. Maries Azalea (Mt. Red Azalea)

From the southeastern coast of China, from the provinces of Kiangsu to Fukien west to southeastern Szechwan and Formosa. Discovered by Fortune and later by Charles Maries in 1878, a collector for Veitch Nursery. Seed introduced into England in 1886, and later by USDA from England and China between 1929 and 1948. A tall upright shrub to 10′, young shoots with yellowish hairs. Leaves 2–3 at branch tip, ovate lanceolate 1½–2″ across, purplish pink, with darker blotch, 10 stamens. Not common. Similar to *R. farrerae.* Hardy in zones 7a-9a.

R. reticulatum D. Don. Rose Azalea (Kobane Mitsiba Tsutsuji)

A common, medium to tall shrub thoughout most of Japan at elevations from 5,000 to 6,000 feet, but not along the warm sea coasts or the northernmost islands of Hokkaido. A large shrub up to 20 feet in thickets in high gorges and dwarf on Yakushima. First described in England in 1834, introduced into Europe 1865 as both *R. dilatatum* and *R. rhombicum*. Leaves 2–3 at branch tips, 1–2½" rhombic or broad ovate. Flowers before the leaves, usually in pairs, 1½–2" across, usually 10 stamens, strong purple, 78A, with a few darker spots. Variety *albiflorum* has white flowers. *R. reticulatum* is quite variable and has many geographical forms. Many of these forms are now given species rank. Hardy in zones 6b-8a. Introduced to Arnold Arboretum as seed by E. H. Wilson in 1914 and also the USDA at various times after 1927. *R. dilatatum (R. reticulatum* f. *pentandrum)* often described as a separate species is generally included within *R. reticulatum*. Usually with 5 stamens, but this is not constant. *R. reticulatum* has usually 10 stamens.

Ohwi's *Flora of Japan* lists additional deciduous species all very similar to *R. reticulatum*, that were often included under this species. *R. dilatatum* is reported to have 5 stamens, but this is not constant. The other species are *decandrum, Kiyosumense, lagopus, mayebarae, viscistylum,* and *wadanum*.

R. weyrichii Maximowicz. Weyrich Azalea (Tsukushi Aka Tsutsuji)

Discovered in 1853 on the Goto Islands by Dr. Weyrich, a Russian Naval surgeon. A large shrub to small tree on the islands of Shikoku, Kyushu, and Quelpaert, Japan. Flowers strong red, with purplish blotch, usually after the leaves, stamens usually 10. *Shikokianum* is a dwarf hardier form with red flowers. A white form in cultivation on Hirado Island is thought to have been wild on Goto Island. *R. weyrichii*, first brought by E. H. Wilson to the Arnold Arboretum in 1914 and later distributed to England. Seed collected by USDA between 1932 and 1940 and later in 1961. Hardy in zones 7b-8a.

R. sanctum Nakai. Shrine Azalea (Jungu Tsutsuji)

Found on southern Honshu, Japan in the sacred area of the great shrine of Ise. Up to 15' with lustrous rhombic leaves. Flowers after the leaves, strong purplish pink. Rare. Hardy in zones 7a–8a.

R. nudipes Nakai. Nudipe Azalea (Saikoku Mitsuba Tsutsuji)

A large shrub of the mountains of Kyushu and Honshu, Japan, with rhombic leaves. Flowers, 1½–2" across are borne usually in pairs, strong yellowish pink. Seedlings have proven hardier than others in this subseries, zones 5a–8a.

DAURICUM SERIES (Subgenera *Rhodorastum*)

R. mucronulatum Turcz.

A large deciduous shrub often called an azalea. However, differs from azaleas by having lepidote leaves or scales on the upper and lower surfaces of the leaves. Flowers are borne singly from individual bud at the end of twigs and occasionally from axillary flower buds.

R. mucronulatum is one of the earliest rhododendrons to bloom often with Forsythia and early daffodils. The wide funnel shaped flowers are light reddish purple to purplish pink, 1¾" wide. 'Cornell Pink' is a strong pink popular selection made by the late Henry Skinner.

The deciduous leaves are elliptic-lanceolate to lanceolate, up to 4" long, to 1¼" wide; with scales on both upper and lower surfaces. The fall color is reddish orange to red.

First described in 1837 and introduced to the Arnold Arboretum, U.S.A., in 1882 from Peking by Dr. Bretschneider. Native of northern China, Korea, and Japan and an excellent plant for its early spring flowers and to use with azaleas in the garden. Hardy to zones 5–9.

DECIDUOUS AZALEA HYBRID GROUPS

The hybrid groups of deciduous azaleas are arranged into six major groups. An alphabetical list of azaleas cross-referenced to the groups, varieties and pages will be found in the Index of Azaleas.

The groups are:

Ghent Hybrids
Mollis Hybrids
Occidental Hybrids
Knap Hill Hybrids
 Exbury, Ilam, Windsor and others
Eastern North America Hybrids
Interspecific Hybrids

GHENT HYBRIDS

Ghent, Belgium was the center of azalea hybridizing in Europe in the early 1800's. Mr. P. Mortier, a Ghent baker, crossed the Flame and Pinxter-bloom Azalea *(R. calendulaceum* × *R. nudiflorum)* and produced the Mortier Hybrids. In 1834 Mr. Mortier sold his entire stock to Louis Verschaffelt, a nurseryman of Ghent. News of these hardy Azaleas reached England in 1835, and Mr. T. Rivers, a famous nurseryman of Sawbridgeworth, England, advertised them in 1843.

Also in England around 1820 Mr. J. R. Gowen, a genteel gardener highly respected in London society, crossed *R. calendulaceum* and *R. luteum,* and also *R. viscosum* and *R. luteum.* The latter hybrid group became known as the Ornatum Hybrids.

The Viscosepalum Hybrids *(R. molle* × *viscosum)* comprise another early group represented by the variety 'Altaclerense' produced by J. R. Gowen. 'Viscosepalum' introduced in 1842 by Anthony Waterer (doubtful if still available) was one of the first hybrids and became the parent of other plants. Isaac Davies of Ormskirk in Lancashire, introduced 'Daviesii' *(R. viscosum* × *molle)* in 1879, a stoloniferous and durable plant very similar to 'Viscosepalum' and still popular today; but is essentially sterile and hence, difficult as a parent in hybridizing.

M. L. Verschaffelt of Ghent, crossed a large number of Mortier's seedlings and Ornatum Hybrids obtained from Gowen with Pontic *(R. luteum),* Flame, Pinxter-bloom *(R. periclymenoides),* and Swamp Azaleas *(R. viscosum).* Over a hundred of these hybrids were named, including the well known cultivars 'Coccinea Speciosa', 'Glora Mundi', and 'Grandeur Triomphante'.

Anthony Waterer of England made similar crosses and produced the cultivars 'Unique' and 'Nancy Waterer'. The latter is reported to be a hybrid of *R. molle* × *calendulaceum,* but its delightful fragrance is possibly from *R. luteum.*

All of these and similar hybrids of other breeders have been consolidated and called the hardy Ghent Hybrids. In Holland they are called Pontic Azaleas. An artificial species name "*R. gandavense*" has been used for all the cultivars of the Ghent Hybrids and is often found in catalogs and literature.

The Double Ghent Hybrids (× *gandavense plenum*) or Rustica Azaleas originated about 1858, when Louis Van Houtte of Belgium found a double flowered seedling of a Mortier hybrid. By 1873 he had bred and named several doubles such as 'Narcissiflora' and 'Graf von Moran'. He later introduced 'Corneille', 'Fenelon', 'Quentin Metsys', 'Racine', and 'Teniers', all doubles.

Later, in 1890, Charles Vuylsteke of Belgium introduced several well-known double forms called the Rustica Flora Plena Hybrids. Their origin is unknown but are possibly Double Ghent Hybrids × *R. japonicum.* The term 'Rustica' or Rustica Flora Plena Hybrids has created some confusion, for the Double Ghent Hybrids, which have no infusion of genes from the Chinese and Japanese azaleas, have also been called Rustica Azalea.

It is interesting to note in 1850 there were over 500 different named Ghent Hybrids. Over 100 are included in the Description of list, of which probably fewer than 25 are commonly grown today.

The Ghent Hybrids are tall upright shrubs up to 6–10′ high and 6–8′ wide, broadening with age. They usually bloom mid-season to late. They prefer a cool climate and are very hardy, withstanding −15 to −25°F. (−26 to −32°C.), hardiness zones 5b–8a. At one time many of the Ghents were produced by grafting and were less adaptable to both cold and warm areas than the plants grown by cuttings today. The flowers are 1½–2¼″ wide, funnel-shaped with a long tube, and many are fragrant. The colors range from off-white to pale yellow to purplish red often flushed or shaded another color. The flowers are both single and double.

A more detailed story of the development of the Ghent and Mollis Hybrids is found in Herman J. Grootendorst, *Rhododendrons or Azaleas,* published in Holland in 1954. His list of Ghents, Mollis, and others include varieties not commonly available today.

Frederick Street's book *Azaleas* published in England in 1959 gives an excellent account of the hybrid deciduous azaleas.

The following Ghent Hybrids include many of the original introductions and those introduced up to 1960. Unfortunately the origin and hybridizer is not available for all cultivars. See Appendix I.

'Adolphe' (in cultivation Sunningdale Nur. since 1898): Pink, blotch orange, large.

'Agatha': pink, blotch orange.

'Altaclerense' (*molle* × *viscosum;* Gowen): white, blotch orange; upright tall. A Viscosepalum Hybrid. Plant sold as 'Altaclarensis' (syn. 'Aureum grandiflorum') has yellow flower, blotch orange. Is possibly a Mollis hybrid.

'Amber Rain': light orange yellow 16C, blotch orange.

'Arethusa' (J. Rinz, before 1885): pale yellow, striped pale yellowish pink, double.

'Ariel': white, blotch yellow, with deep orange flare. late.

'Auguste Mechelynck' (L. van Houtte, 1873): white.

'Aurore de Rooighem': strong pink, blotch yellow; late, upright, tall.

'Bartholo Lazzari' (J. Rinz, 1869): moderate yellow shaded reddish orange, double, 2″, upright, tall; late mid-season.

'Beaute Celeste' (syn. 'Cardinal' before 1882): soft yellowish pink tinted orange, 1″, scented; upright, tall; late mid-season.

'Bijou de Amateurs' (before 1872): strong pink 49A, blotch yellow, late; upright, tall.

'Bijou de Gentbrugge' (L. van Houtte, 1872): vivid pink, double; late.

'Bouquet de Flora' (A. Verschaffelt, before 1869): vivid red, blotch yellow, frilled, 2″, late; upright, tall.

'Charlemagne': light orange 28C, and light yellowish pink 31D, blotch yellow, 2″, late; upright, tall.

'Chieftain' (Standishii × late Ghent H. White): strong reddish orange 31B.

'Coccinea Grandiflora' (before 1922): deep yellowish pink, blotch orange.

'Coccinea Speciosa' (L. Sènèclause before 1846): vivid yellowish pink 30C, blotch strong orange 24A.

'Comte de Flandre' (Byls before 1869): vivid red, blotch orange, 2″, late; upright, tall.

'Corneille' (C. Vuylsteke): pink, double, late mid-season.

'Crimson King': vivid purplish red.

'Cuprea Ardens' (in cultivation Sunningdale Nur. since 1898): strong reddish orange, blotch orange.

'Cuprea Pulchella': reddish orange, tips reddish, large blotch.

'Cymodocee': strong pink 49A, 2½″, late, upright, tall.

'Daviesi' (J. Davies about 1840): pale yellow to white, 2½″, late; upright tall, a Viscosepalum Hybrid.

'Decorator': pale purplish pink.

'Decus Hortorum' (before 1871): strong pink 48C, blotch brilliant orange yellow 21A.

'Delicata': light yellowish pink.

'Dr. Chas. Baumann' (syn. 'Ann Louise' before 1882): vivid red, blotch yellow. frilled; late.

'Dulcinae' (C. Vuylsteke about 1886): reddish orange, yellow blotch.

'Electa' (Standish and Noble before 1854): deep yellowish pink 39B, midportion of petals light orange yellow; blotch vivid yellow 15B to strong orange 30D.

'Emile' (Belgium before 1854): pink flushed reddish orange.

'Emma' (before 1922): strong yellowish pink, blotch orange yellow.

'Fanny' (syn of 'Pucella'): pale purplish pink, orange blotch; long tube, petals revolute, 2¼", early mid-season, upright, tall.

'Fenelon': light yellow, flushed strong orange at tips, double, 1¾"; early mid-season, upright, tall.

'Flamboyant': deep yellowish pink 39A, light yellowish pink 31D, and light greenish yellow 4B.

'Flora' (before 1875): strong yellowish pink 38A, 1½", late; upright, tall.

'Furst Camille von Rohan' (before 1874): light orange, tipped white, deep orange blotch.

'General Chasse' (before 1869): vivid red.

'Gloria Mundi' (L. Sènèclause, 1846): vivid orange 30C, blotch orange yellow, 2½", frilled.

'Goldlack' (Hesse, 1900): strong orange yellow, early mid-season.

'Graf Alfred von Niepperg' (before 1875): light yellowish pink, spotted yellow, edged red.

'Graf von Meran' (J. Rinz before 1854): light purplish pink 55C, double, late mid-season; upright tall.

'Grandeur Triomphante' (L. van Houtte before 1872): deep purplish red, late.

'Grand Monarque' (before 1874): strong yellowish pink, blotch yellow.

'Guelder Rose' (before 1872): yellow, flushed strong orange yellow, blotch yellowish.

'Heroine Plena' (J. Rinz before 1871): white, flushed pink, double.

'Heureuse Surprise' (before 1869): light purplish pink 62C, 1¾", late; upright, tall.

'Hollandia' (*luteum* × japonicum: P. M. Koster 1902): orange yellow, double, early mid-season.

'Ignaea' (syn. 'Ignoea Nova'; 'Ignea Nova', before 1876): deep yellowish orange 43C, blotch strong orange, 2½", late; upright tall.

'Joseph Baumann' (before 1875): vivid purplish red, blotch orange yellow; late.

'Josephine Klinger' (before 1875): strong, yellowish pink 38A, 1¾"; late, upright, tall.

'Julia Schipp': pink.

'Julie DuPont' (Sunningdale Nur. since 1808): strong purplish pink, deep yellow flare, red stamens.

'Julius Caesar' (before 1872): vivid red, blotch orange yellow.

'Laelia': pink and orange.

'Leibnitz' (J. Rinz before 1871): yellow, double.

'Lelia' (Sunningdale Nur. since 1895): pale yellow, flushed, moderate purplish red at edges, deep yellow flare.

'Louis Hellebuyck': moderate purplish red, white striping, yellow blotch;

'Marie Verschaffelt' (before 1871): probably the same as 'Bouquet de Flare'. light pink, late.

'Melanie' (before 1875): deep pink, late mid-season.

'Meteor': red.

'Minerva' (before 1861): deep pink, flushed yellow, 2¼", late; upright, tall.

'Miniata Floribunda' (Sunningdale Nur. since 1898): light purplish pink, similar to 'Rembrandt'.

'Mme. Gustave Guillemot' (syn. 'Roi de Belges'): deep red 53B, 2¼".

'Mme. Moser' (Moser & Fils before 1902): deep pink with white stripes, blotch yellow; late midseason.

'Mrs. Harry White' (late Ghent × 'Standishii'; H. White): white suffused light purplish pink 62C, blotch vivid yellow; late.

'Nancy Waterer' (A. Waterer before 1876): vivid yellow large, fragrant, late midseason.

'Narcissiflora' (L. van Houtte before 1871): light yellow 15D, double, 1¾", late mid-season; upright, tall.

'Nivalis Striata' (Sunningdale Nur. since 1898): deep pink and white.

'Nosegay': pink.

'Orange Man' (Waterer, Sons & Crisp): orange yellow 21B, strong orange blotch.

'Oscar I': light yellowish pink, blotch orange.

'Pallas' (before 1875): flushed, light yellowish pink, blotch brilliant orange yellow, 2¼", early mid-season; upright, tall.

'Prince Henri de Pays-Bas' (Sunningdale Nur. before 1854): strong orange 24A, and vivid red, 2¼", late; upright, tall.

'Puchella Roseola' (before 1815): pink, yellow blotch.

'Queen of England' (Sunningdale Nur. before 1854): moderate purplish red, orange blotch.

'Quentin Metsys': white, flushed strong yellowish pink, blotch, vivid yellow, double, 1½" early midseason; upright, tall.

'Racine' (C. Vuylsteke): white, flushed, moderate yellowish pink, double 1½", late midseason; upright, tall.

'Raphael de Smet' (before 1889): white, edged light pink 49C, double, 1¾", late midseason; upright, tall.

'Reine des Rouges': vivid red, orange flare.

'Rembrandt': deep red 53B, 1½", late; upright, tall.

'Richardissima': light pink.

'Roi des Feux' (before 1873): light purplish pink 55C, 2", late, upright, tall.

'Rosea Plena' (Moser before 1914): pale pink, double.

'Sang de Gentbrugge' (L. van Houtte 1873): deep yellowish pink 43C, late; upright tall.

'Sessostris' (Ghent × 'Standishi'; H. White): strong yellowish pink, blotch orange.

'Souvenir du President Carnot': light orange yellow and strong reddish orange, semidouble, 1½", early mid-season; upright, tall.

'Standishi' (Standish & Noble before 1854): deep yellow, darker blotch.

'Sully' (Sunningdale Nur. 1898): light purplish pink, yellow flare.

'Taylor's Red' (Sunningdale Nur. 1898): red.

'Teniers': strong orange yellow, flushed light pink, double 2¼", early midseason; upright, tall.

'Unique' (before 1875): strong orange yellow 24B, 2", late midseason, upright, tall.

'Variegata' (Sunningdale Nurs. since 1898): pink shaded white.

'Versicolor' (Before 1885): light yellowish pink, deeper stripes, blotch yellow.

'Volcano' (Standish & Noble): strong reddish orange, blotch deep orange yellow.

'Vulcan' (Waterer & Sons. before 1929): strong red 45D, blotch vivid orange yellow 23A.

'Vurida' (before 1875): red, blotch yellow.

'Willem III' (syn. 'William III'): strong yellowish pink 32C, 2½", early midseason; upright, tall.

MOLLIS HYBRIDS

The Mollis hybrids are a complex group derived mainly from *R. japonicum* but confusing due to the vicissitudes of the names of the Chinese and Japanese Azaleas and the early history of their introduction and breeding. The Japanese Azalea was first called the Mollis Azalea (*A. mollis*). The Chinese Azalea was known botanically as *A. sinensis.* Plant names are not engraved in stone, but are changed to correctly reflect plant relationships. In keeping with this evolving understanding of the plant world, the botanical name of the Chinese Azalea was first changed to *A. molle* and subsequently to *R. molle*. The name of the Japanese Azalea was changed from *A. mollis* to *R. japonicum,* and there is rumbling to the effect that this name may be changed again. (Heaven forbid!)

Many cultivars of the Japanese Azalea were developed and called Mollis Azaleas. Hybrids were soon thereafter developed from crosses of the Japanese and Chinese Azaleas and called Mollis × Sinensis Hybrids. Yet today the various forms of the Japanese azalea and the hybrids are grouped together as Mollis and Mollis × Sinensis Hybrids in Europe. An artificial name *R.* × *kosterianum* is often used for this collective group.

For simplicity's sake the whole group is now called the Mollis Hybrids, with the full understanding that some of the plants may be selected forms of the Japanese Azalea (*R. japonicum*) and not hybrids.

The origin of the Mollis Hybrids begins with Louis van Houtte of Ghent, Belgium who bought Japanese Azalea seedlings from P. F. von Siebold's Nursery in Leiden, Holland, derived from seeds obtained from Japan in 1861. By 1873 L. van Houtte had selected and named over 20 forms, many still grown today, for example: 'Alphonse Lavallee', 'Chevalier de Reali', 'Comte de Quincey', and 'W. E. Gumbleton'. It has been argued that van Houtte's azaleas were really the result of 30 years of breeding. If this is true, their origin goes back to the early 1840's. Possibly the Mollis Hybrids derived from some of the first *R. japonicum* plants brought in by von Siebold in 1830, but which he had mis-labeled as (*A. sinensis.*) (Confusion compounded!)

The color range of van Houtte's azaleas is typical of a breeding group developed over a long period of time, ranging from pale yellow to rose, orange and reddish orange, and even some which are fragrant. This wide range of characteristics indicates the possible use of (*A. sinensis* var. *alba,*) reported to be a hybrid of *R. molle* × *viscosum*. *R. viscosum* is also thought to have been used in the Mollis Hybrids, possibly through a small white azalea introduced by Charles Vuylsteke, of Belgium, called 'Elegantissima Odorata'.

Ambrose Verschaffelt of Ghent and others added to the group. About 1890 he introduced two cultivars: 'J. C. van Tol' and 'Machteline Alberts', which he crossed in turn to produce 'Hugo Hardijzer'.

Frederik de Coninck, a Belgian, crossed the Japanese with the Chinese Azalea in the 1880's. In 1892 M. Koster and Sons of Holland acquired a collection of de Coninck's hybrids and named eight varieties: 'Anthony Koster', 'Dr. Reichenbach', 'Frans Van der Bom', 'Emil Liebig', 'Hortulanus H. Witte', 'Hugo Koster', 'Nicolaas Beets', and 'T. J. Seidel'. The early hybrids of Japanese and Chinese Azaleas were yellow, orange, and reddish orange. The later hybrids were deep orange and reds.

The Kersbergen Brothers of Holland in 1899 acquired a large number of seedlings from various Belgian and Dutch sources, mostly forms of pure Japanese Azalea, but also some hybrids with the Chinese Azalea. They named 120 varieties which largely replaced the early Japanese Azaleas developed by van Houtte and his successors. The Kersbergen Nursery introduced 'Babeuff', 'Dante G. Rossetti', 'Multatuli', and 'Professor Donders'.

By the turn of the century the pure lines of Japanese Azalea selections and hybrids of the Japanese and Chinese Azaleas had been merged. Many Dutch breeders working with this mixed bag continued hybridizing and introduced varieties such as 'Koster's Brilliant Red', 'Adriaan Koster', 'John Ruskin', 'Prof. Amundsen', 'Koningin Emma', 'Directeur Moerlands', 'Mathilda', and others still familiar today.

Some of the Mollis Hybrid varieties are not true clones, but are seedlings of plants that come fairly true when selfed or from isolated plants; and some are line-hybrids produced by repeated crossing of two selected strains. 'J. C. van Tol' produces about three quarters reds when selfed. The reds in the second generation produced one-third true breeding reds and two-thirds resembling the parent. Other varieties similarly handled are 'C. B. van Nes', a reddish orange selection from 'J. C. van Tol', 'Dr. M. Oosthoek', a vivid reddish orange, and 'Babeuff', a strong orange.

'Koster's Brilliant Red' was originally a line hybrid, but some of the seedlings are not propagated vegetatively and given the same name. One should be aware that some seedling strains and line hybrids are sold under clonal names while others are sold under a color designation.

The Mollis Hybrids are deciduous, tall, upright plants, up to 8′ high and 6′ wide but generally not as hardy as the Ghents; hardiness zones 5b–8a. They are best on their own roots. They bloom in mid to late season and best in slight shade to full sun. The colors range from white-yellow, orange, to red and pinkish shades, and some are fragrant. The flowers are usually larger than the Ghents, 2–2½″, in clusters 7 to 13, all singles, with shorter tubes, and more striking colors.

While the Mollis and Ghents were first used as forcing plants, they have found a place in the garden. New introductions are still appearing even though they have to compete with the Knap Hill Hybrids. They are often more heat resistant than the Knap Hills and are being used by breeders in warm climates with North American azaleas. Very few of these new hybrids have been named, but there are some interesting plants under observation.

The following Mollis hybrids include many of the original introductions and those introduced up to 1960. Unfortunately the origin and hybridizer is not available for all the cultivars. See Appendix I.

'Adelaide' (Mollis × *x kosterianum:* M. Koster & Sons before 1939): orange-yellow, red blotch.

'Admirable' (*japonicum* cl. from Belg.): light orange, blotch orange.

'Adriaan Koster' (Mollis × *x kosterianum:* M. Koster & Sons 1901): deep yellow.

'Alice de Stuers' (Mollis × *x kosterianum:* M. Koster & Sons before 1939): strong yellowish pink, blotch deep orange.

'Alma Tadema': light pink, blotch red.

'Alphonse Lavallèe' (*japonicum* cl. L. van Houtte 1873): orange flushed pink.

'Altaclarensis Sunbeam': brilliant yellow 20B, flushed pale orange yellow 24C, blotch strong orange 24A, 2½".

'Ambrose Verschaffelt' (*japonicum* cl.; Verschaffelt before 1910): moderate reddish orange, blotch vivid orange, 2".

'Anna': vivid yellow.

'Anthony Koster' (*x kosterianum* × ?; M. Koster & Sons 1892): brilliant yellow 20B, blotch brilliant orange yellow 17B, 2¾".

'Apple Blossom' (K. Wezelenburg & Son): light pink.

'Babeuff' (G. Kersbergen 1918): strong orange.

'Baron Constant de Rebecque' (*japonicum* cl.; L. van Houtte 1872): yellow, blotch orange.

'Baron Edmund de Rothschild' (syn. 'Charles Kekule') (*japonicum* cl.; L. van Houtte 1873): strong yellowish pink.

'Baron Krayenhoff' (Felix & Dijkhuis 1950): vivid reddish orange, orange blotch.

'Bataaf Felix' ('Anthony Koster' × red *japonicum;* Felix & Dijkhuis): brilliant yellow.

'Benelux' (red *japonicum* × 'Koster's Brilliant Red'; Felix & Dijkhuis): vivid reddish orange, darker blotch.

'Betsy de Bruin' (*x kosterianum:* M. Koster & Sons): light yellow and light orange yellow, tips of lobes moderate reddish orange, blotch vivid reddish orange.

'Bouquet d'Orange' (*japonicum* cl.; M. Koster & Sons 1876): deep red 47D, blotch strong orange 30D, 2¼".

'Catherine Rinke' ('Floradora' × a Mollis Hybrid): strong yellowish pink 33C, blotch orange, 4".

'C. B. van Nes' (C. B. van Nes & Sons): reddish orange.

'Charles Rogier' (dbl Ghent × *japonicum* C. Vuylsteke 1892): pale purplish pink, orange blotch.

'Chevalier de Reali' (*japonicum* cl. (L. van Houtte 1875): light yellow, fading to off-white, 1½".

'Chicago' (*x kosterianum:* G. Kersbergen 1918): light reddish orange.

'Christopher Wren' (syn. 'Goldball'; L. J. Endtz & Co.): brilliant yellow 15C, blotch strong orange 24A, large flowers. There is a seedling plant available as 'Altaclerense' (syn. 'Aureum Grandiflorum') which is much superior. See 'Altaclerense' under Ghents.

'Clara Butt' (*japonicum* cl.; K. Wezelenburg & Sons 1912): strong yellowish pink.

'Colonel F. R. Durham' (L. J. Endtz & Co. 1930): brilliant yellow.

'Comte de Gomer' (syn. 'Consul Ceresole'; J. Waterer): moderate purplish pink 62B, blotch vivid orange yellow 23A to vivid yellow 15A, 2½".

'Comte de Kerckhove' (Belgium): moderate yellowish pink shaded moderate reddish orange, blotch orange, 2¼".

'Comte de Papadopoli' (*japonicum* cl.; L. van Houtte 1873): deep yellowish pink, blotch strong orange, 3".

'Comte de Quincy' (*japonicum* cl. L. van Houtte 1873): light yellow 14D, 2½".

'Consul Pêcher' (*japonicum* cl. L. van Houtte 1873): strong yellowish pink, orange blotch.

'Dante Gabriel Rossetti' (*japonicum* cl.; G. Kersbergen): white with yellowish pink, blotch, 2¾".

'David Teniers' (G. Kersbergen): moderate reddish orange.

'Directeur Moerlands' (syn. 'Golden Sunlight'; 'Anthony Koster' × ?; P. L. Binken): strong yellow, darker throat.

'Dr. A. Plesman' (Felix & Dijkhuis 1950): vivid reddish orange, blotch orange.

'Dr. Benesj' (Felix & Dijkhuis 1950): vivid reddish orange, blotch orange.

'Dr. H. Colyn' (Felix & Dijkhuis 1950): strong orange yellow, blotch yellow.

'Dr. Jacobi' (W. Hardijzer & Co. 1944): deep red.

'Dr. Leon Vignes' (*japonicum* cl.; L. van Houtte 1873): light yellow.

'Dr. M. Oosthoek' (syn. 'Mevrouw van Krugten') (*x kosterianum;* P. J. C. Oosthoek & Co. 1920): vivid reddish orange, lighter blotch, 3".

R. albrechtii. CREECH

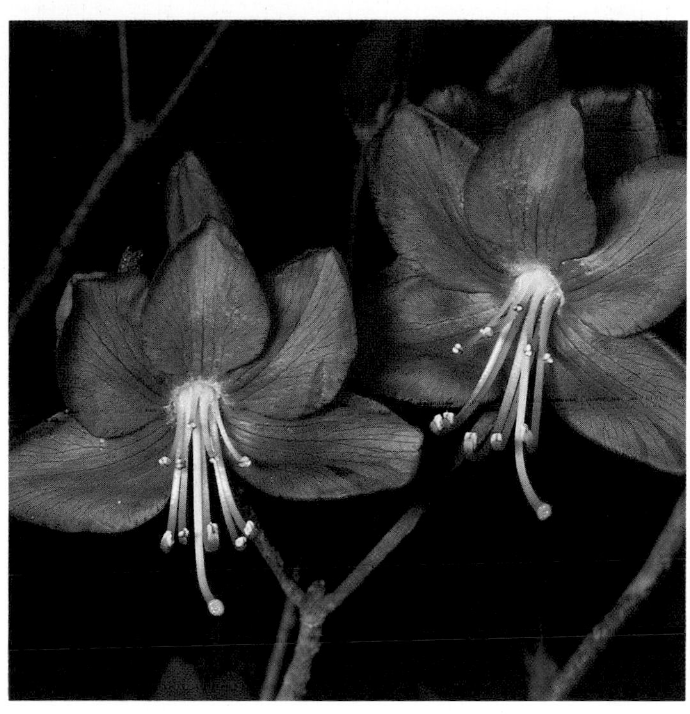

R. albrechtii Albrecht Azalea. GREER

R. sanctum Shrine Azalea. GREER

R. farrerae. CREECH

Plate 10

R. calendulaceum Flame Azalea. GALLE

R. bakeri Cumberland Azalea. GALLE

R. prunifolium Plumleaf Azalea. GALLE

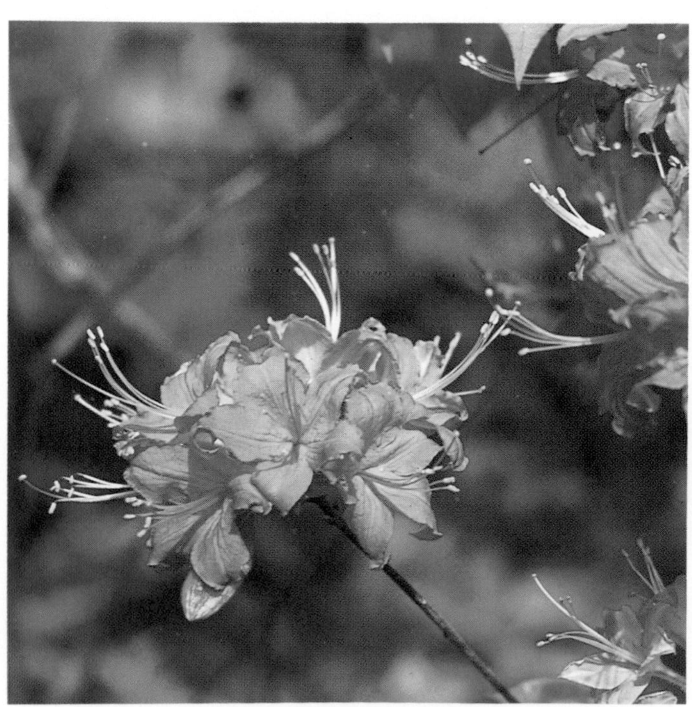

R. flammeum (speciosum) Oconee Azalea. GALLE

R. austrinum Florida Azalea. GALLE

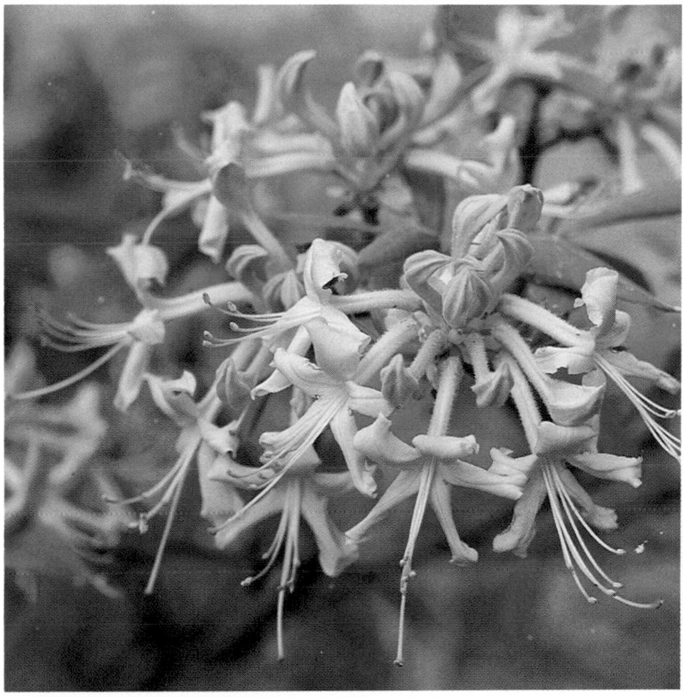

R. luteum. Pontica Azalea. GALLE

R. atlanticum Coastal Azalea. GALLE

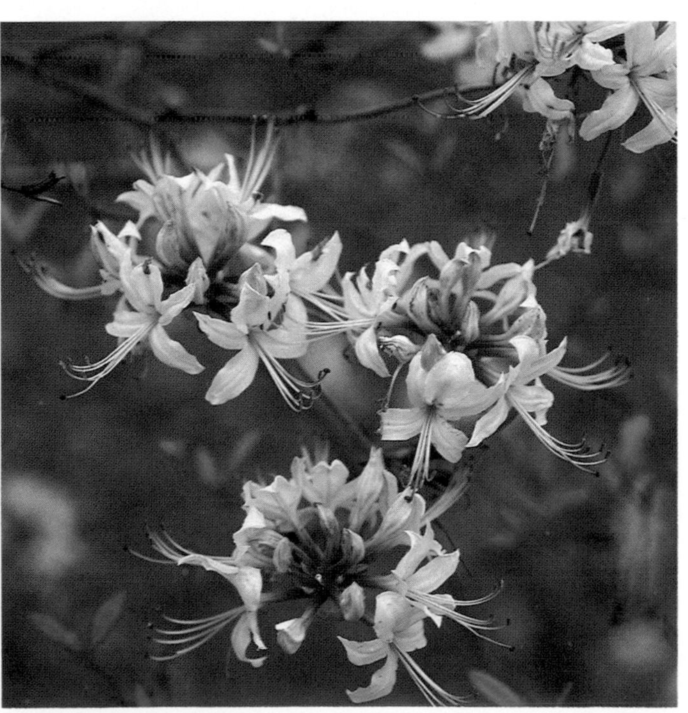

R. periclymenoides (nudiflorum), Pinxterbloom Azalea. GALLE

Plate 12

R. alabamense Alabama Azalea. GALLE

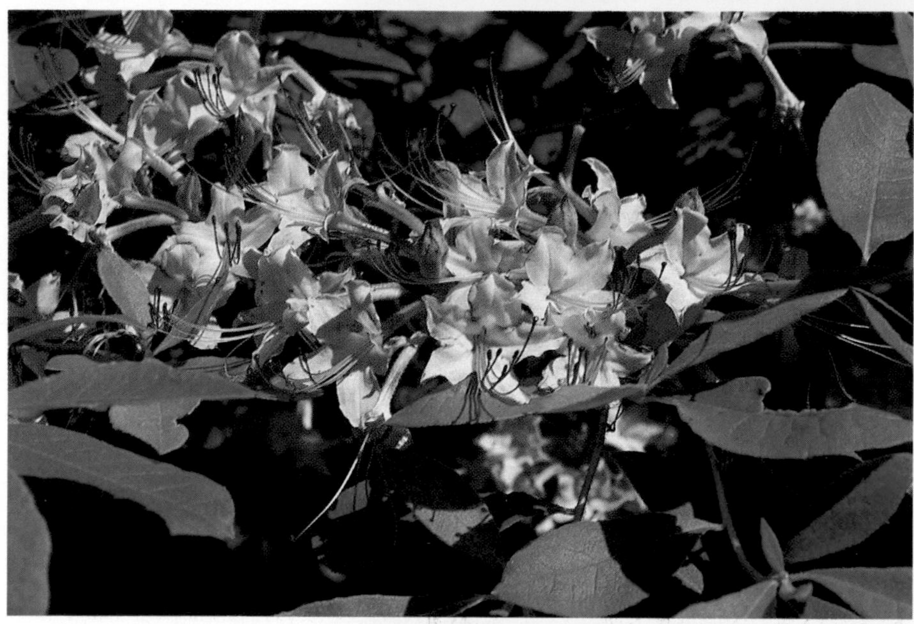

R. alabamense Alabama Azalea. GALLE

R. prinophyllum (roseum) Roseshell Azalea. GALLE

R. occidentale Western Azalea. Stage Coach Ridge, California; Pacific Ocean in background. B. SMITH

R. canescens Piedmont Azalea. GALLE

R. occidentale #305 Western Azalea. B. SMITH

Plate 14

R. vaseyi. Pink shell Azalea. GALLE

R. canadense albiflorum White Rhodora. GREER

R. arborescens Sweet Azalea. GALLE

R. viscosum Swamp Azalea. GALLE

Plate 15

R. japonicum. Japanese Azalea. GALLE

R. japonicum Japanese Azalea orange phase. CREECH

R. japonicum Japanese Azalea red phase, Hokkaido, Japan. CREECH

Plate 16

R. canadense Rhodora. GREER

R. schlippenbachii Royal Azalea. GREER

R. schlippenbachii alba White Royal Azalea. GREER

'Dr. Reichenbach' (*x kosterianum;* M. Koster & Sons 1896): strong yellow, shaded strong orange, blotch moderate reddish orange, 2½". Similar to 'Emil Liebig', 'Frans van der Bom' and 'T. J. Seidel'.

'Duchess of Portland' (*x kosterianum;* K. Wezelenburg & Son 1911): light yellowish pink.

'Elizabeth' (*japonicum* cl.; M. Koster & Sons before 1896): vivid pink, yellow spots.

'Ellen Cuthbert' (syn. 'E. Cuthbert'; *x kosterianum;* M. Koster & Sons 1895): brilliant orange yellow 23B, blotch deep orange.

'Emil Liebig': (*japonicum* cl.; M. Koster & Sons 1892): strong orange, blotch deep orange, 2¾".

'Enchantress' (*japonicum* cl.; M. Koster & Sons before 1889): brilliant orange.

'Ernest Bach' (syn. 'E. Bach'; *japonicum* cl.; L. van Houtte 1873): pale yellow, tinted light orange.

'Esmeralda' (*japonicum* × dbl. Ghent; C. Vuylsteke 1892): deep pink, blotch vivid yellow.

'Evening Glow' (*x kosterianum* cl.; M. Koster & Sons 1920): deep red.

'Fairy Queen' (K. Wezelenburg & Son 1912): strong yellowish pink.

'Firebrand' (H. White): vivid reddish orange.

'Fireflame': vivid reddish orange.

'Flambeau' (intro. to U.S.A. by Domoto Bros.): deep pink, darker blotch.

'Floradora' (syn. 'Florodora') (*x kosterianum* cl.; M. Koster & Sons 1910): brilliant orange 2C, blotch strong reddish orange 31A.

'Floralia' (M. Koster & Sons before 1939): pink, red blotch.

'Flying Enterprise' (*x kosterianum* cl.; Straver 1950): light yellow, shaded pink.

'Franklin D. Roosevelt' (Felix & Dijkhuis 1950): vivid reddish orange, blotch orange.

'Frans van der Bom' (*x kosterianum* cl.; M. Koster & Sons 1892): strong orange yellow to moderate reddish orange, 2½".

'Fraternite' (G. Kersbergen 1922): strong yellowish pink.

'Fred de Coninck' (syn. 'de Konick'; from Belgium): strong orange yellow, edges darker, blotch vivid orange, 2¾".

'General Goffinet' (*japonicum* × dbl. Ghent; C. Vuylsteke 1892): pale purplish pink, yellow blotch.

'General Vetter' (*x kosterianum* cl.; M. Koster & Sons 1896): strong orange yellow to strong yellowish pink, 2½".

'Guillaume Caillet' (*x kosterianum* cl.; G. Kersbergen): light yellow, edged pink.

'Hamlet' (*x kosterianum* cl.; M. Koster & Sons 1936): strong yellowish pink, blotch reddish orange.

'Henri Conscience' (*japonicum* × dbl. Ghent; C. Vuylsteke 1892): moderate red, blotch yellow.

'Hortulanus A. Fiet' (*japonicum* clone): vivid red, blotch reddish purple.

'Hortulanus H. Witte' (*x kosterianum* cl.; M. Koster & Sons 1892): moderate orange yellow, strong orange blotch, 2¼".

'Hugo de Groot' (*x kosterianum* cl.; L. J. Endtz & Co.): strong orange, late.

'Hugo Hardijzer' (P. W. Hardijzer): strong yellowish pink 38A, blotch reddish orange 31A, 2¼".

'Hugo Koster' (*x kosterianum* cl.; M. Koster & Sons 1892): vivid reddish orange, blotch orange.

'Imperator' (*x kosterianum* cl.; K. Wezelenburg & Son before 1885): orange, late.

'Isabella van Houtte' (*japonicum* cl.; L. van Houtte 1873): light yellow.

'J. C. van Tol' (J. C. van Tol): deep yellowish pink, blotch vivid orange, 2¾".

'Jeanne': reddish orange.

'J. J. de Vink' (*x kosterianum* cl.; M. Koster & Sons 1896): light yellow 18A, to moderate reddish orange 33C, orange blotch.

'John Ball' (G. Kersbergen 1918): vivid red, early midseason.

'John Kersbergen' (G. Kersbergen 1918): deep yellowish pink 41B, blotch orange.

'John Ruskin' (*x kosterianum* cl.; G. Kersbergen): vivid pink, late.

'Joseph Ditzen': dark red.

'Koersbergen': moderate reddish orange, flushed yellowish pink, blotch strong orange yellow, 3".

'King Albert' (*x kosterianum* cl.; G. Kersbergen, intro. Wallace 1921): vivid yellow.

'Koningin Emma' (syn. 'Queen Emma'; *x kosterianum* cl.; K. Wezelenburg & Son): light orange yellow 21D, to strong orange 25C, suffused yellowish pink 38A, blotch strong orange, 2½".

'Koningin Wilhelmina' (syn. 'Queen Wilhelmina'; *x kosterianum* cl.; Ottolander & Hooftman 1896): moderate orange, blotch moderate red, 2½".

'Koster's Brilliant Red' (syn. 'Brilliant Red'; *x kosterianum* cl.; M. Koster & Sons 1918): moderate reddish orange, 2½".

'Koster's Orange' (*x kosterianum* cl.; M. Koster & Sons 1920):

'Koster's Yellow' (*x kosterianum* cl.; M. Koster & Sons 1920): strong orange yellow, blotch orange, 3½".

'Lemonora' (syn. 'Dr. L. N. Deckers'; K. Wezelenburg & Son 1920): moderate yellow, tinted pink.

'Liberty' (G. Kersbergen): dark pink.

'Madame Anthony Koster' (*x kosterianum* cl.; M. Koster & Sons 1898): light orange, tinged pink at margin.

'Marconi' (*x kosterianum* cl.; M. Koster & Sons before 1924): strong reddish orange, blotch reddish orange.

'Marmion' (*x kosterianum* cl.; M. Koster & Sons 1936): yellow.

'Mathilda' (*x kosterianum* cl.; P. L. Binken 1940): deep pink, and deep yellowish pink, shaded red.

'Mevrouw G. van Noordt' (syn: 'Mrs. G. van Noordt', 'Jeanne Oosthoek'; *x kosterianum* cl.; P. van Noordt & Son): strong yellowish pink, throat orange yellow, large flowers.

'Mina den Ouden' (H. den Ouden & Son 1924): deep pink.

'Minister Thorbecke' (before 1890): deep orange.

'Miss Louisa Hunnewell' (*x kosterianum;* T. D. Hatfield 1920): vivid orange yellow 21A, 3"; true clone may not exist. Seedlings frequently substituted.

'Mme. Arthur de Warelles' (*japonicum* cl.; L. van Houtte 1873): moderate orange.

'Mme. Caroline Legrelle d'Hanis' (*japonicum* cl.; L. van Houtte 1872): moderate purplish red.

'Mme. Jules Buyssens' (*x kosterianum* cl.; M. Koster & Sons): orange.

'Mollis Alba': pale yellow.

'Mr. D. Webster' (*x kosterianum* cl.; H. den Ouden & Son 1924): light yellow, tinted pink.

'Mrs. A. E. Endtz' (*x kosterianum* cl.; L. J. Endtz & Co. 1900): vivid yellow, flushed orange.

'Mrs. H. den Ouden' (*x kosterianum* cl.; H. den Ouden & Son 1924): deep orange.

'Mrs. Helen Koster' (*x kosterianum* cl.; M. Koster & Sons): deep orange.

'Mrs. J. Dijkhuis' (*x kosterianum* cl.; Felix & Dijkhuis): strong orange, late.

'Mrs. John Russell' (*x kosterianum* cl.; M. Koster & Sons before 1939): pink with yellow.

'Mrs. L. J. Endtz' (L. J. Endtz & Co. 1900): moderate yellow, orange, blotch yellow, 3".

'Mrs. Norman Luff' (*molle* × *japonicum;* M. Koster & Sons before 1939): orange, blotch yellow.

'Mrs. Oliver Slocock' (*x kosterinum* cl.; W. C. Slocock 1933): orange yellow, flushed orange.

'Mrs. Peter Koster' (*x kosterianum* cl.; M. Koster & Sons): deep reddish orange 43B, blotch strong reddish orange 31B.

'Mrs. Walter': brilliant orange.

'Mrs. Will Paterson': yellow with pink edge.

'Multatuli' (*x kosterianum* cl.; G. Kersbergen 1918): strong yellowish pink 31C, blotch strong orange yellow 24B, 3¼".

'Nicolaas Beets' (*x kosterianum* cl.; M. Koster & Sons 1892): strong yellow to strong orange yellow, 2¼".

'Oranea' (*x kosterianum* cl.; Kromhout & Co.): deep reddish orange.

'Orange Glow': strong yellowish pink 40D, blotch vivid yellowish pink 30C, 3½"; selection from 'J. C. van Tol'.

'Paul Harris' (Mrs. J. Dijkhuis' × red *japonicum;* Felix & Dijkhuis): deep reddish orange.

'Peter Kersbergen': moderate reddish orange, blotch orange yellow.

'Peter Koster' (M. Koster & Sons 1895): orange, darker blotch.

'Polly Claessens' (*x kosterianum* cl.; M. Koster & Sons 1954): orange.

'Prince Baudouin' (*japonicum* × dbl. Ghent; C. Vuylsteke 1892): light red, yellow blotch.

'Prins Frederik' (*japonicum* cl.): vivid purplish red 55A, blotch orange yellow, 2¾".

'Prinses Juliana' (*x kosterianum* cl.; C. Frets & Sons): vivid yellow, edged yellowish pink.

'Prof. Amundsen' (*x kosterianum* cl.; L. J. Endtz & Co.): light purplish pink, red border, yellow blotch.

'Prof. Donders' (G. Kersbergen): light red.

'Prominent' ('Anthony Koster' × 'Alphonse Lavallee'): strong yellowish pink 41C, 3¼".

'Queen Sophia' (syn. 'Koningin Sophia' from Belgium): strong pink 52D, blotch vivid yellow 15A, 2".

'Radiant' (*x kosterianum* cl.; Kromhout & Co.): reddish orange.

'Robespierre' (syn. 'Prof. H. Lorentz'; G. Kersbergen 1918): deep yellowish pink, edges paler, 2½".

'Rosy' (*x kosterianum* cl.; Ottolander & Hooftman 1900): light pink, blotch light yellow.

'Rudyard Kipling' (*x kosterianum* cl.; M. Koster & Sons): reddish orange, dark spots.

'Salmon Glow' (*x kosterianum* cl.; H. den Ouden & Son): strong orange.
'Salmon Queen' (*x kosterianum* cl.; A. Vuyk): light orange 25D, blotch vivid orange yellow 23A.
'Samuel Taylor Coleridge' (*x kosterianum* cl.; G. Kersbergen): light purplish pink, vivid orange blotch, 2¾".
'Saturnus' (Boskoop Sta. before 1967): reddish orange, large.
'Sebastopol' (*x kosterianum* cl.; M. Koster & Sons 1896): vivid reddish orange.
'Shakespeare' (G. Kersbergen): orange yellow 21B, blotch vivid yellow 2¼".
'Snowdrift' (H. White): very pale yellow, yellow green stripes and spotting.
'Southgate Wonder' (*x kosterianum* cl.; K. Wezelenburg & Son): light reddish orange.
'Spinoza' (L. J. Endtz & Co.): light orange yellow 21D, suffused strong yellowish pink 38A, blotch yellowish green.
'Suzanne Loef' (M. Koster & Sons): vivid purplish red, blotch vivid orange.
'Therese' (syn. 'Afterglow', 'Pink Beauty', 'Ebenezer Pyeke'; *japonicum* cl.; M. Koster & Sons 1872): pink with darker pink stripes.
'Thomas A. Edison' (syn. 'Edison'; *japonicum* × dbl. Ghent; C. Vuylsteke 1892): dark yellow.
'T. J. Seidel' (*x kosterianum* cl.; M. Koster & Sons 1892): vivid yellowish pink 30C, darker blotch, 2½".
'Tubantia' (P. M. Koster & Co. before 1939): deep pink with darker dots.
'U.N.R.R.A.' (Felix & Dijkhuis 1950): deep reddish orange, vivid reddish orange blotch.
'Victoria' (L. van Houtte 1869): brilliant orange; early midseason.
'Viscosepala' (*molle* × *viscosum;* M. Waterer before 1848): pale yellowish white, yellow blotch, fragrant, 2" good truss; still popular today.
'Von Gneist' (syn. 'Edward Henry') (*x kosterianum* cl.; P. van Noordt & Son): strong reddish orange, light orange glow.
'W. E. Gumbleton' (*japonicum* cl.; L. van Houtte 1872): light yellow, faint greenish blotch 2¼".
'W. F. Raiffeisen' (*x kosterianum* cl.; P. L. Binken 1940): light reddish orange.
'Willem II' (M. Koster & Sons): reddish orange, early midseason.
'Willem Hardijzer' (W. Hardijzer & Co. 1944): deep red.
'Winston Churchill' ('Koster's Brilliant Red' × seedling; Felix & Dijkhuis 1949): vivid reddish orange, vivid red blotch.
'Yellow Prince' (*x kosterianum* cl.; M. Koster & Sons before 1939): yellow.

PUYALLUP VALLEY HYBRIDS

These are Mollis Hybrid seedlings from the Gregg McKinnon Garden, Sumner, Washington, U.S.A., selected and named by Leonard F. Frisbie, Puyallup, Washington. Hardiness zone 5b–8a. Height 6–8' width 4–6'. Blooming period April-May. Otherwise like the Mollis Hybrids.

'Annie Laurie': strong yellowish orange, edged deep pink, orange yellow blotch.
'Gypsy Lass': orange with flush of pink.
'Indian Chief': orange and yellow.
'Irish Lass': pink, orange, and yellow.
'Orange Princess': orange.
'Signal Light': deep reddish orange.

RUSTICA FLORA PLENO HYBRIDS

The Rustica Flora Peno hybrids were introduced in Belgium about 1890 by Charles Vuylsteke, who acquired them from Louis de Smet also of Belgium. Their origin is unknown, possibly Double Ghent azaleas crossed with the Japanese Azalea. The term "Rustica" involves some confusion, for at times the Double Ghents which have no infusion from the Chinese and Japanese Azaleas have also been known as Rusticas. The Double Ghents Hybrids and Mollis Hybrids were also named Mixtum Hybrids (× Mixtum) by Alfred Rehder. They are commonly called Rustica Flora Pleno Hybrids or Rustica, and all flowers are mid to late blooming and double. Plants are upright and tall, 6–8′ to 4–6′ wide, and hardy in zone 6b–8.

'Aida': faintly tinged pink.
'Byron' (syn. 'Garten Inspektor C. Ohrt'): white tinged deep pink 52D, hose-in-hose, 2½″.
'Freya': light yellowish pink 37C, tipped strong pink 52D, hose-in-hose, 1½″.
'Il Tasso': reddish orange, paler edges, 1½″.
'Milton': white with orange yellow blotch, 2″.
'Murrillo': deep pink, with light orange glow.
'Norma': reddish orange, edged deep pink, 1¼″.
'Phebe': deep yellow.
'Phidias': pale yellow 8D, 1½″.
'Ribera': deep pink.
'Velasquez': pale yellowish white, tinged pink, fading to white.

RECENT GHENT AND MOLLIS HYBRIDS

The recent lack of interest in working with the superb and historically important Ghent and Mollis Hybrids is unfortunate. Only the few hybrids listed below have been introduced since 1958.

'Apricot Glory' (*molle* × *japonicum;* Shammarello): light orange.
'Deep Rose' (Ghent; Mezitt): pink, fragrant, 1¼″.
'Dinie Metselaar' (Mollis; Metselaar, '69): pink, faint yellow blotch, midseason, 2⅜–3½″, broad habit, very hardy.
'Early Orange' (Mollis; N.Z. & Aust.): reddish orange.
'Fragrante Delicto' (Ghent; Carlson): pale pink, star shaped, furrowed petals, fragrant, buds deep pink, late May.
'Henry Allanson' (Mollis; Keshishian, '72): vivid yellow, frilled, 2″, large truss; 6 ft. in 11 yrs., hardy to 0°F.
'Mademoiselle Sue' (Ghent; Carlson): white flushed pink, fragrant, early June.
'Phoebe' (Ghent; N.Z. & Aust.): deep yellow, double, hose-in-hose.
'Red King' (*molle* × *japonicum;* Shammarello): red.
'Red Perfection' (Mollis; A. deBats, introd. W. deJong): dark red, dense truss; vigorous, very hardy.
'Spek's Brilliant' (Mollis × x kosterianum; Spek): vivid red, tinged reddish orange, blotch orange yellow, 4½″, 9 in truss; 4×4′, compact habit.
'Spek's Orange' (Mollis × x kosterianum; Spek, '58): vivid red, tinged orange, blotch orange, 4½″, 9 in truss; 4×4 ft. compact.
'Susan Monyeen' (Mollis; Carlson): light pink, dark pink ribs, large, mid May.
'Willem Hardijzer' (Mollis; Hardijzer, '67): dark yellowish pink, flushed reddish orange, blotch strong orange, wavy, 4¾″, 14 in truss.
'Yellow Bouquet': (*molle* × *japonicum;* Shammarello): yellow.

EARLY OCCIDENTALE HYBRIDS

The Western Azalea *R. occidentale* from the Pacific Coast was discovered in 1827, and seed was sent to the Veitch Nursery in the 1850's. A description of this species is found earlier in this chapter. The Western Azalea is rarely successful on the east coast of North America but has been used in hybridizing abroad and is now being crossed with other azaleas.

In 1870 the Western Azalea was crossed with the Chinese Azalea and later with the Mollis Hybrids by Anthony Waterer in England. This group is known as the Albican Hybrids. While unknown today, they were used by Mr. Waterer in future hybridizing.

Around 1895, selections of the Western Azalea x Mollis Hybrids were introduced by M. Koster & Sons of Holland, John Waterer & Sons, and Crisp Ltd. of England. The clone 'Mrs. Anthony Waterer', introduced in 1892, should possibly be included as an Occidentale Hybrid rather then a Knap Hill. The plants are usually 8 to 10 feet in height. The flowers are usually light colors with a yellow blotch like *R. occidentale,* 2 to 3" wide, fragrant, and bloom mid to late season. Hardiness zone 7a–9.

'Advance': deep pink, yellow blotch.

'Albicans' (*molle* × *occidentale;* A. Waterer 1894): white with yellow blotch, fragrant. Used by L. de Rothschild to introduce *R. occidentale* to the Exbury azaleas.

'Bridesmaid': white, yellow blotch.

'Cinderella' (M. Koster & Sons 1952): pale yellow, brown dots in blotch, large.

'Dainty': white flushed pink, yellow blotch.

'Delicatissima': pale yellowish white, flushed pink, yellow blotch.

'Exquisita': white flushed pink, orange yellow blotch, frilled, scented, 2¼".

'Graciosa': pale orange yellow 19D, suffused strong pink, blotch orange.

'Irene Koster': white flushed strong pink, scented, 2½".

'Joan Paton': orange flushed pink.

'Magnifica': moderate purplish red 55C, blotch orange yellow.

'Mrs. Anthony Waterer' (A. Waterer hybrid introd. 1892, often listed as a Knap Hill): white, suffused moderate pink 50D, blotch vivid yellow 13B, fragrant, late; tall upright.

'Primavera': deep pink and pale white.

'Rosea': pink and white.

'Superba': dark pink, orange blotch, frilled.

'Westminster': pink, scented.

RECENT OCCIDENTALE SELECTIONS AND HYBRIDS

In the early to mid-1900's Leonard F. Frisbie of Tacoma, Washington, U.S.A., made numerous selections of *R. occidentale* from the wild and used them in crosses with other species. In the 1950's Ben Lancaster of Lackamas Gardens, Camas Washington, introduced the Lackamas Hybrids from crosses of *R. occidentale* 'Graciosa' × various Ghent Hybrids. The flowers are 3–4" wide, fragrant, and in large trusses.

Continuing the study of the native forms of *R. occidentale,* Dr. Frank D. Mossman and Mr. Britt Smith both from Washington have evaluated and numbered over 200 selected types throughout the natural range of the species. Reports of their on-going study are often reported in the A. R. S. *Journal.* The *R. occidentale* selections and hybrids do very well on the West Coast but have not been successful or evaluated extensively on the East Coast. Hopefully, in the future we will have reports of successful Occidentale Hybrids in the East. The author has a group of interesting 7 year old seedlings of *R. prunifolium* × *occidentale* in Georgia that are heat tolerant with a range of colors from yellow to pink. These hybrids are still being evaluated and have not been propagated or named. The following Occidentale selections and hybrids have been named. The name of the hybridizer or introducer has been included in parenthesis. In some cases the number used by the hybridizer has been included as a synonym.

'Brimfield Pink' (Spaargaren): light purplish pink on outside to purplish red tube, 2¼", 12–17 in truss, fragrant.

'Calico' ('Coquille' × *bakeri;* Frisbie): pink, yellow, and white, 3", June.

'Calicoette' (Frisbie): same as 'Calico' except 2" flowers.

'Coquille' (Frisbie): white with yellow blotch, 3".

'Crazy Quilt' (Frisbie): white with red and pink stripes, orange blotch, 2½".

'Crescent City Double' (syn. SM-28-2; Smith & Mossman): white to pale pink, orange tint on upper petals, double; mature plants have up to 15 petals, pistil present.

'Crescent City Gold' (syn. SM-30; Smith & Mossman): white with gold stripe on each petal.

'Foggy Dew' (Frisbie): white with pink and yellow, 2".

'Hartman' (Kraus): pink.

'Hazle Smith' ('Corona' × *occidentale;* Wyatt '66): white, large deep red blotch, 2", large truss; 5×5 ft. in 14 yrs.

'Honeydew' (*occidentale* seedling; A. J. Knuttel): brilliant orange, very prolific.

'Humboldt Peppermint' (Frisbie): white with pink stripe down center of each lobe, 2¼".

'Humboldt Picotee' (syn. SM-502; Smith & Mossman): variable, 3 distinct forms, white with purple red margin, normal leaves; red flowers, small pigmented recurved leaves; the third intermediate between the above two; rooted cuttings produce all three forms.

'Jock Brydon' (*molle* × *occidentale;* Clausen, introd. Beneschoen Gardens, '68): white, suffused pink, speckled reddish orange blotch, wavy, ruffled, 3¾", fragrant, 7×7 ft. in 7 yrs.

'July Charm' (*prunifolium* × 'Coquille'; Frisbie): light orange, 2", late.

'June Delight' (Frisbie): orange tinted pink, 2", late.

'Kalama' (Lancaster): orange tinted pink.

'Lackamas Bouquet' (Graciosa' × *luteum;* Lancaster): pale yellowish white and pink, fragrant.

'Langlois Milk Maid' (Frisbie): flushed pink, yellow blotch, 24 flowers in truss all opening at once.

'Leonard Frisbie' (natural selection; Mossman & Smith '69): light red 51B, orange yellow 17A flare, tubular funnel, 3½", 22 florets, compact; 4×4 ft., hardy to −15°F.

'Mazama' (Lancaster): white.

'Miniskirt' (natural selection; Mossman & Smith): white, corolla small ⅜", normal red pistil, filaments very short, anthers small; leaves small.

'Mollala' (Lancaster): no description available.

'Multnomah' (Lancaster): reddish orange.

'Myeena' (Lancaster): pink.

'Ocean Gold' (Frisbie): yellowish white with deep pink markings, orange blotch, 2½".

'Ocean Mist' (Frisbie): white, pink stripes, yellow blotch, 2½".

'Oryx' ((*bakeri* × *occidentale*) × 'Kilauea'; D. Waterer, '75): pale yellowish white, opening white.

'Pistil Packin Mama' (natural selection; Slonecker): pistillate form, flower small ¼–⅜" across × ⅝" long, 5 lobes separate, 1/16–⅛" wide, light yellowish green 145C, tinged pink, slightly fragrant, styles deep red 53B, 10–12 in truss.

'Pistil Pete' (natural selection; Slonecker): pistillate form, lobes small and cut to base, densely hairy, ⅜" long, 1" wide, pale greenish yellow 150D, no stamens, pistil 2½", style purplish red 54B, 17–21 in truss; plant upright 6×4 ft.; hardy to 0°F.

'Prunifolium Junior' (*prunifolium* × 'Ocean Mist'; Frisbie): orange and white 2½"; very late.

'Rogue River Belle' (Frisbie): white with pink markings, yellow blotch, 2½".

'Sacajewea' (Lancaster): orange tinted pink.

'Stagecoach Frills' (natural selection; Mossman & Smith): white, strong yellow blotch, attractive frilled margins.

'Summer Fragrance' (*occidentale* × *luteum;* Pratt, '63): pale yellow 13D, blotch vivid yellow 13A, 10–12 in. truss.

'Summer Tan' (*prunifolium* × 'Foggy Dew'; Frisbie): light orange, 2", late.

'Tahoma' (Lancaster): white.

'Tamsen Donner' (*bakeri* × 'Rogue River Belle'; Frisbie): red, orange and yellow, 2½", late.

'Wallowa' (Lancaster): pale yellowish white.

'Wapata' (Lancaster): pink.

'Winona' (Lancaster):

'Yaquina' (Lancaster): pink.

KNAP HILL HYBRIDS

The history of the Knap Hill azaleas goes back to 1870 when Anthony Waterer and his son at the Knap Hill Nursery of Knap Hill, Woking, England, undertook the improvement of the Ghent Hybrids by crossing them with the Chinese azalea and other species. Anthony Waterer, Sr. described as "The Father of the Deciduous Hybrid Azaleas" did "Good by raising azaleas that were nearly perfect and harm in destroying those that were not" (an excellent practice to be strongly recommended to all breeders).

The Waterer seedlings had large, late blooming flowers with a rich variety of color and substance. Ironically, they named no seedlings save for 'Nancy Waterer'. Very few of their seedling azaleas left the nursery until the death of the younger Anthony in 1924. At that time the seedlings were acquired and developed further by the Slocock, Bagshot and Sunningdale Nurseries of Surrey, England.

In 1922 Lionel de Rothschild of Exbury, Southampton, England, obtained several Knap Hill seedlings including one named 'George Reynolds'. This was one of the parents of 'Hotspur' introduced in 1934. Many of the Exbury seedlings were nearly lost during World War II. Fortunately the restoration of the Gardens and the azaleas was done by Peter Barber and his staff. Many of the Exbury Azaleas have been named and large numbers are sold as seedlings by color.

The Ilam hybrids were developed by the late Edgar Stead at the Ilam Estate, Christchurch, New Zealand with stock derived from the original Knap Hill strains. The Windsor hybrids resulted from Knap Hill seedlings developed by Sir Eric Savill in the Savill Gardens in Windsor Great Park and introduced into the United States by James Wells of New Jersey.

There are five major sub-groups of Knap Hill Azaleas—the Knap Hill, Slocock, Ilam, Exbury, and Windsor. New named clones of the Knap Hill group continue to be developed and introduced. Seedlings are also sold either as to color or as seedlings of a particular clone such as 'Gibraltar' or 'Hotspur'. Seedlings are cheaper and available in quantity, with flowers often only slightly inferior to the named clone.

Knap Hill Azaleas are generally medium to large shrubs, (4–10 feet high, 4–6 feet wide) with a few having a dwarf, spreading habit. Hardy in zones 5a–8a. Young foliage often has a reddish orange tint and many have excellent fall color. The large, wide tubular flowers, 2–3", are usually fragrant and some are doubles. Trusses are often very large, 18–30 flowers, and vary from rounded to spreading in form. Colors range from near whites, to yellow, orange, pink to vivid red. They bloom mid to late mid-season.

The abbreviations following the cultivar names indicate the breeder or source of each of the Knap Hill subgroups.

KH = Knap Hill Nursery
Ex = Exbury Nursery
Sl = Slocock Nursery
Win = Windsor Park

The names of other nurseries breeding Knap Hill type Azaleas are spelled out.

'Ada Brunieres' (KH): white, lightly suffused light purplish pink 56A, blotch vivid yellow 13A.
'Albacore' (KH): white.
'Albatross' (KH '41): white suffused pink.
'Annabella' (Ex '47): strong orange yellow.
'Ann Callingham' (KH): moderate red 50B.
'Aurora' (Ex '47): strong yellowish pink, blotch orange.
'Avocet' (KH): white, tinged pink.
'Ballerina' (Ex): white.
'Balzac' (Ex): reddish orange, fragrant.
'Basilisk' (Ex): pinkish white, blotch yellow.
'Bazaar' (Ex): strong reddish orange.
'Beaulieu' (Ex): pink with orange blotch.

'Berryrose' (Ex): vivid red, blotch vivid yellow, spotted vivid orange, fragrant.
'Betty Kelly' (KH): deep reddish orange.
'Brazil' (Ex '34): vivid reddish orange.
'Brazil' (Ex; A selection of 'Brazil'): strong reddish orange 31A, frilled.
'Bright Forecast' (Ex): light yellowish orange, deep orange blotch, fragrant.
'Bright Straw' (Ex): deep yellow, deeper blotch.
'Brimstone' (Ex): pale yellow.
'Bullfinch' (KH '49): deep red.
'Buzzard' (KH '47): pale yellow tinged pink, fragrant.
'Canasta' (Ex): strong orange yellow, fragrant.
'Cecile' (Ex '47): vivid red, blotch vivid orange yellow.
'Chaka' (KH): deep red.
'Chaffinch' (KH): deep pink.
'Cockatoo' (KH): vivid orange yellow.
'Coos' (KH; 'Hugh Wormald' × 'Marion Merriman'): pale pink yellow blotch.
'Coquette' (KH): deep pink.
'Coronation' (Ex): strong yellowish pink.
'Corringe' (Ex): reddish orange.
'Corston's Yellow' (KH): yellow, derived mainly from *luteum,* strongly scented.
'Crinoline' (Ex): white, flushed pink, frilled.
'Daybreak' (Ex): strong orange yellow, suffused reddish orange, blotch vivid orange to yellow.
'Debutante' (Ex): light purplish pink, lower lobes lighter, orange blotch.
'Desert Pink' (Ex): deep yellowish pink, orange blotch.
'Devon' (Sl '52): strong red 45D, orange shading at throat.
'Diabolo' (KH): strong orange.
'Double Damask' (KH): pinkish white.
'Drift' (KH): white.
'Eisenhower' (Ex '52): vivid reddish orange, blotch strong orange.
'Embley Crimson' (Ex): red.
'Eva Goude' (KH '41): vivid yellow.
'Exbury Apricot' (Ex): strong orange yellow, blotch orange.
'Exbury Cream-Yellow' (Ex): pale yellow.
'Exbury Pink' (Ex): deep pink, small orange blotch.
'Exbury Salmon-Orange' (Ex): reddish orange.
'Exbury White' (Ex): large white with orange yellow blotch.
'Exbury Yellow' (Ex): vivid greenish yellow, blotch orange.
'Fancy Free' (Ex '51): light pink, blotch yellow.
'Farall Pink' (KH; Haworth-Booth): pink, a Knap Hill × Exbury hybrid.
'Farall Yellow' (KH; 'Marion Merriman' × 'Marmalade'; Haworth-Booth): brilliant yellow 4A, blotch vivid yellow 15B.
'Favor Major' (Ex '47): orange yellow.
'Fawley' (Ex '47): white, flushed pink.
'Fireball' (Ex '51): deep red, foliage reddish.
'Firecracker' (KH; Waterer, Sons & Crisp): vivid reddish orange.
'Firecrest' (KH '44): vivid reddish orange.
'Firefly' (Ex '47): vivid purplish red, slight orange flare.
'Fireglow' (Knap Hill sold to Slocock '26): strong reddish orange, 2½".
'Flaming June' (KH '50): deep pink 52C, blotch orange yellow to vivid yellow.
'Flamingo' (KH): deep pink, blotch orange, 2½"; midseason; upright tall.
'Flarepath' (KH): deep red. June.
'Florence Pilkington' (KH '52): white tinged pink.
'Frances Jenkinson' (KH): moderate orange.
'Frills' (Ex '51): reddish orange, frilled.
'Gallipoli' (Ex '47): strong, yellowish pink, orange blotch.

'Gannet' (KH '37): pale pink, suffused pale yellow.
'George Reynolds' (KH; raised by A. Waterer, intro. Rothschild): yellow.
'Gibraltar' (Ex '47): vivid orange, popular; 2½"; midseason.
'Gilbury' (Ex): pink.
'Ginger' (Ex): strong orange 30D.
'Glowing Embers' (Ex; Rothschild sold to Waterer, Sons & Crisp): vivid reddish orange, blotch vivid orange.
'Gog' (Knap Hill sold to Slocock '26): strong orange.
'Gold Crest' (KH '35): brilliant yellow 15C, blotch brilliant orange yellow 17B; 2¾".
'Gold Dust' (Ex '51): deep yellow.
'Golden Dream' (Ex '51): strong orange yellow.
'Golden Eagle' (KH; *calendulaceum* × ?; Knap Hill Nur. '49): strong reddish orange 32B, with orange yellow mid rib, blotch, vivid orange.
'Golden Eve' (KH): reddish orange, orange blotch.
'Golden Eye' (KH '49): vivid reddish orange, blotch strong orange, 2½".
'Golden Girl' (KH '51): yellow deep blotch.
'Golden Guinea' (KH): deep yellow, occasionally petaloid.
'Golden Horn' (Ex '47): strong orange yellow.
'Golden Oriole' (KH '39): brilliant yellow, deep orange blotch, early midseason.
'Golden Slippers': (said to be *R. schlippenbachii* × 'George Reynolds'; R. Henry): vivid orange, 25A, shaded to reddish orange in throat.
'Golden Sunset' (KH; Rothschild, sold to Waterer, Sons & Crisp '48): vivid yellow 16C.
'Goldfinch' (KH '41): light yellow 15D, blotch vivid yellow 15A, slight tinge of reddish orange.
'Gwenda Kitcat' (KH): pink and white, fragrant.
'Gwyneth' (KH): orange.
'Harvest Moon' (Sl, Knap Hill Nur.,–Slocock '38): brilliant yellow 18A, blotch darker, frilled, 2½".
'Heron' (KH '52): strong reddish orange 35A, blotch orange yellow.
'H. H. Hunnewell' (Sl, A. Waterer sold to Slocock '20): vivid purplish red.
'Hiawatha' (KH '52): vivid reddish orange, darker blotch, early midseason.
'Homebush' (KH; Knap Hill, named by H. Waterer sold to Slocock '26): vivid purplish red 55A, semidouble, 1¼".
'Honeysuckle' (Ex): pale pink, orange blotch.
'Hoopoe' (KH '35): moderate pink.
'Hotspur' (Ex): reddish orange.
'Hotspur Orange' (Ex): reddish orange.
'Hotspur Red' (Ex): strong reddish orange 32B, blotch vivid orange 25B.
'Hotspur Salmon Buff' (Ex): light yellowish pink, deep orange blotch.
'Hotspur Yellow' (Ex; Rothschild '47): yellow, blotch orange.
'Hugh Wormald' (Ex): vivid yellow 13B, blotch orange yellow 23A.
'Imago' (KH): deep yellow, tinged purplish red.
'Iora' (KH): yellow.
'Javelin' (KH): strong orange yellow and red, late.
'J. J. Jennings' (Ex): red.
'Joy Bentall' (KH): orange, flushed orange yellow.
'Kathleen' (Ex '47): light orange, darker blotch.
'Kentucky Minstrel' (KH): strong orange yellow, and orange: 'Golden Eagle' × Knap Hill seedling.
'Kestrel' (KH; probably a hybrid of *R. calendulaceum;* '52): orange.
'Kilauea' (KH): reddish orange, blotch orange, late.
'Kipps' (Ex '43): vivid reddish orange, blotch orange.
'Klondyke' (Ex '47): strong orange 24A, blotch orange yellow 23A.
'Knap Hill Apricot' (KH '50): moderate yellow, early midseason.
'Knap Hill Orange' (KH '51): vivid orange.
'Knap Hill Pink' (KH; named by H. Waterer '25): moderate purplish pink 62B, blotch orange yellow 21B.
'Knap Hill Red' (KH '48): deep red.

'Knap Hill Tangerine (KH): strong orange.

'Knap Hill White' (KH; named by H. Waterer '25): very pale pink, fading white.

'Knap Hill Yellow' (KH '51): vivid yellow, tinged orange.

'Knighthood' (Ex): strong yellowish pink 40D.

"Krakatoa' (KH): red.

'Lady Derby' (KH '37): pale yellowish pink, tinged pink, orange blotch.

'Lady Rosebery' (KH '44): vivid red.

'Lapwing' (KH '35): brilliant yellow, blotch brilliant orange, 2".

'Leo Kelly' (KH): orange yellow.

'Lila' (KH): pale purplish pink.

'Lorelei' (KH): pale purplish pink.

'Madeleine' (Ex): pale pink, blotch yellow.

'Marina' (Ex '51): pale yellow, deeper blotch.

'Marion Merriman' (KH; Knap Hill Nur. named by H. Waterer, '25): brilliant yellow 15C, flushed orange yellow 17C, blotch vivid orange yellow 23A, frilled, 6 petals, 3½". Late midseason.

'Marionette' (KH): pink, orange blotch, fragrant.

'Mary Claire' (Ex '51): pink, yellow blotch.

'Mauna Loa' (KH): red with orange blotch.

'Mauve Pink' (KH): purplish pink, semidouble.

'Mazurka' (KH): light yellowish pink, fragrant.

'Mephistopheles' (KH): deep red 46A.

'Merlin' (KH '41): strong yellowish pink, blotch orange, wrinkled.

'Middle East' (Ex '51): deep orange.

'Minuet' (KH): pink, white and yellow.

'Mrs. Anthony Waterer' (KH): white suffused moderate pink 50D, blotch vivid yellow 13B fragrant, very late; upright tall. This is one of A. Waterer's hybrids of *R. occidentale* introduced in 1892 (See Occidentale List).

'Mrs. Gomer Waterer' (KH '50): pinkish white, and pale purplish pink, semidouble.

'Nam Khan' (Ex): deep pink.

'Nancy Buchanan' (Ex '47): white, yellow blotch.

'Old Gold' (Ex '51): light orange yellow, flushed pink.

'Orangeade' (KH): orange.

'Orient' (Ex '51): strong reddish orange, blotch orange.

'Osprey' (KH): white.

'Oxydol' (Ex '47): white, blotch of yellowish dots.

'Paramount' (KH): yellow, double; late.

'Pastiche' (KH): yellow and pink.

'Pavane' (KH): light yellowish pink, fragrant.

'Peregrine' (KH '49): orange.

'Persil' (Sl, Knap Hill sold to Slocock): white, pale yellow blotch.

'Petrouchka' (KH): strong orange yellow and yellow.

'Pink Delight' (Ex '51): deep pink.

'Pink Ruffles' (Ex; named by Rothschild; sold to Waterer, Sons & Crisp): pink, orange blotch.

'Pompadour' (KH): moderate pink, orange blotch, fragrant.

'Princess' (Sl '36): deep pink, 52C, orange yellow blotch 21B.

'Princess Royal' (Ex): white flushed pink, yellow blotch.

'Quaker Maid' (Ex; Rothschild sold to Waterer, Sons & Crisp): light pinkish white, edged pink, orange blotch.

'Radiance' (Ex): light orange yellow 21D to yellowish pink 41B, blotch orange yellow 17B.

'Red Brazil' (Ex): similar to 'Brazil' but deeper red.

'Red Indian' (KH; derived from *R. calendulaceum;* '51): reddish orange, yellow blotch.

'Redshank' (KH '47): light orange yellow 24C, flushed reddish orange 32B, blotch orange yellow 17C; 2½".

'Renne' (Ex): vivid red, suffused yellow.

'Robin' (KH '41): reddish orange, late; spreading, medium height.

'Rocket' (Ex; 'Hotspur' × orange seedling; Rothschild sold to Waterer, Sons & Crisp): strong orange yellow, blotch yellow.
'Rosella' (KH): white, purplish red margin 55C, blotch orange yellow.
'Royal Lodge' (Ex; '47): red, long protruding stamens.
'Ruddy Duck' (KH '41): reddish orange, blotch orange yellow.
'Rumba' (KH): vivid orange, red tubes.
'Ruth Davies' (KH): orange.
'Sahara' (KH): yellow, late.
'Salmon Orange' (Ex): strong yellowish pink, orange blotch.
'Sand Dune' (Ex): light pink, suffused orange yellow.
'Sandpiper' (KH '41): pale yellow, flushed pink, orange blotch, 3"; late midseason; tall.
'Saskia' (KH): pink, late.
'Satan' (Sl; Knap Hill Nur. sold to Slocock '26): vivid red.
'Scarlet Pimpernel' (Ex '47): red.
'Sceptre' (KH; Knap Hill seedling × 'Mrs. Anthony Waterer'): pinkish white, tinged purplish pink.
'Severn' (Wisley): strong pink, blotch orange yellow.
'Seville' (Sl; Knap Hill Nur. sold to Slocock '26): orange.
'Silver Slipper' (Ex; Rothschild sold to Waterer, Sons & Crisp '48): light pink 39D, blotch vivid yellow 15B, 3¼"; late.
'Siskin' (KH): yellow, (*luteum* × *molle*), buds tender, appears a fine form of *luteum*.
'Soft Lips' (Ex '51): flushed yellow, with blotch.
'Sonia' (Ex '51): white flushed pink.
'Strawberry Ice' (Ex '47): strong yellowish pink, overlay deep yellow pink, blotch orange yellow.
'Stromboli' (KH): red.
'Sugared Almond' (Ex '51): pale pink.
'Sun Chariot' (Ex; Rothschild sold to Waterer, Sons & Crisp): vivid yellow 16C, blotch orange yellow 33A.
'Sunset' (KH): orange, flushed purplish pink.
'Sunset Pink' (Ex '51): vivid red, yellow blotch.
'Surprise' (KH): vivid orange yellow, frilled, fragrant, large.
'Swallow' (Ex): strong orange yellow.
'Sydney Firth' (KH): pink, orange blotch, frilled, fragrant.
'Sylphides' (KH '50): purplish pink 12B, blotch vivid yellow 15B, 2½".
'Syncopation' (KH): yellow and moderate red.
'Tangiers' (Ex): strong orange.
'Tessa' (Ex '47): strong orange flushed reddish orange at tips.
'Toucan' (KH '41): pale pinkish white 3½". Late midseason, upright open.
'Troupial' (KH): reddish orange 31A, outside of tube strong red 47A.
'Tunis' (Sl; Knap Hill Nur. sold to Slocock '26): dark red 53C, blotch reddish orange 31B.
'Tyrol' (KH): pale pinkish white, late.
'Venetia' (KH): moderate yellowish pink, late.
'Whitethroat' (KH '41): white, double 2", late midseason; spreading medium height.
'White Yellow Eye' (Ex): white, yellow blotch, fragrant.
'Wryneck' (KH): vivid yellow, edged pink.
'Yaffle' (KH; *prunifolium* × ?; '41): reddish orange, late, spreading medium height.
'Zanzibar' (KH): vivid yellow, splashed yellow pink.

KNAP HILL AND EXBURY AZALEAS INTRODUCED SINCE 1959

Unfortunately complete information on size of flowers, habit of growth, and hardiness of all cultivars is not available. See Appendix I.

'Alice' (KH; Pride): pale yellowish white; compact habit.
'Altair' (Ex): pale yellow, blotch yellow.
'Amber Rain' (Ex; Rothschild-Waterer '62): vivid yellow, blotch orange.

'Anna Pavlova' (KH; Kraus, intr. by Beneschoen Gar. '67): white, double, ruffled, 2½", fragrant, 9 in truss, midseason; 42×42" in 8 yrs.

'Annelies' ('Gibraltar' seedling; A. Knuttel): deep orange, large truss, very fragrant.

'Ann Ione' (KH; Girard, raised & reg; Peters '81): light purplish pink 65C, wavy, fragrant, 3½"; 7×6 ft. in 17 yrs.; hardy to −25°F.

'Anquistas' (KH): light yellow, outlined in pink, fragrant.

'Arctic Sun' ('Cecile' selfed; Childers): white, blotch orange yellow 17A–B, margins light yellow 16D, buds orange yellow; 4×8 ft. in 22 yrs., hardy to 0°F.

'Avon' (KH; R. H. S. Wisley '62): light yellow, darker spotting in blotch, wavy, yellow stamens.

'Bakkarat' ('Coccinea Speciosa' × 'Gibraltar'; Hachmann, Ger. '78): orange, blotch yellow, wavy, 2–2½", 5–11 in truss, late; low.

'Balkis' (Ex): pale yellowish white, yellow blotch.

'Banana Split' (Cecile' × 'Sylphides'; A. J. Knuttel): pale yellowish white, flushed pink, vivid yellow blotch, ruffled, vivid red throat, loose truss.

'Barbara Jenkinson' (KH): moderate orange.

'Big Girl' (White Knap Hill × 'Avocet'; Phipps): pale purplish pink, orange green blotch. 3".

'Brides Bouquet' (Ex): white, flushed pale pink.

'Brinnon Beauty' (Knap Hill) parents unknown; Bailey, '85: deep yellowish pink 39A, prominent orange blotch, throat strong reddish orange 32B; reverse deep reddish orange 42A, 4", wavy frilled recurved lobes, buds gray reddish orange 182A, ball shaped truss up to 17; broad rounded 6×6" in 14 yrs.; hardy to 0.

'Buttercream' (KH; Cummins): pale yellow, 2", early.

'Buttercup' (K. H. van Gelderen Holland): yellow.

'Buttons and Bows' (Knap Hill): open pollinated 'Strawberry Ice'; Bailey, '85: light yellow 20B with ± ½" strong reddish orange 32B to deep yellowish pink 39B edging, with blotch same color, 7 frilled lobes, 3" fragrant, compact truss up to 15; upright rounded 5×5½" in 14 yrs; leaves red in fall; hardy to 0.

'Calder' (KH; R. H. S. Wisley '69): deep pink 52C, flushed & veined moderate red 50A, fading to almost white, slight yellow blotch, 2½", 12–15 in truss.

'Calico' (KH; Waterer '75): vivid yellow.

'Cam' (KH; R. H. S. Wisley '62): light purplish pink 56A, deepening to strong purplish pink 55B on wavy margins, yellow blotch, 16–20 in truss.

'Canary Yellow' ('Cecile' selfed; Henny '70): vivid yellow, fades lighter, 2 faint yellow streaks, star shaped, 3½".

'Cannon's Double' (Ex): pale yellowish white, lobes pink, double.

'Caprice' (Ex): deep pink.

'Caterina' (Exbury seedling; Kern): pale yellow, flushed pink, frilled, 3–4", large trusses, early; low, hardy −5°F.

'Cheerful Giant' (Whitethroat' × yellow seedling; Sorenson '84): light yellow 13C, double, 3½", 12 in truss; leaves reddish in fall; 3½–4 ft. in 8 yrs; hardy to −20°F.

'Chelsea Reach' (Rozanne Waterer' × ?; KH '72): pale yellowish white, flushed purplish pink.

'Chenille' (KH; Waterer-Knap Hill '75): vivid red.

'Chorister' (KH; Knap Hill '62): light yellowish white, double, foliage tinted reddish.

'Chocolate Ice' ('Donald Waterer' × 'Whitethroat'; Waterer '74): white.

'Clarice' (Ex): light yellowish pink, blotch orange.

'Clyde' (KH; R. H. S. Wisley '60): white tinted pink, orange blotch, crinkled, 12 in truss.

'Coral Queen' (KH; Pride): yellowish pink, orange flush; dense growth.

'Coral Red' (KH; Pride): deep yellowish pink, flushed red, fragrant.

'Coronation Lady' (KH): yellowish pink, blotch orange yellow.

'Colin Kenrick' (KH; Knap Hill Nur.): pale pink, fragrant.

'Crimson Tide', see 'Girard's Crimson Tide'.

'Cynthia Ann' (KH; Peters '81):moderate orange yellow 24C, blotch yellow, frilled, fragrant, 3"; 5×7 ft. in 17 yrs.; hardy to −25°F.

'Dart' (KH; R. H. S. Wisley '62): deep pink, yellow blotch, 4¾", 12 in truss; some stamens petaloid.

'Dawn's Chorus' ('Strawberry Ice' × 'Persil'; Sorenson '84): light pink 49C, tinted white, yellow blotch, frilled, 3", fragrant, bud reddish orange; 5×5 ft. in 10 yrs; hardy to −20°F.

'Deben' (KH; R. H. S. Wisley '66): brilliant yellow 15C, tinged vivid yellow 15B, large orange yellow blotch, frilled, 2½", 15–18 in truss.

'Deborah Alice' (KH; Girard, intr. by Peters '83): white, blotch vivid yellow 14A, buds yellow 11A, wavy, fragrant, 2½". 12 in truss; upright compact, 2½×4 ft. in 10 yrs.; hardy to −25°F.

'Dee' (KH; R. H. S. Wisley '62): white flushed pink on reverse of 3 upper petals, blotch orange yellow, 3", 14–17 in truss.

'Del's Choice' ('Cecile' × F-2; Childer '71): deep pink, to purplish red, orange blotch, squarish flowers, 4", mid May; 3½ ft. in 12 yrs.

'Derwent' (KH; R. H. S. Wisley '67): white, veined and flushed moderate pink 54D, blotch orange, 2¾", frilled, wavy, 16 in truss.

'Doctor Lee Shields' (KH; Girard, raised & reg. Peters '81): pale orange yellow 19B, yellow wash 39A at edges, wavy, fragrant, 3", 9–17 in truss; 6×6 ft. in 17 yrs.; hardy to −25°F.

'Doctor Rudolph Henny' ('Cecile' selfed; Henny '68): reddish orange, fading pink, yellow spotting, semidouble, 6 lobes, 4", 6–10 in truss.

'Donald Waterer' (Knap Hill Nur.): deep yellow, reddish orange outside.

'Dorothy Corston' (KH; Knap Hill '67): deep red, leaves tinted red; dense growth.

'Dosewallips Gold' (Knap Hill): 'Old Gold' selfed; Bailey '85: light orange yellow 19A, orange blotch with ±¼" strong reddish orange 31B edging, 3½", 5 wavy reflexed lobes, fragrant, ball shaped truss up to 12; new leaves vivid purplish red 57A; broad rounded 5½×6" wide in 14 yrs.; hardy to 0.

'Dracula' (KH; Hillier '71): strong reddish orange 32B, strong red 52A overlay, frilled, buds dark red.

'Elsie Pratt' ('Sylphides' × ?; M. C. Pratt, intr. by deJong): deep pink, orange blotch, stamens & tube red, 2⅜–3"; 8–16 in truss; upright spreading, very hardy.

'Edwina Mountbatten' (Ex): deep yellow.

'Evening Glow' (KH): pale pink, tinged light yellow, throat yellow.

'Ezra J. Kraus' ('Cecile' × 'Strawberry Ice'; Beneschoen Gar. '67): moderate pink 49C, wavy, fragrant, 3½", 11 in truss; 4×4 ft. in 6 yrs.

'Fal' (KH; R. H. S. Wisley '72): light yellow 18B, and light yellowish pink 29C, flushed red, blotch orange yellow.

'Farall Flamingo' (KH; Haworth-Booth '62): strong orange 24A, suffused vivid orange 30C, 5–7 in truss.

'Farall Mandarine' ('Farall Yellow' × 'Farall Pink'; Haworth-Booth '69): pale reddish orange, square shaped flowers.

'Farall Orangea' ('Exquisita' × 'Mrs. Oliver Slocock'; Haworth-Booth '69): orange yellow, fragrant, 3", late May.

'Fasching' ('Royal Command' × 'Gilbraltar'; Hachmann '78): brilliant orange 25C with yellowish pink 28A–B, marked vivid yellowish pink 30C, 5–6 lobes, 2", 18–21 in truss.

'Feuerwerk' ('Cecile' × 'Fireball': Hachmann, Ger. '77): deep reddish orange 32A–B to 33A, blotch vivid orange 28A–B, fringed, 4½–5", 7–10 in truss, late; upright.

'Fragrant Gold' (KH; de Wilde, intr. by Magruder '74): light yellow 17A, darker spots, fragrant, 5–6 wavy lobes, 2½–2¾", 15–20 in truss; 42×52" in 12 yrs.; hardy to −10°F.

'France' (Ex seedling; Kern): light yellow fades to pale yellow, flushed pink, 3"; very late; medium; hardy −10°F.

'Frome' (KH; R. H. S. Wisley '62): strong orange yellow, overlaid reddish orange in throat, wavy frilled, 2¾", 12–14 in truss.

'Gallipoli Red' (Ex): reddish orange.

'Gilda' (Ex; Marty, Aust, '73): strong reddish orange 32C, blotch orange.

'Gladngay' ('Cecile F2'; Childers '71): moderate orange yellow 24C, overlay of reddish orange 40C, blotch orange 26A, 6 squarish petals, 4", 11 in truss.

'Glockenspiel' (KH; Waterer, introd. Knap Hill '75): yellowish pink.

'Glorious Orange' ('Gilbraltar' seedling; A. Knuttel): light orange, large truss, prolific.

'Goldflamme' ('Gibraltar' × 'Royal Command'; Hachmann, Ger. '79): brilliant orange 25C, suffused reddish orange 30A–D, reverse side orange 25C, tinted deep pink 52B, 3⅛–3⅝", late.

'Golden Flare' ('Aurea Grandiflora' seedling; Metselaar, '69): vivid yellow, blotch reddish orange, 2½", 12–14 in truss; tall; very hardy.

'Golden Glory' (Ex): yellow, blotch darker.

'Golden Peace' (Ex; Conard Pyle Nur.): yellow, large strong orange blotch; upright habit.

'Golden Superior' (KH; Bruns): vivid orange yellow 21A.

'Gwynnid Lloyd' (Ex): white, flushed pink, blotch yellow.

'Hachman Juanita' ('Cecile' × 'Gibraltar'; Hachmann, Ger. '79): deep to strong pink 52B–C, blotch vivid orange 25A to orange yellow 21A, 2⅛–3", 5–11 in truss; upright.

'Harwell' ('Sylphides' × 'Pomadour'; Knap Hill Nur. '68): deep pink, large, good truss.

'Hell's Fire' ('Big Red' × red Exbury; Childers '71): strong red, light overlay reddish orange, squarish, 6 lobes, 4½", 7–9 in truss, mid May; 3 ft. in 8 yrs.

'High Fashion' (KH): deep pink, blotch orange.

'Holly's Yellow' (seedling from 'Penny'; Holly, reg. by Dosser '83): orange yellow 21C with vivid orange yellow flare 23A, 3", 11–13 in truss.

'Hotspur Salmon' (Ex.): moderate yellowish pink, blotch orange.

'Hotspur White' (Ex): white, blotch deep yellow.

'Humber' (KH; R. H. S. Wisley '64): vivid yellow, edged yellowish pink, blotch orange yellow.

'Icarus' (Ex): yellowish pink and orange.

'Impala' (Knap Hill × 'Satan'; Waterer-Knap Hill '75): deep red.

'Isolde' (Exbury seedling; Kern): brilliant yellow, 3–4", long stamens; midseason; tall; hardy −10°F.

'Jack A. Sand' ('Homebush' × 'Cecile F2'; Sand, introd. Eichelser '80): vivid purplish red 55A at edges to lighter yellowish pink 36A toward throat, orange yellow blotch 17A, frilled, petaloid, (double), fragrant, 30×36" in 7 yrs.

'Jackie Parton' (KH): light reddish orange, striped orange, double.

'Janet Baker' (Ex; E. de Rothschild '82): yellowish white 158D, flare orange yellow 23A.

'Jessica Lynn' ('Gilbraltar' seedling; A. Knuttel): orange, ruffled, small truss, prolific.

'John Chappell' (KH; Bovee, intr. by Chappell '75): vivid yellow 14A, blotch orange 24A, wavy, 3¼", 8–12 in truss; 30×36" in 9 yrs.; hardy to 5°F.

'John F. Kennedy' ('Corringe' × 'Knighthood'; Beneschoen Gar. '68): dark reddish orange 43A, ruffled, fragrant, 3", 9 in truss; 3½×5 ft. in 6 yrs.

'Juliette' (Exbury seedling; Kern): light orange, 3", early; hardy −10°F.

'Karl Korn' ('Basilisk' × 'Ginger'; Korn '66): moderate orange yellow, 4", 15 in truss; 4×4 ft. in 10 yrs.

'Katanga' (Ex; Rothschild '82): deep pink, darker throat.

'Kensey' (KH; R. H. S. Wisley '64): light yellow, overlay of yellowish pink 37C and reddish orange, blotch yellow.

'Kern's Pride' (Exbury seedling; Kern): dark pink, orange undertone, frilled, 3–4", midseason, fragrant; tall; hardy −10°F.

'King Red' (Ex; King, intr. by Kehr '83): vivid red, slightly ruffled, large ball truss; leaves bullate, difficult from cuttings, propagated by tissue culture.

'Knap Hill Gog' (KH: N. Z. & Aust.): reddish orange.

'Lady Cynthia Colville' (Ex): deep pink, blotch yellow.

'Lady Jayne' (Exbury × 'Klondyke'; Elliot '77): vivid yellow 15A, suffused reddish orange 33B, blotch orange yellow 21A, wavy fragrant, 3½", 8–9 in truss; 3×3½ ft. in 8 yrs.; hardy to 0°F.

'Langley' (Ex): pink, blotch yellow.

'Leigh' ('Gibraltar' seedling; A. Knuttel): reddish orange, pointed petals, loose truss.

'Lemon Ice' (Ex; Serbin): pale yellow; 4 ft. in 10 yrs.

'Liffey' (KH; R. H. S. Wisley '72): white, blotch strong orange.

'Lindy Lou' ('Cecile' × 'Sylphides'; A. J. Knuttel): pink fading to yellowish pink, large truss; vigorous.

'Lucky Lady' (Ex; Zimmerman '66): vivid yellow, blotch reddish, 2½", 30–34 in truss.

'Mandarin Maid' (KH; Hyatt '82): strong orange 29A, fading to light yellowish pink 29A, veined and suffusion of yellowish pink 37B, blotch orange yellow, 5–7 wavy lobes, 3½", fragrant; 3×5½ ft. in 10 yrs.; hardy to −5°F.

'Margaret Olive' (KH; Girard, intr. by Peters '83): brilliant yellow 11A, orange yellow edging on two lobes, blotch vivid yellow 14A, wavy, fragrant, funnel shaped, 3"; upright, 4×7 ft. in 17 yrs; hardy to −25°F.

'Marie' (Ex;N.Z.): purplish pink.

'Marlies' (KH; Pratt, intr. by deJong); deep pink, large blotch orange yellow, late; very hardy.

'Mary Holman' (KH; Pride): red, 2", slightly fragrant; very hardy.

'Mavis' (KH): moderate pink.

'Medway' (KH; R. H. S. Wisley '62): light purplish pink 56A, wavy frilled darker margins, blotch yellow.

'Mermaid' (Exbury seedling; Kern): white with yellow throat, early; medium; hardy −10°F.

'Mernda Yellow' (Ex; Marty): orange yellow.

'Mersey' (KH; R. H. S. Wisley '64): deep pink 48B, blotch yellow, wavy, 4", 12 in truss.

'Middle East' (Ex): deep orange.

'Mildred Alfarata' (KH; Girard, intr. by Peters '81): brilliant yellow 11A, blotch vivid yellow, wavy, frilled, buds reddish orange; upright, 5×7 ft. in 17 yrs.; hardy to −25°F.

'Moonlight Rose' (Ex): pale shades of pink.

'Musette' (Exbury seedling; Kern): dark reddish orange, large round truss, late; tall, hardy −5°F. Requires shade.

'Nene' (KH; R. H. S. Wisley '64): light pink 49C, deep yellowish pink overlay, blotch light yellow.

'Night Light' (KH): white.

'One-O-One' ('Cecile' selfed; Childers '78): deep orange 43D, marbled or veined lighter, blotch orange yellow, 6 wavy lobes, fragrant, 4"; upright 4×8 ft. in 21 yrs.; hardy to −10°F.

'Orange Supreme' (Ex; Marty, Aust. '73): strong orange 30D, flushed deep reddish orange 33A, blotch vivid orange.

'Orange Truffles' (KH; Hiller & Son '67): strong orange yellow, brilliant yellow outside, flushed reddish orange on tube and back of petals, double, frilled, crinkled, 1½–2".

'Orientale' (Exbury seedling; Kern): orange yellow flushed pink, 5–7 petals, 3–4", late; medium compact; hardy −10°F.

'Orwell' (KH; R. H. S. Wisley '68): strong pink 51C, 2½", 11 in truss.

'Papoose' (KH; Waterer-Knap Hill '75): pale pink.

'Patti' (Exbury seedling; Kern): vivid yellow, frilled, late; medium; hardy −10°F.

'Painted Desert' (Exbury × 'Primrose'; Garrett): light orange yellow 19B, variegated light yellowish pink 33D, blotch orange yellow 17B, pinkish tube, 1½" long, midseason.

'Peppermint' (KH): pink with lighter striped, midribs, yellow blotch.

'Peach Sherbet' (KH; Pride): yellowish pink, mildew resistant, very hardy.

'Peach Sunset' (KH): deep yellowish pink.

'Piccolo' (KH; Waterer-Knap Hill '75): very pale yellow, tinged pink.

'Pink Balloon' (Ex; White Flower): light pink.

'Pink Cloud' (Exbury seedling; Kern): strong pink, good truss, midseason; medium; hardy −10°F.

'Pink Gem' (KH; Herbert): yellowish pink to pink, 3", open truss; 5 ft. in 10 yrs.; hardy to −15°F; reddish fall foliage.

'Pink Sherbet' (KH): pink.

'Plectrum' (KH; D. Waterer, intro. Knap Hill '75): light reddish orange.

'Pom Pom' ('Cecile F2': Childers '71): deep pink to moderate orange, blotch strong red, 8 ruffled petals, 2¾", 11–13 in truss; 6 ft. in 11 yrs.

'Pot of Gold' (Knap Hill seedling; Kern '58): vivid yellow, 6 petals, midseason; 12×7 ft. tall in 30 yrs.; hardy to −15°F.

'Primrose' (Ex): pale yellow.

'Princess Margaret of Windsor' (Ex; Rothschild '81): orange yellow 21C, flushed orange yellow 21A.

'Pumpkin' (KH; Johnson): deep orange yellow.

'Pure Gold' ('Cecile F2'; Childers '71): light orange, blotch orange, pink overlay, 7 petals, 4", 11–12 in truss; 4 ft. in 12 yrs.

'Queen Louise' (Ex): pale pink, yellow throat.

'Rachel Dacre' (Ex; Rothschild '82): vivid yellow 14C, blotch orange yellow 21A, 14 in truss.

'Rapunzel' ('Golden Sunset' × ruffled yellow seedling; Sorenson '84): light yellow 10B, darker shading 11B, inconsistent orange spotting, 6–8 wavy, frilled lobes, fragrant, 3", modified 0–5 stamens; fall leaf color; upright rounded 5×5 ft. in 12 yrs.; hardy to −20°F.

'Redder Than' (KH; Pride): red, slightly fragrant, 2", very hardy.

'Redder Yet' (KH; Leach, intr. by Pride): strong purplish red 54A, brown spotting.

'Red Sizzler' (KH; Pride): red, slightly fragrant, 2", very hardy.

'Ribble' (KH; R. H. S. Wisley '62): between strong pink 52D and strong purplish pink 55B, orange blotch, frilled, 3½".

'Rio D'oro' (KH): orange yellow, striped orange.

'Rothschild Supreme' (KH): yellow, double.

'Royal Command' (Ex): vivid reddish orange.

'Rozanne Waterer' (Knap Hill Nur. '62): white, tinged red, deep pink tube, double, midseason.

'Saint Ruan' (KH; Knap Hill Nur. '62): white, large yellow blotch.

'Sampler' (KH): white, pink tips, blotch yellow.

'Sarina' ('Cecile' × 'Gibraltar'; Hachmann, Ger. '80): moderate to deep red 47C-D, blotch vivid orange 28B, 3⅛–4", late; upright.

'Satan's Choice' (KH; Sorenson '84): vivid reddish orange, tinged orange yellow, vivid orange blotch, semidouble 7–10 frilled, reflexed petals, no stamens, 2½"; 3½×5 ft. in 10 yrs.; hardy to −20°F; leaves reddish brown in fall.

'Scarlatti, (KH; Knap Hill Nur. '72): red.

'Scarlet O'Hara' (Ex): red.

'Scarlet Supreme' (Ex): vivid red.

'Sham's Yellow' (KH; Shammarello): light yellow, fragrant.

'Shanty' (KH; Knap Hill Nur. '75): pale yellowish pink.

'Snowwhite' (KH): white, blotch yellow, fragrant.

'St. Jee' (KH): light purplish pink; tall.

'Stour' (KH; R. H. S. Wisley '62): vivid reddish orange, blotch vivid orange, wavy, 2¾", 1–3 in truss.

'Summer Day' (Exbury seedling; Kern): strong yellow, fragrant, midseason; tall, hardy −10°F.

'Sunburst' ('George Reynolds' × 'Klondyke'; Henny & Wennekamp '75): vivid yellow, wavy, fragrant, 2½", 15–20 in truss; 4×6 ft. in 10 yrs.; hardy to −25°F.

'Sunburst' (Exbury seedling; Kern): brilliant yellow, fragrant; very late; medium; hardy −10°F; heat resistant.

'Sunset Boulevard' (Ex): pale pink.

'Sunte Nectarine' (Ex): deep orange, blotch yellow.

'Sweet Caroline' (Ex; A. J. Knuttel): light pink, deeper pink ruffled edges, yellow flare, mild fragrance.

'Sweet Christy' (KH; de Wilde, intr. by Magruder '77): brilliant yellow, fading light to near white, blotch yellow, frilled, fragrant, 2½–3", 11–14 in truss; mildew resistant; 36×45" in 13 yrs.; hardy to 10°F.

'Tamar' (KH; R. H. S. Wisley '64): vivid yellow, blotch orange yellow.

'Tam O'shanter' (Ex; Caperci, intr. by McDonald '83): strong orange 26B, blotch orange yellow 23A, throat light yellow 18A, frilled, 3"; upright 3×5 ft. in 15 yrs.; hardy to 0°F.

'Tay' (KH; R. H. S. Wisley '62): brilliant yellow, blotch orange, frilled, 3½", 10–14 in truss.

'Tees' (KH; R. H. S. Wisley '64): deep pink, vivid yellow blotch.

'Thomas Jefferson' ('Kathleen' × 'Firefly'; Beneschoen Gar. '67): moderate reddish orange 32D, 6 ruffled petals, fragrant, 4", 10 in truss; 42×42" in 6 yrs.

'Thumbelina' (KH): pink, double.

'Tonga' (Ex; Baldsiefen '74): vivid reddish orange, semi hose-in-hose, funnel shaped, 5–7 frilled lobes, 3", 10 in truss; 2½×3 ft. in 10 yrs.; hardy to −25°F.

'Torcia' ('Cecile' selfed; Childers '78): strong red 52D, veined darker, shading at tips to reddish orange, blotch orange 25A–23A, wavy frilled, fragrant, 3½", 13 in truss; 3½×7 ft. in 21 yrs. hardy to −10°F.

'Trent' (KH; R. H. S. Wisley '59): light yellow, wavy fringed orange margins, blotch orange yellow, 3", 10 in truss.

'Tweed' (KH; R. H. S. Wisley '64): vivid red with strong red overlay.

'Tyne' (KH; R. H. S. Wisley '62): between deep and light pink 52C–50D, blotch orange, 3", 11 in truss.

'Umpqua Queen' (KH; Schoneman, intr. by Theiss A. G. '79):brilliant yellow 11A, blotch vivid yellow 14A, 4", 12 in truss; 40×50" in 8 yrs.; hardy to 0°F.

'Verulam' (Ex): pale yellow, blotch yellow.

'Victoria Elizabeth' (KH; Girard, intr. by Peters '82): pale orange yellow 19B, reddish orange wash on 2 lobes, blotch orange yellow 22B, wavy, fragrant, 2½", buds reddish orange 40C; 6×6 ft. in 17 yrs.; hardy to −25°F.

'Vineland Flame' ('Gibraltar' × 'Favor Major'; Henry, intr. by H. R. I. O. V. S. '78): vivid red to reddish orange 44A–B, fragrant, 2⅜", 10–12 in truss; upright, 4×5 ft. in 16 yrs.; hardy to −15°F.

'Vineland Flare' ('Klondyke' × 'George Reynolds'; Henry, intr. by H. R. I. O. V. S. '78): vivid yellow 15B, wavy, fragrant, 2⅜", 10–12 in truss; upright 4×6 ft. in 16 yrs.; hardy to −15°F.

'Vineland Glow' ('Gibraltar' × 'Favor Major'; Henry, intr. by H. R. I. O. V. S. '78): deep reddish orange 33A, wavy, fragrant, 2⅜", 10–12 in truss, upright 3½×4½ ft. in 16 yrs.; hardy to −15°F.

'Violet Gordon' (KH): vivid orange, yellowish blotch; reddish foliage.

'Vivienne Waterer' (KH; Knight '75): strong yellow.

'Waveney' (KH; R. H. S. Wisley '62): vivid yellow, blotch orange yellow, wavy, 3½".

'Westminster' (KH): light pink.

'White Swan' (Ex): white, yellow blotch.

'White Top' (Ex; Teese, Aust.): white, blotch yellow.

'Windrush' (KH; R. H. S. Wisley '71): vivid purplish pink 55A, flushed and veined white, blotch orange yellow, 3", 10 in truss.

'Wryneck' (KH; N.Z.): vivid yellow, edged pink.

'Wye' (KH; R. H. S. Wisley '62): yellow 15C–15D, wavy margin flushed strong pink 52D, blotch orange, 3¼", 10–14 in truss.

'Yellow Bird' (KH; Pride): yellow, very hardy.

'Yellow Cloud' (KH; Hyatt '80): light yellow 10A, deepening to brilliant yellow 12B, blotch vivid yellow 14A, fragrant, 3¾", 12 in truss; 3½×5 ft. in 10 yrs. hardy to −0°F.

'Yellow Giant' (Ex; Pride): brilliant yellow, 3½", large truss.

'Yoga' (Waterer-Knap Hill '75): reddish orange.

ILAM HYBRIDS

This group was developed by the late Edgar Stead of Ilam, a suburb of Christchurch, New Zealand from Knap Hill azaleas. Mr. Stead recombined the Knap Hills with *R. calendulaceum, R. viscosum,* and *R. molle* in the early development of the Ilam hybrids, for new colors, increased truss size and fragrance. Only the lighter colored hybrids were fragrant. The first introductions were numbered plants: numbers 1, 2, 3, 4, 7, and 8 were yellow and red; number 5, red, now 'Ilam Cardinal'; number 6, orange; number 12, yellow. Some of these have been named by others and seedlings from them introduced.

Dr. J. S. Yeates of Palmerston North, New Zealand continued the work, starting in 1950, and is still breeding and selecting azaleas, up to 3,000 plants in a single year. He is also actively involved in breeding lilies and rhododendrons. Dr. Yeates named many of his selections Melford for, as he stated, his azaleas cannot fairly be called Ilams. While Ilam plants were mostly used in the breeding, Exbury Hybrids have been used extensively in crossing, including 'Gallipoli', 'Princess Royal', 'Berryrose' and others. The Melford name has also been given to seedlings and cuttings obtained from Dr. Yeates and named by others.

Over the years the name Ilam has been extended to include all deciduous azaleas originating in New Zealand or for seedlings grown from seed obtained in New Zealand. Many of the plants, based on their parentage, could be called Knap Hills, but due to their source, are grouped as Ilams.

David Leach, one of the first to work with Ilam seedlings from Dr. Yeates, reported that the flowers have heavy substance and on the average are more durable in hot weather. Mr. Jim Wells reported the same characteristic. Unfortunately, these remarks have been misconstrued to mean that the plants are "heat tolerant". David Leach reported no consistent superiority of the Ilams over Knap Hills and Exburys in heat tolerance. Our early observations and evaluation at Callaway Gardens, zone 8a, indicated as with other hybrid groups that there is considerable variation among cultivars. Additional evaluation is needed for these plants in zones 8 and 9, particularly under extended periods of high temperature. While often recommended for open sites, in southerly latitudes light to moderate shade from noon on is advised. Extra water during drought periods must be supplied. The cold hardiness of Ilams should be similar to Knap Hill azaleas. There is considerable variation among clones as to bud hardiness, and some are reported not bud hardy in zone 5a.

Dr. Yeates sent seed and cuttings of his azaleas to many friends and nurserymen in New Zealand and throughout the world. Plants named by Dr. Yeates are indicated by adding his name, for example: 'Ilam Chartreuse'; Dr. Yeates, 'Melford Red Letter'; Dr. Yeates, etc. The Melford clones not so indicated have been named by others. When definitely known that the plants originated as seed or cuttings from Dr. Yeates, they will be marked as follows (Dr. Yeates). Also Ilam hybrids developed in New Zealand, when known, will be indicated by N. Z.

'Bourbon Supreme' (('Melford Chief' × 'Melford Glory'); B. Badger, introduced R. Hacanson 1971): vivid reddish orange 28A, blotch orange-yellow 23A, 2¾"; 15" truss, fragrant; 5 ft. in 10 years.

'Brickdust' (Dr. Yeates; D. G. Leach): reddish orange, extra large flowers.

'Canterbury': reddish orange, 4½".

'Carlson's Strawberry Glow' (Carlson): vivid pink, to reddish orange, late May.

'Cherokee': yellowish orange, blotch reddish orange, 4".

'Comanche': reddish orange, 2".

'Darkey' (Dr. Yeates): red, compact plant.

'Gillian's Gold': vivid yellow.

'Ilam Cardinal' (original Ilam #5 named by L. Frisbie): deep red, 3".

'Ilam Carmen' (Dr. Yeates; syn. 'Carmen'): yellowish pink, gold flare, early.

'Ilam Center' (Bush, N. Z.): orange.

'Ilam Chartreuse' (Dr. Yeates; syn. 'Chartreuse'): pale yellow, light orange flare, 3", late; buds greenish.

'Ilam Copper Cloud' (Leach; introduced by J. Wells; syn. 'Copper Cloud'): orange, frilled.

'Ilam Jasper' (Dr. Yeates, N. Z.; syn. 'Jasper'): reddish orange, frilled, 3", late.

'Ilam Louie Williams' (Dr. Yeates; syn. 'Louie Williams'): light pink, suffused pale yellowish white, orange flare, 3", early to midseason.

'Ilam Martie' (Dr. Yeates; syn. 'Martie'): dark red, frilled, 2½", late.

'Ilam Melford Beauty' (syn. 'Melford Beauty'): 3"; no description available.

'Ilam Melford Flame' (Dr. Yeates; syn. 'Melford Flame'): vivid reddish orange, frilled, 3", midseason.

'Ilam Melford Gold' (Dr. Yeates; syn. 'Melford Gold'): vivid orange red overlay, 3", compact truss of 7–9 large florets, midseason.

'Ilam Melford Lemon' (syn. 'Melford Lemon'): strong orange-yellow, orange flare, 3¼", large truss, early.

'Ilam Melford Red' (Dr. Yeates; syn. 'Melford Red'): vivid reddish orange with orange flare, 2¾", midseason.

'Ilam Melford Salmon' (syn. 'Melford Salmon'): vivid yellowish pink, orange flare, large, 2¾", frilled; compact habit.

'Ilam Melford Yellow' (syn. 'Melford Yellow'): vivid orange-yellow flare, frilled, mid to late.

'Ilam Ming' (Dr. Yeates; syn. 'Ming'): vivid orange with yellow flare, large, 3¼", early.

'Ilam Peachy Keen' (Leach; introduced by J. Wells; syn. 'Peachy Keen'): light pink, suffused red; compact.

'Ilam Persian Melon' (Wells; syn. 'Persian Melon'): orange-yellow, large truss; compact habit.

'Ilam Persian Rose' (T. C. Davies, N. Z.; syn. 'Persian Rose'): deep purplish pink, prominent orange flare, 3¼", frilled, midseason.

'Ilam Pink. Williams' (Wells; syn. 'Louis Williams' and 'Pink Williams'): light pink, large truss, fragrant.

'Ilam Primrose' (Wells; syn. 'Primrose'): pale yellow.

'Ilam Red Ball' (Dr. Yeates; syn. 'Melford Red Ball'): vivid red, frilled, late.

'Ilam Red Frills' (N. Z.; syn. 'Red Frills'): reddish orange, large, 2¾", frilled, early.

'Ilam Red Gem' (N. Z.; syn. 'Red Gem'): red, orange flare, yellow stamens, 2½", early midseason.

'Ilam Red Giant' (syn. 'Red Giant' and 'Melford Red Giant'): dark red with orange flare and white stamens, 2¾", large, frilled, early midseason.

'Ilam Red Velvet' (Wells; syn. 'Red Velvet'): deep red, petals slightly turned back.

'Ilam Yellow Beauty' (Dr. Yeates; syn. 'Yellow Beauty' and 'Melford Yellow Beauty'): brilliant orange-yellow, faint blotch, frilled, early to midseason.

'Ilam Yellow Giant' (Dr. Yeates; syn. 'Yellow Giant' and 'Melford Yellow Giant'): brilliant yellow, darker flare, 3¼", mid to late.

'Maori' (seed from Dr. Yeates; Leach 1964): strong reddish orange 33A; 5–6 lobes, 10" truss, 33 × 48" tall in 13 years.

'Mary Lou' (Ilam; H. Van der Ven, Australia 1966): brilliant orange-yellow 17C, flushed pink on tips.

'Melford Chief': no description available.

'Melford Glory' (named by Frisbie, seed from Yeates): strong orange, lobes tipped reddish orange, 8" truss.

'Melford Orange': orange.

'Melford Red Letter' (Dr. Yeates; syn. 'Red Letter'): vivid red.

'Orange Ball' (Wells): vivid orange, compact ball truss; 6 × 6" in 12 years.
'Peach Sunset' (Wells): orange suffused pink, early.
'Red Hot' (cross of 2 Ilams; Wright): deep red; strong grower.
'Rufus' (Wells): dark red.
'Spring Salvo' (seed from Dr. Yeates; Leach 1964): strong reddish orange, orange blotch, 3½", 7" truss, dense foliage; 32 × 42" high in 13 years.
'Sunrise' (Wells): orange, deeply frilled, large.
'Supreme' (Wells): reddish orange, deeply frilled, late May.
'Tintoretto' (Wells): reddish orange, blotch orange, frilled.
'Whakanui' (parentage unknown; A. Pinney, N. Z. 1975): strong to moderate pink 49B-D.
'White Cap': white with yellow blotch, 2½".

The following azaleas named by Dr. Yeates are being propagated by Thermal Nurseries, Rotorua, New Zealand for release in the future. Unfortunately descriptions are not available for all:

'Angus Red': vivid red
'Awapuni Red'
'Coffee'
'Frilled Orange'
'Golden Bell'
'Irene Harris'
'James Deans': deep orange
'Ken Buons': strong orange
'Ken Mitchell': strong orange, late, heavy texture
'Kimbolten Orange'
'Kimbolten Pink'
'Kimbolten Red': vivid reddish orange
'Melford Rose'
'Peggy's Pink'
'Picture': yellow, pink blush
'Pink Beauty'
'Red Peter': good red
'Red Rag'
'Stuert's Red': good red
'Yellow Ball': large truss

BOVEE KNAP HILL HYBRIDS

The Bovees Nursery, a garden spot among fir trees, was started in 1954 by Mr. and Mrs. Robert (Bob) Bovee of Portland, Oregon, U.S.A. From imported Knap Hill seed they grew and bloomed 8000 seedlings, discarded most and selected the following 19 from 66 numbered seedlings. The small but diverse nursery is now owned by Lucie Sorenson and George Watson. The Bovee Hybrids after 1972 were named and introduced by them. The plants should be hardy in zones 6–8. They grow from 4–10 feet high and 3–5 feet wide.

'Agnes Harvey', '72: white flushed pale pink 49C, frilled, 3½".
'Balls of Fire', '61: vivid red 43A, squarish, 3"; 4 ft. in 10 years.
'Bryon Mayo', '63: strong reddish orange 33A, frilled, 3".
'Cathye Mayo', '62: pale orange yellow 19B, flushed yellow, blotch vivid yellow 14A, 4½–5", 12–14 in truss.
'Chimes', '62: strong pink 49A, deep pink 52C stripe on back of petals, 3", 4 ft. in 10 years.
'Goldflakes', '62: vivid yellow 14A, strong orange blotch, 2½"; 12–14 in truss; low compact growth, 4 × 4' in 15 yrs.
'High Sierras', '70: white, blotch yellowish green, squarish, 3½", 9–12 in truss, late May; 4–5 ft. in 20 years.
'King Midas', '76: light yellow 13C, darker throat, paler blotch orange yellow 17A, 2¾", 13 in truss; 8 ft. in 23 years.
'Lace Valentine', '76: white, shaded to purplish pink 56B, blotch yellow, ruffled, fragrant, 3", 11 in truss; upright.
'Leilani', '76: moderate orange 168C, changing to light pink, white and yellow, blotch orange yellow, wavy, fragrant, 3", 13 in truss; upright.
'Lila', '76: very pale yellow to white, large deep yellow blotch, 4", heavy substance.
'Lilikoi', '76: pale yellow 5D, faint blotch 5C, frilled, 4"; good substance.
'Maui Peach', '76: pink with reddish blush 31C, yellowish white center, yellow blotch 17A, 3½" buds reddish orange 39D.

'Maui Sunset': Deep orange, no blotch, squarish, ruffled, 3½"; 5' in 20 yrs.

'Nevada', '68: white, flushed moderate pink 49B, blotch orange yellow, 3½"; 6 ft. in 20 years.

'Sandra Marie', '59: pale orange yellow 19B, flushed strong yellowish pink, 31B, blotch orange yellow 22B, 3½–4", 12–14 in truss.

'Scotty', '61: deep to moderate yellowish pink 39B to38B, flushed pale to moderate orange yellow with a strong yellow blotch, 3", 15–18 in truss; 4 ft. in 10 years.

'Suez', '63: strong orange blend 28A and 26A, 2½"; 3 ft. spreading.

'Sweet Sue', '61: strong purplish pink 55B, with deep yellow blotch, ruffled, 3½–4", 8–12 in truss; 4 ft. in 10 years.

CARLSON-EXBURY HYBRIDS

Selected and named by Bob and Jan Carlson at Carlson's Gardens, South Salem, New York, U.S.A. They should be hardy zones 6–8. 4–10 feet tall and 3–5 feet wide.

'Bob's Buttercup': light yellow, darker flare; late May.

'Carlson's Canary': brilliant yellow, fragrant, late May.

'Carlson's Double Dip': pale yellow tinged with pink, double.

'Carlson's Full Moon': large, light yellow, late May.

'Carlson's Gold Nuggets': vivid yellow, fragrant, mid-May.

'Chartreuse': yellow with greenish tinge, mid-May.

'Fall Guy': yellow, deeper blotch, fragrant, occasional September blooming.

'Golden Goose': vivid yellow, deep yelllow flare.

'Heaven Scent': white, flushed pink, light yellow on upper lobe, fragrant, late May.

'Honey's Lovin' Arms': multicolored, light yellow to strong orange, petaloid, 2¼", tight trusses, early June.

'Janice Monyeen': pale yellow, tipped pink, blotch darker, frilled, fragrant, 3½", late May.

'Pink Pachyderm': light pink, large, in large trusses, late May.

'Sunny-Side-Up': white, upper petal strong yellow, large, late May.

'Tiger Lil': moderate reddish orange, late May; low growing.

'Towering Inferno': deep reddish orange, mid-May; tall vigorous.

FLEISCHMANN HYBRIDS

The following deciduous azaleas derived from Knap Hill Hybrids were introduced in 1970 by the late Carl Fleischmann of Weismoor, W. Germany. All are hardy in zones 6–8. They are 4–10 feet high and 3–5 feet wide.

'Fridtjof Nansen' ('Gibraltar' × 'Cecile'): vivid reddish orange, late; upright habit.

'Friedrich Wohler' ('Gibraltar' × 'Cecile'): orange, large, late; upright.

'Gemini' ('Cecile' × 'Gibraltar'): vivid orange yellow, blotch yellow, 2½", mid to late; low compact.

'Gnom' ('Harvest Moon' × 'Johann Sebastian Bach'): vivid red, blotch yellow, 2", late; compact dwarf.

'Hans Spemann' ('Gibraltar' × 'Cecile'): reddish orange, mid to late, upright.

'Kobold' ('Harvest Moon' × 'Johann Sebastian Bach'): orange, 2½", mid to late; dwarf compact.

'Max Planck' ('Gibraltar' × 'Cecile'): vivid orange yellow, mid to late; upright.

'Otto Hahn' ('Gibraltar' × 'Cecile'): vivid reddish orange, blotch yellow, midseason to late; upright.

'Paul Ehrlich' ('Gibraltar' × 'Cecile'): vivid orange, blotch orange, 7 wavy lobes, 4", 10–15 in truss; late; upright.

'Perkeo' ('Harvest Moon' × 'Johann Sebastian Bach'): orange, 2", late; compact habit.

'Robert Koch' ('Gibraltar' × 'Cecile'): vivid reddish orange, blotch dark yellow, 2½–3¼", 12–16 in truss.

'Wilhelm Roentgen' ('Gibraltar' × 'Cecile'): pink, blotch orange, wavy, 3"; late; upright.

GIRARD HYBRIDS (DECIDUOUS)

Peter E. Girard of Geneva, Ohio, U.S.A., has been breeding *Rhododendron* since the 1940's. His deciduous azalea breeding objectives are mildew resistance, ability to withstand heat and cold, ease in propagation, landscape plants, and adaptable for container culture, He has worked principally with the Knap Hill Hybrids in his breeding of deciduous azaleas. Many are double with a good range of colors and good orange to yellow fall foliage. (See also Evergreen Azaleas).

'Apple Blossom Delight' ('Homebush' × 'White Cloud'): white, tinted pink, and splashes of pink on each petal, yellow blotch, 1½–2", truss of 20–30; slightly fragrant; upright growth. Hardy to −20°F.

'Arista' ('Homebush' ('117K Homebush' × 'Strawberry Rose'): deep pink 52B, flushed light pink 55D, blotch orange yellow 21B, 2½–3", wavy ruffled, truss 18–28; dense growth habit. Hardy to −20°F.

'Constance Burnett' ('White Swan' × 'Nancy Waterer'): light yellow 13C, slight flush of strong orange 24B,hose-in-hose, no stamens, 2¼", truss of 21–25; leaves orange yellow in fall. 30 × 18" wide in 4 years. Hardy to −20°F. Registered as 'Crimson Tide'.

'Girard's Crimson Tide' ('Homebush' × 'Red Letter'): strong red 47B, outside deep yellowish pink 39A, double petaloid, 0–3 stamens, 2¼"; truss 20–40; leaves yellow to orange in fall; 3 × 2' wide in 5 years. Hardy to −20°F. Registered as 'Crimson Tide'.

'Girard's Mount Saint Helen' ('Cecile' × Knap Hill clone G-181): blend of moderate to strong yellowish pink 38D and 38A, large blotch of vivid orange reddish 32A, wavy, fragrant, 2½", truss of 12–15; upright 3 × 2' in 4 years. Hardy to −25°F. Registered as 'Mount Saint Helen'.

'Girard's Orange Lace' ('Gibraltar' × 'Klondyke'): vivid orange 25A, blending to vivid yellow 15A toward laced edges, 2½–3", 18–28 in truss; leaves orange yellow in fall; broad upright. Hardy to −20°F.

'Girard's Parfait' ('Homebush' × 'Cecile'): white, with lobes edged, strong pink 49A, and vivid yellow 14A blotch, 2½"; fragrant; 36 × 24' wide in 5 years. Hardy to −20°F.

'Golden Pom Pom' ('Homebush × 'Klondyke') (F_2): vivid yellow, 9A, with darker blotch 14B, 2½", no stamens, fragrant, truss 18–24; 30 × 30 in 5 years. Hardy to −30°F.

'Moonlight Rose' ('Homebush' × 'Strawberry Ice'): light pink 50C, vivid yellow blotch, wavy, 2½", truss 5–9; upright 30 × 19" wide in 5 years. Hardy to −20°F.

'Orange Cape' (OK–141 orange × 'Gibraltar'): vivid orange, 3–3½", petaloid tuft in center, truss of 18–20. Hardy to −25°F.

'Orange Cloak' (('Gibraltar' × 'Klondyke') × 'Gibraltar'): string reddish orange 32B; petaloid tuft in center, 2–4 stamens, lobes frilled, fragrant, truss of 18–20; upright 24 × 18" in 4 years. Hardy to −25°F.

'Orange Flash' ('Gibraltar' × orange clone): strong reddish orange 32B splashed vivid yellow, 2"; wavy, tips rolled back, anthers white, truss 8–12, leaves orange yellow 123A, in fall. Hardy to −10°F.

'Orange Jolly' ('Homebush' × 'Gibraltar'): vivid orange 25A, flushed light orange 29B, hose-in-hose, no stamens, fragrant, 3"; truss of 18–24; upright 30 × 24" in 4 years. Hardy to −20°F.

'Pink Delight' ('Homebush' × 'Cecile'): vivid yellowish pink hose-in-hose, double, 2½"; truss of 20–24, fragrant; tall. Hardy to −20°F.

'Pink Jolly' ('Homebush' × ' (HB–14G Rose)): strong pink, fragrant, petaloid, 2½"; upright, Hardy to −25°F.

'Salmon Delight' ('Pink Delight' × 'Klondyke'): strong pink 50C flushed yellowish pink 32C, semidouble, 2–2½", wavy ruffled; truss 25–30, upright habit; leaves yellow 15D tinged orange in fall; very hardy to −25°F.

'Sister Alice' ('Strawberry Ice' × 'Moonlight Rose'): unusual color combination, rolled back upper lobes white, yellow and orange at base, lower lobes white bordered light purplish pink 62B, 2", frilled and ruffled; truss to 30; broad upright habit. Hardy to −20°F.

'Sun Frolic' ('Golden Oriole' × 'Nancy Waterer'): brilliant orange yellow, 17B, flushed vivid orange 25B, fragrant, 3"; truss of 15–18; upright 30 × 18" wide in 4 years. Hardy to −20°F.

'Wedding Bouquet' ('Homebush' × ('White Swan' × 'Persil')): white flushed strong pink 49B, short tufted petaloid center, fragrant, 2¼". Upright broad 30 × 24" wide in 4 years. Hardy to −25°F.

'White Cloud' ('White Swan' × 'Persil'): white, faint touch of yellow 8C, 2", 20–40 in truss, leaves light yellow green in fall; low bushy habit. Hardy to −20°F.

'Yellow Pom Pom' (('1129 White Swan' × 'Klondyke' × ('Homebush' × '1129')): vivid yellow 12A, occasionally tinged orange yellow 21A, hose-in-hose, 2"–2½"; truss 18–24; leaves vivid yellow 14A in fall; bushy low habit. Hardy to −25°F.

'Yellow Stars' ('Narcissiflora' × 'Nancy Waterer'): vivid greenish yellow 5A, flushed light orange yellow 24C, hose-in-hose, no stamens, fragrant, 2', truss of 22–28. Upright 42 × 18" wide in 5 years. Hardy to −20°F.

SLONECKER HYBRIDS

Starting in the 1960's Mr. Howard Slonecker developed a number of azaleas adapted to the West Coast of North America from crosses of Knap Hill Hybrids. Some were introduced by Mr. Arthur Wright, Sr. of Canby, Oregon, U.S.A. All have withstood +3°F. in Oregon, but should be hardy to −10°F. They range from 4–8 feet in height and 3–5 feet in width.

'Alsea' ('Hugh Wormald' × 'Marion Merriman'; '68): vivid yellow 13A, blotch vivid orange 23A, 3½", midseason; upright.

'Calapooya' ('Hugh Wormald' × 'Marion Merriman'; '68): brilliant yellow 11A, fades to light yellow 11D, tinged light pink, blotch vivid orange 23A, occasionally 6 to 8 petals, 3½"; midseason.

'Chetco' ('Hugh Wormald' × 'Marion Merriman'; introduced by A. Wright, '65): vivid yellow 13A, blotch, vivid orange 23A, outside corolla tube orange red 42B, 3½", rounded habit.

'Clackamas' ('Klondyke' × 'Marion Merriman'; '68): vivid orange yellow 23B in center and suffused reddish orange 28A, margins strong yellowish pink 37B, blotch vivid orange 24A, 3½", midseason; low and upright habit.

'Coquille' ('Hugh Wormald' × 'Marion Merriman'; introduced by A Wright, '65): vivid yellow 13B, blotch vivid orange 23A, 3½", occasionally 6 petals, tall upright.

'Ochoco' ('Hugh Wormald' × 'Marion Merriman'; '64): pale pink, deep yellow blotch, midseason; upright.

'Santiam' ('Hugh Wormald' × 'Marion Merriman'; '68): vivid yellow 14A, blotch vivid orange 23A, margins frimbricated, 3½", occasionally 6 lobes, midseason; tall upright.

'Siletz' ('Hugh Wormald' × 'Klondyke'; introduced by A. Wright, '65): brilliant orange yellow 17B, suffused pink blotch, vivid orange 23A, 3½", 80% 6 petals, midseason; new foliage bronzy; tall upright.

'Siuslaw' ('Hugh Wormald' × 'Marion Merriman'; '68): vivid yellow 13A, blotch, vivid orange yellow 21A, 3½", 50% 6 petals, early midseason; upright.

'Tillamook' ('Hugh Wormald' × 'Marion Merriman'; '63): light yellow, fading white, orange blotch, 3½"; late midseason.

'Tualatin' ('Hugh Wormald' × 'Marion Merriman'; '68): pale yellow 11D, heavily tinged moderate pink 49B, blotch vivid orange, 23B, 3½", occasionally petaloid; rounded habit.

'Umatilla' ('Hugh Wormald' × 'Marion Merriman'; '68): brilliant yellow 21C, tinged red, blotch strong orange 24A, 3¾"; occasionally 6 petals, midseason; tall upright.

'Umpqua' ('Hugh Wormald' × 'Klondyke'; '68): brilliant orange yellow 21C, tinged red, blotch vivid orange 23A, 3½", 70% are 6 petaled occasionally 7, midseason; new foliage bronze; upright.

'Wallowa Red' (syn. 'Red Hot'; seed of Ilam hybrid from J. Yeates N.Z.); introduced by A. Wright '68, selected from 400 seedlings): deep red 46A, 2¾", occasional 6 petals, midseason; open round with arching branches.

'Winchuk' ('Hugh Wormald' × 'Marion Merriman'): deep yellow, blotch orange, midseason.

'Yachats' ('Hugh Wormald' × 'Marion Merriman'; '68): vivid yellow 13A, blotch vivid orange 23A, 4", late midseason, tall, larger leaves than other.

'Yaquina' ('Hugh Wormald' × 'Marion Merriman' introduced by A. Wright): vivid yellow 13B, blotch vivid orange 23A, midseason; tall upright.

WINDSOR HYBRIDS

Sir Eric Savill around 1932 obtained azalea seedlings from the Exbury Estate for landscaping the Savill and Valley Gardens in Windsor Great Park. In need of additional plants, Mr. Findley under the direction of Sir Eric crossed some of the best Exbury seedlings. From some 10,000 seedlings raised each year for 25 years, a few of the best were selected each year and planted in the Savill and Valley Gardens.

Mr. Jim Wells of New Jersey, U.S.A., formerly of England, visited Windsor in 1970. He revisited in 1971 and, with the assistance of Mr. Bond and the approval of Sir Eric, selected about 30 outstanding plants. The first group of plants were called the V Group. Seedlings that came later were designated the W.S.-Windsor Seedlings. The original plants are at the home of Jim Wells in New Jersey. Propagation and introduction are being carried on by his son, Jeremy, at the Wells Nursery in Penrose, N.C.

The original Windsor hybrids were selected for clearness of color, size of flower and truss, growth habits, and commercial value. All are hardy to −20°F. They range in size from 4–10 feet in height and 3–5 feet in width. The following five plants have been introduced:

'Windsor Apple Blossom' (V35); multicolored, very pale, pink to deep pink, orange blotch.
'Windsor Buttercup' (V3): brilliant yellow.
'Windsor Daybreak' (V9): yellowish pink, orange yellow blotch.
'Windsor Peach Glo' (WS56): vivid orange yellow.
'Windsor Sunbeam' (WS1): vivid yellow.

The following will be released in the future:

'Windsor Pink Souffle' (W8): pink.
'Windsor Ruby' (V2): deep red.

EASTERN AMERICAN SPECIES AND HYBRIDS

The eastern North America native azaleas have long been neglected by North American breeders and gardeners. Often called "wild honeysuckle", they were seldom used in landscaping except in native gardens. Interest began to develop in the early to late 50's and subsequently many large collections were formed in botanical gardens such as Biltmore, Callaway, Morris, USDA National Arboretum, and others.

The Herbarium of the USDA National Arboretum has, on loan from the Smithsonian Institution, the Beadle Collection from the Biltmore Estates of 2400 herbarium specimens and accompanying water color paintings of the Eastern native azaleas by Mrs. Luella Porche Johnson. The 8000 herbarium specimens of the Skinner collection are maintained at the Morris Arboretum.

Selected clones of the eastern North American species collected from the wild and seedlings are being named. In addition, interspecific crosses of various species are being made and clones of these hybrids selected and named. These azaleas are often difficult to propagate asexually so many are grown by seed and some as line hybrids. In addition, they are being crossed with Asiatic species and other group hybrids. The latter will be listed in the Interhybrid Group List.

The following Eastern North American Deciduous Azalea Groups are the work of American breeders.

ABBOTT HYBRIDS

Frank L. Abbott of Bellows Falls, Vermont, U.S.A., developed a group of very cold hardy azaleas, to −25°F and lower. Many of his plants were sold as seedlings and often named by others. The following were named by Abbott. For other Abbott hybrids see Carlson and Weston Hybrids.

'Jane Abbott' (*roseum* × 'Miss Louisa Hunnewell'): pink.
'Margaret Abbott' (*roseum* × *calendulaceum*): white with yellow blotch, flower larger than parents.

BEASLEY HYBRIDS

A love of native plants led to the selection and hybridizing of native azaleas by George and Mary Beasley and their son, Jeffrey, of Transplant Nursery, Lavonia, Georgia, U.S.A. All plants hardy to −10° to −15°F.

'Austrinum Gold' (selected form of *R. austrinum*): strong yellow, darker blotch, light pink tube, fragrant, 1½".

'Chattooga' (Natural hybrid *R. calendulaceum* × *nudiflorum*): bicolor effect, pink ruffled, matures to all yellow, large blotch brilliant yellow, 2", midseason; 2 × 4' in 10 years.

'Choptank C1' (seedling of 'Choptank River Hyb.'): white with purplish pink blush, buds purplish pink, fragrant.

'Fairy Speciosum' (natural hybrid): light pink and white, slightly fragrant.

'Frilly Dilly' (*R. calendulaceum* seedling): two tone, pale orange yellow 19B, and light yellowish pink 27A, ruffled 2", late June, 5'.

'Jeff' (*R. prunifolium* × *arborescens*) Jeffery B.: white, overlay with light pink 50D to strong purplish pink 55B, dark border, white filaments, pink anthers, 2", July; good fall foliage, 5 feet.

'Joseph's Coat' (possible *bakeri* × *viscosum* hybrid): variable colors, yellow turning to other colors, slightly fragrant.

'Lemon Drop' (selection of *viscosum*): pale yellow, fragrant.

'My Mary' ('Nacooche' × 'Austrinum Gold'): light brilliant yellow 11A, 2½", fragrant, late April, stoloniferous, 50" × 52".

'Nacoochee' (*R. atlanticum* × *nudiflorum* selected from Choptank Hyb.): white with wash veining of pale purplish pink 65C, 2½", fragrant, late April; stoloniferous, 5 × 5'.

'Nugget' (*R. calendulaceum* yellow × *R. calendulaceum* pink): brilliant yellow 11A, blotch moderate orange yellow 22B, hose-in-hose, double, 2", round full truss, midseason, 4 × 4' in 10 years.

'Paxton Blue' (*R. periclymenoides* selection by B. Bower & J. Paxton from SC, U.S.A.): light purplish blue, fragrant.

'Peaches and Cream' (*R. viscosum* var. *montanum* × *bakeri*): yellowish white center, margin of strong purplish pink 55B, yellow blotch, 1¾", mid-June; low stoloniferous. 3 × 4' wide; leaves leathery.

'R. Pennington' (parentage unknown; from R. Pennington): orange yellow, orange blotch.

'Richard Bielski' (*R calendulaceum* seedling): light brilliant yellow 11A blotch brilliant yellow, 3½", early June, 5 × 5'.

'Rose Choptank' ('Choptank Cl' selfed seedling): deep pink, fragrant; vigorous grower.

'Running Arborescens' (selection of *arborescens*): white with red stamens and pistil, fragrant, 1½"; low stoloniferous habit.

'Top of the Mountain' (selected form of *bakeri*): deep orange, no distinct blotch.

'Twiggy' (seedling of 'Choptank C1'): white with pink blush and tube; small leaves; dense habit.

'Velvet Red' (*R. Bakeri* × *arborescens*): deep reddish orange 43A, velvety texture, red filaments, crinkly, 2½", late June; 3 × 3' in 10 years.

'Yellow Delight' (*R. atlanticum* OP seedling): pale yellow, fragrant; good plant habit.

'Yellow Surprise' (*R. atlanticum* OP seedling): light yellow, fragrant.

'Yonah Mountain' (*R. bakeri* selection): deep reddish orange 43A, red filament, yellow anthers, 2", late June, 2 × 3' tall in 10 years.

CARLSON HYBRIDS

Post Script Azaleas are clones selected by Bob and Jan Carlson from North American species at Carlson's Garden, South Salem, New York, U.S.A. The objective of their work has been to extend the blooming season into June and July. All are hardy to −25°F. The height and width are the same as the Beasley Hybrids. See Appendix I.

'Balls of Fire' (*R. bakeri*): reddish orange, frilled, tight ball-like trusses, late June.

'Bright and Lively' (*R. calendulaceum*): strong, orange yellow, large, early June.

'Butterscotch' (*R. calendulaceum*): vivid orange yellow, early June.

'Butter Up' (*R. calendulaceum*): yellow, mid-June.

'Can't Elope' ('Colossus' × *R. luteum*): yellow orange, large, mid-June.

'Carlson's Red Hot' (*R. bakeri*): vivid reddish orange, late June.

'Come Quickly' (*R. bakeri*): orange, late June.
'Come Running' (*R. bakeri*): vivid reddish orange, late June.
'Delectable' (*R. calendulaceum*): orange, yellow flare, late June.
'Fringe on Top' (*R. arborescens*): white, fine serrated margins, fragrant, late June.
'G. H. C.' (*R. bakeri*): dark red, early June.
'Gosh' (*R. bakeri*): vivid reddish orange, flat face, mid-June.
'Heavenly' (*R. calendulaceum*): pale yellowish white, flushed yellow, pale pink edge, mid-June.
'Honey Do' (*R. calendulaceum*): light orange, mid-June.
'Hot Ginger and Dynamite' (*R. arborescens*): white, large, pink stamens, very fragrant, mid-June.
'Hot Vibes' (*R. bakeri*): vivid red, late June.
'Melony' (*R. calendulaceum*): orange, large, early June.
'Moon Melons' ('Colossus' × *R. luteum*): light yellow, large, red stamens, mid-June.
'Pinkadilly' (*R. prunifolium*): light pink, yellow flare, late June.
'Pinkerbell' (selected form of *vaseyi*): deep pink, 1½–2"; 6 to 8 ft. high; colorful fall foliage; hardy to −15°F.
'Plumb Beautiful' (*R. prunifolium*): vivid red, late July.
'Pumpkin 3.1416' ('Colossus' × *R. luteum*): light orange yellow, large, mid-June.
'Scrumptious' (*R. calendulaceum*): multicolored, orange yellow, mid-June.
'Summer Spice' (*R. arborescens*): white, pink tinge, fragrant, late blooming, July.
'Vibrant' (*R. bakeri*): vivid reddish orange, late June.
'Wow' (*R calendulaceum*): vivid orange, large, mid-June.

Carlson's Gardens' selection of Abbot Azaleas bred by F. Abbott of Saxton's River, Vermont, U.S.A. Crosses of *R calendulaceum* and *R. japonicum* with *R. roseum*. All are hardy to −25°F.

'Abbott's Orange Glow': light translucent orange, large, late May.
'Abbott's Rose Ruffles': frilled, saucer-shaped, deep yellowish pink, early June.
'Bit O'Honey': multicolored yellow-orange, small, late May; low growing.
'Coral Sands': yellowish pink, fragrant, mid-June.
'Doin' My Thing': mixed, yellow and orange, early June.
'Double Dip': orange yellow, double, fragrant, early June.
'Gold Chip': strong yellow, orange edges, small, mid-June.
'Sparkle Plenty': pale yellow, dark yellow flare, red stamens; buds striped with red, late May.
'Starfire': yellowish pink, orange yellow blotch, pink edges, tubular, low growing mid-May.
'Starlight': white, yellow throat, pink striping, low growing, late May.
'Strawberry Blonde': multicolored, pink, early June.
'Vermont Gold': light yellow, early June.
'White Star': white, star-shaped, tubular, mid-June.

Miscellaneous Carlson Selections of Other North American Species Plus Luteum Hybrids

'Baby's Bottom' (*R nudiflorum*): light pink, late May.
'Choptank River Belle' (*R. atlanticum* × *R. nudiflorum*): pink flush, fragrant, late May.
'Lemon Popsickle' (*R. speciosum*): yellow, mid-May.
'Orange Popsickle' (*R. speciosum*): orange, mid-May.
'Pincushion' (*R. nudiflorum*): pale pink, showy, long stamens, tight trusses, mid-May.
'Strawberry Popsickle' (*R. speciosum*): deep pink, mid-May.

Selections of *R. luteum* by Bob Carlson of Carlson's Gardens, South Salem, New York, U.S.A. All are hardy −10°F., 6 feet high and 4 feet wide.

'Bee High': yellow, long narrow petals, fragrant, mid-May.
'Bee Loved': yellow fragrant, late May.
'Bee Witched': pale yellowish white, yellow flare, fragrant, late May.
'Big-Leif-Carlson': yellow, fragrant, large strap-like leaves, mid-May.
'Precocious': brilliant yellow, fragrant, large, mid-May.

CHEROKEE HYBRIDS

Olin Holsomback of Chickamauga, Georgia, U.S.A., began selecting native azaleas in the late '40's and followed by crossing many of his favorite plants. All have proven hardy to 5°F. They are 6–8 feet high and 3–5 feet wide.

Cherokee Series

'Altanuwa' (*bakeri* × *viscosum*): strong yellowish pink 38A, pointed lobes, faint yellow blotch, 1½"; late.

'Big Chief' (*calendulaceum* × 'Hortulanus H. Witte'): strong yellowish pink, orange blotch, lower petals light yellowish pink, orange veins; buds, tube and stamens reddish orange, 1½"; 8 in truss, midseason; tall upright.

'Cheulah' (*bakeri* × *bakeri*): strong red 52A, orange blotch, 1½"; late.

'Chief Yonaguska' (Gregory Bald seedling × *bakeri*): strong red 52A, orange blotch, late, 1½".

'Nikwasi' (Gregory Bald seedling × *viscosum*): strong red 47B, faint blotch, 1½"; late.

'Tagu' (*bakeri* × *viscosum*): light orange 29A, pink blush, petals reflexed, 1½"; late.

'Tsikamagi' (Gregory Bald seedling × *bakeri*): strong orange 24B, flushed pink, blotch orange, 1¾".

Miscellaneous Group

'Burning Bush' ('Satan' × red *calendulaceum*): strong red, late.

'July Joy' (*bakeri* × *prunifolium*): deep pink, light yellow blotch, early July.

'Salmon Spectacle' (*arborescens* × *calendulaceum* orange): deep yellowish pink.

CHINQUAPIN HILL HYBRIDS

Developed by the late Augustus (Gus) Elmer, Jr., of Chinquapin Hill, Pass Christian, Mississippi, U.S.A., by crossing Exbury azaleas with *R. austrinum*. The objectives were to breed heat tolerance into large flowered deciduous azaleas, The plants have proven adaptable in the Southern U.S.A. and withstood winter temperatures in New Jersey to −10°F.; 6–10 ft. tall, 4–6 ft. wide. Registered in 1984.

'Bebita' (#11; 'Orangeade' × *R. austrinum*): strong reddish orange 31A, blotch strong orange 24A, 2¼", 12–14 in truss, fragrant.

'Bob Elmer' (#8; 'Orangeade' × *R. austrinum*): brilliant orange 29A, margins reddish orange 33A, blotch orange yellow 23A, 6 petals, 2¼", 10–12 in truss, fragrant.

'Jonathan' (#10; 'Orangeade' × *R. austrinum*): brilliant orange yellow 23B, blotch vivid orange yellow 23A, 12 in truss, fragrant.

'Julian Elmer' (#9; 'Orangeade' × *R. austrinum*): light orange yellow 23C, blotch and tips of petals reddish orange 30A, 2½–3" 12–14 in truss, fragrant.

'Mary Anne Elmer' (#1; 'Orangeade' × *R. austrinum*): strong orange yellow 24B, tips yellowish pink 30C, outside reddish orange 33B, blotch orange 25A, 2½, 10 in truss, fragrant.

'Pudding' (#3; 'Orangeade' × *R. austrinum*): strong yellowish pink, 38A, shading to deep yellowish pink, 39B, blotch orange yellow 23A, 2½", 15–16 in truss, fragrant.

'Rusty Keller' (#2; 'Orangeade' × *R. austrinum*): strong reddish orange 32B, blotch orange 25A, 2½–2¾", 10–12 in truss, fragrant.

'Saint Stanislaus' (#7; 'Orangeade' × *R. austrinum*): strong reddish orange 31A, blotch orange yellow, 23A, 2", 15 in truss, fragrant.

'Shy Girl' (#12; 'George Reynolds' × *R. austrinum*): light yellow 18A, blotch orange yellow 23A, 2½", 14–16 in truss, fragrant.

'Terre's Delight' (#6; 'George Reynolds' × R. austrinum): pale yellowish pink 27D, blotch orange yellow 23A, 2¼", 15–16 in truss, fragrant.

'Terre's Yellow' (#13, 'George Reynolds' × *austrinum*): vivid yellow 13A, throat and blotch orange yellow 23A, 6 petals, 2", 8–10 in truss, fragrant.

'Therese Elmer' (#5; 'Orangeade' × *R. austrinum*): bicolor, light yellow 18A to vivid reddish orange 30B, blotch orange yellow 23B, 6 to 7 petals, 2½", 15 in truss, fragrant.

'Yellow Sand' (#4; 'George Reynolds' × *R. austrinum*): light yellow 11B, blotch orange yellow 17A, 2¾", 10–14 in truss, fragrant.

DOSSER HYBRIDS

Lillie Dosser of Centralia, Washington introduced the following azaleas. The parentage is unknown except that the parents were native species. *The International Rhododendron Register* lists these as either Mollis or Ghent hybrids.

'Apricot Queen' (Mollis hyb.): orange yellow, blotch orange.

'Fluted Gold' (Ghent hyb.): pale yellow, frilled.

'Golden Gleam' (Ghent hyb.): pale yellow, dark yellow blotch, frilled.

'Goldspot' (Mollis hyb.): white, orange blotch.

'Pink Glow' (Ghent hyb.): light pink, orange blotch, frilled.

'Pinkie' (Ghent hyb.): pink, orange blotch, frilled.

'Ruffled Beauty' (Mollis hyb.): white, flushed pink, yellow blotch, frilled.

GALLE HYBRIDS AND SELECTIONS

Starting in 1954, the author made intraspecific crosses of North American deciduous azaleas at Callaway Gardens. The breeding objective was to develop color forms and hybrids often found in the wild. Thousands of seedlings were raised and numbered, some with a Knap Hill as one parent. The following were registered in 1984. They are all hardy to 0°F.

'Choice Cream' (*austrinum* × *atlanticum*): light yellow 10B fades to pale yellow 11C, tube pink 48D, yellow blotch 13A, wavy, fragrant, 1½", early; 5×5 ft. in 12 yrs., partially stoloniferous.

'Galle's Choice' (*calendulaceum* × *alabamense*): light yellow 11B, white throat, light pink on tips of wavy lobes, fragrant, 1¾"; midseason; 10 × 10 ft. in 15 yrs.

'Katy's Plum' (Knap Hill ? × *speciosum*): strong pink 50C, flushed red, orange blotch, wavy, fragrant, 2½", late April; 6×5 ft. tall in 15 yrs.; heat tolerant.

'Kelly's Orange' (*speciosum* × 'Cecile'): vivid reddish orange 30A, yellow blotch 2½"; 5 × 5 ft. in 11 yrs; heat resistant.

'White Flakes' (selection of wild *canescens* from Haralson Co. Ga.): white, pale to light pink on tips of lobes, double, 20 or more petals, fragrant, 1⅜"; 5 × 5 ft. in 10 yrs.

LEACH HYBRIDS

Selections and hybrids of North American Deciduous Azaleas by David G. Leach of North Madison, Ohio, U.S.A., well known for his book, *Rhododendrons of the World,* and his hybridizing work with *Rhododendron* to develop cold hardy cultivars. All his azalea selections are hardy. They are 6 to 8 ft. high and 4 to 6 wide.

'Chamois' (advance generation hybrid of *R. bakeri* × *arborescens*): brilliant yellow 11a, darker blotch. Hardy −20°F.

'Coloratura' (advance generation hybrid of *R bakeri* × *arborescens*): strong purplish red 51A, blotch, orange, late. Hardy −20°F.

'Colossus' (large flowered selection of *R. calendulaceum* collected near Burning Town Gap, N.C.): deep reddish orange 32A with red lines, blotch orange 26A, frilled; 4" when collected, 2⅜" in cultivation; upright, 3 × 1½" wide in 10 years. Hardy −20°F.

'Cream Puff' (advance generation hybrid of *R bakeri* × *arborescens*): brilliant yellow 11a, blotch orange yellow, 2¼"; late. Hardy −15°F.

'Flower Girl' (advance generation hybrid of *R. arborescens* × *bakeri*): pale pink; mid June. Hardy −15°F.

'July Jester' ('S. D. Coleman' × 'Scarlet Salute'): vivid reddish orange 40B, orange blotch 30B, lobes rounded, 1¾", 5 to 6 in truss; upright, 4½ × 3' in 16 years. Hardy −20°F.

'July Jewel' ('S. D. Coleman' × 'Scarlet Salute'): deep reddish orange 33A, blotch vivid reddish orange, lobes rounded 1⅝", late, 5 to 7 in truss; broad semidwarf 20 × 26" in 16 years. Hardy −20°F.

'July Jingle' ('S. D. Coleman' × *R. arborescens*): moderate purplish pink, suffused deep pink, blotch pale orange, lobes rounded, 1⅝", fragrant, late, 5–7 in truss; broad 36 × 52" in 16 years. Hardy −20°F.

'July Jubilation' ('S. D. Coleman' × 'Cream Puff'): strong reddish orange 40D, darker flush, blotch orange yellow 25C, lobes rounded, fragrant, 1⅝", late, 6–7 in truss; broad 28 × 36" in 16 years. Hardy −20°F.

'July Julep' ('S. D. Coleman' × 'Cream Puff'): strong reddish orange 40D, suffused darker, aging to moderate orange 32D, blotch orange, lobes rounded 2", fragrant, late, 6–7 in truss; rounded habit 42 × 46" in 16 years. Hardy −20°F.

'June Bride' (natural hybrid of *R. arborescens*): white, forked blotch, orange yellow 22B, red to pink, stigma, 2"; 4–5 in truss; broad spreading 6½ × 4½' tall in 12 years. Hardy −15°F.

'Maid of Honor' ('Scarlet Salute' × *arborescens*): deep pink 52C, blotch reddish orange 30A, 1¾", 6–7 in truss, style and stamens red, late June. Hardy −20°F.

'Pink Fire' (*R. bakeri* selection from the Cumberland Mountains): pink flushed strong reddish orange 33A, blotch reddish orange, 2⅛". Hardy −10°F.

'Pink Plush' (natural hybrid of *R. bakeri* × *arborescens*): strong pink 52C tipped darker pink, blotch faint orange, 2¼", late. Hardy −10°F.

'Pink Puff' (natural hybrid of *R.bakeri* × *arborescens*): strong yellowish pink, blotch yellow, 2½"; late. Hardy −15°F.

'Scarlet Salute' (*R bakeri* selection from the Cumberland Mountains): brilliant red, with reddish orange blotch, 1⅞", 5–6 in truss, late June. Hardy −15°F.

'S. D. Coleman' (*R. prunifolium* selection re-named, original plant lost): deep reddish orange 43B, lobes rounded 1½"; late, broad habit, 4½' × 6' in 20 years. Hardy 0°F.

'Spring Party' (*R. vaseyi* selection): deep pink, flat and widely open, 1¾", 8–9 in truss; 4 × 4' in 10 years. Hardy to −25°F.

'Tang' ('Scarlet Salute' × 'Red King'): strong orange, suffused reddish orange becoming strong reddish orange 33A, margins darker, 2⅜", 9–11 in truss; upright 3 × 6' in 11 years. Hardy −25°F.

WESTON HYBRIDS

After the killing winter of 1933–34 Ed Mezitt of Weston Nurseries of Hopkinton, Massachusetts, U.S.A., started selecting and breeding for very hardy azaleas. They have used a wide variety of plants as parents. Weston Nurseries is noted as an excellent source of unusual plants and for its hardy hybrid rhododendrons including 'P. J. M.' and others. All azaleas are hardy to −25°F. The average size of plants is 6 to 8 ft. high and 4–6 ft. wide. See Appendix II.

'Bonfire' (parentage unknown): deep reddish orange 43B, 1¾" mid July; upright.

'Cotton Candy' (*R. bakeri* × *viscosum*): strong pink 52D, 1" fragrant, 10 July.

'Deep Rose' (Ghent): pink, fragrant, 1¼".

'Frank Abbott' (*R. molle* × *roseum*): vivid purplish red 58B, 1½", fragrant, mid-season; tall upright, very hardy.

'Golden Showers' (parentage unknown): light orange yellow 24C, buds light orange, 1¾", slightly fragrant, broad habit.

'Independence' (*R. bakeri* × *viscosum*): moderate red, 50B, buds deep red 53B, 1", fragrant, July.

'Iridescent' (*R. bakeri* × *arborescens*): moderate pink, 54C, 1"fragrant; late June.

'Jane Abbott Hybrids' (*R. roseum* × *mollis*): pink, fragrant, very hardy.

'Lemonade' (parentage unknown): very pale yellow 160C; 1", early July; glossy foliage.

'Lemon Drop' (parentage unknown): vivid yellow, fragrant, late June.

'Lollipop' (parentage unknown): moderate pink, fragrant, late June.

'Parade' (*R. bakeri* × *viscosum arborescens*): moderate red, 50B, 1½" fragrant, July; tall.

'Pink and Sweet' ((*R. bakeri* × *viscosum*) × *arborescens*): moderate purplish pink, 55C, 1", fragrant, July.

'Popsicle' (*R. viscosum* × *arborescens*): moderate red, 47C, line of glandular hairs, sticky on underside, 1½".

'Ribbon Candy' (*viscosum* × *arborescens*): vivid purplish red 55A, yellow blotch, white throat, white stripes up center of each lobe to rounded and reflexed tips, 1½", fragrant; upright habit.

'Salute' (*R. viscosum* × *prunifolium*): strong red 47B, buds vivid red 44A, 1½", mid July; upright habit.

'Trumpeter' (parentage unknown): yellowish pink.

'Weston's Innocence' (parentage unknown): white, 155D, 1½", fragrant, mid June.

OTHER DECIDUOUS EASTERN AZALEAS

Unfortunately complete information is not available on all plants. See Appendix I.

'Alhambra' (*bakeri* seedling; Gable, introd. by Baldsiefen): vivid reddish orange, late; resistant to heat and powdery mildew.

'Apple Blossom' (selection of wild *canescens*, Troup Co. Ga.; Jacobs): white, flushed pink, buds white tipped pink, faint yellow blotch, fragrant, 1½", mid April; 7 to 8 ft.

'Betty Cummins' (*viscosum* selection; Lewis): pink, fragrant.

'Burning Light' (form of *calendulaceum;* Crown Est. Comm '66): moderate reddish orange 32D, throat vivid orange, 2⅛", 6 in truss.

'Buttercup' (*austrinum* selection; Varnadoe): vivid yellow, 1¼", large truss, fragrant, very early.

'Camp's Red' (*bakeri* selection, Big Black Mt. Ky.; Skinner): strong red 45D to vivid red on Mt., lighter in cultivation, 1½", June; propagates readily; tall. Honors Dr. W. H. Camp.

'Chattahoochee' (selection of wild *speciosum* hybrid, Fulton Co. Ga.; Seiferle): 5 to 7 very narrow petals split to base, 1¼" long, light pink 49C, stamens short; 8 × 8 ft. in 15 yrs.; hardy to 0°F.

'Chauncey Beadle': deep pink, yellow blotch; semidwarf; natural hybrid in Biltmore Gardens.

'Choptank River Hybrids' (*atlanticum* × *periclymenoides;* natural seedling in Delaware at headwater of Choptank River, collected by Hill, '57): pale pink, fragrant; stoloniferous; glaucous bluish leaves. Often sold as seedlings. See 'Marydel'.

'Coleman's Early Yellow' (Coleman): light yellow, possible hybrid of *austrinum* and *alabamense*.

'Debbie Ann' (*atlanticum* × *bakeri;* Coe): pink with yellow blotch.

'Delaware Blue' (selected form of *R. viscosum* var. *glaucum*, Piersons Corner, Dela.; Hill '84): whiter than 155D, red tipped glandular hairs on tube, 1¼" across, June early July, buds faintly pink, fragrant; leaves dull dark green, greyed greenish blue and glaucous beneath; 5 × 10 ft. tall in 7 yrs.; hardy to −10°F.

'Diorama' (*viscosum* hybrid; Holland): red, fragrant.

'Doughoregan' (selection of *R. nudiflorum*, Howard Co., Md.; Gambrill): uniform pink, later than species; low habit under 3 ft.

'Escatawpa' (selection of wild *austrinum;* Escatawpa river area, Ala.; B. Dodd): brilliant yellow, 1½", large truss, fragrant.

'Greenville Gold' (selection of wild *austrinum*): Greenville Co. Ala.; B. Dodd): vivid yellow, 1½", large truss, fragrant.

'Harrison Red' (selection of wild *austrinum*, So. of Chipley Fla.; Robertson): dark reddish flowers, fragrant, very early; compact.

'Hohman' (*prunifolium* seedling; Hohman, reg. by Skinner '79): deep reddish orange 39A, rounded lobes lighter, 1½"; upright 6 × 10 ft. in 15 yrs.; new stems purplish red; hardy to 0°F.

'Kentucky Colonel' (*bakeri* selection; Frisbie): reddish orange.

'Lemon Rind' (*arborescens* × *bakeri*, natural hybrid; Gable, introd. by Herbert '76): light greenish yellow 154D to 4D, yellow blotch 5C, brownish spotting 176A, 6 wavy lobes, 3", 10 in truss; hardy to −15°F.

'Marita' (*prunifolium* × *viscosum:* Rothschild '45): moderate reddish orange to pink.

'Marydel' (selection natural hybrid *atlanticum* × *nudiflorum;* Hill '78): white, margin and base of tube deep purplish pink, buds purplish red to pink, lobes rounded and curved, 1¾", fragrant, 8–11 in truss; semi-dwarf, 3 × 3 ft. in 10 yrs.; hardy to −10°F.

'Millie Mac' (selection of wild *austrinum;* Escambia Co. Ala., McConnell '78): vivid yellow 17B, white margin, wavy & recurved, 1⅛–1½", 17–20 in truss, fragrant, buds reddish orange 34B; 48 × 78" in 11 yrs., hardy to 0°F.

'Patricia Burton' (*prunifolium* × *serrulatum:* Early): light pink, 2", late; tall habit.

'Pauline Neeley' (*prunifolium* × *serrulatum;* Early): deep pink, 2", late; medium tall.

'Philip Holmes' (form of *prinophyllum;* Anne, Countess of Rosse & The Natl. Trust '81): white, flushed pink 62B, throat darker 63B, 9 in truss.

'Pink Peppermint' (selection of wild *arborescens;* Pride): light pink, fragrant; very vigorous.

'Pink Smokey' (selection of wild *arborescens;* Pride '55): light to strong pink, fragrant, late; 2 ft. in 10 yrs.; hardy to −35°F.

'Sara Copeland' (selection of wild *canescens* from Terrell Co. Ga.; Copeland '84): double, petaloid form, anemone center; white, pink tube, 5 normal petals, 1¼", remnant brown anthers, fragrant.

'Sizzler' (selection of *R. bakeri,* collected Gregory Bald N.C., U.S.A. by Holsomback, intro. Hill '84): vivid yellowish pink 40A and deep reddish orange 42B, blotch insignificant, 5 rarely 6 wavy lobes, dorsal is frilled and often reflexed, 2", 5–6 in truss, late June early July; semi-dwarf 4 × 5 ft. wide in 16 yrs.; hardy to −10°F. Very difficult to propagate.

'Smoky Mountaineer' (open pollinated seedling of *calendulaceum,* probably hybrid, introd. by Arnold Arboretum): reddish orange.

'Snowbird' (*atlanticum* × *canescens*): white, fragrant, compact; natural hybrid in Biltmore Gardens.

'Summer Perfume' (*arborescens* × *prunifolium;* Jacobs): strong orange, 2", clove scented, late; 7–8 ft.

'Summer Sunset' (*prunifolium* selection; Crown Est. comml '62): vivid red.

'Sunlight' (selection of *bakeri* seed from Gregory Bald N.C.; Hill): deep reddish orange 43B, to deep yellowish pink 42B, edged red 45D, throat orange yellow 24B, frilled, 2"; broad upright 6 × 6 ft. in 14 yrs.; hardy to −5°F.

'Suva' (*vaseyi* seedling; L. de Rothschild '70): strong purplish pink 62A, opening to light purplish pink 62C, throat white, sparse spotting of reddish purple, 2", 6–7 in truss.

'Varnadoe's Moonbeam' (selection of *R. austrinum;* Varnadoe): yellow, fragrant, 1½"; 5 ft. in 10 yrs.

'Virginia Callaway' (selection of wild *alabamense;* Coleman): white, pink border, 1¼", fragrant.

'White Find' (selection of wild *vaseyi* from Mts. of N.C.; La Bar Nur.): white, greenish yellow blotch, 1½", fragrant; leaves light green.

'Yellow River' (selected natural hybrid of *austrinum* × *canescens;* from Okaloosa Co. Fla.; Skinner): brilliant yellow 11A, lower half of tube moderate orange yellow 24C, 1⅛"; leaves hold late; upright rounded 11 × 9 ft. in 20 yrs.; hardy to 5°F.; easily propagated.

INTERGROUP HYBRIDS AND MISCELLANEOUS DECIDUOUS HYBRIDS

The following hybrids are not included in the previous groups. Many are miscellaneous hybrids with no information on parentages available. The hardiness and mature size of plants are not available for many of these plants.

'Appalachia' (parentage ?; Neal, '67): brilliant to vivid yellow 11A to 14A, red on outside, fragrant, 3", 20 in truss; 3–4 ft. in 10 yrs. Possibly a Knap Hill hybrid.

'April Showers' (New Race Hybrid; J. Waterer, '67): pale yellow, center orange yellow with slight blotch, early; compact.

'Carat' ((*viscosum* × 'Koster's Brilliant Red') × 'Satan'): Research Station for Arboreous Crops, Boskoop Holland: reddish orange, blotch orange, 1½"–2", fragrant, 7–9 in truss; mid season broad upright, very hardy.

'Celeste Terry' (*arborescens* × *x Kosterianum;* Forbes, '69): white, flushed deep pink, fragrant, 1½", 8 in truss.

'Diorama' ((*viscosum* × 'Koster's Brilliant Red') × 'Fireglow'): Research Station for Arboreous Crops, Boskoop Holland: strong red 45D, 2", 9–12 in truss, fragrant; mid to late, very hardy.

'Double Delight' ('Narcissiflora' × selected unnamed seedling; Bunnell '84): vivid yellow 15A-B, 2¼", hose-in-hose, rounded lobes, petals irregular and/or aborted, no stamens, very fragrant; mid May; 46" × 55" wide in 10 yrs.; good fall foliage; hardy to −5°F.

'Double Pleasure' ('Rosea Plena' × *R. albrechtii;* Bunnell '84): strong red 53C-D, reverse deep red 53A, buds deep red 46A, hose-in-hose, slightly wavy lobes, 2" across, no stamens; early May; 63" × 70" tall in 10 yrs.; good fall color; hardy to −5°F.

'Double Salmon' (Knap Hill N2 × *austrinum*): deep yellowish pink, double.

'Five Arrows' (*quinquefolium* seedling; E. de Rothschild, '68): white 155B, throat spotted and flecked green, 1½–1¾", 10 stamens.

Fraseri (syn. *R. fraseri; R. canadense* × *japonicum;* G. Fraser, B.C. 1912): purplish pink, deeply two lipped, tube funnel-form, early, low shrub of twiggy habit. Available in Canada.

'Fred Neeley' ('Hugh Wormald' × *austrinum;* Early): strong orange yellow, 2½"; medium habit.

'Frontier Gold' (Exbury × *austrinum;* Aromi '81): brilliant orange 23A, 2⅜", 15–21 in truss, fragrant, early midseason; upright to 6 ft. in 10 yrs.; heat tolerant in zone 9A.

'Jolie Madame' ((*viscosum* × 'Koster's Brilliant Red') × 'Satan'): Research Station for Arboreous Crops, Boskoop Holland, '71): pink, blotch orange yellow, 2¾–3½", 7–9 in truss, late midseason; broad upright, very hardy.

'June Fire' (*prunifolium* × 'Royal Lodge'; Pratt, '75): deep red 45D, 4–5 in truss.

'Montrose' (Lovett Nur.): deep pink.

'Morris Gold' (*japonicum* × *luteum;* Skinner, introd. Morris Arb., '80): light yellow 13C, buds 13A, blotch orange, wavy, fragrant, 2¼"; easily propagated; 6 × 8 ft., in 12 yrs.; stoloniferous; hardy to −10°F.

'Pathfinder (Exbury × *austrinum;* Aromi, '81): brilliant orange yellow 23B, flushed yellowish pink 39A, blotch orange yellow, fragrant, 2⅝", 11–16 in truss, early to midseason; upright to 6 ft. in 10 yrs.; heat tolerant in zone 9a.

'Rising Star' (Mollis × Exbury; Landauer): light yellowish pink, large reddish orange blotch 2–2½".

'Schlippenbleachy' (selection of *schlippenbachii;* Carlson): white, brownish dots in blotch, 2½–3", slightly fragrant.

'Sea King' (form of *reticulatum;* Rokujo, introd. by Hyden Nur., '82): deep purplish pink 74A, upper lobe slightly paler and sparingly spotted; solitary or in pairs.

'Spring Melody' ('Goldie' × yellow Mollis; Pride, introd. by Baldsiefen, '75): vivid yellow, blotch orange yellow, 3", 10–12 in truss, 4 × 4½ ft. in 10 yrs.; hardy to −25°F.

'Totally Awesome' (cross of 2 selected unnamed seedling; Bunnell '84): brilliant yellow 14G and light yellow 15D, shaded vivid reddish orange 40C on edges, spotted blotch of vivid yellow 15A, deep reddish orange buds 42A; 0–7 stamens some irregular petal-like aborted stamens 4" across, 7 in truss, no fragrance; mid May; 41" × 43" wide in 7 yrs.; good fall color; hardy to −5°F.

NORTHERN LIGHTS SERIES

The breeding program for cold hardy azaleas was initiated by the late Albert Johnson at the University of Minnesota Landscape Arboretum in 1957. Robert Mullin from the Horticulture Dept.was also involved in the project for a few years. Dr. Harold Pellett started in the project in the 1970's and has been project leader since 1978. The current goal of the breeding program is to develop cultivars representing a wide range of deciduous azaleas that are bud hardy in Minnesota and other northern states. Current breeding and selecting involves mildew resistance, better foliage quality, and later flowering season.

'Northern Lights F/1 hybrids' (controlled crosses of selected strains of *R. prinophyllum* × Mollis hybrids; introd. '78): seedlings are quite uniform in size and form; colors range from light pink to dark pink. Flower bud hardiness is consistent at −45°F; most of the F/1 hybrids are sterile.

The following cultivars are clonally propagated.

'Golden Lights' (seedling selection of *R. atlanticum* × unknown Exbury hybrid; introd. '87): light orange-yellow 16C, suffused with strong reddish orange 31B, strong orange-yellow 17A blotch, 2¾", dorsal lobes frilled, lower lobes wavy, 10 in truss, late May, very fragrant, buds strong reddish orange 31B; flowers are sterile; plant habit rounded, 36 × 42" tall in 6 yrs. Hardy to −35°F.

'Orchid Lights' (*R. canadense* × Mollis hybrid; introd. '86): moderate purplish pink 68C, with moderate yellow 161A spotting in dorsal lobe, bottom 2 lobes deeply cut, zygomorphic flowers, 1¾", tubular funnel shaped, skunky odor, up to 9 in truss; semidwarf rounded 20 × 26" wide in 5 yrs.; flower buds very hardy to −45°F. Flowers somewhat obscured by new foliage; stamens and pistils present but plant is sterile; no seed pods formed.

'Pink Lights' (Mollis hybrid × *prinophyllum;* introd. '83): moderate pink 54D, dorsal lobe vivid orange 30C spotting, rounded lobes, floriferous, fragrant, 2"; broad spreading habit to 6–8 ft.; flower buds hardy to −45°F.

'Rosy Lights' (Mollis hybrid × *prinophyllum;* introd. '83): vivid purplish red 55A, reddish orange spotting 33B in blotch, lobes rounded, 2⅜"; broad habit 6 × 4 ft. high in 24 yrs.; flowers are sterile; buds hardy to −45°F.

'Spicy Lights' (open pollinated *prinophyllum;* introd. '85): strong yellowish pink 37B with gray red 180B veining, blotch orange yellow 22B, 2", 11 in truss, slight fragrance, broad spreading habit 5 × 6 ft. wide in 20 yrs. Flowers are sterile no seed pods, and buds are hardy to −35°F.

'White Lights' (seedling possibly *prinophyllum* × white Exbury; introd. '83): buds pale pink, open very pale pink fading to near white, 1¾", rounded spreading habit of 4–5 ft. Flowers are sterile; buds hardy to −35°F.

Plate 17

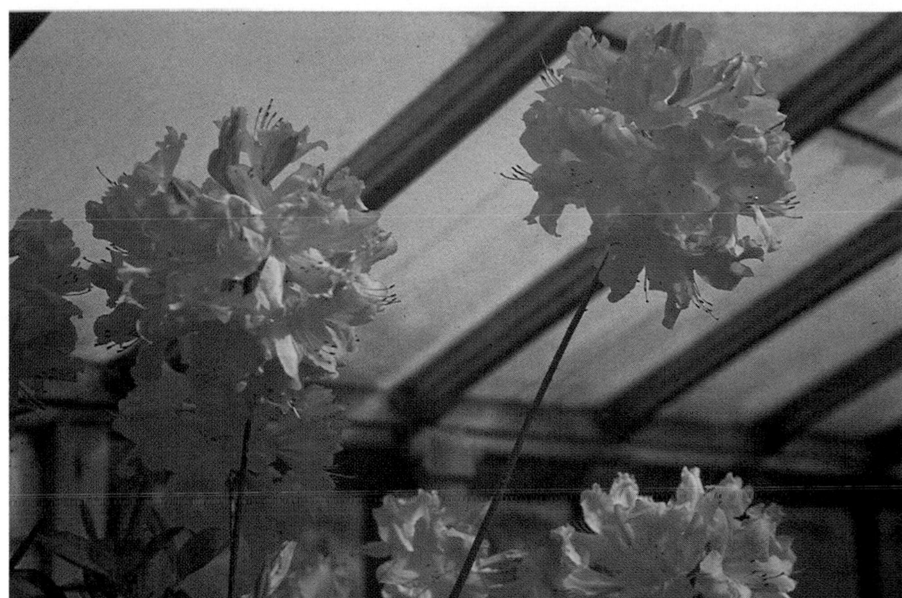

R. molle. Chinese Azalea.
CREECH

R. quinquefolium. Cork Azalea.
CREECH

R. quinquefolium Cork Azalea.
GREER

Plate 18

R. reticulatum. Rose Azalea.
CREECH

R. reticulatum albiflorum.
CREECH

R. reticulatum in the wild, Japan. GALLE

Fall foliage of *R. reticulatum.* GREER

Fall foliage color of 'Persil' Knap Hill Azalea. GREER

Variegated Sims Azalea *R. simsii variegata.* GREER

"Winter Jewels" glisten ice on a deciduous azalea. GALLE

Plate 20

R. wadanum = *R. reticulatum.*
GALLE

R. reticulatum × *komiyamae,*
natural hybrid in Japan. GALLE

R. wadanum = *R. reticulatum.*
CREECH

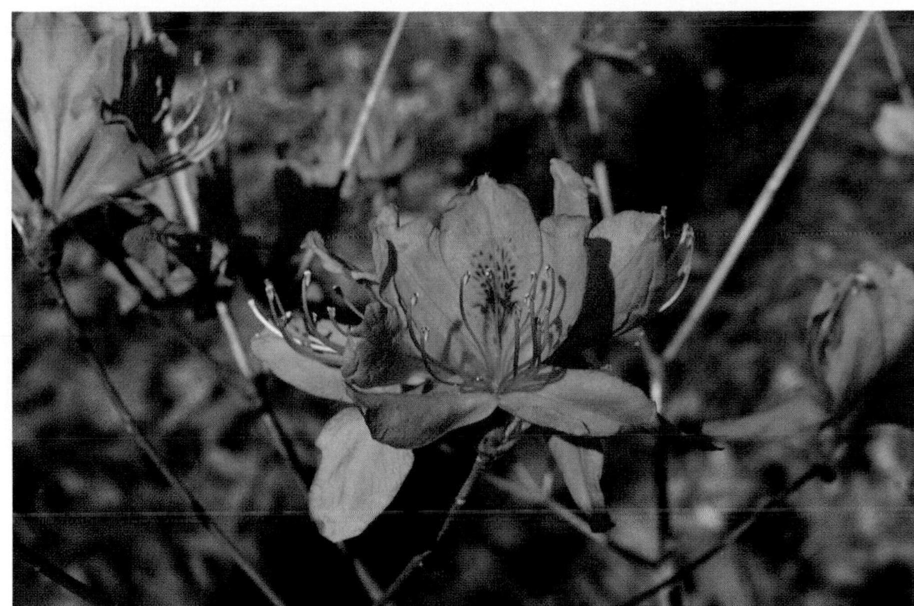

R. nudipes. GALLE

R. amagianum Mt. Amagi Azalea. GREER

R. weyrichii. CREECH

Plate 22

'Corneille' Ghent Hybrid. GREER

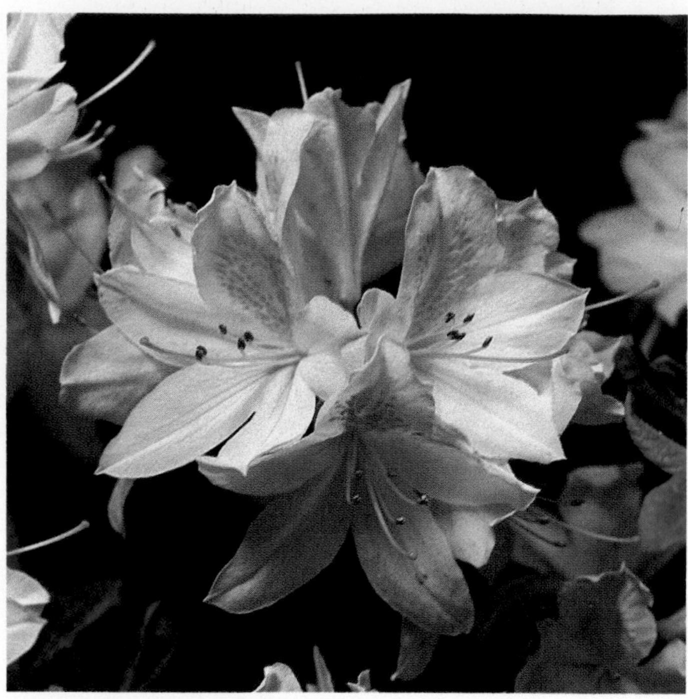

'Dante Gabriel Rossetti' Mollis Hybrid. GREER

'Narcissiflora' old Ghent Hybrid and still popular. GREER

'Susan Monyeen' Mollis Hybrid. B. CARLSON

'Alice de Steurs' Mollis Hybrid. GREER

'Apple Blossom' Mollis Hybrid. GREER

'Salmon Queen' Mollis Hybrid. GREER

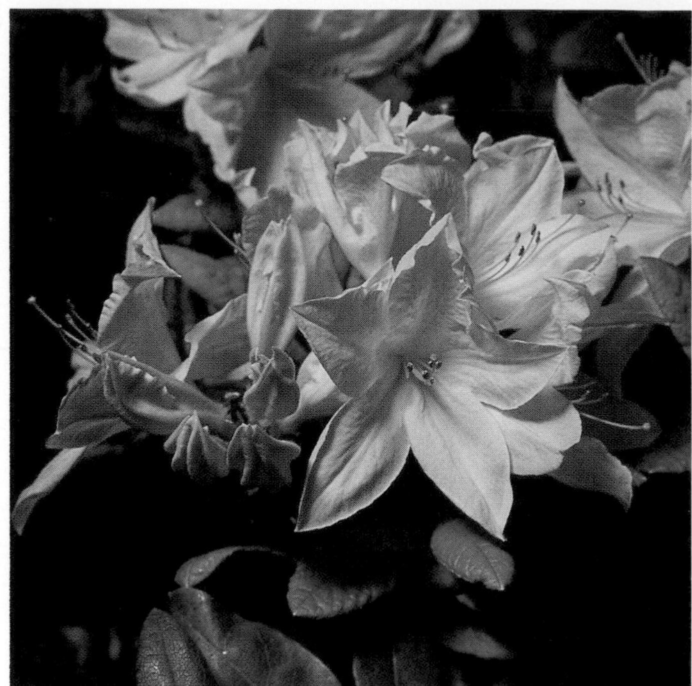

'Colonel F.R. Durham' Mollis Hybrid. GREER

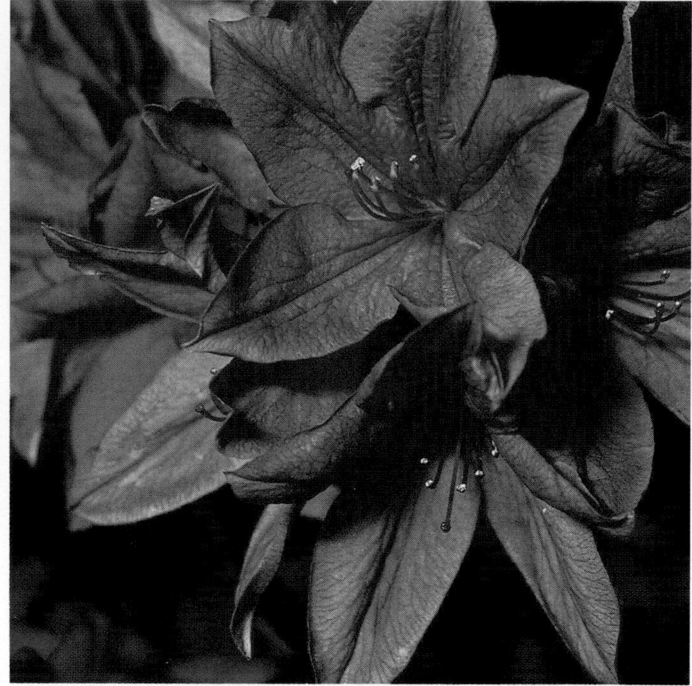

'Hugo Hardijzer' Mollis Hybrid. GREER

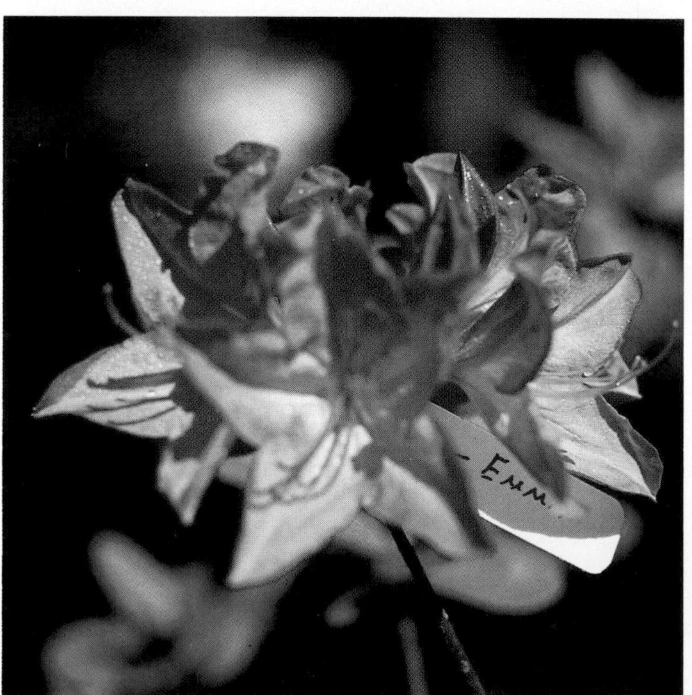

'Köningen Emma' syn. 'Queen Emma' Mollis Hybrid. BARRY

'Adriaan Koster' Mollis Hybrid. B. CARLSON

FELIZ AND DIJKHUIS VISCOSUM HYBRIDS

Messrs. Felix and Dijkhuis of Boskoop, NL, have been actively hybridizing both deciduous and evergreen azaleas for many years. The Viscosum Hybrids (*R. viscosum* × Mollis hybrid) registered in the 1960s are gaining popularity in Europe and North America. Plants are noted for their fragrance and clarity of color. Hardiness, while not completely known, should be zone 6 or hardier.

For other Felix & Dijkhuis deciduous hybrids see the Mollis list. For evergreen hybrids see the Feldyk Hybrids and the Kurume list.

'Antilope' (*viscosum* × Mollis, '63): moderate pink 49B, darker median lines, faint yellow blotch, 2", 10 in truss, fragrant.

'Arpege' (*viscosum* × 'Koster's Brilliant Red', '69); vivid yellow 20B, tube tinged yellowish pink, 1½–1¾", 10 per truss, fragrant, late; upright habit.

'Chanel' (reg. '65): light yellow 18B on outside lobes, on median lines suffused with pink inside, dark yellow blotch, 2¼", tubular funnel-shaped, fragrant.

'Pink Mimosa' (reg. '65): deep purplish pink, tubular funnel-shaped, 1¾", fragrant.

'Replique' (reg. '65): white suffused moderate purplish pink 62B, spotted yellow blotch, tubular funnel-shaped, 2¼", fragrant.

'Reve d'Amour' (reg. '65): light purplish pink 62C, with darker median lines, pale orange blotch, tubular funnel-shaped, 1¾", fragrant.

'Rosata' (*viscosum* × 'Koster's Brilliant Red', '67): deep pink, ribs darker, 1¾", 10 in truss, fragrant, broad upright habit.

'Soir de Paris' (reg. '65): moderate purplish pink, orange blotch, darker median lines, 2", 7–9 in truss, fragrant.

Sapporo
HOKKAIDO
Aomori
Akita
Yamagata
Sendai
Toyama
Nikko
Utsunomiya
Kyoto
HONSHU
Tokyo
Hiroshima
Yokohama
Mt. Fuji
Shizuoka
Sakai
KYUSHU
Kagoshima

8. EVERGREEN AZALEAS

The evergreen azaleas are often called Japanese Azaleas because the majority of the species are native to Japan and the oldest hybrids were developed in Japan.

Azaleas are deeply embedded in the history and culture of Japan. But the literature on the origin and development of evergreen azaleas in Japan is not as readily available in the Western World as is the literature for the deciduous azaleas. Azaleas were mentioned in an ancient Mannyoshu book of poems (A.D. 759). The first horticultural book written in Japan was Kadan Komoku (1681). In it over 317 different varieties and 15 species of azaleas are described. In 1692 the first monograph on azaleas, *Kinshu Makura* by Ito Ihei a nurseryman of old Japan, appeared. *Kinshu Makura* (Brocade Pillow) was published in five volumes and described 332 azaleas, 171 classed as Tsutsuji and 161 as Satsuki. Relatively few books on azaleas appeared thereafter. *Kinshu Makura* was reprinted in 1733 under the name *Cho Sei Karin Sho* and again in 1849, both reprintings using the original wood block illustrations. The descriptions and illustrations of azaleas in *Kinshu Makura* are the first accurate picture of the scope and sophisticated understanding of azaleas by early Japanese horticulturists.

It is important to understand that the Japanese to this day basically classify azaleas as either Tsutsuji or Satsuki. *Rhododendron kiusianum* is one exception and is called Miyama Kirishima. In general the Tsutsuji Azaleas include all the early spring azaleas flowering before or with the new leaves or azaleas flowering 30 days after the spring equinox. Satsuki means "fifth month" referring to an old lunar calendar which was used in Japan until 1873. The fifth month of the old lunar calendar corresponds to June, and the Satsuki flower about one month later than Tsutsuji Azaleas. The Satsuki Azaleas include both *R. indicum* and *R. tamurae (R. eriocarpum)* and their hybrids.

Japanese Azaleas were cultivated in China and elsewhere in Asia as a result of the pilgrimages of Buddhist monks. The same monks were largely responsible for the introduction into Japan of such plants as the *Ginkgo*, tea, Chrysanthemums, Bamboos, Peony, and Nandina. The Japanese *Cryptomeria*, Azalea, Camellia japonica, black Pine, and Hinoki Cypress reached China by the reverse intermediation of the same Buddhist pilgrims.

With the arrival of Western science under the auspices of the Jesuits and Dutch physicians, Latin names were appended to Japanese names which resulted in multiple synonomous names. Confusion was further compounded when plants were introduced into Europe under a variety of yet other names. For example, *R. indicum* was first brought to Holland by the Dutch in 1680 but, unfortunately, was lost. However, the name *A. indica*, established by Linnaeus in *Species Plantarum* (1753), was based on the Dutch descriptions. In 1833 it was reintroduced into England as *A. indica laterita* at approximately the same time as *A. danielsiana, A. macrantha,* and *A. decumbens.* (Curiously, since most of the Dutch ships came from the East Indies [Batavia], it was thought that *R. indicum* was native to the East Indies.) When *R. simsii,* the most important evergreen azalea native to China, was first introduced into England in 1808, it was described as *A. indica*.

Between 1790 and 1853 (Perry's voyages to Japan) more than 125 foreign merchant vessels and war ships touched Japan's shores and brought additional azaleas to Europe. Although 25 American vessels reached Japan during this period, no azaleas were brought directly to America. Robert Fortune brought *A. obtusa* to England in 1844 as plants collected in gardens near Shanghai, China.

It is most likely that the azaleas introduced into Europe during this period represented selections cultivated in Japanese gardens and because of the language difficulty were assigned westernized names. Both 'Indica Alba' and 'Phoeniceum' were introduced to England from China in 1809 and 1824 respectively. 'Indica Alba' is an old cultivar found in Japanese gardens over 300 years ago, but never in the wild. The origin of 'Phoeniceum' is unknown, but has not been collected in the wild. Since *R. simsii* had already been introduced to England (1808) and later to the continent, it figured in the early breeding of azaleas in Europe. This is a departure from the direction followed by the Japanese, for to the best of our knowledge *R. simsii* was introduced into Japan within only the last 30 years.

All of these early azaleas individually, collectively, and with their hybrids have been called the Indian Azaleas. In the mid to late 1800's the Indian Azaleas and their hybrids were popular greenhouse and indoor container plants. Hybridization continued, and the Belgian Hybrids or Belgian Indian Hybrids were developed mainly in Belgium but also in England, France, and Germany.

The first Indian Hybrid Azaleas came to Boston from England in 1838 and were soon distributed to New York and Philadelphia.

Southern Indian Hybrid was the name given to the early Indian Azalea grown outdoors in the southern U.S. The first Southern Indian Azaleas were planted by the Rev. John G. Drayton at Magnolia Gardens, near Charleston, S.C., about 1848. The plants were probably obtained from the David Lambreth Co. in Philadelphia. The P. J. Berckman Co. (Fruitland Nursery) of Augusta, Georgia, also played an important role in introducing the Southern Indian Azaleas to southern gardens.

The Kurume Hybrids, as they are known today, have a long and confusing history. The plants were originally called forms of *R. obtusum*. This plant is now considered of hybrid origin, and its name should only be used in conjunction with the Kurume Azaleas. By 1692, many azaleas of the Kurume type were grown in Japan. Some varieties were introduced to England by the mid-1800's, but the major thrust of interest came in 1918 when E. H. Wilson introduced 50 of the over 250 cultivars grown by Mr. Kijiro Akashi in Kurume, Japan. The Kurume Azaleas were, like the Indian Hybrids, first used as greenhouse or indoor plants, but they proved hardier than the Indian Hybrids and soon became an important landscape plant.

R. kaempferi, a cold-hardy azalea of Japan, was introduced by Professor Sargent to the Arnold Arboretum in 1892 and then to Kew Gardens in 1894. The Kaempferi Hybrids have proved to be more cold-hardy plants than the Kurumes and so became popular garden plants.

The later hybrid lines, such as Glenn Dale, Back Acres, Robin Hill, Greenwood, Gerard, and others are the offspring of these earlier hybrids.

EVERGREEN SPECIES AND VARIETIES

All the evergreen azaleas are classified in two subseries *Obtusum* and *Tashiroi.* The *Tashiroi* subseries is monotypic containing only one species *R. tashiroi.* Over 40 species are in the *Obtusum* subseries.

The term "evergreen" is not absolute for all these species. Even the term "persistent" is not always true. The leaves of these azaleas are dimorphic, that is, having two types of leaves referred to as "spring" leaves and "summer" leaves. The new leaves in the spring are thinner and larger than the summer leaves, turn yellow in the fall, and drop off. The summer leaves are smaller, thicker and more leathery, and usually persistent. The number of persistent leaves retained depends upon the species, clone, and the weather. For more information see Chapter 4.

All of the evergreen azaleas are native to eastern Asia: Japan; south to the Ryukyu Islands, Taiwan and the Philippines; east to Korea and central and southeastern China; and south to central Vietnam. Over 20 of these species are rare and little is known about them save for botanical descriptions.

Species of the *Obtusum* series (Section *Tsutsutsi*) are arranged into eight groups emphasizing basic geographical relationships rather than alphabetically:

1. Kyushu Group
   R. kaempferi, R. kiusianum, R. sataense, R. komiyamae (R. 'Obtusum')
2. Ryukyu Group
   R. macrosepalum, R. ripense, R. scabrum
3. Chinese Azalea
   R. simsii
4. Indica Group
   R. indicum, R. tamurae (R. eriocarpum)
5. Taiwan (Formosa) Group
   R. oldhamii, R. rubropilosum, R. nakaharai
6. Korean Azalea
   R. poukhanense
7. Small Leaf Group
   R. serpyllifolium, R. tosaense, R. tschonoskii, R. microphyton
8. Uncommon or recently introduced species

KYUSHU GROUP

One or more species from the island of Kyushu are probably the parents of the Kurume Hybrids. These species are set forth below:

R. kaempferi Planchon. Kaempfer Azalea ('Yama Tsutsuji').

R. kaempferi is the most common native azalea of Japan, from the southern island of Kyushu to Honshu, the main island, and central Hokkaido. It is now treated as a species, but was first thought to be a variety of *R. indicum,* and later by E. H. Wilson, as a variety of *R. obtusum.* The Kaempfer Azalea is named after Engelbert Kaempfer, a Dutch merchant who introduced many Japanese plants in 1690. Professor Sargent introduced the plant to the Arnold Arboretum in 1892 and to Kew Gardens two years later.

Kaempfer Azalea is one of the hardiest evergreen or semievergreen azaleas, zones 5b–9a. Its range of distribution is from sea level to 4,000 feet. It is most abundant in thickets or on open hillsides as an upright shrub eight to ten feet in height. It is intermediate in persistent leaves between *R. kiusianum*, the least, and *R. sataense*, the most persistent. In northern areas, zone 5, it is generally deciduous but is fully evergreen in warmer climates. The leaves are generally oblong to broadly ovate, one to two inches in length.

The flowers are funnel-shaped, 1½–2" long with five stamens in a small two to four flowered truss. The color is typically various shades of red to yellowish pink with a darker blotch; usually single but hose-in-hose and semidouble flowers are found. In full sun, the flowers often fade to a lighter shade. Flowers are borne before the new leaves, but individual plants may bloom very late. 'Indian Summer', a Gable hybrid, and 'Dorsett', named by E. A. Hollowell, are fall blooming clones. *R. kaempferi* has been an important parent in the development of hardy evergreen azaleas.

The following varieties and forms have been reported:

R. kaempferi var. *albiflorum:* white flowers.

R. kaempferi var. *angustisectum:* a red petaloid flower. An old clone is called 'Bon Fire'.

R. kaempferi var. *tubiflorum:* a small, persistent open tubular flower, white throat and reddish pink at the margin. A Japanese clone is called 'Eijyuho' (longevity treasure).

R. kaempferi f. *kinshibe (cryptopetalum):* (literally, golden stamens), has red stamens and no petals.

R. kaempferi f. *multicolor:* varicolored flowers ranging from pale pink to purple.

R. kaempferi 'Tachisene': double form.

R. kaempferi 'Komatsui': hose-in-hose.

R. kaempferi 'Monstrosum': white, hose-in-hose with petaloid calyx, aborted stamens, and abnormal pistil.

R. kaempferi 'Mikado' or 'Daimio' (syn. 'Daimyo'): a late low growing type. The form *R. kaempferi* f. *mikawanum* is now classified by most botanists as the species *R. komiyamae*, while others consider *R. mikawanum* a separate species.

R. kiusianum syn: *R. indicum amoenum* and *R. obtusum* f. *japonicum* Makino. Kyushu Azalea ('Miyama Kirishama')

A low, dense, twiggy, often prostrate, shrub up to two to three feet. Native to open mountain tops over 2,400 feet in Kyushu Island, Japan. Introduced from seed by E. H. Wilson in 1918. The leaves are dimorphic, semievergreen to deciduous, and more deciduous than *R. kaempferi*. The summer leaves are obovate ½ to ¾". The flowers are borne in terminal umbels of two to three, 1" across, flat with a very short flaring tube, five stamens, usually single, but hose-in-hose and doubles are reported. Color variable, typically shades of purple, varying to red, pink, and white. Hardy in Zones 7a to 8b in well drained soils. Hybridizes in the wild with other species such as *R. kaempferi* producing a greater range in flower color, plant form, and leaf size.

In 1976 Dr. Creech, Director, and Mr. Sylvester March, Horticulturist, of the U.S.D.A. National Arboretum collected azaleas from several of the small nurseries on Kyushu Island.

The following plants were obtained from the Kyoma Yokata Nursery near Mt. Unzen:

'Aya nohomare'	NA 40825	purple
'Fugen no tsuki'	NA 40818	deep to moderate purplish red light center, style red, ¾–1"
'Fujiko machi'	NA 40823	light reddish purple 75B, ¾–1¼"
'Harunoumi'	NA 40815	moderate to deep purplish pink, ¾–1¼"
'Mado no tsuki'	NA 40828	light purple

'Maiogi'	NA 40836	strong purplish red, ¾–1"
'Miyamakikoshi'	NA 40825	moderate purplish red
'Miyama no kasumi'	NA 40820	light reddish purple 78C, throat lighter, ¾–1⅛"
'Miyama murasaki'	NA 40821	strong reddish purple, red style, ¾"
'Otome gokora'	NA 40817	deep purplish pink, style pink, ¾"
'Shogetsu'	NA 40822	white
'Tenshi'	NA 40824	deep purplish pink, lighter throat, 1–1⅛"
'Unzen zakura'	NA 40819	strong purplish pink, ¾"
'Zuiko'	NA 40814	strong red 52A, 1", partially evergreen

The following plants were obtained from the Miyami-en Nursery near Kurume:

'Beni suzume'	NA 40425	reddish orange 43B, ¾", partially evergreen
'Beni zakura'	NA 40439	pale pink
'Beni zuru'	NA 40427	deep reddish orange, 43B, 1⅛"
'Ekubo'	NA 40449	vivid reddish purple 74B, 1⅛", partially evergreen
'Fuji musume'	NA 40429	light purplish pink to near white, ¾"
'Hakutsura'	NA 40420	white, 1–1⅛"
'Hane otome'	NA 40442	pale pink, ¾"
'Hane komachi'	NA 40426	pale reddish orange, ¾"
'Hanshiro'	NA 40421	white, ¾–1"
'Haruno sato'	NA 40445	deep pink
'Haru no yoi'	NA 40450	deep purplish pink, ¾–1", partially evergreen
'Harusame'	NA 40438	deep purplish pink 68A, 1"
'Hina zakura'	NA 40443	strong purplish red 57D, 1"
'Hinode'	NA 40424	vivid purplish red 58B, 1"
'Kiyohime'	NA 40422	reddish orange, 1¾", open habit
'Kuroi wahaku'	NA 40418	small flowers
'Maioogi'	NA 40447	strong purplish red, pale center
'Miyama no kasumi'	NA 40435	reddish purple 78A
'Miyama no katsura'	NA 40434	vivid reddish purple 78A, 1"
'Miyama shikibu'	NA 40431	purplish pink, ¾"
'Miyama susogo'	NA 40433	deep purplish red, style pale red, 1–1⅛"
'Sakon'	NA 40436	strong red 52A
'Takochiko'	NA 40437	strong purplish red, 59D–60C, 1"
'Taisen haku'	NA 40419	thick stems
'Tatsuta'	NA 40423	pale reddish orange 1¼"
'Tenshi'	NA 40432	light purple, lighter throat, 1"
'Tsukushi komachi'	NA 40446	deep pink
'Tsurami'	NA 40428	strong reddish purple, style red, ¾–1"
'Ukon'	NA 40444	strong to deep purplish pink, style red, ¾–1"
'Yakae'	NA 40441	strong purplish red 63B
'Yufu zakura'	NA 40440	strong to moderate purplish red, style red, ¾"
'Yuugiri'	NA 40448	strong reddish purple, lighter center, style red
'Yuzuki'	NA 40430	deep purplish pink, ¾"

Dr. Masaki Kunishige, formerly of the Kurume Ornamental Crops Research Station and now director of the research station at Mie-ken, Japan, advises that most of the forms of *R. kiusianum* available in Japanese nurseries come from the following three locations: #1, Mt. Kuju, the highest mountain southeast of Kurume, where typical *R. kiusuanum* is found; #2, Mt. Unzen southeast of Kurume; and #3, Mt. Haneyama adjacent to Mt. Kuju where most of the plants are compact and vary in flower color, attributing the variability to hybridization, with *R. kaempferi*.

The following *R. kiusianum* clones are also available in the West.

'Album': white flowers.

'Benichidori': strong, reddish orange, 1"

'Benisuzume': reddish orange, 42B, ¾"

'Best Pink': pink.

'Good Times': strong purplish red, hose-in-hose, ¾"

'Hana Aka' (introduced from Japan by Greer): pink
'Hanejiro' (introduced from Japan by Greer): white.
'Hano komachi': pink
'Hiller's Pink'; Hillier Nursery, U. K.: light purplish pink
'Kermesina' (syn. 'Pink Kiusianum'): old variety in Boskoop, vivid purplish red 57B, ¾"
'Kokonoe': double, pale reddish purple, very popular in Japan.
'Komo kulshan': strong purplish red, 57B, pale, pink center, 1"
'Mai Ohgi': deep pink, ¾–1"
'Miyama Komachi' (introduced from Japan by Greer): pink.
'Mountain Gem' (Crown Est., Comm. U.K.): deep purplish pink 68A
'Murasaki Shikibu': reddish purple, hose-in-hose
'Pink Clusters': Weston; hose-in-hose, light, yellowish pink, 38C
'Pink Leach': selection pink
'Shoi Pink': purplish pink

For other *Kiusianum* hybrids such as the Aronense and Diamant Hybrids see the Hybrid Lists.

R. komiyamae Makino. Ashitaka Azalea ('Ashi Taka Tsutsuji')

An obscure azalea restricted to the summit of Mt. Ashi-taka (4,950 ft.) a volcanic cone in the Fuji Hakone range of central Honshu, Japan. Originally classified by the Japanese as *R. indicum* var. *mikawanum* and by E. H. Wilson as *R. obtusum* var. *kaempferi* f. *makawanum* based on its 10 stamens.

A medium to large shrub with persistent leaves. The flowers appear before the leaves in small, one to four, terminal clusters, reddish purple, ¾–1¼", with 10 stamens, *R. kaempferi* has five stamens. With *R. kaempferi* it is the most northern of the large evergreen azaleas of Japan and should be important for breeding. Hardiness zones 7a–9a. On Mt. Ashi-taka, *R. kaempferi* occurs up to 2,970 ft. while *R. komiyamae* is found at higher elevations. Between the two localities, hybrid populations have been observed with a color range from pink to purple and five to 10 stamens. Plants are uncommon in the West but have been introduced by John Creech to the U.S.D.A. National Arboretum.

R. sataense Nakai. Sata Azalea ('Sata Tsutsuji')

An isolated species from open meadows and woodlands of Mt. Takakuma on the island of Kyushu. In Ohwi's *Flora of Japan*, 1965, it was still included under *R. kiusianum*. It closely resembles the Kurume Hybrids and is thought now to be the most influential parent of this group. In fact one can see in the wild, on Mt. Takakuma, so many forms of the plant that appear to be almost identical with selected Kurumes as we know them. In open sites the plants are dense and bushy, three to six feet in height. In the woodland areas it is more open, reaching 10 feet. It is not as compact as *R. kiusianum*, or as leggy as *R. kaempferi*. The summer leaves are elliptic ¾ to 1½", usually larger than *R. kiusianum* and smaller than the oblong to ovate leaves of *R. kaempferi*.

The flowers range from pink and red to purple, clustered at the ends of the branches and dispersed throughout the foliage as in many cultivated Kurumes. This relatively new species more nearly approximates the Kurume Azaleas than does either *R. kaempferi* or *R. kiusianum*. Plants and seeds were brought into the United States by Dr. J. Creech in 1961 but are still uncommon. Plants are hardy in Zones 7a–9a and should be important in future hybridizing.

R. 'Obtusum' Kirishima Azalea ('Kirishima tsutsuji')

This is now regarded as a hybrid within the orbits of *R. satense, R. kiusianum,* and *R. kaempferi,* and not the wild species *A. obtusa* Lindley which was first introduced into England by Fortune in 1844 collected in a garden near Shanghai, China. The original plants came from Japan, possibly several hundred years earlier. Thus, *R. 'Obtusum'* is a garden clone derived from natural hybrids and gardens. E. H. Wilson considered the wild form of the species to be *R. obtusum japonicum* (which included *R. kiusianum*) from Kirishima Mountain on the island of Kyushu. He also placed *R. kaempferi* as a variety *R. obtusum kaempferi*. Both Japanese and Western botanists have recently separated *R. kiusianum* and *R. kaempferi* as species and regard *R. 'Obtusum'* of hybrid origin.

There are several important clones of *R. 'Obtusum'*:

'Obtusum Album' ('Ramentacea'): a tall upright plant; flowers single white, late.

'Amoenum': upright, spreading 6–8 ft., very dense; flowers hose-in-hose 7/8", vivid purplish red 57B, early. Hardier than similar clones, zones 6b–9b. Introduced into England from a Shanghai garden by Robert Fortune in 1850 or '51. Originally thought to be of Chinese origin, it is a Japanese plant and a form of the complex *R. 'Obtusum'*. Wisley Gardens has a plant over 60 years of age with a spread of over 15ft. Occasionally has branch sports with darker flowers deep purplish red 70A; also vivid red. See 'Coccinea'. The small flowered 'Amoenum' phase suggests relatively close relationship with *R. kiusianum*.

'Amoenum Obtusifolium': dwarf form, only 3–4 feet high.

'Normale': single flowered form.

'Kochonomai': Japanese name for 'Amoenum' in Kurume. The plant introduced by the U.S.D.A. Plant Introduction Section in 1939 by this name is single, 1½", vivid purple with a faint darker blotch.

'Macrostemon' (PI 77690): low spreading, flowers strong orange, 1½", exserted stamens.

'Kokinshita' (PI 78379 & 1146720): possibly a selected clone of 'Macrostemon'.

See also Amoena Hybrids.

RYUKYU AZALEA GROUP

There are three related wild species from southern Japan and the Ryukyu (Riukiu and Liukiu) Islands: *R. scabrum, R. ripense,* and *R. macrosepalum*. Unfortunately, garden forms of these species, derived nearly 300 years ago, were described by botanists before the wild forms. These garden forms 'Sublanceolatum', 'Linearifolium', 'Mucronatum', and 'Phoeniceum' were given species designations and will be included here.

Many fine azaleas come from this group of species and played a part in the parentage of the Indica Hybrids. While many clones are tender, they do well in zones 7–9.

R. scabrum G. Don. Luchu Azalea ('Kerama Tsutsuji')

A large evergreen shrub endemic in Okinawa and other Ryukyu Islands. It has been in gardens of southern Japan around Kagoshima for over 250 years. It was first named *R. sublanceolatum* and often referred to as the Chinese Azalea, but it is not native to China or Japan proper.

A large, vigorous, loose shrub, with lanceolate leaves two to four inches long. The large flowers up to 4" are larger than other evergreen species. The wide, funnel-shaped flowers are reddish orange to rosy purple with a darker blotch, 10 stamens, and sepals ½" long. The Luchu Azalea is tender, possibly best in zones 8b to 9b. E. H. Wilson introduced plants to the Arnold Arboretum in 1915, but it had been introduced before.

'Sublanceolatum' (syn. *R. scabrum*), garden form first introduced as a species, has deep pink flowers and blooms a month later.

'Coccineum' ('Kwazan-jima') with vivid red frilled flowers is similar. The form with narrow leaves and smaller flowers from the island of Amamioshima, the northern limits of the species, may have been the one described by early botanists as *R. sublanceolatum*. Wada has crossed the Luchu Azaleas with Kurumes and called them the Scabrum Group.

R. ripense Makino. Riverbank Azalea ('Kishi Tsutsuji')

A medium shrub to six feet found growing along river banks of southern Honshu, S. Koku, and Kyushu, Japan. It is a common cultivated plant and the true parent of 'Mucronatum'. The flowers are light purple, three to four inches, with 10 stamens; white forms are found. The true species *R. ripense* is rare in the West.

'Mucronatum' (syn. *R. indica* var. *alba, R. ledifolia* var. *alba, R. rosmarinifolium*)

A popular cultivated azalea found in Japanese gardens over 300 years ago, but not known in the wild and should not be given a specific rank. Commonly called 'Indica Alba' or 'Ledifolia Alba', it was introduced from China into England in 1819 by Joseph Poole, a plant collector. It was called 'Jedogawa Tsutsuji' and described as white flowered by Kaempfer in 1712. The botanist Burmann called it *A. rosmarinifolia* in 1768. Lindley in 1824 named it *A. ledifolia*, meaning leaves like *Ledum*, a genus in the Heath Family. In 1834 G. Don renamed it *A. mucronatum* for its mucronate leaves with small stiff points at the ends. It is sometimes called Snow Azalea, but is not to be confused with the Kurume clone 'Snow'.

A double white form of 'Mucronatum' was introduced to England from China by Fortune about 1850 under the name *A. narcissiflorum*. This form was cultivated in Japan for hundreds of years as 'Shiro-manyo Tsutsuji'. A reddish purple, double form known as *A. indica* var. *plenum* or 'Fujimanyo' was introduced into England from Chinese gardens in 1819 by J. Poole. Both may still be seen in old gardens. It is a medium to large shrub six to 10 feet in height, broad and spreading. Flowers are pure white, 2½–3", 10 stamens, sepals about ½" long, with a delicate fragrance and sticky on the outside. The leaves are lanceolate to ovate, lanceolate 1½–2½" long and hairy on both surfaces.

Commonly sold as 'Indica Alba' or 'Ledifolia Alba', it is hardy in zones 7a to 9b.

'Mucronatum' and its derivative, the Southern Indian Azalea 'Fielder's White' (tenderer), are excellent early midseason white azaleas.

The following clones which differ from the usually cultivated form:

'Amethystinum', 'Indica Rosea', 'Damask Rose' and 'Magnifica': all similar: 'Indica Rosea' often more flushed; 'Magnifica' has a conspicuous blotch; and 'Amethystinum' has smaller, more starry flowers, a faint blotch and flowers earlier. Considerable variation in this group, better clones are excellent.

'Bulstrode' (syn. 'Mattapan', 'America', 'Maxwell White'): white with a faint greenish yellow blotch.

'Delaware Valley White': white, like 'Indica Alba': reported to be hardier.

'Fujimoyo': light purple 54B, double petaloid, 2", earlier writers listed it as a Kurume, and may be the same as 'Plenum'.

'Hatsushima' (PI 77138): flushed lightly purplish pink 55C, white edges and darker blotch, 2", early; often listed as Kurume but possibly a 'Mucronatum' × *indicum* hybrid.

'Ho oden': white flushed moderate purplish pink 70D, white edges and dark stripes, hose-in-hose, 2", often listed as a Kurume, but possibly a 'Mucronatum' × *indicum* hybrid.

'Japonica Alba': pure white, but flowers scantily.

'Lilacina' (syn. Purpureum): light reddish purple with red blotch 2¼–4" and 10 stamens. This may be closer to *R. phoeniceum* f. *calycinum* than to 'Mucronatum'. 'Lady Lilac' similar, but smaller flowers and blooms earlier and longer in warm climates; deeper color and only five stamens. 'Rubra' and 'Salmonea' vary a little in color. 'Lady Mulberry' very pale violet with darker blotch, flatter and smaller flowers.

'Noordtianum': larger white, occasionally striped purplish red

'Plenum' (syn. 'Fujimanyo', 'Murasaki Botan'): semidouble, numerous stamens, changed to petals and some green tipped or fringed, 'Ira Asabi' (PI 77097) is similar. 'Narcissiflorum' ('Shiro-manyo') is a similar white double.

'Ryukyu' (PI 77074) and 'Shiro Ryukyu' (PI 77085): white and similar to 'Mucronatum'. 'Laughing Water', a Coolidge Rare Plant Garden introduction is similar with smaller flowers.

'Sekidera', 'Ryukyu Shibori' and 'Kanaka': white flushed vivid purplish red, with blotch of same color, sometimes striped [Ryukyu Shibori] or flecked [Kanoka] and sometimes frilled.

'Shishoren' (PI 77131): deep purplish pink, 1½"

'Shishu' (PI 77141): semidouble, to double, petals separate, deep purplish pink 68A.

'Phoeniceum', an early well known evergreen garden azalea, was introduced to England from Canton, China in 1824 and given a specified name *A. indica*. Following this it was given other names including *A. punica* and *A. rawsonii*. In 1834 it was given the name *A. phoeniceum* by G. Don for its phoeniceus (dark red) flowers, that actually are purplish red. Although first given species rank, it has not been found in the wild and should not be given this status. Known only as a garden form, 'Phoeniceum' is probably a form of *R. scabrum* or a hybrid of *R. scabrum* and 'Mucronatum'.

Other forms commonly attributed to 'Phoeniceum' are:

'Akebono' (syn. *R. pulchrum* or *R. phoeniceum* var. *calycinum* 'Akebono'): flowers broadly funnel-form, 3" light purple (PI 276290).

'Omurasaki': (syn. *R. p.* var. *calycinum*, 'O-omurasaki', PI 77095, 'Kumagi-yodogawa'): Similar to 'Phoeniceum' but more vigorous and hardier, possibly a *R. scabrum* × 'Mucronatum' hybrid. The common 'Formosa' azalea has larger and less rounded flowers, and is tall spreading; flowers vivid purplish red, 3½" with darker blotch. Some variation among clones of this name. Introduced before 1851 by R. Fortune.

'Tebatan': double with small green leaves coming up out of the center, more double than 'Mucronatum Plenum' which is often a substitute name.

'Maxwell' (Syn. 'Aka-yodogawa', *R. phoeniceum* var. *calycinum* f. *maxwelli*): medium upright shrub, vivid purplish red, with darker blotch, late midseason, much hardier zone 6b, probably a hybrid. 'Maxwell Alba' is possibly a form of 'Mucronatum', white with greenish throat, 2½", early midseason.

'Smithi' (syn. *R. phoeniceum* var. *Smithi*): a form of 'Phoeniceum' compact growth to 6 feet, purplish red, 2½". Introduced into America in 1835.

'Shirotae' (syn. *R. pulchrum* var. *Shirotae*) white, 3", similar to 'Indica Alba' possibly a sport of 'Smithi'.

R. macrosepalum Maximowicz. Big Sepal Azalea ('Mochi Tsutsuji') (syn. *R. linearifolium* var. *macrosepalum*).

This is another case where a garden form was introduced as a species, *R. linearifolium* in 1846 and the wild form *R. macrosepalum* not described under later, although both are described in *Kinshu Makura* in 1692.

The Big Sepal Azalea is found south of Tokyo on the main island of Honshu and on Shikoku, in woodlands and open thickets in well drained soils. A low to medium shrub three to six feet. It is distinguished by its hairy leaves, 1½ to 2½ inches long, and its large conspicuous sepals about 1½ inches long. The fragrant flowers are broadly funnel-shaped, 2", five stamens, early to midseason, light purple to light reddish purple with a reddish blotch. Hardy in zones 7a to 8b. It was introduced into Europe by Maximowicz in 1879 but did not reach England until 1914. See 'Lady Locks' p. 274.

'Linearifolium'. Spider Azalea ('Seigai Tsutsuji') (syn. *R. linearifolium*)

An unusual azalea with narrow strap-like leaves and the flowers divided into narrow strap-like petals, 1½" long, strong purplish pink to strong purplish red. The foliage has a reddish cast in winter. It was introduced into England in 1869 and reported to have flowered in 1876 in the Honeywell Garden in Wellesley, Massachusetts. 'Seigai Tsutsuji' is an old Japanese name for 'Linearifolium'. A clone 'Seigai' is reported to have purple flowers, but it is very similar to the type 'Linearifolium'.

The following forms of *R. macrosepalum* are:

'Hahaguruma' (syn. 'Oye Yame'): 'Amagashita' and 'Rhodoroides' Japanese selections of other narrow petal and leaf forms. All are purplish red types. 'Surugamanyo' is a double form.

'Koromo Shikibu' (PI 77142): usually listed as a Kurume Hybrid is more like a *R. macrosepalum* hybrid. The hairy leaves are of normal size; petals are divided and strap-like, ½" wide, 1½" long, light purplish pink with darker tips and dark spots at the base.

R. tectum Koidz. ('Miyaki Tsutsuji')

Natural hybrids of *R. kaempferi* and *R. macrosepalum* not known in the West.

CHINESE AZALEAS

Of the over 12 evergreen azaleas native to China only *R. simsii* is commonly known but still rare as a species in the West. Other species have been introduced including *R. microphyton*, *R. mariesii*, and others, but generally are still not available. A brief description of the lesser known species is covered later. Now that the "doors are open" to China, the introduction of these and other species hopefully will increase.

R. simsii Plachon. Sims Azalea ('Yin-shan-hung')

Native to the temperate regions of southern and central China, east of Taiwan, Burma, and Thailand. An important garden plant in China, it was introduced around 1793 to Europe and first described by J. Sims as *A. indica* in 1812. It was cultivated as a greenhouse or tub plant as *A. indica* var. *ignescens* and was flowered in 1847 by M. P. Wilder of Dorchester, Massachusetts. Sims Azalea played an important part in the development of the Indian and Belgian hybrid azaleas in Belgium, Holland, and England.

A medium shrub six to eight feet with elliptic ovate leaves, up to 3" long. The flowers are in small trusses two to six, broadly funnel-shaped, usually 10 stamens, occasionally eight, 1½–2", yellowish pink to various shades of red with darker blotch. The plants are tender outside of zones 8a to 9a.

The Sims Azalea sports freely, and from these a number of new varieties or clones have developed:

'Vittatum' (syn. 'Vittata Fortunei', 'Vittata Punctata'): flowers white flaked or striped purplish red 66A. Also pure white and purplish red selfs, 2". 'Vittatum Beale' has reddish stripes and flakes. These are two old clones and were collected by Fortune in Shanghai, China around 1850.

'Vittatum Fortunei Purpurea' (syn. 'Vittata Purple'): large flowers 2¾", purplish red as in 'Vittatum'.

INDICA AZALEA GROUP

The Indica Azalea Group consists of two late-blooming evergreen species, *R. indicum* and *R. tamurae* (syn. *R. eriocarpum*). For over three hundred years the Japanese have divided azaleas into two groups according to their time of flowering.

1. Tsutsuji: early spring flowering azalea before or with the new leaves.
2. Satsuki: late flowering azaleas, the fifth month azalea under the old Chinese calendar Satsuki.

R. indicum and *R. tamurae* are called Satsuki and likewise their hybrids, the Satsuki Hybrid azaleas.

R. indicum (L.) Sweet Indica Azalea ('Satsuki')

The Indica Azalea should not be confused with hybrids called Indica or Southern Indian Azaleas. *R. indicum* is native to southern Japan south of Tokyo on Honshu, and the more southern islands of Shikoku, Kyushu, and Yakushima.

R. indicum was first introduced into Holland in 1680 as *A. indica* by Dutch merchants, citing the plant as from (Jaccarta) Batavia, Indonesia (Java). Plants doubtlessly were taken by Dutch trading ships from Japan to Batavia and then to Holland. In 1833 it was re-introduced to England as *A. indica* var. *lateriti.* About the same time different color forms were brought to England from China under various names, *A. danielsana, A. macrantha, A. decumbens,* and others. A white-flowered form with reddish stripes called *A. indica* var. *variegata* was introduced by Mr. M. Killigan in 1833. In 1838 the indica azalea came to Boston from England as both *R. danielsiana* and *R. lateritia.* Between 1840 and 1870 Magnolia Gardens in South Carolina had received it under the names *A. lateritia, A. danielsiana, A. indica,* and also the var. *variegata.*

R. indicum is a densely branched, low to medium shrub up to six feet. The leaves are lanceolate to oblanceolate ¾ to 1½" long by ¼ to ½" wide; and smaller than *R. simsii.* They are larger than *R. tamurae* and have a reddish color in the winter. The broad funnel-shaped flowers are solitary or in pairs, 2–2½" wide with stamens, and open late. The colors range from pink, purplish red to vivid red and even white. Today the Indica Azalea is commonly sold as 'Macrantha', 'Balsaminaeflora' and other varieties. Small plants often are tender, but mature plants are as hardy as Kurumes, zones 7a–10a. *R. indicum* does not force well, and it is doubtful if it was important in the development of the Indican and Belgium greenhouse hybrids. However, both *R. indicum* and *R. tamurae* and possibly others are important in the Satsuki Hybrids which are dealt with later.

The following clones of *R. indicum* have been in cultivation for many years:

'Balsaminaeflorum' (syn. 'Rosaeflora' 'Komanyo Satsuki'): low compact, flowers late, very double, about 40 petals, no pistil or stamens, 1½", moderate red 47C. A very old but popular clone. Introduced to France from Japan in 1877. 'Kinnozai' is similar but less double. 'Pink Beauty' is a similar pink variety. A double white form has been reported but must be very rare.

'Crispiflorum': a deep pink to strong red with frilled petals. Leaves thicker than the type. Another old clone introduced to England in 1851. Other color forms have been introduced by U.S.D.A.P.I.S. as 'Crispiflorum Mauve', 'Crispiflorum Orange' and 'Crispiflorum Pink'.

'Flame Creeper': low and spreading, reddish orange.

'Hakata Shiro': white with yellowish green throat, earlier than *R. indicum* and more tender. 'Gledstanesi', introduced in the 1840's into England and then to the United States, is late blooming, white and low. 'Shiro Satsuki' (PI 77117). 'Macrantha Alba' and the Southern Indian Hybrid, 'Lantana Alba' are similar.

'J. T. Lovett': low, dense, strong red 50A, with darker blotch 2½". *R. indicum* PI 78382 is about the same.

'Laciniatum' (syn. 'Shide Satsuki'; *augustipetalum*): low, dense. Strong red, five narrow strap-like, widely separated petals. 'Polypetalum' has five or more strap-like petals and normal leaves. Wilson's form of 'Polypetalum', with no corolla but petaloid laciniate calyx, is very rare.

'Kinsai' is a Satsuki with similar strap-like flowers and very small narrow leaves.

'Macrantha' (syn. 'Macrantha Orange'): A reddish orange clone of *R. indicum*, low and compact.
- 'Macrantha Pink': deep pink flowers
- 'Macrantha Double': deep pink double flowers.
- 'Macrantha Dwarf': a semidouble deep pink, compact.

'Okina-Nishiki': low, hose-in-hose, reddish orange.

'Salmonea': deep pink, with darker throat 2½".

'Satsuki' (PI 77104): purplish red 63A, darker blotch; low spreading

'Tamino no yuki' (syn. 'Coral Ivory'): a Satsuki hybrid with red to purplish red flowers and white throat.

'Variegatum' (syn. 'Matsushima', 'Shiki Takane satsuki'): white with red stripes or flakes. It was the parent of the best Indian Azaleas cultivated up to about 1850 such as 'Iveryana' and 'Charles Encke'.

R. tamurae Masamune (syn. *R. eriocarpum* Nakai). Dwarf Indica Azalea ('Maruba-satsuki')

R. tamurae is a rare azalea both in the wild and in cultivation. It is found on the islands south of Kyushu including Yakushima, Tanegashima, and Tokara Islands. Due to the limited distribution, the classification has varied. It was first described by Japanese botanists as *R. indicum* var. *eriocarpum*, later by E. H. Wilson as *R. Simsii* var. *eriocarpum*, then as a separate species *R. eriocarpum* and now *R. tamurae*. The Japanese name 'Maruba satsuki' means "The Satsuki with round leaves", and like *R. indicum* is a late blooming species. It grows at low elevations from sea level to rocky hillsides. The plants are typically low and compact, but upright growth habits are reported. The summer leaves are orbiculate to obovate about 1" long and remain green in the winter. The flowers vary from red to purplish red to pink and occasionally white, 1½–2" with eight to 10 stamens. *R. indicum* differs in being a mountainous plant with narrow elliptic to lanceolate leaves, and pink to red flowers with five stamens. *R. tamurae* is hardy in zones 7a–10a.

On Yakushima Island both *R. indicum* and *R. tamurae* occur together with their natural hybrids. Early horticultural clones of the Satsuki Azaleas were selected from these natural hybrids. (See Satsuki Hybrids). *R. tamurae* is still uncommon in the West, but should be important in future azalea breeding. Previously 'Gumpo' and its clones have been included under *R. tamurae*, *R. eriocarpum*, or *R. tamurae*; however, it is best to include these under Satsuki Hybrids.

TAIWAN (FORMOSA) GROUP

Taiwan is the home of many wild evergreen azalea species including *R. simsii* and *R. tashiroi* whose ranges extend to Taiwan. Three Taiwanian azaleas are now found in the western world: *R. oldhamii*, *R. rubropilosum*, and *R. nakaharai*. The following species are still rare in cultivation: *R. breviperulatum, R. kanehirai, R. lasiostylum, R. longiperulatum, R. mariesii, R. noriakianum, R. sikayotaizanenis,* and *R. taiwanalpinum.*

R. nakaharai Hayata.

A low, prostrate shrub, one to two feet, endemic to northern Taiwan in grassland at elevations of 2,300 to 3,300 feet. First reported to be similar and described as *R. serpyllifolium (sensu)* but easily distinguished by its oblong ovate to oblanceolate leaves ½ to ¾" long, larger flowers and 10 stamens. The flowers are in small one- to three-terminal clusters, reddish orange to red, 1½" wide. Hardy in zones 6b–9a. Seeds were first introduced into the U.S.A. in 1960 by R. Bovee of Oregon, and Mrs. J. Hill of Delaware brought in plants in 1961 and later introduced the clone 'Mount Seven Star' plus *R. nakaharai* hybrids. (See North Tisbury Hybrids.) Dr. T. Rokujo from Tokyo, Japan introduced to England a clone 'Mariko'. While the species is still uncommon, the above clones and hybrids are good dwarf garden azaleas.

R. oldhamii Maximowicz (syn. *R. ovatosepalum* Yamamota). Oldham Azalea

An upright open branched shrub to 10 feet, endemic to northern Taiwan from sea level to 9,000 feet. The twigs and leaves 1–3" long are densely covered with reddish, glandular hair. The flowers are in small two to four terminal clusters, reddish orange with darker dots, 1½–2", and 10 stamens. Flowering is in late spring and is sporadic throughout the summer. A tender species hardy to zones 8a–9a. It was first discovered in 1864 by R. Oldham of Kew and introduced into England in 1878 by C. Maries, but was later reported lost. Reintroduced by E. H. Wilson in 1918 to the United States and England. Being tender it was used in England as a greenhouse plant and as a parent of an Evergreen Exbury Hybrid as well as others later in the U.S.A. It should be used in warmer climate for its summer flowers.

R. rubropilosum Hyata (syn. *R. caryophyllum* Hayata). Redhair Azalea

A medium to tall shrub to 10 feet, endemic to grassy mountain slopes east of Arisan, Taiwan, at elevations between 1,000 to 3,500 feet. The stems and leaves are covered with grey to reddish brown hairs. The flowers are pink with dark spots, eight to 10 stamens, 1–1½" wide. Hardy in zones 7b–8b. Introduced by E. H. Wilson in 1918 and again by J. L. Creech in 1968, still uncommon.

KOREAN AZALEAS

The hardiest azaleas of the *Obtusum* subseries, both native to Korea, are *R. yedoense* var. *poukhanense* and *R. tschonoskii,* a small-leaved azalea described later.

R. yedoense Maximowicz (syn. *R. poukhanense* var. *Yodogawa).* Yodogawa Azalea ('Botan Tsutsuji')

In 1866 Maximowicz gave a species name to a double flowered garden form of an azalea that grows wild in Korea. Yodogawa Azalea was known in Japan for hundreds of years and was mentioned in *Kinshu Makura,* 1692. It was introduced into England from Japan in 1884.

Unfortunately the wild, single flowered plant was not described until later and botanically must be treated as a variety of the cultivated offspring. Unfortunately, this adds to confusion, for in most horticultural literature the wild single flowered plant is treated as a species, and in many cases throughout this book it will be handled as such.

Yodogawa Azalea is often described as a monstrous form, but it is an attractive garden plant with sterile flowers and must be propagated vegetatively. The plant is of medium height 4 to 6 feet. The fragrant double flowers are light purple, 2" across and persist longer than the single flowers. Very hardy in zones 6a–9b, it is often semievergreen to deciduous in colder climates.

R. yedoense var. **poukhanense** Nakai (syn. *R. poukhanense)*. Korean Azalea ('Chosen Yama Tsutsuji')

The Korean Azalea was first described as *R. poukhanense* by Leveille in 1908, and as *R. coreanum* by Rehder in 1913; but changed to a variety of *R. yedoense* in 1920 by Nakai, due to priority as mentioned earlier.

It is often said that the double Yodogawa preceded the single wild type, but the Korean Azalea is mentioned in *Kinshu Makura,* 1692, as 'Shiki Murasaki' (syn. 'Chosen Shileu'). It is not a question of which came first, like the chicken and the egg, but which was botanically described first.

R. yedoense var. *poukhanense* is the common azalea of Korea. A low to medium shrub, 5 to 6 feet, in southern to central Korea and on the Japanese island of Tsushima, south of Korea. It is partial to open grassy slopes from sea level to over 5,000 feet and forms dense masses.

The Korean Azalea is persistent-leaved, but loses all of its leaves in colder climates. The ovate to lanceolate leaves, 1½ to 3", have impressed veins on the upper surface and are covered with soft straight gray to brownish hairs. The single flowers are in small trusses of 2 to 4, light to moderate purple with a reddish blotch, 10 stamens, mildly fragrant, and 1½–2" wide.

It was introduced into the Arnold Arboretum by J. H. Jack in 1905 and then to England in 1913. Very hardy in zones 6a–9a and widely distributed in colder areas. It has also played an important role in the development of hardier evergreen azaleas both in Europe and in the United States. There is a pink flowered form called 'Poukhanense Pink' and 'Munchkin', a dwarf selection introduced by Carlson's Gardens. White form available.

SMALL LEAF AZALEA GROUP

There are six small leaf azaleas cultivated in Japan, Korea, and China. *R. nakaharai* could be included in this group but was discussed with the Taiwan azaleas. Their leaves are small from 1/16–1½" long, with small flowers usually less than 1" wide. They are all hardy but often unsatisfactory in areas of hot humid summers.

R. serpyllifolium Miguel. Wild Thyme Azalea ('Unzen Tsutsuji')

A small, dense, spreading shrub three to four feet, on the southern half of Honshu and on the island of Shikoku and Kyushu, Japan, usually confined to volcanic, well drained soils. The leaves are ¼ to ¾" long, ⅛ to ¼" wide. The small flowers are light pink, ¾" wide. Hardy in zones 6a–8b. Introduced into England by C. Maries around 1880 and later to the United States.

R. serpyllifolium var. **albiflorum** often labelled var. *alba* is a white flowered form, usually more common in cultivation than the species.

R. tosaense Makino, (*R. miyazawe*). Tosa Azalea ('Fuji Tsutsuji')

A low shrub three to six feet on the southern tip of Honshu and in Shikoku and Kyushu, Japan. Spring leaves are usually lanceolate, ⅓ to 1½" long, 1/16 to 2/5" wide. The summer leaves are similar to but smaller and narrower than *R. serpyllifolium.* Flowers in trusses of one to six, moderate purplish red, 1", early, five stamens. Hardy in zones 7a–8a. E. H. Wilson introduced seed to the Arnold Arboretum in 1914, but plants were not hardy. The U.S.D.A. Plant Introduction Section obtained plants in 1940 and seed in 1950. Tosa Azalea is still rare in the West. *R. komiyamae* from central Honshu is similar in leaf but flowers later with six to nine stamens.

R. tschonoskii Maximowicz. Tschonoski Azalea('Kume Tsutsuji')

A spreading low, dense, alpine shrub, three to six feet, from central Hokkaido, south through the mountains of Honshu, Shikoku, and Kyushu, Japan, and also in southern

Korea. One of the hardiest evergreen azaleas, although it usually loses its leaves in the winter. Hardy in zones 5a–8a. The leaves are lanceolate, 1/3 to 1½" long, 1/6 to 5/8" wide, reddish orange in winter. Small white flowers ½", four to five lobes, and stamens, bloom late, in trusses 2–6, often hidden by leaves. Introduced into England by C. Maries in 1878. C. S. Sargent sent seed to the Arnold Arboretum in 1892 and E. H. Wilson in 1917. The Plant Introduction Section obtained seeds from England, Scotland, and Japan over a number of years, but the plant is still rare.

A variety once listed as a separate species *(R. trinerve)* is now *R. tschonoskii* var. *trinerve* being larger in all its parts.

R. microphyton Franchot. Pinkflush Azalea, 'Liang mao dujuan', 'Shining Hair Azalea'

The Chinese analogue to *R. tschonoskii.* An alpine plant from the provinces of Yunnan and southwest Sichuan, China. A low, shrub three to six feet, twigs with dense reddish brown hairs. The leaves are elliptic ½ to 1¼" long. The small, pink to white flowers have reddish spots in the throat, ½–1½" and five stamens. It was discovered by the Abbe Delavay about 1884 and introduced into England by Forrest in 1913. It is still very rare. Its adaptability and hardiness are not known.

R. tsusiophyllum Sugimoto (syn. *R. tanakae* & *Tsusiophyllum tanakae).*

A low, prostrate shrub to two feet from the mountains of Honshu and Taiwan. Leaves elliptic to obovate 1/3 to ¾" long. Small flowers are tubular, four to five lobed, 3/8 to ½" long and 2¼" wide, white, five stamens. A rare plant, hardy in zones 6b–8a. Often listed as a separate genus *Tsusiophyllum tanakae* Maximowicz, due to its tubular flowers.

R. yakuinsulare Masam.

This is not to be confused with the linear-leaved plant often given this name in the United States that is correctly called *R. otakumii. R. yakuinsulare* is from the island of Yakushima. The spring leaves are elliptic or ovate-oblong ¾" to 2" long, 3/8"–¾" wide. The summer leaves are smaller. The funnel-shaped pink to red flowers are 5 petaled, not polypetaled, with 5 stamens. The plant is very similar to *R. simsii* but very rare in cultivation.

R. otakumii Yamazaki.

This plant was introduced into the United States as *R. yakuinsulare* and is being propagated and sold as such. *R. otakumii* is a relatively newly identified species collected on the banks of the Otakumi River on the island of Yakushima. The spring leaves are narrow linear ½–1" long, 3/16–¼" wide. The summer leaves are generally smaller ½" or less in length. Winter coloration is reddish. The small flowers reddish orange are polypetaled, 5–6 strap-like petals. The plant resembles a *R. indicum* type and is similar to the 'Kinzai' Satsuki which has more elliptical leaves and usually 10 narrow, strap-like petals.

Mr. Hideo Suzuki of Japan has been of great assistance in the correct identification of these two plants.

It should also be pointed out that neither *R. otakumii* nor *R. yakuinsulare* is included in the *Flora of Japan* by J. Ohwi so the names may be changed with further study.

TASHIROI SUBSERIES

This is a montotypic subseries. The single species *R. tashiroi* serves to link subseries *Farrerae* and *Obtusum.* It shares the characteristics of both, the persistent leaves are in threes, flattened, bristles, naked seed and vegetative buds included in the inflorescence buds. Some botanists feel that *R. tashiroi* should be placed in the *Obtusum* subseries. However, the finger-like hairs on the margins of the cotyledons are found only in the subseries *Farrerae.*

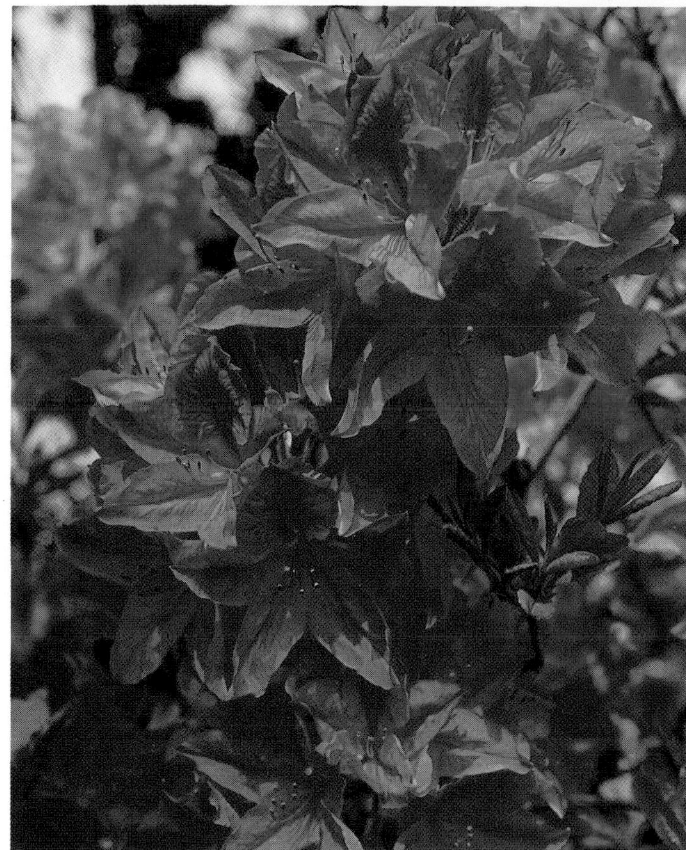

'W.F. Raiffeisen' Mollis Hybrid. GREER

'Gloria Mundi' Ghent Hybrid. PLANTING FIELDS

'Ignaea Nova' Ghent Hybrid. CARLSON

'Hamlet' Mollis Hybrid. GREER

Plate 26

'Dr. M. Oosthoek' Mollis Hybrid. B. CARLSON

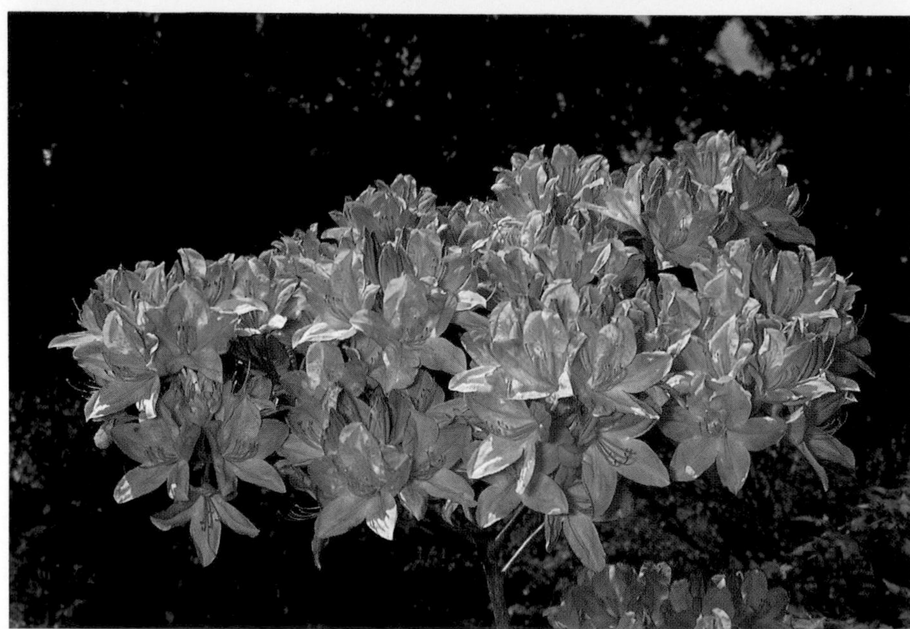

'Hortulanus H. Witte' Mollis Hybrid. GREER

'Prominent' Mollis Hybrid. GREER

'Pathfinder' (Exbury × *austrinum*) heat resistant Hybrid. GIORDANE

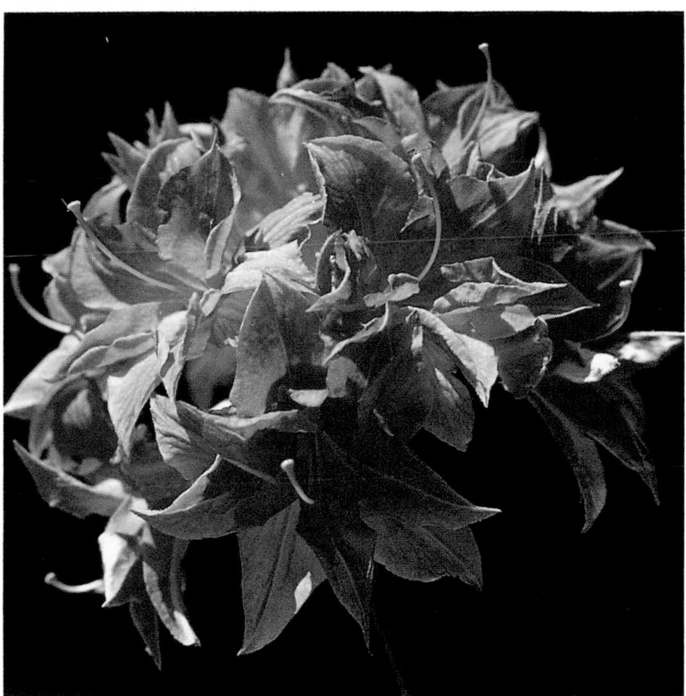

'Norma' Rustica Flore Pleno Hybrid. E. HAGER

'Graciosa' Occidentale Hybrid. GREER

'Jolie Madame' *R. viscosum* × 'Koster's Brilliant Red' Hybrid. GREER

Plate 28

'Exquisita' Occidentale Hybrid. GREER

'Jock Brydon' Mollis × Occidentale Hybrid. GREER

'Rosita' *R. viscosum* × 'Koster's Brilliant Red' Hybrid. GREER

'Irene Koster' Occidentale Hybrid. GREER

'Arpege' *R. viscosum* × 'Koster's Brilliant Red' Hybrid. GREER

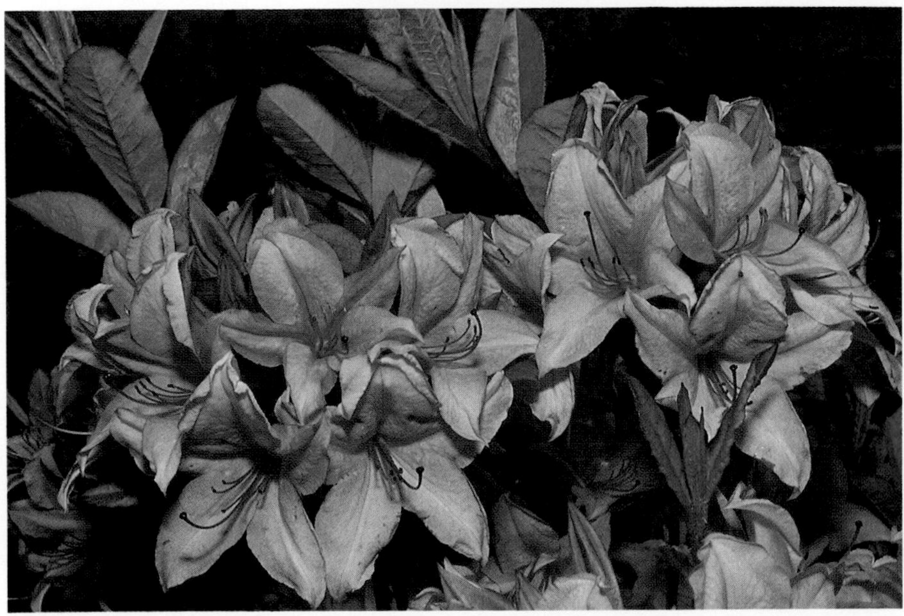

'Soir de Paris' *R. viscosum* × Mollis Hybrid. GREER

Plate 30

'Garden scene with Knap Hill Azaleas. GALLE

'Cecile' Exbury Azalea. D. HYATT

'Gallipoli Red' Exbury Azalea. GREER

'Balzac' Exbury Azalea. GREER

'Goldfinch' Exbury Azalea. GREER

'Exbury White' Exbury Azalea. GREER

'Gibraltar' Exbury Azalea. GREER

Plate 32

'Sunset Pink' Exbury Azalea. GREER

'Bright Forecast' Exbury Azalea. GREER

'Sun Chariot' Exbury Azalea. GREER

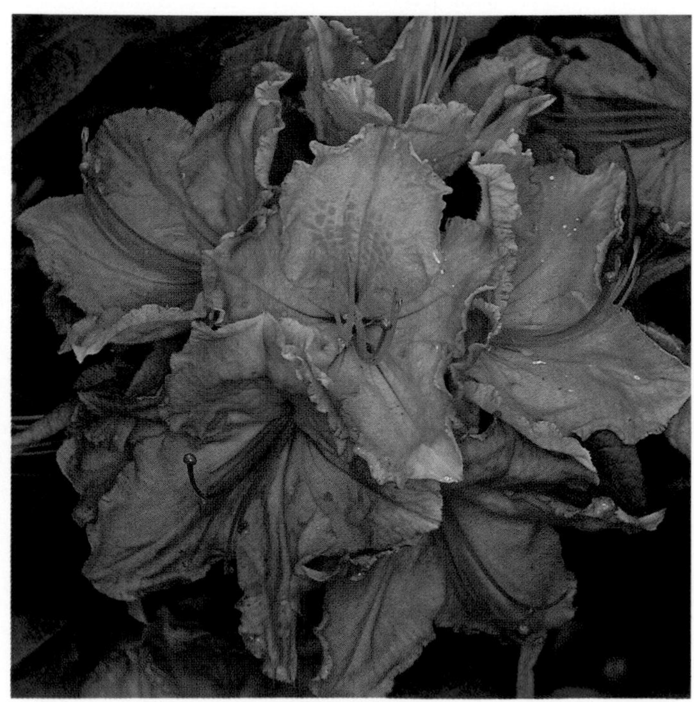

'Strawberry Ice' Exbury Azalea. GREER

R. tashiroi Maximowicz ('Sakura tsutsuji')

A tall, twiggy plant up to 15 feet; a montana plant in southern Kyushu and south through the Ryukyu Island to Taiwan. The elliptic obovate leaves are 1½–2½" long and are usually in pairs or in threes. The flowers are in trusses of two to three, bell-shaped, funnelform, pale reddish purple with darker spots, 1–1½" wide, 10 to rarely 12 stamens.

Plants were brought into the United States in 1955 by the U.S.D.A. Plant Introduction Section, but are very rare in cultivation. K. Wada of Japan reported hybrids of *R. tashiroi* × *R. weyrichii,* eight to 10 feet tall, yellowish pink to deep pink flowers, 4" wide. One selection has been named 'Tashiroi Pink Pearl'. Wada also crossed *R. tashiroi* × *R. reticulatum* var. *roseum.*

UNCOMMON OR UNINTRODUCED SPECIES

The following azalea species are uncommon. Very few have been evaluated for cultural adaptability and hardiness. The brief descriptions are taken for the most part from various botanical manuals.

R. annamense Rehder: the southern-most azalea from central Vietnam; flowers purplish red, 1½" long, 10 stamens; leaves persistent oblanceolate 1–2½" long, with rust colored hairs. Similar to *R. hainanense* but smaller leaves and flowers.

R. atrovirens Franchet: large shrub or small tree from Yunnan, China; flowers red with darker blotch 1½" wide, 10 stamens; leaves persistent, ovate lanceolate 1–3" long.

R. boninense Nakai: medium shrub, Bonin Island, Japan, 600 miles south of Tokyo; flowers white 2" wide, 10 stamens; leaves persistent, oblong lanceolate 1–1¾" long; branches with dense rufous hairs. Collected by Dr. J. L. Creech for the National Arboretum.

R. breviperulatum Hayata: small twiggy shrub from mountain forest of Taiwan; flowers reddish, 1" wide, 5 stamens; leaves persistent, oblong ovate 1–1½" long.

R. chrysocalyx Levl. et Vant; 'Jine dujuan', Golden Calyx Azalea: medium shrub, Guizhou, N. Guangxi, and W. Hubei Prov., China; flowers purple, 5 stamens, calyx and ovary with yellowish hairs; leaves deciduous or semi-evergreen, lanceolate ¾–1½" long.

R. chunii Fang; 'Su zhu dujuan', Persistent Style Azalea: large shrub from N. Guangdong Prov., China; flowers purplish pink, purple dots on upper lobes, 5 stamens; leaves persistent, elliptic ⅜–¾" long with reddish brown hairs.

R. flumineum Fang et M. Y. He; 'Hebian dujuan', Riverside Azalea: Yunnan Prov., China; shrub with brownish red hairs on branches; flowers red, dark red spotted upper lobe, 5 exserted stamens; leaves 1½–2½" long. Similar to *R. rufohirtum* with smaller leaves and longer stamens and style.

R. glandulostylum Fang et M. Y. He; 'Xianzhu dujuan', Glandular Style Azalea: small shrub, Guangxi Prov., China; flowers red with purple dots on upper lobe. 1½" wide; leaves deciduous 1–1⅜" long, lower surface whitish. Similar to *R. chunii* but with larger narrow elliptic leaves, and style with hairs and glands.

R. hainanense Merrill; 'Hai nan dujuan', Hainan Azalea: low to medium shrub, Hainan Prov., China, and Vietnam; flowers red, 10 stamens; leaves semievergreen, linear lanceolate ¾–1½" long.

R. jinpingense Fang et M. Y. He; 'Jinping dujuan', Jinping Azalea: shrub with slender branches, Yunnan Prov., China; flowers red, purple dots on upper lobes 5 stamens; leaves elliptic, 1⅜–1¾" long. Similar to *R. microphyton* with larger leaves and glandular style. Similar to *R. adenostylum* with larger thicker leaves and long curved style.

R. jinxiuense Fang et M. Y. He; 'Jinxiu dujuan', Jinxiu Azalea: large shrub, Guangxi Prov., China; flowers purple, 1½" wide, 5 stamens; leaves semievergreen, oblong ovate 2¾–4" long. Similar to *R. rivulare* but with shorter petioled, thick leaves and longer exserted stamens and style.

R. kanehirai Wilson; 'Tai bei dujuan', Taibei Azalea: medium shrub, hilly areas of Taiwan; flowers red, Wilson reported 5 stamens, others 10; leaves semievergreen linear lanceolate ¾–1½" long. Similar to *R. indicum.*

R. kwangsiense Hu; 'Guangxi dujuan', Guangxi Azalea: medium shrub, hill areas of Guangxi and Quandong Prov., China; flowers light purple 1" long; 4 stamens; leaves semievergreen ellipticlanceolate ¾–1¾" long.

R. kwangtungense Merr. et Chun; 'Guang dong dujuan', Guangdong Azalea: medium shrub, Guangdong, Guangxi and Hunan Prov., China; flowers purple 1" long, 10–12 in truss, 5 stamens; leaves evergreen oblong lanceolate 1½–3" long.

R. lasiostylum Hayata *(R. sasakii):* low shrub of Taiwan; flowers pink 1½" long, 5 stamens; leaves evergreen oblong lanceolate 1½–2" long: Collected by Dr. J. L. Creech for the U.S.D.A. National Arboretum.

R. lingii Chun; 'Ru yuan dujuan', Ruyuan Azalea: medium shrub, rocky hill sides in N. Guangdong Prov., China; flowers purplish pink, ¾" wide, 8–10 in cluster, 5 stamens; leaves semi-evergreen elliptic-lanceolate 1½–2½" long.

R. longiperulatum Hayata: erect shrub of Northern Taiwan; flowers red, 1¼" long, 9–10 stamens; leaves semievergreen ovate ½–1" long.

R. macrogemmum Nakai *(R. kaempferi* var. *macrogemmum);* Large Bud Azalea: medium shrub, Japan; flowers purple.

R. mariae Hance; 'Ling nan dujuan', Lingnan Azalea: medium shrub, Guangdong, Jiangxi and Hunan Prov., China; flowers light purple with darker spots, ¾" wide, fragrant, 5 stamens; leaves evergreen elliptic lanceolate 1½–3" long.

R. mariesii Hemsl. et Wilson; 'Man shan hong', Maries Azalea: a deciduous shrub up to 10 feet tall, distributed through Southeast and Central China to Taiwan. Leaves 2–3 in terminal whorls, ovate lanceolate, 1½–3" long, ¾–2" wide. Twigs with yellowish silky hairs. Flowers before the leaves, pale reddish purple with darker spots, 1½–2" wide.

R. minutiflorum Hu; 'Xiao hua dujuan', Small-flowered Azalea: medium shrub in hilly areas of Guangxi, Guangdong and Hunan Prov., China; flowers white, ⅜" wide, 5 stamens; leaves evergreen oblong to ovate ½" long.

R. myrsinifolium Ching; 'Tieziye dujuan', Myrsine-leaved Azalea: small shrub of Guangxi Prov., China; flowers purple, ⅜–½" wide, 3 stamens; leaves elliptic, ¼–⅜" long. Similar to *R. minutiflorum* with smaller elliptic leaves and purple flowers with 3 stamens.

R. naamkwanense Merrill; 'Nan kun dujuan', Nankun Azalea: low shrub on shady rocky cliffs in Guangdong Prov., China; flowers purplish pink, 1" wide, 5 stamens; leaves semievergreen oblong obovate ½–1" long.

R. noriakianum T. Suzuki: low shrub of Northern Taiwan; flowers red, 1" wide, 7–10 stamens; leaves evergreen ovate to oblong ⅜–⅝" long.

R. rivulare Hand.-Mazz.; 'Xi pan dujuan', Streambank Azalea: medium shrub, Hunan, Guangxi, Guizhou and Sichuan Prov., China; flowers reddish purple, 1" wide, 10 stamens; leaves evergreen ovate lanceolate 2–3½" long. Similar to *R. oldhamii* with large truss, 10 stamens and glandular ovary.

R. rufohirtum Handel-Mazzetti: low shrub of Yunnan Prov., China; flowers purplish pink, 1" wide, 10 stamens; slender hirsute branches; leaves evergreen ovate lanceolate 1–2½" long. Similar to *R. oldhamii* with smaller flowers and eglandular branches. Collected by Dr. J. L. Creech for U.S.D.A. National Arboretum.

R. saisiuense Nakai: very low shrub from Cheju (formerly Quelpaert Island off Korea); flowers purplish pink; leaves evergreen.

R. seniavinii Maximowicz; 'Mao guo dujuan', Hairy Fruit Azalea: medium shrub, in hilly areas of Fukien, Hunan and Guizhou Prov., China; flowers white with purple spots on upper lobes, ⅝" wide, 5 stamens; leaves semievergreen ovate, ½–2" long.

R sikayotaizanense Masamune: low evergreen shrub, Taiwan; flowers red 1" wide, 4–6 stamens; leaves ovate oblong ½" long. Similar to *R. nakaharai* with smaller leaves and 4–6 stamens.

R. subsessile Rendle: medium shrub, mountains of Luzon, Philippines; flowers light purple, 1" wide, 6–10 stamens; leaves evergreen oval to lanceolate ½–1¼" long, with grayish hairs. Similar to *R. rubropilosum* with purple flowers.

R. taiwanalpinum Ohwi: low alpine shrub, Northern Taiwan; flowers pink with red dots in upper lobes, ¾" wide, 9–10 stamens; leaves semievergreen, oblong ⅓–¾" long.

R. tenue Ching; 'Xishou dujuan', Slender Azalea: shrub with slender branchlets, Guangxi Prov., China; flora characteristics unknown; leaves elliptic-ovate, 1¼–1½" long. Similar to *R. minutiflorum* with delicate slender branches and thin leaves.

R. tsoi Merrill; 'Liang dujuan', Two Guang Azalea: low shrub, Guangxi and N. Guangdong Prov., China; flowers pink, ¾" wide, 5 stamens; leaves semievergreen, obovate, ½" long.

BELGIAN INDIAN HYBRIDS

The development of the Belgian Indian or Indian Hybrids is shrouded in confusion beginning in the early 1800's when *R. simsii* was introduced into England in 1808 as *A. indica.* The misidentification of this plant with the true *R. indicum* created a muddle which lasted for nearly a century. *R. indicum* had been introduced into Holland in the 17th century but was lost. In the meantime 'Indica Alba' or 'Mucronatum' came to England in 1819 from gardens in China, followed by 'Phoeniceum' in 1824. Wm. Smith of England began raising seedlings or hybrids of these early introductions in the mid-1830's, calling them 'Indica'. In 1833 several forms of *R. indicum* reached England under the name *A. indica lateritia,* along with the sportive *R. indicum variegatum* which proved to be a valuable parent. So now the fat was entirely in the fire not to be recovered until the turn of the century.

In the 1840's these early English Indian Hybrids became popular indoor and greenhouse plants. While many of them were lost, 'Indica Alba' proved to be good for forcing and has survived, as did 'Fielder's White', a seedling of 'Mucronatum'. Some of these early English Indian Hybrids such as 'Fielder's White', 'Flag of Truce', 'Prince of Orange', and 'Iveryana' reached the U.S.A. and became known as the Southern Indians.

The major parents of the Belgian Indians were three forms of *R. simsii* collected by Robert Fortune in a Shanghai nursery and sent to England in 1851, but again under the incorrect name of 'Indica'. These plants were named 'Vittata', 'Vittata Punctata', and 'Bealii' ('Vittata Bealii'), all with white flowers striped and flecked with red. By 1854 these three varieties reached Belgium, launching an enormous breeding and growing program. By 1860 the English Indians had been almost entirely replaced by the superior Belgian Indian Hybrids exported from Belgium. By 1864 'Vittata Punctata' was a popular forcing azalea in France. Indeed all of Europe was flooded with Belgian Indian Hybrids. Since most of the plants were bred for greenhouse growing and the florist trade, they were bred for forcing. But the true *R. indicum* does not force readily. So despite the popular name, the species was not incorporated into the breeding lines.

Hybridizing intensified in Belgium as the Belgian Indians became widely popular as greenhouse and indoor plants in Europe. They were grown by the millions and exported to all parts of the world. Before 1914 more than two and a half million were exported annually from Belgium alone.

The most successful breeder was Joseph Vervaene of Ghent, Belgium, who developed such hybrids as 'Vervaeneana' and 'Vervaeneana Alba'. Other outstanding breeders contributing to the development of the Belgian Hybrids were Louis Van Houtte, L. Eeckhaute, A. Haerens, A. Verschaffelt, A. Van Queert, E. Van der Cruyssen, and J. de Kneef of Belgium; J. P. Knight, Perry, Ivery, and Rollisson of England; L. Truffaut, H. de May, and Mabire in France; and C. Schultz, Liebig, T. Seidel, R. Ambrosius, and Rose in Germany.

The best selection of first class "Indian Azaleas" were sent out in the early 1900's by Louis Van Houtte, the Royal Nurseries La Pinte near Ghent, Belgium. The original list did not indicate the name of the hybridizer or introducer so I have added them. Information on some of the parentage of 'Boclens', 'Louise Culvelier', and 'Henrich Hass' is unknown. The list included the following varieties:

EARLY FLOWERING VARIETIES IN EARLY 1900s

'Deutsche Perle' (Rose, Ger): double, pure white.
'Madame Petrick' (possibly cross of 'Deutsche Perle' × 'Sigismund Rucker'; C. Petrick, 1901): double, brilliant pink.

'Madame Romain de Smet' (sport of 'Eborina Plena'; L. de Smet Duviver): double, pink bordered white.
'Petrick Superba': pink bordered white.
'Pharailde Mathide' ('Comte Charles de Kerckhove' × 'Konigin de Weisse'; Vervaene, 1887): double, white striped red and spotted yellow.
'Simon Mardner' (Rose, 1878): double, brilliant pink.
'Talisman' (de May, 1897): double, salmon, bordered white.
'Vervaeneana' (sport of 'Pharaild Mathide'; Vervaene, 1886): double, pink bordered white, very large flowers.
'Vervaeneana Alba' (sport of 'Vervaeneana'; Vervaenae, 1903): pure white.
'Van Houtte's Pink Pearl' (sport of 'Pharaide Mathide'; Van Houtte, 1914): double, delicate pink blush, very large flowers.

MEDIUM EARLY VARIETIES IN EARLY 1900s

'Apollo' (Knight, 1843): semidouble, deep scarlet.
'Blushing Bride' (de Mont-Saint Amand, 1911): double, salmon pink.
'Haerensiana' (sport of 'Louise culvelier'; Haerens, Belg. 1898): double, salmon bordered white.
'Helen Theleman' (Mardner, Ger. 1863): double of a charming pink.
'Jean Peeters' (syn. 'Madame Peeters'; Van Houtte, 1878): double, rose carmine.
'John T. D. Lewelyn' (Van Houtte, 1887): double, delicate flesh-pink bordered white.
'Mme. Jos. Vervaene' (Vervaene, 1892): double, salmon bordered white.
'Mme. van der Cruyssen' (Van der Cruyssen, 1867): semidouble, bright pink, large blotch.
'President O. de Kerchove' (sport of 'Mme Herman Seidel'; J. de Kneef): double, bright pink with white edges.
'Sacountala': double, alabaster-white.
'Spitfire' (Vervaene, 1896): double, bright vermillion.
'Professeur Wolters' (sport of 'Baronne de Vriere'; Van Houtte, 1871): single, brilliant pink bordered white.

LATE FLOWERING VARIETIES IN EARLY 1900s

'Chicago' (Van Houtte, 1893): double, deep pink bordered white.
'De Schryveriana' (sport of 'Gartendirecteur Krause'; Schryver 1888): double, rosy carmine bordered white.
'Ernest Eeckhaute' ('Phoebus' × Souvenir du Recteur Kickx'; Eeckhaute, 1903): double, bright red with undulating edges.
'Empress of India' (Van Geert, 1879): double, salmon-pink bordered white.
'Empereur du Bresil' (sport of 'Reine de Portugal'; Verschaffelt, 1876): double, pink striped with deep pink and white.
'Mlle Emma Eeckhaute' (sport of 'Madame Louis Eeckhaute'; Eeckhaute, 1898): double, carmine striped and bordered white.
'Madame Moreux' (sport of 'Empress of India'; Moreux, 1898): double, salmon bordered white with undulating edges.
'Niobe' (Schultz, before 1879): double, pure white.
'Paul Weber' (sport of 'Henrich Hass'; Haas, 1893): double, brilliant pink bordered white.
'Temperance' (E. de Cock, 1890): double, delicate lilac.

In this enormous burst of activity some of the most beautiful and spectacular evergreen azaleas ever developed emerged. The popularity of the Belgian Indian Azaleas was not confined to greenhouse potted plants, but also extended to widespread use in the florist trade as a cut flower. As a consequence cultivars emphasizing flowers, semi to full doubles and many frilled petals, for forcing by the florist were developed.

The *Tuinbouw Encyclopedia* by H. Scheerlinck, published in Antwerp, Belgium in 1928, listed some 800 clones, over two-thirds of which were introduced after 1880. Many of these clones have been distributed widely around the world. Development of new Belgian

Indian Hybrids still continues.

The Belgian Indian Hybrids are considered tender so are sometimes called Tender Ghents to distinguish them from the Hardy Ghents or the deciduous Ghent Hybrids. There is considerable variation in the hardiness. As a group the hardiness range is zones 8a to 10a; however, without extensive outdoor trials the reputation for tenderness may not apply to all cultivars. Hardiness trials in zones 7a and 7b might well prove that many would be found hardy as in this case of the early importations that became the Southern Indian Hybrids.

The Belgian Indian Hybrids are medium size plants ranging from 4 to 6 ft. high, and usually well branched. The evergreen leaves are medium in size usually 1¼ to 1¾" long and are a dark glossy green.

The following article on Belgian Evergreen Azaleas by Dr. J. Heursel describes many of the popular Belgian Indian Hybrids in Europe. The information prefacing the azalea descriptions offers in detail the method used in data collecting done on azaleas at the Research Institute in Belgium. Basically this is the same as used in the U.S.A. and Europe. It is of interest in *Flower Diameter,* that the flower diameter increases with the stem diameter and that pinching of vegetative growth to induce branching has a negative influence on the stem diameter and on the flower size.

The "Sports Series" discussed in *Occurrence of Sports* is seldom used in the U.S.A. Since the Belgian Indian Hybrids sport freely, all the named sports derived from a single parent plant become a "Series". To readily recognize the importance of a "Sport Series", one has only to look at two important series and the number of plants resulting.

Vervaeneana Series includes the following named sports: 'Albert-Elizabeth', 'Haerwille Pink Pearl', 'Pink Pearle Fonce', 'Vervaeneana Alba', 'Vervaeneana Rosea', 'Vervaeneana Rubra', and 'Vervaeneana Saumona'.

Paul Schaeme Series: 'Eri', 'Doberlug', 'Dresden', 'Madame Bourlard', 'Memoire Reine Astrid', 'Princess Beatrix', 'Schaeme Frise', and 'Schaeme Alba'.

DESCRIPTION OF BELGIAN EVERGREEN INDIAN HYBRIDS GROWN IN WESTERN EUROPE

Dr. J. Heursel
Certified Senior Assistant
Institute of Ornamental Plant Growing
B-9230 Melle, Belgium

1. FLOWER DIAMETER

Diameter is determined as follows: Azalea flowers are funnel-shaped and, with only a few exceptions, have five petals. One of these petals displays a blotch. This petal is counted as number one after which the corolla is opened between the third and fourth petal, recurved petals flattened and measured.

At least 100 flowers of most cultivars are measured in order to compute the standard deviation. This method was adopted by U.P.O.V. (International Union for the Protection of New Varieties of Plants) but we found that the size of flowers can vary to a much greater degree than would be expected on the basis of this standard deviation.

The diameter of a flower increases with the diameter of the stem and the number of pinchings. The flowers become successively smaller the longer the plant remains in flower. An increasing number of pinchings has a negative influence on the diameter of the stem. The largest flowers are obtained on young plants, i.e, those not yet heavily pinched, if the interval between the last pinch and flowering is sufficiently long. In this way the stems become thicker so maximum bud formation is possible.

2. FLOWER COLOR

The flower colors are assigned to conform to those of the Royal Horticultural Society Colour chart 1966. To visualize these numbers I have added a color name derived from the U.S. National Bureau of Standards Special Publication 440.

Qualitative chromatographic analysis of anthocyans and flavonols in azalea flowers clearly proves that flavonols, (azaleatin and quercetin) result in a purplish tinge being given to the anthocyans present in the flowers. We can say that the color numbers 39A to 53C are flavonol deficient. Numbers 53D to 77D are rich in flavonols.

3. FLOWER TYPE

Eight different evergreen azalea flower types can be distinguished. The most common is a double flower with green calyx. Doubleness results from the metamorphosis of all, or nearly all, the stamens into petals, (petaloid).

Doubled flowers rotate through an angle of about 36 degrees, resulting in a "star-shaped" flower, which occurs as a sport on many cultivars. Azaleas bearing star-shaped flowers are now uncommon as gardeners today have little interest in them.

Semidouble flowers result when only some stamens have metamorphosed. The remaining stamens are free as in a single flower.

The fourth type is the common single flower with 5 sepals and petals, and 5 to 10 stamens.

The fifth type develops when the green and unspectacular calyx becomes much enlarged and has taken on the color of the corolla. In addition, it is rotated through an angle of 36 degrees with respect to the corolla. This type of flower is called "hose-in-hose".

The other three flower types are double, star-shaped and semidouble flowers with a "hose-in-hose" calyx.

4. EARLINESS

Four flowering periods can be distinguished.
Very early—October 15 to December 25.
Early—December 25 to January 31.
Mid-season—February 1 to March 31.
Late—April 1 to May 15.

The assumption underlying these dates is that the last pinching is done about mid-May. Obviously, therefore, changing the timing of the last pinching or use of growth regulators can markedly alter these dates.

5. OCCURRENCE OF SPORTS

Azaleas are a genetically very unstable group of plants and so produce many sports. Sports occur both in species and cultivars grown from seed. Azalea breeders, responding to public demand, are only interested in flower color sports provided that the mother plant's basic characteristics such as flowering period and growth habit are not lost. It is safe to say that sports have all the characteristics of the mother plant grown from seed save for flower color.

Flower color sports arise following a regular pattern, resulting in "sports series". Many gardeners have difficulty in identifying the series to which a sport belongs. To help the reader, I have mentioned in the description whether or not a cultivar has produced sports, or to what series a cultivar belongs.

Sports with variegated leaves may occur in several cultivars, e.g. on 'Ambrosiana', 'Madame Auguste Haerens alba' and 'Marie Claude Truffaut'. Only the variegated sport of 'Ambrosiana' is grown under the name of 'Ambrosiana variegated'.

'Adinda' (Sport obtained by irradiation of 'Karl Glaser'. Breeder Irradiation Laboratory of the I.W.O.N.L. (Institute for Scientific Research in Industry and Agriculture), Belg. 1976): flower color strong red 46D. Other characteristics as 'Karl Glaser'.

'Adolf Grille' ('Ernst Thiers' × 'Hexe'; R. Ambrosius, Ger. 1928): Flower color strong red 50B. Semi-double flower with green calyx.

'Adrien Steyaert' (Seedling, parents unknown; A. Steyaert, Belg. 1928): Flower diameter 3½" ± ¼". Flower color vivid reddish purple 72C. Double flower with green calyx. Flowers late. Irradiation produced several sports with colors purplish red 57D and vivid purplish red 67BC.

'Adventglocke' (Syn. 'Chimes'; 'Paul Schäme' × 'Fritz Sander'; R. Ambrosius, Ger. 1934): Flower diameter 3¾" ± ⅛". Flower color strong purplish red 54A. Semidouble cup-shaped flower with an average of 2 stamens, green calyx. Flowers early. Fairly vertical growth. Very sturdy leaves but sensitive to sunlight. Has produced sports. Also spelled 'Adventglockchen'.

'Albert-Elizabeth' (Sport of the 'Vervaeneana' series. Haerens and Wille, Belg. 1921): Flower color white with pink edge 52C. Flowers late. The leaves are slightly different otherwise identical to 'Vervaeneana'.

'Alex De Somer' Sport of 'Haerensiana' ('Mademoiselle Louise Culvelier's sport); A. De Schrijver, Belg. 1942): Flower color moderate red 47D. Other characteristics as 'Mademoiselle Louise Cuvelier'.

'Alice Erauw' (Sport of 'Eclaireur'; J. Sonneville, Belg. 1944): Flower color vivid red 53C. Other characteristics as 'Eclaireur'.

'Ambrosiana' (Seedling, parents unknown. R. Ambrosius, Ger. 1948): Shown for the first time in Belgium by F. Sonneville and Sons, 1958. Flower diameter 3⅝" ± ⅛". Flower color strong purplish red 58B. Double flower with green calyx. Flowers very early. Grows rapidly but somewhat irregularly. Very suitable for propagation from cuttings. Shows a tendency to form vegetative shoots at its base which bud with greater difficulty and have to be removed. Resembles 'Reinhold Ambrosius' closely, in 'Ambrosiana' the leaf veins lie a little deeper, the flower is slightly frilled and has a blue tinge. Has produced sports.

'Ambrosiana Variegated' (Sport of 'Ambrosiana' with variegated leaves. Several discoverers): Due to its slow vegetative growth it has never been shown (as far as we know) at a horticultural show, and is bred as rarity only. Its flower is identical to that of 'Ambrosiana' but proportionally smaller.

'Ambrosiana White' (Sport of 'Dicky' ('Ambrosiana' sport). Discovered independently by R. De Bruyne and irradiation Laboratory of the I.W.O.N.L. (Institute for Scientific Research in Industry and Agriculture), Belg. 1980): Flower color white with purplish red flakes. Other characteristics 'Ambrosiana'.

'Ambrosius Superba': Parent of 'Prinses Maria Pia'.

'Ammy Maarse' (Sport of 'Reinhold Ambrosius'. Fr. A. Maarse, Netherlands 1973): Flower color vivid red 53B. Other characteristics as 'Reinhold Ambrosius'.

'Andenken an Hugo Muller' (Sport of 'Andenken an Vater Drewitz', F. J. Muller, G.F.R. 1954): Flower color red. Other characteristics as 'Andenken an Vater Drewitz'.

'Andenken an Vater Drewitz' (syn. Vater Drewitz; Seedling 'Paul Schaeme' × 'Fritz Sander'. R. Ambrosius, Ger. 1936): Flower diameter 3⅜" ± ¼". Flower color strong purplish red 53D. Double flower with slightly frilled edge, green calyx. Leaf oblong on a long stem. Flowers mid-season. 'Reinhold Ambrosius' is superior. Has produced a sport.

'Anton Kobisch = 'Madame Cyrille Van Gele'.

'Apollo' (Origin unknown; C. Schultz, Ger. 1878): Flower diameter 3–3/16" ± ¼". Flower color vivid red 44C. Semidouble flower with an average of 0.43 stamens, green calyx. Flowers late.

'Armand Haerens': Parent of 'Leopold-Astrid' and parent of 'Guido Gezelle'.

'Avenir' (Seedling 'John T. D. Lewelyn' × 'Madame Royer', A. Haerens, Belg. 1911): Flower diameter 3–3/16" ± ⅜". Flower color pink 52BC. Double flower with green calyx. Flowers mid-season. Grows very well when grafted. Has produced several sports.

'Baronne de Vriere': Parent of 'Professor Wolters'.

'Benelux' Sport of 'Madame Petrick'; S. Van Damme, Belg. 1948: Flower color red 50B. Other characteristics same as 'Madame Petrick'. Subsequently, several red sports of the 'Madame Petrick' series made their appearance. 'Madame Emile Van de Sompel' 1952 sport of 'Findeisen'; 'Lumineux' 1955 sport of 'Kees Bier'; 'Madame Coty' or 'President Coty' 1955. They do not differ sufficiently from 'Benelux' to be considered separate cultivars.

'Bergmann Feu' Sport of 'Doctor Bergmann'. C. Van Gele and Son, Belg. 1938: Flower diameter 3¾" ± ⅜". Flower color strong red 39A–44D. Semidouble flower with an average of 2 stamens, green calyx. Flowers mid-season. Flowers keep very well. Strong vertical growth.

'Berlinerin' (Sport of 'Reinhold Ambrosius'. E. and W. Scherf, Ger., circa. 1968. Introduced by G. Boese Fa. Klattenberg-Kulturen, F.R.G. 1973): Flower color reddish purple 63C with white edge. Grows a little slower than 'Reinhold Ambrosius'. A few strong purplish red flowers on each plant.

'Bertina' (Seedling 'Hermann Klusmann' × seedling. O. Stahnke, F.R.G. 1972. Patented 1981): Flower diameter 4⅞" ± ⅜". Flower color yellowish pink 48D. Single flower with an average of 4 ± 1.33 stamens, green calyx. Flowers early.

'Breslau' (Seedling, parents unknown. A. Steyaert, Belg. 1934): Flower diameter 2¾ ± 3/16". Flower color strong purplish red 58B. Double flower with calyx colored, hose-in-hose.

'Bruno Kaerger' (Seedling, parents unknown. R. Ambrosius, Ger. 1940): Flower diameter 2⅞" ± ¼". Flower color red 51A. Double flower with green calyx.

'California Sunset' = 'Haerens Saumona'.

'Camille Vervaene': Parent of 'Lentegroet'.

'Capitaine Gau' (Sport of 'Madame Gau' ('Madame Petrick' sport). C. Van Gele and Son, Belg. 1941): Flower color purplish red 58D, gradually changing into purplish red 55C towards the edges. Other characteristics as 'Madame Petrick'.

'Carmen' (Seedling 'Madame A. D'Haene' × 'Avenir'. A. Truffaut, Fr. Introduced by G. J. Bier and Sons, Belg. 1958): Flower diameter 3⅛" ± ¼". Flower color vivid red 53C. When the flowers are opening the color is more bluish 55A–58B. Semidouble flower with an average of 0.19 stamens, green calyx. Flowers mid-season. Slow growth and irregular shape. Both irradiation and spontaneous mutation produced a sport.

'Casablanca Tetra' (Tetraploid resulting from 'Casablanca' (*R. indicum* × 'Snow') by colchicine. R. L. Pryor, U.S.A. 1961. Imported into Belgium by the Institute of Ornamental Plant Growing, 1974): Flower color white. Single flower with 5 stamens, calyx colored, hose-in-hose.

'Charles Encke' (Sport of 'Marie Louise'. A. Verschaffelt, Belg. 1819): Flower diameter 3¼" ± 7/16". Flower color pink 52CD with white edge. Single flower with 5 stamens. Flowers late. Has produced several sports. Other characteristics as 'Marie Louise'.

'Charles Encke Alba' (Sport of 'Charles Encke' ('Marie Louise' sport)): Never presented (as far as we know) at a horticultural show. Flower color white. Other characteristics as 'Marie Louise'.

'Charly' (Sport of 'Lucie'; K. Glaser, G.F.R. 1978): Flower color strong purplish red 58B. Other characteristics as 'Lucie'.

'Charme de Noel' (Sport of 'Ideal' ('Madame Petrick' sport). A. Haerens, Belg. 1911): Flower color reddish purple 67D. Other characteristics as 'Madame Petrick'.

'Chimes' = 'Adventglockchen'.

'Christina' (Sport of 'Carmen'. A. Truffaut, France 1972): Flower color pink with white edge. Other characteristics as 'Carmen'.

'Christina' (Seedling 'Leuchtfeuer' × 'Schnee'. R. Mayer, G.F.R. 1977): Flower color reddish purple 67CD. Semidouble flower with green calyx. Flowers mid-season.

'Coelestine' (Very old cultivar, of unknown origin but probably from Ger.): Small flowers. Flower diameter 2½" ± 3/16". Flower color strong purplish red 58B. Single flower with an average of 7 stamens, green calyx. Flowers late. Small leaves. Branches abundantly, low growth. Has the habit of *R. kiusianum.*

'Coelestine Superba': Parent of 'Gruss aus Holzhausen'.

'Coelestine White' (Seedling 'Dresdener Coelestine' × seedling; K. Glaser, G.F.R. 1958): Flower diameter 3" ± ¼". Flower color white. Single flower with an average of 6 stamens.

'Comte Charles de Kerchove': Parent of 'Vervaeneana'.

'Comtesse de Kerchove' (Parents unknown. J. B. Haerens and Son, Belg. 1938): Flower diameter 3¼" ± 3/16". Flower color deep pink 48C. Double flower with green calyx. Flowers mid-season. Bud formation is sometimes poor. Young branches green. Has produced several sports.

'Dame Blanche' (syn. 'Dame Melanie White', 'Dame Melanie Alba'; Sport of 'Dame Melanie' ('Roi Leopold' sport). L. Van Roye, Belg. 1942): Flower color white. Other characteristics as 'Roi Leopold'. Better known as 'Dame Melanie White'.

'Dame Melanie' (syn. 'Melanie', 'Mistress Turner'; Sport of 'Roi Leopold'. Van De Male and Van Coppenolle, Belg. 1867): Flower color deep pink 52D with white edge. Other characteristics as 'Roi Leopold'.

'Dame Melanie Saumona' (syn. 'Melanie Saumona'; Sport of 'Dame Melanie'. C. Van Gele and Son, Belg. 1935): Flower color deep pink 52D gradually changing into white towards the edges. Other characteristics as 'Roi Leopold'.

'Dame Melanie White' = 'Dame Blanche'.

'De Coninck's Favorite' (Sport of 'Emiel De Coninck' ('Jean Haerens' sport). R. De Coninck, Belg. 1969): Flower color white with red blotches and red, irregularly distributed, 50B flower edge. Other characteristics as 'John Haerens Sport'.

'Delicatesse' (Seedling 'Frau Reinhold Ambrosius' × 'Memoire de Louis Van Houtte'; R. De Meyer, Belg. 1938): Flower color white with a few red flakes. Double flower with green calyx, filled flower edge. Flowers mid-season. Has produced sports.

'Delicatesse Rubra' (Sport of 'Delicatesse'; R. De Meyer, Belg. 1950): Flower color deep pink 43C. Other characteristics as 'Delicatesse'.

'Delicatesse Saumona' (Sport of 'Delicatesse'. R. De Meyer, Belg. 1965): Flower color pink with white edge. Other characteristics as 'Delicatesse'.

'Denise Gau' (Sport of 'Capitaine Gau'. ('Madame Petrick' sport)). C. Van Gele and Son, Belg. 1947): Flower color deep pink 52D. A more intense color than that of 'Suzanne Moreux'. Other characteristics as 'Madame Petrick'.

'Deutsche Perle': Parent of 'Paul Schaeme'.

'De Waeles Favorite' (Sport of 'Knut Erwen'. F. De Waele, Belg. 1958): Flower color purplish pink 61D with white edge. Other characteristics as 'Knut Erwen'.

'Diablo' = 'Madame Bier'. American name for 'Madame Bier'. H. Kerrigan, U.S.A.

'Dicky' (Sport of 'Ambrosiana'; W. Oosterom, Netherlands, 1978): Flower color purplish red 57CD with white edge. Other characteristics as 'Ambrosiana'.

'Dirk Bosch' (syn. 'Jan Bosch', 'Red Dream'; Sport of 'Pink Dream'. Fr. A. Maarse Kzn, Netherlands, 1968): Flower color reddish purple 68B. Other characteristics as 'Pink Dream'.

'Doberlug' (syn. 'Hermann's Eri'; Sport of 'Eri' ('Paul Schaeme' sport). E. Hermann, Ger. 1928. The name 'Doberlug' given 1963): Flower color moderate red 47D with white edge. The color is more intense than that of 'Eri'. The young branches are a light pink distinguishing this cultivar from 'Jan Bier'. The branches of 'Doberlug' are a little firmer and bud formation a little better.

'Doctor Arnold' (Seedling 'Vervaeneana' × 'Pink Dream'. K. Glaser, F. R. G. 1963): Flower diameter 3–13/16" ± ⅛". Flower color vivid purplish red 66D. Semidouble flower with an average of 2 stamens, green calyx. Flowers early. After last pinching it only produces short twigs and forms buds. Unpinched branches flower at an earlier date. Flowering is somewhat irregular.

'Doctor Bergmann' (Seedling, parents unknown. J. De Kneef, Belg. 1890): Flower color moderate red 47D, somewhat darker towards the edge red 50B. Only its sports are grown.

'Doctor Bergmann Alba' (Sport of the 'Doctor Bergmann' series. G. J. Bier and Sons, Belg. 1953): Flower color white with a few blotches. Semidouble flower with an average of 3 stamens.

'Doctor Bergmann's Saumonea' (Sport of 'Doctor Bergmann'. Bullens and Van Gele, Belg. 1925): Flower color deep pink 52D with a fading edge purplish pink 55D. Other characteristics as 'Doctor Bergmann'.

'Doctor Heimann' (syn. 'Heimann'; Seedling, parents unknown. Breeder Thieme, G.D.R., ca. 1955, Introduced by K. Glaser, G.F.R.): Flower color vivid purplish red 66C. Flowering is at its best in October and February.

'Doctor Koester' (Seedling 'Friedhelm Scherrer' × seedling. O. Stahnke, F.R.G. 1980. Patented 1981): Flower color vivid red 42A. Double flower with green calyx. Flowers mid-season.

'Doctor Sven Hedin' (Seedling 'Julius Roehrs' × 'Memoire de Louis Van Houtte'. R. De Meyer, Belg. 1950): Flower color vivid red 46AB. Double flower with green calyx.

'Doctor Van Hove' (Origin unknown. J. Wille, Belg. 1950): Flower diameter 3 7/16" ± 3/16". Flower color vivid purplish red 57C. Double flower with green calyx. Flowers late. Has produced a red sport in Denmark which has no separate name.

'Doctor Van Hove Red' (Sport of 'Doctor Van Hove'. Discoverer unknown. Imported by the Institute of Ornamental Plant Growing into Belgium in 1966): Flower color red 50B. Other characteristics as 'Doctor Van Hove'.

'Dorothy Gish' (Seedling, parents unknown. Bobbink and Atkins, U.S.A. 1935): Flower color moderate red 47C with darker blotches. Belongs to the 'Rutherfordiana' group. Parent of 'Gloria'.

'Dresden' (Sport of 'Paul Schaeme'. W. Voight, Ger. 1936): Introduced in Belgium by F. Sonneville and Sons 1943. Flower color deep pink 43C with darker red edge 50B. Other characteristics as 'Paul Schaeme'.

'Dresdener Coelestine': Parent of 'Coelestine White'.

'Eclaireur' (Seedling 'Eggebrecht' × 'Etoile de Noel'. A. Haerens, Belg. 1914): Flower diameter 2 13/16" ± 5/16". Flower color vivid purplish red 57B. Double flower with green calyx. Flowers mid-season. Grows best when grafted. Has produced a few sports.

'Eggebrecht' (syn. 'Louis Spath'; 'Eggebrechtii'; Origin unknown. Different authors mention different breeders. According to Stahn the breeder is F. Eggebrecht, Ger, 1850; Scheerlinck is of the same opinion but according to Schimmler the breeder is T. Seidel, Germany 1890): Flower color red. Semidouble flower with green calyx. Slow growth. Has produced several sports.

'Elkar' (Origin unknown. Seyschab, F. R. G. 1964): Flower color red. Small single flower. Flowers late. Closely resembles 'Glaser number 10'.

'Elsa Kaerger' (syn. 'Kaerger'; Seedling, parents unknown. R. Ambrosius, Ger. 1940): Flower diameter 3" ± ¼". Flower color vivid red 45C. Double flower with green calyx. Flowers mid-season. The flower color is glowing. Grows best as a grafted plant but can be grown from cuttings as well. One of its shortcomings is that it occasionally produces blind buds. Shining leaf.

'Emile de Coninck' (Sport of 'Jean Haerens'; Flandria, Belg. 1938): Flower color white with vivid purplish red blotches and vivid purplish red 57C irregularly distributed flower edges. Other characteristics as 'John Haerens Sport'.

'Eri' (Sport of 'Paul Schaeme'. R. Ambrosius, Ger. 1928): Flower color pink 52C with white edge. In some flowers the pink color extends into the white edge. A selection with a perfectly white edge is offered under the name of 'Souvenir de Theophile Piens' but the difference from 'Eri' is not sufficient to justify a separate name. Other characteristics as 'Paul Schame'.

'Erich Danneberg' (Seedling 'Madame P. B. Van Acker' × 'Paul Schaeme'. E. Herrmann, G.D.R. 1956): Flower color vivid purplish red 61BC. Double flower with green clayx. Flowers early.

'Erika Ambrosius' (Origin unknown. R. Ambrosius, Ger. Imported into Belgium by the Gebroeders Van der Linden, 1963): Flower diameter 3–13/16" ± 3/16". Flower color purplish red 57D–66C. Double flower with green calyx. Flowers mid-season. Strong grower.

'Ernest Eeckhaute' (Seedling 'Phoebus' × 'Souvenir du Recteur Kickx'. L. Eeckhaute, Belg. 1903): Flower diameter 3" ± ¼". Flower color vivid purplish red 57B. Double flower with green calyx. Flowers late.

'Ernst Thiers' (Seedling. According to Vogel 1982 'Hermann Seidel' × 'Liebigs Superba'. According to Schimmler 1935 'Madame Van der Cruyssen' × 'Hermann Seidel'. L. R. Richter, Ger. 1890): Flower diameter 3⅛" ± 3/16". Flower color strong purplish red 63B. Semidouble flower with an average of 2 stamens, green calyx. Flowers late. Susceptible to *Exobasidium* and *Phytophtora*. Has produced a sport.

'Eroica' (syn. 'Knut Erwen Red'; Sport obtained by irradiation of 'Knut Erwen'. Breeder Irradiation Laboratory of the I.W.O.N.L. (Institute for Scientific Research in Industry and Agriculture). Belg. 1976): Introduced 1981. Flower color strong red 52A.

'Etoile de Belgique' (Seedling, parents unknown. A. Haerens, Belgium, 1909): Flower diameter 4¼" ± ½". Flower color strong purplish red 58B. Semidouble flower with an average of 0.16 stamens. Flowers mid-season. Irradiation has produced a red sport.

'Etoile de Noel': Parent of Eclaireur'.

'Euratom' (Seedling, probably 'Apollo' × 'Hexe'; Gijselinck, Belg. Introduced by H. Guyle, 1957): Flower diameter 2⅞" ± 3/16". Flower color strong purplish red 58B. Single flower with an average of 7 stamens, calyx colored hose-in-hose. Flowering late. Rapid growth, the most widely used and a good rootstock. Susceptible to *Exobasidium.* Irradiation produced several sports. A triploid azalea.

'Excelsior' (Origin unknown. J. Haerens and Sons, Belg. 1936): Flower diameter 3⅝" ± ⅜". Flower color vivid red 42A. Double flower with green calyx.

'Feuerzauber' (Seedling 'Friedhelm Scherrer' × 'Kirin' or 'Rex'. O. Stahnke, F.R.G. 1977. Patented 1977): Flower color red 44CD. Single flower with green calyx. Flowers mid-season.

'Fireglow' (Sport of 'Red Wing'. Sand Point Greenhouses, Fort Wayne, Indiana, U.S.A. 1968): Flower color moderate red 47B. Other characteristics as 'Red Wing'.

'Flamenco' (Seedling 'Violacea' × 'Reinhold Ambrosius', Dr. J. Heursel; Institute of Ornamental Plant Growing, Belg. 1971. Introduced 1981): Flower diameter 2¾" ± ⅛". Flower color moderate purplish red 72B. Double with green calyx. The first early flowering purple variety. Flowers last well. Not attractive as big plant. Has produced sports.

'Frau Amalia Riechers' (syn. 'De Schrijveriana'; Sport of 'Gartendirektor Krause'. Imported into Belgium by P. De Schrijver from Germany in 1888): Flower color deep pink 52D with white slightly frilled edge. Flowers late.

'Frau Lina Herrmann (syn. 'Lina Herrmann'; Seedling 'Madame P. B. Van Acker' × 'Paul Schaeme'. E. Herman, G.D.R. 1964): Flower diameter 3⅜" ± 3/16". Flower color vivid purplish red 57C. Double flower with green calyx. Flowers early to mid-season. Upper side of leaf is hairy.

'Frau Reinhold Ambrosius': Parent of 'Delicatesse'.

'Frau Richard Obst' (Sport of 'Richard Obst'. R. De Meyer, Belg. 1958): Flower color purplish red with white edge. Other characteristics as 'Richard Obst'.

'Frau Ursula Herrmann' (syn. 'Ziegelrot'; Seedling 'Madame P. B. Van Acker' × 'Paul Schaeme', E. Herrman, G. D. R. 1964): Flower diameter 2⅞" ± 3/16". Flower color moderate red 47B. Double flower with green calyx. Flowers mid-season.

'Friedhelm Scherrer (Seedling 'Ambrosiana' × seedling from 'Coelestine' crosses. O. Stahnke, F.R.G. 1972): Flower diameter 2–11/16" ± 3/16". Flower color vivid red 53C with some flowers 53D. Semidouble flower with an average of 1 stamen, green calyx. The flower has a very beautiful candle stage. Fast growth, flowers mid-season. Requires low temperatures during the bud resting period. Has produced a sport, 'Puppa'.

'Friedrich Scherrer' (Sport of 'Gerhard Nicolai'. E. Herrmann, G.D.R. 1957): Flower color pink with white edge. Reverts readily to the mother plant. Other characteristics as 'Gerhard Nocolai'.

'Fritz Sander' (Parents unknown. Breeder Sander and son, Belg. 1913): Flower diameter 2¾" ± ¼". Flower color vivid red 53C. Double flower with green calyx. Flowers mid-season.

'Gaby Welvaert' (Sport of 'Gloire de Claude Goyet'. M. Welvaert, Belg. 1978): Flower color vivid red 44A. Other characteristics as 'Gloire de Claude Goyet'.

'Gartendirector Krause': Parent of 'Frau Amalia Riechers'. Also spelled Gartendirecteur Krause.

'Georg Silber' (Seedling 'Reinhold Ambrosius' × 'Erick Danneberg'. O. Stahnke, F.R.G. 1968): Flower color strong purplish red 58B. Double flower with green calyx.

'Georg Struppek' (Seedling 'Friedhelm Scherrer' × 'Kirin' or 'Rex'. O. Stahnke, F.R.G. 1977. Patented 1977): Flower color vivid purplish red to purplish pink 61CD. Single flower with green calyx. Flowers mid-season.

'Gerard J. Bier' (Sport of 'Doctor Bergmann'. G. J. Bier and Sons, 1937): Flower color pink 52C with white edge. Other characteristics as 'Doctor Bergmann'.

'Gerhard Nicolai' (Seedling 'Madame P. B. Van Acker' × 'Paul Schaeme'. E. Herrmann. G.D.R. 1956): Flower diameter 3¼" ± ¼". Flower color purplish red 57D–66C. Double flower with green calyx. Flowers very early and somewhat irregularly. Has produced a sport.

'Glaser Number 10' (syn. 'Manni Lachs'; Seedling, one of the parents is 'Coelestine'. K. Glaser, F.R.G. 1963): Flower diameter 2–11/16" ± 3/16". Flower color moderate red 47C. Single flower with an average of 9 stamens, green calyx. Flowers late. Growth habit is similar to that of 'Coelestine', (i.e. small leaves, low growth and abundant branches). Has produced sports.

'Gloire de Claude Goyet' (syns. 'Claude Goyet' and 'Monsieur Claude Goyet'; Seedling 'Madame Adolf D'Haene' × 'Avenir'. A. Truffaut, France. Imported into Belgium by Franck, 1952): Flower diameter 3–1/16 ± 5/16. Flower color red 51A–53D. Double flower with green calyx. Flowers mid-season. Extremely fast growth. Fertilize sparsely and grow from cuttings to obtain regular shape. Last pinching early June. Is grown for its particularly fine color. The flower does not keep well. Has produced a sport.

'Gloire de Meirelbeke' = 'John T. D. Lewelyn Alba'.

'Gloire de Saint Georges' (syn. 'Hobbie'; Seedling *R. Simsii* cultivar × *Camellia*. A. Steyaert, Belg. Introduced by P. Bekaert, Belg. 1954): Flower color strong purplish red 58B. Not only the stamens but the pistil too are metamorphosed into petals. Green calyx. Flowers late. Flower keeps extremely well. Very irregular growth.

'Gloria' (Sport of 'Dorothy Gish'. Rutherford, U.S.A., year unknown, probably circa. 1969): Flower color purplish red 55C with white edge. Calyx colored, hose-in-hose.

'Gruss aus Holzhausen' (Seedling 'Coelestine Superba' × seedling from 'Coelestine' crosses, K. Glaser, F.R.G. 1954): Flower color strong purplish red 58B. Flowers mid-season. Rapid growth.

'Grussendorf' (Seedling 'Erich Danneberg' × 'Lentegroet'. O. Stahnke, F.R. G. 1968): Flower color vivid purplish red to purplish pink 57C–61CD. Double flower with green calyx.

'Guido Gezelle' (Seedling 'Vervaeneana Pink Pearl' × 'Armand Haerens'. C. Wille, Belg. 1933): Flower diameter 2⅞" ± 3/16". Flower color deep pink 52D to purplish red 55C. Double flower with green calyx. Flowers late. Somewhat loose growth. Has produced a sport.

'Gustav Hacker' (Seedling. One of the parents is 'Coelestine'. K. Glaser, F.R.G. 1966): Flower diameter 3⅝" ± ⅛". Flower color strong purplish red 58B. Single flower with an average of 8 stamens, green calyx. Flowers late. Very compact growth. Has produced sports.

'Guy de Meulemeester' (Seedling, parents unknown. M. De Meulemeester, Belg. 1975): Flower color pink. Double flower with green calyx. Flowers mid-season. Strong growth.

'Guy Yerkes Tetra' (Tetraploid resulting from 'Guy Yerkes' by colchicine. R. L. Pryor, U.S.A. Imported into Belgium by the Institute of Ornamental Plant Growing, 1974): Flower color deep pink 52D. Single flower with 5 stamens; calyx colored, hose-in-hose. Flowers late.

'Haerensiana' (Sport of 'Mademoiselle Louise Cuvelier'. Haerens Brothers, Belg. 1898): Flower color pink 48D, sometimes with stripes moderate red 48A and a white edge. Other characteristics as 'Mademoiselle Louise Cuvelier'.

'Haerensiana Alba' (Sport of 'Mademoiselle Louise Cuvelier'. Haerens and Wille, Belg. 1921): Flower color pure white. Other characteristics as 'Mademoiselle Louise Cuvelier'.

'Haerens Lorraine' (syn.'Lorraine' Seedling 'Charles Encke' × 'Hexe'. A. Haerens, Belg. 1909): Flower diameter 2¾" ± 3/16". Flower color purplish red 57D. Single flower with an average of 5 stamens, calyx colored, hose-in-hose. Flowers late. Irradiation has produced a pink sport 52C. and spontaneous mutation a sport with white edge.

'Haerens Saumona' (syn. 'California Sunset', sport of 'Madame Auguste Haerens' ('Avenir' sport). W. Haerens, Belg. 1944): Flower color moderate red 47D with fading edges pink 50D. Has produced sports. Other characteristics as 'Avenir'.

'Haerewille Pink Pearl' (Sport of the 'Vervaeneana' sports series. Haerens and Wille, Belg. 1913): Flower color pale pink to nearly white. This cultivar has now been replaced by 'Pink Pearl Fonce'.

'Heinrich Luley' (Parents unknown. Found at the H. Luley Nursery, Ger.): Flower diameter 3⅞" ± 5/16". Flower color vivid red 42A. Semidouble flower with an average of 7 stamens, green calyx. Resembles 'Apollo'.

'Helga Kauste' (Seedling from seedlings. K. Glaser, F.R.G. 1972. Put on the market by the firm M. Van Acker, Belg. 1980): Flower color pink 62A. Double flower with green calyx. Resembles 'Prinses Maria Pia' but the growth is more compact.

'Hellmut Vogel' (Seedling 'Ambrosiana' × 'Erich Danneberg'. O. Stahnke, F.R.G. 1967): Flower diameter 3¼" ± ¼". Flower color vivid purplish red 57C. Double flower with green calyx. Flowers very early. This cultivar is a big success in Western Europe because of its rapid growth and excellent forcing properties. Green buds develop in the living room. Grows well from cuttings. Has a low cold requirement for ripening of the buds. When pinched the eyes do not all come up uniformly. Has produced several sports.

'Hermann Klusmann': Parent of 'Bertina'.

'Hermann Seidel': Parent of 'Ernst Thiers' and 'Loelia'.

'Hermann Stahnke' (syns. 'Lach Thiers' and 'Madame Spae'. Sport of 'Ernst Thiers'. H. Stahnke, Ger. 1934): Flower color red 51A. Was also selected in Belgium. Other characteristics as 'Ernst Thiers'.

'Herme' (syn. Hermes, sport of 'Eggebrechtii'; H. Seidel, Ger. 1909): Flower color strong purplish red 58C with large white edge. Semidouble flower with green calyx. Flowers late. Has produced an unnamed pink sport with narrow white edge, and an unnamed white sport. Discoverer Baumgartner, Austria 1964.

'Herrmann's Superba' (Seedling 'Madame P. B. Van Acker' × 'Paul Schaeme'. E. Herrman F.R.G. 1964): Flower diameter 3–1/6" ± ¼". Flower color vivid red 43A. Double flower with green calyx.

'Herzog Adolf von Nassau': Parent of 'Hexe'.

'Hexe' (Seedling 'Herzog Adolf von Nassau' × *(R. obtusum)* 'Amoenum'. O. Forster, Ger. 1878): Flower diameter 2½ ± ¼". Flower color strong purplish red 58B. Single flower with an average of 5 stamens, calyx colored hose-in-hose. Flowers late. Very sturdy plant, good growth, also used as rootstock. Susceptible to *Exobasidium*. Has produced a sport.

'Hexe de Saffelaere' (Seedling 'Apollo' × 'Hexe'. Adolf Van Hecke, Belg. Officially named 'Hexe de Saffelaere' 1934): Was sent to U.S.A. by Kluis and Koning of the Netherlands in 1932 and named 'Red Wing' by A. Pericat. Reintroduced in Belgium as 'Red Wing'.

'Hilde Steyaert' (Seedling, parents unknown. A. Steyaert, Belg. 1959): Flower diameter 3¼" ± 5/16". Flower color deep pink 43C. Semidouble flower with an average of 3 stamens, green calyx. Flowers late. Gives generally only 1 flower per bud. Has produced a sport.

'Hobby' (Seedling from crosses with 'Adventsglocke'. Theime for the firm Thalaker, Ger. Year unknown. First exhibited in Belgium by G. J. Bier and Sons in 1965): Flower color purplish red. Large double flower with green calyx. Flowers mid-season. Strong vertical growth.

'Hollandia' (Seedling, parents unknown. A. Steyaert, Belg. 1928): Flower diameter 3⅛" ± ¼". Flower color red 44D. Double flower with green calyx.

'Ideal' (Sport of 'Madame Petrick'. A. Haerens, Belg. 1911): Flower color pink with white edge. Resembles 'Madame Auguste Mestdagh' but somewhat paler. No longer grown in Belgium.

'Inga' (Sport of 'Hellmut Vogel'. O. Stahnke, F.R.G. 1973): Flower color purplish pink 61D with white edge. Other characteristics as 'Hellmut Vogel'.

'Inga Red Variegated' (Sport of 'Hellmut Vogel'. Lehr and Versuchsanstalt for Gartenbau Bad Zwischenahn, F.R.G. 1973): Flower color purplish pink 61D with small white edge. This cultivar appears regularly but is not in cultivation because the white edge is too small.

'Jacqueline Gau' (Sport of 'Madame Cyrille Van Gele' ('Madame John Haerens' sport): C. Van Gele and Son, Belg. 1942): Flower color red.

'Jan Bier' (Sport of 'Princess Beatrix' ('Paul Schaeme' sport): G. J. Bier and Sons, Belg. 1949): Flower color moderate red 47D with white edge. Resembles the cultivar 'Doverlug' perfectly, except that the young branches are light green instead of pink.

'Jean Haerens' (syn. 'John Haerens', parents unknown; J. Haerens, Belg. 1929): Flower color purplish pink 65C. Only the sports of this cultivar are grown. This cultivar is not to be mixed up with 'Madame John Haerens'.

'John Haerens' = 'Jean Haerens'.

'John Haerens Sport' (syn. 'Memoire John Haerens', sport of 'Jean Haerens'. J. B. Haerens and Son, Belg, 1939): Flower diameter 3–5/16 ± ¼". Flower color white with vivid purplish red edge 57B. Semidouble flower with an average of 2 stamens, green calyx. Dark green shining leaves. This mid-season flowering plant is grown for its striking, slightly frilled flower. Growth is rather unsatisfactory. Must be grafted.

'John T. D. Lewelyn' (Sport from a seedling of unknown parents. L. Van Houtte, Belg. 1887): Flower color pink 48D with white edge. Only the sports of this cultivar are grown.

'John T. D. Lewelyn Alba' (Sport of 'John T. D. Lewelyn'. Discovered independently by Soc. An. Hort. des Flandres and Maenhout, Belg. 1907, who named the sport of 'Glorie de Meirelbeke'. In 1908 there appeared a sport of 'John T. D. Lewelyn' with flaked and striped flowers. Discoverers Haerens and Wille, Belg.): Flower color white with pink flakes and stripes.

'John T. D. Lewelyn Rubra' (Sport of 'John Lewelyn'. J. Kuyck, Belg. Put on the market in 1890): Flower diameter 3–1/16" ± 5/16". Flower color moderate red 47C. Double flower with green calyx. Flowers late.

'Joseph de Meulemeester' (Seedling 'Paul Schaeme' × unknown male parent. M. De Meulemeester, Belg. 1965): Flower color red. Double flower with green calyx. Flowers very early, but slow growth.

'Josiane Maeseele' (Seedling 'Dame Melanie' × unknown male plant. J. De Meulemeester, Belg. 1960): Flower diameter 2–11/16" ± 3/16". Flower color vivid purplish red 66C. Single flower with an average of 6 stamens, calyx colored, hose-in-hose. Flowers late. The flower is slightly fragrant. Vertical growth.

'Jubile' (Sport of 'Triumph'. A. Haerens, Belg. 1935): double.

'Julius Roehrs' (seedling, parents unknown. L. Eeckhaute, Belg. 1903): Flower diameter 3½" ± ⅜". Flower color vivid purplish red 57C. Double flower with green calyx. Flowers late. Has produced a sport.

'Karl Glaser' (Seedling, one of the parents is 'Coelestine'. K. Glaser, F.R.G. 1964): Flower diameter 2⅜ ± ⅛. Flower color vivid purplish red 57C. Single flower with an average of 4 stamens, calyx colored, hose-in-hose. Flowers late. Shining, narrow leaf. Irradiation has produced a sport.

'Kathleen Schepens' (Sport of 'Hilde Steyaert'. M. Schepens, Belg. 1980): Flower color deep pink 49A with white edge. Other characteristics as 'Hilde Steyaert'.

'Katrin' (Seedling, parents unknown. Found at the Plate and Draht Nursery, F.R.G. 1978): Flower color strong purplish red 58B. Semidouble flower with green calyx. Flowers mid-season.

'Kerstin' (Seedling parents unknown. E. Herrmann, G.D.R. circa 1955): Flower color vivid purlish red 61C. Small single flower with green calyx.

'Kingfisher' (A 'Whitewater' hybrid, origin unknown. Motzkau, U.S.A. 1966. Introduced into Western Europe by Van der Meer Brothers, Netherlands 1976): Flower color strong purplish red 58C. Single flower with calyx colored, hose-in-hose. Flowers mid-season. Sinuated leaves.

'Kiwi' (A 'Whitewater' hybrid, origin unknown. Motzkau, U.S.A. 1968. Introduced into Western Europe by Van der Meer Brothers, Netherlands 1976): Flower color purplish red 57D. Single flower with calyx colored, hose-in-hose. Flowers mid-season. Very strong flowers.

'Knut Erwen' (syns. 'Knute Erwin', 'Knute' Seedling. The result of a crossing of the progeny of ('President Oswald de Kerchove' × 'Prof. Wolters') × ('Paul Schaeme' × 'Apollo'). R. De Meyer, Belg. 1934): Flower diameter 3⅜" ± ¼". Flower color strong purplish red 53D. Frilled flower edge. The pistil rises above the flower. If the plant is kept warmer in its last growing year in a glasshouse the flower has diminished doubleness as compared to plants grown in the open. Green calyx. Flowers late. Strong lateral growth and yet well shaped. When grown from cuttings the root system is rather sensitive. Has produced several sports.

'Knut Erwen Orange' (syn. 'Erhard Neuber' Sport of 'Knut Erwen'. P. Buyle, Belg. 1971): Flower color strong red 39A. Other characteristics as 'Knut Erwen'.

'Koli' (Seedling 'Petrick Alba' × 'Rex'. Dr. J. Heursel; Institute of Ornamental Plant Growing, Belg. 1979. Patented 1983): Flower diameter 2⅜" ± ⅛". Flower color purplish pink 61D with almost white stripes 63D. Semidouble flower with an average of 2 stamens, green calyx. Flowers mid-season. Good growth and root formation.

'Koenigin der Weisse': Parent of 'Vervaeneana'.

'Lentegroet' (syns. 'Easter Greetings', 'Lentegruss' and 'Salut Printemps'; 'Camille Vervaene' × 'Hexe'. A. Haerens, Belg. 1909): Flower diameter 3¼" ± 3/16". Flower color strong purplish red 58B. Single flower with an average of 4 stamens, calyx colored, hose-in-hose. Flowers late. Sturdy and irregular growth. Susceptible to *Exobasidium.*

'Leo Captain' (Sport of 'Albert-Elizabeth' ('Vervaeneana' sport). J. Haerens, Belg. 1928): Flower color white with large moderate red edge 47C which extends towards the center. Other characteristics as 'Vervaeneana'.

'Leonore' (Seedling 'Leuchtfeuer' × 'Schnee'. R. Mayer, F.R.G. 1977): Flower color vivid reddish purple 67C. Semidouble flower with green calyx. Flowers late.

'Leopold-Astrid': (Sport of 'Armand Haerens'. J. Haerens and Sons, Belg. 1933): Flower diameter 3" ± ¼". Flower color white with red edge 50B. Double flower with frilled flower edge and green calyx. Flowers midseason. The leaf is highly shining. Grows best when grafted on 'Euratom' or 'Hexe'. Can be grown from cuttings as a small plant. Shows great likeness to the 'Vervaeneana' group. The red flower edge is more pronounced, however, than in 'Albert-Elizabeth' and its growth habit is better. There is fairly great variation between the flowers.

'Leuchtfeuer' (Seedling, parents unknown. R. Ambrosius, Ger. 1940): Flower diameter 2–15/16" ± 3/16". Flower color strong purplish red 53D–58C. Semidouble flower with an average of 3 stamens, green calyx. Flowers late. Irradiation has produced a sport.

'Liebigs Superba': Parent of 'Ernst Thiers'.

'Lieven de Meulemeester' (Seedling 'Madame Van der Cruyssen' × 'Ernst Thiers'. M. De Meulemeester, Belg. 1965): Flower color red. Flowers late.

'Loelia' (Seedling 'Hermann Seidel' × 'Haerensiana'; A. Haerens, Belg. 1928): Flowers diameter 3" ± ¼". Flower color white, double flower.

'Lombardia' (Sport of 'Eggebrechtii'. C. J. Willie and Co. 1933): Flower color pink.

'Lucie' (Seedling, seedling × 'Doctor Arnold'. K. Glaser, F.R.G. 1980). Patented 1981): Flower color vivid purplish red 57C. Flowers very early. The flower color is pink when flowering later.

'Lucifer' (Sport of 'Eclaireur'. J. Wille, Belgium 1943): Flower color vivid purplish red 57B, with small white edge. Other characteristics as 'Eclaireur'.

'Madame Adolf d'Haene': Parent of 'Carmen', 'Gloire de Claude Goyet' and 'Simplet'.

'Madame Auguste Haerens' (Sport of 'Avenir'. A. Haerens and Son, Belg. 1936): Flower diameter 3¾" ± 5/16". Flower color pink 52C with white edge. Other characteristics as 'Avenir'.

'Madame Auguste Haerens Alba' (syns. 'Avenir Alba' and 'Haerens Alba'; Sport of 'Madame Auguste Haerens'. A. Haerens and Son, Belg. 1948): Flower color pure white. There is another form with a slightly pink inner surface of the flowers: 'Mme Auguste Haerens Alba Rosea', R. Haerens, 1947. Other characteristics as 'Avenir'.

'Madame Auguste Mestdagh' (syn. 'Madame Mestdagh', sport of 'Madame Petrick'; A. Mestdagh, Belgium 1925): Flower color reddish purple 63C with purplish pink edge 62C. Other characteristics as 'Madame Petrick'.

'Madame Auguste Van Damme' (Sport of 'Madame Petrick'. A. Van Damme, Belg. 1915): Flower color reddish purple 67D with white edge. This cultivar is being replaced by 'Perle de Noisy' which is slightly more purplish red 55B. Other characteristics as 'Madame Petrick'.

'Madame Auguste Verschueren' (Parents unknown, E. De Meyer, Belg. Put on the market by A. Verschueren, Belg. 1971): Flower color purplish pink 62B. Double flower with green calyx. Flowers late. Has to be grafted. Susceptible to *Botrytis*. Has produced a sport.

'Madame Bier' (syn. 'Diablo', sport of 'Hexe'. G. J. Bier and Sons, Belg. 1935): Flower color strong red 46D. Other characteristics as 'Hexe'.

'Madame Bourlard' (Sport of 'Eri' ('Paul Schaeme' sport). G. J. Bierand Sons, Belg. 1935): Flower color white with many flakes and stripes covering the entire color range of the 'Paul Schaeme' series. Frilled flower. Other characteristics as 'Paul Schaeme'.

'Madame Buyle' (Seedling 'Madame Petrick' × 'Paul Schaeme'. H. Buyle, Belg. 1938): Flower color vivid reddish purple 67C. Double flower with green calyx. Flowers mid-season. Irradiation produced a pink sport.

'Madame Charles Gabert' (syns. 'Ingrid Bergmann' and 'Pink Bergmann' Sport of 'Doctor Bergmann's Saumonea' ('Doctor Bergmann' sport). Mrs. C. Paelinck-De Paepe, Belg. 1935): Flower color purplish red 55C. Other characteristics as 'Doctor Bergmann'.

'Madame Collumbien' (Seedling 'Paul Schaeme' × 'Rubis de Meirelbeke'. J. Collumbien, Belg. 1947): Flower diameter 2⅞" ± 3/16". Flower color red 50B with dark blotch. Semidouble flower with an average of one stamen, green calyx. Dark green shining leaves. Flowers mid-season. Very sturdy cultivar.

'Madame Cyrille Van Gele' (syn. 'Anton Kobisch' Sport of 'Madame John Haerens'. C. Van Gele and Son, Belg. 1936): Was also selected in Germany by A. Kobisch in 1936 under the name of 'Anton Kobisch'. Since, however, the name of the entry is most widely known in Europe, it was classified here. Flower color red 50B. Other characteristics as 'Madame John Haerens'.

'Madame De Cnydt' (Seedling 'Paul Schaeme' × 'Pax'. C. De Cnydt, Belg. 1935): Flower diameter 3½" ± 9/16". Flower color white. Semidouble with an average of one stamen, green calyx.

'Madame de Meulemeester' (Seedling 'Reinhold Ambrosius' × 'Findeisen'. J. De Meulemeester, Belg. 1959): Flower diameter 3⅜" ± ¼". Flower color purplish red 57D. Semidouble flower with an average of 0.43 stamens, green calyx. Flowers mid-season. Has produced a sport.

'Madame De Waele' (syn. 'Knut Alba'. Sport of 'De Waele's Favorite' ('Knut Erwen' sport). F. De Waele, Belg. 1963): Flower color white. Other characteristics as 'Knut Erwen'.

Madame Emile Van de Sompel: see 'Benelux'.

'Madame Flore' (Sport of 'Leopold-Astrid'. Flore, Belg, 1959): Flower color deep pink 52B. This sport is probably a reversion to the mother plant 'Armand Haerens' which is no longer grown. The flowers are sensitive to direct sunlight.

'Madame Gau' (Sport of 'Madame Auguste Mestdagh' ('Madame Petrick' sport). C. Van Gele and Son, Belg. 1934): Flower color purplish red 58D with a purplish red 55C to white edge. Other characteristics as 'Madame Petrick'.

'Madame Gustave De Smet' (Sport of 'Madame Auguste Haerens' ('Avenir' sport). Discoverer G. De Smet, Belg. 1954): Flower color pink with white edge, a little darker than 'Madame Auguste Haerens'. Other characteristics of 'Avenir'. Also as homonym for 'Schaeme Saumona'.

'Madame Gustave Toebaert' (Sport of 'Doctor Bergmann Saumonea' ('Doctor Bergmann' sport). C. Van Gele and Son, Belg. 1941): Flower color deep pink 48B, edge pink 48D with copper colored sheen. Other characteristics as 'Doctor Bergmann'.

'Madame Hartlieb' (Sport of 'Ideal' ('Madame Petrick' sport). A. Haerens and Sons, Belg. 1933): Flower color vivid purplish red 66D with a purplish pink 62B to white edge. Other characteristics as 'Madame Petrick'.

'Madame Henny' (Sport of 'Madame John Haerens'. C. Van Gele and Son, Belg. 1942): Flower color strong purplish red 58BC. Other characteristics as 'Madame John Haerens'.

'Madame Jean de Meyer' (Sport of 'Merveille' ('Delicatesse' × seedling). Discoverer J. De Meyer, Belgium 1965): Flower color red with white edge. Other characteristics as 'Merveille'.

'Madame John Haerens' (syn. 'Madame Jean Haerens', seedling parents unknown; Haerens and Eille, Belg. 1907): Flower diameter 3⅜ ± ¼". Flower color purplish red 57D. Double flower with green calyx. Flowers late. Sturdy and fast grower, grows mainly laterally. Has produced several sports. Not to be mixed up with 'John Haerens'.

'Madame Joseph Maenhout' (syn. 'Madame Maenhout', sport of 'Comtesse de Kerchove'; J. Maenhout, Belg. 1951): Flower color deep pink 48C–62D with strong red blotch 50A. Young branches red. Other characteristics as 'Comtesse de Kerchove'.

'Iora' Knap Hill Azalea.
CARLSON

'Chetco' Knap Hill Azalea.
GREER

'Flamingo' Knap Hill Azalea.
GALLE

'Persil' Knap Hill Azalea. GREER

'Hotspur' Knap Hill Azalea. GREER

'Gold Dust' Exbury Azalea. GREER

'Pink Delight' Exbury Azalea. GREER

'Homebush' Knap Hill Azalea. GALLE

'Honeysuckle' Knap Hill Azalea. GREER

'Beaulieu' Exbury Azalea. GREER

Plate 36

'Princess Royal' Exbury Azalea. GREER

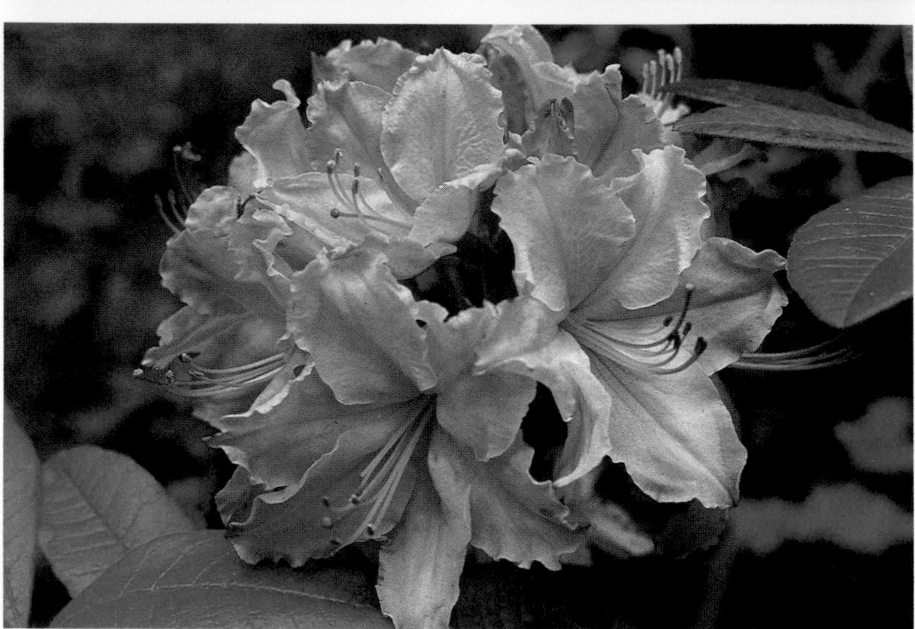

'Mazurka' Knap Hill Azalea. GREER

'Annabella' Exbury Azalea. GREER

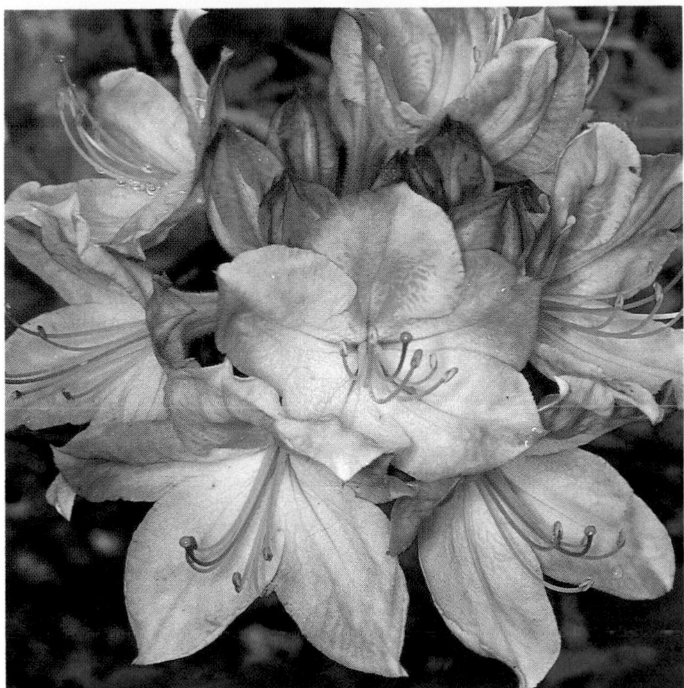

'Quaker Maid' Exbury Azalea. GREER

'Ginger' Exbury Azalea. GREER

'Royal Command' Exbury Azalea. GREER

'Golden Sunset' Exbury Azalea. GREER

Plate 38

'Marion Merriman' Knap Hill Azalea. GREER

'Kathleen' Exbury Azalea. GREER

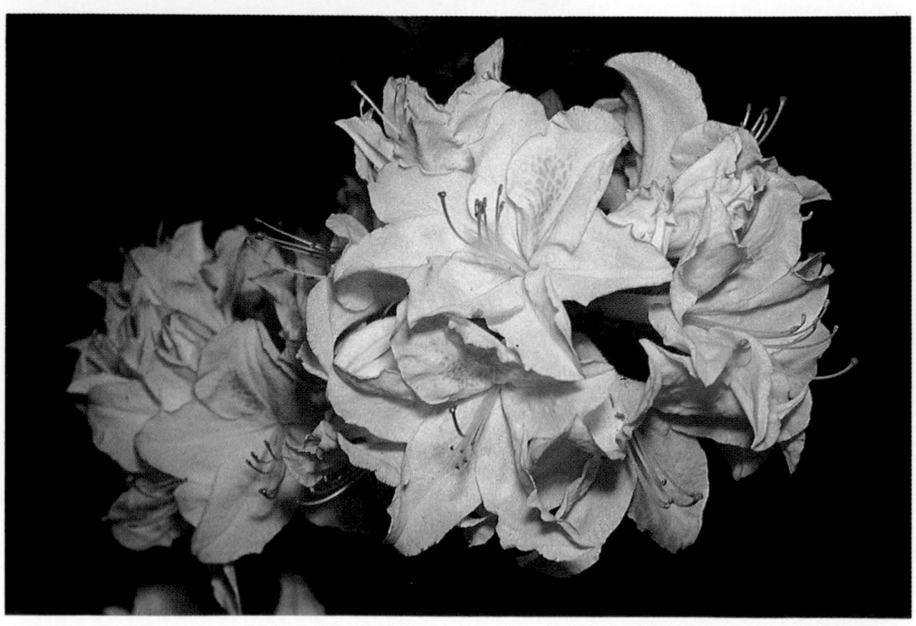

'Oxydol' Exbury Azalea. GREER

'Pot of Gold' Knap Hill KERN

'Colin Kendrick' Knap Hill Azalea. GREER

'Heaven Scent' Carlson Gardens Hybrids. CARLSON

Plate 40

'Scarlet O'Hara' Exbury Azalea. GREER

'Carlson's Canary' Carlson Gardens Hybrid. CARLSON

'Mandarin Maiden' Knap Hill Hybrid. HYATT

'Madame Lemkes' (Sport of 'Julius Roehrs'; M. Cnockaert, Belg. 1944): Flower color strong purplish red 58B. Other characteristics as 'Julius Roehrs'.

'Madame Leon Moreux' (Sport of 'Doctor Bergmann's Saumonea' ('Doctor Bergmann' sport). C. Van Gele and Son, Belg. 1941): Flower color moderate red 47D, edge deep pink 52D. Other characteristics as 'Doctor Bergmann'.

'Madame Lucien de Cock' (Seedling 'Paul Schaeme' × 'Rubis de Meirelbeke'. Breeder Fr. J. Collumbien, Belg. 1950): Flower diameter 3⅝" × 5/16". Flower color purplish red 57D. Double flower with green calyx.

'Madame Marcel De Paepe' (syn. 'White Schaeme', sport of 'Eri' ('Paul Schaeme' sport). M. De Paepe, Belg. 1951): Flower color pure white. Other characteristics as 'Paul Schaeme'.

'Madame Martin' (Seedling 'Guy De Meulemeester' × 'Willem Van Oranje'. M. De Meulemeester, Belgium 1980): Flower color deep pink 43C to red 50B. The flower edge is strongly frilled. Double flower with green calyx.

'Madame Maurice Dhaenens' (Sport of 'Madame De Meulemeester'. M. Dhaenens, Belg. 1975): Flower color strong red 52A. Other characteristics as 'Madame De Meulemeester'.

'Madame Moreau' (Sport of 'Suzanne Moreux' ('Madame Petrick' sport). L. Moreau, Belg. 1975): Flower color purplish pink 65B. Other characteristics as 'Madame Petrick'.

'Madame Oktaaf Gillis' (Sport of 'Eclaireur'. O. Gillis, Belg. 1959): Flower color strong red 46D. Its origin is always a sport but is not grown because its flowers are very sensitive to direct sunlight. Other characteristics as 'Eclaireur'.

'Madame P. B. Van Acker' (Seedling 'Madame Petrick' × 'Spit Fire'. P. B. Van Acker, Belg. 1928): Flower diameter 3⅜" ± ¼". Flower color red 51A. Double flower with green calyx. Flowers early. Forcing must take place at low temperatures (65 F.) Has produced a sport.

'Madame Petrick' (Seedling, parents unknown. S. Mardner, Ger. circa 1880. As a seedling this cultivar was first sold to the amateur, Haas of Wiesbaden, and afterwards to C. Petrick in Belgium who put it on the market): Flower diameter 3½" ± ¼". Flower color purplish red 57D. Double flower with green calyx. Flowers early. Grows rather slowly. Must be grafted. Susceptible to leaf-spot diseases. Its greatest advantage is its forcing properties. Has produced several sports. A selection with a somewhat darker colored flower and which flowers about one week earlier is offered under the name of 'Kees Bier'. It is difficult to consider this selection as a separate cultivar.

'Madame Poelman' (Presumable origin, a cutting from a "witches" broom. Poelman and Son, Belg. 1967): Flower color red. Double flower with green calyx. Flowers early.

'Madame Roger De Meyer' (Seedling 'Paul Schaeme' × 'Vervaeneana rosea'. R. De Meyer, Belgium 1935): Flower color white. Double flower with green calyx. Flowers very early.

'Madame Roggeman' (syn. 'Leopold Liliane'. Sport of 'Comtesse de Kerchove'. Van Houtte, Belg.): First exhibited by A. D'Haenens, Belgium 1966. This mutation has appeared in several firms. Flower color white to deep pink 43D with strong red edge 39B. Other characteristics as 'Comtesse de Kerchove'.

'Madame Royer': Parent of 'Avenir'.

'Madame Van der Cruyssen' (Seedling, parents unknown. E. Van der Cruyssen, Belg. 1967): Flower diameter 3⅛" ± ¼". Flower color reddish purple 67D. Double flower with green calyx. Fragrant. Flowers late.

'Madame Wibier' (Sport of 'Madame Petrick'. C. Wibier, Belg. 1929): Flower color purplish pink 62D. Other characteristics as 'Madame Petrick'.

'Mademoiselle Louise Cuvelier' (Seedling 'Rosa Bonheur' × 'Mademoiselle Marie Planchon'. J. De Kneef, Belg. 1890): Flower diameter 3½" ± ¼". Flower color white with red flakes and stripes. Double flower with green calyx. Flowers late. Produces sports easily. Has produced the 'Haerensiana' series of sports.

'Mademoiselle Marie Planchon': Parent of 'Mademoiselle Louise Cuvelier'.

'Margaret Rose' (Sport of 'Guido Gezelle'. J. Wille, Belg. 1950): Flower color white with deep pink edge 52B. The 'Leopold-Astrid' for very late flowering. Other characteristics 'Guido Gezelle'.

'Marianne Haerig' (Sport of 'Hellmut Vogel'. H. Harig, F.R.G. 1977): Flower color red 50B. Other characteristics as 'Hellmut Vogel'.

'Marie Claire Rodrigue' (Sport of 'Knut Erwen'. C. Rodrigue, Belg. 1977): Flower color purplish red 57D with fading edge vivid purplish red 66D. Other characteristics as 'Knut Erwen'.

'Marie Claude Truffaut' (syn. 'Truffaut'. Sport of 'Haerens Saumona' (Avenir' sport). G. J. Bier and Sons, Belg. 1953): Flower diameter 3½" ± ¼". Flower color pink 52CD. The most widely grown pink cultivar. A somewhat lighter pink selection is 'Souvenir Kathleen Van der Linden'. Other characteristics as 'Avenir'.

'Marie Louise' (Origin unknown, De Marcq, Belg. 1845): Flower color white with pink stripes. Single flower with 5 stamens. Flowers late. Has produced several sports. The red sport has no separate name.

'Marie Rose' (Sport of 'Marie Louise' ('Charles Encke' sport). M. Maenhout, Belg. 1951): Flower color strong purplish red 55C, towards the middle of the petals pink 54C. Other characteristics as 'Marie Louise'.

'Martine Maenhout' (Sport of 'Madame Joseph Maenhout' ('Comtesse de Kerchove' sport). R. Verhaege and Sons, Belg. 1970): Flower color strong red 50C with narrow somewhat lighter edge. Blotch vivid red 46A. Other characteristics as 'Comtesse de Kerchove'.

'Martin Winter' (Seedling, one of the parents is 'Coelestine'. K. Glaser, F.R.G. 1963): Flower color red. Small, single flower with green calyx. Flowers midseason.

'Max Schaeme' (Sport of 'Eri' ('Paul Schaeme' sport). M. Schaeme, Ger. 1935): Flower color deep pink 48C–52D with white edge like 'Eri'. The flower edge is strongly frilled. Other characteristics as 'Schaeme Frise'.

'Memoire de Louis Van Houtte': Parent of 'Delicatesse'.

'Memoire Reine Astrid' (Sport of 'Eri' ('Paul Schaeme' sport). O. Franck and Son, Belg. 1935): Flower color vivid red 44C. Far slower growth than the other 'Paul Schaeme' cultivars.

'Memoria Karl Glaser' (Sport of 'Gustav Hacker'. K. Glaser, F.R.G. 1974): Flower diameter 3⅜ ± ¼". Flower color purplish pink 61D with white edge. Other characteristics as 'Gustav Hacker'.

'Memoria Sander' (Seedling, parents unknown. Sander, Belg. 1923): Flower diameter 3–3/16" ± 5/16". Flower color vivid purplish red 57C. Double flower with green calyx. Flowers very early. Very good forcing properties. Must be grafted. Has a tendency to form vegetative shoots which have to be removed. Must be pinched completely before May 15 in any case, to avoid too early and too irregular flowering. Has produced a sport.

'Merveille' (Seedling 'Delicatesse' × seedling. R. De Meyer, Belg. 1957): Flower color pure white. Double flower with frilled edge, green calyx. Flowers midseason. See also 'Perle de Noisy'.

'Mevrouw Edmond Troch' (Sport of 'Inga' ('Hellmut Vogel' sport). E. Troch, Belg. 1978): Flower color pure white.Other characteristics as 'Hellmut Vogel'.

'Mevrouw Frans Heylbroeck' (Seedling. Seedling × 'Kees Bier'. R. De Meyer, Belg. 1972): Flower color pink. Double flower with green calyx. Flowers midseason.

'Mevrouw Gerard Kint' (Sport of 'Glaser number 10'. M. J. Kint Brothers, Belg. 1978): Put on the market in 1981. Flower color pink 52C with white edge. Other characteristics as 'Glaser number 10'.

'Mevrouw Gerard Kint White' (Sport of 'Mevrouw Gerard Kint' ('Glaser number 10' sport). M. J. Kint Brothers, Belg. 1981): Flower color white with yellow green blotch. Other characteristics as 'Glaser number 10'.

'Mevrouw Jozef Heursel' (Seedling 'Violacea' × 'Hexe'. Dr. J. Heursel; Institute of Ornamental Plant Growing, Belg. 1974): Flower diameter 3⅜" ± 3/16". Flower color vivid reddish purple 74B. Semidouble flower with an average of 3 stamens, green calyx. Flowers midseason. Sturdy grower with big flowers. Last growing year preferably in the open.

'Mevrouw Roger De Loose' (Sport obtained by irradiation of 'De Waele's Favorite' ('Knut Erwen' sport). Breeder Irradiation Laboratory of the I.W.O.N.L. (Institute for Scientific Research in Industry and Agriculture), Belgium 1974): Flower color deep pink 52B with white edge. Other characteristics as 'Knut Erwen'.

'Milda Glaser' (Seedling, parents unknown. K. Glaser, in G.D.R. before 1955): Exhibited by Belgians in England in 1968. Flower diameter 3½" ± 5/16". Flower color vivid purplish red 66C. Semidouble flower with an average of one stamen, calyx colored, hose-in-hose. Flowers late. Irradiation has produced a red sport.

'Mira' (Sport obtained by irradiation of 'Euratom'. Breeder Irradiation Laboratory of the I.W.O.N.L. (Institute for Scientific Research in Industry and Agriculture), Belg. 1976): Flower color strong purplish red 53D. Other characteristics as 'Euratom'.

'Moscou' (Seedling 'Richard Obst' × seedling. De Meyer, Belg. 1961): Flower color vivid red 53C. Flowers late.

'Myriam De Meyer' (Seedling 'Paul Schaeme' × 'Vervaeneana Rosea'. R. De Meyer, Belg. 1935): Flower color white. Double flower with green calyx. Flowers early.

'Nicolette Keessen' (Sport of 'Hellmut Vogel'. De Koninklijke Kwekerij "Terra Nova". W. Keessen Jr. and Sons C. V., Netherlands 1978): Flower color strong purplish red to reddish purple 63BC with darker flakes and stripes strong purplish red 63AB and with purplish pink edge 62B to D. Other characteristics as 'Hellmut Vogel'.

'Niobe' (Origin unknown. C. Schulz, Ger. 1879): Flower diameter 3¼ ± ¼". Flower color white with light green blotch. Double flower with green calyx. Flowers late. Must be grafted.

'Nordlicht' (Sport of 'Hellmut Vogel'. W. Bormann and H. Schoeneman, F.R.G. 1981. Also discovered in Belgium by G. J. Kint Brothers 1981): Flower color vivid red 53C. Other characteristics as 'Hellmut Vogel'.

'Olympia' (Seedling 'Paul Schaeme' × 'Fritz Sander', R. Ambroisius, Ger. 1936): Flower diameter 3⅜" ± 5¼". Flower color strong purplish red 53D. Double flower with green calyx.

'Orange Boven' (Sport of 'Adventsglocke'. G. J. Bier and Sons, Belg. 1948. Also discovered by O. Gerlach, G.F.R.): Flower color strong red 45D. Other characteristics as 'Adventsglocke'.

'Osaka' (Seedling 'Madame Petrick' × 'Pink Dream'. Institute of Ornamental Plant Growing, Belg. 1970): Flower diameter 3⅝ ± 3/16". Flower color reddish purple 67D. Double flower with green calyx. Flowers very early. When opening, the flower is fairly light colored reddish purple 73C. When growing, requires relatively much warmth. Excellent forcing properties.

'Otto Mohrenweiser' (syn. 'Mohrenweiser'. Seedling 'Perle de Noisy' × 'Pink Dream'. G. Boese Fr. Klattenberg Kulturen, G.F.R. 1969): Flower diameter 3⅜" ± 3/16". Flower color purplish red 55C. Double flower with green calyx. Flowers early. The leaves show whitish yellow speckles in the spring (spring chlorosis). Slow growth. The flowers start blanching after about a fortnight.

'Paloma' (Sport of 'Inga' ('Hellmut Vogel' sport). G. Harmsen, F.R.G. 1972): The first flowers were, as with most series of sports, not pure white but yellowish pink 49D to purplish pink 62D. The pure white form was put on the market in the G.F.R. 1978 and found in Belgium by E. Troch. In Belgium the cultivar was named 'Mevrouw Edmond Troch'. Other characteristics as 'Hellmut Vogel'.

'Pastorale' (Sport obtained by irradiation of 'De Waele's Favorite' ('Knut Erwen' sport). Irradiation Laboratory of the I.W.O.N.L. (Institute for Scientific Research in Industry and Agriculture), Belg. 1976): Flower color vivid purplish red 66D with narrow white edge. Other characteristics as 'Knut Erwen'.

'Paul Schaeme' (Seedling 'Wilhelm Scheurer' × 'Deutsche Perle'. J. Schaeme, Ger. circa 1890): Flower diameter 3½" ± ¼". Flower color moderate red 47D. Double flower with green calyx. Flowers early. Not too rapid growth. The leaves are susceptible to leaf-spot diseases and "blue leaf tips". The latter phenomenon is mainly found in autumn when grown in the open. Has produced several sports.

'Pax' (Seedling 'President Oswald de Kerchove' × 'Madame Petrick'. A. Steyaert, Belg. 1923): Flower diameter 2⅞" ± ¼". Flower color white. Double flower with green calyx.

'Perle de Melle' (Sport of 'Aventsglocke'. G. J. Bier and Sons, Belg. 1954): Flower color vivid red 53C to strong purplish red 58C. Other characteristics as 'Adventsglocke'.

'Perle de Noisy' (Sport of 'Madame Auguste Van Damme' ('Madame Petrick' sport). Bullens, Belg. 1933): Flower color purplish red 55B with white edge. Has produced a sport 'Merveille' with small white edge. J. Vercauteren, Belg. 1948. There is not a sufficient difference with 'Perle de Noisy' to consider this selection as a separate cultivar. Other characteristics as 'Madame Petrick'.

'Perle de Saffelaere' (Seedling, one of the parents is 'Sakuntala'. De Reuse Brothers, Belg. 1907): Flower diameter 3⅝" ±¼". Flower color white. Double flower with green calyx. Flowers midseason.

'Perle de Swynaerde' (Syn. 'Perle de Synaude'. Origin unknown. Paelinck Brothers, Belg. 1935): Flower diameter 3⅝" ± ¼". Flower color white. Double flower with green calyx. Flowers midseason.

'Peter Ann' (Sport of 'Madame Auguste Haerens' ('Avenir' sport). R. Verhaege and Sons, Belg. 1969): Flower color red to pink 50BD with narrow white edge. Other characteristics as 'Avenir'.

'Petrick Alba' (Sport of Madame Auguste Van Damme' ('Madame Petrick' sport). Schepens De Baets, Belg. 1920): Flower color white with a light green blotch. Other characteristics as 'Madame Petrick'.

'Phillippe De Meyer (Seedling 'Delicatesse' × 'Knut Erwen'. R. De Meyer, Belg. 1957): Flower color red. Double flower with frilled edge, green calyx. Flowers midseason.

'Phoebus': Parent of 'Ernest Eeckhaute'.

'Pillnitz' (syn. Enzett-Schloss Pillnitz; origin unknown. Put on the market by VEG(S) Zierpflanzen Erfurt, G.D.R. 1976): Flower diameter 3" ± ½". Flower color strong purplish red 58B. Single flower with an average of 6 stamens, green calyx.

'Pink Dream' (Parents unknown. N. V. Louis Van Houtte, Belg. 1948): Flower diameter 3¾" ± 3/16". Flower color purplish pink 65B, slightly blotched. Semidouble to single flower with an average of three stamens, green calyx. Flowers midseason. The leaves are light green. Grows somewhat loosely and has a tendency to drop its flowers when forcing starts too early. Has produced a sport.

'Pink Lady': (American name for 'Werner Muckel'. H. Kerrigan Oakland, Calif., year unknown.).

'Pink Pearl' = 'Pink Pearl Fonce' (Previously a synonym of 'Haerewille Pink Pearl', now of 'Pink Pearl Fonce'.).

'Pink Pearl Fonce' (syn. 'Pink Pearl'. Sport of the 'Vervaeneana' sports series. J. Haerens and Sons, Belg. 1933): Flower color pink 52CD, a darker pink than the original 'Haerewille Pink Pearl'.

'President Oswald de Kerchove': Parent of 'Knut Erwen' and 'Pax'

'Prince Albert' (Sport of 'Madame P. B. Van Acker'. Verschueren Brothers, Belg. 1943): Flower color purplish red 55C. Has produced a white sport 'Princess Josephine Charlotte'.

'Princess Beatrix' (syn. 'Prinses Beatrix'. Sport of 'Paul Schaeme'. G. J. Bier and Sons, Belg. 1941): Flower color red 44D. Other characteristics as 'Paul Schaeme'.

'Princess Josephine Charlotte' (Sport of 'Prince Albert' ('Madame P. B. Van Acker' sport). De Block, Belg. 1952): Flower color pure white. Other characteristics as 'Madame P. B. Van Acker'.

'Princess Margaretha' (syns. 'Avenir Rubra', 'Haerens Feu' and 'Haerens Rubra'. Sport of 'Avenir'. Ets. Horticole, Belg. 1944): Flower color deep pink 43C. Other characteristics as 'Avenir'.

'Princess Maria Pia' (syn. 'Maria Pia'. Seedling 'Temperance' × 'Ambrosius Superba'. C. and J. Wille, Belg. 1940): Flower diameter 2¼" ± 3/16". Flower color purplish pink 62A. Double flower with green calyx. Yellow green, hairy leaves. Very sensitive to pesticides. Vertical growth. Flowers late. Needs more water than average.

'Princess Paola' (Seedling 'Adventsglocke' × 'Reinhold Ambrosius'. J. De Meulemeester, Belg. 1960): Flower color deep purplish pink 55A to deep pink 43D. Double flower with green calyx. Flowers midseason. The name is sometimes erroneously used for 'Madame De Meulemeester'.

'Professor Wolters' (Sport of 'Baronne de Vriere'. J. Lossy, Belg. 1887): Flower diameter 3⅞" ± 7/16". Flower color strong red 46D to pink 48D–52CD with white edge. Single flower with an average of 9 stamens, green calyx. Flowers late.

'Professor Wolters White' (Sport of 'Professor Wolters' ('Baronne de Vriere' sport). R. Van Peteghem P.V.B.A., Belg. 1948): Flower color pure white. Other characteristics as 'Professor Wolters'.

'Prosper Van Den Dael' (syn. Prosper Van Dael; Seedling 'Fritz Sander' × 'Doctor Bergmann'. A. Gijselinck, Belg. 1932): Flower diameter 4¼" ± 5/16". Flower color strong purplish red 58B. Double flower with an average of three stamens, green calyx. Flowers late.

'Puppa' (Sport of 'Friedhelm Scherrer'. W. Streck F.R.G. 1979. Bought into commerce by O. Stahnke F.R.G. 1983): Flower color red. Other characteristics as 'Friedhelm Scherrer'.

'Purdey' (Sport of 'Madame Auguste Verschueren'. E. Verschueren, Belg. 1981): Flower color white with purplish red edge. Other characteristics of 'Madame Auguste Verschueren'.

'Queen Fabiola' (Sport of 'Leopold Astrid'. G. Harmsen, F.R.G. 1980. Patented 1980): A 'Leopold Astrid' with big strong red 52A edge. The middle of the flower is deep pink 50D to white.

'Red Marie' (Sport of 'Marie Louise'. Several discoverers. Put on the market by F. Tollenaere, Belg. 1981): Flower color deep pink 52B. Other characteristics as 'Marie Louise'.

'Red Satin' (Seedling, one of the parents is 'Doctor Bergmann', Lewis, Whittier , Ca., U.S.A. 1967. Imported in the G.F.R. by G. Harmsen, 1969): Flower color strong purplish red 53D-54A. Double flower with calyx colored, hose-in-hose. Gives a beautiful bud. See Red Satin Lewis Hyb.

'Red Wing' (Parents unknown. Imported into Belgium from the U.S.A. by F. Sonneville and Sons, 1957): Flower diameter 2¾" ± 3/16". Flower color strong purplish red 58B. Single flower with five stamens, calyx colored hose-in-hose. Rapid growth. Flowers late. Has produced a sport naturally and by irradiation.

'Reinhold Ambrosius' (syn. 'Ambrosius', seedling, father plant is probably 'Hexe'. R. Ambrosius, Germany circa 1930. The unnamed plant was sent to Belgium and named after the breeder. Shown for the first time in Belgium in 1950, in Germany 1951): Flower diameter 2¾" ± ¼". Flower color strong purplish red 58B. Double flower with green calyx. Flowers mid-season. Good growth, easily propagated from cuttings. A widely grown azalea in Western Europe. Has produced a sport. ('Ambrosia' and 'Ambrosieur' are not correct. 'Ambrosius Superba' is another variety no longer in cultivation in Europe.)

'Renate' (Seedling 'Leuchtfeuer' × 'Schnee'. R. Mayer, F.R.G. 1977): Flower color vivid red 44C. Double flower with green calyx. Flowers mid-season.

'Richard Obst' (Seedling 'Ernest Eeckhaute' × 'Paul Schaeme'. R. De Meyer, Belg. 1938): Flower diameter 3½ ± ¼". Flower color vivid purplish red 61C. Nearly double flower with an average of 0.13 stamens, green calyx. Flowers late.

'Ridder Thim' (Sport of 'Dame Melanie Saumona'. G. J. Bier and Sons, Belg. 1945): Flower color purplish red to purplish pink 55CD. Other characteristics as 'Roi Leopold'.

'Robert De Schrijver' (syn. 'Haerensiana Rubra'. Sport of 'Alex De Somer' ('Mademoiselle Louise Culvelier' sport). A. De Schrijver, Belg. 1942): Flower color red 50B. Other characteristics as 'Mademoiselle Louise Culvelier'.

'Robert Van Oost' (Seedling, probably 'Theodor Findeisen' × 'Paul Schaeme'. G. Van Ooost, Belg. 1941): Flower diameter 3⅝" × ¼". Flower color red 44D. Semidouble flower with an average of two stamens, green calyx. Forms very beautiful buds which are already swollen in the autumn. This cultivar is of the mid-season flowering type and must not be subjected to forcing before January. In young plants dark brown to black spots often appear on the leaves in wintertime. This is a physiological reaction: the spots disappear in the spring.

'Roger De Meyer', (Seedling 'Reinhold Ambrosius' × 'Knut Erwen'. R. De Meyer, Belg. 1962): Flower color purplish red. Double flower with green calyx. Flowers midseason.

'Roi Leopold' (syn. 'Dame Melanie Rubra' or 'Melanie Rubra'. Parents unknown. Van der Cruyssen, Belg. 1958): Flower diameter 2⅞" ± 3/16". Flower color moderate red 47D with dark blotches. Single flower with an average of 7 stamens, green calyx. From this mother plant the widely grown 'Dame Melanie' sports series has descended. Flowers late. Rapid growth. Grows well from cuttings. Habit resembles that of the Japanese azalea. Small leaves.

'Rosabella' (Seedling 'Perle de Noisy' × 'Pink Dream'; G. Boese, F.R.G. 1973): Flower diameter 3⅛" ± 3/16". Flower color purplish pink 62AB. Semidouble flower with an average of 6 stamens, green calyx. Flowers late. Bud formation rather late.

'Rosa Bonheur': Parent of 'Mademoiselle Louise Culvelier'.

'Rosafolia' (Seedling 'Perle de Noisy' × 'Pink Dream'; G. Boese, F.R.G.1973.): Flower diameter 4¼" ± 5/16". Flower color vivid purplish red 66C. The flower color does not fade. Single with an average of six stamens, green calyx. Flowers early.

'Rosali' (Seedling 'Perle de Noisy' × 'Pink Dream'; G. Boese, F.R.G. 1975): Flower diameter 3¼" ± 3/16". Flower color vivid purplish red 66D, inside a little paler. Semidouble flower with an average of two stamens, green calyx. Flowers midseason. Is grown mainly in the Netherlands and Belgium. Has produced a sport.

'Rosa Perle' (Seedling 'Friedhelm Scherrer' × 'Kirin' or 'Rex'. O. Stahnke, F.R.G. 1977.): Flower diameter 2½" ± 3/16". Flower color reddish purple 67D. Semidouble flower with an average of eight stamens, calyx colored, hose-in-hose. Flowers mid-season.

'Rubis De Meirelbeke' (Seedling, parents unknown. C. Vercauteren, Belg. 1927): flower diameter 3¼" ± ¼". Flower color vivid purplish red 57C. Double flower with green calyx. Flowers late. Fragrant flower. Irradiation has produced a sport.

'Saidjah' (Sport obtained by irradiation of 'Euratom'. Irradiation Laboratory of the I.W.O.N.L. (Institute for Scientific Research in Industry and Agriculture), Belg. 1976): Flower color red 50B. Other characteristics as 'Euratom'.

'Sakuntala' (Origin unknown. C. Schulz, Ger. 1878): Flower color white double flower.

'Schaeme Alba' (syn. 'Weisse Schaeme' and 'White Schaeme'. Sport of 'Paul Schaeme'. E. Herrmann, Ger. 1935): Flower color white with purplish pink 56B inner surface. Selected elsewhere in Germany too. From 1947 in Belgium. Discoverer G. Wibier. Is no longer grown because the flower color is not pure white. Now replaced by the pure white 'Madame Marcel De Paepe'.

'Schaeme Frise' (Sport of 'Paul Schaeme'. G. Cnockaert, Belg. 1931): Flower color moderate red 47D to deep pink 52D with a strongly frilled flower edge. The leaves are narrower and more pointed than the other 'Schaeme' cultivars. The flowers are rather heavy, and intolerant of forcing. Other characteristics as 'Paul Schaeme'.

'Schaeme Saumona' (syn. 'Eri Saumona' and 'Madame Dessaert'. Sport of 'Paul Schaeme'. A. Kerckvoorde, Belg. 1944): Flower color moderate red ± 47D with fading edge deep pink 52D. Also a sport from 'Eri'. Other characteristics as 'Paul Schaeme'.

'Schnee' (Origin unknown. C. Schulz, Ger. 1895): Flower diameter 3⅝" ± ¼". Flower color white. Single flower with an average of seven stamens, green calyx. Flowers late. Is grown in Germany.

'Sierra Nevada' (Sport obtained by irradiation of 'De Waele's Favorite' ('Knut Erwen' sport). Irradiation Laboratory of the I.W.O.N.L. (Institute for Scientific Research in Industry and Agriculture), Belg. 1976): Flower color deep pink 48C with narrow white edge and moderate red 47D above the blotch. The leaves are smaller and the growth more compact than 'Knut Erwen'.

'Simplet' ('Madame A. D'Haene' × 'Avenir'; A. Truffaut, France. Put on the market by G. J. Bier and Sons, Belgium 1958): Flower diameter 3⅝" ± ⅜". Flower color deep purplish pink 55A. Double star-shaped flower with green calyx. Flowers mid-season. Has produced sports.

'Simplet Orange' (Sport of 'Simplet'. A. Truffaut, France 1970): Flower color red. Other characteristics as 'Simplet'.

'Snowwhite' (syn. 'Madame Papi'. Seedling, parents unknown. C. J. Wille, Belg. circa 1937): Flower diameter 3⅛" ± ¼". Flower color white. Double flower with green calyx. Flowers very early. Susceptible to *Septoria.*

'Solitaire' (A 'Whitewater' hybrid. Origin unknown. Motzkau, U.S.A. 1971. Introduced into Western Europe by Van der Meer Brothers, Netherlands 1976): Flower color vivid purplish red 66C. Single flower with clayx colored, hose-in-hose. Flowers mid-season.

'Souvenir d'Albert Truffaut' (Sport of 'Simplet', A. Truffaut, France 1971): Flower color purplish red 55B with white edge. Other characteristics as 'Simplet'.

'Souvenir de Theo Piens': see 'Eri'.

'Souvenir du Recteur Kickx': Parent of 'Ernest Eeckhaute'.

'Souvenir Ferdinand Tollenaere' (Sport of 'Comtesse de Kerchove'. T. Tollenaere, Belg. 1963): Flower color deep pink 43C. Other characteristics as 'Comtesse de Kerchove'.

'Souvenir Kathleen Van der Linden' (syn. 'Kathleen Van der Linden'. Sport of 'Haerens Saumona' (Avenir' sport). C. Van der Linden, Belg. 1954): Flower color purplish pink red to purplish 55CD, a little lighter than 'Marie Claude Truffaut'. Other characteristics as 'Avenir'.

'Spit Fire' (Parents unknown. J. Vervaene, Belg. 1896): Flower color vivid red 44C. Double flower with green calyx.

'Sport' (Sport of 'Madame Lucien de Cock'. Fr. J. Collumbien, Belg. 1960): Flower color vivid purplish red 66D with white edge. Other characteristics as 'Madame Lucien de Cock'.

'Stella Maris' (Sport of 'Rosali'. Van der Meer Brothers, Netherlands 1977. Put on the market 1981): Flower color white with moderate purplish red 58A blotch. Other characteristics of 'Rosali'.

'Surprise' (Sport of 'Violacea'. G. J. Bier and Sons, Belg. 1961.): Flower color strong purplish red 60D. This color was not in demand, so the production was discontinued. It reappeared by irradiation. Other characteristics as 'Violacea'.

'Suzanne Moreux' (Sport of 'Madame Gau' ('Madame Petrick' sport). C. Van Gele and Son, Belg. 1938.): Flower color purplish pink 55D. Slower growth than the other 'Madame Petrick' cultivars. There are several pink selections. Other characteristics of 'Madame Petrick'.

'Sverige' (syn. 'Orange Sander' in U.S.A. Sport of 'Memoria Sander'. P. Segers, Belg. 1935.): Flower color strong red 46D. The flowers very sensitive to direct sunlight. Other characteristics as 'Madame Lucien de Cock'.

'Sylvia' (Seedling 'Leuchtfeuer' × 'Schnee', R. Mayer, F.R.G. 1977): Flower color vivid purplish red 57A. Semidouble flower with green calyx. Flowers late.

'Temperance' (Seedling, parents unknown. De Cock, Belg. 1890.): Flower diameter 3¾" ± 3/16". Flower color purple 77D. Double flower with green calyx. Flowers mid-season. Strong vertical growth. Has produced a sport 'Temperance Rose' which is no longer grown.

'Temperance Rose' (Sport of 'Temperance'. A. Haerens, Belg. 1928.): Flower color pink.

'Tendresse' (syn. 'Regina', sport of 'Leopold Astrid' ('Armand Haerens' sport), G. J. Bier and Sons, Belg. 1958): Flower color yellowish pink 49D to nearly white. Other characteristics as 'Leopold Astrid'.

'Theodor Findeisen' (Sport of 'Madame Petrick'. T. Findeisen, Ger. 1920): Flower color purplish pink 61D. Other characteristics as 'Madame Petrick'.

'Tigrina' ('Paul Schaeme' × 'Temperance'. Ch. J. Wille and Co., Belg. 1933): Flower color white with purple and purplish red flakes. Double flower with green calyx.

'Triumph' ('Madame Auguste Haerens' × 'Lentegroet'. August Haerens, Belg. 1923): Flower diameter 3⅛" ± ¼". Flower color vivid purplish red 57C. Double flower with green calyx. Flowers late. White spots appear on the leaves, mainly in spring. Irradiation has produced a deep purplish pink sport 62B with white edges. Other sports are no longer grown.

'Vervaeneana' (syn. 'Vervaeniana,' sport of a seedling named 'Pharailde Mathilde', resulting from a cross of 'Comte Charles de Kerchove' × 'Konigin der Weisse'. J. Vervaene, Belg. 1886): Flower diameter 3⅝" ± ¼". Flower color purplish red 58D with white edge. Flower shows clear blotches. Double flower with green calyx. Flowers late. Fairly strong vertical growth. This cultivar must be grafted. The best results are obtained on 'Euratom' or 'Hexe' because the plants then preserve their leaves better when they have grown bigger. Requires about ⅓ less water than the other cultivars. This group of cultivars is now being grown far less. Pink shades are most in demand because other late cultivars have no pink shades. The flower stem breaks easily. Has produced several sports. See also 'Vervaeneana Rosea'.

'Vervaeneana Alba' (Sport of 'Vervaeneana', J. Vervaene, Belg. 1903): Flower color white. Other characteristics as 'Vervaeneana'.

'Vervaeneana Rosea' (Sport of 'Vervaeneana'. Haerens and Wille, Belg. 1910): The flower color is more intensely pink than in the case of the original 'Vervaeneana', so that what is now being described and marketed as 'Vervaeneana' is actually 'Vervaeneana Rosea'.

'Vervaeneana Rubra' (Sport of 'Vervaeneana'. J. Vervaene, Belg. 1900): Flower color moderate red 47D. Other characteristics as 'Vervaeneana'.

'Vervaeneana Saumona' (Sport of 'Vervaeneana'. Truffaut, France 1926): Flower color pink 52C, fading towards the edges purplish pink 55D. Other characteristics as 'Vervaeneana'.

'Vincent Debernard' (Seedling 'Reinhold Ambrosius' × 'Rubis de Meirelbeke'. M. De Meulemeester, Belg. 1970.): Flower color purplish red. Semidouble flower with green calyx. Flowers late.

'Vinivi' (Sport of 'Flamenco'. Dr. Ir. J. Heursel, Institute of Ornamental Plant Growing Melle, Belg. 1970): Put on the market 1981. Flower color vivid purplish red 66B. Other characteristics as 'Flamenco'. A single branch may mutate back to 'Flamenco'.

'Violacea' (Parents unknown. Probably first known as 'Violacea Multiflora'. C. Schulz, Ger. 1884): Flower diameter 2⅞ ± 3/16". Flower color vivid reddish purple 72C. Double flower with green calyx. Flowers mid-season. Weak growth, weak wood. Is grafted in most cases. Has produced a few sports with not very attractive colors.

'Violacea Lila' (Sport of 'Violacea'. A. Lippens, Belg. 1957): Flower color purplish red, somewhat redder than 'Surprise'. The color is not much in demand, so the production of the sport was discontinued.

'Weinachtsblume' (syn. 'Weihnacht(en)'. Sport of 'Madame Petrick'. M. C. Dierickx, Belg. 1935): This sport differs from the 'Madame Petrick' series because of its somewhat more rounded leaves. Has in turn produced part of the classical 'Petrick' sports such as red and pink with white edges. Its flowering lasts a little longer than the classical 'Petrick'.

'Werner Muckel' (syn. 'Flamingo', 'Pink Lady' and 'Werner Proehl'. Descended from 'Paul Schaeme' as a result of Colchicine treatment. Gartnerische Producktionsgenossenschaft Azalee, G.D.R., year unknown): Flower color purplishred 55C. Other characteristics as 'Paul Schaeme'. Known by the name of 'Werner Muckel' in the G.F.R., circa 1974.

'White Hexe' (Sport of 'Hexe'. G. van der Swaelmen,Belg. 1922): Flower diameter 3" ± ¾". Flower color white. Calyx colored, hose-in-hose. Double flower so it may be questioned whether it is really a 'Hexe' sport. The leaf is a 'Hexe' leaf.

'White Lady' (Sport of 'Memoria Karl Glaser' ('Gustav Hacker' sport). W. Streck, F.R.G. 1977): Flower color white. Other characteristics as 'Gustav Hacker'.

'Whitewater' (Parents unknown. Motzkau, U.S.A. 1965.): Flower diameter 2⅝" ± 3/16". flower color white. Semidouble flower with an average of four stamens, calyx colored, hose-in-hose.

'White Schaeme': If pure white it is a synonym of 'Madame Marcel De Paepe'; if not pure white then it is a synonym of 'Schaeme Alba'.

'Wilhelm Keim' (Seedling. One of the parents is 'Coelestine'. K. Glaser, F.R.G. 1963): flower color vivid red 47A. Small single flower with green calyx. Flowers late. Closely resembles 'Glaser Number 10'.

'Wilhelm Scheurer': Parent of 'Paul Schaeme'.

'Willem Van Oranje' (Seedling 'Madame Petrick' × 'Apollo'. A. Haerens. Belg. 1932): Flower diameter 3⅜" ± 3/16". Flower color red 44D. Semidouble flower with an average of 0.18 stamens, green calyx. Flowers mid-season.

ADDITIONAL BELGIAN INDIAN HYBRIDS

The following Belgian Indian Hybrids include many early cultivars as well as recent introductions from the U.S.A. and Europe. For additional Indian Hybrids see the list Azaleas from Australia and New Zealand. Many of the early Belgian Indian Hybrids developed in Europe as well as some on the list are no longer available.

'Abondance' (syn. 'Abundance', A. Haerens, '28): vivid red, double, 3".

'Alda Lea' ('Eric Schaeme' × 'Prof. Wolter' seedling; Myers, '68): red center with blotch, to pink and white edge, often 5 colors, double, 2½"; compact habit.

'Anytime' (L. Hahn, '65, PP 2568): deep pink, semidouble.

'Big Ben' (S. R. Smith; PP 3041): vivid red, double, 4".

'Blue Angel' ('Perle de Saffelaere' seedling × light purple seedling; Myers, '68): very pale purplish blue; compact plant.

'Blushing Bride' (syn. 'Miss Elza Koelker'; sport of 'Rudolph Seidel'; K. J. Kuyk): pink, semidouble.

'Brillianta Belgica' ('Ernest Eeckhaute' × 'Haerensiana'; Haerens '09): between deep purplish pink and vivid red, double, with a few small petals in center and larger petals, 3".

'California Beauty' (syn. 'My Fair Lady'; sport of 'California Sunset'): vivid yellowish pink, wide white border, double.

'California Peach' (sport of 'California Pink Dawn'): deep yellowish pink.

'California Pink Dawn' (sport of 'California Sunset'): pale pink, large double.

'California Snow' (sport of 'California Sunset'): white double.

'California Sunset' (see 'Haerens Saumona', sport of 'Avenir'): moderate red 47D, edges pale pink to white, 3".

'Candystick' (syn. 'Candy Stick'): red and white variegated, double.

'Chimes' (see 'Adventglocke'): strong purplish red, semidouble, 3¾".

'Christmas Joy' (S. R. Smith; PP 3376): vivid red, double.

'Clare Mae Bell' ('Sweet Sixteen' × 'China Seas'; Phillips): dark pink, double, hose-in-hose, 2".

'Clementine Vervaene' (Vervaene, 1863): white, deep pink stripes and flecks.

'Coe's Pink Beauty': deep pink.

'Columbine': between deep yellowish pink and vivid red, dark blotch, frilled, 3".

'Copper Queen' ('Chimes' seedling × 'Chico'; Myers, '68): strong reddish orange 40C, single to semidouble, 2½–3".

'Coral Redwing' (sport of 'Redwings'): deep yellowish pink.

'Cottage Ruffles' (possible same as 'Miss Cottage Garden'; Cottage Gardens): deep pink, ruffled, 3".

'Deutsche Perle' (Rose, 1978): white, double.

'Dimples': ('Eri' × 'Purple Indica Rosea'; Westfall): double, variegated.

'Eborina Plena' (sport of 'Madame Romain de Smet'; Schultz): white, double.

'Eureka Everlasting': red, semidouble, ruffled, 3".

'Festival Queen': pale yellowish white, large double.

'Firecrown' (Yoder Bros., '69; PP 3370): vivid reddish orange, semidouble, large.

'Fireglow' (sport of 'Redwings'; Yoder Bros., '68): reddish orange, hose-in-hose.

'Florida Beauty' (sport of 'California Sunset'): pink.

'Francois de Vos': dark red, double.

'Freckles' (sport of 'Rose Queen'; Hines, Patent; same as 'White Princess'): white, red spots in throat, hose-in-hose.

'Galaxie': vivid red, double.

'Gartendirecteur Krause' (Rose, 1883): white with red stripes, crisp edges, double. Also spelled Gartendirecktor Krause.

'Gartendirector Krause' (Hart 1891): reddish brown, double.

'Glory of Easter' (sport of 'Jean Haerens'): deep yellowish pink, double.

'Glo Wing' (sport of 'Redwings'; Sand Point Gard.): orange to reddish orange, hose-in-hose.

'Improved Redwings' ('L. J. Bobbink' × 'Miss Cottage Garden'; Nur. Exch., '68, PP 2918): reddish orange, semidouble, hose-in-hose, 3½–4". There are similar sports with the same name: 'Improved Redwing' (rose) and 'Improved Redwing' (pink).

'James Belton' ('Albert-Elizabeth' × 'Schryderi'; E. Kirk, Aust. '64): pink, suffused light purple.

'Juliette' (Van Houtte, 1872): deep pink, double.

'King's White' (Casadaban's Nur.): white.

'Kyoto' (Patent 2248) red.

'Leonora' ('Eri' × purple sport of 'Indica Rosea'; Westfall): light pink.

'Lucille K' (sport of 'Redwings'; Kraus; PP 4275): red, tipped white at edge, ruffled.

'Madonna': white, large semidouble.

'Magnolia Shell Pink': light pink.

'Mamie': light pink, hose-in-hose.

'Mercury': off-white to pale pink, large.

'Miss Cottage Garden' (Cottage Garden Nur.): red, hose-in-hose, ruffled, 3".

'Mission Bells' (R. Yoshimura, '67; PP 2872): vivid red, semidouble to double, ruffled.

'Mme. Alfred Sander' (syn. 'Fred Sanders'): red, double.

'Mme. Joseph Vervaene' (Vervaene, 1892): deep yellowish pink, purplish blotch, double.

'Mme. Louis Van Houtte': (sport of 'Mme. Joseph Lefebvre'; Van Houtte, 1878): deep pink, red stripes, white margins, dark blotch.

'Mme. Memoria Sander': red, double.

'Mme. Moreux' (sport of 'Empress of India'; Moreux, 1898): pink, semidouble, frilled.

'Mme van Oost': reddish orange.

'Morlin B. Bell' ('Crimson Glory' × 'Mr. Charles Vuylsteke'; Phillips): moderate red, double, 3".

'Mr. Charles Vuylsteke' (Vervaene, 1894): vivid red, double, 3½".

'Mr. Jean Peeters' (Vervaene, 1890): vivid red, darker blotch, double.

'Mr. Millaut': vivid red, purplish blotch, single or semidouble, 2¼".

'Mrs. Chas. O. Phillips' (Phillips): dark red, double, 3".

'Mrs. Frederick Sanders' (syn. 'Fred Sanders'): deep yellowish purple, double.

'Nash Pink': vivid pink, late.

'Orange Chimes' (sport of 'Chimes'): deep reddish orange, semidouble; upright habit.

'Orchiphilla' (syn. 'Orchidflora', 'Orchid Lavender'; Haerenst, Wille, '07): moderate pink, semidouble.

'Perle de Ledeberg' ('Pres. Oswald de Kerchove' × 'Vervaeneana'; Vernaene, 1892): white, flushed reddish orange, occasional stripes of same color, yellow green blotch, double or semidouble, frilled, 3".

'Pink Bergmann' (see 'Madame Charles Gabert'; sport of 'Dr. Bergmann'): light pink, darker throat, semidouble.

'Priscilla' ('Berkley red' × lavender sport of 'Indica Rosea'; Westfall): red, double.

'Prize Strawberry': white, striped red, early.

'Red American Beauty' (J. F. Link, '66; PP 2733): vivid reddish orange, hose-in-hose.

'Red Baron' ('Granada' × 'Red Poppy'; S. Barber, '72): between vivid and deep red 46B, double, 3½"; hardy to 25F.

'Red Bird': see 'Red Wing'.

'Red Poppy': red, occasionally semidouble.

'Reine de Portugal' (Verschaffelt, 1872): white, pale green spots on petal edge, occasional pink stripes, semidouble.

'Rosalinda' ('Eri' × lavender sport of 'Indica Rosea'; Westfall): light pink, double.

'Rosa Belton' (sport of 'James Belton'): white, purple margin, ruffled, hose-in-hose, 2½–3"; green calyx.

'Ruffled Giant': deep pink, ruffled, 3–4"; vigorous.

'Ruth Kirk' ('Albert-Elizabeth' × 'Splendens'; E. Kirk, Aust., '64): vivid pink, flushed light pink.

'Saidee Kirk' ('Albert-Elizabeth'× 'Sparkle'; E. Kirk, Aust., '64): light pink, double.

'Salmon Perfection': deep yellowish pink, semidouble. PP 146. Rutherford Hyb.

'Salmon Solomon' (sport of 'Southern Charm'); yellowish pink.

'Santa Fe Red': red.

'Satellite' ('Chimes' × 'John Haerens'; J. Klupenger, '71; PP 3086): white, deep pink variegated: semi to double, frilled, 4", med. to late.

'Sierra Snow': white, semidouble, frilled.

'Sigismund Rucker' (sport of 'Rachel von Varenhagen'; Van Houtte, 1873): purplish pink with white edges and red blotch.

'Silver Glow' (sport of 'Jean Haerens'; Walker, Aust. '72): light purplish pink; variegated foliage.

'Simon Mardner' (Rose, 1878): deep pink, double.

'Snowfall' ('Eri' × purple sport of 'Indica Rosea'; Westfall): white, double.

'Souvenir du Recteur Kickx' ('Charmes' × 'Princess Louise'; Eeckhaute, 1888): purplish red, double, large.

'Spellbound' (sport of 'Orchiphilla'): deep purplish pink, white border.

'Sunday Best' ('Eri' × purple sport of 'Indica Rosea'; Westfall): white, double.

'Super Orange' ('Spit Fire' × 'Paul Schaeme'): deep orange, double.

'Swan': white.

'Sweet Lavender' ('Eri' × purple sport of 'Indica Rosea'; Westfall): light purple.

'Sweet Sixteen' (similar to 'Madame Petrick'; Cottage Garden Nur.): light yellowish pink, 3".

'The Hussy' ('Eri' × purple sport of 'Indica Rosea'; Westfall): deep pink, double.

'Tickled Pink' (sport of 'Purity'): light pink, white margin, hose-in-hose, 3".

'Tilney Red': light red, early midseason.

'Wedding Bells': white, hose-in-hose, frilled.

'White Duc' (sport of 'Duc de Rohan'): white, 2½".

'White Vittati': white.

'Winfried Roelker' (syn. 'Pres. Allexis Callier' and 'Energique'; 'Haerensiana' × 'Ernest Eeckhaute'): vivid red.

'Yuge's Geisha' ('Miss Cottage Garden' × Belgian Indian seedling; Yuge Bros. Nur.; PP 2249): red, semidouble, ruffled.

'Yugi Chimes': dark red, double.

'Yvonne' (sport of 'Jean Haerens'): yellowish pink fading to white center.

OTHER INDIAN HYBRID AZALEAS

The breeding and selection of Belgian Indian Hybrid azaleas was taken up by breeders in the U.S.A., working in parallel with their opposite numbers in Europe and the U.K. Breeding objectives focused primarily on developing plants suitable for florist forcing such as the Rutherford Hybrids, and continuing to the present with the work of Kerrigan, Mossholder, Nuccio, and others. Most of these hybrids have come from the West Coast. They are used both as garden plants and for forcing. Hardiness is generally listed as zones 9–10, but many clones are proving much hardier, so longer term evaluation is needed.

RUTHERFORD HYBRIDS

The Rutherford Hybrids are an American equivalent of the Belgian Indian Hybrids.They originated at the Bobbink and Atkins Nursery of East Rutherford, New Jersey, during the 1920's as greenhouse forcing azaleas. The plant patents state that the single flowers were derived from 'Indica Alba' and 'Omurasaki'. Succeeding generations were derived initially from the Belgian Indian Hybrid, 'Mme. Petrick', and a single 'Macrantha'; and the semidoubles from *R. scabrum* and 'Mme. Petrick'. Still later generations incorporated the Kurume Hybrid, 'Salmon Beauty'; while the doubles arise from further crosses of 'Omurasaki', 'Mme. Petrick', and 'Vervaeneana', and their cultivars. Strangely, *Rhododendron* hybrids were also reported in some of the crosses, but there is no sign of *Rhododendron* influence in surviving plants. Several of the early selections were acquired and named by Charles Coe, Planting Fields, Oyster Bay, New York, and indicated by (Coe) in this list, but from 1934 to 1938 were named by Bobbink and Atkins.

The plants are evergreen, medium in height to 6–8 feet, spreading, compact and floriferous. The blooming range extends from early to late midseason and includes singles, semidoubles, doubles, and hose-in-hose. Many are frilled. The colors range from reddish orange to purple and white, in sizes of 2–3 inches.

They are tender since they were primarily developed as florist pot plants. They are all hardy in zone 9 and so are used out-of-doors in warm climates. Some such as 'Pink Ruffles' and 'Dorothy Gish' are hardy to 7a.

'Alaska': white with yellow green blotch, single to semidouble and double, 2", late midseason.
'Albion': white, green throat, hose-in-hose, 2", late, PP 147.
'Caroline Coe' (Coe): light purple, hose-in-hose.
'Caroline Graham' (Coe): dark orange, double, PP 145.*
'Cherokee Ruby' (Coe): deep pink, red blotch, PP 145.*
'Cherokee White' (Coe) (syn. 'Snowbank'): white, yellow green blotch, frilled, 2½", late midseason, another form 3" with little to no blotch, each have ½" sepals.
'Christmas Red': strong purplish red 57B darker blotch, occasionally semidouble, 2¼".
'Christmas Spirit': vivid red, hose-in-hose.
'Colorado': vivid purplish red 57C, darker blotch, 2¼".
'Conqueror': deep red, double.
'Constance': moderate purplish pink 62B, darker blotch, frilled, 2", early midseason, PP 145.*
'Dorothy Gish': reddish orange 47C, darker blotch, hose-in-hose, frilled, 2½", midseason, PP 146.*
'Early Wonder': strong purplish red 63A, semidouble or double, 2½".
'Firelight': moderate purplish red 63B, semidouble, hose-in-hose, 1½", early midseason, PP 146.*
'F. L. Atkins': purplish red, hose-in-hose, PP 146.*
'Gertrude Bobbink': strong pink, hose-in-hose, frilled.
'Giant': moderate red 50B, darker blotch, frilled, semidouble, hose-in-hose.
'Harlequin': white, flakes and striped red, double.
'Indian Chief': deep pink, hose-in-hose, PP 146.*
'Jewel': deep pink, reddish shades in throat, red blotch, PP 145.*
'J. Horace McFarland': purplish pink, double.

'King': vivid purplish red, very double, extra petals, frilled, 3".
'Lambertus C. Bobbink': strong purplish red, darker blotch, semidouble, frilled, 2¼", late.
'Louise J. Bobbink': vivid reddish purple, lighter throat, occasionally whitish flower, hose-in-hose, frilled, 2".
'Mary Corcoran': vivid purplish red, white throat, darker blotch, tubular, 2", PP 145.*
'Mother Pearl': pale pink, dark blotch, hose-in-hose, PP 146.*
'Mrs. Alice W. Mueller': moderate purplish red, 70A, red blotch, 2½", late, PP 147.*
'Mrs. F. L. Atkins': orange, hose-in-hose.
'Mrs. G. C. White': white, double.
'Mrs. J. D. Eisele': strong pink, hose-in-hose.
'Mrs. W. R. Coe' (Coe): strong pink, PP 145.*
'Natalie Coe Vitetti' (Coe) (syn. 'Crimson Glory'): strong purplish red 63A, brownish blotch, semidouble, extra petals, 2¾", late.
'Natalie Mai Coe' (Coe): light orange yellow, semidouble, PP 145.*
'Orange King': reddish orange, double, PP 147.*
'Orange Queen': moderate red 53A, semidouble, hose-in-hose, 1½".
'Patience': strong red, semidouble.
'Pink Beauty': pink, hose-in-hose, PP 146.*
'Pink Ruffles': deep pink, semidouble, hose-in-hose, 2", PP 146.*
'Planting Fields' (Coe): orange yellow, PP 145.*
'Pocahontas': moderate red 50B, darker blotch, semidouble, hose-in-hose or petaloid sepals, 2½", PP 146.*
'Pres. F. D. Roosevelt': moderate red 50A, semidouble, with petaloid sepals, frilled, 1½".
'Purity': white, hose-in-hose, 2½"; early midseason, PP 147.*
'Red Gish' (syn. 'Red Dorothy Gish'; sport of 'Dorothy Gish'): strong red, other characteristics same as 'Dorothy Gish'.
'Red Ruffles' (sport of 'Pink Ruffles'): strong red, semidouble, hose-in-hose, 2".
'Rhapsody': strong reddish orange, double, PP 147.*
'Rose Queen': deep purplish pink, white, throat, dark blotch, semidouble, hose-in-hose, 1¼"; early midseason, low spreading, PP 147.* 'Improved Rose Queen': darker double flowers.
'White Gish' (syn. 'White Dorothy Gish' sport of 'Dorothy Gish'): very pale pink opening, white, hose-in-hose, 2½".

*In early days, plants were patented in groups; hence some plants have the same PP #.

BROOKS HYBRIDS

This hybrid line was developed by Leonard L. Brooks of Modesto, California, U.S.A. They were derived from various combinations of parents such as 'Willem Van Orange' × 'Hexe', and Belgian or Southern Indian Hybrids × 'Ledifolia Alba', together with Kurume Hybrids. They bloom midseason to late. Many were patented but sold under different names, such as 'Redwings' (syn. 'Red Bird' 'Red Wing' and 'Red Ruffles'). Plants should be hardy in zone 8, but many have not been tested in the eastern U.S.A. Plants are of medium height 4–6 ft. No information available on actual parentage of cultivars as breeding records are no longer in existence.

'Brilliance': orange red, hose-in-hose, PP 1484.
'Capri': white, red stripe, double.
'Dawn': light pink, double.
'Dorothy Ann': purplish pink, double.
'Emelia Gatti': vivid red, hose-in-hose, PP 1866.
'Emily Barton': deep red, double.

'Fairy Queen': pink, double, PP 2224.
'Fantasy': purplish pink, double, PP 1717.
'Flamingo': deep pink, hose-in-hose.
'Flirtation': vivid purplish red, double.
'Ginger': reddish orange, double.
'Grandeur': purplish red, double.
'Hala': pink, semidouble, hose-in-hose.
'Heart's Desire': red, double, PP 1977.
'Madonna': white, double, PP 1819.
'My Valentine': deep pink, double.
'Pinkie': pink, hose-in-hose.
'Pink Splendor': pink, semidouble.
'Princess': light pink, hose-in-hose.
'Rapture': deep pink, double.
'Redwings' (syn. 'Red wing', 'Red Bird' & 'Red Ruffles'; PP 1159): strong red, hose-in-hose, ruffled, 2¾"; very popular.
'Rival': reddish orange; hose-in-hose, PP 1483.
'Romance': yellowish pink double.
'Splendor': purplish red, semidouble.
'Susan Land': reddish orange, double.
'White Grandeur': white, semidouble.

CORNELL HYBRIDS

The azaleas of Phillip B. Cornell of Fort Bragg, California, U.S.A., are hybrids of a Belgian Indian or Rutherford Hybrid as one parent and a Kurume, Kaempferi, or Pericat Hybrid the other. They were introduced around 1960 and may only be available in California. Hardy zone 7, 2–6 feet high.

'Anita': ('Perle de Swynaerde' × 'Fedora'): white, double, 3", early midseason; compact, medium height.
'Cover Girl' ('Twenty Grand' selfed): vivid purplish red, hose-in-hose, 3", early midseason; upright, medium.
'Foxfire' ('Brillianta Belgica' × 'Ward's Ruby'): vivid red, hose-in-hose, 2½", midseason; medium compact.
'Noyo Lilac' ('Fedora' selfed): strong purplish red, 1½", early midseason; upright medium.
'Noyo Pink' ('Alaska' × 'Twenty Grand'): strong red; hose-in-hose, 2", early midseason; upright medium height.
'Noyo Rose' ('Miss Cottage Garden' × 'Fedora'): vivid red, crinkly, 3", early; spreading, medium.
'Pink Cheer' ('Sweet Sixteen' × 'Macrantha'): vivid red, 3", early midseason; low, spreading.
'Rene Cornell' ('Perle de Swynaerde' × 'Sherwood'): vivid reddish purple, 3¼", early midseason; upright, medium.
'Southern Lady' (Kurume type): light pink, early, compact.

KERRIGAN HYBRIDS

Howard Kerrigan of Hayward, California, U.S.A., has been hybridizing azaleas for over 30 years, starting in the early 1950's with the goal of developing good forcing azaleas, but adaptable to the landscape. Some are similar to Belgian Hybrids while others are Kurume Hybrid types. Many of the plants are patented. General hardiness is zones 8b–10; some may be hardier. Plants are upright 3–5 ft. high. Parentage on many of the cultivars is not available.

'Ballerina' ('Paul Schaeme' × 'Mme. Pericat'): deep yellowish pink, double, PP 1881.
'Bride's Bouquet' ('Blushing Bride' × 'Rosebud'): white, very double, PP 3362.
'Bright Eyes' ('L. C. Bobbink' × 'Mme. Butterfly'): vivid red, white center.

'Capitola': yellowish pink, hose-in-hose, ruffled, late.
'Captain Blood': dark red, semidouble.
'Cloud Nine' ('Blushing Bride' × 'Rosebud'): white, double.
'Coral May Queen' (sport of 'May Queen'): yellowish pink, double.
'Diablo' (sport of 'Hexe'): strong red 46D, hose-in-hose, 2¼".
'Envy': very pale green to pale yellow edges.
'Fiesta' ('Shinnyo no Tsuki' × 'Jezebel'): dark red, white center, hose-in-hose, very late.
'Gay Paree' ('Albert-Elizabeth' × 'Capt. Blood'): white with dark red edges, hose-in-hose, PP 2770.
'Geronimo' (('L. C. Bobbink' × 'Rosebud') × 'Rhodalia'): reddish orange, large trusses, very late.
'Goliath' ('Gumpo' × 'L. C. Bobbink'): deep pink, 3¼–4"; flat face, good substance.
'Granada' ('L. C. Bobbink' × 'Miss Cottage Garden'): dark red, early, PP 2505.
'Gypsy Rose' ('Gumpo' × 'L. C. Bobbink'): pink, hose-in-hose, 3½–4".
'Happiness' ('Mrs. Charles Vylsteke' × 'L. C. Bobbink'): vivid red, double, PP 2471.
'Happy Holiday' (sport of 'Eric Schaeme'): no description available.
'Janet Kerrigan' ('Romance' × 'Ballerina'): yellowish pink, double, dark foliage, very floriferous.
'Jezebel': dark red, hose-in-hose, late, dark foliage, PP 2504.
'Kerrigan's Super Red' (('Meg' × 'Vic') × 'Ripples'): red, formal double, very early.
'Lady Fair' (('L. C. Bobbink' × 'Gumpo') × 'Ballerina'): deep yellowish pink, hose-in-hose, ruffled, PP 3356.
'Lucy Star': purple stripe down each petal, white edge, very large.
'Luv' (variegate sport of 'Romance'; (Brook)): with floral pattern of 'Eric Schaeme'.
'Marin' ('Lydia Haerens' × 'Ballerina'): light pink, double.
'Mary Queen' (('Blushing Bride' × 'Rosebud') × unknown): deep pink, full double, very late, PP 3365.
'Mt. Shasta' ('Blushing Bride' × 'Snowdrift'): white, double to semidouble, late, PP 2971.
'Noel': white, double, early.
'Pastel Princess' (('Albert' × 'Elizabeth') × 'Mme. Butterfly'): two tone pink.
'Peace' ('Triumph' × 'Rosebud'): white, formal double.
'Pink Kowkoku' (sport of 'Kowkoku'): pink.
'Pink Lady' (sport of 'Happy Holiday'): light pink, double, PP 2485.
'Prelude' ('Paul Schaeme' × 'Mme. Pericat'): deep yellowish pink, hose-in-hose, midseason.
'Prima Donna' ('Paul Schaeme' × 'Charles Encke'): pale pink, with darker variegation, double, PP 2472.
'Princess Aki' ('Twenty Grand' × '20 Grand' seedling): vivid orange, hose-in-hose.
'Rambling Rose': deep pink, full double, trailing habit.
'Red Poppy': strong purplish red, semidouble.
'Ripples' ('L. C. Bobbink' × 'Rosebud'): full double, ruffled, PP 2929.
'Robin': red, double, PP 2506.
'Salmon Splendor' ('Paul Schaeme' × 'Mme. Pericat'): yellowish pink, hose-in-hose.
'Spring Fever' ('Triumph' × 'Rosebud'): pink, double.
'Starlight' ('Perle de Saffelaere' × 'Ballerina'): light yellowish pink, semidouble, 2½", PP 3364.
'Super Red': vivid red, extra double, large; vigorous growth, PP 4729.
'Trailing Queen' ('Triumph' × 'Gumpo'): yellowish pink; long pendant branches to 5 ft.
'Variegated Kowkoku' (sport of 'Kowkoku'): pink with white tips to petals.
'White Challenge' (('L. C. Bobbink' × 'Rosebud') × (60F21 × 'Baby Jill')): white, formal double.
'Yuletide' ('Mrs. Chas. Vylsteke' × 'Miss Cottage Garden'): vivid red, early.

LEWIS HYBRIDS

Developed by Donald Lewis of Lewis Gardens, Whittier, California, U.S.A., starting in the 1950's. Most of the plants are Belgian hybrids, patented (PP) and for greenhouse forcing. Hardiness zones 8b–10a, not tried outdoors in cooler areas. Upright habit 3 to 5 feet.

'Ablaze' ('Miss Cottage Garden' × 'Firelight'; PP 2312): strong purplish red 63A, semidouble, hose-in-hose, slightly ruffled. 2¾–3¼", early to late season.

'Apple Blossom Time' ('Pink Pearl' B. I. × 'L. J. Bobbink'; (BI Belgium Indian) PP 2307): deep purplish pink edge to lighter center, semidouble, hose-in-hose, 2", multiple bloom clusters.

'Coral Delight' ('Brillianta Belgica' × 'Mme. Pericat'; PP 2305): strong pink to lighter center, semidouble, hose-in-hose, slightly ruffled, 2½–3¼".

'Irresistible' ('Pink Pearl' × 'L. J. Bobbink'; PP 2311): deep purplish pink, semidouble, hose-in-hose, ruffled, 2½".

'Linda Lewis' (parentage unknown): deep pink, with irregular stripes of red occasionally sports solid red, ruffled, hose-in-hose, sometimes with semidouble center, 2–2½".

'Pink Enchantress' ('Sweet Sixteen' × 'Mme. Pericat'; PP 2310): light purplish pink, semidouble, hose-in-hose, 3".

'Pink Frosting' ('Brillianta Belgica' × 'Mme. Pericat'; PP 2309): moderate purplish pink, usually shading to lighter center, appears frosted, semidouble, 2½".

'Red Beauty' ('Chimes' × 'Triumph'; PP 2308) (syn. 'Better Times'): purplish red, semidouble, hose-in-hose, slightly ruffled, 3½–5¼".

'Red Satin' ('Ernest Eeckhaut' × 'Julius Roehrs'; PP 2782): vivid red, double, hose-in-hose, tufted center, 3–3½".

'Ruffled Bergmann' (sport of 'Dr. Bergmann'; PP 2781): light to moderate pink, semidouble, ruffled, 6 petals, 3".

'Sunrise' ('Dr. Bergmann' × unknown; PP 2432): deep purplish pink, semidouble, tufted center, 2", multiple bloom clusters.

'Yum Yum' ('Brillianta Belgica' × 'Mme. Pericat'; PP 2306): vivid pink, shading to white center with pink dots, narrow red margin, semidouble, hose-in-hose, wavy margins, 2½–3¼"; vigorous growth.

MOSSHOLDER—BRISTOW HYBRIDS

This Hybrid line was developed by Owen R. Bristow of San Bernardino, California, U.S.A., and introduced by Mossholder Nursery of Costa Mesa, California, in the 1950's. They are fourth generation hybrids derived from Belgian Indian Hybrids and Rutherford Hybrids. They were developed for florist forcing azaleas, but are hardy in zone 8, withstanding 10°F. Plants are medium size, height 4–6 ft. Unfortunately, no information on parentage is available, but Belgian Indian azaleas are involved. Often called Gold Cup Azaleas.

'Baby Jill': purplish pink, darker veining, semidouble, hose-in-hose, frilled, 3–3½", PP 1706.

'Caprice' (sport of 'Easter Parade'): white bordered vivid yellowish pink, semidouble, hose-in-hose, ruffled margins, 3½".

'Cha Cha' (sport of 'Baby Jill'): white with purplish red frilled margins, semidouble, hose-in-hose, 3–3½".

'Desert Rose': strong pink, lighter throat, and red flecks, frilled, 3½–4", PP 1701.

'Easter Bonnet': purplish pink, white throat, and greenish flecks, frilled, 3", PP 1703.

'Easter Parade': light pink with white marbling, semidouble, hose-in-hose, wavy, 3½", PP 1707.

'Princess Caroline': light yellowish pink, contrasting reddish brown speckling and throat markings, hose-in-hose, ruffled, 3", PP 1702.

'Red Cap': vivid red, hose-in-hose, 2–2½", PP 2315.

'Rose Parade': light pink, double, frilled, 2½–3", PP 1705.

'Sun Valley': white, hose-in-hose, wavy, 2½–3", PP 1708.

'White Orchids': white, with upper half of petals flecked red, semidouble, frilled, 3", PP 1704.

WHITEWATER HYBRIDS

This series was developed by Henry Motzkau in 1943 in Wisconsin, U.S.A., primarily for greenhouse forcing. He has retired three times in Arkansas, Oregon, and recently in Washington, but is still hybridizing. Most are patented by Yoder Bros. of Cleveland, Ohio and Florida. Some are hardy in zone 8. Information on parentage is not available but Belgian Indian Hybrids are involved. Medium size shrubs 4–6'.

'Chickadee': moderate pink, lighter throat, semidouble, ruffled, hose-in-hose.

'Heirloom': purplish pink, double, hose-in-hose,
'Kingfisher': deep pink, hose-in-hose, ruffled, 4".
'Kiwi': deep pink, hose-in-hose.
'Meadowlark': deep pink, semidouble, hose-in-hose, 2½–3".
'Prize': deep pink, semidouble; PP 3795.
'Red Hawk': reddish orange, semidouble, hose-in-hose, 3".
'Rentschler's Rose': purplish pink, semidouble, hose-in-hose.
'Roadrunner': deep pink to red, hose-in-hose.
'Skylark': deep pink, hose-in-hose, ruffled.
'Solitaire': deep purplish pink 66C, hose-in-hose, 2½", PP 3171.
'Valentine': vivid reddish orange 57A, hose-in-hose, 2½". Hardy in zone 8, PP 2492.
'Warbler': light pink, semidouble, hose-in-hose.
'Whistler': purplish pink, double.
'White Christmas': white, greenish throat, semidouble, hose-in-hose, star shaped, PP 2495.
'Whitewater': white, semidouble, hose-in-hose.

SOUTHERN INDIAN HYBRIDS

This hybrid line developed out of the great fondness for Belgian Indian Hybrids which developed in the Deep South of the U. S. A. They were derived from plants purchased by Magnolia Gardens and by Prosper Julius Berckman. Many of these azaleas proved not only hardy but also superior cultivars in this area. They with their sports became known as the Southern Indian Hybrids.

The Reverend John G. Drayton inherited Magnolia Gardens, or Magnolia-on-the-Ashley, in 1840. About 1848 he planted azaleas and camellias that became important to this and other southern gardens. The plants probably came from the David Landreth's Nursery, Philadelphia, 1787, branch store in Charleston, South Carolina.

Mr. P. J. Berckman, a Belgian, established a nursery (Fruitland) about 1856 in Augusta, Georgia. Mr. Berckman was a distinguished horticulturist and introduced many unusual plants. He also played an important role in the development of the Southern Indian Hybrids in the Southeast. It is often said that without Mr. Berckman's interest, azaleas would have made little impression on the gardens of America.

By 1870 Magnolia Gardens had obtained two groups of Belgian Indian Hybrids, totaling some 230 species and clones. Unfortunately, few of the original names survive, but among those that do are 'A. Borsig', 'Ceres', 'Charles Encke', 'Criterion', 'Duke of Wellington', 'Fielder's White', 'Flag of Truce', 'Formosa', 'Glory of Sunninghill', 'Louise Margottin', 'Mme. Dominique Vervaene', 'Phoenicea', 'Praestantissima', and 'Vittata'.

Some of the early acquisitions such as 'President Claeys' and 'Triumphe de Ledeberg' do not conform to the plant descriptions in the *Tuinbouw Encyclopedia* and may be color sports under the original name. Other old standard clones of the Southern Indian Hybrids of Belgian and English origin prior to 1870 are 'Brilliantiana', 'Coccinea Major', 'Eulalie Van Geert', 'Iveryana', 'Marie Louise', 'Miltonia', 'Pluto', 'Prince of Orange', 'Venus', 'Violacea' and 'William Bull'. There is some duplication of names as 'Lawsal' ('Pride of Summerville', 'Daphne Salmon'), 'Elegans Superba' ('Pride of Mobile'), 'Cavendishii' ('Cavendishiana', 'Lady Cavendish').

The Southern Indian Hybrids are not all hybrids, but reflect the parentage of the earlier Belgian Hybrids and the species included in the early acquisitions at Magnolia Gardens and Fruitland Nursery, such as 'Indica Alba'; 'Mucronatum Narcissiflora', a double form of Mucronatum; *R. indicum* ('Macrantha', *A. danielsiana, A. lateritia, A. indica* var. *variegata*); 'Amoenum' and 'Album' ('Ramentacca') 'Obtusum' forms; *R. simsii,* and various forms of 'Villata', 'Villata Fortunei', 'Coccinea', 'Phoeniceum'.

P. J. Berckmans' Spring Catalogue. 19

AZALEA INDICA.

These beautiful early spring flowering shrubs are perfectly hardy in this latitude; they succeed best in a shady situation and in a light soil, containing an abundance of leaf mould. Few plants are more desirable for the decoration of conservatories or for blooming in rooms. When pot grown plants are through their period of blooming, plunge the pots in the ground in a shady situation. The beauty of this plant is only realized when planted in masses in open ground.

PRICES OF PLANTS.

2 years, with flower buds, 25c.
3 and 4 years, very strong and well set with buds, 50c. to $1 each.
12 Plants, our selection of varieties, 2 years, $2 50; 3 and 4 years, $5.

The following are the most distinct out of our collection of upwards of one hundred varieties. Amateurs desiring a larger selection can be supplied with some fifty additional varieties:

ADMIRATION—White, striped carmine.
ALBA MACULATA—White.
ALBA ILLUSTRIS—White, semi-double.
AMŒNA—Purple, double, small flowers, early.
BARON DE ROTHSCHILD—Rosy lilac, striped.
BRILLIANT—Vivid scarlet.
BIANCA—White.
BROUGHTONII—White, rose striped.
CRITERION—White, striped salmon.
CARMINOSA—Carmine.
CRYSTALLINA—Rose.
COLUMBIA—White, variegated.
COCCINEA MAJOR—Scarlet, late.
COLORIS NOVA—Vivid crimson.
COMTE DE THOLL—Scarlet, large.
DUKE OF WELLINGTON—Bright red.
EULALIE VAN GEERT—Carmine.
" " Variegated; var. leaves.
FORMOSA—Lilac pink, large.
INDICA ALBA—White.
IVERYANA—White, striped rose.
LATERITA SUPERBA—Scarlet, late.
LATERITA ALBA SUPREMA—White, late.
MR. LEROY—White, striped lilac.
MARIE LOUISE—Salmon rose.
MARIE VERVAENE—White, variegated.
OBTUSA—Scarlet, small, early.
OSBOURNII—Scarlet rose, late.
PHŒNICEA—Lilac pink, large, early.
PRÆSTANTISSIMA—Brilliant crimson.
PRINCE OF WALES—Rosy carmine.
PROF. LEMOINE—White, striped red.
PRIDE OF DORKING—Bright carmine.
QUEEN VICTORIA—White, variegated.
REINE DES ROSES—Bright rose.
ROSEA PURPUREA—Rosy carmine.
REFULGENS—Fiery scarlet.
SOUVENIR DU PRINCE ALBERT—Double salmon, striped white.
VITATA FORTUNII—White and lilac, early.
WM. BULL—Double scarlet.

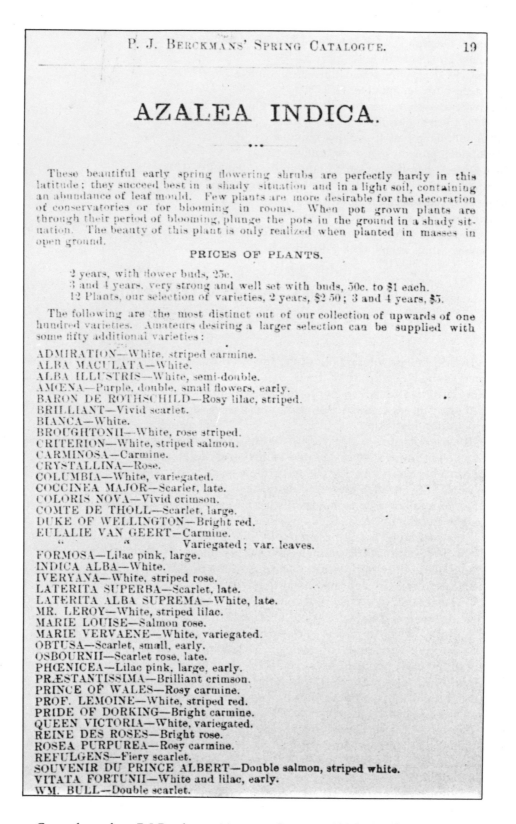

Copy of page from P. J. Berckmans' Augusta, Georgia, 1883 Spring Catalog. Most of the azaleas listed are Southern Indians except for 'Amoena' and 'Obtusa.'

'Janice Monyeen' Carlson Gardens Hybrid. CARLSON

'Thomas Jefferson' Exbury Hybrid. GREER

'Yellow Cloud' Knap Hill Hybrid. HYATT

Plate 42

Ilam Hybrids in Dr. Yeates' Garden, New Zealand. YEATES

'Brickdust' Ilam, CARLSON

'Leilani' Knap Hill Hybrid. BOVEE

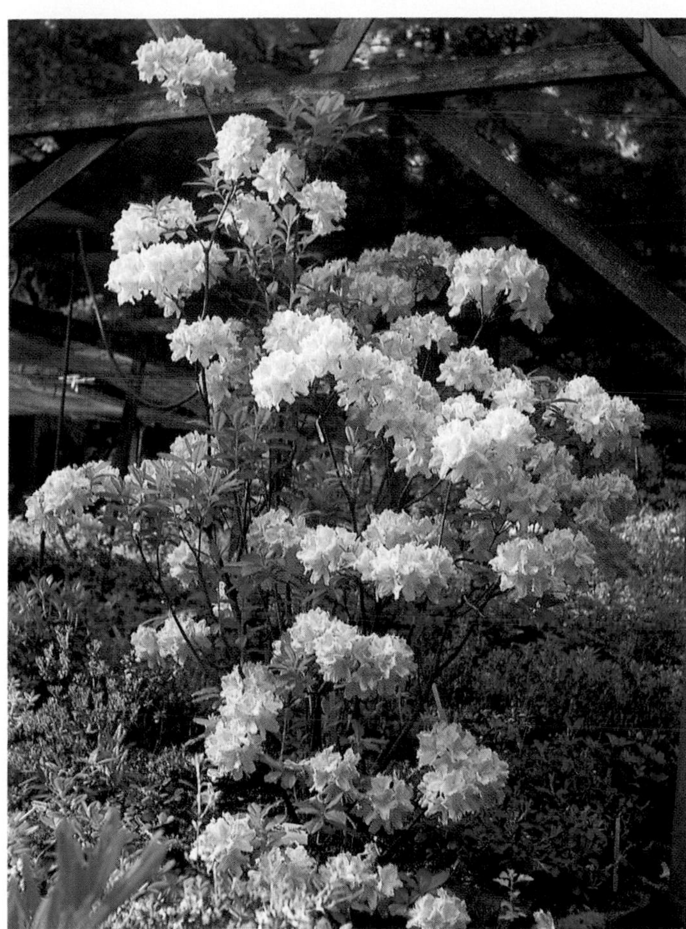

'Sandra Marie' Knap Hill Hybrid. BOVEE

'Moonlight Rose' Girard Hybrid. GIRARD

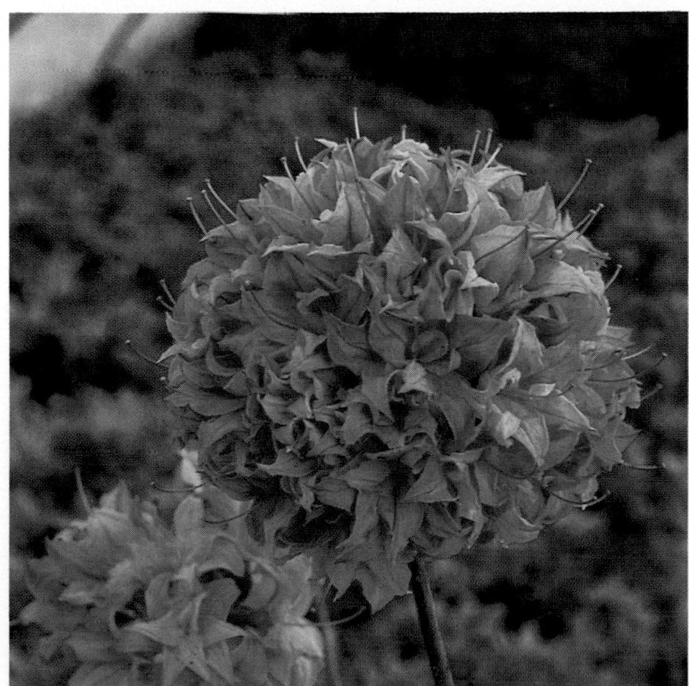

'Pink Delight' Girard Hybrid. GIRARD

'Yellow Pom Pom' Girard Hybrid. GIRARD

Plate 44

'Orange Flash' Girard Hybrid. GIRARD

'Sandra Marie' Knap Hill Hybrid. HYATT

'Yellow Ball' Ilam YEATES

'Girard's Orange Lace' Girard Hybrid. GIRARD

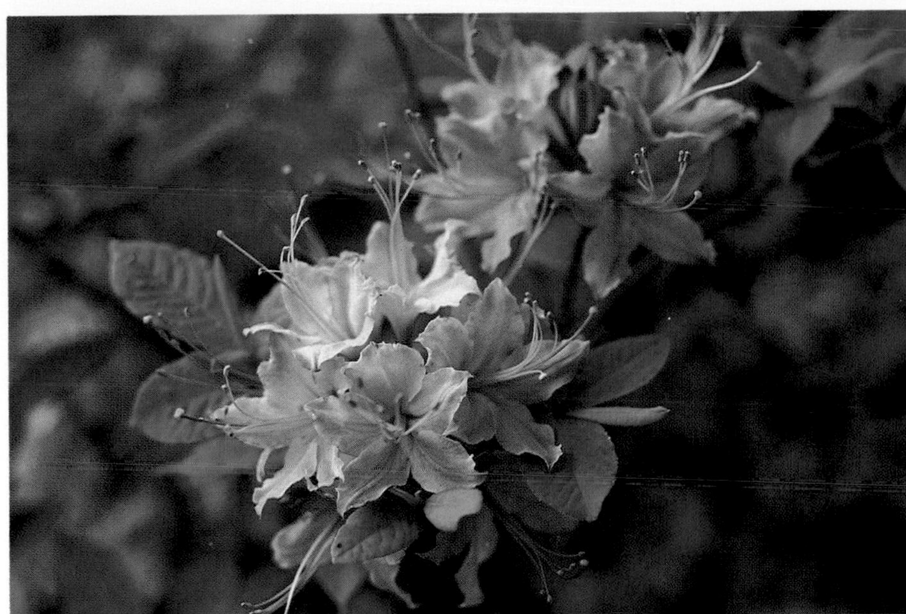

'Chatooga' Beasley Hybrid. BEASLEY

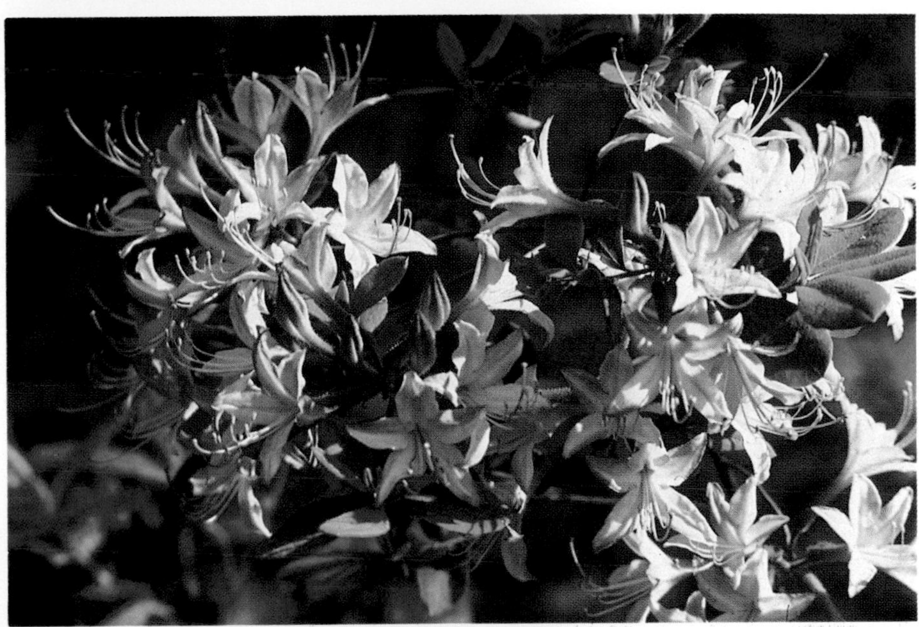

'Marydel' natural selection of *R. atlanticum* × *nudiflorum.* CARLSON

'White Find' *R. vaseyi* selection. GREER

Plate 46

'Chattahoochee' *R. flammeum* hybrid. GALLE

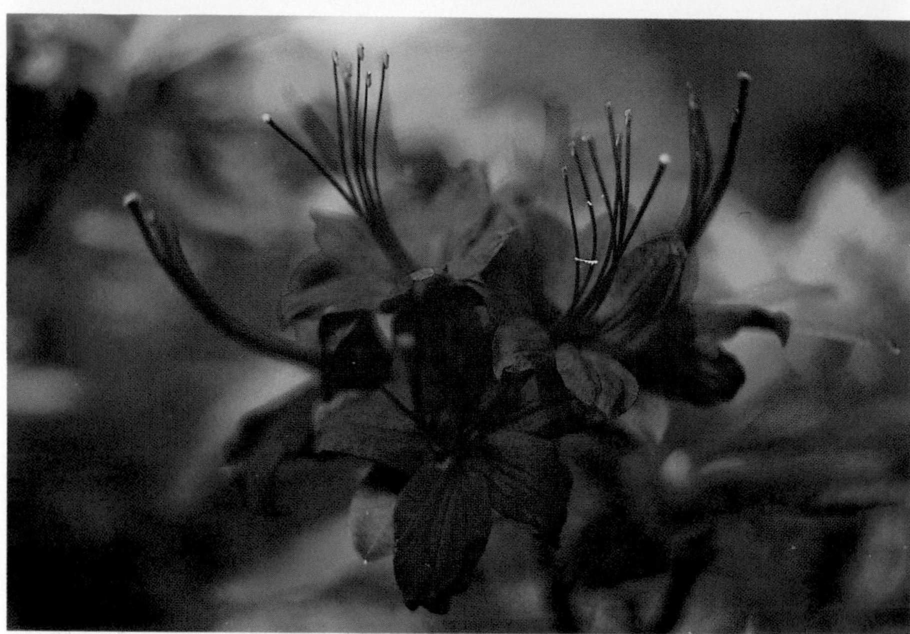

'Yonah Mt.' Beasley Hybrid. BEASLEY

'Richard Bielski' Beasley Hybrid. BEASLEY

'Peaches and Cream' Beasley Hybrid. BEASLEY

'Snowbird' *R. atlanticum* × *canescens* hybrid. GREER

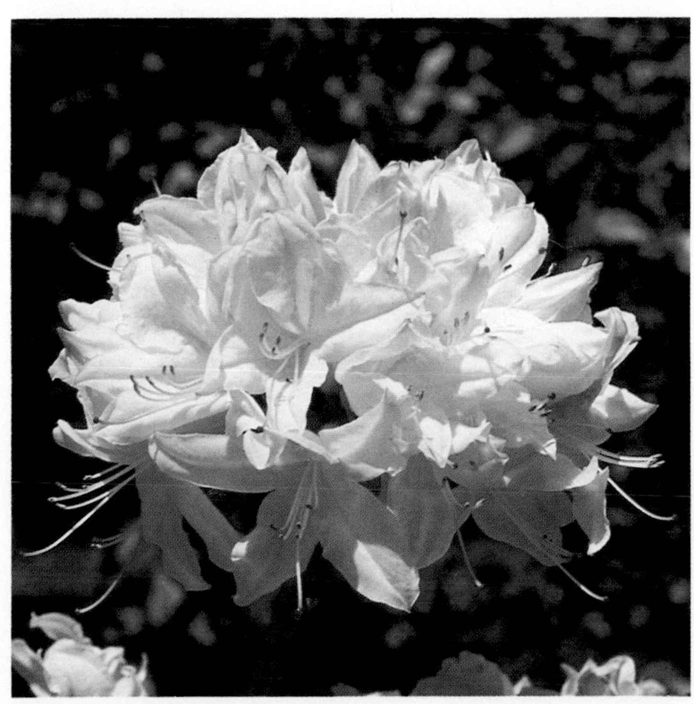

'White Lights' cold resistant hybrid. L MAINQUIST

'Nugget' Beasley Hybrid. BEASLEY

'White Flakes' Galle Hybrid. GALLE

'Precocious' Carlson Luteum Hybrid. CARLSON

'Galle's Choice' Galle Hybrid. GALLE

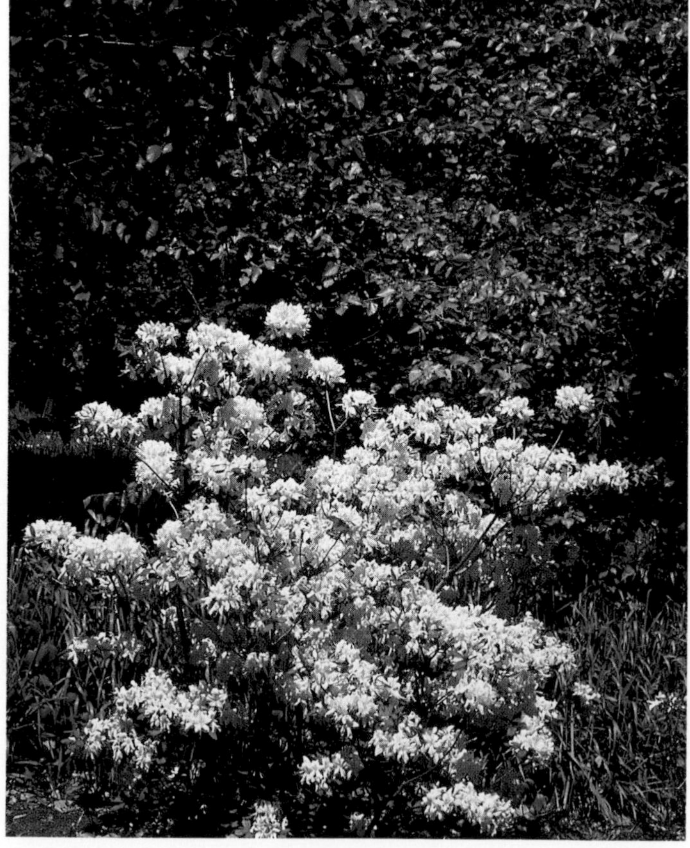

'White Lights' cold resistant hybrid. L MAINQUIST

Thus the Southern Indian Hybrids are a mixed group including forms of the above plants and hybrids of *R. indicum* × *R. simsii* and 'Mucronatum' forms × *R. indicum.*

Based on habit of growth and blooming period, the Southern Indian Hybrids can be divided into two groups. The first, and most common, include the tall, to 8 to 10 feet, more open, faster growing, and earlier blooming plants of which 'Elegans', 'Elegans Superba', 'Fielder's White', 'Formosa', 'George Lindley Taber' and 'President Claeys' are typical. The second group are dense, compact, slow growing, low to medium 6 to 8 feet shrubs, usually late blooming, and showing charateristics of *R. indicum.* This group includes 'Alba Punctata', 'Anthenon', 'Cavendishii', 'Charles Encke', 'Coccinea Major', 'Criterion', 'Duc de Rohan', Duke of Wellington', 'Flag of Truce', 'Glory of Sunninghill' ('Glorisa'), 'Harry Weitch', 'Iveryana', 'Mme. Margottin', 'Modele' ('de Marcq'), 'Miltoni', 'Perfection' ('de Rentz'), 'Pluto', 'Supreme', 'Zeke's Pride', and others.

The flowers of the Southern Indian azaleas are large, from 2 to 3½", mostly single, no hose-in-hose, and a few doubles. Colors range from white through the pinks, reds, and dark purples. Some have stripes and flakes, and bordered flowers which often produce colored selfs showing the influence of the various forms *R. simsii.*

As a group the Southern Indian Hybrids are hardier than the Belgian Hybrids, suitable for zones 8a–10a, and some hardier farther north. The following are generally considered hardier: 'Cavendishi', 'George Lindley Taber', 'Lawsal', 'Mme. Dominique Vervaene', and 'William Bull'.

Most of the newer Southern Indian Hybrids are from sports and will be listed after the old standard varieties. Very little breeding work has been done to improve or develop newer plants of this group. Instead the Southern Indian Hybrids have been used in breeding programs with more cold hardy azaleas to develop larger flowered plants for colder climates.

'A. Borsig' (Mardner, 1865): white, double, late; low.

'Alba Maculata' (syn. 'Alba; probably a form of 'Mucronatum'): white with faint greenish yellow blotch, 3", late midseason; spreading medium height.

'Alba Punctata' (syn. 'Alba Punctulata'; probably a form of *R. indicum*): white flaked reddish purple, 2", late; low spreading. 'Alba Multiflora' is similar.

'Anthenon' (syn. 'Lady Edith'; sport of 'Iveryana'): white with pink throat 2C, light to white margins and darker blotch, 2½", late; low.

'Atropurpurea': vivid reddish purple, thick petals 2½", sepals ⅝"; spreading. Similar to 'Maxwellii'.

'Aurantiaca Superba' (syn. 'Aurantica Splendida'; Knight and Perry, before 1845): vivid red, late; low.

'Brilliantina' (syn. 'Brilliant'; probably a form of *R. indicum*; Vervaene, 1863): deep pink, blotch purplish red, 2¼", late; spreading dense, medium height.

'Catherine Stewart' (Allan, '50): reddish purple, hose-in-hose.

'Cavendishi' (syn. 'Cavendishiana', 'Lady Cavendish'; probably a *R. indicum* × *simsii* hybrid): strong purplish pink, variable, white edges, blotch darker and dark red stripes, 2¾", late; low, dense, spreading. 'Criterion' is similar but late midseason.

'Ceres' (Van der Cruyssen, 1868): pink and white; low.

'Charles Encke' (Verschaffelt, 1861): strong red, blotch darker; or white margined and red striped, 2".

'Coccinea Major' (probably a form of *R. indicum*): reddish orange, 2½", late; low dense spreading.

'Comtesse Eugenie de Kerckhove': white striped reddish orange.

'Crescent City Pink': dark pink.

'Criterion' ('Exquisite' × 'Iveryana'; Ivery, before 1853): vivid purplish red flush, white edges, darker blotch, and a few dark stripes and flakes, 2¼", some stamens partially petaloid; low dense. Similar to 'Cavendishi'.

'Croemina': light reddish purplish; early midseason; tall.

'Daphne Red': reddish orange, purple spots.

'Daphne Salmon' (syn. 'Lawsal', 'Pride of Summerville'): strong yellowish pink, blotch darker, 2½"; tall, rangy plant.

'Dixie' (probably form of *R. simsii*): dark yellowish pink, blotch purplish red 2½", early; tall upright.

'Dr. Augustin': deep red, blotch darker.

'Du de Rohan' (probably form of *R. indicum*): deep yellowish pink 44D, blotch purplish red, 2¼", early midseason; medium height.

'Duke of Wellington' (probably a *R. indicum* × *simsii* hybrid): reddish orange, blotch purplish red, 3", late; spreading medium height.

'Duke of Windsor': strong reddish orange.

'Early Lavender' (probably 'Mucronatum' × *R. simsii* hybrid): light reddish purplish, 2½", early midseason; tall spreading.

'Elegans' (probably a 'Mucronatum' × *R. simsii* hybrid): light purplish pink, blotch purplish red, 3", early midseason; tall upright.

'Elegans Superba' (commonly called 'Pride of Mobile' or 'Watermelon Pink' in U.S.A.; probably a hybrid of 'Phoeniceum'): strong pink, blotch darker, 2½", midseason; upright tall.

'Eulalie van Geert' (Van Geert, 1854): reddish orange, white margin and red flecks, 2½, early; tall upright.

'Fielder's White' (probably form of 'Mucronatum' but blooms earlier and tenderer): white with faint light greenish yellow blotch, frilled, 2¾", early midseason; spreading, medium height.

'Fisher Pink' (syn. 'Dodd's Pink', 'Perfection'): light pink, midseason.

'Flag of Truce' (Smith, 1861): white, semidouble, frilled, 2", late midseason; medium upright.

'Formosa' (probably a 'Phoeniceum' hybrid): deep purplish red, 74B, blotch darker, 3", midseason; tall, upright.

'Frederick the Great': light reddish orange, late; low.

'George Franc': (probably a *R. simsii* × *indicum* hybrid): strong pink, blotch purplish red, early midseason; medium, spreading.

'George Lindley Taber' (sport of 'Omurasaki', selected by Dr. H. Hume): white flushed light to strong purplish pink, blotch darker, 3½", midseason; medium height.

'Gervin Pink': light pink.

'Glory of Sunninghill' (syn. 'Gloriosa'; probably a *R. indicum* × *simsii* hybrid): vivid red, 2", late; spreading, dense, medium height.

'Gulf Pride' (sport of 'Mucronatum', K. Sawada, '35): light purple, faint blotch of strong purple.

'Harry Veitch': light pink, frilled; low.

'Iveryana' (probably a form of*R. indicum*; Ivery, before 1849): white with deep red flecks or deep red selfs, 3", late; low.

'Judge Solomon' (sport of 'Formosa'): strong purplish red, blotch darker, 2½"; tall. Darker than 'Pride of Mobile'.

'Lawsal': see 'Daphne Salmon'.

'Lilac': light reddish purple.

'Louise Margottin': see 'Mme. Margottin'.

'Magnolia Alba' (syn. 'Magnolia White'; Magnolia Gardens): white, 2½".

'Miltoni' (probably a form of *R. indicum*): vivid purplish red, blotch darker, 2½", very late; low.

'Mme. Dominique Vervaene' (probably a 'Mucronatum' × *R. indicum* hybrid): white flushed yellowish pink 39A, white margins, blotch purplish red, 2¼", late midseason; spreading, medium height. Two plants with same name; other is purplish red or red with purplish red stripes and white margins.

'Mme. Frey': strong yellowish pink, late; medium height.

'Mme. Margottin' (syn. 'Louise Margottin'; probably a form of *R. indicum*, Margottin, 1866): white with occasional flecks and stripes of purplish red, 2¼", late; low, spreading.

'Modele' (syn. 'Modele de Marcq'; Marcq, 1857): deep purplish pink.

'Moss Point Late Salmon': deep yellowish pink.

'Mrs. Frederick Sanders' (syn. 'Fred Sanders'): yellowish pink, double.

'Mrs. G. G. Gerbing' (sport of 'George Lindsey Taber'): white, 3½".

'Mrs. P. F. Smith' (Allan, '52): white flushed light purple.

'Mrs. Walker': pink.

'New White': white, 2¼". Similar to 'Fielders White' but smaller flowers.

'Nora Lee': deep yellowish pink; low.

'Omurasaki' (syn. 'O-Omurasaki', *R. phoeniceum* var. *calycinum; R. scabrum* × 'Mucronatum' hybrid, Japan; intro. as form of 'Phoeniceum' by Beattie '29, PI 276290): deep purplish red with darker blotch, rounded lobes, 3½". Very similar to 'Formosa' but darker and not as rank in growth.

'Orchid': light purplish pink.

'Pax' (Steyaert, '26): white with occasional red stripes, semidouble.

'Perfection' (syn. 'Perfection de Rentz'; probably a *R. simsii* × *indicum* hybrid): white with faint light greenish yellow blotch, 2½", late midseason; spreading, medium height.

'Pluto' (probably a form of *R. indicum;* Schultz): reddish orange, blotch darker, 2½", late; spreading, medium height, PP 3247.

'Praestantissima' (probably a hybrid of 'Phoeniceum'): strong purplish red, blotch darker, 2½", late; upright, medium height.

'President' (Kinghorn, 1861): deep yellowish pink, darker throat, early midseason; medium height.

'President Claeys' (syn. 'President Clay'; probably a *R. indicum* × *simsii* hybrid): strong red 52A, darker blotch, 2¼", early midseason; tall upright.

'Pride of Dorking': deep pink, late; medium height.

'Pride of Kingstreet' (Allan, '52): pink.

'Pride of Mobile' (popular name for 'Elegans Superba', syn. 'Watermelon'; probably a 'Phoeniceum' hybrid): strong pink, blotch darker, 2½", midseason; tall upright.
'Pride of Orange': deep orange, blotch purplish red, ruffled 2½", late; low.
'Pride of Orangeburg' (Allan, '52): reddish orange; original plant at Edisto Garden, Orangeburg, South Carolina.
'Prince of Orange' (probably a *R. simsii* × *indicum* hybrid): reddish orange, 2¼", late midseason; spreading, medium height.
'Prince of Wales': vivid red, early midseason; mediun height.
'Princess Marie Jose' (Haerens & Wille, '10): dark red, semidouble.
'Red Flame': red; tall.
'Rosea Elegans' (Ivery, 1846): light pink, late midseason; medium height.
'Rosea Purpurea': strong reddish purple, late midseason; medium height.
'Sanders Special': red.
'Southern Charm' (sport of 'Formosa'): light pink, blotch darker, 2½". Similar to 'Pride of Mobile'.
'Supreme': white with light greenish yellow throat, late; low, spreading.
'Triomphe de Lederberg' (syn. 'Moss Point Red'; probably a *R. simsii* × *indicum* hybrid, Vervaene, 1863): strong red, blotch deep red, ruffled, late; dense, spreading, medium height.
'Venus': white with pink stripes; low.
'Vicomte de Nieuport': vivid purplish red, 2" early midseason; spreading, lax, medium height.
'Violacea Rubra' (probably a 'Phoeniceum' hybrid): vivid purplish red, 2½", frilled, late midseason; spreading, medium height.
'William Bull' (Verschaffelt, 1862): deep reddish orange 42B, very double, 2", midseason; buds like rosebuds; spreading, medium to tall.
'Wine': deep red, large flowers.
'Zeke's Pride' (probably a *R. simsii* × *indicum* hybrid): deep pink, shaded yellowish pink, blotch purplish red, 2¾", early midseason; tall upright.

SOUTHERN INDIAN HYBRIDS Never Recorded or Introduced Since 1960 (including 'MUCRONATUM' HYBRIDS)

All hardy in zone 8–10; some may be more hardy. Medium to large shrubs 6–8 ft. Unfortunately parentage not available on all cultivars.

'Comanche' ('Phoeniceum' × ?; K. Marsh, Aust. 69): vivid yellowish pink.
'Crinkle Cut' ('Agnes Gault' × 'Mucronatum'; Langdon, '79): white, spotted yellowish green.
'Delaware Valley White' ('Mucronatum' hybrid): white, 2½", hardy to 5°F.
'Dixie Beauty': purple, late.
'Duchess of Cypress' (sport of 'Duc de Rohan'; Peterson and Stabler, intro. by Cypress Gardens): light pink, white streaks, reddish blotch, 2½", early; low, compact, hardy to 5°F.
'Dwarf Formosa' (syn. 'Phoeniceum Lavender' and 'California Formosa'; sport of 'Lavender Formosa'): light purple, 3½"; low, compact.
'Evelyn Hyde' ('Mucronatum' × ?; Hyde '80): strong purplish red 63C, margins slightly darker, blotch spotted darker.
'Florida Beauty' (sport of 'Ruffled Giant'): purplish pink, 4"; leaves variegated; compact.
'Fuchsia' (sport of 'Formosa'; Thompson): deep purplish red, darker blotch, 2½", midseason; hardy 8b–9b.
'Giant Ruffles': deep pink, early; possibly same as 'Ruffled Giant'.
'Gloria' ('Pride of Mobile' × 'Hino Supreme'; Sawada): deep pink, white blotching, early.
'Green Goddess' (pink and white Dbl. × 'Damask Rose'; Harrington 70): white, yellow green blotch, wavy, 3", midseason; 5 ft. in 10 yrs.; hardy to −5°F.
'Helen' ('Sekidera' seedling × 'Purple King'): deep purple, large.
'Highlander' (pink and white dbl. × 'Damask Rose'; Harrington 70): vivid purplish red, darker blotch, wavy, frilled, 3½". midseason; 5 ft. in 10 yrs.; hardy to −5°F.
'Iveryana Royal' (sport of 'Iveryana'): deep purple.
'Iveryana Silver' (sport of 'Iveryana'): white with occasional purple stripes.
'Jennifer' ('Pride of Mobile' seedling; T. Dodd '63): moderate red 50A, 2½", early; 4 × 5' high in 10 yrs.
'Kate Arendall' (Dodd): white, hose-in-hose, ruffled, early.
'Little Giant' (sport of 'Ray's Ruby'): deep purplish red; leaves with reddish cast; hardy in zones 9–10.
'Little John' (second generation sport of 'Ray's Ruby'; G. Jones): reddish purple, 3½", reddish foliage, rose in shade; hardy in zones 9–10.
'Mardi Gras': white, striped purple, 2½".
'Margaret Palmer' ('Phoeniceum' × ?; Marsh, Aust. '64): deep pink, darker throat.
'Min's Choice' ('Agnes Gault' × 'Mucronatum'; Langdon, '79): moderate purplish pink 70D, blotch red spots.

'Moon Maiden' (*simsii* × 'Mucronatum'; Haworth-Booth, U. K. '68): white occasional purple streaks, blotch yellow, 4".
'Mucronatum' (cultivated in Japan for over 300 years., not found in wild; registered '66): white, very pale pink on upper lobe, 2½"; leaves hairy below.
'Mucronatum Pastel' ('Mucronatum' hybrid; Lancaster): pale purple.
'Mucronatum Rosea' ('Mucronatum' hybrid; Lancaster): reddish purple.
'Noordtiana Rosea' (syn. 'Ledifolia Noordtiana'; sport of 'Mucronatum'; P. van Noordt Nur., '04): white, often sports to reddish purple and pink.
'North Carolina Red' ('Mucronatum' hybrid): deep pink.
'North Carolina White' ('Mucronatum' hybrid): white, 2", similar to 'Delaware Valley White'.
'Orange Delight': orange, 4–5", midseason; compact.
'Orange Flair' (possibly a 'Mayo Hybrid'): reddish orange, 2½".
'Orange Pride of Dorking' (sport of 'Pride of Dorking'): moderate red, late, midseason, 2½".
'Phyllis Marsh' ('Phoeniceum' × ?; Marsh, Aust. '69): light purple.
'Pierre Du Pont' (Longwood Gardens '62): white, yellowish green spotting, fading greenish.
'Pink Champagne' ('Ruffled Giant' × 'Rosebud'; Thompson): deep purplish pink 73A, blotch purplish red 71A, double 2½", late; hardy in zones 7a to 9b.
'Pink Formosa': pink; tall.
'Pink Lace' (sport of 'Duc de Rohan'; Milfeld; PP 2757, '66): light pink with moderate red blotch, variegated white edge, 2¼–2½"; branches vigorously.
'Pride of Brunswick': red, 4", late; spreading habit.
'Pride of Orlando' (Meridith): white; zone 9.
'Pride of Prichard' (syn. 'Opal's Pride'; Petry): purplish pink, frilled, hose-in-hose, 2¾".
'Primitive Beauty' (seedling; Dobb '84): white, 5 separate individual petals, 2 × ½" wide, 3–5 in truss, early; hardy to 0°F.
'Purple George Taber' (sport of 'George Lindley Taber'): strong reddish purple blotch.
'Purple Queen' (Petry): vivid purplish red, hose-in-hose, 2½".
'Purple Supreme' (Petry): vivid purplish red, hose-in-hose, 1½"; low.
'Purple Taber' (origin unknown): light purple; variegated leaves with pale yellowish white margin.
'Ray's Rubra' (sport of 'Formosa'): deep purplish red 61A.
'Red Formosa' (sport of 'Formosa'): reddish purple, 3".
'Red Ribbons' ('Giant Ruffles' × 'Pride of Prichard'; E. Aromi '81): vivid purplish red 58B, blotch deep red 53A, semidouble, hose-in-hose, 3½", early to midseason; 52 × 48" tall in 10 yrs.
'Red Ruffles': red, hose-in-hose.
'Red Ruffles Variegated' (sport of 'Red Ruffles'; Nuccio): leaves variegated, pale white margin.
'Reverie': deep pink, midseason; upright habit.
'Robin Hood' (sport of 'Formosa'): reddish purple, 3"; leaves with reddish blotches and variegations.
'Rosea' (Orchard Nur.): deep pink, semidouble.
'Rosemary Hyde' ('Maxwellii' × 'Sir William Lawrence'; Hyde): pink.
'Ruffles' ('Mucronatum' hybrid; Lancaster): deep purple, frilled.
'Shipley' ('California Sunset' × 'Gloria'; Aromi, '81): moderate purplish pink 63B, blotch purplish red 61A, hose-in-hose, 2¼", 3 × 3 ft. in 10 yrs.
'Silver Wings' ('Mucronatum' hybrid; Lancaster): white.
'Snow Hill' (*wadai* × 'Mucronatum'; Crown Est. Comm., U. K. '74): white with green eye.
'Snow Queen' (Bobbink and Atkins; PP 147, '30): white, blotch yellow green, hose-in-hose.
'Southern Belle' (sport of 'Pink Ruffles'; Mitchell '80, PP): strong purplish pink, darker blotch, hose-in-hose, 2½"; leaves variegated, fine whitish margin; hardy zone 7a–9.
'Southern Charm Variegated' (sport of 'Southern Charm'; Milfeld): pink; leaves variegated, with numerous small yellowish spots.
'Thompson Rosea' ('Ruffled Giant' × 'Rosebud'; Thompson): strong purplish red, double, 25 petals, 2½", late; hardy zones 7a–9b.
'Variegated Ruffled Giant' (sport of 'Ruffled Giant'; Boling): deep pink, 2½–3"; distorted leaves, with pale yellow margin. keep in shade.
'Watermelon Red': deep pink, early.
'West's Superba' (dbl. red greenhouse var. × 'Dragon'; West): light pink, darker pink on reverse side, rounded, 2¼", slight blotch; compact, 24 × 18" high in 10 yrs.
'White April': white, late midseason; upright habit.
'White Grandeur': white double, midseason.
'White Lace' (sport of 'Pink Lace'; Milfeld, PP 2994): white with pale green throat, 2¼–2½"; vigorous habit.
'White Swan': white, greenish throat, 2½", early.
'Winterset' ('Mucronatum' seedling; Grothaus, intro. by Brockenbrough '71): light pink 55D, light yellow green blotch.
'Winterthur' (sport of 'Mucronatum Magnifica'; du Pont): light purple, 2½", late midseason, fragrant.

KURUME HYBRID AZALEAS

Kurume, an industrial/agricultural inland city on the Island of Kyushu, is the home of this large group of azaleas. Accounts of the origin of the Kurume hybrid are given by E. H. Wilson in his book, *Plant Hunting,* Vol. II and *A Monograph of Azaleas* by Wilson, E. H. and A. Rehder. Mr. Motozo Sakamoto, a Japanese samurai, is regarded as the originator of these hybrids in the 19th century. The parent stock was reportedly collected by the sacred Mt. Kirishima, whether collected by or given to Mr. Sakamoto is not certain. He cultivated several forms and raised seedlings including 'Azuma Kagami' (syn. 'Pink Pearl') from which it is claimed all the pink color forms have descended. Mr. Sakamoto had difficulty in germinating seeds and observed they were growing naturally in moss beneath parent plants. Thus, he discovered the method of germinating seeds on moss. After his death, Sakamoto's collection was passed on into the hands of Kojiro Akashi, a nurseryman in Kurume.

However, there are reports that the breeding of Kurume Hybrids began over 300 years ago, and by 1860 there were 15 varieties of *R.* × *obtusum* listed in Japan. Recent Japanese research indicates that the number of Kurume Hybrid cultivars reached 700 in the past 200 years of which about 300 cultivars survive today. Kirishima Tsutsuji was the name used for centuries for this plant grown in Japanese gardens. The origin and ancestral background of these beautiful plants has been of interest to both American and Japanese horticulturists for many years but we may never know the true story.

In 1844 Robert Fortune collected the Kirishima Azalea, *R.* × *obtusum* and several forms in gardens from Shanghai, China. There is no doubt that the original plants came from Japan. *A. obtusa* Lindley was the species name given to these gardens forms collected by Fortune. Since these plants were garden forms and not collected in the wild, the plants should be named as clones of *R.* × *obtusum* and not a single wild species.

E. H. Wilson, on his visit to Kurume in 1918, climbed the Kirishima Mountains, but did not find the typical Kirishima Azalea. He found what he considered a form of it with flowers of numerous colors which he named *R. obtusum* f. *japonicum*. The Kaempfer Azalea was also found at the base of the mountains, so Wilson concluded that the Kurume Hybrid Azaleas were all derivatives of *R. obtusum* f. *japonicum* and that the Kaempfer Azalea was only a variety of *R. obtusum* var. *kaempferi*.

Interest and curiosity about the Kurume Hybrids continued; and in 1924 J. G. Millais of England in his book *Rhododendrons Second Series* made this prophetic comment: "It seems difficult to understand, however, how such diverse plants as *R. kaempferi, R. obtusum, R. amoenum,* and all the hose-in-hose varieties came from an original stock found wild on Mt. Kirishima without some crossing or other species and hybrids and of whose history we are unacquainted."

There is little doubt that the original Kurume Hybrids were derived from the evergreen azalea species of the southern part of the island of Kyushu. John Creech made extensive exploration trips in Japan in 1955, 1956, 1961, and again in 1978 and 1980, retracing Wilson's steps and in other areas, investigating extensively the azalea species on Kysuhu. He concluded, as had many Japanese botanists, that the Kurume Hybrids were not derived solely from Wilson's *R. obtusum* f. *japonicum.*

Involved in the story are three mountains near the city of Kogashima: Sakurajima, an active volcano; Takatoge, a mountain on Osumi penninsula; and Kirishima, a group of high volcanic cones famous for their hot springs. The three species found on these mountains that are of special significance in the development of the Kurume Hybrid Azaleas are *R. kaempferi (R. obtusum* var. *kaempferi), R. kiusianum (R. obtusum* f. *japonicum),* and *R. sataense,* the Sata Azalea. *R. sataense* is a relatively new species, unknown to Wilson and included in Ohwi's *Flora of Japan* (1965) under *R. kiusianum.*

On Sakurajima (3189 ft.) the active volcanic mountain, the Kaempfer Azalea is the most prevalent species distinguished by its habit of growth and orange-red flowers, up to two inches. A swarm of azaleas closely resembling the Kurume Hybrid Azalea in flower color and plant habit also grows here. There is also an azalea with lavender flowers similar to *R. kaempferi*. Some Japanese botanists refer to this as *R.* × *obtusum*, but the status of this plant is still in question. Japanese horticulturists suggest that the majority of azaleas on Sakurajima are hybrids between this azalea and *R. kaempferi*. No azaleas similar to *R. kiusianum* are found, and unfortunately no one will probably ever know if it or another azalea was once growing on top of Sakurajima since it is now covered with fresh lava rock.

In the Kirishima Mountains (5600 ft.) the Kaempfer Azalea grows from sea level to approximately 2600 ft. At higher elevations, 4,000 ft. and above, the Kyushu Azalea, *R. kiusianum*, with its small semi-evergreen and small purplish pink flowers, is found in alpine settings above timberline, such as Oonami-dake.

When *R. kiusianum* hybridizes with *R. kaempferi* at lower elevations, a complex array of plants is formed with pink, scarlet, crimson and purple flowers together with variations in foliage. It is this group of hybrids that are mentioned in older literature in the development of the Kurume Hybrid Azaleas. It should be pointed out that *R. kaempferi* flowers through May while *R. kiusianum* does not bloom at high elevations until June.

On Takatuge (4078 ft.) the Kaempfer Azalea grows from sea level to about 1600 ft. Above it, at higher elevations, *R. sataense* appears in open areas with a dense mound-like habit, flowers ranging from pink to purple as found in the Kurume Hybrids, and with overlapping petals. The elliptic to ovate shiny leaves are flat to convex. The leaves are usually larger than leaves of *R. kiusianum* and smaller than the oblong to ovate leaves of *R. kaempferi*. This relatively new species more nearly approximates the cultivated Kurume Hybrids than does *R. kaempferi* and *R. kiusianum* or their hybrids.

Thus, the ancestral species of the Kurume Hybrids is now thought to be more closely allied to *R. sataense* and its hybrids possibly crossed with the natural hybrids from the other two mountains. It is questionable if *R. kaempferi*, as we know it today, has any role in the Kurume Hybrid line. Rather they were probably crosses of *R. sataense* and *R. kiusianum* with the emphasis on *R. sataense* all along the way. Dr. Kenichi Arisumi from the University of Kagoshima in Japan has been working on the relationship of the flower colors of *R. kiusianum*, *R. kaempferi*, and *R. sataense*. In a personal communication received in 1983, he points out the importance of *R. sataense* in the development of the Kurume Hybrids.

Now back to the history of the introduction of the Kurume Hybrids. By 1918 when Wilson visited Mr. Akashi to see his Kurume Hybrids, Japanese experts recognized 250 cultivars. Wilson first became acquainted with Kurume Hybrids in 1914 and 1917, when he visited Yokohama Nursery Company which trained azaleas in an umbrella shape in a full range of colors. The Yokohama Nursery first listed these plants in their English language catalog as *Azalea indicum*; but in 1912 changed it to *Azalea indicum* Kurume, and in 1918 to *Azalea obtusum* Kurume. In 1916 at Wilson's suggestion, John S. Ames of North Easton, Massachusetts, procured a number of small azaleas from the Yokohama Nursery Company.

In 1915 Mr. Akashi of Kurume, Japan, received a gold medal for an exhibit of 12 Kurume cultivars consisting of 31 plants at the Panama Pacific Exposition in San Francisco. Following the Exposition, some of the plants were purchased by the Domoto Brothers Nurserymen of Hayward, California. The elder Toichi Domoto's father visited Japan in 1917 and obtained exclusive rights to propagate and sell Kurume Hybrids in the United States, and they imported large numbers of plants in the succeeding years. Many of the plants imported by the Domoto Brothers were sold to Cottage Gardens on Long Island and by them to Bobbink and Atkins in New Jersey. The Domotos also sold azaleas to the old Henry A. Dreer Company of Riverton, New Jersey, and some found their way to Henry F. du Pont of Winterthur, Delaware. The last importation by the Domotos, 5,000 plants of 25 cultivars in 1920, arrived after the U.S.D.A. plant quarantine regulations came into effect. Only bare root specimens were permitted to enter. A good portion of this last shipment was lost. The intensive domestic propagation of cultivars previously imported nearly stopped further imports from Japan.

Henry Dreer, with the agreement of Bobbink and Atkins and Cottage Gardens, substituted English names (not translations) for the Japanese names of the Domoto Introductions. The records relating the Japanese names to the English have been lost.

Prior to the general introduction of Kurume Hybrid, several clones were being grown in England and Holland, from which they were exported to the United States. They were probably imported by Dutch nurserymen from the Yokohama Nursery Company. There were 'Hinode Giri', 'Hinomayo', 'Yage Giri' and 'Benigiri'.

WILSON'S FIFTY

The Kurume Hybrids became widely known in the West through the popular and enthusiastic writings of Ernest H. Wilson. His assessments are as enticing now as they were then: "The Kurume Azaleas are the loveliest of all azaleas. The colors are so pure and exquisite and of every hue and shade from white, pink, and salmon to scarlet, crimson and the richest of magenta. They are extremely floriferous and in season the blossoms often completely hide the leaves."

In 1917 a small group of Kurumes were obtained by Wilson from the Oishi Gardens at Hatageya, north of Tokyo, and sent to John S. Ames of North Easton, Massachusetts. Following his visit with Mr. Akashi in Kurume in 1918, Wilson selected 50 cultivars in duplicate of the Kurume Hybrids. The shipment safely reached the Arnold Arboretum in 1919. Thus, a complete range of these beautiful azaleas became known in the Western World. Wilson gave English names to his Fifty Kurumes that are not translations from the Japanese but coined by him. See Wilson's Fifty, p. 174. Unfortunately, many of the Wilson's Fifty are very uncommon in gardens today, and it is doubtful if a complete set of his introductions is available in this country. Many of the Kurume varieties introduced by the Domoto Brothers are more widely known and grown than are the Wilson's.

The Kurume Hybrids were first grown as greenhouse and potted plants in Boston, New York, and Philadelphia then gradually tried outdoors. They soon became popular landscape plants and are the best known azalea group.

In 1929 R. K. Beattie, while traveling in the orient for the U.S. Department of Agriculture, introduced from Japan numerous azalea clones for the Plant Introduction Section. Beattie brought in 127 azaleas; 60 were Kurumes, 49 were new clones, while 11 were collected previously by Wilson or Domoto. The seven other azaleas were hybrids of other species. Many of the Beattie azaleas are very good but unfortunately are unknown and overlooked. His Kurume introductions and their P.I. numbers will be included in the descriptive list of the older Kurumes.

Before 1938, J. B. Stevenson of England introduced, from Yokohama Nurseries and K. Wada of Japan, a group of Kurume Hybrids to England. Many of these plants were grown by the now defunct Sunningdale Nursery, Surrey, England, and are no longer available. A collection of many of these is maintained by James Russell at Castle Howard Estates, York, England. Many of the Kurumes suffer winter damage in England apparently from improper hardening off in the fall. Hardy forms are grown in Europe and used in breeding with Kaempferi and other hybrids to develop hardier strains.

KURUME HYBRIDS

The Kurume Hybrids, while often described as dwarf azaleas, are upright medium to tall shrubs, 6 to 12 ft. at maturity, and usually dense and shapely plants. They bloom early or early midseason. Flowers are mostly single with some hose-in-hose, ranging from ½ to 1½" wide and a full range of colors from pink, red, purple and white, and occasional striped or flecked flowers.

A description of the older Kurumes introduced by Domoto Brothers, Wilson, Beattie, Stevenson and other follows.

DOMOTO INTRODUCTIONS

English names were given to many of the Domoto introductions by H. Dreer and are among the best known Kurumes. Many of the same Kurume varieties were introduced by E. H. Wilson in 1917 and 1918.

'Admiration'
'Akebono'
'Appleblossom' (syn. 'Ho o')
'Apricot'
'Avalanche'
'Ayagoromo'
'Azuma Kagami' (syn. 'Pink Pearl')
'Bouquet Rose'
'Bridesmaid'
'Brilliant'
'Cattleya'
'Cheerfulness'
'Cherryblossom' (syn. 'Takasago')
'Chiyono Akebono'
'Christmas Cheer' (syn. 'Imashojo')
'Daphne'
'Debutante'
'Delicatissima'
'Exquisite'
'Fairy'
'Flame' (syn. 'Suetsumu')
'Flamingo' (syn. 'Tama no Utena')
'Fudestesan'
'Gosho Sakura' (syn. 'Vanity')
'Gunecho'
'Hagoromo'
'Hanaikada'
'Hortensia'
'Iwato Kagami'
'Kasumi Gaseki' (syn. 'Elf')
'Kiono Kami'
'Kirin' (syn. 'Daybreak', 'Coral Bells')
'Kumo no Homare'
'Kurenosuki'
'Lavender Queen'
'Mauve Beauty'
'Miyagino'
'Morning Glow'
'Mountain Laurel'
'Nani Wagata' (syn. 'Painted Lady')
'Oimatsu'
'Orange Beauty' (syn. 'Tsutamomiji')
'Peach Blossom' (syn. 'Saotome')
'Rose'
'Sakura Tsukasa' (syn. 'All-a-glow')
'Salmon Beauty'
'Shojyo'
'Snow'
'Sun Star'
'Terukimi'
'Ummu'
'Vesuvius'
'Wuchiwa Kasane'
'Yaehime'

WILSON'S FIFTY

'Agemaki' (No. 41, 'Jose')
'Aioi' (No. 43, 'Fairy Queen')
'Asa Gasumi' (No. 14, 'Rosy Morn')
'Aya Kammuri' (No. 19, 'Pinkie')
'Azuma Kagami' (No. 16, 'Pink Pearl')*
'Benifude' (No. 30, 'Sunbeam')
'Bijinsui' (No. 13, 'Little Imp')
'Fudesute Yama' (No. 35, 'Poppy')
'Gosho Zakura' (No. 46, 'Vanity')
'Hachika Tsugi' (No. 7, 'Prudence')
'Hana Asobi' (No. 50, 'Sultan')
'Hinode Giri' (No. 42, 'Red Hussar')
'Hinode no Taka' (No. 48, 'Ruby')
'Ho o' (No. 9, 'Apple Blossom')
'Ima Shojo' (No. 36, 'Fascination')
'Iro Hayama' (No. 8, 'Dainty')
'Kasane Kagaribi' (No. 32, 'Rosita')
'Kasumi Gaseki' (No. 12, 'Elf')
'Katsura no Hana' (No. 27, 'Ruth')
'Kimigayo' (No. 15, 'Cherub')
'Kirin' (No. 22, 'Daybreak')*
'Kiritsubo' (No. 24, 'Twilight')
'Kumo no Ito' (syn. 'Suga no Ito'; No. 31, 'Betty')
'Kumo no Uye' (No. 28, 'Salmon Prince')*
'Kurai no Himo' (No. 40, 'Carmine Queen')*
'Kureno Yuki' (No. 2, 'Snowflake')*
'Nani Wagata' (No. 5, 'Painted Lady')
'Oino Mezame' (No. 25, 'Melody')
'Omoine' (No. 26, 'Dame Lavender')
'Osaraku' (No. 17, 'Penelope')
'Osaraku' seedling (No. 49, 'Winsome')
'Otome' (No. 18, 'Maiden's Blush')
'Rasho Mon' (No. 37, Meteor')
'Sakura Tsukara' (No. 44, 'All-a-Glow')
'Saotome' (No. 21, 'Peachblossom')
'Seikai' (No. 1, 'Madonna')
'Shin Seikai' (No. 3, 'Old Ivory')
'Shintoki no Hagasane' (No. 20, 'Rose Taffetas')
'Shin Utena' (No. 28, 'Santoi')
'Suetsumu' (No. 34, 'Flame')
'Sui Yohi' (No. 10, 'Sprite')
'Takasago' (No. 11, 'Cherryblossom')*
'Tamafuyo' (No. 23, 'Fancy')
'Tama' no Utena' (No. 45, 'Flamingo')
'Tancho' (No. 6, 'Seraphim')
'Tsuta Momiji' (No. 33, 'Cardinal')
'Ukamuse' (No. 47, 'Princess Delight')
'Waka Kayede' (No. 38, 'Red Robin')
'Yaye Hiryu' (syn. 'Yayi Giri'; No. 39, 'Scarlet Prince')
'Yoro Zuyo' (No. 4, 'Purity')

*At Mr. Wilsons suggestion, the two leading experts, Messrs. Akashi and Kuwano selected these 6 as the pick of them all.

OLD KURUME HYBRIDS FROM JAPAN

The following Kurume Hybrids were brought into the United States and England in the early 1900's. Many of the old Kurumes brought in by Beattie, Stevenson, and others are oddly spelled and appear as a scrambled attempt at a translation. This has been confirmed by Wm. T. Turner of Atlanta and by Dr. M. Kunishige of Japan. Minor changes will be incorporated in the name. Questionable names will be in parentheses such as (Gaeshi), (Harumiji), and others. Some of these were from Stevenson, and others. Synonymous names are included in the description followed by the introducers such as Domoto, Wilson, Beattie, Stevenson and others. The numbers following Wilson are the numbers assigned to these plants when they were introduced. U.S.D.A. Plant Introduction Section Plant numbers will be included for plants collected by the section and known to be the same plant.

'Admiration' (Domoto): pink.

'Agemaki' (syn. 'Jose', Wilson #41): vivid purplish red, similar to 'Hinode Giri'.

'Aioi' (syn. 'Fairy Queen', Wilson #43): pale yellowish pink 36D, blotch strong red, hose-in-hose.

'Akebono' (Domoto): pink.

('Akebono Ryukyu') (Beattie, PI 77071): not a Kurume; no description available.

('Ao umi') (Beattie, PI 77081): see 'Seikai'.

'Appleblossom' (syn. 'Ho o', Domoto): white tinged strong pink 62B, blotch darker, occasional red stripes.

'Apricot' (Domoto): white throat, edges strong pink 43D, blotch darker hose-in-hose.

'Asa Gasumi' (syn. 'Rosy Morn', Wilson #14): vivid purplish pink 55B, hose-in-hose, 1–1¼".

'Asahi' (Beattie, PI 77089): moderate purplish pink.

'Avalanche' (Domoto): white, hose-in-hose.

'Ayagoromo' (Domoto): pink.

'Aya Kammuri' (syn. 'Pinkie', Wilson #19): deep yellowish pink 39B, dark spots, 1".

'Aya no Kamuri' (Beattie, PI 77121): same as 'Aya Kammuri'.

'Azuma Kagami' (syn. 'Pink Pearl', Wilson #16, Domoto): strong pink 49B, lighter center, hose-in-hose, 1¼".

'Azuma Shibori' (Beattie, PI 77076): white, hose-in-hose.

'Benifude' (syn. 'Sunbeam', Wilson #30): strong yellowish pink 41C, 1".

'Beni Giri' (C. B. van Nes): vivid purplish red 57A, 1¼", similar to 'Hinode Giri'.

'Bijinsui' (syn. 'Little Imp', Wilson #13): light yellowish pink 36A, ¾–1".

'Bouquet Rose' (Domoto): vivid purplish red 55A, hose-in-hose, 1".

'Bridesmaid' (Domoto): moderate reddish orange 44D, prominent stamens. 1½".

'Brilliant' (Domoto): strong pink, edges darker.

'Cattleya' (Domoto): white, flushed reddish purple, blotch darker.

'Cheerfulness' (Domoto): strong purplish red 55B, darker center, hose-in-hose, 1½".

'Cherryblossom' (syn. 'Takasago', Domoto): white, deep red flush 53C, dark spots, hose-in-hose, 1¼".

'Cherry Ripe' (Domoto): vivid red, tubular, hose-in-hose; low, compact.

'Chiyono Akebono' (Domoto): vivid purplish pink 55A, hose-in-hose, 1".

('Choraku') (Stevenson): strong purplish pink 55B, darker spots, 1¼".

'Christmas Cheer' (syn. 'Ima Shojo', Domoto): Strong red 53D, hose-in-hose, 1", upright to 7 feet.

'Coral Bells' (syn. 'Kirin', 'Daybreak'; Domoto): strong pink 54C, hose-in-hose, 1½".

'Daphne' (Domoto): white with strong reddish purple edge 78B, 1¼", perhaps same as 'Iroha Yama'.

'Debutante' (Domoto): strong yellowish pink 38A margin, lighter center darker blotch 39A, occasionally semidouble and partially petaloid, 1½".

'Delicatissima' (Domoto): white, flushed moderate purplish pink 55C, 1¼".

'Ecstasy' (Domoto): strong pink, 1½".

'Exquisite' (Domoto): deep purplish pink, hose-in-hose, 1½"; low, spreading.

'Fairy' (Domoto): white, flushed deep reddish orange 34A, darker blotch, 1".

'Firebird': strong red 46D, hose-in-hose, 1½". 'Yaye Giri' similar. 'Yaeshojo' and 'Suetsumu' similar with smaller flowers.

'Flame' (syn. 'Suetsumu', Domoto): strong red 45C blotch darker 46A.
'Flamingo' (syn. 'Tama no Utena', Domoto): deep yellowish pink 41C, hose-in-hose, ¾".
'Fudesutesan' (Domoto): deep yellowish pink, possibly same as 'Fudesute Yama' with incorrect color.
'Fudesute Yama' (syn. 'Poppy', Wilson #35): vivid purplish red 54D, ¾".
'Fude Tsukata' (Stevenson): pink paling to greenish white.
('Fujibotan') (Beattie, PI 77092): light purplish pink and reddish purple, small flowers.
('Fuji Murasaki') (Beattie, PI 77079): large flowers.
'Fuji no Asahi': white flushed yellowish pink on edges 38A, hose-in-hose, 1".
'Fukuhiko' (Stevenson): strong purplish red stripes, ¾–1".
('Gaeshi') (Stevenson): deep purplish pink 73A, petals spaced, 1¼".
'Gibiyama' (Beattie, PI 77091): light purple 77C, 1¾"; low, compact.
'Gloria Mundi' ('Apollo × Kurume; A. van Hecke, '38; syn. 'Orange Coral Bells'): vivid reddish orange to red, hose-in-hose, occasionally semidouble, 1½".
'Gosho Zakura' (syn. 'Vanity', Wilson #46; Domoto): white, striped yellowish pink.
'Gunecho' (Domoto): purplish pink.
'Hachika Tsugi' (syn. 'Prudence', Wilson #7): white, suffused light purple.
'Haru no Sato' (syn. 'Had no Sato', Stevenson): purplish pink, 1".
'Hagoromo' (Domoto): light pink.
'Hana Asobi' (syn. 'Sultan', Wilson #50; Beattie, PI 77016): strong purplish pink 58D, ¾–1".
'Hanaikada' (Domoto): moderate pink.
('Hana no Seki') (Beattie, PI 77065)
('Haru no Kyokii') (Stevenson): white, light greenish buds, irregular, ragged, 1".
('Harumiji') (Stevenson): white, ¾–1".
'Haru no Akebono' (Stevenson): moderate yellowish pink, pale center, dark blotch, hose-in-hose, ¾".
'Hatsunami' (Beattie, PI 77075): deep purplish pink with blotch.
'Hatsushimo' (Beattie, PI 77138; previously listed as a Kurume, possibly a *indicum* × 'Mucronatum' hybrid.): light purplish pink, white edges and darker center, 2".
'Hime Kagami' (Domoto): white, occasional pink stripes, hose-in-hose,1¼".
'Hino Crimson' ('Amoenum' × 'Hinode Giri'; Vermeulen): strong red 52A, 1¼".
'Hinode' (Beattie, PI 77101): deep purplish pink, small flowers.
'Hinode Giri' (syn. 'Hino', 'Red Hussar', Wilson #42): vivid purplish red 58B, 1½. Very common azalea and one of the hardiest. 'Carminata Splendens', an 'Amoenum' derivation is similar. 'Hinode Giri Double' is a hose-in-hose, not double. 'Hino Supreme' is a 'Hinode Giri' seedling, vivid red, and slightly larger.
'Hinode no Taka' (syn. 'Ruby', Wilson #48): vivid red 46C, hose-in-hose, 1½".
'Hino Hakama' (Beattie, PI 77126): strong red, semidouble, 1½".
'Hinomayo': strong purplish pink 68B, 1¼"; tall, upright. An old variety one of first introduced to Holland by C. B. van Nes & Sons about 1910. In Japan the name is 'Hinamoyo'.
'Hinomayo Fl. Pl'.: similar to 'Hinomayo' with partially petaloid sepals, not double.
'Hiyakasen' (syn. 'Hikkasen', Stevenson): light yellowish pink, pink center, dark blotch.
'Hokorobi' (Beattie, PI 77125): white, faintly touched with purplish red.
'Ho o' (syn. 'Appleblossom', Wilson #9): white, tinged strong pink 62B, blotch darker, some stripes of strong red.
'Ho oden' (Beattie, PI 77101): previously listed as a Kurume, see Mucronatum hybrids.
'Hortensia' (Domoto): light pink; broad as tall.
'Ima Shojo' (syn. 'Christmas cheer', Domoto; 'Fascination', Wilson #36; Beattie, PI 77111): strong red 53D, hose-in-hose, 1¼"; dense, upright to 7 feet.
'Ima Zuma' (syn. 'Chi no Ito'), (Stevenson): pale purplish pink, red striped, tips darker.
'Iroha Yama' (syn. 'Dainty', Wilson #8): white with margins of deep yellowish pink 39B, 1½".
'Itten' (Stevenson): pale purplish red.
'Iwato Kagami' (Domoto): vivid purplish pink 55A, hose-in-hose.
'Izumigawa' (Stevenson): moderate purplish red 55C, pale throat, reddish blotch, 1¼".
'Juhachiko' (syn. 'Yukachiko', Stevenson): reddish orange.
'Kagaribi' (Beattie, PI 77102): vivid red, tinged strong red, 2".
'Kamakura': moderate pink, occasional darker stripes; low.

('Kan') (Beattie, PI 77078): no description available.

'Karan Nishiki' (Beattie, PI 77084): pale red with darker stripes.

('Karenka') (Beattie, PI 77084): deep purplish pink, 1".

'Kasane Kagaribi' (syn. 'Rositi', Wilson #32): deep yellowish pink 39A, 1½".

'Kasumi Gaseki' (syn. 'Elf', Wilson #12; Domoto): vivid purplish red 55A on edges, with lighter center, spots darker, 1¼".

'Katsura no Hana' (syn. 'Ruth', Wilson #27): strong purplish red 55B, 1¼".

('Keinohana') (syn. 'Ishiyama', Stevenson): deep purplish pink, white anthers.

'Kimigayo' (syn. 'Cherub', Wilson #15): deep pink 52C, white throat, 1¼".

'Kinjo Tama' (Stevenson): deep yellowish pink, hose-in-hose.

('Kiono Kami') (Domoto): pink.

'Kirin' (syn. 'Coral Bells', Domoto; 'Daybreak', Wilson #22; 'Pink Beauty'): strong pink, 54C, hose-in-hose, tubular, 1½"; low spreading.

'Kiritsubo' (syn. 'Twilight', Wilson #24): strong reddish purple 78A, ¾".

'Ko Asobi' (Beattie, PI 77089): no description available.

('Kocha no Kawa') (Beattie, PI 77077): moderate purplish red 63B, blotch darker, 1¼", very late, spreading.

'Kocho no Mai' (syn. 'Butterfly Dance', Beattie, PI 77136): deep purplish pink 72D, with lighter throat and darker spots, 1¼". E. H. Wilson states that a plant of this name is typical of the hose-in-hose form of 'Amoenum'. However, the plant PI 77136 does not resemble 'Amoenum' as commonly known in this country.

'Kogasane' (Beattie, PI 77116): light purplish pink, hose-in-hose.

'Kojo no Odorikaraka' (Stevenson): vivid red, small.

'Komachi' (Stevenson): pale pink with darker margin.

'Komurasaki' (Beattie, PI 77127): deep purplish pink.

('Koraini') (Beattie, PI 77137): strong purplish red 63B, darker blotch, 1½".

'Koshikibu' (Beattie, PI 77139): white, flushed light pink margin 49C, 1¼".

'Kotsubo' (Beattie, PI 77133): deep purplish pink, small flowers.

'Kumagaya' (Stevenson): strong pink 52D, 1¼".

'Kumo Giri' (Beattie, PI 77120): deep yellowish pink 41B, spots darker, 1½".

'Kumoi' (Domoto): vivid red, paler throat, hose-in-hose.

'Kumo no Ito' (syn. 'Suga no Ito', 'Betty', Wilson #31): strong pink 49C, darker center, hose-in-hose, 1".

('Kumo no Homare') (Domoto): deep pink.

'Kumo no Uye' (syn. 'Salmon Prince', Wilson #29; Beattie, PI 77123): reddish orange, 1". A red hose-in-hose plant is also found with the same name.

'Kurai no Himo' (syn. 'Carmine Queen', Wilson #40): vivid red, hose-in-hose.

'Kure no Yuki' (syn. 'Snowflake', Wilson #2): white, hose-in-hose.

('Kyo no Tsumibana') (Beattie, PI 77118): vivid red to vivid purplish red, 1½"; similar to 'Hinode Giri'.

'Kyu Miyagino' (Beattie, PI 77114): strong purplish pink hose-in-hose, 1¼".

'Lavender Queen' (Domoto): vivid purplish red, 1¼"; broader than tall.

('Manyoki') (Beattie, PI 77068): no description available.

'Mauve Beauty' (Domoto): vivid reddish purple, hose-in-hose, 1¼".

'Mikaera Zakura' (Stevenson): pink.

('Misu no Uchi') (Beattie, PI 77066): no description available.

'Miyagino' (Domoto; Beattie, PI 77144): strong purplish red 54A, 1".

'Miyako Shibori' (Beattie, PI 77070): white, with red stripes.

'Momiji Gasane' (Beattie, PI 77124): deep pink, hose-in-hose.

'Momo Zono' (Beattie, PI 77108): vivid purplish red 55B, spots darker, hose-in-hose.

'Morning Glow' (Domoto): deep to strong purplish pink, hose-in-hose, 1".

'Mountain Laurel' (Domoto): pale pink shading to moderate pink 49B, dark spots, 1".

'Murasame' (Beattie, PI 77090): white with purple stripes.

'Nani Wagata' (syn. 'Painted lady', Wilson #5; Domoto): white suffused purplish pink 55C, darker spots, 1¼".

'Ogikasane'(syn. 'Cherryblossom', Beattie, PI 77086): white flushed purplish hose-in-hose, 1¼".

'Ogi no Odorikaraki' (syn. 'Kojo no Odorikaraki', Stevenson): deep reddish orange 42B, 1¼".
'Oino Mezame' (syn. 'Melody', Wilson #25; Beattie, PI 77135): light to deep rose pink, 1".
'Omoine' (syn. 'Dame Lavender', Wilson #26): light purplish violet.
'Orange Beauty' (syn. 'Tsuta Momiji', 'Cardinal', Domoto): deep red 53C, 1".
'Orange Coral Bell' (syn. 'Gloria Mundi'): vivid reddish orange to red, hose-in-hose, occasionally semidouble, 1½".
('Ore Beni'), Domoto: white flushed purplish pink 55B, darker spots, 1¾".
'Osaraku' (syn. 'Penelope', Wilson #17): white suffused and margined light purple.
'Osaraku Seedling'; (syn. 'Winsome', Wilson #49): white suffused light purple.
'Otome' (syn. 'Maiden's Blush', Wilson #18): blush pink.
('Ouchiyama') (Stevenson): light purplish red.
'Ozora': deep purplish pink 70C, 1".
('Paikune') (Stevenson): pink, star shaped.
'Peach Blossom' (syn. 'Saotome', Domoto): light purplish pink 55C.
'Peach Blow': flushed strong pink 48D, with darker blotch 58A, 1¼". The Sawada hybrid 'Twilight' is a seedling, white, flushed pink.
'Pink Jewel' (Allan '50; received from Fruitland Nur.): strong purplish pink 55B, hose-in-hose.
'Pink Pearl' (syn. 'Azuma Kagami', Domoto): strong pink 49B, lighter center, hose-in-hose, 1¼".
'Rangyoku' (Beattie, PI 77109): no description available.
('Rankyoken') (Stevenson): vivid reddish orange, ¾".
'Rasho Mon' (syn. 'Meteor', Wilson #37): vivid red.
'Rose' (Domoto): deep pink, stamens almost red, hose-in-hose.
'Sahohime' (Stevenson): white flushed purplish pink, darker spotting, partially petaloid.
('Sakura Kagami') (Beattie, PI 77115): white flushed purplish pink 55C, brownish spots, 1½".
'Sakura Tsukasa' (syn. 'All-a-Glow', Wilson #44; Domoto; Beattie, PI 77129): light reddish purple 75A, hose-in-hose, ¾".
'Salmon Beauty' (Domoto): deep yellowish pink, 39B, darker throat, hose-in-hose, 1¾".
'Salmon Queen': strong yellowish pink 41C, spots darker, 1½".
'Saotome' (syn. 'Peachblossom', Wilson #21; Domoto): light purplish pink 55C, 1¼".
'Seikai' (syn. 'Madonna', Wilson #1): white, hose-in-hose, 1¼".
('Senju') (Stevenson): pale purplish pink, flushed, darker blotch.
('Senka') (Stevenson): strong yellowish pink 41C, whitish throat, blotch darker, 1".
'Shikishima' (Stevenson): purplish red 55A, darker spots, light center, 1½".
('Shikizaki') (Beattie, PI 77073): no description available.
'Shi no Nome' (Stevenson): pale greenish white, pink margins.
'Shino Miyagino' (Stevenson): purplish red, white anthers, hose-in-hose, ¾".
('Shinsagino Kagasana') (Stevenson): purplish red, pale throat, reddish blotch.
'Shin Seikai' (syn. 'Old Ivory', Wilson #3): yellowish white to white, hose-in-hose, 1"; low.
'Shintoki no Hagasane' (syn. 'Rose Taffetas', Wilson #20): deep pink, shading to light pink, hose-in-hose.
'Shin Utena' (syn. 'Santoi', Wilson #28): white, flushed strong yellowish pink 37B, darker blotch, 1½".
'Shirataki' (Beattie, PI 77103): no description available.
('Shjuchuke') (Stevenson): no description available.
'Shojyo' (Domoto): vivid red.
('Shoshobeni') (Beattie, PI 77067): strong yellowish pink 41C, hose-in-hose.
'Snow' (Domoto): white, very light yellowish blotch, hose-in-hose, 1½". Very common, but still popular, dead flowers persist.
'Sorai': white, flushed and edged strong purplish pink 55B, 1".
'Suetsumu' (syn. 'Suetsumu Hana', 'Flame', Wilson #10): strong red 45C, blotch darker 46A. 'Hardy Firefly' and 'Vesuvius' are similar.
'Sui Yohi' (syn. 'Sprite', Wilson #10): white flushed pink, strong pink tips 49B, hose-in-hose, 1".
'Sun Star' (Domoto): strong purplish red 58C, darker blotch, 1".
'Surisumi' (Beattie, PI 77143): moderate reddish purple 78B, 1¼".
'Sweet Briar': strong purplish red 55B, ¾". Often confused with 'Eleanor Allan'.

'Takamakie' (Stevenson): white, with greenish blotch.

'Takasago' (syn. 'Cherryblossom', Wilson #11): white, flushed deep red 53C, dark spots, hose-in-hose, 1¼".

'Tamafuyo' (syn. 'Fancy', Wilson #23): white, striped and selfs of moderate red 63B, 1¼".

'Tama no Yukari' (syn. 'Tama no Midori', Beattie, PI 77093): vivid purplish pink 55D, ¾".

'Tama no Utena' (syn. 'Flamingo', Wilson #45): deep yellowish pink 41C, hose-in-hose, ¾".

'Tancho' (syn. 'Seraphim', Wilson #6): white flushed and edges moderate pink 39B, hose-in-hose, 1".

('Tarasa') (Beattie, PI 77082): no description available.

'Terukimi' (Domoto): pink.

'Torch': see Kaempferi Hybrids.

('Toun') (Steventon): white faint pink blush, reddish purple spots, 1½".

'Tsuta Momiji' (syn. 'Cardinal', Wilson #33; Beattie, PI 77110): deep red 53C, 1".

'Ukamuse' (syn. 'Princess Delight', Wilson #47): deep purplish pink 72D, darker blotch, hose-in-hose, 1¾"; low.

('Ummu') (Domoto): pink, very large.

'Usugukari' (Stevenson): white, pale purple edges.

'Vesuvius' (Domoto): strong red 50A, blotch darker, 1¼".

'Waka Kayede' (syn. 'Red Robin', Wilson #38): strong red 52, ¾–1".

('Warai Gao') (Beattie, PI 77130): strong pink, hose-in-hose.

'Ward's Ruby' (Domoto): strong red, 1¼". One of best reds, but less hardy than most Kurumes.

('Wasegiri') (Beattie, PI 77080): moderate reddish orange.

('Wuchiwa Kasane') (Domoto): pink.

('Yaehime') (Domoto): pink, double.

'Yaeshojo' (Beattie, PI 77100): deep reddish orange 44B, hose-in-hose, 1¼". Similar to 'Firebird', 'Suetsumi', and 'Vesuvius'.

'Yakumo': moderate pink 39B, dark spots, hose-in-hose, 1¼".

'Yatsu Hashi' (Beattie, PI 77119): deep pink.

'Yaye Hiryu' (syn. 'Yaye Giri', 'Scarlet Prince', Wilson #39): moderate reddish orange 43C, hose-in-hose, tubular, 1½". Similar to 'Firebird'.

'Yezo Nishiki' (Stevenson): white, red stripes and selfs of purplish red 57C, 1".

"Yorozuyo' (syn. 'Purity', Wilson #4): white, greenish base, tubular, 1¼".

'Yoshi Migatake' (Stevenson): purplish red, ¾".

'Yozakura' (Stevenson): reddish purple, 2". Possibly a Satsuki Hybrid.

('Yukachiko') (Stevenson): strong yellowish pink 38A, center whiter, darker spots, 1½".

OTHER KURUME HYBRIDS

The following Kurume azaleas were developed and introduced for the most part outside of Japan, by growers in the United States, England, or Europe. The number of Kurume azaleas registered for Belgium, England, and Germany is very small, undoubtedly due to the lack of hardinesss in these countries. The Kurumes are used in hybridizing with other more cold-hardy species and cultivars, and these registered are listed under Miscellaneous and Intergroup Evergreen Hybrids. The hybridizer and/or introducer when known is given. See Appendix J.

'Addy Wery' (syn. 'Mrs. Wery' ('Malvatica' × 'Flame'); Ouden): strong red 45D, dull orange blotch, 1¾", early; upright.

'Adonis' (Felix and Dijkhuis): white, hose-in-hose, frilled.

'Aladdin' (Hage '43): vivid red.

'Aladdin' × 'Amoena' (Research Station for Arboreous Crops Boskoop, Holland '64): purplish pink, margins lighter, 1⅛", early; upright, very hardy.

'Amy' ('Elizabeth Gable' × seedling; L. Yavorsky): pink, double; compact, glossy foliage.

'Anne Frank' ('Mother's Day' × 'Multiflorum'; W. Nagel, Ger.): pink, faint reddish markings, 5 to 6 lobes, 1½", late; low broad, rounded.

'Antony Roland' (Kurume seedling, G. Langdon '79): strong purplish red 55B, spotted deep red, hose-in-hose.

'Becky' (sport of 'Hinode Giri'; Voster Nur.): deep pink, blended with strong purplish pink, blotch darker, 2", PP 1699.

'Besse A. Dodd' (Kurume seedling; T. Dodd): light pink, lighter center, hose-in-hose, 2", early mid season; compact.

'Betsy': white, fringed pink.

'Bikini'('Hinomayo' seedling; M. Haworth-Booth, U.K. '79): moderate purplish red 55C, flushed 55B, shading to almost white, faint spotting 2¾", upright, spreading.

'Blaauw's Pink'; (Blaauw): strong yellowish pink, darker blotch, hose-in-hose, 1¼"; very similar or the same as 'Glory'.

'Canyalo' (Koppeschaar): strong pink.

'Cardinal' (sport of 'Mother's Day'; Schepens): vivid reddish orange, 2", compact habit.

'Catherine Stewart' (Allan): moderate purple, hose-in-hose.

'Chloris' (Felix and Dijkhuis): pink.

'Colyer' (Kurume seedling; C. E. Brown, introd. by Stewart, U.K. '62): deep purple 74B, spotted red at throat, large flowers.

'Coral Bell Supreme': vivid purplish red, hose-in-hose, PP 1515.

'Crepuscule' (Hage): light purple.

'Dark Mahogany' (H. Hohman): deep red, 1", early mid-season; rounded habit.

'Decision' (Hage): light reddish orange.

'Dee Dee' (Wildwood Gar.): pink, 1", compact.

'Diana' (Felix and Dijkhuis): yellowish pink, hose-in-hose.

'Diane Robin' (seedling; Langdon '79): strong purplish red, 55B.

'Double Hinode Giri' (syn. 'Hinode Giri Double'): vivid purplish red, hose-in-hose.

'Duke of Connaught' ('Amoena' form; Waterer 1879): purplish red, light center.

'Edna B' ('Elizabeth Gable' × seedling; Yavorsky): pink, large flowers.

'Eleanor Allan' (Allan): pink, 2".

'El Frida': light purple, white throat, hose-in-hose, 2".

'Esmeralda' (Koppeschaar): pale pink to near white.

'Etna' (Hage): moderate red.

'Freesia': white, tubular; low; from Japan.

'Firestar' (introd. by Mrs. Schepens): reddish orange, mid-season.

'Gabriele' ('Mother's Day' × 'Kermesina'; H. Hachmann, Ger. '79): vivid purplish red 58B, 1¼"–1½", late; very hardy.

'Gina Hohman' (Hohman): light reddish orange, hose-in-hose, 1½", early mid-season.

'Glory': strong yellowish pink, hose-in-hose, darker blotch, 1¼", may be same as 'Blaauw's Pink'.

'Greenway' (Williams, U.K. '75): pink.

'Hahn's Red' (Hahn): vivid red, 2", similar to 'Mother's Day'.

'Hatsu Giri': vivid reddish purple, pink spotting in throat, 1¼".

'Heather': strong purplish red 63B, hose-in-hose, 1½".

'Helene' (Felix and Dijkhuis): pink, semidouble.

'Hexe Supreme': dark red, double.

'Hino Supreme' (K. Sawada, U.S.A.): improved dark red 'Hinode Giri'.

'Illustre' (Hage '43): reddish orange.

'Irresistible' (syn. 'My-o'; 'Hino Crimson' × 'Salmon Elf'; R. Pryor U.S.D.A. '67): strong purplish pink, hose-in-hose, 1½", 5–7 stamens; leaves with white margin; dwarf compact.

'Jennifer': deep purplish pink.

'Jimmy Allan' (Allan): reddish orange.

'Jubile' ('Kirin' × 'Hinomayo'; A. van Hecke, Belg. '45): light purplish pink, hose-in-hose, very early; good for forcing.

'Julie Ann' (Langdon '79): strong purplish red 55B.

'Karens' ('Hinode Giri' × *poukhanense;* A. Pederson '79): deep reddish purple, darker spotting, wavy, fragrant, 1¾'; semi-evergreen, 4×4 ft. in 6 yrs.; tolerates pH 7; hardy to −25°F.

'Kermesina' (old variety in Boskoop, parentage unknown): strong purplish red; very hardy. Also listed as a *R. kiusianum.*

'King's Luminous Pink' ('Pink Pearl' × 'Eleanor Allan'; King, introduced by Partain): pink with white rays, and darker margin, throat white, 1½"; 4×5 ft. in 10 yrs.; hardy −10°F.

'Kinsey White' (Kinsey Gar.): white, 1½"; hardy to at least 0°F.
'Kirishima': white, with pale red center.
'Laura': vivid purplish red 57C, dark spots, hose-in-hose, 1½".
'Linda Stuart' (Yavorsky): deep yellowish pink, paler center, hose-in-hose, 2".
'Little Beauty' ('Amoenum' × 'Favorite'; van Nes '50): purplish red, hose-in-hose.
'Lysander' ('Mother's Day' × 'Else Karger'; U. Schumacher, Ger.): vivid red, shaded orange, brown markings, 1½–2¼", mid to late season;; broad; hardy; leaves reddish in winter.
'Martin's White' (J. Martin): white, hose-in-hose, 1".
'Mary Frances Hohman' (Hohman): reddish orange, partially petaloid, late midseason; low.
'Maryland Purple' (Tingle): purple.
'Massasoit' (Allan): dark red.
'Matador' (Hage '39): strong reddish orange.
'Mauve Beauty': strong purple.
'May Glory' (deWilde): red.
'Merle Finimore' ('Hinode Giri' × 'Tancho'; K. M. March, Aust. '73): deep red 47D.
'Midinette' (Hahe '52): yellowish pink.
'Miss Prim' (Yavorsky): deep pink, semidouble, midseason; low compact.
'Mother's Day' (syn. 'Muttertag', 'Moederkesdag'; ('Prof. Wolters' × 'Hinode Giri'; A. van Hecke, Belg. '32): vivid red, faint brown spotting, hose-in-hose to semidouble, 2"; very popular. Introduced from Belgium, by M. G. Schepens, Conn.
'Nancy Plent' ('Edna B' × pink seedling; Yavorsky): vivid pink, 3–3½", mid May; wide as tall.
'Nicole Joy' (Langdon '79): moderate purplish red 55C; spotted dark red.
'Orange Cup': strong orange, hose-in-hose.
'Orion' (Felix and Dijkhuis): deep pink.
'Ozora': deep yellowish pink 39A, 1¼".
'Perfection' (Hage '39): reddish orange.
'Pink Jewel' (Allan): pink.
'Pink Lady' (Hage '50): vivid pink, darker center.
'Pink Progress' (deWilde): pink.
'Pixie Petticoat': purple, frilled, hose-in-hose, 1¼"; low.
'Psyche' (Felix and Dijkhuis): pink.
'Red Progress' (deWilde): deep pink, dark throat, 2".
'Red Seal' (Hage '52): vivid red.
'Rex' ('Kirin' × 'Hinomayo'; A. van Hecke, Belg. '45): light reddish orange, early, good for forcing.
'Rubinetta' ('Kermesina' × 'Mother's Day'; H. Hachmann, Ger. '74): vivid purplish red 58B, faint reddish markings, 1½", late; leaves reddish in winter; very hardy.
'Ruhrfeuer' ('Kermesina' × 'Mother's Day'; U. Schumacher, Ger. '70): strong red 53D, dark brown markings, ¾–1⅛", late; dwarf, round; hardy.
'Ruth May' ('Pink Pearl' × 'Indica Alba'; Oliver): moderate pink, white stripes, lighter margin, 1½".
'Sakata Blush' (Koppeschaar): light pink to near white.
'Sakata Red' (Koppeschaar): vivid red, 1¾".
'Sakata Rose' (Koppeschaar): deep pink.
'Salmon Bells'(sport of 'Coral Bells', R. Talley, '54): yellowish pink, hose-in-hose, PP1267.
'Salmon Princess' (Hage): yellowish pink.
'Salmon Sander': deep yellowish; low.
'Salmon Special': yellowish pink, hose-in-hose, ruffled.
'Salmon Spray' (Hage '52): light yellowish pink.
'Sharon Kathleen' (R. James '79): light purplish pink 56A, spots dark red.
'Sherwood Cerise' ('Hinode Giri' × Kurume Hybrid, Sherwood Nur., Ore.): vivid purplish red 54A, 1½".
'Sherwoodi' (syn. 'Sherwood Orchid'; 'Hinode Giri' × 'Kurume', Sherwood Nur., Ore '35): vivid reddish purple, darker blotch, 2".
'Sherwood Red' ('Hinode Giri' × Kurume Hybrid, Sherwood Nur., Ore. '49): vivid red 45B, 1¾", early.
'Silvester' ('Aladdin' × 'Amoena'; Research Station for Arboreous Crops Boskoop, Holland '64): vivid purplish red, margins lighter, 1¼", very early; very hardy, good for forcing.

'Snow #125': white, hose-in-hose; similar to 'Snow', but blooms later.

'Snowball' (J. Martin): white, hose-in-hose; self cleaning, low compact.

'Snowball' (sport of 'Snow'; J. Cagle): white, double, hose-in-hose, small brown remanent stamens gives spotting effect, 1½"; compact.

'Sorrento' (T. Lelliot, Aust. '67): purplish pink, hose-in-hose, yellow flush in throat.

'Tilly' (sport of 'Hino Crimson'; Yavorsky): reddish orange.

'Torch' Azalea: see *R. kaempferi.*

'Tracy T' (Thompson): pale pink.

'Tradition': (possibly same as 'Roehr's Tradition'): deep pink, hose-in-hose, mid-season; medium growth.

'Tropic Sun' (sport of 'Hino Crimson'; Akehurst Nur. '74): reddish orange, 8 in truss, PP3048.

'Twilight' (seedling of 'Peach Blow': K. Sawada): white flushed pink, 1¼".

'Velvet Gown' ('Pink Perfection' × Kurume Hybrid; J. Waterer, U.K. '67): vivid reddish purple, red speckling on lower throat, 1¾", slightly wavy.

'Victoire' (Hage): brilliant orange.

'Victorine Hetling' (seedling of 'Hinomayo'; Adr. van Nes): vivid purplish red, 2½".

'Wendy': white.

'Wintertime' (syn. 'Midwinter'; 'Aladdin' × 'Amoena'; Research Station for Arboreous Crops Boskoop, Holland '65): vivid red, 1½", early; broad upright, good for forcing.

'Yukumo': moderate red, double; low.

RECENT KURUME HYBRID INTRODUCTIONS FROM JAPAN

The U.S.D.A. National Arboretum released 33 new Kurume Hybrid azalea cultivars in the fall of 1983, to cooperating nurserymen and arboreta, for future distribution. Some 50 varieties were collected from two trips, 1976 and 1978 by Drs. John L. Creech, and Frederick G. Meyer and Mr. Sylvester G. March from the Kurume Branch, Vegetable and Ornamental Research Station, Kurume, Fukuoka Prefecture, Japan. They are reported to be the finest Kurume Azaleas in Japan and should be available commercially in a few years. The balance of the collection should be released in the future. Specific hardiness and individual plant habit are not available, but the plants should be like other Kurume Hybrids. The flowers are single and the stamens are as long as the petals unless described differently.

'Aratama' (NA 45406): vivid red, darker blotch on upper petals, 1¾".

'Atsumi Zakura' (NA 45404): pale light pink with purplish white throat, hose-in-hose, 1⅜–1½.

'Ayahime' (NA 45405): strong purplish red to paler throat, with darker blotches on the upper petals, 1⅜".

'Ezoishiki' (NA 45415): nearly pure white with red stripes, 1⅛.

'Fuji Asahi' (NA 45438): strong purplish pink ruffled edges, hose-in-hose, 1½"; stamens longer than petals.

'Fukuhiko' (NA 45440): variable from strong purplish red to light purplish pink, striated with strong purplish red stripes, 1½".

'Gunki' (NA 45422): white, with deep purplish red stripes on upper petals, ruffled edges, 1⅛", stamens half as long as petals.

'Hakuo Nishiki' (NA 45436): yellowish white with dark red stripes, hose-in-hose, 1¾".

'Haru no Sato' (NA 45435): deep purplish pink, lighter throat, darker blotch on upper petals, 1⅛"; stamens shorter than petals.

'Hino Tsukasa' (NA 45436): vivid strong red, 1⅛", stamens longer than petals.

'Ima Murasaki' (NA 45408): strong reddish purplish, darker blotch, tube lighter red, 1½", stamens slightly longer than petals.

'Itten' (NA 45410): white, some with purplish pink edges to a white throat, 1½–1⅜", stamens very short, ⅛–¼" long.

'Iwato Kagami' (NA 45411): deep pink, throat white, 1½".

'Kagura' (NA 45419): strong purplish pink, whitish throat, darker blotch, hose-in-hose, 1", stamens slightly longer than petals.

'Kara Nishiki' (NA 45420): deep pink to strong purplish red, with darker stripes, 1½".

R. kaempferi Torch Azalea in the wild, Japan. GALLE

R. kaempferi alba. CREECH

R. kaempferi 'Tachisene'. GREER

'Komatsu' hose-in-hose Kaempferi Hybrid. PLANTING FIELDS

Plate 50

R. sataense Sata Azalea on Mt. Takatoge, Kyushu, Japan. GALLE

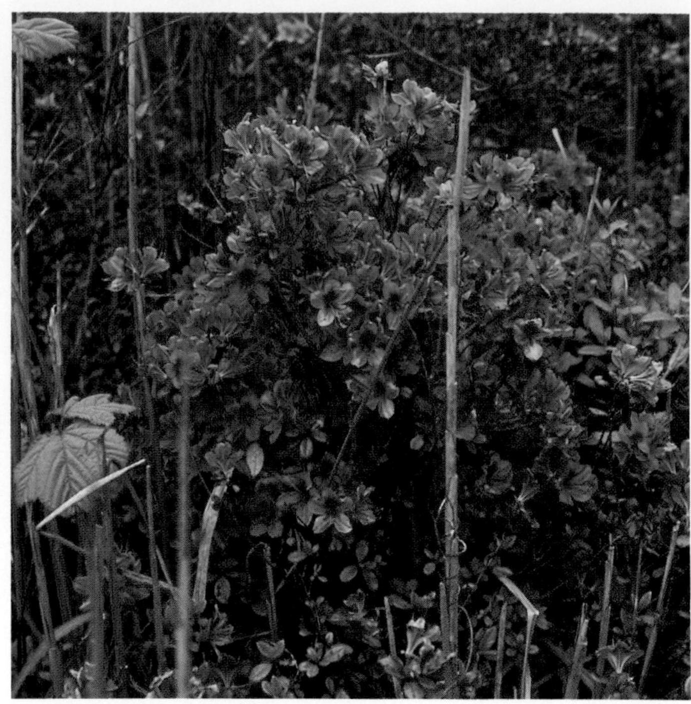

R. sataense. Sata Azalea CREECH

'Amoenum'. GREER

R. kiusianum. Kyushu GALLE

'Benichidori' Kuisianum Hybrid. GALLE

R. nakaharai 'Mount Seven Star'. GALLE

R. tamurae. Dwarf Indica Azalea. CREECH

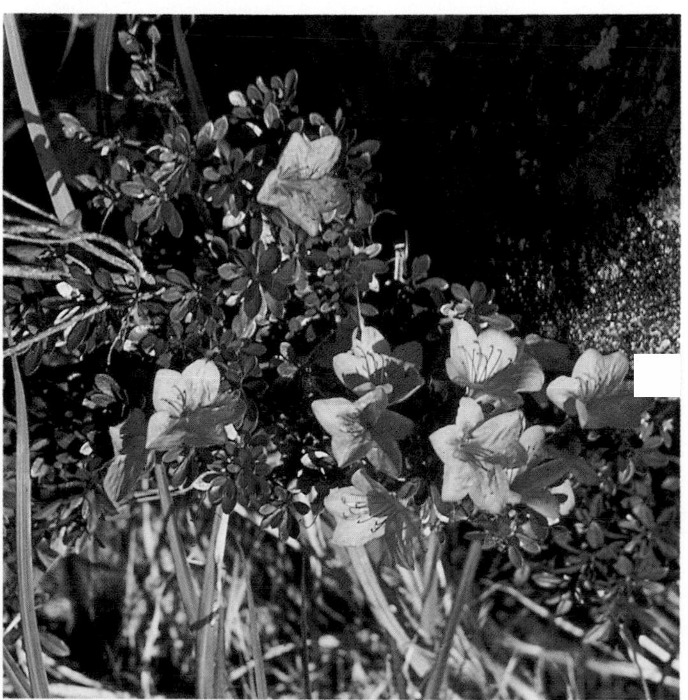

R. indicum. Indica Azalea. CREECH

Plate 52

R. scabrum, Luchu Azalea Iso Garden, Japan. GALLE

R. scabrum. Luchu Azalea. CREECH

R. macrosepalum Big Sepal Azalea. GALLE

R. macrosepalum linearifolium Spider Azalea. GREER

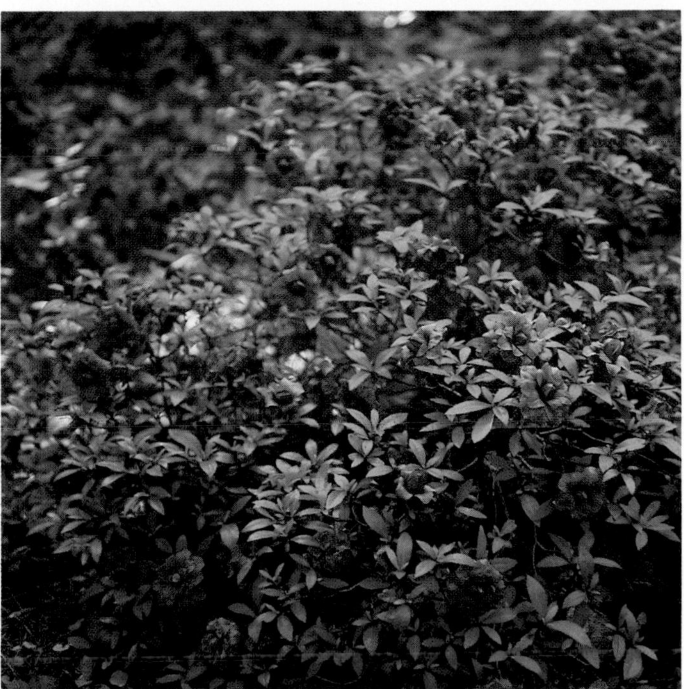

R. indicum 'Balsaminaeflorum'. GALLE

R. indicum 'Balsaminaeflorum'. GALLE

R. serphyllifolium var. *albiflorum*. GALLE

R. indicum 'Polypetalum'. GALLE

Plate 54

R. indicum 'Flame Creeper'. GALLE

R. indicum 'Macrantha'. GALLE

R. indicum 'Macrantha Double Pink'. GALLE

R. tschonoskii. Tschonoski Azalea. GALLE

R. yakuinsulare. H. SUZUKI

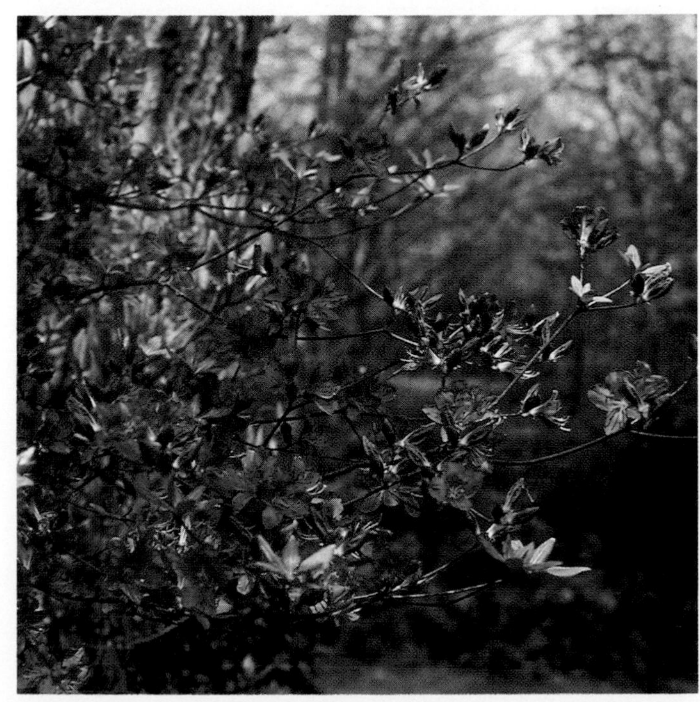

R. komiyamae. Ashitaka Azalea. CREECH

R. komiyamae. Ashitaka Azalea. GALLE

Plate 56

Munchkin' dwarf form of *R. yedoense poukhanense.* CARLSON

R. rubropilosum. Red hair Azalea. GALLE

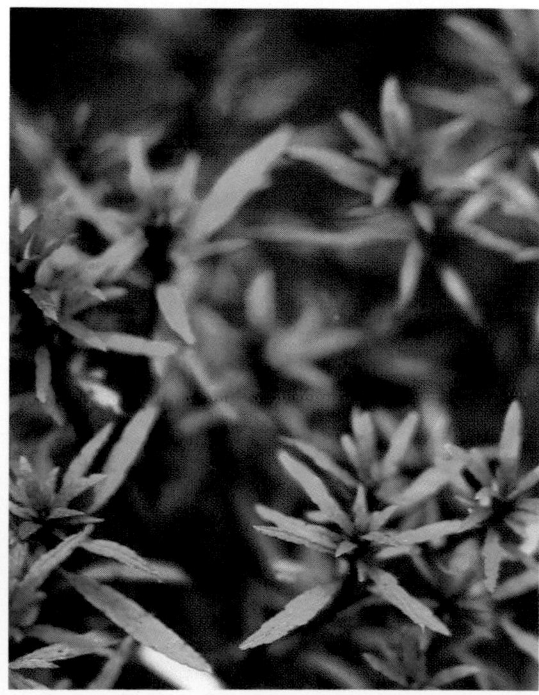

R. otakumii (yakuinsulare). GALLE

R. kanehirae. Taibei Azalea. GREER

'Konohana' (NA 45425): deep yellowish pink, with dark purplish blotches, 1⅜".
'Kunimitsu' (NA 45423): strong purplish red, white center, hose-in-hose to semidouble, 1⅜–1½', some stamens polypetaloid.
'Maya Fujin' (NA 45443): deep purplish red edges, darker blotch, 1⅜".
'Oogocho' (NA 45418): strong purplish red, darker blotch, variable hose-in-hose, to semidouble, 1¾".
'Oouchi Yama' (NA 45416): strong reddish purple, whitish throat, darker blotch, 1⅛".
'Rikyugonomi' (NA 45450): moderate red, very pale throat, darker blotch, hose-in-hose, 1".
'Shizu no Mai' (NA 45426): pale red, dark stripes, hose-in-hose, 1⅛", stamens very short, ⅛".
'Tago no Ura' (NA 45429): white, very faint yellowish blotch, or absent, hose-in-hose, 1¾", stamens nearly as long as petals.
'Tama Beni' (NA 45427): vivid red, darker blotch, 1", stamens nearly as long as petals.
'Tennyo no Mai' (NA 45430): deep purplish pink, whitish throat, dark pink blotch, 1¾", stamens longer than petals.
'Tokoharu' (NA 45433): white, strong purplish red striping, hose-in-hose, 1⅜".
'Tokonatsu' (NA 45432): white, strong purplish red stripes, 1⅜", stamens longer than petals.
'Tsuki Minoen' (NA 45431): deep purplish pink edges, slightly ruffled, white throat 1½", stamens as long or slightly longer than petals.
'Usuyukari' (NA 45413): strong purple edges changing to white, throat white, 1⅜", stamens longer than petals.
'Wakaebisu' (NA 45450): moderate red, very pale throat, dark blotch, 1".
'Yomei Nishiki' (NA 45446): white, purplish pink stripes, nearly white throat, with dark blotch, 1⅛".
'Yoro' (NA 45447): white, 1⅜", stamens 1½ times longer than petals.
'Yoshi' Migatake' (NA 45445): deep purplish pink edges, white throat, no blotching, 1⅜".

ADDITIONAL KURUME HYBRIDS

AICHELE HYBRIDS

The development of these hybrids started in 1948 with Mr. C. F. Aichele, Sr., owner of Carolina Floral Nursery at Mt. Holly, South Carolina, U.S.A., and his son, James. The objective was to develop hardy greenhouse forcing garden cultivars. Over 10,000 seedlings were produced and after eight years, six varieties were introduced.

'Clemson' (chance seedling of 'Caroline Graham', Rutherford): deep yellowish pink, hose-in-hose, 3"; midseason, good for forcing and hardy in zone 8. 5 ft. Not a Kurume.
'Eric the Red' ('Daphne Salmon' × 'Hexe'): vivid red, hose-in-hose, 2", mid season; compact growth, hardy in zones 6b to 9.
'Fritz Aichele' (parentage unknown): white, hose-in-hose, ruffled, 3"; good for forcing, compact form. Hardy in zones 8–9.
'Laura' ('Daphne Salmon' × 'Hexe'): deep pink, hose-in-hose, 2"; compact, hardy in zones 6b–9b. Good for forcing.
'Mary Lynn' (seedling of 'Sweetbriar'): vivid purplish pink, hose-in-hose, 2"; compact habit. Hardy in zones 6b–9a. Good for forcing.
'Posaeman' ('Bridesmaid' × 'Mother Pearl', Rutherford hybrid): light yellowish pink, hose-in-hose, 3", midseason, compact habit. Hardy in zones 8–9. Good for forcing.

AMOENA HYBRIDS

The Amoena Hybrids are derivatives of the 'Amoenum' Azalea introduced from Shanghai by Robert Fortune around 1850 or 1851. It is a Japanese azalea and not Chinese as first believed. The typical 'Amoenum' or 'Amoena' Azalea has small, purplish red, hose-in-hose flowers on a dense, twiggy, compact plant, and is noted for its hardiness. It is also notable in its capacity to produce color sports, particularly when crossed with other species—*R. indicum*, etc. Many of the early Amoena Hybrids are undoubtedly just color sports.

Unfortunately, the origin of the Amoena Hybrids is not well understood. One of the first hybridizers or introducers was Mr. Carmichael, gardener for the Prince of Wales at Sandringham around 1860. Others early associated with the Amoena Hybrids were Charles Smith of Guernsey and B. S. Williams of Holloway England.

The 'Amoenum' Azalea soon reached Belgium, Germany, and France and was introduced to the U.S.A. by C. M. Hovey of Boston, Mass., in 1855. By 1879 Pynaert (*Rev. Hort. Belg.* V 277) mentioned the cultivar 'Mrs. Carmichael' and five others derived from the 'Amoenum' Azalea that were in commerce.

The Amoena Hybrids are hardy in zones 6b to 9. One must assume that the flowers of these old cultivars are all hose-in-hose, as old descriptions often do not mention the type of flower. The PI numbers in parentheses are the U.S.D.A. Plant Introduction Section numbers assigned to plants.

'Amoena Coccinea' (syn. 'Coccinea', sport of 'Amoena'): vivid red, hose-in-hose, reverts back.
'Caldwelli' (syn. 'Bidwelli', B. S. Williams 1880: (PI 102161)): pale pink, hose-in-hose.
'Carminata Splendens' (Sunningdale Nur.; (PI 78376)): vivid purplish red.
'Cheniston' (Sunningdale Nur.): deep reddish brown, a more recent derivative.
'Duke of Connaught'; (J. Waterer 1879): moderate red, lighter center.
'Flambeau' (originated in France late 1800's): dark red.
'Forsterianum' (O. F. Lebank, Austria 1892): reddish orange, late, hose-in-hose.
'H. O. Carre' (PI 78377): vivid red, semidouble.
'Holfordi': red, late.
'Illuminata' (received F.C.C. in 1885, PI 78378): reddish purple.
'La France' (Sunningdale Nur.): pink, flushed red, hose-in-hose.
'Marvel': vivid red, hose-in-hose.
'Miss Buist' (Bull 1885): white.
'Mrs. Carmichael' (Williams 1879 (PI 78381)): reddish purple, dark blotch, semidouble, late; less hardy.
'Optima': deep pink, large; late.
'Prime Minister': pink.
'Princess Maude' (Carmichael 1879: (PI 78383)): deep pink.
'Pulchellum' (PI 78237): description not available.
'Roseum' (PI 78237): purplish pink, dark blotch, hose-in-hose.
'Splendens' (Wisley Trials 1957) (PI 78385): pale purple.
'Superba': dark purple, hose-in-hose.

BELTSVILLE (YERKES-PRYOR) HYBRIDS

These azaleas are also known as the Yerkes-Pryor Azaleas of U.S.D.A. Azaleas. From 1950 to 1959, the Horticultural Crops Research Division, United States Department of Agriculture, introduced 47 azaleas using cultivars, particularly 'Snow', 'Firefly', 'Indica Alba', 'Maxwell', and the species *R. kaempferi*, as parents. The work was commenced at the Beltsville, Maryland Station by the late Guy E. Yerkes of the Ornamental Plant Section and subsequent to his retirement in 1946 was carried on by Robert L. Pryor at the Plant Introduction Station. The objectives were the production of hardy outdoor evergreen azaleas and plants suitable for forcing by the florist. Three hundred seedlings were saved from approximately 50,000 grown.

A condensed description of these cultivars follows. The numbers in parenthesis are the plant test numbers. All plants are hardy in Zones 7a to 8b.

'Alpine' (836) (Selfed unnamed seedling of a Southern Indian Hybrid × *kaempferi*): white, hose-in-hose, 2½"; in clusters of 2 to 3; compact, about as wide as high.
'Animation' (145) (Kaempferi Hybrid × 'Obtusum'): vivid red throat with darker dots, hose-in-hose, slightly wavy, 1⅜", stamens 5+; erect growth.

'Bacchus' (49) ('Firefly' × 'Snow'): pink, hose-in-hose, 1½", wide petals ½", flowers in clusters of 8 to 20; bushy, about one and a half times as tall as wide.

'Blush' (180) (Kaempferi Hybrid × 'Snow'): light purplish pink, dark dots, hose-in-hose, 1¾"; stamens 5 to 7; erect similar to *kaempferi*.

'Brandywine' (81) ('Maxwelli' × 'Snow'): yellowish pink 2¼–2½", in clusters of 2 or 3; bushy plant about one and a half times as wide as tall.

'Carillon' (91) ('Maxwelli' × *kaempferi* × 'Kumonoe'): reddish orange dark spots, 3–3½", in clusters of 2 to 3; about as wide as tall.

'Carol' (61) ('Firefly' × 'Snow'): white, hose-in-hose, slightly wavy, 1–1½", in clusters of 3 to 5, branches freely from the base.

'Casablanca' (228) ('Indica Alba' × 'Snow'): white, 1½ to 2¼", in clusters of 3 to 7; well branched, wider than high.

'Cindy' (205) (Kaempferi Hybrid × 'Obtusum'): purplish pink, red dots in throat, hose-in-hose, 1¾"; 2 to 4 in cluster; compact, rounded.

'Comet' (83) ('Maxwelli × 'Snow'): pink, hose-in-hose, 2 to 2¼", in clusters of 3 or 4; bushy, plant wide as high.

'Eureka' (117) (Kaempferi × 'Snow'): light purplish pink, hose-in-hose, 1½ to 1¾", in clusters of 3 to 5; spreading, one third wider than high.

'Flash' (429) ('Pride of Mobile' × sport of 'Flame' (syn. 'Suetsumu')): dark red, 1 to 1½" in clusters of 3 to 9; dense growth, one and half times as wide as tall.

'Flirtation' (88) ('Maxwelli' × 'Snow'): purple, hose-in-hose, 2½", in clusters of 3 or 4; erect growth.

'Foam' (11) ('Firefly' × 'Snow'): white, hose-in-hose, slightly wavy, 1¾", 2 to 4 per cluster; low branching.

'Frosty' (127) (Kaempferi Hybrid × 'Snow'): white, hose-in-hose, slightly wavy, 2½", stamens 5+; moderately branched.

'Green Eyes' (784) (Cross of two unnamed seedlings of Kurume, 'Maxwelli' and Southern Indian Hybrid): white, green blotch, hose-in-hose, 3 to 4", in clusters of 3; compact, two times as wide as high.

'Guy Yerkes' (135) (Kaempferi Hybrid × 'Snow'): yellowish pink to dark pink, fading to light pink, hose-in-hose, dark pink dots in throat, 1¾ to 2¼", in clusters of 3 to 5; profusely branched.

'H. H. Hume' (224) ('Indica Alba' × 'Snow'): white, faint yellow throat, hose-in-hose, 2", in clusters of 3 to 5; erect spreading. Hardy zone 7–9.

'Ibis' (71) ('Maxwelli' × 'Snow'): yellowish pink, 1½ to 1¾", bushy plant, wide as high.

'Innocence' (17) ('Firefly' × 'Snow'): white, with faint greenish yellow throat, hose-in-hose, 1¾"; medium spreading, compact.

'Irma' (80) ('Maxwelli' × 'Snow'): purple, hose-in-hose, 2¼–2½", in clusters of 3; low, bushy, wide as high.

'Lark' (22) ('Firefly' × 'Snow'): white, faint yellowish green throat, hose-in-hose, 1½"; moderately spreading.

'Lucia' (25) ('Firefly' × 'Snow'): white, hose-in-hose, 1½", margin crimped; erect, moderately branched.

'Lucinda' (203) (Kaempferi Hybrid × 'Snow'): deep pink, lighter at base, hose-in-hose, 1¾", 5 per cluster; well branched, rounded and compact.

'Majestic Pink' (168) (Kaempferi Hybrid × 'Snow'): deep pink, faint dark dots, hose-in-hose, 1¾"; semi-erect.

'Mithra' (74) ('Firefly' × 'Snow'): white, light yellow throat, hose-in-hose, 1¾", in clusters of 2 to 3; well branched compact plant.

'Northland' (133) (Kaempferi Hybrid × 'Snow'): white, crenate margin, 1¾"; in clusters of 2; dense growth, wide as high.

'Pink Banner' (200) (syn. 'White Mountain'; Kaempferi Hybrid × 'Snow'): moderate reddish orange 43C with darker dots, hose-in-hose, 2", filament and style darker pink; erect spreading.

'Pink Profusion' (47) (Sister seedling of 'Polar Bear'): pink fading to light pink, dark pink spots, hose-in-hose, 1½ to 2"; vigorous, height one and a half time the spread.

'Placid' (123) (Kaempferi Hybrid × 'Snow'): white with slight greenish tint, hose-in-hose, 1¾", slightly wavy, low and compact.

'Polar Bear' (20) ('Firefly' × 'Snow'): white, slight yellowish green throat, hose-in-hose, 1¾", margins slightly serrated, moderately branched, erect.

'Purple Glory' (193) (Kaempferi Hybrid × 'Snow'): purple fading to light purple, dark spots, hose-in-hose, 2"; erect with long shoots.

'Rose Banner' (126) (Kaempferi Hybrid × 'Snow'): purplish pink, dark spots, hose-in-hose, 1½"; open type growth, wide as high.

'Rose Glory' (142) (Sister seedling of 'Rose Banner' and 'White Banner'): purplish pink, dark red spots, hose-in-hose, 1½ to 1¾"; spreading, tall as it is wide.

'Roxanne' (150) (Kaempferi Hybrid × 'Snow'): vivid pink 44D, fading to yellowish pink, faint spots, hose-in-hose, 1½"; erect, moderate branching.

'Sanguinaire' (271) ('Pride of Mobile' × sport of 'Flame'): dark red and darker spots, 1½", in clusters of 2 or 3; branches freely with erect growth.

'Shocking Pink' (833) (cross of two unnamed seedlings of 'Maxwelli', and Kurume, Kaempferi, and Southern Indian Hybrids): vivid pink, 3", in clusters of 2 to 5; medium growth.

'Snowhite' (226) (sister seedling of 'White Perfection'): white, faint tinged yellowish green throat, hose-in-hose, 2"; spreading wider than tall.

'Twilight' (48) ('Firefly' × 'Obtusum'): light pink, dark spots, hose-in-hose, 2½"; compact, branching freely.

'White Banner' (1366) (Sister seedling of 'Rose Banner'): white, faint yellowish tint in throat, hose-in-hose, 1 to 1¼"; vigorous, low spreading twice as wide as tall.

'White Cap' (221A) ('Indica Alba' × 'Snow'): white, 2½", in clusters of 2 to 3; moderately branched, wide as tall.

'White Cloud' (121) (Kaempferi Hybrid × 'Snow'): light purplish pink, few darker spots, hose-in-hose, 1½"; slightly wavy; erect, well branched.

'White Cluster' (30) ('Firefly' × 'Snow'): white, hose-in-hose, 1¼"; slightly wavy; erect, branching low.

'White Habit' (125) (Kaempferi Hybrid × 'Snow'): white, hose-in-hose, 1¾"; erect, sparsely branched while young.

'White Perfection' (221) ('Indica Alba' × 'Snow'): white, throat partly greenish yellow, hose-in-hose, 2"; moderately branched, erect spreading.

'White Squall' (128) (Kaempferi Hybrid × 'Snow'): white, faint spots, 1⅔ to 1¾"; stamens light brown; compact low branching.

'Whitney' (138) (Kaempferi Hybrid × 'Snow'): white, faint greenish yellow throat, 1⅔ to 2"; in clusters of 2 to 3; low branching, twice as wide as high.

BELTSVILLE DWARFS

A race of true genetic dwarfs, selected by Robert L. Pryor, resulting from the Yerkes-Pryor hybrids. The dwarfs are very low growing with a compact spreading habit, early blooming with characteristics of Kurume Hybrids with normal size flowers. Plants after 15 years vary from 16 to 24" wide, and 12 to 30" in height, with an average growth of about 1½" a year. Nineteen dwarfs were introduced in 1959 and 1960. They are excellent for the small garden or as foundation plants in front of taller plants. They all bloom profusely and cover the entire plant. They are excellent for container culture and bonsai. All are hardy in Zones 7b to 9a.

'Boutonniere' (604) ('Maxwelli' × 'Snow') × (*kaempferi* × 'Snow'): white with creamy throat, hose-in-hose, 1½ to 1¾"; compact, about one third wider than high.

'Dainty Rose' (682) (*kaempferi* × 'Snow') × (*kaempferi* × 'Snow'): light purplish pink, 1 to 1¼" in clusters of 2 to 3; about one and a half times as wide as high.

'Flower Girl' (689) (*kaempferi* × 'Snow') × (*kaempferi* × 'Snow'): deep purplish red 67C, 1¾"; very dwarf about two and half times as wide as high.

'Lavender Elf' (608) ('Maxwelli' × 'Snow') × (*kaempferi* × 'Snow'): light purple, hose-in-hose, 1½–1¾"; about as wide as high.

'Leprechaun' (504) (cross of two seedlings of Kaempferi, Kurume and Southern Indian Hybrids): light purple, 77C, 1½" in clusters of 2 to 7; compact habit, twice as wide as high.

'Little White Lie' (553) (cross of a Kaempferi Hybrid × 'Snow' × 'Firefly'): white, hose-in-hose, 1", in clusters of 2 to 3; very dwarf, one and a half times as wide as high.

'Orchid Belle' (551) (cross of two unnamed seedlings of *kaempferi* × 'Snow' × 'Firefly'): light purple, with deeper throat, 1½" usually in clusters of 3; very dwarf, about as tall as wide.

'Pequeno' (552) (cross of two unnamed seedlings of *kaempferi* × 'Snow' × 'Firefly'): deep yellowish pink 39B, hose-in-hose, ¾"; bunched in clusters of 3; compact, twice as wide as high.

'Ping Pong' (606) ('Maxwelli' × 'Snow') × (*kaempferi* × 'Snow'): white, creamy throat, hose-in-hose, 1¼ to 1½" in clusters of 3 to 5; very dwarf about one and a half times as wide as high.

'Pink Elf' (601) ('Maxwelli' × 'Snow') × (*kaempferi* × 'Snow'): strong pink 43D, hose-in-hose, ¾ to 1"; very dwarf about three times as wide as high.

'Pinkette' (499) (cross of two unnamed seedlings of Southern Indian × Kurume Hybrids × 'Maxwelli'): strong purplish red 55B, 1 to 1½" in clusters of 3 to 9; compact, spreading to one and a half times its height.

'Purple Cushion' (688) (*kaempferi* × 'Snow') × (*kaempferi* × 'Snow'): vivid reddish purple, 1½"; very dwarf, about two times as wide as high.

'Rose Elf' (485) ('Mucronatum' × 'Snow' × 'Salmon Beauty'): strong pink, 1"; very dwarf about one and half times as wide as high.

'Salmon Elf' (528) (cross of two unnamed seedlings of *kaempferi* × 'Snow' × 'Firefly'): deep yellowish pink, dark blotch, hose-in-hose, 1¼"; in clusters of 2 or 3; very dwarf about as wide as high.

'Snowdrop' (602) ('Maxwelli' × 'Snow') × (*kaempferi* × 'Snow'): white, hose-in-hose, 1–1½"; in clusters of 2 to 7; very dwarf, about 3 times as wide as high.

'Snow Flurry' (611) ('Firefly' × 'Snow') × (*kaempferi* × 'Snow'): white, hose-in-hose, 1–1½"; very dwarf, about two times as wide as high.

'White Doll' (502) (cross of two unnamed seedlings of 'Maxwelli' × Kurume × Southern Indian Hybrids): white, 1½", in clusters of 2 or 3; dwarf and compact, spreading to twice its height.

'White Elf' (494) (cross of two unnamed seedlings of 'Maxwelli' × Kurume × Southern Indian Hybrids): white, 1 to 1½"; young plants often sparse in flower; very dwarf and dense, about 3 times as wide as high.

'White Nymph' (610) ('Firefly' × 'Snow') × (*kaempferi* × 'Snow'): white, 1 to 1½"; profuse; dwarf, 1½" times as wide as high.

CHISOLM-MERRITT HYBRIDS

The Chisolm-Merritt Hybrids were introduced around 1947, from crosses made in 1934 by the late Julian J. Chisolm, a nurseryman of Garret Park, Maryland. The plants were subsequently turned over to the late Dr. E. I. Merritt, Chevy Chase, Maryland, who named and introduced them. The seed parents were *R. poukhanense* and 'Cleopatra'; the pollen parents, 'Mme. Alphonse Pericat', 'Azuma Kagami', 'Salmon Beauty', 'Snow', and 'Yaye Giri'. The hybrids bloom early to midseason, along with Kurume Hybrids, and are medium to tall compact plants. Hardy in zones 7a–9. Many of the flowers are very similar in color and are single unless noted to the contrary. The flower sizes are usually 1½ to 1¾" across. The actual parents of the various cultivars are unknown.

'Alaska': yellowish pink.
'Alice Perry': moderate yellowish pink.
'Asia': deep pink, hose-in-hose.
'Augusta Brez': moderate yellowish pink, hose-in-hose.
'Begonia Rose': purplish pink 55B, hose-in-hose.
'Canton': light pink, hose-in-hose.
'Cella Costa': deep pink.
'Charlotte Weiss': deep pink, hose-in-hose.
'Charmer': deep yellowish pink.
'Chesapeake': strong pink.
'Chevy Chase': strong pink.
'China Girl': vivid red.
'Colorado': strong pink 48C, hose-in-hose.
'Columbia': deep pink.
'Coral Cluster': yellowish pink.
'Coral Sea': light yellowish pink.
'Cornelia': deep pink, flushed orange.
'Dessa Merritt': deep yellowish pink 41B, partially petaloid.
'Dorothy': light pink.
'Dr. E. A. Merritt' (syn. 'China'): strong red, 2½", large sepals.
'Eagle Heart': strong red.
'E. H. Wilson': vivid red.
'Eleanor': deep purplish pink.
'Enchantress': strong pink.
'Evening Star': light yellowish pink.
'Fascination': light pink.
'Flower Queen': deep purplish pink.
'Gloriosa': deep purplish pink.
'Gunji': deep purplish pink.
'Henry Wallace': deep pink.
'Isabel Chisolm': reddish orange.
'Jessica': strong red.
'Jewell': strong reddish orange.
'Kiska': purplish red, dark blotch, 2¼".
'Leah Coe': deep pink, flushed orange.
'Lizette': purplish pink 55B, hose-in-hose.
'Mary': strong pink.
'Maryland': strong red.
'May Day': light yellowish pink.

'Mickey Chisolm': moderate reddish orange.
'Millicent': purplish pink 55C.
'Ohio': deep pink, hose-in-hose.
'Pandora': light pink.
'Pink Lady': yellowish pink, dark blotch.
'Portia': light pink.
'Potomac': deep pink, hose-in-hose.
'Princess': pink with reddish flush.
'Printemps': light yellowish pink.
'Rosebud': pink.
'Rouge': light reddish orange.
'Ruth Stillwell': reddish orange.
'Sachem': reddish orange.
'Seminole': strong pink.
'Spring Splendor': strong pink.
'Sun Girl': yellowish pink.
'Suzanne': reddish orange.
'Virginia Merritt'; deep pink.
'Winston': pink, flushed light purple.
'Yoshino': deep reddish orange.

COOLIDGE HYBRIDS

Hybridized and introduced by the Coolidge Rare Plant Garden of Pasadena, California in the 1930's, some appear to have 'Mucronatum' as well as Kurume parentage, but parentage of individual cultivars is unknown. All are single unless noted hose-in-hose. About 100 were named, but information is only available on the following. The plants are seldom available except on the West Coast and should be hardy in zones 7–9. The shape and form of the plants are unknown, but should be similar to Kurume Hybrids. Actual parentage of plants is unknown.

'Algiers': deep pink, ¾".
'Ameratsu': deep yellowish pink, shaded orange red, 1¼".
'American Beauty': strong reddish purple, 1¼".
'Avalanche': white.
'Batik': orange with purplish cast, dark blotch.
'Bells of Arcady' (Mucronatum hybrid): white, 3".
'Bonny Kay': vivid red.
'Botticelli': pink with orange margin.
'Candlelight': pale yellowish pink.
'Coralie': deep yellowish pink, hose-in-hose, 1¼".
'Crabapple': pink, hose-in-hose.
'Dark Spring' (Mucronatum hybrid): vivid reddish purple, 1¾".
'Darling of the Gods': purplish pink.
'Evening Star': white, shaded violet.
'Flamboyant': purple.
'Flamingo: yellowish pink, 1½".
'Geisha: deep yellowish pink, ruffled, 1¼".
'General MacArthur': reddish purple.
'Her Majesty': purple.
'Hummingbird: light purple.
'Lantern Parade' (Mucronatum hybrid): vivid reddish purple, 2¼".
'Lavender and Old Lace': light purple.
'Misty': purplish pink.
'Muezzin': strong yellowish pink, hose-in-hose.
'Ning Po': strong pink.
'Old Wine': deep yellowish pink.
'Orchis': light purple.
'Pagentry' (Mucronatum hybrid): reddish purple 1¾", similar but less red than 'Dark Spring' and 'Lantern Parade'.
'Pagoda': purplish pink.
'Peacock': light purple.
'Pink Perfection': pink.
'Pink Window': deep pink, 2".
'Pitti Sing': light purplish pink, edges darker, 1½".
'Porcelain': pink, hose-in-hose.
'Red Lustre': strong red.
'Red Ruby: ruby.
'Salmon Tints': vivid to moderate red.
'Shimmer': deep pink.
'Silver Tears': light reddish purple.
'Singing Fountain': strong pink 49A, 1¾".
'Snowbird': white.
'Sunset': yellowish pink.
'Surprise': reddish purple, hose-in-hose.
'Twilight': reddish purple.
'Valo': deep purplish pink petals strap shaped, 2–2½"; low compact.
'Vanessa': violet.
'Violetta': violet, hose-in-hose.
'White April': white.
'Wood Dove': light purple, hose-in-hose.

DEERFIELD HYBRIDS

Hybridized and introduced by the Deerfield Nursery of New Jersey at the Philadelphia Flower Show in 1950, they were developed by the nursery between 1936 and 1940. All should be hardy in zones 7–9.

'Banks Land' (parentage unknown): pink, hose-in-hose, 1¼", early midseason, spreading, medium height.

'Eskimo' ('Hinomayo' hybrid): pink, hose-in-hose, 2", late midseason; spreading medium height.

'Frigid' ('Hinomayo' hybrid × 'Coral Bells'): white, 1½", early, upright, medium height.

'Iceberg' ('Hinode Giri' × 'Mucronatum'): white, 2¼", late midseason; low, spreading.

'Iceland' ('Mucronatum' × 'Hinode Giri'): white, 2¼", late midseason; low, spreading.

'Ivory I': (parentage unknown) white.

'Ivory II': (Hinomayo' × 'Mucronatum'): white, 1½", early midseason, spreading, medium height.

'Mme. Butterfly' ('Fedora' × 'Mucronatum'): white flushed light purple, 2½", late midseason; low spreading.

'Nome' ('Hinomayo' × 'Coral Bells'): pink, hose-in-hose, 1½", early midseason, upright, medium height.

'Polar' ('Salmon Beauty' × 'Othello'): white, hose-in-hose, 1½", early; upright medium height.

'Zero' ('Hinode Giri' × 'Mucronatum'): white, 1½", early midseason; upright, medium height.

FERNDOWN HYBRIDS

Introduced by D. Stewart and Son, Ltd., Ferndown, Dorset, England. Some of the plants were raised by C. E. Brown in England. Unfortunately most of the records on parentage were lost during World War II. They are hardy in zones 7–9. Most of the cultivars are medium-size shrubs 4 to 6 ft. unless otherwise noted.

'Andrew Elphinstone': orange.
'Armada': deep pink.
'Bournemouth Belle': yellowish pink.
'Cerita': reddish orange.
'Clarissa': yellowish pink, hose-in-hose, frilled.
'Crown Jewel': reddish orange, hose-in-hose, low.
'Fenella': white.
'Ferndown Beauty': strong purple.
'Galleon': orange.
'Ida': deep pink; low.
'Kilimanjaro': white with greenish blotch.
'Kilimari': strong pink 43C; compact.
'Lady Elphinstone': deep pink 52C, margins darker, deep red blotch, 2½".
'Margot': reddish orange.
'Martin Stewart': red, hose-in-hose.
'Master of Elphinstone': strong red.
'Nettie': light orange yellow.
'Selina': strong red.
'Vida Brown': strong purplish red 54B, hose-in-hose, ruffled, 1½"; late, low compact plant; popular in England but not widely known in the United States.
'Virginia': pale yellowish white, shaded pale green.

HERSHEY AZALEAS

The Hershey Azalea Farm in Gap, Pennsylvania was started in 1936 by the late Ralph Hershey and continued by his son Everett. Most of the azaleas are Kurume Hybrids, but parentage is unknown. Some have been used for greenhouse forcing. Hardy in zones 6b–9b. Plants are similar in form to other Kurume Hybrids.

'Chris': Purplish pink.
'Crossroad': Purplish pink.
'Double Hinode Giri' (probably syn. for 'Hinode Giri Double'): Very similar to 'Hinode Giri', hose-in-hose, not double; compact habit; fall foilage.
'G. G.': pink, hose-in-hose.
'Hershey's Red' (syn. 'Hershey's Bright Red'): strong red 52A.
'Hershey's Gold' (sport of 'Hershey's Red): reddish orange, hose-in-hose.
'Hershey's Orange': reddish orange

44B, hose-in-hose, 1½".
'Hershey's Pink': purplish pink, hose-in-hose.
'Hershey's Salmon': deep yellowish pink.
'Hershey's Salmon #2': reddish orange.
'Janny' (syn. 'Corner'): purplish pink, hose-in-hose, very hardy.
'Little Purple': purple, fast grower.
'Memorial Day': deep reddish orange, hose-in-hose, 1½", late.
'Red Sunrise': red, hose-in-hose.
'Red Sunset': red, hose-in-hose.
'Wood's White': white to light pink, with pink flare.

MAYO HYBRIDS

Developed by R. P. Mayo of Augusta, Georgia. The nursery is no longer in existence, but many of the Mayo Hybrids are still available. Most of the plants are early midseason, blooming later than Kurume Hybrids or *R. kaempferi*, with larger flowers, and hardy in zone 8 and possibly 7b.

'Bo-Peep' (Kurume hybrid × *kaempferi*): light reddish orange, hose-in-hose, 1¼"; medium upright.
'Fairy Queen' (*indicum* × *kaempferi*): white, flushed pink, 2"; tall, upright.
'Fireglow' ('Hinode Giri' hybrid): reddish orange 1½", upright.
'Flaming Beacon' (*indicum* × *kaempferi*): reddish orange, blotch darker, 1¾" upright, tall.
'Gypsy Rose' (*kaempferi* hybrid): purplish red, darker blotch, 2"; upright tall.
'Indian Sunset' (Kurume hybrid × *kaempferi*): strong yellowish pink, hose-in-hose, 1½"; upright, tall.
'May Firelight' (Kurume hybrid × *kaempferi*): reddish orange, 1¾"; upright, tall.
'Mayo's Magic Lily' (parentage unknown): pale purplish pink, blotch darker, partially petaloid sepal, petals divided, 2¼"; medium upright.
'Mayo's Perfection' (Kurume hybrid × *kaempferi*; an improved 'Hinodi Giri'): reddish orange; medium upright.
'Mayo's Pride' (parentage unknown): strong red, hose-in-hose, 2", upright tall.
'Orange King' ('Hinode Giri' hybrid): reddish orange, 2"; medium, spreading.
'Orange Surprise' (parentage unknown): deep yellowish pink 43C, dark spots in blotch, hose-in-hose, 2½".
'Pink Imperial' (Kurume hybrid × Indicum hybrid): vivid purplish red, frilled, 2¼"; upright, medium.
'Pink Lustre' (Kurume hybrid × *kaempferi*): purplish red, 1½", upright, medium.
'Princess Augusta' (parentage unknown, possibly a Mucronatum hybrid): light pink, hose-in-hose, 2½", very popular.
'Queen of Augusta' (Kurume hybrid ?): strong yellowish pink, hose-in-hose, 2"; spreading, medium.
'Salmon Monarch' (Kurume hybrid × *kaempferi*): yellowish pink, blotch darker, 2½"; spreading, medium.
'Salmon Splendor' (Kaempferi hybrid): strong red, 2¼"; upright tall.

PENDER HYBRIDS

Developed by Dave Pender, Jr., Garner, N. C., since WWII. The parentage is unknown but possibly Kurume and 'Mucronatum' hybrids. The plants are of medium habit, 4 to 6 ft. tall.

'Dixie Red': Vivid purplish red, 2¼–2½"; bushy dense growth, late midseason. Hardy Zone 6.
'Mable Andrews': Light purplish pink, 3"; medium strong grower, late midseason. Hardy Zones 6–7.
'Mary Cabell': Light purplish pink with purplish blotch, 3"; midseason; strong open growth, leaves elliptic. Hardy Zone 7.
'Maude Grimes': Moderate pink, petaloid, 2½–3"; foliage semi-persistent; strong growth, late midseason. Hardy Zone 6.
'Mishew Edgerton': Deep pink, purplish undertones, 3"; late midseason, rapid grower. Hardy Zone 6.
'Rhea Pender': Moderate purplish pink, hose-in-hose, ruffled, 2½"; medium compact growth. Hardy Zone 5.

SANDER AND FORSTER AZALEAS

These two groups were developed around 1885 from some of the early introductions of evergreen azaleas to the United States and Austria.

The Sander Hybrids were developed by Charles Sander, gardener at Holm Lea, Brookline, Mass. the home of the late Professor C. S. Sargent of Arnold Arboretum. The Indian Azalea 'Decora' introduced in 1847 is thought to be the parent of two dwarf compact plants raised, one named 'Garnet'. 'Garnet' was then crossed with an unknown Kurume (*R.* 'Obtusum')and a white form, both probably 'Amoena' selections, and later with 'Hinode Giri'. Three decades were taken to develop a group of azalea with compact twiggy habit and flowers of various colors ranging from 1 to 1¾" wide. Ernest Wilson predicted a great future for these plants as mentioned in *A Monograph of Azaleas* (1921, p. 44) by Wilson, E. H. and Alfred Rehder.

Unfortunately, most of the named Sander Hybrids have been lost. Occasionally one can find a 'Sander White', 'Sander Red', or 'Sander Orchid', but there is no way to determine their original names.

Otto Forster of Lebenhof, Austria, also around 1885, made a similar cross of the 'Amoena' Azalea × 'Duc de Nassau' an Indian hybrid, from which 'Hexe' was derived. 'Hexe' was extensively cultivated around Dresden and was used as a stock plant to graft commercial Indian Azaleas. It soon became popular on its own merits and was sent as a greenhouse plant to England and the U.S.A.

Another race of hose-in-hose azaleas with large colorful red flowers 1¾–2½" wide was developed at Holm Lea from the cross 'Flambeau' × 'Vuylestekeana', which has also been reported as a cross of 'Hexe' × 'Vuylestekeana'. Unfortunately no other information is available on these hybrids.

'Hexe' (syn. 'Firefly'; 'Amoena' × 'Duc de Nassau'; Forster): strong purplish red 63A, hose-in-hose, 1¾", late midseason; low dense spreading. The 'Hexe' from Blaauw Nursery in Holland has a different flower; deep red, semidouble, frilled and 1½" wide.

SANDER HYBRIDS

'Alice Sargent': vivid reddish orange.
'Brookline': vivid red.
'Garnet': vivid red, 1¼".
'Havemeyer': vivid red.
'Hebe': white with red stripes.
'Helene': deep pink.
'Hermione': deep reddish orange.
'Hilda Hedlund': deep pink.
'Holm Lea': vivid red.
'Jupiter': deep reddish orange.
'Mars': vivid red.
'Muriel': vivid red.
'Natalie: deep yellowish pink.
'Rose Queen': deep pink.
'Ruby': strong red 46D with darker blotch, ¾"; upright tall. Not to be confused with 'Ward's Ruby' which is a dwarf, compact plant. 'Ruby' has been considered one of the best early blooming red Kurume azaleas.
'Suzuki': deep red.
'Uncas': dark reddish orange.
'Venus': deep purplish red.
'Vivid': strong red, 50A, 1¾"; early midseason; low, dense spreading.

KAEMPFERI HYBRIDS

The Kaempferi Hybrids comprise cultivars in which *R. kaempferi* is one of the important parents. Prof. C. S. Sargent of Arnold Arboretum first introduced *R. kaempferi* to the U.S.A. from seed collected in the mountains of Japan in 1892 and sent seed to Kew Gardens in England in 1894. The plant had been known earlier in England, introduced by Charles Maries in 1887, but only apparently with a few plants. It became better known from the seed sent by Sargent.

Its hardiness was a surprise and delight to American gardeners, when it proved hardy in Boston and flowered there from the first time in 1897. The same hardiness as well as the plant's attractiveness was also recognized in England and Belgium. For the colder areas of Europe, *R. kaempferi* was a better plant than the Kurume Azalea. Its easy propagation by cuttings increased the popularity of selected seedlings, and soon thereafter it became an important plant in the hybridizing being done at Exbury and elsewhere in England.

Hybrids were developed in Holland during World War I by P. M. Koster of Boskoop. They were crosses of *R. kaempferi* with 'Malvatica' and often referred to in Europe as the Malvatica Hybrids. The origin and history of the plant 'Malvatica' is vague, but apparently came in with a shipment of 'Mucronatum' azaleas from Japan to Koster Nursery in the mid to late 1800's. It is doubtful if the true 'Malvatica' still exists, but the original plant was reported to have purplish flowers and dark shiny leaves. Mr. Koster named some of his selections after operas and their characters, such as 'Carmen', 'Oberon', and 'Othello', before leaving Holland in 1921 to establish a nursery in Bridgetown, New Jersey, U.S.A. The C. B. van Nes and Sons Nursery in Holland obtained the first seedlings in 1921 and put them into commerce. Selections by Van Nes were given girls' names such as 'Anny', 'Betty', and 'Gretchen'. The firm Koster and Co. also sold small lots of seedlings to L. J. Endtz and Hugo T. Hooftman of Boskoop. These were probably second generation seedlings of Koster's original lot. Endtz and Hooftman each introduced selections such as 'Anne Maria' and 'John Cairens'. It is believed that the Maxwell Azalea (*R. phoeniceum* var. *calycinum* f. *maxwelli*) may have been included in the parentage of these later introductions.

The Vuyk Hybrids were introduced by Aart Vuyk of the Vuyk Van Nes Nursery in Boskoop. The first crosses were made in 1921 with an evergreen azalea, presumably *R. kaempferi* and reportedly a Mollis Hybrid 'J. C. van Tol'. The hybrids show no evidence of the Mollis Azalea and are possibly just *R. kaempferi* seedlings or crosses with 'Maxwell' and 'Mucronatum'. The plants were named after musical composers and introduced in 1926. Other azaleas of the same origin were introduced by Felix and Dijkhuis of Boskoop and called the Feldyk Hybrids.

Following the original introduction of the Kaempferi Hybrids from Europe, hybridizing began in the United States. Early introductions were the Arnold Hybrids developed by Jackson T. Dawson of the Arnold Arboretum; the Dawson Hybrids by Henry S. Dawson of Eastern Nurseries, Holliston, Mass., and others.

The Gable Hybrids by Joseph Gable of Stewartstown, Pennsylvania, were first introduced in 1927 and were basically hybrids of *R. y. poukhanense* and *R. kaempferi*. These were very hardy evergreen azaleas and received wide acceptance throughout the northeast and the mid-west. Following Gable and often starting with Gable Hybrids were the following hybridizers: Girard, Pride, Shammarello, Stanton, and others.

The original Kaempferi Hybrids are usually medium to tall shrubs (4–10 feet) with flowers usually larger than Kurume Kybrids, 1½–2½", and in general the plants are hardier. They are hardy in zones 5b–9a. The flowers range from pink through reds and purples and a few are white, and bear early to mid-season after the Kurume Hybrids. Some of the orange and red flowered clones fade in hot sunny weather. The leaves are generally persistent; however, in the lower hardiness range they may be deciduous. Many have beautiful fall and winter colors.

The following are *R. kaempferi* or related hybrids. Some are old varieties, while others have been introduced in the past 20 years. Many are available only in Europe. See Appendix I.

'Adele' (W. C. Hage, 1952): deep pink, early.

'Ageeth' (sport of 'Vuyk's Scarlet'; Hooftman '70): strong red 47d, faint brown blotch, frilled, 2½", midseason; compact broad upright.

'Aleida' (sports of 'Vuyk's Scarlet'; R.S.A.N.C. '80): deep reddish orange 44C, faint brown red blotch, 2½", midseason; broad upright.

'Alice' ('Malvatica' × *kaempferi*; Vyuk van Nes '21): vivid yellowish pink, blotch darker.

'Annamaria' (syn. 'Frau Dakens'; Hooftman about 1950): white.

'Ann Rothwell' ('Nanki-Poo' × *kaempferi*; George '66): strong purplish red 71C.

'Anny' (*kaempferi* × 'Malvatica'; van Nes Son '22): strong red.

'Apotheose' (Van Hecke '40): red, small, early.

'Arabesk' (van Nes '70): vivid red; compact.

'Atlanta' (*kaempferi* × 'Malvatica'; C. B. van Nes): vivid reddish purple, 2"; low grower.

'Beattie' ('Mucronatum' × 'Betty'; Woodland Garden '73): purplish pink.

'Bengal Star' ('Red Star' × 'Bengal Fire'; Larson '65): dark red 53B, 2¾", buds red, late midseason; 3 ft. in 10 yrs.

'Betty' (*kaempferi* × 'Malvatica'; C. B. van Nes '22): strong purplish red, darker throat, 2".

'Blue Danube' (old variety in Boskoop; Van Hecke, Belg. registered '69): strong purplish red 72B, midribs deep purplish red 74B, blotch spotted deep red 60A, 1½", midseason; upright, spreading.

'Brazier' (old var. in Boskoop; Van Hecke, Belg., registered '69): deep pink, tinged reddish orange, 1¾" early midseason.

'Bycendron' (old var. in Boskoop; Wuyt, Belg., registered '69): vivid purplish red 55A, 2", midseason.

'Cameo' (grown and reg. in Boskoop '69): vivid reddish purple, 1½".

'Carmen': vivid red, darker throat, 2½"; upright tall.

'Charlotte': dark reddish orange.

'Christina' ('Florida' × 'Louise Gable'; van Nes '69): moderate red, hose-in-hose, occasionally double, large, midseason; broad; good for forcing.

'Cleopatra': deep yellowish pink, 2½"; upright tall.

'Dawn' (Hage '69): moderate yellowish pink, very early; good for forcing.

'Decoration': dark pink, blotch red, late; spreading habit.

'Dorsett' (selection of *kaempferi*, seed from PI 85871, Japan; Hollowell; NA 273481): strong yellowish pink 41C, purplish red blotch 58B, 1⅔". Selected for consistent fall flowering Oct., early Nov., few flowers in spring; hardy in zones 7b.

'Double Beauty' (dbl. seedling × 'Vuyk's Scarlet'; van Nes '66): strong purplish red 55D, hose-in-hose, midseason; low compact; hardy zone 6.

'Dusty Rose': light pink.

'Eastern Fire' (a *R. kaempferi* selection, by Crown Est. Comm. '66): deep yellowish pink, funnel-shaped.

'Eira' ('Kirishima' × 'Malvatica'; Stevenson '51): different shades of purplish pink and reddish purple.

'Elisabeth' (Hooftman '35): pale yellowish pink.

'Ethel Orme' (sport of 'Linwood E 30'; Borme): deep purplish pink, hose-in-hose, midseason; low compact; hardy zone 6.

'Eva' (van Nes '22): strong purple.

'Excelsior' ('Mother's Day' × ?; van Hecke, Belg.): large red leaves, purplish in fall.

'Explorer' ('Hinomayo' × ?; van Hecke, Belg., registered in Boskoop '69): deep pink, 1⅛, early, midseason; compact; good for forcing.

'Favorite' ('Hinode Giri' × *kaempferi*, van Nes about 1920): deep pink, frilled.

'Fedora' (*kaempferi* × 'Malvatica', van Nes '22): deep purplish pink, 2".

'Fidelio' (*kaempferi* × 'Malvatica'; van Nes '22): moderate purplish red.

'Fireball'; vivid pink.

'Frieda' (van Nes '52): strong purple.

'Frits Hooftman' (Hooftman '35): light red.

'Frostburg' ('Desiree' × 'Rose Greeley'; Yates '69): white, spotted flare light yellowish green 45C, hose-in-hose, 3", fragrant; 3×3 ft. in 10 yrs.

'Gabriele' ('Mother's Day' × 'Kermesina'; Hachmann '79): vivid purplish red 58B, 1½", late; very hardy.

'Garda Joy' (Gable seedling H–12–G; registered by Griswold '68): yellowish pink, semidouble, 2¼", late May; leaves reddish in fall; 24×18" high in 10 yrs.

'Garden Beauty' (syn. 'Gartenshoenheit'; van Nes '22): light pink.

'Gingy': vivid pink, 43D, darker blotch; need shade, sun burns.

'Glow Worm': reddish orange.

'Goblin' (Hage): deep purplish pink, early.

'Gretchen' (van Nes, '22): vivid reddish purple, darker blotch, 2"; late midseason, upright.

'Heather Macleod' ('Eria' × *kaempferi*; Hydon '73): strong purplish pink 63A.

'Hino Scarlet' (syn. 'Campfire'; Peters '66): deep red 53D, yellowish cast in throat, hose-in-hose. 1½"; upright compact, very hardy, zone 6b–9.

'Holland Red' (syn. 'Holland'): vivid red, 1½".

'H. Whitelegg' (Endtz '31): vivid red.

'Ivette' (Vuyk van Nes '22): pink.

'Janka' (witches broom sport of 'Johanna'; Nozal): red; low compact.

'Jan Wellen' ('Aladdin' × 'Amoena') × 'Vuyk's Scarlet'; R.S.A.N.C. '78): vivid pink, blotch dark red, 2½", early; tall spreading, good for forcing.

'Jeanette' (van Nes '20): deep purplish pink, darker blotch, 2". Similar to 'Fedora'.

'Joe's Charmer' ('Martha Hitchcock' × 'James Gable'; Folding '71): strong purplish pink 62A, white center 155A, midseason; hardy to −4°F.

'Joe's Showpiece' ('Martha Hitchcock' × 'James Gable'; Folding '71): vivid red 45A, white center 155A, late; dark fall foliage; hardy to −4°F.

'Joe's White' ('Martha Hitchcock' × 'James Gable'; Folding '71): white 155D, 3", midseason; hardy zone 6.

'Johanna' ('Florida' seedling; van Nes '69): deep red.

'John Cairns' (Endtz '40): vivid red, 1½".

'John P. Albert' (Boer '70): deep pink, late; good for forcing.

'Juliana': deep pink.

'Kakiemon' ('Nanki-Poo' × *kaempferi*; George '70): moderate red 50B, dark spotting.

'Kathleen' (van Nes '22): strong purplish pink.

'Katisha' ('Kirishima' × 'Malvatica'; Stevenson, intro. by Hydon '69): light purplish pink, dark spotting, white stamens; compact habit.

'Lakme' (P. M. Koster): light purplish red; low. Similar to 'Mary' but lighter and lower.

'Leon's Red' (Vuyk's Red' × 'Gable R49'; Yavorsky): vivid red, 2", early to midseason.

'Leon's Sport' (sport of 'Leon's Red'; Yavorsky): deep pink, hose-in-hose, 1½".

'L'Hirondelle' (Hage '69): deep pink, tinged yellowish pink, early.

'Lilac Time' (Endtz): light purple.

'Lily Marleen' (syn. 'Marlene Vuyk'; 'Little Ruby' × 'Dr. W. F. Wery'; van Nes '69): vivid purplish pink 57B, hose-in-hose, double, frilled, 1¾", early midseason; broad and low; very hardy, to −10°F.

'Linda Stuart' (? × 'Blaauw's Pink'; Yavorsky): deep yellowish pink margin, center paler, hose-in-hose, 2", midseason; taller than wide.

'Lohengrin' (P. M. Koster about 1920): deep pink.

'Louise' (van Nes '22): vivid purplish red, 1¼". Similar to 'Mary'.

'Luzi' (*kaempferi* × ('Malvatica' × Kurume Hybrid; Mittendorf '69): white, no markings, 2–2¾", early; upright; hardy.

'Mahler' (seedling × 'Vuyk's Rosyred'; van Nes '69): reddish purple, blotch dark dots, 2¾", late; low and broad.

'Margaret George' ('Eira' × *kaempferi*; Hydon '73): vivid purplish red 61D.

'Martin Stewart' (parentage ?; Stewart '62): vivid red, hose-in-hose, tubular.

'Mary' (van Nes '22): strong pink, 2½", early midseason; upright, medium height.

'Mary King' (syn. 'Mikado'; van Hecke '40): deep pink.

'Mary Meredith' ('Eiria' × *kaempferi*; Hydon '73): vivid purplish red 67B.

'Meister's Double Pink': pink double.

'Mercator' ('Blue Danube' × 'Amoena'; van Hecke): reddish purple, late; vigorous.

'Mimi' (*kaempferi* selection; Bunshoten '62): pale purplish pink 61D, darker blotch.

'Mme. Albert Van Hecke' ('Willy' × ?; Van Hecke '60): light pink; good grower.

'Myosotis' (old variety in Boskoop, Wuyt, Belg., registered '69): red, 1¾", early.

'Nanki-Poo' ('Kirishima' × 'Malvatica'; Stevenson; intro. Hydon '67): vivid red petals and stamens.

'Nordlicht' ('Vuyk's Scarlet' × 'Aladdin'; Hachmann '77): deep reddish orange 42A, brown markings, 1½–2⅛", early; dwarf, fairly hardy.

'Norma' (P. M. Koster): strong reddish purple, light throat, darker blotch, 2½", early; upright, medium height.

'Oberon' (Koster about 1920): pale pink.

'Ophelia' ('Hinomayo' × ?; van Hecke): pink; sunburn resistant.

'Orange Beauty' ('Hinode Giri' × *kaempferi*): light orange.

'Orange Giant' (*yedoense* × 'Louise Gable'; van Nes '70): vivid orange, large.

'Orange King' (Endtz): reddish orange.

'Othello' (Koster about 1920): strong red, 2", early midseason; upright, medium height; superior to the Kurume Hybrid 'Hinode Giri'.

'Parfait' (Schepens): pink, hose-in-hose, ruffled; hardy to −10°F.

'Peep-Bo' ('Kirishima' × 'Malvatica'; × ?; Hindla '78): strong purplish pink 55A, darker spotting, rounded spaced lobes, 2½", 6×7 ft. in 15 yrs., hardy −5°F.

'Pink Radiance' (Fedora × ?; Hindla '78): strong purplish pink 55A, darker spotting, rounded spaced lobes, 2½"; 6×7 ft. in 15 yrs, hardy −5°F.

'Pink Treasure' (van Nes): deep pink.

'Pooh-Bah' ('Kirishima' × 'Malvatica'; Stevenson, intro. Hydon '67): reddish purple, darker spotting, red stamens, large.

'Pouffe' (*kaempferi* × *indicum*; Haworth-Booth '64): strong yellowish orange 38A, 1¼" low compact spreading.

'Pretty Girl' (Schepens): dark red, hose-in-hose; hardy to −10°F.

'Princess Ida' ('Kirishima' × 'Malvatica'; Stevenson, intro. Hydon '68): purplish pink, red stamens.

'Purple King': deep purplish pink, 1¾".

'Red Pimpernel' (Endtz): reddish orange.

'Regina' (Hooftman '35): light yellowish pink.

'Riponia' ('Violacea' × 'Tropper'; Meyer '68): light purple, double, frilled; compact.

'Roehr's Mother's Day' (Kurume Hybrid × *kaempferi*: Bauman, intro. Roehr'55): deep pink, hose-in-hose, frilled, 2–2½", late; hardy zone 6b.

'Roehr's Peggy Ann' (syn. 'Peggy Ann', 'Peggy Ann Rodino'; Bauman, intro. Roehr'55): white, purplish pink edge, hose-in-hose, 2", late; hardy zone 6b.

'Roehr's Tradition' (syn. 'Tradition', Kurume Hybrid × *kaempferi*; Bauman, intro. Roehr '55): moderate pink, hose-in-hose, 1¼" late; low broad habit, hardy zone 6.

'Royal Pink' (syn. 'May Queen'; 'Hinomayo' × ?; vanHecke '69): strong purplish pink, 62A, 1½", long stamens; tall.

'Salmon King' (Endtz): strong orange.

'Schneeglanz' ('Kermesina' × 'Leanette'; Hachmann'78): white 155D, marked yellow green 150A-B, 2", 2–4 in truss.

'Schneewittchen' ('Kermesina' × 'John Cairns'; Hachmann '83): white 155D with no markings, 2¼–2½", 3–6 in truss.

'Sikorsky' (old variety in Boskoop, imported from U.K. '67): reddish orange, large, late; other varieties better.

'Silbersee' ('Arendsii' × 'Amoena'; Schumacher): white, yellow markings, ¾–1⅛", late; dwarf; hardy to −5°.

'Silver Sword' (sport of 'Girard's Rose'; Meivogel, intro. Cottage Gardens '80): deep red 53D, 5–7 frilled wavy lobes, 2½"; variegated foliage, fine white margin, reddish in fall; 18×24" in 5 yrs.; hardy zone 6.

'Sunrise' (Hooftman '39): light reddish orange.

'Swan White': white, faint yellowish green throat, hose-in-hose, 1¾"; early midseason; upright, medium height.

'Tanja' (witches broom of 'Christina'; Nozal): moderate red, hose-in-hose; low compact.

'Thais' (P. M. Koster): strong pink, yellowish pink throat; low growing. Similar to 'Mary'.

'Titipu' ('Kirishima' × 'Malvatica'; Stevenson, intro. Hydon '68): deep purple.

'Tit-Willow' ('Kirishima' × 'Malvatica': Stevenson, intro. Hydon '67): very pale purple, long white stamens.

'Toreador' (syn. 'Leontientje'; van Hecke; old variety in Boskoop '69): vivid purplish red 57C, 1–1⅛", early.

'Treasure': strong pink, double.
'Verne's Red' (seedling of 'James Gable'; Wood): vivid red, hose-in-hose, red stamens and pistil, small; 5×6 ft. in 16 yrs.
'White Lady' (Endtz): white.
'Whitelegg': deep pink.
'Wilhelmina' (van Ness): deep pink.
'Willy' (van Nes): vivid pink.
'Yankee Doodle' ('F. Abbott' seedling, intro. Carlson): pink; very hardy.
'Zampa' (van Nes '22): deep purplish pink, 2¼".

SMALL GROUPS OF KAEMPFERI OR RELATED HYBRIDS

ARNOLD HYBRIDS

Developed by Jackson T. Dawson from a chance 'Amoenum' × *kaempferi* hybrid at the Arnold Arboretum about 1910. The plants are very hardy, −10°F., for evergreen azaleas, medium to tall 6–10 feet, but more spreading than *R. kaempferi;* and bloom in early midseason.

'Briarcliffe': deep purplish pink, 1¼".
'Cardinalis': deep purplish pink, 1¼".
'Dexter's Pink': deep purplish pink, 1½".
'Early Dawn': vivid purplish red, 1¼".
'Mello-Glo': vivid purplish red, 1".
'Mossieanum': deep purplish pink.

DAWSON HYBRIDS

Henry J. Dawson of the Eastern Nurseries, Holleston, Mass., about 1923 crossed *R. kaempferi* × 'Indica Alba'. They are noteworthy as the first of the large flowered, 3¼", hardier hybrids to zone 6 and one of the many progenitors of the Glenn Dale Hybrids. The plants are tall, 6–10 ft.

'Hazel Dawson': vivid reddish purple, 3¼", late midseason; upright, tall.
'Helen Dawson': moderate purplish red, 3¼", late midseason; upright, tall.

EXBURY EVERGREEN HYBRIDS

Introduced by the late Lionel de Rothschild, Exbury, Southhampton, England, around 1933. The plants were first registered and reported *R. oldhamii* as one of the parents. *R. oldhamii* was introduced to England in 1878 but was lost, and was later introduced by Wilson to Kew Gardens in 1918. It is pointed out in the book *The Rothschild Rhododendrons* that *R. oldhamii* was used only to produce 'Bengal Fire'. The source of some of the other parents is unknown; 'Bassett Wood' may have come from Knap Hill Nursery but was never registered. 'Kanaho' is a form of *R. scabrum* from Wada in Japan. The *R. scabrum* 'Mikado' is unknown and is possibly the kaempferi selection 'Mikado' from Japan. Most of the Exbury Evergreen Hybrids should be hardy in zones 6 to 8. They are medium to tall plants, 6 to 8 ft.

'Audrey Wynniatt' ('Bassett Wood' × *kaempferi*): purplish red, large, produced freely; shrubby plant to 4 ft.
'Bengal Fire' (*kaempferi* × *oldhamii* '34): vivid red, 2½", late; tall spreading.
'Eddy' (*kaempferi* × 'Apollo' '33): deep red 34A, 3", late midseason; upright tall.
'Imbros' (*simsii* cultivar): deep reddish orange, 3".
'Lady Ivor Churchill' (parentage ?): pink, hose-in-hose, 3 ft. high.
'Leo' ('Malvatica' × *kaempferi* '33): vivid orange, 2½", late midseason; low compact.

'Louise' (*kaempferi* × Indian Hybrid): vivid red, 2½", early midseason; upright medium height.
'Marie' (*kaempferi* × Indian Hybrid): purplish red, hose-on-hose, 3", early midseason; upright medium height.
'Naomi' ('Malvatica' × *kaempferi*): strong pink, 2½", late midseason; upright medium height.
'Nigella' (*scabrum* 'Kanabo' × 'Louise'): purplish red, hose-in-hose.
'Nimrod' (same parentage as 'Nigella'): light orange.
'Pekoe' ('Malvatica' × *kaempferi*): vivid pink; more spreading than others.
'Pippa' (*kaempferi* × 'Mucronatum'): moderate red, large; semidwarf, spreading habit.
'Sir William Lawrence' ('Hinode Giri' × *kaempferi*): pale pink, 2", late midseason; upright medium height.
'Tamarisk' (*scabrum* 'Mikado' × *kaempferi*): strong yellowish pink; compact medium height.

FELDYK HYBRIDS

Introduced by Felix and Dijkhuis, Boskoop, Holland, around 1930 and called the Feldyk Hybrids. Plants should be hardy in zones 6–9. No information is available on parentage and age of plants. They are of the same origin as the Vuyk Hybrids.

'Aartje': deep pink, darkly spotted.
'Hanny': reddish orange.
'Jeanne': moderate purple.
'Margo': deep pink.
'Prinses Marijke' (syn. 'Princess Marijke'): deep purplish pink, purplish outside.
'Truus': white.

TEN OAKS HYBRIDS

Selections of *R. kaempferi* seedlings introduced in the 1950's by the Ten Oaks Nursery, Clarksville, Maryland, U.S.A. Hardiness and habit of growth similar to other Kaempferi Hybrids.

'Bette': deep orange yellow.
'Connie': moderate reddish orange 43C, early.
'Roberta': vivid red.

VUYK HYBRIDS

Developed by Aart Vuyk of the Vuyk van Nes Nursery, Boskoop Holland starting in 1921. The objective was hardier evergreen azaleas with large flowers. A few of the hybrids were introduced into the U.S.A. in 1926, with extensive importations beginning in 1945. The crosses with 'J. C. van Tol', a deciduous Mollis Hybrid, as the male parent are doubtful, showing no characteristic of the deciduous parent. The appearance, habit of growth, and hardiness are all characteristic of the female parent.

'Beethoven' (*maxwelli* × Mollis hybrid, '41): strong purplish red 70B, deeper blotch, fringed lobes, 2¾".
'Chopin' (syn. 'Mrs. Vuyk van Nes'; 'Schubert' × unknown seedling, '54): strong purplish pink 58C, dark blotch, 2½".
'Florida' (unknown seedling × 'Vuyk's Scarlet', '62): deep red, hose-in-hose, with some petaloids.
'Geraldina' (around 1960): deep yellowish pink.
'Geraldine Vuyk' (Kaempferi hybrid × 'J. C. van Tol'): strong purplish pink 58D, deeper blotch, 2".
'Helene Vuyk' (syn. 'P. W. Hardijzer'; 'Maxwelli' × 'J. C. van Tol'): deep purplish pink, deep red blotch, 2½".
'Johann Sebastian Bach' ('Maxwelli' × 'J. C. van Tol'): vivid reddish purple 74B, 2½".
'Johann Strauss' (Kaempferi hybrid × 'J. C. van Tol', van Tol): vivid purplish red 61D, darker blotch, 2½".
'Joseph Haydn' ('Mucronatum' × 'J. C. van Tol'): light purple 74B, brownish blotch, 2¾".

'Koningin' Wilhelmina' (syn. 'Queen Wilhelmina'): vivid reddish orange, 2".
'Lilac Beethoven' (around 1960): moderate purple with red blotch.
'Mozart' (Kaempferi hybrid × 'J. C. van Tol'): deep purplish pink, 2½".
'Palestrina' (syn. 'Wilhelmina Vuyk'; Kaempferi × 'J. C. van Tol', '26): white with light greenish yellow blotch, 2¼". Good hardy white.
'Prins Bernhard' (syn. 'Prince Bernhard'): reddish orange; low.
'Prinses Irene' (syn. 'Princess Irene'; van Nes): moderate red.
'Prinses Juliana' (syn. 'Princess Juliana'): orange; low.
'Purple Triumph': purple.
'Schubert' (Kaempferi hyb. × 'J. C. van Tol'): moderate purplish pink 62B, 2".
'Sibelius' ('Maxwelli' × 'J. C. van Tol'): deep yellowish pink 39B, with brown-purple blotch, 2".
'Vuyk's Rosyred' (about '54): deep pink, PP 1325.
'Vuyk's Scarlet' (about '54): deep red, PP 1283.
'Wilhelmina Vuyk': see 'Palestrina'.

GABLE HYBRIDS

These hardy evergreen azaleas were introduced by the late Joseph B. Gable, a nurseryman of Stewartstown, Pennsylvania; best known for his azalea and rhododendron hybrids. Basic objectives were for hardy evergreen azaleas. Hardiness is obtained from the Korean Azalea, *R. poukhanense*, and the Kaempfer Azalea, *R. kaempferi*. There are however a wide range of other crosses and recrosses involved including Kurume hybrids 'Hinode Giri', 'Yaye Giri', Forster's 'Hexe', 'Mucronatum', *R. macrosepalum*, and 'Beni Kirishima', a red double form of *R. indicum*, and possibly 'Macrantha'. The cultivar 'Forest Fire' is the only known hybrid of *R. tschonoskii*. The crosses of Kaempferi × 'Maxwelli' were not found reliably hardy. The Gable Hybrids are some of the hardiest evergreen azaleas, zones 6b and 8b for most, and the plants are of medium height 6 to 8 ft. tall. They have achieved wide acceptance and been used by other hybridizers in their crosses. Some of Gable's seedlings have been introduced by others under names or numbers as Gable Hybrids, often without Gable's consent. They will follow the plants named by Gable.

'Apricot' (probably *poukhanense* × 'Hexe'): strong orange yellow, fades; very hardy.
'Barbara Hille' (parentage unknown): deep yellowish pink; slow grower.
'Big Joe' (*poukhanense* × *kaempferi*): strong purplish pink, blotch brownish, 2½", early midseason; spreading medium habit. One of the first hybrids selected and still popular.
'Campfire' ('Caroline Gable' × 'Purple Splendor'): strong red 52A, blotch darker, hose-in-hose, late midseason; tall.
'Carol' ('Louise Gable' × 'Caroline Gable'): vivid purplish red 57C, hose-in-hose, late midseason; low very hardy.
'Caroline Gable' ((*poukhanense* × 'Hexe') × (*poukhanense* × *kaempferi*)): vivid red 55A, blotch darker, 1¾", late midseason.
'Charlotte' (*poukhanense* × 'Mucronatum'): vivid reddish purple, blotch red, early midseason; spreading medium dense.
'Cherokee' (*kaempferi* × 'Hinode Giri'): strong red, 1¾", late; low to medium height.
'Chinook' (parentage unknown): deep yellowish pink, 2"; similar to 'Mary Dalton'.
'Claret' ((*poukhanense* × 'Hexe') × (*poukhanense* × 'Hexe')): dark red, 1½"; low dwarf, poor grower.
'Elizabeth Gable' (*indicum* × (*poukhanense* × *kaempferi*): deep red 53B, frilled, darker blotch, 2½", late; spreading medium habit.
'Ethelwyn' (parentage unknown): pink; tender.
'Forest Fire' (*tschonoskii* × 'Caroline Gable'): deep pink, hose-in-hose, 1".
'Fuchsia' (*macrosepalum* × 'Caroline Gable'): vivid purplish red, hose-in-hose, 1½", late midseason.
'Gable's Flame' (syn. 'Gable's Scarlet'; parentage unknown): strong red, hose-in-hose, frilled, 1¾", late midseason; spreading medium habit.
'Glow of Dawn' (*poukhanense* × *kaempferi*): similar to 'Springtime' and 'Kathleen'.
'Herbert' (*poukhanense* × 'Hexe'): vivid reddish purple, darker blotch, hose-in-hose, frilled 1¾", early midseason; spreading low to medium height.

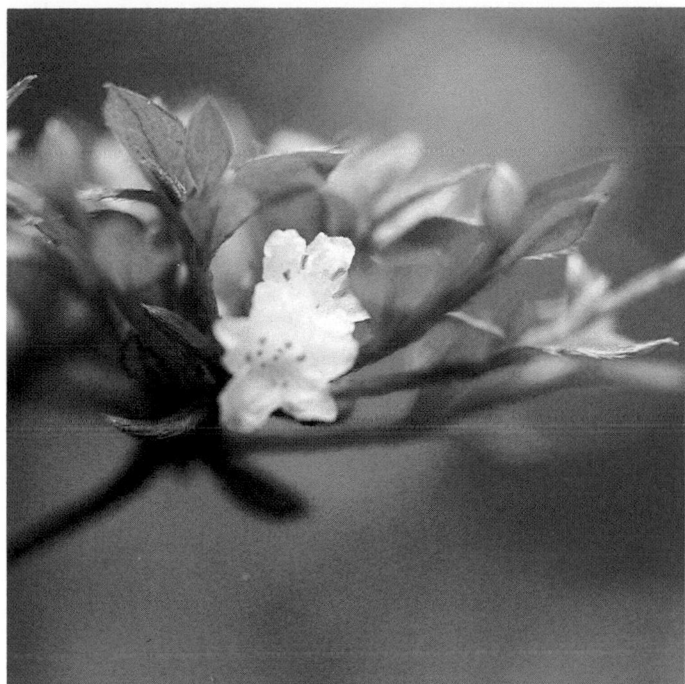

R. tsusiophyllum. GALLE

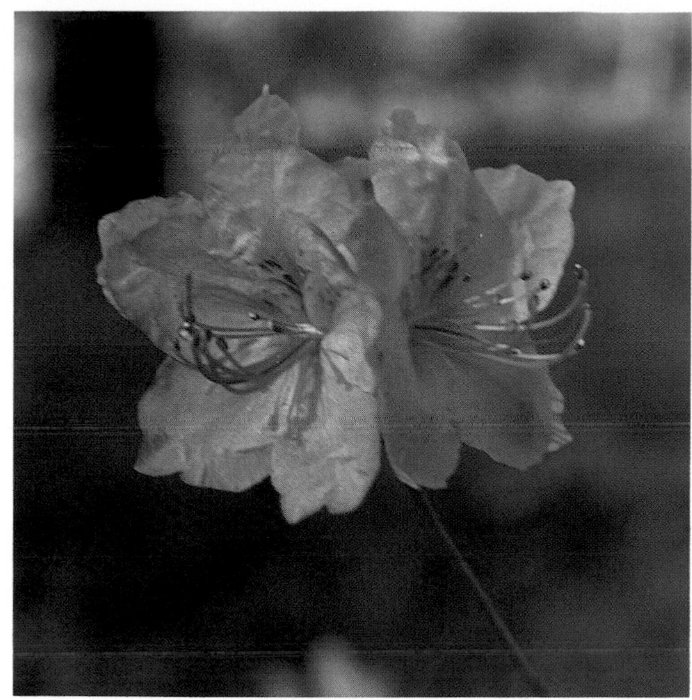

R. mucronulatum 'Cornell Pink'. GALLE

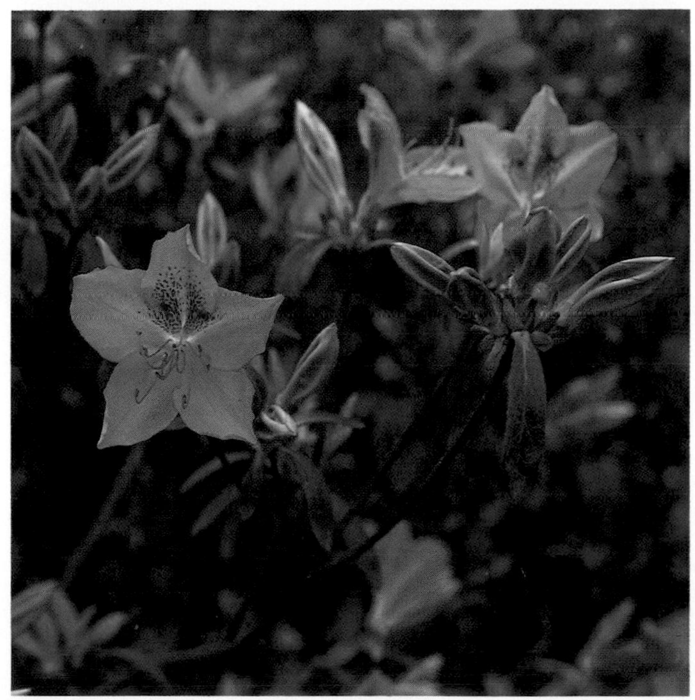

R. yedoense poukhanense. Yodogawa Azalea. G. MILLER

R. oldhamii. Oldham Azalea. GALLE

'Eri' syn. 'Eri Schaeme' Belgian Indian Hybrid. GALLE

'Rosa Belton' Belgian Indian Hybrid. GALLE

'Easter Parade' Mossholder Bristow Hybrid. BARRY

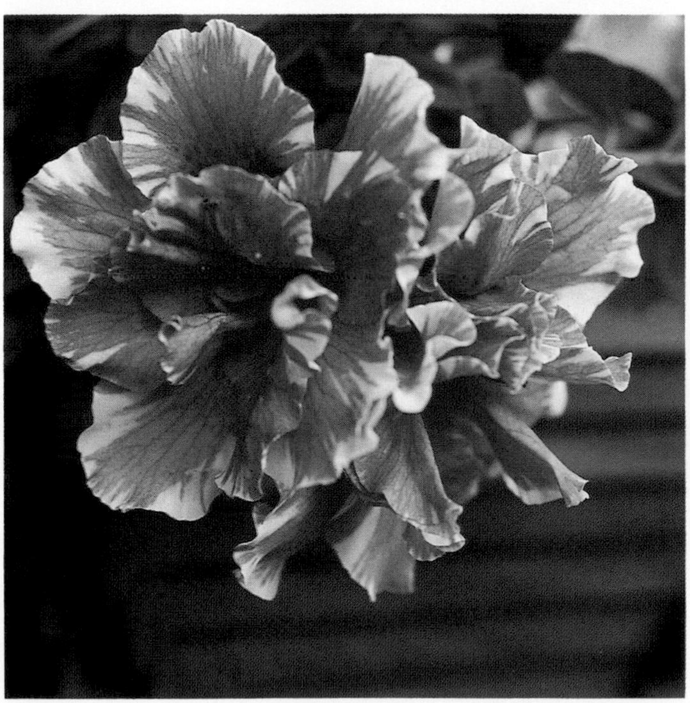

'Haerens Saumona' syn. 'California Sunset' Belgian Indian Hybrid. GALLE

'Nuccio's Variegated Red Ruffles' Belgian Indian Hybrid. GALLE

'Nuccio's Wild Cherry' Belgian Indian Hybrid. GALLE

'Madonna' Belgian Indian Hybrid. GALLE

'Tickled Pink' Belgian Indian Hybrid. GALLE

Plate 60

'Starlight' Kerrigan Hybrid. GALLE

'Elegans Superba' syn. 'Pride of Mobile' Southern Indian Hybrid. GALLE

'Anthenon' Southern Indian Hybrid. GALLE

'Primitive Beauty' Southern Indian Hybrid. GALLE

'George Lindley Taber' Southern Indian Hybrid. GALLE

'Koromo Shikibu' Macrosepalum Hybrid often listed as a Kurume. GALLE

'Satellite' Belgian Indian Hybrid. GALLE

'William Bull' Southern Indian Hybrid. GALLE

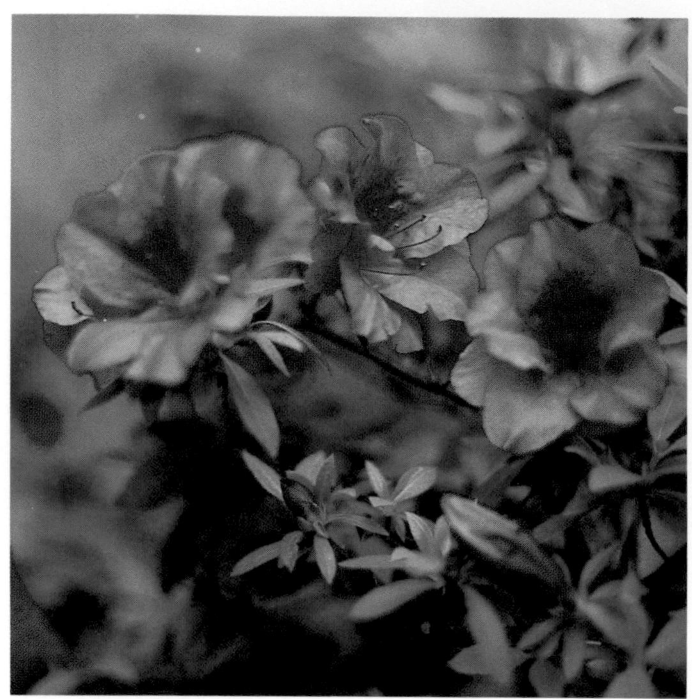

'Shipley' Southern Indian Hybrid. GALLE

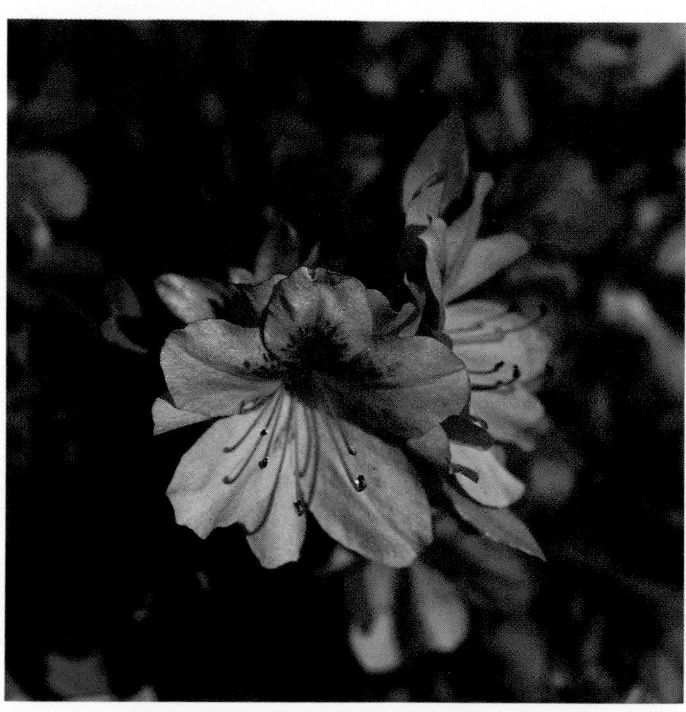

'Mrs. L.C. Fisher' Bobbink Atkins Macrantha Hybrid. GALLE

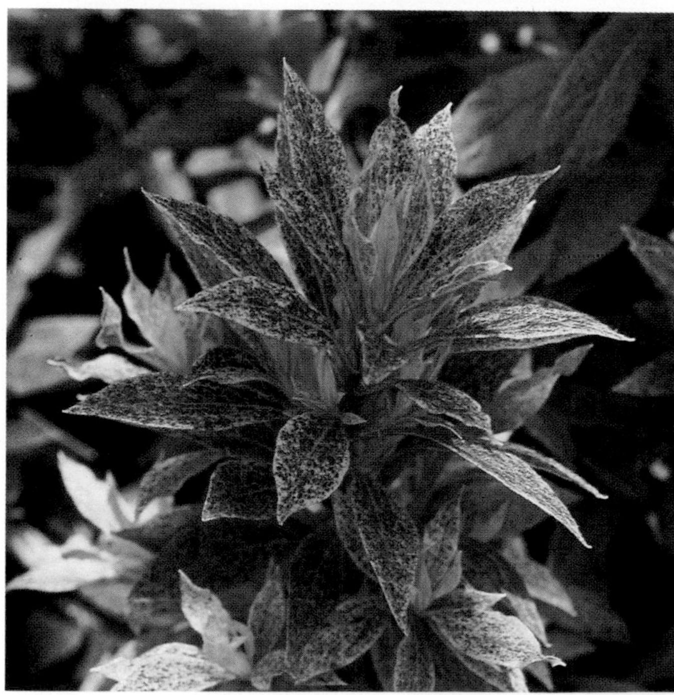

'Southern Charm Variegated' sport of Southern Charm'. GALLE

'Benifude' syn. 'Sunbeam' Kurume Hybrid. GALLE

'Aya Kammuri' syn. 'Pinkie' Kurume Hybrid. GALLE

'Kirin' syn. 'Coral Bells' Kurume. GALLE

White sport of 'Chiyono Akebono' Kurume Hybrid. GALLE

'Hinode Giri' old standard Kurume Hybrid. GALLE

'Glory' Kurume Hybrid. GALLE

'Mountain Laurel' Kurume Hybrid. GALLE

'Kasane Kagaribi' syn. 'Rosita' Kurume Hybrid. GALLE

'Howard Anderson' (syn. 'H. W. Anderson'; probably a 'Mucronatum' hybrid): white flushed pink; spreading low dense.

'Indian Summer' (form of *kaempferi*): strong yellowish pink, fall flowering, and also in the spring.

'Iroquois' (*kaempferi* × 'Maxwelli'): moderate reddish orange, 2¼"; tender.

'James Gable' ('Caroline Gable' × 'Purple Splendor'): strong red 52A, hose-in-hose, darker blotch; like a dwarf 'Campfire'.

'J. C. Bowman' (possible seedling of a 'Mucronatum' hybrid): pink; vigorous growth.

'Jessie Coover' ('Louise Gable' × 'Caroline Gable'): deep reddish purple, hose-in-hose, double; low spreading. Similar to 'Rosebud', with larger darker flowers and freer growth.

'Jimmy Coover' (*indicum* hybrid, possibly 'Macrantha'): red, sometimes semidouble, late; low, very hardy.

'Judy' (parentage unknown): vivid red, hose-in-hose.

'Kathleen' (*poukhanense* × *kaempferi*): light pink.

'La Lumiere' ('Hinode Giri' × (*poukhanense* × *kaempferi*)): strong red, 1½"; similar to 'Cherokee'.

'La Premiere' ((*poukhanense* × *kaempferi*) × dbl. *indicum*, 'Beni Kirishima'): deep purplish pink, very double, 1¾", late; spreading medium height.

'La Roche' (*poukhanense* × 'Hinode Giri'): vivid purplish red, early midseason; hardy.

'Little Indian' (parentage unknown): dark red; similar to 'Claret'.

'Lorna' ('Louise Gable' × 'Caroline Gable'): similar to 'Rosebud' with freer growth and lighter purplish pink color.

'Louise Gable' (*indicum* × (*poukhanense* × *kaempferi*)): deep pink, darker blotch, semidouble, 2¼", late; spreading low dense.

'Margie' (*poukhanense* × 'Hexe'): deep pink, late; low, similar to 'Carol'.

'Maryann' (*indicum* × (*poukhanense* × *kaempferi*)): deep pink; similar to 'Louise Gable'.

'Mary Dalton' (*kaempferi* × 'Yaye Giri'): reddish orange, hose-in-hose, 1½", early midseason; upright tall.

'Mary Frances Hawkins' (parentage unknown): moderate pink, hose-in-hose; tall grower; hardy.

'Mildred Mae' (*poukhanense* × 'Mucronatum'): vivid reddish purple; spreading low compact; similar to 'Viola' but more compact and slower growing.

'Miriam' (*poukhanense* × *kaempferi*): vivid purplish red, darker blotch, 1¾", early midseason.

'Old Faithful' (parentage unknown): vivid purplish red, darker blotch, 2¼", early midseason: similar to 'Big Joe', 'Springtime', and 'Miriam'.

'Polaris' ('Springtime' × 'Snow'): white, faint light greenish throat, hose-in-hose, 2¼", late midseason.

'Purple Splendor' (*poukhanense* × 'Hexe'): vivid reddish purple; similar to 'Herbert'.

'Pyxie' (syn. 'Pixie'): deep pink; similar to 'Forest Fire'.

'Rosebud' ('Louise Gable' × 'Caroline Gable'): deep purplish pink, double hose-in-hose, 1¾", mid to late season; spreading low dense, slow growth. Several different cultivars called 'Rosebud'.

'Rose Greeley' ((*poukhanense* × 'Mucronatum' cross) × (*poukhanense* × 'Hexe') × *poukhanense*): white, blotch yellowish green, hose-in-hose, 2½", sweet scented, early; spreading low dense; good hardy early white.

'Springtime' (*poukhanense* × *kaempferi*): vivid purplish red, blotch darker, 2", early midseason; upright tall.

'Stewartstonian' (parentage unknown): vivid red, 2"; medium to tall; reddish winter foliage; very hardy.

'Viola' (*poukhanense* × 'Mucronatum'): vivid reddish purple, blotch dark red, 2¾", early midseason; spreading large tall plant.

'White Star' (parentage unknown): white, hose-in-hose; similar to 'Polaris', possibly more tender.

The following plants are Gable Hybrid seedlings but named and introduced by others including Old Kent Nursery (Cannon), Tingle Nursery, and others. Some Gable azaleas are still grown under number such as 'C–12–9', 'A–12–9', 'U–19', 'J–3–9', etc. Unfortunately, as Gable seedlings the parentage is not always known.

'Billy' (*poukhanense* × *kaempferi*): strong pink; low dense.

'Boudoir': strong purplish red, darker blotch, 1½".

'Cameo': light pink, hose-in-hose, 1½", late.

'Cameroon' ((*poukhanense* × 'Hexe') × (*poukhanense* × *kaempferi*)): strong purplish red, darker blotch, 2", late midseason.

'Corsage': purple, 2½", fragrant.

'Edna' (34G): vivid purplish red, similar to 'Carol', large flower and not as hardy.

'Fringed Beauty': pink.

'Gillin's Red': very deep red.

'Grenadier': vivid red, 1½".

'Isabel': light purplish pink, hose-in-hose, 1½"; registered in Boskoop.

'Linda Ann': pink, double.

'Pink Rosette': red, double.

'Robert Lee': white; low.

'Royalty': vivid reddish purple, partially petaloid sepals, 1½", late; low spreading.

'Susan': pink.

'Swan': white, hose-in-hose, small.

'Yorktowne' (A-17-G; possibly *poukhanense* × *kaempferi;* Dauber's Nur.): red.

GIRARD EVERGREEN HYBRIDS

The breeding and selecting of azaleas by Peter E. Girard, Sr. of Geneva, Ohio, U.S.A., started in the late 1940's. The goal was to develop attractive hardy azaleas, with good compact growth suitable for landscaping and container growing. Mr. Girard started hybridizing with the Gable Hybrids and then crossing his own seedlings and named Hybrids. Some parents only listed as numbers such as Ev 1689 are Girard seedlings used in breeding. The plants are hardy for zones 6 to 9 and are medium shrubs 4 to 6 feet in height.

'Angel' (parents unknown): pure white, ruffled, 2".

'Bula' (Gable Hybrid ? × *poukhanense*): reddish purple, 2".

'Christina Marie' (parentage unknown): pink, 2½", moderately ruffled; tall open growth.

'Christine Ann' (Gable Hybrid ? × *poukhanense*): pale pink, 2", heavily ruffled; low dense. Hardy to −10°F.

'Clare Marie' (parents unknown): white, slightly ruffled, 2½", dense upright grower. Hardy to −10°F.

'Custom White' (parents unknown): pure white, slightly wavy 2½–3", semi-upright. Hardy to −15°F.

'Donna Mae' ('Orchid Lace' × white seedling): white, slightly ruffled, 2½". Hardy to −10°F.

'Dorothy Woodworth' (syn. G–106; 'Boudoir' × 'Gumpo Pink'): light pink, ruffled, 2½–3½"; broad dense growth. Hardy to −5°F.

'Double Shot' ('El Capitan' × 'Aladdin', '76): dark reddish orange with dark red spots, hose-in-hose, 2½"; semidwarf 2×2½ feet wide in 6 yrs. Hardy to −15°F.

'Downy Pink' ('Geneva' × ('Kathleen' × 'Pink Beauty')): deep pink 52C, hose-in-hose, ruffled, 2½–3"; semidwarf, 18"×18" in 8 years. Hardy to −10°F.

'El Capitan' ('Aladdin' × red Kurume Hybrid seedling): vivid red, petals rounded, 2"; semi-upright 24×18" wide.

'Eriedell' ('Robert Ann' × 'Boudoir') × 'Boudoir')): strong purplish pink, 5B, hose-in-hose, no stamens, wavy lobes, 2½"; 36"×36" in 5 years. Hardy to −10°F.

'Geneva' (scarlet seedling × *poukhanense*): yellowish pink, ruffled; low and spreading. Hardy to −10°F.

'Girard's Border Gem' (sport of 'Girard's Rose'): deep pink 52C, 1–1½"; leaves small ⅜×¾" long; dwarf, dense growth.

'Girard's Chiara' ('Pink Dawn' × 'Boudoir'): deep purplish pink 57C, with deep reddish orange blotch 44C, hose-in-hose, ruffled, 2½"; semidwarf, 16"×16" in 4 years. Hardy to −15°F.

'Girard's Crimson' (('Boudoir' × 'Aladdin') × ('Boudoir' × 'Corporal')): strong purplish red, 59D, with vivid red 46B blotch, (5R 4/12, 2½") lobes rounded; dwarf 18" × 24" wide in 8 years. Hardy to −5°F.

'Girard's Deep Salmon' (('Robert Ann' × 'Girard's Hot Shot') × 'Roberta Ann'): vivid reddish orange 41B, hose-in-hose, wavy lobes, 24"×18" wide in 4 years. Hardy to −10°F.

'Girard's Fuchsia' (('Sandra Ann' × 'Ev 1689' Girard seedling) × ('Herbert' × 'Hot Shot') × 'Sandra Ann')): deep reddish purple 71A, lighter spotting, wavy lobes, 2½–3"; 24"×30" wide in 4 years; leaves reddish in winter. Hardy to −10°F.

'Girard's Hot Shot' ('El Capitan' × 'Aladdin'): dark reddish orange, 24A, with dark red spotting, wavy lobes, 2½" semidwarf 24"×30" wide in 8 years. Hardy to −15°F.

'Girard's National Beauty' (parentage unknown): deep pink, ruffled margins, 2–2½"; glossy foliage reddish in fall; low spreading habit, 18"–24" in 5 years; hardy to −10°F.

'Girard's Pink' ('Girard's Crimson' × 'Girard's Rose'): strong red, 52A, with deep purplish red blotch 58A, rounded lobes, 1¾"; 15"×18" wide in 4 years. Hardy to −10°F.

'Girard's Purple' ('Sandra Ann' × 'Girard's Scarlet'): deep purplish red 74B, darker spotting, lobes wavy, prolific 2½"; 24"×18" wide in 4 years. Hardy to −10°F.

'Girard's Rose' (('Fedora' × 'El Capitan') × ('Boudoir') × 'Boudoir')): deep pink 52C, reverse deep yellowish pink, wavy lobes, 2½", 24"×24" in 7 years; leaves reddish orange in winter. Hardy to −10°F.

'Girard's Scarlet' ('Aladdin' × 'El Capitan'): strong red 46B, deep blotch, rounded lobes, slightly wavy, 22"; 24"×30" wide in 9 years. Hardy to −15°F.

'Girard's Variegated Gem' (sport of 'Girard's Border Gem'): variegated leaves with brilliant yellow 14C margin; ⅜–1¼" long; deep pink 52C, 1–1½"; dwarf, compact habit.

'Girard's Variegated Hot Shot' (sport of 'Girard's Hot Shot'): variegated foliage, very pale yellow margins, slightly smaller foliage; flowers dark reddish orange 24A with dark red spotting, wavy margins, 2½"; low, compact, spreading habit, 18" high in 8 years; hardy to −10°F. Release date 1988.

'Jeremiah' (('Pink Dawn' × 'Girard's Rose') × 'Girard's Rose'): deep pink 52C, hose-in-hose, ruffled 2½"; semidwarf 30"×30" in 5 years. Hardy to −10°F.

'Joshua Jeffrey' ('Girard's Crimson' × 'Girard's Hot Shot'): strong red 47A, slightly ruffled, prolific, 2"; low, dense. Hardy to −10°F.

'Kathy Ann' (syn. 'Kathy') (Cross of 2 white unknown seedlings): white, slightly ruffled, 3", semi-upright; 36"×30" wide.

'Lavender Bouquet' (Cross of 2 *R. poukhanense* seedlings): light purple, hose-in-hose, 2"; 2'×2'.

'Leslie's Purple' ('Elizabeth Gable' × 'Boudoir'): strong purplish red with dark spotting, lobes wavy, 2½"; semidwarf, 19"×18" in 3 years. Hardy to −10°F.

'Luxury Rose' ('Roberta Ann' × 'Girard's Pink'): deep pink 52B, triple hose-in-hose, wavy, funnel-shaped, 2½", 3–5 stamens; 15"×20" wide in 5 years; hardy to −5°F.

'Mitey White' ('Kathy Ann' × 'Clara Marie'): white, faint spotting, hose-in-hose, lobes wavy 2½"; 24"×18" wide in 4 years. Hardy to −10°F.

'Orchid Lace' (Gable Hybrid × 'Palestrima'): light purple with white throat.

'Pink Dawn' (('Geneva' × 'Kathleen') × 'Pink Boudoir'): deep pink 52C, hose-in-hose, wavy 2½", dense upright habit. Hardy to −15°F.

'Pleasant White' ('Kathy Ann' × 'Clara Marie'): white, rounded wavy lobes, 2½–3"; 24" × 18" wide in 7 years. Hardy to −10°F.

'Purple Robe' (*R. poukhanense* × 'Purple Triumph'): moderate purple, hose-in-hose, wavy, 2"; semi-upright 18"×24" wide.

'Renee Michelle' ('Boudoir' × 'Gumpo Pink'): deep pink 52C, light red spotting, rounded ruffled lobes; 20"×18" wide in 6 years. Hardy to −10°F.

'Roberta' ('Elizabeth Gable' × 'Girard's Pink'): deep pink, double, ruffled, 2¾–3", 18" × 24" wide in 4 years; good for forcing. Hardy to −5°F.

'Rose Perfecta' ('Roberta' × 'Girard's Pink'): strong red 52D, hose-in-hose 6 lobes; low, compact; good for forcing. Hardy to −10°F.

'Ruby Glow' ('Pink Dawn' × 'Hot Shot'): strong purplish pink, reverse is deep yellowish pink, hose-in-hose, 2½"; compact dense, 18" × 24" wide in 5 years. Hardy to −10°F.

'Sandra Ann' (*R. poukhanense* × ('Herbert' × 'Purple Splendor')): reddish purple, wavy and ruffled, 3"; dense habit. 18"×24" wide in 4 years. Hardy to −15°F.

'Saybrook Glory' ('Robert Ann' × 'Fedora'): vivid purplish pink 58C, purplish red blotch, wavy, 3½"; 18"×18" in 4 years. Hardy to −20°F.

'Scarlet Glory' ('Aladdin' × 'Red Seedling'): vivid red, 2" semi-upright, 24"×18" wide.

'Unsurpassable' (parents unknown): deep pink 52B, wavy, 2½–2¾"; broad, dense habit; hardy to −15°F.

'Villa' (*R. poukhanense* × 'Kathleen'): light purple with violet case and dark violet blotch, slightly wavy, 2½"; 30" × 30". Hardy to −15°F.

'White Princess' ((white Kurume seedling × *R. poukhanense*) × 'Orchid Lace'): white, slightly ruffled, 2½"; 2'×3' wide. Hardy to −15°F.

LINWOOD HARDY AZALEAS

Dr. Charles Fisher, Jr. started in 1950 to develop hardy azaleas for greenhouse forcing in Linwood, NJ, U.S.A. In 1953 G. Albert (Al) Reid took over the project to develop hardy azaleas with good plant habit, foliage, flower quality life, and for forcing. In 1967 Al Reid retired and took over the project to continue developing hardy azaleas. Accordingly Dr. Fisher kept the Linwood varieties best suited for the commercial florist needs. There is no common background for the Linwoods. They are a heterogenous conglomeration of azalea crosses including back and sibling crosses, and the records are incomplete. Hardy parents included Kurume and Kaempferi Hybrids plus Indian greenhouse forcing varieties.

Many of the Linwoods were distributed under number for testing such as 0–9, C–14, L18, and these numbers follow the cultivar name. Numbered Linwood seedlings are listed as parents, but the actual parents of the numbered seedling is unknown; with information only on the following K28: a hardy 'Macrantha' from Bobbink and Atkins, K7: 'Salmon Spray', A3: Fisher hybrid azalea and E9: a 'Hexe' × 'Vervaeneana' seedling. Others such as N4, N3, Gables 38G are numbered seedlings with no information available. Others such as 'Konia' and 'Koenig' may be incomplete names for Indian greenhouse azaleas.

'Bess Hallock' (0–9) (Parents unknown): strong purplish red 63A, hose-in-hose, semidouble, 2"; 12 × 24" wide in 5 years. Hardy to 0°F.

'Dr. Curtis Alderfer' (C–24) ('Crimson King' × 'Konia'): red, semidouble, 2¾"; 16 × 12" wide in 3 years, greenhouse. Hardy to 15°F. PP 2016.

'Dr. Franklin West' (0–5) (parents unknown): strong red 46D, with purple blotch, double, 2¼"; 14 × 18" wide in 4 years. Hardy to 10°F.

'Edward M. Boehm' (L–18) (A–3 × E): vivid purplish red, with large blotch streaked brown, hose-in-hose, 2¾", 18 × 30" wide in 6 years. Hardy to −5°F.

'Emma Reid' (0–19) (Parents unknown): strong purplish red, 58D, 2½", 12 × 14" wide in 4 years. Hardy to −5°F.

'Garden State Garnet' (Parents unknown): strong purplish red 58D, hose-in-hose, 2¼"; 30 × 40" wide in 6 years. Hardy to 0°F.

'Garden State Glow' (E–26) ('Salmon Spray' × 'Hino Crimson'): strong purplish red 58D, hose-in-hose, 1¼"; 26 × 24" wide in 4 years. Hardy to 0°F.

'Garden State Pink' (E–30) ('Dawn' × 'Hino Crimson'): strong purplish red 58D, hose-in-hose, 1½"; 20 × 18" wide in 4 years. Hardy to 5°F.

'Garden State Red' (N–3) (L–21 seedling × 3–9) ('Hexe' × 'Vervaeneana'): vivid purplish red 57A, hose-in-hose, 2¼"; 15 × 24" wide in 6 years. Hardy to 5°F.

'Garden State Salmon' (C–36) ('Koenig' × 'Orange Cup'): vivid red 45B, hose-in-hose, 1¾"; 20 × 16" wide in 4 years. Hardy to 0°F.

'Garden State White' (H–11) ('Salmon Glow' × 'A–3'): white with light greenish yellow blotch, hose-in-hose, 2¼"; 18 × 24" wide in 4 years. Hardy to 0°F.

'Hardy Gardenia' (L–30) ('A–3' × 'E–9'): white, hose-in-hose, double 2½"; 14 × 30" wide in 8 years. Hardy to 10°F.

'James Dunlop' (0–13) (Parents unknown): vivid purplish red 66C, hose-in-hose, semidouble, 2¼"; 20 × 18" in 5 years. Hardy to 5°F.

'Janet Rhea' (N4+) (Sports of N4) (Sister of N–3): strong purplish red 65A, with white edge ⅛ to ¼", hose-in-hose, semidouble, 2½"; 16 × 24" wide in 4 years. Hardy to 0°F.

'Linwood Blush' (E–4) ('Jean Haerns' × 'Salmon Spray'): light yellowish pink, hose-in-hose, double 2¼"; 12 × 10" wide in 3 years. Good for forcing. Hardy to 15°F.

'Linwood Charm' (0–2) (Parents unknown): deep purplish pink 62B, hose-in-hose, semidouble, 2¼"; 18 × 30" wide in 6 years. Hardy to 0°F.

'Linwood Lavender' (H–1) ('Salmon Glow' × 'A–3'): vivid purplish red, 67A, purple and brown spotting, hose-in-hose, semidouble, 2½"; 24 × 24" wide in 5 years. Hardy to 0°F.

'Linwood Lilac' (E–15) ('Albion' × 'Gables 38G'): light violet, hose-in-hose, 2½"; 14 × 10" wide in 3 years. Good for forcing. Hardy to 15°F.

'Linwood Lustre' (H–4) (syn. 'Improved Linwood White'; 'Crimson King' × 'A–3'): white, with light greenish yellow blotch, hose-in-hose, semidouble, 2½"; 20 × 18" wide in 5 years. Hardy to 5°F.

'Linwood Pink Giant' (K–11) (syn. 'Improved Linwood Pink'; A–3 × C14): strong purplish red 61C, hose-in-hose, 2½"; 4' × 5' wide in 7 years. Hardy to −10°F.

'Linwood Pink #1' (C28) ('Salmon Special' × 'Mother of Pearl'): strong pink, hose-in-hose, 2¼"; 14 × 12" wide in 3 years, forcing. Hardy to 15°F. Patented.

'Linwood Pink #2' (K–2) ('C–14' × 'A–3'): strong pink, hose-in-hose, 2¼"; 12 × 14" wide in 3 years. Hardy to 0°F.

'Linwood Ruby' (0–7) (Parents unknown): vivid purplish red 57B, hose-in-hose, semidouble, 2¼"; 30 × 36" wide in 6 years. Hardy to 0°F.

'Linwood Salmon' (K–10) ('A–3' × 'C–14'): strong red 46D, hose-in-hose, frilled, 2½", 22 × 28" in 6 years, requires shade. Hardy to −5°F.

'Linwood White' (H–5) ('Salmon Glow' × 'A–3'): white, hose-in-hose, double, 2¼"; 40 × 30" wide in 7 years, requires shade. Hardy to 0°F.

'Mary Elizabeth' (0–24) (Parents unknown): deep purplish pink 68A, hose-in-hose, 2½"; 24 × 30" wide in 4 years. Hardy to 0°F.

'Nellie' (C–4) ('Prince George' × 'M. R. Mulford'): moderate pink, hose-in-hose, semidouble, 2"; 12 × 12" in 3 years. Good for forcing. Hardy to 15°F.

'Opal' (L–1) ('A–3' × 'K–28'): vivid purplish red 67B, double, 2½"; fall flowering, 2 × 2' in 4 years. Hardy to 0°F.

'Orchid Beauty' (E–52) ('Glory BA' × 'Gable 38G'): vivid purplish red, 58D, hose-in-hose, double, 2¼" 20 × 18" wide in 4 years. Hardy to 0°F.

'Peach Fuzz' (L–34) ('A–3' × 'K–28'): deep pink, 52C, double, 1½"; 20 × 30" wide in 5 years. Hardy to −10°F.

'Pink Pincushion' (L–8) ('A–3' × 'K–28'): vivid purplish red 61D, double, 1¾"; 26× 24" wide in 4 years. Hardy to 10°F.

'Reid Red' (0–1) ('Hershey Red' × unknown): vivid purplish red, 58B, semidouble, 2"; 20 × 18" wide in 4 years. Hardy to 10°F.

'Salmon Pincushion' (L–4) ('A–3' × 'K–28'): vivid red, double, 1¾"; 20 × 22" wide in 4 years. Hardy to 0°F.

'Slim Jim' (L–14) ('A–3 × 'K–28'): light pink, very double, 2¼" × 36" in 4 years, rounded, foliage poor. Hardy to 0°F.

'Tiny' (L–28) ('A–3' × 'E–9'): vivid purplish red, hose-in-hose, double, 1"; 9 × 16" wide in 7 years. Hardy to −5°F.

'Victoria Hohman' (0–3) (Parents unknown): vivid purplish red, hose-in-hose, double, 2½"; 14 × 16" wide in 4 years. Hardy to 0°F.

'White Squatter' (0–22) (Parents unknown): white 155D, light green blotch, hose-in-hose, wavy, 2½"; 10 × 18" wide in 4 years. Hardy to 5°F.

The following plants have now all been registered. All are from the cross, 'Nellie' × 'Opal', with the exception of 'Carol Kitchen'.

'Carol Kitchen' (0-25) (parentage unknown): vivid purplish red 57C, hose-in-hose.
'Dimsdale' (S–3): deep purplish pink 68A, hose-in-hose, frilled.
'Doctor Thomas McMillan' (S-13): deep purplish pink 68A, double, hose-in-hose. PP 2021.
'Edward W. Collins' (S-55): deep pink 52C, double hose-in-hose, ruffled.
'Evelyn Hart' (S-2): pale purplish pink 68B, double, hose-in-hose.
'George School' (SX-8): vivid purplish red 55A hose-in-hose, ruffled.
'John Brockett' (S-1): vivid purplish red 61D, double.
'Lorna Carter' (S-56): strong purplish red 54B, double, hose-in-hose.
'Lotta Burke' (S-54): deep pink 52C, hose-in-hose, frilled.
'Theodore S. Stecki' (S-26): vivid purplish red 61D, double, hose-in-hose.
'Thomas Rose' (S-43): moderate red 47C, double, hose-in-hose, ruffled.
'Walter Kern' (SX-2): deep purplish pink 68A, double, hose-in-hose.

PRIDE HYBRIDS

Orlando Pride, a landscape architect and nurseryman of Butler, Pennsylvania, U.S.A., first learned of *Rhododendrons* from Joe Gable in 1928. One of his first seedlings obtained from Gable he named 'Nadine'. All of his later selections were 'Nadine' seedlings unless noted otherwise. Mr. Pride and Tony Shammarello concurred that it takes 15 to 30 years to really test a plant. The plants marked with an asterisk are still being observed and have not been released; the others may only be seen in or available from private gardens. The Pride Hybrids are hardy in zones 6 to 8 and are medium to tall plants 6–8 feet in height.

'Arlene Leach': vivid pink.
'Arthur Pride': white.
'Ben Smith': light pink.
'Carl Brosch': strong yellowish pink.
'Chal McElvain': moderate pink.
'Charles A. Pride': strong yellowish pink.*
'Clark Adams': deep pink.
'Dan Bush': pink.
'David Leach': deep pink.
'Deep Pink' (Kaempferi Hybrid × *poukhanense*): dark pink.
'Dell Cribbs': deep pink.*
'Doc Fleming': reddish purple.
'Dr. Kottraba': vivid pink.
'Ed Howard': moderate pink.
'Edith Pride': moderate reddish orange.
'Eleanor Lord': deep pink.
'Ellen Mac Mullan': pale pink.*
'Esther Reiber': light reddish purple.*
'Evan Wimer': purple.
'Frank Curto': light pink.
'Grace Pride': deep pink.
'Harry Scanlon': light pink.
'Jack Jamison': moderate red.*
'Jack Stewart': vivid pink.
'Jean Brandt': moderate yellowish pink.
'John Bracken' (*poukhanense* type): red.
'John Hill': moderate red.
'Joseph Gable' ('Rose Greeley' × 'Nadine' × 'Nadine'): white, hose-in-hose; very hardy.*
'Judy McIntire': light pink.
'Kay Greer': strong pink.
'Margaret Pride': moderate red.
'Marianne Holman': pale pink.
'Marjorie': reddish purple.*
'Mary Holman' (*kaempferi* × *poukhanense*): strong yellowish pink.
'Mary Llewellyn': deep pink.
'Mauve' (*kaempferi* × *poukhanense*): vivid reddish purple.
'Mrs. Paul Brandt': vivid red.
'Nadine' (*kaempferi* × *poukhanense*): light pink.*
'Norbert': moderate red.
'Pale Lilac' (*kaempferi* × *poukhanense*): very pale purple.
'Paul Brandt': vivid pink.
'Peach' (*kaempferi* × *poukhanense*): light yellowish pink.
'Peg Howard': reddish orange.
'Pride Red': dark red, late.*
'Prof. Newins': reddish orange.
'Richard Holman': light pink.
'Ruth McElvain': deep pink.
'Sally Bush': light reddish purple.
'Sam': red.
'Sam Greer': vivid red.*
'Shell' (*kaempferi* × *poukhanense*): light yellowish pink.
'Ted Jamison': deep pink.
'Ted Kottraba': dark pink.
'Thor': reddish purple.
'Vickie' (*kaempferi* × *poukhanense*): strong yellowish pink.*
'Victoria' (*kaempferi* × *poukhanense*): reddish orange.
'Watermelon' (*kaempferi* × *poukhanense*): moderate pink.*
'Wheeler Lord': reddish orange.
'Winifred Greer': vivid red.*
'Winny': red.
'Wm. McElvain': white, small.

Recent introductions (see also Appendix I):

'Pride-Linwood' unknown ('Linwood' × 'Snowball'): white, very hardy.
'Pride's White' unknown ('Linwood × 'Snowball'): white.
'Sue Paterno': purplish pink.
'Susan Page': yellowish pink, hose-in-hose.

SHAMMARELLO HYBRIDS

Introduced by the late A. M. (Tony) Shammarello of South Euclid, Ohio, U.S.A. Similar to Gable Hybrids and hardy in zone 5, to −15°F.

'Cascade' (*poukhanense* × 'Indica Alba', '61): white, 1½", midseason; 2 × 3½' wide in 10 years. Extremely hardy.

'Desiree' ((*poukhananse* × 'Indica Alba')) × (*poukhanense* × 'Indica Alba') PP 2068, '61): white, frilled, 2½", early midseason; spreading, medium height.

'Elsie Lee' ('Desiree' × 'Rosebud', '68): light reddish purple 78C, semidouble, 10 lobes, 2½"; semidwarf, 3 × 3' in 15 years. Very hardy.

'Helen Curtis' ('Desiree' × 'Rosebud', PP 2837, '68): white, no marking, semidouble 10 frilled lobes, 2½"; semidwarf 2 × 3'wide in 15 years. Very hardy.

'Hino-Pink' (('Hino Crimson' × *poukhanense*) × ('Fedora' × 'Louise Gable') '65): strong purplish pink 55B, 2"; early; low 18 × 36" wide in 10 years.

'Hino-Red' (('Hino-Crimson' × *poukhanense*) × (Kaempferi × 'James Gable') PP 2507, '65): moderate red 53B, 1¾, early; spreading, compact, 18 × 36" wide in 10 years.

'Hino-White' (('Hino Crimson' × *poukhanense*) × 'Desiree', PP 2508, '65): white , 2", early; spreading, 15 × 36" wide in 10 years.

'Marie's Choice' (('Hino-Crimson' × *poukhanense*) × 'Desiree', '70): white, 2½", midseason; 2½' × 3' wide in 10 years.

'May Belle' (('Helen Curtis' × 'Hino Red') PP 3827, '77): deep pink 52C, to strong purplish red 51A, semidouble 2½"; broad, semidwarf; 1½' × 3' wide in 12 years.

'Pink Gem' ('Sherwoodi' × 'Fedora'): pink, 2", early midseason; medium height, spreading.

'Red Red' (('Hino-Red' × 'Ward's Ruby') PP 3465, '74): strong red 47B, 2", midseason; 2' × 3' wide in 10 years.

'Sham's Flame' (Kaempferi hyb. × 'James Gable'): reddish orange, 2", early midseason; medium height and spreading.

'Sparkle' (red Kaempferi hyb. × 'Gable's Flame', '60): strong red 45D, round lobes, funnel-shaped, 1¾"; new leaves and mature growth reddish; semidwarf, 2½–3' wide in 10 years.

'Wintergreen' (('Hino Crimson' × *poukhanense*) × 'Desiree', '65): white, 1½", midseason; 15 × 30" wide in 10 years. Good leaf retention.

STANTON HYBRIDS

Ernest Stanton of Grosse Isle, Michigan, U.S.A., developed a number of hybrids that are selections of *R. poukhanense* × *R. kaempferi* F2's. They are hardy in zone 6b and have a good fall leaf color of red to reddish orange.

'Cadmium Red': reddish orange, late midseason, 3 × 3½' in 10 years.

'Cherado' (syn. 'McClosky's Pink'): yellowish pink, semidouble, late midseason, 3½ × 5' tall in 10 years.

'Lake Erie': deep pink, blotch spotted reddish orange; midseason; 2½ × 3½' wide in 10 years.

'Lake Michigan': purplish pink, midseason; 4 × 2½' wide in 10 years.

'Lake Ontario': light purplish pink, early; spreading 2½' high in 10 years.

'Lake St. Clair': light purple, early; upright 3' in 10 years.

'Lake Superior': deep purplish pink, midseason, 3 × 3' in 10 years.

'Myrtle Leaf': yellowish pink, semidouble, late; 3 × 3' tall in 10 years, not as hardy.

'Shawnee': reddish orange, late; 3 × 3' tall in 10 years, not as hardy.

'Upright Red': reddish orange, early, 3 × 3' tall in 10 years.

'Wyandot': deep pink, large, early; 3 × 3½' tall in 10 years.

SATSUKI AZALEAS

In Japan, the Satsuki Azalea is the most beloved. They are a notable contribution by Japanese horticulturists to gardeners the world around. The range of flower color, form, leaf shape and color, and habit of growth is greater than in any other group of azaleas. The word *Satsuki* means "Fifth Month" (Japanese/Oriental lunar calendar).The preferred Japanese pronunciation is 'sat-ski'; with an unvoiced "u", however, 'sat-su-ki' is also used and is not incorrect.

Since the time of *Kinshu Makura (A Brocade Pillow)* (1692), the classic treatise on azaleas by Ito Ihei, the Japanese have divided azaleas into two groups: 1. Tsutsuji and 2. Satsuki.

1. Tsutsuji includes all species and hybrids which flower 30 days or so after the spring equinox (flowering before or with the new leaves).
2. Satsuki includes azaleas which flower 30 days or so after the Tsutsuji.

Any cultivar derived primarily from *R. indicum* and/or *R. tamurae (R. eriocarpum)*, with occasional other species contributing, is a Satsuki.

The Japanese have a deep understanding of what is meant by Satsuki, and there is much to be learned by Western gardeners about this important group of plants. For simplicity, we can divide the Satsukis into two groups, knowing that the Japanese use other more complex groupings.

The first, Mie Satsuki or hedge-type Satsuki, is a *R. indicum* type plant while the second is the container culture Satsuki.

The Mie Satsuki are cultivars of *R. indicum* used in the landscape for sheared hedges in boxwood-like form or evergreen mounds, made to resemble and recall rocks. The small leaves and the rich, purplish red coloration in the winter are essential features of this use. While flowers may vary from white through pink to red, the Japanese do not consider flower color essential. The foliage and shape of the plant are the important features. Only a few cultivars are used in this way, for the heavy shearing removes many of the flower buds. Since we in the West tend to equate azaleas with their flowers, we have yet to appreciate and learn to use the Mie Satsuki in landscaping as do the Japanese. We Occidentals generally use the container culture Satsuki as landscape plants. Here again we are just beginning to learn of the many forms of Satsuki selected by the Japanese for the varied and satisfying practices of container culture or bonsai culture. In Japan the Satsuki Azaleas are the prize plants for Bonsai work, of which many treasured specimens several hundred years old are displayed in Bonsai gardens and occasionally exhibited in exquisite and extensive private collections. Satsuki exhibitions in Japan are usually held in early June, displaying both new and old cultivars accompanied by demonstrations of pruning methods to achieve profound esthetic effects. The most notable exhibit is held in Utsunomiya, not far from Nikko. Several large Satsuki nurseries are located in this area and nearby is Kanuma, the source of the popular kanuma potting soil. Kanuma is a soft, yellowish, inert volcanic rock used in potting soil. For additional information on Bonsai, see Chapter 10.

The history of the development of Satsuki Azaleas is shrouded in mystery. The old Japanese texts name only some of the most noteworthy cultivars. We know that 'Musashino' and 'Takasago' were in existence several hundred years ago. The cultivar 'Shokko Nishiki' is said to be four or five hundred years old. The general view at present is that the first Satsuki Azaleas developed as natural interspecific hybrids of *R. indicum* and *R. tamurae (R. eriocarpum)*. Collection and selection of these natural hybrids were followed by cultural crosses of these two species, their natural hybrids with further desirable characteristics introduced from breeding with other species.

The following outline is derived from the observations and notes of Dr. John Creech, Dr. Masaaki Kunishige, Barry Yinger, and others.

R. indicum is native to southern Japan on Honshu and the southern islands of Shikoku, Kyushu, and Yakushima. *R. tamurae* is found on the islands south of Kyushu including Yukushima, Tanegashima, Kuchierabujoma, and Tokara. The native range of *R. indicum* and *R. tamurae* overlap on Yakushima Island, a small mountainous point of land 70 kilometers south of the island of Kyushu. The highest peak Miyanouradake is 6,350 ft. in elevation. Rainfall is very heavy, averaging 158 inches at sea level to 390 inches at high altitudes. The lowland is frostfree, but the peaks are snow-covered and frozen in winter.

The narrow-leafed *R. indicum* is a mountainous plant with flowers of five stamens and colors ranging from pink to reddish and occasionally white. *R. indicum* inhabits rocky crevices on steep mountain slopes along mountain streams.

R. tamurae, called Maruba Satsuki, the Satsuki with round leaves, is generally found at sea level near Nagata on the northwestern coast of Yakushima. Dr. Creech notes it to be more extensive on nearby Erabu Island. The plants grow in a harsh exposed habitat in shallow gravelly or rocky soil and sand. The leaves of *R. tamurae* are broad elliptic in the spring, followed by thick, persistent, obovate leaves in the summer. The flowers with eight to ten stamens are typically red to purple with white to various shades of pink. The plants are generally low-growing and form thick masses. Some seedlings have a vigorous upright growth habit.

R. indicum and *R. tamurae* are seldom found in the same habitat. However, at Isso and other locations near Anbo on Yakushima Island, natural hybrids do occur with the range of flower colors of Satsuki Hybrids. Barry Yinger reported that the most interesting hybrids are no longer seen in the wild, for most of them have been dug and moved to the gardens of local farmers. It is in these gardens with extremely large old plants that the potential of the hybrids can by appreciated.

The origin and parentage of all the Satsuki clones are not known. Some such as 'Gunbi' and 'Gunrei' are sports of 'Gumpo'; while others are crosses of Satsuki cultivars. Other species and cultivars were possibly used in producing some of the Satsuki Hybrids. The well known 'Shinnyo no Tsuki' is considered a sport of 'Kusadama', but also a cross of 'Sakuragata' × 'Zetsurin'. 'Zetsurin' is reportedly a cross of 'Kyokko Nishiki' × 'Mme. Moreux', a Belgian Indian Hybrid. The now defunct Chugai Nursery announced 'Kibabu' as a hybrid of 'Macrantha' × 'Mme. Moreux Alba'. It is interesting to note that the florist Belgian Indian Hybrids were introduced into Japan quite some years ago. The following are considered as crosses with 'Mme. Moreux': 'Gyokurei' ('Kaho' × 'Mme. Moreux') and 'Koka' ('Kyokko Nishiki' × 'Mme. Moreux').

Satsuki Hybrids have come to play an important role for hybridizers not only in Japan but in the West as well. B. Y. Morrison used Satsuki Azaleas as parents in 150 of the Glenn Dale Hybrids and 46 of the Back Acres Hybrids for example. Both Robert Gartrell in his Robin Hill Hybrids and James Harris in his Harris Hybrids have used Satsuki Hybrids in their crosses. Satsuki Hybrids are now being crossed with other species such as the cultivar 'Kaempo', a cross of *R. kaempferi* × 'Gumpo'. Mr. Takeo Kuwana in Kurume has introduced two early flowering hybrids, 'Hoshikagami' and 'Suzaku', both hybrids of Kurume hybrid × Satsuki hybrid. For additional intraspecific Satsuki Hybrids see Additional Satsuki Azalea List.

While some few Satsuki Hybrids were introduced to the West in the early 1900's, the first major introductions were made in 1938 and 1939 by the Plant Introduction Section of the U.S.D.A. A total of 53 clones were chosen at random by B. Y. Morrison from the Chugai Nursery and introduced as Chugai Hybrids, later changed to Satsuki Hybrids. All were propagated and distributed to cooperating nurseries and arboreta. Unfortunately, not all have survived so some cultivars are no longer available. The original spelling of the clonal names as introduced was taken from the "English Speaking" Chugai Nursery catalog of 1936–1937. Many of the names have been changed in the meantime—'Adzuma no Hana' = 'Azuma no Hana', 'Bankwa' = 'Banka', 'Johga' = 'Joga' and others. Check the Index for present day spelling. The following clones were introduced:

Satsuki Introductions in 1938

'Adzuma no Hana' (PI 127653)
'Bankwa' (PI 127654)
'Chichibu' (PI 127655)
'Chojuraku' (PI 127656)
'Eikwan' (PI 127657)
'Eiten' (PI 127658)
'Fuji no Koshi' (PI 127659)
'Fukuju' (PI 127660)
'Fuku Musume' (PI 127661)
'Fukurokuju' (PI 127662)
'Gosho Zakura' (PI 127663)
'Gunbi' (PI 127664)
'Ginrei' (PI 127665)
'Ginsei' (PI 127666)
'Gyokurin' (PI 127667)
'Gyokushin' (PI 127668)
'Gyokuyo' (PI 127669)
'Hatsu Gasumi' (PI 127670)
'Heiwa no Hikari' (PI 127671)
'How Raku' (PI 127672)
'How Zan' (PI 127673)
'Jindai' (PI 127674)
'Johga' (PI 127675)
'Kagetsu' (PI 127676)
'Kaigetsu' (PI 127677)
'Keisetsu' (PI 127678)

Satsuki Introductions in 1939

'Kikaru' (PI 131295)
'Kingetsu' (PI 131296)
'Kongo' (PI 131297)
'Kow How' (PI 131298)
'Kow Koku' (PI 131299)
'Kaho' (PI 131300)
'Mai Hime' (PI 131301)
'Musahina' (PI 131302)
'Myogi' (PI 131303)
'Otome' (PI 131304)
'Reihow' (PI 131305)
'Rimpu' (PI 131306)
'Row Getsu' (PI 131307)
'Sakura Yama' (PI 131308)
'Seigetsu' (PI 131309)
'Seium' (PI 131311)
'Shi How' (PI 131310)
'Shikun ow (PI 131317)
'Shinnyo no Tsuki' (PI 13112)
'Shinsei' (PI 131313)
'Shin-sei' (PI 131315)
'Shumpow' (PI 131314)
'Sohow' (PI 131316)
'Takara Bune' (PI 131318)
'Tama Giku' (PI 131319)
'Tama Sugata' (PI 131320)
'Ten Meikai' (PI 131321)

The Satsuki Azaleas are evergreen and late blooming, usually mid-May and June, varying according to climatic conditions. The flowers are generally single; however, there are hose-in-hose such as 'Wakebisu', semidouble such as 'Gyokurin', and doubles such as 'Beni Botan' and 'Tama Botan'. The flowers range in size from less than one inch to over five inches. The flower shapes vary from rounded with large rounded overlapping five or more lobes to widely spaced lobes giving a "star-like" effect. Petals of some are divided completely to the base while others are very narrow and linear or even absent, with only stamens and stamenoid filaments present. The lobes can be smooth or frilled on the edges and flat or varied. The flower colors vary from white to solid "self" colors of various shades of pink, yellowish pink, red, reddish orange, and purple. They can be striped or with flakes to sectors of solid colors against a white or light background, and even bordered 'tsuki' forms with a margin of contrasting color.

Often the complete range of color patterns can appear on one plant. A plant with striped, dotted, flecked, bordered, or sectored flowers is not fixed except in the sense that it will continue to produce a known range of variants. Few countries describe in detail the color patterns as do the Japanese.

They distinguish twenty or more different color patterns in the Satsuki Azaleas. The flecked and striped patterns are called "shibori" (tie dye pattern) while the white throated flowers are called "sokojiro".

The Japanese were describing color patterns of azaleas dating back to *A Brocade Pillow* written in 1692. Many of the old terms are no longer used in modern Japanese. The recurring term *shibori* refers to varied "tie-dyed" patterns of which there are several styles. Japanese gardening books describe 12 or more color patterns. The color patterns were redrawn by Dr. Charles Hiers, and the transliteration made by Dr. Hiers and his wife Sheba (Setska) fro' 'he book *Satsuki Taikan* by H. & M. Suzuki, Tokyo, Japan, 1972.

2
3
4
5
6
7
8
9
10
11a
11b
12
13
14
15
16
17
18
19
20
21
22
23
24

JAPANESE COLOR PATTERNS IN THE SATSUKI AZALEAS

Adapted from *Satsuki Taikan* by H. & M. Suzuki, Tokyo, 1972.

A. Solid (base) Colors

1. **Shiromuji** [base color white]: Solid white, with or without green mottling in the center.
2. **Akamuji** [base color red]: Solid red or purple, with or without red mottling in center.

B. Color-Ring Variegation

3. **Sokojiro (white throat).** White spreading evenly from the center of the blossom. The effect is a solid rim of color, often called "picottee" in America. Type flower: 'Seidai'.
4. **Shirofukurin (white jewel-border).** The reverse of sokojiro, with the darker color in the inner part of the flower. The petals are bordered in white. Sokojiro has the effect of a darker border of color around the flower. Shirofukurin has more of a border around the petals, with color brushed out from the middle of the flower. The inner white margin is scalloped/serrate in color. There are two variations: one with a prominent border, the other with a very narrow margin of white. Type flowers: 'Chiyo no Homarre', 'Eiko'.
5. **Shibori sokojiro (variegated sokojiro).** Flowers are a mixture of sokojiro with variegations, usually with variegation subordinate to the sokojiro. Also may have bordered flowers mixed in. Type flower: 'Kagetsu'.
6. **Janome shibori (bulls eye variegation).** A sokojiro flower with shirofukurin and variegations superimposed. Type flower: 'Sogen no Tsuki'.

C. Dabs and Daubs

7. **Shirotamafu (white jewel spot).** A lighter smudge of color in the very center of the petals. When this spot becomes larger, it is referred to as otamafu. Type flower: 'Yata no kagami'.
8. **Tsumajiro (white fingernail).** White marking only at the tip of the petals. Type flower: 'Gyokudo'.

D. Stripes and Sectors

9. **Tsumabeni (crimson fingernail).** Opposite of Tsumajiro, with darker color only at the very tip of the petal. Type flower: 'Gekkeikan'.
10. **Oshibori (major variegation/sector)** One petal or as much as half the petal colored. Type flower: 'Kogetsu', 'Reiko'. When half or more of the flower is a solid red/purple, it is called Hanzome (half-colored). Type flowers: 'Kaho', 'Kinkazan'.
11. **Koshibori (11a, minor variegation/sector).** Flower is sharply divided from the edge of the petal to the center by a line of color (covers less than half of the petal). Two half-colored petals side by side are still considered koshibori. Type flower: 'Kotobuki', 'Kogetsu'. When both Oshibori and Koshibori occur on the same petal, as is common, the variegation is called Daishoshibori, (11b, major+minor variegations). Jiai shibori (combination color from two base colors (Jiai) with variegation): pale base color with variegation of darker color. Jiai flowers are usually a pale pink mixture of the two colors, white and red. The base colors are usually present on the same plant. The superimposed variegations run the gamut between a light dusting to major sectors. Type flower: 'Yamo no Hikari'. When a Jiai flower has a white variation, it is called Jiai shiroshibori. Type flower: 'Heiwa', 'Reiko'.
12. **Data shibori (showy variegation).** White crowded with variegations of color, uniform outline extending from the edge of the petals to the base. Type flower: 'Matsunami', 'Namba Nishiki'.
13. **Tate shibori (lengthwise variegation).** Similar to Data shibori, but this variegation is narrow and does not extend the length of the flower. Often 12 and 13 combine. Type flower: 'Kiri no Hikari', 'Mansaku'.
14. **Shiro shibori (white variegation).** White variegation on an otherwise red or purple flower. Type flower: 'Shinkyo'.

E. Speckles and Sprays

15. **Fukiage shibori (fountain variegation).** Fine sprays and streaks of color extending in a feathery pattern from the center of the petal toward the edge (like spray from a fountain). Type flower: 'Seiun'.
16. **Fukkake shibori (spray variegation).** In contrast to 15, a fine spray of many specks originating at the edges, trending toward the center of the petal. Type flower: 'Ogon Nishiki', 'Kinkazan'.
17. **Arare shibori (hail variegation).** Inumerable large specks and streaks all over the petals. Type flower: 'Matsu no Homare'.

18. **Mijin shibori (fine particle variegation).** A heavy fog of countless, extremely small particles of color all over the petals, heavy enough to give the flower a decided pink cast. Type flower: 'Gobi Nishiki'.

A note comparing 15, 16, 17, and 18:
15. Definite spray pattern is heaviest along the center line of the petal.
16. Color heaviest near the edges, especially the apices.
17. Larger streak size, of even distribution. No long lines of color like 12, 13, and 14.
18. A real fog of tiny particles, entirely coloring the flower.

19. **Hakeme shibori.** Numerous fine parallel lines. Type flower: 'Reiko'.
20. **Tobiiri shibori. (patchy variegation).** Irregular large and small splashes of color, here and there on the flower. Type flower: 'Chiyo no Hikari'.
21. **Harusame (Spring rain variegation).** Numerous dots and very small lines over all the petals.
22. **Sarasa shibori.** Fine parallel lines with few interspersed thicker lines. Type flower: 'Matsushima', 'Komei', 'Ue no Yama Kirin', 'Tokiwa'.
23. **Hanzome shibori.** A flashy shibori that is divided into two major segments of red and white. Type flower: 'Shinsen', 'Hatsu no Hana', 'Kaho', 'Shintayo'.
24. **Kano shibori.** A spotted shibori resembling the markings of a lily. Type flower: 'Komei', 'Ue no Yama Kirin'.

Note: since one plant can have many types of flowers, several have similar patterns, thus double listings such as 'Ue no Yama Kirin' for both Kano shibori and Sarasa shibori.

An old 1936–37 catalog of Chugai Nursery Company stated that "The flowers are of the most noble and refined beauty . . . we recommend with confidence their real value of highest attainable grade which is totally unknown outside of Japan." For more information on azalea colors and color patterns as used in this book, please refer to the chapter on Azalea—Plants, Habits, Flowers and Leaves.

Not all Satsuki Azaleas are dwarf as is commonly believed. Most clones are slow-growing, and plants range from low-spreading habit to a medium height of five to six feet in ten to fifteen years. The plants in general are rounded in shape with compact twiggy growth, while some few are pendulous and some have a upright branching habit.

As a group the Satsuki Azaleas are generally not as hardy as Kurume Azaleas so are best used in zones 7a to 9b. However, some are hardy to −10°F. Because they bloom late, it is best to site the plant in partial shade protected from noon to mid-afternoon sun.

The leaves of Satsuki Hybrids are extremely variable ranging from lanceolate shapes 1½ to 2" long like *R. indicum* to orbiculate to obovate shapes favoring *R. tamurae.* Many clones have distinct foliage such as the small narrow lanceolate, 1–1¼" long leaves of 'Kinsai'. 'Kokinsai', a sport of 'Kinsai', has even smaller leaves about ½" long. 'Kazan' ('Rukizon') has small, broad, ovate or 'heart-shaped' leaves about ½" long. 'Rinpu' or contorted and twisted leaf Satsukis are often used for Bonsai. Several clones with contorted leaves are available: 'Rinpu', 'Shuangetsu', and 'Tsuki no Shino'. Blotched and variegated leaves add an interesting feature to a Satsuki plant. The first yellow blotched leaf type introduced was 'Keisetsu', one of the 1938 collected plants. Other blotched leaf Satsukis are 'Shinnyo no Hikari' and 'Uki Nishiki'. Marginal variegated leaves with fine yellowish margin are found on 'Shira Fuji', 'Murasaki Fuji', and 'Tancho'. 'Ryusei', a Satsuki in Japan, has a combination of leaf forms with leaves that are both curled and blotched.

Satsuki azaleas are usually diploids but some including 'Banka', 'Taihei', and 'Wako' are tetraploids with 52 chromosomes.

In the United States 'Gumpo' and its sports are popular Satsukis in the landscape. However, there is an increasing interest in other Satsuki azaleas supported by the specialty growers and collectors, with over 500 clones now available. The plants are being used for Bonsai following the Japanese practice. There is no question that the Satsuki Hybrids will play an increasingly important role in both Azalea culture and the landscape in Western countries.

The descriptive list of Satsuki clones includes those introduced by the U.S.D.A. Plant Introduction Section (with the PI numbers) and by others, but does not include those available only in Japan. All those included are in private or public collections in the West, and many are being grown commercially. The color names are from the ISCC-NBS; other color numbers or designation are given when known.

The Japanese names are transliterations from Japanese Kanji to the English alphabet and conform to the correct and accepted registered names in Japan. In brackets following the Japanese name is the English meaning when known, which has been added for interest and *should not* be construed as the correct Japanese name.

The spelling of the Japanese name varies depending upon the system used by the person making transliteration. For example, the synonyms for 'Kinsai' are 'Kinzai', 'Kin no Sai' and 'Kin no Zai', 'Gumpo' or 'Gunpo'; 'Bunka' or 'Bunkwa'; 'Joga' or 'Johga'; 'Waraijishi' or 'Waraigishi' or 'Waraishishi'; and 'Eikan' or 'Eikwan'. A few of the common synonyms are included in the lists; the others will be found in the index. For more information on transliteration, the pronounciation and meaning of some Japanese words, please refer to Appendix D.

Azaleas are an important element in the collections of Brookside Gardens, The Maryland National Capital Park and Planning Commission in Silver Spring, Maryland. Due to the keen interest shown by the public, Barry R. Yinger, under the sponsorship of Carl R. Hahn, Chief Horticulturist, selected a superlative collection of Satsuki cultivars to be imported. The cuttings, most of which were selected at Kairyo Nursery in Japan, were imported in 1978 and 1979. Cuttings of the entire collection of 387 plants have been released to the Azalea Society of America for propagation, evaluation, and distribution through commercial nurserymen who are ASA members. The Brookside collection is designated in the Listing by a 'BG' number following the description. A few of the cultivars have not yet been described. The description will be published in the Azalea Society of America Journal after several blooming cycles have occurred. See Appendix J.

SATSUKI HYBRIDS

'Aigyoku' [Love jewel]: dark pink with white tips, dark pink blotch, lobes rounded, early, 1½–2". BG 1110.

'Aikoku' [Patriotism] ('Koho' × 'Tanima no Yuki'): white with occasional stripes of deep purplish pink, some solid deep purplish pink edged white, and white center bordered purplish pink, 2½–3"; low spreading. PI 227066, '55. BG 1221.

'Ai no Nishiki' [Brocade of love]: white with many variations of vivid reddish orange flecks, stripes and sectors, to blushes of pale yellowish pink, and solid dark, round slightly spaced lobes, 2½–3". BG 1122.

'Ai no Tsuki' [Moon of love] ('Aikoku' seedling): white with purplish stripes, occasionally pink with white center, some light purplish pink and bordered white, 2½–3". BG 0868.

'Aishifu': white with flakes and sectors of strong reddish purple, greenish blotch 1½–2". BG 0871.

'Akanagi' [Red harmony]: white with many streaks of pale pink, occasional sectors of darker pink, light green throat, round wavy overlapping lobes, 2½". BG 1026.

'Akatsuki no Zao' [Moon at dawn on Mt. Zao]: white to strong pink with pink sectors, lobes slightly separate, 2½–3". BG 0859.

'Akebono' [Daybreak] (sport of 'Zuio'): white with blush of pale purplish pink with scant pink variegations, 6 wide overlapping lobes, 4–4½". BG 1314.

'Akita Nishiki' [Akita brocade]: white to deep yellowish pink with deep pink stripes, deep pink spotted throat, wavy lobes, 2½–3". BG 0977.

'Akita Shibori' [Akita striped] (sport of 'Akita Nishiki'): strong pink with white margins, deep pink markings, wavy lobes, 2½–3".

'Akoyo Hime' [Princess Akoya]: white, 5 to 9 large lobes, with moderate purplish red stripes, and wavy hairline stripes.

'Amagasa' [Umbrella] (syn. 'Tengasa'; seedling of 'Huzan'): vivid red, darker spots on upper lobe, wide overlapping lobes, 3–4". PI 227067, '55. BG 0930.

'Aoi' [Asarum—Tokugawa Family Crest] (sport of 'Nikko'): pale yellowish pink with deep yellowish pink and reddish marking, some white blushed pink, small pointed lobes, 2–2½", late; slow compact. BG 0994.

'Aozora' [Blue sky]: very pale pink with dark pink stripes and flecks, occasional dark pink sports, overlapping lobes, 2", early; low spreading. BG 1189.

'Appare' [Splendid] ('Kikenjo' × 'Kimimaru'): white with red sectors and selfs, or dots in throat, some white centered with red margin, 2½", midseason. BG 1213.

'Asafuji' [Morning Wisteria]: white with yellowish pink flecks, dots stripes and sectors, occasional pink selfs, long lobes, early, 2". BG 1274.

'Asahi' [Morning sun] ('Kusudama' × 'Banka'): white with scattered flakes and stripes of deep pink, some pink self, wavy, rounded, overlapping lobes, to 4".

'Asahi no Hikari' [The light of dawn] (sport of 'Eikan'): pale pink fading to white, to deep pink margin, round ruffled lobes, 2½–3", late; upright growth. BG 0919.

'Asahi no Izumi' [Morning spring-water]: white with red specks and vivid red sectors and stripes, green blotch, round overlapping lobes, 2", early. BG 1294.

'Asahi Zuru' [Morning Crane]: light yellowish pink with red flecks in throat, occasionally with white margins and orange red selfs, rounded lobes, 2½–3", midseason; upright growth. Old variety. Two distinct plants have same name.

'Asahi Zuru': white with pink blush and prominent red dotted blotch. See description of previous cultivar.

'Azuma Kagami' [Mirror of the East] ('Yata no Kagami' × 'Shiun no Tsuki'): light pink shading to deeper pink edges, many variations of mottling and toning of blush to deep pink, dark blotch, rounded lobes, 2½–3", vigorous upright habit. BG 0506.

'Azuma no Hana' [Flower of the East]: white, relatively fine dots, occasional sectorial flakes of strong reddish orange, round overlapping lobes, 2 to 4". PI 127653, '38.

'Azuma Nishiki' [Oriental brocade]: white with flakes and stripes to selfs of moderate red, 5–8 lobes, 2–2½", midseason.

'Baiho' [Plum treasure] ('Kozan' × 'Matsunami'): variegated white with deep pink to strong red stripes, many variations, occasional selfs, and white rimmed pink, round lobes, 1½–2", midseason; upright habit. BG 0945.

'Baisetsu' [Plum snow]: white with reddish purple stripes, 2½–3".

'Bandai' [Ten-thousand generations]: white with red stripes to red selfs, up to 9 lobes spaced with a slight twist, 2½–3". BG 1011.

'Bangaku' [Ten-thousand peaks] ('Shozui' × 'Shomei'): white with green throat, light purple spotting and stripes to purple selfs, wide lobes, 3–4". PI 227069, '55. BG 1135.

'Banjo' [Universe]: white with strong pink to deep red flakes, occasionally marginal and pink selfs, usually 6 or more, round ruffled lobes, 3–4".

'Banjo no Tsuki' [The moon of the universe] ('Zuio' × 'Shinnyo no Tsuki'): white bordered strong pink, with occcasional faint white edge, many variations only with red flakes and stripes, 5–6 wide overlapping lobes, 3–4". PI 227072, '55.

'Banka' [Myriad flowers] (sport of 'Banjo'): white with flakes of light pink to solid deep pink, 6 rounded lobes, to 4". PI 228103, '55. PI 230608, '56. BG 1298.

'Banko' [Eternity] (seedling of 'Bunka'): white flushed light pink, sectors and flakes of light pink, wide wavy lobes, 3-4". PI 228104, '55. PI 230609, '56.

'Bano': white with few tiny green dots in blotch, usually 6 overlappink lobes, 3-3½". PI 227074, '55.

'Banshin' [Ten-thousand hearts]: white with stripes and sectors of deep pink, no blotch, wide round overlapping lobes, 2½-3", late. BG 0920.

'Banzai' [Ten-thousand years] ('Izayoi' × 'Tamaori Hime'): white with flakes of strong pink, occasional pale pink center with darker margins, 5–6 wavy lobes, 2½-3", BG 0364/0996.

'Beni Botan' [Red Peony] (old variety from Osaka): strong red, double, round lobes, 2½-3", midseason; vigorous upright bushy.

'Benigasa' [Red umbrella] (sport of 'Amagasa'): strong red to vivid red, rounded lobes, 3–4", early to midseason; slow to medium spreading habit. BG 1148.

'Beni Kagami' [Red mirror]: white with deep reddish orange stripes, many variations, occasional red selfs, rounded lobes, 2-2½"; midseason; upright habit. BG 0940.

'Beni Kirin' [Red giraffe]: formal double, strong to vivid reddish orange, with few dark dots in blotch, small overlapping lobes decreasing in size to the center, 2½-3".

'Beni Kirishima' [Red Kirishima]: double (rosebud), strong reddish orange, darker blotch, 2", late. PI 77113, 77128, '29.

'Beni Tsubame' [Red swallow] (seedling of 'Kikoshi'): moderate red with white blotches on lobes, bellshaped, lobes spaced, 2–2½", midseason. BG 0502/1176.

'Benizume' [Red Fingernail]: no description available.

'Biho' [Beautiful peak] ('Gekkeikan' × 'Kozan'): white with many variations of flecks, dots and sectors to selfs of dark reddish orange, spaced pointed lobes, 2–2½", mideason; leaves yellowish green. BG 0875.

'Biko' [Pretty light] ('Onyo' × 'Kozan'): white with greenish throat, many variations of light to deep pink stripes and selfs, 2", spaced pointed lobes, slightly tubular, 2".

'Buho no Tsuki': deep reddish purplish with faint white throat, faint red blotch, rounded lobes, 2½–3"; upright vigorous habit. BG 0947.

'Buncho' [Java Sparrow]: dark pink to red, 1½", anthers brown; BG 0854.

'Bunka' [Cultured] (seedling of 'Yata no Kagami'): light pink, some with white center, upper 3 lobes overlap, lower 2 free, 2½–3", PI 127654, '38. BG 1102.

'Cain' (Satsuki hybrid, Spartanburg Nursery): light pink fading to pale to white in the center, greenish yellow blotch in throat, rounded lobes, 3", late; compact habit; hardy in zone 7.

'Chichibu' [proper noun]: white, frilled, occasional light purple colors, 5–6 lobes, 3". PI 127655, '38.

'Chidori' [Plover]: deep pink with light star in center, wide vivid reddish purple margins, crinkled edges, 3–3½", early. BG 1157.

'Chigo Sugata' [Celestial child figure] ('Hogetsu' × 'Taihei'): white center, wide border of deep pink, round wavy overlapping lobes, 2½–3", midseason.

'Chikyuho' [Treasure of the Earth] ('Yata no Kagami' × 'Yushigure'): white center shading to vivid yellowish pink on margins, irregular double, many variations, in form, 2–2½", midseason; upright spreading habit.

'Chikyu Nishiki': white with pale green center or with stripes and sectors of pale to moderate pink, some selfs of pale or moderate pink, round wavy lobes, 2½–3". BG 1200.

'Chinei' (syn. 'Chinyeyi'; sport of 'Gumpo'): white with pink dots and flakes and slight green blotch, round wavy overlapping lobes, 2½–3". BG 1021.

'Chinrei': vivid purplish pink with darker margins, blushes of white toward center, reddish purple blotch, 3–3½". BG 1056.

'Chinsai' [Rare color] (sport of 'Kotobuki'): white with strong and deep pink variations, occasional pink selfs, long narrow petals, many unusual forms, 1½–2", late; spreading habit.

'Chinsei' [Tranquillity]: vivid purplish pink, darker blotch, 1½–2"; leaves small and narrow; compact habit.

'Chinzan' [Rare mountain] (sport of 'Osakazuki'): vivid pink with darker blotch, rounded lobes 1½–2"; leaves elliptical 1" long; compact growth. Popular for bonsai; some disagree with color, appears deep pink, but with a faint purplish cast. BG 1025.

'Chitose Gawa': [Thousand-year river]: white with dots and sectors of light purplish pink, rounded spaced lobes, 1½–2". BG 1188.

'Chitose Nishiki' [Brocade of a thousand years): white with stripes of light to strong purplish pink, many variations to pink selfs rounded lobes, 1½–2¼", midseason; slow to medium spreading habit.

'Chiyodo Nishiki' [Chiyodo brocade]: white with pink stripes, 2½–3".

'Choyo no Hagoromo' [Celestial of a Thousand Years]: no description available.

'Chiyo no Haru' [Spring of a thousand-years] (sport of 'Sakura Yama'): white with some broad stripes, flakes and narrow lines of strong red to deep pink, red dot in blotch, often 6 overlapping lobes, 4"; low compact. PI 227077, '59.

'Chiyo no Hikari' [Light of a thousand-years]: white with light purplish pink stripes to pink selfs, and white rimmed pink, slightly funnel-shaped, long narrow spaced lobes, 2–2½". BG 0510.

'Chiyo no Homare' [Glory of a thousand-years] (seedling of 'Tomari Hime'): white with stripes of strong to vivid purplish pink, many variations to purplish pink self, broad rounded notched lobes, 3–4", mid to late. BG 0402/0874.

'Chiyo no Mine' [Summit of a thousand-years] (seedling of 'Yama Biko'): pale pink, dots and sectors deep pink, tube white at base, 3".

'Chiyo no Tsuki' [Moon of a thousand-years] ('Matsunami' × 'Kikoshi'): heavily variegated, white with border of pink, and deep pink, many variations, slightly pointed lobes, 1½–2".

'Choei' [Long prosperity] (syn. 'Shichihenge'): white with prominent green blotch, occasional stripes and blush of deep pink, wide overlapping lobes, 3½–4". BG 0890.

'Choeiraku' [Joy of long prosperity] ('Yata no Kagami' × 'Seium'): white, faint pale yellow blotch (unusual), lobes rounded, 2", stamens and pistil white.

'Chojuho' [Treasure of longevity]: deep red changing to strong reddish orange to brownish orange, occasionally with large yellowish blotches, small narrow strap-like lobes, 1–1½", prominent stamens; early to late; flowers persist; upright spreading habit.

'Shinseikai' syn. 'Old Ivory' Kurume Hybrid. GALLE

'Orange Cup' Kurume Hybrid. GALLE

'Yaye Hiryu' syn. 'Yaye Giri', 'Scarlet Prince' Kurume Hybrid. GALLE

'Cattleya' Kurume Hybrid. MILLER

Plate 66

'Azuma Kagami' syn. 'Pink Pearl' Kurume Hybrid. GALLE

'Sakura Tsukasa' syn. 'All a Glow' Kurume Hybrid. GALLE

'Ima Shojo' syn. 'Christmas Cheer' Kurume Hybrid. GALLE

'Snowball' Double Kurume Hybrid. GALLE

'Sherwood Red' Kurume Hybrid. GALLE

'Amoenum' Kurume Hybrid. GALLE

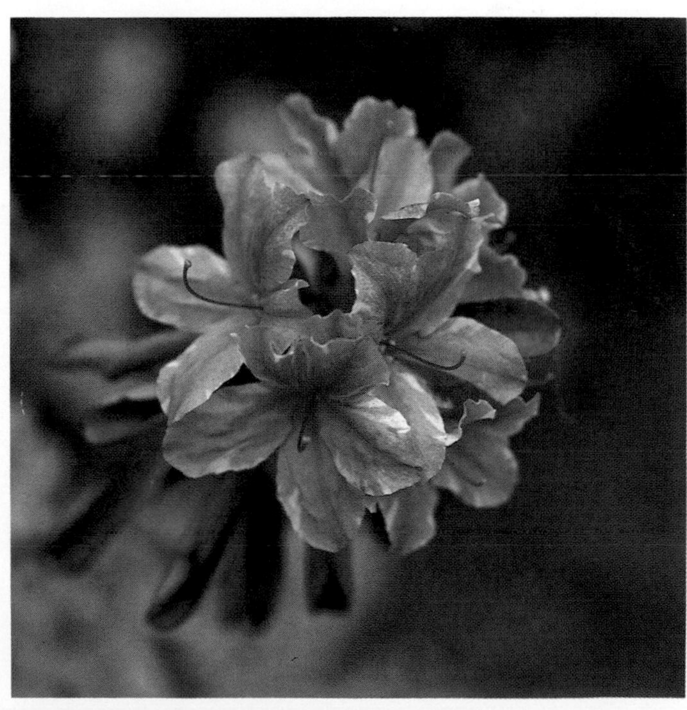

'Gunki' new Kurume Hybrid from Japan. GALLE

Plate 68

'Hershey Red' Hershey Kurume Hybrid. MC DONALD

'Eureka' Beltsville Hybrid. GALLE

'White Nymph' Beltsville Dwarf. GALLE

'Tennyo no Mai' new Kurume Hybrid from Japan. GALLE

'Mayo's Magic Lily' Mayo Hybrid. GALLE

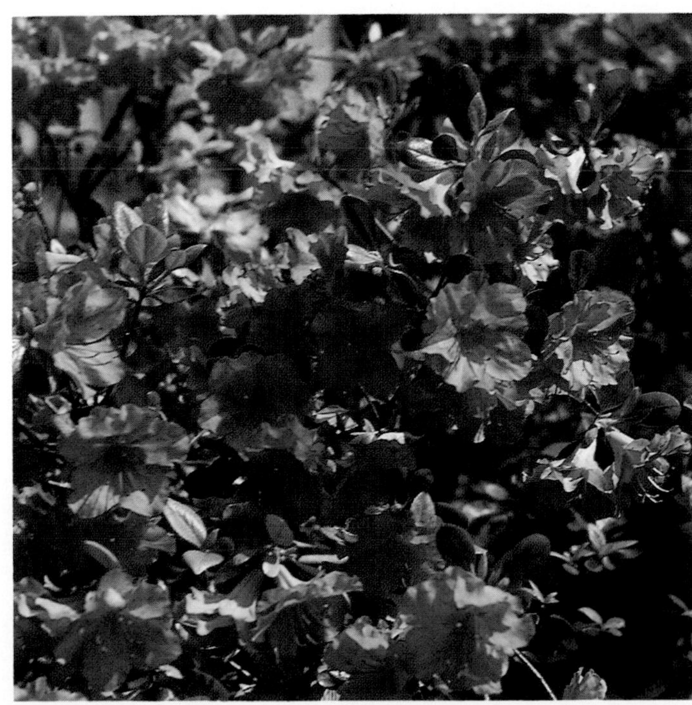

'Printemps' Chisolm Merritt Hybrid. GALLE

'Wilhelmina Vuyk' syn. 'Palestrina' Kaempferi Hybrid. MILLER

Plate 70

'James Gable' Gable Hybrid. B. S. HARDING

'Rosebud' Gable Hybrid. D. F. SAUER

'Pleasant White' Girard Hybrid. GIRARD

'Girard's Rose' Girard Hybrid. GIRARD

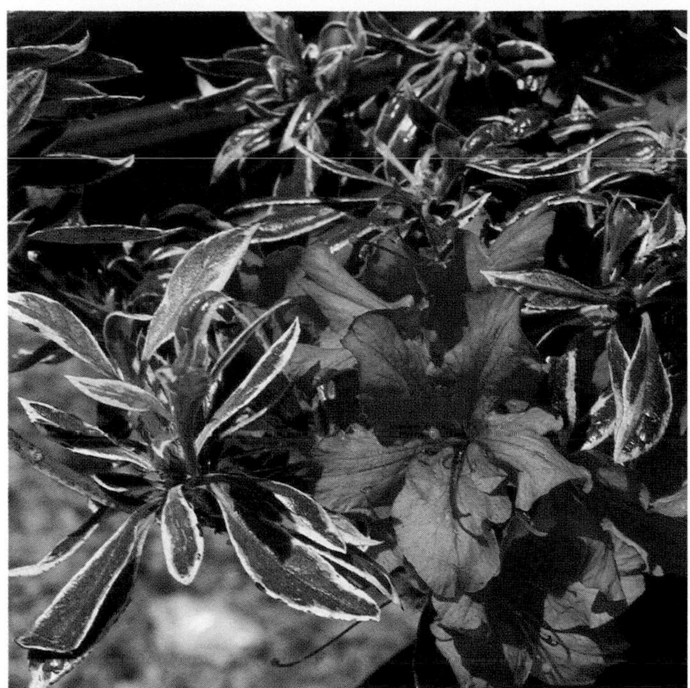

'Silver Sword' sport of 'Girard's Rose' Kaempferi Hybrid. GALLE

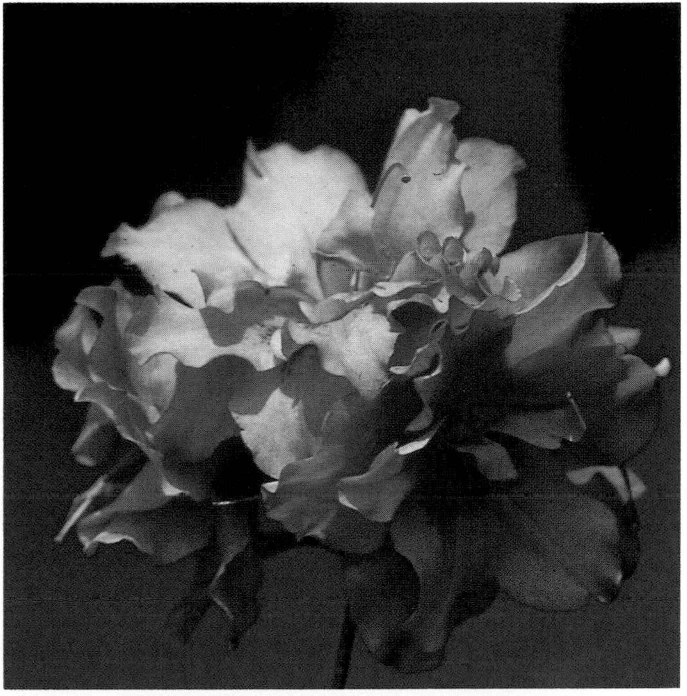

'Salmon Pincushion' Linwood Hybrid. HARDING

'Girard's Hot Shot' Girard Hybrid. GIRARD

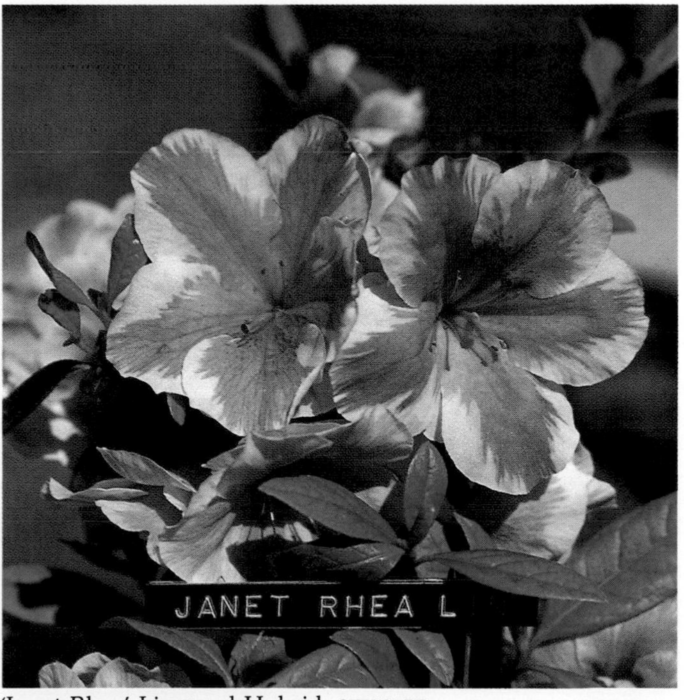

'Janet Rhea' Linwood Hybrid. STEWART

Plate 72

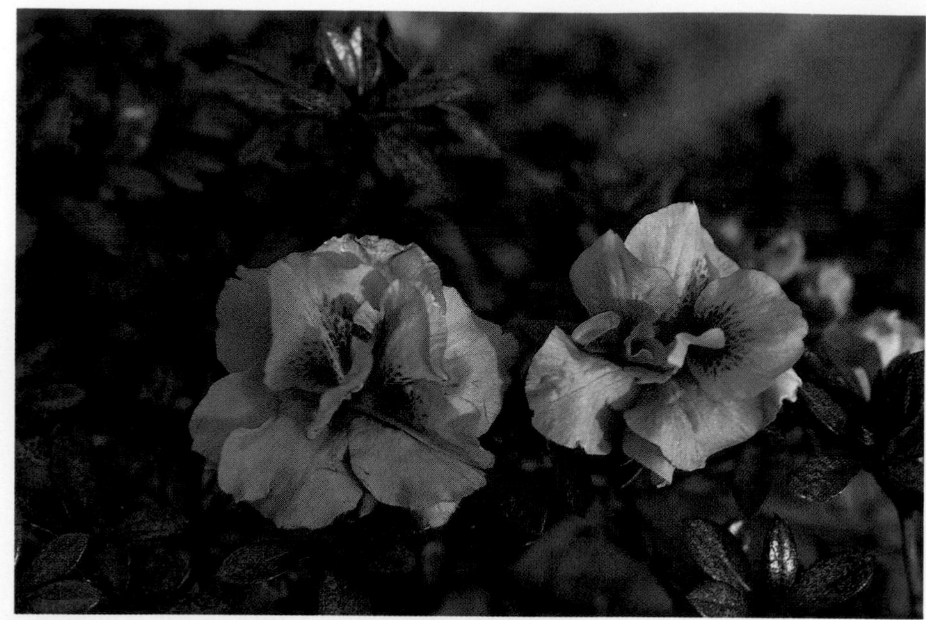

'Opal' Linwood Hybrid.
G. HARDING

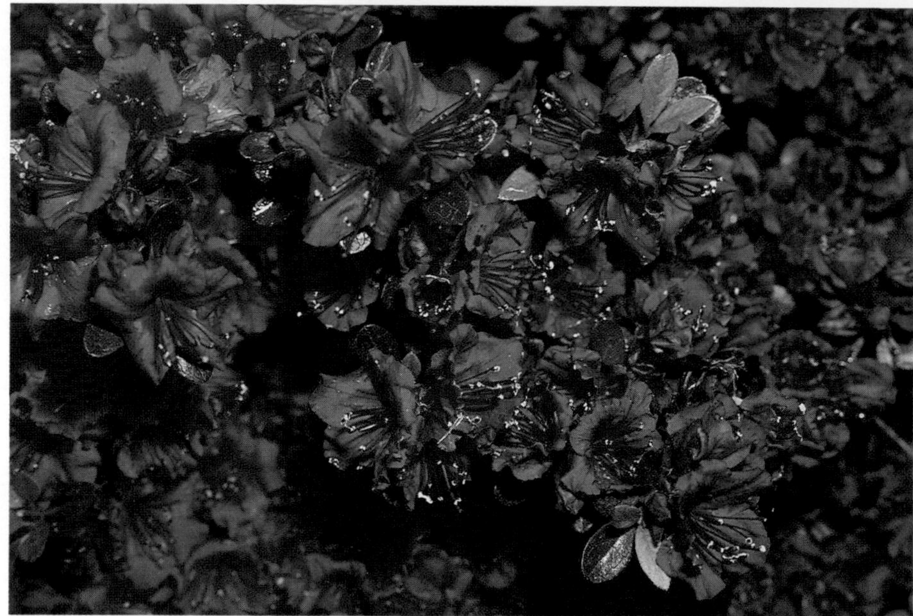

'Girard's Scarlet' Girard Hybrid. GIRARD

'Baiho' [Plum Treasure] Satsuki Hybrid. GALLE

'Choju no Iwai' [Celebration of long life]: white, many sectors and flakes of deep pink and occasional reddish orange selfs, often 6 wavy overlapping lobes, 3–4". PI 227076, '55.

'Chojuraku' [Pleasure of long life]: white with pink to vivid red variegations, occasionally pale pink center with reddish orange margins, 3–4". PI 127656.

'Cho no Hagoromo': white with flecks and sectors of yellowish pink, light green blotch, 2½". BG 1324.

'Daigokuden' [Great jewel palace]: vivid pink with star-center and reddish purple blotch, hose-in-hose, semidouble, petaloid, 2½-3"; upright habit. BG 1075.

'Dainanko' (seedling of 'Hakato Jiro'): variegated, white with purplish red speckles and stripes, occasional pale purple to selfs of deep pink, lobes spaced, 2–2½", late; slow compact habit.

'Daiseiko' [Great starlight] (sport of 'Gobi Nishiki'): white variegated with occasional stripes of deep pink, to pink selfs with white edge, wide spaced pointed lobes, turned back at ends, 2–2½", very late; slow compact habit.

'Daisetsuzan' [Great snow mountain]: white with yellow green center, 5 to 9 large rounded lobes, 4–5", early to midseason; vigorous upright habit.

'Daishuhai' [Great vermilion cup] (syn. 'Taishuhai'): deep yellowish pink, lighter to white in center, round lobes, 2½–3", early; open habit. PI 226145, 227078, '55. BG 0488.

'Eikan' [A garland] (seedling of 'Asahi Zuru'): extremely variable, white with many variations of stripes and selfs of strong to deep pink to yellowish pink, large round, often 6–9 ruffled lobes, 3–4", mid to late; vigorous spreading habit. PI 127657, PI 227079, '38 & '55. BG 1256.

'Eiko' [Glory] (seedling of 'Shinkigen'): white with occasional stripes of pink, and selfs of pink to strong red, many variations, wide rounded lobes, 3–4", early to midseason; vigorous low spreading. BG 0955.

'Eishi' ('Fuji Nishiki' × 'Homare no Kokka'): white with occasional stripes of deep purplish pink, to selfs of light to deep pink, flowers slightly tubular, round wavy lobes, 2–2½"; low spreading. BG 1217.

'Eiten' [Honors] ('Fuji Nishiki' × 'Yume'): white with stripes, or more often light purple selfs, overlapping lobes, 3–3½". PI 127658, '38.

'Fuji' [Wisteria]: white, vivid purplish pink margin, round wavy lobes, 2½–3". BG 1152.

'Fuji Hime' [Wisteria Princess]: white with stripes and sectors of purplish pink, round wavy overlapping lobes, 2½–3". BG 0931.

'Fuji Mori' [Wisteria woods]: vivid pink, long narrow lobes, 2–2½", early, white stamens and pistil; low spreading. BG 0466.

'Fuji Nami' [Wisteria wave]: white with flecks and sectors of dark purplish pink, long round lobes, 2½–3". BG 1004.

'Fuji Nishiki' [Peerless brocade] (natural seedling): white, striped and flecked with shades of strong purplish red, many variations, wavy lobes, 2½–3", late. BG 1291

'Fuji no Koshi' [Base of Mt. Fuji]: white with deep purple variegations, some with white center or margins, 5–6 lobes, 3". PI 127659, '38.

'Fuji no Mine' [Peak of Mt. Fuji] strong pink, darker center, 2½"; leaves variegated with numerous flecks and blotched yellow.

'Fuji Zakura' [Cherry blossom of Mt. Fuji] (seedling of 'Chiyo no Hikari'): white usually with numerous fine pink stripes with larger stripes and flakes to pink selfs, pointed lobes, 2–2½", mid to late; slow compact habit.

'Fukuju' [Happiness and longevity] ('Kyokko Nishiki' × 'Mme. Moreux'): white, stripes, sectors and selfs of deep yellowish pink, greenish blotch, 5–7 round overlapping lobes, 4–4½"; large leaves, PI 127660, '38. BG 0900.

'Fukuju Jiai' (sport of 'Fukuju'; Jiai means colored): light reddish purple with darker stripes, spotting and selfs, or white spotting to lobes with lighter edge; leaves large.

'Fuku Munsume' [Wealthy maid]: white, variable, flakes of deep reddish purple from margin inward, self of light purple, dark ruffled margins, 2½". PI 127661, '38.

'Fuku no Hana' [Flower of wealth] ('Kozan' × 'Tamari Hime'): white with stripes and sectors of deep pink to red, rounded lobes, 2½". BG 0877.

'Fukurakuya': no description available.

'Fukurokuju' [proper noun; Japanese Goddess]: white with few flakes of light pink, variable with occasional pink sectors, upper lobes overlap well apart from 2 lower overlapping lobes, 3". PI 127662, '38. BG 0912.

'Fuku Suzume' [Wealthy sparrow] ('Fuji Nishiki' × 'Tamaori Hime'): white with numerous red flakes, occasionally red with small white center. 1½–2". BG 0873.

'Futaba no Tsuki' [Two leaf moon]: deep yellowish pink with red blotch, ruffled lobes, 2½–3", early. BG 1117.

'Gaho' [Refined fragrance]: white with purplish pink stripes, flecks and sectors, 2–2½", pale pink stamens and pistil. BG 1232.

'Geigetsu': no description available.

'Gekka': white with flakes of deep pink and flushes of light pink, occasionally margins and selfs of pink, overlapping lobes, 3".

'Gekkeikan' [Laurel crown] ('Yata no Kagami' × 'Shozui'): white with occasional deep yellowish pink stripes to pink selfs, also pale pink centers and vivid yellowish pink wide margins, 6 or more rounded spaced lobes, 3–4", late; slow, upright. BG 0368/1198.

'Gekko' [Moonlight] (sport of 'Haru Gasumi'): white with numerous flakes of pink, often light to vivid purplish pink with white centers, round overlapping lobes, 2–2½". BG 0367.

'Genjiguruma' [Genji wheel]: white to light pink with deep pink flakes to pink selfs, some petaloidy, 3–4".

'Getsu Keikan': pale purplish pink to brighter pink edges, occasional fleck of deep pink, dark purple blotch, 6 pointed lobes, 2½–3", early, white stamens and red pistil. BG 0468.

'Getsu Rei': white with occasional flecks of deep pink, wide round slightly wavy lobes, 3½–4". BG 0404.

'Getsutoku' [Moon of virtue] (syn. 'Gettoku' BG 1074; 'Banka' × 'Shinnyo no Tsuki'): white with strong pink and red stripes, many variations to pink selfs, often 6, wavy overlapping lobes, 3–4", late; spreading habit. PI 227080, 230610, '56. BG 1214.

'Ginga' [Silver river] (sport of 'Mine no Hikari'): white with many variations of deep pink stripes and sectors, red blotch, round spaced lobes 2–2½"; long narrow leaves. BG 1101.

'Ginrei' (sport of 'Sanko no Tsuki'): white blushed light to deep pink, sometimes with dark red blotch, or pale pink center with dark margins and no blotch, very variable, 5–6 round lobes, 2–2½". BG 1139.

'Ginsei' [Silver star] ('Meiko' × 'Kozan'): white with green blotch, occasional blush of pink, rounded lobes, 2", white stamens and pistil. BG 0954.

'Ginsekai' [Silver world]: white with slight greenish blotch, round spaced lobes, 1–1½", early. BG 1015.

'Gobi Nishiki' [Defender of beauty brocade]: white with vivid red flakes stripes and sectors to red selfs, often light pink with white edges, and red speckled throat, rounded lobes, 2½–3".

'Godaishu' [Five great states] ('Kyokko Nishiki' × 'Tenshiho'): white with occasional dark red sectors, faint greenish blotch, wide round irregular lobes, 2½". BG 1228.

'Goko' [Five lights] (sport of 'Nikko'): pale yellowish pink with many variations of stripes and sectors of dark yellowish pink and occasional sectors of white, round spaced lobes, 2–2½". BG 0891.

'Gorin Nishiki' [Five ring glory] (seedling of 'Kami no Yamakirin'): white, variegated usually heavily speckled and striped with strong reddish purple to selfs, rounded lobes, 2½–3", mid. to late.

'Gosai no Hikari': white with yellowish pink sectors, occasional flecks and blush of deep yellowish pink, rounded lobes, 2–2½", mid-season. BG 0863.

'Gosho Guruma' [Court carrriage] (seedling from Domoto): white with pink variegations, 2–2½", slightly pendulous habit.

'Gosho no Tsuki' [Moon of Imperial Palace] ('Aikoku' × 'Seiko no Tsuki'): white with occasionally delicate blushes, stripes or sectors of purplish pink, 6 rounded overlapping lobes, 2–2½". BG 1154.

'Gosho Zakura' [Cherry of Imperial Palace]: light purplish pink, center pale pink to whitish, occasionally with pale pink margins, ruffled lobes, 2–2½". PI 127663, '38.

'Gumpo' [A group of phoenixes] (syn. 'Gunpo'; origin unknown, early 1900's): white with occasional small flakes of purplish pink, blotch area light green, lobes equal, overlapping and ruffled, 2½–3"; compact growth; popular landscape plant. Named sports: 'Pink Gumpo': light pink; 'Rose Gumpo': strong pink; 'Fancy Gumpo': pink, with white margin; and 'Tuki Gumpo': yellowish pink. The following are witches broom sports: 'Dwarf' and 'Mini' 'Gumpo', and are labeled as such until proper names are given.

'Gunbi' [Beauty of the group] (sport of 'Gumpo'): white with purplish red flecks, stripes, or tips, also white with purplish red blotch, lobes ruffled, 2½–3"; compact habit. PI 127664, '38. Same as 'Gunrei'.

'Gunbo Nishiki' [Gunbo brocade] (syn. 'Akatsuki no Zoa'): white, variable with stripes, sectors and margins in strong purplish pink, also light pink and white margin, lobes wavy, 2½–3"; leaves oval 1¼–1½". BG 0469.

'Gunjo' [Ultramarine]: red with darker spots in blotch, 2".

'Gunki' [Joy of the masses]: white with many variations heavily striped, flecked, and sectored reddish orange, 6 lobes and petaloid, 3–3½". BG 1111.

'Gunno' [Ruler of the masses]: deep violet, large wavy lobes.

'Gunrei' [Beautiful group] (sport of 'Gumpo'): pale pink with light pink flakes and small sectors, lobes overlapping, frilled, 2–2½". PI 127665, '38. Sold as 'Gunbi' on the West Coast of the U.S.A.

'Gunsei' [Voice of the masses] ('Gunno' × 'Gumpo'): white with some dots and flakes of purplish pink, occasional light pink selfs, ruffled equal overlapping lobes, 2–2½". PI 127666, '38.

'Gyokka no Kagayaki': light purplish pink center with dark purplish pink margins, occasional light purplish pink star in center with wide dark pink margins, occasionally white with dark purplish pink stripes and flecks, 1½–2", early. BG 1114.

'Gyoko' [Dawn light] ('Gomi Nishiki' × 'Shokko Nishiki'): white heavily variegated with large stripes and sectors of strong reddish orange, occasionally reddish orange with white center, lobes rounded occasionally 5 to 7, 3–4". BG 1098.

'Gyokokan' [Crown of the dawn] (seedling of 'Gyoko'): white heavily striped with vivid reddish orange, some wide sectors, to reddish selfs, rounded lobes, 2½–3"; long narrow leaves. BG 0883.

'Gyoko no Kagayaki' (seedling of 'Gyoko'): white with various types of deep purplish pink stripes, or vivid purplish pink with pale pink center, 2–2½". BG 1326.

'Gyokudo' [Gem temple] ('Gekkeikan' × 'Sangosai'): white to light pink base, long rounded lobes tipped with strong red and white 2–3", star-shaped; vigorous open. BG 0486/1180.

'Gyokuho': white with vivid pink sectors and flecks, white stamens and pistil, 2½–3"; low spreading with large leaves, BG 0896.

'Gyokurei' [Gem] ('Kaho' × 'Mme. Moreux'): white often speckled vivid purplish red to purplish red self, irregular double, round lobes, 2½–3"; early to midseason; upright growth.

'Gyokuren' [Gem forest]: strong reddish purple some lobes with white blotches, semidouble, tubular flowers do not open fully, 1–2". PI 127667, '38.

'Gyokuryu' [Gem dragon]: vivid purplish red with dark spots in throat, lobes spaced, 3"; leaves narrow and twisted. BG 1145.

'Gyokushin' [Nodding jewel] (seedling of 'Ashai Zuru'): white with some light to strong purplish pink selfs, flakes of deep pink and dots in blotch, some light or colored margins, 5–6 round ruffled lobes, 2½–3". PI 127668, '38. BG 1045.

'Gyokusui': white, dotted striped and sectors of purplish pink, tubular, star-shaped; low spreading.

'Gyokuyo' [Gem sun]: white, few tiny flakes of vivid violet, blotch area washed yellow, frilled equal lobes, 3½–3¾". PI 127669, '38.

'Gyoten' [Dawn sky] (sport of 'Kaho'); light pink with feathered white edges, vivid yellowish pink blotch and strong red stripes or white tipped vivid yellowish pink, round wavy lobes, 2½–3", late; slow growing and bushy. PI 227082, '55 & '59. BG 0888.

'Gyotoku': white with flakes of moderate orange and pink flushes, blotch reddish purple, 2¾".

'Hagoromo no Hikari' [Light of the feather cloak] ('Gekkeikan' × 'Sangosai'): pale yellowish pink center bordered deep reddish orange, some selfs, pointed spaced lobes, 1½–2". BG 1352.

'Hagoromo no Mai' [The dance of the feather cloak]: white with pink tint, and purple spotting, 6 wavy lobes, 2½–3".

'Hakatajiro' [White Hakata]: white with pale green dots in throat, rounded lobes, 2½–3"; upright habit. BG 1275.

'Hakatahako': white with faint yellow green blotch, 3 upper lobes overlapping, 2–2¾.

'Hakata Shiro': white with faint greenish blotch, wavy lobes, 2½".

'Hakko' [White light] (sport of 'Nikko'): white with slight greenish throat, long-pointed spaced lobes, 1½". BG 1105.

'Hakuho' [White peak] ('Hakurei' × 'Chiyo no Hikari'): white with faint green center, spaced pointed lobes, 1½", prominent white stamens and pistil. BG 0967.

'Hakurei' [White excellence] ('Kozan' × 'Osakazuki'): white, narrow pointed lobes, star shaped, 1½–2"; slow, bushy habit.

'Hakusen no Mai' [Dance of the white fawn] ('Miyuki Nishiki' × 'Hakatajiro'): white, pale green center, semidouble, inner lobes strap-like outer lobes round overlapping, 2½–3", white stamens and pistil; spreading habit. BG 1130.

'Hakushin' [White faith] (sport of 'Matsu Kagami'): white to pale pink, rounded lobes, 2–2½"; bushy habit.

'Hakutsuru' [White crane]: white, spaced pointed lobes, margins serrated, 2".

'Hama Chidori' [Plover]: white with small and large reddish purple stripes or small spotting to reddish purple selfs, 2"; small curled leaves. BG 1009.

'Hanamoyo': white with stripes and sectors of purplish red, wavy lobes. BG 1202.

'Hana no Kagami' [Flower mirror] ('Kozan' × 'Reigetsu'): white, variable with flecks, stripes and sectors to selfs reddish orange, occasional white center, 2". BG 1046.

'Hanazono' [Flower garden] ('Kaho' × 'Kotobuki'): white with stripes and flecks of purplish red, medium size. BG 1086.

'Haresugata' [Dressed in one's best]: white, variable with large and small purplish pink stripes, margins lightly colored or white throat, 5–6 widely spaced lobes, 2½–3". BG 1296.

'Haru Gasumi' [Spring mist] (sport of 'Kagetsu'): white with margin of vivid purplish pink, many variations and stripes of pink, slightly wavy rounded lobes, 2½–3"; vigorous open growth. PI 127670, '38. BG 0491.

'Harukaze' [Spring breeze]: white with green blotch, many variations with blushes, flecks, tips and sectors of pale yellowish pink, often star-like centers with wide margins of vivid yellowish pink. 2½–3". BG 1005.

'Haru no Hikari' [Light of spring] (sport of 'Soko'): white and pink, variegations of deep pink, round lobes, often 6, 3–4"; vigorous.

'Haru no Mai' [Dance of spring]: white with pale green blotch, dots, flecks and sectors of purplish pink, 6 lobes, 2". BG 1138.

'Haru no Sono' [Garden of spring] (sport of 'Issho no Haru'); pale purplish pink, many variations of vivid purplish pink and selfs, to pink with white margins and pale green blotch, round lobes, 3–4"; compact. BG 1220.

'Haru no Uta' [Song of spring]: BG 1123.

'Hatsu Gasumi' [New mist]: white with stripes to selfs of very light purple, conspicuous blotch, 2½–3". PI 127670, '38.

'Hatsuhigumo' ('Gumpo' × 'Kagetsu'): white with light yellow throat and fine edge of purplish pink, 6 wide round ruffled lobes, 2½–3". BG 1245.

'Hatsu Kagami' [First mirror]: BG 1071.

'Hatsu no Hana' [The first flower] ('Tatsumi no Hikari' × 'Kusudama'): white, many variations with large and small pale purplish pink stripes and spotting, to pale pink centers with pink margins, 6 round wavy lobes, 3". BG 1187.

'Hatsu Shimada' ('Hokyo' × 'Taihe'): very light greenish white with yellowish green blotch, occasional deep pink dots, 6 wide rounded wavy overlapping lobes, 2½–3". BG 0884.

'Heiwa' [Peace] (sport of 'Wako'): white flushed light purplish pink with flakes of light purple to deep pink selfs, and light pink with white margins, upper 3 lobes nearly flat and notched, 5–6 lobes, 3–3¾". PI 227083, '55; 230611, '56. BG 1272.

'Heiwa no Hikari' [Light of peace]: white to pale pink centers, bordered pink, many variations, 2½–3". PI 127671, '38; 235979, '56. BG 1199.

'Heiwa no Kagami' [Mirror of peace]: pale yellowish pink to vivid orange tips, spaced pointed lobes, 2", pale yellowish pink stamens and pistil BG 1249.

'Higasa' [Parasol] ('Banko' × 'Shinnyo no Tsuki'): purplish pink, prominent reddish purple blotch, large wide overlapping wavy laid back lobes, 4–5". PI 227084, '55. BG 0917.

'Higata Kirin': no description available.

'Hikari' [Light] (sport of 'Soko'): white with flakes, sectors and dots of light pink, occasional selfs of strong pink, and white margined pink, large round overlapping lobes, 3–4".

'Hikari no Tsukasa' [Official light] (sport of 'Nikko'): white to light pink, variations with stripes, sectors and selfs of strong red, narrowly spaced and pointed lobes, star-shaped, 1½–2". BG 1023.

'Hikarugenji' [Proper name] ('Ishiyama' × 'Kinzai'): purplish pink with dark spots, separate narrow petals, 1½–2".

'Himearukuma': white to pale greenish white, unusually variable, occasional vivid pink sectors and selfs, green blotch, sometimes pink with darker pink stripes and flecks, occasionally all white flowered branch, trumpet-flowers, spaced pointed lobes uneven with notched tips, 2½–3". BG 1053.

'Hime' [Princess]: no description available.

'Hime Kikoshi' [Noble princess]: BG 1225.

'Hime Nakahara': small reddish orange trumpet-like flowers with tiny leaves ¾–1" long; low spreading ground hugger. BG 0849. Possibly a form of *R. nakaharai*.

'Hime Nishiki' [Princes brocade] ('Chitose Nishiki' × 'Gumpo'): white with sectors, flecks and dots of purplish red, occasional selfs, and lighter edges, irregular round wavy lobes, 2½–3". BG 1230.

'Hime no Hana' [Flower of Princess]: no description available.

'Himeshishin Nishiki': pale pink with green throat, occasionally white with greenish tips, round overlapping lobes, 1½", early. BG 1183.

'Hino Tsukasa' [Vermilion official]: dark reddish orange, lobes slightly pointed, 2–2½"; compact growth. Purportedly one of original Satsukis.

'Hiodoshi' [Scarlet-threaded suit of armor] ('Ishiyama' × 'Shuchuka'): vivid red many with pale pink to white centers, slightly bell-shaped, round pointed spaced lobes, 2–2½.

'Hio Ogi' [Scarlet threaded fan]: reddish orange with dark red blotch, round wavy slightly crinkled lobes, 3¾–4", early, prominent red stamens tipped black and red pistil; spreading habit. BG 1253.

'Hiraku': white with sectors and dots of reddish purple, occasional selfs of purplish red, wavy overlapping lobes, 3½".

'Hitachi': white with sectors of purplish pink, some all white, occasionally with pink border, 2"; low spreading habit. BG 1223.

'Hitomaru' [named after a poet of the seventh century]: light pink, occasionally with sectors of white and flakes of deep pink, rounded lobes, slightly tubular, 2–2½". Very old variety, popular for bonsai. BG 0898.

'Hogetsu' [Prosperous moon] ('Izayoi' × 'Seida'): white with light pink edge, occasionally moderate red with white to pale pink centers, margins crinkled, 1½–2". Two distinct plants with same name.

'Hogetsu': light pink with reddish throat, rinpu type with twisted lobes and leaves. See description of previous cultivar.

'Hoju no Hikari' [Light of precious jewel] ('Hosei' × 'Kokusei'): white with pale yellowish green blotch, occasional dots of dark pink, 6 overlapping lobes, 3–3½", early. BG 1186.

'Hoko' [Abundant light] (sport of 'Honen'): white with flecks and stripes of light purplish pink, usually 6 wide round wavy lobes, 3–4", one lobe often irregular and smaller. BG 0876.

'Hokoku' [syn. 'How Koku'): extremely variable, deep yellowish pink with blotch of reddish dots, occasionally with white border, lobes often overlapping 2".

'Homare' [Pride]: white with yellowish pink sectors, deep pink flecks to solid white flowers, overlapping ruffled lobes, 2½", early. BG 1155.

'Homare no Hana' [Praiseworthy flower] (sport of 'Banka'): white to strong pink with many reddish stripes, flakes and dots, often appears stippled, usually 6 lobes, 3¼–4". PI 228106, '56. BG 1129.

'Homare Matsunami' [Proud pine wave]: BG 1353.

'Homei' [Fragrant dawn]: white with large red spots on the tips, 2½–3".

'Homo no Haru': no description available.

'Honen' [Year of plenty] ('Izayo' × 'Gobi Nishiki'): white with stripes, flakes, sectors and selfs of strong red, margin sinuate and slightly irregular round lobes, 3–4".

'Horaizan' [Mount Horai]: white with occasional flakes of dark purplish pink, rounded lobes, tubular, 2½–3".

'Horaku' [Pleasure of a virtuous life]: light purplish pink, variable with white border to solid white to light purplish pink, 5–7 large ruffled round lobes, 3–4"; blooms heavily. PI 127672, '38.

'Hosai' [Rich color] (origin unknown): white, separate narrow petals, tubular. Two distinct plants with the same name.

'Hosai': reddish orange with inconspicuous red blotch, overlapping lobes, 4". See description of previous cultivar.

'Hosei' [Sweet voiced] ('Kumo no Ue' × 'Kyokko Nishiki'): white, variable with stripes, sectors and selfs of deep purplish pink, wide rounded notched lobes, 2½–3". BG 1348. Two distinct plants with same name.

'Hosei' [Star of the Phoenix] ('Nikko' × 'Hakurei'): light pink some petals white, star shaped petals, 1½–2"; low spreading. BG 1348. See description of previous cultivar. Possibly 'Hosi'.

'Hoshi': white with light green throat, purplish pink flakes to purplish pink tips and pale to white center, rounded spaced lobes.

'Hoshi no Sato': BG 1282.

'Hoshizukiyo': white suffused light yellowish pink, occasional sectors, rounded lobes. 2½–3". BG 1127.

'Hoshun': yellowish pink throat fading to deep yellowish pink tips, occasional orange selfs, spaced pointed lobes, 2"; very dense, low spreading. BG 1346.

'Hototogisu' [Cuckoo] (seedling of 'Kikoshi'): variable, white with deep pink flakes, some deep pink with white center, rounded spaced lobes, slightly tubular, 2–2½". BG 0501. Possibly two plants with same name.

'Hoto no Kagami': no description available.

'Hozan': white with red variegations, heavy substance, flowers up to 5". PI 127673, '38.

'Ikoi no Tomo' [Friend of relaxation]: extremely variable, white to purplish pink with or without white margins or flakes, usually 6 lobes, 2½–2¾".

'Ikoma': White with very pale blush of yellowish pink, occasional flecks and sectors of vivid yellowish pink, rounded lobes, 2–2½"; low spreading. BG 0411.

'Ishiyama' [Stone mountain]: Light purple center to darker purple edge, reddish purple blotch, occasional dark purple dots and fleck, white stamens and pistil, 2½–3". early; vigorous upright spreading habit. BG 1267.

'Isochidori' [Beach Plover]: no description available.

'Issho no Hana' [Flower of a lifetime]: light purplish pink, purple spots in blotch, anthers dark and showy, 2½–2¾".

'Issho no Haru' [Spring of one life] (syn. 'Haisai'; sport of 'Yamato no Hikari'): pale to light purplish pink with purple stripes and flakes to solid reddish purple, large round lobes, 3–4"; compact habit. PI 227085, '55. BG 0484/1216.

'Issho no Hikari' [Light of a life time]: light pink with greenish blotch, lobes overlapping, 3–3½".

'Iwa no Tsuki' [Moon crag]: white with faint yellow green blotch, some flecks and stripes of yellowish pink, 3". BG 0490.

'Iwai no Tsuki' [Moon of celebration] ('Banrai' × 'Bangaku'): white to light pink with off-white margin, to white with red margin, occasional stripes and sectors, usually 6 overlapping rounded lobes, 2½–3"; broad spreading. BG 1335.

'Izayoi' [Sixteenth night]: deep pink, blotch heavily dotted strong red, occasional moderate red flowers, round wavy lobes, 2½–3"; old cultivar. BG 0476/1266.

'Izumi' [Fountain or spring] ('Aikoku' × 'Kozan'): white with greenish blotch, many variations with stripes, dots, flecks and sectors of purplish red. Lobes rounded or slightly pointed, 2". BG 0935.

'Jindai' [Divine age]: white to light pink, many dots and flakes of strong purplish pink, large flakes darker, many variations, 4–4½". PI 127674, '38.

'Joga' [proper name] (syn. 'Johga'; sport of 'Izayoi'): white to light purple or light pink, occasional flakes of purplish pink, reddish dots in blotch, wide rounded lobes, 2¼–3". PI 127675, '38.

'Juko' [Congratulatory light] ('Kotobuki' × 'Gyoten') light purplish pink with white center, to dark pink with pale pink to white center, many variations, wide lobes, 2½–3". BG 1033.

'Junbi': white with greenish blotch, and deep pink stripes flecks and sectors, 3½–4". BG 1104.

'Kagamijishi' [Lion mirror]: white with flecks and stripes of strong pink, some selfs of deep pink, others heavily speckled, small rounded lobes, 1–1¼", late; low growing, narrow leaves. BG 1339.

'Kagayaki no Matsu' [Proud pine]: white with pale green blotch, flecks of deep pink, rounded lobes, trumpet-shaped, 2–2½". BG 1280.

'Kagetsu' [Flowery moon]: white with occasional purplish pink stripes, and white centered with deep purplish pink margin, round wavy lobes, 2½–3". PI 127676, '38. BG 0978.

'Kagetsu Muji' [Unmarked flower]: two distinct cultivars introduced under the same name. (#1) deep purplish pink, occasionally with white centers. (#2) white rarely with dots or flakes of deep purplish pink from margin inward, also selfs of deep purplish pink, 2½–3". PI 226147, '59.

'Kaho' [Floral treasure] (seedling of 'Asahizura'): white with occasional deep pink stripes, and some light to deep pink selfs, also light pink with white border, wavy round lobes, 3"; vigorous upright spreading habit. PI 131300, '39. BG 0850/1209.

'Kahoku no Tsuki' [Moon of Kahoku] ('Aikoku' × 'Reigetsu'): pale yellowish white with stripes and pink variations to solid colors, many variations, round lobes, 2½–3". BG 1030.

'Kaho no Hikari' [Light of floral treasure] (sport of 'Kaho'): white with occasional deep yellowish pink stripes with some light and deep pink selfs, small narrow spatulate spaced petals, 1½–2". BG 1063.

'Kaigetsu' [Full moon]: white with light reddish purple margin, large. PI 127677, '38; 228007, '55. Possibly same as 'Kagetsu'.

'Kairaku' [Joint pleasure]: strong purplish pink with lighter to near white centers, round wavy lobes, 2½–3". BG 1124.

'Kako' [Deer lake]: white, occasional light pink sports with margins of deeper pink, rounded lobes, 2–2½. PI 227086, '55.

'Kakyo no Hikari': very pale purplish pink, faintly white throat, rounded spaced lobes, 2"; pale pink stamens and pistil. BG 1167.

'Kami no Hikari' [Divine light]: white, flakes spots and blotches of deep purplish pink, 2½–3".

'Kami no Yama Kirin' [Kirin of the sacred mountain]: white, heavily spotted, flakes and selfs of deep purplish pink, rounded lobes. BG 1177.

'Kamiyo Goromo' [Robe from the age of the gods]: white, heavily striped strong purplish pink, occasional pink selfs, round lobes, 2½–3".

'Kanki' [Delight] (seedling of 'Meisei'): white with large and small flakes of deep purplish pink, occasional selfs, 5 to 6 overlapping lobes, 3–4", PI 227088, '55. BG 1118.

'Kanuma no Hikari' [Light of Kanuma] ('Gyoko' × 'Hoshi'): white, flaked, striped or dotted reddish orange, occasionally reddish orange tipped white, with greenish throat, lobes slightly pointed, 2–2½".

'Karaito' [Chinese thread]: dark pink, hose-in-hose with petaloid sepals, petals narrow thread-like, with spatulate ends, appears lacy, 2".

'Kashin' [Flower God]: white to light purplish pink, many variations, some tips vivid purplish red, 5–6 rounded spaced lobes, 2½–3"; small leaves; low spreading habit. BG 1218.

'Kasho' [Flower prize] ('Kaho' × 'Taihei'): white with pale green blotch, purplish pink flakes and sectors to solid selfs, 6 overlapping ruffled lobes, 2½–3"; vigorous broad spreading. BG 1142.

'Kasugano' [The Moor of Kasuga]: deep red, 2–2½".

'Katsurayama no Tsuki' [Moon of Mt. Katsura]: white with deep pink to strong red stripes, many variations and reddish selfs, round lobes, 2½–3".

'Kayo no Homare' [Honor of melody]: white center bordered yellowish pink, occasionally white with deep pink stripes and selfs, slightly pointed lobes, 1–1½". BG 0862.

'Kazan' [Deer mountain] (sport of 'Taihai'; syn. 'Rukizon'; in U.S. also 'Kakuba Chinzan'): lighter than strong red, blotch dotted, small lobes, 1½–2"; small dark glossy green leaves, ½" or less, broad ovate; compact habit. Propagators please note; there are several different 'Kazan' azaleas.

'Kazan' [Flower mountain] ('Bandai' seedling): white with sectors of light to dark pink, sometimes suffused to irregular white margins, or white centers with vivid pink margins, rounded lobes, bell-shaped, 2½–3". BG 1325. See description of previous cultivar.

'Kazan no Homare' [Glory of Kazan]: white with pale to light pink margins, occasional pink stripes and sectors, 5–6 rounded lobes, upright habit.

'Kazan no Tsuki': vivid reddish orange, 5–7 round spreading lobes, 2½–3"; low spreading growth. BG 0946.

'Kaze' [Breeze]: white with purplish pink dots and sectors, rounded lobes, 2". BG 1236.

'Keisetsu' [Student days]: strong red, center light pink to nearly white, (often does not show up on young plants), 3", early; leaves variegated with fine network of yellowish lines and small blotches. PI 127678, '38. Also found with deep pink margin.

'Keishuku' [Celebration]: white with green blotch, 6 round overlapping lobes with pointed tips, 2–2½", early. BG 1064.

'Kenbishi' [Diamond-shaped sword] ('Chiyo no Hikari' × 'Shinnyo no Tsuki'): pink often with white center to white selfs, narrow spaced lobes star-shaped, trumpet-like, 2". BG 1001.

'Kesho Kagami' [Make-up mirror]: light red with white border and touches of red, white throat, 3–3½".

'Kesui': no description available.

'Kietsu': no description available.

'Kifujin' [Lady]: white with occasional flecks and blush of light yellowish pink, some selfs, rounded lobes, 2". BG 1226.

'Kijo' [Tortoise castle]: white with fine stripes and small spotting of purple, to purple selfs, 5–6 ruffled lobes, 3–3½".

'Kikaku' [Tortoise crane] ('Macrantum' × 'Mme. Moreux Alba'): white with purple variegations, 5–8 wide rounded lobes, 1½–2". PI 131295, '39. BG 0973.

'Kiko' [Kikyo=*Platycodon grandiflorum*]: vivid red with white throat. Chinese Balloon (*P. grandiflorum*) flower-like in shape, small, late. BG 0895.

'Kikoshi' [Young noble] (sport of 'Kyushu'): deep to light pink with pale pink to white centers, and tipped light pink, pointed lobes, 1¼–2". PI 228108, '55. BG 0924.

'Kikusui' [Floating Chrysanthemun crest] ('Matsunami' × 'Hakatajiro'): white, many variations of purplish pink stripes to light and deep purplish pink selfs, round overlapping lobes, 2½".

'Kimimaru' [Proper Name] ('Kimi no Hana' × 'Hitomaru'): white with blush of pale yellowish pink to darker sectors, occasional white throat with dark yellowish pink margins to white selfs, round wavy dimpled lobes, 2½–3". BG 0992.

'Kimi no Hana [Recorded beauty] ('Tamaori Hime' × 'Yata no Kagami'): white with occasional deep pink sectors, many variations, and white to deep pink with white centers, round lobes, 2–2½". BG 0487/1212.

'Kimi no Hikari' [Light of noble beauty] ('Kozan' × 'Kikoshi'): white, variable with deep pink sectors to pink selfs, some pale pink with dark pink blotch. 1½–2". BG 1224.

'Kingetsu' [Brocade moon]: white with sectors, stripes, flakes and selfs of pink and occasional white centers, lobes overlapping, 2–2½". PI 131296, '39.

'Kinkazan' [Golden Luster Mountain]: white, flaked and striped reddish orange, green throat, pale pink blotch, 6–8 wide rounded lobes slightly rolled back, 2–2½". BG 0958.

'Kinmei' [Brocade of light]: light to strong purplish pink with occasional blush of white, spaced lobes, tubular, 1½–2". BG 1044.

'Kin Nishiki' [Golden brocade] (sport of 'Shokko Nishiki'): light pink with red stripes and small spotting to light pink rimmed white, many variations, throat greenish, wide round lobes, 2½–3". BG 0378.

'Kinno no Hikari': no description available.

'Kinpa' [Golden waves] (sport of 'Matsunami'): white with stripes, flecks , sectors and selfs of yellowish pink, 2"; very small leaves. BG 0916.

'Kinpai' [Golden cup] (sport of 'Yata no Kagami'): white center with reddish orange border, occasional selfs of light to strong reddish orange, round lobes, 2½–3"; foliage sunburns. BG 0909.

'Kinpo' [Golden treasure] (sport of 'Gumpo'): white with very pale yellow center, round wavy lobes, 2–2½". Two distinct plants with same name.

'Kin po': purplish red not as above; variegated leaves with yellow spots and blotches: See description of previous cultivar.

'Kinpo Nishiki' [Golden treasure brocade] ('Sakurayama' × 'Kono'): light to deep yellowish pink with darker stripes, occasional pink selfs, or pink with narrow white margin or white center with pink margin, 6 or more round overlapping lobes, 2½-3". BG 1239.

'Kinsai' [Distinguished gold] (syn. 'Kinzai'): deep reddish orange, separate and distinct long narrow petals, 1½–2½"; leaves small oblanceolate ¼ × 1¼" long, plant low spreading. Popular for bonsai. PI 227090, 228109, '55. BG 0360/1052.

'Kinsei' [Golden star] (seedling of 'Chiyo no Hikari'): white with pale pink stamens and pistil, round lobes, 2". BG 0991.

'Kintaro': BG 0963.

'Kinu no Hikari' [Light of Kinu]: white, very variable with flecks stripes and sectors of deep pink, occasionally suffused pale pink with narrow white edges and dark red blotch, irregularly rounded or pointed to spaced lobes, 1½–2½". BG 0950.

'Kinu no Tsuki' [Moon of silk] (natural seedling): purplish pink with white throat, occasional white suffused purplish pink, and sectors of purplish pink, 1½–2", midseason. BG 1197.

'Kippo no Hikari' [Light of lucky peak] ('Kozan' × 'Mine no Hikari'): white with occasional reddish orange sectors, some dark red selfs, slightly pointed spaced lobes, 2–2½". BG 1306.

'Kirinkan': light purple with reddish purple stripes flecks and sectors, red blotch, round lobes, 2¼–2½", early. BG 1316.

'Kisarazu' ('Kohan no Tsuki' × 'Matsunami'): white blushed very pale pink with narrow margin of deep yellowish pink, occasionally striped pink, 6 round spaced lobes, 3". BG 1334.

'Kisarazu no Sokojiro': white with vivid reddish orange border, round lobes, 2–2½"; compact habit.

'Kobai' [Red Plum] ('Sanko no Tsuki' × 'Yata no Kagami'): deep pink with distinct white blotches, 6 round overlapping lobes, 1½–2".

'Kogane Nishiki' [Gold coin brocade]: white with slight green blotch, round overlapping lobes, 2–2½", early. BG 1295.

'Kogen no Hikari': white with occasional flecks of reddish orange, many margined reddish orange, broad wavy lobes. BG 0921.

'Kogetsu' [Monthly tribute] ('Matsunami' × 'Tamaori Hime'): white with flakes and sectors to borders of strong red, occasionally light pink with dark dots and narrow white border, wide overlapping lobes, 2–2½", many beautiful variations; low spreading with fine twigs. BG 1018/1191.

'Kohan no Tsuki' [Moon of the lake] ('Gyoko' × 'Seidai') white to very pale pink center with wide reddish orange border; 5 to 6 wide round lobes, 2½–3". BG 0847/1301.

'Koho' [Phoenix of light] ('Gobi Nishiki' × 'Takasa'; syn. 'Kow How'): white to very pale purplish pink with flecks, small sectors and selfs of deep purplish pink, 3". PI 131298, '39.

'Kojo no Hikari' [Light over the ruined castle]: white with green blotch and deep pink stripes and dots, 2". BG 1344.

'Kojo no Homare': BG 0902.

'Kojo no Tsuki' [Moon over the ruined castle]: white with slight green blotch and reddish purple stripes, flecks, sectors and dots, 5–7 rounded lobes, 3–3½", early. BG 1096.

'Koka' [Light of flowers] ('Kyokko Nishiki' × 'Mme. Moreux'): white, occasional flakes, sectors and selfs of deep pink, light yellow green dots in throat, wide spaced lobes, 3–4". BG 0885.

'Koki': pale light purple with slight stripe in center of long pointed lobes, 1¾", early. BG 1022.

'Kokin': strong red, rounded lobes, 1½. BG 0971.

'Kokin Nishiki' [Fine gold brocade]: white with flakes, sectors and selfs of moderate red, yellow green dots in throat; 5 to 6 overlapping lobes, 2½–3". BG 0518.

'Kokinsai' [Small 'Kinsai'] (sport of 'Kinsai'): deep reddish orange, small, single, narrowly spaced petals, spider type; leaves smaller than 'Kinsai'; slower grower.

'Kokko no Bi' [Beauty of national light] ('Karafune' × 'Gyoko'): very dark red, 2–2½" BG 1207.

'Kokoku' [Empire]: (syn. 'Kow Koku';'Gumpo' × 'Fuji Nishiki'): white with vivid red variegations, ruffled, 2–2½. PI 131299, '39.

'Kokyo Ko': pale yellowish pink, 2".

'Komachi Warai' [Laughter of pretty maiden] ('Izayoi' × 'Gobi Nishiki'): white many variations, some sectors of suffused light purplish pink to pink with white edge, round overlapping lobes, white stamens and pistil, 2–2½. BG 1133.

'Komadori' [Robin]: white with occasional short narrow flecked stripes of light reddish purple, round wavy lobes, 3–3½". BG 0922.

'Komeno no Hikari' [Light of Komeno]: no description available.

'Komeno no Yuki' [Snow of Komeno]: no description available.

'Komei' [Brilliant light] ('Kozan' × 'Tamaori Hime'): white with many variations, of flakes and sectors to selfs of deep pink, some light pink with darker blotch, round spaced lobes, 2–2½". BG 0987.

'Kongo' [Diamond]: white with purple variations or white margined purple, 2". PI 131297, '39.

'Kongo no Hikari' [Light of the diamond]: white, variable with flakes and sectors to selfs of deep pink with white centers, spaced pointed lobes, 2–2½". BG 0886.

'Koraku' [Great pleasure]: white with large border of deep purplish pink, overlapping wavy lobes, 2½–3". BG 0846/0937.

'Korin' [proper name] ('Kozan' × 'Osakazuki'): deep pink, star-shaped pointed lobes, 1½–2"; compact habit.

'Koryu' [Radiant willow] ('Kozan' × 'Meikyo'): strong yellowish pink with occasional darker stripes to light pink with white rim, narrowly spaced lobes, 1½–2". BG 1078.

'Koshi no Nami' [Waves of Koshi] ('Suio' × 'Shinnyo no Tsuki'): white with speckles and stripes of vivid purplish red, sometimes slight purplish pink blotch, round wavy 5–7 overlapping lobes, 4–4½"; leaves small. BG 0878.

'Koshi no Tsuki' [Moon of noble child] ('Kikoshi' seedling): pale to moderate pink center with vivid yellowish pink tipped margins, some with white centers to moderate yellowish pink margins, long spaced pointed lobes, 2–2½"; fairly low spreading habit. BG 0953.

'Koshuku no Aki': deep pink with occasional white centers, semidouble, round lobes, 2–2½"; compact habit.

'Kosui' [Water of the lake]: white with light yellow green dots in blotch, occasional strong pink flakes, spaced lobes, 2½". BG 1000.

'Koten' [Classics]: white with green blotch, round spaced, 2½", early. BG 1174.

'Kotobuki' [Congratulations]: white, variable flakes and selfs in strong to deep purplish pink with white centers and purplish pink with faint white edge, occasional irregular lobes, 2½"; compact habit PI 227092, 228110, '55. BG 1141.

'Kotobuki Hime' [Princess Kotobuki] ('Shinsen' × 'Kotobuki'): white, variable with occasional red stripes and selfs of deep pink to strong red, and some with white margins, round lobes, 2–2½": low spreading habit. BG 1311.

'Kotobuki no Izumi' [Fountain of celebration]: white with slight light brown blotch, round overlapping lobes, 2½", early. BG 1300.

'Kotobuki no Sono' [Garden of celebration] (sport of 'Kotobuki'): white with flakes and self of strong purplish pink, occasionally bordered, wide lobes, 2½–3". BG 1120.

'Koyo': pale pink with strong purple stripes and sectors or no stripes, wide wavy overlapping lobes, large and thick texture. BG 0872.

'Kozan' [Brilliant mountain]: very pale pink to off-white, small spaced lobes, 1–1½"; slow, bushy habit. PI 227091, '55.

'Kozan no Hikari' [Light of Kozan] (sport of 'Kozan'): light pink, long narrow strap-like lobes, star-shaped, 2".

'Kozan no Homare' [Honor of brilliant mountain] (seedling of 'Kozan'): pale pink occasional stripe and wide sector of deep pink, many variations, spaced lobes, 1½–2"; small leaves; low spreading habit. BG 1219.

'Kozan no Tsuki [Moon of brilliant mountain] ('Kozan' × 'Matsunami'): light pink with darker pink stripes to pink selfs small round lobes, 1½–2"; slow grower. BG 0946.

'Kumano': red, 2½". BG 0979.

'Kunpu' [Fragrant breeze]; pale to light purplish pink, wavy lobes, 2–2½"; upright habit. BG 1093.

'Kusudama' [Camphor-tree gem] (sport of 'Shinnyo no Tsuki'): pale pink, many variations of speckles, flakes and selfs of deep pink to moderate red, some with white centers, wide rounded lobes, 2½–3"; vigorous. PI 227094, 228111, '55. BG 1351.

'Maigesho' [Dance make-up] ('Aikoku' × 'Seiko no Tsuki'): white with occasional flecks and dots of vivid reddish orange or white with wide margins or wide tips of reddish orange with red blotch, wide round overlapping irregular lobes, 3–3½". BG 1072.

'Mai Hime' [Dancing princess]: many variations, white with sectors and selfs of light or strong purplish pink, some with white margins, other with white blotch, 5–8 round ruffled lobes, 2½–3". PI 131301, '39.

'Mai Ogi' [Dancing fan] (sport of 'Shogetsu'): white with flakes, speckles and sectors of deep pink to strong red, many variations and selfs to pink with white rim, rounded lobes, 2½–3". BG 1051.

'Mansaku' [Abundant harvest] (sport of 'Honen'): strong pink with occasional white and deep pink stripes, wavy round lobes, 2½–3"; upright habit. BG 1185.

'Matsu Kagami' [Pine mirror] ('Matsunami' × 'Yata no Kagami'): white with speckles, stripes and sectors of strong red, some selfs and some with light centers, rounded lobes, 2–2½"; upright habit.

'Matsunami' [Pine wave]: white with stripes and sectors of vivid reddish orange, some selfs of reddish orange, occasional light yellowish pink self with faint light edge, narrow lobes slightly spaced and rounded, 2–2½"; very old hybrid. PI 227095, 228112, '55. BG 0505.

'Matsu no Hikari' [Light of the pine] ('Seidai' × 'Shinnyo no Tsuki'): white, many variations with stripes, sectors and selfs of deep pink, some light pink with dark blotch and lighter margins, round wavy overlapping lobes 2½–3". Two distinct plants with same name.

'Matsu no Hikari' ('Banka' × 'Shinnyo no Tsuki'): white with deep yellowish pink variations, ruffled overlapping lobes, 3". See description of previous cultivar.

'Matsu no Homare' [Proud pine] ('Matsunami' × 'Kozan'): white with stripes, sectors and selfs of light yellowish pink many variations, narrow spaced lobes, 1½–2", early; upright bushy habit. BG 1070.

'Matsu no Mei': reddish orange, 3 upper lobes overlapping , round lobes, 2½".

'Matsu no Tsukasa' [Chief of pines] (sport of 'Matsukagami'): white with flecks, stripes, sectors and some selfs of light to strong yellowish pink, 2–2½", two bottom lobes hang low. BG 1208.

'Matsushima' [Pine island]: white with pale green blotch, occasional flecks of vivid pink, round overlapping lobes, 3½–4". BG 1037. Very old cultivar.

'Meicho' [Sunny morning] (seedling of 'Soko'): white, many variations with stripes, sectors and selfs of light to strong pink, wide round overlapping lobes, 3–4", early.

'Meigetsu' [Full moon] ('Kozan' × 'Tamaori Hime'): white, with many variations of speckles, stripes and selfs of strong to deep pink, some with lighter centers, wide lobes, 2–2½"; upright habit.

'Meiho': white with pale purplish pink blotch, round wavy lobes, 2½–3". BG 0887/0908.

'Meiko' [Fine light]: pale to light pink, occasional white margins, red dots in blotch, large, 4–5". BG 0959/1192. Two distinct plants with same name.

'Meiko': white with pale green dots in blotch, also light to deep pink sectors and selfs with red dots in blotch. See description of previous cultivar.

'Meikyo' [Clear mirror] (seedling of 'Yata no Kagami'): white, variable with stripes, sectors and selfs of strong red, also off whites bordered pink, round divided lobes, 2½"; vigorous spreading BG. 0492/1171.

'Meisei' [Good reputation] ('Izayoi' × 'Gobi Nishiki'): white, heavily striped flaked and dots to selfs varying from deep pink to vivid red, wavy overlapping lobes, somewhat funnel-shaped, 2½–3"; low compact spreading. BG 1126.

'Meisho': white with dark pink stripes, flecks and blotch, occasional pink with white border and red blotch, 6 overlapping lobes, 3–4", early; upright habit. BG 1080.

'Meizan' [Beautiful mountain]: white with strong yellowish pink dots and stripes, very variable, round lobes, 3"; leaves spotted and flaked with yellow; low compact habit. BG 1012.

'Meoto Nishiki': white with flecks, sectors and some selfs of vivid purplish pink, occasionally pale pink with stripes and sectors, petaloid, hose-in-hose, trumpet-like blossoms in cluster, 2", early. BG 1162.

'Minato' [Harbor]: white center with strong purplish pink border, some without light center, single to semidouble, wavy lobes, 2–2½"; upright habit; good for bonsai. BG 1156.

'Mine no Hana' [Flowers of the peak] (sport of 'Naniwa Nishiki'): pale pink with stripes and sectors of deep pink, occasionally lighter edges, long lobes, some with irregular scalloped edges, 2". BG 0858.

'Mine no Hikari' [Light of the peak] ('Kozan' x 'Matsunami'): white with stripes, sectors and selfs of strong red, some light to deep pink with darker blotch, spaced pointed lobes, 2½–3"; vigorous low spreading. BG 1166.

'Mine no Hoshi' [Star of the peak]: pale to light pink to vivid yellowish pink with reddish purple blotch, occasional narrow white margins, prominent dark pink blotch, long pointed spaced lobes, 3–3½". BG 0948.

'Miyako' [old name for Kyoto]: white with occasional stripes and flecks of purplish pink, some white with purplish pink margins, rounded lobes. BG 0893.

'Miyako no Hikari' [Light of Kyoto]: white blushed very pale yellowish pink with pale yellowish blotch, and flecks, dots and sectors of vivid reddish orange, 2½–3", white stamens and yellowish pink pistil. BG 1241.

'Miyako no Homare' [Glory of a capital]: no description available.

'Miyako no Tsuki' [Moon of Kyoto]: white, heavily striped deep pink, occasional pink sectors, sometimes dark pink blotch or pale green center at base, rounded lobes, 2½–3", early. BG 0867.

'Miyo Chiyo': white with yellowish green tint at base of upper lobe, many dots and flakes of strong red and some stippling, 3¼–4".

'Miyo no Tsuki' [Moon of era] ('Kozan' x 'Soho'): white with stripes and marked with pink to deep yellowish pink, wide round lobes, 2–2½".

'Miyo Tiyo': white with faint green blotch, many small dots and flakes of light red, 3¼–4".

'Miyuno no Kagami' [Mirror of Miyuno]: no description available.

'Miyuno no Tsuki': white with dots of light yellow green in throat and stripes and sectors of strong red, 10 stamens short and red; probably not a Satsuki Hybrid. PI 226144 '55.

'Mizuho no Kagami' [Mirror of ancient Japan] (seedling of 'Shinkyo'): white with deep pink dots and stripes, occasional pink selfs, some with pale pink centers and deep pink margins, 5–6 wide overlapping notched lobes, 2½–3"; spreading cascade habit. BG 0861.

'Momo no Haru' [Spring of peach]: vivid purplish red, lobes slightly separate and pointed 1–1½". BG 0860.

'Mori no Miyako' [Kyoto with woods]: deep purplish pink with reddish purple blotch, wide round slightly overlapping lobes, 3", very thin stamens and prominent white pistils. BG 1147.

'Murasaki Fuji' [Purple Fuji] (sport of 'Shira Fuji'): white with strong purplish pink border, irregular lobes, some curled, 1½–2"; leaves variegated with fine yellowish margins.

'Murasaki no Hoshi' [Purple star]: deep purplish pink with faint white center, no blotch, trumpet-like blossom, 2"; low spreading. BG 0975.

'Musashi no Homare' [Ancient pride]: white with light reddish purple stripes to darker selfs, wide round overlapping lobes. BG 0911.

'Musashino': white with few small flakes of strong purplish red, throat flushed with pale yellow green, round wavy overlapping lobes, 3", late; very old variety. PI 131302 '39.

'Myocho': white with few flakes and sectors of deep pink, often 6 lobes, 3–3½".

'Myogi' [proper name]: white with few tiny flakes of purplish pink, ruffled irregular lobes, 2½–3"; very compact habit. PI 131303 '39.

'Myojo' [Morning star] (seedling of 'Chiyo no Hikari'): white with purplish pink dots in blotch, occasional sectors and selfs of purplish pink. BG 1178.

'Nachi no Tsuki' [Moon of Nachi] ('Shiko no Tsuki' × 'Chiyo no Tsuki'): white, speckled and striped strong purplish red, many variations to purplish red selfs, narrowly spaced lobes, bell-shaped, 1½–2"; compact habit.

'Nakano Nishiki' [Nakano brocade]: BG 1329.

'Nakatsu no Hikari': white with reddish purple stripes, flecks and sectors, round spaced lobes, 2½" early. BG 1151.

'Nami' [Wave]: white with yellowish pink flecks, stripes and many dots, 2½". BG 1205.

'Nanba Nishiki' [Nanba brocade]: white heavily striped with vivid red, many variations, and red selfs, narrowly spaced ragged lobes, slightly spatulate, 1½–2"; slow spreading.

'Narihira' [Proper Name] ('Chinzan' × 'Mai Sugata'): yellowish pink to light yellowish pink center, semidouble, petaloid, round lobes, 2½–3"; low open spreading habit, BG 0477. Two distinct plants with same name.

'Narihira': white center, vivid purplish pink wide margins, semidouble, petaloid, round spaced lobes, 2½"; small leaves; dense habit. BG 1354. See description of previous cultivar.

'Narumi Shibori': BG 1050.

'Nichirin': white with large green blotch, occasional yellowish pink flecks and sectors, round lobes, 3½", early; wide round leaf, low spreading. BG 0927.

'Nihon no Hana' [Flower of Japan]: white with occasional stripes and selfs of deep pink to strong red, large wide wavy lobes, 4–5"; vigorous.

'Nihon no Hikari' [Light of Japan]: white with few flakes of light pink and yellow green blotch, overlapping lobes, 2½".

'Niigata Kirin' [Niigata giraffe]: white with pale green throat, blush and sectors of purplish pink, 2", midseason; low spreading. BG 1048.

'Niji' [Rainbow]: light pink with flecks, stripes and sectors of reddish orange, long oval lobes, 1½". BG 0974.

'Nikko' [Sunlight] (sport of 'Kozan'): strong pink with occasional white stripes to light pink, occasional selfs of deep pink, spaced lobes, 1½–2", prominent pistil; compact habit. BG 0511.

'Niroku no Iwai' [Celebration of Niroku]: purplish pink, 1½–3"; leaves variegated with white margins. BG 0981.

'Nisei' [Second generation]: no description available.

'Nishiki' [Brocade]: white with some purplish pink small flecks, 6 wide round wavy overlapping lobes, 3½–4", heavy texture, early. BG 1269.

'Nishiki Boshi' [Brocade hat]: BG 0951.

'Nishiki no Yama' [Brocade mountain]: suffused pale yellowish pink to white margin, reddish purple blotch and sectors of vivid yellowish pink, 2½–3", white stamens and colored pistil. BG 1252.

'Nyohozan' [Mount Nyoho] (sport of 'Kozan'): pale pink with strong red blotch, spaced lobes, 1½–2; extremelly slow grower.

'Oboro Tsuki' [Misty moon]: BG 0961.

'Ogon no Mai' [Golden dance]: pale pink, small 1½".

'Ogon no Tsuki' [Golden moon] (seedling of 'Tamaori Hime'): white, heavily speckled and striped deep pink to strong red, many variations, to red selfs, and some with white centers and colored borders, round spaced lobes, 1½–2". BG 1017.

'Okina Nishiki' [Brocade of the old man]: deep reddish orange, hose-in-hose, 2½–3": compact habit.

'Omoi no Maku': white blushed with purplish pink, rounded spaced lobes, 2½", pale pink stamens and pistil. BG 1181.

'Onsho' [Reward] ('Katoi' × 'Kyokku Nishiki'): white with purplish pink blush toward edge, occasional purplish pink flecks and sectors, rounded overlapping lobes, 2", early. BG 1034.

'Osakazuki' [Large sake cup]: deep pink with darker blotch, round slightly overlapping lobes, 2–2½"; bushy growth; old cultivar.

'Otome' [Maiden] ('Izayoi' × 'Kyokko Nishiki'): off white with many light pink and yellowish pink variations to pink selfs, slightly pointed lobes, 2½–3". PI 131304, '39.

'Otome no Mai' [Dance of the maiden] (seedling of 'Aikoku'): whitish to pale pink center, and irregular purplish pink margin, rounded lobes, 2½–3". BG 0848.

'Otome Zakura' [Maiden's cherry blossom]: pale pink center, deep pink margins, round lobes, 2", pink stamens and red pistil. BG 1317.

'Raiko' [Coming light]: (seedling of 'Hitomaru'): white to very pale pink with occasional stripes to edge and selfs of strong to deep pink, wide wavy spaced lobes, 2½–3". BG 0986.

'Rakuzan' [Pleasure mountain]: white with occasional stripes, sectors, selfs and feathered margin of deep pink, 4–4½". BG 1131.

'Reigetsu' [Beautiful moon] ('Shozui' × 'Yata no Kagami'): white, heavily variegated with numerous red flakes, to red with pale center, round lobes, 2½–3".

'Reiho' [Place name] (sport of 'Hakurei'): very pale pink, heavy spotting of dark pink in upper lobe, narrow spaced pointed lobes, 1½–2". BG 1340. Two distinct plants with same name.

'Reiho' (seedling of 'Takasago'): white with sectors and selfs of deep purplish red, round lobes, 2½". PI 131305, '39. See description of previous cultivar.

'Reijin' [Beauty] ('Banka' × 'Kusudama'): white to very pale pink with stripes, sectors and selfs of deep pink, overlapping slightly wavy lobes, 3–4"; compact.

'Reiko' [Beautiful light] ('Hotogisu' × 'Ungetsu'): white to pale pink with stripes sectors and margins of moderate purplish red, some white centers with deep pink borders, wide pointed lobes, 2–2½. BG 0988.

'Ringetsu': no description available.

'Rinpu' [Long lasting wind]: moderate purplish pink with darker blotch, flowers tubular, 1½–2"; narrow leaves rolled axially, twisted and contorted; slow grower. PI 131306, '39. BG 0390.

'Roche no Mai': no description available.

'Rogetsu' [Wax moon]: white to light purplish pink center, margins deep purplish pink, some selfs, 2½–3"; more tender than most. PI 131307, '39.

'Sachi' [Colorful crown] (Sport of 'Setchu no Matsu'): moderate purplish pink; wide lobes slightly tubular, 1½–2"; leaves very narrow and twisted (rinpu).

'Sachi no Hana' [Flower of good fortune]: light pink with occasional stripes to selfs of deep pink, small narrow pointed separate petals, star-like, 1–1½"; small leaves; slow grower. BG 1271.

'Sakuragata' [Cherry blossom shape]: white center with deep pink to deep purplish pink borders, extremely variable; wide wavy lobes, 2–2½"; upright spreading habit. BG 1347.

"Sakura Kagami' [Cherry blossom mirror] (sport of 'Meikyo'): strong pink, lighter toward center, many variations of speckles, stripes and pink selfs, even occasional white flowers, 2–2½". BG 1168.

'Sakura Yama' [Cherry blossom mountain] (seedling of 'Sejun'): pale to moderate reddish orange with vivid red variations to red selfs, 2½–3". PI 131308, '39. BG 0870.

'Sankatsu' [Three victories]: white with occasional stripes flakes and sectors of vivid purplish pink, and white with green blotch, round wavy lobes, 2½". BG 1250.

'Sanko' [Three lights]: yellowish pink to white edges, deeper sectors and reddish purple blotch, wide wavy overlapping lobes, 3½–4, stamens and pistil lightly colored, early. BG 1265.

'Sanko Nishiki' [Three lights brocade]: BG 1222.

'Sanko no Kagayaki' [Splendor of three lights]: white with pale yellow-green blotch, wide round overlapping lobes, 2". BG 1297.

'Sanko no Tsuki' [Moon of three lights] ('Shyozui' × 'Fukumusume'): white with speckles, stripes to selfs of strong to deep purplish pink some with white blotches in center; wide round lobes, 2½–3".

'Sanyo' (Seedling of 'Kyokko Nishiki'): white, many variations of spots, flakes, sectors and selfs of deep purplish pink, 5–6 rounded spaced lobes, 2½. BG 0933.

'Sato no Hikari' [Light of the village]: white with yellow green blotch, occasional yellowish pink flecks, stripes, sectors and selfs, long pointed lobes lower two lobes separate, 2–2½". BG 1277.

'Sayotsuki': white blushed light purple, sometimes pale center with vivid purplish pink margins, 2". BG 1330.

'Seidai' [Glorious reign]: white centers with deep pink to strong red border, occasional red selfs; wavy rounded lobes, 2½–3"; low spreading habit. PI 227097, '55. BG 0401.

'Seigetsu' [Holy month] ('Kozan' × 'Onshi'): many variations of very pale to pale reddish purple with darker margins, occasional speckles and stripes darker; overlapping lobes, 2½–3"; upright habit. PI 131309, '39. BH 1060/1309.

'Seiho' [Blue peak] ('Kozan' × 'Matsunami'): white, many variations of heavy purplish pink margins to purplish pink selfs or white with sectors of dark pink, petaloid, 2", early; upright habit; good for bonsai. BG 1106.

'Seika' [Saintly flower] ('Tamino no Yuki' × 'Asahi Nishiki'): white to buff center with strong red tips and margin, other variations to off white or pale pink, wide round lobes, 2–2½"; compact habit. BG 1002/1312. Two distinct plants with the same name.

'Seika' [Refreshing flower] ('Kusudama' × 'Banka'): white to pale pink with red blotches, occasional stripes, ruffled lobes, 2½". See description of previous cultivar.

'Seiko no Hikari' [Green moon light] ('Banrai' × 'Kaho'): white with deep pink stripes, many variations of sectors and selfs from light to deep pink, round wavy lobes, 1½–2". BG 1203.

'Seiko no Tsuki' [Moon of green light]: white center with deep purplish pink margin, many variations of white with stripes, wide 5–6 round lobes, 2½–3". PI 227098, 228114, '55.

'Seiqua': white to tinted center with narrow pink margin, 2".

'Seirin' [Blue storm] ('Shyozui' × 'Kaho'): strong purplish pink with darker blotch, pointed spaced lobes, bell-shaped, 2", early. BG 1196.

'Seisho no Tsuki': white with light yellow green blotch and tips of deep pink, overlapping lobes, 2".

'Seito no Hana' [Flower of sacred city] ('Nihon no Hikari' × 'Taihei'): white with green throat; occasionally blushed pink with reddish stripes and sectors of purplish pink, reddish blotch, wide round wavy overlapping lobes, 4–4½". BG 0932.

'Seiun' [Divine destiny] (seedling of 'Gohi Nishiki'): white with many variations of deep reddish orange flakes and sectors, greenish throat, 5–6 round lobes, 2½–3". PI 131311, '39. BG 1238.

'Seizan': white with deep pink stripes and sectors, wavy overlapping lobes, 3", early. BG 1173.

'Sekai no Hikari' [Moon of the world] (sport of 'Tatsumi no Hikari'): extremely variable, white with speckles, stripes and sectors to selfs of strong purplish pink; often 6 wide rounded overlapping lobes, 4–5". BG 1029.

'Sharaku' [Proper name] ('Gyoko' × 'Shogetsu'): white with green throat and vivid yellowish pink flecks, dots and sectors, some white star-centers with wide margins of vivid yellowish pink, wavy overlapping lobes, 2½", early. BG 1043.

'Shibori Asagao' [Striped Morning Glory]: white with pink blush and purplish pink blotch rounded lobes, 2", early; vigorous upright. BG 1003.

'Shichifufuju' [Seven happiness] ('Izayoi' × 'Kinkazan') white, heavily striped deep pink, many variations to selfs of deep pink, round lobes, 2–2½"; upright habit.

'Shein no Tsuki': white with reddish purple blotch, heavily flecked yellowish pink, sometimes suffused pink to feathered white margins, large prominent reddish purple blotch, long spaced rounded lobes, 3–3½". BG 1020.

'Shifuki' [New wealth]: pale pink center to vivid pink wide margins, round lobes, 3–3½". BG 0879.

'Shiho' [Purple treasure] (seedling of 'Taihei'): white with purplish pink speckles and stripes, occasional selfs of pale to light purplish pink with white edge; wide round ruffled lobes, 3–4"; spreading habit. PI 131310, '39. BG 0385/1089.

'Shiki no Haru': no description available.

'Shiko' [Purple light] (sport of 'Shiho'): light purplish pink with occasional darker stripes; 5–6 wide round lobes, 3–4"; spreading habit. BG 1065.

'Shiko no Kagami' [Mirror of purple light] (seedling of 'Kami no Yama'): very light purplish pink center, tipped darker on ends of round pointed lobes, many tones of light purple with occasional strong purple, 2–2½"; compact habit.

'Shiko no Tsuki' [Moon of purple light]: purplish pink with white throat, reddish purple blotch, round petals, 2–2½", early; low spreading. BG 0965/0969.

'Shikokan': vivid purplish pink with white deep in center, slightly darker purplish pink blotch, trumpet-like flowers, 2–2½", early, purplish stamens and pistil. BG 0997

'Shikun Ow': vivid purplish red, double at center, large 4". PI 131317, '39.

'Shinju no Hikari': white with blush of pale purplish pink, light green blotch, rounded spaced lobes, trumpet-like, 2½". BG 1338.

'Shinkigen' [New era] ('Bangaku' × 'Sumida'): white, many variations, sectors and selfs of red to white with light yellow green blotch, often 6 round overlapping lobes, 3–4". PI 227099, '55. BG 1140.

'Shinkotobuki' [New happiness] (sport of 'Kotobuki'): white to light pink, occasional stripes of deep pink, blotch darker, 5–6 round lobes, 2–2½"; low bushy habit.

'Shinkyo' [Divine mirror] (sport of 'Yata no Kagami'): light to strong pink, to white or light pink with pale center, round slightly spaced lobes, 2–2½"; upright bushy. BG 1024.

'Shinmatsu Kagami' [New pine mirror] (sport of 'Matsu Kagami'): white, many variations with flecks stripes, dots, and blushes from very light yellowish pink to vivid and dark, sometimes selfs with yellow star in center, round spaced lobes, slightly irregular, 2–2½". BG 1201.

'Shinnen' [New year]: white with vivid pink fleck and sectors, pale green blotch, 6, wide round overlapping lobes, 3½–4", early. BG 1240.

'Shinnyo no Hikari' [Eternal light] (sport of 'Shinnyo no Tsuki'): white with flakes, stripes, margins and sectors of vivid purplish pink, with occasional pink selfs, wide round overlapping lobes, 2½–3"; variegated foliage with yellow dot and blotches on the leaves. PI 227101, 228115, '55.

'Shinnyo no Tsuki' [Eternal moon] ('Sakuragata' × 'Zetsurin'): white centers with margin of vivid purplish red with occasional reddish selfs, wide overlapping lobes, 3–3½". PI 131312, '39; 227102, 226148, 228116, '59. Popular cultivar.

'Shinsei' [Divinity] (sport of 'Chitose Nishiki'): pale to deep pink, some with white stripes and sectors, variable and late, wide round slightly overlapping lobes, 2½–3". PI 131315, '39. BG 1125. Two distinct plants with same name.

'Shinsei': white with purple splash and variegations, large fringed lobes, PI 131313, '39. May just be a variation of above.

'Shinsen' [Divine selection] (sport of 'Gyoko'): white with deep pink and red speckles and stripes, many variations, to red selfs, slightly bell-shaped folded lobes, 2½–3". BG 1028.

'Shintaiyo' [New sun] ('Banka' × 'Shinnyo no Tsuki'): white with stripes and sectors of vivid yellowish pink, prominent yellowish pink blotch, occasionally suffused with light yellowish pink to white margins, wide wavy overlapping lobes, 3½–4" early. BG 0381.

'Shinyomo no Haru': pale pink, occasional deeper pink blotch, large ruffled petals. BG 1010.

'Shinyo no Ko': white center reddish orange border, 5–6 round wavy overlapping lobes, 2½–3"; leaves variegated with mottled yellow spots. BG 0840.

'Shira Fuji' [White Mt. Fiji] (sport of 'Aikoku'): variable, white with stripes of purplish pink and blush of light purplish pink, occasional white center with margin of strong purplish red to purplish red selfs, slightly irregular curled lobes, 1½–2"; noted for variegated foliage with fine yellowish white margin. BG 1349.

'Shiraito no Taki' [Waterfall of white thread] (sport of 'Reiho'): white with occasional purplish stripes, flower irregular, petals ragged and split to base or absent with only white stamens and pistil present, 1½–2".

'Shiraito no Tsuki' [Moon of Shiraito]: white ragged spaced petals, often just stamens and pistil; very low spreading. BG 0410.

'Shirasumi': white wavy round lobes, 2½–3″, prominent white stamens and pistil. Good for bonsai. BG 1235.

'Shiryu no Mai' [Dance of the purple dragon]: purplish red, single to semidouble, 2½–3″.

'Shishin Nishiki': vivid purplish pink, slightly darker blotch, 2″, reddish purple stamens and pistil; low spreading. BG 1161.

'Shisui' [Purple water] ('Karaito' × 'Ishiyama'): deep purplish pink, petals ragged spatulate and divided, petals often lacking with only stamens and pistil present, 1½–2″.

'Shogetsu' [Shining moon]: white with moderate red flakes, blotch light green, occasional broad red margin, overlapping sinuate lobes, 3″. BG 1254.

'Shoji Kuruma': BG 1259.

'Shoka': pale pink with yellowish pink margin, unequal lobes, upper 3 apart from lower 2, starry, 2″.

'Shokko Nishiki' [Shokko brocade]: white with many variations of stripes, flecks and sectors of vivid yellowish pink, some self and some dark center to light pink suffused to white margins, rounded lobes, 2–2½″. BG 1069. One of oldest varieties, said to be 4–500 years old.

'Shoqua': pale pink with deep pink margin, lobes not equal, upper 3 stand apart from lower 2, starry and tubular, 2″.

'Shoshi no Hana': strong pink with upper lobes touched with deep pink, lobes pointed and tubular, 2″. PI 227100, '55, '59.

'Showa no Homare ' [Pride of Showa Era]: white with greenish yellow blotch stripes and sectors of pale yellowish pink, round overlapping wavy lobes, 3½–4″. BG 1270.

'Showa no Kagayaki' [Glory of Showa Era]: white with red stripes and sectors, occasional red selfs, rounded lobes, 2″. BG 1278.

'Shozui' [Good omen] ('Kyokka Nishiki' × 'Izayo'): yellowish pink with dots, flecks and sectors of dark yellowish pink, slight red blotch, wide pointed lobes, 2–2½″. BG 1039.

'Shuchuka': variable, light purple to white center with deep pink margin, red dots in blotch, 3″.

'Shugetsu' [Autumn moon] (sport of 'Aikoku'): white or blush center with vivid purplish red border, occasional purplish red selfs, or white with sectors of light to dark purple, rounded lobes, 2½–3″. BG 0852.

'Shuho no Hikari' [Light of excellent peak] (sport of 'Kozan no Hikari'): strong pink often with white edge or tips of lobes, blotch red, narrow spaced pointed lobes, star-shaped, 1½–2″.

'Shuko no Tsuki' [Moon of vermilion light] (seedling of 'Kosan no Kikari'): white to blush-pink center with border of strong reddish orange, round spaced lobes, 2–2½″; compact habit. BG 1055.

'Shukubai': yellowish pink, occasional white selfs or white with sectors of vivid yellowish pink, round spaced lobes, 2–2½″, early, white stamens and colored pistil; upright habit. BG 1175. Good for bonsai.

'Shukufuku' [Celebration]: white to deep pink with many variations and markings of strong red, wide round lobe, 3–4″.

'Shungetsu' [Spring moon] ('Setchu no Matsu' × 'Hokutose'): very pale purplish pink blushed and tipped with light purplish pink, lobes slightly separate, 1½–2″; leaves narrow and twisted. BG 1076.

'Shunpo' [Spring treasure]: white with purplish red variations, wavy lobes, 3½″. PI 131314, '39.

'Shunraku': white, extremely variable with light purplish pink margins, some pink with white margin, upper 3 lobes large.

'Shunrei' [Beautiful spring]: white with red stripes, 5–8 lobes, 3″.

'Siho': white with faint blotch of yellow green and tiny flakes of light purple, 6 imbricated lobes, 3½″.

'Sogon Nishiki' [Magnificent brocade] (seedling of 'Matsunami'): white, many variations of strong to deep purplish pink speckles stripes sectors and selfs, rounded lobes slightly tubular, 2–2½″; compact habit. BG 1047.

'Soho' [The peak of the So plant]: white with vivid red variations, sometimes vivid red with white margins, 3½–4″. PI 131316, '39. BG 0855/1227.

'Sono no Homare' ('Taiho' × 'Seidai'): white with reddish purple stripes, large wavy rounded lobes. BG 0869.

'Suifu': white with occasional stripes and selfs of strong pink, 6–7 overlapping lobes, 4″.

'Suigetsu' [Water moon]: white with light green throat, blushes and sectors of pale to vivid purplish pink, 3½–4″, pale pink stamens and pistil. BG 0962.

'Suikan' [Water crown] ('Gekkeikan' × 'Ungetsu'): white with green blotch, stripes and sectors of deep pink, to light pink with deep pink sectors, 5–6 long pointed spaced lobes, 3″. BG 1006.

'Suisen' [Green fan] ('Reiko' × 'Komei'): white with green blotch and yellowish pink stripes, dots and flecks, occasional selfs of vivid yellowish pink, rounded lobes, 2–2½", early. BG 1061.

'Suisho': white with flecks and occasional stripes of purplish pink, 6 rounded lobes, 2½–3". BG 0897.

'Suishoho': white with green blotch, rounded spaced lobes, 2". BG 1195.

'Sumizome' [Black ink dye] (sport of 'Shinnyo no Tsuki): pale pink center with darker pink margin, round wavy lobes, 2½–3", early, pale pink stamens and pistil; low spreading. BG 1119.

'Suzu' [Bell] (seedling of 'Tamaori Hime'): white many variations of strong pink to purplish pink speckles, stripes, sectors and selfs, some with white edges, wide round lobes. 2½–3".

'Suzumushi': deep pink center to pale pink margins and dark pink stripes in center of petals, vivid pink blotch, occasional white with dark pink stripes and sectors, hose-in-hose, 2–2½", early, white stamens and pistil. BG 1159.

'Tagoto no Tsuki' [Moon reflected in paddy fields]: white with strong purplish red flecks, sectors, and selfs, occasional pink with white margin, wide rounded lobes, 2½–3". BG 0941.

'Tai Fuki': white with blush of purplish pink, blotch deep purplish pink, round ruffled lobes, 4–4½". PI 227104, '55, '59.

'Taihei' [Tranquility]: light purplish pink with small white throat, occasionally all white selfs, often 6 wide overlapping ruffled lobes, PI 227105, 228118, '55.

'Taiheikan' [Tranquil crown]: white center with pale to darker purplish pink on edges, dark pink blotch, rounded lobes, 2½", early. BG 0995.

'Taigoto no Tsuki': no description available.

'Taiho' [Abundance]: light to deep pink with stripes of strong red, occasional white center with deep pink margins, round slightly overlapping 6–7 lobes, 2½–3", very late BG 0899.

'Taikan' [Large crown]: white with deep pink to strong red sectors and selfs, white with red blotch, also deep pink with white center, 5–7 lobes, 2–2½".

'Taisanhaku': white round wavy lobes, 2", mid-season, BG 1092.

'Taka no Hana' [Hawk's flower[: white with red spots, stripes, sectors and selfs, pointed spaced lobes, 2–2½"; vigorous low spreading. BG 0480/1255.

'Taka no Tsukasa': pale purplish pink, white towards center, slight yellowish brown blotch, rounded spaced lobes, 2", white stamens, colored pistil. BG 1343.

'Takara' [Treasure] ('Kaho' × 'Kinkazan'): white with occasional deep pink to strong red stripes sectors and selfs, to pink with white edges. 5–6 wide wavy rounded lobes, 2½–3"; low compact. BG 0881.

'Takarabune' [Treasure ship] ('Kyokko Nishiki' × 'Mme. Moreux'): white with strong red stripes, greenish throat, 5–7 overlapping wavy lobes, 2½–3". PI 131318, '39 . BG 1016.

'Takara no Hikari' [Treasure's light]: white, upper lobes with wash of pink, lower lobes striped red, 3". BG 0914.

'Takara no Yama' [Treasure's mountain]: white with vivid red stripes, 2½". BG 1284.

'Takasago' [Celebration of happiness]: light purplish pink with purplish pink blotch, wavy lobes, 2½–3", upright habit. BG 0366/856/1054.

'Tamabotan' [Peony jewel]: white to light pink, double, buds rose-like, occasional sectors and selfs of reddish orange many variations, 12–15 wavy lobes, 3–3½". Vigorous plant. BG 1113.

'Tama Giku' [Jewel chrysanthemum]: deep purplish pink with darker dots in blotch, 5–12 narrow lobes, 3–3½". PI 131319, '39.

'Tama Hime' [Little jewel]: white with vivid pink flecks, 2–2½", early, white stamens and pistil. BG 1244.

'Tamahota': white with a few stripes of strong purplish pink and often blushed with light pink, somewhat tubular, 2". PI 227107, '55.

'Tama Kagami' [Jewel mirror]: white with yellowish pink stripes and sectors, slight green blotch, occasional pink self with reddish purplish blotch, round lobes, 2–2½" early. BG 1247.

'Tama no Hada' [Pearl complexion]: white with deep pink stripes, occasional strong to deep pink selfs and white margins, wide round lobes, 4–5".

'Tama no Hikari' [Jewel light] ('Hitomaru' × 'Yata no Kagami'): light to strong pink with red stripes, narrow spaced lobes, star-shaped, some tips rolled back, 1½–2". BG 0966.

'Tama no Yuki' [Snow jewel]: white with light purple border, 2½", white stamens.

'Tamaori Hime' [Princess Tamaori]: white, flaked deep pink with occasional spots and stripes, greenish throat, wide overlapping lobes, slightly tubular, 2–2½". BG 0865.

'Tama Sugata' [Jewel shape]: white to blush center with border of moderate red, occasional solid colors, slightly overlapping lobes, 3–3½". PI 131320, '39.

'Chiyo no Homare' [Glory of a Thousand Years] Satsuki Hybrid. GALLE

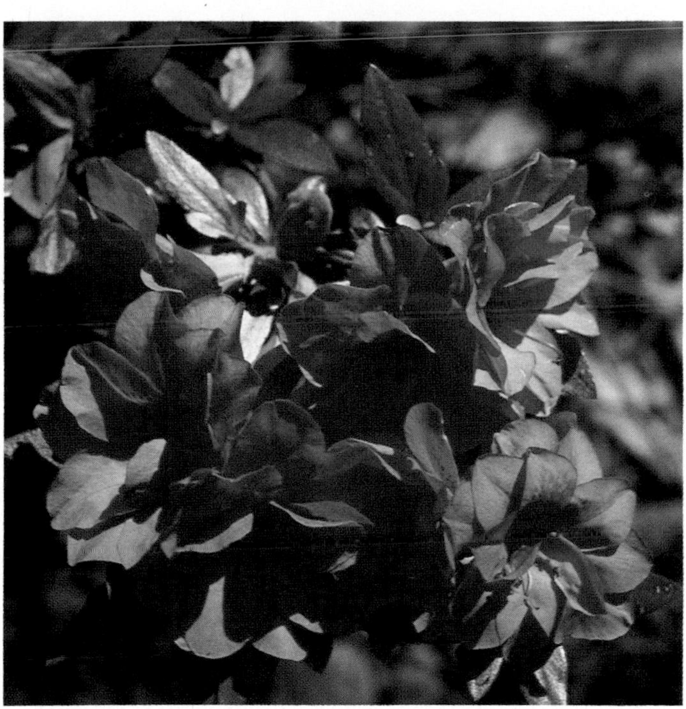

'Beni Kirin' [Red Giraffe] Satsuki Hybrid. GALLE

'Chojuho' [Treasure of Longevity] Satsuki Hybrid. GALLE

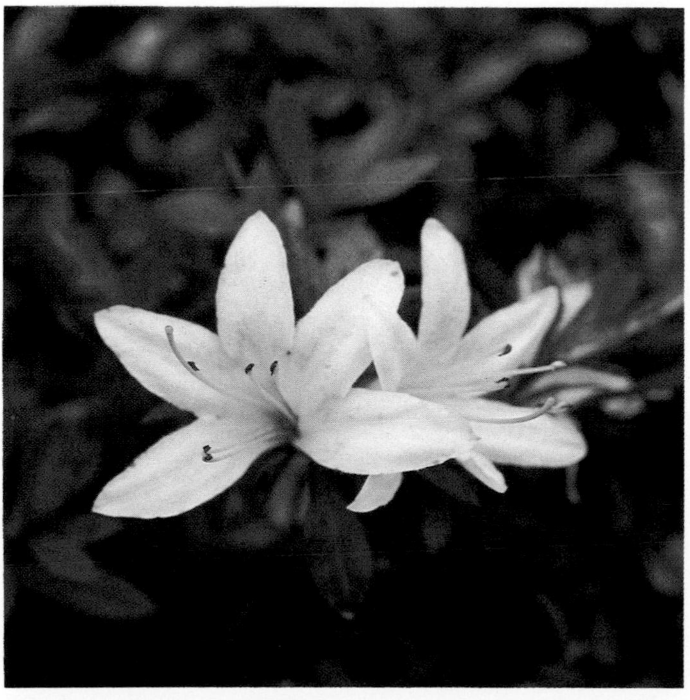

'Hakurei' [White Excellence] Satsuki Hybrid. GALLE

Plate 74

'Kimi no Hana' [Recorded Beauty] Satsuki Hybrid. GALLE

'Otome' [Maiden] Satsuki Hybrid. GALLE

'Shinnyo no Hikari' [Eternal Light] Satsuki Hybrid. STEWART

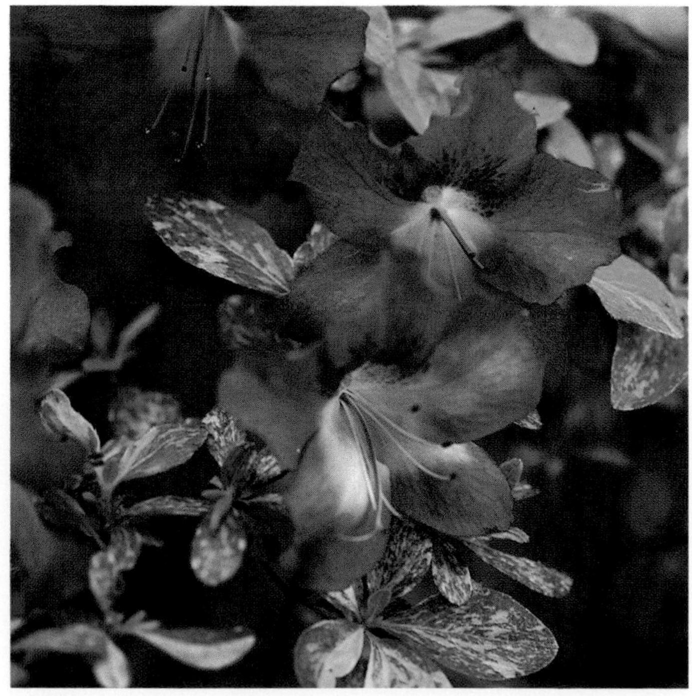

'Keisetsu' [Student Days] Satsuki Hybrid. GALLE

'Gorin Nishiki' [Five Ring Glory] Satsuki Hybrid. GALLE

'Daishuhai' [Great Vermilion Cup] Satsuki Hybrid. GALLE

'Pink Gumpo' Satsuki Hybrid. GALLE

Plate 76

'Daishuhai' [Great Vermilion Cup] Satsuki Hybrid.
STEWART

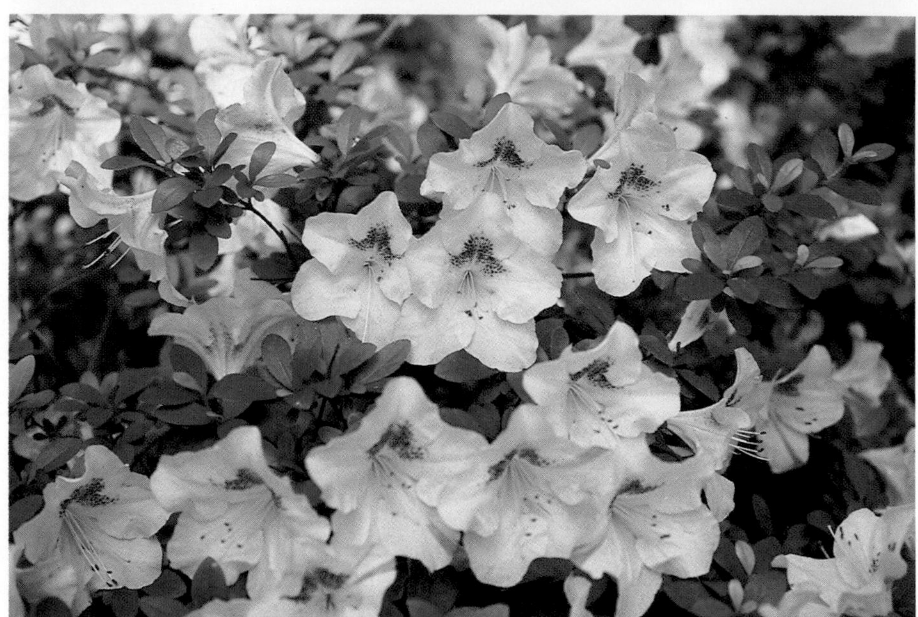

'Joga' Satsuki Hybrid. GALLE

'Gumpo' [A group of Phoenixes] Satsuki Hybrid.
GALLE

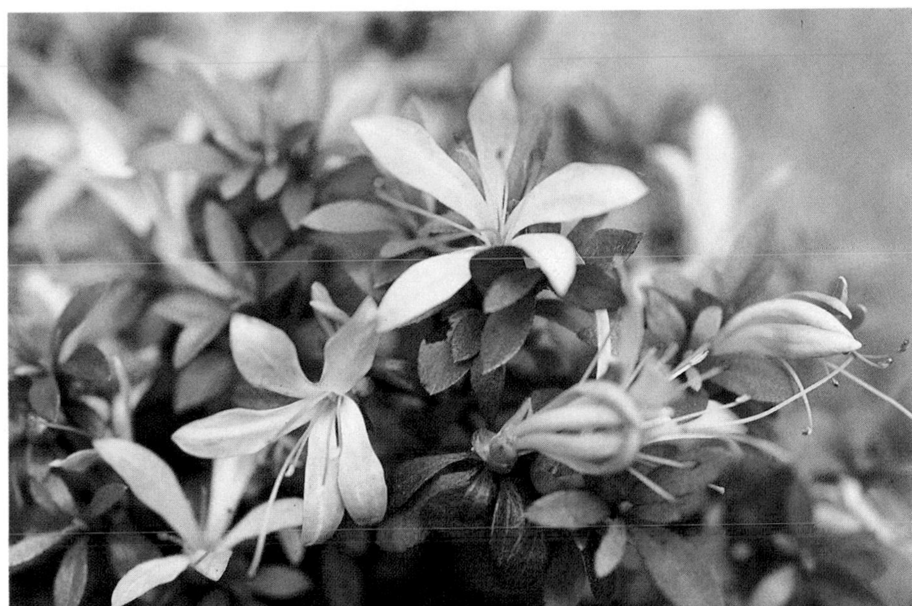

'Sachi no Hana' [Flower of Good Fortune] Satsuki Hybrid. GALLE

'Shinsen' [Divine Selection] Satsuki Hybrid. GALLE

'Joga' Satsuki Hybrid. GALLE

Plate 78

'Izayoi' [Sixteenth Night] Satsuki Hybrid. GALLE

'Shira Fuji' [White Mt. Fuji] Satsuki Hybrid. GALLE

'Gekko' [Moon Light] Satsuki Hybrid. GALLE

'Wakaebisu' [Young Goddess] Satsuki Hybrid. GALLE

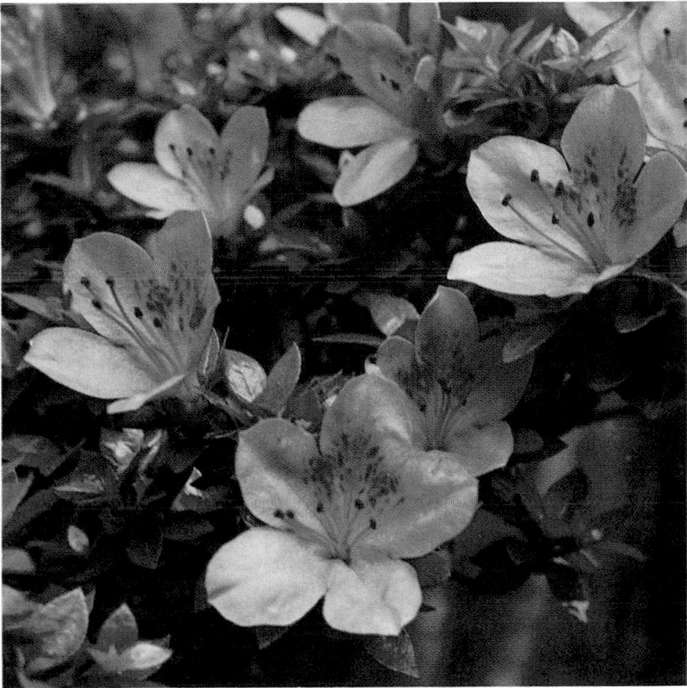
'Kazan' syn. 'Rukizon' Satsuki Hybrid. GALLE

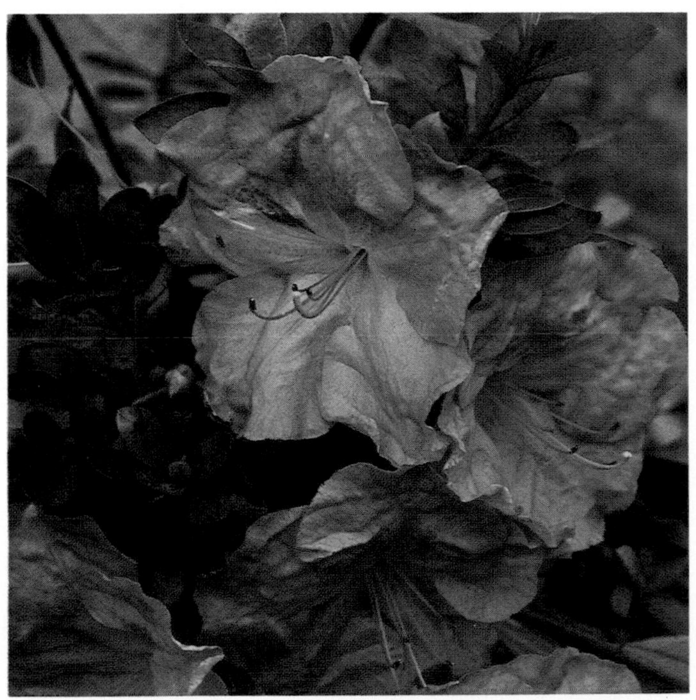
'Tama no Hada' [Pearl Complexion] Satsuki Hybrid. GALLE

'Beth Bullard' Satsuki Hybrid. GALLE

'Dayspring' Glenn Dale Hybrid. B. S. HARDING

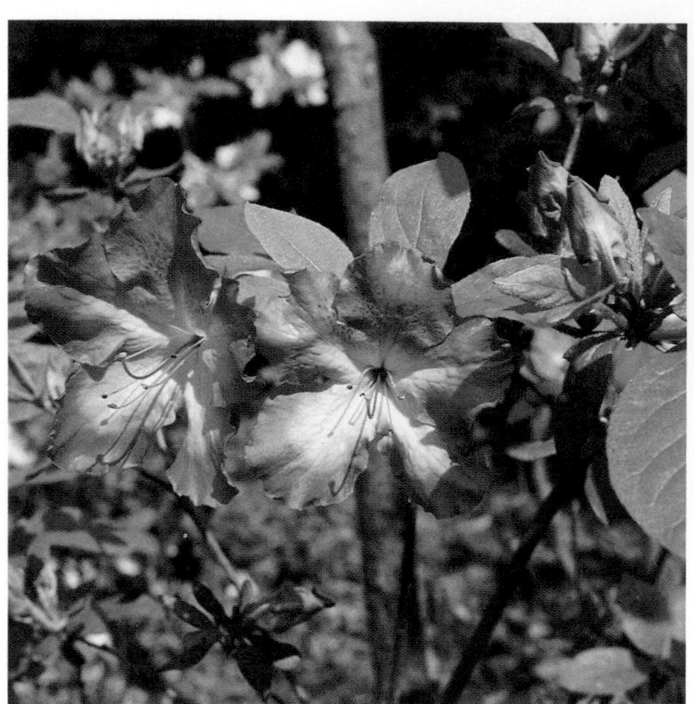

'Martha Hitchcock' Glenn Dale Hybrid. MILLER

'Ambrosia' Glenn Dale Hybrid. GALLE

'Geisha' Glenn Dale Hybrid. MILLER

'Tancho' [Redtop] (seedling of 'Aya Nishiki'): purplish pink, spaced lobes; variegated leaves with fine yellow margin. BG 1112.

'Tatsumi no Hikari' [Light of the southeast] (seedling of 'Banjo'): white with speckles, stripes and selfs of strong purplish pink, occasional strong pink with white margins, blotch darker, 5–6 round wavy lobes usually notched at tip and crinkly, 3½–4". PI 227109, 210613, '53. BG 0853.

'Teikan': white with purplish pink flecks, 6 overlapping lobes, 3–3½", early, prominent white pistil. BG 0913. Possibly same as 'Taikan'.

'Tenjiku': reddish orange with faint blotch, overlapping lobes, 3½".

'Ten Meikai': white with vivid red variations, double flower, 2–3". PI 131321, '39.

'Tennyo no Hikari' [Light of the celestial nymph]: deep reddish orange with lighter centers, narrow spaced lobes, 2–2½".

'Tennyo no Sugata' [Figure of the celestial nymph]: white with many flecks and dots of dark pink, green throat, wavy round lobes, 2½", early. BG 1243.

'Tenshi' ('Gyoko' × 'Sanko no Tsuki'): white with occasional pale red stripes, heavy texture, 2½". BG 1165.

'Tenshoko': white with deep pink stripes and sectors to colored margins and white throat, rounded lobes. BG 1204.

'Tensho no Hikari' [Light of Heaven]: white, many variations with speckles, stripes, and selfs of deep yellowish pink to deep reddish orange, some with white centers, wide rounded lobes, 2½–3".

'Tochi Gumpo': no description available.

'Tochi no Hikari' (sport of 'Banko'): white with light purplish pink stripes, darker dots in blotch, round wavy overlapping lobes, 4–4½". PI 227111, '58, '59. BG 0976.

'Tochi no Homare' (sport of 'Banko'): pale purple, deep purple stripes, very large, early. BG 0901.

'Tokai': white with purplish pink spots, flecks and sectors, slightly pointed lobes, 2½". BG 1194.

'Tokiwa' [Rabbit]: vivid reddish orange, also white with stripes and sectors of reddish orange, 6 wide round overlapping lobes; 2½–3". BG 0944.

'Toko Nishiki': white with yellowish pink flecks and sectors, occasionally white suffused pink to white edge with reddish purple blotch, 2½–3", early. BG 1143.

'Tomei Nishiki' [Brocade of eastern light]: white to light yellowish pink, numerous fine stripes, speckles and sectors of yellowish pink to strong reddish orange, round spaced lobes, 2–2½"; low spreading. BG 0929.

'Tosho no Hikari' [Light shining in the east] (sport of 'Nikko'): light yellowish pink, occasional selfs of white and pink, narrowly spaced lobes, 1½–2".

'Towa no Kagami': vivid purplish red with slight red blotch, round overlapping lobes, 1½", early, pink stamens and red pistil. BG 1179.

'Tsukasa' [Official] (sport of 'Gekkeikan'): white with sectors of deep pink to pale pink centers and wide deep pink margins, 6 rounded lobes, 3–3½". BG 0500/0982.

'Tsuki' [Moon] ('Heiwa' × 'Seiko no Tsuki'): pale pink to white with occasional darker margins, often 6 lobes, 2½–3".

'Tsukihime' [Little moon]: white with many variations of flecks and sectors of yellowish pink, sometimes wide margins of dark yellowish pink with lighter center, green blotch, round wavy lobes, 3½–4". BG 0923.

'Tsuki no Hitomaru' [Moon's 'Hitomaru'] ('Hototogisu' × 'Hitomaru'): light yellowish pink with occasional white stripes or blotches, some white tipped pink or bordered pink to solid white, slightly spaced lobes, 2–2½".

'Tsuki no Shimo' [Frosty moon]: white to light pink, occasionally white tipped or bordered light pink, purplish pink blotch, round irregular overlapping lobes, 2–2½"; leaves curved inward; compact habit.

'Tsuki no Tsukasa' [Moon official] (seedling of 'Kagatsu'): white with reddish purple irregular dots and flakes, yellowish green dots in blotch, 3". BG 0926.

'Tsuki Shama': no description available.

'Tsukuba no Akebono' [Dawn of Tsukuba] ('Chiyo no Nishiki' × 'Issho no Haru'): white with faint green blotch and occasional flecks of vivid yellowish pink, round spaced lobes, 1½", early. BG 1066.

'Tsuyu no Hikari' [Light of the rainy season]: white to light yellowish pink, heavily speckled, striped and selfs of deep red, many variations, spaced pointed lobes, 1½–2".

'Tsuyu no Tama' [Jewel of the rainy season]: BG 1210.

'Tukishiro': no description available.

'Uchu no Hikari' [Light of the universe]: white with speckled and stripes of light to vivid reddish orange, blotch heavily dotted red, pointed spaced lobes, 2–2½". BG 1206.

'Ugigumo no Tsuki': white with pale to vivid yellowish pink dots, flecks and sectors, wide overlapping round petals, 2–2½", early. BG 0882.

'Ukigumo no Tsuki': white to reddish orange with slight white edge and white sectors, blotch purplish red, 3".

'Uki Nishiki' [Floating brocade] (seedling of 'Matsunami'): white, many variations with speckles, stripes, sectors and selfs of strong purplish pink, round wavy lobes, 2½–3"; leaves with yellow blotches and stripes.

'Ume no Hikari' [Plum's light]: BG 1013.

'Ungetsu' [Cloudy moon]: white with green blotch, occasional sectors of reddish orange, long oval spaced lobes, 3", prominent white stamens and pistil. BG 0943.

'Ungetsu no Hana' [Clouded moon's flower]: vivid reddish purple with dark red blotch, occasional white and light pink flecks, rounded lobes, 1½", early. BG 0972.

'Ungetsu no Hikari' [Light of a cloudy moon]: light yellowish pink with narrow margins and sectors of vivid yellowish pink, blotch heavily dotted with red, long spaced petals, 2–2½". BG 0952.

'Unryu' [Cloud dragon]: very light purple with white centers and light to strong purple margins, lobes funnel-shaped, 1½–2"; leaves narrow and twisted; compact habit.

'Usshu no Hikari': no description available.

'Usugesho' [Light make-up]: pale to light pink with speckles and flakes of deep pink, many variations, 5–6 wavy overlapping lobes, 2–3". BG 0857.

'Usuginu' [Thin silk] (seedling of 'Hitomaru'): very pale yellowish pink with flecks of deep pink, blotch deep pink, some small sectors of white, round notched lobes, 2", small leaves. BG 0892.

'Utage no Hana': yellowish pink with slight white center, slight green throat with dark pink blotch, rounded lobes, 3", early. BG 1242.

'Uyo no Tsuki' [Moon of Uyo] ('Banzai' × 'Yato no Kagami'): white with green blotch, reddish purple sectors, flecks and dots, overlapping lobes trumpet-like, 3–3½", early. BG 1260.

'Wakaebisu' [Young goddess]: deep yellowish pink with deep pink dots in blotch, hose-in-hose, rounded lobes, 2–2½"; popular landscape and container plant.

'Wakakoma' [Young colt] ('Gumpo' × 'Gyokushin'): white with blushes of pale reddish orange or heavily blushed with prominent reddish orange blotch and stripes, round wavy ruffled lobes, 2½–3". BG 1341.

'Waka Matsu' [Young pine]: pale white to light pink with deep pink dots in blotch, round wavy lobes, 2½–3".

'Wako': white with many variations of purplish pink sectors and reddish blotch. PI 227112, 230614, '55.

'Warai Jishi' [Laughing lion]: deep purplish pink, dots in blotch darker but not too conspicuous, double but irregular in amount of doubling, spaced pointed lobes, 2½–3". PI 77132, '29.

'Yachiyo' [Eternity]: white to light pink, variable with stripes, sectors and selfs of strong red, often with white centers, slightly spaced pointed lobes, 2½–3". PI 320028. Another 'Yachiyo' azalea is a Wada Hybrid; deep yellowish pink, hose-in-hose, and early.

'Yae no Tsuki' [Double moon] ('Narihira' × 'Kikoshi'): very pale pink with margins tipped deep purplish pink, irregular hose-in-hose, round lobes, 2–2½". BG 0880.

'Yakata no Tsuki' [Moon of the mansion] ('Kohan' × 'Kohan no Tsuki'): pale yellowish pink with slight flush of white on edge, veins in petals slightly darker reddish orange but prominent, occasional selfs or reddish orange, 6 spaced lobes star shaped, 2½", white stamens and pistil. BG 1215.

'Yakura Yama' [Mount Yakura]: no description available.

'Yakushin': white to blushed purplish pink to light purple tips, round dimpled lobes, 3", early. BG 0942.

'Yamaji no Tomoshiba': white suffused vivid purplish pink with white edges, reddish purple blotch, round wavy lobes, 3", pink stamens and white pistil. BG 1137. Flowers early.

'Yamakawa no Tsuki' [Moon of the mountain river] ('Gyoko' × 'Kohan no Tsuki'): white with stripes and sectors of deep reddish orange, also deep pink with white marked edges and deep reddish orange selfs, occasionally with lighter centers, often 6 lobes, 2½–3".

'Yama no Akebono' [Mountain's dawn]: white with pale yellowish green blotch, many variations of dark pink stripes, dots and sectors to solid selfs, wide rounded lobes, 3–3½", early. BG 0889.

'Yama no Haru' [Spring of mountain]: pale purplish pink with white towards center, blotch light yellowish brown, occasional stripe of darker purplish pink, wide round lobes, 2½–3", midseason, white stamens and pistil. BG 1158.

'Yama no Hikari' [Light of the mountain] (sport of 'Kazan'): white to light and deep pink, many variations of stripes sectors and solid selfs of deep pink, lobes rounded, 2½". BG 1283.

'Yama no Takara' [Treasure mountain]: pink to pale pink margins very light yellowish pink tint, dark pink blotch, round overlapping lobes, 2½", early. BG 1099.

'Yamato' [Old name for Japan]: white with pale yellow green blotch, some flecks and stripes to solid selfs of deep pink, wide round overlapping lobes, 3½–4", late, upright habit. BG 1345.

'Yamato no Hikari' [Light of Japan] ('Hozan' × 'Eiten'): white with green blotch, speckled and striped with deep purplish pink, some pink selfs, wavy overlapping lobes, 3–4". BG 1160.

'Yata no Kagami' [Sacred mirror]: light yellowish pink with white 'jewel' spot spreading from center in varying degrees to nearly all off white, with red blotch, spaced lobes, 2–2½"; low spreading habit. BG 1193.

'Yata no Sai' [Eight colors] (sport of 'Yata no Kagami'): pale pink shading to deep pink on margins, long round spaced lobes rolled inward, star-shaped 2–2½". Occasionally reverts back to 'Yata no Kagami'.

'Yatsubusa no Ushi': no description available.

'Yatsubusa no Ushi': BG 1073.

'Yatsubusa Seirin': deep pink with darker pink blotch, long spaced lobes, trumpet-shaped, 1½–1¾", early, dark pink stamens and pistil. BG 1088.

'Yatsubusa Ukigami': BG 1190.

'Yayoi no Hikari' [Light of Japan]: white center, vivid purplish pink margins, some pale pink with green center and occasional pink stripes rounded lobes, 2–2½', early, white stamens and pistil. BG 1153.

'Yayoi no Tsuki' [March moon] (sport of 'Reigetsu'): white to pale pink with many variations of stripes and sectors of deep purplish pink, some with white star center and wide dark pink margins, round overlapping lobes, 2½".

'Yorokobi': white with occasional dark reddish sectors, some selfs reddish orange, red blotch, pointed spaced lobes, 1½", early. BG 1304.

'Yorozo no Kagami': pale pink with faint green blotch and thin margin of deep pink, overlapping lobes, 3".

'Yoshimitsu' [Personal name of a Tokugawa Shogun]: white with green blotch, overlapping lobes, 2½–3". early. BG 1257.

'Yosoi' [Attire]: white with margins of deep pink, variable, some only blotched with pink, rounded lobes, 2–3".

'Yozakura' [Evening cherry]: reddish purple with darker blotch, round spaced lobes, 3".

'Yugetsu' [Elegant moon] (sport of 'Aikoku'): white usually with margins of deep purplish pink, but varies from white to stripes and blotches of pink, lobes rounded, 2½–3".

'Yugiri' [Evening mist]: pale purplish pink, overlapping ruffled petals, 2½–3". Reported to be 'Pink Gumpo' but looks like 'Rose Gumpo'. BG 0918.

'Yuho' [Elegant phoenix] (sport of 'Gumpo'): deep pink to slight white margin, heavily spotted deep pink blotch, occasional white sectors, overlapping ruffled lobes, 2½–3". BG 0392/0851/0998.

'Yukata Yama' [Mount Yukata]: no description available.

'Yuki no Myojo' [Venice in snow]: pale yellowish white, with light to strong purple flakes, pointed lobes, 1½–2".

'Yukishiro' [White snow]: BG 1042.

'Yume' [A vision] ('Matsunami' × 'Tamaori Hime'): white with many variations of stripes, sectors and selfs of deep yellowish pink to vivid reddish orange, some selfs with white margins, round lobes, 2–2½"; spreading habit. BG 0956.

'Yuta': no description available.

'Yuwai no Tsuki': BG 0409.

'Zetsurin' ('Kyokko Nishiki' × 'Mme Moreux'): No description available.

'Zuigetsu' ('Kagetsu' × 'Kasei'): white with long and short vivid red stripes, rounded lobes, 2½". BG 0906.

'Zuio' [Proper name] (sport of 'Shyozuki'); white with occasional deep purplish pink stripes and light yellowish green dots in blotch, round wavy overlapping lobes, 2–2½"; compact habit. BG 1103.

ADDITIONAL SATSUKI AZALEAS

The following Satsuki azaleas were named and introduced in countries other than Japan. Some of the plants listed came as cuttings from Japan but were named in the United States or other countries.

Several plants are listed from New Zealand and Australia (N.Z. & Aust.). They have Japanese names but are not found in the Japanese literature on Satsuki Azaleas. Hardiness and dimensions are typical of the Satsuki Group.

'Aiden' (see 'Sakuragata'): light purple, white margin.

'April Showers' (syn. 'Apricot Falls'; 'Purple Weeper' × 'Trailing Queen'; Domoto): strong pink 49A, hose-in-hose, 2¼"; pendulous growth.

'Avalon Exquisite': strong pink 49A, dark spots in blotch, double. 2¼".

'Benizuki' (N.Z. & Aust.): white with deep pink border.

'Benzikari' (N.Z. & Aust.): white with red margin. Possibly 'Beni Hikari'.

'Clara Brown' ('Macrantha Orange' × 'Caldwellii'; D. Stewart '62): strong reddish orange.

'D.J.O.' ('Pink Gumpo' × 'Hexe'; PP 4688; Branigan): strong red 45D, hose-in-hose, early midseason, 1¼–1½"; dwarf compact; good for forcing; hardy in zone 6b.

'Dwarf Geisha': white marked with red.

'Early Bright' (N.Z. & Aust.): light pink with darker margin.

'Eiko San'=North Tisbury Hybrids.

'Farrall Ruby' ('Macrantha' × 'Hinode Giri'; Haworth-Booth '62): reddish orange 43C, 1¾".

'Firmament' (Coolidge): white center with border of strong yellowish pink, lobes rounded 2–2½"; vigorous bushy; occasional sports with light purple border.

'Geisha Girl': white center bordered strong red to red selfs, rounded lobes, 2–2½"; vigorous bushy.

'General Wavell' ('Glory of Numazu' × *indicum;* Ingram '60): deep yellowish pink suffused yellow at the base, red spotting in the blotch, ruffled lobes, 3¾".

Gumpo sports:

'Dwarf Gumpo' (witches broom of 'Gumpo'; Cross): white with pink stripes and flakes, 1½", leaves small ⅜–½"; compact habit.

'Gumpo Fancy': pink with white margin.

'Gumpo Pink': light pink.

'Gumpo Rose': strong pink.

'Gumpo White Sport' (Bowhan): strong pink, improved foliage.

'Mini Gumpo' (Cross): white and pink, 1¼", very small leaves, ¼–⅜", very compact; not stable.

'Wood's White Gumpo' (Woods): white, heavier texture; narrow petals; low.

'Hana Fubuki': see 'Chinsai'

'Hatsu Shimada' (N.Z. & Aust.): white with red stripes.

'Hikari no Affinity': light pink, deep orange margin, many variations.

'Hohman' (Domoto): reddish orange, 2½", partially petaloid; pendulous growth.

'Isshu no Tsuki' (N.Z. & Aust.): white with deep pink border.

'Itsi Gishi' (sport of 'Warai Jishi'; Cross): small leaf sport and more compact habit, flowers the same; often reverts back.

'Jack's Picotee' (Greer): white center with moderate purple margin.

'Kashu no Hikari' (syn. 'California Sunshine'; Ogawa): white with stripes, sectors and selfs of light to deep pink; many variations, double, 3".

'Kwo' (possibly 'Kow koku'='Kokoku'): light pink with white throat; low compact.

'Lateritia Alba' (old clone from U.S., not Japan): white with faint flush of yellow green in blotch, wavy overlapping lobes, 2½".

'Lavender Lady' (Domoto): light violet, wavy lobes, 2–2½"; compact cascading growth.

'Linda R.' (sport of 'Eikan'; Curtis): deep yellowish pink, 6–9 round ruffled lobes, 3–4".

'Lotte': deep pink; glossy foliage and compact habit.

'Lynn Stieglitz' ('Myu no Tsuki' × 'Corsage'; Handcock): large purple, star-shaped, slightly fragrant.

'Macrantha Fl. PL': reddish orange, double; low compact.

'Madame Margotten' (form of *indicum*): white with occasional flecks and stripes of reddish purple, 2½".

'Matsuyo'=North Tisbury Hybrids.

'Meiro' (N.Z. & Aust.): white with pink dots, also sectors and selfs of reddish orange.

'Midori'=North Tisbury Hybrids.

'Midsummer Beauty' ('Kokinshota' × 'Macrantha'; Haworth-Booth '75): yellowish pink suffused red, 2½".

'Mini Hakata' (sport of 'Hakatashiro'; Nosal): white with faint flush of pale yellow green in blotch; plant has smaller leaves and compact habit; often reverts back.

'Moira Pink' (Wada hybrid introd. to Eng.): pink.

'Moira Salmon' (Wada hybrid introd. to Eng.): deep yellowish pink.

'Nichola' ('Fidelio' × 'Gumpo Red'; Waterer & Son '65): pale purplish pink, 2"; compact spreading.

'Oh My' (introd. by Beattie): light purplish pink with white margin and darker blotch, 2½–3"; dwarf. PI 77087, '29.

'Paradise Pink' ('Fidelio' × 'Gumpo Red'; Waterer & Son '65): vivid purplish pink, 2½"; compact low spreading.

'Patches' ('Chichibu' self'; Caperci '77): white, with many variations of blotches, stripes, sectors and selfs of deep yellowish pink 39A, round wavy lobes 2"; broad dwarf, 13×32" in 20 yrs; hardy to 0°F.

'Polypetalum' (Macrantha type): reddish orange, narrow petals split to base, 2"; narrow linear leaves; upright bushy habit.

'Pouffe' (*kaempferi* × *indicum*: Haworth-Booth '64): deep yellowish pink; low compact spreading.

'Purple Weeper' (seedling of 'Daikagura'; Domoto): light purple, rounded lobes, 2"; pendulous habit.

'Rukizon': see 'Kazan'.

'Ryde Heron' (form of 'Macrantha'; Knap Hill '62): vivid purplish red with darker spotting, funnel-shaped, 2¼".

'Solstice' ('Glory of Numazu' × *indicum*; Ingram '70): strong pink 52C, faint reddish orange on central veins, blotch purplish red 57A, 4".

'Summer Sun' (Coolidge): deep reddish orange 43A, pointed lobes, semidouble 2–2½".

'Summer Time' (Sawada seedling; Nuccio): deep yellowish pink 43C, semidouble to double, 2–2½".

'Uki Funei' (Greer): white with red stripes, 2½"; leaves variegated with spots and blotches of yellow.

'Yoshimi' (sport of 'Shinnyo no Tsuki'; Ogawa): white with deep yellowish pink border, round overlapping lobes, 3½".

'Yachiyo Red' (from Japan; Greer): white with numerous variations of light pink blotches, stripes and sectors to pink selfs, some with white centers, rounded lobes, 1½–2"; compact growth. Flowers not red.

'Yaye'=North Tisbury Hybrids.

'Yuka'=North Tisbury Hybrids.

INTER-GROUP EVERGREEN HYBRIDS

The Inter-Group Evergreen Hybrids are a relatively new grouping of azaleas, starting with the introduction of the Glenn Dale Hybrids by B. Y. Morrison in the late 1940's and early 1950's. The interest in hybridizing with the Glenn Dales and inter-crosses with plants from other groups such as Satsuki, Kurumes, Kaempferi Hybrids, and others has given rise to the Inter-Group Evergreen Hybrids. At least 75% of the azaleas introduced in the past twenty years are from inter-group crosses. The interest in crossing azaleas with such a mixed parentage undoubtedly will continue for years to come as many unusual and hitherto unconceived breeding objectives may be realized. Some Hybrid lines such as the Arendsii Hybrids might have been included with the Kaempferi Hybrids; but as they were developed by George Arends as part of his Inter-Group work, they have been included here.

GLENN DALE HYBRIDS

In the annals of azalea breeding the development of the Glenn Dale Hybrids is unsurpassed. Hybridizing was begun in 1935 by B. Y. Morrison, horticulturist and plant breeder, former Chief of the Plant Introduction Section and Director of the National Arboretum, United States Department of Agriculture. The hybrid group takes its name from the location of the Plant Introduction Station at Glenn Dale, Maryland.

Morrison had several objectives in developing the Glenn Dale Hybrids. The first was to develop plants with flowers as large and varied as those of the Southern Indian Hybrids but, secondly, to be cold hardy. Lastly, they were planned to provide flowers from mid-April to mid-June, filling the mid-May flowering gap then typical of evergreen azaleas. The Glenn Dales are now grown around the world. As a group they are hardy in zones 6b to 9a, though some clones can withstand winter temperatures to −10°F. and occasionally lower.

A few clones were introduced in 1941, just before World War II, but most appeared from 1947 to 1949, with a few following in 1952. The 440 clones introduced were selections from over 70,000 seedlings arising out of the breeding work. The clonal introductions vary in flowering period—early, early midseason, late midseason, and late; in habit—from dwarf 3 ft. to large 8 ft. in height; in color—from white through pink to red and purple, and include variations in color form as stripes, flecks and variegated margins and throats; in flower size—from 1½ inches to 4½ inches. Most flowers are single, some hose-in-hose, and a few semidouble and double. The wide diversity of the Glenn Dale Hybrids is the direct outcome of the many species and hybrid groups in the subseries *Obtusum* used. The principal species and clones used include:

a. the Indian Azalea (*R. indicum*) and a number of its cultivars;
b. selected Satsuki Hybrids;
c. the Kaempfer Azalea (*R. kaempferi*), Kaempferi Hybrids ('Malvatica'), mainly clones 'Alice', 'Louise', and 'Willy', also 'Malvatica' of unknown origin;
d. the Sims Azalea (*R. simsii*) particularly 'Vittata Fortunei';
e. 'Indica Alba' and 'Lilacina', syn 'Lilacinum'.
f. the Kurume Hybrids and 'Amoena';
g. the Maxwell Azalea (*R. phoeniceum* var. *calycinum* f. *maxwelli*), the Dawson Hybrid, clone 'Hazel Dawson';
h. the Southern Indian Hybrid clones 'Modele', 'Madame Margottin', and 'Miltoni',
i. the Korean Azalea (*R. yedoense poukhanense*) and others.

The Department of Agriculture in October, 1953 published an extensive, illustrated account of these azaleas entitled *The Glenn Dale Azaleas*, by B. Y. Morrison, Agriculture Monograph No. 20. The late Dr. Roy Magruder (U.S.D.A., retired), after considerable research, concluded that the following clones were never introduced:

'Alexandria'	'Candlelight'	'Orpheus'
'Aries'	'Etna'	'Pontiff'
'Barchester'	'Horus'	'Touchstone'
'Berceuse'		

In addition the Azalea Society of America, using the findings of George Harding and Dr. Neil Campbell, suggested corrections to several of the azalea descriptions contained in *Monograph 20*. These corrections have been incorporated into this book for the following azaleas:

'Alight'	'Cranford'	'Marmora'
'Angelus'	'Cygnet'	'Modesty'
'Anthem'	'Delight'	'Paprika'
'Aztec'	'Delos'	'Picotee'
'Beacon'	'Dimity'	'Pied Piper'
'Bopeep'	'Dream'	'Stunner'
'Bravura'	'Grace Freeman'	'Tanager'
'Burgundy'	'Jubilant'	'Winner'
'Celestial'	'Louise Dowdel'	'Wildfire'
'Chum'		

In 1980 the Azalea Society of America, under the direction of Frank White, conducted an "eye catcher/good-doer" poll on the Glenn Dale Hybrids contacting over 100 growers in 20 states. The complete results of the survey were published in the *Azalean*, April 1981. The four most highly rated Glenn Dale Hybrids were 'Martha Hitchcock', 'Glacier', 'Buccaneer', and 'Dayspring'.

The most highly rated eighteen cultivars, receiving seventy or more nominations were:

'Ambrosia'	'Dream'	'Glamour'
'Boldface'	'Fashion'	'Helen Close'
'Buccaneer'	'Festive'	'Martha Hitchcock'
'Copperman'	'Gaiety'	'Refrain'
'Dayspring'	'Geisha'	'Treasure'
'Delos'	'Glacier'	'Sagittarius'

The second ranking eleven with 10–19 nominations were:

'Aphrodite'	'Gorgeous'	'Moonbeam'
'Ben Morrison' *	'Grace Freeman'	'Surprise'
'Camp Fire'	'Greeting'	'Zulu'
'Fawn'	'Louise Dowdle'	

*'Ben Morrison' is not a bona-fide Glenn Dale even though included in the list. B. Y. Morrison propagated, but did not register it. It was registered and introduced only after Morrison's death by the Plant Introduction Station, U.S.D.A.

The following description of the Glenn Dale Hybrids is derived from the information contained in Monograph 20 with corrections.

The original color descriptions were based on the Ridgeway Color Standard and are no longer available. I have used corresponding ISCC–NBS color designation in *Color, Universal Language and Dictionary of Names*, (see Chapter 4). The size of flowers follows the color description. The season of flowering (early, midseason or late) is based on the Washington, D.C., area but relates in a straightforward way to other parts of the world. The majority of the Glenn Dale flowers are borne two to three in a truss, so will not be noted unless the truss is larger such as two to four, three to five, etc.

The basic habit of all the Glenn Dales is an upright rounded plant. The height of the plant after 10 years is based on observations in the Washington, D.C., area and may be larger or smaller in other places. Established plants 20 years and older are usually much larger than the size given. The Monograph makes numerous admonitions to cut branches of solid colors out of the striped, flaked and variegated clones such as 'Boldface', 'Fawn', and

'Ben Morrison' Azalea

others. I will only suggest removing branch sports. The following cultivars frequently produce branch sports.

'Altair'
'Boldface'
'Cadenza'
'Chum'
'Cinnabar'
'Dowager'
'Fawn'
'Furbelow'
'Geisha'
'Goblin'
'Harlequin'
'Helen Gunning'
'Herald'
'Memento'
'Moira'
'Moonstone'
'Oriflamme'
'Paprika'
'Picotee'
'Pied Piper'
'Pinocchio'
'Pinto'
'Puck'
'Satrap'
'Shimmer'
'Silver Mist'
'Sonata'
'Susannah'
'Swagger'

Many other clones derived from 'Vittata Fortunei' or Satsuki Hybrids will sport with age, particularly white flowering cultivars. Also, many described as "white"with stripes, sectors or spots may eventually become solid white or colored.

The U.S.D.A. Plant Introduction Number follows the cultivar name.

Glenn Dale Azaleas

'Abbott' (PI 160069; *indicum* × 'Hatsushimo'): deep purplish pinks paler at base, dots vivid purplish red, lobes undulated, 2½–3" across, 1 to 4 in head; early; vigorous, erect to wide spreading to 5 ft. high.

'Acme' (PI 160141; 'Fielder's White' × *kaempferi*): deep purplish pink at center to dark pink near margins, dots in blotch not conspicuous, 2¼–3" across, 2 to 3 in head; erect with ascending branches to 6 to 7 ft. high.

'Acrobat' (PI 163879; ('Lilacinum' × 'Willy') × ('Mrs. Carmichael' × 'Willy')): white, heavily sanded, few stripes of vivid purplish red, 2½" across, midseason, 1 to 3 in head; broad spreading to 4 ft. high.

'Adorable' (PI 163765; 'Mucronatum Roseum' × *indicum*): light purple dot in blotch, vivid purplish pink, 3–3¾" across, 3 to 4 in head mid season; somewhat spreading up to 5 ft. high.

'Advance' (PI 163876; ('Lilacinum' × 'Willy') × ('Mrs. Carmichael' × 'Willy')): between vivid purplish pink and vivid red: 2" across, 2 to 4 in head; midseason; dense twiggy to 5 ft. high.

'Afterglow' (PI 160100; 'Mrs. Carmichael' × 'Alice'): vivid purplish red, blotch darker, base of tube lighter, 1¾–2" across, early; strong erect growth to 7 ft. high.

'Alabaster' (PI 141770; 'Vittata Fortunei' × 'Amoena'): white, flakes of purplish pink, irregularly hose-in-hose, 2–2½" across, 2 to 4 in head, mid season May; broad spreading to 5 ft. high.

'Aladdin' (PI 160126; 'Multiflora' × *kaempferi*): deep pink, white base, few darker dots, early; erect habit to 5 to 6 ft. high; almost deciduous.

'Alexandria' (PI 141796; 'Mucronatum' × *simsii*): deep pink, 2–2¾" across, early; vigorous with ascending branches 6 ft. high. Not introduced.

'Alight' (PI 163942; 'Mucronatum' × 'Kagetsu'): strong purple pink, lighter center, small plants are solid color, 2½" across, midseason; broad spreading to 5 ft. high.

'Allegory' (PI 163785; ('Lilacinum' × 'Willy') × ('Mrs. Carmichael' × 'Willy')): white, greenish blotch, few purplish pink stripes, 2¾–3" across, midseason; broad spreading 5 ft. high.

'Allure' (PI 163896; *simsii* × 'Mucronatum'): light purplish pink, 2–2¾" across, early; spreading habit to 5 ft. high.

'Altair' (PI 163824; (*kaempferi* × 'Mucronatum') × 'Kagetsu'): white, few dots of purple, 3" midseason; broad spreading 4 ft. high. Remove branch sports.

'Ambrosia' (PI 163899; 'Vittata Fortunei' × 'HEA #34'): deep yellowish pink, aging to light orange yellow, 1¾–2" across, 2 to 5 in head, early; erect somewhat spreading to 8 ft. high.

'Anchorite' (PI 141900; 'Malvatica' × *indicum*): deep pink, orange undertone, 2" across, early; erect to broad spreading to 4 ft. high.

'Andros' (PI 141805; 'Vittata Fortunei' × 'Warai Gishi'): strong purplish pink, double, bud - "rose buds", 2–2½" across, midseason; erect to broad spreading to 6 ft. high.

'Angela Place' (PI 163960; (*kaempferi* × 'Mucronatum') × 'Shinnyo no Tsuki'): white, 3" across, 2 to 4 in head, midseason; broad spreading to 4 ft. high.

'Angelus' (PI 160110; 'Lilacinum' × 'Willy'): white with rare flush of pale purple when first opens, 2–2½" across, 3 to 5 in head, early; vigorous spreading to 5 ft. high.

'Antares' (PI 160063; 'Vittata Fortunei' × 'Alice'): strong red, large blotch purplish red, base of tube white, 2½–2¾", early; erect, with ascending branches to 8 ft. high.

'Anthem' (PI 163936; 'Malvatica' × 'Yosakura'): pale purplish pink, dots darker in blotch, 2–3½" across, midseason; strong upright growth to 5 ft. high.

'Antique' (PI 163766; 'Mucronatum' × 'Fukuju'): white, stripes of reddish purple, 2¾–3" across, late; broad spreading to 6 ft. high.

'Aphrodite(PI 141898; 'Malvatica' × *indicum*): light purplish pink, inconspicuous blotch, 2" across, midseason; erect to broad spreading to 5 ft. high.

'Araby' (PI 160119; 'Kagaribi' × *indicum*): between moderate and strong red, blotch purplish red, 2¾–3" across, early; erect to spreading to 5 ft. high.

'Arcadia' (PI 160053; 'Malvatica' × *indicum*): deep pink, blotch purplish red dots, 3" across, early; erect to wide spreading to 7 ft. high.

'Arctic' (PI 163810; 'Mucronatum' × 'Kagetsu'): white, green blotch, often 6 lobes, 2½–3" across, midseason; low broad spreading to 3 ft. high.

'Argosy' (PI 160095; 'Vittata Fortunei' × 'Maxwellii'): deep pink, upper lobes deep yellowish pink, blotch darker, 3–3½" across, early; erect to spreading to 5 ft. high.

'Aries' (PI 141806; 'Vittata Fortunei' × 'Warai Gishi'): strong purplish pink, blotch purplish red dots, semi to double, 3" across, late; spreading habit, 3 ft. high. Not introduced.

'Astarte' (PI 160078; 'Osakazuki' × 'Kagaribi'): deep purplish pink, shading to reddish purple, blotch purplish red, base of tube white, 2¾–3½" across, early; erect to spreading to 6 ft. high.

'Astra' (PI 160123; *indicum* × 'Hatsushimo'): between vivid purplish red and reddish purple, blotch darker, base of tube white, 2½–3" across, early; leaves narrow; upright to spreading to 5 ft. high.

'Ave Maria' (PI 163771; 'Mucronatum' × 'Fukuju'): white, yellow green blotch, sanded or flaked reddish purple, ruffled, 2½–3" across, midseason; low broad spreading 5 ft. high.

'Aviator' (PI 163869; ('Vittata Fortunei' × 'Louise') × 'Adzuma no Hana'): white green blotch, striped red 2½", midseason; dense twiggy to 4 ft. high.

'Aztec' (PI 163906; *indicum* × 'Tamasugata'): between yellowish pink and reddish orange, blotch purplish pink dots, 3" across, late; broad spreading to, 3 ft. high. Not dependable for having a white eye or center.

'Bacchante' (PI 163898; 'Vittata Fortunei' × 'Louise'): upper petals strong purplish red, lower petals lighter, blotch purplish red dots, 2½–3" across, early; erect with ascending branches, 7 ft. high.

'Bagatelle' (PI 160115; *kaempferi* × 'Maxwell'): deep yellowish pink, sinuate margins, faint blotch, white at base of tube, 2¾–3½" across, 3 to 5 in head, early; open erect to 7 ft. high.

'Bagdad' (PI 163985; (*indicum* × 'Momozono') × (*indicum* × 'Hazel Dawson')): deep pink, blotch purplish red, 2½–3" across, midseason; vigorous upright to, 5 ft. high.

'Ballet Girl' (PI 160043; 'Vittata Fortunei' × 'Miyagimo'): deep pink, blotch purplish red, hose-in-hose, 2" across, early to midseason; upright, open habit to, 5 ft. high.

'Barchester' (PI 141808; 'Shishu' × 'Hatsushimo'): white, green dots deep in throat, double, 2" across, early; erect, to 5 ft. high. Not introduced.

'Baroque' (PI 163778; ('Lilacinum' × 'Willy') × ('Mrs. Carmichael' × 'Willy')): white, great variation of stripes and sanding of reddish pink, 2½–3" across, midseason; broad spreading to 5 ft. high.

'Beacon' (PI 160085; 'Osakazuki' × 'Kagaribi'): deep yellowish pink, effect is reddish orange, 1¾" across, midseason; 5 ft. high; erect to overarching growth.

'Berceuse' (PI 141801; 'Vittata Fortunei' × 'Warai Gishi'): between purplish and deep pink, 2–2½" across, early; broader that tall to, 5 ft. high. Not introduced.

'Bettina' (PI 182866; 'Vittata Fortunei' × 'Hinode Giri'): vivid red 1½–2" across, 2 to 4 in head, early; erect with ascending branches, to 5 ft. high.

'Bishop' (PI 160120; 'Hinode Giri' × 'Alice'): deep purplish pink, dots purplish red in blotch, underlying tone of yellow, anthers dark, 1¼–1½" across, 2 to 5 in head, midseason; erect, to 5 ft. high.

'Blizzard' (PI 163784; ('Lilacinum × 'Willy') × ('Mrs. Carmichael' × 'Willy')): white, yellow green throat, ruffled, few reddish purple stripes, 2¾–3' across; mid season; broad spreading, to 5 ft. high.

'Blushing Maid' (PI 160114; *kaempferi* × 'Maxwell'): between purplish pink and strong purplish red, 2–2½" across, sinuate margins, early; upright open habit, to 7 ft. high.

'Bohemian' (PI 163796; (*kaempferi* × 'Mucronatum') × 'Shinnyo no Tsuki'): deep purplish pink, 2½" across, mid season; broad spreading 4 ft. high.

'Boldface' (PI 163847; 'Mucronatum' × 'Keisetsu'): white center, deep purplish pink margin, red blotch, 3" across, midseason; broad spreading 4 ft. high. Remove branch sports.

'Bolivar' (PI 163928; *indicum* × 'Hazel Dawson'): strong purplish pink, blotch of small purplish red dots, 2¾" across, broad lobes, midseason; spreading habit, to 4 ft. high.

'Bonanza' (PI 163807; 'Mucronatum' × 'Kagetsu'): vivid purplish red, blotch darker, 2½" across, midseason; broad spreading, to 4 ft. high.

'Bopeep' (PI 160009; 'Vittata Fortunei' × 'Amoena'): white, tinted from margin light purplish pink, blotch, purplish pink dots, 2–2½", 2 to 4 in head, very early; erect to spreading, to 5 ft. high.

'Bountiful' (PI 113956; 'Mucronatum' × 'Keisetsu'): strong reddish purple, blotch purplish red, frilled, 3" across, midseason; broad spreading, to 4 ft. high.

'Bowman' (PI 163764; 'Osakazuki' × 'Flame'): deep pink, blotch of purplish red dots, 2–2½" across, early; dense twiggy, broader than height, to 5 ft. high.

'Brangaene' (PI 182868; 'Vittata Fortunei' × 'Alice'): light pink with yellow undertone, blotch darker, 2–2½" across, early; erect with ascending branches, to 7 ft. high.

'Bravo' (PI 163811; ('Lilacinum' × 'Willy') × ('Mrs. Carmichael' × 'Willy')): strong reddish purple, blotch purplish red, tube red, 1½" across, 2 to 4 in head, midseason; erect, to 5 ft. high.

'Bravura' (PI 163908; *indicum* × 'Tamasugata'): light purplish pink, white center with age, 2½–3" across, midseason; broader than tall, to 4 ft. high.

'Bridal Veil' (PI 160006; 'Vittata Fortunei' × 'Louise'): white, yellow green blotch, 3" across, early; open upright, to 5 ft. high.

'Buccaneer' (PI 141903; 'Hinode Giri' × 'Late Salmon'): vivid reddish orange, upper lobe darker, 2" across, 2 to 4 in head, early; erect to tall spreading, to 5 ft. high. Sunburns in open.

'Burgundy' (PI 160003; 'Vittata Fortunei' × 'Hinode Giri'): deep yellowish pink, darker margins, strong red, blotch purplish red, 2" across, early; upright, spreading with age, to 6 ft. high.

'Cadenza' (PI 163884; 'Mucronatum' × 'Shinnyo no Tsuki'): white ruffled, few stripes of reddish purple, 2" across, midseason; low, broad spreading to 4 ft. high. Remove branch sports.

'Camelot' (PI 163930; 'Lilacinum' × *indicum*): strong purplish red, margins darker, blotch darker, 2¾–3" across, early; upright spreading, to 5 ft. high.

'Campfire' (PI 163871; ('Lilacinum' × 'Willy') × ('Mrs. Carmichael' × 'Willy')): deep purplish red, tube purplish pink, 1½" across, 2 to 4 in head, midseason; dense twiggy, to 5 ft. high.

'Candlelight' (PI 141782; *indicum* × 'Azuma Shibori'): dull purplish pink, hose-in-hose, 1½" across, early; spreading, to 4 ft. high. Not introduced.

'Cantabile' (PI 163897; 'Splendens' × 'Vittata Fortunei'): white, 2–2½" across, early; broader than tall, to 5 ft. high.

'Capella' (PI 160037; *kaempferi* × 'Willy'): white, rare flakes of strong purple, irregularly hose-in-hose, 2–2½" across, early; erect, dense habit, to 6 ft. high.

'Caprice' (PI 141792; 'Splendens' × 'Vittata Fortunei'): white, rayed and flaked red, bell-shaped, 2" across, 2 to 4 in head, early; erect, to 5 ft. high.

'Captivation' (PI 160020; *indicum* × 'Momozomo'): between deep pink and yellowish pink, blotch purplish red, base of tube nearly white, hose-in-hose, 1¾–2" across, 2 to 4 in head, early; broad spreading, to 5 ft. high.

'Caraval' (PI 163806; 'Mucronatum' × 'Kagetsu'): strong purplish red, flushed darker, undertone yellow, 3" across, midseason; broad spreading, to 5 ft. high.

'Carbineer' (PI 160098; 'Jeanette' × *kaempferi*): between light strong purplish pink, undertone yellow, filaments red, 2–2½" across, early; tall, with ascending branches, to 8 ft. semi evergreen.

'Caress' (PI 141769: 'Vittata Fortunei' × 'Marta'): white center to pale pink margins, 2–2¼" across, 2 to 4 in head, early; erect to broad spreading, to 5 ft. high.

'Carmel' (PI 1417760; 'Madame Margottin' × 'Splendens'): strong purplish red, blotch red, 2" across, early; tall to spreading habit, to 5 ft. high.

'Carnival' (PI 163097; *indicum* × 'Hazel Dawson'): yellowish pink, undertone orange, blotch red, 3½–4" across, early; upright to spreading, to 4 ft. high.

'Carrara' (PI 163798; (*kaempferi* × 'Mucronatum') × 'Shinnyo no Tsuki'): white, yellow blotch, some petaloidy, 2½–3" across, midseason; dwarf broad spreading, to 2 ft. high.

'Cascade' (PI 182864; 'Willy' × 'Momozomo'): white, few flakes of purplish pink, hose-in-hose, 1½" across, 2 to 4 in head, early; upright broad spreading 4 ft. high.

'Catawba' (PI 163983; *kaempferi* × 'Fuji no Koshi'): strong reddish purple, large blotch, purplish red, 2–2½" across, late; broad spreading, to 4 ft. high.

'Cathay' (PI 160046; 'Madame Margottin' × 'Kagaribi'): deep yellowish pink, blotch of purplish red dots, 2" across, 2–4" in head, early; broad spreading, to 5 ft. high.

'Cavalier' (PI 160068; 'Kagaribi' × 'Hinode Giri'): deep yellowish pink, orange undertone, 1½–1¾" across, 2–4 in head, early; erect, dense bushy, to 6 ft. high.

'Cavatina' (PI 163791; ('Lilacinum' × 'Willy') × ('Mrs. Carmichael' × 'Willy')): white, striped reddish purple, 2¾"–3½" across, late; broad spreading, to 5 ft. high.

'Celestial' (PI 160081; 'Malvatica' × *indicum*): deep purplish pink, yellow untertone, blotch reddish, white center on older plants, 2½–2¾" across, early; stiff upright, to 4 ft. high.

'Challenger' (PI 160124; *indicum* × 'Hatsushimo'): deep yellowish pink wash of pale purple, blotch showy dark dots, 2¾–3", flat face, imbricated lobes, early; leaves narrow; erect spreading, to 5 ft. high.

'Chameleon' (PI 163825; (*kaempferi* × 'Mucronatum') × 'Kagetsu'): white, blotch yellow, few stripes purplish pink, 2–3½" across, midseason; broad spreading, to 4 ft. high.

'Chanticleer' (PI 163872; ('Lilacinum' × 'Willy') × ('Mrs. Carmichael' × 'Willy')): deep purplish red tube yellowish pink, 2" across, 2–4 in head, midseason; dense twiggy, to 5 ft. high.

'Cherry Spot' (PI 160132; 'Vittata Fortunei' × 'Osakazuki'): between brilliant purple and reddish purple, blotch reddish purple dots, 2–2½" across, rounded lobes, early; erect to spreading, to 6 ft. high.

'Chloe' (PI 160049; *simsii* × 'Mucronatum'): vivid purplish red, faint darker blotch, 2¾–3" across, early leaves pubescent; upright spreading, to 6–8 ft. high.

'Chum' (PI 163862; ('Vittata Fortunei' × 'Louise') × 'Adzuma no Hana'): white, blotch green, striped moderate red, 2" across, 2 to 4 in head, midseason; dense twiggy, to 4 ft. high. Remove branch sports.

'Cinderella' (PI 201897; 'Vittata Fortunei' × 'Louise'): white, heavily striped red, 2–2½", early, semi deciduous; tall, flat topped, to 6 ft. high.

'Cinnabar' (PI 163855; ('Vittata Fortunei' × 'Louise') × 'Adzuma no Hana'): white with stripes and sanding of purplish red, 3" across; dense twiggy, to 4 ft. high. Remove branch sports.

'Circe' (PI 182881; *simsii* × 'Mucronatum'): light purplish pink, 2–2¾" across, early; leaves pubescent; spreading, to 5 ft. high.

'Clarion' (PI 160094; *kaempferi* × 'Maxwell'): between deep yellowish pink and scarlet red, blotch inconspicuous, 2¾–3" across, early; erect, to 8 ft. high.

'Cocktail' (PI 163839; ('Lilacinum' × 'Willy') × ('Mrs. Carmichael' × 'Willy')): white, with moderate red stripes and some sports, 2" across, midseason; compact, dense, to 5 ft. high.

'Colleen' (PI 160112; *kaempferi* × 'Maxwell'): deep pink, blotch variable, 2" across, 3 to 10 in head, early; tall, open, to 7 ft. high.

'Commando' (PI 163832; (*kaempferi* × 'Mucronatum') × 'Kagetsu'): brilliant purple, blotch purplish pink, 2–2½" across, 2 to 4 in head, midseason; broad spreading, to 5 ft. high.

'Commodore' (PI 160111; 'Kagaribi' × *indicum*): vivid red, blotch purple dots, 2¾–3", early; leaves narrow; spreading, to 4 ft. high.

'Con Amore' (PI 163940; 'Osakazuki' × 'Kagaribi'): between strong and deep purplish pink, lighter margins, blotch few dots, round imbricated lobes, 2½–3" across, early; dense spreading, to 5 ft. high.

'Concordia' (PI 160106; 'Mucronatum' × *simsii*): strong purplish pink, faint blotch purplish red; leaves long narrow; errect with ascending 2" across, early; branches, to 5 ft. high.

'Conquest' (PI 163987; (*indicum* × 'Momozomo') × (*indicum* × 'Hazel Dawson')): white, few short lines of purplish red, 2½–2¾" across, midseason; leaves small; spreading, to 3 ft. high.

'Consolation' (PI 163772; 'Mucronatum' × 'Fukurokuju'): white with purple stripes, ruffled, occasionally deep pink with light center, 2½–3" across, late; broad spreading, to 5 ft. high.

'Constance' (PI 160089; 'Vittata Fortunei' × 'Osakazuki'): deep purplish pink, large blotch of darker dots, 3–3½" across, early; vigorous erect, to 6 ft. high.

'Consuela' (PI 160082; 'Malvatica' × *indicum*): deep purplish pink, lighter center, blotch not conspicuous, 2½–3", early; erect to broad spreading, to 5 ft. high.

'Content' (PI 160136; 'Malvatica' × 'Yozakura'): light purple, dots purplish red, imbricated lobes, 2¾–3"across, early; erect to broad spreading, to 5 ft. high.

'Copperman' (PI 163927; *indicum* × 'Hazel Dawson'): deep yellowish pink, shaded orange, blotch purplish pink, 2¾–3" across, overlapping lobes, late; dense spreading, to 4 ft. high.

'Coquette' (PI 160036; *indicum* × 'Momozono'): deep purplish pink, few dots of purplish red in blotch, red pistil, hose-in-hose, 2" across, early; erect to overarching habit, to 5 ft. high.

'Coralie' (PI 160017; *indicum* × 'Momozono'): deep pink, flushed yellowish, pink, blotch purplish red, irregularly hose-in-hose, 1½–1¾" across, midseason; erect to overarching habit, to 5 ft. high.

'Coral Sea' (PI 163819; (*kaempferi* × 'Mucronatum') × 'Keisetsu'): between strong and deep purplish pink, strong blotch of purplish red dots, 2½–3"across, midseason; broad spreading 4 ft. high.

'Cordial' (PI 163818; (*kaempferi* × 'Mucronatum') × 'Keisetsu'): strong purplish red, darker blotch, frilled, 2½–3" across, 2 to 4 in head, midseason; broad spreading, to 4 ft. high.

'Corsair' (PI 160138; 'Osakazuki' × 'Kagaribi'): strong purplish pink, blotch purplish red, 2½" across, early; broad spreading, to 5 ft. high.

'Corydon' (PI 160074; 'Yozakura' × 'Kagaribi'): strong purplish pink, few dots in blotch, overlapping lobes, 2–2¼" across, early; erect to broad spreading, to 4 ft. across.

'Cranford' (PI 163910; *indicum* × 'Tamasugata'): strong purplish pink, blotch slightly darker, white center in old plants, 3" across, late; spreading to 3 ft. high.

'Cream Cup' (PI 163842; ('Lilacinum' × 'Willy') × ('Mrs. Carmichael' × 'Willy')): white heavily suffused yellowish green, few red flakes, 2" across, midseason; compact dense, to 5 ft. high.

'Cremona' (PI 163901; *indicum* × 'Hazel Dawson'): deep purplish pink, blotch purplish red dots, tube yellowish, wavy margin, 3" across, late; broad spreading, to 4 ft. high.

'Crinoline' (PI 163943; 'Mucronatum' × 'Kagetsu'): strong reddish purple, frequently with white eye, ruffled, 3" midseason; broad spreading, to 5 ft. high.

'Crusader' (PI 163909; *indicum* × 'Tamasugata'): deep pink, showy blotch purplish red, imbricated, 2¾" across, late; spreading habit, to 3 ft. high.

'Cupid' (PI 163799; (*kaempferi* × 'Mucronatum') × 'Shinnyo no Tsuki'): light purple, fades lighter, 3" across, midseason; broad spreading, to 4 ft. high.

'Cygnet' (PI 163954; 'Mucronatum' × 'Shinnyo no Tsuki'): white, blotch pale yellow, 1½" across, midseason; dense twiggy, to 4 ft. high.

'Cytherea' (PI 163934; 'Malvatica' × 'Yozakura'): deep purplish pink, midseason; broader than tall, to 4 ft. high.

'Damaris' (PI 160099; 'Mrs. Carmichael' × 'Alice'): vivid purplish red, wash purplish pink, heavy dark blotch, 2–2¾" across, midseason; upright growth 6 ft. high.

'Damask' (PI 163959; 'Mucronatum' × 'Chojakuru'): white wash of greenish yellow, hose-in-hose, 2" across, midseason; broad spreading, to 4 ft. high.

'Damozel' (PI 160031; *indicum* × 'Momozono'): deep yellowish pink, blotch purplish red, base of tube white, 2" across, early; erect to overarching habit, to 5 ft. high.

'Dandy' (PI 163803; 'Mucronatum' × ('Splendens' × 'Vittata Fortunei')): vivid purplish red, reddish orange tube, 2½" across, 2 to 4 in head, midseason; upright bushy habit, to 5 ft. high.

'Daphnis' (PI 160070; *indicum* × 'Hatsushimo'): strong reddish purple, few dots, 2–2½" across, early; small narrow leaves; erect to spreading habit, to 5 ft. high.

'Darkness' (PI 163815; ('Lilacinum' × 'Willy') × ('Mrs. Carmichael' × 'Willy')): moderate red, with darker blotch, 3" across, 2 to 4 in head, midseason; compact twiggy, to 4 ft. high.

'Darling' (PI 160113; *kaempferi* × 'Maxwell'): deep purplish pink, darker dots at base, 2–2½" across, early; erect dense shrub, to 5 ft. high.

'Dauntless' (PI 163852; ('Lilacinum' × 'Willy') × ('Mrs. Carmichael' × 'Willy')): deep purplish red, base of tube reddish orange, 2" across, 2 to 4 in head, midseason; low, dense twiggy, to 2 ft. high.

'Dawning' (PI 182862; 'Mucronatum' × *simsii*): pale purplish pink, 2–2¾" across, early; leaves pubescent; spreading habit, to 5 ft. high.

'Dayspring' (PI 141780; 'Vittata Fortunei' × 'Marta'): white center shading to light purplish pink margin, blotch greenish yellow, 1¾–2" across, 2 to 4 in head, midseason; broad spreading, to 6 ft. high.

'Dazzler' (PI 163797; (*kaempferi* × 'Mucronatum') × 'Shinnyo no Tsuki'): strong purplish pink, dark blotch, frilled, 3" across, midseason; broad spreading, to 3 ft. high.

'Defiance' (PI 163870; ('Vittata Fortunei' × 'Louise') × 'Adzuma no Hana'): white, heavily striped moderate red, 2" across, 2 to 4 in head, midseason; dense twiggy, to 4 ft. high.

'Delight' (PI 160000; 'Vittata Fortunei' × 'Mucronatum'): white, flakes of reddish purple occasionaly heavy stripes to purple sports, 3–4" across, 3 to 4 in head, early; vigorous, erect to 7 ft. high.

'Delilah' (PI 163952; *indicum* × 'Hatsushimo'): deep pink, 2–2½" across, early; spreading with ascending branches, to 6 ft. high.

'Delos' (PI 141803; 'Vittata Fortunei' × 'Warai-gishi'): light purplish pink, double, 2½" across, midseason; cannot support masses of flowers, occasionally fall flowered; erect to spreading with overarching habits, to 7 ft. high, heavier texture.

'Demure' (PI 160014; *indicum* × 'Momozono'): deep purplish pink, blotch purplish pink dots, 2" across, early; erect to overarching, to 5 ft. high.

'Desire' (PI 141778; 'Mucronatum' × *simsii*): light purplish pink, toned orange, 2–2¾" across, early; spreading, up to 5 ft. high.

'Dimity' (PI 141766; 'Vittata Fortunei' × *kaempferi*): white, flaked and striped purplish red, 1½–2" across, 2 to 4 in head, early; semideciduous; upright open habit to 6 ft. high. Solid 'Divinity sport' hardier.

'Dowager' (PI 163978; 'Mucronatum' × 'Fukwokuju'): white, flaked and striped purplish red, 3" across, 2 to 4 in head, late; low compact to spreading, to 4 ft. high. Remove branch sports.

'Dragon' (PI 163874; ('Lilacinum' × 'Willy') × ('Mrs. Carmichael' × 'Willy')): vivid purplish red to purplish pink, 2" across, 2 to 4 in head, midseason; dense twiggy, up to 5 ft. high.

'Dream' (PI 160047; *simsii* × 'Mucronatum'): strong purplish pink, blotch darker dots, frilled, 2¾–3" across, early; spreading, to 6 ft. high.

'Driven Snow' (PI 163933; 'Malvatica' × 'Yozakura'): white, 3" across, late; erect to broad spreading, to 6 ft. high. Similar to 'Snowscape'.

'Duenna' (PI 160022; 'Mucronatum' × 'Vittata Fortunei'): white, numerous stripes of purplish pink, 1–1½" across, early; spreading, to 5 ft. high.

'Dulcimer' (PI 160076; 'Osakazuki' × 'Kagaribi'): deep yellowish pink, blotch purplish red dots, 2–2½" across, early; erect to spreading, to 5 ft. high.

'Echo' (PI 163895; *simsii* × 'Mucronatum'): vivid purplish red, dots of blotch not showy, 2–2¾" across, early; spreading habit, to 5 ft. high.

'Effective' (PI 160090; 'Vittata Fortunei' × 'Osakazuki'): Deep purplish pink, very faint blotch, 2½–3" across, early; upright growth, to 4 ft. high.

'Egoist' (PI 163783; ('Lilacinum' × 'Willy') × ('Mrs. Carmichael' × 'Willy')): white, few stripes and much sanding of reddish purple, 2½–3" across, late; broad spreading, to 5 ft. high.

'Elizabeth' (PI 163923; *indicum* × 'Hazel Dawson'): deep yellowish pink, heavy blotch of purplish red, 3" across, late; spreading habit, to 4 ft. high.

'Ember' (PI 163801; (*kaempferi* × 'Mucronatum') × 'Shinnyo no Tsuki')): deep purplish pink, darker blotch, yellow undertone, frilled, 3" across, midseason; broad spreading, to 4 ft. high.

'Emblem' (PI 160013; 'Hinode Giri' × 'Willy'): between vivid red and reddish orange, blotch deep sanding, 1¾–2" across, early; erect habit, to 6 ft. high.

'Enchantment' (PI 160029; *indicum* × 'Momozono'): deep pink, heavy blotch purplish red, hose-in-hose, 1½–1¾" across, early; erect to overarching growth, to 5 ft. high.

'Epicure' (PI 163907; *indicum* × 'Tamasugata'): deep pink, small blotch purplish red, late; spreading somewhat open growth, to 3 ft. high.

'Epilogue' (PI 141785) clone of PI 81661: light purplish pink, blotch and style, purplish red, 1–1¼" across, late; semievergreen, straggling growth, to 5 ft. high.

'Eros' (PI 163902; *indicum* × 'Joga'): deep pink fading lighter, small dark blotch, 2½–3" across, overlapping lobes, late; low spreading, to 3 ft. high.

'Etna' (PI 163875; ('Lilacinum' × 'Willy') × ('Mrs. Carmichael' × 'Willy')): between vivid and deep purplish red, tube pink, 2" across, midseason; dense twiggy, to 5 ft. high. Not introduced.

'Eucharis' (PI 163802; (*kaempferi* × 'Mucronatum') × 'Shinnyo no Tsuki'): white, greenish yellow blotch, frilled, 3" across, midseason; broad spreading, to 3 ft. high.

'Evangeline' (PI 160065; 'Vittata Fortunei' × 'Alice'): deep purplish pink, blotch purplish red dots, 2½–3" across, early; semideciduous, strong upright habit, to 7 ft. high.

'Evensong' (PI 160032; *indicum* × 'Momozono'): deep purplish pink, faint blotch, purplish red, 1¾–2¼" across, midseason; erect to overarching habit, to 5 ft. high.

'Everest' (PI 163953; 'Mucronatum' × 'Shinnyo no Tsuki'): white blotch pale greenish yellow, 2" across, midseason; broad spreading, to 5 ft. high.

'Fairy Bells' (PI 160075; 'Yozakura' × 'Kagaribi'): strong purplish red, few darker dots, hose-in-hose, pendant, 2–2½" across, midseason; upright to spreading habit, to 6 ft. high.

'Faith' (PI 160117; 'Jeanette' × *kaempferi*): strong purplish pink, darker blotch, imbricated, 3" across, matures lighter, early; nearly deciduous; upright open habit, to 6 ft. high.

'Fakir' (PI 163914; *indicum* × 'Hazel Dawson'): deep purplish pink, yellow undertone, blotch heavy dots of purplish red, 3" across, rounded lobes, late; spreading habit, to 4 ft. high.

'Fandango' (PI 163816; ('Lilacinum' × 'Willy') × ('Mrs. Carmichael' × 'Willy')): strong purplish pink, blotch vivid red, reverse of corolla and stamens reddish orange, 3" across, 2 to 4 in head, midseason; compact twiggy, to 4 ft. high.

'Fanfare' (PI 160021; *indicum* × 'Momozono'): deep pink, large darker blotch, irregularly hose-in-hose, 1¾–2" across, early; leaves narrow; erect to overarching habit, to 5 ft. high.

'Fantasy' (PI 141775; 'Splendens' × 'Vittata Fortunei'): white, broadly flaked and striped red, 2" across, early; spreading habit, to 4 ft. high.

'Fashion' (PI 141788; *indicum* × 'Momozono'): deep yellowish pink, blotch purplish red, dark anthers, hose-in-hose, 2" across, 2 to 4 in head, early; erect to overarching habit, to 6 ft. high.

'Favorite' (PI 160035; *indicum* × 'Momozono'): deep pink, orange undertone, heavy blotch red, irregular hose-in-hose, 1¼–1½" across, early; erect to overarching habit, to 5 ft. high.

'Fawn' (PI 163844; ('Lilacinum' × 'Willy') × ('Mrs. Carmichael' × 'Willy')): White center, purplish pink margins, 2–2½" across, midseason; broad spreading, to 5 ft. high. Remove branch sports.

'F. C. Bradford' (PI 160071; 'Hinode Giri' × 'Miltoni'): deep purplish pink, edges darker, blotch purplish red dots, 2–2½" across; spreading with ascending branches, to 5 ft. high.

'Felicity' (PI 160040; 'Fielder's White' × *kaempferi*): strong purplish pink, margins darker, blotch purplish red dots, 2¾–3" across, late midseason; erect, to 8 ft. high.

'Fenelon' (PI 141809; 'Fielder's White' × *kaempferi*): strong purlish red, blotch light olive dots; midseason; upright broad habit, to 6 ft. high.

'Festive' (PI 141779; 'Vittata Fortunei' × 'Ho Oden'): white, no blotch, sanded and striped purplish red, 2–2½", 2 to 4 in head, early; erect spreading, to 6 ft. high.

'Firedance' (PI 163835; ('Lilacinum' × 'Willy') × ('Mrs. Carmichael' × 'Willy')): strong purplish pink, purplish red spots, frilled, tendency to doubling, 2" across, 2 to 4 in head, mid to late; broad spreading, to 5 ft. high.

'Folly' (PI 163790; ('Lilacinum' × 'Willy') × ('Mrs. Carmichael' × 'Willy')): white, striped reddish purple 2¾–3" across, late; broad spreading, to 4 ft. high.

'Fountain' (PI 163913; *indicum* × 'Tamasugata'): light purplish pink, broad blotch of dark striate lines, 3" across, pointed lobes, late; spreading habit, to 3 ft. high.

'Freedom' (PI 163931; 'Vittata Fortunei' × 'Osakazuki'): deep pink, shaded yellowish pink, blotch small dots of purplish pink, 2–2½" across, broad lobes, early; moderately dense with ascending branches, to 5 ft. high.

'Frivolity' (PI 163868; ('Vittata Fortunei' × 'Louise') × 'Adzuma no Hana'): white, yellow blotch, few reddish stripes, 2½" across, 2–4 in head, midseason; dense twiggy, to 4 ft. high.

'Furbelow' (PI 163970; ('Vittata Fortunei' × 'Mucronatum') × 'Shinnyo no Tsuki'): white heavily sanded, flaked and stripes of strong red, anthers blackish, 2" across, 2–4 in head, midseason; broad spreading, to 5 ft. high. Remove branch sports.

'Futurity' (PI 163851; 'Mucronatum' × 'Chojuraku'): white, with stripes purplish pink, hose-in-hose, 2½" across, 2–4 in head, midseason; broad spreading, to 3 ft. high.

'Gaiety' (PI 141910; *indicum* × 'Hazel Dawson'): light purplish pink, blotch darker, 2–3" across, early midseason; erect to broad spreading, to 5 ft. high.

'Galathea' (PI 160097; 'Mrs. Carmichael' × 'Alice'): grayish red, few dots in blotch, 1½" across, early; erect with twiggy branching, to 5 ft. high.

'Galaxy' (PI 163786; ('Lilacinum' × 'Willy') × ('Mrs. Carmichael' × 'Willy')): white, sanding of deep purplish pink, 2½–3" across, occasionally sports reddish purple pink, white center, 2½–3" across, late; broad spreading, to 5 ft. high.

'Gallant' (PI 163866; ('Vittata' × 'Louise') × 'Adzuma no Hana'): very pale, yellowish white, few red flakes, 2½" across, midseason; dense twiggy, to 4 ft. high.

'Ganymede' (PI 182878; 'Fielder's White' × *kaempferi*): light purplish pink, 2–2½" across, early midseason; tall habit, to 6 ft. high.

'Gawain' (PI 182875; *poukhanense* × 'Modele'): light purple, blotch of distinct dark purple, shaped marks, 2–2½" across, early; nearly deciduous; broad spreading, densely twiggy, to 5 ft. high.

'Geisha' (PI 141774; 'Vittata Fortunei' × 'Miyagimo'): white, blotch yellowish green, flaked and striped reddish purple, 1½–2" across, early; tall to spreading habit, to 6 ft. high. Remove branch sports.

'Glacier' (PI 160073; 'Malvatica' × 'Yozakura'): white with faint green tone, 2½–3" across, early; leaves lustrous dark green; vigorous, erect to spreading habit, to 6 ft. high.

'Gladiator' (PI 160024; 'Vittata Fortunei' × 'Hinode Giri'): strong red, blotch purplish red dots, 1¾" across, 3 to 4 in head, early; upright with dense twigs, to 5 ft. high.

'Glamour' (PI 141908; *indicum* × 'Hazel Dawson'): strong purplish pink, 2–3" across, early; leaves narrow; erect to broad spreading, to 5 ft. high.

'Glee' (PI 163881; ('Lilacinum' × 'Willy') × ('Mrs. Carmichael' × 'Willy')): striped and flaked purplish red, very faint greenish blotch, 2–2½" across, early; broad spreading, to 5 ft. high.

'Gnome' (PI 163861; ('Vittata Fortunei' × 'Louise') × 'Adzuma no Hana'): white, blotch green, striped red, 2½" across, midseason; dense twiggy habit, to 4 ft. high.

'Goblin' (PI 163974; ('Vittata Fortunei' × 'Louise') × 'Adzumo no Hana'): white, flaked and striped red, 2" across, 2 to 4 in head, midseason; broad spreading, to 5 ft. high. Remove branch sports.

'Gorgeous' (PI 160116; 'Vittata Fortunei' × 'Maxwell'): deep yellowish pink, heavy blotch of shaped purplish pink marks, over 4" across, 3 to 4 in head, midseason; erect to spreading, to 5 ft. high.

'Grace Freeman' (PI 202128; sport of seedling from ('Vittata Fortunei' × 'Mucronatum') × 'Shinnyo no Tsuki'): vivid pink, few dark spots in blotch, 3¾–4" across, midseason; dense broad spreading, to 6 ft. high.

'Gracious' (PI 160028; *indicum* × 'Momozono'): between reddish purple and deep purplish pink, blotch darker, 2" across, early; brighter than 'Evensong'; erect to overarching branches, to 5 ft. high.

'Granat' (PI 160091; 'Vittata Fortunei' × 'Osakazuki'): moderate red, large inconspicuous blotch of purplish red dots, 2" across, early midseason; erect growth, to 6 ft. high.

'Grandam' (PI 163981; 'Mucronatum' × 'Fukuju'): white with very little sanding and few stripes of reddish purple, 3" across, ruffled margin, midseason; low twiggy habit, up to 3 ft. high.

'Grandee' (PI 160054; 'Yozakura' × 'Kagaribi'): deep pink, blotch of purplish red dots, 2¾" across, early midseason; broad spreading, to 4 ft. high.

'Greeting' (PI 141901; 'Malvatica' × *indicum*): deep pink, ruffled margin, 1¾" across, early; erect to broad spreading, to 4 ft. high.

'Grenadier' (PI 160105; 'Reddish Salmon' × *kaempferi*): moderate reddish orange, blotch purplish red dots, not conspicuous, 1¾–2" across, early, semideciduous; tall open habit, to 5 ft. high.

'Guerdon' (PI 163779; ('Lilacinum' × 'Willy') × ('Mrs. Carmichael' × 'Willy')): deep purplish pink, blotch purplish red, orange tube, 2½–3" across, often 6 lobes, midseason; low spreading habit, to 2 ft. high.

'Gypsy' (PI 160058; 'Lilacinum' × 'Willy'): between purplish red and deep purplish pink, 3–3¼" across, early; erect to spreading habit, to 8 ft. high.

'Harbinger' (PI 163794; (*kaempferi* × 'Mucronatum') × 'Shinnyo no Tsuki'): deep purplish pink, blotch purplish red, yellow tone at base of tube; 3" across, midseason; broad spreading 3 ft. high.

'Harlequin' (PI 163958; 'Mucronatum' × 'Chojuraku'): white, flaked and striped reddish purple, 2" across, overlapping lobes, 2–4 in head, midseason; broad spreading, to 5 ft. high.

'Helen Close' (PI 163961; (*kaempferi* × 'Mucronatum') × 'Shinnyo no Tsuki'): white, blotch pale yellow, fading to white, 2½–3" across, 2 to 4 in head, midseason; dense twiggy, to 4 ft. high.

'Helen Fox' (PI 163859; ('Vittata Fortunei' × 'Louise') × 'Adzuma no Hana'): moderate red flushed yellowish pink, blotch darker, margins irregularly white, 2–2½" across, midseason; dense twiggy, to 3 ft. high.

'Helen Gunning' (PI 163967; ('Vittata Fortunei' × 'Mucronatum') × 'Shinnyo no Suki'): white center, margins strong reddish purple, ruffled, 2½" across, midseason; broad spreading, to 5 ft. high. Remove branch sports.

'Herald' (PI 163980; 'Mucronatum' × 'Fukuju'): white with reddish purple stripes, distinguished by blotch of dull red dots, on upper lobes and pale reddish purple flush, 2" across, midseason; broad spreading, up to 6 ft. high. Remove branch sports.

'Hopeful' (PI 160016; *indicum* × 'Momozono'): deep purplish pink blotch inconspicuous, 1½–1¾" across, early; erect to overarching branching, to 6 ft. high.

'Horus' (PI 141798; 'Osakazuki' × 'Flame'): pale purplish pink, starry, 2–2¾" across, early; twiggy, broad topped, to 6 ft. high. Not introduced.

'Illusions' (PI 160018; *indicum* × 'Momozono'): strong purplish pink, blotch purplish red, 2½" across, early midseason; dense upright spreading, to 7 ft. high.

'Isolde' (PI 182869; 'Vittata Fortunei' × 'Alice'): moderate red, heavy conspicuous blotch, purplish red with darker dots, early midseason; vigorous with ascending branches, to 7 ft. high.

'Ivory' (PI 160060; (*kaempferi* × 'Mucronatum') × 'Mucronatum'): white, flowers 3" wide by 4", early; broad spreading, to 5 ft. high.

'Jamboree' (PI 160077; 'Osakazuki' × 'Kajaribi'): between vivid red and deep yellowish pink, faint blotch, 2–2½", early; erect, spreading habit, to 5 ft. high.

'Janet Noyes' (PI 163965; (*kaempferi* × 'Mucronatum') × 'Kagetsu'): deep purplish pink, reddish orange tube and throat, 2" across, midseason; compact twiggy, to 5 ft. high.

'Jeannin' (PI 160137; 'Osakazuki' × 'Flame'): deep purplish pink, blotch purplish red, base of tube reddish orange, 1¾"–2" across, early; wide spreading, up to 5 ft. high.

'Jessica' (PI 163918; *indicum* × 'Hazel Dawson'): strong purplish pink, small blotch of purplish red dots, 3" across, midseason; spreading habit, up to 4 ft. high.

'Jingle' (PI 182867; 'Vittata Fortunei' × 'Hinode Giri'): strong purplish pink, 1½–2" across, 2–4 in head, early; 3 ft. high.

'Joker' (PI 163826; (*kaempferi* × 'Mucronatum') × 'Kagetsu'): changing, much sanded and striped, purplish pink, 3–3½" across, midseason; broad spreading, to 4 ft. high.

'Jongleur' (PI 141797; 'Vittata Fortunei' × 'Alice'): strong purplish pink, undertone of red, blotch purplish red dots, 2–2¾" across, early; upright spreading, to 6 ft. high.

'Joya' (PI 141905; 'Mucronatum' × 'Maxwell'): light purplish pink, 2½–3" across, early; broad spreading, to 4 ft. high. Best show when mature.

'Jubilant' (PI 141781; 'Mrs. Carmichael' × 'Willy'): strong reddish brown, not purplish red, 2–2½" across, early; erect habit, to 6 ft. high.

'Jubilee' (PI 163890; (*indicum* × 'Momozono') × (*indicum* × 'Hazel Dawson')): deep purplish pink, blotch few dots of purplish red, 2–2½" across, midseason; spreading habit, up to 3 ft. high.

'Juneglow' (PI 141773; clone of PI 81661, seed collected in Japan in 1929): strong orange, 1–1¼" across, 3 to 4 in head, late; straggling habit, up to 5 ft. high.

'Kashmir' (PI 160084; 'Osakazuki' × 'Kagaribi'): deep yellowish pink, broken blotch of purplish red dots, 3" across, 3 to 5 in head, early; leaves narrow; erect spreading, to 6 ft. high.

'Kathleen' (PI 163921; *indicum* × 'Hazel Dawson'): deep yellowish pink to lighter, blotch small dots purplish red, 2½" across, late; spreading habit, to 4 ft. high.

'Katinka' (PI 182871; 'Mucronatum' "Butheana" × *indicum*): light purplish pink, lightly suffused orange, 2" across, early; spreading erect, up to 5 ft. high.

'Kenwood' (PI 141800; 'Vittata Fortunei' × 'Warai Gishi'): dark pink, double, 2–2¾" across, early; broader than tall, to 5 ft. high.

'Killarney' (PI 163792; ('Lilacinum' × 'Willy') × ('Mrs. Carmichael' × 'Willy')): white, blotch greenish yellow, few reddish purple flakes, 2¾–3¼" across, late; broad spreading, to 5 ft. high.

'Kobold' (PI 163877; ('Mucronatum' × 'Willy') × ('Mrs. Carmichael' × 'Willy')): between moderate and deep purplish red, 2" across, 2 to 4 in head, midseason; dense twiggy, up to 5 ft. high.

'Kohinoor' (PI 163885; ('Vittata Fortunei' × 'Louise') × 'Adzuma no Hana'): white, greenish yellow blotch, few reddish stripes and flakes, ruffled, 3" across, midseason; broad spreading, up to 5 ft. high.

'Allure' Glenn Dale Hybrid.
HAGER

'Allure' Glenn Dale Hybrid.
HAGER

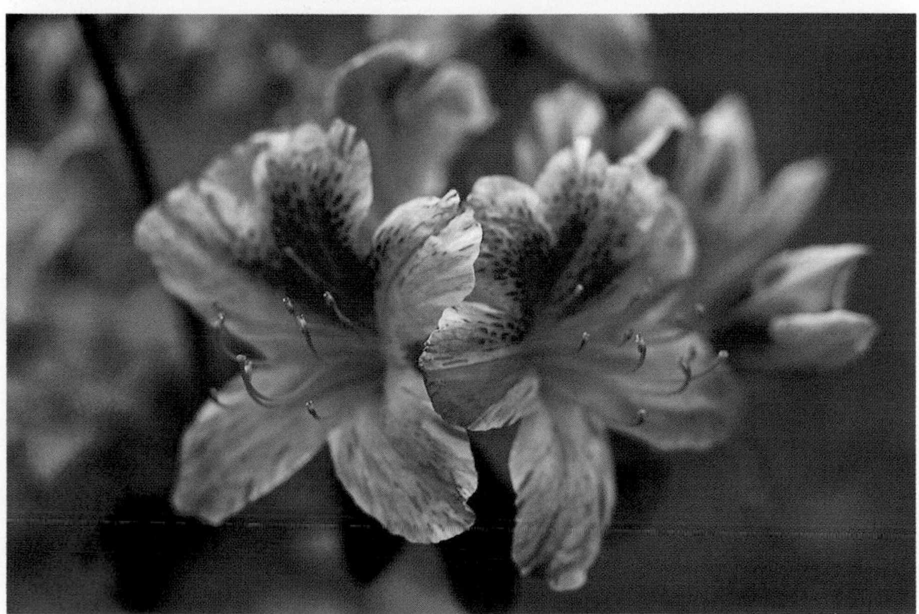

'Satrap' Glenn Dale Hybrid.
HARDING

Plate 82

'Cinderella' Glenn Dale Hybrid. HARDING

'Epicure' Glenn Dale Hybrid. HARDING

'Rhapsody' Glenn Dale Hybrid. SAUER

'Advance' Glenn Dale Hybrid. HARDING

'Glacier' Glenn Dale Hybrid. GALLE

'Fawn' Glenn Dale Hybrid. SAUER

'Pippin' Glenn Dale Hybrid. SAUER

Plate 84

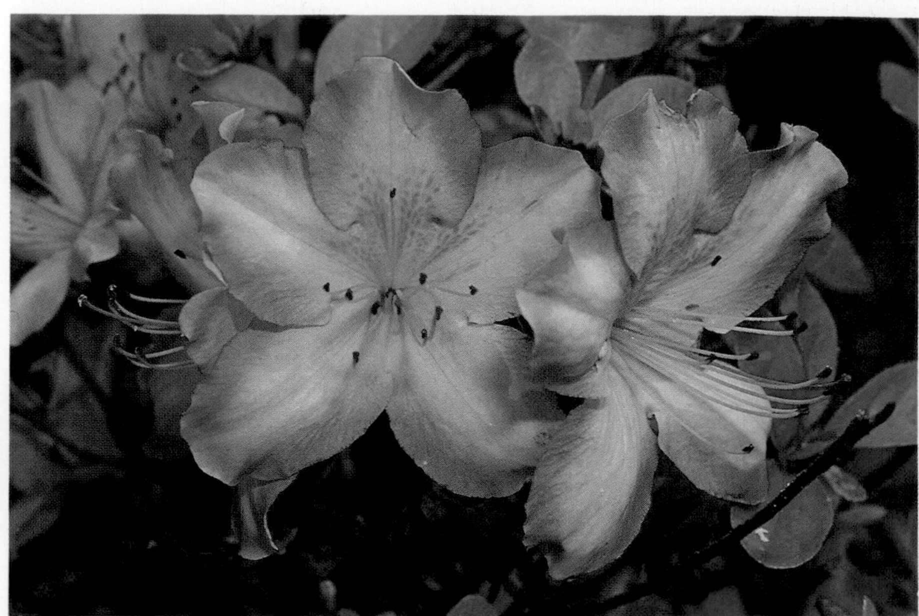

'Grace Freeman' Glenn Dale Hybrid. SAUER

'Gypsy' Glenn Dale Hybrid. B. S. HARDING

'Acrobat' Glenn Dale Hybrid. SAUER

'Ben Morrison' Glenn Dale seedling. Very popular and excellent plant in memory of a great horticulturist and friend. GALLE

'Refrain' Glenn Dale Hybrid. GALLE

'Gorgeous' Glenn Dale Hybrid. GALLE

Plate 86

'Zephyr' Glenn Dale Hybrid. HARDING

'B.Y. Morrison' parentage unknown, named by Henry Hohman. MILLER

'Saint James' Back Acres Hybrid. GALLE

'Keepsake' Back Acres Hybrid. STEWART

'Red Tip' Back Acres Hybrid. STEWART

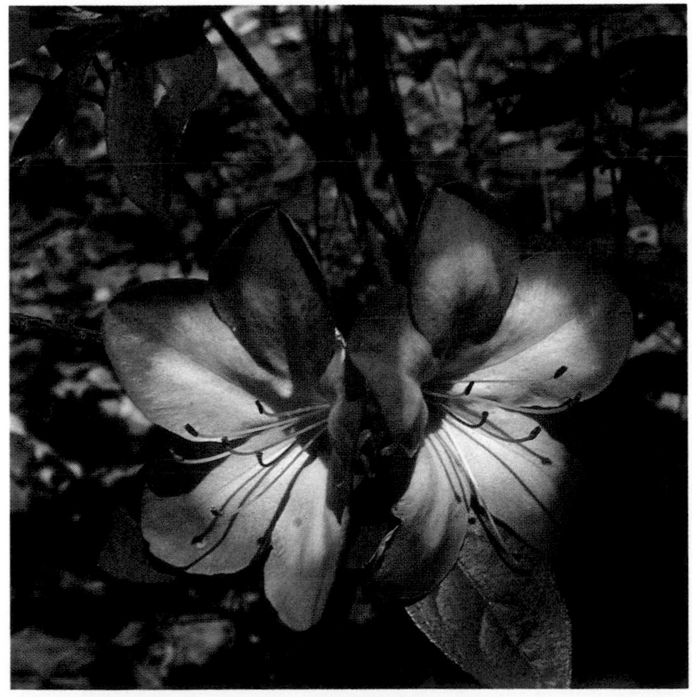
'Elsie Norfleet' Back Acres Hybrid. GALLE

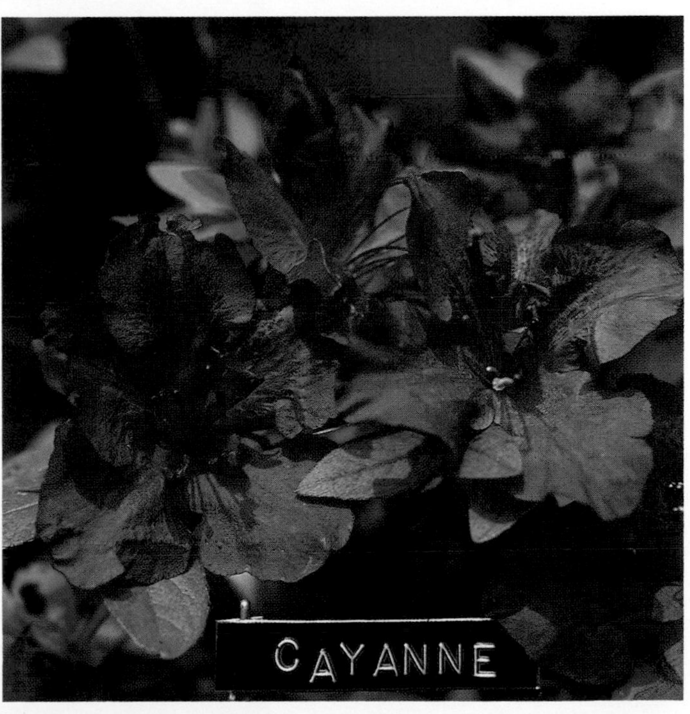

'Cayenne' Back Acres Hybrid. STEWART

Plate 88

'Marian Lee' Back Acres Hybrid. STEWART

'Spring Bonnet' Back Acres Hybrid. STEWART

'Margret Douglas' Back Acres Hybrid. GALLE

'Lacquer' (PI 163856; ('Vittata Fortunei' × 'Louise') × 'Adzuma no Hana'): white, with stripes and sanding moderate red, 3" across, early midseason; dwarf dense twiggy, up to 3 ft. high.

'Ladylove' (PI 160131; 'Vittata Fortunei' × 'Osakazuki'): between light and strong purplish pink, darker margins, blotch purplish red dots, 3" across, early; erect to wide spreading, to 6 ft. high.

'Leonore' (PI 163922; *indicum* × 'Hazel Dawson'): strong purplish pink to off white at base of tube, blotch shaped purplish red dots, 2" across, early midseason; spreading, to 4 ft. high.

'Lillie Maude' (PI 163968; ('Vittata Fortunei' × 'Mucronatum') × 'Shinnyo no Tsuki'): strong reddish purple, frilled, 3" across, late; broad spreading, to 5 ft. high.

'Limerick' (PI 141767; 'Vittata Fortunei' × *kaempferi*): white, striped purplish red, 1½–2" across, 2 to 5 in head, early; semideciduous; upright open, to 6 ft. high.

'Litany' (PI 160083; 'Malvatica' × *indicum*): deep purplish pink, blotch darker dots 2–2¾" across, early; dense twiggy, broader than tall, to 5 ft. high.

'Louise Dowdle' (PI 163969; ('Vittata Fortunei' × 'Mucronatum') × 'Shinnyo no Tsuki'): strong reddish purple, blotch purplish red, produced unstable sports with white centers, 3" across, late; broad to wide spreading, to 5 ft. high.

'Loveliness' (PI 160033; 'Fielder's White' × *kaempferi*): strong purplish pink, pale yellow undertone, to make vivid pink, ruffled, 2–2¾" across, midseason; leaves narrow; erect with ascending branches, to 6 ft. high.

'Lucette' (PI 160055; 'Yozakura' × 'Kagaribi'): strong, reddish purple, blotch purplish red dots, base of tube yellowish, wavy, 2" across, early midseason; erect habit, to 3 to 4 ft. high.

'Lullaby' (PI 141794; 'Willy' × 'Momozono'): deep purplish pink, blotch purplish red, hose-in-hose, 1½" across, early; upright broad spreading, to 4 ft. high.

'Luminary' (PI 163823; (*kaempferi* × 'Mucronatum') × 'Keisetsu'): strong purplish red, throat purplish pink, yellow base of tube, often 6 lobes, 2–2¾" across, midseason; broad spreading, to 4 ft. high.

'Luna' (PI 201896; *kaempferi* × 'Shinnyo no Tsuki'): vivid purplish red, with darker blotch and white eye, 3½" across, late; spreading habit, up to 5 ft. high.

'Lustre' (PI 141802; 'Vittata Fortunei' × 'Warai Gishi'): deep purplish pink, 2–2½" across, early midseason; erect to spreading, up to 5 ft. high.

'Lyric' (PI 163891; (*indicum* × 'Monozono') × ('Osakazuki' × 'Flame')): white, greenish yellow blotch, 2½–3" across, midseason; broad spreading, to 5 ft. high.

'Madcap' (PI 163973; ('Vittata Fortunei' × 'Louise') × 'Adzuma no Hana'): white, flaked and striped, moderate red, with yellow tone, 2" across, 2 to 4 in head, midseason; broad spreading, to 5 ft. high.

'Madeira' (PI 160093; 'Vittata Fortunei' × 'Osakazuki'): strong purplish pink, darker spots in blotch, anthers brown, funnel shaped, 3" across, early; vigorous, erect to eventually spreading, to 7 ft. high.

'Madrigal' (PI 163096; *indicum* × 'Momozono'): deep yellowish pink, flushed red, blotch purplish red, 3½" across, early; early; leaves slender; vigorous spreading habit, up to 3½ ft. high.

'Magic' (PI 141789; *indicum* × 'Momozono'): deep yellowish pink, blotch purplish red, irregular hose-in-hose, 1¾" across, 2 to 5 in head, early midseason; erect to overarching branches, to 5 ft. high.

'Mandarin' (PI 163986; *indicum* × (*indicum* × 'Hazel Dawson')): deep pink, blotch purplish red dots, 2½–2¾", midseason; spreading habit, to 3 ft. high.

'Manhattan' (PI 163917; *indicum* × 'Hazel Dawson'): between deep purplish pink and reddish purple, blotch purplish red, 2½" across, late; spreading habit, to 4 ft. high.

'Marionette' (PI 160066; 'Vittata Fortunei' × 'Alice'): deep purplish pink, shading to deep pink on margins, blotch purplish red, overlapping lobes, 1½–2" across, early; vigorous upright growth, to 8 ft. high.

'Marjorie' (PI 163924; *indicum* × 'Hazel Dawson'): deep puplish pink, blotch purplish red, 3" across, late; spreading habit, up to 4 ft. high.

'Marmora' (PI 160051; 'Madame Margottin' × 'Warai Goa') white, occasionally has red stripes, hose-in-hose, 2–2½" across, 2 to 4 in head, early; erect to spreading habit, up to 7 ft. high.

'Martha Hitchcock' (PI 163955; 'Mucronatum' × 'Shinnyo no Tsuki'): white, with reddish purple margins, 3" across, early midseason; broad spreading, to 4 ft. high.

'Marvel' (PI 160007; 'Vittata Fortunei' × 'Maxwell'): deep purplish pink, blotch purplish red, 3–3½" across, early; erect to broad spreading, to 5 ft. high.

'Mary Helen' (PI 163888; ('Mucronatum' × 'Vittata Fortunei') × 'Kagetsu'): white, greenish yellow blotch, anthers brown, 2" across, midseason; broad spreading, to 5 ft. high.

'Mary Margaret' (PI 163920; *indicum* × 'Hazel Dawson'): deep yellowish pink, heavy blotch purplish red dots, lobes imbricated, 3" across, late; spreading habit, to 4 ft. high.

'Mascot' (PI 160039; 'Alice' × 'Vittata Fortunei'): deep yellowish pink, blotch purplish red, 2–2½" across, 2 to 4 in head, early; vigorous upright growth, to 8 ft. high.

'Masquerade' (PI 163963; (*kaempferi* × 'Mucronatum') × 'Kagetsu'): white, sanded, flaked and striped reddish purple, 2½" across, midseason; low spreading, compact twiggy, to 3 ft. high.

'Masterpiece' (PI 163821; (*kaempferi* × 'Mucronatum') × 'Keisetsu'): deep purplish pink, blotch purplish red, 3–3½" across, midseason; broad spreading, to 4 ft. high.

'Matins' (PI 182883; (*kaempferi* × 'Mucronatum') × 'Mucronatum'): very pale violet, 2–2" across; early; spreading, up to 5 ft. high.

'Mavis' (PI 163962; (*kaempferi* × 'Mucronatum') × 'Keisetsu'): strong purplish red, blotch darker, tube yellowish, stamens exserted, 2" across, midseason; low spreading, compact twiggy, up to 3 ft. high.

'Mavourneen' (PI 141768; 'Vittata Fortunei' × 'Omurasaki'): light purplish pink, 2–2½" across, 2 to 4 in head, early; erect, eventually broading, to 5 ft. high.

'Mayflower' (PI 141793; 'Willy' × 'Momozono'): vivid pink, blotch few purplish red dots, hose-in-hose, 1½–2" across, early midseason; erect to overarching habit, to 5 ft. high.

'Medea' (PI 182882; 'Vittata Fortunei' × HEA #34): light reddish purple, 1½–2" across, 2 to 4 in head, early; full erect habit, up to 5 ft.

'Megan' (PI 163900; *indicum* × 'Hazel Dawson'): deep purplish pink, blotch purplish dots, 2¾–3" across, late; broad spreading, dense twiggy, to 5 ft. high.

'Melanie' (PI 141783; *indicum* × 'Azuma Shibori'): light purplish pink, blotch, few purplish red dots, hose-in-hose, 1½" across, early; upright spreading, to 5 ft. high.

'Memento' (PI 163977; ('Lilacinum' × 'Willy') × ('Mrs. Carmichael' × 'Willy')): white heavily sanded, striped and flaked, reddish purple, 2" across, 2 to 4 in head, midseason; dwarf spreading, compact twiggy, to 2 ft. high. Remove branch sports.

'Merlin' (PI 182876; *poukhanense* × 'Modele'): light reddish purple, 2½–3" across, midseason; nearly deciduous; broad spreading densely twigged, to 5 ft. high.

'Meteor' (PI 163804; 'Mucronatum' × 'Kagetsu'): between strong reddish purple and purple red, red tube, frilled, 3" across, midseason; broad spreading to 4 ft. high.

'Minstrel' (PI 16008; 'Vittata Fortunei' × 'Willy'): strong red, blotch purplish red, 3" across, 3 to 5 in head; early; vigorous spreading, to 6 ft. high.

'Minuet' (PI 141772; 'Vittata Fortunei' × 'Amoena'): white, greenish yellow blotch, occasional purple line or dot, crinkled petals, early; tall open habit, to 6 ft. high.

'Modesty' (PI 160048; *simsii* × 'Mucronatum'): vivid purplish red, flushed purplish pink from center, 2½–3" across, early; erect slighty spreading, to 5 ft. high.

'Moira' (PI 163843; ('Lilacinum' × 'Willy') × ('Mrs. Carmichael' × 'Willy')): white, heavy sanded, striped and sectioned, moderate red, 2" across, midseason; dense compact, up to 5 ft. high.

'Moonbeam' (PI 163836; ('Lilacinum' × 'Willy') × ('Mrs. Carmichael' × 'Willy')): white, some frilling on margins, 4–5" across, midseason; broad spreading, to 5 ft. high.

'Moonstone' (PI 163768; 'Mucronatum' × 'Fukurokuju'): white, greenish yellow throat, 2½–3" across, late; broad spreading, to 5 ft. high. Remove branch sports.

'Morgana' (PI 182877; 'Fielder's White' × *kaempferi*): light purplish pink, 2–2¾" across, early midseason; nearly deciduous; broad spreading, to 6 ft. high.

'Morning Star' (PI 160062; 'Vittata Fortunei' × 'Hinodegiri'): deep purplish pink, yellowish undertone, 2" across, early; erect, slighty spreading, to 6 ft. high.

'Mother of Pearl' (PI 160127; 'Fielder's White' × 'Exquisite'): white, with light purplish pink margin, blotch few reddish purple dots, irregularly hose-in-hose, 1½–1¾" across, early; erect to somewhat spreading, to 6 ft. high.

'Motley' (PI 163975; ('Mucronatum' × 'Vittata Fortunei') × 'Kagetsu'): white, sanded and striped reddish purple, blotch greenish yellow 2" across, midseason; compact twiggy habit, up to 3 ft. high.

'Mountebank' (PI 163911; *indicum* × 'Tamasugata'): strong purplish pink, blotch darker dots, wavy, 3" across, late; spreading with ascending branches, to 3 ft. high.

'Muscadine' (PI 160122; *poukhanense* × 'Modele'): brilliant purple to paler, blotch distinct shaped reddish purple, 3½–3¾" across, imbricated; early midseason; semi to nearly deciduous; broad spreading, to 6 ft. high.

'Nativity' (PI 160045; (*indicum* × 'Momozono') × ('Osakazuki' × 'Flame')): white, pale yellow greenish blotch, 2–2½" across, early midseason; spreading habit, to 5 ft. high.

'Naxos' (PI 141804; 'Vittata Fortunei' × 'Warai Gishi'): light purplish pink, 2–2¾" across, early midseason; broader than tall, to 5 ft. high.

'Nectar' (PI 160088; 'Vittata Fortunei' × 'Osakazuki'): deep yellowish pink, pale at edges, 2½–2¾"; early; erect eventually spreading, to 5 ft. high.

'Nerissa' (PI 160103; *indicum* × 'Momozono'): strong purplish pink, lighter edges, blotch purplish pink dots, yellow undertone, 1½–1¾" across, early midseason; erect to eventually overarching, to 4 ft. high.

'Niagara' (PI 163853; ('Lilacinum' × 'Willy') × ('Mrs. Carmichael' × 'Willy')): white, yellow green blotch, frilled, 2½" across, midseason; dense twiggy habit, up to 3 ft. high.

'Niphetos' (PI 163769; 'Mucronatum' × 'Fukurokuju'): white, blotch yellow green, few stripes reddish purple, late; broad spreading, to 5 ft. high.

'Nobility' (PI 163880; ('Lilacinum' × 'Willy) × ('Mrs. Carmichael' × 'Willy'): light purple, with irregular white margin, heavy blotch purplish pink dots, occasional purplish stripe, 2½" across, late; broad spreading, to 4 ft. high.

'Nocturne' (PI 163950; 'Mucronatum' × 'Shinnyo no Tsuki'): between vivid and deep purplish red, blotch darker, tube reddish orange, 3" across, early midseason; broad spreading, to 5 ft. high.

'Noreen' (PI 160102; *indicum* × 'Azuma Shibori'): strong purplish pink, blotch dark purplish red, hose-in-hose, 1¾–2" across, 2–5 in head, early; spreading habit, to 5 ft.

'Novelty' (PI 163944; 'Mucronatum' × 'Kagetsu'): white, blotch yellow green, light shading and few stripes, reddish purple, 2" across, early midseason; dense twiggy, to 4 ft. high.

'Nubian' (PI 163812; ('Lilacinum' × 'Willy') × ('Mrs. Carmichael' × 'Willy')): moderate purplish red, blotch dark reddish brown, 1½" across, color fades in sun; 2 to 4 in head, midseason; low growing, compact twiggy, to 3 ft. high.

'Omen' (PI 202127; (*indicum* × 'Momozono') × ('Osakazuki' × 'Flame')): white, blotch yellow green, 2–2½" across, midseason; spreading, up to 5 ft. high.

'Opera' (PI 141911; *indicum* × 'Momozono'): deep yellowish pink, small blotch of red dots, irregular hose-in-hose, 1½" across, early midseason; erect to eventually overarching habit, to 5 ft. high.

'Oracle' (PI 160107; *indicum* × 'Mikawa Murasaki'): strong purplish pink, blotch purplish red dots, 2½–3", early; wide spreading, to 5 ft. high.

'Oriflamme' (PI 163781; ('Lilacinum' × 'Willy') × ('Mrs. Carmichael' × 'Willy')): vivid purplish red, irregular white margin, blotch of darker dots, 2½–3" across, late; broad spreading to 5 ft. high. Remove branch sports.

'Orison' (PI 163979; 'Mucronatum' × 'Fukuju'): white, flaked and few stripes of reddish purple, 2½" across, late; broad spreading, to 5 ft. high.

'Orpheus' (PI 160001; 'Malvatica' × *indicum*): light purplish pink, 2" across, early midseason; broad spreading, to 5 ft. high. Not introduced.

'Padre' (PI 160041; 'Mrs. Carmichael' × 'Willy'): strong reddish purple, 2–2½" across, sinuate margins, early; erect habit, to 7 ft. high.

'Paladin' (PI 163948; 'Mucronatum' × 'Shinnyo no Tsuki'): vivid reddish purple, ruffled, 2½" across, late; broad spreading 5 ft. high.

'Paprika' (PI 163838; ('Lilacinum' × 'Willy') × ('Mrs. Carmichael' × 'Willy')): white with moderate red stripes and flakes, green blotch; 2" across, midseason; compact dense habit, to 5 ft. high; produces numerous unstable sports of solid red. Remove branch sports.

'Parade' (PI 163822; (*kaempferi* × 'Mucronatum') × 'Keisetsu'): vivid purplish red, blotch darker, tube reddish, 3–3½" across, midseason; broad spreading, to 4 ft. high.

'Paradise' (PI 160012; *indicum* × 'Asuma Shibori'): deep yellowish pink, wide blotch of purplish red dots, hose-in-hose, 2" across, 2 to 5 in head, early midseason; erect to overarching growth, to 5 ft. high.

'Pastel' (PI 141790; 'Vittata Fortunei' × 'Kyu Miyagimo'): white, few stripes purplish pink, dots of purplish red on upper lobe, hose-in-hose, 1½–2" across, 2 to 4 in head, early; upright with ascending branches, to 6 ft. high.

'Patriot' (PI 163787; ('Lilacinum' × 'Willy') × ('Mrs. Carmichael' × 'Willy')): white, greenish blotch, few stripes reddish purple, 2¾–3" across, late; broad spreading, to 5 ft. high.

'Pearl Bradford' (PI 163904; *indicum* × 'Johga'): strong purplish pink, blotch purplish red dots, 3" across, late; broad spreading, to 4 ft. high.

'Peerless' (PI 160104; *indicum* × 'Momozono'): deep pink, darker center, blotch reddish, irregular hose-in-hose, 1¾" across, early midseason; erect to over arching habit, to 5 ft. high.

'Peter Pan' (PI 163941; (*indicum* × 'Momozono'): strong purplish pink, reddish undertone, faint blotch, starry, 1½–1¾", early midseason; wide spreading and over arching, to 5 ft. high.

'Phoebe' (PI 182874; *indicum* × 'Hazel Dawson'): deep pink, flushed red, blotch purplish pink, 2½–3" across, early midseason; broad spreading, to 4 ft. high.

'Picador' (PI 141899; 'Osakazuki' × 'Kagaribi'): deep yellowish pink, flushed reddish orange, heavy blotch of red dots, 2–2½" across, early midseason; broad spreading, to 4 ft. high.

'Picotee' (PI 163834; (*kaempferi* × 'Mucronatum') × 'Kagetsu'): white center, reddish purple edge, 2" across, midseason; broad spreading, to 4 ft. across. Cut out self colored sports.

'Pied Piper' (PI 163763; 'Vittata Fortunei' × 'Louise'): white, flushed pale purplish pink, stripes and flakes purplish pink, blotch purplish red dots, usually 6 petals, 2¾–3" across, early; dense twiggy, compact, to 5 ft. high. Remove branch sports.

'Pilgrim' (PI 141904; 'Mucronatum' × 'Maxwell'): light purplish pink, blotch not showy, 2–2½" across, early; broad spreading, to 4 ft. high.

'Pinkie' (PI 160092; 'Vittata Fortunei' × 'Osakazuki'): strong purplish pink, blotch purplish red dots, faint yellow suffusion, 2½" across, early midseason; wide branching habit, to 6 ft. high.

'Pink Star' (PI 163916; *indicum* × 'Hazel Dawson'): deep yellowish pink, blotch purplish red, narrow lobes, 2½" across; early, spreading habit, to 4 ft. high.

'Pinocchio' (PI 163971; ('Vittata Fortunei' × 'Louise') × 'Adzuma'): white with stripes of vivid red, 2–2½" across, early midseason; dense twiggy habit, up to 5 ft. high. Remove branch sports.

'Pinto' (PI 163840; ('Lilacinum' × 'Willy') × ('Mrs. Carmichael' × 'Willy')): white, stripes and flakes, moderate red, 2½" across, midseason; compact dense, to 5 ft. high. Remove branch sports.

'Pippin' (PI 163937; 'Osakazuki' × 'Kagaribi'): between deep pink and yellowish pink, base of tube white, starry, 2–2½" across, early; leaves narrow; erect to spreading, to 5 ft. high.

'Pirate' (PI 141787; *indicum* × 'Momozono'): vivid red, heavy blotch darker, irregular hose-in-hose, 1¾–2" across, early midseason; erect to over arching habit, to 6 ft. high.

'Pixie' (PI 141777; 'Vittata Fortunei' × 'Miyagimo'): white, central rays of purplish red, blotch purplish red, occasional stripes, 1¾–2½" across, early; broad spreading, to 5 ft. high.

'Polar Sea' (PI 163795; (*kaempferi* × 'Mucronatum') × 'Shinnyo no Tsuki'): white, yellow green blotch, frilled, 3" across, midseason; broad spreading, to 3 ft. high.

'Polonaise' (PI 163946 'Mucronatum' × 'Kagetsu'): white, yellow green blotch, very rare reddish purple stripes, 2" across, early midseason; broad spreading, to 5 ft. high.

'Pontiff' (PI 141795; *kaempferi* × 'Maxwell'): deep yellowish pink to red, blotch purplish pink dots, 2–2½" across, 2 to 4 in head, early; erect to wide spreading, to 6 ft. high. Not introduced.

'Portent' (PI 182865 'Vittata Fortunei' × 'HEA #34'): white, flaked reddish purple, 1–1½" across, 2–4 in head, early midseason; erect with ascending branches, to 4 to 5 ft. high.

'Prelate' (PI 160052; *kaempferi* × 'Maxwell'): strong purplish pink, few purplish red dots, some 6 petals, 2½" across, early; dense, with strong ascending branches, to 6 ft. high.

'Presto' (PI 163867; ('Vittata Fortunei' × 'Louise') × 'Adzuma no Hana'): heavily striped and sanded red, 2½" across, 2 to 4 in head, midseason; dense twiggy, up to 4 ft. high.

'Prodigal' (PI 163774; ('Lilacinum' × 'Willy') × ('Mrs. Carmichael' × 'Willy')): white, sanded and striped reddish purple; occasional sports of light purple, white edges, 2¾–3" across, late; low spreading, to 3 ft. high.

'Progress' (PI 163957; 'Mucronatum' × 'Keisetsu'): vivid purplish red, some with white centers, 2" across, early midseason; dense twiggy, to 4 ft. high.

'Prosperity' (PI 163976; ('Mucronatum' × 'Vittata Fortunei') × 'Kagetsu'): strong reddish purple, 2½–3" across, early midseason; dense round top, to 5 ft. high.

'Prudence' (PI 160034; *indicum* × 'Momozono'): deep purplish pink, 2 to 4 in head, early midseason; erect to over arching branches, to 5 ft. high.

'Puck' (PI 163972; ('Vittata Fortunei' × 'Louise') × 'Adzuma no Hana'): white, sanded and striped, grey red, blotch greenish yellow, 2½–3" across, 2 to 4 in head, midseason; broad spreading, to 5 ft. high. Remove branch sports.

'Punchinello' (PI 163827; (*kaempferi* × 'Mucronatum') × 'Kagetsu'): white, sanded purplish pink, frilled, 3–3½" across, midseason; broad spreading, to 4 ft. high.

'Quakeress' (PI 160002; 'Mucronatum' × 'Vittata Fortunei'): white, few flakes, reddish purple, many different flowers, 2–2¾" across, 2 to 7 in head, early; erect to spreading, to 6 ft. high.

'Quest' (PI 182872; 'Mucronatum' × 'Alice'): pale purplish pink, 2½–3" across, early; broad spreading, to 4 ft. high.

'Radiance' (PI 163800; (*kaempferi* × 'Mucronatum') × 'Shinnyo no Tsuki'): strong purplish pink, blotch darker, frilled, 3" across, midseason; broad spreading, up to 3 ft. high.

'Ranger' (PI 141807; 'Shishu' × 'Hatsushimo'): white slight yellow green, double, 2–2½" across, early midseason; erect, to 5 ft. high.

'Red Bird' (PI 160010; 'Mrs. Carmichael' × 'Alice'): vivid red, blotch purplish red dots, 2–2½" across, early; semievergreen, upright slow growth, to 5 ft. high.

'Red Hussar' (PI 160118; 'Mrs. Carmichael' × 'Willy'): deep purplish pink, blotch few dots, base of tube reddish orange, 1¼–1½" across, 2 to 4 in head, early; erect with broad top, to 5 ft. high.

'Red Robe' (PI 160038 'Vittata Fortunei' × 'Koraini'): strong red, large blotch purplish red dots, 2¾" across, early; vigorous upright growth, to 5 ft. high.

'Refrain' (PI 163762; 'Vittata Fortunei' × 'Miyagimo'): margins white, suffused purplish pink, few stripes, purplish pink, dark blotch dots, hose-in-hose, 1¾–2" across, early; tall, well branched, to 7 ft. high.

'Refulgence' (PI 160096; 'Mrs. Carmichael' × 'Willy'): deep purplish pink, blotch purplish red, faint yellow tinge at base, 1½–1¾" across, early; leaves narrow; dwarf twiggy habit to 3 ft. high.

'Regina' (PI 163925; *indicum*' × 'Hazel Dawson'): strong purplish pink, small blotch purplish red, 2¾" across, late; spreading habit, to 4 ft. high.

'Remembrance' (PI 141909; *indicum* × 'Hazel Dawson'): purplish red, blotch tiny purplish pink dots, early midseason; erect to broad spreading, to 5 ft. high.

'Requiem' (PI 163945; 'Mucronatum' × 'Kagetsu'): white, yellow green blotch, very rare reddish stripes, 2" across, early midseason; dense twiggy, up to 4 ft. high.

'Revery' (PI 141902; 'Mucronatum' × *indicum*): light purplish pink, 2–2½" across, early midseason; erect to broad spreading to 4 ft. high.

'Reward' (PI 182873; 'Mucronatum' × 'Alice'): pale purplish pink, 2½–3" across, early; broad spreading, to 4 ft. high.

'Rhapsody' (PI 163805 'Mucronatum' × 'Kagetsu'): light purplish pink, blotch darker, frilled, 3" across, midseason; broad spreading, to 4 ft. high.

'Rising Sun' (PI 160133 'Vittata Fortunei' × 'Osakazuki'): strong purplish pink, margins darker, blotch small dots, 3–3½" across, early; erect to spreading habit, to 6 ft. high.

'Robinhood' (PI 160086; 'George Franc' × 'Yae Shojo'): strong purplish pink, heavy dotting in blotch, 3½–4" across, early; upright habit, to 5 ft. high.

'Rogue' (PI 163808; 'Mucronatum' × 'Kagetsu'): white, yellow green blotch, few fine flakes of purplish pink, 3" across, midseason; broad spreading, to 5 ft. high.

'Romance' (PI 141784; *indicum* × 'Azuma Shibori'): light purplish pink, hose-in-hoes, 1½" across, early; upright spreading to 5 ft. high.

'Rosalie' (PI 163919; *indicum* × 'Hazel Dawson'): strong reddish purple, washed over with yellowish pink, blotch shaped purplish dots, 3" across; late; spreading habit, to 4 ft. high.

'Rose Ash' (PI 163939; 'Vittata Fortunei' × 'Osakazuki'): deep pink to yellowish pink, blotch darker, 2½–3" across, late; erect to spreading habit, to 4 ft. high.

'Roselight' (PI 182861; *simsii* × 'Mucronatum'): clear pink, 2–2¾" across, early; spreading, up to 5 ft. high.

'Rosette' (PI 160135; 'Vittata Fortunei' × 'Warai Gishi'): light purplish pink, blotch not showy, double sometimes semidouble, 3½–4" across, early midseason; upright habit, to 5 ft. high.

'Roundelay' (PI 163767; 'Mucronatum' × 'Fukuju'): white, few stripes of reddish purple, 2¾–3" across, late; low, broad spreading, up to 3 ft. high.

'Safrano' (PI 163850; 'Mucronatum' × 'Keisetsu'): white, yellow green on upper lobe, 3½" across, midseason; broad open spreading, to 5 ft. high.

'Saga' (PI 163793; (*kaempferi* × 'Mucronatum') × 'Shinnyo no Tsuki'): deep purplish pink, strong purplish red blotch frilled, 3" across, late; broad spreading, to 3 ft. high.

'Sagittarius' (PI 163905; *indicum* × 'Joga'): vivid pink, orange undertone, white at base of tube, blotch darker, 3" across, late; dense broad spreading, to 3 ft. high.

'Sambo' (PI 163873; ('Lilacinum' × 'Willy') × ('Mrs. Carmichael' × 'Willy')): moderate to dark purplish red, 2" across, 2 to 4 in head, midseason; dense twiggy habit, to 5 ft. high.

'Samite' (PI 141791; 'Vittata Fortunei' × 'Kyu Miyagimo'): white, irregular hose-in-hose, 2" across, 2 to 4 in head; late; upright open habit, to 7 ft. high.

'Samson' (PI 163926; *indicum* × 'Hazel Dawson'): deep purplish pink, yellow undertone, darker blotch, 3" across, late; spreading habit, to 4 ft. high.

'Sappho' (PI 160042; 'Mrs. Carmichael' × 'Willy'): vivid purplish red, blotch darker, 2–2½" across, 3–5 in head, early; upright with spreading crown, to 6 ft. high.

'Sarabande' (PI 163789; ('Lilacinum' × 'Willy') × ('Mrs. Carmichael' × 'Willy')): white center edges of purplish pink, 2¾–3" across, late; broad spreading, to 5 ft. high.

'Satin Robe' (PI 141786; *indicum* × 'Momozono'): between vivid and deep pink, heavy blotch of purplish red, hose-in-hose, 2½" across, 2 to 4 in head, early midseason; leaves narrow; erect to overarching, to 5 ft. high.

'Satrap' (PI 201898; 'Vittata Fortunei' × 'Louise'): exactly like 'Cinderella', with lighter stripes, for peppermint effect, early; tall, flat topped, to 4 ft. high.

'Satyr' (PI 163809; 'Mucronatum' × 'Kagetsu'): white, with purplish red flakes, almost yellow blotch, 3" across, midseason; broad spreading, to 5 ft. high.

'Scherzo' (PI 163770; 'Mucronatum' × 'Fukurokuju'): white, with purple stripes, 2½–3" across, occasional sport pale purple center and darker margin, late; broad spreading, to 5 ft. high.

'Scholar' (PI 163782; ('Lilacinum' × 'Willy') × ('Mrs. Carmichael' × 'Willy')): white, green botch, very fine light purple stripes, 2½–3" across, late; broad spreading, to 5 ft. high.

'Scout' (PI 163938; 'Malvatica' × *indicum*): light purplish pink, 2" across, early; broader than tall, up to 5 ft. high.

'Seafoam' (PI 163837; ('Lilacinum' × 'Willy') × ('Mrs. Carmichael' × 'Willy')): white, yellow green blotch, frilled, 3" across, midseason; to broad, low growing, to 3 ft. high.

'Seashell' (PI 163915; *indicum* × 'Hazel Dawson'): strong purplish pink, almost white at base of tube, 3" across, late; spreading with ascending branches, to 4 ft. high.

'Sebastian' (PI 160044; 'Vittata Fortunei' × 'Kyu Miyagimo'): deep purplish pink, faint blotch, hose-in-hose, early; upright open habit, to 7 ft. high.

'Seneca' (PI 160067; 'Vittata Fortunei' × 'Alice'): strong purple, showy blotch of dark shaped marks, 3–3½" across, early; very erect, with ascending branches, to 6 ft. high.

'Sentinel' (PI 160142; 'Fielder's White' × *kaempferi*): deep purplish pink, washed purplish red, blotch fine dark dots, imbricated lobes, 2¾–3" across, early midseason; spreading, to 7 ft. high.

'Serenade' (PI 160027; 'Mucronatum' × *simsii*): light purplish pink, 2–3" across, early; erect to tall spreading, to 8 ft. high.

'Serenity' (PI 182879; *simsii* × 'Mucronatum'): vivid pink, 2–2¾" across, early; spreading, to 5 ft. high.

'Shannon' (PI 163892; 'Vittata Fortunei' × 'Maxwell'): deep yellowish pink, 2–2¼" across, 2 to 4 in head, early midseason; erect to spreading, to 5 ft. high.

'Sheila' (PI 160140; 'Fielder's White' × *kaempferi*): vivid pink, margins darker, pale center, 3–3½" across, early; erect with ascending branches, to 6 ft. high. Sister seedling to 'Treasure'.

'Shimmer' (PI 163964; (*kaempferi* × 'Mucronatum') × 'Kagetsu'): white, sanded, flaked and striped, deep purplish pink, 2" across, midseason; broad spreading, to 5 ft. high. Remove branch sports.

'Signal' (PI 160056; *indicum* × 'Mikawa Murasaki'): deep purplish pink, blotch purplish red, starry, 2–2¼" across, early; upright to overarching growth, to 5 ft. high.

'Silver Cup' (PI 163773; 'Mucronatum' × 'Fukurokuju'): white, fine flakes of purple, 2¾–3¼" across, late; broad spreading, to 5 ft. high.

'Silver Lace' (PI 163788; ('Lilacinum' × 'Willy') × ('Mrs. Carmichael' × 'Willy')): white, green blotch, very few purple stripes, 2¾–3" across, late; broad spreading, to 5 ft. high.

'Silver Mist' (PI 163883; 'Mucronatum' × 'Kagetsu'): white, lightly sanded, flaked and few stripes of reddish purple, 2" across, midseason; low spreading, to 4 ft. high. Remove branch sports.

'Silver Moon' (PI 163845; ('Lilacinum' × 'Willy') × ('Mrs. Carmichael' × 'Willy')): white, yellow green blotch, frilled, 3" across, midseason; broad spreading, to 5 ft. high.

'Simplicity' (PI 160059; 'Lilacinum' × 'Willy'): light purplish pink washed light purple, 2½–3" across, 3 to 5 in head, early; erect to wide spreading, to 7 ft. high.

'Sligo' (PI 163894; 'Vittata Fortunei' × 'Kyu Miyagimo'): light purplish pink, hose-in-hose, 1½" across, 1 to 4 in head, early; erect, up to 7 ft. high.

'Snowclad' (PI 163949; 'Mucronatum' × 'Shinnyo no Tsuki'): white, yellow green blotch, ruffled, 3–3½" across, midseason; broad spreading, to 5 ft. high.

'Snowscape' (PI 163932; 'Malvatica' × 'Yozakura'): greenish white, no blotch, 2" across; 3 to 5 in head, late; erect, broad spreading top, to 6 ft. high.

'Snow Wreath' (PI 163882; 'Mucronatum' × 'Kagetsu'): white, faint, yellow green blotch, 3½" across, midseason; low spreading up to 4 ft. high.

'Sonata' (PI 163947; 'Mucronatum' × 'Kagetsu'): white, sanded and flaked reddish purple, ruffled 2½" across, early midseason; broad spreading, to 5 ft. Remove branch sports.

'Sorcerer' (PI 163828; (*kaempferi* × 'Mucronatum') × 'Kagetsu'): white, sanded and striped purplish pink, 2" across, midseason; broad spreading, very twiggy, up to 4 ft. high.

'Souvenir' (PI 160015; *indicum* × 'Momozono'): deep pink, blotch yellowish pink, irregular hose-in-hose, 1¼" across, 2 to 4 in head, early; erect to overarching growth, to 5 ft. high.

'Spangles' (PI 163858; ('Vittata Fortunei' × 'Louise') × 'Adzuma no Hana'): white, light reddish orange flakes, 3" across, 2 to 4 in head, midseason; dense twiggy habit, to 4 ft. high.

'Sprite' (PI 163929; 'Lilacinum' × *indicum*): strong purplish pink, lightly sanded to margin, blotch reddish purple, starry, 2½–3" across, early; vigorous spreading habit, to 5 ft. high.

'Stampede' (PI 160129; 'Beni Giri' × 'Mrs. Carmichael'): deep yellowish pink, blotch purplish red, 2–2½", midseason; erect to spreading habit, to 5 ft. high.

'Stardust' (PI 141771; 'Vittata Fortunei' × 'Amoena'): white, few purple flakes, 2–2¼" across, 2 to 4 in head, early; broad spreading, to 6 ft. high.

'Sterling' (PI 163903; *indicum* × 'Joga'): strong purplish pink, small blotch, starry, 3" across, late; broad spreading, to 2 ft. high.

'Stunner' (PI 163912; *indicum* × 'Tamasugata'): strong purplish pink, white center not dependable, 3" across, late; spreading growth, to 3 ft. high.

'Surprise' (PI 163857; ('Vittata Fortunei' × 'Louise') × 'Adzuma no Hana'): moderate red, margins irregular white, 2½–3" across, midseason; to dense twiggy, rather upright, 3 ft. high.

'Susannah' (PI 163846; ('Lilacinum' × 'Willy') × ('Mrs. Carmichael' × 'Willy')): white, with broad purplish red edges, 2½" across, midseason; broad spreading, to 5 ft. high. Remove branch sports.

'Suwanee' (PI 160139; 'Yozakura' × 'Kagaribi'): light purplish pink, darker dots shaped, 3" across, early; erect to spreading habit to 5 ft. high.

'Swagger' (PI 163860; ('Vittata Fortunei' × 'Louise') × 'Adzuma no Hana'): white, sanded and striped red, 2½" across, 2 to 4 in head, midseason; dense twiggy, to 4 ft. high. Remove branch sports.

'Swansong' (PI 163854; ('Lilacinum' × 'Willy') × ('Mrs. Carmichael' × 'Willy')): white, with yellow blotch, 3½–4" across, midseason; dwarf, dense twiggy, to 3 ft. high.

'Swashbuckler' (PI 160080; 'Malvatica' × *indicum*): deep yellowish pink, blotch, stamens and pistil red, 2–2¾" across, early midseason; vigorous upright to spreading habit, to 5 ft. high.

'Taffeta' (PI 163829; (*kaempferi* × 'Mucronatum') × 'Kagetsu'): white, sanded and striped, purplish pink, frilled, 2–2½" across, midseason; broad spreading very twiggy, to 4 ft. high.

'Talisman' (PI 163864; ('Vittata Fortunei' × 'Louise') × 'Adzuma no Hana'): white, no blotch, but red stripes and sanding, 2½" across; 2 to 4 in head, midseason; very dense and twiggy, to 4 ft. high.

'Tanager' (PI 141907; *indicum* × 'Hazel Dawson'): vivid purplish red, dark blotch, early midseason; erect to broad spreading, to 5 ft. high.

'Tango' (PI 160064; 'Vittata Fortunei' × 'Alice'): lower part of flower deep pink, upper 3 lobes purplish pink, blotch purplish red, 3" across, early; very erect with ascending branches, to 7 ft. high.

'Tartar' (PI 182863; 'Reddish Salmon' × 'Ogi Kasane'): deep pink, blotch not showy, hose-in-hose, 2" across, 2 to 4 in head, early; wide spreading, up to 5 ft. high.

'Templar' (PI 160130; *poukhanense* × 'Modele'): light purplish pink, blotch purplish red not showy, 2¾–3" across, imbricated, early; erect to wide spreading, to 6 ft. high.

'Temptation' (PI 182860; *simsii* × 'Mucronatum'): deep purplish pink darket at tips, dots purplish red, 2–2½" across, early; spreading habit, up to 5 ft. high.

'Teresa' (PI 163982; ('Mucronatum' × 'Vittata Fortunei') × 'Kagetsu'): top half of 3 upper petals deep pink, bottom half and 2 lower petals pale pink, flaked and striped purplish pink, white stripes around margin, dark heavy blotch, 2–2½" across, midseason; to broad spreading, 4 ft. high.

'Thisbe' (PI 160025; *indicum* × 'Momozono'): deep pink, blotch yellowish pink, irregular hose-in-hose, 1–1½" across, 2 to 4 in head, early midseason; broad and over arching habit, to 5 ft. high.

'Tokay' (PI 160011; 'Jeanette' × *kaempferi*): darker than light purplish pink, blotch darker with brownish overtone, 2–2½" across, early; vigorous erect growth, to 8 ft. high. Best when plant fully matured.

'Token' (PI 163814; ('Lilacinum' × 'Willy') × ('Mrs. Carmichael' × 'Willy')): moderate red, heavy blotch, purplish red, 3" across, 2 to 4 in head, midseason; very compact and twiggy, to 4 ft. high; sunburns.

'Tomboy' (PI 163841; ('Lilacinum' × 'Willy') × ('Mrs. Carmichael' × 'Willy')): white, yellow blotch, striped and heavily sanded red, 2" across, midseason; very compact and dense, to 5 ft. high.

'Touchstone' (PI 141799; 'Mucronatum Roseum' × *indicum*): strong yellowish pink, 2½–3" across, early; broader than tall, 6 ft. high. Not introduced.

'Treasure' (PI 160125; 'Fielder's White' × *kaempferi*): buds pale pink, white, very pale pink on margins and in blotch, 3½–4½" across, early; vigorous broad spreading, to 5 ft. high.

'Trilby' (PI 141906; 'Lilacinum' × *indicum*): deep purplish pink, blotch dark dots, 2½–3", early; broad spreading, to 5 ft. high.

'Trinket' (PI 163777; ('Lilacinum' × 'Willy') × ('Mrs. Carmichael' × 'Willy)): white, few flakes of purplish pink, 2½–3" across, late; broad spreading, to 5 ft. high.

'Tristan' (PI 182870; 'Vittata Fortunei' × 'Alice'): deep purplish pink, heavy blotch purplish red, 2–2½" across, early; erect with ascending branches, to 7 ft. high.

'Trophy' (PI 163820; (*kaempferi* × 'Mucronatum') × 'Keisetsu'): light purplish pink, showy blotch reddish purple dots, 3–3½" across, midseason; broad spreading, to 4 ft. high.

'Troubador' (PI 160005; 'Vittata Fortunei' × 'Willy'): deep yellowish pink, few purplish red dots, imbricated lobes, 2" across, early; erect open growth, to 8 ft. high.

'Trouper' (PI 160121; 'Kagaribi' × 'Hinode Giri'): strong red, blotch not showy, 1¼–1½" across; early; dense upright, to 5 ft. high.

'Trousseau' (PI 163849; 'Mucronatum' × 'Keisetsu'): white, yellow green blotch, few purplish red stripes, frilled, 3" across, midseason; broad open spreading, to 4 ft. high.

'Twinkles' (PI 160108; 'Phoeniceum' × *kaempferi*): deep purplish pink, yellow suffusion at base of tube, small blotch, 2" across, early; broad spreading to 5 ft. high.

'Undine' (PI 160087; (*indicum* × 'Momozono') × ('Osakazuki' × 'Flame')): white, green dots in blotch, 2–2½" across, midseason; spreading, to 5 ft. high.

'Ursula' (PI 160026; (*indicum* × 'Momozono') × (*indicum* × 'Hazel')): vivid pink, darker margins, heavy blotch of purplish red dots, 2–2½" across, early midseason; spreading, to 5 ft. high.

'Valentine' (PI 163830; (*'kaempferi* × 'Mucronatum') × 'Kagetsu'): pale purplish pink with white margins, midseason; broad spreading, to 4 ft. high.

'Valkyrie' (PI 160057; 'Lilacinum' × 'Willy'): vivid purplish red, margins darker, 3" across, early; somewhat spreading, to 5 ft. high.

'Vanguard' (PI 163863; ('Vittata Fortunei × 'Louise') × 'Adzuma no Hana'): white, blotch yellow, stripes and sanding of red, 2½" across, 2 to 4 in head, midseason; very dense and twiggy to 4 ft. high.

'Vanity' (PI 160030; *indicum* × 'Momozono'): strong purplish pink, blotch not conspicuous, 1½–1¾" across, late April, early midseason; erect to overarching, to 5 ft. high.

'Velvet' (PI 160134; 'Vittata Fortunei' × 'Osakazuki'): deep yellowish pink, blotch purplish pink, flowers bell-shaped, early; very erect with ascending branching, to 6 ft. high.

'Vespers' (PI 163848; 'Mucronatum' × 'Keisetsu'): white, yellow green throat, occasional purplish red stripes, 3" across, midseason; broad spreading, to 5 ft. high.

'Vestal' (PI 163833; (*kaempferi* × 'Mucronatum') × 'Kagetsu'): white, yellow green blotch, 2–2½" across, midseason; broad to wide spreading, to 4 ft. high. Produces semi and double sports.

'Veteran' (PI 163889; 'Vittata Fortunei' × 'Warai Gishi'): deep purplish pink, blotch purplish red dots, 2½–3" across, mid to late; broad spreading, to 4 to 5 ft. high.

'Viking' (PI 160128; *poukhanense* × 'Modele'): light purplish pink, small blotch of purplish red, 2½–2¾" across, early; semideciduous; broad spreading, to 4 ft. high.

'Vintage' (PI 160072; 'Malvatica' × 'Yozakura'): deep purplish pink, no blotch, 2" across, imbricated, early; wide spreading, to 4 ft. high.

'Violetta' (PI 160079; 'Malvatica' × *indicum*): light purplish pink, blotch purplish red, 2–2¼" across, early; erect to wide spreading, to 4 ft. high.

'Vision' (PI 160050; 'Mucronatum' × *simsii*): strong reddish purple, paler in center, few dots in blotch, 3" across, early; erect to wide spreading, to 8 ft. high.

'Volcan' (PI 160061; 'Vittata Fortunei' × 'Hinode Giri'): strong reddish purple, blotch not conspicuous but definite, purplish red dots, 1½–2" across, midseason; erect with spreading top, to 5 ft. high.

'Wanderer' (PI 160004; (*indicum* × 'Momozono') × ('Osakazuki' × 'Flame')): strong purplish pink, heavy blotch of purplish red dots, starry, 2½" across, early midseason; spreading, to 5 ft. high.

'Warrior' (PI 160202; 'Mrs. Carmichael' × 'Alice'): vivid purplish red, blotch purplish pink, 2" across, 3–5 in head, early; strong, erect habit, to 7 ft. high.

'Wavelet' (PI 163951; 'Mucronatum' × 'Shinnyo no Tsuki'): white, yellow blotch, 2½" across, mid to late; broad spreading, to 5 ft. high.

'Welcome' (PI 163886; ('Vittata Fortunei' × 'Mucronatum') × 'Shinnyo no Tsuki'): strong purplish pink, darker center, white throat, in 4 lower petals, blotch purplish red dots, occasional sports with white centers, 2½–3" across, late; broad spreading to 5 ft. high.

'Whimsical' (PI 163878; 'Mucronatum' × 'Fukurokuju'): white, very small yellow green blotch, flakes of reddish purple, 2" across, late; broad spreading, up to 4 ft. high.

'Whirlwind' (PI 160029; 'Willy' × 'Momozono'): light purplish pink, hose-in-hose, 1½" across, 2 to 4 in head, early; upright to broad spreading, to 5 ft. high.

'Wildfire' (PI 163984; *kaempferi* × 'Keisetsu'): ruffled margins between yellowish pink, and reddish orange, base of tube white, few dots in blotch, 2–2½" across, early; spreading up to 3 ft. high.

'Winedrop' (PI 163775; ('Lilacinum' × 'Willy') × ('Mrs. Carmichael' × 'Willy')): white, sanded and striped reddish purple, 2¾–3" across, late; broad spreading, not over 5 ft. high.

'Winner' (PI 160023; *indicum* × 'Momozono'): deep purplish pink, blotch purple dots, 1¾–2" across, early; erect and spreading to over arching, to 5 ft. high.

'Wisdom' (PI 163887; ('Mucronatum' × 'Vittata Fortunei') × Kagetsu'): white, yellow green blotch, brown anthers, 2" across, late; dense twiggy habit, up to 4 ft. high.

'Witchery' (PI 182880; *simsii* × 'Mucronatum'): clear pink, 2–2¾" across, early; spreading up to 5 ft. high; leaves pubescent.

'Yeoman' (PI 163865; ('Vittata Fortunei' × 'Louise') × 'Adzuma no Hana'): white, wide yellow green blotch, red striping, 2½" across, 2 to 4 in head, midseason; dense twiggy habit, to 4 ft. high.

'Youth' (PI 163966; ('Mucronatum' × 'Vittata Fortunei') × 'Kagetsu'): strong reddish purple, 2" across, late; broad spreading, up to 5 ft. high.

'Zealot' (PI 163813; ('Lilacinum' × 'Willy') × ('Mrs. Carmichael' × 'Willy')): strong reddish purple, red blotch, showy purplish red blotch, 2" across, 2 to 4 in head; midseason; compact erect, to 4 ft. high.

'Zephyr' (PI 163776; ('Lilacinum' × 'Willy') × ('Mrs. Carmichael' × 'Willy')): white, great variations in flakes of purplish pink, some sanding; 2¾–3" across, late; broad spreading, up to 5 ft. high.

'Zingari' (PI 160109; 'Lilacinum' × 'Willy'): strong yellowish pink, small blotch pink, 2" across, early; erect, to 6 ft. high; semideciduous.

'Zulu' (PI 163935; *poukhanense* × 'Modele'): vivid purplish red, distinct purple blotch, 3–3½" across, early; broad spreading, to 5 ft. high, partial semievergreen.

The following plants were developed by B. Y. Morrison but are not Glenn Dale Hybrids as they were introduced by others.

'Ben Morrison' (Possibly ('Vittata Fortunei' × 'Louise') × 'Adzuma no Hana') or it may be a numbered Belgian-Glenn Dale Hybrid; J. Creech, 1972): deep yellowish pink 39B, blotch purplish red, irregular white margin, 2½" across, early to midseason; upright twiggy habit. White margins not pronounced until plants mature. Very popular and excellent plant in memory of a great horticulturist and friend. 4 to 6 feet high.

'B. Y. Morrison' (Parentage unknown—named by Henry Hohman): Reddish orange, midseason; not reliably bud hardy; see misc. hybrids.

SWEET PEA GROUP

A group of unnumbered Glenn Dale seedlings are now being tested and evaluated for possible introductions. Most of them are reportedly light to pastel shades.

BACK ACRES HYBRIDS

This group of hybrids was developed by B. Y. Morrison at Pass Christian, Mississippi, following his retirement from the U.S. Dept. of Agriculture. Clones were first introduced in 1964 and registered in 1964–65.

The breeding work was largely an extension of work with the Glenn Dale Hybrids based on a continuing interest in late blooming and double flowering clones. 124 flats of seedlings were moved from Maryland to Morrison's home, Back Acres, in Mississippi in 1951. Over 500 crosses were made with 370 numbered clones selected for testing and evaluation. Many of the unnamed numbered clones are still being grown and evaluated by collectors and friends.

Foliage is of heavy texture and tolerant of high air temperatures. The flowers are of equally heavy texture and generally appear in mid to late midseason. The plants with a few exceptions are as cold resistant as the Glenn Dale Hybrids-zone 7a, but the flowers are not as cold resistant.

'Apricot Honey' (('Kagetsu' × *Indicum*) × ('Mucronatum' × *Kaempferi*) × 'Tamasugata'): Light center between strong pink and white, margins broad between strong and deep pink, dots almost vivid red, 2 to 2-¾",2 to 3 in head; upright, 30" in about 10 years.

'Badinage' (('Vittata Fortunei' × 'Mucronatum') × (*Kaempferi* × 'Shinnyo no Tsuki')): irregular white center, broad margin of strong purplish pink washed with strong pink, double, 2½–3", 4' high and broad in 10 years.

'Bergerette' (seedling #32666 × 'Musashino'): tinted white, washed from edges of petals between vivid pink and light yellowish pink, towards white, dots inconspicuous but a little darker, 2–2½"; 4.5' tall in ten years.

'Bouffant' ('Dream' ('Mucronatum' × 'Simcil' pink clone) × 'Gunrei'): near white margin shading inward to strong purplish pink in center, dots small but distinct reddish purple, 2–2½", 2 to 3 per head; 36" tall and wide in ten years.

'Bourdon' (('Vittata Fortunei' × 'Warai Gishi') × 'Pluto'): deep to moderate purplish red, dots darker, double, pistil usually present, 9 to 12 petals, 1¼–1½", early, 4' in 10 years.

'Bride's Bouquet' (('Warai Gishi' × 'Kagetsu') × ' Rogetsu'): white, double, 15 to 20 petals, pistil normal, 2–2½", early; columnar habit.

'Cayenne' (('Vittata Fortunei' × 'Warai Gishi') × 'Pluto'): deep yellowish pink, dots purplish red, buds almost vivid red, double, 12 to 16 pointed petals, 1½–1¾"; early; 4' rounded in 10 years.

'Cora Brandt' ('Kagetsu' × 'Warai Gishi'): strong reddish orange, with brownish dots, double, 12 to 20 petals; late 3' tall in 10 years.

'Coral Ace' ('Troubadour' × #158057): white center, margin brighter than moderate red, dots darker; 2½–2¾".

'Corinne Murrah' ('Kagetsu' × ('Hazel Dawson' × *indicum*)): white center, shading to margin of strong to deep purplish pink, ruffled, 3 to 3½", late midseason; 4' in 10 years.

'Crescendo' (Parentage unknown): between strong to moderate reddish orange, double, 10 to 16 petals, imbricated, late. Probably not available.

'Debonaire' ('Copperman' × 'Hakata Shiro'): vivid pink, edges deep pink; center lighter and faintly greenish, 2½ to 3"; 3' in 10 years.

'Elise Norfleet' ('Kagetsu' × 'Warai Gishi'): light pink in center, wide border of vivid red, dots darker, 2 to 2½", variable until plants mature; 3' in 10 years.

'Encore' ('Kagetsu' × 'Warai Gishi'): deep purplish pink, undertone of yellow, dots not conspicous, double, 14 to 18 petals, 2¾" to 3"; 3½ × 4' wide in ten years.

'Extravaganza' (seedling #32629 × 'Tama Sugata'): variable, white, heavily striped flaked and dotted strong reddish purple, overlapping petals 3¼ to 3½"; 4½' × 3'wide in ten years.

'Fire Magic' (('Vittata Fortunei' × 'Warai Gishi') × 'Pluto'): deep yellowish pink, dots vivid red, double, 16 to 22 narrow pointed petals, 1¼ to 1½"; 4' tall in 10 years.

'Folksong' (seedling 36/45 × 'Shikuno'): white, heavy showy dotted blotch of deep pink occasional tinting and rare stripe between purplish pink and moderate red, overlapping petals, 2 to 2¾"; 2½' tall in 10 years.

'Friendship' ('Kagetsu' × 'Copperman'): deep purplish pink, dots slightly darker, petals overlapping, 2¾ to 3"; mid to late.

'Garnet Royal' (('Vittata Fortunei' × 'Warai Gishi') × 'Pluto'): moderate purplish red, toning to grayish red, base lighter, double, 16 to 20 petals, 1¼ to 1¾"; early; 4' in 10 years.

'Gratitude' ('Kagetsu' × 'Warai Gishi'): strong purplish pink, few dots of reddish purple, double, 10 to 15 petals, imbricated, late; low, spreading; 14 × 24" wide in 10 years.

'Habanera' ((*indicum* orange clone × 'Hatsusime') × 'Tama Sugata'): irregular white center, margin strong reddish purple, conspicuous blotch purplish red, 2 to 2¼", twiggy; 4' in 10 years.

'Hearthglow' ('Kagetsu' × 'Warai Gishi'): deep yellowish pink, flushed, strong reddish orange from center, double, 10 to 15 petals, imbricated, late; 4' in 10 years.

'Heigh-Ho' (seedling #32629 × 'Tama Sugata'): deep purplish pink, conspicuous blotch across 2 upper lobes of vivid to deep purplish red; overlapping lobes, 2½–3".

'Heirloom' ('Kagetsu' × seedling 32666 (*indicum* × 'Hazel Dawson')): white center, margin vivid purplish red, dots in blotch conspicuous; 3"; 4 ft. in 10 years.

'Ivan Anderson' (('Warai Gishi' × 'Horaku') × 'Kokoku'): white center, margin of vivid to deep, purplish red, double, 10 to 15 petals, some petaloid, 2½ to 2¾"; 2½' in 7 years.

'Keepsake' ('Kagetsu' × seedling 32666 (*indicum* × 'Hazel Dawson')): white, margin vivid purplish red, conspicuous dots in blotch; 2½ to 3¼"; 4½ × 3' wide in 10 years.

'Largesse' ('Kagetsu' × 'Warai Gishi'): strong purplish pink, few dots on base of upper lobes, double, 15 to 20 petals, 2¼"; 4' in 10 years.

'Lost Chord' ('Dream' × 'Luna' ('Mucronatum' × *simsii*) × (*Kaempferi* × 'Shinnyo no Tsuki')): margin strong purplish pink, center pale purplish pink, distinct dots in blotch, 10 stamens, 3"; columnar; 5' in 10 years.

'Malaguena' (('Vittata Fortunei' × 'Warai Gishi') × 'Pluto'): deep yellowish pink, dot on upper petal vivid purplish red, double, 12 to 16 petals, pistil present, 1¼–1½".

'Margaret Douglas' ((*indicum'* × 'Hatsushimo') × ' Shinsei'): large center area light pink, margin, deep yellowish pink, 2¾–3"; 4' in 10 years.

'Marian Lee' ('Kagetsu' × ('Hazel Dawson' × *indicum*)): white center with tint of purple; border strong red, dots in blotch not conspicuous, 2½–3"; 4' in 10 years.

'Marion Armstrong' ('Kagetsu' × 'Warai Gishi'): deep yellowish pink, few dots, double, 14 to 20 petals, 2½"; 5' × 3½' wide in 10 years.

'Maude Jacobs' ('Kagetsu' × 'Warai Gishi'): strong reddish purple, few dots, double, 15 to 20 overlapping petals, pistil present, 3 to 3¼; low 24" × 24" in 15 years.

'May Blaine' ('Kagetsu' × 'Warai Gishi'): light purple, few dots, double, 12 to 16 imbricated petals, pistil present, 2½ to 3"; rounded, 3½' tall in 10 years.

'Merrymaker' ('Kagetsu' × 'Warai Gishi'): between strong and moderate reddish orange, double, 10 to 15 petals, 2¼–2⅜"; late.

'Miss Jane' ('Kagetsu' × 'Warai Gishi'): white center, border between light and strong purplish pink, double, petaloid stamens 2 to 2½"; late, 2' in 10 years.

'Misty Plum' ('Kagetsu' × seedling 32666 (*indicum* × 'Hazel Dawson')): white, margins, vivid purplish red, dots purplish red with greenish wash in blotch, 2½ to 2¾"; funnel-shaped.

'Moresea' (('Vittata Fortunei' × 'Warai Gishi') × 'Pluto'): deep purplish pink, dot purplish red, double, 15 to 20 petals, 1¼–1½", early; 4' in 10 years.

'Orange Flare' ('Kagetsu' × 'Warai Gishi'): vivid pink at base of petals, tips between deep pink and deep yellowish pink, double petals narrow and cut to base, tassel-like form, 2½–3"; dwarf; 18" in 10 years.

'Painted Tips' (seedling 79/49 (seedling 38/45 × 'Cavendish') × 'Shinnyo no Tsuki'): off white, with flush of vivid pink near tips, that are blotched with spots of deep yellowish pink, blotch distinct but not showy, 5 stamens, 2 to 3"; late; low spreading 20" in 10 years.

'Pat Kraft' ('Copperman' × 'Hakatashiro'): vivid red, dots purplish red, often 6 lobes; 3 to 3¼", very late; 20" to 2½' tall in 10 years.

'Rachel Cunningham' (seedling 32619 × 'Pluto'): deep yellowish pink to vivid red at center, double, pistil present, 17 to 20 petals, 2¾ to 3"; 4' tall in 10 years.

'Red Slippers' (('Andros' × 'Parade') × 'Keisetsu' = ('Vittata Fortunei' × 'Warai Gishi') × (*kaempferi* × 'Mucronatum') × 'Keisetsu'): strong purplish red dots purplish red, 5 stamens, some petaloidy, 2½ to 3"; 24" in 10 years.

'Rejoice' ('Kagetsu' × 'Warai Gishi'): between light and deep purplish pink, few purplish red dots, double, 15 to 20 broad overlapping petals, 2½ to 3"; 4' in 10 years.

'Rose Brocade' ('Kagetsu' × 'Warai Gishi'): deep purplish pink, few purplish red dots, double, 15 to 20 broad overlapping petals, 2½ to 3"; 4' in 10 years.

'Saint James' (cross 23/45): deep yellowish pink washed with moderate reddish orange, blotches are purplish red, white center, 2¾ to 3"; 4' in 10 years.

'Spring Bonnet' (Parentage unknown): off white center, strong purplish pink to margin, blotch area reddish purple, overlapping petals 2 to 2¾"; open habit, 4–5' in 10 years; excellent foliage.

'Starfire' (('Vittata Fortunei' × 'Warai Gishi') × 'Pluto'): deep pink, dots, purplish red, double, 16 to 18 petals 1½ to 1⅜"; 4' in 10 years.

'Stormcloud' ('Kagetsu' × 'Warai Gishi'): vivid reddish purple blotch purplish red at base, double, crest of irregular inner petals, some vestiges of anthers showing; 2¾"; 4' in 10 years.

'Target' (Parentage not reported): deep yellowish pink shading to vivid red, blotch strong red 2½ to 2¾", late midseason; 4' in 10 years.

'Tharon Perkins' (Parentage not reported): deep pink to deep yellowish pink on margins, blotch vivid red dots, 2½ to 2¾"; late; 3' in 10 years.

'Waltz Time' ('Kagetsu' × 'Warai Gishi'): white center on mature plants, margin moderate red, double, 16 to 20 narrow petals, 2¾–3"; late; low, broader than tall.

'White Jade' ('Helen Gunning' × 'Rei Ro'): white, pale green flush on upper lobe, ruffled, 2½ to 3"; 4' in 10 years.

The following Back Acres Azaleas are named but not registered. Some were seedlings given to friends by B. Y. Morrison and may have been named by them or others.

'Armstrong's White' (Named by Armstrong, introd. by H. Hill): white, semidouble 3"; low, compact.

'B. Y. Morrison' (syn. 'B. Y. M'.; parentage unknown, introduced by H. Hohman): reddish orange, 2½–3", late May, dense bushy; buds tender.

'Caroline Dorman': white with stripes, dots, and splashes of light pink to purplish pink, variable single to double, 2½"; low compact.

'Fred Lee': strong red 50A, semidouble, darker blotch, 2½–3"; petaloidy in center often white, no stamens.

'Helen Hill' (Named by Armstrong, introd. by H. Hill): pale pink center with variable margin or just tips of lobes deep yellowish pink, 2¾".

'Lila Stapleton': pale yellowish white, double to semidouble, imbricated; low, compact. Believed to have been named by Morrison and given to Mrs. Murrah.

'Louise Morrow' (sold by B. Y. Morrison to Morrow, named and introduced by Murrah): light pink, often with white center, 3–4".

'Margaret Slaughter' (believed to have been named by Morrison): light reddish orange, double, 2½".

'Nils Hansen' (believed to have been named by Armstrong): white with purplish red stripes, semi-double, 2½"; large trusses. Less hardy, zones 8–9.

'Stewart Armstrong': reddish orange, occasional white blotch, semidouble, 2½".

'Takoma Park' ('Sheila' × 'Seattle White'; introduced by S. M. Armstrong, a close friend of B. Y. Morrison): white, yellow green blotch, crinkly, 3¼" across; mid-May; hardy to 8°F.

Sweet Pea Group: Rejects from the Glenn Dale Hybrids work; no numbers, light pastel shades, none named at present.

ARENDSII HYBRIDS

Developed by George Arends of Wuppertal-Ronsdorf, Germany, using 'Mucronatum' × *kaempferi* in the early 1950's. Plants are intermediate between parents in size and flowers. Should be hardy to at least −5° to −10°F. Plants are usually all upright spreading 4 to 5 feet with average flower size of 2".

'Agger': light purple.

'Bever': light reddish purple.

'Bigge': light purple with darker spotting, 2½"–3".

'Diemel': light yellowish pink.

'Eder': purplish pink with yellowish pink tint.

'Ennepe': strong purplish pink 54B.

'Gloer': strong purplish red 64C, faint reddish markings.

'Kerspe': reddish orange.

'Lingese': reddish orange.

'Lister': strong purplish red 63B.

'Moehne': vivid red.

'Neye': vivid red.

'Oester': purplish pink.

'Sorpe': purple.

'Uelfe' (syn. 'Ulfe'): purple.

'Violme': purplish pink.

'Wipper': moderate purple, lighter throat, reddish marking; late.

ARONENSE HYBRIDS

A group of low compact plants developed from a seedling of unknown origin called 'Multiflorum' (syn. 'Multiflora') around 1950 by George Arends of Wuppertal-Ronsdorf, Germany. They are very hardy and have been tested to 0°F. Parentage of plants not known; may be crossed with *R. kiusianum* or Arendsii Hybrids. Plants basically have small hairy leaves and low mounding habit, 18 to 24" high. They were first introduced in Germany in the early 1960's.

'Aronensis' (Misnamed in the U.S.-does not exist in Germany): pale purple 74C; low mounding, loose growth, taller than others.

'Fumiko' (syn. 'Geisha Purpurrosa'): strong purple 77D, ¾"; dense compact.

'Hanako' (syn. 'Geisha Lilarosa'): purplish pink.

'Haruko' (syn. 'Geisha Dunkellila'): deep purplish red 74B, lighter throat, red dots hose-in-hose, ¾"; low compact.

'Hiroko' (syn. 'Geisha Purpurrosa'): moderate reddish purple 78B, ruffled, 1¼"; low compact.

'Hisako' (syn. 'Geisha Weiss'): white, ¾"; low compact.

'Kazuko' (syn. 'Geisha Karminrot'): deep purplish red 67C, hose-in-hose, 3/4"; low compact.
'Kumiko' (syn. 'Geisha Lachskarmin'): vivid purplish red 61D, slight blotch, 3/4"; low compact.
'Michiko' (syn. 'Geisha Dunkellachsrot'): dark reddish orange, dark buds.
'Momoko' (syn. 'Geisha Rosa'): pink, 3/4".
'Multiflorum' (syn. 'Multiflora'; seedling of unknown origin, not a *R. kiusianum*):
'Noriko' (syn. 'Geisha Karmin'): vivid red.
'Satschiko' (syn. 'Geisha Orangerot'): reddish orange.
'Takako' (syn. 'Geisha Lilarosa'): light purple, faint red marking, 3/4"; dense, mounding; leaves very hairy.

AUGUST KEHR HYBRIDS

Dr. August Kehr, a plant geneticist for the U.S. Dept. of Agriculture and now retired in Hendersonville, N.C., has been working with *Rhododendron* and other genera his entire life. In all the years of hybridizing of *Rhododendron*, he has been very selective and named only the following four azalea cultivars—a very good practice to follow for many hybridizers.

'Anna Kehr' ('Triumphe' × 'Rosebud', '78): Strong purplish pink 55C, double, 40 wavy lobes, no stamens, calyx present, 1¾"; 2½ × 2' high in 10 years; hardy to 0°F.

'Great Expectations' ('Anytime Tetra' × *R. nakaharai* 'Mariko', 306–1, '84): vivid reddish orange, double, 2"; slow growing; hardy to −5F°. Released at the A.R.S. convention in 1984.

'Mary Lou Kehr' (Gable's Macrosepalum hybrid #2 × 'Heiwa no Hikari'); light pink, semidouble, very fragrant; 5 ft. in 15 yrs.; hardy to −5°F.

'White Rosebud' ('Vervaeneana Alba' × 'Rosebud', '73): white, green throat, double + or − 40 lobes, 1¾–2": bud rosebud form, no calyx, mid-May; hardy to −10°F.

BELGIAN—GLENN DALE HYBRIDS

This group was developed by B. Y. Morrison and John L. Creech of the USDA at the Plant Introduction Station, Glenn Dale, Maryland. Crosses were made in 1947 to incorporate some of the flower qualities of the Belgian Indian Hybrids into the hardier Glenn Dale Hybrids. Five were selected from trials of 96 and introduced in 1962 by the Plant Introduction Section. The five cultivars introduced were from a cross of a double pink forcing azalea × 'Treasure', a Glenn Dale. They bloom in midseason and are hardy in zone 8 and possibly 7B. Plants are upright rounded 4 to 6 feet.

'Bayou' (PI 279405): white with occasional reddish flakes and stripes, occasionally petaloid stamens, 2½"; spreading.
'Green Mist' (PI 279406): white, greenish blotch, 2½"; upright.
'Petite' (PI 279407): vivid reddish purple, wavy overlapping, round petals, 3"; spreading.
'Pink Ice' (PI 279408): light reddish purple, with occasional purple flakes, double, 3"; spreading.
'Whitehouse' (PI 279409): white, wavy overlapping roundish petals, 3¾"; spreading.

ADDITIONAL BELGIAN—GLENN DALE HYBRIDS

The following 15 hybrids were never officially released, but some are available in the trade. The B or Bell Number was a working number assigned to the crosses. The seed parent in all crosses was an unknown Double Belgian florist pink azalea abbreviated Fls Pk. Very little information is available. They should be hardy in zones 8, possibly 7b; upright rounded 4 to 6 feet tall.

'Ballero' (B44819–184; Fls Pk. × 'Clarion'): strong purplish red, deep pink blotch, 3½" wavy overlapping petals.
'Butterfly' (B44842–267; Fls Pk. × 'Treasure'): strong purplish pink 65A, purple flakes, 3", wavy.
'Climax' (B44815–51; Fls Pk. × 'Clarion'): vivid purplish red 57C, darker blotch, funnel-shaped sometime 6 overlapping petals.
'Dancing Waters' (B44802–40; Fls Pk. × 'Treasure'): white occasional flakes of purplish pink, green blotch, 3¼" overlapping petals.
'Honeymoon' (B44762–4; Fls Pk. × 'Argosy'): purplish red 54, semidouble, rose bud effect, 2¼".

'Lagoon' (B44772–341; Fls Pk. × 'Treasure'): strong purplish pink 65A, 3" ruffled double.

'Limelight' (B44838–250; Fls Pk. × 'Treasure'): white green blotch, semidouble, large ovoid petals, 2½".

'Pink Frills' (B44782–29; Fls Pk. × 'Treasure'): vivid purplish red, blotch red; frilled, 3¼", occasional petaloid stamens.

'Risque' (B44783–82; Fls Pk. × 'Argosy'): deep purplish pink 66B, blotch purplish red, semidouble, 2¾", mostly petaloid stamens.

'Satellite' (B44834–218; Fls Pk. × 'Treasure'): white, yellow green blotch, some petaloid stamens, 3½", funnel-shaped, smooth margins.

'Starfire' (B44775–57: Fls Pk. × 'Argosy'): white, many flakes and stripes of purplish red, distinct yellow blotch, 3¾", broad petals, squarish.

'Sultrey' (B44774–33; Fls Pk. × 'Afterglow'): strong red 50A, semidouble, rosette center, ovoid petals 4", prolific.

BOBBINK AND ATKINS MACRANTHA HYBRIDS

Bobbink and Atkins Nursery, East Rutherford, New Jersey, introduced the Bobbink and Atkins Macrantha Hybrids in the 1940's. They were hybrids of Kurume or Kaempferi Hybrids × *R. indicum*. The flowers are single, some hose-in-hose, or frilled, 1¾–2½", and bloom from early midseason to very late. The plants are medium in height, 4 to 6 ft., dense, upright and hardy in zone 7a. Descriptions are not available for all varieties named.

'Amber Glow' (K-1): moderate red 47C, hose-in-hose, 1¾", late midseason.

'Americana'

'Carmine King': red

'Chippewa' (K–4): strong purplish red 54B, with darker blotch, frilled, 2½", very late.

'Crimson King' (K–18): pink, hose-in-hose, 1¾", late midseason.

'Dainty' (K–l7): strong red, with darker blotch, frilled, 2", late midseaon.

'Elite' (K–32)

'Glory' (K–10): deep pink 52D, hose-in-hose, 2", early midseason. There are other cultivars with the name 'Glory', PP 146.

'Hiawatha' (K–36)

'Jersey Belle': deep yellowish pink, hose-in-hose, 1½": early midseason; low dense spreading. May not be a B. and A. hybrid.

'Jubilee' (K–19): strong purplish red; very similar to 'Chippewa'.

'June Dawn': reddish orange with red flakes.

'June Skies': deep yellowish pink with pink blotch, rounded lobes, 2½", very late; dense, spreading. May not be a B. and A. hybrid.

'Mrs. L. C. Fisher' (K–4): strong pink 49A, with reddish blotch, hose-in-hose, 1¾", late midseason.

'Ruby Dust'

'Salmon Joy'

'Salmon King': strong pink; similar to 'Mrs. L. C. Fisher'.

'Salmon Spray' (K–7)

CARLA HYBRIDS

A breeding program was started at North Carolina State University in 1960 by Dr. R. J. Stadtherr and H. M. Singletary using Kurume, Kaempferi, Belgian Indian, and Satsuki Hybrids. In 1968, Dr. Stadtherr moved to Louisiana State University but continued to cooperate on the project until his retirement in 1982 while the work was continued by Drs. F. D. Cochran, D. M. Benson, and V. P. Bonaminio. Azaleas released from the ongoing program are being introduced as Carla (North Carolina-Louisiana) Hybrids. Basic objectives of the program are the development of hybrids with superior resistance to root rot diseases, cold hardiness, floriferousness, and drought tolerance. In 1976 seven cultivars were released from N. C. State Univ. In 1981 four cultivars were released from N. C. State Univ. and six were released from Louisiana State Univ. The breeding program continues at N. C. State Univ.

'Adelaine Pope' ('Sherwood Red' × 'Ruffled Giant', 1979): deep purplish red 51A, deep purplish red blotch 53A, 2–3"; dense oval upright 4 to 5 ft. Hardy to 5°F.

'Autumn Sun' ('Ruby' × 'Hexe', 1981): strong reddish orange 33A, hose-in-hose, 7–8 stamens, 1¼–1¾"; upright, spreading to 3½ ft. Hardy to 5°F.

'Baton Rouge' (('Morning Glow' × 'Amagasa') × 'Wakaebisu', 1981): deep reddish orange, white throat, hose-in-hose, mid-season, 2½"; dwarf rounded plant two ft. in six years. Small leaves bronzing in fall. Hardy to 5°F.

'Carla' ('Anytime' × 'Amagasa', 1981): strong reddish orange 40C, double cushion type, 2½–4", no stamens. Mid-season; medium, compact plant. Hardy to 15°F.

'Carror' ('Anytime' × 'Morning Glow', 1976): deep purplish pink 55A, darker blotch semidouble, 0–3 stamens, mid to late, 2–2½"; low to 3½ ft. Hardy to 0°F.

'Cochran's Lavender' ('Hampton' × 'Herbert', 1981): moderate purplish pink 75B, darker blotch 9 to 10 stamens, 3 to 3½"; dense, spreading, up to 4 ft. high. Hardy to 5°F.

'Dixie Rhythm' ('Morning Glow' × 'Kathleen', 1981): deep purplish pink 55A, double; ruffled, no stamens, 3 to 4"; small oval spreading. Hardy to 20°F.

'Dixie Rose' ('Morning Glow' × 'Kathleen', 1981): deep purplish pink 55A, faint blotch, double, no stamens, 3–4"; small oval spreading, to 4 ft. Leaves occasionally variegated with light blotches. Hardy to 15°F.

'Elaine' ('Anytime' × 'Delos', 1976): light purplish pink 55D, double, rosebud type, opening wide, no stamens or pistil, 2–3"; low 3 to 4 ft. Hardy to 10°F.

'Emily' ('Ruby' × 'Hexe', 1976): moderate red 53B, hose-in-hose, 1½–2"; semi-dwarf, compact to 3 ft. Leaves reddish in winter. Hardy to 5°F.

'Ione Burden' (('Ruffled Giant' × 'N. C. Red') × 'R. Ashomon', 1981): deep pink.

'Jane Spalding' ('Kathleen' × 'Hahn's Red', 1976): strong, purplish pink 55B, blotch strong purplish 59D, rounded lobes, 2–3"; growth irregular, broad to 4 ft. Leaves reddish in winter. Hardy to 5°F.

'Pink Camellia' ('Morning Glow' × 'Kathleen', 1981): light purplish pink 65C, double, rose type opens wide, stamens and pistil seldom present, 2½–3½"; mid-season, plant to 4½ ft. Hardy to 5°F.

'Pink Cloud' ('Morning Glow' × 'Kathleen', 1976): light purplish pink, 65C, blotch strong purplish red, 59D, some petalloidy, 3–5 stamens, 2½–3½"; medium, spreading to 4 ft. Hardy to 5°F.

'Rose Dawn' ('Anytime' × 'Amagasa', 1981): light purplish pink 15C double, ruffled, stamens seldom present, 2½–3"; oval spreading to 3½ ft. Hardy to 10°F.

'Sunglow' ('Stewartstonian' × 'Ruffled Giant', 1976): strong purplish red 51A, 2½–3"; rounded upright to 5 ft.; leaves reddish in winter. Hardy to 5°F.

'Wolfpack Red' ('Sherwood Red' × 'Ruby Red', 1981): strong red 46B, 1–1⅛ to 1⅜"; dense, semi-dwarf to 3 ft. Hardy to 5°F.

CARLSON HYBRIDS

Face 'Em Down Hybrids of 'Mucronatum' were selected by Bob and Jan Carlson at Carlson's Gardens, South Salem, New York, since the 1960's for their low spreading habit and as facing plants. Flowers star-shaped, in mid-May; plants are wider than tall, 2 to 3 feet in 14 years. Plants are hardy in zone 7 and with protection in zone 6. Hardy to −10°F.

'Baby's Blush': white, light pink speckling in blotch, whiter and smaller than 'Maiden's Blush'.

'Early Errol': white, contrasting dark tipped white stamens, slight blotch, fine light purple specks, early May.

'Foamy': white, flushed light pink.

'In The Pink': light pink, mid-May; hardiest of the group.

'Maiden's Blush': white, conspicuous reddish purple speckling in blotch, flushed light reddish purple.

'Missy': white, flushed pink, conspicuous reddish blotch, early May.

'Pink Patootie': pink, deeper throat, pink stamens.

'Raspberry Parfait': moderate pink.

'Supersuds': white, very faint greenish yellow blotch, white stamens.

CZECHOSLOVAKIAN HYBRIDS

The following azalea hybrids were developed in Czechoslovakia. They are probably hybrids of a Kurume azalea and *R. yedoense* var. *poukhanense*. Generally frost-proof;

however, young plants should have winter protection. Plants should be hardy to 0°F. See Appendix J.

'Blanice' (Kavka 1969): light pink, funnel-shaped, 1½–1¾"; low flat mound, 36 × 18" high.

'Cylava': vivid pink, funnel-shaped, 1½", late; persistent leaves; rounded habit, 24" high.

'Labe' (B. Bavka 1970): vivid red, funnel-shaped, 1⅜–1½", rounded habit, 32" high, slow.

'Morava' (Dvorak 1970): moderate yellowish pink, 1⅜–1½"; low mounding, 28 × 18" high.

'Sazava' (B. Bavka 1970): purplish pink with a silvery tinge, 1¼"; low compact, 36 × 24" high.

'Vltava' (Jelinck 1962): vivid pink, 1⅛"; low dense, 20" high.

DECKERT HYBRIDS

Developed by Emile Deckert of Hampstead, Maryland, in the 1970's. Hardy in zone 7.

'Alpenrose' (syn. 'Jutta'; 'Marion Lee' × 'Glacier'): white, many variations, blotches, and margins of deep yellowish pink 3½"; midseason; low.

'Duke of Alsace' (syn. 'SS. #5'; 'Marion Lee' × 'Glacier'): light purplish pink, white center, blotch deep red, wavy, 2¾"; late, upright habit.

'Germanique' (syn. 'Sam Moller'; 'Geisha' × 'Mitsu no Yamabuki'): white, variable with dots, stripes and sectors of dark red, 2¼"; early.

'Maid of Orleans' (syn. #3'; 'Marion Lee' × 'Glacier'): white, with wavy, narrow margins of deep yellowish pink 2½"; late; upright.

'Omega' (syn. 'Antoine'; 'Marion Lee' × 'Glacier'): deep pink with darker blotch and occasional white areas, 3½"; midseason; low rounded.

'Orage' (syn. 'SS #7'; 'Marion Lee' × 'Glacier'): moderate purplish red with white center and flushed purplish red, wavy, 2½–3", mid-May; upright.

'Sangraal' (syn. #6'; 'Marion Lee' × 'Glacier'): deep purplish pink, large darker blotch, starry spaced petals, 3"; late.

'Saturnalia' ('Geisha' × 'Mitsu no Yamabuki'): white, with stripes of pale purple, 3½"; very early; upright.

DIAMANT HYBRIDS

Developed by the late Carl Fleischmann, Wiesmoor, Germany, with small flowers ⅞ to 1¼", and low dense mound growth. They were developed by crossing 'Multiflorum' × *R. kiusianum*. They were first introduced in Germany in 1969. Hardy in zones 6 to 8.

'Diamant Dunkellila' (syn. 'Dark Lilac Diamond'): moderate purple.

'Diamant Enzianblau' (syn. 'Gentian Blue Diamond'): moderate purplish pink, 1".

'Diamant Hellila' (syn. 'Lilac Diamond'): light purple.

'Diamant Himmelblau' (syn. 'Skyblue Diamond'): purplish pink, 1".

'Diamant Lachs' (syn. 'Salmon Diamond'): deep pink 51B, 1".

'Diamant Lachsviolett' (syn. 'Salmon Purple Diamond'): light purplish red.

'Diamant Purpur' (syn. 'Purple Diamond'): light purple 73A, faint reddish marking, 1–1¼".

'Diamant Rosa' (syn. 'Red Diamond'): strong purplish pink 55B, faint darker blotch, 1¼".

'Diamant Rot' (syn. 'Red Diamond'): vivid purplish red 57B, ⅞".

'Diamant Violett' (syn. 'Violet Diamond'): pale purple, 1".

EDEN HYBRIDS

Developed by W. David Smith at Spring Grove in the Pocono Mountains of Pennsylvania, U.S.A. The Eden Hybrids, over 500 named clones, represent the fruits of over 120,000 seedlings raised by Mr. Smith who since 1947 has devoted his life to hybridizing azaleas and *Rhododendron*. His main objectives were to develop plants that are hardy at Spring Grove, which is located in zone 6, and blooms of a wide color spectrum and large size. The clones introduced so far include (see also Appendix J):

'Alice Holland' ('Eden Mark Bittinger' × 'Eden Y3'): vivid reddish purple 78A; strong purplish red spotting, 4"; 3' in 6 years.

'Alimo' (('Eden Jane Alcott' × 'Pink Pearl') × ('Eden Frank Preston' × 'How Raku')): two tone strong red deep pink, 50A, B; especially strong spotting; 4"; bronze winter foliage; 4' in 8 years.

'Amy Bittinger' ('Delaware Valley White' × *calendulaceum*): pure white; frilled; 2"; 4' in 6 years.

'Hearthglow' Back Acres Hybrid. GALLE

'Debonaire' Back Acres Hybrid. GALLE

'Red Slipper' Back Acres Hybrid. GALLE

Plate 90

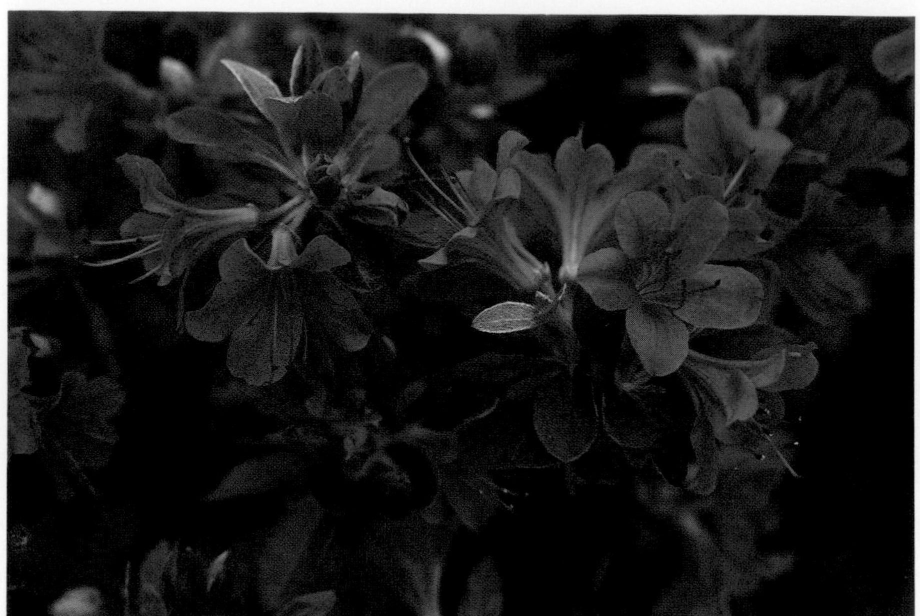

'Kumiko' Aronense Hybrid. GALLE

'Haruko' Aronense Hybrid. GALLE

'Pink Ice' Belgian Glenn Dale Hybrid. BARRY

'Anna Kehr' August Kehr Hybrid. HAGER

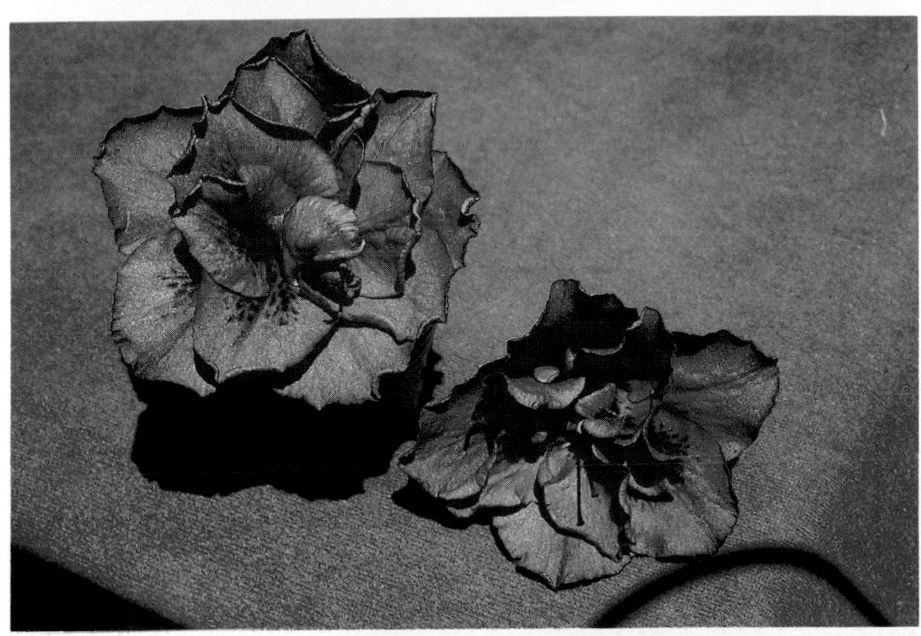

'Great Expectations' August Kehr Hybrid. KEHR

'White Rosebud' August Kehr Hybrid. KEHR

Plate 92

'Greta' Carlo Hybrid. GALLE

'Elaine' Carlo Hybrid. GALLE

'Missy' Carlson Hybrid. CARLSON

'Pink Cloud' Carlo Hybrid. GALLE

'Emile Decherd' Decherd Hybrid. GALLE

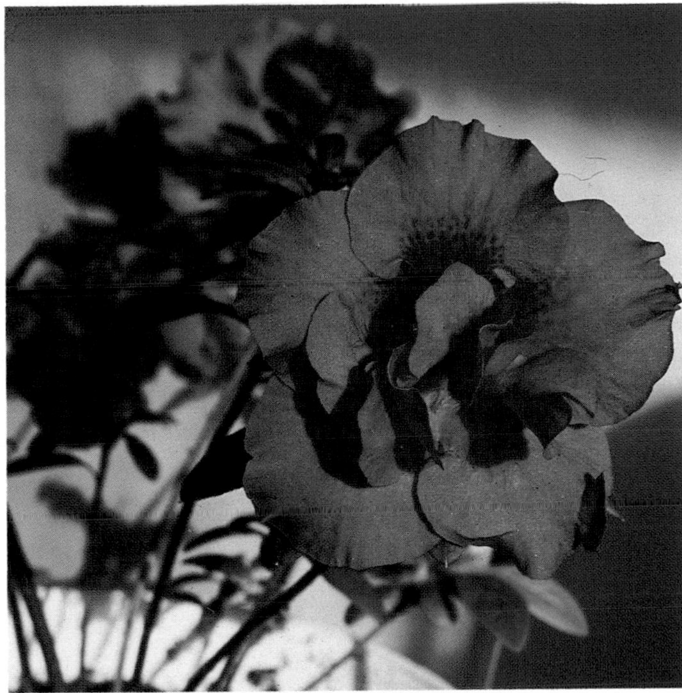

'Carol Ann Fiery' Eden Hybrid. D. SMITH

'Hersh Eden' Eden Hybrid. D. SMITH

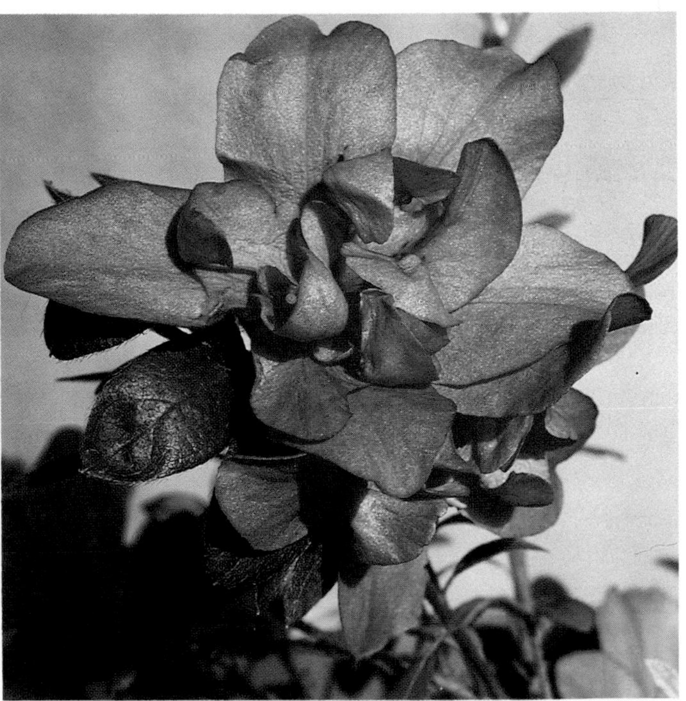

'Trudy Alcott' Eden Hybrid. D. SMITH

'Cotton Top' Greenwood Hybrid. GUTTORMSEN

'Dolores' Greenwood Hybrid. GUTTORMSEN

'Greenwood Rosebud' Greenwood Hybrid. GUTTORMSEN

'Greenwood Pink' Greenwood Hybrid. GUTTORMSEN

'June' Greenwood Hybrid. GUTTORMSEN

'Star' Greenwood Hybrid. GUTTORMSEN

'White Splendor' Greenwood Hybrid. GUTTORMSEN

'Crimson Crest' Greenwood Hybrid. GUTTORMSEN

'Joan Garrett' Harris Hybrid. MILLER

'Miss Suzie' Harris Hybrid. HARDING

'River Mist' Harris Hybrid. MILLER

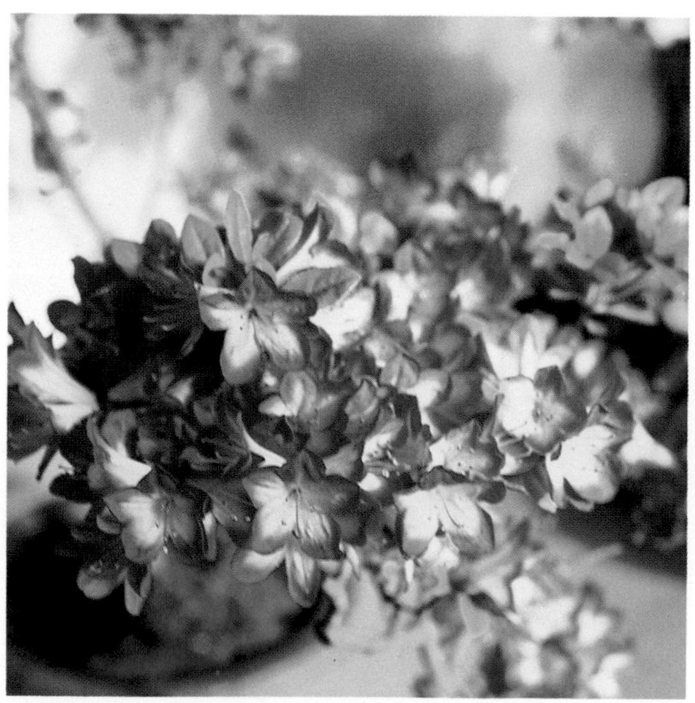
'Izami no Mai' Kuwana Hybrid. KUWANA

'Andrew Leuttgen' (parentage unknown): white, rounded lobes, rosette center, 10 stamens, 3–4", upright 3 × 4" in 8 years.

'Angelica' (Bittinger grex): white hose-in-hose; frilled; green blotch, 3"; 4' in 7 years.

'Barry Bittinger': white, hose-in-hose, 3"; mid-May; 3 × 4' tall in 8 years.

'Bismark' (*Kaempferi* × 'Eden Janea'): purplish red 66B; deep red spotting; 2⅓" frilled, 3' in 7 years.

'Capitola' (('Eden Janea' × 'Pink Pearl') × ('Eden Frank Preston', selfed)): vivid reddish purple, more red than 78A; reddish purple blotch 74A; 3"; 4' in 7 years.

'Carol Ann Fiery' ('Eden Frank Preston' × ('Eden Jane Alcott' × 'Pink Pearl')): deep yellowish pink; rosette center; strong red blotch; 3"; 4' in 7 years.

'Carol Brown' (parents unknown): deep red 46A; dark red blotch, 2½"; red winter foliage; 4' in 7 years.

'Charles Susinski' (Hinckley grex): frilled deep purplish pink 68A; purplish spotting; 2¼"; red winter foliage; 3' in 7 years.

'Christian Bowman' (Bowman grex): pale purplish pink; faint darker blotch; 3'; 3' in 7 years.

'Colleen Becker' (Hinckley grex): strong purplish red 54A; strong red blotch 53C; 3¼"; 4' in 8 years.

'Dancing Butterfly' ('Haskel' grex): white; heavy deep red spotting 3 lobes; deep reddish purple stripes; 3"; 5' in 9 years.

'Daniel Buranich' ('Eden Jennifer' × 'George L. Taber'): strong reddish orange; rosette center; 3½"; 4½' in 9 years.

'Daphne' ('Eden White' × 'Eden Y1'): strong purplish pink to deep purplish pink; rosette center is a neatly formed ring of ½" lobes; 3¼"; 6 stamens, with black anthers, (protrude from rear of rosette); 4' in 8 years.

'David Haskell' (Haskell grex): white; deep pink specks and stripes; 3½"; 4' in 7 years.

'Deborah Buranich' (Fiery grex): deep yellowish pink 43C; reddish orange blotch 43A; 2¼"; very heavy bloomer; bronze winter foliage; hose-in-hose; 4' in 7 years.

'Dianne Hersh' ('Mark Bittinger' × 'Eden Y2'): deep purplish pink 68A; very light blotch 66C; 3½"; 3' in 6 years.

'Dorothy Miller' (Hinckley grex): between deep and strong red 53C, B; blotch purplish red 67A; hose-in-hose, 3½"; 4' in 7 years.

'Dr. Neil Bathon' ('Eden Mark Bittinger' × 'Eden Y2'): deep purplish pink 68A; purplish red blotch 67A; 3¾"; heavy bloomer; 3' in 6 years.

'Dr. Neil Campbell' ('Eden Mark Bittinger' × 'Eden Y2'): white with strong reddish purple 78B; prominent purplish red 67A, spotting on 3 lobes; 3"; very frilled; heavy bloomer; 3' in 6 years.

'Estellen' (Stiner grex): between strong and vivid purplish red 61C, B; blotch darker 61A; 1½"; very heavy bloomer; 4' in 8 years.

'Eva Zaner' (Stewart grex): between strong and moderate purplish pink 68C, B; white edging; 3"; 4' in 7 years.

'Fido' ('Delaware Valley White' × 'Shinkigen'): strong purplish red; blotch strong purplish red 59D; 3¼"; 3' in 7 years.

'Freda' (Rose grex): vivid purplish red 57B, C; prominent spotting on 3 lobes purplish red 61A; 2½"; 4' in 7 years.

'Fred Fuchs' ('Mark Bittinger' × 'Eden Y2'): two tone strong purplish red 55B, A: spotting strong red 53C; 3¼"; 3' in 7 years.

'Fred Stiner' ('Helenm' × 'Amoena'): strong reddish purple 70A; blotch strong purplish red 53C; rosetter center; 4"; 3' in 7 years.

'Gene Miller' (*kaempferi* × 'Eden G2'): hose-in-hose; deep purplish pink 68A; purplish red blotch; 2½"; 3½'; in 8 years.

'Gretchen Kellas' (Hinckley grex): strong reddish orange; light blotch 45B; 3"; heavy bloomer; 3½' in 8 years.

'Hannah Kessler' ('Eden Frank Preston' × 'Ella Grainger'): moderate red 47C; hose-in-hose; spotting vivid red 46C; 3½"; heavy bloomer; 4' in 7 years.

'Hector' ('Delaware Valley White' × 'Shinkigen'): purplish pink, double; 3"; 3½' in 7 years.

'Helena' ('Eden Jane Alcott' × 'Pink Pearl'): strong yellowish pink 38A; blotch vivid red 43A; 4"; 4' in 7 years.

'Helenm' (*calendulaceum* × 'Pink Pearl'): white with deep pink 52C tips of lobes; hose-in-hose; 2"; 4' in 8 years.

'Ida Harmon' ('Pink Pearl' × 'Sherwood Red'): deep purplish pink 67C; blotch 67A; 2½" hose-in-hose; 4' in 7 years.

'Jane Geiselman' ('Helenm' × 'Magorie'): strong purplish pink 55B, slight yellowish cast in throat, hose-in-hose, 2"; 6 × 6' in 8 years.

'Jean Botscheller' ('Eden Helenm' × 'Amoena'): deep yellowish pink 39B; blotch faint strong red 45D; 3"; 4' in 8 years.

'Jethro' ('Eden Midas 3' × 'Eden Midas 1'): strong red; blotch reddish brown; 3"; 4' in 7 years.

'Jonathon' ('Eden Mark Bittinger' × 'Eden Y3'): between reddish purple and purplish pink 74D, C; no blotch showing; 3½"; 3' in 6 years.

'John Shaffer' ('Eden Mark Bittinger' × 'Y3'): strong purplish red between 63C, B; blotch purplish red 66B; 3½"; 4' in 7 years.

'John Stiner' (Stiner grex): strong purplish red 63A, purplish red blotch 61A; hose-in-hose; 3"; 4' in 8 years.

'Joseph Chiodo' (Stiner grex): deep purplish pink 67C to 67B; blotch 67A; 2½"; 4' in 7 years.

'Mae Knapper' (Haskell grex): white striped and spotted deep yellowish pink 39A and 39B; 3¼"; very frilled; 4' in 7 years.

'Marguerite Sheehan' (parents unknown): deep red 47D; strong blotch 47A on 3 lobes; 3½"; 3½' in 8 years.

'Mark Bittinger' (Bittinger grex): pure white; 3½"; 4' in 9 years.

'Mary Stewart' (('Vervaeneana' × 'Eden Mummert') × 'Eden Frank Preston'): deep pink with rosette center; 3"; red winter foliage; 4' in 8 years.

'Mary Hoffman' ('Eden Jane Alcott' × 'Pink Pearl'): between light and strong pink 50C and 50B; 2½"; hose-in-hose: very heavy bloomer; 4' in 6 years.

'Minnie Hatta' ('Eden AK' cross): deep purplish pink 73A, strong blotch on 3 lobes, purplish pink 74B, heavy bloomer, 3"; 3' in 7 years.

'Orange Delight' (*kaempferi* × 'Eden Janea'): strong reddish orange 33A; 3"; 3' in 7 years.

'Paschal' (('Eden Jane Alcott' × 'Pink Pearl') × ('Eden Frank Preston' × 'How Raku')): strong purplish pink 55B; spotting deep red 53B; 3"; 4' in 6 years.

'Pearl Jarman' ('Eden A.L.' × 'Eden Y1'): vivid reddish purple 74A; rosette center; 3¼"; 4' in 6 years.

'Pink Perfection' (('Eden Jane Alcott' × 'Pink Pearl') × ('Eden Frank Preston' × 'How Raku')): deep purplish pink; deep red blotch 53B; 4"; 3' in 6 years.

'Reba' ('Eden Rasputin' × 'Eden Sheba'): vivid purplish red 58A; hose-in-hose; 3"; 3½' in 5 years.

'Red Flame' (Hinckley grex): strong red 47A; spotting vivid red 45A; 2"; bronze winter foliage; 4' in 8 years.

'Rover' ('Delaware Valley White' × ' Shinkigen'): between strong and vivid purplish red 61C and 61B; spotting 60B; 3"; bronze winter foliage; 3½" in 7 years.

'Ruth' ('Eden Mark Bittinger' × 'Eden Y2'): between reddish and moderate purplish pink 74D and 74C; strong blotch on 3 lobes reddish purple 74A; 3"; 3' in 7 years.

'Sandy Hook' ('Eden Jane Alcott' × 'Pink Pearl'): moderate purplish red 58A; dark red blotch 59A; 3½"; 4' in 8 years.

'Sarah' ('Eden Helenm' × 'Amoena'): deep purplish pink 55A; blotch purplish red 60C; 2¼"; 4' in years.

'Sarah Ivy' ('Eden Rasputin' × 'Eden Sheba'): vivid reddish purple 74B; orange throat; spotting purplish red 63B; 3"; 3' in 5 years.

'Seaford' (*kaempferi* × 'Eden Janea'): between purplish red and deep purplish pink 66B and 66C; spotting light 66A; 2½"; red winter foliage; 4' in 8 years.

'Somerset' (parents unknown): deep purplish pink 68A; light green blotch; 2¾"; bronze winter foliage; 4' in 8 years.

'Sue Bittinger' (Bittinger grex): white, hose-in-hose; frilled, no blotch; 2½"; 4' in 8 years.

'Susanah' ('Eden Mummert' × 'Vervaeneana'): two-tone pale pink 49C; to white; spotting deep purplish pink 73B; 3"; heavy bloomer; long lasting blooms; 3½' in 7 years.

'Susanna Silcox' (Hinckley grex): strong purplish red 63A; blotch purplish red 66A; 3¾" hose-in-hose; 3' in 7 years.

'Trudy Alcott' ('Eden Frank Preston' × 'Eden Marguerite'): deep purplish pink 67C; rosette center; 2¾"; 3' in 7 years.

'Walter David' ('Eden Jennifer' × 'George L. Taber'): deep purplish pink 68A; slight spotting 67C; 4"; heavy bloomer; 4' in 8 years.

GARRETT RAINBOW HYBRIDS

Joan and Dewey Garrett of Anderson, South Carolina, started in 1975 hybridizing azaleas as a hobby and will devote full time after retirement. Objectives include size and clarity of color of flowers, length of blooming period, and two-season flowering. The parentage includes evergreen species such as *R. indicum*, *macrosepalum*, and the following hybrid groups: Back Acres, Glenn Dale, Robin Hill, Satsuki, Kaempferi, and others. The following three plants, 'Dr. Steven Garrett', 'Jeff Garrett' and 'Mrs. Bertha Crawford', were grown from open pollinated seed from Myashi Oyama of Japan. All are hardy in zones 6b–9.

'Artie Julia Garrett' (299–49–1 B.A. × T49–9 R.H.): white streaks and flakes purplish red, darker blotch, 3–3¼″, midseason; spreading habit.

'Calypso' ('Pink Star' × 'Saint James'): dark yellowish pink, washed reddish orange, darker blotch, occasional white throat with age, 3–3¼″, late midseason; spreading habit.

'Dr. Alex Garrett' (('Mrs. Villars' × 'Chanson') × ?): pink white, variegation, faint blotch, frilled, 3¼″, late.

Dr. Steven Garrett ('Hibotan' ('Hirado' Belgian hyb.) Open pollinated): white, yellow green throat, fragrant, 3″, mid-late April; upright.

'Fan Dancer' ('Lady Robin' × 'Miyo no Sakae'): deep pink, darker blotch, 3–3½″, midseason; spreading habit.

'Foxy Lady' ('Miyo no Sakae' × 'Corsage'): vivid pink, margin moderate reddish purple, starry darker blotch, 2¾″, midseason; spreading habit.

'Gum Drop' ('Malvatica' × *indicum*): moderate yellowish pink, darker blotch, ruffled, 1″, mid-late April; dwarf, spreading; leaves reddish in winter.

'Jeff Garrett' ('Yume Dona' ('Hirado' 'Tectum' hyb.) Open pollinated): dark reddish orange, darker blotch, 3″, mid-late April; spreading habit.

'Moulin Rouge' ('Issho no Haru' × ?): strong, purplish red, darker blotch, 2¾–3″, late; upright spreading.

'Mrs. Bertha Crawford' (*macrosepalum* f. *rhodorides* 'Kochozaria' × 'Misima Tuluji') Open pollinated): dark purplish red, darker blotch, fragrant, 3½″, midlate April; spreading habit.

'Mrs. Emma Jones' (*kaempferi* × 'Vittata Fortunei'): white, purplish pink 74D flakes, streaks and dots, blotch purplish red 54B, funnel-shaped, 2½″, upper 3 petals attached, 2 lower petals spaced, stamens and pistil pinkish, very early; spreading habit.

'Salmon Floret' (*indicum* × 'Momozono'): deep yellowish pink, blotch vivid purplish red, hose-in-hose, 1½″, midseason; dwarf, spreading; dark green leaves in fall; reddish purple beneath.

'Tom Garrett' (*kaempferi* × ('Yaeshojo' × 'Hinode Giri')): vivid reddish orange, small dark blotch, hose-in-hose, 1½″, profuse, early, dense, slow growth.

GEORGE RING SERIES

George Ring of Fairfax, Virginia, U.S.A., has been active since the 1960's in hybridizing both *Rhododendron* and azaleas. The objectives for the azalea breeding are plants with good root systems, hardiness, and floriferousness. All are hardy to at least −5°F. The parents of some hybrids are unknown; others include Glenn Dales, Belgian Indians, Gable, and Back Acres Hybrids.

The following plants were registered in 1984.

'Fairfax' ('Polar Seas' × 'Debonaire'): strong purplish pink 62A fading to large white center, wavy, 3½″, 6 stamens, late midseason; dense, 2′ × 4′ wide in 10 years.

'Lucent' ('Dream' × 'James Gable'): between deep and strong pink 52C-D with orange flair, strong red speckles 45C, hose-in-hose, 2¼, 6 stamens, midseason; upright, spreading, 5′ in 10 years.

'Orchido' ('Polar Seas' × 'Debonaire'): light purplish pink 69A, paler center, few dark spots on upper lobe, 2½″, late midseason; 3½ × 3′ wide in 10 years.

'Taenzer' ('Moonbeam' × 'Beacon'): pale purplish pink 62D, paler center, numerous purplish red speckles 61C on upper 3 lobes, midseason; upright, spreading to 5′ in 10 years.

VIRGINIA ROYALTY SERIES

Seedlings of George Ring, named and introduced by Don Hager in the 1980's.

'Coral Red': deep reddish orange, red blotch, 2½", early midseason; upright, to 5 ft.

'Oakton': deep pink, red blotch, 2½–3", midseason; dense, spreading, to 3 ft.

'Virginia': pale, yellowish white, shading to pale green center, rounded incomplete hose-in-hose, 3–3½", midseason; compact, spreading, to 3 ft.

'Virginia Baroness': white, small yellowish green blotch, fine pink stripes and flecks, hose-in-hose, 3", early midseason, broad, spreading, to 4 ft.

'Virginia Duchess' ('Moonbeam' × 'Beacon'): white, washed deep yellowish pink at tips, semi-double, 3½", midseason; broad, spreading, to 4 ft.

'Virginia Duke' ('Vervaeneana' × 'James Gable'): reddish orange, dark blotch, funnel-shaped, 2½–3" midseason; broad, spreading, to 3–3½ ft.

'Virginia King': dark reddish orange, darker blotch, funnel shaped, 3", midseason; upright, spreading, to 4 ft.

'Virginia Knight' (parents unknown): moderate pink, light red blotch, deep funnel-shape, hose-in-hose, 3" midseason; broad, spreading, to 4 ft.

'Virginia Lady' (parents unknown) moderate pink, semi-tubular, 3–3½", midseason; broad, spreading, to 4 ft.

'Virginia Prince' ('Dream' × 'Polar Bear'): deep pink, light red blotch, tubular, incomplete hose-in-hose, 3", early midseason; upright, spreading, to 5 ft.

'Virginia Princess' (parents unknown): pale pink, deep blotch, ruffled, 4", midseason; broad, spreading, to 5 ft.

'Virginia Queen' (parents unknown): light pink, deep pink blotch, 4", early midseason; broad, spreading, to 5 ft.

GREENWOOD HYBRIDS

The Greenwood Hybrids breeding program was started in 1960 by Bill Guttormsen, Canby, Oregon, U.S.A. The goal is to develop compact, well-shaped plants for temperate, moist climates. The hybrid groups involved are basically Kurumes, Glenn Dale, and Gable hybrids. Flowers are single except where noted. All plants hardy to at least 0°F. unless noted. Size of plants after 10 years is given. The plants adapted well in other areas and retain their shape and form but plant size may be larger. See also Appendix J.

'Baby Rosebud' ('Linda Jean' × 'Springtime'): light purplish pink 62C, double hose-in-hose, rosebud form, 1½"; late May, 20 × 24" upright.

'Bingo' ('Helen Close' × 'Purple Splendor'): strong, purplish red 53C 2¾'; late May, 20 × 24", rounded.

'Blazon' (('Louise Gable' × 'Ward's Ruby') × 'James Gable'): deep red 53B, hose-in-hose, 2", early May, 24 × 18" wide, upright.

'Bolero' ('Addy Wery' × 'Salmon Elf'): strong red 50A, hose-in-hose, 2", late April; 24 × 24", rounded.

'Bright Star' ('Linda Jean' × 'Hahn's Red'): white 155D, long narrow petals, starlike, 2½", mid-May; 18 × 24", upright.

'Calienta' ('Addy Wery' × 'Salmon Elf'): vivid red 43A, hose-in-hose, 2"; early May; 24 × 18", upright.

'Calusa' ('Helen Close' × 'Purple Splendor'): deep purplish pink 55A, hose-in-hose, 2½", early May; 30 × 22"; upright.

'Can Can' ('Louise Gable' × 'Helen Close'): moderate purplish red 64D, semidouble to double, frilled, 3", late May; 24 × 30", rounded and compact.

'Candice' ('Linda Jean' × 'Springtime'): moderate purplish pink, 55C, double, 2", mid-May' 18 × 24", rounded.

'Cantico' ('Helen Close' × 'Purple Splendor'): white with light purple edge 82D, late May; 30 × 24"; upright.

'Capri' ('Louise Gable' × 'Helen Close'): deep purplish pink 73B, 3¾", early May; 36 × 30"; upright.

'Cathy Lynn' ('Louise Gable' × 'Helen Close'): strong purplish pink 67D, double, 3", late May, 24 × 24", rounded.

'Cayuga' ('Helen Close' × 'Purple Splendor'): deep purplish pink 73B, sports white throat, hose-in-hose, 2¼", mid-May; 20 × 24"; upright.

'Chiffon' ('Helen Close' × 'Purple Splendor'): moderate purplish pink 64D, hose-in-hose, 2", mid-May; 18 × 18" low, rounded. Hardy to 5°F.

'Clipper' ('Louise Gable' × 'Ward's Ruby'): white to deep and strong purplish pink 68B and 68C, 3", late May, semidouble to double; 20 × 26", rounded: winter foliage very deep purplish red 187A

'Cloud Cap' ('Helen Close' × 'Madrigal'): white, pale yellow blotch, partially petaloid stamens, 2¾", mid May; 18 × 26', low, spreading, Hardy to 5°F.

'Concho' ('Helen Close' × 'Purple Splendor'): strong reddish purple 64D, 2½", prolific, late May; 16 × 24", low dwarf. Hardy to 5°F.

'Confetti' ('Boudoir' × 'Rose Greeley'): deep purplish pink 68B, hose-in-hose, 2", early May; 20 × 20" rounded.

'Cottontail' ('Linda Jean' × 'Satanta'): white, pale yellow throat, double, 2¼, late April; 18 × 24" wide.

'Cotton Top' ('Linda Jean' × 'Springtime'): white, partially petaloid stamens, 2", 1ate April; 16 × 20", low, spreading.

'Cover Girl' ('Linda Jean' × 'Hahn's Red'): deep pink 52C, double, hose-in-hose, 1¾", early May; 18 × 24", rounded.

'Crimson Crest' ('BV 6' ('Louise Gable' × 'Ward's Ruby') × 'James Gable'): deep red 53A, hose-in-hose, 2", mid to late April; 16 × 14" in 8 years, rounded.

'Crystal' ('Linda Jean' × 'Springtime'): moderate purplish pink, 73C, with a thin lighter pink edge, double, 2½", mid-May; 20 × 24", rounded.

'Deep Purple' ('Violacea' × 'Purple Splendor'): deep purplish red 72B, hose-in-hose, 2¾", mid-April; 22 × 22", rounded. Hardy to 5°F.

'Deseronto' ('Rose Greely' × 'Ward's Ruby'): strong purplish red 53C, 2¾", mid-May; 36 × 24", tall, upright. Hardy to 5°F.

'Dolores' ('Helen Close' × 'Campfire'): deep purplish pink 55A, double, 3", mid-May; 36 × 24", upright.

'Dorian' ('Louise Gable' × 'Helen Close'): light reddish purple 78C, 4", late May; 20 × 20", rounded.

'Estrellita' ('Louise Gable' × 'Ward's Ruby'): deep red 46B, 2¼", mid-May; 24 × 20, upright. Hardy to 5°F.

'Fire Chief' ('Helen Close' × 'Purple Splendor'): strong purplish red 51A, 3", mid-May; 18 × 20" rounded. Hardy to 5°F.

'Fire Sprite' (('Louise Gable' × 'Ward's Ruby') × 'James Gable'): deep red 53C, hose-in-hose, 2¼", late April; 28 × 26", upright.

'Frolic' ('Helen Close' × 'Campfire'): strong purplish red 48B, hose-in-hose, 3", early May; 36 × 24", tall upright. Hardy to 5°F.

'Gemini' ('Helen Close' × 'Purple Splendor'): light reddish purple 77C, semidouble 2½", late May; 22 × 22", rounded.

'Genie Magic' (('Rose Greeley' × 'Ward's Ruby') × 'Kirin'): moderate red 47C, hose-in-hose, 2", mid-April; 20 × 24", broad rounded.

'Geronomo' ('Helen Close' × 'Purple Splendor'): strong reddish purple 70B, hose-in-hose, 2¼", early May; 24 × 30", rounded.

'Greenwood Cherry' ('Linda Jean' × 'Hahn's Red'; syn. 'Cherry'): moderate red 46D, hose-in-hose, petaloid stamens, 2", early May; 16 × 16", rounded.

'Greenwood Jackpot' ('Maria Elena' × 'Linda Jean'; syn. 'Jackpot'): deep pink 47D, double, 2", early June; 12 × 30", broad, semi-dwarf, creeping.

'Greenwood Orange' ('Louise Gable' × 'Ward's Ruby'): moderate reddish orange 43C, double, 2", mid-May; 30 × 24", upright, open.

'Greenwood Orchid' ('Helen Close' × 'Purple Splendor'): strong reddish purple 77B, hose-in-hose, 2¼", mid-May; 30 × 24", rounded.

'Greenwood Pink' ('Louise Gable' × 'Helen Close'): moderate purplish pink, 62B, double, 3", mid-May; 36 × 24", upright, open.

'Greenwood Popcorn' ('Linda Jean' × 'Springtime'; syn. 'Popcorn'): pure white, semidouble, hose-in-hose, 2", mid-May; 20 × 30", upright, broad.

'Greenwood Rose Queen' ('Linda Jean' × 'Springtime'; syn. 'Rose Queen'); deep purplish pink 64D, double, 2½", early May; 16 × 18", broad, rounded.

'Greenwood Rosebud' ('Linda Jean' × 'Hahn's Red'): deep purplish pink 6B8, double, hose-in-hose, 2¼", early May; 14 × 20", low, upright.

'Greenwood Rosy-red' ('Linda Jean' × 'Hexe'): strong purplish red 58B, deeper red throat, double, hose-in-hose, 2¼", early May; 15 × 20", low, upright.

'Greenwood Showboat' ('Linda Jean' × 'Hexe'; syn. 'Showboat'): deep purplish pink 57D, semidouble, hose-in-hose, 2", late May; 14 × 24", low, compact, spreading.

'Greenwood White' ('Linda Jean' × 'Hahn's Red'): whiter than 155D, pale yellow throat, hose-in-hose, 2", mid-May; 15 × 20", rounded.

'Greenwood Yukon' ('Linda Jean' × 'Hahn's Red'; syn. 'Yukon'): pure white, pale yellowish geen throat, double, 2"; 20 × 24", broad, rounded.

'Halo' ('Linda Jean' × 'Springtime'): pure white, pale yellow throat, hose-in-hose, 2½", early May; 16 × 22", upright, broad.

'Hardy Hexe' ('Linda Jean' × 'Hexe'): strong purplish red 58B, hose-in-hose, 2", late May; 24 × 20", upright.

'Irene Cook' ('Linda Jean' × 'Springtime'): strong purplish pink 62A, semidouble, 2", early May; 20 × 36", broad, upright.

'Jan' ('Helen Close' × 'Purple Splendor'): moderate purplish red 72C, hose-in-hose, 2½", mid-May; 24 × 24", rounded, compact.

'Jet Fire' ('Helen Close' × 'Glamour'): strong purplish red 67C, 2½", late April; 36 × 24", tall, upright.

'June' ('Maria Elena' × 'Linda Jean'): moderate red 50B, double, 2¼", early June; 18 × 20", broad, spreading.

'Kachina' ('Rose Greeley' × 'Ward's Ruby'): strong purplish red 59D, hose-in-hose, 1½", early May; 20 × 20", rounded. Hardy to 5°F.

'Katie' ('Helen Close' × 'Purple Splendor'): deep purplish red 72B, hose-in-hose, 2½", mid-May; 20 × 20", compact, rounded. Hardy to −10°F.

'Linda Jean' ('Helen Close' × 'Glamour'): deep purplish pink 68B, double, hose-in-hose, 3", no stamens, mid May; 18 × 24", rounded, broad.

'Lindean' ('Helen Close' × 'Purple Splendor'): strong reddish purple 64D, hose-in-hose, 2½", early May; 22 × 22", rounded.

'Lunar Sea' ('Helen Close' × 'Purple Splendor'): light purple 75A, hose-in-hose, 3", early May; 24 × 24", rounded.

'Maria Elena' ('Louise Gable' × 'Helen Close'): strong purplish pink 62A, double, 2¾", late May; 24 × 30", broad, rounded.

'Marianne' ('Linda Jean' × 'Hahn's Red'): strong pink, 48C, semidouble, hose-in-hose, 2", late April; 18 × 22", rounded.

'Marvee' ('Louise Gable' × 'Ward's Ruby'): strong purplish red 61C, double, no stamens, 2", mid-May; 30 × 24", stiff upright. Hardy to 5°F.

'Mary Allen' ('Linda Jean' × 'Springtime-Kur'.): light purplish pink 56A, double, 1¾", late April; 18 × 24", open, rounded.

'Misty' ('Linda Jean' × 'Hahn's Red'): white base, changing gradually to light purplish pink at edge 55B, C, D, hose-in-hose, 2¾", late April; 24 × 20", upright.

'Mona Lisa' ('Louise Gable' × 'Helen Close'): deep purplish pink, 68B, double, 3", mid-May; 36 × 24", tall, upright.

'Montezuma' ('Helen Close' × 'Purple Splendor'): moderate purplish red 72D, white throat, hose-in-hose, 3", late May; 36 × 24", upright.

'Mt. Adams' ('Linda Jean' × 'Springtime-Kur'): white, double, hose-in-hose, 2¼", mid-May; 30 × 24", upright.

'North Pole' ('Linda Jean' × 'Springtime'): pure white, semidouble, hose-in-hose, 2", late May; 22 × 36", upright.

'Orange Sherbet' ('Linda Jean' × 'Hexe'): vivid red 44A, double, 2¾", mid-May; 12 × 20", low, semi-dwarf, spreading.

'Paleface' ('Helen Close' × 'Madrigal'): white, 2½", late May; 18 × 22", rounded, compact.

'Paluna' ('Helen Close' × 'Purple Splendor'): strong purplish red 53C, 2½", mid-May; 18 × 18", low, rounded. Hardy to 5°F.

'Pawnee' ('Helen Close' × 'Purple Splendor'): strong purplish red, 59D, hose-in-hose, 2¼", late May; 18 × 22", upright. Hardy to 5°F.

'Pink Annette' (syn. 'Annette';('Rose Greeley' × 'Ward's Ruby') × 'Kirin'): vivid purplish red 61A, hose-in-hose, 1¼", mid-April; 16 20"; compact, low, rounded. Hardy to 0°F.

'Pink Cloud' ('Helen Close' × 'Glamour'): moderate purplish red 72D, double, 3¾", late May; 36 × 24", upright.

'Pink Fancy' ('Helen Close' × 'Purple Splendor'): strong purplish pink 55B, hose-in-hose, 2½", early May; leaf variegated; 18 × 18", rounded. Hardy to 5°F.

'Pink Lace' ('Helen Close' × 'Purple Splendor'): deep purplish pink 55A, hose-in-hose, 3", mid-May; 24 × 24", rounded.

'Pollyanna' ('Helen Close' × 'Purple Splendor'): white, edged deep purplish pink 73B, red throat, 2½", mid May; 24 × 24", rounded, open.

'Puff' ('Louise Gable' × 'Helen Close'): deep purplish pink 68B, double, frilled, 3", mid-May; 36 × 24", upright, open.

'Red Beauty' (('Louise Gable' × 'Ward's Ruby') × 'James Gable'): deep red 53C, hose-in-hose,2¼", mid-April; 24 × 18", upright.

'Red Blaze' ('Linda Jean' × 'Hexe'): deep red 53B, 2", late May; 20 × 24", upright, broad.

'Red Feather' ('Louise Gable' × 'Ward's Ruby'): moderate to reddish orange 43C, double, 2", early May; dark red winter foliage 187A; 26 × 24", upright. Hardy to 5°F.

'Redland' ('Linda Jean' × 'Hahn's Red'): strong, purplish red 54A, hose-in-hose, 2", mid-May; 24 × 24", rounded.

'Rimfire' (('Louise Gable' × 'Ward's Ruby') × 'James Gable'): strong purplish red 60C, hose-in-hose, 2", late May; 36 × 24".

'Robin Cook' ('Linda Jean' × 'Springtime'): moderate purplish red 63B, double, hose-in-hose, 2", early May; 12 × 16"; low, compact, spreading.

'Rose Parade' ('Linda Jean' × 'Hahn's Red'): vivid purplish red, 55A, double, hose-in-hose, 2¼", early May; 20 × 20", rounded.

'Royal Crown' ('Violacea' × 'Katie'): deep purplish red, 72A, semidouble, hose-in-hose, 3½", late May: 12 × 21", dwarf, spreading. Hardy to 5° F.

'Royal Robe' ('Helen Close' × 'Purple Splendor'): deep purplish red 70B, hose-in-hose, 3½", late May; 16 × 24", low compact, rounded.

'Ruth Ticknor' ('Linda Jean' × 'Springtime'): deep pink 52B, semidouble, hose-in-hose, 1¾", late April; 20 × 30", broad, rounded.

'Salishan' ('Rose Greeley' × 'Ward's Ruby'): moderate purplish red 64D, hose-in-hose, 1½", early May; 30 × 34", upright. Hardy to 5°F.

'Santee' ('Helen Close' × 'Purple Splendor'): strong purplish red 66C, hose-in-hose, 4", mid-May; 24 × 24", rounded.

'Sarrano' ('Helen Close' × 'Purple Splendor'): deep purplish pink 68B, hose-in-hose, mid-May; 24 × 24", rounded.

'Satanta' ('Rose Greeley' × 'Ward's Ruby'): strong purplish red 63A, hose-in-hose, 1¾", mid-April; 36 × 24", upright, stiff. Hardy to 5°F.

'Shawna' ('Louise Gable' × 'Helen Close'): deep purplish pink 73B, double, 3", mid-May; 34 × 24", rounded.

'Sherry' (('Louise Gable' × 'Ward's Ruby') × 'James Gable'): deep red 53C, hose-in-hose, 2¼", late April; 20 × 24", rounded.

'Show Time' (('Louise Gable' × 'Ward's Ruby') × 'James Gable'): strong purplish red, 63A, hose-in-hose, 2¼", mid-May; 30 × 20", upright.

'Si-lin' (('Louise Gable' × 'Ward's Ruby') × 'James Gable'): deep red 53B, hose-in-hose, 2½", early May; 26 × 20", upright.

'Silver Star' ('Louise Gable' × 'Helen Close'): white, shaded moderate purplish red, 71D, double, 3", late May; 30 × 20", upright.

'Silver Streak' (sport of 'Deep Purple'): deep purplish red 72B, hose-in-hose, 2", mid-April; leaf variegated, pale white margin, and mottling; 20 × 20", rounded. Hardy to 5°F.

'Sleigh Bells' ('Helen Close' × 'Madrigal'): pure white with pale yellow blotch, 2¼", late May; 20 × 24", rounded, broad to spreading.

'Snow Cloud' ('Linda Jean' × 'Springtime'): pure white with pale yellow blotch, semidouble, hose-in-hose, 2½", late April; 14 × 18:, low, spreading.

'Snow Mound' ('Linda Jean' × 'Hahn's Red'): pure white, with pale green throat, hose-in-hose, 2¼", late April; 16 × 30", low, spreading.

'Snow Puff' ('Linda Jean' × 'Springtime'): pure white with pale yellow throat, hose-in-hose, 2", early May; 14 × 24", low, spreading.

'Star' ('Linda Jean' × 'Springtime'): pure white, 2½", long narrow curved petals, forming a twisted star, 24 × 18", upright.

'Star Fire' ('Helen Close' × 'Purple Splendor'): moderate purplish red 63B, hose-in-hose, 2", mid-May; 20 × 18", rounded.

'Star Ruby' ('Addy Wery' × 'Salmon Elf'): deep red, 46A, hose-in-hose, 1½", early May; 36 × 24", upright.

'St. Helens' ('Linda Jean' × 'Satanta'): pure white with yellow throat, double, hose-in-hose, 2½", early May; 30 × 24", upright.

'Sundance' ('Helen Close' × 'Purple Splendor'): deep purplish pink 57D, hose-in-hose, 2", mid-May; 20 × 20", rounded.

'Susie Cook' ('Boudoir' × 'Rose Greeley'): strong purplish pink 67D, 3", mid-April; 24 × 36", rounded, open, spreading.

'Tamara' ('Violacea' × 'Sundance'): strong purplish red 58B, hose-in-hose, 2¼", early May; 20 × 24", rounded.

'Tami' ('Boudoir' × 'Rose Greeley'): strong purplish pink 55B, fragrant, hose-in-hose, 1¾", mid-April; 20 × 20", rounded.

'Tara' ('Helen Close' × 'Glamour'): strong purplish red, 57C, 3½", late May; 20 × 24:, rounded.

'Tat' ('Helen Close' × 'Glamour'): strong purplish pink 55B, double, 3" mid-May; 20 × 24", rounded.

'Tenino' ('Helen Close' × 'Purple Splendor'): moderate reddish purple, 78B, hose-in-hose, 3", late May; 16 × 36", low, spreading, very compact.

'Tico Tico' ('Helen Close' × 'Purple Splendor'): moderate purplish red 72C, hose-in-hose, 2½", mid-May; 20 × 24", rounded.

'Tina' (('Rose Greeley' × 'Ward's Ruby') × 'Kirin'): strong purplish pink 58D, hose-in-hose, 1", early April; 12 × 16", rounded dwarf, very compact.

'Torchlight' ('Helen Close' × 'Purple Splendor'): strong purplish pink, 67B, hose-in-hose, 2¼", mid-May; 18 × 24", compact, spreading.

'Trisha' ('Dorothy Gish' × 'Purple Splendor'): strong purplish pink, 67C, hose-in-hose, 3", late April; 30 × 24", upright open.

'Vera Cook' ('Linda Jean' × 'Springtime'): vivid purplish pink, 54B, double 1¾", early May; 20 × 24", rounded.

'White Ermine' ('Linda Jean' × 'Satanta'): pure white, with yellowish green throat, lobes rounded, spotted effect with 9 distinct brown anthers, 1¾" early May; 15 × 15", low, rounded.

'Winter Hawk' ('Linda Jean' × 'Hahn's Red'): pure white, with pale yellow blotch, hose-in-hose, 2", mid-May; 20 × 24" rounded.

'Zig Zag' ('Addy Wery' × 'Salmon Elf'): deep pink, 52B, hose-in-hose, 1½", early May; 22 × 18", upright.

HAGER HYBRIDS

Developed by Don Hager of Hager Nurseries in Spotsylvania, Virginia, U.S.A. The prime objectives are to develop low plants with good foliage and early to midseason blooms with flowers with clear colors, size, and substances to withstand the natural elements. Several deciduous azaleas are to be released in the future. The parentage includes Kurume, Gable, Glenn Dale, and Satsuki Hybrids. Plants are hardy in zones 7–9 and may prove hardier with further testing.

'Alvera Hager' (('Pink Pearl' × 'Mandarin') × 'Mother of Pearl'): light pink, white variegation toward margin, tubular, 2", early midseason; upright, spreading to 5 ft.

'Barbara Workman' (('Bowman' × 'Stewartstonian') × 'Mrs. Dorenbos'): strong reddish orange, light red blotch, hose-in-hose, rounded, red stamens and pistil, 2½", early midseason; dense, spreading to 4 ft.

'Clara Lee Hager' (('Gyokushin' × 'Beni Giri') × ('Gunrei' × 'Louis Koster')): pale pink, fine pink stripes and rays, green base, rounded ruffled, 3", midseason; low, spreading to 2 ft.

'Hager White' ('Aikoku' (white form) × 'Leprechaum'): white, exserted stamens and pistil, 3½", late; very dense, spreading to 1½–2 ft.

'Jeffie Moss' ('Stewartstonian' × 'Illusion'): moderate reddish orange, light red blotch, funnel shaped, hose-in-hose, 2½", early midseason; dense, twiggy, to 4' ft.

'Lovable' ('Glacier' × 'Alight'): white, light pin, margins, rounded, slightly ruffled, large truss, 3", late midseason; broad, spreading, to 4' ft.

'Lozenge' (('Madeira' × 'Nocturne') × 'Warai Gishi'): strong pink, rounded, hose-in-hose, 2½", early midseason; erect, spreading to 7 ft.

'Magic Lily' ('Mother of Pearl' × 'Mandarin'): pink and white variegation, white tube, somewhat funnel shaped, hose-in-hose, 1½–2", early midseason; spreading ascending branches, to 3 ft.

'Mary Ellen Hager' (('Tharon Perkins' × 'Niagara') × 'Debonaire'): deep yellowish pink, slightly tubular, 2", midseason; dense, broad, spreading, to 3 ft.; leaves dark reddish brown in fall.

'Mom' ('Eucharis' × 'Mrs. G. G. Gerbing'): white rounded, to 5" as plant matures, midseason; upright, spreading, to 5 ft.

'Musical' (('Hinode Giri' × 'Amoena Purple') × 'Camelot'): moderate pink, slight blue tint, dark blotch, slightly tubular, 2", early midseason; broad, spreading, to 4 ft., leaves dark reddish brown in fall.

'Patti Ann Hames' ('Lilacina' × 'Gable Poukhanense'): light purple, reddish brown blotch, somewhat starry, 4–5" with age, early midseason; broad, open, spreading to 6 ft.

'Rosalie Nachman' (('Macrantha Rose' × 'Pat Kraft' × 'Orange Beauty'): light pink, orange tone, vivid pink blotch, 3–3½", late; low, spreading, to 2–2½ ft.

HAGER FUN SERIES

'Angel' (('Getsutoku' × 'Dream') × 'Glacier'): yellowish pink, red pistil, stamens, and blotch, overlapping rounded petals, 3–3½", late; semidwarf, dense, compact to 1½–2 ft.

'Fooey' (('Dream' × 'Blizzard') × 'Surprise'): vivid red center, fading to moderate yellowish pink, irregular white border, 2½–3", midseason; vigorous, upright, to 6 ft.

'Gee Whiz' (('Aviator' × 'Veteran') × 'Gyokushin'): pale pink, numerous fine light pink rays, greenish throat, 3", late; low, dense, spreading, to 2 ft.

'Gosh Darn It' (('Salmon Spray' × 'Salmon Bells') × 'Blauuw's Pink'): deep yellowish pink, red blotch, tubular, 2", early; broad, spreading, to 3 ft.

'Grabbit' ('Harbinger × 'Hatsushima'): deep yellowish pink red blotch, white rays at margin, slightly funnel-shaped, 3", late midseason; medium, spreading, to 5 ft.

'I'll Be Damned' (('Polar Sea' × 'Corrine Murrah') × 'Debonaire'): light pink, shading to white center, light green at base, deeply ruffled, white pistil and stamens, semidouble, 4½–5½, mid to late midseason; dense, compact, to 3 ft.

'Kelly' ('Arctic' × 'Aerobat'): white, irregular, purple striping, slightly ruffled, 2½:, midseason; upright, spreading, to 4 ft.

'Oh Heavens' (('Kagetsu' × 'Silver Cup') × 'Masterpiece'): flushed purplish pink, striped and sectored purplish red, round petals 2½–3", midseason; broad, spreading, to 4 ft.

'O Nuts' ('Harbinger' × 'Hatsushima'): light reddish orange to dark red center, some white edging, rounded, 3", midseason; broad, spreading, to 5 ft.

'Son of a Gun' (('Geisha' × 'Rose Greeley') × ('Cadenza' × 'Capella')): white, light purple striping, rounded and ruffled, 2½ × 3", midseason; dense, spreading, to 3 ft.

'Wow' (('Warai Gishi' × 'Gunbi') × 'Macrantha Pink'): moderate pink, double, rosette type, 2½", late midseason; narrow leaves; low spreading to 2½–3 ft.

HARRIS HYBRIDS

Developed by James Harris of Lawrenceville, Georgia, starting in 1970. Plants are evergreen hybrids of Glenn Dales, Satsuki, and Kaempferi Hybrid parents, large flowered and most are late-mid-season. 'Pink Cascade' is excellent as a hanging basket plant. All plants are hardy in zones 7a–9a.

'Ann Lee McPhail' ('Chikyo no Haru' × 'Surprise'): light pink 55C, 6 lobes, 3"; 44 × 33" wide in 10 years.

'Betsy Monnen' ('Delos' × 'Amagasa'): deep purplish pink 68A, double, 3½"; 24 × 21" wide in 19 years.

'Betty Hemmingway' ('Delos' × 'Amagasa'): white double, 3½ to 4'; tall grower.

'Bruce Hancock' (*Azaleodendron*: 'White Gumpo' × *R. keiskei*): white with pink border, 3½", cascading 4' down in 5 years.

'Bryan Harris' ('Pink Gumpo' × 'Grace Freeman'): light pink, lighter center, 3½"; 'Gumpo' foliage, 3' × 3' in 9 years.

'Buddy McMakin' ('Grace Freeman #2' × 'Amagasa'): pale purplish pink, 65C, border vivid purplish red 66B, 3½"; 28 × 24" wide in 10 years.

'Cille Shaw' ('Amagasa' × 'Grace Freeman #2'): pale purplish pink 65D, bordered, deep purplish red, 3¼"; 18 × 26" wide in 10 years.

'Dorothy Clark' ('Grace Freeman' × 'Amagasa'): light pink with light red border, 4½"; 3 × 3' in 9 years.

'Edith Henderson' ('Banka' × 'Target'): yellowish pink, red blotch, 4½"; 42" × 42" in 9 years.

'Ellie Harris' ('Sherwood Orchid' × 'Fedora'): light pink, hose-in-hose, 2"; 42 × 36" wide in 10 years.

'Fascination' ('Grace Freeman' × 'Amagasa'): pink with red border, 4½"; 42 × 42" in 9 years.

'Francis E. Seidler' ('Amagasa' × 'Grace Freeman #2'): pale purplish pink 62D, moderated red 51A border, 3¼"; 18 × 26" wide in 10 years.

'Frosted Orange' ('Bunkwa' × 'Target'): white with strong reddish orange border, 3½" very late; 30 × 36" in 9 years.

'Georgia Giant' ('Moonbeam' × 'Lilacina'): white, large star-shaped, 4–5½", fragrant; 54 × 42" wide in 8 years.

'Gloria Still' ('Albert & Elizabeth' × 'Fedora'): variegated pink and white, 2¾"; large truss; forces easily, 2 × 3' wide in 6 years.

'Harris Purple' ('Martha Hitchcock' × 'Wakaebisu'): dark purple, hose-in-hose, 3½"; 42 × 42" in 9 years.

'Joan Garrett' ('Banka' × 'Target'): yellowish pink, red blotch, large 5 to 6"; 36 × 48" wide in 9 years.

'Lee Thomas' ('Banka' × 'Target'): pink with red blotch, 5"; 21 × 34" wide in 10 years.

'Margaret Rowell' ('Mother's Day' × 'Red Slippers'): deep red 53B, hose-in-hose, semidouble, 3" wide, mid to late April: 14 × 19" wide in 10 years.

'Mary Ann Egan' ('Amagasa' × 'Grace Freeman #2'): pale purplish pink, bordered deep pink 52B, 3¼"; 28 × 36" in 10 years.

'Mattie Barron' ('Caroline Dorman' × 'Grace Freeman #2'): white, double, 23 petals, stripes of light reddish purple 186C, 3"; 20 × 34" wide in 10 years.

'Ming Chuen' (Satasuki hybrid): white with many variations; stripes, flakes, and sectors of light purplish pink, 2½"; low compact habit.

'Miss Suzie' ('Hershey Orange' × 'Hershey Red'): strong red 53D, hose-in-hose, 2"; 24 × 36" wide in 10 years, compact.

'Parfait' ('Sherwood Orchid' × 'Fedora'): pink with white center, red dots, 2", slight fragrance; 42 × 42" wide in 10 years.

'Pink Cascade' (*R. nakaharai* × 'Bunka'): deep yellowish pink, red blotch, 2", 30 × 36" spreading, cascading, basket plant.

'Pride of Lawrenceville' ('Bunka' × 'Hinode Giri'): pink, with red border, 2", 42 × 60" wide in 10 years.

'Rain Fire' ('Moonbeam' × 'Lilacina'): vivid red 3"; sun tolerant; 24 × 30" wide in 8 years.

'Rhonda Stiteler' ('Delos' × 'Amagasa'): pink, double, 20 petals, 2½"; foliage variegated with yellow blotches, 30 × 24" wide in 9 years.

'Rivermist' ('Sherwood Orchid' × 'Fedora'): light reddish purple 78D, up to 30 in truss; 42" height in 9 years.

'Seven Dwarfs' ('Okina Nishiki' × 'Grace Freeman'): white with numerous variations, stripes, flakes and sectors of light purplish pink; 7 different blooms, 2¼"; leaves variegated and yellow blotches; 24 × 60" wide in 9 years.

'Sue Bell' ('Amagasa' × 'Grace Freeman #2'): light purplish pink 56B, border deep pink 47C, 3", 30 × 28" wide in 10 years.

'Vibrant' ('Grace Freeman' × 'Amagasa'): white with pink border, 4"; 24 × 36" wide in 9 years.

HOLMES HYBRIDS

Introduced by Holmes Nurseries, Tampa, Florida, in the late 1950's. May not be available outside of Florida or under different name. Parentage unknown.

'Cherry Flip': pink, double, hose-in-hose, 3".
'Frosted Lavender': white, stripped light purple 3".
'Jelly Bean': orange, double; low spreading.
'Lipstick': red.
'Shocking Pink': purplish pink.
'Vivitone': yellowish pink, 3".

KUWANA HYBRIDS

For nearly 20 years Mr. Takeo Kuwana, a nurseryman of Kurume, Japan, has been hybridizing Satsuki × Kurume Hybrids. The hybrids named are early midseason flowering, suitable for bonsai and landscaping. Plants are not available in the U.S. at this time.

'Hoshi Kagami' [Star Reflection] (F4 reverse cross of 'Izumi no Mai' × 'Tennyo no Mai'): vivid red 45B with white or pale pink center, 1¼"; registered as a Kurume in Japan.

'Izumi no Mai' [Spring Dance]: vivid purplish red with white center, 1¼".

'Sazaku' [Red Sparrow]: deep yellowish pink with white center, pistil present but stamens absent, 1".

LOBLOLLY BAY HYBRIDS

This hybrid group was selected principally from seedlings of Glenn Dale Azaleas by I. Lee Amann of Loblolly Bay, Bozman, Maryland, U.S.A. The seedlings are naturals collected in the proximity of the seed parents when so designated. Seedlings are mostly from 'Buccaneer', 'Day Spring', 'Geisha', 'Glacier', and 'Merlin'. Possible pollen parents, based on inherited characteristics, include Kurume, Pericat, Glenn Dale, Indicum, and Gable Hybrids. Plants listed range in age from 7 to 18 years of age and have proven hardy in Zone 6, with many definitely hardier. The following plants currently being grown for distribution bear single flowers unless stated otherwise:

'Angeletta': white with a greenish throat and blotch, 3" rather flat florets, early midseason; upright, branched, 4'.

'Baby Salmon' ('Glacier'): strong reddish orange 40D, 3", midseason, spreading; 2' to 3'.

'Becky Curtis' ('Day Spring'): deep yellowish pink 37A, purplish blotch, hose-in-hose, to semidouble, 1½", early midseason; erect, branched; leaves shiny rounded; flowers long lasting.

'Brightly' ('Glacier'): deep purplish pink 58D, darker blotch, 2½", late midseason; vigorous, sprawling 3'. Leaves like 'Glacier'.

'Bucklow' ('Buccaneer'): vivid reddish orange 41B, 2½", midseason, compact 3'; dark ovate leaves.

'Cheerful': bright reddish purple 75A, 2"; upright, compact, somewhat twiggy, 3', midseason.

'Cocoa Path': deep red 46A, 2½", late; tall; compact, upright, branched 5'.

'Coral Day' ('Day Spring'): strong yellowish pink 40D, evident blotch, hose-in-hose 1½", early; upright, compact, branched, 5'.

'Crinkles' ('Glacier'): vivid red to reddish orange 43B, 2½", midseason; upright with broad top, 3'. Petals variously waved and crinkled.

'Dainty Lady' ('Day Spring'): light purplish pink 66B, darker blotch, hose-in-hose to semidouble 1½", early; upright, spreading, 3'. Glossy foliage, long lasting flowers turn darker with age.

'Day Dream' ('Day Spring'): moderate purplish pink 68C, 2¼", early; very broad spreading, 4'. Strong hardy foliage.

'Double Day' ('Day Spring'): pale purplish pink 65D, hose-in-hose 2", late midseason; very erect, 5'. Very hardy with limited winter foliage.

'Dreamboat': margin light reddish purple 75B shades to white throat and midrib, 2½" rippled edge, early midseason; broad spreading, 3'.

'Dreamy': moderate purple 82B, 2¼", early midseason; upright to spreading, 4'. Delicate pale pink effect.

'Gaily': white with greenish throat 1C, rounded wavy petals, 2¼", early midseason; low, spreading, 2+'. Very floriferous. Tufted foliage.

'Geisha, Too' ('Geisha'): white with slight stripes, deep purplish pink 55A, 2½", early; upright, spreading, 3'. Throws solid color branches.

'George, Jr.' ('G. L. Taber'): pale purplish pink 65C, shading to white margin, 4", heavy spotted blotch, midseason; upright, broad, spreading but compact 3'. Similar to 'Taber' flowers but larger, flatter and lighter.

'Georgette' ('G. L. Taber' Mutant): light purplish pink 65B with white edge, darker blotch, 1¾", early, open, develops flat umbrella branches 3'. Appeared in a group of 'G. L. Taber' cuttings.

'Glacier Beauty' ('Glacier'): extremely variable color, from solid reddish orange phase to white phase very pale pink shading to darker tips 50D, darker blotch, wavy petals, 2½", late midseason; vertical angular vigorous growth, 7'. Typical foliage, prominent feathered calyx turns red in the fall. Tolerates full sun.

'Glacier Stripe' ('Glacier'): white with occasional deep purplish pink 57C stripes, yellowish green blotch, 2", midseason; upright spreading 3'.

'Green Star': white with greenish cast and vivid yellowish green blotch 143A, 1¾" pointed petals, star-shaped florets, late midseason; open, upright, branched, 5'.

'Happy Face': moderate purplish pink 63D, heavy midrib and strong heavily dotted blotch, 2¼", midseason, very upright, erect, 7'. Pansy face.

'Lapin': strong purplish pink 58D, darker blotch, 2¼", late; compact, twiggy; spreading with small evergreen leaves, 3'.

'Lavender Day' ('Day Spring'): deep purplish pink 67B, 1½–2", very early; upright branched, spreading, 5'. Blanketed with flowers.

'Lavender Glow' ('Indica Rosea'): moderate purple 78C, 2", very early; upright branched, spreading 4'. Blooms in fall also.

'Lavender Light': deep purplish pink 68B, 2½", midseason; upright spreading, 5'.

'Lavender Pearl' ('Day Spring' × 'Pink Pearl'): light purplish pink 75A to lighter midribs and white throat, reddish purple blotch, hose-in-hose, 2–2¼", early, midseason; erect branched, 6'. Larger lavender copy of 'Pink Pearl'.

'Li'l Lavender': ('Day Spring'): strong reddish purple 68B, hose-in-hose, 1¼", early midseason; upright spreading, 3'.

'Loverly': moderate red 57A, darker blotch, 3", early midseason; upright branched, 3+'.

'Ma Belle' ('Merlin'): strong purplish pink 54B, moderate blotch, 2¼", midseason; upright branched, spreading 4'. Cold hardy and salt spray tolerant.

'Maid Marion': pale yellowish pink 24D, deeper rose margin gives overall buff effect, 2", midseason; tall, erect branched at top, 6'.

'Mimi Ball' ('Day Spring'): strong red 46B, darker blotch, hose-in-hose 2", early; fairly fat florets, branched 2 to 3'.

'Misty Pink' ('Day Spring'): white throat and midribs shade to strong purplish pink margin, darker blotch, 2" midseason; upright, spreading broad top, 6'.

'Moonlight': light purple 77D, shading to white throat, darker blotch, 2½", midseason; upright, wide spreading, 4 to 5'.

'Mystery': strong purplish pink 63C, margin, shades to white to vivid yellow throat, reddish blotch, 2½" narrow (½") petals, early midseason; upright branched 3 to 4'.

'New Baby': deep purplish pink 68B, margin shades to pale purplish pink midribs and throat, darker spotted blotch, 2", midseason; upright branched, 3'.

'Pam' ('Glacier'): strong purplish red 58B, 2½" narrow petals, darker blotch, midseason; spreading, 4'.

'Paula' ('Peter Pan'): strong purplish pink 68B, darker blotch, 2", late midseason; upright spreading, 3'.

'Pink Cloud, Too' ('Day Spring'): moderate pink to pale pink throat 68D, darker blotch, hose-in-hose to semidouble 1½", early, upright branched, 5'. Long lasting florets turn darker with age.

'Pink Glee' ('Peter Pan'): strong pink 52C, blotch strong purplish red, 2½", midseason; upright branched, spreading 3'.

'Pink Reward' ('Reward'): deep purplish pink 54A, 2½–3", midseason; upright spreading, 4'.

'Purple Path': strong reddish purple 72D, heavy midrib, twisted petals; 2¼", late midseason; erect branched, twiggy flat top, 2'. Leaves form twisted evergreen rosettes. Unique.

'Red by the Tree': strong reddish orange 41B, purplish blotch, 1½", midseason; upright, spreading, 3'.

'Red Glacier' ('Glacier'): deep purplish red 57C, darker blotch, 2¼", midseason; spreading open growth, 4'.

'Rosemary White' ('Day Spring'): white with greenish blotch 149B, 2½", early; vertical columnar, 8'.

'Rosie': deep yellowish pink shades to moderate pink edged 50B to 51D, cherry blotch, 2½" rounded petals, midseason; upright branched, 4+'.

'Ruby Lee' ('Merlin'): strong reddish purple 82B, reddish blotch, 2¼", midseason; upright, spreading 3'.

'Salmon Day' ('Day Spring'): deep pink 49A, upper petal deep purplish pink 63B, no blotch, hose-in-hose to semidouble 1½", early, erect, somewhat columnar, 7'. Good foliage.

'Spiraea': white, greenish throat 149B, large prominent anthers, strong brown, with white filaments, 1¼", early midseason; upright spreading, 4'. Resembles Spiraea in appearance.

'Spring Day' ('Day Spring'): strong purplish red 54A, darker blotch, back lighter, hose-in-hose 2", early; upright branched, 3'. Showy.

'White Frills' ('Day Spring'): white, pale yellow green blotch 145C, hose-in-hose 1½" outer floret deeply cleft, early; upright spreading, 5'.

'White Rug' ('Day Spring'): white, faint yellowish green blotch, 1¾", early; wide spreading, 3'. Florets persist well.

'White Spring' ('Day Spring'): white, bright yellow green blotch, 1¾", early; upright, spreading, 6'.

'Willa Owens' ('Merlin'): deep purplish pink 54A, deeper blotch, 2", early midseason; upright, spreading, 5'. Hardy, tolerates salt spray.

MARLBANK FARMS HYBRIDS

Starting in the 1970's these hybrids were developed by Dick J. Cole on Marlbank Farms, York County, Yorktown, Virginia, U.S.A. Unless otherwise noted, they are seedlings of 'Sweetheart Supreme'. Flowers usually in clusters of 1 to 3. Hardy in zones 6b–9. Plants are similar in habit to Kurumes; dense, broad round plants 3–5 ft. in height.

'Ann Koman' ('Hino Crimson' seedling): red, 1¼"; dwarf.

'Betty Bailey' ('Flame' seedling): reddish orange, mid-April.

'Bob Gregorie' ('Flame' seedling): light reddish orange, 1½", mid-May.

'Crestwood' ('Hino Crimson' seedling): light red, 1½", mid-April.

'David Crocket': deep purple with faint darker blotch, hose-in-hose, mid-May.

'Dick Cole': white, brownish blotch, ruffled, 3", late April.

'Dr. Rives Bailey': strong yellowish pink, purplish red blotch, hose-in-hose, late April.

'Eleanor Cole': yellowish pink, darker blotch, hose-in-hose, ruffled, 1½", persistent, mid-April.

'Gap': deep pink.

'Gretchen Kellas': reddish purple, darker blotch, 2½", mid-April.

'Gusty Cole': purplish pink, hose-in-hose, 1½", late April.

'Heide Hartwiger': white, tinted very pale yellowish green, 2", late May.

'Katie Speirs' (SS–9): purplish pink, single, mid-March, 2".

'Kent Moss': light purple, 2".

'Kimba': deep pink, 1½", mid-April.

'Laura Speirs': light yellowish pink, darker blotch, 2", mid-April.

'Lucie Sproull': light purple, 1½", late April.

'Milt Silvert': white, slightly blushed with light shade of purplish pink, very prominent purplish blotch, slightly wavy, 2½", mid-May.

'Pete Flatley': deep pink, hose-in-hose, 1¾"; mid-April.

'Philip Crocket': purplish pink, hose-in-hose, 1½", mid-April.

'Royce Sproull #2' ('Flame' seedling): reddish orange, 2", mid-May.

'Steve Zalumas': purplish pink, dark purple blotch, 2½", early May.

'Vivian Moss': medium pink, 1½", mid-May.

MARLBANK FARMS "COLONIAL SERIES"

'Baron de Viomenil': deep rose, mid-April.

'Baron von Stuben': strong pink, hose-in-hose, ruffled, 1½", mid-April.

'Betsy Ross' ('Hino Crimson' seedling): light red, hose-in-hose, ruffled, 1½", mid-April.

'Col. Alexander Hamilton': light purple, hose-in-hose, 1½", mid-April.

'Col. John Laurens': light pink, hose-in-hose, mid-April; light green leaves.

'Col. Timothy Pickering' ('Hino Crimson' seedling): light red, single, 1½", small compact.

'Comte de Barras': strong pink, hose-in-hose, 1½", mid-April.

'Comte de Grasse': strong pink, 1½", mid-April.

'Comte de Rochambeau': moderate purplish pink, 1½", mid-April.

'Count William de Deauz Ponts': bright pink, 1½", mid-April.

'Duke de Lauzun': purplish pink with darker blotch, single, 1½", mid-April.

'Gen. Benjamin Lincoln': light pink, hose-in-hose, 1½", mid-April; light green leaves.

'General Choizy': pink, hose-in-hose, slightly ruffled, late April.

'Gen. George Washington': purplish pink, hose-in-hose, late April.

'Gen. Henry Knox' ('Hino Crimson' seedling): light red, hose-in-hose, slightly ruffled, 1½", ruffled, mid-May.

'Gen. James Clinton': purplish pink, hose-in-hose, 1½", mid-April.

'Gen. "Mad" Anthony Wayne': yellowish pink with darker blotch, hose-in-hose, ruffled, 1½", persistent, mid-April.

'Gen. Peter Muhlenberg': purplish pink, 1½", mid-April.

McDONALD HYBRIDS—CAN CAN CHORUS HYBRIDS

Developed by Dr. Sandra McDonald of Le Mac Nurseries, Hampton, Virginia, in late 1970's for forcing azaleas; with flowers of good substance and developing well as pot plants. Plants should be hardy outdoors to 20°F. See also Appendix J.

CAN CAN CHORUS AZALEAS

'Mademoiselle Amy' ('Ambrosiana' × 'Joan's Choice'): deep red 46A, blotch slightly darker, hose-in-hose, 1½" across, early midseason; compact 6 × 10" wide with pruning in 3 years.

'Mademoiselle Bridgette' ('Loelia' × 'Ambrosiana'): vivid purplish red, blotch strong red spotting, 53C, double, ruffled, 3½" across, midseason, pompon center, no stamens; broad 8 × 19" wide with pruning in 3 years.

'Mademoiselle Charlene' ('Loelia' × 'Ambrosiana'): strong purplish red 58C, blotch deep red, double 2¾" across, early midseason; compact spreading, 8 × 12" wide with pruning in 3 years.

'Mademoiselle Gigi' ('Loelia' × 'Ambrosiana'): moderate purplish pink 63B, blotch purplish red, double, pompom center, no stamens, 3", midseason; upright 12 × 12" with pruning in 3 years.

'Mademoiselle Lisette' ('Loelia' × 'Ambrosiana'): moderate purplish pink 62B, blotch purplish red, double, center petals folded, 3", early midseason; 10 × 12" wide with pruning in 3 years.

'Mademoiselle Margot' ('Ambrosiana' × 'Joan's Choice'): deep red 46A, hose-in-hose, wavy margin, 2¾"; 7 × 15" with pruning in 3 years; leaves glossy.

'Mademoiselle Nanette' ('Loelia' × 'Ambrosiana'): vivid purplish red, blotch vivid red, double, no stamens, 2¾", early midseason; broad upright 7 × 15" pruned in 3 years.

'Mademoiselle Yvette' ('Loelia' × 'Ambrosiana'): strong purplish red, blotch deep red, double, 3" diameter, early midseason; broad, 12 × 15" pruned in 3 years.

McDONALD MISCELLANEOUS HYBRIDS

'Blushing Angel' ('Dainty Rose' × 'Ho O'?, open-pollinated, '82.): white, tips moderate pink 49B, hose-in-hose, lobes round, 1½, fragrant; leaves yellow in fall; 24 × 26" in 6 years. Hardy to 5°F.

'Pure Perfection' ('Gumpo' × 'Wakaebisu', '82): white, light green throat, hose-in-hose, wavy, 2½"; late; 20 × 26" wide in 6 years. Hardy to 5°F.

'Salmon Mound' ('Dainty Rose' × 'Salmon Beauty' ? open-pollinated, '82): deep pink to deep yellowish pink 39B, red dots in blotch, white streaks on reverse, hose-in-hose, 1"; low compact, 25" × 13" high in 6 years. Hardy to 5°F.

'Salmon Sunrise' ('Dainty Rose' × 'Salmon Beauty' ? open-pollinated, '82): deep pink to yellowish pink 39B, blotch spotted strong red 45D, hose-in-hose, rounded, 1¼"; low rounded 18 × 22" wide in 6 years. Hardy to 5°F.

MAYO HYBRIDS

Developed by R. P. Mayo of Augusta, Georgia, U.S.A., in the 1940's. The nursery is no longer in existence, but many of the Mayo Hybrids are still available. Most of the plants are early midseason, blooming later than Kurume Hybrids or *R. kaempferi*, with larger flowers, and hardy in zone 8 and possibly 7b. Habit of growth is similar to Kurumes; dense upright spreading 3–5'. Some with *kaempferi* may be taller.

'Bo-Peep' (Kurume hybrid × *kaempferi*): light reddish orange, hose-in-hose, 1¼"; medium, upright.

'Fairy Queen' (*indicum* × *kaempferi*): white, flushed pink, 2"; tall, upright.

'Fireglow' ('Hinode Giri' hybrid): reddish orange, 1½"; upright.

'Flaming Beacon' (*indicum* × *kaempferi*): reddish orange, blotch darker, 1¾"; upright, tall.

'Gypsy Rose' (*kaempferi* hybrid): purplish red, darker blotch, 2"; upright, tall.

'Indian Sunset' (Kurume hybrid × *kaempferi*): strong yellowish pink, hose-in-hose, 1½"; upright, tall.

'May Firelight' (Kurume hybrid × *kaempferi*): reddish orange, 1¾"; upright, tall.

'Mayo's Magic Lily': pale purplish pink, blotch darker, partially petaloid sepal, petals divided, 2¼"; medium upright.

'Mayo's Perfection' (Kurume hybrid × *kaempferi*; an improved 'Hinode Giri'): reddish orange; medium upright.

'Mayo's Pride': strong red, hose-in-hose, 2"; upright tall.

'Orange King' ('Hinode Giri' hybrid): reddish orange, 2"; medium, spreading.

'Orange Surprise': deep yellowish pink 43C, dark spots in blotch, hose-in-hose, 2½".

'Pink Imperial' (Kurume hybrid × indicum hybrid): vivid purplish red, frilled, 2¼"; upright, medium.

'Pink Lustre' (Kurume hybrid × *kaempferi*): purplish red, 1½"; upright, medium.

'Princess Augusta': light pink, hose-in-hose, 2½", very popular.

'Queen of Augusta' (Kurume hybrid ?): strong yellowish pink, hose-in-hose, 2"; spreading, medium.

'Salmon Monarch' (Kurume hybrid × *kaempferi*): yellowish pink, blotch darker, 2½"; spreading, medium.

'Salmon Splendor' (Kaempferi hybrid): strong red, 2¼"; upright, tall.

MONROVIA HYBRIDS

The Monrovia Nursery of Azusa, California, started 1926, has one of the largest wholesale inventories of diverse nursery stock in the United States. They are constantly in search of new plant materials and have introduced the following azaleas. Parentage not available on all cultivars; Indian Hybrids were used including Belgian and Southern Indians. T.M. = Trademark. PP = Plant Patent.

'Christmas Rose' (PP 1212): deep pink, double, large, midseason.

'Fire Dance' (T.M.): vivid red, double, midseason.

The Imperial Series are Laughing Water seedlings, by E. Hudson, introduced by Monrovia as Southern Indian Hybrids:

- 'Imperial Countess' (T.M.): moderate yellowish pink hose-in-hose, petals crinkled, 2½", midseason; compact spreading.
- 'Imperial Duchess' (T.M.): deep pink to light pink, hose-in-hose, double, 2½", compact spreading.
- 'Imperial King' (PP 3031): strong purplish red, double, 2½", vigorous.
- 'Imperial Prince' (PP 3030): vivid reddish orange, double, 2½", compact spreading.
- 'Imperial Princess' (PP 3754): purplish pink, darker blotch, semidouble 2¾–3"; compact habit.
- 'Imperial Queen' (PP 1753): white shading to light purplish pink, darker blotch, hose-in-hose, occasionally semidouble, 3–3½"; compact spreading.

'Pink Charm' (T.M.; Southern Indian Hybrid): pink, semidouble, midseason.

'Plum Crazy' (T.M.; syn. 'Rosa Belton'): deep purplish pink, with white markings on the petals; the petals; 2½"; midseason.

'Red Riot' (T.M.): vivid red.

'Sugar Plum' (T.M; Glenn Dale seedling): vivid pink.

'White Falls' (T.M.): white.

NORTH TISBURY HYBRIDS

Mrs. Julian (Polly) Hill on Martha's Vineyard, Massachusetts, began in the 1960's growing seed and cuttings sent by Dr. Tsuneshige Rokujo, Tokyo, Japan, from crosses he made or seed which he collected in his garden. Some are from *R. nakaharai;* others are crosses of this species and other clones. Many are low mounding, spreading ground cover plants.

'Andante', 'Trill', and 'Hotline' were first introduced as the Music Street Trio, named for a street in West Tisbury, and now included with the North Tisbury Hybrids. They were seeds from a friend's collection of Gumpo azaleas in Tokyo.

'Chinyeyi' is the old Japanese name for 'Chinei'. For her deciduous azaleas such as 'Choptank River', 'Marydel' and others, see the Deciduous List. All plants are hardy to −9°F. unless noted.

'Alexander' (*R. nakaharai* × 'Kin no sai'; by Dr. Rokujo): flowers deep reddish orange 44CD, blotch deep purplish red 63B, 1¾–2¾" wide, very late; plant creeping, dense irregularly mounding, 8 × 36" in 9 years.

'Andante' (open pollinated seed of Gumpo azaleas, collected by Dr. Rokujo): light pink, 2½", late, dwarf compact.

'Gabrielle Hill' ('Chinyeyi' × 'W. Leith'; by Dr. Rokujo): 2½" wide; moderate pink 48D, strong purplish red blotch 54A, ruffled, 2¼", very late; low spreading, 15 × 60" wide.

'Hotline' (open pollinated seed of new dwarf Gumpo. Seed from Dr. Rokujo): vivid purplish red 54B, deep red blotch 53B, 3", late; dwarf branching upward, 28 × 38" in 12 years.

'Jeff Hill' (hand pollinated seed of 'Maruba Osakazuki' by Dr. Rokujo): deep pink 48B, blotch moderate red 51A, 2" wavy, late; semi-dwarf 17 × 26" in 13 years.

'Joseph Hill' (*R. nakaharai* × 'W. Leith'. Seed from Dr. Rokujo): vivid red 44A, 2¼", wavy margin; dwarf creeping, 12 × 42" in 13 years.

'Late Love' ('Chinyeyi' × *R. nakaharai*; by Dr. Rokujo): strong pink 48C, blotch deep purplish red 61B, 2¼", very late; dwarf creeping, 18 × 48" in 14 years.

'Louisa' ('Chinyeyi' × 'W. Leith'; by Dr. Rokujo): deep to moderate pink 50C-D, blotch moderate red 51A, late; low, dwarf spreading 10 × 33" in 10 years.

'Marilee' (*R. nakaharai* seedling; seed from Dr. Rokujo): strong red 50A, blotch moderate red 51A, wavy, 2¼", very late; semidwarf, 16 × 50" in 12 years.

'Michael Hill' ('Chinyeyi' × *R. nakaharai*; by Dr. Rokujo): strong to moderate pink 49A-B, blotch moderate purplish red 63B, 2¾" frilled late; dwarf spreading 17 × 45" in 13 years.

'Mount Seven Star' (*R. nakaharai* seed collected on Mt. Seven Star, Taiwan by C. S. Kuo): vivid red 44A, inconspicuous purplish spotting, lobes wavy, 2"; very low, dense, 4 × 24" in 5 years.

'Pink Pancake' ('Chinyeyi' × *R. nakaharai*; by Dr. Rokujo): strong pink 48C, with purplish red 57A spotting, wavy 2½", late; low creeping 10 × 36" in 14 years.

'Red Fountain' (syn. 'Niobe'; 'W. Leith' × *R. nakaharai*; by Dr. Rokujo): deep reddish orange 42b, with deep red 26A, spotting, wavy, 1¾", late.

'Susannah Hill' ('W. Leith' × *R. nakaharai*; by Dr. Rokujo): strong red 45C with inconspicuous moderate red spotting, wavy, occasionally petaloid, 1¾"; dwarf prostrate 15 × 52" in 13 years.

'Trill' (open pollinated seed of Gumpo collected by Dr. Rokujo): strong reddish orange, 41B, blotch deep red 45A, wavy, 2½", late; semidwarf spreading, 14 × 24" in 12 years.

'Wintergreen' (*R. nakaharai* OP.; seed collected by Dr. Rokujo): moderate red 50B, blotch purplish red 61C, wavy, 2½"; dwarf spreading 15 × 39" in 12 years.

OTHER HYBRIDS

'Corinna Borden' (seed of *R. kaempferi leucanthum* collected by Dr. Rokujo): pale pink 49C, blotch, very light purple 75B; upright. Hardy to −9°F.

'Lady Locks' (seed of *R. macrosepalum* collected by Dr. Rokujo): light reddish purple 77C-D, blotch deep reddish purple 66A, fragrant, 3", frilled, long sepals; upright to 8'.

'Libby' (*R. kaempferi* var. *leucanthum* seed collected by Dr. Rokujo): light purplish pink 68D, blotch deep pink 68A, wavy, 1¾"; upright, 19 × 23" high in 7 years.

'Seigai' (*R. macrosepalum* var. *linearifolium* plant from Dr. Rokujo): 'Seigai' is old Japanese name for this plant; deep purplish pink 68A, 5 separate linear petals 1–12" long, ⅜" wide; leaves also linear, reported semi-dwarf 3 × 6' tall. Can see no difference in 'Seigai' and plants introduced earlier as *R. linearifolium*.

The following plants were cuttings of Satsuki azaleas growing in Japan and sent by Dr. Rokuji. Unfortunately, the cuttings were not labeled and plants have been named for Japanese friends of Mrs. Hill's and registered. All hardy to −9°F.

'Eiko San' (Satsuki cutting from Dr. Rokuji): strong red 47C, double, compact, 15 × 30", in 15 years. Late; hardy to −9°F. Similar to 'Balsaminaeflorum', possibly 'Beni Banyo'.

'Matsuyo' (Satsuki cutting from Dr. Rokujo): white with dots, stripes, sector and selfs of strong red 39B, late; low compact, 16 × 30" in 10 years.

'Midori' (Satsuki cutting from Dr. Rokujo): large, white, wavy, greenish blotch, late; compact.

'Yaye' (Satsuki cutting from Dr. Rokujo): white, many variations of stripes, sectors, selfs and margins of pale pink, blotch light greenish yellow, 6 petals, 4½", late; low loose habit. 19 × 62" in 16 years. Bluish green leaves. Hardy to −9°F.

'Yuka' (Satsuki cutting from Dr. Rokujo): white, occasionally flushed, streaked and selfs of strong pink 52D, blotch deep red, 4" ruffled; mounding 18 × 30" in 10 years. Hardy to −9°F.

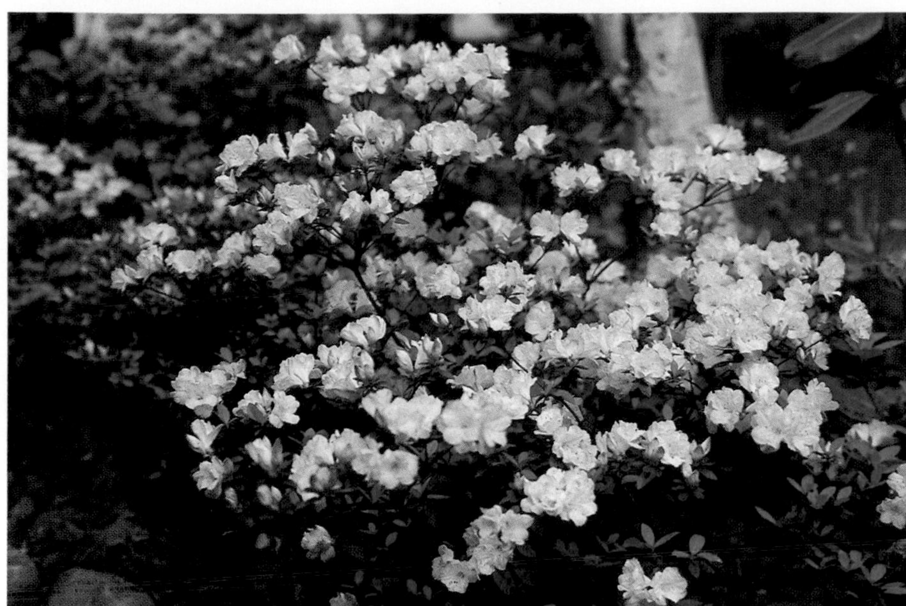

'Blushing Angel' McDonald Hybrid. MC DONALD

'Mademoiselle Nanette' McDonald Hybrid. MC DONALD

'Mademoiselle Gi Gi' McDonald Hybrid. MC DONALD

Plate 98

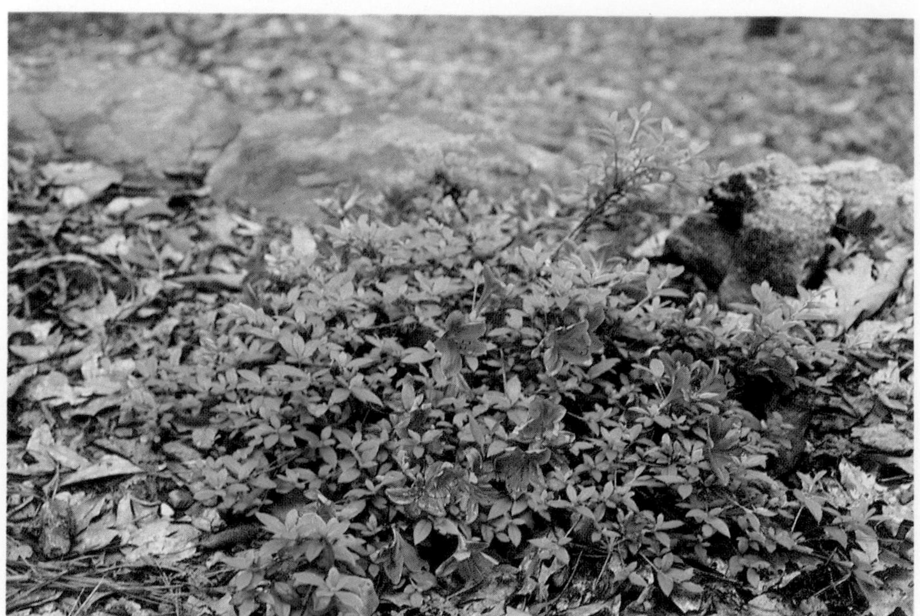

'Wintergreen' North Tisbury Hybrid. GALLE

'Hampton Beauty' Pericat Hybrid. GALLE

'Sweetheart Supreme' Pericat Hybrid. GALLE

'Hiawatha' Pericat Hybrid. GALLE

'Conversation Piece' Robin Hill Hybrid. STEWART

'Mrs. Emil Hager' Robin Hill Hybrid. GALLE

Plate 100

'Nancy of Robin Hill' Robin Hill Hybrid. GALLE

'Wendy' Robin Hill Hybrid. STEWART

'Welmet' Robin Hill Hybrid. HARDING

'Watchet' Robin Hill Hybrid. STEWART

'Madame Mab Chalon' Robin Hill Hybrid. GALLE

'Dogwood' Intergroup Evergreen Hybrid. MILLER

Plate 102

'Otomeno' (*R. kuisianum* × Satsuki) Intergroup Evergreen Hybrid. GALLE

'Broughtonii Aureum' Azaleodendron. GALLE

Hirado Azaleas in Japan. GALLE

Breaking the heavy root ball from a container azalea before planting. MILLER

Azalea planted too deep with a new root system developed at the surface. G. SMITH

Plate 104

Six foot root ball of a deciduous native North American species. GALLE

Less than 40% of the azalea roots intact from a 6-foot balled azalea. GALLE

Cut back North American deciduous species with a new root system developed. GALLE

The following azaleas are numbered North Tisbury seedlings but not named by Mrs. Hill.

'Hills Single Red' (*R. nakaharai* OP; similar to 'North Tisbury Orange' and could be the same or sibling): reddish orange; compact, spreading.

'Mrs. Hill's Flaming Mamie' (61–78 *R. nakaharai* × *R. kaempferi*, crossed by Dr. Rokujo): vivid red; compact, upright to 5 ft. 'Airport Red', a sibling is similar.

'North Tisbury Orange' (61–81C *R. nakaharai*, OP): reddish orange; compact, very dwarf.

NUCCIO HYBRIDS

Started in 1935 by Julius and Joe Nuccio, Altadena, California, U.S.A., this nursery is noted not only for its breeding work with azaleas but also for its work with camellias and the importing of Japanese azaleas, particularly Satsuki Hybrids. Their azalea breeding objectives are to develop hardy and vigorous forcing and garden azaleas. The nursery is family oriented; the work is continuing under the founder's nephew Julius, Jr. and his two sons, Tom and Jim. The following cultivars should be hardy in zones 7b to 9. Habit of growth is compact, twiggy to 3 to 5' high. See also Appendix J.

'Nuccio's Blue Moon' ('Valo' × 'Valo'): brilliant violet, occasionally with white center, 2"; late; compact.

'Nuccio's Harvest Moon' ('Geisha Girl' × 'Summer Sun'): yellowish pink, some with white centers, 2–2½"; late.

'Nuccio's High Sierra' ('Santoi' × 'Laughing Water'): white, hose-in-hose, 1½"; compact.

'Nuccio's Honey Bunch' ('L. J. Bobbink' × 'Duc de Rohan'): white, blending into deep yellowish pink on edges and tips, hose-in-hose, double 2"; compact upright.

'Nuccio's Misty Moon' ('Geisha Girl' × 'Summer Sun'): very pale purple, darker edges, 2–12"; late.

'Nuccio's Mt. Baldy' (seedling of 'Tsuki no Shimo'): white with occasional deep pink throat, 1½–2", late; compact; leaves narrow, curled inward.

'Nuccio's Orchid Queen' (Kurume hybrid seedling): light to pale purple, resembles 'L. J. Bobbink' but blooms longer; strong growth.

'Nuccio's Pink Champagne' ('Triumph' × 'L. J. Bobbink'): light pink, double, hose-in-hose, 3".

'Nuccio's Polka' ('Mme. Alfred Sander' × 'Gumpo'): reddish orange, 2½" midseason; long flowering; compact.

'Nuccio's Variegated Red Ruffles' (sport of 'Ruffled Giant'): leaf with whitish margin, deep pink flower.

'Nuccio's Warm Heart' ('Mme. Alfred Sander' × 'Gumpo'): deep pink, semidouble 2", midseason; compact.

'Nuccio's Wild Cherry' ('Mme. Alfred Sander' × 'Summer Sun'): vivid red, rounded, petals, 2½–3"; dark narrow foliage; compact.

OTHER NUCCIO HYBRIDS

I. 'Snowbird' × 'Rhodelin' hybrids ('Snowbird' = Coolidge 'Mucronatum' seedling, 'Rhodelin' = seedling of *R. scabrum* 'sublaceolatum'). The following cultivars should be hardy in zones 7b to 9, are medium sized shrubs 3 to 5 ft. high.

'Nuccio's Break of Day' (sport of 'California Dawn'): yellowish pink, dark pink spots, 3".

'Nuccio's California Dawn': moderate yellowish pink, 3"; vigorous.

'Nuccio's Friendship': deep pink, single to semidouble, 3".

'Nuccio's Orchid Robe': flowers in terminal clusters; light purple. 3½–4".

'Nuccio's Purple Robe': purple, 3½–4".

'Nuccio's Sunrise': strong yellowish pink, 3".

II. 'Nuccio's California Dawn' × 'Nuccio's Pink Champagne'. The following cultivars are hardy in zones 8–10 and moderate sized plants 3 to 5 ft. high.

'Nuccio's Crown Jewel': white, stripes moderate yellowish pink, semidouble, tubular, 2½–3".

'Nuccio's Magnificence': white, double, 3½–4"; vigorous grower.

'Nuccio's Masterpiece': white, double, ruffled petals 3½–4"; large foliage; extremely vigorous growth.

'Nuccio's Pink Bubbles': light pink, double, 3"; strong growth; large foliage.

'Nuccio's Pink Tiger': moderate purplish pink, purplish red spotting; ruffled, 2½".

'Nuccio's Spring Charm': light yellowish pink, darker edges, 2½–3"; vigorous.
'Nuccio's Spring Delight': light purplish pink, deep pink spotting in upper lobe, 2½–3".
'Nuccio's Vintage Champagne' (sport of 'Pink Champagne'): moderate reddish orange, double hose-in-hose, 3".
'Nuccio's White Champagne' (sport of 'Pink Champagne'; developed by T. Domoto): white with showy red throat, double hose-in-hose, 3".

III. 'Purity' (Rutherford) × 'Louisa J. Bobbink' (Rutherford). The following cultivars are hardy in zones 8–9 and possibly hardier with additional testing. Plants are moderate in size, 3–6 ft. in height.
'Nuccio's Dream Clouds': white with green throat, double hose-in-hose, ruffled, 2½–3"; sun tolerant.
'Nuccio's Garden Party': deep pink, semidouble, 2½–3"; profusion in spring, spot flowering fall and winter.
'Nuccio's Happy Days': light purple, double, hose-in-hose, 2½"; 10 months blooming season.
'Nuccio's Primavera': white with green throat, single to semidouble, 2½–3".
'Nuccio's Mexico': vivid pink, tubular, 1½–2"; long blooming season.

IV. 'Avenir' (Belgium Indian Hybrid) × 'Hexe'. The following cultivars are hardy in zones 8–10 and possibly hardier. Moderate habit of growth, 3 to 6 ft. in height.
'Nuccio's Allegro': strong red, semidouble, 2½".
'Nuccio's Sunburst': vivid reddish orange, semidouble, 2"; compact; leaves small, dark green.

V. 'Red Poppy' (Kerrigan) open pollinated. The following cultivars should be hardy in zones 8–10. Plant habit of moderate growth 3 to 6 ft. high.
'Nuccio's Carnival': deep pink, single to semidouble, 3½–4"; tall.
'Nuccio's Carnival Candy': vivid red, 3½–4"; tall.
'Nuccio's Carnival Clown': vivid purple, ruffled 3"; low.
'Nuccio's Carnival Fanfare': moderate purplish pink, 3½"; low.
'Nuccio's Carnival Firecracker': vivid reddish orange, 2½"; tall.
'Nuccio's Carnival Jackpot': reddish orange, 2"; low.
'Nuccio's Carnival Magic': strong pink, rounded petals, 3"; tall.
'Nuccio's Carnival Parade': purple, 2½"; tall.
'Nuccio's Carnival Queen': strong to vivid pink, semidouble, 2½"; low to medium.
'Nuccio's Carnival Rocket': vivid reddish orange, 2½"; low.
'Nuccio's Carnival Time': vivid purple, 3", tall.

VI. 'Hino Crimson' × 'Laughing Water' (Kurume Hybrid). The following cultivars are hardy in zone 7a, possibly 6b to 9. Dense twiggy growth 3 to 6 ft. high.
'Nuccio's All Glory': vivid pink, 1½".
'Nuccio's Bit of Sunshine': strong red, hose-in-hose, 1½".
'Nuccio's Blue Jay': strong purplish blue, 2–2½".
'Nuccio's Blue Sky': very light violet, 1½".
'Nuccio's Fashion': very pale violet, hose-in-hose, 1½–2"; compact.
'Nuccio's Jewel Box': strong pink, hose-in-hose, 1½"; compact.
'Nuccio's Lilac Lady': light purple, 1½–2".
'Nuccio's Plum Purty': purple, hose-in-hose, 1½'; compact.
'Nuccio's Red Glitters': vivid red, 2"; vigorous, long blooming.
'Nuccio's Rose Glitters': moderate red, 2"; vigorous, long blooming, sun tolerant.

VII. 'Hino Crimson' open pollinated hybrids. The following cultivars should be hardy in zones 6–9. Dense twiggy growth 3 to 6 ft. high.
'Nuccio's Butterfly': yellowish white, hose-in-hose, 1½–2".
'Nuccio's Dancing Doll': strong yellowish pink, double, 1–1½–2"; vigorous.
'Nuccio's First Call': light yellowish pink, hose-in-hose, 1½".
'Nuccio's Limelight': pale yellowish white; 1½–2".
'Nuccio's Little Gem': light pink, 1½"; profuse; compact.
'Nuccio's Little Red Riding Hood': strong reddish orange, 41B, 1½"; vigorous and compact.
'Nuccio's Pink Cloud': light pink, hose-in-hose, 2".

'Nuccio's Pink Smoke': light purplish pink, 1½".
'Nuccio's Popcorn': yellowish white, double, 1½".
'Nuccio's Showgirl': light orange, hose-in-hose, 1–1½".

VIII. 'Duc de Rohan' (Southern Indian Hybrid) × 'Laughing Water' (Kurume Hybrid) hybrids. The following plants should be hardy in zones 7b–10 with moderate habit of growth 3 to 6 ft. high.

'Nuccio's Dew Drop': pale pink to white, reddish spotting, single to semidouble; 1½–2"; vigorous and compact.
'Nuccio's Ivory Tower': white, 1½–2"; very vigorous, tall.
'Nuccio's Melody Lane': light pink, heavily spotted red, 2½–3"; vigorous, upright.
'Nuccio's Pink Snow': light pink, single to semidouble, 1½"; low, compact.
'Nuccio's Rain Drops': white, 2"; compact.

PENNINGTON HYBRIDS

The late Ralph W. Pennington was a collector, nurseryman, and hybridizer from Covington, Georgia, U.S.A. His commercial nursery had one of the largest collections of azaleas in the southeast. The parentage of most of his hybrids is not known. All are hardy to at least 5°F. CNC was Pennington's code for Covington Nursery Co. All of the Satsuki Hybrids are hardy in zones 7b–9; others should be hardy in 6b. All are moderate size shrubs 3 to 6 ft. unless noted.

'Anne Perry' (Satsuki hybrid): reddish orange, midseason; compact habit, good winter foliage.
'Beth Bullard' (Satsuki hybrid): yellowish pink, 4", late; low compact.
'Bill Bullard' (Satsuki hybrid): reddish orange, late; good winter foliage.
'CNC Pinko' (syn. #152): pink.
'Dawn Lovell' (syn.'CNC 2'): purple.
'K. J. P.' (Satsuki hybrid; named for his wife): pink with white edge, variable, with occasional stripes and selfs, mid to late, 4"; open habit.
'Landon' (Pennington seedling, introduced by Landon School, Md. '74): vivid purplish red 66C, darker spotting, 3¼". Hardy in zone 6b.
'Lynn Stieglitz' ('Myu no Isuki' × 'Corsage'; named by B. Hancock): purple, early, slightly fragrant.
'Mary Caroline' (syn. 'CNC 3'; Satsuki hybrid): purplish pink, pale pink center, 3", loose grower.
'Mike Bullard' (sport of 'Festive'): vivid red, early.
'Mike Perry' (Satsuki hybrid): light reddish orange, darker blotch, 2¾", late; low compact.
'Mrs. Anne G. Pennington' (Satsuki hybrid; named for Ralph's mother): variable, pink to white and blotched, 3½–4"; late.
'Mrs. Ralph Pennington' ('Miyuno no Tsuki' × 'Greetings'): light pink, darker margins, 3½".
'Nancy Bullard' ('Rose Gumpo' × 'Pink Gumpo'): deep pink, 3", late; low compact, good winter foliage.
'Pennington Purple' (Kurume hybrid): purple, 2", early, fragrant.
'Pennington White' (Kurume hybrid): white, 2", frilled, early to midseason, fragrant; considered better than 'Snow'. 3 to 5 ft. high.
'Sara Wallace' (chance seedling): deep pink, white center, 2½"; low compact.

PERICAT HYBRIDS

Developed by Alphonse Pericat, a florist, of Collingdale, Pennsylvania, U.S.A., as greenhouse forcing plants. Their parentage is unknown, possibly Belgian Indian Hybrids × Kurume Hybrids. They were first exhibited at the Philadelphia Flower Show in 1931 followed by the introduction of a few named cultivars and a wide distribution of unnamed seedlings. Many of the seedlings were named and introduced by other nurserymen. In parentheses following the cultivar name I have indicated the person naming it.

The plants are generally of medium height, 3 to 5 ft., spreading and dense, but a few are low or tall. The flowers show considerable variation from single, hose-in-hose, semidouble, double and petaloid forms. Many are frilled and the semidouble types give a rosebud effect on opening. The Pericat Hybrids are as hardy as the Kurume Hybrids, zones 7a to 9b.

Many of the clones have excellent qualities in flower and plant habit. Unfortunately many are not readily available.

'Alphonse Pericat' (Pericat): deep pink, hose-in-hose, semidouble, 1¼"; early midseason; spreading, low.

'Anne Chenee' (Pericat): white flushed vivid reddish purple, hose-in-hose, frilled, 2½"; late midseason; spreading, dense, medium height.

'Augusta Beauty' (Mayo): strong yellowish pink, hose-in-hose, 2¼"; early midseason; upright, medium height.

'Augusta Belle' (Mayo): white flushed deep pink with darker blotch, partially petaloid sepals, 1½"; late midseason; upright, dense, medium height.

'Autumn Sunset' (Pericat): dark reddish orange.

'Baby Pericat': light purplish pink, hose-in-hose, small flowers.

'Barbara Gail' (Le-Mac): light purplish pink, hose-in-hose.

'China Seas' (Leach): pink, partially petaloid sepals, semidouble, 2".

'Dawn' (Perkins-de Wilde): deep purplish pink, white center and darker blotch, hose-in-hose, 2¾"; late midseason; spreading, dense, medium height. 'Madame Alphonse Pericat' and 'Morning Glory' are similar.

'Diamen' (Mayo): strong orange, partially petaloid sepals, 2"; early midseason; upright, dense, medium height.

'Eastertide': light yellowish pink, hose-in-hose, frilled.

'Elizabeth Mayo' (Mayo): strong pink, hose-in-hose, 2¼"; early midseason; upright, tall, dense.

'Emile Russave' (syn. 'Emile Rousseau', Pericat): strong red, blotch darker, semidouble, frilled 2¾"; late midseason, spreading, dense, medium height.

'Flanders Field' (syn. 'Cornelia van Herden', Pericat): vivid red, blotch darker, occasionally semidouble; 2¼"; late midseason; spreading, medium height.

'Fortune' (Perkins-de Wilde): strong red, semidouble, 2½"; early midseason, spreading, dense, medium height.

'Gardenia Supreme' (Pericat): white, yellowish green throat, blotch reddish purple, hose-in-hose, semidouble, 1½"; early midseason; spreading, dense, medium height.

'Gem' (Perkins-de Wilde): deep pink, hose-in-hose, frilled, 1½"; early midseason; spreading, dense, medium height. Similar to 'Salmon Beauty' Kur.

'Gloriana' (Pericat): deep purplish pink, blotch darker, petaloid sepals, frilled, 1¾", late; spreading, dense, medium height.

'Glory' (Le-Mac): strong red, hose-in-hose, semidouble, 1¾"; early midseason; spreading, low, dense.

'Hampton Beauty' (Le-Mac): deep pink, blotch darker, partially petaloid sepals, 2"; early midseason; spreading, dense, medium height.

'Hampton Rose' (Le-Mac): vivid purplish red, hose-in-hose, frilled, 1½"; early; spreading, low, dense. May be a Bobbink and Atkins hybrid.

'Harmony' (Le-Mac): deep purplish pink, hose-in-hose, semidouble, 2¼", early midseason.

'Hiawatha' (Robert Craig & Co.): strong red, hose-in-hose, rounded lobes, 1½"; late midseason; spreading, medium height.

'Holiday': strong yellowish pink.

'Lilac Charm' (Mayo): light purple, partially petaloid sepals, 2¼"; upright, dense, medium height.

'Lilac Pearl' (Mayo): pink, 1½"; early midseason; spreading, low, dense.

'Lorraine': deep pink, hose-in-hose.

'Madame Alphonse Pericat' (syn. 'Madame Pericat'; Pericat): purplish pink, dark blotch, light center, 2¾; late midseason.

'Maiden's Blush' (Mayo): deep purplish pink, blotch darker, with partially petaloid sepals, 1¾"; late midseason; spreading, medium height, dense.

'Marjorie Ann' (syn. 'Richesse'; Le-Mac): vivid red, hose-in-hose, semidouble, 1¼"; early midseason; spreading, low, dense.

'Melody' (Le-Mac): strong red, blotch darker, hose-in-hose, 2¼"; late midseason; spreading, medium height, dense.

'Morning Glow': purplish pink, dark blotch, light center, hose-in-hose, 2¾"; late midseason.

'Mme. Pericat Pink' (sport of 'Mme. Pericat'): deep pink, hose-in-hose.

'M. R. Mulford': vivid red, hose-in-hose.

'Mrs. Fisher': light pink, hose-in-hose.

'Nancy Clay' (Mayo): deep pink, hose-in-hose, rounded lobes, 1¾"; early midseason; spreading, medium height, dense.

'New Dawn': strong yellowish pink, double.

'Orchid' (Perkins-deWilde): vivid purplish red, with partially petaloid sepals, 1¾"; early midseason; spreading, mid-height, dense.

'Pericat Orchid' (Pericat): deep purplish pink, hose-in-hose.

'Pericat Pink' (Pericat): pink, hose-in-hose, later than 'Dawn' and with stronger color.

'Pericat Salmon' (Pericat): light yellowish pink, hose-in-hose.

'Pericat White' (Pericat): white, hose-in-hose.

'Pink Enchantress' (Mayo): pink, hose-in-hose, 2", early midseason; spreading, medium height, dense.

'Pink Pericat': light purplish pink, hose-in-hose.

'Pink Supreme': pink, hose-in-hose.

'Pinocchio' (Pericat): deep pink, double.

'Pride' (Perkins-deWilde): strong red, hose-in-hose, 1¾"; late midseason; spreading, medium height.

'Princess Augusta' (Mayo): white, flushed deep purplish pink, blotch darker, hose-in-hose, 2¼"; early midseason; spreading, medium height, dense.

'Rhythm' (Le-Mac): light yellowish pink, blotch darker, semidouble, 2¼"; early midseason; spreading, medium height, dense.

'Rival' (Perkins-deWilde): light red, hose-in-hose; semidouble, 2¼"; late midseason; upright, medium height.

'Sensation' (Perkins-deWilde): vivid purplish red, hose-in-hose, 1¾"; late midseason; spreading, low, dense.

'Splendor' (Perkins-deWilde): deep purplish pink, hose-in-hose, semidouble, 2¼"; early midseason, spreading, medium height, dense. 'Harmony' (LeMac) is similar.

'Spring Beauty' (Mayo): strong yellowish pink, white throat, and deep pink blotch, 2¼"; late midseason; upright, medium height, dense.

'Spring Dawn' (Mayo): white faintly flushed pink, hose-in-hose, semidouble, 1-1'2"; late midseason; upright, medium height, dense.

'Spring Glory' (Mayo): pink, hose-in-hose, frilled, 2½"; early midseason; spreading, low, dense.

'Sunset' (Perkins-deWilde): strong red, semidouble with petaloid sepals, 1¾"; early midseason; upright, medium height.

'Sweetheart' (Perkins-deWilde): strong red, blotch darker, hose-in-hose, frilled, 2"; early midseason; spreading, medium height.

'Sweetheart Supreme' (Robert Craig and Co.): deep pink, blotch darker, hose-in-hose, semidouble, frilled, 1¾"; late midseason; spreading, medium height, dense; more tender than most Pericats. Zone 8a.

'Symphony' (Le-Mac): deep pink, hose-in-hose, 2¼"; late midseason; spreading, medium height.

'Twenty Grand' (Leach): vivid purplish red, semidouble, 2"; early midseason; spreading, medium height.

'Willie Belle Mayo' (Mayo): deep purplish pink, hose-in-hose, frilled, 2½"; late midseason; spreading, medium height, dense.

PETER COX HYBRIDS

These hybrids were developed and introduced by Peter A. Cox of Perth, Scotland, in 1979. Mr. Cox is one of the world's leading growers of, and author dealing with, *Rhododendron*. All are hardy to 0°F.

'Lemur' (*R. nakaharai* 'Mariko' × 'Vuyk's Scarlet'): strong red, 52A, 1¾"; late; dwarf, semi creeping; attractive red winter foliage. Hardy to 0°F.

'Panda' ('Everest' × *R. kiusianum* white): white 1¼", compact dwarf, rounded. Hardy to 0°F.

'Squirrel' ('Galathea' × *R. nakaharai*): deep reddish orange, 42A, 1¼", sun resistant, late; compact dwarf. Hardy to 0°F.

'Wombat' (*R. nakaharai* 'Mariko' × 'Gaiety'): vivid purplish red 55A, 2". late; dwarf prostrate creeping. Hardy to 0°F.

ROBIN HILL HYBRIDS

Robert Gartrell of Wyckoff, New Jersey, started in 1937 to produce hardy, late blooming azaleas comparable in flowering characteristics to the Satsuki Hybrids. By the mid 1960's he had made over 1,000 crosses and grown some 25,000 seedlings. Of the 69 cultivars he named as Robin Hill Hybrids, 29 have been registered and are so marked. The International Registrar has added the prefix 'Robin Hill' to 'Congo', 'Elsa', 'Eric', 'Palmyra', 'Rosanne', and 'Wendy'. Of several hundred additional plants grown under number for testing, some have been distributed and should be referred to as Gartrell Hybrids. Blooming time for New Jersey, mid-May, early June. Hardy in zones 6b–9b. The plants vary in habit of growth, most are moderate size shrubs 3 to 5 ft. in height unless noted.

'Antoine' (syn. U17–3A; sport from U17–3 'Chanson'): light yellowish pink to pink to light pink, 38D–49C, hose-in-hose, petaloidy, wavy, 2¾".

'Betty Anne Voss' (syn. U17–8; 'Lady Louise' × 'Shinnyo no Tsuki') strong to light purplish pink 62A–C, double, hose-in-hose, calyx present, 3"; buds open like a rosebud; compact, broader than tall, 14 × 28" in 5 years. Reg.

'Betty Layman' (syn. T22–7; 'Oakland' × 'Heiwa'): deep yellowish pink to strong yellowish pink 43C–D, 6 petals, 3½".

'Blue Tip' (syn. Z12–2;'Malvatica' open seedling × 'Hosei'): white center, margin reddish purple 78A–78B, often concentrated at tips, 2¾".

'Bob White' (syn. N42–6; 'Oakland' × 'Dr. Bergmann'): white, throat pale yellow green 154D, hose-in-hose, occasionally semidouble, calyx absent, 2¼"; mounding habit.

'Chanson' (syn. U17–3; 'Lady Louise' × 'Shinnyo no Tsuki'): strong purplish pink to light pink 55B–D, occasional hairline edge of purplish red 54B, semidouble to double, calyx present, 3"; mounding habit.

'Christie' (syn. T21–2; 'Lady Louise' × 'Heiwa'): light to pale purplish pink 62C–D, 3".

'Conversation Piece' (syn. T36–6, 'Effie Bunce' ('Emile Russave' × 'Carol') × 'Eikan'): variable, white, moderate purplish pink 68C self, sectored and lighter margin, prominent blotch spotting of purplish red 57B, but not on all flowers, wavy, 3½"; mounding 25 × 28" wide in 16 years.

'Corry' (syn. T21–9; 'Mucronatum' × 'Heiwa'): vivid to strong red 44A to 45C, also reported purple, with variable white margin, wavy, 3".

'Dorothy Hayden' (syn. T5–2; 'Glacier' × ('Louise Gable' × 'Flame') × 'Getsu Toku'): white, with pale yellow green throat 145D, 3½"; dwarf 15 × 34" wide in 13 years.

'Dorothy Rees' (syn. V1–9; 'Glacier' × 'Lady Louise'): white, with light yellow green throat 145D, lobes overlapping, wavy, 3½"; vigorous, mounding 19 × 32" wide in 15 years.

'Early Beni' (syn. N26–6; 'Louise Gable' × ('Oakland' × (Belgian Hybrid × 'Carol')): deep reddish orange 43B, semidouble to double, hose-in-hose, calyx present, 2½"; upright semidwarf 28 × 36" wide in 17 years.

'Eliza Scott' (syn. T23–4; 'Oakland' × 'Heiwa'): strong purplish pink 62A–67D, 5 to 6 lobes, 3¼"; vigorous loose mounding.

'Eric' (syn. P5–2; Belgian Hybrid × 'Margie'): deep yellowish pink 43C, hose-in-hose, wavy, 2¼".

'Eunice Updike' (syn. U22–2; 'Louise Gable' × 'Shinnyo no Tsuki'): deep yellowish pink 43C, double, hose-in-hose, calyx present, 2–2¼"; dwarf 18 × 34" wide in 15 years.

'George Harding' (syn. T38–5; 'Louise Gable' × 'Shinnyo no Hikare'): vivid red 47C, often with white throat, 3".

'Glamora' (syn. V21–1; 'Lady Louise' × 'Wako'): pale purplish pink 62D, slight pale greenish to whitish throat, variably semidouble, calyx present, 3"; semidwarf, 19 × 25" wide in 15 years.

'Glencora' (syn. V5–1; 'Shinnyo no Tsuki' × 'Lady Louise'): moderate red 47C, double, calyx present, 2½"; dwarf, 14 × 24" wide in 15 years.

'Gresham' (syn. T18–3; ('Treasure' × 'Mucronatum' seedling) × 'Getsu Toku'): tinted strong pink 48D, variable with stripes, sectors or selfs of 48C, often 6-lobed, 3¼"; compact, dwarf, 16 × 38" in 10 years.

'Greta' (syn. T13–9; ('Oakland' × (Belgian hybrid × 'Carol')) × 'Getsu Toku'): strong purplish red 58C, 5–6 wavy lobes, 3"; dwarf, mounding, 15 × 39" in 15 years.

'Gwenda' (syn. T37–4; 'Lady Louise' × 'Eikan'): light purplish pink 56B, slightly greenish white in throat, 5 to 6 wavy lobes, 3"; semidwarf, 21" × 36" in 15 years.

'Hilda Niblett' (syn. T17–5; ('Glacier' × 'Tama Giku') × 'Getsu Toku'): tinted moderate pink 52D, edges paler, 5 to 6 very wavy lobes, 3¼"; low spreading.

'Jeanne Weeks' (syn. U7–8; 'Lady Louise' × ('Kaigetsu' × 'Carol')): strong purplish pink 62A to 65A, variable single to fully double, hose-in-hose, calyx absent, 2"; buds open like rose bud; semidwarf, 20 × 34" in 20 years.

'La Belle Helene' (syn. V2–3; 'Glacier' × 'Lady Louise'): white throat, margin strong purplish pink 63C, wavy, 3"; broad, dwarf 18 × 32" in 18 years.

'Lady Louise' (syn. J44–7; 'Louise Gable' × 'Tama Giku'): strong pink 48C, blotch moderate red 51A, double, occasionally semidouble, calyx present, 3"; dwarf mounding 16 × 33" in 18 years.

'Lady Robin' (syn. T14–10; ('Glacier' × 'Tama Giku') × 'Getsu Toku'): white, slightly tinted and variably sectored or striped vivid purplish red 66B, 3½"; semidwarf, 21 × 36" in 15 years.

'Laura Morland' (syn. U4–1, 'Mrs. Morland'; 'Lady Louise' × ('Kaigetsu' × 'Carol')): moderate pink 49B, occasional darker striping or sectoring, variably semidouble, calyx present, 2½"; semidwarf, rounded, 18 × 29" in 15 years.

'Madame Mab Chalon' (T16–7; ('Glacier' × 'Tama Giku') × 'Getsu Toku'): white, tinted strong pink 48D, with some stripling and sectors of strong pink 48C, 5–6 lobes, 3¼"; mounding.

'Maria Derby' (syn. H19–9; 'Jimmy Coover' × 'Glamour'): deep reddish orange 44C, throat paler, double, hose-in-hose, calyx present, 2½".

'Maxine West' (syn. U8–10; 'Lady Louise' × ('Kaigetsu' × 'Carol')): tinted light purplish pink, 69A, slight striping purplish pink 66C, single to semidouble, calyx absent 3½".

'Mrs. Emil Hager' (syn. U14–5, 'Betty Hager'; 'Lady Louise' × 'Shinnyo no Tsuki'): deep purplish pink 68A, semidouble to double, hose-in-hose, calyx present, petaloids often forming a pompon, 2¾"; dwarf, 12 × 25" in 15 years.

'Mrs. Villars' (syn. T23–10; 'Oakland' × 'Heiwa'): variable, white with stripes to sectors and solid selfs of deep yellowish pink 44D, 5 to 6 lobes, ruffled, 3½"; mounding.

'Nancy of Robinhill' (syn. 046–3; 'Vervaeneana' × 'Lady Louise'): light purplish pink 62C, occasional light red blotch, semidouble to double, hose-in-hose, calyx present, 3½"; semidwarf, 20 × 36" in 17 years.

'Nigel' (syn. N33–2; (Belgian Hybrid × 'La Lumiere') × (Belgian Hybrid × 'La Lumiere')): deep yellowish pink 43C to vivid red 44A, 2¼"; broad habit.

'Olga Niblett' (syn. T50–8; 'Oakland' × ('Kaigetsu' × 'Carol')): white, faint yellowish green throat, hose-in-hose, calyx absent, 2¼"; upright habit. A sister seedling T50⅜ has also been introduced as 'Olga Niblett' but it is white hose-in-hose with red flecks in the flower; upright habit.

'Ormsby' (syn. T45–3; 'Louise Gable' × 'Yozakura'): deep yellowish pink 43C, double, calyx present, 2½"; branches freely, dense, upright.

'Papineau' (syn. R8–5; 'Glacier' × 'Swan Song'): white, with pale green throat, 3½"; large leaves; vigorous upright 27 × 36" in 8 years.

'Pat Erb' (syn. T36–3; 'Lady Louise' × 'Tama Sugata'): white shading to light yellowish to light purplish pink, 37C–56B, hose-in-hose, 2".

'Peg Hugger' (syn. U1–8; 'Lady Louise' × ('Kaigetsu' × 'Carol')): strong pink 49A, double , hose-in-hose, calyx present, 2½", mounding.

'Peter Pooker' (syn. U15–1; 'Lady Louise' × 'Shinnyo no Tsuki'): light purplish pink 69A, very wavy, 3¼"; semidwarf, broad.

'Pucken' (syn. T62–6; Belgian Hybrid × 'Carol'): vivid purplish red 61C, hose-in-hose, some petaloid stamens, calyx absent, 2½"; mounding.

'Redmond' (?Syn. T21–1; 'Lady Louise' × 'Heiwa'): deep yellowish pink, 39B, reddish dotting in blotch.

'Red Tip' (syn. W20–10; parentage unknown): white with strong purplish red 58C, margin, often concentrating at tips, short petaloids along with stamens, 2¾".

'Richie' (syn. V3–6; 'Shinnyo no Tsuki' × 'Lady Louise'): deep reddish orange 43B, 2½".

'Robin Dale' (syn. T24–8; 'Oakland' × 'Heiwa'): white, greenish throat, some deep pink splashing, single to occasional doubling, very wavy, 3¼"; broad mounding.

'Robin Hill Congo' (syn. E2–2; parentage unknown; syn. 'Congo'): vivid reddish purple 78B, 3"; dwarf, spreading, 16 × 38" in 10 years.

'Robin Hill Elsa' (syn. T20–7; ('Treasure' × 'Mavis') × 'Getsu Toku'; syn. 'Elsa'): strong to light purplish pink 73B–C, often nearly white, wavy, 3½".

'Robin Hill Frosty' (syn. N31–9, 'Frosty'; ('Oakland' × (Belgian Hybrid × 'Carol')) × 'Lady Louise'): strong purplish pink 62A, purplish red blotch and pale purplish pink narrow margin, 2¾"; semidwarf, mounding 25 × 28" in 19 years.

'Robin Hill Gillie' (syn. T13–5; ('Oakland' × (Belgian Hybrid × 'Carol')) × 'Getsu Toku'): strong reddish orange 42C, 5 to 6 wavy lobes, 3½"; semidwarf, 22 × 21" in 15 years.

'Robin Hill Palmyra' (T49–3; 'Oakland' × 'Lady Louise'; syn. 'Palmyra'): deep to strong purplish pink 67C–D, semidouble, calyx present, 2¾"; vigorous upright.

'Robin Hill Rosanne' (syn. V1–7; 'Glacier' × 'Lady Louise'; syn. 'Rosanne'): white, tinted vivid purplish red 61D, margin slightly darker, 2¾".

'Robin Hill Wendy' (syn. T21–3; 'Lady Louisa' × 'Heiwa'; syn. 'Wendy'): tinted strong pink 52D, with dark pink sectors 52C, very wavy, 3¼", mounding.

'Roddy' (syn. T18–1; ('Treasure' × 'Mucronatum' seedling) × 'Getsu Toku'): white, wavy, 3½".

'Sara Holden' (syn. T22–5; 'Oakland' × 'Heiwa'): white, some stripes and sectors light to deep pink, 49C–52D, 5 to 6 lobes, 2½"; mounding.

'Scott Gartrell' (syn. N31–1; ('Oakland' × (Belgian Hybrid × 'Carol')) × 'Lady Louise'): deep to strong purplish pink, 64D–68B, double, hose-in-hose, calyx present, 2¾".

'Sherbrook' (syn. X55–9; 'Vervaeneana' × ('Lady Louise' × open pollinated)): strong purplish red 78B, irregular double, hose-in-hose, calyx present, 2½"; upright, semidwarf 28 × 38" in 14 years.

'Sir Robert' (syn. T15–8; ('Glacier' × 'Tama Giku') × 'Getsu Toku'): light purplish pink 55C–D, light throat, some stripes and sectoring, 5–6 lobes, 3½"; dwarf 17 × 21" in 12 years.

'Spink' (syn. K34–3; parentage unknown): strong purplish pink 62A, hose-in-hose, calyx absent, 1½"; upright, semidwarf, 29 × 27" in 15 years.

'Talbot' (syn. T16–10; ('Glacier' × 'Tama Giku') × 'Getsu Toku'): light purplish pink 56A–B, greenish white throat, occasional white margin, 3".

'Tamino' (syn. V1–8, 'Rosenkavalier'; 'Kaigetsu' × ('Nancy of Robinhill' × 'Ledifolia Rosea')): white center, strong purplish red 63B to strong purplish pink 63C, margin, 2¾"; dwarf spreading 18 × 54" in 12 years.

'Tan Dilly' (syn. U2–9; 'Lady Louise' × ('Kaigetsu' × 'Carol')): strong pink 48C–D, often shading to light brown 174D at tips, irregular double, calyx present, 2½".

'Turk's Cap' (syn. T60–6; parentage unknown); deep reddish orange 43A, tips of lobes often recurved, 3½".

'Verena' (syn. T49–4; 'Oakland' × 'Lady Louise'): light to pale purplish pink 73C–D, throat lighter, often 6 lobes, 2¾".

'Watchet' (syn. T28–10; 'Amagasa' × 'Lady Louise'): moderate pink 49B, greenish white throat, ruffled, 3½"; broad, dwarf, 15 × 36" in 15 years.

'Wee Willie' (syn. V2–10; 'Shinnyo no Tsuki' × 'Lady Louise'): light purplish pink 56B, greenish white throat, 2½"; dwarf, compact.

'Welmet' (syn. T24–5; 'Oakland' × 'Heiwa'): strong purplish pink 62A, 5–6 lobes, 3½"; slightly loose, mounding.

'White Hart' (syn. J12–1; ('Gumpo' × 'Glacier') × 'Snowclad'): white, pale greenish throat, ruffled, 3½"; stiff mounding.

'Whitehead' (syn. T2–4; 'Glacier' × 'Getsu Toku'): light, purplish pink, 55C, edged with white or variously striped, sectored, or selfed strong pink 50B, often 6 lobed, 3"; mounding.

'White Moon' (syn. T17–7; ('Glacier' × 'Tama Giku') × 'Getsu Toku'): white, occasionally striped, sectored, or selfed deep yellowish pink 43C, 6 lobed, 3½"; semidwarf, 18 × 29" in 15 years.

GARTRELL HYBRIDS

Seedlings grown and numbered by Robert Gartrell but named by others:

'Cherie' (syn. V12–4; ('Jimmy Coover' × 'Glamour') × 'Lady Louise')): deep reddish orange, double, 2".

CRIPPLE CREEK GARTRELL AZALEAS

When Bob Gartrell closed his Robin Hill Nursery in Wyckoff, NJ, in 1981, his stock plants were tagged and many were moved by Fred Rees to his Saluda, NC, nursery.

Terry Wingate and Eddie Coleman of Cripple Creek Nursery of Hawkinsville, Georgia, took cuttings of the named varieties and over 225 numbered crosses including the X, Y, Z, and M series. All are hardy in zones 6b–9b. The following have been named in 1983–84.

'Arrowhead' (X71–6; 'Nancy of Robinhill' × 'Ledifolia Rosea'): strong pink 49A, variable some darker others lighter with faint pastel blending, double, 3", early midseason; broad spreading, to 3 ft.

'Captain's Choice': (Y22–2; ('Nancy of Robinhill' × 'Lady Louise') × ('Glacier' × 'Lady Louise')): light pink with reddish spots in blotch, broad overlapping lobes, 3½", late; dense, broad spreading, to 3 ft.

'Cherokee' (V15–8; 'Oakland' × 'Heiwa'): light pink, variable some with lighter margins, double, wide overlapping lobes, 3½", late; low mounding, to 3½ ft.

'Cherokee Brave' (Z17–1; ('Mai Hime' × 'Jubilee') × 'Getsu Toku'):strong purple 80B with reddish blotch, 6 broad wavy lobes, 3½", late; low mounding, to 2½ ft.

'Cherokee Chief' (X71–9; (('Vervaeneane' × 'Copperman') × ('Jimmy Coover' × 'Picador')) × 'Gartrell R5–9'): deep reddish orange 42A with faint red blotch, broad overlapping lobes, tips recurved, 3½", late; variable upright habit.

'Cherokee Princess' (Z6–8; ('Nancy of Robinhill' × 'Glacier') × 'Lady Louise'): light purplish pink 65B, hose-in-hose, double, broad wavy lobes, 3½", late; similar to 'Nancy of Robinhill' with low compact habit.

'Cherokee Squaw' (Z5–8; 'Wako' × 'Beni' seedling): deep yellowish pink 43C, broad wavy lobes, petaloidy, 3½", late; wider than high, to 2½ ft.

'Cherokee Sunset' (T20–8; 'Lady Louise' × 'Heiwa'): reddish orange with darker blotch, broad ruffled lobes, 4", late; dense-spreading, to 2½ ft.

'Coleman's Candy' (Z12–1; 'Malvatica' × 'Hosei'): strong yellowish pink 38A with strong red blotch, wide frilled tipped lobes, 3", late; dense habit, to 2½ ft.

'Doctor Arthur Pearsall' (X73–8; 'Nancy of Robinhill' × 'Palmyra'): strong pink 48D, broad overlapping wavy lobes, petaloidy, 3½", very late; broad spreading habit.

'Flaming Sally' (V7–1; 'Lady Louis' × unknown): vivid reddish orange 41B, broad ruffled lobes, petaloidy, 3¼", late; broad spreading, to 3 ft.

'Fred C. Galle' (V18–7; 'Nancy of Robinhill' × 'Laura Morland'): strong pink 48D with few inconspicuous dots in blotch, 5 or more flat broad lobes, 3½", late; low dense habit to 2½ ft.

'Fred Rees' (S16–4; parentage unknown): deep pink, hose-in-hose saucer-shaped, 3, midseason, persistent flowers; broad rounded, to 4 ft.

'Indian Mound' (U16–10; 'Lady Louise' × 'Shinnyo no Tsuki'): deep yellowish pink 39A, double petaloidy, 3", late; low mounding to 2½ ft.

'Josephine Coleman' (U18–7; 'Lady Louise' × 'Shinnyo no Tsuki'): strong pink slightly variable and petaloidy, broad wavy lobes, 3½", very late; broad spreading, to 2½ ft.

'Medicine Man' (X77–9; 'Nancy of Robinhill' × 'Gartrell's 042–8'): deep pink 51B with darker red blotch, broad wavy lobes, petaloidy, 3½", late; low broad spreading, to 3 ft.

'Peace Maker' (T37–2; 'Lady Louise' × 'Eikan'): strong yellowish pink 41D, broad wavy curling back lobes, 4", midseason; low, broad spreading, to 2 ft.

'Rain Dance' (X56–1; 'Nancy of Robinhill' × 'Gartrell's Lower Rock'): strong purple 80B with red blotch, broad overlapping lobes, petaloidy, 3", late midseason; broad spreading habit, to 2½ ft.

'Tomahawk' (T38–9; 'Louise Gable' × 'Shinnyo no Hikari'): strong red 47B with red stamens and small red blotch, broad lobes, petaloidy, 3¼", very late; broad spreading, to 2½ ft.

'Warpaint' (X77–6; ('Malvatica' × 'Dainty') × 'Miyuno no Tsuki'): strong purplish pink 63C, variable some with darker margins, some purplish red and variable splashes, numerous variations, broad lobes, saucer-shaped, 3", very late; low to slightly upright, to 3 ft. high.

'White Dove' (X75–8; 'Nancy of Robinhill' × 'Palmyra'): white, very broad rounded lobes, 3½", late; broad mounding, to 3 ft.

'Witch Doctor' (U31–9; 'Louise Gable' × 'Tama Sugata'): light reddish purple 47C with blotch and red stamens, variable, broad flat lobes, 3½", late; low mounding habit.

SONOMA HYBRIDS

The Sonoma Hybrids were introduced by the Sonoma Horticultural Nursery of Sebastopol, California, U.S.A. The plants were developed in the 1960's to early 1970's by Mr. Stewart Barber, the original owner of the nursery. Unfortunately, information on the parentage is no longer available on some cultivars. The plants are generally available in California, with very limited trials elsewhere. All are hardy in zones 7–10 in California, U.S.A.

'Barber's Orange': reddish orange, double, 2"; compact grower to 3 ft. high; usually flowers twice a year.

'Frills': red, double, frilled.

'L. O. M.': red, very large; glossy foliage, red stems; large spreading habit, to 4–5 ft.

'Mimi' ('Madonna' × 'White Grandeur'): white, tinge of green in throat, double, frilled; compact habit, 3 ft. high.

'Orange Baron' ('Granada' × 'L. Brook's seedling 4356a'): reddish orange.

'Red Baron' (Granada' × 'Red Poppy'): red, double, large, usually blooms twice each year.

'Red Orange': orange, semidouble.

'Sonoma Sunset': dark red, semidouble, large; very compact habit, 2–3 ft. high.

SONOMA DWARF HYBRIDS

Mr. Barber developed this group from Satsuki seed received from Japan. Some of the seedlings were used in line breeding or sibling crosses. Introduced in 1974 by color. These plants are available as Sonoma Dwarf and sold by color name.

'Sonoma Dwarf Pink'
'Sonoma Dwarf Vermillion'
'Sonoma Dwarf Red'
'Sonoma Dwarf Rose Bengal'
'Sonoma Dwarf White'
'Sonoma Dwarf Red Plicata'
'Sonoma Dwarf Rose Plicata'
'Sonoma Dwarf Scarlet Plicata'
'Sonoma Dwarf Pink Plicata'

Other Sonoma Dwarfs introduced as plants from Japan; possibly Satsuki hybrids.

'Fuki': deep yellowish pink, darker throat, tubular, narrow twisted leaves; compact grower.

'Komache Hine': light pink, darker flecks, small curled leaves; very compact grower.

WADA HYBRIDS

The late Koichiro Wada of the Hakoneya Nurseries, Yokohamashi, Japan, was a breeder and grower who developed and introduced numerous hybrid azaleas. Most fall into the Satsuki Hybrid group or are closely related. Up to 1943, Wada published an extensive list of azaleas in English. The nursery is still in operation by his son Tomoo, who is concentrating on *Rhododendron* and *Magnolia*. Some of the plants are still available in Japan and are also found in England and used in hybridizing. Most, but not all, other cultivars listed are hybrids or forms developed or introduced by K. Wada. See Appendix J.

I. *R. tamurae (R. eriocarpum)* Forms and Hybrids. If no cross is indicated the cultivar is a selection of the species.

'Akatsuki' (*tamurae* × *kaempferi*): deep pink.

'Album Giganteum': white, yellowish green throat, frilled, 3", very late; low, dense spreading.

'Asagi' (*kaempferi* × *tamurae*)

Pride of Numazu': vivid red, white throat.

'Queen Elizabeth'

'Queen Elizabeth White'

'Rose Glory': deep pink.

'Roseum'

'Terra-cotta Beauty': deep yellowish pink, small flowers.

'Wada's Pink': strong yellowish pink; blooms 2 weeks earlier than 'Gumpo'.

II. Kurumanthum Hybrids (Kurume Hybrids × 'Macranthum'): early blooming with large flowers.

'Fuji no Mime': white.

'Harugasumi': deep pink.

'Hi no Tsukasa': vivid reddish orange.

'Kiju': strong purple, white base.

'Momozono': strong yellowish pink.

'Nomiya': pale red.

'Saigyozakura': light yellowish pink, white base.

'Sekimori': variable strong yellowish pink.

'Tsuki no Katsura': pale purple, white base.

'Ukishima': vivid purple, white base.

'Yomei': vivid red, white base.

III. Indicum Forms —selections of *R. indicum.*

'Anemoniflorum Kagara': pink, large multilobed flowers.

'Compactum': reddish orange, small flowers; very small leaves.

'Fairy Lilac': light purple, white base.

'Orange Beauty': reddish orange, white base, large.

'Otakumi': vivid orange; extremely dwarf.

'Pink Pearl': pale yellowish pink, occasionally reddish orange flowers, large.

'Rakuyo': light yellowish pink, white base.

'Rimpo': moderate reddish orange, tubular; dwarf.

'Rimpu': vivid red, white base, multilobed flowers, early.

'Shihokau': purple, large, multilobed flowers.

IV. Macrindicum Hybrids ('Macranthum' × *R. indicum*). These are hybrids of some form of *R. indicum* with a Belgian Indian Hybrid as the other parent.

'Glory of Numazu': light pink, edged reddish orange, occasional pink selfs, large.

'Matsukasa': pale pink, striped deep pink.

'Pink Delight': white, edged deep pink, large.

V. *R. scabrum* Forms. All cultivars selected from seedlings of the species or hybrids bred for large flowers.

'Kanoka': pink, splashed red.

'Kintaiyo': white, margins and blotch flushed moderate red, petaloid sepals, 2"; one parent is possibly a Kurume Hybrid.

'Purple Beauty': purple; probably 'Hortense' (a garden form of *R. macrosepalum*) and *ripense.*

'Purple Perfection': purple, similar to 'Red Emperor'.

'Red Emperor': red, blooms 2 weeks later than *scabrum.*

'Rose Perfection': deep pink, similar to 'Red Emperor'.

'Scabrica Rose Perfection': (*indicum* 'Rose Belle' × *scabrum*): vivid reddish orange.

'Shell Pink' ('Albert-Elizabeth' × *scabrum*): yellowish pink, semidouble, 3½".

'White Pearl' (Probably *scabrum* × 'Mucronatum'): white, early.

VI. Scabrume Hybrids (*R. scabrum* × Kurume Hybrids): intermediate between parents but larger flowers than Kurume Hybrids.

'Gembu': dark purplish red.

'Hakkei': reddish orange.

'Shium': purple.

'Taikan': reddish orange.

'Tsukiumi': pale yellowish pink, white base.

'Tukasa': pale pink.

WHEELDON INTRODUCTIONS

The late Dr. Thomas Wheeldon, active in A.R.S. and a collector, evaluated many plants in his beautiful Gladsgay Garden in Richmond, Virginia. Some plants can be seen at Winterthur Gardens in Delaware. The source of Dr. Wheeldon's plants is no longer available but may have been seedlings produced by others.

'H. F. du Pont' (parentage unknown, possibly 'Mucronatum' hybrid): vivid reddish orange, hose-in-hose, 1", early midseason, rounded habit; hardy in zone 7A.

'Miss Christine' ('Willy' × 'Momozomo'): white flecked deep pink to selfs of deep pink 52C, hose-in-hose, 2", early midseason.

'Miss Cynthia' (parentage unknown): grey purplish pink; midseason.

'Miss Gertrude' (parentage unknown): strong purplish red 59D; 2¾", open upright.

'Miss Josephine' (parentage unknown): moderate purplish pink 72B, 2", hardy to 0°F.

'Miss Lucy' (parentage unknown): yellowish pink, distinct blotch; early midseason.

'Miss Martha' (parentage unknown): pink, hose-in-hose, rounded petals, 1¾"; late midseason.

'Miss Nancy' (parentage unknown): deep purplish pink 68B, 1¾"; late midseason.

'Miss Patricia': dwarf and spreading.

'Miss Susie' (*simsii* × 'Mucronatum'; Hybridized by Weaver, NC.): deep purplish pink 55A, fades slightly to strong purplish pink 58D, insignificant brown blotch, 2½", ruffled, early midseason; rounded habit; hardy zone 6B.

MISCELLANEOUS INTER-GROUP EVERGREEN HYBRIDS AND MISCELLANEOUS EVERGREEN AZALEAS

This last section might be best labeled as Miscellaneous Inter-Group Evergreen Hybrids and Miscellaneous Evergreen Azaleas. The Miscellaneous Inter-Group Evergreen Hybrids are limited introductions made by a number of different individuals around the world that belong in this basic group.

The Miscellaneous Evergreen Azaleas are plants about which unfortunately insufficient information is available to classify. Having to resort to such a lame and shabby device once again points to the real and critical reason that breeders must register cultivars providing full information on parentage, description, hardiness, etc. Unfortunately the origin and parentage of many of the azaleas in this category are lacking as is information as to dimensions, hardiness, etc.

A listing in the Miscellaneous Group does not mean the plants are of limited or restricted value. More information may in time be forthcoming and permit one to locate some of these cultivars in better defined groupings.

'Alfred Holbrook' (*R. kaempferi* × 'Pink Champagne'; Early): pale pink, semidouble, 2½"; medium habit, hardy in zone 7b.

'Alexander Witches' Broom' (sport of 'Alexander': cross): smaller flowers deep reddish orange, very precocious; small fine leaves; vigorous, very prostrate; good rock garden plant.

'Ambrosier': purplish red, 2¼", leaves with whitish margin.

'Amy' ('Glacier' seedling; Dodd): strong pink 48D, center lighter, strong pink blotch 51C, hose-in-hose, 2½"; hardy in zone 7a.

'Annie Bray' (*R. kaempferi* × 'Pink Champagne'; Early): light pink, semidouble, 2½"; medium habit.

'Arctic Flame' ('Glenn Dale' seedling; C. Herbert, '78): strong red, dark blotch.

'Barbara' (selection of *R. tosaense*; Hillier): pink; narrow 1" leaves.

'Bengal Beauty' ('Diamio' × *R. simsii*; Haworth-Booth, U.K., '64): purplish pink 62B, veined, and flushed vivid purplish pink, light brown dotting, slightly wavy, 2".

'Benifusha' [transliterated from Japanese as 'Red Windmill'] (*R. scabrum* 'Shonoshin Kerama' × *R. indicum* 'Robin'; Kunishige, Tamura, Morishita & Yamaguchi, '82): vivid purplish red 57B, hose-in-hose, wavy, 2¾–3½"; hardy to 5°F., good for forcing.

'Buzi' ('Noordtiana' × *R. poukhanense*; Mittendorf): purplish red 71D to vivid reddish purple 74B, 1–1¾", early midseason; broad habit; hardy in zone 6.

'Congalla': vivid pink.

'Coral Dogwood' (sport of 'Dogwood'; Fessler, intro. Ball, PP 3752): yellowish pink.

'Dave's Pink': bright deep pink, reddish flecks in throat, 1"; compact, wider than high; hardy −10°F.

'Denise': light pink with pale pink margins, double, midseason.

'Dhabi' ('Vuyk's Rosyred' × 'Moonbeam'; G. Griswold, '82): deep purplish pink 68A, strong red spotting in dorsal lobes, 3", mid May; 7" × 8" wide in 3 yrs; hardy to −0°F.

'Dogwood' (unknown seedling; Roberts, intro. Ball, PP 3093,'72): white often stippled moderate red 47C, greenish throat, rounded spaced lobes, recurve with age, 2½"; good for forcing; hardy zone 7.

'Dusty Pink' (*R. simsii* hardy form × 'Daimio'; Haworth-Booth, U.K., '68): light yellowish pink, circular flower.

'Evening Glow': yellowish pink, hose-in-hose; possibly a Girard Hybrid.

'Final Blush' (*R. simsii* hardy form × 'Daimio'; Haworth-Booth, U.K., '68): deep yellowish pink, dark blotch, frilled, 2"; hardy.

'Flam Pearce': light pink, splashed white.

'Flat Out' (parentage ?; Carlson): white, late June; low spreading; hardy zone 6.

'Freesia': white, tubular, small, low habit.

'Gardenia White' (sport of 'Sweetheart Supreme'): white, semidouble, 2½"; hardy in zone 8a.

'Gee Gee': pink.

'Glamour Compacta' (sport of 'Glamour'): strong purplish pink, compact habit.

'Gloskey Pink': strong purplish pink, flushed orange, red dots near throat, double; 3 × 3 ft. in 6 yrs.; hardy to −5°F.

'Gumpkins': pink; low compact habit; good rock garden plant.

'Hexe Supreme': deep red, double.

'Hime Nakahara' (dwarf *R. nakaharai;* from Japan, Brook Green Gardens #0849): vivid reddish orange, reddish purple blotch, 1½–2"; dense compact, small foliage; introduced as a Satsuki Hybrid.

'Judd': reddish orange, hose-in-hose.

'Kaempo' (*R. kaempferi* × 'Gumpo'; H. Fowle intr. about '60): deep purplish pink 66C, darker spots, 1½", midseason; low, compact; hardy in zones 6b to 9.

'Karens' ('Hinode Giri' × *R. poukhanense;* Peterson, introd. Verkades Nur., '79): deep reddish purple, dark spotting, wavy, fragrant, 1¾"; 4 × 4' in 6 yrs.

'King Oluf' (V. Wood): pink, throat and tube yellowish pink, 1", midseason.

'Langmans' (*R. macrosepalum* seedling; Slocock, U.K., '70): moderate pink, small dark spots in blotch.

'Lilliput' ('Diamio' × *R. simsii;* J. Waterer & Sons, U.K., '67): between strong purple 48C, and moderate red 47C, spotting reddish brown, wavy, 3".

'Little Favorite': deep pink, low habit.

'Lotus Porter' (Beneschoen Garden, '67): strong purple, semidouble, 1½", midseason; 21 × 36" wide in 8 yrs.

'Madam Greeley': white with green flecks in throat, 1".

'Marie Louise': white with pink stripes, 1¼", midseason; compact habit.

'Mariko' (*R. nakaharai* seedling; Rokujo): moderate reddish orange 43C, flushed purplish red 54A in blotch, 1".

'Meistag' (grown in Calif.): pale pink, white markings, semidouble, midseason.

'Melba' (grown in Calif.): pale pink, hose-in-hose, 1½"; possibly a Pericat Hybrid.

'Mrs. C.C. Miller' (Gable Hybrid seedling, Billerbeck): reddish orange opens to deep yellowish orange, double, very late. Similar to 'Beni Kirishima'.

'Mrs. Henry Hohman': reddish orange.

'Mrs. LBJ' ('Seattle White' × ?; Close, intro. Creech PI 337619): white, hose-in-hose to double, wavy, 3" late May; hardy zone 7.

'Mrs. L. J. Comer' (*R. kaempferi* × 'Jean Haerens'; Early): moderate red, 3"; tall; hardy in 7b.

'Munchkin' (dwf. selection of *R. poukhanense;* Carlson): light purple, early May; very dwarf 8 × 12" in 14 yrs.

'Multiflorum' (parentage ?; Arends, '40): purplish pink, faint reddish markings, ¾–1"; dwarf compact habit; hardy.

'Myrtle De Friel' (*R. nakaharai* × 'Rosebud'; W. Griswold, '82): strong purplish pink 55B, lighter spotting in lobe, hose-in-hose, with petaloid center may be 2 stamens, early June; semidwarf 4" × 10" wide in 3 yrs.; hardy to −3°F.

'Nanticoke' ('Cora Brandt' × 'White Gumpo'; Nelson): white with light purple flakes and flecks, some shading of pink and light purple, double, 2–2¼", very late; 14" × 4 ft. spread in 10 yrs., tends to cascade; hardy to −5°F.

'Nassau' ('Cora Brandt' × 'White Gumpo'; Nelson): white with light purple flakes and specks, some shading of pink and light purple, center pale green, near pompon double, 2½", very late; 16" × 5 ft. spread in 10 yrs. hardy to −5°F.

'Nellie Gatehouse': deep pink, double, 2½–3", midseason; low habit.

'Nolan's Pink' (seedling; Dodd, '83): deep pink, 2", profuse bloomer; leaves light green 2½" long.

'Otomeno' (*kiusianum* × Satsuki): purplish pink, 2", early; low compact.

'Pamella Malland' (syn. 'Rosy Cheeks'; 'Vuyk's Rosyred' × 'Moonbeam'; G. Griswold,'82): strong purplish pink 55A, pale pink in throat 56C, minor strong red spotting 53C on dorsal lobe, 5–6 deeply cut petals, wavy, overlapping lobes, 3", mid May; 12 × 18" wide in 10 yrs.; hardy to −0°F.

'Pearl Bradford Sport' (witches broom; Wood): deep pink, slow to flower; compact; smaller leaves.

'Pilling': yellowish pink, semidouble.

'Pinkabelle' (*R. simsii* × 'Daimio'; Haworth-Booth, U.K., '68): yellowish pink, 2½", late.

'Pink Charm': vivid pink.

'Pink Discovery' (*R. poukhanense* selection; Mezitt, '73): strong purplish pink 58D, 1"; upright habit, hardy to −25°F.

'Pink Ice #2' (sport of 'Pink Ice'): deeper purple color and larger.

'Pocono Pink' (unknown hybrid, grown in Richmond, Virg.): pink.

'Port Knap' (parentage ?; Knap Hill, '62): light reddish purple 75A, reddish throat, ¾".

'Pink Pearce': light to strong purple, mid-season.

'Pink Snow': light pink, yellow green throat, red spotting.

'Port Wine' (*R. macrosepalum* seedling; Slocock, U.K., '70): purplish red, May, compact, medium height.

'Potts Silver Pink' (Potts): light pink, hose-in-hose, petaloid, 2".

'Red Festive' (sport of 'Festive', Spartanburg Nursery): strong purplish red, 2–2½", early; upright spreading habit; hardy in zone 7.

'Robbins Pink'; (E. Robbins): deep pink, large, late.

'Royal Blazer' (Herbert, '78): strong reddish purple 78A, purple spotting 79D, wavy, 1½", late April; hardy to −5°F.

'Ryde Heron' (form of 'Macrantha'; Knap Hill, '58): vivid purplish red, blotch darker, 2¼".

'Salmon Sander': yellowish pink; low habit.

'Salmon Special': yellowish pink, hose-in-hose, ruffled.

'Shanna Smart' (seedling of 'Advance'; Orme): white base followed by red and ruffled border of purple, 3"; low; hardy zone 6.

'Sir Robert's Witches' Broom' (sport of 'Sir Robert's'; cross): smaller flowers, light purplish pink, with light throats; smaller leaves; low compact, than parent.

'Sleigh Bells': white with yellow green blotch; compact habit.

'Stately Orange' (Bastedo Nur.): orange, medium growth; hardy zone 5.

'Sunstar': reddish orange, darker blotch, midseason; upright growth.

'T. Roosevelt' (grown in Calif.): strong red, 2½–3"; medium grower; prefers light shade.

'Taschkent' ('Multiflorum' × ?; Ger.): deep purplish pink 66C, 1–1⅜", late; low broad rounded; very hardy.

'Tat': deep pink, double; hardy zone 7.

'Variegated Dogwood' (sport of 'Coral Dogwood'; Calif. Camellia Gar., intr. Ball, PP 4455): deep yellowish pink with white blotches.

'Variegated' *R. simsii*: (syn. *R simsii* Variegated; from seed collected in Canton, China; Pl 391401, NA 36749): red with purple blotch, 1½–2"; variegated foliage, fine yellowish white margin; only grown in Calif.

'Variegated Flamingo' (sport of 'Flamingo'): pink and white, double; low compact habit.

'Variegated Heart's Desire' (sport of 'Heart's Desire'): variegated red and white, double, late.

'Vermilion' (grown in Calif.): reddish orange, large, late; vigorous growth.

'Wansbeck' (R. H. S. Wisley, '72): light purplish pink 55C, blotch reddish orange.

'W. Leith' (possible *R. nakaharai* selection from U.K. by Rokujo): red, low compact habit.

AZALEAS FROM AUSTRALIA AND NEW ZEALAND

Deciduous and evergreen azaleas have in recent decades been widely grown in Australia and New Zealand; parts of the former and most of the latter have ideal climates for growing azaleas.

The following azaleas represent only those which are not grown in North America or which have been described nowhere else than in this book. This list should not be construed as descriptions of all the azaleas grown in these two countries for they grow many of the cultivars first introduced and grown in Europe, Japan, and North America.

This list was prepared from numerous growers' catalogs and plant directories published in Australia and New Zealand. I am deeply indebted to Mr. T. C. C. Hutchinson of New Plymouth, New Zealand; Mr. Arthur W. Headlam of Melbourne, Australia; and Mr. Neville McMinn of Victoria, Australia, for their generous assistance in helping to validate these descriptions.

Australian and New Zealand cultivars of the Exbury and Ilam Hybrid groups are included in the Deciduous Azalea Lists, pages 93–105. These lists have been prepared in the following order:

1. Evergreen Azaleas—which have been divided into
   a. Belgian, Indian, or Indica Hybrids
   b. Kurume Hybrids
   c. Miscellaneous.

BELGIAN INDIAN OR INDICA AZALEAS

'Adolphe de Vervaene' (Europe): deep pink, double.

'Advent Bells': see 'Adventglocke' or 'Chimes', p. 142.

'Agnes Neal': light purple, frilled, large, single to semidouble.

'Alabama': deep pink, large.

'Alba Magna' (Forster, 1854; Eur.): white, green throat, fragrant.

'Alba Magnifica' (Forster, 1854; Eur.): white, fragrant, vigorous.

'Alindia': off white, light purple edge.

'Alphonse Anderson': see 'George Lindley Taber', p. 168.

'Ambrosiur': dark pink, double.

'Ambrosius': see 'Ambrosius Superba', p. 143.

'Amethyst': light purple.

'Ann Hazlewood' (Aust.): light purple, frilled.

'Ann Perkes': pink, semidouble, large.

'Ann Perkins': light pink, double.

'Anniversary' ('Mucronatum' × 'Blaauw's Pink'; Van De Ven, '70): light to pale purplish pink, red blotch, hose-in-hose, large.

'Anniversary Joy' (sport of 'Silver Anniversary'; Burbank, '80): pale pink flushed deep pink, white blotch speckled pale green, frilled semidouble.

'Antignonne': yellowish pink, double.

'Apex Flame' (Burbank, '81): reddish orange, hose-in-hose, semidouble.

'Armand Haerens' (syn. 'Red Picotee Red'; Leopold Astrid, Belg.): vivid red, fluted, double, large.

'Auntie Mame' (Greentree-Huntingdale; intro. Burbank, '82): vivid pink with red throat, large semidouble.

'Aurora': light pink, double.

'Autumn Beauty' (sport of 'Searchlight'; Lovegrove; intro. Camellia Grove, '72): light pink, double.

'Baby Jill': purplish pink, large hose-in-hose, midseason.

'Ballerina': see 'Emil de Connick', p. 145.

'Baron Nathaniel de Rothschild' (van Houtte, 1858; Belg.): vivid purple, double.

'Bayou' (Aust. might be same as 'Bayou' PI 279405): very pale pink, semidouble, large.

'Beatrice': reddish orange, double.

'Belgian Beauty' (sport of 'Charles Pynaert'): deep pink, frilled, semidouble, late.

'Bernard Andreae' (Mardner, 1858, Eur.): deep pink, double; compact habit.

'Beryl Eggington': dark red, double, ruffled, large.

'Beverley Haerens' (syn. 'Calif. Snow'): white, occasionally flushed pink, double.

'Big Sister' (Greentree): deep pink flushed purplish pink, very large single to double.

'Blushing Bride' (Europe): pink, double.

'Bobo' ('Mucronatum' × 'Blaauw's Pink'; Van De Ven): buds light reddish purple open to white flushed light purplish pink, hose-in-hose.

'Bonnie McKee' (Greentree, '70): purple, double.

'Bouquet de Roses' (Aust. 'Delmotte', 1861; Eur.): dark red, double.

'Camellia'; yellowish pink, dark blotch, double.

'Cameo' (Holland): yellowish pink, triple hose-in-hose.

'Caroline Bourke' (Greentree): white with pink stripes, frilled double.

'Catherine': light pink, green throat, double.

'Centenary': deep yellowish pink, double.

'Centenary Heritage' ('Dr. Alderfer' × 'Blaauw's Pink'; Burbank, '78): yellowish pink, large.

'Charles de Buck' (Verschaffelt, 1868; Belg.): purplish red, double.
'Charles Pynaert' (Van Geert, 1884; Belg.): pale purplish pink, frilled, white edge, semidouble, large.
'Charmer': see 'William Bull', p. 169.
'Chelsea' (Rothschild, UK): deep reddish orange, ruffled double, mid to late; compact habit.
'Cherry Plum Red': purplish red.
'Christmas Pink': see 'Charme de Noel', p. 144.
'Cliff's Choice' (Burbank, '84): deep yellowish pink, hose-in-hose.
'Cockade' (syn. 'Cockade Orange'; Coppenolle, 1872; Belg.): reddish orange; compact habit.
'Comanche' ('Phoeniceum' × ?; Marsh): deep yellowish pink.
'Comte de Chambord' (J. Aper, 1878): deep yellowish pink, white edges.
'Comte de Keratone' (van Houtte, 1878; Belg.): light pink, dark blotch, white flecks at margin, double.
'Comte de la Torre' (van Houtte, 1878; Belg.): deep pink with white margin, semidouble.
'Concinna' (Smith, 1849; U.K.): purplish red; tall.
'Connellesii': purplish red, double.
'Coronation': deep yellowish pink, double, large.
'Countess of Flanders' (syn. 'Comtesse de Flandre'; Vervaene, 1868; Belg.): deep pink to red.
'Crimson Rose': vivid red, prolific.
'Crinkle Cut' ('Agnes Gault' × 'Mucronatum'; Langdon): white spotted yellowish green.
'Dame Margot Fonteyn' (sport of 'Gretel'; Huntingdale): deep purplish red, large double, mid to late; compact habit.
'Dame Melaine': see 'Dame Melanie', p. 144.
'Dancer': see 'Ballerina', p. 162.
'Daphne' (Seidel, intro '26): white, green blotch, double.
'Day Dawn' (syn. 'Blushing Bride'): pale pink with deep pink markings, double, midseason.
'Debbie': two tone pink.
'Denise' ('Comtesse de Kerchove' × ?; Nichols; intro. Berna Park, '73): pale pink, green throat, pointed petals, 2¾"; bushy habit.
'Dewdrop': see 'Nuccio's Dewdrop', p. 281.
'Dimplesy'(Burbank): pale pink, hose-in-hose, ruffled semidouble.
'Dorothy Jessep' (Greentree): pink, semidouble; medium habit.
'Dr. Arnold' (sport of 'Pink Dream'; from Ger., Burbank): deep pink with white center, red blotch.
'Dr. Glazer' (Europe): dark red, large ruffled double.
'Dreamclouds': see 'Nuccio's Dream Clouds', p. 280.
'Dream Time': pink.
'Drummer Boy' (seedling of 'Spring Magic'; Burbank, '83): purplish pink, hose-in-hose.
'Duc de Nassau' (Mardner 1854; Belg.): reddish purple, semidouble.
'Duchesse Adelaide de Nassau' (Mardner 1854; Belg.): strong red, tinted purple.
'Early Splendor' (sport of 'Searchlight'; Camellia Grove, '76): pink with white margin, double.
'Elizabeth Lawrence': light purple.
'Ellamere' (Europe): reddish orange, fluted semidouble, early to midseason.
'Elsa Karga': see 'Elsa Kaerger', p. 145.
'Elston Neale': red, frilled.
'Emma Greentree' ('Hexe' × 'Vervaeneana'; Greentree): deep pink, hose-in-hose, early.
'Erica' (Greentree, intro. Huntingdale, '70): light pink, double.
'Erica McMinn' (Greentree, intro. Camellia Lodge, '73): pale pink, tips paler, double, midseason.
'Ernest Ecchaut': purplish red, frilled double.
'Esperance' (syn. 'Temperance', p. 156; Haerens, 1907; Belg.): reddish purple, semidouble.
'Euganea' (Greentree; intro. Camellia Lodge, '73): vivid pink.
'Eugene Mazel' (Vervaene, 1865; Belg.): deep yellowish pink, shaded purple.
'Eulalie' (Van Geert, 1854, Belg.): light purple and white; foliage variegated with white margin.
'Eureka' (Burbank): deep pink with white margin, double; low compact.
'Evonne': see 'Southern Aurora', p. 298.
'Excelsior': vivid pink with purplish throat, semidouble.
'Festival Queen' (Camellia Grove, '73): white, large semidouble.

'Fiery Boy' (Burbank '81): vivid red, ruffled, hose-in-hose, semidouble.
'Firefly' (Nelly Kelly): deep red, double.
'Frances Mann': moderate purple.
'Freckleface': white with purplish flecks.
'Frilled Red Line' (Greentree; intro. Camellia Lodge, '73): white, speckled and striped vivid pink, ruffled, double, early.
'Frosty Morn' ('Mucronatum' × 'Blaauw's Pink'; Van De Ven): light to pale purplish pink with darker spots in throat.
'Garden Party': see 'Nuccio's Garden Party', p. 280.
'Gardenia Superba': white, double, early.
'General Bridges': purplish pink, double.
'Gerhard Nicolai': pink, large frilled double.
'Glacier' (Greentree, '69): white with green throat, ruffled, double.
'Glamor Girl' (Burbank, '78): vivid red, ruffled, hose-in-hose semidouble.
'Glory of Newcastle': reddish orange, double, wavy.
'Goyet' (Burbank, '79; imported from Eur.): vivid red, double, large, 4½".
'Green Ice': white with green throat.
'Gretel' (syn. 'John Haerens', Burbank): light pink to white throat, broad margin of deep pink, frilled, double, p. 148.
'Gwen' ('Mucronatum' × 'Blaauw's Pink'; Van De Ven, '72): light purplish pink.
'Happy Birthday' ('Mucronatum' × 'Blaauw's Pink'; Van De Ven): light pink with blotch.
'Happy Days': see 'Nuccio's Happy Days', p. 280.
'Harry Van De Ven' ('Mucronatum' × 'Blaauw's Pink'; Van De Ven, '72): white, light purple edge, hose-in-hose.
'Helen Perkes': vivid pink, bell-shaped, semidouble.
'Helena Theleman' (Mardner, 1863; Eur.): deep pink, fragrant.
'Helen Whalan': red semidouble.
'Iceberg' (sport of 'Vervaeneana', intro. Cheeseman): white with green throat, semidouble; vigorous.
'Impact' (Warren): reddish purple.
'Jack Frost' ('Comtesse de Kerchove' × ?; Nichols; intro. Berna Park, '84): white with yellowish throat, large wavy semidouble.
'Jane Charlesworth' (Greentree; intro. Camellia Lodge, '73): light pink, semidouble.
'Jean Alexandra' (Greentree, '70): light pink, partially petaloid; tall vigorous.
'Jenny Mac' ('Comtesse de Kerchove' × 'Avenir'; Nichols; intro. Berna Park, '73): light reddish orange, double, 2½", early.
'Jessie Lee Cromer' (Greentree): pink, frilled double; medium habit.
'Jezebel': dark red, hose-in-hose, large semidouble; compact habit.
'Jindabyne' (Greentree; intro. Camellia Lodge, '79): deep purple, semidouble, midseason.
'John Crabtree': deep pink, bell-shaped, semidouble.
'Joy Greentree' (Greentree): pink with lighter center, large frilled.
'Jubilee': moderate red, semidouble; dwarf habit.
'Kalimna Beauty' (Boulter): reddish purple, frilled, large.
'Kalimna Gem' (Boulter): purplish red to purple.
'Kalimna Glory' (Boulter): red, ruffled, double.
'Kees Bier' (Bier, '36; Eur.): vivid red, double.
'Kelly's Cerise' (Nelly Kelly): purplish red, double.
'Kosciusko' (Greentree): white, med to large semidouble.
'Lady Bedford': white, double, large.
'Lady Bridges': white, striped purplish red, double, large.
'Lady Constance' (Europe): deep pink, double.
'Lady Poltimore': white.
'La Paix' (Vervaene, 1867; Belg.): purplish red.
'Leith': dark red, late; dwarf habit.
'Les Parkes': light pink, double.
'Little Beauty': vivid purplish red, hose-in-hose, semidouble, early.

'Little Girl' (Burbank, '73): pale pink, hose-in-hose, ruffled, large.

'Lorraine' ('Comtesse de Kerchove' × 'Temperance'; Nichols; intro. Berna Park, '73): deep yellowish pink, double.

'Louis van Houtte' (syn. 'Memoire de Louis van Houtte'; Belg.): purplish red, darker throat, semidouble, large.

'Lynette' (Cheeseman): purplish pink, double.

'Lyn Robinson': pale pink, double.

'Lyn Spencer' (Greentree): white, large frilled.

'Madame Adolphe' (d'Haene; Belg.): pink with white margin, large semi- to double.

'Madame Cavalier': white, hose-in-hose, semidouble, late.

'Madame Gele': see 'Madame Cyrille Van Gele'.

'Madame Henry' (Van Gele, '36): deep yellowish pink, double.

'Madame Herman Seidel' (syn. 'Frau Hermann Seidel'): white, occasional pink flecks, double.

'Madame Iris Lefebvre' (van Houtte, 1870; Belg.): white with pink stripes.

'Madame Joseph de Kneef': white, large.

'Madame Van Gele' (syn. 'Madame Cyrille Van Gele', p. 146): deep pink, double, large.

'Madame Petrique' (Huntingdale): vivid reddish orange, double.

'Mademoiselle Paula Van Acker' (Van Acker, '23; Eur.): purplish red, double.

'Magnet' (Barnes, 1860; U.K.): vivid red.

'Magnifica' ('Mucronatum' form or 'Indica Alba'; Japan): white, fragrant.

'Magnifica Rosea' (Mucronatum form; Japan): deep pink.

'Margaret Palmer' ('Phoeniceum' × ?; Marsh): vivid pink with darker throat.

'Marilyn Kay' ('Elsa Kaerger' × 'Red Ruffles'; Dosser): deep reddish orange.

'Marilyn Monroe' (Greentree; intro. Camellia Lodge, '74): pale pink, flecked pink, double.

'Marquis of Lorne' (van Houtte; Belg.): reddish orange, semidouble.

'Martha Gardner' (Nichols; intro. Berna Park, '74): vivid dark red, very dark buds, double, early; compact habit.

'Martian Boy' (Burbank, '83): white, frilled double.

'Masterpiece': see 'Nuccio's Masterpiece', p. 279.

'Mauve Shryderii' (sport of 'Shryderii'): pale purple, darker throat, fragrant, sun hardy; used in hybridizing.

'Maves': vivid red.

'Mellisa Ray' (Greentree): purple, large double.

'Memoire de Louis van Houtte' (van Houtte: see 'Louis van Houtte', p. 296): double.

'Mexico': see 'Nuccio's Mexico', p. 280.

'Min's Choice' ('Agnes Gault' × 'Mucronatum'; Langdon): moderate purplish pink, red spotting in blotch.

'Miranda Fair' (Bell): pink to pale pink, semidouble.

'Miss Australia' (Greentree, '70): pale pink.

'Mission Bells': red, semidouble.

'Miss Teenager' (Burbank, '75): pale pink, ruffled double.

'M. J. Rose' (syn. 'Mme Joseph Vervaene Rubra'; Vervaene, 1892): deep pink, large.

'M. J. White' (sport of 'M. J. Rose'): white, pink blotch, double.

'Moonglow' (de Rothschild, '46; U.K.): pale pink, semidouble.

'Mortii': white, large.

'Moulin Rouge' (Greentree; intro. Camellia Lodge, '77): reddish orange, semidouble.

'Mrs. Damfus': pink.

'Mrs. Emma Greentree' ('Hexe' × 'Vervaeneana'; Greentree, '68): deep pink, hose-in-hose, large.

'Mrs. Harry Van De Ven' ('Mucronatum' × 'Blaauw's Pink'; Van De Ven, '72): strong to pale purplish pink.

Mrs. Van De Ven' ('Mucronatum' × 'Blaauw's Pink'): light purplish pink, hose-in-hose.

'Mrs. Wright' (Van Houtte, 1872; Belg.): white, red flecks, double.

'Murasaki Ryukyu Rosea' (syn. 'Sekidera', p. 128; Japan): vivid pink.

'My Fair Lady': see 'California Beauty'.

'My Mother's Day' ('Comtesse de Kerchove' × ?; Nichols; intro. Berna Park, '74): white with green throat, wavy double, early; bushy habit.

'Nell Hooper' (Greentree, '70): purple, double, large; compact plant.

'Nellie Gatehouse' ('Comtesse de Kerchove' × 'Madame Auguste Haerens'); Nichols; intro. Berna Park, '73): reddish orange, double, 3½", early to late; upright.

'New Cerise': vivid purplish red, double, early.

'New Red': red double.

'Nicholas Schaure': deep pink with darker blotch, semidouble.

'Niobe Pink' (sport of 'Niobe'): pink flushed red, frilled, double.

'Olinda' (Greentree, '70): light pink, to white center, semidouble; large.

'Olympia': red, ruffled double; low compact.

'Only One Earth' (Burbank, '66): deep purplish pink, ruffled, semidouble, hose-in-hose.

'Orange Sander' (sport of 'Mme. Alfred Sander'): reddish orange, double.

'Orchidflora': see 'Orchiphilla', p. 159.

'Orchidflora Pink' (syn. 'Spellbound', p. 159): light purplish pink, white margin, double large.

'Orchid Gem' (Lovegrove): light purplish red, large ruffled.

'Orchid Pink' (syn. 'Pavlova'; Huntingdale): pale purplish pink, large ruffled double.

'Pacific Twilight' ('Comtesse de Kerchove' × 'Temperance'; Nichols; intro. Berna Park, '73): deep purple, double, 2¾", early; vigorous growth.

'Paddy Nick' ('Comtesse de Kerchove' × 'Pink Champagne'); Nichols; intro. Berna Park, '78): white with white and green flushed throat, double, 2¼", early; compact growth.

'Party Dress' (Greentree; intro. Camellia Lodge, '73): white, frilled, double, late.

'Pauline Mardner' (Mardner, 1860; Belg.): vivid pink, long petaled, double.

'Pavlova' (sport of 'Ballerina'; Huntingdale): pale purplish pink, tipped white, double.

'Peace' (possibly sport of 'Vervaeneana'): pale pink, double.

'Peaches and Cream' (Burbank): strong yellowish pink, edges lighter, slight yellowish blotch, ruffled, hose-in-hose.

'Peter Pan' (Greentree; Camellia Lodge, '73): white, with pink stripes, frilled, double.

'Phil Sherringham' (sport of 'James Belton'; Sherringham, intro. Camellia Lodge): white to light purple center, double.

'Phoebus' (Boelens, 1878; Eur.): reddish orange, light purple blotch, semidouble.

'Phryne': pale yellowish white, frilled, double.

'Phyllis Marsh' ('Phoeniceum' × ?; Marsh): pale purple.

'Piewacket' ('Comtesse de Kerchove' × 'Magnifica'; Nichols, intro. Berna Park, '78): yellowish pink, white lobe tips, yellowish green blotch, double, 2¾", early.

'Pink Bouquet': deep pink, large.

'Pink Dream': pale pink, large.

'Pink Ice': vivid pink, flushed purplish pink, double, early to midseason.

'Pink Iris': deep pink; tall.

'Pink Party Dress' (sport of 'Party Dress'; Greentree, intro. Camellia Lodge, '73): light pink, darker margins, semidouble, hose-in-hose, frilled.

'Pink Pearl': vivid pink, double.

'Pink Phryne' (sport of 'Phryne'): pink, frilled double.

'Pink Ruffles' (sport of 'Eri'; Nelly Kelly): pink and white, frilled, double.

'Pink Snow': see Nuccio's 'Pink Snow'.

'Pink Vervaene' (sport of 'Mme. Joseph Vervaene'; Camellia Lodge, '73): pink, dark throat, double.

'Pixi' (Greentree; intro. Camellia Lodge, '73): white with purple stripes.

'Pride of Kotara': pink; low compact.

'Prince Albert' (Knight, 1843; U.K.): vivid red.

'Princess Caroline': deep yellowish pink, red throat, semidouble, early.

'Princess Maud': purplish red, midseason.

'Princess Sonya' (Burbank, '75): white, frilled semidouble.

'Ralph' ('Mucronatum' × 'Blaauw's Pink'; Van De Ven, '72): strong to deep pink, hose-in-hose.

'Red Devil': vivid red, occasionally petaloid.

'Red Line' (sport of 'Eri'; Edwards, intro. Camellia Lodge): white, speckled pink, double.

'Red Line Frilled' (sport of 'Red Line'; Camellia Lodge, '71): white, striped pink, frilled, double.

'Red Party Dress' (sport of 'Party Dress'): red, semidouble.

'Red Poppy': deep red, petaloid.

'Red Sparks' ('Comtesse de Kerchove' × 'Pink Champagne'; Nichols; intro. Berna Park, '81): opening pale pink, maturing to white, double, narrow pointed petals, 2½", early.

'Rembrandt' (Steyaert, '35; Eur.): light red, fringed semidouble.

'R.G.N.': see 'Comtesse de Kerchove'.

'Roi de Hollande': reddish orange.

'Roi de Rose': pink, large semidouble.

'Rose Avenir' (sport of 'Avenir'): pale pink.

'Rose King' (sport of 'Rose Queen'): deep pink.

'Rose Marsh' ('Leopold Astrid' × 'Hinode Giri'; Marsh, '73): light purplish pink.

'Rose of Heaven': pale pink, semidouble.

'Rose Pearl': deep pink, semidouble.

'Rose Pink Party Dress' (Greentree; Camellia Lodge, '73): deep pink, frilled, semidouble, hose-in-hose.

'Rosina' (Nelly Kelly): pale pink, double.

'Royal Show' ('Comtesse de Kerchove' × 'Magnifica'; Nichols, intro. Berna Park, '78): pale pink, semidouble, 2¾".

'R.S.W.': purplish red, double, large.

'Ruby Glory' (sport of 'Crimson Glory'): vivid reddish orange, semidouble, sun hardy.

'Rudolph Seidel' (de Kneef, 1892; Eur.): deep yellowish pink, dark blotch, semidouble, large.

'Ruth Marian' (Bell): purplish red, white throat, semidouble, hose-in-hose.

'Salmon Rosina' (sport of 'Rosina'): deep yellowish pink, double.

'Schryderii' (sport of 'Lediflora Alba'): spotted purplish pink, throat pink, fragrant.

'Searchlight' (Lovegrove; Camellia Grove, '70): white, occasional pink flecks, greenish throat, double.

'September Bells' (Burbank, not released): deep yellowish pink, hose-in-hose, bell shaped.

'Sharon Joy': white blotched pink, double.

'Show Glory': see 'Madame Auguste Van Damme'.

'Sigismund Rucker' (van Houtte, 1873; Belg.): deep purplish pink, edged white.

'Silver Anniversary' (Burbank, '72): light pink, shading to white tips, frilled, semidouble, hose-in-hose.

'Silver Frills' (Burbank, '66): white, blushed pink, greenish blotch, frilled, double.

'Silver Glow' (sport of 'Jean Haerens'; Van De Ven): purplish red, hose-in-hose; variegated tricolor foliage in spring; compact habit.

'Silver Jubilee' (R. Sparks): deep reddish orange, semidouble; compact habit, very slow, variegated white margined foliage. Victoria Nurseryman's Award of Merit.

'Silver King': pink; variegated foliage.

'Silver Prince' (sport of 'Rose Queen'; Camellia Lodge, '73): pink, hose-in-hose.

'Sinensis Rosea': deep yellowish pink, white markings, large.

'Sir Charles Napier' (Knight, 1852; U.K.); light reddish orange.

'Smithi' (syn. 'Phoeniceum Smithi').

'Snowdrift' (U.K.): white, double; compact habit.

'Snow Girl' ('Comtesse de Kerchove' × ?; Nichols, intro. Berna Park, '73): white, large double.

'Snow Prince' (sport of 'Rose Queen'): white, semidouble to double, sun hardy.

'Snow Queen' (syn. 'Madame Hermann Seidel', p. 296; Rose, 1880; Eur.): white, occasionally flecked pink, double.

'Sophisticated': pale pink, blushed purple, large.

'South Seas' (Greentree, '70): purplish pink, semidouble.

'Southern Aurora' (sport of 'Comtesse de Kerchove'; Huntingdale, '76): light reddish orange, muted white, double.

'Southern Sunset' (sport of 'Southern Aurora'; Camellia Lodge, '83): vivid red-orange, double.

'Souvenier de Monsieur Low': light violet, double.

'Souvenier de Prince Albert': deep pink with white margins, double.

'Souvenier de Theo Piens': see 'Eri', p. 145.

'Sparkle': purplish red.

'Sparkling Burgundy' (Greentree): deep pink large to very large semidouble.
'Splendens': yellowish pink; tall.
'Splendida' (A. Haerens, '28; Belg.): dark red, double.
'Spring Magic' (Alderfer; intro. Burbank, '82): pink, double.
'Spring Time': deep yellowish pink, semidouble, large.
'Springwood' (Greentree; Camellia Lodge, '75): vivid pink, hose-in-hose, midseason.
'Startrek' ('Comtesse de Kerchove' × 'Temperance'; Nichols; intro. Berna Park): white with green throat, double, 2¾", early; compact.
'Stella' (Veitch, 1865; Eur.): reddish orange, upper petals tinged violet.
'Sunburst': see 'Nuccio's Sunburst'.
'Super Star' (Nichols; intro. Berna Park, '73): reddish orange, double, early; bushy pendulous growth.
'Sweet Kiki' (Paradise Garden): pink, variegated white, wavy, double.
'Sweet Nellie' (from USA; intro. Burbank): vivid purplish pink, semidouble to double, hose-in-hose.
'Talisman' (De May, 1897): deep yellowish pink, and white, semidouble.
'Tanya': vivid pink.
'Thelma Bray' (Greentree; Camellia Lodge, '75): purplish pink, white throat, semidouble.
'Theo Captain' (Haerens '28; Belg.): reddish orange, double.
'Theodorus' (Verschaffelt, 1876; Belg,): reddish orange, purplish spot.
'The Teacher' (sport of 'Little Girl'; Burbank '79): white, pink frilled edge, semidouble, hose-in-hose.
'Thredbo' (Greentree; Camellia Lodge, '79): white, flecked and striped purple, hose-in-hose, double.
'Vandercrimson': pink, purplish blotch, semidouble.
'Vanessa': purplish pink with darker throat.
'Variegata' (syn. 'Eulalie'): light purple and white, variegated foliage.
'Vater Druitz': red, double.
'Versicolor'(sport of 'Comte de Kerchove'): white, striped red, double.
'Veronica' (Shultz, 1888; Eur.): purplish pink, double; dwarf, compact.
'Violet Ray: violet.
'White Christmas' (syn. 'Mme. Petrick Alba'): white, large.
'White Cloud' (Camellia Lodge, '79): white, double crested center, large.
'White Crane' (syn. 'Vervaeneana Striata'; sport of 'Vervaeneana Alba'; Ormond): white with greenish throat, pink markings, semidouble.
'White Eureka' (sport of 'Eureka'): white, semidouble.
'White Prince' (sport of 'Rose Queen'; intro. Camellia Lodge, '83): white with red spots in throat, hose-in-hose, large.
'William Selkirk': pink, bordered white.
'William Wylam' ('Mucronatum' hybrid): purple, large.
'Woman's Day' (Greentree; Camellia Lodge, '73): light red, very large frilled, semidouble.
'Wonder Girl' (Burbank, '77): light pink, lighter throat, large.
'Wylam's Surprise' (sport of 'William Wylam'): pale purple, dark purplish throat, large.

KURUME HYBRIDS FROM AUSTRALIA AND NEW ZEALAND

'Amoena Alba Duplex': white, double.
'Anna Gaya: dark red.
'Arabian Knights': yellowish pink.
'Baby Doll' (Greentree): pink, hose-in-hose; medium to tall.
'Betty Cuthbert' (Greentree): pale pink, hose-in-hose.
'Blaze' (Greentree): vivid red, hose-in-hose.
'Bouquet of Roses': deep pink, semidouble.
'Cerise': purplish red.
'Chinko no Shikari': purple.
'Colbertii': red, double.
'Corroboree' (Greentree): dark red, late, semidouble.
'Dancing Doll': see Nuccio's 'Dancing Doll', p. 280.

'Elizabeth Belton' (Hazelwood): deep pink, paler margins, semidouble.
'Emily Knights' (Knights; Camellia Lodge, '73): vivid red, star-shaped.
'Evelyn Utick': purplish pink, mottled throat, midseason.
'Extrante': reddish purple, hose-in-hose; good growth habit.
'Fairy Queen Variegated' (sport of 'Aioi'): vivid pink, hose-in-hose; variegated foliage.
'Fireglow': reddish orange, hose-in-hose.
'Flora': deep yellowish pink, semidouble, hose-in-hose.
'Fred Colbert' (Colbert: Camellia Lodge, '62): vivid red, semidouble, hose-in-hose.
'Frederick Featherstone': light pink, semidouble.
'Fuli Mana': deep yellowish pink.
'Gustav Hacker': dark red.
'International Women' (Greentree): white with deep pink edge, hose-in-hose.
'Isis' (Wille, '33): light pink, darker margins.
'Jacqueline' (Greentree): deep yellowish pink, hose-in-hose.
'Jill Seymour' (Greentree; Camellia Lodge, '73): pink, red stripes, hose-in-hose.
'Kumano Hino': vivid red, hose-in-hose.
'Lisa Broom' ('Hinode Giri' × 'Tancho'; Marsh, '73): moderate purplish pink.
'Lorelei Robins' (Greentree): pink; tall.
'May Queen': pink.
'Miagino': deep pink.
'Momiji no Take': white, purple throat.
'Nola Robbins' (Greentree; Camellia Lodge, '73): vivid pink, hose-in-hose.
'Nulla Nulla' (Greentree): dark red, hose-in-hose; tall.
'October Pink': purplish pink, hose-in-hose.
'Ophelia': pink.
'Orange Red': reddish orange.
'Pauline' (Greentree): vivid red, hose-in-hose; tall.
'Pink Single': pink.
'Rose Pink': pink.
'Roseate': pink, semidouble.
'Sayohime': light purple, pointed spaced petals.
'Scarlet Gem': vivid red, hose-in-hose.
'Sharon Kathleen' (Langdon): strong red, darker spotting, hose-in-hose.
'Snow Storm': white, semidouble.
'Sorrento' (Lelliott): deep purplish pink, darker spotting on upper lobe, yellowish throat.
'Susanne' (Greentree): deep pink, medium habit.
'Toreador' (Japan; similar to 'Hinode Giri'): red.
'Trisha Tilly' (Greentree; Camellia Lodge, '73): pale yellowish white with spotted throat, semidouble, hose-in-hose.
'Vivienne' (Greentree): vivid pink, hose-in-hose.

MISCELLANEOUS AZALEAS FROM AUSTRALIA AND NEW ZEALAND

'Blue Heaven': purplish pink.
'Bonfire': vivid red.
'Burlesque': reddish orange, double.
'C. Sanders': purplish pink, darker throat.
'Candy Stripe': white, fluted, striped reddish orange, double.
'Carl Glazer': red, semidouble.
'Caroline:' deep pink, double.
'Cleopatra': purplish red, hose-in-hose.
'Colwell Pink': pink.
'Del Fluke': white, double.
'Dr. Curtis Aldifer': vivid red, semidouble.

'Fiona': white, hose-in-hose.
'Howard John': purplish red, hose-in-hose.
'Karen': deep yellowish pink, hose-in-hose.
'Karl Glaser': vivid red, hose-in-hose.
'Kellerina': purplish red, double.
'Kotara Golden Jubilee': purplish red, double.
'Lente Groet': purplish red.
'Little Princess': pink, double.
'Lopex': yellowish pink.
'Madame Butterfly': strong purple, double.
'Michael': see 'Michael Hill', p. 278.
'Orange Delight' (syn. 'Mrs. John Ward'): reddish orange.
'Pippa' (Japan): pale violet.
'Polar Hawk': white.
'Rosie O'Dea': purplish pink, double.
'Seagull' (van De Ven, '70): white, spotted green, hose-in-hose, large, fragrant.
'Silver Knight': dark pink, variegated foliage.
'Susanah': dark red, frilled, double.
'Surguri': reddish orange, bell-shaped; small shrub.
'Teena Maree': yellowish pink, hose-in-hose.
'Thurley's Pink': pink.

SATSUKI AZALEAS FROM AUSTRALIA AND NEW ZEALAND

About 20 Satsuki azaleas were found listed in catalogs from New Zealand and Australia. Some are also available in the United States, while others have odd spellings and were not found in Japanese reference books on Satsukis. They will be found in the general Satsuki list. It is also of interest to note that 15 selections of Gumpo azaleas were found in the Norwood Plant Directory from Australia, but all of these will not be listed because some are simply new names assigned previously-named cultivars.

HIRADO HYBRIDS

The Hirado Hybrids were developed on tiny Hirado Island off Japan's southwest coast. Hirado played an important role in Japan's history. Although the main islands of Japan were officially closed to foreign nations until a hundred years ago, this island has been open for the past four hundred years. Ships from China, Portugal, Spain, and Holland used Hirado as a trading post. These voyages brought azaleas to the island from a variety of other countries. Being isolated, the scenic island became a favorite spot for the Japanese samurai. Their palaces, surrounded by elaborate gardens planted with a spectacular array of plants, domestic and exotic, including azaleas, dotted the gentle countryside. Some of these gardens date back more than 300 years from the present. Unfortunately, in recent years many of these old gardens have been abandoned. To preserve the 300 or more named Hirado azalea cultivars, they have been transplanted into special parks scattered across Hirado. So highly regarded are these cultivars the Japanese government has used them extensively in massed highway planting throughout all the islands of Japan.

Their parentage is uncertain, but is generally thought to be hybrids of the Luchu Azalea *R. scabrum*, 'Indica Alba' or 'Mucronatum', and 'Phoeniceum'. The contribution of the Sims Azalea, *R. simsii*, from China is doubtful.

The plants are vigorous, upright to spreading, 6 to 8 feet in height. The foliage is large and coarse, resembling *R. scabrum*. Flower color ranges from white to pink, red and purple. The typical flower is 3 to 4", but some are unusually large, being over 5 to 6". The plants are best suited for warmer climates. While reported to survive in protected locations in Washington, DC, zone 6b, plants at Callaway Gardens, zone 8a, sustained considerable damage at 15°F.

The first plants were introduced by Dr. John Creech in 1963 and 1964 to the United States Plant Introduction Station. In 1976 a cross section of the best cultivars were introduced by Dr. Creech and

S. G. March to the U.S.D.A. National Arboretum. The 1963–64 introductions with their Plant Introduction number include:

'Fukuju' (PI 274706): light purplish pink, 4".
'Hakurakuten' (PI 274707): white, 3-1/5".
'Haru no Hikari' (PI 274708): light, purplish pink, 4".
'Harunoumi' (PI 274709): light, purplish pink, 4".
'Heiwa no Hikari' (PI 274710): reddish purple, blotch, 3¾".
'Hiran' (PI 274726): bright purplish red, 4⅛".
'Horai' (PI 274712): strong red, 4⅛".
'Irihi no Kumo' (PI 274713 and 274727): deep pink, 3½".
'Izaribi' (PI 274714): strong red, 3¾".
'Kintoki' (PI 274715): strong purplish red, 3-1/5".
'Kumo no Ue' (PI 274728): deep purplish pink, 4".
'Korokoshima' (PI 274729): purplish red, 4⅛".
'Matsurahime' (PI 274716): light purplish pink, 4-2/5".
'Momoyama' (PI 274717): strong purplish pink, 3½".
'Myoken' (PI 235981, 274718, and 274719): purplish pink, 4".
'Rakuyo' (PI 274730): moderate pink, 4⅛".
'Ranman' (PI 274731): deep pink, 4".
'Rashomon' (PI 274720): strong red, 4-2/5".
'Reimei' (PI 274721): vivid purplish pink, 4".
'Sekiyo' (PI 274723): strong red, 4½".
'Shinnan' (PI 274724 and 274732): purplish pink, 4-2/5".
'Shinsho' (PI 274733): deep purplish pink, 5-1/5".
'Tai Hai' (PI 274734): deep pink, 4-2/5".
'Tenjin' (PI 274725): deep purplish pink, 2½".
'Tensho' (PI 274735): reddish pink, 3½".

The 1976 Hirado introductions include:

'Ademurasaki' (40455): deep purple.
'Amaogawa' (40458): pale red.
'Fukumusume' (40418): reddish purple.
'Hakuo' (40480): white.
'Hien' (40479): pale red.
'Heiwa no Hikari' (40463): grayish purplish pink.
'Hinode' (40465): reddish purple.
'Hirado no Homari' (40464): pale reddish purple.
'Hiran' (40456): reddish purple.
'Kotobuki' (40473): reddish purple.
'Kurokojima' (40451): grayish reddish purple.
'Megami' (40453): pale purple.
'Maisugata' (40462): reddish purple.
'Momoyama' (40457): deep pink.
'Raijin' (40460): red.
'Rashomon' (40467): reddish purple.
'Saotome' (40474): reddish purple.
'Seibo' (40466): reddish purple.
'Sekiyo' (40461): red.
'Shirogane' (40476): white.

HUANG HYBRIDS FROM CHINA

Little information is available on azalea hybridizing in China, a country rich in native flora including the genus *Rhododendron.* Dr. George F. Drake of Western Washington University and owner of the Big Rock Garden nursery in Bellingham, Washington, obtained information from the Shanghai Botanical Gardens about Mr. Huang, a retired horticulturist who collected and hybridized azaleas for many years. Mr. Huang is now very ill, and many of his records were destroyed in the Cultural Revolution.

Mr. Huang's hybridizing was done with 'Yunnan Jia-tao', an old Chinese late flowering double hybrid, 'Wu Bao Lu Zhu' (Five Precious Stones and a Green Pearl), another old variety 'Yung Gui Fei' (name of a king's wife; a large rose with red margined single flowered cultivar); and Japanese hybrids of Kurume and Satsuki Hybrids.

Dr. Drake obtained cuttings of the Huang Hybrids from the Shanghai Botanical Gardens and has distributed them to other azalea enthusiasts for additional testing. All plants are presently under a number code, for example, 1-3-51. The first number indicates the flowering period, the second number the type of flower, and the third number the color. More information on the Huang Hybrids will appear in the years to come.

TETRAPLOID EVERGREEN AZALEAS

During the early 1970's there was an effort to use colchicine to produce doubled forms of selected cultivars. All these forms were characterized by flowers of much larger size and longer lasting, with a thicker texture than their counterpart diploid cultivars. The colchicine was applied to the growing tips of cuttings forced under lights in the greenhouse. Involved in this project was Dr. Haig Dermen who first discovered the effect of colchicine while still a graduate student at Harvard, Robert Pryor, L. C. Frazier, and Dr. Robert Stewart. To distinguish these clones the official names are coupled with the word "Tetra". Tetraploid forms released were:

'Anytime-Tetra'
'Casablanca-Tetra'
'Chimes-Tetra'
'Guy Yerkes-Tetra'
'Hershey Red-Tetra'
'Pink Gloria-Tetra'
'Road Runner-Tetra'

These plants were distributed to nurserymen, but many were lost because the nurserymen treated them as hardy types, and they were frozen. Some of the hardier clones are still available in specialized collections. These tetraploid clones are especially useful to azalea breeders because they impart their unusually large size flowers to their offspring.

Tetraploid and triploid forms were reported in some of the Satsuki Hybrids by Japanese cytologists. It is likely that tetraploid forms in addition to those below can be found in present day cultivars.

'Banka' — tetraploid
'Tahei' — tetraploid
'Wako' — tetraploid
'Gettsutoku' — behaves as tetraploid in breeding studies.

AZALEODENDRONS

One of the first rhododendron hybrids on record was a difficult and unusual cross of *R. ponticum*, an evergreen rhododendron, with a deciduous azalea, *R. periclymenoides (R. nudiflorum)*. The hybrid was discovered around 1800 at the Thompson Nursery at Miles End near London, England. By 1822 Thompson had four varieties (one with fragrant flowers) under the name *R. azaleoides*. The name was a source of confusion and was used then as is the present day term azaleodendron.

The term 'Azaleodendron' was first coined in 1892 by Rodrigas for hybrids between the Japanese azalea *R. japonicum* and various hardy hybrid rhododendrons. In modern classification it is a botanical subgeneric name. *Azaleodendron* (Rodgrigas) Rehder, designates crosses of Subgenera *Pentanthera* and *Tsutsusi* (the *Azalea* subgenera) with *Hymenanthes*, the elepidote (non-lepidote) rhododendrons. Botanically it is a subgeneric name and should not be used as a generic name. Horticulturally it is also used to include several modern-day crosses such as the Hardijzer Hybrids which botanically would not fall into the subgenus *Azaleodendron*. While they represent a distinct hybrid subgenus, they will be listed under "Azaleodendrons" until a new subgenus is named.

Numerous azaleodendrons have been raised in the past century, but few have survived due to their lack of vigor. Numerous crosses reported either lack seed capsules or bear only a few viable seed that are often lost at an early age. Many of the hybrids are weak plants with odd to ugly foliage and are tolerated as novelties because of their parentage and unusual flowers. These remarks are not intended to discourage the breeding of azaleodendrons, but the production of valuable seedlings unavoidably will be very limited.

Most of the named hybrid azaleodendrons are from elepidote rhododendron crossed with a deciduous azalea or the reciprocal cross. Joseph Gable reported in 1950 a successful cross of *R. ovatum* × a Kurume Azalea, but the plant was later lost. My 10 attempts over a period of several years with different evergreen azaleas produced only one seed capsule, and the few seedlings died at an early age. For a complete listing of records on

Azaleodendrons see the references in appendix—Kehr, August E. 1977 and Schmalscheidt, Walter 1979.

It is doubtful if the first *Azaleodendron* 'Azaleoides' is still in cultivation. However, the following three old hybrids are still available: 'Broughtonii Aureum' and 'Smith's Aureum' developed about 1830 by W. Smith of England; and 'Govenianum' by T. Methven in England about 1868.

The following descriptive list is far from complete, but includes several old and new hybrids along with one unnamed hybrid and the Hardijzer Hybrids at the end.

'Avita' (*occidentale* × 'Margaret Dunn', Brandt, '58): orange-yellow.

'Azaleoides' (*R. ponticum* × *nudiflorum;* Thompson 1800±): light purple, yellow center.

'Broughtonii Aureum' (syn. 'Norbitonense Broughtonianum'; (*R. maximum* × *ponticum*) × *R. molle*, W. Smith, 1830): vivid yellow, reddish brown spots in blotch, 2½" wide, 10 stamens, 8 to 16 in truss; leaves persistent 2" to 6", long, dull green.

'Bruce Hancock' ('Gumpo' × *R. keiskei*): See Harris Hybrids.

'Dr. Masters' ('Prince Camille de Rohan' or 'Leopold' × *japonicum*, G. Vander Meulen, 1892).

'Galloper Light' (parentage unknown, Lionel de Rothchild, '27): reddish, pink with pale yellowish base, 2", 12 in truss; leaves semideciduous, rugose.

'Gemmiferum' (parentage unknown, J. Walker before 1861): purplish pink, funnel-shaped, 1¼" long; leaves 2–3½" long, dark glossy green, pale beneath margins recurved; upright loose habit to 6 feet.

'Glory of Littleworth' (parentage unknown, Henry Mangles before 1880): pale yellowish white fading lighter, blotch orange spots, fragrant, 2", 6 to 8 stamens, 15 to 18 in truss; leaves oblong lanceolate.

'Hazel Smith' (*occidentale* × 'Corona', Wyatt, '65): white with red blotch, 2" wide, up to 18 in truss; leaves 4" × 1½" wide.

'Mary Harmon' ('Mrs. Donald Graham' × *occidentale*, E. Ostbo, '58): white, striped pink outside, funnel-shaped, 2", fragrant, 15 in truss.

'Martha Isaacson' (*occidentale* × 'Mrs. Donald Graham', E. Ostbo, '58): white, occasional pink stripes, slightly fragrant, 8 to 10 stamens, tubular funnel-form, 2½" long; leaves evergreen.

'Nellie' (*occidentale* × unknown, H. White, England): white with large yellow blotch, funnel-shaped, 2½" across, 12 in truss; leaves semideciduous to 4" long.

'Odoratum' (*R. ponticum* × *nudiflorum*, M. Young, before 1875): light purple, fragrant.

'Oregon Queen' (*occidentale* × *macrophyllum*, natural hybrid): light pink.

'Pink Parfait' (parentage unknown, J. Sanko, Oregon, registered '68): pink.

'Smithii Aureum' (syn. 'Norbitonense Aureum', (*maximum* × *ponticum*) × *molle*, W. Smith, 1830): Very similar to 'Broughtonii Aureum' but lighter color, brilliant yellow.

'Tomlonianum' (parentage unknown, possibly *calendulaceum* × *catawbiense*, A. van Geirht before 1845): reddish purple, conspicuous orange blotch, funnel-shaped, 1¾", wide, 9 stamens, 12 in truss; leaves persistent, elliptic glossy.

'Tressa McMurry' (*occidentale* × *ponticum*, McMurry, registered '78): purplish pink with brown dots in blotch, 1½" across, 10 to 14 in truss; semidwarf 20" in 8 years. Hardy to + 14°F.

R. moulmainense × *simsii*, P. G. Valder, Australia, '83: strong purplish pink, darker dots.

Other names are often listed but with no description, such as 'Fortnight', 'Martha', and 'Samurai'.

HARDIJZER HYBRIDS

These "Azaleodendrons" were developed by W. H. Hardijzer of Boskoop, Holland; the first registered in 1958 followed by others in 1964. Horticulturally they are "azaleodendrons" but not in the true botanical sense, since the parent plant is the lepidote *R. racemosum* and the pollen plant, a Kurume Azalea. Listed as an "azaleodendron", but of a distinct hybrid subgenus until named. The plants are evergreen, with small flowers in large axillary inflorescence typical of the seed parent. Hardy in zone 7, but not heat tolerant.

'Hardijzer's Beauty' ((*R. racemosum* × Kurume Hybrid), '65): strong purplish pink 67D, lightly flushed purplish red 66C, spotting darker, 1⅛", 50 to 60 in tight truss; compact habit.

'Lillian Harvey' ((*R. racemosum* × Kurume Hybrid), '65): vivid reddish purple 8 to 10 anthers, 2 to 3 flowers in 8 to 12 lateral trusses.

'Maritime' ((*R. racemosum* × Kurume Hybrid), '65): deep purplish pink darker spots, 1¼"; 2 to 4 flowers in 5 to 10 lateral trusses.

'Ria Hardijzer' ((*R. racemosum* × 'Hinode Giri'), '65): vivid purplish red, faint spots in blotch, 1" across, 8 to 10 stamens, 5 to 10 in truss.

SECTION IV

9. PLANTING AND CARE OF AZALEAS

Azaleas have no cultural mysteries and only a few definite requirements. Understanding these cultural needs will pay dividends in developing the plants into healthy and handsome specimens.

The fundamental considerations include:

1. Garden site: hardiness, climatic zone, and exposure.
2. Soil: aeration, drainage, pH, organic matter, and mycorrhiza.
3. Planting techniques: depth, spacing, and mulching.
4. Nutrition.
5. Pruning.

Successful azalea growing depends upon (1) purchasing quality plants adapted to your area, (2) selecting a garden site with favorable exposure and soil conditions, and (3) following through with proper planting methods.

Azaleas grow best in an acid, well-drained humus soil. Heavy clay soils and sandy sites require physical improvement. The site should be free of frost pockets. High open shade is preferable to a fully exposed area. Light shade is important for azaleas in warmer areas, especially in zones 8 to 10. Morning sun is preferable to noon or afternoon sun. Late flowering azaleas do best with protection from exposure to intense mid-afternoon sun. Coniferous trees such as pines provide a light filtered shade while deciduous trees should be trimmed high to allow sunlight to filter through. Azaleas should be protected from exposure to high winds with a screen planting of large shrubs or trees on the windward side. Avoid planting azaleas near shallow-rooted trees such as Silver Maples and Elms to reduce the competition of the roots for moisture and nutrients. A shady northern exposure is better for tender azaleas than an open site exposed to winter sun.

HARDINESS

Select plants adapted to your plant hardiness zone. Every plant has a temperature limit below and another above which it cannot thrive. The present U.S. Dept. of Agriculture zone rating is an important guide for cold hardiness and indicates how far north a plant may safely be planted. It is, however, equally important to know how far south a plant will survive. Horticulturists have been concerned for many years about adding a designation to indicate the southernmost range in which a plant will satisfactorily grow. While such limits cannot be applied to a specific plant, they can be given in general for each species or hybrid group. It must be recognized that occasionally an aberrant plant within the species or hybrid group may, by reason of its particular genetic makeup, fall outside the behavior of the group as a whole.

Data as to average annual temperature lows for a locality over a period of years can be obtained from the nearest local weather station. Such data also can be obtained from the main office of the United States Weather Bureau in your state and has been summarized on a nation-wide basis by the Plant Hardiness Zone Map prepared by the United States National Arboretum, in cooperation with the American Horticultural Society. The map designates ten temperature zones, through the United States and Canada, each covering a 10 degree F. range of average annual minimum temperatures. Each zone is divided into subzones "a" and "b" showing a 5 degree F. division.

There are several other hardiness zone maps published. However, reference to hardiness zones in this book refers to the U.S.D.A. Plant Hardiness Zone Map No. 814. Simplified hardiness zone maps are printed here. A hardiness map, unfortunately, cannot list all of the local variations or microclimatic areas. For example, city temperatures may be several degrees warmer than the surrounding countryside. Likewise, the city area might also have a higher pollution index than the surrounding areas.

HARDINESS ZONES OF CERTAIN AZALEAS

These are general or approximate ratings for the species and groups. Individual seedlings of a species or hybrid in a group may show greater cold or heat resistance than the ratings given.

	Species	
alabamense	Alabama A.	6b–9a
albrechtii	Albrecht A.	5b–8a
amagianum	Mt. Amagi A.	7a–8a
arborescens	Sweet A.	5a–9a
atlanticum	Coastal A.	6a–9a
austrinum	Florida A.	6b–10a
bakeri	Cumberland A.	5b–8b
calendulaceum	Flame A.	5b–8b
canadense	Rhodora A.	3b–7a
canescens	Piedmont A.	6b–10a
farrerae	Farrer A.	7b–9a
flammeum (speciosum)	Oconee A.	6b–9a
indicum	Indica A.	(6b–7a)–10a
japonicum	Japanese A.	5a–8b
kaempferi	Torch A.	5b–9a
kanehirai		7b–9a
kiusianum	Kyushu A.	6a–8b
komiyamae		7a–9a
luteum (flavum)	Pontic A.	6b–8a
macrosepalum	Big Sepal A.	7b–8b
macrosepalum linearifolium	Spider A.	7b–8b

Bonsai from National Arboretum Bonsai Garden. GALLE

Rock planting of *R. kiusianum,* Bonsai Village, Japan. GALLE

Beltsville Dwarf 'Flower Girl' forced as a pot plant. GALLE

Old Kurume bonsai azalea with leaves picked off after flowering in spring. Private collection in Kurume, Japan. GALLE

Lace bug and residue on the underside of azalea leaf. MILLER

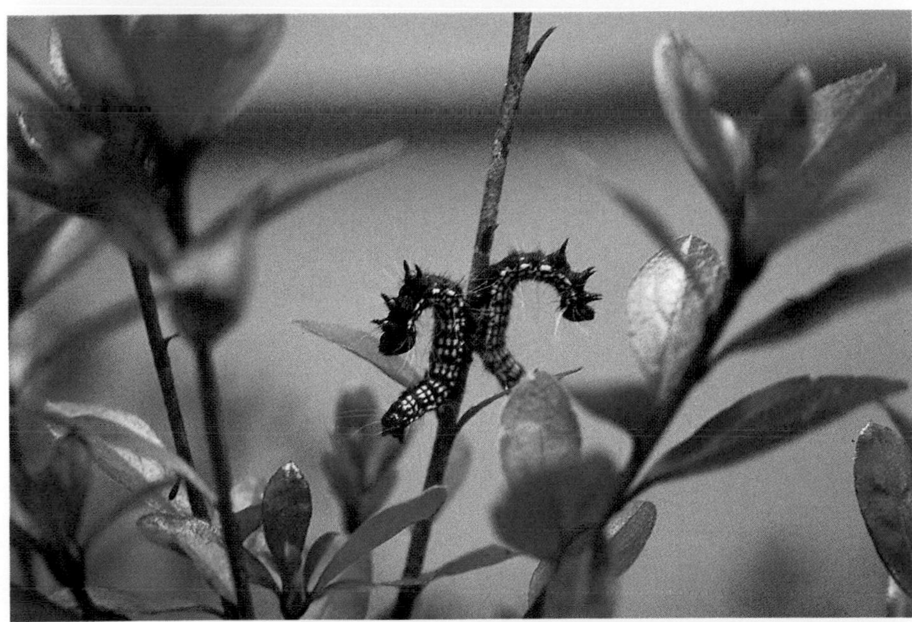

Datana caterpillars on evergreen azaleas. GALLE

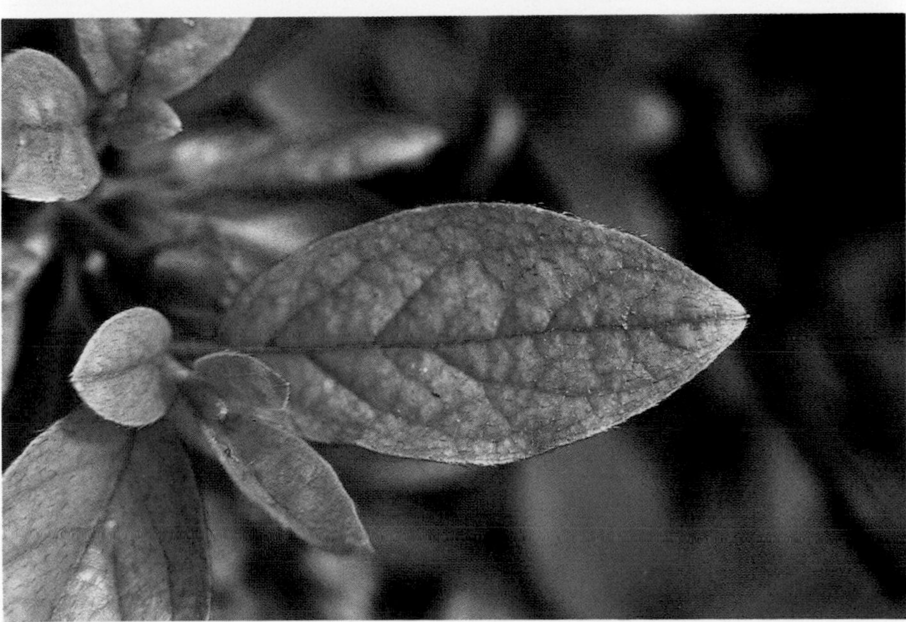

Chlorosis or iron deficiency. MILLER

Ovulinia azalea petal blight. MILLER

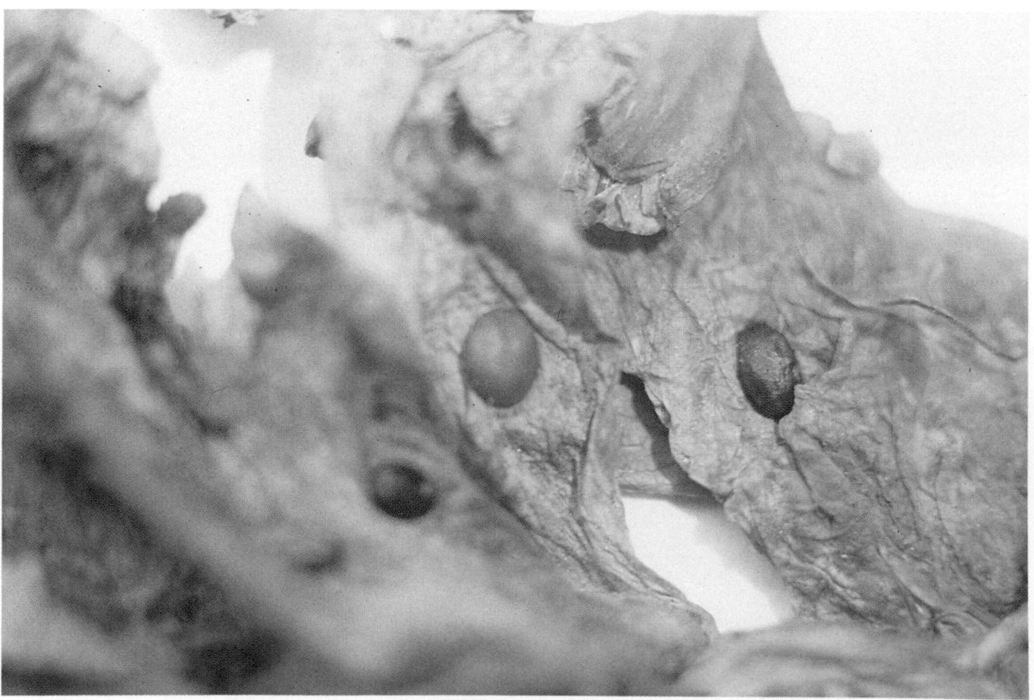

Sclerotia or resting stage of Ovulinia petal blight on blighted petals. GALLE

mariesii	Maries A.	7a–9a
molle	Chinese A.	6b–8a
'Mucronatum'	Ryukyu A.	7a–9b
nakaharai		6b–9a
nipponicum	Nippon A.	6a–8b
nudipes	Nudipe A.	5a-8a
oblongifolium		7a–9a
'Obtusum'	Kirishima A.	7a–9a
'Obtusum amoena'	Amoena A.	6b–9a
occidentale	Western A.	7a–9b West Coast
oldhamii	Oldham A.	8a–9a
otakumii (yakuinsulare)		7b–9a
pentaphyllum	Fiveleaf A.	6b–8b
periclymenoides (nudiflorum)	Pinxterbloom A.	4b–9a
prinophyllum (roseum)	Roseshell A.	4b–8a
prunifolium	Plumleaf A.	7a–9b
quinquefolium	Cork A.	6a–8b
reticulatum	Rose A.	6b–8a
ripense	Riverbank A.	7a–8a
rubropilosum	Redhair A.	7b–8a
sanctum	Shrine A.	7a–8a
sataense	Sata A.	7a–9a
scabrum	Kerama A.	8b–9b
schlippenbachii	Royal A.	5b–9a
serpyllifolium	Wild thyme A.	6a–8b
serrulatum	Hammock Sweet A.	7a–10a
simsii	Sims A.	8a–9a
tamurae (eriocarpum)	Dwarf Indica A.	7b–10a
tosaense	Tosa A.	7a–8a
tschonoskii	Tschonoski A.	5a–8b
vaseyi	Pinkshell A.	5a–9a
viscosum	Swamp A.	4b–9a
weyrichii	Weyrich A.	7b–9a
yedoense	Yodogawa A.	6a–9b
yedoense poukhanense	Korean A.	6a–9b

Hybrid Groups

Arnoldiana	6a–8a	Kurume	7a–9a
Back Acres	6b–9a	Mollis	5b–8a
B. & A. Macrantha	7a–8b	Carla (N.C.S.U.)	6b–8b
Belgian Indian	8a–10b	North Tisbury	6b–8b
Chisolm-Merritt	7a–9a	Occidentale hybrid	7a–9 West Coast
Gable	6b–9a	Pericat	7a–9a
Ghent	5b–8a	Robin Hill	6b–8b
Girard	5a–9a	Rustica Flore Pleno	6b–8a
Glenn Dale	6b–9a	Rutherford	7b–10a
Greenwood	7a–9	Satsuki	7a–9a
Harris	7a–8b	Southern Indian	8a–10a
Kaempferi	5b–9a	Vuyk	5b–9
Knap Hill	5b–8a	Yerkes Pryor	6b–9a

HARDINESS ZONES OF EUROPE

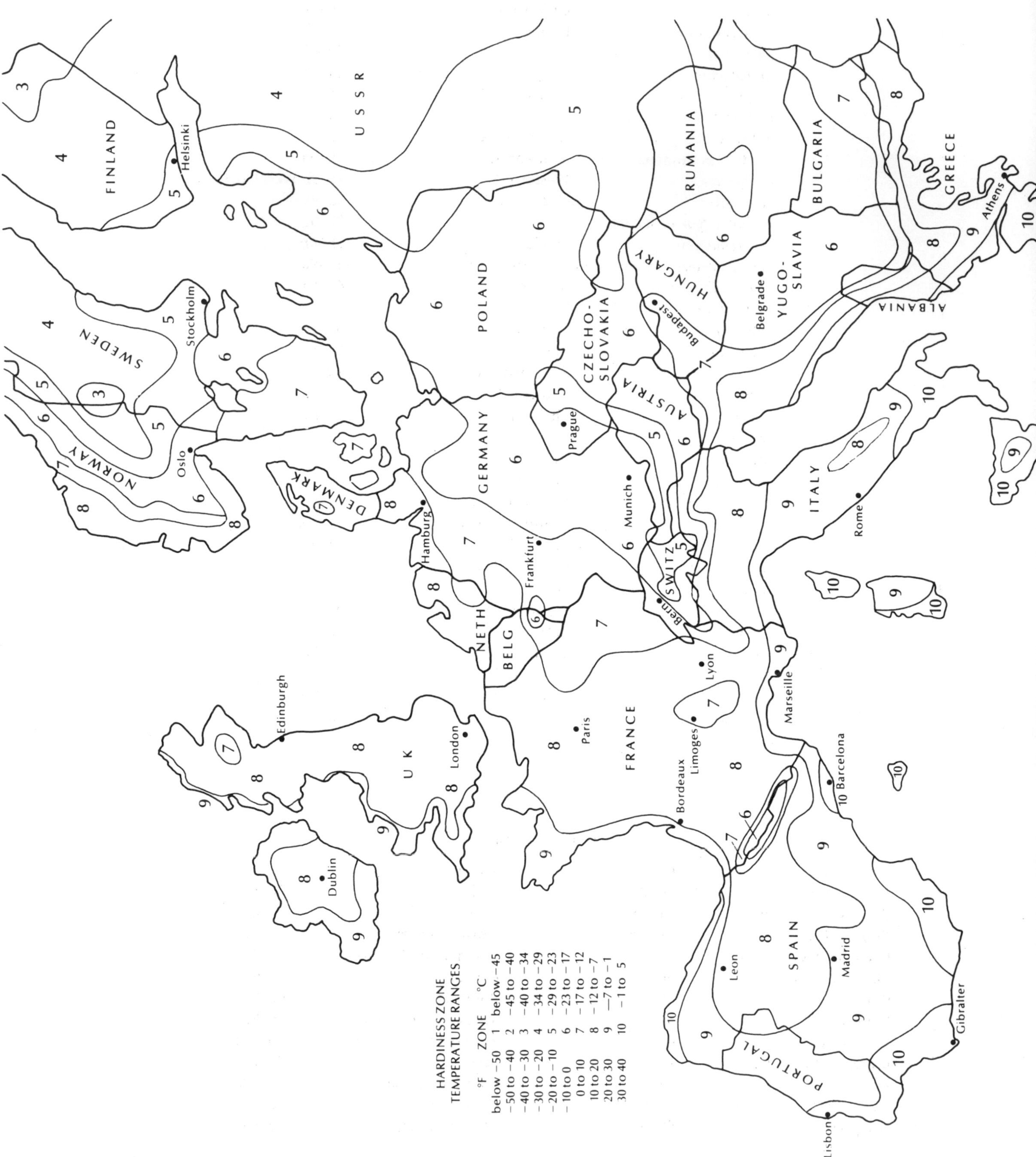

HARDINESS ZONES OF NORTH AMERICA

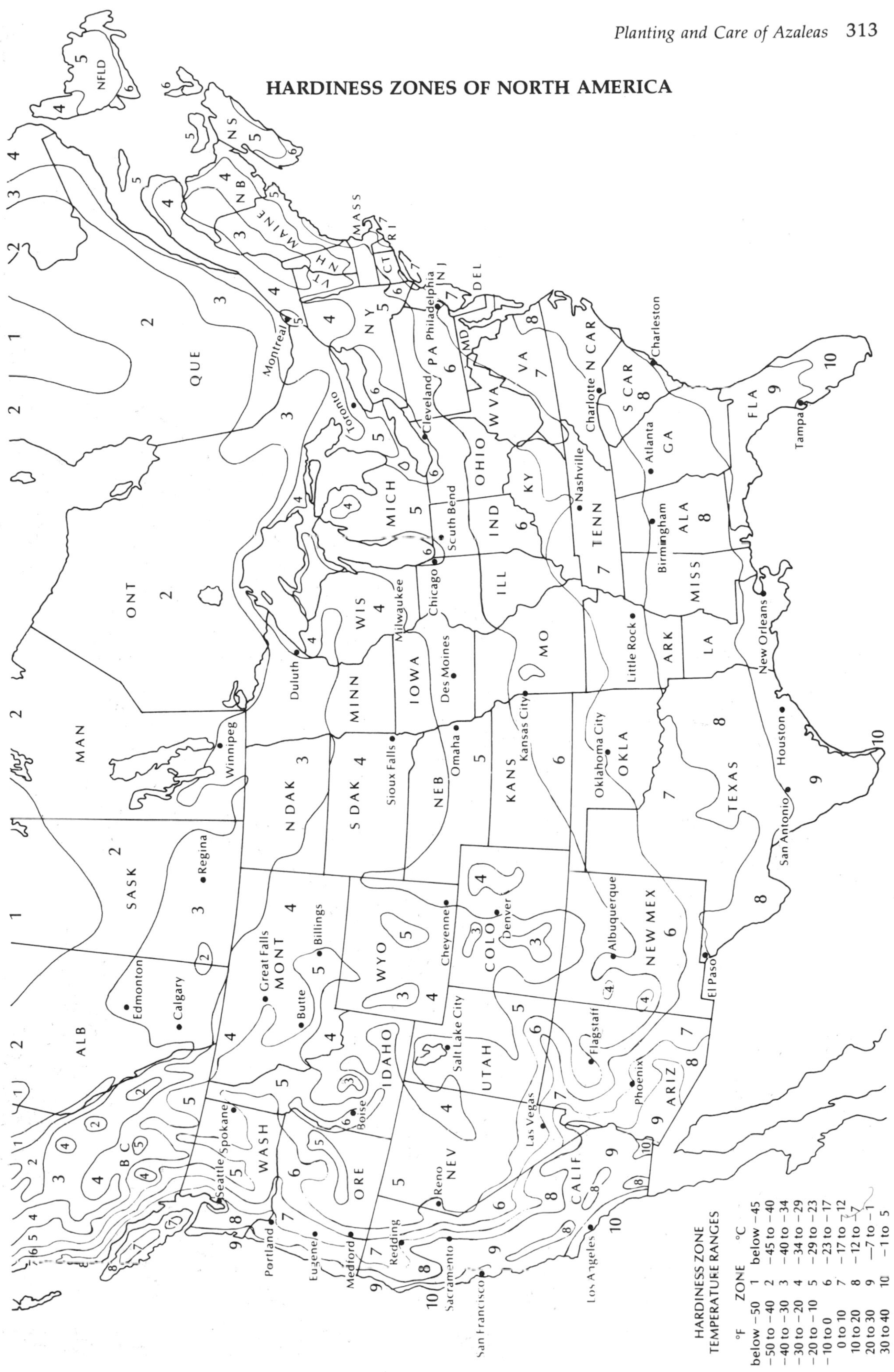

HARDINESS ZONES OF CHINA

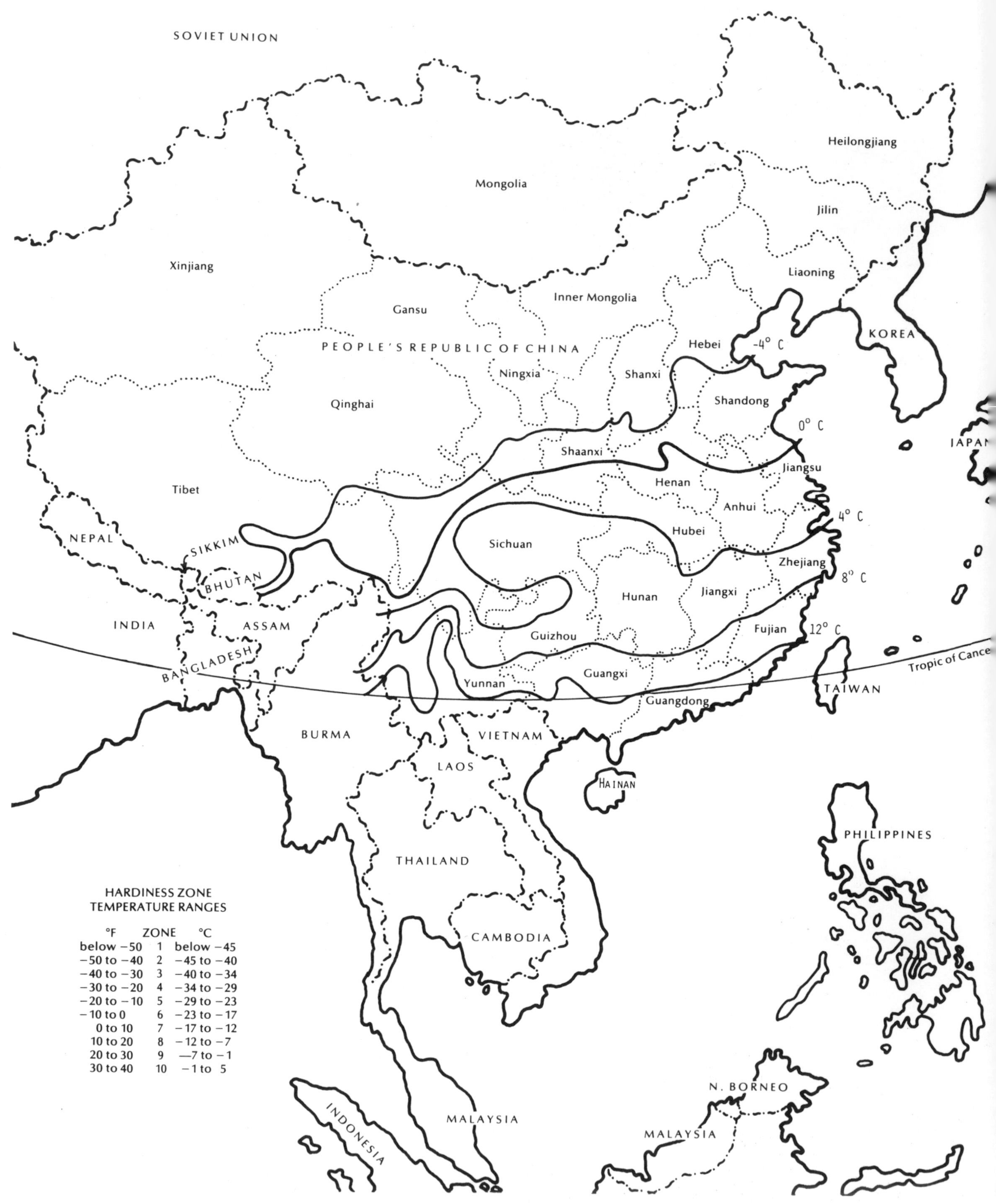
SOVIET UNION
Mongolia
Heilongjiang
Jilin
Xinjiang
Liaoning
Inner Mongolia
Gansu
KOREA
Hebei
-4° C
PEOPLE'S REPUBLIC OF CHINA
Ningxia
Shanxi
Qinghai
Shandong
0° C
JAPAN
Shaanxi
Jiangsu
Tibet
Henan
Anhui
4° C
NEPAL
Hubei
SIKKIM
Sichuan
Zhejiang
BHUTAN
8° C
Hunan
Jiangxi
INDIA
ASSAM
Fujian
12° C
Guizhou
BANGLADESH
Guangxi
Tropic of Cancer
Yunnan
TAIWAN
Guangdong
BURMA
VIETNAM
LAOS
HAINAN
PHILIPPINES
THAILAND
HARDINESS ZONE
TEMPERATURE RANGES
°F ZONE °C
below −50 1 below −45
−50 to −40 2 −45 to −40
−40 to −30 3 −40 to −34
−30 to −20 4 −34 to −29
−20 to −10 5 −29 to −23
−10 to 0 6 −23 to −17
0 to 10 7 −17 to −12
10 to 20 8 −12 to −7
20 to 30 9 —7 to −1
30 to 40 10 −1 to 5
CAMBODIA
N. BORNEO
INDONESIA
MALAYSIA
MALAYSIA

HIGH TEMPERATURE LIMITS

Some deciduous species and hybrids do not thrive in areas where summer temperatures, both of soil and air, are high. As we move into warmer zones, many of the hybrid deciduous azaleas are less successful unless grown at higher elevations to compensate for the heat. Failure probably comes not from the maximum high temperature, but rather from the duration of it, and the associated rapid evaporation of soil moisture. Continuous high night time temperatures are especially harmful. Also the cold period in warmer zones is not constant so winter dormancy is often broken due to fluctuating winter temperatures.

Most of the presently available deciduous azalea hybrids are derived from cool climate species and do not respond uniformly to conditions in zones 8, 9 and 10. Some cultivars, however, are adaptable and often seedlings of these hybrids prove more heat resistant.

Plant breeders are currently developing races of deciduous azaleas involving the combination of some of the Knap Hill and Ilam hybrids with some of the heat tolerant native species.

WINTER INJURY

Winter injury from low temperature may reveal itself in two ways: (1) the bark splits on the stem just above the ground and (2) the flower buds are damaged. If bark splitting is extensive and the stem is girdled, death usually follows, but often not until the next spring or summer. Injured buds usually turn brown. Both may occur during a sudden temperature drop below freezing in early fall before the plant has hardened off. Damage also may occur from a heavy frost after dormancy is broken in spring or during an unseasonable warm spell in winter.

Sometimes plants suffering from bark splitting can be saved. At Callaway Gardens, following a 50 degree drop to 17 degrees in March, 1962, basal bark damage ran up to eighteen inches on over 200 azaleas. Melted paraffin (grafting wax might do as well) was brushed onto the injured portion and pine needles piled up around it. This prevented further injury and bark peeling; all but five plants were saved.

Some azalea plants respond quickly to periods of rising winter temperatures and frequently carry flower buds that appear sound, but do not develop in the spring. Examination usually reveals dead flower buds inside undamaged bud scales. This can happen when a period of mild weather, often in January or February, starts a flow of sap and causes premature development of the buds. This is particularly true with tender varieties that have a short dormant period or with cultivars that frequently give scattered bloom in autumn.

Winter hardiness is not solely a factor of inherent resistance to cold or minimum low temperature. It may also be a product of the duration of the cold periods and the total periods of heat, or of their mutual relationship. Furthermore, winter hardiness is a condition dependent on the age, stage of growth and vigor of the plant, presence of mulches or snow cover, exposure to wind and sun, depth of the root system, and prevalence of early or late frosts or of open periods of rapidly alternating thaws and freezes.

A young plant with stems less than ¼ inch in diameter may be more tender than a four or five year old plant of the same species or cultivar. Twigs and buds able to resist a lower temperature when cooled gradually may die following a sudden drop in temperature. A mulch or snow cover in addition to the soil itself has an insulating effect on the roots so that the soil temperatures lag behind air temperatures. It takes a longer period of the minimum temperature to kill roots of an established plant than the uninsulated branches of the plant above ground mulch, or snow cover. In consequence, where low temperatures are of short duration a plant may be root hardy but not top hardy at a given site. It may revegetate and grow again even though the top is killed.

It is important to know that container grown plants need protection during the winter months for their roots are much more sensitive to cold than the above ground plant parts. Winter winds also cause desiccation of both the tops and roots. Storing of container plants in a polyhouse is a common nursery practice. The home gardener should place containers close together, mulch heavily, or use a cold frame.

Plants not hardened off with a week to ten days of cool weather in the fall before freezing are more subject to cold injury. Loss of azalea flower buds can normally be traced to the first frost, rather than to cold occurring after plants are more adequately hardened. Hardening is characterized by an increase of hydrophilic colloids, which inhibit freezing of the plant cells. Hardening may not have occurred for lack of sufficient cool weather prior to an early frost. Poor growth, a small leaf area, insect injury, disease or mechanical damage and conversely, vegetative growth prolonged into the late fall by late fertilizing, unusual warm weather, or heavy rains all reduce the concentration of hydrophilic colloids and reduce the ability of a plant to harden off.

MULCHES

Mulches on azaleas can have an adverse effect with respect to cold temperature injury to the branches. The air temperature above a mulch may be several degrees lower than the air temperature above bare ground, because the mulch acts as an insulator against the loss of accumulated soil heat to the air above it. This can be more of a problem with mulched plants in an exposed site, and in areas subject to early sudden freezing temperature in the fall. In a wooded garden situation the overhanging branches of the trees effectively slow down the radiation of soil warmth and delay freezing temperatures at or near ground levels until stems and flower buds have developed some cold resistance. Thus, it is important not to reapply mulch in the early fall but instead to wait until the plants are completely dormant.

VIGOR AND WATER SUPPLY

Vigor of a plant may be a factor in hardiness. Unthrifty old plants are killed more quickly than healthy plants when exposed to severe cold. Vigor is, in turn, often affected by water supply during the growing season. In grafted plants an imperfect graft union may be a limiting factor. Thus, own-root deciduous azaleas may be more resistant to cold temperatures than grafted plants.

Inability of roots in winter to absorb sufficient water results in drying out and wilting. A fall or winter drought or frozen soils coupled with high transpiration of moisture from the leaves of evergreen azaleas due to intense winter sun or dry winds are most commonly at the root of winter wilting.

Vapor pressure within a leaf is greater than that of the surrounding area, and moisture will be diffused by the sun from evergreen azalea leaves. Vapor pressure increases with temperature, and the temperature of an evergreen leaf in full sun in the winter may be 20 to 30 degrees F. higher than that of surrounding air. Wind also increases the rate of transpiration of a leaf.

Plants are injured by low temperatures as the result of intracellular freezing or ice crystal formation within the membranes of plant cells. Freezing is always lethal. A slow rate of thawing following freezing of plant tissues seems to have no effect on the amount of injury.

Winter hardiness is only one factor in the adaptability of a plant to a given climatic area. Even when winter temperatures are suitable, the plant may still not do well because it is not adapted to (1) the soil or soil water conditions, (2) the amount of rainfall or its distribution throughout the year, (3) the summer climate or, (4) the amount of light and shade. Unfortunately, these many factors are difficult to define precisely or depict by any readily available graphic means. Although many of these factors are subject to artificial correction, it is still important to study the garden site and select azaleas hardy and adaptable to your area. While it is possible to modify somewhat a site to improve these factors, it is still important to choose the best garden site and select azaleas hardy and adaptable to your area.

SOILS

Soil for azaleas should be of good physical structure, open and friable to provide drainage, and acid with sufficient quantities of organic matter to retain moisture. The best soil for azaleas is one in which native azaleas grow well in the wild. Native soils are loose, crumbly and abundant with organic matter. Such areas are usually found in a humid region under a forest canopy.

Unfortunately, most gardeners do not have such sites and must develop and improve existing soils for their azaleas. Heavy clay soils or pure sand can be improved by the addition of organic matter such as peat, leaf mold, or pine bark. Soil drainage and aeration in most sites can be improved by putting in a tile drain system.

It is usually more practical to use existing soil than to replace it. In some areas, however, where the soil is not sufficiently acid or where building operations either have resulted in removal of top soil or have left additions of trash, mortar or free lime, it will be necessary to substitute a considerable amount of suitable soil. If the soil is low in humus, mix in up to six inches of organic matter, as leaf mold from the woods, well-rotted leaves, sawdust or pine bark, compost, peat moss or other organic matter. Check the soil pH and let the mixture settle a week or so before planting.

SOIL ACIDITY

The soil for azaleas should be acid, somewhere between very strong and medium, that is a pH of 4.5 to 6.0. The acidity or alkalinity of a soil is based on the hydrogen ion concentration expressed as pH. The pH scale is graduated from 0 to 14. A pH of 7.0 is neutral; reactions above 7.0 are alkaline and below 7.0 are acid. The degree of alkalinity or acidity increases or decreases by 10 times the previous level for each whole number change. Thus, a pH of 5.0 is 10 times more acid than a pH of 6.0 and 100 times more acid than a pH of 7.0.

Soils of the forest or originally forested areas are usually suitable for azaleas. Soils originating from limestone are alkaline or close to it. Alkaline soils are usually found in upthrust sedimentary rock formed in ancient oceans. To grow azaleas in such alkaline or neutral soils, it is best to improve the soil by adding large quantities of organic matter.

While there are indicator plants such as Christmas ferns and other acid-loving plants, a soil analysis is the only way to identify correctly soil acidity. Soil testing kits are available, but the results can often be misleading, due to deterioration of the chemical reagents. Your county agent or agricultural officer can provide information on how to have your soil tested for pH and nutrients in a soil analysis lab. The soil test report will indicate if either lime or acid forming materials are needed to adjust the pH of your soil.

Azaleas grow in a wide range of soil acidity. The best range is between 4.5 to 6.0. Azaleas growing in a low pH of 3.5 to 4.5 will be healthy, but will often grow at a slower rate than normal. Foliage of azaleas growing in a soil pH of 6.5 and above may appear yellow, an indication of chlorosis. If the soil pH is above 6, add ground sulfur (flowers of sulfur) not aluminum sulfate, to increase the acidity. Azaleas are harmed by high salts content in the soil so the addition of aluminum sulfate increases the amount of total soil salts. Nor is dusting sulfur recommended since the carrier may be quite alkaline. Approximately 1.5 pounds of ground sulfur per 100 square feet mixed into the soil will lower the pH from 6.0 to 5.5 or ½ point. Sandy soil will require less sulfur, 0.5 pounds per 100 square feet, while heavy clay soils may require up to 2.5 pounds of sulfur, plus the addition of organic material. It is also advisable to add ½ pound per 100 square feet of ferrous sulfate with the ground sulfur. Do not add additional sulfur to the soil until you have had the soil retested.

Chlorosis is caused by a reduction of chlorophyll in the leaves. An improper relationship between soil pH and availability of iron causes chlorosis. Iron is most available to plants in an acid soil of pH 4.5 to pH 6.0. The symptom of azaleas deficient in iron is chlorosis—leaves are yellow with prominent dark green veins. Chlorotic leaves may sometimes have a high iron content, but the iron has been converted to an unusable form due to an excess of calcium carbonate.

Chlorosis may be caused by other factors, however, such as poor root growth, over fertilization, soil nematodes, or poorly drained soils. If the plant is suffering from iron chlorosis, quick but temporary results can be obtained by spraying the foliage with iron sulfate (ferrous sulphate or copperas) at the rate of one ounce per two gallons of water. Chelated iron or iron sequestrenes are also effective as a foliage spray or soil application.

A plant deficient in magnesium looks very similar to one affected by iron chlorosis in the early stages. The yellowish leaves later develop reddish purple blotches, followed by a browning of the tip and margin. Epsom salts (magnesium sulfate) should be applied as a foliage spray at the rate of one ounce per gallon of water.

ORGANIC MATTER

Organic matter is the azalea gardener's elixir, and azaleas respond directly to the amount added to the soil. Humus is the end product of the decomposition of organic matter. Humus makes the soils lighter and open, thus improving aeration. It increases the soil's water holding capacity and reduces leaching of soil nutrients. Humus aids in maintaining an acid soil and provides nutrients for the plant.

Organic matter in the form of humus in the soil or as a mulch around the plant is important for good azalea growth. Organic matter is available from a variety of sources. Leaf mold from shredded and partly decomposed leaves of hardwood and conifers such as oaks and pines is excellent but often difficult to find. Sedge peatmoss is generally of a finer texture and not as good as coarse sphagnum peat. Many gardeners and nurserymen are now replacing fine peatmoss with milled pine bark. Fine graded bark ¼-inch and less in diameter is ideal as a soil amendment. Coarser grades of bark are more useful as a mulch.

Sawdust can also be used as a soil amendment, but fertilizer should be added unless the sawdust is thoroughly decomposed. During the decomposition of sawdust, which is carried out by soil bacteria and fungi, nitrogen is removed from the soil and must be replaced. Additonal nitrogen can be added at the rate of approximately ¼ pound of ammonium sulfate (20% N) or ammonium nitrate (33% N) per bushel of sawdust. Bacteria also use phosphorus while decomposing sawdust. Consequently a small addition of superphosphate to the sawdust is needed to offset phosphorus depletion. A complete fertilizer such as 10-6-4 can be added at the rate of ½ to ¾ pounds per bushel of sawdust. Be sure to mix the soil and organic matter thoroughly before planting.

MYCORRHIZA

Mycorrhizae are symbiotic soil fungi associated with the roots of ericaceous and some other plants. These soil fungi are unlike others such as Phytophthora root rot fungus which are pathogenic in that they infect and destroy roots. Mycorrhizal fungi penetrate root cells but do not kill them. Both the root and fungus derive benefit from this association. Rhododendrons and other ericaceous plants have a fibrous root system but, unlike many plants, do not have root hairs. Substituting for root hairs on many rhododendrons are the microscopic threads of fungi in a mycorrhizal relationship. There are indications that mycorrhizal fungi protect azaleas from harmful pathogenic fungi.

The classification of mycorrhizae is not stable; however, rhododendron mycorrhizae are generally classified as Ericoid Endomycorrhizae; characterized by the fungus penetrating into the cells on the root surface. The invaded root cells continue to function, but contain a mass of fine fungal filaments called hyphae. Outside the cells these hyphae act like a microscopic root system, bringing together the plant roots and the soil particles. The mycorrhizal fungus inside the root cell obtains essential carbohydrates without competing with the microorganisms in the soil. The hyphae outside the plant cell absorb water and minerals some of which are translocated to the hyphae inside the root cell. The rhododendron roots share some of these minerals with the fungus for their own use.

Research in England under laboratory conditions has demonstrated that the mycorrhizal fungi stimulated the growth of cranberry and heather seedlings. They also increased the nitrogen and phosphorus content of the plant when these minerals were not readily available to the plant roots. Dr. Larry Englander of the University of Rhode Island, aided by a grant from the American Rhododendron Society Research Foundation, with the use of radioactive isotopes found a two-way pipeline between rhododendrons and the fruiting bodies of a *Clavaria sp.* fungus. This fungus had the ability to supply phosphorus to the roots of the rhododendron. Dr. Englander has found that several different fungi are capable of forming mycorrhizae. Additional study is going on at Rhode Island, Oregon State and at other universities to better understand the beneficial association of the ericoid mycorrhizae to rhododendron plants.

It has often been suggested that the difficulty of transplanting bare root native azaleas and other plants such as terrestrial orchids is the lack of mycorrhizal fungi. Thus, moving these plants with their native soil or inoculating the new site with soil from areas where the species grow wild is recommenmded. Leaf mold from oaks and pine woodlands may be beneficial in promoting the growth of mycorrhizae. The extensive use of humus to establish plants in poor soils may be in part due to the presence of mycorrhizae.

PLANTS AND PLANTING

Study the site for your azaleas. Check for exposure to winds, soil type, and good drainage. It is advisable to have the soil tested for pH and to make adjustments if necessary in advance of the planting. Prepare the entire area or bed for mass planting by rototilling and working in sufficient organic matter. Good soil preparation is essential for plant growth. Four to six inches of organic matter worked thoroughly into the average garden soil is important.

Azaleas are easy to transplant and container grown plants can be moved or planted at any season of the year if proper care is given. Early spring is ideal in most areas, but the plants can be moved in the fall or early winter. An excellent time to work out color combinations of azaleas is while they are in flower.

Buy your plants from established, reputable nurserymen or garden centers, preferably those specializing in azaleas. In some areas you must rely on your local garden center, which is not a nursery grower of plants, but a retailer who obtains his plants from distant wholesale nurseries. Buy only top quality plants. Misshapen and leggy plants with weak growth and poor foliage color usually sold at discount prices are no bargains. Be sure the plants you purchase are adapted to your area. It is not uncommon to find unknowing garden centers selling plants not adapted to their locality. Frequently the term "suitable for planting", is read in plant advertisements. Many things are "suitable for planting" but the question in point is whether the plant is healthy, hardy, and adapted to your area. You want azaleas best suited for your own climate conditions. Gardening should not be a battle for survival—yours or the plants.

Buy well-shaped plants of good quality. Open, tall, leggy plants are often neglected or leftover plants that appear to be bargains but will need to be drastically pruned back to develop properly. Container grown plants in 1, 2, and 3 to 5 gallon sizes are replacing large balled and burlapped plants (B&B). Container grown plants offer the opportunity to obtain named cultivars at any season of the year. Selecting azaleas while in flower enables one to arrange them in harmonious color combinations. Container grown plants are generally rootbound, so the roots should be broken or washed out to insure that they will develop in the new planting soil. This is important with all container grown material from small liners to established plants. Rootbound plants will have a heavy matting of fine roots around the outer surface of the entire ball. Hold the root mass firmly and cut with a sharp knife to a depth of ½ to one inch at least three times from top to bottom around the circumference of the ball. This may appear drastic but is a safe and necessary procedure. Failure to loosen the tightly bound roots often results in weak or dead plants the first growing season. Soak the root ball well before planting if the root mass appears dry. Remove any old leaves, dead flowers and loose duff that is on the top of the ball and destroy. This will help to eliminate the resting spores of petal blight and other diseases.

When digging holes, be sure to check soil drainage. The old gardeners' adage "Plant a 50 cent plant in a $5.00 hole" is still sound advice. Spending the extra time and effort to satisfy the basic cultural requirements will result in the plants responding tenfold. A two-gallon container plant should have a planting hole approximately 24 inches across and a minimum of 12 inches deep. Add and mix organic matter at the rate of ⅓ to ½ by volume to the transplanting or backfill soil around the plant. A common fault in transplanting azaleas is planting too deep. The top of the root ball or root mass of the container plant should be at the surface of the ground or slightly higher. Except for sandy, well-drained soil, shallow planting for azaleas is recommended. Firm the base of the planting hole; if this soil is left loose and fluffy, it will compress after planting, and the plant will sink into the hole.

In heavy clay soils that may become waterlogged, it is advisable to plant at least half out of the ground, or in extreme cases entirely above ground. The raised beds may be confined by logs or rocks and will require additional maintenance, especially watering during the summer. In the case of large individual plants, a dish-like depression around the plant to retain water is advisable. For mass or bed planting and small plants this depression is not necessary if proper soil preparation and transplanting techniques are followed.

Handle B&B (balled and burlapped) plants in much the same way as container plants. If at all possible, remove the burlap material from the root ball or at least away from the top and peel down. If the ball was bound with nylon cord, cut and remove.

SPACING

Several alternatives present themselves in spacing of plants. Wide spacing allows for future growth, but such a planting will look open and sparse for several years. Setting plants close together will give immediate effect and permit plants to grow into a mass, but individual specimens will not develop to full size or symmetrically. The best solution, since azaleas are easily transplanted, is to set plants reasonably close together and transplant and space them out once or twice as they grow larger.

A general guide for spacing of azaleas is as follows: Kurumes, Satsuki and other low to medium size azaleas—three to four feet minimum; for full development—four to six feet apart. Southern Indian, many of the Glenn Dales and other large azaleas—four to six feet minimum; for full development—six to eight feet apart. (Most deciduous azaleas belong to this group.) Beltsville dwarfs and other very slow growing azaleas—18 to 24 inches. For immediate effect place azaleas even closer than suggested and then transplant as the plants develop.

Azalea hedges are planted close and the following is suggested: Kurume, Satsuki and similar hybrid groups—two to three feet apart; Southern Indian and other large azaleas—three to four feet apart.

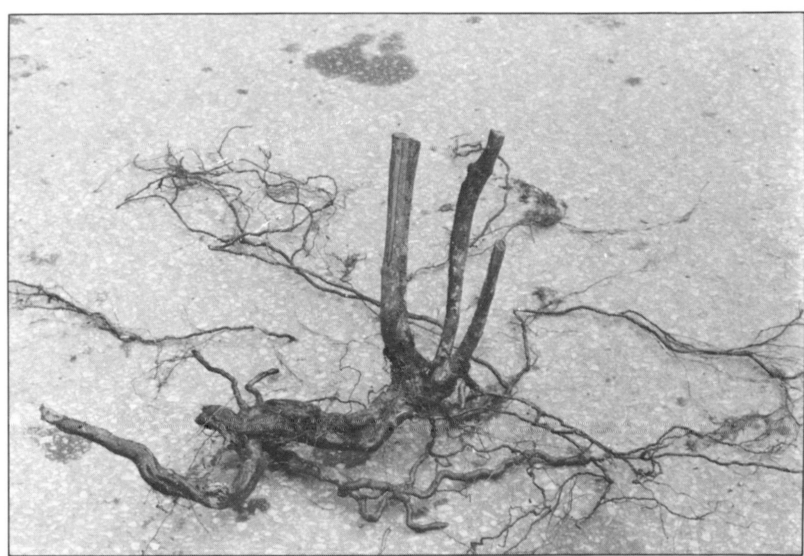

Rhododendron flammeum (R. speciosum) plant showing root system from a 6′ ball. It is estimated that only 40% of the root system was obtained from this large ball.

Root cutting of *R. canescens.*

Two plants of *Rhododendron canescens,* showing new fibrous root systems developing in one growing season. The plants were cut back and heeled-in using a bark compost mix.

TRANSPLANTING AND MOVING PLANTS

Transplant evergreen azaleas at any time, even when in full bloom, but preferably between late summer and late spring, including winter when the ground is not frozen. Avoid moving azaleas during hot, dry summer weather. You may lose next year's blooms if you disturb plants in late spring or summer before flower buds are set.

Move deciduous azaleas and native plants only in the dormant season, in late fall, winter, or early spring. Many states have laws which prohibit the collecting of native plants. Know the laws and regulations in your own area and obtain permission from landowners before collecting plants. Many gardeners are fortunate to have native azaleas on their own property and need only to move them to a more desirable area within the landscape planting. Native azalea plants usually have a poor root system, often widely spread and sparse. It is best to move small plants, for they can better withstand the shock of transplanting. Dig carefully to obtain as many roots as possible. After digging, the plant should be severely pruned to within six to eight inches from the ground. Cutting back the top is very important to compensate for the very poor root system. Wrap the roots in burlap to aid handling the plant and keep the soil intact around the roots. The cut-back plant can be planted to its new site or heeled into a pine bark mixture for one or two years to develop a new root system and new top. Cut-back plants generally produce flower buds after the second season.

WATER AND MULCHING

After a plant is properly planted or transplanted, it should be watered well before applying a mulch. Watering should be thorough to eliminate air pockets. After watering, check to see that the plant is not too deep. If the plant sinks down, it should be lifted and planted higher. Repeat the watering in three to five days, unless nature takes over with ample rains.

New plants, unless receiving at least an inch of rain per week, will require additional watering throughout the first growing season. Spring transplanted azaleas will require more frequent watering to get established than those planted in the fall and winter. Plants should not go into the dormant winter season in a desiccated or dry condition.

Mulching of new plants is very important for it aids in conserving soil mositure. There are a number of good mulching materials; some are also used as a source of organic matter and were discussed previously. Shredded hardwood leaves and leaf mold, as well as shredded pine bark and pine needles, are excellent. Other materials include ground corncobs, peanut hulls, pecan shells, bagasse, wood chips, shingletow, and straw or cotton waste. A good mulch should be two to three inches thick, but loose and airy. Peat moss and sawdust are not desirable mulching materials unless used with other coarser materials because they frequently form a surface crust when dry and shed water. Large dry leaves of hardwood trees, such as maples and oaks, many broadleaf evergreen leaves such as Magnolia, Holly and other will pack and layer very tightly and shed water. Leaves of this type should be shredded first or allowed to decompose before applying as a mulch. The mulch should be at least three inches deep and kept on year-round. Organic mulches decompose, adding humus to the soil and aid in keeping soil acid. Due to this continual decomposition, organic mulches should be renewed at least annually.

Good mulches are essential. In addition to conserving soil moisture they: (1) retard freezing of soil and add protection to the roots during the winter; (2) reduce runoff of rain and increase water penetration; (3) keep the soil aerated; (4) encourage biological action such as mycorrhizae in the soil; (5) aid in keeping down weeds and eliminating the need for cultivation.

Azalea plants should not be cultivated with hand tools, due to their shallow root system. Weeds coming through a mulch are easily controlled by hand pulling or spot treating with a herbicide.

NUTRITIONAL REQUIREMENTS

A soil high in organic matter supplemented with an organic mulch is more important to good azalea growth than fertilizer. Fertilizer, unfortunately, is often regarded as the panacea for all plant problems, but it is not a cure-all. A good fertilization program for azaleas, unique to all ericaceous plants, is based on three factors: (1) they thrive in acid soil; (2) they are easily injured by moderate to high fertilizer applications; and (3) they have low nutritional requirements compared to many other plants.

In their native habitat most ericaceous plants, including rhododendrons and azaleas, are adapted to growing in impoverished soils. Typically the soils have been leached of many minerals such as calcium (Ca), magnesium (Mg), and potassium (K). This leaching characteristic of an acid soil leaves a relatively high level of hydrogen (H), iron (Fe), and aluminum (Al) ions.

Iron is usually available in acid soil. When the pH approaches neutral and becomes alkaline, at pH 7 and above, the availability of iron is reduced. To maintain available iron soils should be acid in the range of 4.5 to 6.0. Azalea growers should avoid using nitrogenous fertilizers that are alkali-forming and should restrict the use of lime as a source of calcium unless the pH is excessively low, below pH 3.0. Calcium sources such as lime (calcium carbonate, calcium oxide or hydroxide) should only be used when it is necessary to raise the soil pH. Calcium, however, is essential for azalea growth—gypsum (calcium sulfate) can be used as a source of calcium without affecting the pH. In some cases chlorosis is corrected by adding calcium to the soil in the form of gypsum. Actual measurement of the pH of your garden and potting soils is an important aid and is generally the first diagnostic test for nutritional disorders.

The tolerance of azaleas to acid soil is in part due to their tolerance of both aluminum and manganese. The solubility and availability of aluminum (Al) and Manganese (Mn) increase in acid soils. Although azaleas have been reported to tolerate high levels of Al up to 60 ppm, and 80 ppm of Mn, concentrations of one to three ppm can be injurious to other genera. While azaleas are tolerant of aluminum and manganese, excessive amounts of these elements are toxic. Repeated use of aluminum sulfate should be avoided.

The nutrient requirements of azaleas are low when compared to other cultivated plants. However, optimum growth is achieved with low to medium applications of fertilizer. Only annual soil testing can serve as a true guide to the type and quantity of fertilizer to use. Remember that, more azaleas are killed by over-fertilizing than through the lack of fertilizer.

Read the fertilizer label, checking for the formulation and the chemicals used. The percent of three major elements—nitrogen (N), phosphorus (P), and potassium (K)—are indicated on all fertilizer containers, by such numbers as 10–6–4, 8–8–8, and other formulations. The first number indicates the percentage of nitrogen, the second the percentage of phosphorus as P_20_5, and the third the percentage of potassium as K_20. There are many fertilizer formulations, including special azalea fertilizers and organic materials.

Soluble fertilizers even of high analysis such as 20–20–20 are completely water soluble and at low concentrations can be used as a foliar application or to the soil at high rates. Slow release fertilizers are also available and can be used by experienced growers in the garden and mixed into potting soils for the production of young plants.

MAJOR PLANT NUTRIENTS

NITROGEN is essential for plant growth. Dark green growth is indicative of ample nitrogen while a deficiency will show up as yellowish green leaves. Ammoniacal forms of N are favored over nitrate forms for fertilizing azaleas and keeping the pH in an acid range. A nitrate source can be used when the pH is below 4.5. The common ammoniacal forms of nitrogen are ammonium nitrate 32.5%, ammonium sulfate 20.5%, and ureaform nitrogen

38%. The first two are water soluble, while ureaform is not and is generally more expensive. The two common nitrate fertilizers generally not recommended for azaleas are sodium or potassium nitrate; both will raise soil pH and the soluble soil salts will cause iron chlorosis.

PHOSPHORUS assists in maturing plants and in flower bud initiation. Phosphorus deficiency symptoms are characterized by dull, dark green foliage, followed by reddening of the under surface of the leaves, especially along the midrib. Phosphorus is available as superphosphate (16 to 20% available phosphoric acid P_20_5) and contains over 50% calcium sulfate; or from triple superphosphate 45% P_20_5 and a small amount of calcium sulfate. These compounds have little effect on soil acidity. Both are slowly soluble and excessive amounts can be detrimental.

POTASSIUM (potash) is important in the formation of starch and sugars, and in the development of roots, leaves, branches, and flowers. Potassium is available from potassium chloride (muriate of potash) which contains 48 to 62% P_20. Both are acid forming. Potassium deficiencies are demonstrated by interveinal chlorosis of young foliage followed by marginal leaf scorch and necrotic lesions on mature leaves.

MICRONUTRIENTS

IRON is one of the most important micronutrients for azaleas and is included in many balanced fertilizers. Most soils contain iron but the question is one of availability and the ability of the plant to make use of the iron which is present. Iron deficiency shows up as chlorosis, splotchy pale green to yellow areas between the veins of the leaves. Later the leaves turn completely yellow, cream colored, or off-white with margin burning and defoliation. Poor root growth by reason of compacted soils, watering, poor drainage, low temperature, over-fertilization, unbalanced fertilization or even excessive soil acidity may result in the inability of a plant to absorb sufficient iron and thus develop iron chlorosis. A deficiency of calcium, potassium, or manganese also apparently makes iron unavailable. Excessive amounts of aluminum, copper, zinc, and even excessive phosphorus also produce iron chlorosis. Iron in the ferric form is generally unavailable to plants, while the ferrous form such as iron (ferrous) sulfate is available and should be used. As a foliage spray use one ounce per gallon of water and add a commercial sticker. Improvement should be noticeable in a week. If not, a second application may be necessary. If no improvement can be seen, try magnesium sulfate, (epsom salts) or a mixture of iron sulfate plus aluminum and magnesium sulfate, ½ ounce each per 2 gallons of water. Soil applications of ferrous sulfate, to which the plant responds more slowly, are made at the rate of 1½ pounds per 100 square feet. In iron deficiency studies, the lack of iron did not appear as chlorosis for five months, indicating that iron is not required in large amounts for azaleas.

CALCIUM is necessary for plant growth, but an excess or deficiency tends to produce chlorosis followed by tip burn and twisting of leaves. Gypsum or calcium sulfate is a safe source of calcium.

Deficiencies of other minor elements seldom occur in garden soils, but can occasionally be a problem in growing forced azaleas in greenhouses. The more common problem is excessive amounts of minor elements. So while micronutrients are commercially available they should be used sparingly and not applied annually in the garden unless indicated by a soil test.

A general recommendation for applying fertilizer is to begin in early spring when new growth starts. Follow soil test recommendations, and apply small amounts of fertilizer at frequent intervals during the growing season. This may involve one to three (or monthly) applications up to midsummer. In areas of long growing seasons fertilizing can be continued later. In the case of container grown plants, due to constant watering and excessive leaching, light applications of liquid fertilizer should be made throughout the growing season and until late fall.

A general rule of application is ½ to 1 pound (½–1 pint) of fertilizer (12–6–6 or 10–5–7) per 100 square feet of bed space. Dry organic fertilizers can be applied evenly on the mulch. Avoid touching the leaves or getting close to the stem. For small plants, 10–12 inches, one teaspoonful of fertilizer per plant is ample. Large individual plants require up to one tablespoon per foot in height. Distribution of dry fertilizer is difficult so it should be thoroughly watered in, and the foliage should be drenched to avoid localized salinity problems.

Fall applications of fertilizer on established plants are recommended for the experienced gardener. The roots of plants in the fall are still active, but the top vegetative parts of the plant are in a semi- to dormant condition.

The fertilizer should be applied generally in mid to late September and early October and before heavy frost. Application of fertilizer in late summer and early fall on active growing plants can stimulate additonal growth that will not be hardened off prior to cold weather; thus resulting in winter damage.

The timing of fall fertilization is important. The experienced gardener with his knowledge of plants and weather patterns should experiment with this new technique and thus give him more time in the spring to devote to other activities.

SOIL SALINITY

A special soil problem is that of saline soil, which occurs throughout the Southwest region of the U.S. and other regions dependent on irrigation. Salinity is also a problem for florist and container grown azaleas where excessive amounts of fertilizer are used and irrigation does not leach the excess out. Irrigation is used to supplement scanty rainfall, particularly during the summer months. The irrigation water, unlike rainfall, often contains large amounts of dissolved salts, as common table salt (sodium chloride), sodium sulfate, sodium carbonate, and the borates. The concentration of these salts in the irrigation water is seldom high enough to cause direct injury to the roots. However, as water is lost by evaporation at the soil surface and by transpiration by the plant, the salts which do not leach out tend to accumulate in the soil-water solution and, to some extent, in the plant. As the soil water salt solution increases in concentration, it becomes increasingly difficult for the roots to absorb water from the soil. Plant roots become damaged, tissues dry out, and leaf burn occurs on the margins of lower leaves, followed by leaf drop.

If the soil drains well, the salts can be washed out by extra heavy irrigation or hand watering. This will remove accumulated salts from the root zone in the upper soil layer and reduce the concentration. The frequency of leaching will depend on the concentration of salts in the irrigation water and the rapidity with which salts build up in the soil water solution. Plants in pots or containers should be watered heavily enough so that water passes out the drainage holes at each watering.

Saline soils are usually alkaline as well as salty. If the salts are sodium salts, the alkalinity may be so strong that organic matter is dissolved and forms a black coating around the soil particles. These are the "black alkali" soils. Use of sulfur, ferrous sulfate, and even gypsum will result in replacing the sodium with calcium. The soil will become less alkaline and soil structure will become crumbly instead of sticky. Acid organic matter can be added and only acid reacting fertilizers should be used.

Soils that have been repeatedly over-fertilized, or are black alkali or alkaline, are best replaced with a good newly prepared soil.

PRUNING

Azaleas require little if any pruning, except for removal of dead wood and shaping and developing into compact plants. Small azaleas should be pinched or pruned repeatedly during the growing season to develop a compact branching system. Large plants can be kept in bounds by cutting flowering branches for decorative use in the home. Tall, leggy plants can be rejuvenated by cutting back to the ground. Open, leggy plants can be "sculpture" pruned; opening up the base, featuring the trunks and making the plant more tree-like. The best period to prune most azaleas is after flowering and before flower buds are initiated in midsummer. Late summer and fall pruning usually results in fewer flowers the next season.

To regenerate some late flowering species, such as *R. prunifolium* and late flowering evergreen cultivars, such as Satsuki azaleas, you may have to sacrifice some flowering because the new flower buds are developing while last year's buds are first flowering. You can stagger the pruning of one plant or of plants in a mass planting. Only prune a third to a half of the plant or plants and follow up in successive years until all the plants are completely shaped.

Some deciduous azalea species and hybrids respond better if older wood is removed as soon as it looks a little unthrifty.

Each species and hybrid has its own particular form and shape and it is best to stay within this pattern than try to change it. It is better to replace a tall vigorous plant in front of a picture window with a slower growing compact plant than to try to keep the tall plant in bounds. Old plants often become open and irregular in shape with long, strong, vigorous branches. The heavy branches should be cut back within the body of the plant and often to the ground. Old plants that are being rejuvenated, and also the tall, leggy bargain sale plants, can be cut back to within six to eight inches from the ground. This should be done following flowering or even before. Adventitious buds will develop on the stem resulting in new strong shoots. These will often require tip pinching to induce additional branching.

Commercial azalea growers are using fatty ester chemicals, such as Off-shoot-O, for chemical pruning. These chemicals are applied to new growth in very precise quantities. There are many variables such as temperature, stage of growth, and varietal variations which must be considered. Treated plants must be watered in 10–15 minutes to stop extensive damage. In most cases chemical pruning is used in conjunction with hand pruning.

Growth retardant chemicals such as B-Nine and Cycocel are used as aids to develop compact plants and to increase flower bud formation.

Neither the chemical pruning nor growth retardants are recommended for the homeowner except for experimental use, and manufacturer's recommendations and advice from your state university should be followed. In an azalea garden of many different varieties each one must be tested separately. For the commercial grower they are labor saving and important tools to use.

10. SPECIAL AZALEA CULTURE

Azaleas are excellent container or pot plants for use outdoors as patio plants or in the house or conservatory. Commercially, azaleas are standard pot plants, flowered from mid-December through May, and in some areas they are flowered year-round.

CARE OF GIFT PLANTS

Upon receiving a forced, potted azalea check the plant to see if it needs water. If so, submerge the pot in a pail of water, or water it thoroughly before displaying. Locate the plant in a well-lighted room of 65 degrees F. or cooler as normal room temperatures of 72 to 75 degrees F. will cause rapid flower loss. Removing the plant to a cooler room at night will retard flower drop. Your own good judgment of temperature and humidity will tell you how much water your plant needs. Azaleas like a moist but not saturated soil so do not allow it to become bone dry. Under home conditions, leaf drop may occur, so the foliage should be syringed lightly every day. Trays or deep saucers filled with gravel beneath the plant will aid in preventing leaf drop.

After flowering, the potted plant must be kept indoors until conditions outside are suitable, if you plan to use it in your garden or save to force the next year. Check to see if it is a variety hardy in your area. Move the plant to a cooler room of 50 to 55 degrees F. Continue to syringe the foliage and keep the soil moist. Remove the old flower heads, and pinch or prune the new growth to maintain a compact plant. Remember, your house plant has been in active growth and even though hardy in your area, it must be kept indoors until there is frost-free weather before planting outdoors. Tender azalea varieties can be discarded or kept to force into bloom next year.

The plant can be planted out in a bed, but it is best to keep it in the container. Check the root system, and if it appears root bound, thin out and repot. Plants can be kept this way for several years before it is necessary to shift to larger containers. Ultimately one reaches a point when it becomes impractical to shift to larger containers due to problems of maintenance and moving the plant. Boxes or containers 18 to 24 inches square or in diameter and 8 to 10 inches deep will hold a very large azalea for many years, by repotting yearly or every two years. Handle the plant as discussed later.

FORCING AZALEAS

All azaleas can be forced to flower out of season. However, the evergreen types are more widely used, having the added feature of handsome foliage. The standard forcing azaleas used by florists are Kurumes, Pericats, Belgian Indian, Rutherford and others. In the book *Growing Azaleas Commercially* edited by Anton M. Kofranek and Roy Larson (Publication 4058, Div. of Agricultural Science, University of California 1975) over 180 commercial cultivars are listed. A few of the common cultivars are 'Coral Bells', 'Dogwood', 'Snow', 'Hershey Red' and 'Pink Pearl' among the Kurumes; 'Madam Pericat' and 'Sweetheart Supreme' among the Pericats. 'Alaska', 'Dorothy Gish', 'White Gish', 'Gloria', 'Easter Parade', 'Kingfisher', 'Mission Bells', 'Roadrunner', 'Snowbank' (or 'Cherokee White'), 'Pink Ruffles', 'Valentine', and 'Red Wings' among the Belgian and Rutherford hybrids. Forcing schedules have been developed by university horticulturists and commercial growers for all of the above azaleas plus others.

An azalea grower, however, is not limited to the standard forcing cultivars unless he is trying to have plants in flower for special dates. The late flowering Glenn Dale and Satsuki hybrids can be forced, but may not flower uniformly, and are seldom used commercially as they are difficult to force in the early winter months. Many of the deciduous azalea species and cultivars can be forced following a cold dormant period. It has been noted, however, that late flowering species such as *R. prunifolium* are affected by photo period and require long days. Thus a Plum Leaf Azalea brought into the greenhouse in January must have additional light equivalent to a 14–16 hour day to force and flower early.

Many commercial companies and university horticulture departments have prepared azalea forcing schedules. A basic summary of such schedules for year-round potted azaleas is as follows:

1. Pinch and give long days (16 hours) for six to 12 weeks at 65 degrees F.
2. Apply a growth retardant five weeks after the final pinch.
3. Allow six weeks of short days.
4. Place plants in a 44 to 48 degrees F. lighted cooler for six weeks with a minimum of seven to 20 footcandles of light 12 hours per day.
5. Force at 60 to 65 degrees F. Flowering occurs in five to six weeks.

   Azaleas for the homeowner can be forced indoors without a greenhouse in a cool 60–65 degrees F. lighted room.

Plants should be established in pots or containers in the spring or summer but no later than early fall. Employ normal pinching to develop well shaped plants. In the fall allow the plants to go dormant. The plants should be protected against hard freezing temperatures in a wind-free area.

In areas of hard freezing plunge the plants into the ground and mulch then. A wire frame or wood structure with a plastic cover will protect the foliage. Protection is very important for tender varieties such as the Belgian and Rutherford hybrids. These varieties will withstand a light frost, but the container plant should not be exposed to temperatures below 25 degrees F. Remember, the roots of an azalea are more susceptible to freeze damage than the top. In zones 7 and 8 container plants with the roots protected can be left outdoors until mid to late December before bringing them in to be forced.

After bringing the plants indoors, syringe the foliage daily and water when necessary. The ideal room temperature for forcing is about 60 degrees F. At warmer temperatures the plants may flower unevenly.

Without cold storage facilities, homeowners will have difficulty in forcing azaleas for Christmas, but can have a pre-spring display of flowering plants indoors in mid to late January until early spring.

Many attractive plant containers are available or you can design and make your own from wood or other material. The container should enhance the plant. Azaleas are more attractive in shallow containers. For example, an 18 inch azalea is more attractive in a container 6–10 inches deep, by 15–18 inches in diameter or square. Wood containers should be treated with copper naphthenate wood preservative, which is available in a clear or green color. Creosote or penta wood preservatives are toxic to plants and should not be used.

Container grown plants require annual pruning and frequent pinching to maintain a desirable shape. They also require more maintenance, particularly in watering and feeding, than plants in the garden. During the growing season container plants require frequent and in mid-summer as the temperatures rise, daily watering. The plants are subject to the same insects, pests, and diseases as in the garden.

Container plants become root bound and require repotting annually or at least every other year. If upon examination the roots are matted on the outside of the ball, repotting is necessary. Cut the matted roots from top to bottom in several places around the circumference. Remove some of the soil and roots. Unless desired, it is not necessary to replant to a larger container. Use organic soil mixture for repotting, firm the soil and water thoroughly. Repotting should be done after the plants finish flowering, or in the spring when the plant is moved outdoors. Do not replant too deeply in the container.

HANGING BASKETS

Hanging basket plants are widely used for the home and patio. Dwarf azaleas and those with a spreading habit of growth are best suited for baskets, rather than tall vigorous varieties. The pendulous varieties of Belgian, Rutherford, and Satsuki hybrids are all good basket plants. Of more recent introduction some of the Harris hybrids such as 'Pink Cascade' and the North Tisbury hybrids have very pendulous growth and are excellent. Hanging baskets do require protection in the winter and should be placed in a cool greenhouse or cold frame to protect the roots from freezing and protect the pendulous branches. The basic care and culture of a hanging basket plant are the same as for any container plant.

STANDARD AND ESPALIER AZALEAS

Any Azalea with a single straight stem can be trained to a standard or tree form. The Southern Indians and some Glenn Dale varieties are suitable for standards in warm climates as are the Kaempferis for cooler areas. Single stem plants grown from cuttings and close together, forcing them to stretch, are preferred. Side branches should be removed with no pinching of the top until the desired height of the standard is obtained. Developing the 'head' is done by pinching of the terminal growth first, followed by pinching of the lateral shoots until a compact head is formed. Leaves and young shoots developing on the main stem should be rubbed off as they occur.

Commercially, special standards of the Belgian and Rutherford hybrids are grafted on a single stem of another single stemmed plant. The green grafting technique is generally used and is usually done in greenhouses or shaded structures in the Deep South or on the West Coast. Unique standards can be made by grafting some of the pendulous azaleas for the top or head.

Loose, open azaleas are ideal for espalier plants, developing into special designs and forms. Constant pruning is required to maintain the desired decorative effect on a wall or trellis.

BONSAI

The history, appreciation, and cultivation of plant miniaturization evolved many centuries ago in China where it is called Penjing and later in Japan where it is called Bonsai, (pronounced "bone-sigh"). Bonsai has become a notable form of gardening in the West in the last 3–4 decades. Bonsai combines creative artistic and horticultural skills in the development of a living art form, a special facet of indoor—outdoor container growing, with emphasis on the art of pruning and training plants. Satsuki azaleas are highly prized for Bonsai or "tray trees" and have been used in the Orient for centuries. Small leaves, good habit of trunk and branches are characteristics of an azalea suitable for Bonsai. Small flowers were formerly considered important, but today the large flowered cultivars are also popular. The Kurumes and other small-leaved cultivars are prized for their finely textured foliage. The Beltsville dwarfs and other dwarf and slow growing cultivars such as some Greenwood hybrids offer great potential as Bonsai as well as small indoor potted plants. Of the evergreen azaleas species both *R. kiusianum* and *R. serpyllifolium* are prized both in Japan and the West as Bonsai subjects. Other evergreen species that have potential include *R. otakumii (R. yakuinsulare), R. nakaharai* cultivars and others. Of the deciduous azaleas *R. quinquefolium* and some of the North American species are being used.

The dwarfing of plants results not from poor soil or starvation, for a well drained potting medium is important; constant watering and a modest fertilization program are all essential.

Plants for bonsai culture can be selected from old plants in the garden, the purchase of a potential plant from a nursery, or grown from a cutting or seedling. Young plants can be trained in two to three years to the trunk style desired and in 5 to 10 years into a fine young Bonsai. The styles or type of Azalea Bonsai are based on the shape of the trunk. The Japanese recognize 12 styles of which the most basic are:

Chokkan	straight trunk
Moyogi	informal upright
Shakan	slanted trunk
Kengai	cascade style
Bunjin	abstract or free style

The other styles include:

Sokan	double trunk
Kabudachi	sprout style
Ikadabuki	raft style
Netsuranari	sprouts from a long surface root
Neagari	above the surface exposed root style
Ishizuki	clinging rock style
Yoseuye	forest or group planting style

Careful examination of plants at Bonsai shows can only lead to a deep appreciation of the art involved in training these plants. In Japan the finest Satsuki Bonsai exhibits are in Utsunomiya not far from Nikko, and are usually held in early June. In the United States Azalea Bonsai exhibits are often included in the Rhododendron and Azalea Chapter Flower Shows. Bonsai Societies are growing in number in Great Britain, Europe, Australia, and New Zealand.

The creating and general care of a Bonsai is an exciting experience. While often time consuming, it offers a restful hobby and a closer look at plants. Training of young plants should be started early to shape the trunks to the desired style. Trunks of young plants are flexible and easy to shape, while older plants are more difficult. Satsuki Azalea whips grown especially for Bonsai are common in Japan and are now available from nurseries in the West. Whips are three to five years old and about 20 inches tall. Some are sold with the trunks sturdily wired while others must be trained by the buyer. Trunks and branches are

'Christmas Cheer' Kurume Azalea—broom style, from a cutting, 7 years in training. Height 4½", width 5", length of pot 3¾"; by Tom Wright, Atlanta, Georgia. Photo: T.G. Wright

R. serpyllifolium—broom style, 5 years in training, purchased as a gal. plant. Height 7", width 10", length of pot 8½"; by Tom Wright, Atlanta, Georgia. Photo: T.G. Wright

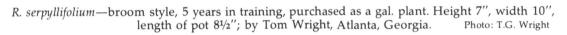

wired to shape the plant into the desired form. Copper or copper-coated aluminum wires are placed in early spring or late summer when the branches are supple. Wires should not be left on indefinitely but must be removed before they become too tight and damage the plant. The shallow and often gnarled root systems of azaleas are as highly esteemed as are the trunk and branching habit.

The soil or potting media for Bonsai should retain moisture but have good drainage and aeration, with a pH of 5 to 6. In Japan the popular kanuma soil, a soft yellowish inert volcanic rock is used in azalea soil mixes. While this material is not available in the West, similar products such as pumice rock and calcinated clays or cat litter make good substitutes. Basic mixes used are 2 to 3 parts perlite, 2 to 5 parts of pine or redwood chips, and one part each of Sphagnum Peat Moss and pumice rock or calcinated clay. All materials except the perlite should be screened to remove very fine particles.

Fertilizer should be applied in small amounts but at regular intervals through the growing season. Either organic mixtures or synthetic slow release fertizers are recommended.

Repotting and root pruning are best done in early spring before or after flowering. Bonsai need be repotted or pruned only when the plant is seriously root bound. Stem and leaf pruning is done throughout the growing season depending on the vigor and growth of the plant. Mature Azalea Bonsai should not be pruned after mid-July to avoid removal of next season's flower buds. Old Kurume Azalea Bonsai in Japan are often pruned following flowering by removing all the leaves, but seldom on Satsuki and other species. This helps develop small leaf size. One only has to do this on a single plant to realize the meticulous detail and time spent by the Japanese on a prize bonsai.

In mild climates Azalea Bonsai can be placed on the ground and mulched in with bark or sawdust for the winter. In colder areas, plants should be stored in pit cold frames or a cool greenhouse.

A Bonsai neophyte will benefit by reading one or more of the excellent books on the subject and studying the styles and forms of prized Bonsai. Excellent books with detailed illustrations on the various styles and techniques include *Bonsai; Its Art, Science History, and Philosophy* by Deborah Koneshoff and *Bonsai Techniques for Satsuki* by John Y. Naka, Richard K. Ota and Kenko Rokkaku.

The development and care of Azalea Bonsai make an excellent hobby offering new challenges in growing azaleas; difficult to give up once started, it requires year-round attention.

11. PROPAGATION OF AZALEAS

Azaleas are generally easy to propagate, but not all species or cultivars may be propagated by the same method. There are many methods or techniques, each having advantages and disadvantages, requiring specific timing procedures. Fundamentally, azaleas can be propagated by seed, stem cuttings, layering, grafting, root cuttings, division, and tissue culture.

The propagation procedures are similar to those used with other woody shrubs. Detailed explanations of various management techniques can be found in articles and books on propagation.

PROPAGATION BY SEED

Propagation by seed is a desirable method for many of the deciduous azaleas and for those cultivars which are difficult to propagate by cuttings or other means. The resulting-seedlings will be variable which is an advantage for the hybridizer seeking new plants. Seedlings where both the seed parent and pollen parent are of the same species show variations natural to the species. Greater variation results from inter-specific crosses and those between different cultivars. 'Line hybrids' are occasionally produced with some of the Exbury hybrids and North American deciduous azaleas. Line hybrids are varieties that have been inbred through repetitive crossing of two strains, or selfing of a cultivar. Their progeny, rogued and selected to a type, results in a fixed strain. Unfortunately, these seedling hybrids may be sold (for example) as 'Gibraltar' resulting from crossing identical cultivars, instead of calling them a Gibraltar strain or Gibraltar 'selfs'.

Seed of many species is available from commercial sources, seed exchanges of various Rhododendron Societies, or by collecting. Seed capsules are normally collected in mid to late fall as they start to turn brown. There is considerable variation among species as to when the seed capsule matures. The seed capsules are plainly visible by midsummer and should be checked periodically for the best time to harvest. Seed capsules can be collected in late summer and early fall while they are still green and allowed to dry. Seed germination may not be as high from early collecting as when collected later. Care should be taken in collecting capsules after they have split open. Some seed may still be lodged in the capsule, but will readily drop out if the plant or branch is shaken.

The seed capsules should be stored at a room temperature in open-top containers or paper envelopes. Be sure to label the seed containers. A week or more may be necessary before the seed can be removed.

Use a small application of an insecticide, such as from an aerosol cannister, if small beetles are observed in the capsules. In nature the seed capsules split open after the first frost and release the seed. Deciduous azalea capsules gathered before frost may not split open on their own so the capsule must be split to release the seed. Evergreen azalea capsules will usually split on drying, requiring only shaking to release the seed. Azalea seeds are small with 100 to 500 seeds per capsule. The seeds can be germinated immediately or stored in a cool dry location for later use.

Seeds are generally germinated by the well-known Sphagnum Moss method. Sphagnum is a true moss bog plant and when dried will absorb 10 to 20 times its weight in water. It is moderately acid (pH 4.5) and contains most of the elements essential to plant growth. Although the quantities are small, they are sufficient to nourish seedlings prior to transplanting. Untransplanted seedlings in pure Sphagnum without soil will keep for over two years without feeding, but growth will be very restricted. Sphagnum Moss is usually sterile so loss of young seedlings to damping-off fungi is reduced.

Clean plastic containers about three inches deep with clear or translucent covers are ideal germinators. The size of the container used will depend on the number of seedlings to be produced. Containers three to four inches wide and long will hold 50 to 100 seedlings. Small holes should be punched in the bottom of the container for drainage. A 10 percent solution of chlorine bleach should be used to sterilize the container.

Sphagnum is a coarse, stringy plant in nature and should be shredded before using. Fortunately, milled or shredded Sphagnum is generally available. The milled Sphagnum should be soaked until thoroughly wet and then squeezed dry before using. Fluff the moss and fill the container within an inch of the top. If media containing peat or soil is used, drench with a solution of captan or similar fungicide. It is not necessary to sterilize Sphagnum Moss with a fungicide. Distribute the seeds over the sphagnum and mist the seeds lightly to settle them. No additional covering is required. Close the container with the lid or with polyethylene film and place under indirect or fluorescent light at a temperature of 60 to 75°F. Alternatively place the uncovered seed container under an intermittent mist system. Germination begins in about two to four weeks. After the second set of leaves appear, the seedlings can gradually be exposed to room temperature. Fertilizing with a weak solution of liquid fertilizer such as a 20–20–20, ¼ to ½ teaspoon per gallon, can be started at this time. Watch the seedlings carefully to prevent drying. Seed germination media other than sphagnum are sometimes used. One is a mixture of one part peat to one part perlite by volume in the bottom of the container, with only ¼ inch milled Sphagnum on top. Another is a 3 to 1 mixture of Sphagnum and perlite.

Transplant the seedlings when they are ½ to 1 inch high into flats or individual containers. The medium used for transplanting should be a 1–1–1 mixture of peat, perlite, and milled sphagnum or a 1–1 of peat and perlite. Drench the medium with fungicide to prevent disease. Transplant the seedlings 1½ inches apart in flat or use 1½ to 2 inch containers. Cover the seedlings for several days to reduce shock. Water carefully to keep the medium evenly moist but not soggy. Excessive moisture and poor air circulation often leads to failure. Keep the seedlings in active growth with light applications of a liquid fertilizer or a fish oil emulsion. Seedlings can be grown under fluorescent lights in a greenhouse or controlled heated rooms of 65–80°F.

Seedlings grown under constant light and good fertilization will equal in one year the size of plants grown outdoors in three years.

Seedlings can be transplanted outdoors from the greenhouse in the spring after danger of frost is over. Raised beds are preferred, and large quantities of peat and organic material should be used in preparing the soil. Slow release fertilizers can be added when preparing the soil. The young seedlings when first transplanted outdoors should be shaded with lath or 50% polyethylene film. They should be grown on under partial shade or gradually exposed to full sun, depending upon the climate. The transplanted seedlings should never be allowed to dry out during the growing season.

EVERGREEN AZALEAS BY CUTTINGS

Propagation by cuttings is generally used for evergreen azaleas. The general concept that cutting-grown plants will develop like the parent plant is basically true. However, bud sports or mutations do occur on rare occasions with azaleas so the cutting-grown progeny may sometimes be different from the parent source. Cuttings randomly taken from some of the variable color forms, particularly the Glenn Dale and Satsuki lines, will often result in plants unlike the type.

Cuttings are made from new wood. Timing will vary seasonally due to climatic differences and condition of the wood. However, cutting wood from a specific species or cultivar is generally ready at the same time each year. New growth suitable for cutting should break with a snap. Soft wood cuttings are difficult to keep turgid, and very hard wood cuttings often are very slow to root. There is an art in timing cuttings which comes with experience. In many areas the first flush of growth begins to firm up in June. The first to mature are the plants with soft or thin leaves, such as Korean Azalea, *R. v.* var. *poukhanense* or hairy leaves such as 'Indica Alba' or the Kaempferi azaleas; followed by plants with the leaf texture of Kurumes and Glenn Dales; and last with the hard foliage of the Satsuki and Indica azaleas.

Cuttings should be taken only from healthy mature stock plants. Cuttings should be three to four inches long from large plants. Cutting stock from dwarf and slow growing plants is often less than one inch in length. Remove all leaves from the lower ⅓ to ½ of the twig. Strip leaves from the base carefully to prevent tearing the bark. Cut the base of the cutting clean with a sharp knife or pruning shears.

Cuttings should be taken when turgid, usually in the morning and not in the heat of a sunny day, or during a long dry spell. If the cuttings cannot be used promptly, they should be wrapped in a moist newspaper, cloth, or sphagnum moss and placed in a polyethylene bag. Cuttings can be refrigerated at 40–45°F. for several days or longer without detrimental results. Rooting hormones are not essential for evergreen azalea cuttings but will hasten and unify rooting, as well as improve the rooting percentage for varieties that are difficult to root. Various rooting hormones such as Hormodin #1 or #2 and quick dip solutions are available; they are usually mixed with a fungicide for disease control.

Cuttings can be rooted in a greenhouse or outdoors where humidity is high, under a mist system, or in shady areas under enclosed plastic structures or a Nearing propagating frame. Commercial nurseries generally use mist systems or high humidity plastic structures. For small quantities, use a plastic box, or enclose a flat in a plastic tent and place in indirect light.

The rooting medium depends upon individual preference and the method of rooting used. The common media vary from equal parts of sand and peat; peat and perlite; to bark, peat and perlite. Porous media mixed with sand are better if propagating under mist. Clean sharp sand should be used. Rooting medium should be used for only one batch of cuttings to prevent disease build-up. The rooting medium should be firmed and moistened thoroughly before sticking cuttings. Flats, pots, or prepared beds are used depending upon the quantity of cuttings and method of propagating.

Cuttings should be stuck to about 1″ in depth if long or ½″ if from dwarf plants and lightly watered. The propagation units should be kept out of direct sunlight unless under mist. Small mist units are available commercially or can be made using mist nozzles on three foot centers at 18 to 24 inches above the bed. The mist units should be in a windfree area such as a greenhouse. The sides should be enclosed and placed in a light shady area if used outdoors.

Self-enclosed plastic structures should be used in full shade under deciduous trees. If necessary, the plastic enclosure should be covered with polyethylene shading material to avoid excessive heat build-up and hot spots.

The Nearing propagating frame was first described as a cold method for propagating plants in 1939. The system works well with rhododendrons, azaleas, and many other plants. The frame constructed of wood with a corrugated aluminum sloped roof should face true north. The open side is covered with cold frame sash, and the north facing inside areas are painted white to reflect light into the beds.

Evergreen azalea cuttings will normally root in four to six weeks. When well rooted, they should be transplanted to soils high in organic matter. Light applications of liquid fertilizer to the rooted cuttings during the growing season will speed up their growth. Use of a liquid fertilizer in the mist system has generally not proved beneficial to azalea cuttings. However, some growers add slow release granular fertilizers and microelements in the rooting medium.

CUTTINGS OF DECIDUOUS AZALEAS

Deciduous azaleas in general are much more difficult to propagate by cuttings than evergreen azaleas. The Ghent, Mollis, Exburys, and other deciduous azaleas can be rooted by cuttings, but there is extreme variability among species and among clones within a species. The stoloniferous North American species such as *R. atlanticum, R. arborescens, R. periclymenoides (nudiflorum),* and *R. viscosum* and hybrids of these often root easier than the nonstoloniferous species. The nonstoloniferous form of *R. periclymenoides* can be very difficult to root. *R. prinophyllum (roseum)* may be notably difficult to root, while within such species as *R. calendulaceum* and *R. bakeri* individual clones may be relatively easy or quite difficult.

There are two problems in rooting deciduous azaleas: first, in rooting the cutting and secondly, in inducing new growth following rooting. Deciduous cuttings failing to develop vegetative growth or a flower bud following rooting have a very low survival rate over the first winter. These problems have been solved for some clones by taking cuttings while the new stem growth is still soft and green to the base. This is usually late May and early June, before evergreen azalea cuttings are taken. Softwood cuttings of deciduous azaleas taken early root more easily, and there is time to produce new vegetative growth before fall. The same type rooting structure and medium recommended for evergreen azaleas are used. The addition of a slow release fertilizer plus microelements to the rooting medium have aided in stimulating new growth. After the cuttings have rooted, they can be left in the flat or potted and given an additional three to four hours of light each night. The light intensity provided by a 75 watt bulb 30 inches above the plants is sufficient.

North American azaleas can also be propagated by root cuttings. This technique was adapted after observing young plants developing from roots left after digging plants in the wild. Root pruning will also promote new vegetative shoots from the severed roots. Root cuttings three to four inches in length and ¼ to ½ inches in diameter can be used at all seasons of the year. The most favorable time, however, is early spring. The root pieces are placed horizontally in a medium of equal parts of peat, perlite, and shredded sphagnum moss and covered with the same. The root pieces develop adventitious shoots and roots within the growing season.

LAYERING

Layering is a modification of the stem cutting technique. Although slow, it is useful if only a few plants are to be propagated, particularly the deciduous types. The three common methods of layering are branch or stem layering, mounding, and air layering.

Practically any azalea will form roots on branches if pegged into a soil suitable for azaleas. Plants heavily mulched frequently layer spontaneously. Layering can be undertaken in any season, but late spring or summer are preferred. Select a one or two year old low and sweeping branch and bend it to the ground. Wound the stem by scraping the bark or making an upward cut one to one and one half inches long on the underside of the branch. Bury the branch three to four inches deep at the point of the cut and twist the top of the branch upward. Peg the buried part of the branch down with wire or with a branch or stone placed on top. Cover the wounded branch with peat or humus and keep moist during the growing season. Layering is slow—often a year or more is required before the new plant can be removed on its own roots. It is preferable to sever the branch from the parent plant in the early fall or spring for transplanting to a lath house or nursery bed until the new plant is well established.

Mound layering is more commonly practiced in Europe for increasing cultivars of deciduous azaleas. The mother plant should be on its own roots. It should have as many shoots as possible from the base, produced if need be by cutting all the existing shoots to within six inches of the soil level to force new shoots from the base. Allow the new shoots to grow one full season. In the fall bury the shoots with just the tips showing above a mound of good soil high in organic matter. The site or prepared beds often referred to as stool blocks, should have a fairly consistent level of moisture. The mounding can be continued in stages as the shoots grow the next spring. The rooted shoots are removed the following spring by clearing away the mound and cutting the shoots just above the old ground level, thus leaving the mother plant with even more stumps for the production of new shoots. The newly rooted shoots should be transplanted to a lath house or nursery bed until the new plant is well established. The number of plants produced by this method increases each year, as the mother plant produces an increasing number of shoots after each operation.

Air layering is a modification of soil layering and can be used on both deciduous and evergreen azaleas. Air layering is usually performed in late spring on last year's wood. Make a shallow upward cut of 1–½ inches long on the underside of the stem. Dust the cut surface with rooting hormone and add damp sphagnum moss around the cut. Pack the shoot above and below the cut with moist sphagnum; tie it in place with cotton string. Seal the mound of sphagnum with plastic and tie lightly at both ends. A plastic sleeve can be made by cutting the bottom off a plastic bag, for the air-tight wrap. It is advisable to cover the plastic wrap with foil to reduce the internal temperature and prevent drying out. Air layers made in the spring are usually rooted in the fall and can be removed. If the layer is not rooted in the fall, it should remain on the branch until the following year. Keep the young plant in a protected location until established.

GRAFTING

Grafting is no longer a common method for propagating azaleas in the United States but is still used in Europe. It is most frequently used for producing an unusual plant which may be difficult to root from cuttings or to produce unusual forms, such as tree azaleas. Grafting has been used with the Ghent, Knap Hill, and evergreen azaleas. The understock or root stock should be in an active state of growth while the scion or top wood should be in a dormant condition. Greenhouse facilities are generally required to force the root stock into growth in the winter or very early spring. It is best to establish the root stock in three or four inch pots for easy handling. In Japan the cultivar 'Omurasaki' is frequently used as root stock. The Dutch usually used *R. luteum* for Ghent and Mollis hybrids.

A modified side graft or wedge is generally used; matching the cambium layers of the scion and understock is necessary before securing with a rubber band. The graft union can be wrapped in damp sphagnum moss and the entire graft covered with a plastic bag, securing it tightly to the container. For large scale operations the potted grafts can be plunged or mounded in peat moss to cover the graft union in a shaded greenhouse bed with high humidity. If individual plastic bags are used for each graft, do not remove too early. After the scion starts to grow, the bag should be punched with a pin hole to slowly increase the volume of air until the scion is hardened off. The top of the understock should then be removed just above the graft union.

Green grafting can be done outdoors or in a greenhouse under mist for tree azaleas. When both scion and understock are in an active state of growth, use a wedge graft and match the cambium layers before wrapping the graft union with damp sphagnum moss. Cover the entire graft union and scion with a plastic bag. Protect the graft from direct sun by shading or cover with a paper bag. The graft should heal in about one month, evidenced by the active growth of the scion. When this is observed, open the plastic bag gradually by punching a few holes in the bag until it can be completely removed. Take care not to remove it too fast, but allow the scion to gradually adjust and harden. The young grafted plant should be handled as carefully as rooted cuttings the first season.

DIVISIONS

The stoloniferous species of North American azaleas and any multiple stemmed plant can be multiplied by divisions. The plants should be divided during their dormant season in late fall or early spring. It is advisable to cut back the top growth of the plant after dividing the root system. The cut back plants propagated by division should produce flower buds within two to three seasons.

MICROPROPAGATION

Considerable research and development have taken place in micropropagation for multiplying plants vegetatively by means of tissue or *in vitro* culture. Tissue culture was developed as a research tool in the early part of this century and has been widely adapted to the production of some horticultural plants, particularly orchids and ferns. Evergreen rhododendrons and deciduous azaleas have been propagated *in vitro* in laboratories, but the technique is rapidly being adapted to commercial production. The potentials of vegetative propagation of plants have been expanded by the application of tissue culture as a faster method and for plants considered difficult to propagate. It has also been used in the control of disease and to produce virus free plants. Tissue culture makes use of small pieces of plant tissue, generally taken from shoot tips or flower buds in the case of azaleas and rhododendrons.

Shoot tips a few millimeters long are excised from the stock plant, and all leaves are removed. The shoot tips are sterilized in a 10 to 15% commercial bleach solution for 10 to 15 minutes and rinsed two to three times in sterile water. All work is performed in a sterile hood. The shoot tip is then placed on a sterile nutrient medium containing the essential elements as well as sucrose, vitamins, hormones, and agar to gel the solution in tubes. The tubes are placed under a cool white fluorescent light for a 16 hour period at a temperature of 26°C. ± 2°, (approximately 80°F.). The exact formulation of the nutrient medium is specific to each plant species or cultivar.

A proper ratio of cytokinin and auxin is necessary to induce shoot growth. This ratio is determined empirically by testing a range of concentrations for both substances. When multiple shoots form, they are divided and transferred to fresh media for continued shoot production or moved to a rooting medium that has no cytokinin but has been supplemented with indolebutyric acid. There are numerous modifications of the rooting process, and some investigators have skipped this step and rooted the young shoots in peat and

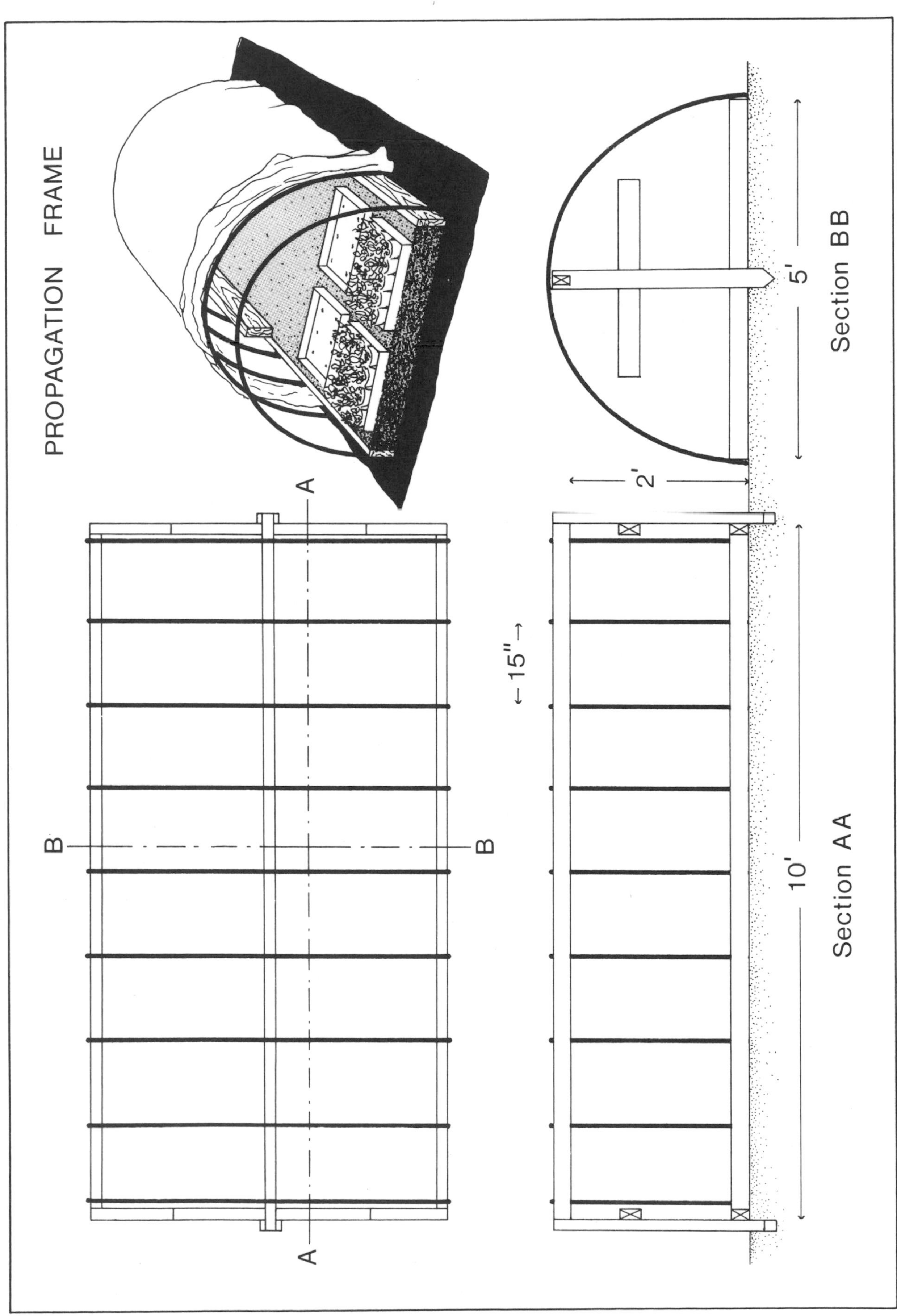
PROPAGATION FRAME
A
A
B
B
← 15" →
2'
5'
10'
Section BB
Section AA

perlite or other suitable media. After rooting, if necessary the tender young plants are acclimatized under mist or in high humidity chambers. Both are reduced over time to properly harden the plants.

Multiplication rates vary according to plant genus, but three to six fold increases every six weeks have been reported. Thus, starting with a single tiny shoot the total number of plantlets increase geometrically in successive subcultures. Research on micropropagation is on-going at many labs, both academic and commercial with many genera. It is to be hoped that the few remaining problems still encountered will shortly be solved. Several nurseries are producing commercial quantities of Rhododendron and Mountain Laurel. In the not too distant future, one might have his favorite hybrid azalea propagated *in vitro* by commercial firms as is now being done with orchids. The gardener might well receive new propagules in a small vial ready to transplant.

Contact local labs or academic institutions for current information and workshops on *in vitro* culture. The *Journal of the International Plant Propagators Society* is a good reference source for current information.

12. HYBRIDIZING AZALEAS

Dr. August Kehr

Hybridizing azaleas can be an engrossing and rewarding hobby for gardeners regardless of background. It can be as simple or as complex as you wish to make it. You must have only a love for plants, patience, curiosity and eagerness to learn, and you must not be discouraged by a few disappointments.

A beginner should heed a word of warning before he embarks on a plant breeding adventure. The progression from rank beginner to full-fledged hybridizer usually runs as follows:

MAKES A FEW CROSSES

INCREASING INTEREST

PERMANENT ADDICTION

This progression, once started, is non-reversible, and the ultimate "disease" is incurable.

Either deciduous or evergreen azaleas are suitable for beginners as both usually flower within two to four years. Waiting and watching for your new creation to flower are a mixed bag. Disappointment can only result if the long awaited flowering reveals a plant of mediocre value. One sometimes hears it said: "A breeder spends years in anticipation but only minutes in disillusionment." However, when you develop a true winner, the saying should be amended to: "A breeder spends years in anticipation, and the rest of his life in satisfaction."

Doing a Good Job: If you intend to hybridize azaleas, plan to start right and do a good job. It is much more satisfying to do a good job than just dabble. To do a good job, you must acquire a thorough knowledge of existing cultivars, in order to judge when you have developed a superior plant worth propagating for further evaluation, to observe how well different cultivars perform, to recognize the differences between them, and to distinguish those which are really outstanding. Superior plants must be general all-round "good-doers" as well as being beautiful, showy, and possessing the characteristics you wished to develop. Extend your ability to identify superior plants by visiting as many gardens as possible and by attending rhododendron shows where the better forms are exhibited. You must build a library of books and study them carefully, especially descriptions and breeding lines, which have stood the test of time, of award-winning plants. Success comes only through choosing the best plants to use as parents in your crosses. Study the pedigrees of the outstanding cultivars to determine which plants have the most potential as parents.

The first requisite of a good breeding program is to establish the purpose for your work. Without definite goals in mind, little progress is likely to be made. Never, never make a cross just because there are two plants available. There should be a reason for every cross. A successful breeder will plan his crosses months ahead of time, often spending the winter months in this pursuit.

Of almost equal importance, concentrate on only a few objectives. Greatest progress is made if you have only one or two primary objectives upon which to concentrate all efforts. A good rule is specialization rather than generalization. It is also a good rule to limit your efforts to only one class of azaleas.

Finally, select only a very few superior plants from the total population of seedlings you grew. Unless you are ruthless in discarding just average (or even above average) plants, you will end up with such a large number of random plants of little or no merit that you will become confused and bogged down with the unrewarding routine of caring for too many plants.

MAKING THE CROSSSES: STEP-BY-STEP PROCEDURE

Mechanically, hybridizing is simple, as the parts of azalea flowers are fairly large and easily handled. This is the procedure:

1. Just before the flower to serve as the female (seed) parent opens, emasculate it by pulling off the stamens with a pair of small tweezers. Fortunately, for hybridizers in most azaleas (but not all), the stigma of the pistil does not usually ripen to receive pollen as early as the pollen of that same flower. In addition remove adjacent flowers to prevent inadvertent pollination caused merely by the branches swaying in the wind.

2. Pull the ripe stamens with their anthers from the flower to be used as the male (pollen) parent. Anthers of the male parent should be used immediately after the flower opens. If it is picked at a later time, after the flower is well open, its pollen may have already been lost or collected by insects. You will quickly recognize the stamens that are still functional, with a little experience.

3. The tip of the pistil which is ripe and ready to receive pollen is covered with a sticky surface to which the pollen will adhere as soon as the pollen touches it. Carry the stamen of the flower to be pollinated and shake out the pollen onto the stigma.

4. Tag the pollinated flower to indicate female (the seed parent) and male parent—in that order, as it is the accepted means of identifying crosses.

It is not necessary to cover pollinated flowers to prevent accidental pollination by insect if you have worked carefully and in a timely way. The really addicted hybridizer doing genetic studies will bag crosses, to absolutely assure that no chance pollination occurs. Examination of numerous crosses has shown that little cross pollination occurs for want of protection against insects. Early spring insects searching for pollen rarely visit emasculated flowers. If stamens have been removed from the flowers you are working with, there is almost no danger of mixture because azalea pollen is not carried by the wind, only by insects.

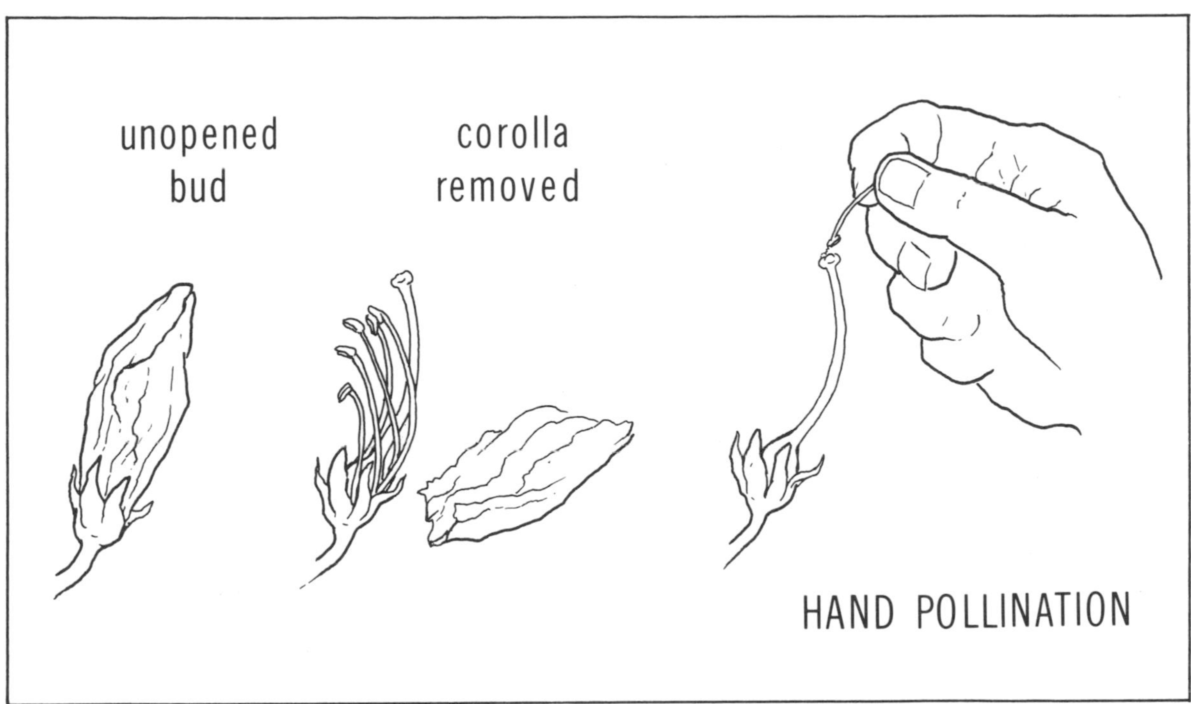

5. If the male plant flowers much earlier than the female plant, you will have to store the pollen as follows.

COLLECTING AND STORING OF POLLEN

Pollen of azaleas can be stored and will remain viable for years if one follows simple but practical techniques. Pollen storage permits you to make almost any cross desired, despite months or years of difference in time of flowering. Briefly, the technique is as follows:

1. Collect anthers, preferably just before the flowers open, and put them into labeled gelatin capsules. Empty capsules can be obtained at most drug stores with a doctor's prescription. Number 1, 0, or 00 are about the right sizes. Avoid sizes larger than 00, as they are difficult to use on small-flowered plants. For labeling, string tags can be glued to the top of the gelatin capsule.

2. Pre-dry the anthers within the capsules for 2 or 3 days in a home refrigerator (not the freezer compartment). Moisture will pass through the gelatin walls. The ideal drying temperature is about 50 degrees F. (10 degrees C.). Pre-drying is imperative before freezing. Anthers that are not completely dried will be damaged.

3. When the anthers are *thoroughly dried,* store the capsules on cotton padding in sealed jars with a dessicant in the bottom of each jar. Calcium chloride or silica gel dessicants can be acquired at a pharmacy. Place the sealed jar in the freezer compartment at about 0 degrees F. (−18 degrees C.).

4. To use the stored pollen, remove the sealed jar from the freezer and warm it in warm water before opening. The sudden warming does not harm dry pollen. Neither does repeated thawing and refreezing which occurs when part of the pollen is used and the balance refrozen. Tap the capsule to loosen the pollen from the dried anthers. Much of the pollen sticks to the walls of the gelatin capsule, making it easier to use in crosses as the pistil of the seed parent can be inserted directly into the capsule.

Effect of Weather: Weather conditions markedly effect the successful crossing of plants. High humidity and rainfall tend to reduce the number of successful crosses. Crosses done out-of-doors, as in the earlier part of the season when temperatures are uniformly low result in a lower rate of success. As the weather warms up, the chances of success improve, especially if the plants are in good health and top growing condition. However, extremely hot, dry conditions usually reduce seed-setting. Greenhouse conditions at 75–85 degrees F. (24–29 degrees C.) are ideal.

NUMBER OF SEEDLINGS TO GROW

In general, the greater the variability of the cross, the more seedlings you should grow to obtain the greatest number of new cultivars. Crosses will range from least variability to greatest variability about as follows:

1. Selfing one clone of one true species.
2. Inter-crossing two clones of one true species.
3. Crossing clones of two different species.
4. Crossing clones of a true species with a hybrid.
5. Selfing one clone of a hybrid.
6. Crossing siblings of the same parental hybrid origin.
7. Crossing two different hybrids of the same color and plant character.
8. Crossing two different hybrids of unlike color and plant character.

It is probable that growing six to ten seedlings in the first category is adequate, while many hundreds would be desirable in the last category.

HARVESTING SEED OF CROSSES

Seed is harvested in the fall of the year at about the time of the first frost. The seed pods at this time contain ripe seed even though the pods are green in color. If one waits too long after the first frost, the seed pods dry out rapidly and much seed may be lost. Collect the seed pods along with the tags marking the cross. Paper muffin cups are ideal for keeping the seed pods of each cross separated. After collecting the ripe pods, dry them for about ten days. Usually dried pods will open and spill out the seeds. Use a pair of pliers to crack open any pods which have not opened. Care must be taken to clean the pliers before working on another cross.

Tea strainers of various sizes are useful in separating the seed from the chaff. Again, care must be taken to clean the strainers between seed of different crosses.

KEEPING RECORDS

Good records are as important for a plant breeder as a road map is to a traveler. They can tell you where you have been and can give you directions for where you are going. Ideally you should be able to know the parentage of every plant you grow. While it is true that labels are easily lost, misplaced, or even stolen by birds for building their nests, or by children for playthings, the objective should be to keep "unk" (unknowns) and "Nolas" (no labels) to a minimum. Likewise, any hybrid with parentage unknown is usually less valuable for other breeders than one of known parentage, regardless of the merit of the individual plant.

RECORDING THE CROSSES

A record book should be kept of the crosses made each year. The entry should record the cross number, the parentage of each cross and any hybridizing notes which may be useful in the future. The crosses of each year should be separated from those of previous and following years. Leave ample space following each cross to record useful informatiom as to the cross which occurs in subsequent years.

SOME WORTHY OBJECTIVES TO CONSIDER IN BREEDING RHODODENDRONS AND AZALEAS

There are so many objectives in a breeding program that only a few can be considered here. Opportunties for further improvement are almost infinite.

There are over 100 species of Azaleas, few of which have been used in developing improved hybrids, to say nothing about improving the species themselves. There is obviously ample opportunity for the breeder to use his ingenuity, skill, and imagination—bound by almost no restrictions.

Most first generation hybrids are only raw material to be used in futher projects. Crossing these hybrids will provide diverse and variable progeny. Selection among second, third, and later generations is needed to remove undesirable characteristics. From among these later generations, especially if valuable new germplasm is introduced from the many species not yet used by hybridizers, new combinations of genetic characteristics will of certainty lead to races of rhododendrons and azaleas not dreamed of today. Hence the objectives mentioned here represent only a *bare beginning* in terms of the potential which exists.

It should be stressed over and over again that there is need to use many more species—especially those which have been little or not used in hybridization.

SOME GENERAL OBJECTIVES

Hardiness: Increased cold hardiness in all azaleas, especially evergreen azaleas, is needed. Perhaps this is one of the most elusive characteristics for which to breed because there are so many factors affecting hardiness. Suffice it to say, the objective should be for clones which consistently flower, year after year, after enduring sub-zero temperatures. Select the most hardy parents, and select from the offspring those most tolerant of cold. In this regard, there is a particular need to develop more cold-hardy clones of the species through continuing cycles of intercrossing individual plants of hardy survivors of a species population.

Good-Doers: Like hardiness, this is a character that is hard to define, and harder yet to breed for. It is probable that good-doers are more deeply rooted, possess genetically controlled vigor, are pest resistant, are tolerant of both high and low temperatures, and grow under diverse and adverse conditions. There are such clones if one really searches.

Compact Growth: Compact growth and dwarf plants are the plants of the future. Fortunately, plants that make good parents for compactness and dwarfness exist in both Rhododendron and Azalea species. In evergreen azaleas there are even prostrate forms, such as in *R. nakaharai* (Cox form 'Mariko'). In general, dwarf plants tend to pass on their dwarfness to such a high level that most plants of a dwarf × tall cross will tend to be much closer to the dwarf parent than the tall parent.

Double Flowers: If you decide to develop double flower types, there is germplasm in many Azalea species and hybrids. These include such plants as 'Rosebud' in the evergreen azaleas and 'Homebush' in the deciduous azaleas. Some of the semidouble and double flowered forms are sterile or semisterile. However, if one carefully inspects plants with such double flowers, he will frequently find functional pistils and pollen. For example, 'Rosebud' has functional pollen which can be found occasionally in anthers adhering to the edges of some petals, along with an occasional deformed anther. Actual trial is the only way to ascertain fertility, since sterility in double flowers may be due to deformities of the pistil or stamens occasioned by the freak character of the flowers rather than to incompatibility. Some double flowers retain a normal pistil which is functional, while in other cases even a normal appearing pistil for some reason is non-functional.

SOME SPECIFIC OBJECTIVES

Evergreen Azaleas: Desirable objectives which should be considered include fragrance, good green winter foliage, colored foliage in winter, fall flowering, frost tolerance of the open flowers ('Dorsett' flowers when fully open withstand 5 to 6 degrees of frost), lasting qualities of the flowers, yellow color (transferred by interspecific crosses from scaly Rhododendron and deciduous Azalea species, or even—some day—from Malesians), and types suitable for areas with very cool summers. The Harris hybrid 'Pink Cascade' is a *R. nakaharai* × 'Bunka' hybrid that can be trained as a beautiful hanging basket plant.

Deciduous Azaleas: One of the most serious problems with deciduous azaleas is the difficulty in propagation from cuttings. However there are species which root rather easily. Hence, breeding for easy rooting is a most worthwhile objective.

In addition, there are many deciduous species that have been used extensively in the improvement of deciduous azaleas. The use of such new germplasm will certainly lead to entirely new races of deciduous hybrids equal to or even of greater merit than the Exbury types.

An informal poll was taken of several azalea breeders and growers* to solicit their choices for parents for some of these specific objectives. As might be expected replies were varied, but significant points of agreement developed. Listed below are some of the plants suggested to realize particular objectives.

EVERGREEN AZALEAS

Most Cold Hardy: 'Corsage', 'Herbert', *R. kiusianum, R. yedoense* var. *poukhanense*
Best Winter Foliage:'Glacier', 'Hot Shot, 'Polar Bear'
Reddest Color: 'Girard's Scarlet', 'Hino Crimson', 'Mothers Day', 'Wards Ruby'
Yellowest-Color: 'Cream Cup', 'Frostburg', 'Mizu no Yuma Buki'
Fragrance: 'Mucronatum', 'Rose Greeley'
Fully Double Flower: 'Anna Kehr', 'Gardenia', 'Elsie Lee', 'Louise Gable, 'Rosebud'
Fall Flowering: 'Dorsett', 'Indian Summer', 'Opal'
Compact Growth: Beltsville Dwarfs, 'Dragon', 'Girard's Border Gem', *R. kiusianum*, 'Myogi'
Lasting Quality of Flowers: 'Ambrosia', 'Chojuho', 'Jeanne', 'Rosebud', 'Scott Gartrell', 'Vuyk's Scarlet'
Best All Around Good-Doer: 'Corsage', 'Herbert', *R. kiusianum*, 'Martha Hitchcock'

DECIDUOUS AZALEAS

Easiest to Root: 'Gibraltar', 'Homebush', *R. austrinum, R. atlanticum*
Mildew Resistance: 'Coccinea', 'Speciosa', 'J. Jennings', 'Persil'
Compact Growth: 'J. Jennings', 'Klondyke', *R. prunifolium*
Red Flower Color: 'Ilam Red Letter'
Yellow Flower Color: 'Klondyke'
Most Floriferous: 'Gibraltar', 'Knap Hill Red'
Double Flowers: 'Homebush', 'Narcissiflora', 'Norma'
Lasting Quality of Flowers: 'Homebush', 'Norma'
Best All Around Good-Doer: 'Gibraltar'

*Weldon Delp, Robert Gartrell, William Guttormsen, Peter Girard, George Harding, James Harris, Edmund Mezitt, Lanny Pride, Albert Reid, Tony Shammarello, Robert Ticknor and Frank White.

APOMIXIS

Sometimes crosses are made between very distinctly different parents (very wide crosses), yet the offspring tend to resemble the seed (or female) parent. These results have most frequently, and erroneously, been attributed to apomixis.

Apomixis in plants is defined as the production of viable true seed by the development of nonsexual cells, usually cells within the ovary walls of the female plant. Such seeds are, therefore, not the result of a true cross—fertilization of the ovules by the pollen of the male parent. In a sense, apomixis is vegetative reproduction, because each apomictic plant will be an exact duplicate of the seed parent, in the same way that cuttings of grafts are exact duplicates. When so defined, there has *never been* a recorded or verified case of true apomixis in the entire *Rhododendron* genus.

In those cases where the offspring tend to resemble the seed or female parent, the explanation is simply this: the plant was self pollenized, through careless technique. It is time that *Rhododendron* and *Azalea* breeders stop covering up their error in technique by calling it apomixis.

Ironically, if true apomixis could ever be found in azaleas, it would create a means of propagation far superior to any method known to date, including tissue culture.

INHERITANCE IN AZALEAS

As a generalization, an azalea breeder need not be overly concerned about the unfortunate scarcity of exact knowledge of the genetics of these plants. Azaleas may be improved through breeding without a knowledge of inheritance; most of our improved economic crops have been developed without knowing much about inheritance of desirable characters. One may say, somewhat facetiously, that *he* may not know the inheritance of genetic characters, but the plants will! In any event, azalea breeding today is largely an art, not a science.

The lack of good genetic information may rise from the fact that much of our azalea germplasm is of hybrid origin. For critical studies of genetic inheritance one should limit his work to a more or less true species. Genetic ratios in largely hybrid material are highly complex and difficult to interpret, while ratios *within* a true species tend to be more easily interpreted.

CROSS-FERTILIZATION

In general, azaleas are self-sterile to a high degree, but readily cross-fertile. Seed most often results from crossing separate individual clones. It is difficult to obtain much seed when pollen from the same flower, or from another on the same plant, or from another plant of the *same* clone is used. However, there is no difficulty when the stigma of a flower is fertilized by pollen from *other* clones of the same species or hybrid group (or of course any unrelated clones).

Furthermore, crosses can rather easily be made between species within the same general taxonomic classification.

Serious hybridizers should study carefully the taxonomic relationships of azaleas and limit cross fertilization to species within a *section.* (See Classification of Azaleas)

Thus *albrechtii, pentaphyllum, vaseyi, canadense,* and *nipponicum* tend to be isolated from the rest of the deciduous group. Likewise, *amagianum, quinquefolium, reticulatum, sanctum, schlippenbachii, weyrichii* and probably *tashiroi* are a group which does not cross readily, if at all, with other azaleas, either evergreen or deciduous.

Differences in chromosome number do not in general create barriers to hybridization; i.e., plants with unlike chromosome numbers will hybridize. However, in the latter case sterility usually results. The exception is hybrids of tetraploid *R. calendulaceum* with diploid deciduous species tend to be fertile.

NAMING AND REGISTERING

Far too many seedlings have been named by enthusiastic breeders not adequately familiar with the great range of clones already in the trade, or named in the past. It bears repeating that if you undertake hybridizing, and especially selecting and naming new plants, it is vital that you be fully familiar with the many species, varieties, forms, and clones now in cultivation. Too often a new creation becomes a wonder that clouds judgment. By all means make certain that the rhododendrons and azaleas you name and introduce are really different, superior and represent an advance over those already in hand. Superior clones are not as easily come by as we might expect. Be discriminating.

As a general rule of thumb, no more than 1% of any given population of seedlings is worthy of selection for further evaluation, and upon several years of careful evaluation and testing less than one tenth of these are worth naming.

However, when a breeder does have a superior plant, he should not only name it but *register* it with the International Registration Authority.

POLYPLOIDY

Azalea species commonly have twenty-six chromosomes, and plants with this number are called diploids i.e., they have thirteen pairs of chromosomes. If they have fifty-two chromosomes (4 times 13), they are considered tetraploids. Thus a hexaploid has 6 times 13 or 78 chromosomes, and so on up to the highest number ever reported in the genus *Rhododendron* of 156 chromosomes (12 times 13).

Among the evergreen azaleas there are a few naturally occuring tetraploids such a 'Banka', 'Taihei', 'Wako', and probably 'Getsutoku'. Likewise, *R. calendulaceum* and *R. canadense* are tetraploids among deciduous azaleas. Hexaploid forms of *R. occidentale* have been reported, although most plants of *R. occidentale* are presently considered to be diploids.

However, very few chromosome counts have been made in the genus, so information is sparse and incomplete. There is much need for such chromosome counts, and such studies should be encouraged. For example, it is probable that many of the Exbury azaleas are polyploids.

Tetraploids in general have much larger flowers than diploids. In addition, the flower texture is thicker, and hence, the lasting quality of the flower is improved. Tetraploid forms of several azalea cultivars have been experimentally developed at the Agricultural Research Center of the U.S. Department of Agriculture at Beltsville, Maryland. When a named clone is developed into a tetraploid, the original clone name should be retained, followed by the word tetra, i.e. 'Corsage Tetra', 'Rose Greely Tetra', etc.

Hybrids between tetraploid deciduous azaleas such as *R. calendulaceum* and diploid deciduous azaleas would (as in other species) normally be expected to be intermediate in chromosome number, i.e., triploids. Plants with triploid chromosome numbers are markedly sterile. Despite this, as mentioned earlier, crosses between tetraploid *R. calendulaceum* and diploid deciduous species are usually fertile, apparently as a result of egg cells or pollen cells in the diploid species acting as functional tetraploids, and hence producing fertile tetraploid offspring.

TECHNIQUE OF DOUBLING CHROMOSOME NUMBER

The technique of doubling chromosome numbers by using colchicine has been known for nearly half a century, but has not been commonly applied to *Rhododendron* and *Azalea* improvement. Colchicine is an alkaloid derived from the autumn-flowering *Colchicum autumnale* and was at one time a commonly used medicine for treating gout in humans. Colchicine may be most successfully applied to (1) stem tissue, (2) sprouting seeds, or (3) seedlings. **Colchicine is poisonous, so avoid getting it into your mouth or eyes.**

Stem treatment: For best results the plants to be treated must be healthy and growing rapidly, preferably under lights in very fertile growing medium. The procedure is as follows:

a. Remove tips of vigorously growing shoots, except for the shoot to be treated.

b. Immediately treat the upper 3 lateral buds of the remaining shoot with 0.5 to 1.0 percent colchicine in a 10% solution of glycerine dispensed from a medicine dropper. The solution must reach the apical growing cells. Other untreated buds or growing tips must be removed from the plant as they emerge to force growth into the treated buds. Keep humidity high to retard drying of the colchicine solution.

c. Treat buds with the colchicine solution daily for one month, placing the solution in the center of the bud. Colchicine effects should be looked for in those buds or shoots whose growth has been retarded as a result of treatment. The effectiveness of the treatment must be judged by the distorted growth of the first leaves emerging from the treated area. If no distortion is observed in the lower leaves of the growing shoot, it can be concluded that the colchicine solution has not penetrated into the buds to reach the growing apical cells. Successful treatment is evident by the leaves which are wider in relation to their length than typical for the plant.

Sprouting Seed: Treatment of sprouting seed is usually the easiest method to induce tetraploidy. The procedure is as follows:
(a) Germinate the seed in covered glass dishes (such as petri dishes) on moistened filter paper or paper towels.
(b) As soon as the seed begins to sprout, place a drop of 0.5 to 1.0% of colchicine in a 10% solution of glycerine on the seed.
(c) Leave the treated seed for 24 to 36 hours. Keep seeds covered with glass or plastic to prevent drying out. Then place them under at least 1,000 footcandles of light for 24 hours a day to speed growth. Plant on regular media as for any other Azalea seedlings.
(d) After growth starts, remove all seedlings which initiate rapid growth. The affected seedlings will be slow to start growth and under close examination will have thick cotyledons. Removal of the unaffected seedlings is critical because the affected seedlings will be crowded out by the faster growing normal seedlings.

Seedlings: Treatment of seedlings has an advantage in that only the shoots are treated, and root growth is normal. In successful treatment the roots will remain diploid while the shoots will be polyploid. The proceedure is as follows:
(a) Germinate seed on sterile growing media such as soilless mixes. Sow very thinly so a good deal of space is allowed between seedlings. Thin the seedlings if necessary. Keep seedlings covered with glass or plastic to prevent drying. Place them under at least 1,000 footcandles of light for 24 hours a day to promote rapid growth.
(b) *Just before* the buds of the first true leaves start to form, place a tiny droplet of 0.5% colchicine in a 10% glycerine solution in the center of the cotyledons, using a micropipette. Repeat daily for three days.
(c) Remove seedlings with initial growth and retain only those which show slowed or distorted growth.
(d) Transplant the treated seedlings to planting beds for further observation.

AN EXPERIMENTAL METHOD OF INDUCING POLYPLOIDY

For the adventuresome person who likes to experiment, another method to induce polyploidy may be tried, using a substance closely related to moth balls. So far, this method has never been used on Rhododendron or Azalea species, but has been more effective than colchicine on plants such as Sugar Beets. The method is very simple, and so there is merit in its trial.

The chemical used is acenaphthene, which comes as white crystals very similar to moth crystals.

Seedlings are grown in flats, covered with a sheet of glass. Just before the first true leaves appear, they are treated as follows:

a. Dissolve the acenaphthene crystals in acetone or ether. Place the solution on the glass cover and allow the ether or acetone to evaporate, leaving a thin film of acenaphthene adhering to the glass.

b. Replace the glass cover with the acenaphthene film side down toward the seedlings. The acenaphthene will vaporize (exactly like moth crystals), and the flat will become saturated with the vapors. Leave for three to five days, then replace the glass cover with clean glass. The temperature inside the flat is the critical factor in this method, and unfortunately no information is available on the optimum temperature for rhododendrons and azaleas. It is recommended that a good starting point is 75 degrees F. (24 degrees C.). A higher temperature increases the biochemical effect, while a lower temperature decreases it.

c. Repeat the treatment in two or three weeks, except that the second treatment should last for only two to four days.

d. If the rate of survival of seedlings is too low, decrease treatment times and reduce temperature.

This method has been successful because the vapor penetrates to the growing point so only the apical point is affected. It also has the advantage of simplicity compared to the colchicine method. If you use this method, you are plowing new ground. Good luck!

WITCHES' BROOMS

In rare instances the growth pattern of an individual branch changes from normal growth to one in which the growth becomes twiggy, multiple-branched, or broom-like as the name implies. Witches' brooms are now believed to be caused by mycoplasma, living organisms which are virus-like but have some characteristics of extra-tiny bacteria. Mycoplasma are introduced into the plant tissue by the mouth parts of leaf hoppers.

Once a witches' broom is formed, it can be perpetuated by vegetative propagation of the affected twigs. Growth from witches' brooms is dwarf, bunchy, and low growing. As such they may become valuable new forms. If they are worthy of naming, they should be given the name of the original plant, followed by the term witches' broom, e.g., 'Rosebud Witches' Broom'.

13. DAMAGE CAUSED BY INSECTS, MITES AND ANIMALS

Fortunately, azaleas are relatively free of insect pests and diseases as compared to other ornamental plants. Azaleas are preeminently a trouble free plant, provided natural preferences as to soil moisture, temperature, and light are respected. Diseases will be covered in more detail in a subsequent Chapter.

No attempt will be made to cover all pests that have been found on azaleas. The report of a new pest does not mean that it is dangerous. Furthermore, the intensity and prevalence of a particular pest may vary from year to year.

Azalea growers should learn to recognize the different kinds of injuries caused by pests and animals. It is important not to confuse winter cold injury which may cause death the following spring or summer, poor growth due to lack of moisture in the summer, or chlorosis and other nutritional problems with injuries from pests.

Specific pesticide and animal controls accepted in 1985 will be found in Table 1. However, continuing attention must be paid to the constant changing of laws and regulations governing the use of chemicals as well as the introduction of new materials. It is not uncommon that a pesticide, licensed for home garden use in one country, state or province, is not approved in others nearby. It is unlawful to use a pesticide for control of a specific pest on a specific genus unless it is specifically labeled for such use. Pesticide recommendations change yearly. Contact a local government horticultural authority for a list of recommended pesticides.

Precautions:

1. Read the pesticide label and observe all recommendations before making an application.
2. Use only recommended pesticides. Contact your local government horticultural

authority for specific recommendations.

3. Follow directions and do not apply in excess of labeled rates.
4. Handle pesticides with care and respect; improperly used they can be injurious to plants, man, and animals.
5. Store pesticides in locked cabinets, away from children, food, fertilizers, and other horticultural materials.
6. Pesticides should not contact nose, eyes, mouth, or skin.
7. Wash skin exposed immediately. Don't eat, drink, or smoke after using pesticides until you have washed.
8. Wear protective clothing if at all possible. Change outer clothing after making pesticide applications.
9. Do not use herbicides (weed killers) in the same sprayer used for other pesticides.
10. Do not tank mix two or more pesticides unless you are sure they are compatible with one another.
11. Dispose of empty containers by placing them in plastic bags before placing in trash or taking to an approved chemical disposal center.

The following information will be given in the discussion of a specific pest:

a. A brief description to aid in identifying the insect or other pest, important points in its life history and habits.
b. The damage it causes.
c. Special treatment.

SUCKING INSECTS

Lace bug. The Azalea Lace bug, *Stephanitis pyrioides* Scott, and the Rhododendron Lace bug, *S. rhododendri* Harv., are common pests of azaleas and rhododendrons grown in sunny places but seldom serious on plants grown in the shade.

The two are similar in appearance, habit and life history, but each species attacks only its respective host with the rhododendron Lace bug found also on Mountain Laurel, *Kalmia latifolia*. These insects are commonly miscalled "lacewing flies", deriving their name from the delicate lace-like appearance of their wings. Adults and immatures both feed from the underside of the leaves and cause a stippled or blanched appearance on the upper leaf surface. The leaves of badly infested plants change from a normal green to an unsightly yellow and lose their vitality The underside of the leaves becomes rust-colored and covered with small dark spots of tar-like excrement and cast skins of the molting nymphs. Lace bugs are most damaging on azaleas in full sunlight and much less so in light or moderate shade.

Lace bugs overwinter as eggs inserted into the leaf tissue along the midrib. Nymphs hatch out in early spring. Adults emerge in about forty days. Most severe damage is done by the second generation and third that develop into adults. A partial third generation develops in September during years of high fall temperature so adults may be present on plants until November. Seriously infested plants go into the winter months in a weakened condition.

To control lace bugs, direct an insecticide spray in a fine but forceful mist to the underside of the leaves to destroy the nymphs hatching from the overwintering eggs before they become adults and lay eggs. Observe the underside of leaves on plants in an open area for the young nymphs. The first spray application should be made at the time the nymphs are hatching. A second application should be made in about 7–10 days with additional applications if needed throughout the summer.

Whitefly. The Azalea Whitefly, *Pealius azaleae* Baker and Moles, is a small four-winged insect about 1/16 inch long. The adults have a white appearance due to a fine powder on the wings and body, and drift from the leaves like snowflakes when they are disturbed. The Azalea Whitefly overwinters as nymphs or pupae on the leaves. The small, flat, oval, pale white nymphs are immobile and usually appear in great number. Both adult flies and nymphs feed by sucking sap from the leaves. Adults emerge as new foliage appears, and several generations develop during the summer. Infested leaves become mottled yellow, and lower leaves often become coated with a black sooty mold that grows on honeydew excreted by the insects. The Azalea Whitefly is a pest only of certain species and cultivars. It may severely damage the cultivar 'Indica Alba' and other Ryukyu azaleas and their hybrids, while other cultivars in the same planting are usually free.

The Rhododendron Whitefly, *Dialeurodes chittendeni* Laing, is similar to the Azalea Whitefly in appearance but only attacks rhododendron plants with a smooth under-leaf surface.

To control whitefly, three or more insecticide applications at 7–10 day intervals may be required. The spray mist must be directed to the underside of the leaves. Whiteflies are attracted to yellow so laying large sheets of yellow heavy paper coated with a sticky glue will trap the flying adults in a greenhouse.

Leaf Miner. The Azalea Leaf Miner, occasionally a problem on azaleas, is the larva of a small moth *Caloptilia (Gracillaira) azaleella* Brants. The adult is a small yellow moth with purple patches on the wings about ⅜ inches long. It lays its eggs on the underside of leaves. Small, yellowish green caterpillars ¼ inches long develop in about four days and mine into leaves, leaving irregularly shaped tunnels and blotches. When partially grown, the larvae emerge and roll under the tips or edges of a new leaf to feed within the roll. The foliage is unsightly when infestations are severe with dead areas in the leaves and wrinkled and deformed leaves. Leaves damaged by the older larvae turn yellow and drop. Three generations develop during the summer while the caterpillar overwinters in rolled leaves.

Spray applications should be repeated at 7–10 day intervals to kill both the moths and caterpillars; hand pick light infestations.

MITES

Spider Mites. The Southern Red Mite or Holly Mite, *Oligonychus ilicis* McGregor, is a common pest on azaleas. The two-spotted mite, *Tetranychus urticae* Koch, is less common but may be a problem on greenhouse plants. Mites are minute (0.5 mm), being just visible to the naked eye, and possess piercing mouth parts. They usually feed on the underside of leaves, withdrawing plant juices. The foliage becomes mottled with a bronzed appearance. Injured foliage turns gray or brown and drops immediately.

The adult females of the Southern Red Mite are dark red, almost black, while immature stages are lighter in color. The males, nymphs, and eggs are red. To detect mites shake suspected leaves over a sheet of white paper, watching for the movement of the small dust-like particles. Overwintering eggs are laid on leaf surfaces and hatch in early spring. Damage is most severe in the spring and fall. Indoor mites reproduce year round.

Approved miticides should be applied at the first sign of infestation. Systemic miticides, if available, are useful for mite control but should only be used in strict compliance with label instructions.

Most miticides are ineffective on eggs and resting stages so two or three applications at weekly intervals are necessary. The number of applications should be governed by the presence of active nymphs and adults.

SCALE INSECTS

Several scale insects reside on azaleas, but in most cases the injury is slight to moderate. Scale occupies leaf axils, forks of twigs and main stems to the ground. Heavily infested plants become unhealthy and ragged in appearance as branches weaken and die.

Adult scales, due to their protective outer surface, are often difficult to control by spraying. Dormant oil emulsion sprays in the winter work best. Pesticide applications should be made in the spring and summer only when the nymphs are active and crawling. Two or more applications 7–10 days apart are recommended.

The following scale insects are the most common on azaleas:

Bark Scale. Azalea Bark Scale, *Eriococcus azaleae* Comstock, a native of Japan, is the most common, and also called Bark Louse. The scale resembles a mealy bug up to ¼ inches long. A white, cotton felt-like sac encloses the dark red female and eggs. The male sac is smaller and elongated. Infested foliage and twigs may become blackened with sooty mold growing on the honeydew excreted by the insect. This bark scale overwinters as partly grown nymphs. In cooler climates only, one generation develops each year from eggs hatched in June. In warmer climates the eggs hatch earlier, often in late March and April and a second generation appears in September.

Peony Scale. Peony Scale, *Pseudaonidia paeoniae* Cockerell, occasionally appears in warmer climates on azaleas and camellias. The insect has only one annual brood from eggs produced in early spring. The purple young scales are covered with a white wax. By means of a sharp tip on the abdomen, the scales cut a circular ring in the outer bark and extend a wax lined chamber beneath the bark with each succeeding molt. The mature scale, covered with the bark of the host plant, appears as a bump or swelling on the stem. When the bark is rubbed off or the scale dies, a conspicuous white waxy patch remains.

Cottony Azalea Scale. *Pulvinaria ericicola* McConnell, a soft scale, has appeared on several species and a few evergreen cultivars. The white egg sac is ¼ to ⅜ inches long and is usually found near the base of the stem. These scales overwinter as fertile but not fully grown females and produce eggs in June.

MISCELLANEOUS PESTS

Stem Borer. The stem borer is a larva of a slender yellow and black beetle, *Oberea myops* Hald. The adult girdles the tips of azaleas, rhododendrons, and other ericaceous plants in two places and inserts an egg into the bark. The tip wilts and dies. The slender one inch, yellow larva bores down the stems to the ground and into the roots. Sawdust or frass is excreted from openings along the stem. It overwinters in the crown of the plant below ground. The adult beetle emerges in June.

Cut out wilted tips and branches and destroy the larvae. Overwintering pupae can be destroyed by probing the tunnel with a soft wire. Apply insecticides in June to control the adult beetles before they deposit eggs.

Caterpillars. The larvae of the Azalea Caterpillar, *Datana major* G. and R., are very gregarious and feed on the foliage of azaleas and related plants. The two inch long larvae are generally brownish black with white or yellowish stripes and a red head. When disturbed, they have a peculiar habit of raising their heads and anal ends in an upright position clinging to a twig with their abdominal legs. The larvae from one egg cluster feed in a colony, usually stripping all the foliage from one small branch before moving to another. The larvae occur during the summer and early fall with generally one generation a year in Northerly latitudes and two generations in Southerly latitudes. Overwintering takes place in the pupal stage in the ground. The adult brownish moths, approximately 1½ inches long, emerge between May and August. The eggs are deposited in a cluster on azalea leaves.

The simplest control in light infestations is to remove and destroy each colony. In heavier infestations insecticides applied to the colonies will give control.

Weevils. Several different kinds of weevils, all characterized by an extended head or snout, attack azaleas and rhododendrons. In feeding the adults cut notches in the margin of the leaves and girdle the stem. The larvae generally feed on the smaller roots and girdle larger ones.

Black vine Weevil, *Otiorhynchus sulcatus* Feb., attacks many hosts and has become a widespread pest in nurseries and gardens. It is a small black weevil about ⅜ inch long, with a broad snout, tufts of yellowish hairs, and hard wing covers. Leaf notching by the adults is readily detected, but root destruction by the small, whitish grubs usually is more damaging. Severely injured plants will die. The larvae overwinter in the soil. Adult weevils emerge in late spring and summer and begin laying eggs in a month. The adults are nocturnal so seldom seen unless trapped, but the leaf notching is all the evidence required for identification. Black vine Weevils are parthenogenetic (reproduce without fertilization) and flightless so that importing a single female from an infected area can result in an infestation.

Control by treating soil for the larvae or by spraying foliage for control of the adults. A foliar spray must remain toxic for at least 48 hours because the weevil may not feed every night.

Similar weevils, the Strawberry Root Weevil, *O. ovatus* Linnaeus, and the Rough Strawberry Root Weevil, *O. rugosostriatus,* also damage azaleas in the same way as the Blackvine Weevil. Control measures are the same.

Other weevils reported feeding on azaleas include the Fuller Rose Beetle, Longhorned Weevil, and the Japanese Weevil.

A small black weevil less than ⅛ inch long is occasionally found with the larvae in and on seed capsules of azaleas. Collected seed capsules should be placed in a plastic bag and treated with an aerosol insecticide.

AZALEA BUD LARVA

Throughout the mid-Atlantic and southern U.S.A., a small larva has been found feeding on the flower buds of both native and evergreen azaleas, resulting in damaged petals and malformed flowers. The insect has been identified as *Orthosia hibisci* (Guence) or Fruitworm Larva. The small, pale green larva, 3/16″ in length, feeds inside the flower bud and is seldom seen after the bud begins to open.

The life cycle of this pest is not completely known. The fruitworm moth probably emerges in the early spring flowers of the Kurume azaleas and early native species such as *R. canescens* and *R. austrinum.* The flower damage continues with the later flowering species and cultivars. Unconfirmed reports indicate that the large leaf rhododendron buds are also infested. Start spraying with Sevin or Malathion early in the spring as soon as feeding is observed.

PESTS OF OCCASIONAL IMPORTANCE

Garden and greenhouse azaleas are occasionally infested with aphids, mealy bugs, and other beetles. Any of the many insecticides registered for these pests will control them.

A new caterpillar has been reported in 1980 feeding on Gumpo Azaleas and junipers in the Southern U.S.A. This insect has been identified as *Autosticha hyotensis.* Most species of the genus are tropical or subtropical. It is not known how this insect entered or its distribution in North America, but it is possible that it is widely distributed in Georgia and Alabama. It is hoped that this insect will only be a very minor pest of azaleas due to its tropical nature. Reports vary as to its control with present pesticides.

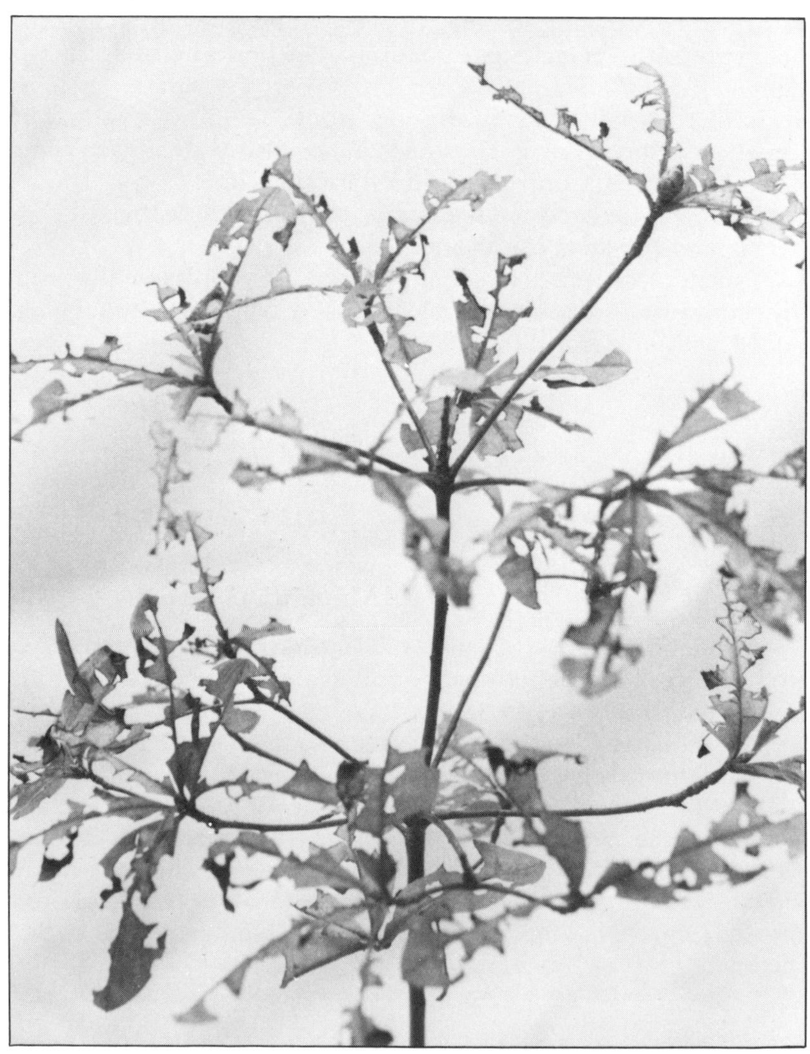

Deciduous azalea leaves skeletonized by larvae. (Galle)

DEER, RODENTS AND DOGS

Azalea growers in suburban and woodland areas must contend with deer and rabbits, which are serious nuisances. Both feed and browse on evergreen and deciduous azaleas. Rabbits have a particular fondness for Gumpo Azaleas and some other Satsukis such as 'Gunbi' but often leave all other azaleas alone. However, when other food sources are short or covered with snow, they will feed on any green shoots projecting above the snow. Rabbits can be captured in a box or "have a heart" trap and moved out of the area. However, like a backyard swimming pool, azaleas are an attractive nuisance and other rabbits will keep coming in. Special plants or beds can be covered or ringed with two foot chicken wire fence.

There are repellent spray materials available both for rabbits and deer. Spray all parts of the plant within reach of the animal, and repeat as needed. Some products have an adhesive added to prevent rain from washing off the repellent. Dog repellents are also available to keep them from spotting and killing portions of plants with urine. These materials must be applied regularly as the odors are diluted by exposure and rain.

Human hair has proved to be a good repellent for deer and wild rabbits. However, if the rabbits are semi-tame or used to being near humans, hair will not work. Small balls of human hair are placed in net sacks and hung from sticks or limbs approximately 15 feet apart in the garden. Just broadcasting hair on plants does not work. The hair, too, will lose its odor after exposure to rain and must be replaced periodically. Another method, but less attractive, is to fasten the sack of hair inside a plastic milk container with the bottom cut off and place them around the garden with the open end down.

As a final resort contact your local game warden for permission to or his assistance in removing animals.

Pine voles, field and wood mice often become pests in cold frames and propagation beds and can be eliminated by trapping and use of poison baits.

14. DIAGNOSING BIOTIC AND ABIOTIC AZALEA PROBLEMS

Symptoms	Probable Cause
Foliage dull green, veins become red in red flowered cultivars, later stages, wilting of leaves	Indicates poor root function. May be one or more of following: Planting when the soil was dry, *Phytophthora* rot, over-fertilization, black vine weevil, root feeding nematode damage.
Leaf drop—slight or severe followed by death of plant	Later stages of above
Uniform light green foliage over entire plant	Nitrogen deficiency
Leaves light yellow-green to intervenal chlorosis; on leaves and shoot tips	Iron deficiency caused by high soil pH. Unavailable iron. Excessive fertilization, poor soil drainage. Root nematode or fungus root rot injury
Chlorosis of older leaves, veins later lose green color	Magnesium deficiency. Root nematode injury
Leaves and flowers become thickened or fleshy; turns, pale green to whitish with white bloom	*Exobasidium* leaf gall disease
Purple or brown spots on leaves	Insect injury. Insecticide injury. Fungus Leaf Spot Disease (Anthracnose, *Colletotrichum*)
White powdery spots on both leaf surfaces, eventually covering the leaves.	Powdery mildew
Small chlorotic spots on upper leaf surface, lower leaf surface later covered with orange spore masses	Leaf rust
Downward cupping of new leaves	Spider mite injury. Herbicide injury
Leaves roll upward from margin	Water stress

Symptoms	Probable Cause
Marginal leaf burn	Water stress on deciduous azaleas. Insecticide injury. Excess fertilizer
Leaf tips fold over, wedded	Azalea leaf miner
Small, round spots on flowers later enlarging, petals, flowers wilt, mushy to the touch, later drying and retained on plant	Petal blight—*Ovulinia azaleae*
Brown spots on flowers, later enlarging, seldom mushy to touch	Flower blight caused by fungus *Botrytis cinerea* (Gray Mold)
Leaves yellowish to gray, blanched or coarse stippled, underside of leaves with black spots	Azalea Lace Bug
Leaves with dull green cast later gray-green or bronze-green	Spider Mite
Wilting of stems, branch or entire plant dying back; cut stem shows brown streaks	*Phomopsis* die-back. Caused by *Phomopsis* fungus
White, cottony scales in leaf axils and twigs or powdery gray insect on leaf axil and buds	Scale and mealy bugs

---

TABLE OF PESTICIDE USE

	Pesticide														Animal Control							
Pest	Bacillus thuringiensis	Lindane	Cygon (dimethoate) #1	Diazinon	Enstar (Kinoprene)	Ficam-Turcam (bendicarb)	Kelthane (dicofol)	Malathion	Orthene (acephate)	Pentac (dienochlor)	Sevin (carbaryl) #2	Vendex (fenbutatin-oxide)	Thiodan (endosulfan)	Superior Oil #3	Dried blood	Hinder (ammonium soap)	Human hair	Tobacco dust	Thiram	BGR—Big game repellant	Zinc phosphide (grain bait)	Box traps
Lacebug			X	X				X	X													
White fly			X	X	X	X																
Spider mites			X	X			X	X		X		X										
Scale			X	X				X	X				X	X								
Azalea bark louse			X	X				X						X								
Stem borers	X	X	X	X				X														
Caterpillars	X		X					X	X		X											
Weevil			X	X				X														
Leaf miner			X	X				X														
Rabbits															X	X	X	X	X			X
Deer																X	X		X	X		
Pine voles																					X	

1. Cygon has shown phytotoxic symptoms on some azalea varieties.
2. Excessive use of sevin can lead to a buildup of mites and aphids.
3. Superior oils are safe in the spring and fall, when temperature is between 42°–85°F.

Symptoms	Probable Cause
Large, bluish black caterpillar feeding on leaves	Datana larvae
Feeding on young leaves and stems, particularly Gumpo and other Satsuki azaleas	Rabbits
Feeding on evergreen azalea leaves and stems	Deer
Bark splitting usually longitudinal, bark often peeling back	Freeze damage
Leaves twisted and lacking vigor, often very narrow and small	Herbicide damage (glyphosate)
Death of center leaves and twigs of cultivars, particularly on Gumpo cultivars	Rhizoctonia web-blight caused by *Rhizoctonia solani* fungus
Leaf and stem blight of cuttings during propagation. Roots turn brown	*Rhizoctonia solani, Cylindrocladium scoparium.* These fungi are common problems during propagation. Cause leaf stem and root rot.
Sudden browning of leaves in late spring and early summer	Look for bark splitting at base of plant

---

TABLES OF DILUTIONS FOR PESTICIDES

1. Quantities of dry materials (wettable powder) for various quantities of water

	Quantity of Material				
Water	1–100	1–200	1–400	1–800	1–1600
100 gal.	4 lb.	2 lb.	1 lb.	8 oz.	4 oz.
50 gal.	4 lb.	1 lb.	8 oz.	4 oz.	2 oz.
5 gal.	12 tbsp.	6 tbsp.	3 tbsp.	1½ tbsp.	2½ tbsp.
1 gal.	8 tsp.	4 tsp.	2 tsp.	1 tsp.	½ tsp.

2. Quantity of liquid materials (emulsion concentrates, etc.) for various quantities of water

	Quantity of Material				
Water	1–100	1–200	1–400	1–800	1–1600
100 gal.	1 gal.	2 qt.	1 qt.	1 pt.	½ pt.
50 gal.	2 qt.	1 qt.	1 pt.	8 fl.oz.	4 fl.oz.
5 gal.	6 fl.oz.	3 fl.oz.	1½ fl.oz.	¾ fl.oz.	1 tbsp.
1 gal.	8 tsp.	4 tsp.	2 tsp.	1 tsp.	½ tsp.

VOLUME & LIQUID MEASURE

3 teaspoon = 1 tablespoon = 14.8 cc

2 tablespoon = 1 fl. ounce = 29.6 cc

8 fl. ounce = 16 tablespoons = 1 cup = 236.6 cc

2 cups = 32 tablespoons = 1 pint = 473.1 cc

2 pints = 64 tablespoons = 1 quart = 946.2 cc

1 gal. = 128 fl. ounces = 231 cu. inches = 3785 cc

Examples: If a mixture calls for 16 oz. of wettable powder per 100 gallons of water, it would take 2 teaspoons per gallon of water or 6 tbsp. per 10 gallon of water to make a spray mixture of the same strength.

If a mixture calls for one pint of liquid per 100 gallons of water, it would take 1 tsp. of the chemical to 1 gallon of water to make a mixture of the same strength.

Abnormal foliage damage of Glyphosate (Roundup) in basal spraying. Herbicide contacted the trunk and pushed up through the thin bark. Damage showed up next season. Plants with severe damage persist, but continue to decline. (Galle)

15. AZALEA DISEASES

R. C. Lambe., W. H. Wills, R. K. Jones, and D. M. Benson*

DISEASES COMMON TO LANDSCAPES

In the landscape azaleas are susceptible to foliar, flower, stem and root rot. The purchase of diseased plants for landscaping has been a common problem. Improper planting and improper care contribute to the development of disease. Frequently the soil around buildings contains large amounts of clay and drains poorly, contributing to root rots. Azaleas that are planted under trees or are crowded are subject to conditions favorable for fungus leaf spots, leaf galls, and petal blight.

Long dry periods during the summer are common in some areas. *Phomopsis* stem dieback of azaleas has been observed to appear during these periods.

Mature azaleas in the landscape will decline due to root injury from nematode feeding. The foliage will become sparse and light in color.

DISEASES COMMON TO NURSERY PRODUCTION

Azalea growers frequently fail to practice adequate sanitation and disease prevention during propagation. As a result, not only do the growers experience economic loss due to disease, but even worse, they move diseased plants into both the retail nurseries and the landscape. Inter-state movement of diseased azaleas is a major problem because diseased but symptomless plants are easily overlooked during plant inspections and so disease is introduced into previously "clean" regions.

*Extension Plant Pathologist and Professor, Plant Pathology, Department of Plant Pathology and Physiology, VPI & SU, Blacksburg, VA 24061, and Plant Pathology and Associate Professor of Plant Pathology, Department of Plant Pathology, North Carolina State University, Raleigh, NC 27650.

DISEASES OF MAJOR IMPORTANCE

***Phytophthora* Root Rot and Wilt.**

The single most important disease of azaleas is probably root rot caused by spp. of *Phytophthora*. The most commonly isolated pathogen is *P. cinnamomi* Rands, a fungus of worldwide distribution and omnivorous habit, attacking more than 1000 known hosts.

The first symptom is slow wilting and bronzing of the foliage, but this is actually preceded by extensive rotting of the fibrous root system. Some browning of the basal portion of the stem may accompany these symptoms. Finally, the foliage turns brown and the leaves drop off. Usually, the entire plant wilts at one time.

Although *P. cinnamomi* is primarily a root pathogen attacking the small feeder roots of the host, it can colonize the larger roots and lower stem to some extent. It is able to survive long periods of time in the soil in the absence of a host. It is also able to compete with other soil micro-organisms for organic nutrients in soil debris. This nutritional versatility makes it a difficult pathogen to control, and one which is unlikely to be eradicated once established. This fungus produces several different types of microscopic reproductive bodies: oospores produced in matings of compatible strains and asexually produced sporangia and chlamydospores. The sporangia produce motile spores that move through the soil on films of water. Chlamydospores are thick-walled resting structures which serve as means of survival during periods unfavorable to active growth of the fungus.

These structures are not produced in any regular sequence making up a life cycle, but are produced in response to environmental and nutritional conditions. Hence, the onset of disease caused by this fungus is highly responsive to environmental influences. The single most important environmental factor favoring disease development is high soil moisture and soggy conditions. Relatively high soil temperatures also favor disease development.

Although *P. cinnamomi* can survive long periods in the soil, the main sources of disease epidemics are plants that are already infected and the media in which they are growing, either soil or potting mixes. Diseased plants may be maintained in apparent good health in a nursery where the plants are subject to minimal moisture and temperature stress. Such diseased plants easily escape detection, are sold, and planted out in nurseries or landscapes. This establishes new centers of disease which under stressful conditions lead to the subsequent death of the already-diseased plants and many of those around them.

Root rot in azaleas may spread rapidly in nurseries when plant containers become immersed in water on top of plastic soil covers, or are otherwise grown in constantly wet environments. The disease may be aggravated by recycling contaminated irrigation water from ponds or reservoirs. The soil where run-off occurs may become infested, and drainage into water sources such as streams and rivers may result in more wide-spread disease development. Azaleas grown in the field die in large numbers from *Phytophthora* when the fields are kept wet or are poorly drained. See Rhododendron Wilt and Root Rot Disease Cycle, page 365.

The first line of defense in control of *Phytophthora* root rot is prevention by maintaining sanitary conditions during propagation.

Fortunately, there are now several very effective protectant and systemic fungicides on the market.

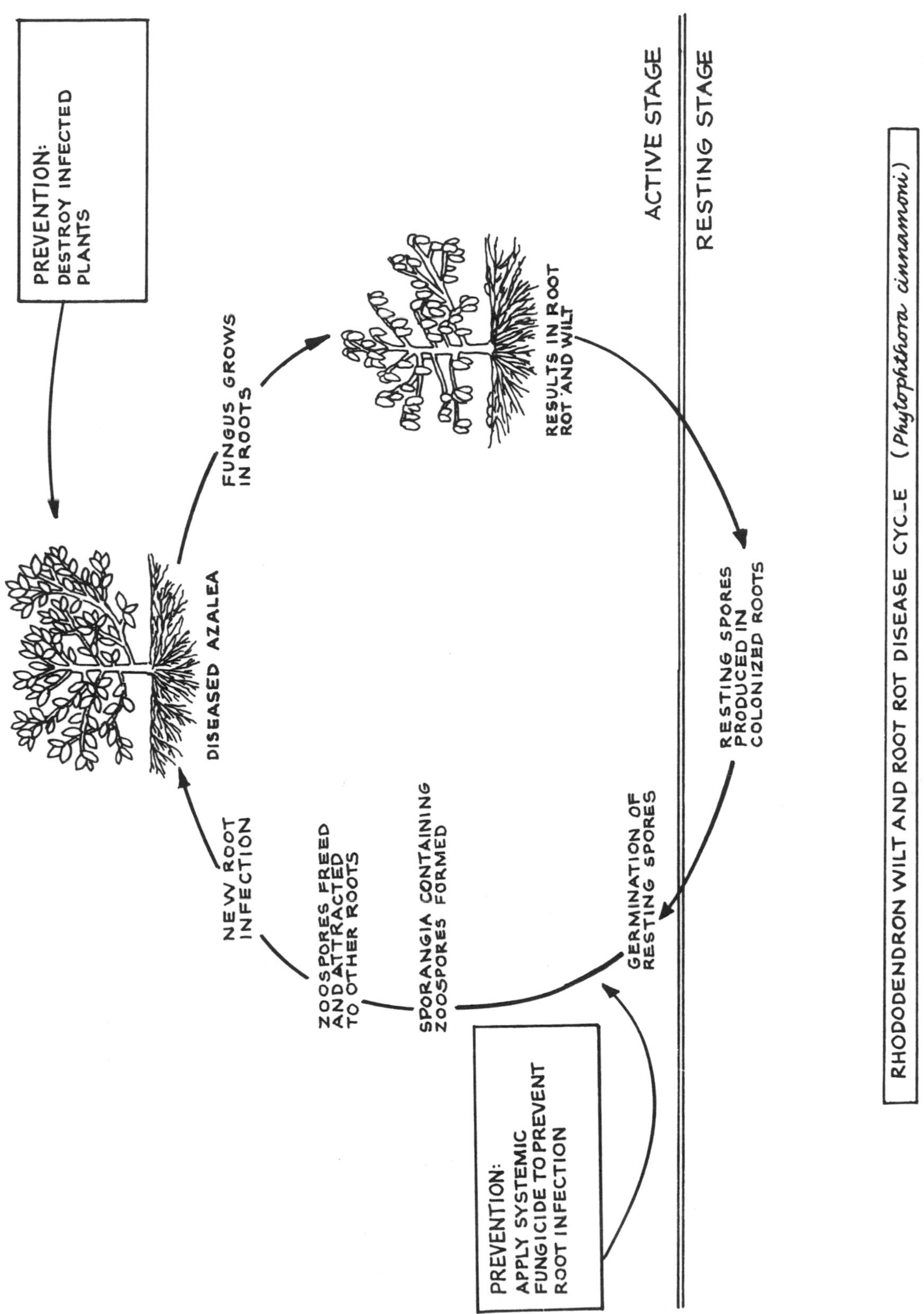

Drawings courtesy of Mrs. Terry Sheuchenko, Lazy S's Farm

Ovulinia petal blight

Petal blight caused by the fungus *Ovulinia azaleae* is a serious disease of azaleas in gardens, but it also occurs on container-grown azaleas in nurseries. Although it is not considered important by nurserymen because they are primarily concerned with the foliage, this is believed to be an important source of disease in home gardens. Indian and Kurume type azaleas are severely affected, but all other azaleas and some rhododendrons are also susceptible. If the environmental conditions are favorable, the disease may spread by conidia so rapidly that flowers are destroyed in 2–4 days.

Petal blight occurs primarily on out-of-door cultivars in warmer regions but the disease has been reported out-of-doors in cooler climates recently. Sclerotia of the fungus may not survive low temperatures so require introduction of infected plants each year to northern latitudes. The disease also attacks azaleas grown in greenhouses.

Spots on the petals are first apparent when they are about the size of a pinhead (Fig. 1). They are pale or whitish on colored flowers, and rust-colored on white flowers. At first they are circular, but they enlarge rapidly into irregular blotches with the affected tissue becoming soft and disorganized. Eventually, the entire corolla collapses. Infected petals are slimy and fall apart readily if rubbed gently between the fingers. This test distinguishes diseased flowers from those injured by low temperature, insects, or other diseases. Diseased flowers dry and cling to the plants for some time, making them ugly whereas healthy flowers of azaleas fall from the plant while still displaying color and normal shape.

Ovulinia produces hard, black bodies of tissue (sclerotia) in the blighted flowers (Fig. 2). Small tan, cup-shaped reproductive structures called apothecia develop from sclerotia on the soil surface during the following spring. Spores are propelled from the apothecia to flower buds initiating primary infections.

Secondary spores is produced in large numbers on the infected petals. These spores are responsible for widespread outbreaks of flower blight. In the greenhouse, an abundance of spores are produced on infected petals. Sclerotia produced in diseased petals drop to the ground and remain undetected. Unsold, container-grown azaleas carrying sclerotia may be held over for forcing again the following year. Fungicides will protect the flower buds from infection if they are applied when the buds start to show color. See Ovulinia Petal Blight Disease Cycle, page 367.

Figure 1. *Ovulinia* petal blight.

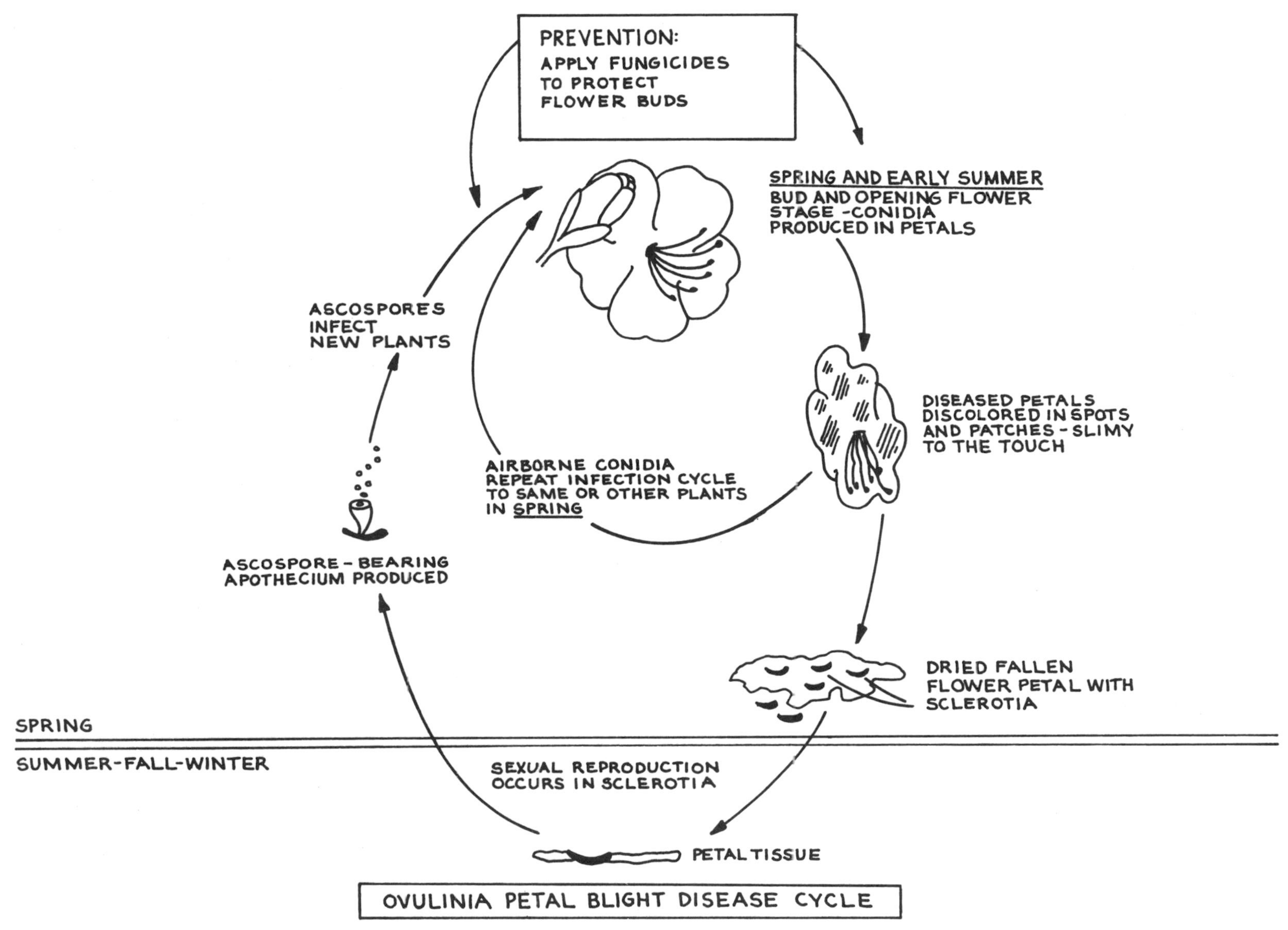
PREVENTION:
APPLY FUNGICIDES
TO PROTECT
FLOWER BUDS
SPRING AND EARLY SUMMER
BUD AND OPENING FLOWER
STAGE -CONIDIA
PRODUCED IN PETALS
DISEASED PETALS
DISCOLORED IN SPOTS
AND PATCHES - SLIMY
TO THE TOUCH
ASCOSPORES
INFECT
NEW PLANTS
AIRBORNE CONIDIA
REPEAT INFECTION CYCLE
TO SAME OR OTHER PLANTS
IN SPRING
ASCOSPORE - BEARING
APOTHECIUM PRODUCED
DRIED FALLEN
FLOWER PETAL WITH
SCLEROTIA
SPRING
SUMMER-FALL-WINTER
SEXUAL REPRODUCTION
OCCURS IN SCLEROTIA
PETAL TISSUE

OVULINIA PETAL BLIGHT DISEASE CYCLE

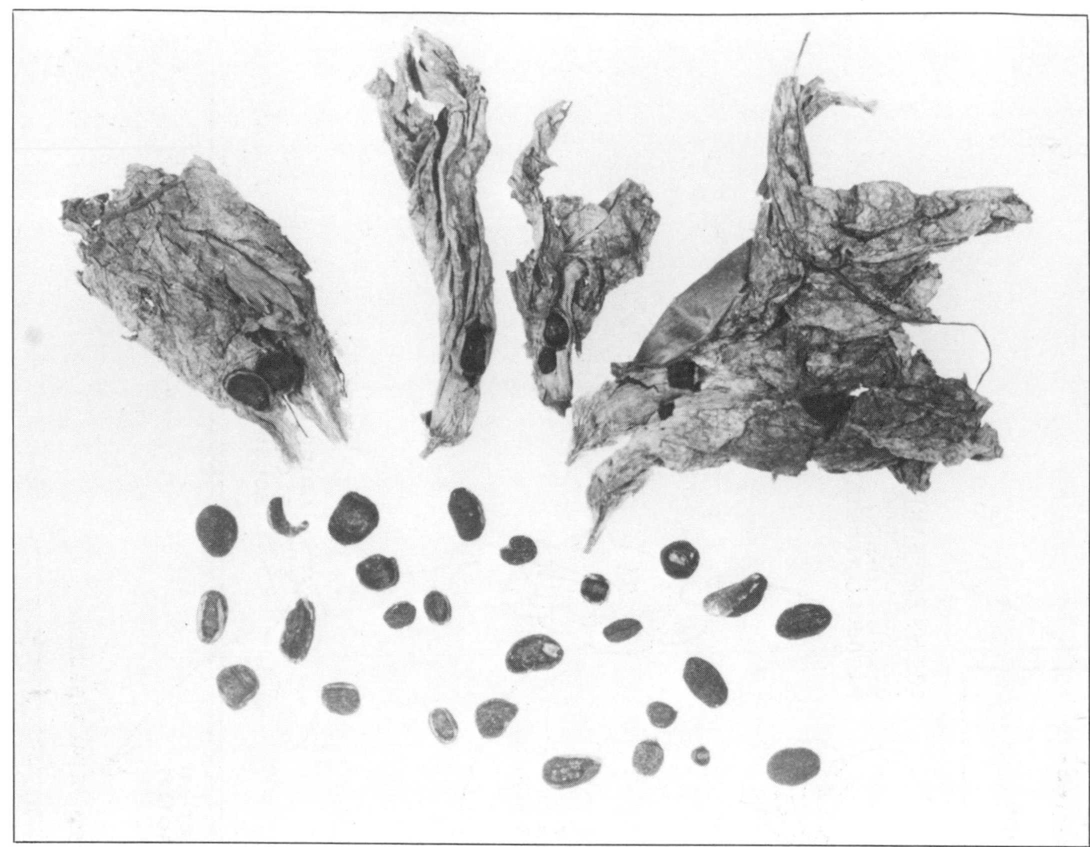

Figure 2. Ovulinia sclerotia

Figure 3. Powdery mildew

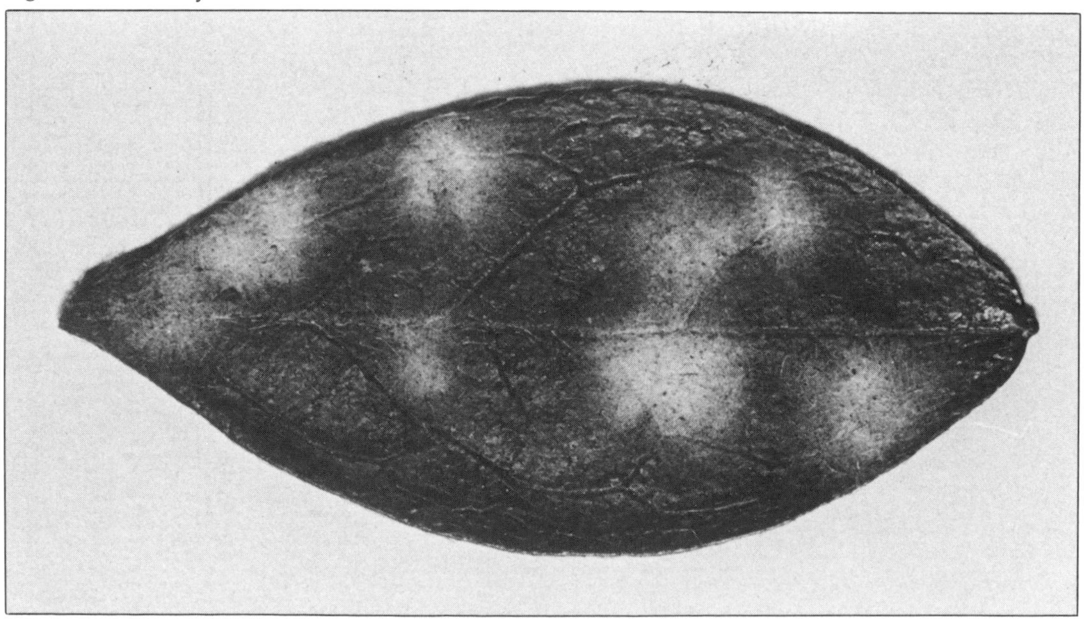

Powdery mildew

Occasionally, evergreen azaleas are infected with powdery mildew caused by either of the fungi *Erysiphe polygoni* or *Microsphaera penicillata;* but, more frequently, certain deciduous azalea cultivars are infected. Cloudy overcast weather conditions favor mildew development. Symptoms on young leaves first appear as white powdery spots, but, with continued favorable environment, the fungus covers the entire lower or upper leaf surface (Fig. 3).

Mildew spores in the white powder on infected leaves are carried by wind or mechanical action to new leaf tissue which in turn is infected. Powdery mildew fungi from azalea can infect rhododendron and vice versa. Mildew develops more rapidly at warm [75°F (25°C) day/60°F (15°C) night] than at cool temperatures [68°F (20°C) day/50°F (10°C) night] but damage to the plant is more severe at lower temperatures. Young foliage is more susceptible than the old. Plants grown in greenhouses under shade are more susceptible.

Newly registered systemic fungicides are frequently applied to protect against powdery mildew. But frequent use may result in fungus resistance. See Azalea Powdery Mildew Disease Cycle, page 366.

Leaf and flower gall

Leaf and flower buds infected by the fungus *Exobasidium vaccinii* result in galls. Under very humid conditions, the galls may become so abundant as to cause considerable damage to plants. Closely related species of the fungus cause the same type of gall on plants such as *Arbutus*, Blueberry, *Camellia, Ledum, Leucothoe,* and *Rhododendron*. The disease causes the leaves to become swollen, curled, and galled (Fig. 5). The fleshy galls are pale green to white or pink in color during the early stages of the disease but turn brown and hard as the season progresses. Infected flowers are fleshy, waxy, and swollen. The lower leaves are usually the most seriously damaged, but, under humid conditions and in shaded locations, galls may occur at the ends of the uppermost branches. Buds of evergreen azaleas are also frequently affected. The galls are covered with a whitish mold-like growth during periods of high humidity.

The occurrence and intensity of this disease are dependent upon favorable cool wet weather conditions and upon a source of the fungal spores. The spores produced in the whitish mold on the surface of the galls are blown and washed to leaf and flower buds causing infections.

Where only a few plants are involved, as in a home planting or a small greenhouse area, the disease is kept in check by picking the galls and destroying them.

Leaf rust

Rust, caused by the fungus *Pucciniastrum myrtilli (P. vaccinii)*, can be a serious disease of deciduous azaleas and particularly the North American *Rhododendron canadense, R. periclymenoides (nudiflorum), R. viscosum,* and *R. ponticum.* The fungus has a host in the hemlock, *Tsuga canadensis*.

The first symptom appears as small circular chlorotic spots on the upper leaf surface. The fungus produces abundant yellow to orange spores on the lower leaf surface. The disease usually appears in late summer and fall in the eastern United States. On highly susceptible deciduous azalea cultivars, lower leaf surfaces can be completely covered with spore masses and early fall defoliation can be severe.

Rust can be controlled by planting resistant cultivars and weekly applications of a fungicide beginning with the first appearance of the disease on susceptible cultivars (Table 2).

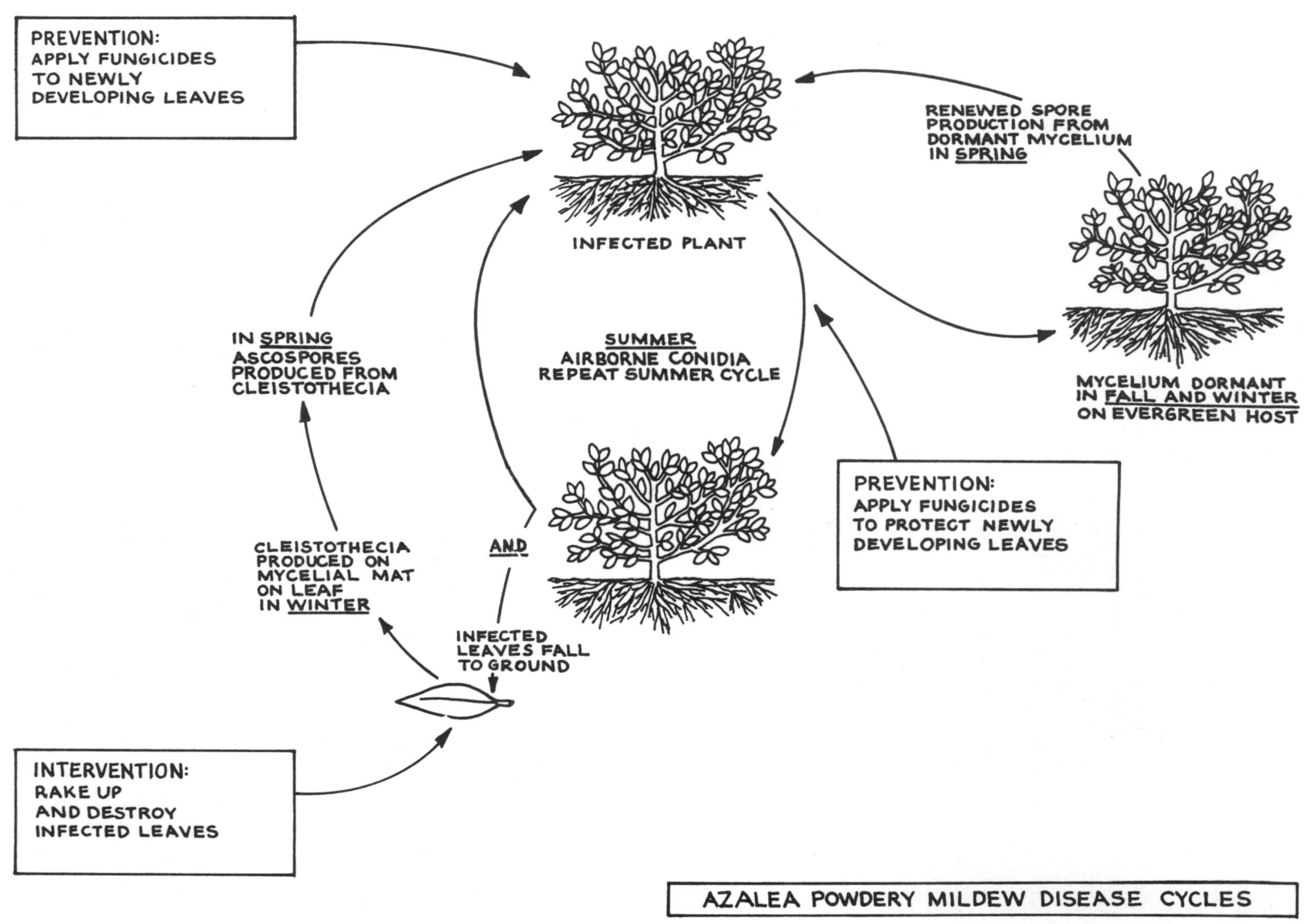
PREVENTION:
APPLY FUNGICIDES
TO NEWLY
DEVELOPING LEAVES
INFECTED PLANT
RENEWED SPORE
PRODUCTION FROM
DORMANT MYCELIUM
IN SPRING
MYCELIUM DORMANT
IN FALL AND WINTER
ON EVERGREEN HOST
IN SPRING
ASCOSPORES
PRODUCED FROM
CLEISTOTHECIA
SUMMER
AIRBORNE CONIDIA
REPEAT SUMMER CYCLE
PREVENTION:
APPLY FUNGICIDES
TO PROTECT NEWLY
DEVELOPING LEAVES
CLEISTOTHECIA
PRODUCED ON
MYCELIAL MAT
ON LEAF
IN WINTER
AND
INFECTED
LEAVES FALL
TO GROUND
INTERVENTION:
RAKE UP
AND DESTROY
INFECTED LEAVES
AZALEA POWDERY MILDEW DISEASE CYCLES

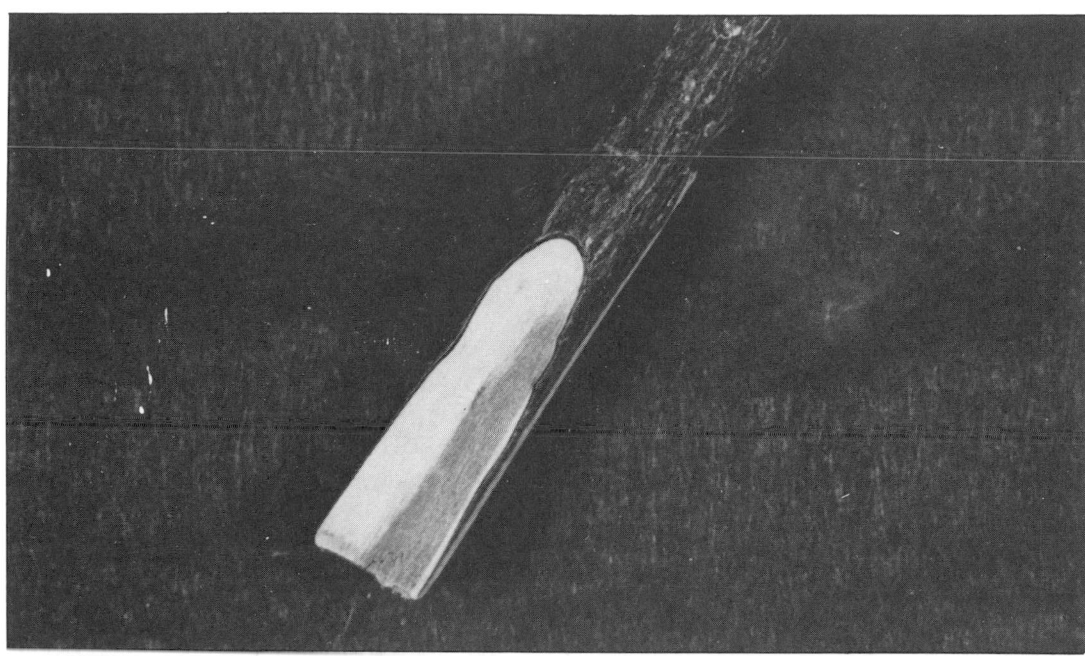

Figure 4. Phomopsis dieback

Figure 5. Leaf and flower gall

Phomopsis die-back

When stressed, as for example by drought, large azaleas in the landscape but also smaller nursery plants become susceptible to infection by the fungus *Phomopsis*. The primary symptoms of die-back or death of leaves and stems on portions of the top and a reddish-brown discoloration of the wood in diseased stems (Fig. 4). *Phomopsis* is chiefly a wound pathogen, and stem tissue is most often affected. Stem wounds up to eight days old are susceptible. After infection living stem tissue is progressively killed, and eventually entire branches die. Pruning wounds are probably the most important cause of infection. Ameliorating moisture stress in the summer and protection from stem splitting due to freezing in the winter are the best methods of control.

Diseases common to propagation

Water molds, root rots, and stem rots caused by pathogenic species of the fungi *Phytophthora, Pythium, Sclerotium,* and *Rhizoctonia* are serious diseases associated with propagation. They are not usually found on cuttings selected to be rooted, but are more commonly present in media rooting containers and propagating benches used a second time for propagation, and not thoroughly disinfected. Consequently, they may also be transmitted to cuttings in irrigation water pumped from ponds used to catch nursery run-off water.

Disease prevention during propagation requires a thoughtful combination of elementary regard for the use of sanitation and fungicides. Unfortunately, propagators usually disregard sound sanitary procedures relying instead on fungicides at rates and intervals frequently in excess of labels to compensate.

Containers, flats, and benches used in propagation should be new or disinfected between crops. Rooting media should be new or pasteurized with steam or chemical fumigants. Mixtures of fungicides or alternating fungicides are recommended by many plant pathologists to prevent infection by the broader spectrum of pathogens and also to avoid the development of fungus resistance to fungicides.

Web blight

Rhizoctonia solani is the causal pathogen of leaf and stem blighting of evergreen azaleas. Symptoms develop very rapidly, characterized by small necrotic lesions on leaves which are initially tan and irregular in outline. These lesions enlarge rapidly and become dark brown to almost black. Typically, the lesions advance along the margin inward toward the midrib until most of the leaf is necrotic by the time abscission occurs. Blighted leaves on container plants usually remain attached to the stems.

This disease most commonly occurs in humid, high temperature propagation and causes up to 100% defoliation. Plants grown in containers are especially susceptible when crowded together and irrigated by overhead sprinklers.

Cylindrocladium blight and root rot

The fungus *Cylindrocladium scoparium* attacks the leaves, stems, and roots of evergreen azaleas. Cuttings become infected during propagation when they are collected from stock plants infected with the fungus. Spots are small, dark brown, and regular in shape. The disease is most severe under humid condition. Although it often appears as a leaf spot, diseased plants may also show root rot and/or a sudden wilting of the top. The wilt phase of the disease is aggravated in plants subjected to over-watering, over-fertilization associated with salt buildup and other stress factors.

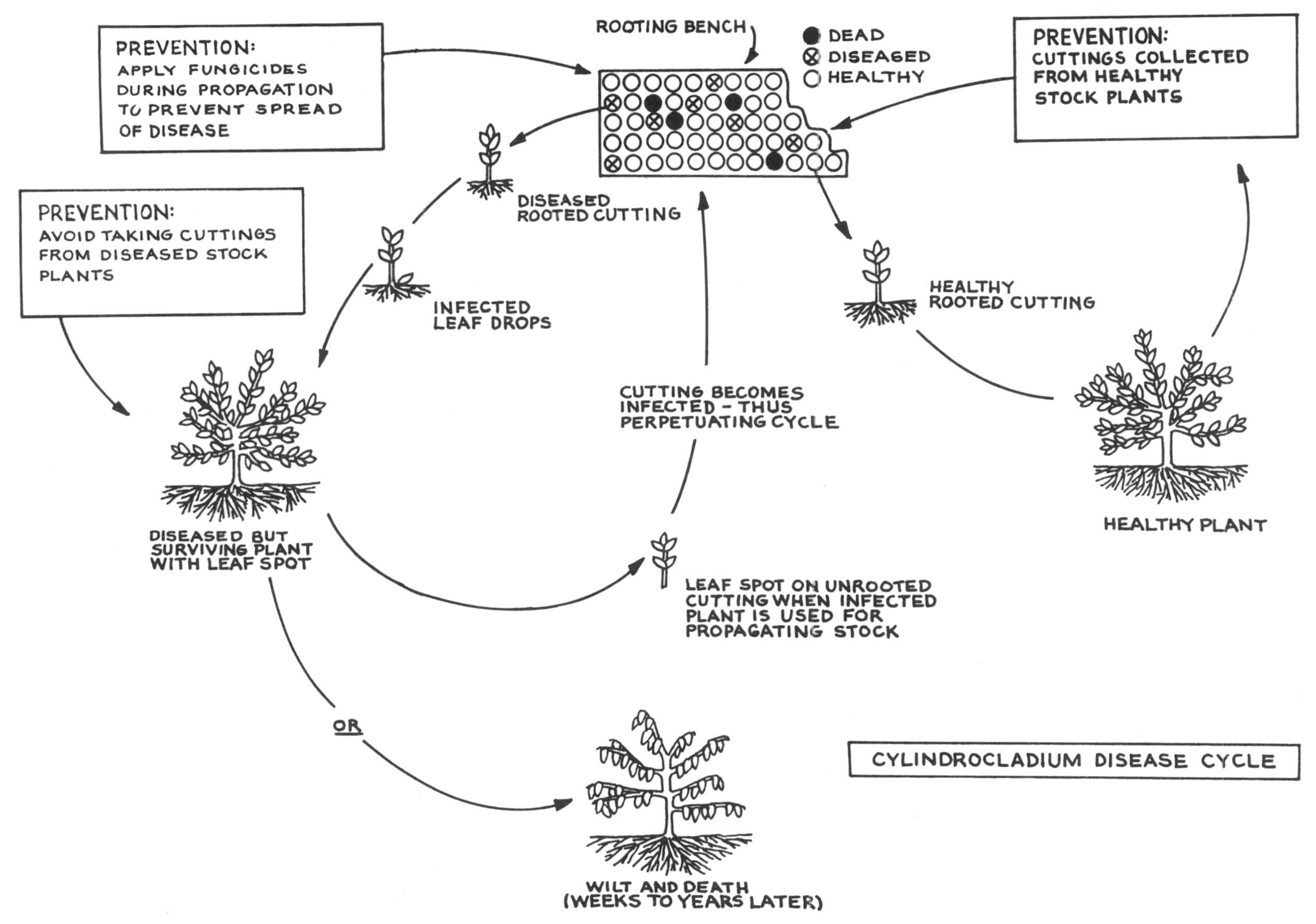
PREVENTION: APPLY FUNGICIDES DURING PROPAGATION TO PREVENT SPREAD OF DISEASE
ROOTING BENCH
DEAD
DISEASED
HEALTHY
PREVENTION: CUTTINGS COLLECTED FROM HEALTHY STOCK PLANTS
PREVENTION: AVOID TAKING CUTTINGS FROM DISEASED STOCK PLANTS
DISEASED ROOTED CUTTING
INFECTED LEAF DROPS
HEALTHY ROOTED CUTTING
CUTTING BECOMES INFECTED – THUS PERPETUATING CYCLE
HEALTHY PLANT
DISEASED BUT SURVIVING PLANT WITH LEAF SPOT
LEAF SPOT ON UNROOTED CUTTING WHEN INFECTED PLANT IS USED FOR PROPAGATING STOCK
OR
CYLINDROCLADIUM DISEASE CYCLE
WILT AND DEATH (WEEKS TO YEARS LATER)

Botrytis petal blight

Propagation undertaken in the spring when the temperatures are low and relative humidity high favors development of gray mold, caused by the fungus *Botrytis cinerea*, on cuttings. Diseased leaves first display water-soaked areas. Gray mold first appears on fully developed flowers and spreads to emerging flowers and leaves causing brown necrotic lesions. Azaleas maintained to protect them from cold injury in unheated structures under humid conditions are particularly susceptible to this disease.

Removing flowers from cuttings and disposal of dead petals and leaves prevent the production of *Botrytis* spores. If all else fails, apply fungicides to prevent infection. Plants wintered out-of-doors should be thoroughly dry before they are covered.

TABLE 1 Response of Azaleas to Inoculation with *Phytophthora cinnamomi**

Resistant	*Moderately Resistant*
'Alaska'	'Amagasa'
'Chimes'	'Barbara Gail'
'Corinne Murrah'	'California Sunset'
'Eikan'	'China Seas'
'Fakir'	'Copperman'
'Formosa'	'Delaware Valley White'
'Glacier'	'Dorothy Gish'
'Hampton Beauty'	'Flanders Field'
'Higasa'	'Gaiety'
'Merlin'	'Gloria'
'Morning Glow'	'Hexe'
'New White'	'Hinode Giri'
'Pink Gumpo'	'Kingfisher'
'Polar Seas'	'Lawsal' ('Pride of Summerville')
'Rachel Cunningham'	'Margaret Douglas'
'Redwings'	'Martha Hitchcock'
'Rose Greeley'	'Massasoit'
'Shinkigan'	'Pink Hiawatha'
'Sweetheart Supreme'	'Prince of Orange'
	'Rentschlers Rose'
	'Sensation'
	'Warbler'
	'White Christmas'
	'White Gumpo'
	'White Jade'

*Benson, D. M. and F. D. Cochran. 1980. Resistance of evergreen hybrid azaleas to root rot caused by *Phytophthora cinnamomi.* Plant Dis. 64:214–215.

TABLE 2 Deciduous azalea cultivar reactions to rust caused by *Pucciniastrum myrtilli**

	Susceptibility Level	
High	*Moderate*	*Low*
'Klondyke'	'Brazil'	'Gibraltar'
'Ilam Peachy Keen'	'Clarice	'Red Letter'
'Ilam Pink William'	'Exbury Crimson'	'Balzac'
'Ilam Primrose'	'Homebush'	
'Rufus'	'Oxydol'	
'Sunrise'	'Peach Sunset'	

*Bir, R. E., R. K. Jones, D. M. Benson. 1981. Susceptibility of selected azalea cultivars to azalea rust. Proceed of Southern Nurserymens Assoc. 26th Ann. Report, pp. 120–121.

Nematodes

Nematodes, particularly Stunt (*Tylenchorhynchus claytoni*), damage landscape and field grown azaleas. They seldom damage azaleas grown in containers with soilless media. Symptoms of nematode damage are reduced plant vigor and lack of dark green foliage color. Nematode problems can be avoided by using nematode-free potting media, selecting nematode-free planting sites, and preplanting soil fumigation. Granular nematicides may be useful in certain situations.

Salt Injury—excess soluble salt

Azaleas are very sensitive to excess soluble salt accumulation in the growing medium. Salt buildups are usually due to excessive use of fertilizer. The symptom of excess salt is burn on the margins of lower leaves, followed by leaf drop. A red coloration of the leaves of some varieties of evergreen azaleas is also a symptom. Some varieties like 'Hexe', 'Lentegroet', and 'Vervaeneana' are reported to be less sensitive than others.

It is important to water azaleas during periods of high temperature to leach salts from the root zone. Fertilizers should be deposited evenly over the medium surface to prevent saline pockets.

FUTURE MEANS OF DEALING WITH DISEASE

The history of chemical plant protection is a story of promising disease control chemicals which for various reasons, usually pathogen resistance, have had a limited useful existence. The newer systemic materials may also follow this pattern. The long-range answer is the breeding of disease and/or insect resistance into the host plant.

Azalea cultivars, for example, differ in resistance to *Phytophthora* root rot. When 73 cultivars in 10 hybrid groups of evergreen azaleas were tested, it was found that a few had high levels of resistance. Resistance ranged from completely susceptible in 'Jane Spaulding' to 'Formosa', 'Fakir', and 18 others of rather high resistance. Of the hybrid groups, the Indians generally had the highest levels of resistance among old recognized groups and the Kurumes the least. The more susceptible was a group developed at North Carolina State University. Some of the popular and commercially available cultivars, including 'Coral Bells', 'Hershey', 'Hino Crimson', 'Purple Splendour', 'Red', 'Rosebud', and 'Snow', were found to be on the low side (Table 1).

Biological control is another potential means of plant protection. *Mycorrhizae* (beneficial fungi growing in association with plant roots) may provide protection against root rot infection if practical methods of use are developed. In view of the inadequacy of genetic resistance and the uncertainty of the future of chemicals, biological control is being investigated in many research centers. Such control measures may be implemented in the future, either alone or in conjunction with other control measures in an integrated plant protection scheme.

FUNGICIDES AND FUMIGANTS

General consideration for chemical disease prevention

Fungicides are used to prevent or eliminate infection on leaves, stems, flowers, and roots. Fumigants are used to eradicate soil-borne fungi and nematodes before planting. Some of the newly registered fungicides are systemics and will provide protection for extended periods of time (weeks or months). Fungicides previously used have had short residual effect and must be reapplied every 7–10 days. It is important that fungicides are not applied in excess of registered rates or applied more frequently than label directions suggest because resistance may develop quickly or plant damage occur.

TABLE 3 **Fungicides and Fumigants**

DISEASES	Banrot (etridiazole + thiophanate methyl)	Bayleton (triadimefon)	Benlate (benomyl)	Chipco 26019 (iprodione)	Daconil 2787 (chlorothalonil)	Lesan (fenaminosulf)	Manzate 200 (mancozeb)	Ornalin (vinclozolin)	Subdue (metalaxyl)	Terrazole (etridiazole)	Truban (etridiazole)	Zineb (zineb)	Zyban (thiophanate methyl + maneb)	FUMIGANTS	Chloropicrin	Methyl bromide	Mylone (mit)	Vapam (mit)
Anthracnose							X											
Nematodes														X				
Botrytis Petal Blight			X	X	X			X					X					
Root Rots														X				
Pythium	X					X			X	X	X							
Rhizoctonia solani	X		X	X														
Cylindrocladium Root Rot	X		X										X					
Phytophthora Root Rot	X					X			X	X	X							
Powdery Mildew		X	X										X					
Leaf and Flower Gall													X					
Ovulinia Petal Blight		X	X		X								X					
Web Blight			X										X					
Leaf Rust		X					X											
Phomopsis Dieback																		

Landscape application

In geographical regions of moderate spring and summer temperatures and frequent rain showers, the petals of most azaleas in the spring and summer are very susceptible to infection by *Ovulinia* petal blight. Fungicides properly applied at the first sign of color in the flower buds will protect the flowers and prolong color. If the landscape site where azaleas are to be planted is known to be infested with *Phytophthora spp.*, soil fumigation with a safe-to-handle fumigant is suggested before planting.

Azaleas should be drenched with a systemic fungicide at the time of planting to insure that the roots will not become infected by *Phytophthora*.

Occasionally following stem injury the large branches of azaleas develop *Phomopsis* Dieback Disease. After all of the diseased stems and limbs have been removed by pruning to healthy wood, application of a fungicide will prevent further infection.

If leaf diseases like *Anthracnose*, Leaf Rust, Powdery Midew, Leaf and Flower Gall and Web Blight appear, apply a fungicide to prevent the spread of the disease to other plant parts. If there is a previous history of these diseases or the cultivars are known to be highly susceptible to disease, a fungicide spray program is suggested. Fungicides registered for the control of diseases of azaleas are listed in Table 3. Because the incidence of azalea diseases will vary in different regions, recommendations for specific disease prevention can be obtained by contacting governmental horticulture authorities or other knowledgeable persons.

Nursery application

Cuttings, containers, water for misting, and propagating media used in rooting of cuttings should be free of pathogens. Fungicides drenched or sprayed after the cuttings have rooted will prevent infection of newly formed roots, leaves, and stems. Some fungicides can inhibit rooting of cuttings. However, most fungicides can be safely applied after the cuttings are rooted. Systemic fungicides may be drenched in water or incorporated as granules into the growing media to give protection against water mold root rots.

SELECTED REFERENCES

Cox, R. S. 1969. *Cylindrocladium scoparium* on azalea in south Florida. Plant Dis. Reptr. 53:139.

Coyier, D. L. 1980. Disease Control on Rhododendron. *In* J. L. Luteyn & M. E. O'Brien (eds.), Contributions toward a Classification of Rhododendrons. New York Botanical Garden, New York. Pages 289–304.

Coyier D. L. and Martha K. Roane 1986. Compendium of Rhododendron and Azalea Diseases. The American Phytopathological Society, St. Paul, MN. 65 pages, illustrated.

Lambe, R. C., W. H. Wills and L. A. Bower. 1979. Control of *Phytophthora* root rot of azalea with a new systemic fungicide. SNA Nursery Research Journal 6:(2)1–7.

Linderman, R. G. 1972. Occurrence of azalea petal blight in Connecticut. Plant Dis. Reptr. 56:1101–1102.

Miller, Sharon B. and L. W. Baxter, Jr. 1970. Die back in azaleas caused by *Phomopsis* sp. Phytopathology 60:387–388.

Stathis, P. D. and A. G. Plakidas. 1958. Anthracnose of azaleas. Phytopathology 48:256–260.

Strider, D. L. 1976. Increased prevalence of powdery mildew of azalea and rhododendron in North Carolina. Plant Dis. Reptr. 60:149–151.

Wehlburg, C. and R. S. Cox. 1966. Rhizoctonia leaf blight of azalea. Plant Dis. Reptr. 50:354–355.

APPENDICES

Appendix A
AZALEA HYBRIDIZERS AND INTRODUCERS

Improved selections of Azalea spp. and better Azalea cultivars both in the past and in the future rests with growers and hybridizers world wide. A knowledge of the work of azalea hybridizers is central not only for an appreciation of the numerous plants now available but also to the work of future hybridizers and growers in bringing more variety and better plants. Horticultural books all too frequently ignore the work of numerous people who have made fine plant material available to us. This shortcoming in part is due to the difficulty and sometimes hopeless task presented to horticultural writers by the failure of growers and hybridizers to record and register the results of their work. It is hoped that in the future hybridizers and introducers of azaleas will register their plants with the American Rhododendron Society or the International Rhododendron Register.

In the list which follows I have tried to identify all those who in the past or present have introduced new azaleas. Enormous effort, often frustrated, has been spent to make the list complete. Any omissions are unintentional and I hope not too numerous.

Abbott, Frank L.; Bellows Falls, Ver., U.S.A.: hardy deciduous & evergreen hybrids.

Aichele, C. F.; Mount Holly, S.C., U.S.A.: Aichele's Hybrids.

Akashi, Kojiro; Kurume, Japan (deceased): early Kurume nurseryman in Japan.

Akehurst Nursery Inc.; Perry Hall, Md., U.S.A.: Kurume Hyb.; 'Tropic Sun'.

Alderfer, Dr. A.; Aust: Indian Hybrids.

Allen, Walter; Summerville, S.C., U.S.A. (deceased): Southern Indian & Kurume Hybrids.

Amann, I. Lee; Loblolly Bay, Bozman, Md., U.S.A.: Loblolly Bay Hybrids.

Amateis, A.; Fla., U.S.A.: deciduous azaleas.

Ambrosius, R.; Germany (deceased): Indian Hybrids.

Ames, J. S.; North Easton, Mass., U.S.A. (deceased): procured collection of Kurumes in 1916 from Japan.

Anderson, E. T.; Longview, Wa., U.S.A.: evergreen hybrids.

Anne, Countess of Rosse & Natl. Trust; England: deciduous species.

Aper, J.; Belg. (deceased): Indian Hybrids.

Arends, George; Wuppertal-Ronsdorf, W. Ger.: Arends & Aronense Hybrids.

Armstrong, Stewart; Silver Springs, Md., U.S.A. (deceased): Back Acre Hybrids.

Aromi, Dr. Eugene, Jr.; Mobile, Ala., U.S.A.: evergreen & deciduous azaleas.

Astrid, L.; Belg.: Indian Hybrids.

Badger, Robert; Tacoma, Wash., U.S.A.: Ilam Hybrids.

Bailey, Mr. and Mrs. H. L.; Brinnon, Wash., U.S.A.: Knapp Hill azaleas.

Baldsiefen, Warren; Bellvale, N Y., U.S.A.: deciduous N.A. sp. 'Alhambra'.

Banister, John;: missionary in Virg., U.S.A. in late 1600's and sent seed of *R. viscosum* to England.

Barnes, E.; UK; (deceased): Indian Hybrids.

Bastedo Nursery; Freehold, N.J., U.S.A.: 'Stately Orange'.

Ball, George J. Inc.; West Chicago, Ill., U.S.A.: introd. 'Dogwood' series.

Barber, Stewart; Sebastopol, Calif., U.S.A.: Sonoma Hybrids.

Bartram, John; Phila. Pa., U.S.A.: outstanding N.A. plantsman; collected plants for Peter Collinson of England in early & mid 1700's.

Bauman; N.J., U.S.A.: hybridizer of Roehr's Azaleas.

Beasley, George; Lavonia, Ga., U.S.A. (deceased): Beasley Hybrids.
Beasley, Jeff; Lavonia, Ga., U.S.A.: Beasley Hybrids.
Beattie, B. K.; U.S.A. (deceased): U.S.D.A. introd. Japanese Azaleas.
Bell, A.; New South Wales, Aust.: Indian Hybrids.
Beneschoen Gardens; Myrtle Creek, Or., U.S.A.: Occidentale & Knap Hill Hybrids.
Benesh, Otto; Or., U.S.A.: Knap Hill Hybrids.
Benson, D. M.; Raleigh, N.C., U.S.A.: Carla Hybrids.
Berckman, P. J.; Augusta, Ga., U.S.A. (deceased): introd. many azaleas to S.E. U.S.A.
Berna Park Nursery; Victoria, Aust.: Indian Hybrids.
Billerbeck, Wilford. J.; Waynesboro, Pa., U.S.A. (deceased): evergreen hybrids.
Bier, G. J. & Sons; Belg.: Indian Hybrids.
Bier, P. & Sons; Belg.: Indian Hybrids.
Binken, P. L.; Holland (deceased): Mollis Hybrids.
Blaauw, J.; Boskoop, Holland: evergreen hybrids.
Boer, J. A.; Boskoop, Holland.
Bobbink & Atkins; East Rutherford, N.J., U.S.A. (deceased): Rutherford Hybrids.
Boike, A. J.; Decatur, Ala., U.S.A.: evergreen hybrids.
Boling, Ed, Boling Farms Inc.; Longwood, Fla., U.S.A.: Southern Indian Hybrids.
Bonaminio, Dr. V. P.; Raleigh, N.C., U.S.A.: Carla Hybrids.
Bormann, W. & H. Schoemann; W. Ger.: Belgian Indian Hybrids.
Borme, L.; Okla., U.S.A.: Kaempferi Hybrids.
Boulter, V. J.; Australia.
Bovee, Robert; Portland, Or., U.S.A. (deceased): Bovee Hybrids.
Bovee Nursery, L. Sorenson & Geo. Watson; Portland, Or., U.S.A.: Bovee Hybrids.
Bowhan, Tom & Emma; Eugene, Or., U.S.A.: evergreen hybrids.
Brandt, Cora R.; Calif., U.S.A.
Brandt, Lester E.; Tacoma, Wash., U.S.A.: Azaleodendron 'Avita'.
Branigan, Jenni; Arlington, Virg., U.S.A.: 'D.J.O.' Satsuki Hybrid.
Bristow, O. R.; San Bernardino, Calif., U.S.A. (deceased).
Brockenbrough, Dr. E. C.; Bellevue, Wash., U.S.A.: Indian Hybrids.
Brooks, Leonard L.; Modesto, Calif., U.S.A.: Brooks Hybrids.
Brown, C. E.; UK.: Kurume Azaleas.
Bruns, John; W. Ger.: Knap Hill Azaleas.
Bullens & Van Gele; Belg.: Belgian Indian Hybrids.
Bunnell, J. O.; Olympia, Wash., U.S.A.
Bunshoten; Boskoop, Holland: Kaempferi Hybrids.
Buyle, H.; Belg. (deceased): Belgian Indian Hybrids.
Burbank Nursery, G. Taylor; New South Wales, Aust.: Indian Hybrids.
Byls; Belg. (deceased): early hybridizer.
Byrkit, Dr. M. F.; Williamsport, Md., U.S.A.: evergreen hybrids.
Cagle, James; Seagrove, N.C., U.S.A.: 'Snowball' Kurume Azalea.
California Camellia Garden; San Fernando, Calif., U.S.A.: 'Variegated Dogwood'.
Camellia Grove Nursery, P. Campbell; New South Wales, Aust.: Indian Hybrids.
Camellia Lodge Nursery; N. McMinn; Victoria, Aust.: Indian Hybrids.
Caperci, Jim & Betty; Seattle, Wash., U.S.A.: Knap Hill & Satsuki Hybrids.
Carlson, Bob and Jan; South Salem, N.Y., U.S.A.: Carlson deciduous & evergreen hybrids.
Carmichael; UK. (deceased): Amoena Hybrids.
Carter, Raymond I.; Aspers, Pa., U.S.A.: Knap Hill Hybrids.
Casadaban's Nursery; Calif., U.S.A.: 'Kings White' Belg. Indian Hybrid.
Casadevall, Joseph; Whippany, N.J., U.S.A.
Chapman, Dr. A. W.; Ala., U.S.A. (deceased): discovered *R. austrinum* before 1865.
Chappel, J. L. Durham, N.C., U.S.A.: Knap Hill Hybrids.
Cheeseman R. and Son; Victoria, Aust.: Indian Hybrids.
Childers, Mr. & Mrs. Arthur A.; Vida, Ore., U.S.A.: Knap Hill Hybrids.

Chisolm, Julian J., Garret Park, Md., U.S.A. (deceased): Chisolm-Merritt Hybrids.
Clausen, Dr.; Ore., U.S.A.: Occidentale Hybrids.
Close, A.; Beltsville, Md., U.S.A. (deceased): evergreen Azaleas.
Cnockaert, M.; Belg. : Belgian Indian Hybrids.
Coe, Dr. Fred W.; Ross, Calif., U.S.A.: N.A. deciduous hybrids.
Cockran, F. D.; Raleigh, N.C., U.S.A.: Carla Hybrids.
Colbert, F.; New South Wales, Aust.: Kurume Hybrids.
Cole, Dick J.; Yorktown, Va., U.S.A.: Marlbank Farm Hybrids.
Coleman, S. D.; Fort Gaines, Ga., U.S.A. (deceased).
Collumbien, J. Fr.; Belg. (deceased): Belgian Indian Hybrids.
Collumbien, M.; Belg.
Compton, Bishop H.; UK.: first to grow *R. viscosum* in England in 1680.
Conard-Pyle Nursery Co.; West Grove, Pa., U.S.A.: Knap Hill Hybrids.
Coolidge Rare Plant Garden; Pasadena, Calif., U.S.A.: Coolidge Hybrids.
Copeland, Vernon; Bronwood, Ga., U.S.A.: 'Sara Copeland' N.A. deciduous sp.
Coppenolle, V.; Belg. (deceased): Indian Hybrids.
Cornell, Phillip; Fort Bragg, Calif., U.S.A.: Cornell Hybrids.
Cottage Gardens; Eureka, Calif., U.S.A.: Belgian Indian Hybrids.
Cottage Gardens; Perry, Oh., U.S.A.: 'Silver Sword' sport.
Cox, Peter A.; Perth, Scotland: Peter Cox Hybrids.
Creech, Dr. John L.; Hendersonville, N.C., U.S.A.: plant explorer for U.S.D.A., introduced many species and cultivars from Japan & China.
Cross, Jim; Cutchogue, N.Y., U.S.A.: evergreen Azaleas.
Crown Estate Commissioners; Windsor Great Park, Eng.: Knap Hill Hybrids.
Cummins, Elizabeth; Marlboro, N.J., U.S.A.: Knap Hill Hybrids.
Curtis, William; Sherwood, Or., U.S.A.: deciduous & evergreen, 'Linda R'.
Cypress Gardens; Winterhaven, Fla., U.S.A.: intro. 'Duchess of Cypress'.
Davies, I.; Belg. (deceased): 'Daviesi' Ghent Hybrid.
Davies, Trevor C.; New Zealand: Ilam Hybrids.
Dawson, J. T.; Arnold Arb., Mass., U.S.A. (deceased): Arnold Hybrids.
De Block; Belg.: Belgian Indian Hybrids.
De Bats, A.H.O.W.; The Hague, Holland: Mollis Hybrids.
Deckert, Emile; Hampstead, Md., U.S.A.: Dechert Hybrids.
De Coninck, R.; Belg.: Belgian Indian Hybrids.
De Bruyne, R.; Belg.: Belgian Indian Hybrids.
Deerfield Nursery; N.J., U.S.A.: Deerfield Hybrids.
De Cock, E.; Belg. (deceased): Belgian Indian Hybrids.
De Jong W. & Sons; Boskoop, Holland: Mollis Hybrids.
De Kneef, J.; Belg. (deceased): Belgian Indian Hybrids.
Delmotte; Europe (deceased): Indian Hybrids.
De May, V. & V. Coppennolle; Belg. (deceased): Belgian Indian Hybrids.
De Meulemeester, M.; Belg.: Belgian Indian Hybrids.
De Meyer, R.; Belg.: Belgian Indian Hybrids.
Den Ouden H.; Holland (deceased): Mollis & Evergreens 'Addy Wery'.
De Paepe, M.; Belg.: Belgian Indian Hybrids.
Dermen, Dr. Haig; Md., U.S.A.: Tetraploid Evergreen Hybrids.
De Reuse Bros. Belg. (deceased): Belgian Indian Hybrids.
De Rothchild, Edmond; Exbury, Eng.: Exbury Hybrids.
De Rothchild, Lionel; Exbury, Eng. (deceased): Exbury & Exbury Evergreen Hybrids.
De Schrijyer, P.; Belg. (deceased): Belgian Indian Hybrids.
De Smet, G.; Belg.: Belgian Indian Hybrids.
De Waele; Belg.: Belgian Indian Hybrids.
De Wilde, Roland; Bridgeton, N.J., U.S.A.: Knap Hill & De Wilde Hybrids.
Dhaenens, M.; Belg.: Belgian Indian Hybrids.

Dierickx, M. C.; Belg.: Belgian Indian Hybrids.
Dodd, Tom Jr.; Semmes, Ala., U.S.A.: evergreen hybrids.
Dodd, Wm. (Bill); Mobile, Ala., U.S.A.: deciduous N.A. species.
Doleshy, F.; Edmond, Wa., U.S.A.: plant explorer in Japan.
Domoto Bros.; Hayward, Calif., U.S.A. (deceased): early introducers of Kurume Azaleas.
Domoto, Toichi; Hayward, Calif., U.S.A.: Kurume & Satsuki Hybrids.
Dosser, D.; Victoria, Aust.
Dosser, Miss Lillie; Centralia, Wa., U.S.A.: Knap Hill & Occidentale Hybrids.
Du Pont, H. F.; Winterthur, Dela., U.S.A. (deceased): introduced many Azaleas.
Early, S. C.; Atlanta, Ga., U.S.A.: Evergreen & deciduous Azaleas.
Edwards, B.; Victoria, Aust.: Indian Hybrids.
Eeckhaute; Belg. (deceased): Belgian Indian Hybrids.
Eggebrecht, F.; Ger. (deceased): Belgian Indian Hybrids.
Eichelser, John; Olympia, Wa., U.S.A.: Knap Hill Hybrids.
Elliot, James A.; Astoria, Or., U.S.A.: Knap Hill Hybrids.
Elmer, Augustus, Jr.; Pass Christian, Miss., U.S.A. (deceased): Chinquapin Hill Hybrids.
Endtz, L J. & Co.; Holland: Mollis & Kaempferi Hybrids.
Felix and Dijkhuis; Boskoop, Holland: evergreen & deciduous hybrids.
Fessler Nursery; Woodburn, Or., U.S.A.: 'Coral Dogwood' sport.
Findeisen, T.; Ger.: Belgian Indian Hybrids.
Fischer, C. W.; Linwood, N.J., U.S.A. (deceased): Linwood Hybrids.
Flandria; Belg.: Belgian Indian Hybrids.
Fleischmann, Carl; Ostfriedland, Ger. (deceased): Fleischmann & Diamant Hybrids.
Folding, Joseph; Woodcliff Lake, N.J., U.S.A. (deceased): Kaempferi Hybrid.
Forbes, Howard M.; Weston, Mass., U.S.A.: Intergroup Deciduous Hybrids.
Forrest, G.; Scotland (deceased): plant collector in early 1900's.
Forster, O.; Ger. (deceased); 'Hexe' Azalea.
Fortune, Robt.; UK. (deceased): early collector of plants from China,1850's.
Fowle, Herbert; Newberryport, Mass., U.S.A. (deceased): Kaempo Azalea.
Franck, O. & Sons; Belg.: Belgian Indian Hybrids.
Frazier, L. C.; Md., U.S.A.: Tetraploid Evergreen Hybrids.
Frisbie, Leonard F.; Tacoma, Wa., U.S.A. (deceased): Occidentale & Puyallup Valley Hybrids.
Fruitland Nur.; Augusta, Ga., U.S.A. (defunct): intro. many azaleas.
Gable, Joseph B.; Stewartstown, Pa., U.S.A. (deceased): Gable Hybrids.
Galle, Fred C.; Hamilton, Ga., U.S.A.: Galle Hybrids.
Garrett, Thomas; Anderson, S.C., U.S.A.: Garrett Rainbow Hybrids.
Gartrell, Robert D.; Black Mountain, N.C., U.S.A. (deceased): Robin Hill Hybrids.
George, A. F., Hydon Nursey; Surrey, Eng.: Kaempferi Hybrids.
Gijselinck, A.; Belg. Belgian Indian Hybrids.
Gillis, O.; Belg.; Belgian Indian Hybrids.
Giordano, Dr. John M.; Chickasaw, Ala., U.S.A.: deciduous azaleas.
Girard, Peter Sr.; Geneva, Oh., U.S.A. (deceased): Girard evergreen & deciduous hybrids.
Glaser, K.; W. Ger.: Belgian Indian Hybrids.
Gowen, J. R.; UK.: early hybridizer in 1820's, Ornatum Hybrids.
Greentree, M. E. (Jack); New South Wales, Aust.: Indian & Kurume Azalea.
Greer, Harold; Eugene, Or., U.S.A.: evergreen & deciduous hybrids.
Griswold, Wm. (Bill); Kirkland, Wa., U.S.A.: evergreen hybrids.
Griswold, Garda; Kirkland, Wa., U.S.A.: evergreen hybrids.
Grothaus, Louis; Lake Oswego, Or., U.S.A.: evergreen hybrids.
Guttormsen, Wm. L.; Canby, Or., U.S.A.: Greenwood Hybrids.
Hacanson, Ray; Puyallup, Wa., U.S.A.: Ilam Hybrids.
Hachmann, Hans; W. Ger.: Kaempferi & Kurume Hybrids.
Haerens, Aug; Belg. (deceased): Belgian Indian Hybrids.
Haerens, W.; Belg.: Belgian Indian Hybrids.

Hage, W. C. & Co.; Boskoop, Holland: Kurume Hybrids.
Hager, Don; Spotsylvania, Va., U.S.A.: Hager Hybrids.
Hahn, C.; Wheaton, Md., U.S.A.: introduced large collection of Satsuki cultivars from Japan to Brookside Gardens, U.S.A.
Hahn, Louis & Sons; Pittsburgh, Pa., U.S.A.: Belgian & Kurume Hybrids.
Handcock, Bruce; Social Circle, Ga., U.S.A.: evergreen hybrids.
Hardijzer, W.; Boskoop, Holland: deciduous, evergreen & azaleodendrons.
Harig, H.; W. Ger.: Belgian Indian Hybrids.
Harmsen, G.; E. Ger.: Belgian Indian Hybrid.
Harrington, R.; unknown: 'Highlander' azalea.
Harris, James; Lawrenceville, Ga., U.S.A.: Harris Hybrids.
Hatfield, T. D.; (deceased): Mollis Hybrids.
Haworth-Booth, Michael; Surrey, Eng.: evergreen hybrids.
Hazelwood Nursery; New South Wales, Aust.: Indian Hybrids.
Henny, Rudolph; Brooks, Or., U.S.A. (deceased): Knap Hill Hybrids.
Henny & Wennekamp, Inc.; Brooks, Or., U.S.A.: Knap Hill Hybrids.
Henry, J.; Canada: Knap Hill Hybrids.
Herbert, Charles; Phoenixville, Pa., U.S.A. (deceased): evergreen hybrids.
Hermann, E.; Ger. (deceased): Belgian Indian Hybrids.
Hershey, Everett; Gap, Pa., U.S.A.: Hershey Azaleas.
Hesse; (deceased): early hybridizer of Ghents.
Heursel, Jozef; Belg.: Research Scientist for Institute of Ornamental Plant Growing.
Hicklin, C.; Stone Mt., Ga., U.S.A.: evergreen hybrids.
Hiers, C. J.; Auburn, Al., U.S.A.
Hill, Mrs. Julian (Polly); Wilmington, Del., U.S.A.: North Tisbury & deciduous species.
Hill, Helen, Hill Nursery; Arlington, Va., U.S.A.: evergreen hybrids.
Hillier & Sons Nursery; Winchester, Eng.: Knap Hills, introd. many azaleas.
Hindla, L.; Bohemia, N.Y., U.S.A.: Kaempferi Hybrid, 'Pink Radiance'.
Hohman, Henry J.; Kingsville, Md., U.S.A. (deceased): evergreen hybrids.
Hollowell, E. A.; Port Republic, Md., U.S.A. (deceased): "Dorsett" Kaempferi.
Holly, V. B.; Victoria, Aust.: Knap Hill Hybrids.
Holmes Nursery; Tampa, Fla., U.S.A.: Holmes Hybrids.
Holmsomback, Olin; Chickamauga, Ga., U.S.A.: Cherokee Hybrids.
Hooftman, Hugo T.; Boskoop, Holland: 'Ageeth' Kaempferi Hybrids.
Horticok, E. & S.; Belg.: Belgian Indian Hybrids.
H. R. I. O., V. S., Horticultural Research Institute of Ontario, Vineland Station; Ontario, Canada: Knap Hill Hybrids.
Huang; Shanghai, China: Huang Azaleas.
Hudson, Earl D.; Hemet, Calif., U.S.A. (deceased): Belgian Indian Hybrids.
Hume, H.: Fla., U.S.A. (deceased): author, 'George Lindley Taber'.
Huntingdale Nursery, Eric Crawford; Victoria, Aust.: Indian Hybrids.
Hyatt, Donald W.; McLean, Va., U.S.A.: Knap Hill Hybrids.
Hyde, W. G.; Eng.: Indian Hybrids.
Hydon Nursery Ltd.; Surrey, Eng.: Kaempferi Hybrids.
Ingram, Capt. Collingwood; Kent, Eng.: 'General Wavell' Azalea.
I. O. P. G., Institute for Ornamental Plant Growing; Melle, Belg.: Plant Research Station.
I. W. O. N. L. Institute for Scientific Research in Industry & Agriculture; Belg.
Jack, J. H.; Arnold Arboretum, Mass., U.S.A.: Plant collector for Arnold around 1905.
Jacobs, Donald,, Atlanta, Ga., U.S.A.: N.A. deciduous species.
Ivery; Eng. (deceased): Indian Hybrids.
James, Ray; Hawthorne, Or., U.S.A.: Kurume Hybrid, 'Sharon Kathleen'.
Janouch, B.; Czechoslovakia: evergreen hybrids.
Jelinch, Prof.; Pruhonice, Czech.: Czechoslovakian Hybrids.
Jelinek, J.; Czechoslovakia: evergreen hybrids.

Johnson, Albert; Chanhassen, Minn., U.S.A. (deceased).
Johnson, M.; Conn., U.S.A.
Jones, Germaine; Longwood, Fla., U.S.A.: 'Little John' Southern Indian.
Kaus: evergreen hybrids.
Kavka, B.; Czechoslovakia: evergreen & deciduous hybrids.
Kehr, August E.; Hendersonville, N.C., U.S.A.: August Kehr Hybrids.
Kerrigan, Howard; Hayward, Calif., U.S.A.: Kerrigan Hybrids.
Kern, Walter; Woodlyn, Pa., U.S.A.: Knap Hill Hybrids.
Kerckvoorde, A.; Belg.: Belgian Indian Hybrids.
Kersbergen, G.; (deceased): Mollis Hybrids.
Keshishian, Dr. J. M.; Wash., D.C., U.S.A.: Mollis Hybrids.
Kessen, W., Jr. & Sons; Holland: Belgian Indian Hybrids.
King, Edward; Alexander, Va., U.S.A. (deceased): Knap Hill Hybrids.
Kinghorn; (deceased): Indian Hybrids.
Kint, M. J. Bros.; Belg.: Belgian Indian Hybrids.
Kirk, E.; New South Wales, Aust.
Kinsey Gardens; Knoxville, Tn., U.S.A.: 'Kinsey White' & other evergreen hybrids.
Klupenger, Joe; Aurora, Or., U.S.A.: 'Satellite' evergreen hybrids.
Knap Hill Nursery Company; Eng.: Knap Hill Hybrids.
Knight & Perry; Eng. (deceased): Indian Hybrids.
Knight, C.; New South Wales, Aust.: Knap Hill Hybrids.
Knight, J. P.; Eng. (deceased): Indian Hybrids.
Knuttel, Adrian; East Windsor, Conn., U.S.A.: Knap Hill Hybrids.
Knuttel, Anna J.; East Windsor Conn., U.S.A.: Knap Hill & Occidentale Hybrids.
Koppeschaar, W. F.; Boskoop, Holland: Kurume Hybrids.
Korn, Robert C.; Renton, Wa., U.S.A.: Knap Hill Hybrids.
Koster, M.; Belg. (deceased): Mollis Hybrids.
Kraus, E. J.; Corvallis, Or., U.S.A. (deceased).
Kromhout & Co.; Boskoop, Holland: Mollis Hybrids.
Kunishige M., Tamura, T., Morishita, M., and Yamaguchi, S.; Kurume, Japan: 'Benifusha' Azalea.
Kuwana, Takeo; Kurume, Japan.
Kuyck, J.; Belg. (deceased): Belgian Indian Hybrids.
Kuyk, K. J.; (deceased).
La Bar Nursery; Va., U.S.A.: 'White Find' deciduous azalea.
Laessle, Albert; Gainesville, Fla., U.S.A. (deceased): evergreen hybrids.
Lancaster, Ben; Camas, Wa., U.S.A. (deceased): Indian Hybrids.
Landauer, Mr. & Mrs. H.; Forest Grove, Or., U.S.A.: Intergroup Dec. Hybrids.
Langdon, G.; Aust.: Indian & Kurume Hybrids.
Larson, H.L.; Tacoma, Wa., U.S.A.: evergreen hybrids.
Leach, Dr. David G.; North Madison, Oh., U.S.A.: Leach Hybrids & others.
Lebank, O.F.; Austria (deceased): Amoena hybrids.
Lehr & Versuchsanstalt; W. Ger.: Belgian Indian Hybrids.
Lelliott, T.; Boronia, Victoria, Aust.: Kurume Hybrids.
Lewis, Dr. David; Colts Neck, N.J., U.S.A.: N.A. deciduous species.
Lewis, Donald; Whittier, Calif., U.S.A. (deceased): Lewis Hybrids.
Link, John F., Jr.: Calif., U.S.A.: Belgian Indian Hybrids.
Loder, Sir Giles; Leonardslee, Eng.: Knap Hill Hybrids.
Longwood Gardens; Kennet Square, Pa., U.S.A.: evergreen hybrids.
Lossy, J.; Belg. (deceased): Belgian Indian Hybrids.
Lovegrove, F.; Aust.: Indian Hybrids.
Luley, H.: Ger.: Belgian Indian Hybrids.
Maarse, Fr. A.; Holland: Belgian Indian Hybrids.
Mabire; France (deceased): Belgian Indian Hybrids.
Mackay, M.; New South Wales, Austr.: evergreen hybrids.

Maenhout, J.; Belg.: Belgian Indian Hybrids.
Magruder, Dr. Roy; Silver Springs, Md., U.S.A. (deceased): Knap Hill Hybrids & worked on Glenn Dale Hybrids.
Mangles, H. (deceased): Azaleodendron.
March, S.; Wash., D.C., U.S.A.: plant explorations for National Arboretum.
Maries, C., Eng. (deceased): plant collector for Veitch Nur. in late 1800's.
Marsh, K. M.; Aust.: Kurume Hybrids.
Magnolia Gardens; Charleston, S.C., U.S.A.: Southern Indian Hybrids.
Mardner, S.; Ger. (deceased): Belgian Indian Hybrids.
Margo, H.; (deceased): Indian Hybrids.
Marog; (deceased): Indian Hybrids.
Martin, Dr. A. C.; Los Gatos, Calif., U.S.A.
Martin, Joe; Lake Co., Oh., U.S.A. (deceased): Kurume Hybrids.
Marty, J. A.; Olmda, Victoria, Aust.: Knap Hill Hybrids.
Matous, J.; Czechoslovakia: evergreen hybrids.
Mauritsen, S.; Kent, Wa., U.S.A.: Maritsen hybrids.
Mayer, R.; W. Ger.: Belgian Indian Hybrids.
Mayo, R. P.; Augusta, Ga., U.S.A. (deceased): Mayo Hybrids.
Maximowicz, C. J.; Russia (deceased): introduced species to Europe in 1879.
McConnell, F. T.; Mobile, Ala., U.S.A.: 'Millie Mac' deciduous selection.
McDonald, Mrs. V. R.; Seattle, Wa., U.S.A.: Knap Hill Hybrids.
McDonald, Dr. Sandra; Hampton, Va., U.S.A.: McDonald & Can Can Chorus Hybrids.
McQuiness, P. J.; West Haven, Conn., U.S.A.: Knap Hill Hybrids.
Mehlquist, Dr. Gustav A.L.; Storrs, Conn, U.S.A.: Knap Hill Hybrids.
Melselaar; Holland: Mollis Hybrids.
Meridith, W. V.; Winter Park, Fla., U.S.A.: evergreen hybrids.
Merritt, Dr. E.; Chevy Chase, Md., U.S.A.: Chisolm-Merritt Hybrids.
Mestdagh,A.; Belg.: Belgian Indian Hybrids.
Metselaar, A. C. H.; Boskoop, Holland: Mollis & Knap Hill Hybrids.
Meyer, F. G.; Wash., D.C., U.S.A.: plant taxonomist for National Arboretum, introduced cultivars from Japan.
Mezitt, Edmund V.; Hopkinton, Ma., U.S.A. (deceased): Weston Hybrids.
Milfeld, Raymond M.; Monrovia, Calif., U.S.A.: Evergreen Azaleas.
Mitchell, Luther; Oxford, Ala., U.S.A.: 'Southern Belle' Azalea.
Mittendorf, Gerhard; Magdeburg, Ger.: 'Buzi' Kaempferi Hybrid.
Monrovia Nursery; Azusa, Calif., U.S.A.: Monrovia Azaleas.
Moreux, L.; Belg.: Belgian Indian Hybrids.
Morrison, Ben Y.; Pass Christian, Miss., U.S.A. (deceased): Glenn Dale & Back Acres Hybrids, and introducer of Satsuki Hybrids and others to U.S.A.
Mortier, P.; Ghent, Belg.: produced Mortier Hybrids, early 1800's forerunner of Ghent Hybrids.
Moser & Fils; (deceased): early hybridizers of Ghents.
Mossholder, J. Lynn; Costa Mesa, Calif., U.S.A.: Mossholder-Bristow Hybrids.
Mossman, Dr. Frank D.; Vancover, Wa., U.S.A.: Occidentale Azaleas.
Motzkau, Henry; Seattle, Wa., U.S.A.: Whitewater Hybrids.
Muller, F. J.; Ger.: Belgian Indian Hybrids.
Murrah, Corinne; Memphis, Tn., U.S.A. (deceased): Back Acres Hybrids.
Myers, Walter A.; Ripon, Calif., U.S.A.: Belgian Indian Hybrids.
Nagel, W.; Germany: 'Anne Frank' evergreen hybrid.
Neal, O. M.; W. Va., U.S.A.: 'Appalachia' Intergroup Deciduous Hybrid.
Nelly Kelly Nursery; Victoria, Aust.: Indian Hybrids.
Nelson, Nels; Millsboro, Del., U.S.A.: evergreen hybrids.
Nichols, Ian; Victoria, Aust.: Indian Hybrids.
Nosal, Mathew; Calverton, N.Y., U.S.A.: Witches Broom of evergreen hybrids.
Nuccio, Julius and Joe; Altadena, Calif., U.S.A.: Nuccio Hybrids.

Ogawa, Mrs. Tsuriu; Danville, Calif., U.S.A.: 'Yoshimi' Satsuki Hybrid.
Oliver, J.; Fairfield, Conn., U.S.A. (deceased): 'Ruth May' evergreen hybrid.
Orme, Mrs. L. B.; Oklahoma City, Okla., U.S.A.: 'Shanna Smart' evergreen hybrid.
Ormond Plant Farm; Victoria, Aust.: Indian Hybrids.
Ostbo, Endre; Bellevue, Wa., U.S.A. (deceased): Knap Hills & Azaleodendron.
Pallas, P. S.; Berlin, Ger.: sent seed of *R. luteum* to England in 1793.
Paradise Garden Nursery; Victoria, Aust.: Indian Hybrids.
Parks, J.; Dover, N.H., U.S.A.: 'Concord Cemetery' azalea.
Partain, Lloyd; Pottstown, Pa., U.S.A.: Knap Hill & evergreen hybrids.
Pedersen, A. & A.; Wayne, N.J., U.S.A.: 'Karens' Evergreen Hybrid.
Pellett, Dr. Harold; Chanhassen, Mn., U.S.A.: Intergroup Dec. Hybrids.
Pender, David J.; Garner, N.C., U.S.A.: Pender Hybrids.
Pennington, Ralph W.; Covington, Ga., U.S.A. (deceased): Pennington Hybrids.
Pericat, Alphonse; Collingdale, Pa., U.S.A. (deceased): Pericat Hybrids.
Peters, H. M.; Boskoop, Holland.
Peters, Robert K.; Benderville, Pa., U.S.A.: Knap Hill & Kaempferi Hybrids.
Peterson, N. C. & D. Stabler; Fla., U.S.A.: 'Duchess of Cypress' Southern Indian Hybrid.
Petry, Mrs. Frank; Prichard, Ala., U.S.A. (deceased): Southern Indian Hybrids.
Phillips, C. O.; Oakland, Ca., U.S.A.: Belgian Indian Hybrids.
Phipps, Howard; Tacoma, Wa., U.S.A.: Knap Hill Hybrids.
Pinney, Mrs. Ann; South Canterbury, New Zealand: Ilam Hybrids.
Plate & Draht Nur.; W. Ger.: Belgian Indian Hybrids.
Poelman & Sons; Belg.: Belgian Indian Hybrids.
Potts J.; Pa., U.S.A.: 'Potts Silver Pink'.
Pratt, M. C.; Pulborough, Eng.: Occidentale & Knap Hill Hybrids.
Pride, Orlando S. (Lanny); Butler, Pa., U.S.A. (deceased): Pride Hybrids.
Pryor, Robert L.; Beltsville, Md., U.S.A.: Beltsville Dwarfs and others.
Raustein, A. A.; Holbrook, L.I., N.Y., U.S.A.: evergreen hybrids.
Redder, David; Clarksville, Md., U.S.A.
Rees, Fred; Saluda, N.C., U.S.A.: Robin Hill Hybrids.
Reid, Albert G.; Linwood, N.J., U.S.A. (deceased): Linwood Hybrids.
Richter, L. R.; Ger. (deceased): Belgian Indian Hybrids.
Ring, George W.; Fairfax, Va., U.S.A.: George Ring Series.
Roberts Al. N.; Corvallis, Or., U.S.A.: 'Dogwood' Azalea.
Robbins, Evert; Conn., U.S.A. (deceased): 'Robbins Pink'.
Rodrigue, C.; Belg.
Robertson, Ola; Chipley, Fla., U.S.A.: N.A. deciduous species.
Roehrs Company; Rutherford, N.J., U.S.A.: Roehr's Kaempferi Hybrids.
Rokujo, Dr. Tsuneshige; Tokyo, Japan: Azalea hybridizer and collector.
Rose, J.; Ger. (deceased): Belgian Indian Hybrids.
Royal Horticultural Society; Wisley, Eng.: deciduous & evergreen hybrids.
R. S. A. N. C., Research Station for Arboreous Crops; Boskoop, Holland.
Sakamoto, M.; Kurume, Japan (deceased): originator of Kurume Hybrids.
Sander & Sons; Belg.: Belgian Hybrids.
Sander, F.; Belg. (deceased).
Sanders, Charles; Brookline, Mass., U.S.A. (deceased): Sander & Forster Azaleas.
Sand, Jack A.; Wa., U.S.A.: Knap Hill Hybrids.
Sand Point Greenhouses; Fort Wayne, Ind., U.S.A.: Indian Hybrids.
Sanko, J.: Or., U.S.A.: Azaleodendron.
Sargent, Prof. C. S.; Arnold Arboretum, Boston Mass., U.S.A.: introduced *R. kaempferi* in 1892, and other species to U.S.A. and England.
Savill, Sir Eric; Eng.: Knap Hill Hybrids.
Sawada, K.; Mobile, Ala., U.S.A. (deceased): evergreen hybrids, 'Hino Supreme' and 'Gloria'.
Scarbeck, J.; Oakdale, N.Y., U.S.A.: evergreen hybrids.

Scheclause, L.; (deceased): early hybridizer.
Schepens, de Basts; Belg.: Belgian Indian Hybrids.
Schepens, M.; Belg.: Belgian Indian Hybrids.
Schepens, M. G.; Clinton, Conn., U.S.A. (deceased): Kurume Hybrids.
Schepens, Mrs. M. G.; Clinton, Conn., U.S.A.: Kurume Hybrids.
Scherf, E. & W.; Ger.: Belgian Indian Hybrids.
Schoneman, Ralph; Or., U.S.A.: Knap Hill Hybrids.
Schroeder, S.; Evansville, Ind., U.S.A.: Schroeder Hybrids.
Schulz, C.; Ger. (deceased): Belgian Indian Hybrids.
Schumacher, U.; Germany: Kurume & Kaempferi Hybrids.
Scott, L.: College Park, Md., U.S.A.: evergreen hybrids.
Segers, P.; Belg.: Belgian Indian Hybrids.
Seidel, H.; Ger. (deceased): Belgian Indian Hybrids.
Seidel, R.; Ger. (deceased): Belgian Indian Hybrids.
Seiferle, Mrs. Edward; Atlanta, Ga., U.S.A.: 'Chattahoochee' N.A. dec. species.
Serbin, Dr. F. A.; Hartford, Conn., U.S.A.: Kaempferi Hybrids.
Sestak, J.: Czechoslovakia: evergreen hybrids.
Seyschab; W. Ger.: Belgian Indian Hybrids.
Schaeme, M.; Ger.: Belgian Indian Hybrids.
Shammarello, A. M. (Tony); Euclid, Oh., U.S.A. (deceased): Shammarello Hybrids.
Shanks, J. and C. Link: Univ. Maryland, College Park, Md., U.S.A.: evergreen hybrids.
Sherringham Nursery, L. McDonald; New South Wales, Aust.: Indian Hybrids.
Singletary, H. M.; Raleigh, N.C., U.S.A.: Carla Hybrids.
Skinner, Henry; Hendersonville, N.C., U.S.A. (deceased): 'Cornell Pink' & N.A. species.
Slocock, W. C.; Surrey, Eng.: Mollis, evergreen & Slocock Knap Hill Hybrids.
Slonecker, Howard; Milwaukee, Or., U.S.A.: Occidentale & Slonecker Hybrids.
Smith; Engl. (deceased): Indian Hybrids & Azaleodendrons.
Smith, Britt; Kent, Wa., U.S.A.; Occidentale selections.
Smith, Spencer R., Post Gardens Inc.; Calif., U.S.A.: Belgian Indian Hybrids.
Smith W. David; (deceased): Spring Grove, Pa., U.S.A.: Eden Hybrids.
Sonneville, J.; Belg.: Belgian Indian Hybrids.
Sorenson, S. E.; Clayburn, British Columbia, Canada: Knap Hill Hybrids.
Sorenson & Watson (Bovee Nursery); Portland, Or., U.S.A.: Bovee Knap Hill Hybrids.
Spartanburg Nursery; Spartanburg, S.C., U.S.A.
Sparks R.; Victoria, Aust.: Indian Hybrids.
Spaargaren, W.J. & Sons; Boskoop, Holland: Occidentale Hybrids.
Spek, Jan; Holland: Mollis Hybrids.
Srpkova, M.; Czechoslovakia: evergreen hybrids.
Stabler, Dave; Winterhaven, Fla., U.S.A.: Evergreen Hybrids 'Cypress Gardens'.
Stadherr, Dr. Richard; Baton Rouge, La., U.S.A.: Carla Hybrids.
Stahnke, O.; W. Ger.: Belgian Indian Hybrids.
Standish & Noble; Eng. (deceased): early hybridizers of Ghents.
Stanton, Ernest H.; Grosse Isl.e, Mi., U.S.A.: Stanton Hybrids.
Stead, Edgar; Christchurch, New Zealand (deceased): Ilam Hybrids.
Stevenson, J. B.; Eng. (deceased): introduced Kurumes from Japan and hybridized evergreen hybrids.
Stewart, D.; Dorset, Eng. (deceased): Ferndown Hybrids.
Stewart, Dr. Robert; Maryland, U.S.A.: Tetraploid Evergreen Hybrids.
Steyaert, A.; Belg. (deceased): Belgian Indian Hybrids.
Stiborek, Z.; Czechoslovakia: evergreen hybrids.
Stokes, Warren E.; Butler, Pa., U.S.A.: Knap Hill Hybrids.
Straver, J. M.; Boskoop, Holland (deceased): Mollis Hybrids.
Streck, W.; W. Ger.: Belgian Indian Hybrids.
Sunningdale Nur.; Eng.: imported many azaleas.

Talley, Robert; Wachapreague, Va., U.S.A. (deceased): 'Salmon Bells' Kurume Hybrid.
Taylor, G.; Springfield, Va., U.S.A.: 'Marj T' hybrid.
Teese, A.; Victoria, Aust.: Knap Hill Hybrids.
Theiss Azalea Garden; Canyonville, Or., U.S.A.: Knap Hill Hybrids.
Thompson, James G.; Mobile, Ala., U.S.A. (deceased): Southern Indian Hybrids.
Thompson, Ross C.; Salinas, Calif., U.S.A.: Kurume Hybrids.
Ticknor, Dr. Robert L.; Canby, Or., U.S.A.: Knap Hill Hybrids.
Tingle Nursery Company; Pittsville, Md., U.S.A.: introduced numerous azaleas.
Tollenaere, C.; Belg.: Belgian Indian Hybrids.
Tolstead, W. L.; Elkins, W. Va., U.S.A.: Hardy species.
Towe, C.; Walhalla, S.C., U.S.A.: Appalachian Series.
Truffaut, A.; France: Belgian Indian Hybrids.
Univ. Mn. Landscape Arboretum; Chanhassen, Minn., U.S.A.: Northern Light Deciduous Hybrids.
Van Acker, L. and P.; Belg. (deceased): Belgian Indian Hybrids.
Van Damme, S.; Belg.: Belgian Indian Hybrids.
Van De Ven, H.; Toolangi, Victoria, Aust.: Indian & Ilam Hybrids.
Van Der Cruyssen, E.; Belg. (deceased): Belgian Indian Hybrids.
Van Der Linden, C.; Belg.: Belgian Indian Hybrids.
Van Der Swaelmen; Belg.: Belgian Indian Hybrids.
Van Geert, A.; Belg. (deceased): Indian Hybrids.
Van Geirht, A.; Belg. (deceased): Azaleodendron.
Van Gele, C.; Belg. (deceased): Belgian Indian Hybrids.
Van Gele, G.; Belg.: Belgian Indian hybrids.
Van Houtte, L.; Belg.: father of Mollis Hybrids in 1800's.
Van Nes, Adr; Boskoop, Holland: Kurume Hybrids.
Van Nes, C. B. & Sons; Boskoop, Holland: Mollis Hybrids.
Van Nes, Vuyk; Boskoop, Holland: Kurume Hybrids.
Van Noordt P. Nur.; Holland: Mollis Hybrids.
Van Oost, R.; Belg. (deceased) Belgian Indian Hybrids.
Van Peteghem, R.; Belg.: Belgian Indian Hybrids.
Varnadoe, Aaron; Colquitt, Ga., U.S.A.: N.A. deciduous species.
Veitch Nur., England: sponsored and received many plants from China & Japan in late 1800's.
Vercanteren, C.: Belgian Indian Hybrids.
Verhaege, R. & Son; Belg.: Belgian Indian Hybrids.
Verkade Nur.; Lincoln Park, N.J., U.S.A.: Kaempferi Hybrids.
Vermeulen, J.; Bridgetown, N.J., U.S.A.: Kurume Hybrids.
Verschuren Bros.; Belg.: Belgian Indian Hybrids.
Verschaffelt, A.; Belg. (deceased): early hybridizer of Ghents & Belgian Indian Hybrids.
Verschaffelt, J.; Belg. (deceased): Belgian Indian Hybrids.
Vervaene, D.; Belg. (deceased): Belgian Indian Hybrids.
Vervaene, Jean; Belg. (deceased): Belgian Indian Hybrids.
Voight, A.; Ger. (deceased): Belgian Indian Hybrids.
Voight, W.; Ger. (deceased): Belgian Indian Hybrids.
Von Siebold, Dr. P.; Ger.: collected *R. japonicum* in 1830.
Vosters Nursery; Pa., U.S.A.: Kurume Hybrids.
Vuyk, A.; Boskoop, Holland: Vuyk Hybrids.
Vuylsteke, C.; Belg. (deceased): Ghent Hybrids.
Wada, Koichiro; Yokamashi, Japan (deceased): Wada Hybrids.
Walker, J.; Eng. (deceased): early hybridizer of Ghents.
Walker Nursery; Aust.: Indian Hybrids.
Wallen, D. W. and V. A.; Aust: Indian Hybrids.
Waterer, A., Sr.; Eng. (deceased): Father of Deciduous Hybrids Azaleas in 1800's.
Waterer, John & Son; Eng.: deciduous & evergreen hybrids.
Weaver; N.C., U.S.A.

Well, Jim; Red Bank, N.J., U.S.A.: Knap Hill, Ilam & Windsor Hybrids.
West, Dr. Franklin; Penn Valley, Pa., U.S.A.: 'West's Superba'.
Westfall, Q. R.; Calif., U.S.A.: Belgian Indian Hybrids.
Wheeldon, Dr. Thomas; Richmond, Va., U.S.A. (deceased): evergreen hybrids.
White Flower Farm; Litchfield, Conn., U.S.A.: Knap Hill Hybrids.
White, H.; Eng. (deceased): early hybridizer of Ghents.
Whittier, L.; U.S.A.: Belgian Indian Hybrids.
Wibier, C.; Belg. Belgian Indian Hybrids.
Wille, C. J.; Belg.: Belgian Indian Hybrids.
Williams, F. J.; Eng.: Amoena Hybrids.
Wilson, E. H.; Boston, Mass., U.S.A. (deceased): introduced Wilson's Kurume Azaleas in 1918, and many species from China.
Wingate, T. and E. Coleman; Hawkinsville, Ga., U.S.A.: Cripple Creek Gartrell Hybrids.
Wood, Ed; Canby, Or., U.S.A.: introduced 'Bradford Sport'.
Wood, Verne L.; Tacoma, Wa., U.S.A.: Kaempferi Hybrids.
Woodland Nursery Garden; Eng.: Kaempferi Hybrids.
Wright; Aust.: Ilam Hybrids.
Wyatt, Vernon; Union, Wa., U.S.A.: Azaleodendrons.
Yates, H. R.; Frostburg, Md., U.S.A.: Kaempferi Hybrids.
Yavorsky, Leon; Freehold, N.J., U.S.A.: Kaempferi & Kurume Hybrids.
Yeates, Dr. J. S.; Palmerston North, New Zealand: Ilam Hybrids.
Yerkes, Dr. Guy E.; Md., U.S.A. (deceased): Beltsville Hybrids.
Yinger, B. and C. Hahn; Wheaton, Md., U.S.A.: introduced large collection of Satsuki cultivars to Brookside Garden. U.S.A.
Yoder Bros.; Barberton, Oh., U.S.A.: introduced many evergreen florist azaleas.
Yoshimura, R.; Japan: 'Mission Bells'.
Young, M.; U.S.A. (deceased): Azaleodendron.
Yuge Bros. Nursery; Altadena, Calif., U.S.A.: Belgian Indian Hybrids.
Zimmerman, J. D.; Rockville Center, N.Y., U.S.A.: Knap Hill Hybrids.

Appendix B
AZALEA INTRODUCTIONS

Plants introduced by
the United States Department of Agriculture,
New Crops Research Branch and the National Arboretum

The U.S. Department of Agriculture first established an Office of Foreign Seed and Plant Introduction in 1898. Today, coordination of plant introductions and exchange of plant germplasm is handled by the Plant Introduction Office (PIO), Germplasm Resources Laboratory, Agricultural Research Service, Beltsville Agricultural Research Center. The Plant Exploration and Taxonomy Laboratory participates and assists with direct field explorations.

Introductions are obtained from plant explorers, botanical gardens, scientists of research institutes, travelers, nurserymen, and other channels. As appropriate, the available passport data are documented and PI (Plant Introduction) numbers assigned by PIO. The National Arboretum actively participates in plant introduction activities in close cooperation with PIO.

Plant materials are introduced through the Plant Germplasm Quarantine Center for inspection and compliance with quarantine regulations. PI number assignments are usually completed after quarantine requirements are met. Distribution to government, scientific institutions, and cooperative organizations is the next step. The PIO coordinates the introduction of a broad range of plant material including ornamentals, crop and crop-related species especially field and vegetable crops. The National Arboretum introductions are mainly ornamental plants.

The following azaleas are introductions made since the Glenn Dale Plant Garden was established in 1919. The PI numbers after 1930 are all 6 digit numbers. The National Arboretum introductions are those with NA numbers. Following the source of the plants the U.S.D.A. after a name means the individual was an explorer, a collector or plant breeder for the New Crops Research Branch or the National Arboretum.

PI Number	Material	Source	Date
Alabamense, Rehder Alabama Azalea:			
196535	plants	United States; C.O. Erlanson, U.S.D.A.	1936
Albrechtii, Maxim. Albrecht Azalea:			
30850	seed	Japan; Tohoku Imperial Univ.	1911
80304	seed	England; Rev. J.F. Anderson	1929
83815	seed and scions	Japan; Botanic Gardens Imperial University, Sapporo Hokushu	1930
86749	seed	Japan; Phytotechnical Institute, Miyazaki College of Agriculture	1930
114671	plants	England; Hillier & Sons	1936
117066	seed	Japan; Botanic Garden, University of Tokyo	1936
123418	seed	North Wales; Lord Aberconway	1937
227183	plants	Japan; J. L. Creech, U.S.D.A.	1955

PI Number	Material	Source	Date
276091	plants	Japan; J. L. Creech, U.S.D.A.	1961
NA 44440	seed	Japan; Mr. M. Matsuyama Tayomsken	1979
479543–44	seed	Japan; Kawasi, M., Nielson, D., Meyer R., Ohio Agr. Res. Sta.	1983
Amagianum, Makino/Mt. Amagi Azaleas:			
263849	seed	Japan; Yokohama Plant Protection Station, Tokyo	1960
289553	seed	Great Britain; Royal Horticultural Society, Surrey, England	1963
NA 31200	plants	Japan; Dr. Taro Sukegawa, Tokyo	1969
Arborescens, Torr./Sweet Azaleas:			
442923	seed	Wayah Bald, N.C.; N.E. Pellett, Univ. Vt.	1980
442924	seed	Randolph Co., Va., N.E. Pellett, Univ. Vt.	1980
Atlanticum, Rehder/Coast Azalea:			
184842	seed	United States; S. F. Balke, U.S.D.A.	1940
196536	plants	United States; C. O. Erlanson, U.S.D.A.	1936
Balsamaeflorum Hybrids, Veitch:			
273268	plants	England; Royal Botanic Garden	1961
Beltsville (Yerkes-Pryor) Hybrids:			
293689–707	plants	United States; Plant Industry Station, U.S.D.A.	1963
Calendulaceum (Michx) Torr./Flame Azalea:			
442925	seed	Wayah Bald, N.C.; N.E. Pellet, Univ. Vt.	1980
442926	seed	Mt. Pisgah, N.C.; N.E. Pellett, Univ. Vt.	1980
442927	seed	Blue Ridge Pkwy 338 N.C.; N.E. Pellett, Univ. Vt.	1980
442928	seed	Tucker Co. W. Va.; N.E.	1980
442929	seed	Pellett, Univ. Vt.	
Canadense (L.) Torr./Rhodora Azalea:			
203694	seed	United States; Yale Univ.	1929
442930	seed	Pelham, Ma.; N.E. Pellett, Univ. Vt.	1978
442931	seed	N. Island Pond, Vt.; N.E. Pellett, Univ. Vt.	1978
NA 45804	seed	Canada; Montreal Bot. Gardens	1980
Canescens, Michx. Sweet/Florida Pinxter Azalea:			
203696	plants	United States; C. O. Erlanson, U.S.D.A.	1936
Canescens var. *Candidum* (Small) Rehd:			
203697	plants	United States; C. O. Erlandson, U.S.D.A.	1936
Dilatatum, Miquel:			
163850	seed	Japan; Yokohama Plant Protection Station, Tokyo	1960
39988	seed	Japan; Wada Hakoneya Nur., Yokohama	1976
45012	seed	Mt. Daisen, Japan; J. L. Creech & S. March, U.S.D.A.	1978
46383	seed	Mt. Ashitaka, Japan; J. L. Creech, & S. March, U.S.D.A.	1961

PI Number	Material	Source	Date
Farrerae, Tate ex Sweet/Farrer Azalea:			
276257	cuttings	Hong Kong; J. L. Creech, U.S.D.A.	1961
Glenn Dale Hybrids:			
141766–809	plants	United States; B. Y. Morrison, U.S.D.A. breeding project	1941
160000–86 and 160088–142	plants	United States; B. Y. Morrison, U.S.D.A. breeding project	1947
163762–987	plants	United States; B. Y. Morrison, U.S.D.A. breeding project	1948
182860–83	plants	United States; B. Y. Morrison, U.S.D.A. breeding project	1949
201896–8 and 202127–8	plants	United States; B. Y. Morrison, U.S.D.A. breeding project	1952
Ghent Hybrids:			
231390–92	plants	Surrey, England; Sunningdale Nurseries	1965
231395	plants	England; Sunningdale Nurseries	1956
231400	plants	England; Sunningdale Nurseries	1956
231404–5	plants	England; Sunningdale Nurseries	1956
279405–9	plants	United States; J. L. Creech, U.S.D.A.	1962
337187	plants	England; Sunningdale Nurseries	1968
NA 30821	plants	England; Sunningdale Nurseries	
Hirado Hybrids:			
235977–83	plants	Kurume, Japan; J. L. Creech, U.S.D.A.	1956
274705–25	cuttings	Japan; J. L. Creech, U.S.D.A.	1961
NA 40451–480	plants	Japan; Hisata Nur., Hirado Island; Creech, J. L. & S. March, U.S.D.A.	1976
46391	plants	Japan; Shibanich Garden Ctr.; Creech, J. L. & S. March, U.S.D.A.	1980
Hybrids:			
319926–29563	plants	Surrey, England; Sunningdale Nur.	1966
319942–29564	plants	England; Exbury Ev. Hyb.	1966
319987–29565	plants	England; Exbury Ev. Hyb.	1966
319983–29566	plants	England; Exbury Ev. Hyb.	1966
320001–29567	plants	England; Exbury Ev. Hyb.	1966
320002–3–29575–7	plants	England; Sunningdale Nur.	1966
320008–29578	plants	England; Sunningdale Nur.	1966
319916–29579	plants	England; Sunningdale Nur.	1966
319930–29580	plants	England; Sunningdale Nur.	1966
319934–29581	plants	England; Sunningdale Nur.	1966
319964–29582	plants	England; Sunningdale Nur.	1966
320038–29583	plants	England; Sunningdale Nur.	1966
319922–29554	plants	England; Sunningdale Nur.	1966
31909–320033	plants	England; Sunningdale Nur.	1967
337618–619	plants	United States; 'Ben Morrison', 'Mrs. L.B.J.' Glenn Dale Sta.	1968
364495–35823	plants	United States; 'Casablanca Tetra', Nat. Arb.	1974
364496–35824	plants	United States; 'Guy Yerkes Tetra', Nat. Arb.	1974

PI Number	Material	Source	Date
39886–93	plants	England; Hydon Nurs. Ltd.	1976
29395	plants	England; Hydon Nurs. Ltd.	1976
39398	plants	England; Hydon Nurs. Ltd.	1976
39400	plants	England; Hydon Nurs. Ltd.	1976
39402–4	plants	England; Hydon Nurs. Ltd.	1976
400055	plants	Japan; Watanabe Nur., Nodo City	1976
44783	cuttings	Japan; Mr. Hirose, Tokyo	1978
45590–93	plants	Japan; Shibahato Bonsai Nursery	1978
53585–6	plants	England; Bransford Nursery	1979
Hybrids-Natural Deciduous Hybrids:			
442937	seed	Gregory Bald Terra, N.C.; N.E. Pellett, Univ. Vt.	1979
442938	seed	Blue Ridge Pkwy 322.9, N.C.; N.E. Pellett, Univ. Vt.	1979
446759	seed	R. L. Pryor cross, U.S.D.A.	1983
Indicum (L.) Sweet/Indica Azalea:			
77087	cuttings	Japan; R. K. Beattie, U.S.D.A.	1928
77094	cuttings	Japan; R. K. Beattie, U.S.D.A.	1928
77104	cuttings	Japan; R. K. Beattie, U.S.D.A.	1928
77113	cuttings	Japan; R. K. Beattie, U.S.D.A.	1928
78379	plants	England; G. Reuthe	1928
78380	plants	England; G. Reuthe	1928
78382	plants	England; G. Reuthe	1928
85685	seed	Japan; Chugai Shokubutsu Yen Nurserymen	1930
114672–73	plants	England; Hillier Sons	1936
133426	plants	Brazil; Jardim Botanico, Rio de Janeiro	1939
199300	cuttings	Formosa; N. H. Fritz	1952
235758	plants	Japan; Yakushima, J. L. Creech, U.S.D.A.	1956
238598	plants	Japan; Kofu-En Bonsai Nursery, Tokyo	1957
246457	plants	Brazil; Llewelyn Williams, U.S.D.A.	1958
276288	plants	Japan; J. L. Creech, U.S.D.A.	1961
NA 40015	plants	Japan; Mr. Fususis Garden, Tochigi City, J. L. Creech & S. March, U.S.D.A.	1976
NA 40029	plants	Japan; Mr. Fususis Garden, Tochigi City, J. L. Creech & S. March, U.S.D.A.	1976
NA 41051	plants	Japan; Nagata, Yakushima, J. L. Creech & S. March, U.S.D.A.	1976
NA 40227	seed	Japan; Nagata, Yakushima, J. L. Creech & S. March, U.S.D.A.	1976
NA 40229	plants	Japan; Nagata, Yakushima, J. L. Creech & S. March, U.S.D.A.	1976
NA 40231	cuttings	Japan; Kosugedani, Yakushima, J. L. Creech & S. March, U.S.D.A.	1976
39188–9	cuttings	Japan; Imperial Household, Tokyo, J. L. Creech & S. March, U.S.D.A.	1976
Japonicum (Gray) Schneid/Japanese Azaleas:			
188995	seed	South Africa, Union of South Africa Dept. of Agriculture, Pretoria	1950
227184	plants	Japan; J. L. Creech, U.S.D.A.	1953
227277	plants	Japan; J. L. Creech, U.S.D.A.	1953
227278	plants	Japan; J. L. Creech, U.S.D.A.	1955

PI Number	Material	Source	Date
227572	plants	Japan; J. L. Creech, U.S.D.A.	1955
234949	plants	Japan; J. L. Creech, U.S.D.A.	1956
235138	seed	Japan; J. L. Creech, U.S.D.A.	1956
235139	plants	Japan; J. L. Creech, U.S.D.A.	1956
232011	seed	Japan; J. L. Creech, U.S.D.A.	1956
232011	seed	Japan; Botanical Garden, Osaka	1956
235138–9	seed	Japan; J. L. Creech, U.S.D.A.	1956
266180	seed	Japan; Sanwa Trading Co. Ltd.	1960
266357	seed	Japan; H. Kubota, Nikko	1960
275029–31	seedlings	Japan; J. L. Creech, U.S.D.A.	1961
275081–2	seed	Japan; J. L. Creech, U.S.D.A.	1961
275401	plants	Japan; J. L. Creech, U.S.D.A.	1961
275532	seedlings	Japan; J. L. Creech, U.S.D.A.	1961
275811	plants	Japan; J. L. Creech, U.S.D.A.	1961
277728–9	seed	Japan; Kyushu Agricultural Exp. Station, J. L. Creech, U.S.D.A.	1961
277732	seed	Japan; Munato Regional Forestry Office, J. L. Creech, U.S.D.A.	1961
277735	seed	Japan; Ministry of Agriculture and Forestry, Tokyo, J. L. Creech, U.S.D.A.	1961
278156	seed	Japan; Tanichi National Forest, J. L. Creech, U.S.D.A.	1962
315027	seed	Japan; above Kusatsu, F. L Doleshy	1966
318657 & NA 29132	seed	Japan; Kurume Res. Station	1967
303064	seed	Japan; F. L. Doleshy	1968
303065	seed	Japan; var. *glaucophyllum*, F. L. Doleshy	1968
NA 45358	seed	Japan; Seidagawa, Fukucho Pref., J. L. Creech & S. March, U.S.D.A.	1978
453382–a–c	plants	Japan; Kujiware Nur., J. L. Creech & S. March, U.S.D.A.	1978
479552	seed	Japan; Kawasi, Mij Nielson, D., Meyer F.; Ohio Agri. Res. Station	1983
Kaempferi, Planch./Kaempfer Azaleas:			
227183–86	plants	Japan; No. Honshu, J. L. Creech, U.S.D.A.	1955
227279	plants	Japan; Honshu, J. L. Creech, U.S.D.A.	1955
227573	plants	Japan; Hokkaido, J. L. Creech, U.S.D.A.	1955
228037	seed	Japan; Shikoku, J. L. Creech, U.S.D.A.	1955
227185	plants	Japan; Honshu, J. L. Creech, U.S.D.A.	1955
227186	plants	Japan; Honshu, J. L. Creech, U.S.D.A.	1955
227279	plants	Japan; Honshu, J. L. Creech, U.S.D.A.	1955
227573	plants	Japan; Hokkaido, J. L. Creech, U.S.D.A.	1955
228037	plants	Japan; Shikoku, J. L. Creech, U.S.D.A.	1955
266359	seed	Japan; H. Kubota, Nikko	1960
274542–4	plants	Japan; J. L. Creech, U.S.D.A.	1961

PI Number	Material	Source	Date
274736	seedlings	Japan; J. L. Creech, U.S.D.A.	1961
274875	plants	Japan; J. L. Creech, U.S.D.A.	1961
275032–4	seedlings	Japan; J. L. Creech, U.S.D.A.	1961
275060–1	seedlings	Japan; J. L. Creech, U.S.D.A.	1961
275402–3	plants	Japan; J. L. Creech, U.S.D.A.	1961
275533–5	plants	Japan; J. L. Creech, U.S.D.A.	1961
275812	seedlings	Japan; J. L. Creech, U.S.D.A.	1961
276093–7	plants	Japan; J. L. Creech, U.S.D.A.	1961
276141–2	plants	Japan; J. L. Creech, U.S.D.A.	1961
276289	plants	Japan; J. L. Creech, U.S.D.A.	1961
269227–231	plants	Germany; G. Arends	1960
274875	plants	Japan; J. L. Creech, U.S.D.A.	1961
275832–032	plants	Japan; J. L. Creech, U.S.D.A.	1961
275402	plants	Japan; J. L. Creech, U.S.D.A.	1961
275533–35	plants	Japan; J. L. Creech, U.S.D.A.	1961
275812	plants	Japan; J. L. Creech, U.S.D.A.	1961
2756093–97	plants	Japan; J. L. Creech, U.S.D.A.	1961
319989–NA 29466	plants	England; Sunningdale Nurs., Surrey	1966
319918–NA 29472	plants	England; Sunningdale Nurs.	1966
319968–72/NA 29474	plants	England; Sunningdale Nurs.	1966
319992–NA 29478	plants	England; Sunningdale Nurs.	1966
319995–NA 29479	plants	England; Sunningdale Nurs.	1966
320000–NA 29481	plants	England; Sunningdale Nurs.	1966
410704	plants	Japan; Nippon Bonsai Assoc., J. L. Creech & S. March, U.S.D.A.	1976
NA 90823	plants	Japan; Mr. Tamura Garden, J. L. Creech & S. March, U.S.D.A.	1976
NA 40829	plants	Japan; Mr. Tamura Garden, J. L. Creech & S. March, U.S.D.A.	1976
NA 44993	seed	Japan; Mt. Daisen, J. L. Creech & S. March, U.S.D.A.	1978
NA 44877	seed	Japan; Suzu City, J. L. Creech & S. March, U.S.D.A.	1978
NA 45301	cutting	Japan; Fukui Island, J. L. Creech & S. March, U.S.D.A.	1978
NA 45582	seed	Japan; Forestry Agency Toyuma, J. L. Creech & S. March, U.S.D.A.	1978
NA 45145	seed	Japan; Kyoga-Oaku, J. L. Creech & S. March, U.S.D.A.	1978
NA 44962	seed	Japan; Hakura Shrine Totteri, J. L. Creech & S. March, U.S.D.A.	1978
479553	seed	Japan; Kawase, M.; Nielson, D.; Meyer F.; Ohio Ag. Res. Station	1983
479554–6	seed	Japan; Kawase, M.; Nielson, D.; Meyer, F.; Ohio Ag. Res. Station	1983
Kaempferi × *Komiyamae:*			
274872–3	seedlings	Japan; J. L. Creech, U.S.D.A.	1961
Kanehirae			
325026	seed	Taiwan; J. L. Creech, U.S.D.A.	1968
Kiusianum, Makino/Kyushu Azalea:			
231951	plants	Japan; Kyushu Ag. Exp. Stat., J. L. Creech, U.S.D.A.	1956
235976	plants	Japan; J. L. Creech, U.S.D.A.	1956
261746	plants	Japan; Tsuneshige Rokuto, Tokyo	1959
40419	plants	Japan; Miyami-en Nur. near Kurume, J. L. Creech & S. March, U.S.D.A.	1976

PI Number	Material	Source	Date
40424–28	plants	Japan; Miyami-en Nur. near Kurume, J. L. Creech & S. March, U.S.D.A.	1976
40432–36	plants	Japan; Miyami-en Nur. near Kurume, J. L. Creech & S. March, U.S.D.A.	1976
40438–44	plants	Japan; Miyami-en Nur. near Kurume, J. L. Creech & S. March, U.S.D.A.	1976
40447–48	plants	Japan; Miyami-en Nur. near Kurume, J. L. Creech & S. March, U.S.D.A.	1976
404501	plants	Japan; Miyami-en Nur. near Kurume, J. L. Creech & S. March, U.S.D.A.	1976
40814–16	plants	Japan; Kyoma Yokato Nurs. near Mt. Unzen, J. L. Creech & S. March, U.S.D.A.	1976
40818–21	plants	Japan; Kyoma Yokato Nurs. near Mt. Unzen, J. L. Creech & S. March, U.S.D.A.	1976
40823–26	plants	Japan; Kyoma Yokato Nurs. near Mt. Unzen, J. L. Creech & S. March, U.S.D.A.	1976
40828	plants	Japan; Kyoma Yokato Nurs. near Mt. Unzen, J. L. Creech & S. March, U.S.D.A.	1976
40976	plants	Japan; Shibamichi Nurs., Angyo, J. L. Creech & S. March, U.S.D.A.	1976
45329–31	seed	Japan; Fuhue Island, Nagasaki Pref., J. L. Creech & S. March, U.S.D.A.	1976
45151	seed	Japan; Hagosaki Pref., J. L. Creech & S. March, U.S.D.A.	1978
45366–67	seed & cuttings	Japan; Mt. Haneyama, Oita Pref., J. L. Creech & S. March, U.S.D.A.	1978
45371	plants	Japan; Kyoma Yokato Nur., Fukioki Pref., J. L. Creech & S. March, U.S.D.A.	1978
45372–78	plants	Japan; Manami-en Nur., J. L. Creech & S. March, U.S.D.A.	1978
45382	plants	Japan; Minamataki Nur. Nagasaki Pref., J. L. Creech & S. March, U.S.D.A.	1978
45461	cuttings	Japan; Kurume Agr. Res. Sta., J. L. Creech & S. March, U.S.D.A.	1978
46383	seed	Japan; Jyurigi near Mt. Ashitaka, J. L. Creech, U.S.D.A.	1980
46393	plants	Japan; Tomozo Mozuda, J. L. Creech, U.S.D.A.	1980
Knap Hill & Exbury Hybrids:			
210918/4585	plants	England; Exbury Estate	1953
210920–1/4588–9	plants	England; Exbury Estate	1953
210925–4593	plants	England; Exbury Estate	1953
213418–4811	plants	England; John Waterer & Son Nursery	1954
213421–4813	plants	England; John Waterer & Son Nursery	1954
213427–28	plants	England; John Waterer & Son Nursery	1954

PI Number	Material	Source	Date
213431–33	plants	England; John Waterer & Son Nursery	1954
223039–41	plants	England; Knap Hill Nursery	1955
230012–13	plants	England; Knap Hill Nursery	1955
323077	plants	England; Knap hill Nursery	1955
223080	plants	England; Knap Hill Nursery	1955
230027–39	plants	England; Knap Hill Nursery	1955
243996–9	cuttings	England; F. G. Meyer, U.S.D.A.	1957
253699–702	plants	England; Waterer & Sons & Crisp, Ltd.	1958
266448–52	plants	Netherland; Old Farm Nurseries, Boskoop	1960
273265–7	plants	England; Royal Botanic Garden	1961
337195–30841	plants	England; Sunningdale Nurs.	1968
337205–30851	plants	England; Sunningdale Nurs.	1968
337220–30861	plants	England; Sunningdale Nurs.	1968
337225–30931	plants	England; Sunningdale Nurs.	1968
337240–30869	plants	England; Sunningdale Nurs.	1968
337173–244	plants	England; Sunningdale Nurs.	1968
Komiyamae, Makino/Ashitaka Azalea:			
227685	seed	Japan; National Agricultural Research Institute, J. L Creech, U.S.D.A.	1961
41046–7	seed	Japan; Watanabe Nurs., Gotemba, J. L. Creech & S. March, U.S.D.A.	1976
40869–10	cuttings & seed	Japan; Ashitaka Yama near Gotemba, J. L. Creech & S. March, U.S.D.A.	1976
40863	cuttings	Japan; Shizuoka Agr. Exp. Sta., J. L. Creech & S. March, U.S.D.A.	1976
Kurume hybrids:			
319909–911 and 29483–85	plants	England; Sunningdale Nurs., Surrey	1966
319925, 29491	plants	England; Sunningdale Nurs.	1966
319939, 29494	plants	England; Sunningdale Nurs.	1966
319944, 29496	plants	England; Sunningdale Nurs.	1966
319948, 29496	plants	England; Sunningdale Nurs.	1966
319950–967 and 29496–29513	plants	England; Sunningdale Nurs.	1966
319977–78/29520–21	plants	England; Sunningdale Nurs.	1966
319980–83/29523–25	plants	England; Sunningdale Nurs.	1966
319984–85/29527–28	plants	England; Sunningdale Nurs.	1966
319991–29530	plants	England; Sunningdale Nurs.	1966
319998–29532	plants	England; Sunningdale Nurs.	1966
319921–29533	plants	England; Sunningdale Nurs.	1966
320004–5 and 29534–35	plants	England; Sunningdale Nurs.	1966
320009–11/29536–38	plants	England; Sunningdale Nurs.	1966
320013–15/29541–43	plants	England; Sunningdale Nurs.	1966
220017–29544	plants	England; Sunningdale Nurs.	1966
320020–25/29545–50	plants	England; Sunningdale Nurs.	1966
320029–29551	plants	England; Sunningdale Nurs.	1966
320031–29553	plants	England; Sunningdale Nurs.	1966
NA 39386–91	plants	England; Hydon Nurs. Surrey	1976
NA 39390–404	plants	England; Hydon Nurs. Surrey	1976
40489	cuttings	Japan; Kyushu Agr. Exp. Sta., J. L. Creech & S. March, U.S.D.A.	1976
49493–95	cuttings	Japan; Kyushu Agr. Exp. Sta., Kurume	1976

PI Number	Material	Source	Date
40498	cuttings	Japan; Kyushu Agr. Exp. Sta., Kurume	1976
40500	cuttings	Japan; Kyushu Agr. Exp. Sta., Kurume	1976
40501	cuttings	Japan; Kyushu Agr. Exp. Sta., Kurume	1976
40505	cuttings	Japan; Kyushu Agr. Exp. Sta., Kurume	1976
40508	cuttings	Japan; Kyushu Agr. Exp. Sta., Kurume	1976
40510	cuttings	Japan; Kyushu Agr. Exp. Sta., Kurume	1976
40511	cuttings	Japan; Kyushu Agr. Exp. Sta., Kurume	1976
40514	cuttings	Japan; Kyushu Agr. Exp. Sta., Kurume	1976
40515	cuttings	Japan; Kyushu agr. Exp. Sta., Kurume	1976
40522	cuttings	Japan; Kyushu Agr. Exp. Sta., Kurume	1976
40525	cuttings	Japan; Kyushu Agr. Exp. Sta., Kurume	1976
40533	cuttings	Japan; Kyushyu Agr. Exp. Sta., Kurume	1976
40055	plants	Japan; Watanoki Nurs., Noda City	1976
319931–2/29450–1	plants	England; *Amoena* hyb., Sunningdale Nurs.	1966
319914–29463	plants	England; *Amoena* hyb., Sunningdale Nurs.	1966
39397	plants	England; Hyden Nurs., Surrey	1976
39191	cuttings	Japan; Fujinaasahi, Imperial Household, Tokyo, J. L. Creech & S. March, U.S.D.A.	1976
39192	cuttings	Japan; Hanaasobi, Imperial Household Tokyo, J. L. Creech & S. March, U.S.D.A.	1976
45404–50	cuttings	Japan; Kurume Agr. Res. Sta., J. L. Creech & S. March, U.S.D.A.	1978
Luteum, Sweet (flavum)/Pontic Azalea:			
78875	seed	Ireland; Daisy Hill Nursery	1929
108801	seed	U.S.S.R.; Union of Socialist Republics Garden, Tifflis, Caucasus	1935
114516	seed	Sweden; Botanic Garden, Goteborg	1936
122709	seed	Turkey; H. H. Westover & F. L. Wellman, U.S.D.A.	1937
206469	seed	Turkey; R. K. Godrey, U.S.D.A.	1953
238715	cuttings	Portugal; F. G. Meyer, U.S.D.A.	1957
238780	cuttings	Portugal; F. G. Meyer, U.S.D.A.	1957
274593	seed	Hortus Botanicus Batumensis, Batum	1961
274592	seed	Hortus Botanicus Batumensis, Batum	1961
324054	seed	U.S.S.R.; H. J. Brooks, U.S.D.A.	1967
324055	seed	U.S.S.R.; H. J. Brooks, U.S.D.A.	1967

PI Number	Material	Source	Date
325472	seed	U.S.S.R.; W. H. Skrdla	1968
331008	seed	U.S.S.R.; Main Botanic Garden	1968
331015/30498	seed	U.S.S.R.; Main Botanic Garden	1968
331090	seed	U.S.S.R.; Bot. Garden Subtropical Sta.	1968
399405	seed	Yugoslavia; Lav Rajevski Acad Seit Art	1975
36377	seed	U.S.S.R.; J. March, U.S.D.A.	1973
Macrosepalum, Maxim, M./Big Sepal Azalea:			
85687	seed	Japan; Chugai Shokumutsu yen Nurserymen	1930
136143	seed	Japan; Chugai Nursery Co.	1940
199302	cuttings	Formosa; N. H. Fritz	1952
274874	seedlings	Japan; J. L. Creech, U.S.D.A.	1961
Macrosepalum linearifolium/Spider Azalea:			
274890	plants	Japan; H. Kubota, Nikko	1961
319903/29452	plants	England; Sunningdale Nurs.	1966
Macrostemon, Max.:			
77690	plants	France; Leon Chenault & Son	1928
Mariesii Hemsl. & Wils./Maries Azalea:			
80306	seed	England; Rev. J. F. Anderson	1929
87475–76	seed	England; Rev. J. F. Anderson	1930
124718	seed	China; Lu-Shan Botanical Garden	1937
158036	seed	China; Lu-Shan Botanical Garden	1947
162487	seed	China; Lu-Shan Botanical Garden	1948
162602	seed	China; Botanic Garden, Nanking	1948
Microphyton, Franch:			
101232	plants	United States; Arnold Arboretum	1932
162966	seed	China; Lu-Shan Botanical Garden	1938
182657	seed	China; Lu-Shan Botannical Garden	1949
Molle (Blume) Don./Chinese Azalea:			
59226	seed	China; National Geographic Society	1924
159034	seed	China; Lu-Shan Botanical Garden	1947
171381	seed	Hong Kong; Andrew Tse	1954
Mollis Hybrids:			
230062/6373	plants	England; Knap Hill Nurs.	1955
224331/6405	plants	England; Sunningdale Nurs.	1955
224341/6415	plants	England; Sunningdale Nurs.	1955
231393–4	plants	England; Sunningdale Nurs.	1956
231397	plants	England; Sunningdale Nurs.	1956
231399	plants	England; Sunningdale Nurs.	1956
231401–3	plants	England; Sunningdale Nurs.	1956
231406–7	plants	England; Sunningdale Nurs.	1956
337249–50	plants	England; Sunningdale Nurs.	1968
337251–264	plants	England; Sunningdale Nurs.	1968
337256/30887	plants	England; Sunningdale Nurs.	1968
'Mucronatum' syn. 'Indica Alba' Azalea:			
77074	cuttings	Japan; R. K. Beattie, U.S.D.A.	1928
77084	cuttings	Japan; R. K. Beattie, U.S.D.A.	1928
77131	cuttings	Japan; R. K. Beattie, U.S.D.A.	1928
199299	cuttings	Formosa; N. H. Fritz	1952

PI Number	Material	Source	Date
274891–2	plants	Japan; H. Kutota, Nikko	1961
41170	seed	Belgium; The Arboretum Kalmthout	1977
41176	seed	Belgium; The Arboretum Kalmthout	1977
45201	seed	Japan; Mt. Shiratake, Nagasaki Pref., J. L. Creech & S. March, U.S.D.A.	1978
45204	seed	Japan; Mt. Shiratake, Nagasaki Pref., J. L. Creech & S. March, U.S.D.A.	1978
45206	seed	Japan; Mt. Shiratake, Nagasaki Pref., J. L. Creech & S. March, U.S.D.A.	1978
45195–6	seed	Japan; Mt. Shiratake, J. L. Creech & S. March, U.S.D.A.	1978
45452	cuttings	Japan; Kurume Orn. Res. Sta., J. L. Creech & S. March, U.S.D.A.	1978
45172	plants	Japan; Tsushima Is., Nagasaki Pref., J. L. Creech & S. March, U.S.D.A.	1978
48206	seed	Korea; C. F. Miller, Chollipo Arboretum	1981
'Mucronatum' Bulstrode:			
319929/29561	seed	England; Sunningdale Nurs.	1966
Nakaharai, Hayata:			
325035	seed	Taiwan; J. L. Creech, U.S.D.A.	1968
Nipponicum, Matsum. Nippon Azalea:			
209097	seed	England; Royal Horticultural Society	1953
229408	seed	England; F. Griffin	1954
Nudipes, Nakai:			
228244	seed	Japan; J. L. Creech, U.S.D.A.	1955
44887	seed	Japan; Noto Peninsula, Ishikawa Pref., J. L Creech, U.S.D.A.	1978
44968	seed	Japan; Mt. Daisen, To Hori Pref., J. L. Creech, U.S.D.A.	1978
Oblongifolium, Millais:			
337265	plants	England; Sunningdale Nurs.	1968
× 'Obtusum', Kirishima A.:			
226139	plants	Japan; Kirishima, J. L. Creech, U.S.D.A.	1955
231951–2	plants	Japan; Kirishima, J. L. Creech, U.S.D.A.	1956
231952	plants	Japan; Kyushu Agricultural Experiment Station, J. L. Creech, U.S.D.A.	1956
374076	seed	Japan; Mt. Mtyshi, Shime Univ.	1972
× 'Obtusum' F. *Amoenum,* Lindl Rehd. Amoena Azalea:			
102161–62	plants	England; Keener's Hill Nursery	1933
× 'Obtusum' F. *Japonicum,* Wil. Kurume Azalea:			
235813–7	plants	Japan; J. L. Creech, U.S.D.A.	1956
Occidentale Hybrids:			
231396	plants	England; Sunningdale Nurseries, Surrey	1956
231398	plants	England; Sunningdale Nursries	1956
337261–271	plants	England; Sunningdale Nurseries	1956

PI Number	Material	Source	Date
Oldhamii, Maxim. Oldham Azalea:			
78540	seed	Japan; Miyazaki College of Agriculture	1929
101225	plants	United States; Arnold Arboretum	1932
242477	cuttings	Scotland; F. G. Meyer, U.S.D.A.	1957
335036–39	seed	Taiwan	1968
Parvifolium, Adams:			
377739	seed	U.S.S.R.; Main Bot. Garden, Leningrad	1972
Pentaphyllum, Maxim. Fiveleaf Azalea:			
85688	seed	Japan; Chugai Shokubutsu Yen Nurserymen	1930
91247 92033	seed	Japan; Chugai Shodubutsu Yen Nurserymen	1931
97626	seed	Scotland; Royal Botanic Garden, Edinburgh	1932
101961	seed	Scotland; Royal Botanic Garden, Edinburgh	1933
117069	seed	Japan; Botanic Garden, Univ. of Tokyo	1936
127627	seed	Scotland; Royal Botanic Garden, Edinburgh	1938
131926	seed	Scotland; Royal Botanic Garden, Edinburgh	1939
137494	plants	England; Hillier & Sons	1940
227999	plants	Japan; Shikoku, J. L. Creech, U.S.D.A.	1955
46748	seedlings	Japan; Rakko Falls, Nikko, J. L. Creech, U.S.D.A.	1980
Pentaphyllum var. *nikoense,* Kobatsu Nakai:			
2988060	seed	Japan; H. Kubota, Nikko	1964
40002	seed	Japan;	
Periclymenoides, Shinn (*nudiflorum,* Torr.) Pinxter Bloom Azalea:			
203698	plants	United States; C. O. Erlanson, U.S.D.A.	1952
Periclymenoides (nudiflorum) f. *glandiferium* (Porter) Fern:			
203699	plants	United States; C. O. Erlanson, U.S.D.A.	1952
Perrclymenoides (nudiflorum) × *Sinense* (molle):			
28377	plants	United States; Walter Van Fleet, U.S.D.A.	1910
Prinophyllum, Millars (*Roseum,* Rehd) Roseshell Azalea:			
209098	plants	United States; C. O. Erlanson, U.S.D.A.	1953
442941	seed	United States; Summit, N.Y., N.E. Pellett, Univ. Vt.	1978
442940	seed	United States; Tucker Co., W. Virg.; N.E. Pellett, Univ. Vt.	1979
442939	seed	United States; Vermont, West of Johnson; N.E. Pellett, Univ. Vt.	1980
Pulchrum, Sweet (*phoeniceum* F. *smithi*):			
78541	seed	Japan; Miyazaki College of Ag.	1929
117070	seed	Japan; Botanic Garden, Univ. of Tokyo	1936
235984	plants	Japan; J. L. Creech, U.S.D.A.	1956
275026	cuttings	Japan; H. Kubota, Nikko	1961

PI Number	Material	Source	Date
Phoeniceum var. *calycinum* (Lindl.) Rehd.:			
77095	cuttings	Japan; R. K. Beattie, U.S.D.A.	1928
276290–1	plants	Japan; J. L. Creech, U.S.D.A.	1961
Prunifolium, Millais Plumleaf A. Azalea:			
	plants	United States; C. O. Erlanson, U.S.D.A.	1936
Pulchrum var. *calycinum* × *Scabrum*:			
101226	plants	United States; Arnold Arboretum	1932
Pulchrum var. *calycinum* f. *Maxwelli* Maxwell Azalea:			
101231	plants	United States; Arnold Arboretum	1932
32039	plants	England; Sunningdale Nursery	1967
Pulchrum var. *tebotan* (Komatsu), Rehd:			
101238	plants	United States, Arnold Arboretum	1932
Quinquefolium, Boiss & Moore Cork Azalea:			
114674	plants	England; Hillier & Sons	1936
117071	seed	Japan; Botanic Garden, Univ. of Tokyo	1963
228000	seed	Japan; Shikoku, J. L. Creech, U.S.D.A.	1955
275062	seedlings	Japan; J. L. Creech, U.S.D.A.	1961
298061	seed	Japan; H. Kubota, Nikko	1964
NA 40001	seed	Japan; Nikko, J. L. Creech, U.S.D.A.	1976
46744	seed	Japan; Kanaya Hotel, Nikko	1980
47182	seed	Japan; Kanaya Hotel, Nikko	1980
47196	seedlings	Japan; Lake Chuzenji, Tochigi Pref.	1980
47211	seed	Japan; Nikko Bot. Garden, Nikko	1980
Reticulatum, D. Don ex G. Don Rose Azalea:			
855789–90	seed	Japan; Chungai Shokubutsu Yen Nurserymen	1930
91245–46	seed	Japan; Chugai Shokubutsu Yen Nurserymen	1931
95542	seed	Japan; Chugai Shokubutsu Yen Nurserymen	1931
96525	seed	Japan; Chugai Shodubutsu Yen Nurserymen	1932
97401	seed	North Wales; Henry McLaren	1932
117076	seed	Japan; Botanic Garden, Univ. of Tokyo	1936
266360	seed	Japan; H. Kubota, Nikko	1960
318656	seed	Japan; Kurume Hort. Res. Station	1967
NA 455225	seed	Japan; Mt. Mitaki, J. L. Creech & S. March, U.S.D.A.	1978
45202	seed	Japan; Mt. Mitaki, J. L. Creech & S. March, U.S.D.A.	1978
45583	seed	Japan; Toyama Forestry Agency	1978
45237	seed	Japan; Tsushima Island, J. L. Creech, U.S.D.A.	1978
45259	seed	Japan; Tsushima Island, J. L. Creech, U.S.D.A.	1978
45182	seed	Japan; Tsushima Island, J. L. Creech, U.S.D.A.	1978
45192	seed	Japan; Tsushima Island, J. L. Creech, U.S.D.A.	1978

PI Number	Material	Source	Date
45153	seed	Japan; Tsushima Island, J. L. Creech, U.S.D.A.	1978
50973	seed	Japan; Mikio Matsuyana Toayama-shi	1982
Ripense, Makino Riverbank Azalea:			
78542	seed	Japan; Miyazaki College of Agr.	1929
45959	plants	Japan; Kurume Orn. Res. Sta.	1978
Rubropilosum, Hyata Redhair Azalea:			
325042–049	seed	Taiwan; J. L. Creech, U.S.D.A.	1968
325582	plants	Taiwan; J. L. Creech, U.S.D.A.	1968
Sataense, Nakai Sata Azalea:			
274541	plants	Japan; J. L. Creech, U.S.D.A.	1961
45460	cuttings	Japan; Kurume Orn. Res. Sta., J. L. Creech & S. March, U.S.D.A.	1978
Satsuki Hybrids:			
127653–678 & 131295–321		Japan; Chugai Nursery Co.	1938/39
228103–18	plants	Japan; Rokuji Kai Aichi, J. L. Creech, U.S.D.A.	1955
227066–112	plants	Japan; Rokuji Kai Aichi, J. L. Creech, U.S.D.A.	1955
410699–02/37823–27	plants	Japan; Nippon Bonsai Assoc. (150) J. L. Creech & S. March, (150), (Izayai 21 yrs.) (Hatatashiro 60 yrs.) (Shio, 150 yrs.); (Kaho 50 yrs.)	1976
320063/29573	plants	England; Sunningdale Nurs.	1966
319954/29570	plants	England; Sunningdale Nurs.	1966
319959/29571	plants	England; Sunningdale Nurs.	1966
319937/29556	plants	England; Sunningdale Nurs.	1966
319939/29558	plants	England; Sunningdale Nurs.	1966
319941/29560	plants	England; Sunningdale Nurs.	1966
41021–38	plants	Japan; Mr. Yoshiyuki Angyo, J. L. Creech & S. March, U.S.D.A.	1976
41001–3	plants	Japan; Mr. Yoshiyuki Angyo, J. L. Creech & S. March, U.S.D.A.	1976
41005–17	plants	Japan; Mr. Yoshiyuki Angyo, J. L. Creech & S. March, U.S.D.A.	1976
41019	plants	Japan; Mr. Yoshiyuki Angyo, J. L. Creech & S. March, U.S.D.A.	1976
40795	plants	Japan; Hirata Nurs., Kurume, J. L. Creech & S. March, U.S.D.A.	1976
39190	cuttings	Japan; Imperial Household, Tokyo, J. L. Creech & S. March, U.S.D.A.	1976
40799	plants	Japan; Manuyama-en, Kurume, J. L. Creech & S. March, U.S.D.A.	1976
40802	plants	Japan; Manuydama-en, Kurume, J. L. Creech & S. March, U.S.D.A.	1976
45484	cuttings	Japan; Higashiyama Gardens, J. L. Creech & S. March, U.S.D.A.	1978
45391	plants	Japan; Mt. Shunsulu, Kurume, J. L. Creech & S. March, U.S.D.A.	1978

PI Number	Material	Source	Date
Scabrum, Don Luchu Azalea:			
188541	seed	Japan; Hakoneya Nurseries	1950
242478	cuttings	Scotland; F. G. Meyer, U.S.D.A.	1957
418265–273	cuttings	Japan; Okinawa, Prof. W. D. Ackerman, U.S.D.A.	1977
418269–72	cuttings	Japan; Okinawa, Prof. W. D. Ackerman, U.S.D.A.	1981
46917–19	cuttings	Japan; Okinawa, Prof. W. D. Ackerman, U.S.D.A.	1981
Scabrum × *Pulchrum* var. *calycinum:*			
101234	plants	United States; Arnold Arboretum	1932
Scabrum × Kurume 'Yayehiru' ('Scarlet Prince') × Oldhamii:			
101235	plants	United States; Arnold Arboretum	1932
Scabrum × Kurume 'Yayehiru' ('Scarlet Prince'):			
101236	plants	United States; Arnold Arboretum	1932
Scabrum × Kurume 'Kureno-yuki' ('Snowflake'):			
101237	plants	United States; Arnold Arboretum	1932
Schlippenbachii, Maxim. Royal Azalea:			
17727	seed	Korea; Keijo Forestry Experiment Station	1927
78411	seed	Korea; Keijo Forestry Experiment Station	1928
82163	seed	Korea; P. H. Dorsett & W. J. Morse, U.S.D.A.	1929
82164	seed	Korea; P. H. Dorsett & W. J. Morse, U.S.D.A.	1929
82485	seed	Korea; Keijo Forestry Experiment Sta.	1929
83817	seed & scions	Japan; Botanic Gardens, Imperial Univ., Sapporo, Hokushu	1930
266361	seed	Japan; H. Kubota, Nikko	1960
316934	seed	Korea; E. G. Corbett & R. W. Light	1966
317380	seed	Korea; Mt. Kwan Ak, E. G. Corbett & R. W. Light	1966
39853	seed	U.S.S.R.; Mortus Bot. Garden	1976
40013	seed	Japan; Nikko Bot. Garden, J. L. Creech & S. March, U.S.D.A.	1976
45844–6	seed	Korea; Chollipo Arboretum	1980
Serpyllifolium (A. Gray) Miguel/Wildthyme Azalea:			
85691	seed	Japan; Chugai Shokobutsu Yen Nurserymen	1930
199303	cuttings	Formosa: N. H. Fritz	1952
202749	cuttings	United States; E. A. Hollowell	1952
235327	plants	Japan; J. L. Creech, U.S.D.A.	1956
274545–6	plants	Japan; J. L. Creech, U.S.D.A.	1961
Simsii Planch. Sims Azalea			
124720	seed	China; Lu-Shan Botanical Garden	1937
158037	seed	China; Lu-Shan Botanical Garden	1947
161483	seed	Hong Kong; Andrew Tse	1947
161687	seed	Hong Kong; Andrew Tse	1948
162425	seed	Hong Kong; Andrew Tse	1948
162489	seed	China; Lu-Shan Botanical Garden	1948

PI Number	Material	Source	Date
163370	seed	China; National Forestry Research Bureau, Nanking	1948
171382	seed	Hong Kong; Andrew Tse	1948
276258–9	cuttings	Hong Kong; J. L. Creech, U.S.D.A.	1961
276343	seed	Hong Kong; J. L. Creech, U.S.D.A.	1961
391401	seed	China; Chinese Acad. Agrt. Forestry	1974
418274–279	seed	Okinawa; W. D. Ackerman, U.S.D.A.	1977
Subsessile, Rendle:			
105041	seed	Phillippine Islands; Bureau of Forestry, Manila	1934
Tamurae, Masam (*Eriocarpum,* Nakai)/Dwarf Indica Azalea:			
42541–5	seed	Japan; Nagata, Yakushima	1976
42578	seed	Japan; Nagata, Yakushima	1976
45454	seed	Japan; Kurume Orn. Res. Sta.	1978
Tashiroi, Maxim:			
226714	seed	Okinawa; J. L. Creech, U.S.D.A.	1955
418280–282	cuttings	Okinawa; W. L. Ackerman, U.S.D.A.	1971
40199	seed	Japan, Ambu, Yakushima, J. L. Creech & S. March, U.S.D.A.	1976
45356	seed	Japan; Kyushu, Agr. Exp. Sta., J. L. Creech & S. March, U.S.D.A.	1978
Tosaense, Makino/Tosa Azalea:			
137495	plants	England; Hillier & Sons	1940
186515	seed	England; George Johnstone	1950
45357	cuttings	Japan; Kyushu, Agr. Exp. Sta., J. L. Creech & S. March, U.S.D.A.	1978
Tschonoskii, Maxim./Tschonoski Azalea:			
79043	seed	England; Royal Botanic Garden, London	1929
80307	seed	England; Rev. J. F. Anderson	1929
85859	seed	Scotland; Royal Botanic Garden, Edinburgh	1930
114675	plants	England; Hillier & Sons	1936
117075	seed	Japan; Botanic Garden, Univ. of Tokyo	1936
127630	seed	Scotland; Royal Botanic Garden, Edinburgh	1938
131927	seed	Scotland; Royal Botanic Garden, Edinburgh	1939
228001	plants	Japan; J. L. Creech, U.S.D.A.	1955
296122	plants	United States; Glenn Dale	1964
44806	seed	Japan; Tatayama, Toyame Pref., J. L. Creech & S. March, U.S.D.A.	1978
44807Aa–d	seed	Japan; Tatayama, Toyame Pref., J. L. Creech & S. March, U.S.D.A.	1978
Tashiroi × *Weyrichii:*			
39960	seed	Japan; Wada Nurs., J. L. Creech, U.S.D.A.	1976
39987	cuttings	Japan; Wada Nurs., J. L. Creech, U.S.D.A.	1976
39986	cuttings	Japan; Wada Nurs., J. L. Creech, U.S.D.A.	1976
39990	seed	Japan; Wada Nurs., J. L. Creech, U.S.D.A.	1976

PI Number	Material	Source	Date
Vaseyi Gray Pink Shell Azalea:			
443942	seed	United States; Blue Ridge Pkwy, 417; N.E. Pellett, Univ. of Vt.	1979
× *Viscosepalum*	plants	England; Sunningdale Nurs.	1968
Viscosum glaucum, Torrey/Swamp Azalea:			
337276	plants	England; Sunningdale Nurs.	1968
Viscosum nitidum:			
337277	plants	England; Sunningdale Nurs.	1968
Viscosum rhodanthum:			
337278	plants	England; Sunningdale Nurs.	1968
Wadanum, Makino:			
276294	plants	Japan; J. L. Creech, U.S.D.A.	1961
Weyrichii, Maxim. Weyrich Azalea:			
98479	plants	England; Sunningdale Nurs.	1932
102741	seed	Manchuria; Manshu Nosan Shokai, Inc., Dairen	1933
117073	seed	Japan; Botanic Garden, Univ. of Tokyo	1936
137496	seed	England; Hillier & Sons	1940
228002–003	plants	Shikoku; Japan, J. L. Creech U.S.D.A.	1955
228038	seed	Shikoku; Japan, J. L. Creech U.S.D.A.	1955
274737	cuttings	Japan; J. L. Creech, U.S.D.A.	1961
274839	seed	Japan; J. L. Creech, U.S.D.A.	1961
317273	seed	Korea; E. G. Corbett & R. W. Lighty	1966
40805	seed	Japan; Hoyashi Farms, Ushibiso Mirado	1976
40837	seed	Japan; Hoyashi Farms, Ushibiso Mirado	1976
40388	seed	England; Hillier's Nursery	1977
45320	seed	Japan; Nantsu-Iake, Nagasaki Pref.	1978
45317	seed	Japan; Shimayama Asagii, Nagasaki Pref.	1978
45300	seed	Japan; Shimayama Asagii, Nagasaki Pref.	1978
45295	seed	Japan; Shimayama Asagii, Nagasaki Pref.	1978
45309	seed	Japan; Shimayama Asagii, Nagasaki Pref.	1978
45291	seed	Japan; Shimayama Asagii, Nagasaki Pref.	1978
Yedoense Maxim. Yodagawa Azalea:			
82166	seed	Korea; P. H. Corsett & W. J. Morse, U.S.D.A.	1929
R. yedoense var. *poukhanense* Nakai Korean Azalea:			
319908/29458	plants	England; Sunningdale Nursery	1966
317272	seed	Korea; E. G. Corbett & R. W. Lighty	1966
318576	cuttings	Korea; Mt. Halla, E. G. Corbett & R. W. Lighty	1967
319321	cuttings	Korea; Mt. Chiri, E. G. Corbett & R. W. Lighty	1967
479557	seed	Japan; Kawase M; D. Nielsen, F. Meyer, Ohio Agr. Res. Sta.	1983
43745	plants	England; Bransford Nur., Worcester	1979

PI Number	Material	Source	Date
43584	plants	England; Bransford Nur., Worcester	1979
46399	plants	Japan; Watanake Nur.	1980

Appendix C
THE INHERITANCE OF FLOWER COLOR IN AZALEAS

Dr. J. Heursel
Institute of Ornamental Plant Growing
B-9230, Melle, Belgium

Flower colors of evergreen azaleas may be divided into four types: Purple ('Mevrouw J. Heursel', 'Violacea'): Purplish red ('Red Wings', 'Reinhold Ambrosius'); Red ('Elsa Kärger', 'Paul Schäme') and White ('Perle de Swynaerde', 'Niobe'). Specific genes control the production of pigments known as anthocyanins and flavonols. Genes are discrete sequences of a nucleotide commonly called DNA (deoxyribo nucleic acid) situated in the chromosomes.

In evergreen azaleas one pair of genes controls the production or expression of all colors except white, which is colorless. This pair we refer to as W for color and w for colorless. We believe three other pairs of genes control the production of specific anthocyanin pigments. All these genes will be described under inheritance of anthocyanins. There are still other pairs of genes, Q and q and M and m, which determine the production of flavonols. Additional research in the genetics of flower color in azaleas is still needed to explain the expression of other colors such as pink, bicolors, etc.

In azaleas all colors are dominant over white. Red is dominant only over white. Purplish red is dominant over red, and purple is dominant over all other colors. These relationships are shown in Table 1.

Table 1. Summary of the Inheritance of Colors in Azaleas.

purple × purple	= purple
purplish red × purple	= purple
purplish red × purplish red	= purplish red
red × purple	= purple
red × purplish red	= purplish red
red × red	= red
white × color	= color
white × white	= white

Anyone who regularly carries out crosses will have found that in practice results other than these indicated in Table 1 are obtained. In order to obtain the results in Table 1, both parents must be homozygous or non-hybrid for color genes. If we represent "Color" by W, then we can represent color homozygously by WW, that is to say, the gene W was contributed by each of the two parents. Thus, for example, 'Apollo' (red) × 'Wilhelm Scheurer' (red) are homozygous, and crosses between these two cultivars therefore always produce 100% WW progeny, consistent with Table 1.

Many azaleas are not homozygous for color. The red 'Paul Schäme', for example, inherited color (W) from one parent and colorless (or white) w from the other parent. We call this heterozygous and represent it as Ww. 'Paul Schäme' originated by crossing 'Deutsche Perle' by 'Wilhelm Scheurer' as follows:

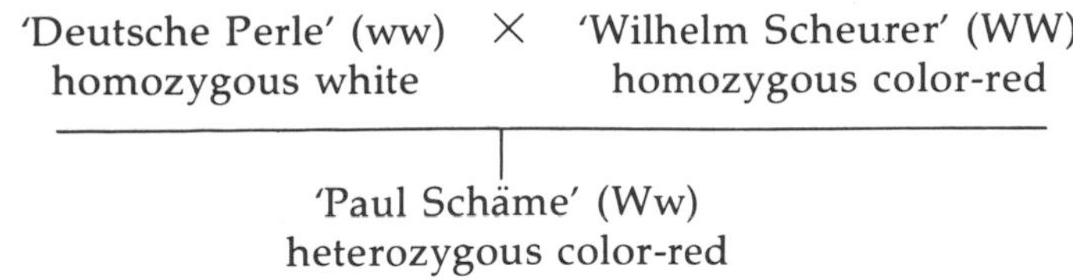

In appearance 'Wilhelm Scheurer' (WW) homozygous red and 'Paul Schäme' (Ww) heterozygous red are identical, but they do not impart identical color to their offspring. This is why Table 1 is just a guide, and the results shown there are accurate only if both parents are homozygous.

If we cross heterozygous plants as 'Paul Schäme' (Ww) and 'Avenir' (Ww), both of which are red, we obtain reds and whites in the progeny as follows:

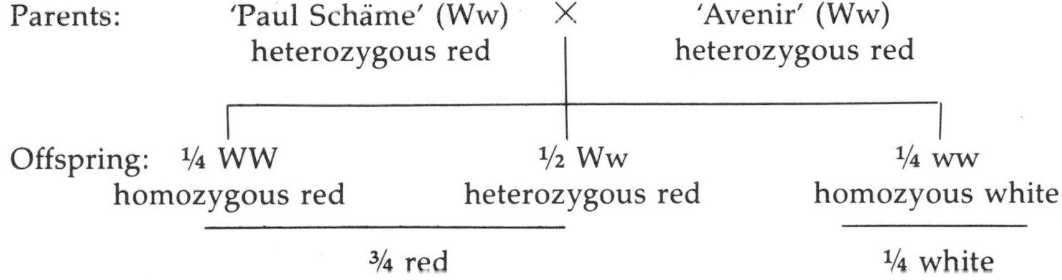

Because azaleas are largely cross pollinated, they are most commonly heterozygous in their breeding behavior.

Genetic of Specific Anthocyanin Pigments

We have studied the inheritance of four specific anthocyanin pigments and believe their production is controlled by two genes, P and O (See Fig. 1). These are summarized as follows:

P = methylation at 3′–5′ position in presence of gene O
p = no methylation even in the presence of gene O
O = oxidation of position 5′
o = no oxidation

Combinations of these two pairs of genes we believe result in the production of the four above pigments as shown in Fig. 3 as follows:

OOPP = production of malvidin (purple)
ooPP = production of peonidin (red)
OOpp = production of delphinidin (blue)
oopp = production of cyanidin (red)

'Violacea' is an example of a purple cultivar which contains malvidin. 'Vervaeneana' is a red containing peonidin. 'Paul Schäme' is a red containing cyanidin. There is no known named cultivar containing only delphinidin.

Genetics of Flavonols

Flavonols in high concentrations produce yellow flowers. In evergreen azaleas the concentrations are very low and flowers containing flavonols can hardly be distinguished with the bare eye from white flowers without flavonols. There are azalea cultivars that contain only flavonols, such as 'White Hexe' and 'White Water' which contain quercetin as the only flavonol (see Fig. 3).

One pair of genes appear to control the production of the flavonol quercetin. The action of these genes can be summarized as follows:

Q = production of quercetin
q = no flavonols produced

If the gene Q is recessive to qq then we no longer find any flavonols.

Other flavonols found are azaleatin, myricetin, and myricetin–5–methylether. One gene O is responsible for the oxidation quercetin (see Fig. 2).The resulting flavonol is myricetin. Another gene M can methylate quercetin and myricetin into azaleatin and myricetin–5–methylether respectively.

Anthocyanins and Flavonols Together

If flavonols occur together with anthocyanins, there is a purpling effect. Purplish red is produced by the addition of flavonols to the red pigments cyanidin or peonidin. 'Friedhelm Scheurer' contains the same anthocyanins as 'Elsa Kärger' but the purplish effect is produced by the addition of flavonols in 'Friedhelm Scherrer'.

For another example, the white 'Mucronatum' ('Ledifolia Alba') crossed with a red flowered plant results in 100% purple progeny. This fact was observed by Wada (1968) and also undoubtedly by Joseph Gable. 'Mucronatum' is white because it carries the genes for non-expression of color (ww). However, it is homozygous for anthocyanin genes PP, and flavonol genes MM, QQ. The anthocyanins and flavonols, however, are not expressed because they are suppressed by the colorless ww, which prevents production of anthocyanin pigments, and the flavonol is essentially colorless.

For further details on the proposed inheritance formula of 30 cultivars, see Table 2 taken from Heursel and Horn (1977).

Flower Color and Inheritance of Hose-in-Hose Character

From numerous crosses with hose-in-hose azaleas, such as 'Hexe' and 'Kirin' the following results have occurred. Crosses with parents having green calyces always produce progeny with green calyces.

Crosses of a mother plant having a green calyx (homozygous) with a father plant with a hose-in-hose calyx (heterozygous) produce 50 per cent hose-in-hose and 50 per cent green calyces. On the other hand, crossing a mother plant having a hose-in-hose calyx with a father plant having a green calyx almost never produces any progeny. Hose-in-hose × hose-in-hose, too, was unsuccessful. We may conclude that the green calyx is recessive with respect to the hose-in-hose calyx. Let us represent the recessive green calyx by hh and the hose-in-hose calyx by Hh. Homozygous hose-in-hose plants (HH) do not occur. Crossing of a green calyx (hh) × hose-in-hose (Hh) explains the one-to-one ratio.

These relationships may be shown as follows:

hh = single flowers with green calyx
Hh = hose-in-hose
HH =lethal or sterile

female single flower	×	hose-in-hose male → half single and half hose-in-hose
female hose-in-hose	×	male single flower → sterile
female hose-in-hose	×	male hose-in-hose → sterile

The hose-in-hose character turns out to be linked to the Q gene involved in the production of quercetin. This means the hose-in-hose character and genes are sited on the same chromosome. (See Fig. 4.)

In a coupling phase, as in the case of 'Hexe', the progeny of the cross purplish red, hose-in-hose × red, green calyx are purplish red, hose-in-hose and red, green calyx.

In a repulsion phase, as in the case of 'Kirin', the progeny of the cross purplish red, hose-in-hose × red, green calyx are purplish red, green calyx and red, hose-in-hose.

Table 2. Genotype suggested for a number of R. obtusum, R. scabrum and R. simsii hybrids

Cultivar	R.H.S. C.C.	W	Q	M	O	P	G
'Adventsglocke'	54A	WW	Qq	Mm	oo	pp	gg
'Apollo'	44C	WW	qq	Mm	oo	Pp	gg
'Avenir'	52BC	Ww	qq	mm	oo	pp	Gg
'Carmen'	55A	Ww	Qq	M.*)	oo	pp	gg
'Coelestine'	58B	WW	Qq	Mm	oo	Pp	gg
'Constance'	67D	Ww	Qq	M.	oo	Pp	Gg
'Dame Melanie'	52D–WE**)	Ww	qq	mm	oo	pp	Gg
'Dr. Bergmann'	43C	Ww	qq	MM	oo	pp	Gg
'Eclaireur'	57B	Ww	Qq	Mm	oo	Pp	Gg
'Elsa Kärger'	45C	W.	qq	?	oo	Pp	gg
'Ernst Thiers'	63B	W.	Qq	mm	oo	pp	Gg
'Hexe'	58B	WW	Qq	mm	oo	Pp	Gg
'Josiane Maeseele'	66C	WW	Q.	M.	oo	pp	GG
'Julius Roehrs'	57C	W.	Qq	Mm	oo	Pp	Gg
'Kirin'	62B	Ww	Qq	mm	oo	pp	gg
'Knut Erwén'	53D	Ww	Qq	Mm	oo	pp	gg
'Niobe'	white	ww	Qq	M.	oo	—	—
'Mme Petrick'	57D	Ww	Qq	MM	oo	pp	gg
'Paul Schäme'	47D	Ww	qq	MM	oo	pp	GG
'Perle de Swijnaerde'	white	ww	qq	MM	oo	—	—
'Pink Dream'	65B	Ww	Qq	Mm	oo	pp	Gg
'Prof. Wolters'	46 D-WE	Ww	qq	Mm	oo	Pp	Gg
'Reinhold Ambrosius'	58B	WW	QQ	MM	oo	pp	gg
'Rex'	48C	WW	qq	?	oo	pp	gg
R. kiusianum	72C	Ww	Q.	M.	OO	P.	G.
'Mucronatum'	white	ww	QQ	MM	OO	(PP)	—
R. scabrum 'Ademurasaki'	71D	W.	Qq	mm	Oo	Pp	G.
R. pulchrum 'Maxwellii'	66C	WW	Q.	M.	oo	P.	Gg
'Tempérance'	77D	Ww	QQ	Mm	Oo	Pp	G.
'Violacea'	72BC	WW	QQ	MM	Oo	Pp	G.

*) Dominant or recessive allel. **) WE means: White edge.

LITERATURE

Heursel J. & Horn W. A hypothesis on the inheritance of flower colors and favonols in *R. simsii* Planch. Z. Pflanzenzuchtg., 1977, *79:* 238–249.

Wada, K., 1967. *R. mucronatum.* In: The Rhododendron and Camellia year book 1968, 143–146. Roy. Hort. Soc., London.

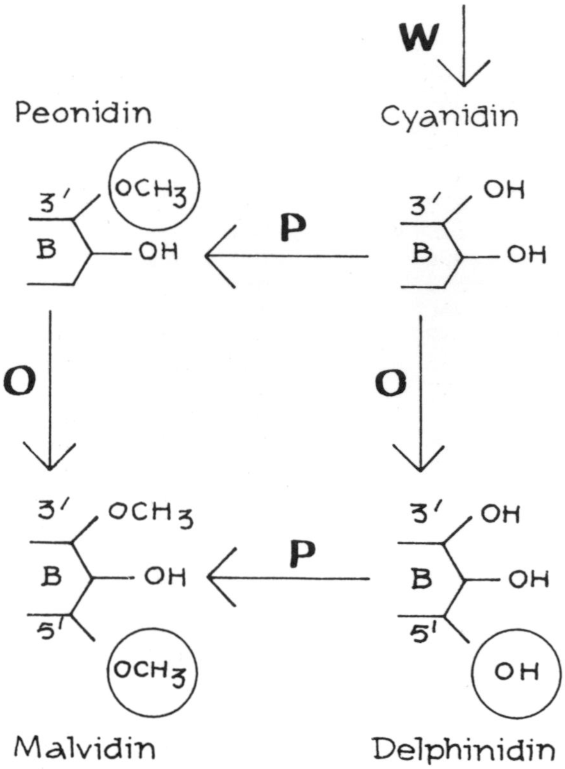

W

Peonidin

Cyanidin

P

O

O

P

Malvidin

Delphinidin

Figure 1. Anthocyanins in Azalea flowers.

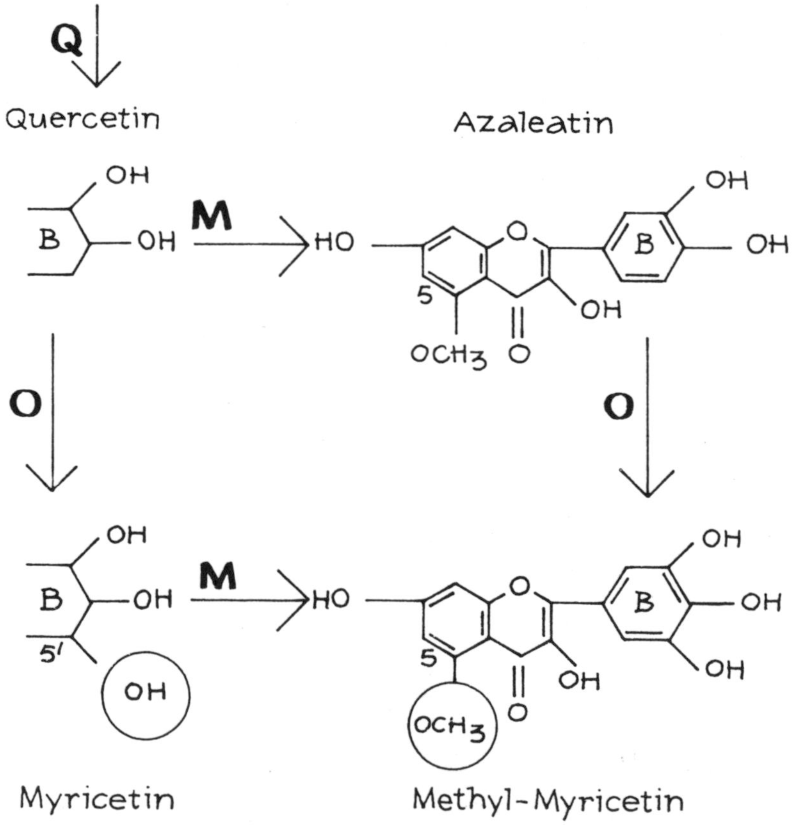

Q

Quercetin

Azaleatin

M

O

O

M

Myricetin

Methyl-Myricetin

Figure 2. Flavonols in azalea flowers.

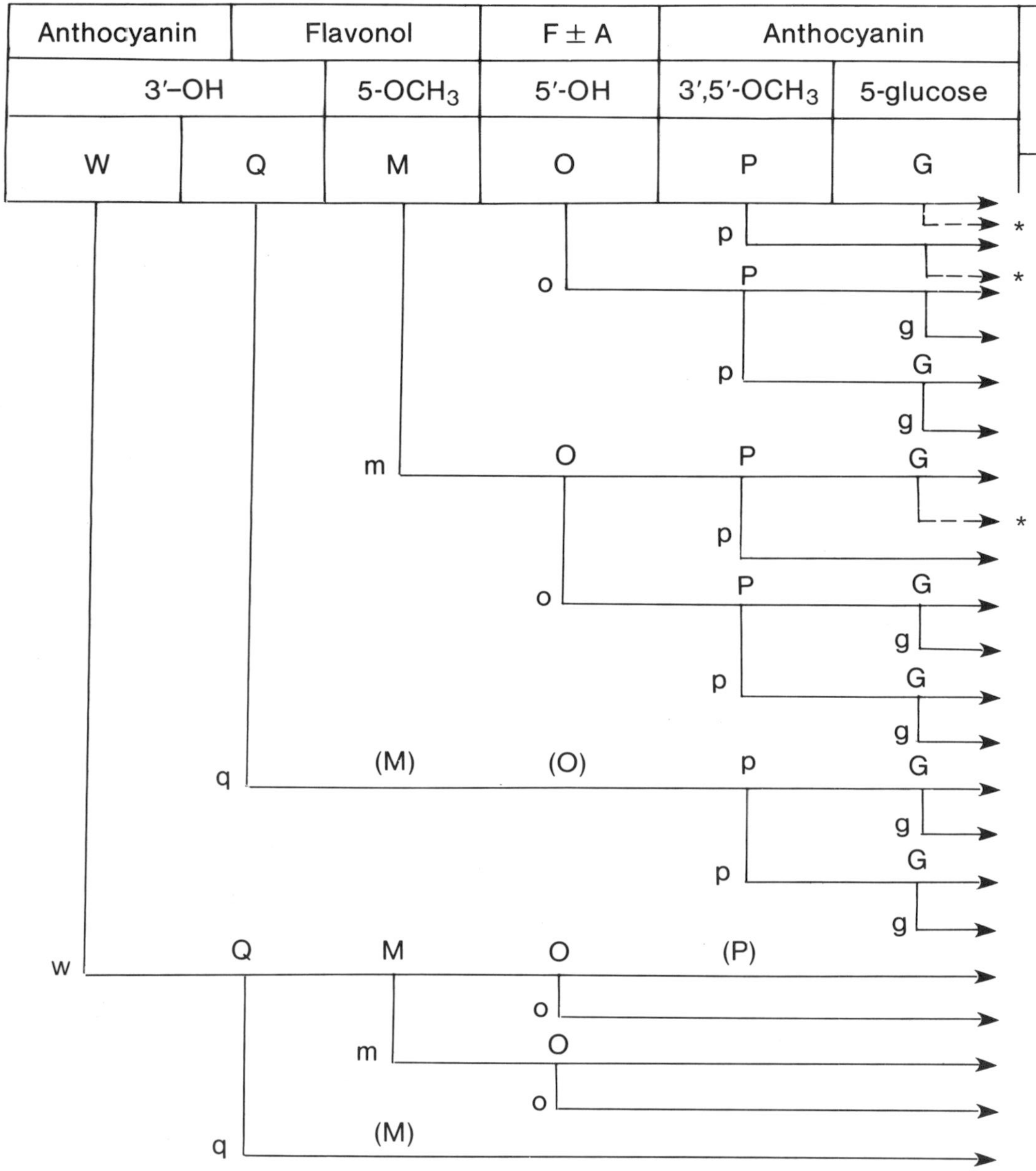

Anthocyanin	Flavonol		F ± A	Anthocyanin					
3′-OH		5-OCH_3	5′-OH	3′,5′-OCH_3	5-glucose	Flavonol	Anthocyanin	R.H.S.C.C.	Cultivar
W	Q	M	O	P	G				
						Myr-5-met	Malv. di	72BC	'Violacea'
				p		* Myr-5-met	Delf. di	71 CD	Seedlings
			o	P		* Azal.	Peo. di	58 B	'Coelestine'
					g	Azal.	Peo. mon.	53 CD	'Friedhelm Scherrer'
				p	G	Azal.	Cya. di	58 B	'Euratom'
					g	Azal.	Cya. mon	58 B	'Reinhold Ambrosius'
		m	O	P	G	Myr.	Malv. di	71 D	*Rh. scabrum* 'Ademurasaki'
						*			
				p		Myr.	Delf. di	68 A	Seedlings
			o	P	G	Quer.	Peo. di.	58 B	'Hexe'
					g	Quer.	Peo. mon.	62 B	'Kirin'
				p	G	Quer.	Cya. di.	66 B	'Cangallo'
					g	Quer.	Cya. mon.	62 A	*Rh. indicum*
	q	(M)	(O)	p	G	—	Peo. di	52 B	'Vervaeneana rubra'
					g	—	Peo. mon.	45 C	'Elsa Kärger'
				p	G	—	Cya. di.	47 D	'Paul Schäme'
					g	—	Cya. mon.	44 D	'Prinses Beatrix'
w	Q	M	O	(P)		Myr.-5-met	—	white	*Rh. mucronatum*
			o			Azal.	—	white	'Niobe'
		m	O			Myr.	—	white	—
			o			Quer.	—	white	'White Water'
	q	(M)				—	—	white	'Perle de Swynaerde'

*We also found seedlings in which monoglycosides dominated. The flowers did not differ from diglycosides phenotypically.

Fig. 3. Inheritance of flower pigments in azaleas.

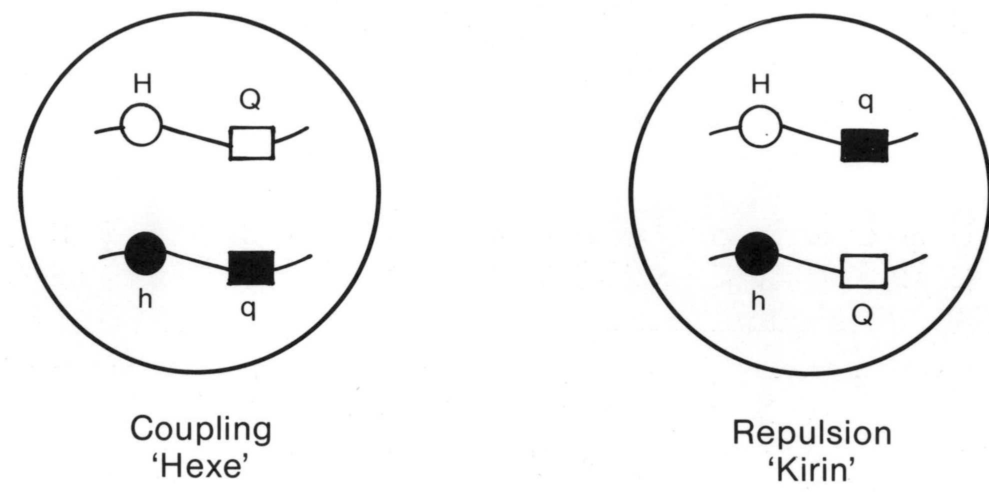

Figure 4. Linkage of the hose in hose character.

Appendix D
TRANSLITERATION AND PRONUNCIATION OF JAPANESE

Japanese is often described as a difficult language, and this assertion is seldom questioned. It has such features as a large vocabulary, coining of new words, and unfamiliar idioms and sentence structure. The written system is very difficult for most westerners. St. Francis Xavier, an early missionary, declared that the language was devised by the devil to confound the faithful and to obstruct the spread of the gospel.

The written Japanese language uses characters (Kanji) borrowed from the Chinese. So a system is necessary to transliterate the Kanji characters to the characters of the Roman alphabet. Several systems have been developed but are unfortunately often used interchangeably. Many azalea names consequently will be spelled differently by different translators using one or more transliteration systems. Kinsai and Kinzai, Kin no sai and Kinno zai; Bunka and Bunkwa are three examples.

The most commonly used system of Romanization is the Hepburn (Hebon-shiki Romanization) System found in most Japanese-English dictionaries and study aids. This system is most convenient for English-speaking people since it is based on the pronunciation of English for consonants and Italian for vowels.

Japanese is what some philologists call an agglutinative language, because many suffixes and particles are tacked on to a word to form a string of words. Therefore, it is difficult to determine whether a certain sound-group is a single word or a compound of several words.

For this reason names of plants that have been passed on by word of mouth and written directly into a Roman based script are sometimes broken into word sounds by one author and spelled as a single word by another, such as Akatsukinozoa—Akatsuki no Zoa; Fujinotsuki—Fuji no Tsuki; Sakurayama—Sakura Yama, etc.

The phonic (or sound) system of the Japanese is comparatively simple, containing only a fraction of the number of sounds found in the English language. Consequently, there are many "sound homonyms" in the Japanese language. For readers of Japanese who have the Chinese characters to help them differentiate, it is no problem, but for a translator who has only the Romanized spelling, it becomes a guessing game with several different meanings for each word-sound.

Fortunate is one to have friends skilled in the Japanese language as are Dr. Charles Hiers and his Japanese wife at Auburn University, William Turner in Atlanta, and Dr. Terry Davis in Gainesville, Florida. The reader may find assistance in pronouncing the Japanese names of azaleas following ideas based on the work of Professor Samuel E. Martin and published in his book, *Essential Japanese, Revised Edition* by the Charles E. Tuttle Co., Inc., Rutland, Vermont.

Pronunciation

There are five vowels in Japanese. Each vowel may be long or short. They are approximately the same as the following, but much shorter:

a = as in f*a*ther
i = as in mach*i*ne or pol*i*ce
u = as in oo in t*oo*l
e = as in *e*ffort or s*e*t
o = as in b*o*ne or s*o*ld

Consonants are all approximately the same as in English with the "g" sound always hard as in garden. The soft "g" sound is always represented by "j" as in jade. The *important* thing is that each letter transliterated into Roman has only one sound.

In Romanized spelling an "h" sometimes designates a nasal quality after "g", as in Amaghasa (Amagasa), but it is best to leave out the "h".

One important rule is that Japanese words have no accented syllable, but are spoken in metronomic fashion. There is no bouncing or heavy stress on some syllables or irregular rhythm as in English. The Japanese give each syllable a moderate even stress, allowing about the same time for each of the syllables, regardless of the apparent prominence, such as tsuki—tsu-ki. With a double consonant, such as in the Hirado hybrid Shi*nn*an, both consonants must be spoken, Shi*n*-*n*an. This is similar to our English work Boo*k*case, where the two k sounds are clear and distinct.

When two words are compounded to form another word, the initial sound of the second component is frequently modified in the interest of euphony. Thus K becomes G; S becomes Z; Sh and Ch become J; T becomes D; and F and H become B or P. Examples:

Gosho Sakura	= Gosho Zakura
Tama kawa	= Tamagawa
Iwo shima	= Iwojima

This may at first seem confusing, but it is not; with a little practice the modified sounds come naturally.

Another common change occurs when a word ending in "tsu" is followed by a syllable beginning with t, s, k, or p: the "tsu" is dropped and the consonant doubled. Among azaleas, this is often seen with combinations of "getsu" (moon/month).

Getsu & toku	= Gettoku
Getsu & keikan	= Gekkeikan
Getsu & sho	= Gessho

Unlike the previously mentioned consonant change, this is invariant; Getsutoku has always been an incorrect reading of the azalea Gettoku.

There is one other vowel change which has led to confusion in azalea names: an "n" followed by a "p" or "b" is pronounced as "m". For instance, the azalea pronounced "Goompoh" is written in Japan as Gunpo and Gumpo in the United States. Gunbo and Gumpo, both pronounced with m's, are different plants.

A final word about translations: they are anything but straightforward. Some name parts such as "sei" can refer to any one of hundreds of Japanese characters (Kanji) with that reading, and each has its own meaning. Ultimately the identity of a plant is unequivocally specified by Kanji.

The Transliteration of a Few Common Words Used in Azalea Names

aka: red
akebono: dawn
aki: fall, autumn
asahi: morning, rising sun
azuma: east
beni: red, vermilion
botan: peony (button)
chiyo: eternal
cho: butterfly
fubuki: snowstorm
fuji: wisteria, peerless, as in Mt. Fuji
gasa/kasa: parasol
gin: silver
gyoko: luck, good fortune
hagoromo: a rope of feathers (as worn by celestial beings)
hana or bana: flower
haru: spring
hikari: light
hime: princess
homare: honor, glory, fame
juni: twelve
kagami: mirror
kasa/gasa: parasol
kasumi: morning mist
ko: small, bright, shining
kin: gold
kiri/giri: fog, mist
kongo: in the future
kotobuki: congratulations
kozan: a mine, high mountain
kumo: cloud
kuruma: wagon or carriage; wheel
mai: dance
minato: harbor
mine: peak
miyo: reign
mizu/sui: water
muji: plain, unfigured
murasaki: purple (also proper name)
musume: girl
nani: many, number
nishiki: brocade
no: "of" or as apostrophe's (possessive particle)
ogi: fan
otome: maiden
sakura/zakura: cherry
san/zan: mountain
shakunage: rhododendron
shin: new
shinzan: remote mountain, newcomer, or novice
shiro/jiro: white
sugata: figure, form
takara: treasure, heirloom
tama: ball or pearl, gem or jewel
te: hand
tsuki or zuki/getsu: moon or month
tsutsuji: azalea
umi: ocean
yama: mountain
yuki: snow
yume: dream

Appendix E
GOOD DOER AZALEAS

In 1980 the American Rhododendron Society published, in the book *American Rhododendron Hybrids,* a list of Good Doer Rhododendron species and cultivars recommended by the Chapters throughout the country. Following the same approach the A.R.S. and the Azalea Society of America (A.S.A.) chapters were asked to provide the same information on Good Doer Azaleas for their areas.

Some azaleas perform well in many areas of the country. However, it should be noted that recommendations vary from chapter to chapter and region to region depending on grower experience and preference, climate, soils, and source of plants.

The organization of the lists vary from chapter to chapter. Most are listed by season of bloom; however, one is by color of flower. The exchange of azalea information is important and useful. Information on local plant preferences, cultures, availability, and sources can be used to good effect by all gardeners. The challenge in trying azaleas not common in the region is part of the fun in growing them.

More information can be obtained from the national societies by writing to the executive secretaries:

American Rhododendron Society
Mrs. Paula L. Cash
Executive Secretary
14885 SW Sunrise Lane
Tigard, Oregon 97224
U.S.A.

Azalea Society of America
P.O. Box 6244
Silver Spring, Maryland 20906
U.S.A.

The Secretary
Royal Horticultural Society
Vincent Square
London, S.W. 1
England

AZALEA CHAPTER A.R.S.
Atlanta, Georgia

DECIDUOUS

All North American Azalea species do well in this area except *R. canadense, R. roseum,* and *R. occidentale.* The following hybrids are the best growers:

Early	Midseason	Late
'Cecile'	'Brazil'	'Orangeade'
'Daviesi'	Windsor Hybrids	'Silver Slippers'
'Gibraltar'	'Marion Merriman'	'Ilam Rufus'
'Hotspot'	'Ilam Primrose'	'Leilane'
'Corringe'		

EVERGREEN

Early	Midseason	Late
'Mother's Day'	'Delilah'	'Martha Hitchcock'
'Red Slipper'	'Frosted Orange'	'Delaware Valley White'
'Ward's Ruby'	'Glory'	'Glacier'
'Amagasa'	'Wakaebisu'	'Mrs. G. G. Gerbing'
'Buccaneer'	'Ben Morrison'	'Festive'
'Fashion'	'Caroline Dorman'	'Mizu no Yamabuki'
'Orange Cup'	'Eikan'	'Isho no Haru'
'Hershey's Red'	'Grace Freeman'	'Gyokushin'
'Hinode Giri'	'George L. Tabor'	'Blue Danube'
'Princess Augusta'	'Helen Fox'	'Shimmer'
'Sunglow'	'H. H. Hume'	'Hardy Gardenia'
'Pink Ruffles'	'Snow'	'Fascination'
'Coral Bells'	'Margaret Douglas'	'Mt. Seven Star'
'Easter Parade'	'Marion Lee'	'Pink Pancake'
'Heiwa no Hikari'	'St. James'	'Red Fountain'
'Pink Pearl'	'Formosa'	'Meicho'
'Beth Bullard'		'Gumpo' & varieties

BROOKSIDE GARDENS (BETHESDA, MARYLAND) CHAPTER A.S.A.

DECIDUOUS

Early	Mid Season	Late
R. vaseyi	Mollis	'Coccinea Speciosa'
R. nudiflorum	*R. calendulaceum*	'Corneille'
R. japonicum	*R. arborescens*	'Narcissiflora'
	'Persil'	*R. prunifolium*
	'Strawberry Ice'	*R. bakeri*
	'Balzac'	
	'George Reynolds'	
	'Tunis'	
	'Gibraltar'	

EVERGREEN

Early	Mid Season	Late
'Corsage'	'Palestrina'	'Debonaire'
'Morning Star'	'Ben Morrrison'	'Beni-Kirishima'
'Vespers'	'Martha Hitchcock'	'Flame Creeper'
'Festive'	'Stewartstonian'	'J. T. Lovett'
'Dream'	'Louise Gable'	'Margaret Douglas'
'Rose Greeley'	'Kintaiyo'	'Sagittarius'
'Ambrosia'	'Amoena'	'Gumpo' & varieties
'Glacier'	'Koromo Shikibu'	'Copperman'
'Zulu'	'Cavendishii'	'Nocturne'
'Dayspring'		'Eikan'

CALIFORNIA CHAPTER A.R.S.

DECIDUOUS

Early

'Adrian Koster'
'Beaulieu'
'Brightstraw'
'Christopher Wren'
'Desert Pink'
'Hotspur Yellow'
'Irene Koster'
'Marion Merriman'
'Orangeade'
R. schlippenbachii
'Surprise'

Mid Season

'Antelope'
R. austrinum
'Balzac'
'Berry Rose'
'Corringe'
'Gallipoli Red'
'Golden Horn'
'Goldfinch'
'Jolie Madame'
'Old Gold'
R. pentaphyllum
'Princess Royal'
'Red Hot'
'Sugared Almond'

Late

'Cecile'
'Fawley'
'Homebush'
'Kathleen'
'Klondyke'
'Narcissiflora'
'Strawberry Ice'
'Sun Chariot'
'Sylphides'

EVERGREEN

Early

'Addy Wery'
'Appleblossom'
'Ballerina'
'Ballet Girl'
'Cora Brandt'
'Coral Bells'
'Crinoline'
'Day Spring'
'Delicatissima'
'Dr. Bergmann'
'Firefly'
'Hino Crimson'
'Hino Mayo'
'Kintayo'
R. kiusianum
'Lavender Elf'
'L. J. Bobbink'
'Melba'
'Mizu no Yomabuki'
'Nuccio's Pink Showgirl'
'Orange Cup'
'Orchid Cup'
'Pixie'
'Pitti Sing'
'Revery'
'Salmon Queen'
'Santoi'
'Sherwood Red'
'Shimmer'
R. simsii
'Snow'
'Stewartstonian'
R. tashiroi
'T. Roosevelt'
'Twilight'
'Vivid'

Mid Season

'Avalanche'
'Ballerina'
'Blue Danube'
'Campfire'
'Cloud Nine'
'Coral Dogwood'
'Crinoline'
'Dogwood'
'Flower Girl'
'Freedom'
'Lavender Elf'
'Lawsal'
R. macrosepalum
'Madonna'
'Mucronatum Lilacinum'
'Mucronatum Rosebud'
'Pinkie'
'Prof. Walters'
'Purple Splendor'
'Red Luster'
'Rose Greeley'
R. sataense
R. serpyllifolium
'Sherwood Red'
'Singing Fountain'
'Snowbird'
'Sweet Briar'
'Twilight'
'Vuyk's Scarlet'
'Ward's Ruby'

Late

'Bride's Bouquet'
'Cameo'
'Copperman'
'Flame Creeper'
'Glacier'
'Gumpo'
'Guy Yerkes'
R. indicum
R. kaempferi
'Mary Margaret'
'Mary Queen'
'Meistag'
R. nakaharai
'Nocturne'
R. obtusum
R. oldhamii
R. prunifolium
'Sonoma'
'Spring Charm'
'Sun Valley'
'Vermilion'
'William Bull'
'Youth'
'Zulu'

CENTRAL GULF COAST (MOBILE AREA) CHAPTER A.R.S.

Yellow
R. austrinum
R. calendulaceum selections
R. molle selections

Red and Orange
R. bakeri selections
R. japonicum selections
R. prunifolium
R. speciosum
R. weyrichii

White
R. alabamense
R. atlanticum
R. × *coryi*
R. oblongifolium
R. serrulatum
R. viscosum

Pink
R. arborescens
R. canescens
R. japonicum selections
R. nudiflorum selections
R. roseum selections

DECIDUOUS HYBRIDS

'Gibraltar'
'Hiawatha'
'Sylphides'
'Brazil'

'Fireball'
'Orangeade'
'Klondyke'

A. Elmer hybrids
'Pathfinder'
'Frontier Gold'

EVERGREEN

Most evergreen azaleas do well in the Middle Atlantic area.

Indicas

'Criterion'
'Elegans'
'Elegans Superba'
'El Frida'
'Fielder's White'
'George L. Taber'
'Giant Ruffles'
'Mrs. G. G. Gerbing'
'Pride of Prichard'
'Southern Charm'

Gables, Girards, Shammarellos & Prides
'Elsie Lee'
'Girard's Scarlet'
'Herbert'
'Rosebud'
'Stewartstonian'
'Sam'

Kurumes, Beltsvilles, etc.
'Azuma Kagami'-'Pink Pearl'
'Guy Yerkes'
'H. H. Hume'
'Ho-o' 'Appleblossom'
'Massasoit'
'Salmon Beauty'
'Sherwood Red'

Belgian Indians, Rutherfords, etc.
'Albert-Elizabeth'
'Dorothy Gish'
'Pink Ruffles'
'Redwings'
'Triomphe'
'Vervaeneana'

Satsukis
'Eikan'
'Fuji no Koshi'
'Getsutoku'
'Wakaebisu'
'Gumpo' & varieties

Glen Dales
'Ambrosia'
'Boldface'
'Coralie'
'Festive'
'Glacier'
'Martha Hitchcock'

Pericats
'Gardenia Supreme'
'Hampton Beauty'
'Madame Pericat'

Back Acres
'Margaret Douglas'
'Red Slipper'

DANISH CHAPTER A.R.S.

Denmark

DECIDUOUS

Early	Mid Season	Late
R. albrechtii	*R. luteum*	*R. atlanticum*
R. schlippenbachii	*R. prinophyllum*	*R. calendulaceum*
R. reticulatum	*R. occidentale* (not all)	'Coccinea Speciosa'
R. canadense	'Nancy Waterer'	*R. arborescens*
R. vaseyi	'Narcissiflora'	
R. periclymenoides	'Daviesi'	
	'Irene Koster'	
	'Persil'	
	'Gibraltar'	
	'Directeur Moerlands'	

EVERGREEN

Mid Season		Late
R. kiusianum	'Hino Scarlet'	*R. nakaharai*
R. kaempferi	'Diamant' hybrids	*R. nakaharai* v. 'Mariko'
'Orange Beauty'		

GREAT LAKES CHAPTER A.R.S.

(Holden Arboretum)

Includes northeastern Pennsylvania, northern Ohio, and Michigan

DECIDUOUS

Early	Mid Season	Late
'Knap Hill Apricot'	'Narcissiflora'	*R. calendulaceum*
R. vaseyi	'Knap Hill Apricot'	'Satan'
R. schlippenbachii	'Crimson Tide'	'Phebe'
R. vaseyi 'White Find'	'Homebush'	*R. arborescens*
R. yedoense	*R. prinophyllum*	'Daviesi'
R. prinophyllum	'Cecile'	*R. furbishii*
R. canadense	'Golden Eagle'	*R. bakeri*
R. luteum	*R. periclymenoides*	'Coccinea Speciosa'
R. yedoense poukhanense	*R. atlanticum*	*R. atlanticum*
R. periclymenoides	'George Reynolds'	*R. viscosum*

EVERGREEN

Early	Mid Season	Late
'Cascade'	'Snowball'	'Snowball'
'Hino-Red'	'Hino-Red'	'Elsie Lee'
'Mme. Butteryfly'	'Mme. Butterfly'	'Rosebud'
'Stewartstonian'	'Hino-White'	'May Belle'
Sherwood hybrids	'Mucronatum'	'Red Red'
'Delaware Valley White'	'Desiree'	'Helen Curtis'
	'Red Red'	'Renee Michelle'
	'Karens'	'Wilhelmina Vuyk'
	'Favorite'	'Pink Gem'
	'Dave's Pink'	'Gloskey Pink'

INDIANA CHAPTER A.R.S.

DECIDUOUS

Early	Mid Season	Late
'Balzac'	'Gibraltar'	*R. bakeri*
'Banana Split'	'Klondyke'	'Cecile'
'Cockatoo'	Mollis hybrids	'Hot Ginger'
R. vaseyi	'Persian Melon'	'Summer Spice'
R. roseum	'Pink William'	*R. viscosum*

EVERGREEN

Early	Mid Season	Late
'Campfire'	'Herbert'	'Gumpo'
'Mildred Mae'	'Snowball'	'Cherokee'
'Boudoir'	'White Swan'	'Takako'
'Gable A-27'	'Nancy of Robin Hill'	'Louise Gable'
'Formosa'	'Diamant Rot'	'Rosebud'
R. y. poukhanense	'Haruko'	
	'Fedora'	
	'Indica Alba'	
	'Blauuw's Pink'	
	'Sham's Flame'	
	'Cascade'	
	'Hino White'	
	'May Belle'	
	'Delaware Valley White'	

JUAN DE FUCA CHAPTER A.R.S.

Port Angeles, Washington

DECIDUOUS

Early	Mid Season	Late
R. schlippenbachii	*R. calendulaceum*	'Cecile'
	R. luteum	'Berry Rose'
	R. molle	'Klondyke'
	'Marion Merriman'	'Gallipoli'
		'Graciosa'
		'George Reynolds'
		'Oxydol'
		'Gibraltar'
		R. bakeri
		'Goldfinch'
		R. atlanticum
		'Homebush'
		'Satan'
		'Strawberry Ice'
		'Scarlet Pimpernel'

EVERGREEN

Early	Mid Season	Late
'Purple Splendor'	'Caroline Gable'	'Glamour'
	'Hino Crimson'	'J. L. Lovett'
	'Sweet Briar'	'Rosebud'
	R. y. poukhanense	'Lorna'
	'Vuyk's Scarlet'	'Polypetalum'
	'Ward's Ruby'	*R. nakaharai*
	R. albrechtii	*R. yedoense*
	R. kiusianum & varieties	

LOUISIANA AZALEA CHAPTER A.R.S.

DECIDUOUS

Early	Mid Season	*Late*
R. canescens	*R. alabamense*	*R. prunifolium*
R. austrinum	*R. speciosum*	*R. serrulatum*
'My Mary'		*R. viscosum*
		R. arborescens

EVERGREEN

Early	Mid Season	Late
'Formosa'	'Fashion'	'Wakaebisu'
'Coral Bells'	'Pink Pearl'	'Gyokushin'
'George L. Taber'	'Hampton Beauty'	'Pink Gumpo'
'Red Ruffles'	'Cavendishi'	'Eikan'
'Snow'	'Madame Pericat'	'White Gumpo'
'Judge Solomon'	'Prince of Orange'	'Getsutoku'
'Pride of Mobile'	'Watchet'	'Flame Creeper'
'Fritz Aichele'	'Peter Pooker'	'Marion Lee'
'Pink Ruffles'	'Hahn's Red'	'Izayoi'
'Cheer'	'Trouper'	'Heiwa'

MASON/DIXON CHAPTER A.R.S.

This chapter covers central Maryland and south-central Pennsylvania.

DECIDUOUS

Early	Mid Season	Late
R. canadense	*R. nudiflorum*	'Golden Peace'
R. y. poukhanense	*R. bakeri*	'Berry Rose'
R. vaseyi	*R. bakeri* 'Kentucky Colonel'	'Peach Sunset'
	R. roseum	*R. viscosum*
	R. austrinum	*R. prunifolium*
	'Gibraltar'	*R. arborescens*
	'Homebush'	
	R. calendulaceum	

EVERGREEN

Early	Mid Season	Late
'La Roche'	'Mildred Mae'	'Kaempo'
'Springtime'	'Dream'	'White Gumpo'
'Caroline Gable'	'Rose Greeley'	'Beni Kirishima'
'Lorna'	'Stewartstonian'	'Flame Creeper'
'Rosebud'	'Girard's Hot Shot'	'Eikan'
'H. H. Hume'	'Delaware Valley White'	'Pat Kraft'
'Herbert'	'Helen Curtis'	'Gumpo' varieties
'Kathleen'	'Elsie Lee'	All N. Tisbury hybrids
'Gaiety'	'Louise Gable'	'Tochi no Hikari'
'Hino Crimson'	'Purple Splendor'	'Elizabeth Gable'

MASSACHUSETTS CHAPTER A.R.S.

Two lists are included, one for the northern area zone 5 and another for zone 6, the southern area.

USDA ZONE 6

DECIDUOUS

Early	Mid Season	Late
R. vaseyi	'Gibraltar'	*R. calendulaceum*
R. vaseyi 'White Find'	'Daviesi'	'Homebush'
R. schlippenbachii	'Narcissiflora'	*R. bakeri*
R. canadense albiflorum	*R. japonicum*	*R. arborescens*
	'Klondyke'	'Satan'
	'Golden Eagle'	'Toucan'
	'Pink Sherbet'	'Girard's Crimson Tide'
	'Coral Queen'	'Old Gold'
	'Yellow Giant'	'Troupial'
	'Nicolaas Beets'	'Fireball'
	'Evening Glow'	'Tunis'

EVERGREEN

Early	Mid Season	Late
R. kaempferi	*R. kiusianum*	*R. kiusianum* 'Album'
'Buccaneer'	'Hino Crimson'	'Fedora'
'Eureka'	'Mother's Day'	'Louise Gable'
R. y. poukhansense	'Delaware Valley White'	'Lorna'
	'Stewartstonian'	'Yuka'
	'Herbert'	*R. nakaharai*
	'Rosebud'	'Betty Ann Voss'
	'Ledifolia Alba'	'Dorothy Reese'
	'Blauuw's Pink'	'Louisa'
	'Rosebud White'	'Peter Pooker'
	'Boudoir'	'Turk Cap'
	'Girard's Hot Shot'	'Alexander'
	'Hooden'	'Joseph Hill'
	'Polar Bear'	'Shubert'
	'Vuyk's Scarlet'	'Hardy Gardenia'
	'Nancy of Robin Hill'	'Yaye'
	'Kate Waterer'	'Michael Hill'
	'Desiree'	'Wintergreen'
	'Blue Danube'	'Mariko'
	'Purple Splendor'	
	'Girard's Rose'	
	'Girard's Purple'	
	'Girard's White'	

USDA ZONE 5

DECIDUOUS

Early	Mid Season	Late
R. vaseyi	'Gibraltar'	*R. calendulaceum*
R. schlippenbachii	'Klondyke'	*R. viscosum*
'Toucan'	'Daviesi'	*R. prinophyllum*
'Sham's Yellow'	'Jane Abbott'	*R. arborescens*
'Flamingo'	'Cecile'	*R. japonicum*
	'Tang'	'Brazil'
	'Brazil'	'Debutante'

'Golden Oriole'
'Persil'
'J. J. Jenkins'
'Flarepath'
'Hotspur'
'Golden Eagle'
'Satan'

'Deville'
'Harvest Moon'
Exbury × *atlanticum*

EVERGREEN

Early	Mid Season	Late
'Springtime'	*R. kiusianum* 'Album'	'Alexander'
R. y. poukhanense	'Palestrina'	'Lady Robin'
'Ledifolia Alba'	'Herbert'	'Conversation Piece'
'Kathleen'	'Guy Yerkes'	'Marilee'
	'Lorna'	'Michael Hill'
	'Helen Curtis'	'Trill'
	'Stewartstonian'	
	'Girard's Scarlet'	
	'Girard's Rose'	
	'Jeanne Weeks'	
	'Kathy'	
	'Pride's White'	
	'Louise Gable'	

MIDDLE ATLANTIC CHAPTER A.R.S.

The list is recommended for tide water areas of Norfolk and Hampton, Virginia and should also apply to Richmond. More cold hardy evergreen and more deciduous varieties are used in the colder areas of Virginia.

DECIDUOUS

Early	Mid Season	Late
R. atlanticum	*R. nudiflorum*	*R. viscosum*
R. canescens	'Bullfinch'	*R. prunifolium*
R. austrinum	'Toucan'	*R. arborescens*
'Gold Crest'	'Rhumba'	*R. bakeri*
'Gog'	'Klondyke'	*R. calendulaceum*
'Roxanne Waterer'	'Cecile'	
'Hiawatha'	'Knap Hill Red'	
'Sahara'	'Golden Eagle'	
'Petrouchka'	'Golden Sunset'	
'Golden Peace'	'Homebush'	
'Kilauea'	'Narcissiflora'	
'Gibraltar'	'Orient'	
'Brazil'		

EVERGREEN

Early	Mid Season	Late
R. kiusianum	'Gloria'	*R. nakaharai*
R. serpyllifolium	'Elsie Lee'	'Wakaebisu'
'Coral Bells'	'Helen Curtis'	'Gumpo'
'Hershey Red'	'H. H. Hume'	'Buccaneer'
'Dayspring'	'Glacier'	'Nancy of Robin Hill'
'Yaeshojo'	'Hampton Beauty'	'Laura Moreland'
'Hino Crimson'	'Flamingo'	'Beni Kirishima'
'Hinode Giri'	'Cavalier'	'Margaret Douglas'
'Ho o'	'Tradition'	'Youth'
'Salmon Beauty'	'Herbert'	'Lorna'
'Bridesmaid'	'Girard's Rose'	'Marion Lee'
'Majorie Ann'	'Rose Greeley'	'Keepsake'
'Mary Lynn'		
'Snow'		

MIDWEST CHAPTER A.R.S.

A large area covering Indiana, Illinois, Wisconsin, and Minnesota with distinct sub-climatic areas.

NORTHERN ZONE | CENTRAL ZONE

DECIDUOUS

NORTHERN ZONE		CENTRAL ZONE
'Northern Lights'	'Aurora'	'Pink William'
'Pink Lights'	*R. bakeri*	'Princess Royal'
'Rosy Lights'	'Cecile'	'Royal Lodge'
'White Lights'	'Cockatoo'	'Strawberry Ice'
R. canadense	'Gallipoli Red'	'Sunte Nectarine'
	'Gibraltar'	'Tang'
	'Kathleen'	'Tunis'
	'Old Gold'	*R. vaseyi*
	'Oxydol'	'Westminister'
	'Peachy Keen'	*R. molle*

EVERGREEN

'Hino Red'	'Pride's Pale Lilac'
'Hino Pink'	'Cardinalis'
'Elise Lee'	'Cherado' (Westcroft)
'May Belle'	'Pride's Joe Gable'
'Red-Red'	'Candy Apple'
'Delaware Valley White'	*R. kiusianum*
'Helen Curtis'	

NEW YORK CHAPTER A.R.S.

DECIDUOUS

Early	Mid Season	Late
R. schlippenbachii	*R. calendulaceum*	*R. viscosum*
R. vaseyi	'Gibraltar'	*R. prunifolium*
'Cockatoo'	'Nancy Waterer'	'Seville'
'Christopher Wren'	*R. roseum*	'Toucan'
R. albrechtii	*R. nudiflorum*	'Oxydol'
R. reticulatum	*R. atlanticum*	'Homebush'
'Hotspur Yellow'	'Cecile'	'Fireball'
'Peach Sunset'	'Strawberry Ice'	'Bouquet de Flore'
	'Daviesi'	'Gloria Mundi'
	'Berry Rose'	'Coccinea Speciosa'

EVERGREEN

Early	Mid Season	Late
'Allure'	*R. kiusianum* & hybrids	'Aphrodite'
'Dayspring'	'Rose Greeley'	'Kaempo'
'Fedora'	'Stewartstonian'	'Rosebud'
'Geisha'	'Peggy Ann'	'Buccaneer'
R. kaempferi	'James Gable'	'Renee Michelle'
'Purple Splendor'	'Mucronatum' & varieties	'Lorna'
'Hinode Giri' & 'Hino Crimson'	'Treasure'	*R. nakaharai*
'Daphne'	'Girard's Rose'	'Gaiety'
'Cattleya'	'Blaauw's Pink'	'Glamour'
'Springtime'	'Hershey's Red'	'Betty Ann Voss'

NORTHERN VIRGINIA CHAPTER A.R.S.

DECIDUOUS

Early	Mid Season	Late
R. schlippenbachii, white & pink	'Gibraltar'	*R. calendulaceum*
R. vaseyi	'Cecile'	*R. prunifolium*
R. vaseyi 'White Find'	'Old Gold'	*R. bakeri*
R. nudiflorum	'Brightstraw'	*R. arborescens*
R. speciosum	'Queen Emma'	
R. luteum	'Sun Chariot'	
R. austrinum	'Yellow Cloud'	
	'Klondyke'	
	'Marina'	
	'Peachy Keen'	

EVERGREEN

Early	Mid Season	Late
'Dayspring'	'Margaret Douglas'	'Gumpo' varieties
'Dream'	'Martha Hitchcock'	'Wakaebisu'
'Rose Greeley'	'Nancy of Robin Hill'	'Debonaire'
'Hershey's Red'	'Glacier'	'Beni Kirishima'
'Ambrosia'	'Marion Lee'	'Balsaminaeflorum'
'Geisha'	'Moonbeam'	'Higasa'
'Festive'	'Betty Ann Voss'	'Jindai'
'Herbert'	'Delos'	'Tochi no hikari'
'Buccaneer'	'Rosebud'	'White Jade'
'Quakeress'	'Treasure'	'Saint James'

Evergreen azaleas are more popular in this area than deciduous azaleas.

NORTHWEST CHAPTER A.S.A. and EUGENE CHAPTER, A.R.S. OREGON

DECIDUOUS

Most deciduous azaleas do well in this area, and the following represent only a partial list:

Early	Mid Season	Late
'Gibraltar'	'Strawberry Ice'	'Bright Stream'
'Homebush'	'Cecile'	'George Reynolds'
'Klondyke'	'Corringe'	'Basilisk'
	'Ballerina'	

EVERGREEN

Early	Mid Season	Late
'Hino Crimson'	'Redmond'	'Beni Kirishima'
'Dayspring'	'Betty Ann Voss'	'Gumpo Pink Fancy'
'Twenty Grand'	'Blue Danube'	'Flame Creeper'
'Purple Splendor'	'Helen Close'	'Shinnyo-no-Tsuki'
'Coral Bells'	'Caroline Gable'	'Gunrei'
'Buccaneer'	'Vuyk's Scarlet'	'Pearl Bradford'
'Stewartstonian'	'Everest'	'Rukizon'
'Glamour'	'Gaiety'	'Gumpo' varieties
'Amoenum'	'Amagasa'	'Macrantha' varieties
'Sherwood Orchid'	'Ben Morrison'	*R. nakarahai*
'Festive'	'Glacier'	'Balsaminaeflora'
'Corsage'	'Rosebud'	'Keisetsu'
'Refrain'	'Louise Gable'	'Eikan'
'Howard Anderson'	'Mothers Day'	'Tamino no Yuki'
'Sebastian'	'Burgundy'	'Cayuga'
'Betty'	'Aphrodite'	'Red Fountain'
	'Treasure'	

The Greenwood hybrids will become important in this area.

NOYO CHAPTER A. R. S.

Fort Bragg, California

DECIDUOUS

All deciduous azaleas do well when planted in full sun.

EVERGREEN

Early	Mid Season
'Amoenum'	'Aphrodite'
'Christmas Cheer'	'Edna'
'Corsage'	'Ethelwyn'
'Dainty'	'Lorna'
'Delicatissma'	*R. poukhanense*
'Day Spring'	'Snowbird'
'Everest'	'Snowscape'
'Firebird'	
'Flower Girl'	
'Sweetbrier'	
'Swan'	

PHILADELPHIA/VALLEY FORGE CHAPTERS A.R.S.

DECIDUOUS

Early	Mid Season	Late
R. schlippenbachii	'Gibraltar'	*R. viscosum*
R. vaseyi (pink)	'Cecile'	*R. bakeri*
R. nudiflorum	'Klondyke'	*R. prunifolium*
R. vaseyi	'Golden Oriole'	*R. arborescens*
'White Find'	'Homebush'	*R. calendulaceum*
'Pink Gem'	'Strawberry Ice'	'Royal Lodge'
R. luteum	'Pot of Gold'	*R. roseum*
R. canescens	'Narcissiflora'	'Daviesi'
R. alabamense	'Brazil'	*R. viscosum*
	'Renne'	*R. atlanticum*
	R. atlanticum (Choptank River hybrid)	'Pink Smokey'
	'Toucan'	
	'Sugared Almond'	
	'Oxydol'	
	R. speciosum	
	'Sham's Yellow'	
	'Appalachia'	
	'Renne'	

EVERGREEN

Early	Mid Season	Late	Very Late
'Ambrosia'	'Delaware Valley White'	'Copperman'	'Louise'
'Springtime'	'Palestrina'	'Everest'	'Marilee'
'Dayspring'	'Polaris'	'Buccaneer'	'Alexander'
'Rose Greeley'	'Martha Hitchcock'	'Snowclad'	'Yuka'
'Samite'	'Treasure'	'Swansong'	'Mt. Seven Star'
'Mildred Mae'	'Dragon'	'Beni Kirishima'	'Matsuyo'
'Karen'	'Hershey's Red'	'Lillie Maude'	
'Dream'	'Hardy Gardenia'	'Pearl Bradford'	
'Guy Yerkes'	'Stewartstonian'	'Chinsayi'	
'Spink' (Robin Hill)	'Dream'	'Macrantha Flore Plena'	
R. y. poukhanense	'Lady Louise'	'Sagittarius'	
'Corsage'	'Gwenda'	'Cora Brandt'	
'Mary Dalton'	'Sara Holden'	'Gwenda'	
'James Gable'	'Conversation Piece'	'Betty Ann Voss'	
'Geisha'	'Watchet'	'Betty Layman'	
'Big Joe'	'Betty Ann Voss'	'Laura Morland'	
'Helen Close'	'Elsie Lee'	'Wavelet'	
'Polar Bear'	'Helen Curtis'	'Sarabande'	
R. kiusianum	'Surprise'	'Balsaminaeflorum'	
'Treasure'	'Bo Peep'	'Eiko San'	
'Eleanor Allen'	'Silver Moon'	'Louisa'	
'Libby' (Kaempferi)	'Moonbeam'	'Wintergreen'	'Yuka'
'Anna Kehr'	'Jeff Hill'	'Alexander'	'Matsuyo'
'Blushing Bride'	'Joseph Hill'	'Marilee'	'Mt. Seven Star'
'Lady Locks' (macrosepalum)	'Placid'	'Michael Hill'	'Mariko'
	'King's Luminous Pink'	'Late Love'	'Angela Place'
		'Pink Pancake'	'Dauntless'
	'Aphrodite'	'Trill'	'Mary Ann'
	'White Lady'	'Hot Line'	'Helen Close'

PORTLAND, OREGON CHAPTER A.R.S.

DECIDUOUS

Early	Mid Season	Late
'Altaclarensis'	'Homebush'	'Klondyke'
'Desert Pink'	'Silver Slipper'	*R. bakeri*
'Strawberry Ice'	'Agnes Harvey'	*R. occidentale*
'Flamingo'	'Sugared Almond'	'Royal Lodge'
'Sunset Pink'	'Sun Chariot'	'Sweet Sue'
'Mollis'	'Cecile'	'Corneille'
'Old Gold'	'Narcissiflora'	'Kathleen'
'Irene Koster'	Viscosepalum hybrids	'Jock Brydon'
'George Reynolds'	'Whitethroat'	'Chocolate Ice'
'Sylphides'	'Marion Merriman'	'Imago'
'Mrs. L. H. Endtz'	'Floradora'	
R. schlippenbachii	'Spek's Brilliant'	
R. albrechtii'	'Ginger'	
	'Cecile'	
	'Chetco'	
	'Homebush'	
	'Beautica'	
	'Yaquina'	

EVERGREEN

Early	Mid Season	Late
'James Gable'	'Higasa'	*R. nakaharai* hybrids
'Hershey's Red'	'Maria Derby'	'Macrantha'
'Ward's Ruby'	'Gumpo'	'Sir Robert'
'Sekidera'	'Hexe'	'Aiden'
'Pink Ice'	'Rosebud'	'Beni Kirishima'
'Mother's Day'	'Eikan'	'Pearl Bradford'
'Treasure'	'Glamour'	'Keisetsu'
'Takasago'	'Aphrodite'	'Robin Dale'
'Sarrona'	'Everest'	'General Wavell'
'Anchorite'	'Torchlight'	'Joseph Hill'
'Hinomayo'	'Palestrina'	'Gumpo'
'James Cairns'	'Lorna'	
'Hino Crimson'	'Purple Splendor'	
'Rose Greeley'	'Treasure'	
'Sherwood Orchid'	'Fedora'	
'Geisha'	'Caroline Gable'	
	'James Gable'	

PRINCETON (NEW JERSEY) CHAPTER A.R.S.

DECIDUOUS

Early	Mid Season	Late
R. schlippenbachii	'Daviesi'	'Royal Lodge'
R. vaseyi	'Klondyke'	*R. sanctum*
R. austrinum	'Gibraltar'	*R. arborescens*
R. speciosum	'Tunis'	*R. viscosum*
'Flamingo'	'Annabelle'	*R. atlanticum*
'Knap Hill Apricot'	'Debutante'	*R. calendulaceum*
'Persil'	'Golden Eagle'	*R. prunifolium*
R. canescens	'Strawberry Ice'	
	R. calendulaceum	

EVERGREEN

Early	Mid Season	Late
'Dayspring'	'Sherwood Orchid'	'Balsaminaeflorum'
'Springtime'	'Amoena'	'Snow Clad'
'Karen'	'Peggy Ann'	'Saggitarius'
'Rose Greeley'	'Rosebud'	'Gumpo' varieties
'Coral Bells'	'Treasure'	'J. T. Lovett'
'Geisha'	'Vestal & Vespers'	'Macrantha'
'La Roche'	'Mme. Butterfly'	'Chinsay'
'Herbert'	'Glory'	'Oriflammae'
'Hino Crimson'	'Guy Yerkes'	'Beni Kirishima'
R. y. poukhanense	'Caroline Gable'	'Buccaneer'

RALPH PENNINGTON CHAPTER A.S.A.

Piedmont area of South Carolina and Georgia

DECIDUOUS

Early	Mid Season	Late
R. austrinum	*R. arborescens*	*R. bakeri*
R. canescens	'Brazil'	'My Lady'
R. atlanticum	'Windsor Buttercup'	*R. prunifolium*
'Klondyke'	*R. calendulaceum*	*R. quinquefolium*
R. vaseyi	'Gibraltar'	*R. viscosum*
	'Golden Eagle'	
	'Homebush'	
	'Peachy Keen'	
	'Primrose'	
	R. speciosum	

EVERGREEN

Early	Mid Season	Late
'Blaauw's Pink'	'Ambrosia'	'Aztec'
'Corsage'	'Boldface'	'Beni-kirishima'
'Dayspring'	'Carillon'	'Ben Morrison'
'Dream'	'Easter Parade'	'Beth Bullard'
'Hershey's Red'	'Elsie Lee'	'Charles Encke'
'Hiawatha'	'Grace Freeman'	'Debonaire'
'H. H. Hume'	'Kehr's White Rosebud'	'Eikan'
'Massasoit'	'Martha Hitchcock'	'Gumpo Fancy'
'Miss Suzie'	'Mother's Day'	'Gunrei'
'Mrs. G. G. Gerbing'	'Opal'	'Ivan Anderson'
'Palestrina'	'Red Slippers'	'Higasa'
'Peach Bloosom'	'Surprise'	'Kikoshi'
'Red Ruffles'	'Treasure'	'Sagittarius'
'Rose Greeley'		'Shinkigen'
		'Saint James'
		'Swansong'
		'Shinnyo no Tsuki'
		'Yaye'
		'Yuka'

ROBERT D. GARTRELL CHAPTER A.S.A.

New Jersey

DECIDUOUS

Early	Mid Season	Late
R. schlippenbachii	'Brazil'	*R. calendulaceum*
'Flamingo'	*R. vaseyi*	'Klondyke'
'Hiawatha'	'Beaulieu'	'Coronation Lady'
	'Debutante'	'Berry Rose'
	'Gallipoli Pink'	'Devon'
	'High Fashion'	'Mephistopheles'
	'Homebush'	'Oxydol'
	'Old Gold'	'Yaffle'
	'Orange Ball'	'Satan'
		'Royal Lodge'

EVERGREEN

Early	Mid Season	Late
'Dayspring'	'Guy Yerkes'	'Jimmy Coover'
'Mary Dalton'	'Vestal'	'Martha Hitchcock'
'Geisha'	'Oriflamme'	'Gaiety'
'Eureka'	'Louise Gable'	'Copperman'
'Springtime'	'Stewartstonian'	'La Belle Helene'
'Ambrosia'	'Pixie'	'Blue Tip'
'Snowball'	'Ben Morrison'	'Gwenda'
'Allure'	'Linwood Lustre'	
'Rosebud'	'Helen Curtis'	
'Rose Greeley'	'Refrain'	

SEATTLE RHODODENDRON SOCIETY A.R.S.

In the Puget Sound area of Washington State, with its various climates, one can grow nearly all of the deciduous and evergreen azalea species except for the tender. The species are not listed, but the list from this area is generally larger than most other areas.

DECIDUOUS

Knap Hill

Reds
'Brazil'
'Corringe'
'Gibraltar'
'Ginger'
'Hot Spur Red'
'Krakatoa'
'Renne'
'Satan'
'Comanche'
'Ilam Cardinal'
'Bright Forecast'
'Cecile'
'Homebush'
'Princess Royal'
'Silver Slipper'
'Strawberry Ice'

Yellows
'Annabella'
'Basilisk'
'George Reynolds'
'Golden Oriole'
'Harvest Moon'
'Klondyke'
'Marina'
'Marion Merriman'
'Sun Chariot'
'Cherokee'

Whites
'Ballerina'
'Mrs. Anthony Waterer'
'Oxydol'

Mollis, Ghents and Others

'J. C. van Tol'
'Dr. M. Oosthoek'
'Koster's Brilliant Red'
'C. B. Van Nes'
'Spek's Brilliant'
'Mevrouw G. van Noordt'
'Directeur Moerlands'
'Adrian Koster'
'Atlaclarensis'
'Coccinea Speciosa'
'Corneille'
'Narcissiflora'
'Norma'
'Aida'
'Il Tasso'
'Magnifica'
'Irene Koster'
'Exquisita'

EVERGREEN

Kurume Hybrids

'Coral Bells'
'Hinode Giri'
'Hinomayo'
'Pink Pearl'
'Hino Crimson'
'Sherwood Red'
'Snow'
'Hershey's Red'
'Sherwood Orchid'
'Hexe'

Glen Dale Hybrids

'Buccaneer'
'Everest'
'Gaiety'
'Glacier'
'Glamour'
'Helen Close'
'Martha Hitchcock'
'Pearl Bradford'
'Treasure'
'Aphrodite'
'Captivation'
'Moonbeam'

Satsuki Hybrids

'Beni'
'Bunka'
'Chinzan'
'Gumpo'
'Gunrei'
'Hakata Shiro'
'Gyokushin'
'Jindai'
'Kirishima'
'Shinnyo no Tsuki'
'Pink Gumpo'
'Shogetsu'

Robin Hill Hybrids

'Lady Louise'
'Greta'
'Dorothy Reese'
'Eunice Updyke'
'Mrs. Emil Hager'
'Nancy of Robinhill'
'Redmond'
'Robin Hill Gillie'
'Watchet'
'Sir Robert'
'Robindale'
'Ormsby'
'Sara Holden'
'White Hart'

Gable Hybrids

'Campfire'
'Lorna'
'Louise Gable'
'Purple Splendor'
'Rose Greeley'
'James Gable'
'Rosebud'
'Stewartstonian'
'Herbert'
'Caroline Gable'

Miscellaneous Hybrids

'Palestrina'
'Vuyk's Rosyred'
'Vuyk's Scarlet'
'Flame Creeper'
'Balsaminaeflorum'
'J. T. Lovett'

SOUTHERN CALIFORNIA CHAPTER A.R.S.

DECIDUOUS

More emphasis is placed on evergreen azaleas in this area. The southern forms of *R. occidentale* should do well.

EVERGREEN

Many azalea varieties do well in southern California and the list is endless; most Kurumes, Southern Indians, Rutherford, Gold Cup, Kerrigan, and most of the Satsukis are the major groups. Many of the Belgian hybrids are also popular plants.

Early	Mid Season	Late
'Nuccio's Happy Days'	'Nuccio's Pink Bubbles'	'Caprice'
'Nuccio's Garden Party'	'Starlight'	'Sun Valley'
'Madonna'	'Gay Paree'	'Content'
'Nuccio's Carnival Queen'	'Nuccio's Carnival'	'Pride of Dorking'
'Easter Bonnet'	'Nuccio's Carnival Candy'	'Benigasa'
'Rose Glitters'	'Nuccio's Carnival Firecracker'	'Gumpo' & sports
'Rose Queen' & sports	'Hexe'	'Tama no Hada'
'Red Poppy'	'Phoeniceum'	
'Red Wings'	'L. J. Bobbink'	
'White Orchids'	'Hino Crimson'	
	'Easter Parade'	
	'Nuccio's Allegro'	

TACOMA CHAPTER A.R.S.

Tacoma, Washington

DECIDUOUS

Most deciduous species and hybrids do well in this area.

Early	Mid Season	Late
R. albrechtii	'Gallipoli'	'Cecile'
R. roseum	'Gibraltar'	*R. occidentale*
'Kathleen'	'Oxydol'	*R. bakeri*
'Old Gala'		

EVERGREEN

Early	Mid Season	Late
'Annette'	'Refrain'	'Kenwood'
'Hinomayo'	'Daphne'	'Elsie Lee'
'Vuyk's Scarlet'	'Tat'	'Polaris'
'Mother's Day'		

TAPPAN ZEE (NEW JERSEY) CHAPTER A.R.S.

DECIDUOUS

Early	Mid season	Late
R. schlippenbachii	*R. japonicum*	*R. arborescens*
R. nudiflorum	*R. molle*	*R. calendulaceum*
R. vaseyi	*R. kaempferi*	*R. prunifolium*
R. atlanticum	*R. prinophyllum* 'Avocet'	*R. viscosum*
R. canadense	'Oxydol'	'Cecile'
R. yedoense poukhanense	'Coccinea Speciosa'	'Klondyke'
R. daricum	'Gibraltar'	'Homebush'
R. mucronulatum	'Persil'	'Daviesi'
'Cornell Pink'		'Narcissiflora'
		R. bakeri

EVERGREEN

'Springtime'	*R. kiusianum*	'Balsaminaeflorum'
'Tradition'	'Delaware Valley White'	'J. T. Lovett'
'Peggy Ann'	'Louise Gable'	'Macrantha'
'Blaauw's Pink'	'Rosebud'	'Wintergreen'
'Dream'	'Hershey's Red'	
'Treasure'	'Martha Hitchcock'	
'Christmas Cheer'	'Vuyk's Scarlet'	
'Coral Bells'	'Palestrina'	
'Hinode Giri'		

TRI-STATE AZALEA CHAPTER A.S.A.

Southern Illinois, southern Indiana, and western Kentucky

DECIDUOUS

Early	Mid Season	Late
R. canescens	'Gibraltar'	'Lady Roseberry'
R. vaseyi 'White Find'	'Klondyke'	'Bouquet de Flore'
R. vaseyi 'Pink'	'Crimson Tide'	'Tunis'
R. austrinum 'Yellow'	'Cecile'	'Royal Lodge'
'Golden Peace'	*R. roseum*	'J. J. Jennings'
'Daviesi'	*R. calendulaceum*	*R. atlanticum*
R. periclymenoides	'Kathleen'	*R. bakeri* 'Alhambra'
R. alabamense	'Old Gold'	*R. viscosum*
'Primrose'	'Coral Queen'	*R. serrulatum*
R. mucronulatum 'Cornell Pink'	'Flamingo'	*R. arborescens*

EVERGREEN

Early	Mid Season	Late
'Hino Crimson'	'Elsie Lee'	'Susan'
'Mildred Mae'	'May Belle'	'Rosebud'
R. y. poukhanense & varieties	'Cascade' (Sham's)	'Lady Louise'
'Karen'	'Fedora'	'Frosty'
'Boudoir'	'Palestrina'	'Purple Splendor'
'Stewartstonian'	'Hino Red'	'Louise Gable'
'Herbert'	'Delaware Valley White'	'Maryann'
'Hino White'	'Helen Curtis'	'Jimmy Coover'
'Othello'	'Betty'	'Johann Straus'
'Springtime'	'John Cairns'	'Vestal'

VALLEY FORGE (PENNSYLVANIA) CHAPTER A.R.S.

DECIDUOUS

Early	Mid Season	Late
R. schlippenbachii	'Daviesi'	*R. calendulaceum*
R. vaseyi 'Pink'	'Narcissiflora'	'Royal Lodge'
R. vaseyi 'White Find'	'Golden Oriole'	*R. bakeri*
R. nudiflorium	'Gibraltar'	*R. arborescens*
R. canescens	'Cecile'	*R. atlanticum*
'Pink Gem'	'Klondyke'	'Pink Smokey'
	'Homebush'	*R. viscosum*
	'Strawberry Ice'	*R. prunifolium*
	'Renne'	
	'Pot of Gold'	

EVERGREEN

Early	Mid Season	Late
'Springtime'	'Placid'	'Angela Place'
'Dayspring'	'Palestrina'	'Swansong'
'Samite'	'Delaware Valley White'	'Copperman'
'Rose Greeley'	'Polaris'	'Pearl Bradford'
'Mildred Mae'	'Hershey's Red'	'Beni Kirishima'
'Karen'	'Treasure'	'Everest'
'Dream'	'King's Luminous Pink'	'Lillie Maude'
'Ambrosia'	'Stewartstonian'	'Dauntless'
'Eleanor Allen'	'Buccaneer'	'Maryann'
'Guy Yerkes'	'Louise Gable'	'Helen Close'
	'James Gable'	'Snowclad'

WILLIAM BARTRAM CHAPTER A.R.S.

This chapter covers the area at the junction of North Carolina, South Carolina, and northeast Georgia.

DECIDUOUS

Early	Mid Season	Late
R. canescens	*R. japonicum*	*R. viscosum*
R. austrinum	*R. speciosum*	*R. arborescens*
R. canescens × *speciosum* hybrids	*R. vaseyi*	*R. bakeri*
'Primrose'	*R. nudiflorum*	*R. calendulaceum*
	R. calendulaceum	*R. prunifolium*
	'Gibraltar'	*R. serrulatum*
	'Klondyke'	*R. prunifolium* × *arborescens* hybrids
	'Windsor Buttercup'	*R. bakeri* × *arborescens* hybrids
	Choptank hybrids	

EVERGREEN

Early	Mid Season	Late
'Dayspring'	'Kehr's White Rosebud'	All Robin Hill varieties except 'Spink'
'Festive'	'Anna Kehr'	'Beth Bullard'
'Mike Bullard'	'Frosted Orange'	'Hill's Single Red'
'Coral Bells'	'Pride of Lawrenceville'	'Trill'
'Pink Pearl'	'Miss Susie'	'Andante'
'Hershey's Red'	'Margaret Douglas'	'Eikan'
'Mother's Day'	'Marion Lee'	'Gunrei'
'Daphne'	'Ben Morrison'	'Fukirokuju'
'Orange Cup'	'Easter Parade'	'Issho no Haru'
'Pennington White'	'Janet Rhea'	'Gumpo' varieties

Appendix F
SELECTED REFERENCES

American Rhododendron Society Journal, American Rhododendron Society.

A Brocade Pillow, Azaleas of Old Japan, Kinshu Makura, Ito Chei 1692, translation by Kaname Kato, Introduction and Commentary by John L. Creech, Weatherhill, N.Y., Tokyo, 1984.

Asen, S., R. N. Stewart and K. H. Norris, "Co pigmentation effect of quercetin glycosides on absorption characteristics of cyanidens, glycosides and color of 'Red Wing' azalea", *Phytochemistry* 10: 171–175, 1971.

Bowers, Clement G., *Rhododendrons and Azaleas, Their Origins, Cultivation and Development* 2nd ed., Macmillan, N.Y., 1960.

Clark, D. L. and G. Taylor editor, *W. J. Bean, Trees and Shrubs, Hardy in the British Isles* Vol. III, 8th edition, London, Butler and Tanner, Ltd., 1976.

Clarke, J. Harold, *Getting Started with Rhododendrons and Azaleas,* reprint ISBS/Timber Press, Portland, Ore., 1983.

Color, Universal Language and Dictionary of Names, Special Publication 440, U.S. Department of Commerce, National Bureau of Standards, Washington, D.C., 1976.

Contributions Toward a Classification of Rhododendrons, N.Y. Bot, Gardens, 1980.

Cox, Peter A., *Dwarf Rhododendrons;* Macmillan, 1973.

Dodd, John H. and Lorin W. Roberts, *Experiments in Plant Tissue Culture,* Cambridge Press, N.Y.; 1982.

Fletcher H. R., comp. *The International Rhododendron Register.* London Royal Horticultural Society, 1958.

Flora of Taiwan, Vol. IV, Epoch Publishing Co. Ltd., Taiwan.

Galle, F. C., "Native and some Introduced Azaleas for Southern Gardens: Kind and Culture". Cason Callaway Foundation *Bull.* #2, 1956.

Galle, F. C., *Southern Living Azaleas,* Oxmoor House Inc., Ala., 1974.

Grootendorst, Herman J., *Rhododendrons en Azaleas,* Vereniging Voir Boskoopse Culturen, 1954.

Harborne, J. B.; "Flavonid Pigments as both Taxonomic and Phyletic Markers in the Genus Rhododendron" *Contributions Toward a Classification of Rhododendrons,* N.Y. Botanical Garden, 1980.

Hartmann, Hudson T. and Dale E. Kester, *Plant Propagation; Principles and Practice,* 4th Ed. Prentice-Hall, Inc., Englewood Cliffs, N.J.; 1983.

Hedegaard, Johannes, *Studies in the Genus Rhododendron Dealing with Fruits, Seedling and Their Associated Hairs,* 2 vols., G. E. C. Gads Publishing House, Denmark, 1980.

Hortus Third, Macmillan, N.Y., 1976.

ISCC-NBS Color-Name Charts illustrated with Centroid Colors, Supplement to NBS Circular 553, U.S. Department of Commerce, National Bureau of Standards. Washington D.C.

Jones, S. B. and A. E. Luchsinger, *Plant Systematics,* McGraw-Hill Book Co., N.Y., 1979.

Kaufman, Peter; T. L. Mellicamp; J. Glimm-Lacy; J. D. LaCroix; *Practical Botany;* Reston Publishing Co., 1983.

Kehr, August, "Azaleodendron Breeding", American Rhododendron Society *Bulletin,* Vol. 31, 1977 #4.

Kelly, K. L. and D. B. Judd, *Color Universal Language and Dictionary of Names,* U.S. Dept. of Commerce National Bureau of Standards, Special Pub. 440, 1976.

King, B. L., "Flavonoid Analysis of Hybridization in Rhododendron Seed in Pentanthera". Syst. *Botany* 2; 14–27, 1977.

King, B. L., "The Flavonoids of the Deciduous Rhododendrons of North America", *Amer. Jour. Botany* 64: 350–360, 1977.

King, B. L., "The Systematic Implications of Flavonoids in Rhododendron Subgenus Pentanthera": *Contributions Toward a Classification of Rhododendrons,* N.Y. Botanical Gardens, 1980.

Kofranek, A. M. and R. A. Larson eds. "Growing Azaleas Commercially", Davis, Ca. Univ. Calif. Div. of Agr. Sc., 1975 (Pub. #4058).

Koreshoff, D. R. *Bonsai, Its Art, Science, History, and Philosophy,* Timber Press, Portland, Or., 1984.

Krüssman, Gerd., *Rhododendrons: Their History, Geographical Distribution, Hybridization and Culture,* London, Ward Lock, 1970.

Kunishige, M. and Y. Kogayashi, "Chromatographic Identification of Japanese Azalea Species and Their Hybrids", *Contributions Toward a Classification of Rhododendrons,* N.Y. Botanical Gardens, 1984.

Lawrence, George H. M., *Taxonomy of Vascular Plants,* Macmillan Co., N.Y., 1951.

Leach, David G., "That's Why the Lady is a Tramp", American Rhododendron Society *Bulletin,* Vol. 36, #4, 151–52, 1982.

Leach, David G., "Two Thousand Year Curse of the Rhododendron", *Rhododron Information* 1967:146.

Lee, Fredric P., *The Azalea Book,* 2nd ed., Princeton, N.J., Van Nostrand, 1965.

Leslie, Alan comp. *The Rhododendron Handbook Rhododendron Species in Cultivation,* 1980, London, The Royal Horticultural Society.

Leslie, Alan, *The International Rhododendron Register,* Royal Horticultural Society, U.K., expected publication date, 1985.

Li, Hui-lin, "Chromosome Studies in the Azaleas of Eastern North America", *Amer. Journal Botany,* 44:8–14, 1957.

Livingston, Philip A. and F. H. West, *Hybrids and Hybridizers: Rhododendrons and Azaleas for Eastern North America,* Harrowood Books, Newton Square, Pa., 1978.

Luteyn, James L. editor. *Contributions Toward a Classification of Rhododendrons, Int. Rhododendron Conference,* 1978, New York Botanical Gardens, Bronx, N.Y., 1980.

Millais, John G., *Rhododendrons and the Various Hybrids,* London, Longmans, Green Vol. 1, 1917, Vol. 2, 1924.

Morrison, B. Y., "The Glenn Dale Azaleas", U.S.D.A. Agricultural Monograph, #20, 1953.

Naka, John Y., R. K. Ota and K. Rokkatu, *Bonsai Techniques for Satusuki,* Printed in Japan, published by Ota Bonsai Nursery, Orange, California, 1979.

Ohwi, Jisaburo, *Flora of Japan,* Smithsonian Institution, Washington, D.C., 1965.

Phillips, C. E. Lucas and Peter N. Barber, *Rhododendrons: A Record of the Gardens of Exbury,* Cassel, London, 1967.

Phillipson, William B.; "Problems in the Classification of the Azalea Complex"; *Contr. Toward a Classification of Rhododendrons,* N.Y. Botanical Garden, 1980.

Rhododendron Year Books; The Royal Horticultural Soc., London.

Roane, M. K. and J. D. Henry, "The Species of Rhododendron Native to North America". *Virginia Journal of Science,* Vol. 32 #2, 1981.

Salley, Homer and Harold Greer, *Rhododendron Hybrids,* Timber Press, Portland, Or., 1986.

Satsuki Encyclopedia (Bantam), In Japanese, cultivar names in English, Tokyo.

Schenk, George; *The Complete Shade Gardener;* Houghton Miffin Co., 1984.

Schmalscheidt, Walter, "More on Azaleodendrons", American Rhododendron Society *Bulletin,* Vol. 33, 1979, #3.

Skinner, H. T., *Classification of the Native American Azaleas, Proceeding of the International Rhododendron Conference, Portland, Oregon.* The American Rhododendron Society, May 11–14, 1961.

Skinner, H. T., "In Search of Native Azaleas", Morris Arboretum *Bulletin* (Univ. of Penn.) Philadelphia, Morris Arboretum, 1955, Vol. 6, No. 1 and No. 2.

Solymosy, S. L., "A Treatise on Native Azaleas", Louisiana Society for Horticulture Research, Vol. IV, #2, 1976.

Spethmann, W.; "Flavonoids and Carotenoids of Rhododendron Flowers"; *Contributions Toward a Classification of Rhododendrons,* N.Y. Bot. Garden, 1980.

Stevenson, J. F. ed. *The Species of Rhododendron,* Edinburgh Rhododendron Society, 1930.

Street, Frederick, *Azaleas,* Cassel, London, 1959.

Suzuki, H. & M. *Satsuki Taikan.* Tokyo, 1972.

"The Azalean", *Journal* of the Azalea Society of America.

Wetherell, Donald, *Introduction to In Vitro Propagation,* Avery Publishing Group, Inc., Wayne, N.J. 96 pp., 1981.

Wilson, Ernest H. and A. Rehder. *A Monograph of Azaleas; Rhododendron Subgenus Anthodendron,* Cambridge, Ma., Harvard University Press, 1921.

Wilson, Ernest H.; *Plant Hunting,* Boston, Ma., Stratford, 1927.

Young, Judy, Dr. In-Shong Chang Trans.; *Rhododendrons of China,* Amer. Rhododendron Society and Rhododendron Species Foundation, Binford and Mort, Oregon, 1980.

Appendix G
GLOSSARY

ACUMINATE: An acute apex, tapered to a protruded point.

ACUTE: Sharp, ending in a point.

APEX: Tip or distal end.

ARISTATE: Bristle-like or elongated apex.

APOMICT: A plant produced without fertilization.

BRISTLY: Having stiff strong hairs or bristles.

CALYX: Outer whorl of floral envelope, composed of sepals.

CAMPANULATE: Bell shaped.

CILIATE: Marginally fringed with hairs.

CONNATE: United or joined; as in connate petals or lobes.

COROLLA: Inner circle of a floral envelope, composed of petals.

DECIDUOUS: Falling at the end of one season's growth.

DIPLOID: Two similar complements of chromosomes—Rhododendrons ($n = 13$) ($2n = 26$).

EGLANDULAR: Without glands.

ELEPIDOTE: Without scales.

ELLIPTIC: Oval in outline, narrow to rounded units, widest at or above the middle.

EXSERTED: Sticking out or projecting out, as stamens from the petals.

GAMOPETALOUS: With petals united or sympetalous.

GLABRESCENT: Becoming nearly glabrous with age.

GLABROUS: Not hairy.

GLANDULAR: Bearing glands or gland-like appendages or protuberances.

GLANDULAR-PUBESCENT: With glands and hairs intermixed or hairs terminated by pin-head-like glands.

GLAUCESCENT: Slightly glaucous.

GLAUCOUS: Covered with a whitish substance that rubs off.

HIRSUTE: With rough or coarse hairs.

HOSE-IN-HOSE: One corolla superimposed inside another, or two circles of petals, the calyx may or may not be present.

IRREGULAR FLOWER: Having some parts different from other parts and incapable of being divided into two equal halves.

IMBRICATED: Overlapping.

INDUMENTUM: A heavy hairy or pubescent covering.

LANCEOLATE: Lance-shaped, much longer than broad, widening above the base and tapering to the apex.

LEPIDOTE: Surface with small scales.

LINEAR: Long and narrow, sides parallel or nearly so.

LOBE: Any part or segment of a corolla (as a petal).

MIDRIB: The main rib of a leaf.

MUCRONATE: Terminated abruptly by a short and sharp point.

OBLANCEOLATE: Reverse of lanceolate, leaf broader beyond the middle.

OBOVATE: Reverse of ovate, the terminal half broader than the basal.

OBTUSE: Blunt, rounded.

OVATE: Outline like a hen's egg, the broader end below the middle.

PERIANTH: The floral envelope consisting of calyx and corolla (when present).

PERSISTENT: Remaining attached.

PETALS: Division or lobe of the corolla.

PILOSE: Having soft, long, straight hairs.

POLYPETALOUS: A corolla of separtate petals; as contrasted with gamopetalous.

PUBESCENT: Covered with soft short hairs; downy.

ROTATE: Wheel-shaped.

SETA: A bristle.

SINUATE: Indented or wavy margin of a leaf or petal.

SPATULATE: Spoon-shaped.

STIPITATE: Borne on a short stalk.

STOLONIFEROUS: Producing runners on basal branches that are inclined to root and give rise to new plants.

STRIGOSE: With sharp oppressed straight stiff hairs, often swollen at the base.

TAXON (pl. taxa): General term applied to any taxonomic element of a population or group; i.e. species, cultivar breeding line, etc.

TETRAPLOID: Complement of chromosomes four times the usual—Rhododendrons ($2n = 26$) ($4n = 52$).

TOMENTOSE: Densely woolly or pubescent.

VILLOUS: Bearing long and short hairs.

VISCID: Sticky.

Appendix H
LIST OF REGISTERED AZALEAS

In 1958 the Royal Horticultural Society as the International Registration Authority for rhododendron cultivars, including azaleas, published the *International Rhododendron Register.* The *Register* listed with a condensed description all known horticultural varieties of azaleas or clones up to that date. Since 1958 a registration procedure has been set up for all new azalea cultivars by the International Registration Authority, provided the cultivar has a validly published name and is adequately described. A new *International Rhododendron Register* is expected to be published in 1988.

The following list of azaleas has been registered in the period since the publication of the *International Rhododendron Register* in 1958, through the spring of 1984. Descriptions of these azaleas can be found in the plant description chapters.

The abbreviation 'dec.' following the azalea denotes a deciduous azalea.

'Agnes Harvey'-dec.
'Albacore'-dec.
'Alclara'
'Alda Lea'
'Aleida'
'Alexander'
'Allotria'
'Alpine'
'Alsea'-dec.
'Amber Rain'-dec.
'Andrew Leuttgen'
'Annabella'-dec.
'Anna Kehr'
'Anna Pavlova'-dec.
'Anneke'-dec.
'Ann Ione'-dec.
'Antilope'-dec.
'Antony Roland'
'Appalachia'-dec.
'Apple Blossom Delight'-dec.
'Apricot Honey'-dec.
'April Showers'-dec.
'Arcadia'-dec.
'Arctic Flame'
'Arctic Sun'-dec.
'Arpege'-dec.
'Aurora'
'Avon'

'Baby Rosebud'
'Badinage'
'Bakkarat'-dec.
'Balkis'-dec.
'Ballerina'-dec.
'Balls of Fire'-dec.
'Balzac'-dec.
'Barry Bittinger'
'Basilisk'-dec.
'Bayou'
'Bazaar'-dec.
'Beattie'
'Beaulieu'-dec.
'Bebita'-dec.
'Becky'
'Bengal Beauty'
'Bengal Star'
'Bergerette'
'Berryrose'-dec.
'Bess Hallock'
'Betty Anne Voss'
'Betty Kelly'-dec.
'Betty Layman'
'Big Girl'-dec.
'Bikini'
'Bingo'
'Blazon'
'Blue Angel'
'Blue Danube'
'Blushing Angel'
'Bob Elmer'-dec.
'Bobo'
'Bob White'
'Bolero'
'Bouffant'
'Bourdon'
'Bourbon Supreme'
'Boutonniere'
'Brazier'
'Brazil'-dec.
'Brides Bouquet'
'Bridesmaid'
'Bright Forecast'-dec.
'Bright Straw'-dec.
'Brimfield Pink'-dec.
'Brimstone'-dec.
'Brinnon Beauty'
'Bryan Mayo'-dec.
'Burning Light'-dec.
'Buttons and Bows'
'Bycendron'

'Calapooya'-dec.
'Calder'-dec.
'Calico'-dec.
'Calienta'
'Calusa'
'Cam'-dec.
'Cameo'
'Camp's Red'-dec.
'Canary Yellow'-dec.
'Canasta'-dec.
'Can Can'
'Candice'
'Canterbury'-dec.
'Cantico'
'Capri'
'Caprice'-dec.
'Carat'-dec.
'Carol Kitchen'
'Casablanca'
'Catherina Rinke'-dec.
'Cathye Mayo'-dec.
'Cathy Lynn'
'Cayenne'
'Cayuga'
'Cecile'-dec.
'Celeste Terry'-dec.
'Chaka'-dec.

'Chamois'-dec.
'Chanel'-dec.
'Chanson'
'Chartreuse'-dec.
'Chattahoochee'-dec.
'Cheerful Giant'-dec.
'Chelsea Reach'-dec.
'Chenille'-dec.
'Chetco'-dec.
'Chiara'
'Chiffon'
'Chimes'-dec.
'Choice Cream'-dec.
'Chorister'-dec.
'Christina'
'Clackamas'-dec.
'Clara Brown'
'Clara Marie'
'Clarice'-dec.
'Clipper'
'Cloud Cap'-dec.
'Clyde'-dec.
'Coloratura'-dec.
'Colossus'-dec.
'Colyer'
'Comanche'
'Concho'
'Constance Brunett'-dec.
'Conversation Piece'
'Coos'-dec.
'Copper Queen'
'Coquille'-dec.
'Cora Brandt'
'Coral Ace'
'Corinna Borden'
'Corinne Murrah'
'Coronation'-dec.
'Corringe'-dec.
'Corston's Yellow'-dec.
'Cottontail'
'Cotton Top'
'Cover Girl'
'Cream Puff'-dec.
'Crescendo'
'Crimson Crest'
'Crimson Tide'-dec.
'Crinkle Cut'
'Crinoline'-dec.
'Cynthia Ann'-dec.

'Dainty Rose'
'Dancing Butterfly'
'Dart'-dec.
'Dawn'
'Dawn's Chorus'
'Deben'-dec.
'Debonaire'
'Deborah Alice'-dec.
'Debutante'-dec.
'Dee'-dec.
'Deep Purple'
'Delaware Blue'
'Del's Choice'-dec.
'Derwent'-dec.
'Deseronto'
'Desert Pink'-dec.
'Desiree'
'Devonia'-dec.
'Dhabi'
'Diana Trask'
'Diane Robin'
'Dimsdale'
'Dinie Metselaar'-dec.
'Diorama'-dec.
'Doctor James Hitchner'
'Doctor Lee Shields'-dec.
'Doctor Rudolph Henny'-dec.
'Doctor Thomas McMillan'
'Dolores'
'Dorian'
'Dorothy Corston'-dec.
'Dorothy Hayden'
'Dorothy Rees'
'Dorothy Woodworth'
'Dosewallips Gold'
'Double Beauty'
'Double Damask'-dec.
'Double Delight'
'Double Eagle'-dec.
'Double Pleasure'
'Double Shot'
'Downy Pink'
'Dracula'-dec.
'Dr. Franklin West'
'Dusty Pink'

'Early Beni'
'Eastern Fire'
'Edward M. Boehm'
'Edward W. Collins'
'Eiko-san'
'Eisenhower'-dec.
'El Capitan'
'Elsie Lee'
'Elise Norfleet'
'Eliza Scott'
'Ellen Zora'
'Elsie Pratt'-dec.
'Emma Reid'
'Encore'
'Eriedell'
'Estrellita'
'Ethel Le Frak'-dec.
'Eunice Ann'-dec.
'Eunice Updike'
'Evelyn Hart'
'Evelyn Hyde'
'Exbury Pink'-dec.
'Exbury White'-dec.
'Exbury Yellow'-dec.
'Explorer'
'Extravaganza'
'Ezra J. Kraus'-dec.

'Fal'-dec.
'Fanal'-dec.
'Fancy Free'-dec.
'Farrall Flamingo'-dec.
'Farrall Mandarine'-dec.
'Farrall Orangea'-dec.
'Farrall Ruby'
'Fasching'-dec.
'Fashing'
'Favor Major'-dec.
'Fawley'-dec.
'Feuerwerk'-dec.
'Final Blush'
'Fireball'-dec.
'Fire Chief'
'Firefly'-dec.
'Fire Magic'-dec.
'Fire Sprite'
'Five Arrows'-dec.
'Flash'
'Flirtation'
'Florida'
'Flower Girl'
'Folksong'
'Foxfire'
'Fragrant Gold'-dec.
'Friendship'
'Frills'-dec.
'Frolic'
'Frome'-dec.
'Frostburg'
'Frosty Morn'

'Gabriele'
'Gabrielle Hill'
'Galle's Choice'-dec.
'Gallipoli'-dec.
'Garda Joy'
'Garden State Garnet'
'Garden State Glow'
'Garden State Pink'
'Garden State Red'
'Garden State Salmon'
'Garden State White'
'Garnet Royal'
'Gemini'
'General Wavell'
'Genie Magic'
'George Harding'
'George Reynolds'-dec.
'George School'
'Geronimo'
'Gibraltar'-dec.
'Gilbury'-dec.
'Gilda'-dec.
'Ginger'-dec.
'Girard's Crimson'
'Girard's Crimson Tide'
'Girard's Deep Salmon'
'Girard's Fuchsia'
'Girard's Hot Shot'
'Girard's Parfait'-dec.
'Girard's Pink'
'Girard's Purple'
'Girard's Rose'
'Girard's Scarlet'
'Gladngay'-dec.
'Glamora'
'Glencora'
'Glockenspiel'-dec.
'Glowing Embers'-dec.

'Gold Dust'-dec.
'Golden Dream'-dec.
'Golden Flare'-dec.
'Golden Girl'-dec.
'Golden Glory'-dec.
'Golden Guinea'-dec.
'Golden Horn'-dec.
'Golden Pom Pom'-dec.
'Golden Sunset'-dec.
'Golden Superior'-dec.
'Goldflake'-dec.
'Goldflamme'-dec.
'Goldpracht'-dec.
'Goldtopas'-dec.
'Gratitude'
'Great Expectations'
'Green Eyes'
'Green Mist'
'Greenway'
'Greenwood Cherry'
'Greenwood Jackpot'
'Greenwood Orange'
'Greenwood Orchid'
'Greenwood Pink'
'Greenwood Popcorn'
'Greenwood Rosebud'
'Greenwood Rose Queen'
'Greenwood Rosy-Red'
'Greenwood Showboat'
'Greenwood White'
'Greenwood Yukon'
'Gresham'
'Greta'
'Gwen'
'Gwenda'
'Gwenda Lloyd'-dec.

'Habanera'
'Halo'
'Happy Birthday'
'Hardijzer Beauty'
'Hardy Hexe'
'Harry Van de Ven'
'Harwell'-dec.
'Hatsu Giri'
'Hazel Smith'-dec.
'Hearthglow'
'Heather Macleod'
'Heigh-Ho'
'Heirloom'
'Helen Curtis'
'Hell's Fire'-dec.
'Henry Allanson'-dec.
'High Sierras'-dec.
'Hino-Pink'
'Hino-Red'
'Hino-Scarlet'
'Hino-White'
'Hohman'
'Holly's Yellow'-dec.
'Honeysuckle'-dec.
'Hotline'
'Hotspur'-dec.
'Hotspur Orange'-dec.
'Hotspur Red'-dec.
'Hotspur Salmon'-dec.
'Hotspur Yellow'-dec.
'Hugh Wormald'-dec.
'Humber'-dec.

'Ilam Carmen'-dec.
'Ilam Chartreuse'-dec.
'Ilam Copper Cloud'-dec.
'Ilam Jasper'-dec.
'Ilam Louie Williams'-dec.
'Ilam Martie'-dec.
'Ilam Melford Beauty'-dec.
'Ilam Melford Flame'-dec.
'Ilam Melford Gold'-dec.
'Ilam Melford Lemon'-dec.
'Ilam Melford Red'-dec.
'Ilam Melford Salmon'-dec.
'Ilam Melford Yellow'-dec.
'Ilam Ming'-dec.
'Ilam Peachy Keen'-dec.
'Ilam Persian Melon'-dec.
'Ilam Persian Rose'-dec.
'Ilam Pink Williams'-dec.
'Ilam Primrose'-dec.
'Ilam Red Ball'-dec.
'Ilam Red Frills'-dec.
'Ilam Red Gem'-dec.
'Ilam Red Giant'-dec.
'Ilam Red Velvet'-dec.
'Ilam Yellow Beauty'-dec.
'Ilam Yellow Giant'-dec.
'Imago'-dec.
'Impala'-dec.
'Irene Cook'
'Irresistible' (syn. 'My-o')
'Isabel'
'Ivan Anderson'

'Jack A. Sand'-dec.
'James Belton'
'James Dunlop'-dec.
'Jan'
'Jan Wellen'
'Jane Geiselman'
'Janet Baker'-dec.
'Janet Rhea'
'Javelin'-dec.
'Jeanne Weeks'
'Jeff Hill'
'Jeremiah'
'Jet Fire'
'J. J. Jennings'
'Jock Brydon'-dec.
'Johanna'
'John Brockett'-dec.
'John Chappell'-dec.
'John F. Kennedy'-dec.
'John Yeates'-dec.
'Jolie Madame'-dec.
'Jonathan'-dec.
'Joseph Hill'
'Joshua Jefferey'
'Julian Elmer'-dec.
'Julie Ann'
'July Jester'-dec.
'July Jewel'-dec.
'July Jingle'-dec.
'July Joy'-dec.
'July Jubilation'-dec.
'July Julep'-dec.
'June'
'June Bride'-dec.
'June Fire'-dec.

'Kachina'
'Kakiemon'
'Karen'
'Karl Korn'-dec.
'Katanga'
'Kathleen'
'Kathy Ann'
'Katie'
'Katisha'
'Katy's Plum'-dec.
'Keepsake'
'Kelly's Orange'
'Kensey'
'Kentucky Minstrel'-dec.
'Kermesina'
'Kilauea'-dec.
'King Midas'-dec.
'King Oluf'
'Kipps'-dec.
'Klondyke'-dec.
'Knighthood'-dec.

'La Belle Helene'
'Lace Valentine'-dec.
'Lady Elphinstone'-dec.
'Lady Jayne'-dec.
'Lady Locks'
'Lady Louise'
'Lady Robin'
'Lady Rosebery'-dec.
'Landon'
'Langmans'
'Largesse'
'Late Love'
'Laura Morland'
'Lavender Bouquet'
'Lavender Delight'
'Lavender Elf'
'Leilani'-dec.
'Lemon Rind'-dec.
'Lemur'
'Leonard Frisbie'-dec.
'Leprechaun'
'Leslie's Purple'
'L'Hirondelle'
'Libby'
'Liffey'-dec.
'Lilian Harvey'
'Lilliput'
'Lily Marleen'
'Linda Jean'
'Lindean'
'Linwood Charm'
'Linwood Lavender'
'Linwood Lustre'

'Linwood Pink Giant'
'Linwood Ruby'
'Linwood Salmon'
'Linwood White'
'Lisa Broom'
'Little White Lie'
'Lorelei'-dec.
'Lorna'
'Lorna Carter'
'Lost Chord'
'Lotta Burke'
'Lotus Porter'
'Louisa'
'Lucky Lady'-dec.
'Lunar Sea'
'Luxury Rose'

'Madame Loth'
'Madame Mab Chalon'
'Madame Margotten'
'Madeleine'-dec.
'Mahler'
'Maid of Honor'-dec.
'Malaguena'
'Mandarin Maid'-dec.
'Maori'-dec.
'Margaret Douglas'
'Margaret Einarson'
'Margaret George'
'Margaret Olive'-dec.
'Margaret Palmer'
'Maria Derby'
'Marian Lee'
'Marie Elena'
'Marie's Choice'
'Mariko'
'Marilee'-dec.
'Marina'-dec.
'Marion Armstrong'
'Marlies'-dec.
'Martha Isaacson'-dec.
'Martine'
'Martin Stewart'
'Marvee'
'Mary Allen'
'Mary Anne Elmer'-dec.
'Mary Claire'-dec.
'Mary Dalton'
'Mary Elizabeth'
'Mary Harmon'-dec.
'Mary Lou'-dec.
'Mary Meredith'
'Marydel'-dec.
'Matsuyo'
'Maud Jacobs'
'Mauna Loa'-dec.
'Maxine West'
'May Belle'
'May Blaine'
'Medway'-dec.
'Melford Glory'
'Merle Finimore'
'Merrymaker'
'Mersey'-dec.
'Mevrouw Jozef Heursel'
'Mevrouw Roger de Loose'
'Michael Hill'
'Middle East'
'Midori'
'Midsummer Beauty'
'Mildred Alfarata'-dec.
'Millie Mac'-dec.
'Mimi'
'Min's Choice'
'Miss Jane'
'Misty Plum'
'Mitey White'
'Mona Lisa'
'Montezuma'
'Moonlight Rose'-dec.
'Moon Maiden'
'Moresea'
'Morris Gold'-dec.
'Mountain Gem'
'Mount Saint Helens'-dec.
'Mount Seven Star'
'Mucronatum'
'Mrs. Emil Hager'
'Mrs. Van de Ven'
'Mrs. Villars'
'My Mary'
'Myeena'-dec.
'Myosotis'
'Myrtle de Friel'

'Nacoochee'-dec.
'Nambucca Princess'
'Nam Khan'-dec.
'Nancy Buchanan'-dec.
'Nancy of Robinhill'
'Nanki-Poo'
'Nene'-dec.
'Nevada'-dec.
'Nichola'
'Nicole Joy'
'Nigel'
'Night Light'-dec.
'Northland'
'North Pole'
'Noyo Pink'

'Ochoco'-dec.
'Old Gold'-dec.
'Olga Niblett'
'One-O-One'-dec.
'Opal'
'Orange Cloak'-dec.
'Orange Flair'
'Orange Glow'-dec.
'Orange Jolly'-dec.
'Orange Sherbet'
'Orange Supreme'-dec.
'Orange Truffles'-dec.
'Orchid Beauty'
'Orchid Belle'
'Orchid Lights'-dec.
'Orient'-dec.
'Ormsby'
'Orwell'-dec.
'Oryx'-dec.
'Osaka'
'Osprey'-dec.
'Oxydol'-dec.

'Painted Tips'
'Paleface'
'Paluna'
'Pamela Malland'
'Panda'
'Papineau'
'Papoose'
'Paradise Pink'
'Paramount'-dec.
'Parkfeuer'-dec.
'Pastiche'-dec.
'Patches'
'Pat Kraft'
'Patrick's Supreme'-dec.
'Pawnee'
'Peep-Bo'
'Peg Hugger'
'Pequeno'
'Persil'-dec.
'Peter Pooker'
'Petite'
'Petrouchka'-dec.
'Pettychaps'
'Philip Holmes'-dec.
'Phyllis Marsh'
'Piccolo'-dec.
'Pierre Du Pont'
'Ping Pong'
'Pinkabelle'
'Pink Annette'
'Pink Ball'-dec.
'Pink Delight'-dec.
'Pink Elf'
'Pinkette'
'Pink Fancy'
'Pink Fire'-dec.
'Pink Ice'
'Pink Jolly'-dec.
'Pink Lace'
'Pink Lights'-dec.
'Pink Mimosa'-dec.
'Pink Pancake'
'Pink Parfait'
'Pink Pincushion'
'Pink Plush'-dec.
'Pink Puff'-dec.
'Pink Radiance'
'Pink Ripples'
'Pink Ruffles'-dec.
'Pistil Packing Mama'-dec.
'Pistil Pete'-dec.
'Pleasant White'
'Plectrum'-dec.
'Pollyanna'
'Pom Pom'-dec.
'Pooh-Bah'
'Popsicle'-dec.
'Port Knap'
'Port Wine'
'Pouffe'
'Pride of Nambucca'

'Primitive Beauty'
'Prince Charming'-dec.
'Princess Ida'
'Princess Margaret of Windsor'-dec.
'Princess Royal'-dec.
'Prominent'-dec.
'Pucken'
'Pudding'-dec.
'Puff'
'Pure Gold'-dec.
'Pure Perfection'
'Purple Cushion'
'Purple Robe'

'Quaker Maid'-dec.

'Rachel Cunningham'
'Rachel Dacre'-dec.
'Radiance'-dec.
'Ralph'
'Rapunzel'-dec.
'Red Baron'
'Red Beauty'
'Redder Yet'-dec.
'Red Feather'
'Red Fountain'
'Redmond'
'Red Red'
'Red Slippers'
'Red Tip'
'Reid Red'
'Rejoice'
'Renee Michelle'
'Renne'-dec.
'Replique'-dec.
'Reve d'Amour'-dec.
'Ria Hardijzer'
'Ribble'-dec.
'Ribbon Candy'-dec.
'Rimfire'
'Riponia'
'Roberta'
'Robin Cook'
'Robin Hill Congo'
'Robin Hill Elsa'
'Robin Hill Frosty'
'Robin Hill Gillie'
'Robin Hill Palmyra'
'Robin Hill Rosanne'
'Robin Hill Wendy'
'Rocket'-dec.
'Roddy'
'Rose Brocade'
'Rose Elf'
'Rose Marsh'
'Rosemary Hyde'
'Rose Parade'
'Rose Perfecta'
'Rosita'-dec.
'Rosy Lights'
'Royal Blazer'
'Royal Command'-dec.
'Royal Crown'
'Royal Lodge'-dec.
'Royal Pink'
'Royal Robe'
'Rozanne Waterer'-dec.
'Rubinstern'
'Ruby Glow'
'Rusty Keller'
'Ruth Kirk'
'Ruth May'
'Ruth Ticknor'
'Ryde Heron'

'Sahara'-dec.
'Saidee Kirk'
'Saint James'
'Saint Ruan'-dec.
'Saint Stanislaus'-dec.
'Salishan'
'Salmon Elf'
'Salmon Mound'
'Salmon Pincushion'
'Salmon Sunrise'
'Samurai'-dec.
'Sand Dune'-dec.
'Sandra Ann'
'Sandra Marie'-dec.
'Sanquinare'
'Santee'
'Santiam'-dec.
'Sara Copeland'-dec.
'Sara Holden'
'Sarina'-dec.
'Sarrano'
'Saskia'-dec.
'Satan's Choice'
'Satanta'
'Saybrook Glory'
'Scarlatti'-dec.
'Scarlet Glory'
'Scarlet O'Hara'-dec.
'Scarlet Pimpernel'-dec.
'Scarlet Salute'-dec.
'Sceptre'-dec.
'Scheegold'-dec.
'Schneeglanz'
'Schneewittchen'
'Scott Gartrell'
'Scotty'-dec.
'S. D. Coleman'-dec.
'Sea King'
'Seigai'
'Shanty'-dec.
'Sharon Kathleen'
'Shawna'
'Sherbrook'
'Sherry'
'Sherwoodi'
'Shocking Pink'
'Show Time'
'Shy Girl'-dec.
'Sikorsky'
'Siletz'-dec.
'Silver Glow'
'Silver Slipper'
'Silver Star'
'Silver Streak'
'Silver Sword'
'Silvester'
'Sir Robert'
'Siskin'-dec.
'Siuslaw'-dec.
'Sizzler'-dec.
'Sleigh Bells'
'Smoky Mountaineer'-dec.
'Snow Cloud'
'Snowdrop'
'Snow Flurry'
'Snow Hill'
'Snow Mound'
'Snow Puff'
'Soft Lips'
'Soir de Paris'-dec.
'Solstice'
'Sorrento'
'Southern Sunset'
'Sparkle'
'Spek's Brilliant'-dec.
'Spicy Lights'
'Spicy Lights'-dec.
'Spink'
'Spring Bonnet'
'Spring Melody'
'Spring Party'-dec.
'Spring Salvo'-dec.
'Spring Spangle'-dec.
'Squirrel'
'Star Fire'
'Star Ruby'
'Stormcloud'
'Stour'-dec.
'Strawberry Ice'-dec.
'Stromboli'-dec.
'Suez'-dec.
'Sugared Almond'-dec.
'Su-Lin'
'Summer Evening'-dec.
'Summer Fragrance'-dec.
'Summer Sunset'-dec.
'Sunburst'-dec.
'Sun Chariot'-dec.
'Sundance'
'Sun Frolic'-dec.
'Sunlight'-dec.
'Sunset Boulevard'-dec.
'Sunset Pink'-dec.
'Surprise'-dec.
'Susannah Hill'
'Susie Cook'
'Suva'-dec.
'Suzanne Loef'-dec.
'Swallow'-dec.
'Sweet Cristy'-dec.
'Sweet Sue'-dec.
'Syncopation'-dec.

'Takoma Park'
'Talbot'
'Tamar'-dec.
'Tamino'
'Tam-O'-Shanter'-dec.
'Tan Dilly'
'Tang'-dec.

'Tangiers'-dec.
'Target'
'Tat'
'Tay'-dec.
'Tees'-dec.
'Tenino'
'Terre's Delight'-dec.
'Tessa'-dec.
'Tharon Perkins'
'Theodore S. Stechki'
'Therese Elmer'-dec.
'Thomas Jefferson'-dec.
'Thomas Rose'
'Tico Tico'
'Tina'
'Tiny'
'Tillamook'-dec.
'Titipu'
'Tit-willow'
'Tonga'-dec.
'Torchlight'
'Torcia'-dec.
'Toreador'
'Totally Awesome'
'Trent'-dec.
'Tressa McMurry'
'Trill'
'Trisha'
'Tropic Sun'
'Tsuneshige Rokujo'-dec.
'Tualatin'-dec.
'Tweed'-dec.
'Tyne'-dec.
'Tyrol'-dec.

'Umatilla'-dec.
'Umpqua'-dec.
'Umpqua Queen'-dec.
'Velvet Gown'
'Venetia'-dec.
'Vera Cook'
'Verena'
'Verne's Red'
'Victoria Elizabeth'-dec.
'Victoria Hohman'
'Victorine Hetling'
'Vida Brown'
'Villa'
'Vineland Flame'-dec.
'Vineland Flare'-dec.
'Vineland Glow'-dec.
'Vivienne Waterer'-dec.

'Wallowa Red'-dec.
'Walter Kern'
'Waltz Time'
'Wansbeck'-dec.
'Watchet'
'Waverney'-dec.
'Wedding Bouquet'-dec.
'Welmet'
'Whakanni'-dec.
'Whitecap'
'White Doll'
'White Elf'
'White Ermine'
'White Find'-dec.
'White Flakes'-dec.
'Whitehead'
'Whitehouse'
'White Jade'
'White Lights'-dec.
'White Moon'
'White Nymph'
'White Princess'
'White Rosebud'
'White Squatter'
'White Top'
'Willem Hardijzer'-dec.
'Winchuk'-dec.
'Windrush'-dec.
'Windsor Apple Blossom'-dec.
'Windsor Buttercup'-dec.
'Windsor Daybreak'-dec.
'Windsor Peach Glo'-dec.
'Wintergreen'
'Winter Hawk'
'Winterset'
'Wintertime'
'Womat'
'Wye'-dec.

'Yachats'-dec.
'Yaquina'-dec.
'Yaye'
'Yellow Cloud'-dec.
'Yellow River'-dec.
'Yellow Sand'-dec.
'Yellow Stars'-dec.
'Yoga'-dec.
'Yuge's Geisha'
'Yuka'

'Zanzibar'-dec.
'Zig-Zag'

Appendix I
ADDITIONAL DECIDUOUS AZALEAS

Additional Ghent and Mollis Hybrids

Many of the following Ghent and Mollis Hybrids were introduced before 1900 and are still available in Europe.

OLD GHENT HYBRIDS

'Admiraal de Ruyter' (before 1855): deep reddish orange, yellow blotch, large, late.
'Admiral Tromp' (Ghent hyb. × *japonicum;* Vuylsteke).
'Alba Odorata' (Boskoop Nurs. Assoc. 1889): white.
'Alba Plena Odorata' (before 1896): pinkish white, double.
'Alba Violacea' (before 1875): white, rose tinted, yellow blotch.
'Amabilis' (Sunningdale Nur. since 1898): yellowish white, flushed pale pink, margins deep pink, large yellow flare.
'Baron van Heekeren': light yellowish pink, yellow blotch.
'Belle Merveille' (syn. 'Belle Verveille'; before 1881): pink, yellow blotch.
'Brilliant' (before 1896): deep reddish orange.
'Bronze Unique' (before 1874): vivid red, orange blotch.
'Cardoniana' (syn. 'Cardon'; before 1874): moderate red, orange blotch.
'Chromatella' (J. Rinz before 1872): light yellow, double, buds pink.
'Coccinea Major' (before 1875): dark red.
'Comtesse de Saint-Crieg' (J. Moser before 1914): yellow, deep yellow blotch.
'Cottage Maid' (A. Waterer 1909): pink, with light center.
'Crocea Tricolor' (Sunningdale Nur. since 1898): yellowish white, broad yellowish white band down each petal, orange yellow flare, flushed pink on margins.
'Cuprea Grandiflora' (before 1875): strong orange, blotched orange yellow.
'Cuprea Splendens' (Sunningdale Nur. since 1898): pale pink, with dark line down each petal, small deep yellowish pink flare, long deep pink tube.
'Dominico Scassi' (L. van Houtte 1873): light pink with faint yellow markings on lighter underside.
'Dr. Auguste Cambier' (L. van Houtte before 1875): reddish orange, tinted violet, orange blotch.
'Duc de Provence' (before 1874): reddish orange, spotted yellowish green.
'Duchesse de Chatres' (Moser before 1914): vivid red, orange blotch.
'Duchesse de Melzi' (Moser before 1914): violet, double.
'Eugenie' (Verschaffelt before 1855): dark red, shaded reddish orange.
'Favorita' (before 1875): light yellowish pink.
'Fidele Mechelynck' (L. van Houtte before 1875): moderate pink, shaded reddish orange, yellow blotch.
'Frederic de Merode' (*japonicum* × Ghent hyb.; Vuylsteke 1892): deep reddish orange, yellow blotch.
'Fritz Benary' (Moser before 1914): double.
'Fritz Quihou' (before 1873): deep red.
'Fulgida' (A. Waterer 1870): reddish orange.
'General Trauff' (before 1874): light reddish purple, paler lines on petals, yellow flare, edged white; small flowers.

'Gloire d'un Parterre' (before 1874): pale pinkish white, upper lobes yellow.

'Gloriosa' (Mollis hyb. × *occidentale*): white flushed pink, orange blotch.

'Gloriosa Perfecta' (before 1851): reddish orange, deep yellow blotch.

'Guillaume II' (before 1874): orange yellow, shaded yellowish pink.

'Honneur de la Belgique' (Verschaffelt before 1855): orange, yellow blotch.

'Imperatrix' (syn. 'Imperatrice', 'L'Imperatrice', 'Imperatrice de France'; before 1881): moderate yellow, shaded light orange.

'Lady Pigott': vivid yellow.

'La Surprise' (Sunningdale Nur. since 1898): pale yellowish pink, flushed deeper with a few lines, upper petals deep yellow, orange at base; unusual and attractive.

'L'Esperance' (before 1875): vivid orange, blotch deep orange.

'Louis Aimée van Houtte' (L. van Houtte 1873): red, double.

'Lucifer' (Moser before 1914): reddish orange, double.

'M. Chaguerand' (Moser before 1914): reddish orange with white star.

'Madame Alexander Hardy' (L. van Houtte before 1875): white bordered reddish purple, pale yellow blotch.

'Madame Ernest Saintin' (Moser before 1914): pink with orange blotch.

'Madame Georges Berger' (Moser before 1914): pink with yellow blotch, double.

'Madame Joseph Baumann' (before 1875): yellowish pink, center of petals striped white, orange blotch.

'Madame Paul Gervais' (Moser before 1914): vivid red, orange blotch.

'Mademoiselle Jeanne Siere' (Moser before 1914): pinkish white.

'Mademoiselle Jeanne Tissarand' (Moser before 1914): pink with frilled petals, double.

'Magnifica' (Rollison Nur. before 1873): pale red.

'Magnifica Albicans' (before 1903): yellowish white.

'Maja' (S. & J. Rinz before 1871): pale purplish pink, double.

'Max Petit' (Moser before 1914): vivid reddish orange, orange blotch, white line in center of each petal.

'Mignon' (*japonicum* × Ghent hyb.; Vuylsteke 1892): pale red, yellow blotch.

'Mirabilis (before 1875): purplish yellow on moderate pink.

'Monsieur Desbois' (*japonicum* × Ghent hyb.; Vuylsteke 1892): reddish orange.

'Nereide': moderate pink.

'Nero' (before 1896): light reddish orange.

'Nobilis' (A. Verschaffelt before 1881): deep reddish orange with dark orange blotch.

'Ochroleuca' (before 1871): yellowish white.

'Optima' (before 1878): yellowish white, edged reddish orange, yellow blotch.

'Opherie' (J. Rinz before 1871): light yellow, edged pink, semidouble.

'Orpheus' (Waterer, Sons & Crisp Ltd.): reddish orange, deep orange blotch; upright habit, good fall color.

'Perfecta': reddish orange.

'Phoenica': white with a faint pink line down each petal, very faint yellow blotch, margins and tubes flushed pink; long glandular tubes like *R. viscosum.*

'President Carnot' (Moser before 1914): reddish orange.

'Prestantissima' (Sunningdale Nur. since 1889): vivid reddish orange, upper petal orange yellow to vivid orange.

'Princess Adrienne' (before 1896): dark red.

'Princess Marie Gortsehakow' (Croux before 1905): light pink, white center, double.

'Proteus' (A. Waterer before 1909): moderate pink, yellow blotch.

'Puchella Roseola' (before 1875): purplish pink, yellow blotch.

'Queen Victoria' (before 1896): purplish pink, throat lighter, small yellow blotch.

'Reine Louise' (before 1875): vivid reddish orange, yellow blotch.

'Remarquable' (before 1875): deep yellowish pink, spotted dark yellow.

'Rose d'Amour': light pink flushed deep pink, reddish orange blotch.

'Rose de Flandre' (van Houtte before 1875): vivid pink, flaked white, orange blotch.

'Rose de Hollande' (J. Rinz before 1872): deep yellowish pink.

'Rose Marie' (before 1875): dark red.
'Rosetta' (J. Rinz before 1872): moderate pink and yellow, double.
'Rubens' (before 1875): deep yellowish pink, yellow blotch.
'Sally' (van Houtte 1869): deep yellowish orange.
'Saturne' (J. Waterer, Sons & Crisp Ltd.): purplish red shading to pink, white center.
'Schöne von Gressen' (*arborescens* × *molle*): deep pink.
'Soleil d'Or' (Moser before 1914): pale yellow, deep yellow blotch.
'Thalie' (before 1908): double.
'Thisbe' (A. Waterer about 1909): vivid pink, orange blotch.
'Tower Beauty' (syn. 'Cote' var. 'Tower Beauty'; *atlanticum* × unknown; Stevenson cross 1937, intro. 1955): very pale yellowish pink, scented.
'Tower Dainty' (syn. 'Cote' var. 'Tower Dainty'; *atlanticum* × unknown; Stevenson cross 1937, intro. 1955): very pale pink, scented.
'Tricolor van Aken': white, shaded pale purple, small flowers.
'Van Dyck' (syn. 'Van Dyke'; before 1875): dark red; in another clone light yellow shaded light pink.
'Van Houttei Flore Pleno' (before 1862): moderate red with orange yellow flecks, double. Also spelled 'Plena'.
'Verna Bergen' (*arborescens* × *japonicum*): white flushed pink.
'Vesta': dark yellow, flushed pink.
'Vestale' (Moser before 1914): vivid orange, blotched orange yellow.

ADDITIONAL MOLLIS HYBRIDS

'A. Abels' (Koster): pink, yellow blotch.
'Adriaan Brouwer' (Kersbergen): reddish orange, small flowers.
'Alfred Mame' (G. Croux before 1905): reddish purple.
'Arthur de Warrelles' (L. van Houtte 1876): blotched orange.
'Aurora': orange.
'Baron L. von Wolff': pale yellow.
'Beethoven' (H. Knepper 1896): strong orange.
'Bismarck' (Ottlander & Hooftman 1896): orange yellow tinted pink.
'Candew' (Moser before 1914): white, yellow blotch.
'C. Esveld' (G. Kersbergen): orange.
'C. Maarschalk' (*R. japonicum* cl.; Koster 1896): orange with purple blotch.
'Charles Dickens' (*R. japonicum* selection; Koster): reddish orange.
'Charles Francois Luppis' (L. van Houtte 1872): pink shaded purple, orange blotch.
'Columbus' (G. Kersbergen 1918): red.
'Copernicus' (G. Kersbergen): reddish orange.
'Countess of Donoughmore': pale yellowish white, blotched.
'Danton L. van Beethoven' (*japonicum* cl.; G. Kersbergen): dark pink.
'Davonia' (K. Wezelenburg & Son): moderate pink.
'Dazzler': vivid orange.
'Devonia': reddish orange.
'Dr. Pasteur' (Koster 1886): orange with purplish red blotch.
'E. Cuthbert': orange yellow.
'Edward Jenner' (G. Kersbergen): light orange yellow, reddish margin.
'Eisenhower' (Felix & Dijkhuis 1950): strong orange, veined red outside, orange blotch. Also Exbury hybrid with same name.
'Faust' (× *kosterianum* cl; H. Knepper & Son 1896): light orange.
'Favorite' (× *kosterianum* cl; Koster): red or deep pink.
'Frau L. Helmann' (× *kosterianum* cl.): color ?
'Fred Engels' (G. Kersbergen 1918): red.
'Frisia' (G. Kersbergen): yellowish pink.
'Gartendirector Walter' (syn. 'Hofgärten Director Walter'; *japonicum* cl., before 1896): moderate pink, heavily blotched purple.

'General Brialmont' (*japonicum* × *gandavense;* Vuylsteke 1892): deep reddish purple, yellow blotch.
'General Goffinet' (*japonicum* × *gandavense;* Vuylsteke 1892): purplish red, yellow blotch.
'George Cuthbert' (× *kosterianum* cl.): orange yellow, red blotch.
'George Stephenson' (× *kosterianum* cl; Kersbergen 1918): pale pink.
'Glory of Boskoop' (× *kosterianum* cl; Koster & Son 1896): orange, red blotch.
'Golden Queen': yellow.
'Gold Star': yellow.
'Goldsworth Red' (Slocock): vivid red.
'Guillaume Caillet' (× *kosterianum* cl; Kersbergen): light yellow, edged with pink.
'Gypsy Lass' (G. McKinnon): brownish orange.
'Hanny Felix' ('Mrs. J. Dijkhuis' × *japonicum* seedling; Felix & Dijkhuis 1967): light pink, border of reddish orange, large orange blotch. Another cultivar exists with same name but no description available.
'Helena de Groot' (*japonicum* cl; Koster & Son): orange, shaded light yellow.
'Helena Oosthoek' (P. J. C. Oosthoek & Co. 1925): reddish orange.
'Hugo Oosthoek' (× *kosterianum* cl; P. J. C. Oosthoek & Co. 1925): light reddish orange.
'Jack Straw' (G. Kersbergen): pink, yellow blotch.
'James H. Laing' (first clones of *japonicum* × *mollis* (× *kosterianum*) group; F. de Coninck, described by E. Pynaertvan Geert 1891): no description available.
'Jan Steen' (G. Kersbergen): very pale yellow.
'Jeanne A. Koster' (Koster & Son 1900): yellow.
'King Lear' (× *kosterianum* cl.): dark red, orange blotch.
'King Leopold' (× *kosterianum* cl.): strong yellowish orange.
'Lady of the Rose': vivid pink.
'Lonnie Smit' (*kosterianum* cl; P. van Noordt & Sons 1905): reddish orange.
'Lord Lister' (G. Kersbergen): pink.
'Louis Endtz' (*japonicum* cl; before 1908): orange yellow.
'M. Charles van Wambeke' (before 1875): orange shaded, dark pink, yellow-green blotch.
'M. Jules Putzeys' (*japonicum* × before 1875): red, shaded purplish pink, orange blotch.
'M. Koster' (*japonicum* × Koster & Sons before 1896): light orange.
'M. Lebandy' (*japonicum* × *molle;* Croux before 1905): reddish orange with yellow blotch.
'Madame Ambroise Verschaffelt' (Verschaffelt before 1905): deep reddish orange with yellow blotch.
'Madame Bocquet' (Croux before 1905): red, orange center.
'Mademoiselle Sieber' (Croux before 1905): deep pink with yellow blotch and red veining.
'Margaretha' (G. Kersbergen): dark pink.
'Marshall Blücher' (*kosterianum* cl.): orange yellow.
'Mary Koster': blotched form of 'Anthony Koster'.
'Mignon' (Vuylsteke about 1888): pink, upper lobes purplish red, dark yellow blotch.
'Miss E. Cavell' (G. Kersbergen 1918): greenish yellow, flushed pink.
'Mrs. C. C. Page' (K. Wezelenburg & Son): strong red.
'Mrs. J. Patterson' (× *kosterianum* cl; L. J. Endtz & Co.): light pink, darker margins, yellow blotch.
'Mrs. Oosthoek' (P. J. C. Oosthoek & Co. 1925): deep red.
'Mrs. T. Wezelenburg': dark reddish orange, blotched dark red.
'Mrs. Whitelegg' (× *kosterianum* cl; L. J. Endtz & Co.): light pink, yellow blotch.
'Mrs. Wm. Urie' (× *kosterianum* cl; L. J. Endtz & Co.): light pink, yellow blotch.
'Multiflora' (from Belgium): deep yellowish pink.
'Nelly Hardijzer' (W. Hardijzer & Co.): reddish orange, yellow blotch.
'Obergärtner Nietner' (syn. 'Oberhofgärtner Nietner'; *japonicum* × *molle,* before 1896): vivid red, spotted reddish purple.
'Odin' (× *kosterianum* cl; W. Wezelenburg & Son): orange yellow, rose tint.
'Ophelia' (Koster & Son 1905): deep orange.
'Oswald de Kerchove' (Vuylsteke about 1888): moderate pink, upper petal shaded pale yellow.
'Otto Lilienthal' (G. Kersbergen 1918); pale yellow.
'Paragon': orange yellow, yellow center.

'Paul Kruger' (before 1938): red.
'Peach Blossom': light yellowish pink.
'Peggy O'Neil': deep yellowish pink.
'Percy Bysshe Shelley' (G. Kersbergen 1918): reddish orange.
'Peter van Noordt' (*japonicum* cl; G. van Noordt & Son 1895): yellow.
'Picture': orange yellow.
'President Carnot' (× *kosterianum* cl; Ottolander & Hooftman 1896): orange yellow.
'President Cleveland' (× *kosterianum* cl; Ottolander & Hooftman 1896): orange yellow with reddish glow.
'President Grevy' (× *kosterianum* cl; Ottolander & Hooftman 1896): orange yellow.
'Prince Albert' (*japonicum* × *molle;* Vuylsteke about 1888): yellowish pink, shaded yellowish white.
'Prins Alexander' (before 1903): moderate pink, small flowers.
'Prins Frederik' (*japonicum* cl.): yellowish pink, small flowers.
'Prins Hendrik' (*japonicum* cl.): yellow.
'Prins Maurits' (× *kosterianum* cl; L. J. Endtz & Co.): red; late flowering.
'Prins van Oranje' (× *kosterianum* cl; H. Knepper & Zonen, before 1886): orange.
'Professor Aug. Forel' (G. Kersbergen): deep reddish orange.
'Professor M. Koster' (before 1896): red.
'Professor Roentgen' (Koster & Son 1896): pale orange, purplish blotch.
'Professor W. Koster' (before 1896): red.
'Psyche': pale yellowish white, tinted pink.
'Queen Alexandra' (Koster & Sons 1935): pale yellowish white, tinged strong pink.
'Queen Victoria' (× *kosterianum* cl; Ottolander & Hooftman before 1896): light yellow, tinted pink, with yellow blotch.
'Radiancy': yellowish pink, shaded yellow.
'Rembrandt' (G. Kersbergen): deep yellowish pink.
'Rose Queen': moderate pink.
'Saffron': yellowish pink, shaded orange yellow.
'Salmonea Rubra' (syn. 'Salmoniana Rubra'; before 1896): deep yellowish pink.
'Sensation': pale yellowish pink, darker blotch.
'Souvenir de J. C. van Tol' (× *kosterianum* cl.): orange yellow.
'Stadtgartner Machtig' (*japonicum* × *molle;* V. Noordt 1900): yellow, shaded orange.
'Sunbeam' ('Alaclarense' hybrid; Koster & Sons 1895): orange yellow.
'Sunray': light reddish orange.
'Sunset' (× *kosterianum* cl; Wezelenburg & Son 1912): strong red.
'Sybil': vivid orange yellow.
'Thomas Moore' (G. Kersbergen): yellowish pink.
'Thomas Newcomen' (G. Kersbergen 1918): strong red.
'W. E. Gladstone' (× *kosterianum* cl; Koster & Sons 1902): orange yellow.
'Walter Crane' (G. Kersbergen 1918): vivid orange.
'Watt. Tyler' (G. Kersbergen): reddish orange.
'Yellow van Tol': light yellow.
'Zeelandia' (Koster & Sons before 1939): reddish orange.

Additional Knap Hill Hybrids

'Anneke' (syn. 'Gold N'; parentage unknown; Pratt, named & introd. F. de Long '85): brilliant yellow to light yellow 14C-D, darker on tube externally, dorsal spotting vivid yellow, tubular funnel-shaped, 3–4", 9 in truss.
'Dairymaid' (parentage and source unknown): white with yellow blotch.
'Ethel Le Frak' (parentage unknown; E. L. de Rothschild '84): brilliant orange yellow 23B, shaded vivid orange 28B towards edges, aging to vivid orange yellow 23A with vivid orange 25A shading between veins, 2⅜", 9 in truss.
'Eunice Ann' ('Elsie Pratt' × 'Cecile'; Pratt '84): deep purplish pink 55A, paler at center, throat and dorsal blotch strong orange 24A, partially petaloid, 1–3 stamens, 3–4", 8–10 in truss.

'Fanal' ('Satan' × 'Gilbraltar'; Hachmann '84): vivid reddish orange 33A-B, unmarked, 2⅜", 12–14 in truss.

'Goldpracht' (('Cecile' × 'Klondyke') × 'Marion Merriman'; Hachmann '84): vivid yellow 16A to light orange yellow 16B, blotch strong orange 25B, 2–2¾", 9–10 (–12) in truss.

'Goldtopas' (('Cecile' × 'Klondyke') × 'Marion Merriman'; Hachmann '84): vivid yellow 15A-B, strongly blotched of strong orange 24A, 2½–3", 7–9 in truss.

'Jimmy Come Lately' (parents unknown, Bailey): buds vivid red 45A, opening to vivid reddish orange 33A, dorsal lobe strong reddish orange 31A, wavy and frilled lobes, 3", fragrant, 9–11 in truss; upright rounded habit 5 × 4' tall in 15 yrs.; hardy to −0°F. Fall foliage deep red.

'Marlies' (parents unknown; Pratt & de Jong '85): strong red 52A in bud with white midribs to lower lobes, opening deep pink 52B with strong orange 24A blotch, 3–3½", 9 in truss.

'Parkfeuer' ('Feuerwerk' × 'Feuerwerk'; Hachmann '84): deep reddish orange 34A with deep reddish orange 42A & vivid red 44A, unmarked, 2¼", 9–11 in truss.

'Pink Ball' ('Homebush' × unknown; K. Van de Van): vivid purplish red 57D, dorsal lobes flushed vivid orange yellow 23A, 2¾", 15 in truss.

'Schneegold' ('Saint Ruan' × 'Cecile'; Hachmann '84): yellowish white 155D, blotch vivid orange yellow 23A-B, 3–3¾", 9 in truss; often several trusses together.

'Spanish Gold' (Slocock): vivid yellow.

American Deciduous Species, Hybrids and Miscellaneous Deciduous Hybrids

'Cullowhee' (selection of *calendulaceum* collected near Cullowhee, N.C., U.S.A., by B. Clark, described by D. Pitillo, named by Kehr): unusual petaloid flowers with petals totally lacking, reddish filaments with five additional filaments, each truss has ten flowers with a total of 100 filaments packed tightly together; upright spreading habit; hardy to −20°F. Original plant moved to Western Carolina Univ., Cullowhee, N.C.

'Mrs. Betty Oliver' (*occidentale* × unknown; seedling from Edwards Nur. raised & reg. by H. W. Oliver '86): moderate pink with deeper pink veining, prominent orange blotch, buds deep yellowish pink, wavy margins, 3", 14 in truss, midseason, fragrant; vigorous, stiff upright habit, 9 × 13 ft. high in 21 yrs.; heat resistant and adaptable in S. Calif.; leaves turn red in fall; hardy to −10°F.

'Spring Spangle' (*vaseyi* × 'Spring Party'; Leach, reg. '85): deep purplish pink 73A, spotting strong purplish red 61B in blotch, 1¾", 6–8 in truss; hardy to −25°F.

'Summer Evening' ('Sang de Genthrugge' × *austrinum;* Hardy '85): reddish orange with orange blotch.

'Tsuneshige Rokujo' (*serrulatum* × *prunifolium;* Skinner, named & reg. Hill '86): buds deep purplish pink 55A, with glandular hairy pale purplish pink ribs 55D; opening strong purplish pink 55B, some flowers light to pale purplish pink 55C-D, stripes pale purplish pink 55D to white down center of each lobe, 1½", 6 in truss, late August; rounded plant 5' high in 13 yrs.

'Washington Centennial' ((*occidentale* × *bakeri*) × 'Santiam'; Mossman, reg. '86): buds variable orange, yellow to red, opening light orange yellow 16C paling to white, blotch vivid orange yellow 17A, veins and variable margins up to ¼" of strong pink 50C, 3½", 10–11 in truss, stamens orange yellow 165C, style strong pink 50C, fragrant; leaves very shiny, resistant to mildew and good fall color of red to yellow; hardy to −10°F.; propagation by tissue culture. Scheduled for release in 1989 Washington State Centennial.

Appalachian Series

Clarence Towe of Walhalla, SC., U.S.A., has been selecting superior and unusual forms of native azaleas since 1975. He has now started hybridizing to develop better colors and flower forms with the native azaleas.

'Appalachian Spectrum' (natural hybrid of *calendulaceum* × *periclymenoides;* collected in Oconee Co., S.C.): color ranges from yellow to orange, light pink to deep pink with several pastel colors of yellowish pink, blotched yellow or orange, different colored flowers in each truss, 1¾", semidouble with partially petaloid stamens, midseason; upright spreading habit; hardy to −15°F.

'Chameleon' (natural hybrid of *calendulaceum* × *periclymenoides;* collected in Oconee Co., S.C.): pale yellowish white with yellow-green blotch, fades to light pink with yellow blotch, with lobes edges in light purple, 1¾", midseason, fragrant at pink stage; vigorous, upright spreading habit; hardy to −15°F.

'Cherokee Sun' (natural hybrid of *arborescens,* or *arborescens* × *bakerii;* collected in Snowbird Mtns. near Franklin, S.C.): light yellow, with contrasting red glands and purplish red pistils, 1¾", mid to late season, very fragrant; arborescens-like foliage; upright spreading habit; hardy to −25°F.

'Fool's Gold' (natural hybrid of *calendulaceum* × *periclymenoides;* collected in Oconee Co., S.C.): white, with orange yellow throat and upper petal, upper petal with white margin, pink pistils and white filaments, large, 1¾", midseason, slightly fragrant; upright spreading habit; hardy to −15°F.

'Indian Warbonnet' (selection of *calendulaceum,* collected in Oconee Co., S.C.): vivid orange yellow, 5 distinct, separate, narrow petals 3/16 to ¼" wide, midseason, stamens and pistil present; upright spreading habit, hardy to −15°F.

'Keowee Sunset' (natural hybrid of *calendulaceum* × *periclymenoides;* collected in Oconee Co., S.C.): moderate pink, with orange yellow upper petal, pistils and filaments moderate red, large 2¼", flowers, early to midseason; wide oval foliage; upright spreading habit; hardy to −15°F.

Oconee Arrow' (selection of *calendulaceum* collected in Oconee Co., S.C.): orange, unusual flowers, corolla tube present ¾ to 1" in length, but petals are lacking, pistils and filaments present; upright spreading habit; hardy to −15°F.

'Pisgah Rose' (natural selection of *vaseyi,* collected on Mt. Pisgah, N.C.): moderate pink, small, 1¼" flowers, midseason; lower growth habit than typical forms; hardy to −25°F.

'Smoky Rose' (natural hybrid of *calendulaceum* × *periclymenoides;* collected in Oconee Co., S.C.): deep rose with reddish orange throat and upper petal, 2", midseason; upright spreading habit; hardy to −15°F.

'Sundance Yellow' (natural hybrid of *calendulaceum* × *periclymenoides;* collected in Oconee Co., S.C.): vivid yellow with orange yellow blotch, 1½", midseason, small leaves; very compact habit to 4 ft. high; hardy to −15°F.

'Wayah Crest' (natural hybrid of *arborescens* × *bakerii;* collected in the Snowbird Mtns. near Franklin, N.C.): deep pink, 2", very fragrant, mid to late season; upright spreading habit; hardy to −25°F.

'White Lightning' (natural hybrid of *arborescens* or *arborescens* × *bakerii;* collected in the Snowbird Mtns. near Franklin, N.C.): white, with distinct yellow blotch, large lily-like 2½" flowers, waxy heavy substance, very fragrant, mid to late season; upright spreading habit; hardy to −25°F.

Additional Carlson Deciduous Azaleas

CARLSON'S POST SCRIPT AZALEAS

Advance generation of *R. bakeri* × *R. arborescens.* See pages 108–109.

'Dream Lover': moderate yellowish pink with large orange yellow flare, late June.

'Dreamer's Holiday': yellowish pink with large yellow flare, late June.

'Embraceable You': light yellowish pink with orange yellow blotch, early June.

'Fine & Dandy': vivid pink, early July.

'Get Happy': pink with yellow flare, floriferous, early to mid-June.

'Glad Rag Doll': deep yellowish pink, yellow upper petal, late June.

'Let's Dance': light pink with light yellow upper petal, fragrant, mid-June.

'Makin' Whoopee': vivid pink with orange yellow flare on upper petal, late June to early July.

'Mexicali Rose': red buds open to reddish orange, mid-June.

'Moonlight Bay': pale yellow with deeper yellow blotch, spicy fragrance, late June to early July.

'Moonlight Becomes You': light yellow with orange yellow upper petal, fragrant, late June to early July.

'Moonlight Cocktail': light yellowish pink with orange yellow flare, late June.

'Moonlight Serenade': pale pink with pale yellow undertones, light yellow flare, mid-June.

'Rose of Washington Square': deep pink with orange yellow flare, mid-June.

'Salmon Chanted Evening': yellowish pink with yellow flare, late June.

'Satin Doll': deep pink with orange yellow flare, large, early July.

"S Marvelous': deep pink with large orange flare, late June–early July.

"S Wonderful': vivid pink with orange yellow flare, mid-June.

'Schaum Torte': very pale yellow tinged greenish yellow, deep yellow flare, very fragrant, late June.

'Sing, Sing, Sing': yellowish pink with orange yellow upper petal, late June.

'Sophisticated Lady': light pink with bluish white ribs, a hint of yellow in the pale yellow flare, delicate fragrance, early to mid-July.

'Southern Nights': pale yellowish pink with yellow upper petal, early July.

'Such A Night': light pink, with a yellow flare, large, late June.

'Summer Affair': pale pink with faint yellow flare, early July.

Summer Bouquet': pink with yellow flare, fragrant, early July.

'Summer Fancy': strong pink with yellow flare, late July.

'Summer Sachet': yellowish pink with deep yellow upper petal, fragrant, early July.

'Thou Swell': strong pink, mid-July.

'Uncle Salmon': pale yellowish pink with large yellow flare, late June.

SELECTIONS OF DECIDUOUS SPECIES

'Alabammy Bound' (*R. alabamense*): white flushed pink, fragrant.

'Beeguiling' (*R. luteum*): pale yellow, deep yellow upper petal.

'Carlson's Coral Flameboyant' (*R. calendulaceum*): vivid shades of yellowish pink, large, early blooming form.

'Carlson's Golden Flameboyant' (*R. calendulaceum*): orange yellow, large.

'Carlson's Orange Flameboyant' (*R. calendulaceum*): vivid orange, large.

'Carlson's Yellow Flame' (*R. calendulaceum*): yellow.

'Carlson's Yellow Flameboyant' (*R. calendulaceum*): yellow, large.

'Choptank River Doll' (*R. atlanticum* × *R. periclymenoides*): light yellow with reddish tube, deeper yellow flare, fragrant.

'Choptank River Dutchess' (*R. atlanticum* × *R. periclymenoides*): deep pink buds open to white with deep pink on the reverse of petals, very fragrant.

'Choptank River Queen' (*R. atlanticum* × *R. periclymenoides*): pink striped buds open white with pink tips at ends of petals, tight trusses, fragrant.

'Deed I Do' (*R. arborescens*): pink with yellow flare, fragrant.

'Delectable' (*R. calendulaceum*): bright shades of orange and yellow.

'Good Old Summertime' (*R. viscosum*): large white, very fragrant, mid-July.

'Jazz' (*R. calendulaceum*): orange yellow, large.

'Lovey Mine' (*R. arborescens*): light pink, fragrant.

'Milenberg Joys' (*R. atlanticum*): pale pink, orange yellow flare.

'Opus One' (*R. prinophyllum*): pale pink, large, in large trusses, fragrant.

'Party Girl' (*R. flammeum* hybrid): pale pink, deeper pink margins, orange yellow flare, very fragrant.

'Party Popsickle' (*R. flammeum* hybrid): pink, yellow flare.

'Pink Lady Schlipper' (*R. schlippenbachii*): deep pink.

'Schlippink und Schlyedink' (*R. schlippenbachii*): deep pink.

'Summer Parasol' (*R. arborescens*): white, fragrant, early July; low mounding habit, 4 ft. in 15 yrs.

'The Cat's Pajamas' (*R. calendulaceum*): mixed yellow and orange.

'The Pearls' (*R. atlanticum*): very pale yellow with yellow blotch, fragrant.

'Yes, Indeed' (*R. prinophyllum*): pale pink tinged with yellow, fragrant.

CARLSON'S GARDENS SELECTIONS OF ABBOTT AZALEAS

see also page 109.

'Blue Nun': vivid pink form of *R. prinophyllum,* fragrant; bluish green foliage.
'Carlson's Chameleon': deep yellowish pink, aging to vivid pink.
'Carlson's Yellow Scentsation': vivid yellow, very fragrant.
'Fragrant Delicto II': deep pink with lighter ribs, very fragrant.
'Honey Hush': light yellow.
'Later On': yellow with distinct pale orange stripes, large, late June.
'Little Queenie': off white; low growing.
'Love Explosion': orange, frilled.
'Over the Rainbow': multicolored yellowish pink and orange.
'Peach Luscious': light yellowish pink, with yellow overtones.
'Sheer Joy': changing shades of yellowish pink.
'Sweet Little Sixteen': multicolored yellowish pink, fragrant.
'The Killer': strong pink, orange yellow flare, very fragrant.
'Vermont Nugget': orange yellow.
'Vermont Picotee': white with vivid pink edges, yellow blotch.
'Yvonne': pale pink with faint yellow flare.

Varnadoe Azalea Selections

A south Georgia farmer and now nurseryman with his sons in Colquitt, Ga., with a keen interest in native plants, Aaron Varnadoe started with native azaleas by seed; now propagating many of his selected plants by cuttings. Plants should be hardy to zone 6.

'Beatrice Varnadoe's Appleblossom' (selection of *R. canescens* collected in Randolph Co., Ga.): white with a light pink margin on each petal, 1½", fragrant, early. Easy to root.

'Varnadoe's Apricot' (*austrinum* hybrid): deep yellow, pink tube and stripes on petals, 1½".

'Varnadoe's Lilac' (selected seedling of a *R. flammeum* (*speciosum*) hybrid): pale reddish purple, no blotch, 1½", flowers persist, midseason. Difficult to root.

'Varnadoe's Salmon' (selected seedling of a *R. canescens* × *flammeum* hybrid): strong yellowish pink, no blotch, 1½", midseason. Roots well.
See also 'Varnadoe's Moonbeam' p. 114.

Additional Weston Hybrids

The following are for release in 1986 and hardy to −25°F. For other Weston Hybrids, see p. 112.

'Lobster' (*prunifolium* hybrid): reddish orange, late July, nonfading flowers.

'Pink Rocket' (*viscosum* × pink *arborescens*): pink flowers in clusters, 1½", fragrant, early July; leaves bluish green, light gray underneath, reddish fall color.

'Sparkler' (*viscosum* × pink *arborescens*): large pink, 1½–2", crinkled edges, fragrant; bluish green rounded leaves, light gray underneath.

Appendix J
ADDITIONAL EVERGREEN AZALEAS

Additional Kurume Azaleas

'Cangallo' (Koppeschaar): moderate red, early; spreading habit.
'Cherry Pink' (Knap Hill Nur.): vivid pink.
'Futami Akebono' (Beattie, PI 77134): deep pink, 1½".
'Iro Sobi' (Beattie, PI 77097): light reddish purple, 2".
'Kokonaye' (Knap Hill Nur.): white to yellowish white with greenish throat, broad margin of light purplish pink, reddish spotting. Resembles 'Azuma Kagami'.
'La Perle': yellowish pink, hose-in-hose.
'Marj T' ('Coral Bell' × 'Hinode Giri'; G. Taylor): deep pink, slightly tubular, 1½–1⅝"; compact habit; hardy in zone 6b.
'Mikawa Murasaki' (Beattie, PI 77072, 77083): vivid reddish purple, 1½."
'Mizu no Yamabuki' (introd. Domoto; Stevenson): pale yellowish white 11D, parially petaloid sepals, 1"; upright habit. Similar to 'Shin Sekai'.
'Oimatsu' (Domoto 1920): deep red.
'Peter' (Stewart 1952): yellowish pink with deeper blotch.
'Phyllis Elliot' (C. Elliot): light pink.

Kaempferi Additions

'Allotria' ('Rubinette' × 'Vuyk's Scarlet'; Hachmann 1984): moderate purplish red 58A, with strong purplish red 63A, marked dark red 59A, 2–2¼".
'Gerda' (C. B. van Nes 1922): yellowish pink.
'Helvetia' (Hooftman 1935): red.
'Kitty' (C. B. van Nes 1922): orange.
'Little Ruby' ('Amoenum' × 'Favorite'; V. van Nes 1953): deep reddish orange, hose-in-hose.
'Orange Favorite' (sport of 'Favorite'; V. van Nes 1953): deep yellowish orange.
'Oregon Pride': deep yellowish pink.

Stevenson Kurume Introductions

The late J. B. Stevenson of England, well known in the Rhododendron world, introduced a group of Kurume azaleas before 1938 from the Yokohama Nurseries and K. Wada of Japan. Many of these azaleas were available from the now defunct Sunningdale Nursery in Surrey, England. Many of the plant weres moved to the Castle Howard Estate Ltd., Castle Howard, York, England. A few were grown at Callaway Gardens, but most are uncommon in the U.S.A. They may be available under different names, and some have questionable spelling.

'Arziemakie': vivid yellowish pink, darker spotting, large.
'Augigasana': pale pink with deeper margins, brown spotting in blotch; tall upright habit.
'Chigo no Mai': deep pink with lighter center, red spotting, white anthers.
'Chiyo no Akebono': purplish pink.

'Choraku': strong purplish red, with stripes, ¾–1".
'Fude Tsukata': pink paling to greenish white.
'Fukuhiko': strong purplish red, with stripes, ¾–1".
'Gaeshi': deep purplish pink 73A, petals spaced, 1¼".
'Harumiji': white, ¾–1".
'Haru no Akebono': moderate yellowish pink, pale center, dark blotch, hose-in-hose, ¾".
'Haru no Kyokii': white, light greenish buds, irregular, ragged, 1".
'Haru no Sato' (syn. 'Had no Sato'): purplish pink, 1".
'Haru no Shiou': pale throat, purple margins, hose-in-hose, anthers pale.
'Hatsuoti': purple blush, large.
'Hiyakasen' (syn. 'Hikkasen'): light yellowish pink, pink center, dark blotch.
'Hinode no Kumo': no description available.
'Ima Zuma' (syn. 'Chi no Ito'): pale purplish pink, red stripes, tips darker.
'Itten': pale purplish red.
'Izumigawa': moderate purplish red 55C, pale throat, reddish blotch, 1¼".
'Juhachiko' (syn. 'Yukachiko'): reddish orange.
'Keinohana' (syn. 'Ishiyama'): deep purplish pink, long narrow shaped flowers, white anthers.
'Kinjo Tama': deep yellowish pink, hose-in-hose.
'Kodai Nishiki': white, hose-in-hose.
'Kojo no Odorikaraka': vivid red, small.
'Kokinran': yellowish pink, white throat, with red spots, 6 petals.
'Kokonaye': white to yellowish white, green throat, broad margins of light purplish pink, red spotting.
'Komachi': pale pink with darker margins.
'Koran Yuki': reddish orange, small. May be the same as 'Kojo no Oderikaraka.'
'Kumagaya': strong pink 52D, 1¼".
'Maikojaku': no description available.
'Maimsode': purplish pink, late.
'Metake': vivid red, small, late; dwarf, compact habit.
'Mikaera Zakura': pink.
'Ogi no Odorikaraski' (syn. 'Kojo no Odorikaraski'): deep reddish orange 42B, 1¼".
'Onno Sora': light purple, narrow petals, anthers white, occasional reddish brown spots.
'Ouchiyama': light purplish red.
'Paikune': pink, star shaped.
'Rankyoken': vivid reddish orange, ¾".
'Sahohime': white flushed purplish pink, darker spotting, partially petaloid.
'Saroi': white, flushed and edged pink, anthers white, no spotting.
'Senju': pale purplish pink, flushed darker, red spotting, anthers pale.
'Senka': unusual color pattern from tiny dots and small blotches of strong yellowish pink 41C, whitish throat, blotch of darker spots, 1".
'Shikishima': purplish red 55A, darker spots, light center, 1½".
'Shinimiagagino': purplish pink, hose-in-hose, anthers white, small.
'Shinoito': yellowish white, flushed light purple.
'Shi no Nome': (syn. 'Shi no Noe'): pale greenish white with pink margins.
'Shino Miagagino': purplish red, white anthers, hose-in-hose.
'Shi no Uye': white with reddish brown spotting, large.
'Shinsagino Kagasane': purplish red pale throat, reddish blotch.
'Shintsune': white, frilly margins, anthers greenish, no blotch, tends to sport.
'Shjuchuke': no description available.
'Takamakie': white with greenish blotch.
'Tonkonatsu': white, large.
'Toun': white with faint pink blush, reddish purple spots, 1½".
'Usugukari': white to pale purplish pink, with pale purple margins, anthers white.
'Wakalia': strong orange, small, anthers pale.
'Yezo Nishiki': white, variable with red stripes and selfs of purplish red 57C, 1".

'Yoshi Migatake': purplish red, 3/4".
'Yozakura': reddish purple, 2". Possibly a Satsuki Hybrid.
'Yukachiko': strong yellowish pink 38A, center white, darker spots, 1½".

Additional Pride Azaleas

The late Orlando Pride tested and evaluated many azaleas and rhododendrons for cold hardiness. Records on parentages are often not known, and descriptions of cultivars are often confusing or lacking. The Pride Azaleas have proven the test of time, often not named and released without 15 or 20 years of evaluation. The following are possibly some of Lanny's last releases. Unfortunately, descriptions are very brief and there is confusion with azalea and rhododendron names. For additional information see pages 199–200.

'Betty Pride': moderate pink, midseason.
'Dr. Clarence Lewis': pink.
'Edith': moderate reddish orange. Possibly same as the azalea 'Edith Pride' or a rhododendron.
'Everbloom': no description available.
'Gordon Greer': no description available.
'Joe Paterno': white. Given as an azalea; however, there is a Pride rhododendron with the same name.
'Ling Close': strong red. Also called 'Ling'.
'Mrs. Cribbs': pink.
'Mrs. John Wilson': light pink.
'Nudiflora Pink': moderate pink. Listed earlier as a Knap Hill.
'Pride's Old Faithful': no description available.
'Pride's Pink': pink, late.
'Pride's Pride': red, late.
'Pride's Super Hino-Red': reddish orange.
'Red Poukhanense': red.
'Red Satin': moderate red.
'Susan Pride': yellowish pink, hose-in-hose.
'Winnie Greer': vivid red. Possibly the same as 'Winifred Greer'.

Additional Satsuki Growing in the U.S.A.

'Aya Nishiki': white with red spotting, distinct dissected petals.
'Haku Oden': white with red spots and markings, 7–14 petals.
'Komachi Hime': no description available.
'Kyokko Nishiki': no description available.
'Macrantha Ovata Rokuzan': deep red, small broad ovate leaves. Very similar to 'Kazan' or 'Rukizon'.
'Matsu Nami': white, variable with stripes, flecks, sectors, and selfs of deep yellowish pink, rounded lobes, 3".
'Muffett' ('General Wavell' × 'Glory of Numazu', syn. 'General Wavell var. Muffett'; Ingram): vivid red, large.
'Muffineer' ('General Wavell' × 'Glory of Numazu', syn. 'General Wavell var. Muffineer'; Ingram): vivid red, large.
'Naniwa Nishiki': white with deep reddish orange markings, many variations; narrow elliptic leaves.
'Onyo': very pale pink, many variations, stripes, blotches, and selfs of deep yellowish pink, rounded lobes.
'Shiki Magaki': white with stripes, sectors, and selfs of reddish orange, double.
'Tamori Hime': white with purplish red stripes and sanding, white throat.
'Tenkei': white with stripes, splotches, and selfs of purplish red, 3½".
'Tenritsu': no description available.
'Uyo no Hikari': white with deep red spots and mottling.
'Yuki no Akebono': white with stripes, sectors, and selfs of reddish purple; cupped shaped leaves.

Miscellaneous Inter-Group Evergreen Hybrids

'Alclara' ('Snowclad' × 'Coccinea'; Raustein, named and reg. by Scarbeck 1985): buds strong red 45D, open vivid purplish red 57D, with heavy strong purplish red 58B spotting in blotch, wavy lobes, 3", midseason; rounded spreading habit, 2½ × 4' wide in 21 yrs; hardy to −5°F.

'Alice W. Muller' (Macrantha hybrid; Bobbink Atkins 1935): vivid pink, with reddish sheen, hose-in-hose.

'Armstrong's Fall' (Kaempferi hyb., origin unknown): reddish orange, fall flowering; hardy in zone 7.

'Aztec Joy' (probably a Belgian hyb. from Japan, introd. to U.S.A. by Nuccio): large, unusual flower, light to strong yellowish pink, double hose-in-hose, margins deeply scalloped or fringed, 3–3½"; upright spreading habit; hardiness not known. See 'Pink Joy'.

'Chesapeake' ('Vervaeneana' × 'Mucronatum'; syn 'Scott's White'; Shanks and Link, named by Scott): white with faint yellow throat, 3"; large, medium dense, rounded habit, 6 × 6 ft. in 15 yrs; hardy in zone 7.

'Concord Cemetery' (selection of *poukhanense* in Blossom Hill Cemetery, Concord, NH, U.S.A., named by J. Parks): medium purplish pink, large blotch of dark red spots on upper petal, mildly fragrant, 2½ to 2¾", usually 3 per truss; original plant low spreading, 72 × 30" high in 25 years; hardy to at least −25°F. Deciduous below −13°F, possibly a hybrid of *R. y. poukhanense.*

'Coral Cascade': (syn. 'Bruce Hancock'; TM. Monrovia Nur.): pink with white border, 3½"; cascading habit. In Calif. reported to be only pink in fall.

'Crimson Tide' ('Beth Bullard' × 'Red Slippers'; Boike 1986): vivid red 44A, blotch of darker spots, 3–3¼"; hardy to −10°F.

'Diana Trask' ('Marilyn Kay' × 'Rosanna'; Dosser 1985): vivid red 44A, hose-in-hose, 2¾"; low shrub 20" high.

'Ellen Zora' ('Elsie Lee' × 'Purple Splendor'; syn. 'Ell'; Byrkit, introd. Anderson 1985): very light purple 74C, with strong purplish red 61C spotting on dorsal half of all whorls, double, 5–8 wavy lobes, rose bud shape when opening, 2"; semidwarf, stiff upright branches 30–18" high in 10 yrs.; hardy to 0°F.

'Irene' ('Elsie Lee' × 'Amagasa'; Schroeder, raised and introd. C. Hicklin): strong purplish pink 68B, with purplish red dots in blotch, slightly ruffled, 3", double; upright rounded habit, 30" in 5 yrs.; hardy in zone 8, possibly hardier.

'Julia Scott' ('Elsie Lee' × 'Amagasa'; Schroeder, raised and introd. Hicklin): white, double, 2½–3", heavy bloomer, shiny foliage; rounded compact plant, 24" in 5 yrs.; hardy in zone 8, possibly hardier.

'King's Orange Red' (parentage unknown, King): reddish orange, 3–3½", flowers intermittently; upright spreading habit; hardy in zone 7.

'Lalla' (parentage unknown, white × peach color, A.R.S. seed ex.; raised and introd. Hicklin): buds moderate purplish pink 70D, open pale purple 75D, shading light purple 75A–B, green in throat, 2½–3", 21 in truss; 4 × 4' in 5 yrs.; hardy in zone 8, possibly hardier.

'Lavender Delight' ('Gretel' × 'Purple Triump'; Mackay): pale purplish pink 56A, fading lighter, 2¾"; compact shrub to 18".

'Maggie Powell' ('Saint James' × 'Red Slippers'; Boike 1986): wide margin of vivid reddish orange 44B, throat pale to light pink 49D–C, spotting in blotch deep red, 2¾–3"; medium size shrub; hardy to −10°F.

'Marge Alexander' (('Shinnyo no Tsuki' × 'Grace Freeman') × 'Foxy Lady'; Garrett 1986): light pink with dark pink margins, 3½", midseason; upright spreading habit; hardy to 0°F.

'Martha's Double' (parentage unknown, available in Knoxville, Tn. and N. Georgia): white, semidouble, occasionally some petaloidy, lobes rounded, ruffled, 2½–3"; upright rounded habit; hardy to −15°F. Possibly an Aichele hybrid.

'Maryland Orange' ('Vervaeneana' × 'Pink Pearl' × 'Vervaeana' × 'Coral Bells'; Shanks and Link): deep reddish orange, throat vivid red, numerous petaloid anthers, hose-in-hose, 3"; medium dense compact habit with large leaves, 3 ft. in 15 yrs.; hardy in zone 8; susceptible to bleaching and disease.

'Mount Fuji' (*tamaurae* × *kaempferi;* Wada): white.

'Morning Mist' (*rubropilosum* × *poukhanense,* Ingram 1945): purplish pink to pink.

'Nambucca Princess' ('Elsa Karga' × 'Silver Anniversary'; Mackay): vivid red 45B, bunch of petaloids in center, 2¾", shrub to 28".

'Pettychaps' (parentage unknown; Reuthe 1985): light to deep purplish pink 55A, B–C, with darker spots in blotch, hose-in-hose, 1¼–1¾", compact shrub to 18".

'Phyllis Moore' (parentage and origin unknown): white, hose-in-hose, 1¾"; upright spreading habit; hardy in zone 6. Popular in Canada around Vinelands, Ontario as a hardy evergreen white.

'Pink Joy' (probably a Belgian hyb. from Japan, introduced to U.S.A. by Nuccio): large unusual flower, pale to light pink with darker pink flecks, double, hose-in-hose, margins deeply scalloped or fringed; upright spreading habit; hardiness unknown.

'Pride of Nambucca' ('Rosa Belton' × 'Sweet Nellie'; Mackay 1985): vivid purplish red 57C, some petaloid stamens, 2¾"; compact shrub to 18".

'Pryored' (by-product, 4th generation controlled crossing for developing yellow flowered evergreen; 62% *prunifolium*, 19% *indicum* and 19% yellow Mollis Hybrid; Pryor, Na 36544, PI 476758): deep reddish orange 42A, with dark red spotting, hose-in-hose, 2–2⅜", wavy margins; upright habit, 24 × 36" high in 10 yrs.; leaves elliptic 1¾" long, ⅛" wide; hardy in zone 5b.

'R. N. Pennington' (Pennington): white, blushed pale pink, prominent green throat, 2"; upright rounded habit; hardy to −15°F.

'Red Star' ('Berkeley Red' × light purple sport of 'Indica Rosa'; Westfall, introd. Brant 1950): deep red.

'Ring #1' (parentage unknown; Ring 1986): strong purplish pink 73B, light purplish pink 73C outside, hose-in-hose, pendant flowers, 1¾", midseason; upright spreading habit, 4 × 4½ ft. high in 12 yrs.; hardy to −5°F.

'Rubinstern' ('Mother's Day' × 'Kermesina'; Hachmann 1984): moderate purplish red 58B, sometimes marked moderate red 184B to moderate purplish red 184C, 5–7 lobes, 1½–1¾"; shrub to 36" high.

'Scott's Lavender' ('Vervaeneana' × 'Mucronatum'; Shanks and Link, named by Scott): light violet with clearly marked purplish red throat, 3"; vigorous dense spreading habit, 8 ft. in 15 yrs.; hardy in zone 7.

'Seattle White' (florist plant obtained by B. Y. Morrison in Seattle, Wa.; one existing greenhouse plant at U.S.D.A. Glenn Dale, Md.): white, with greenish yellow blotch, semidouble to double, 3", green calyces present, early May. Used in several crosses such as 'Mrs. LBJ' and 'Takoma Park'.

'Tama no Ito' (Beattie PI 77107): light reddish purple, dark green foliage. Possibly an Indica Azalea (*indicum*).

'Usuyo' (Beattie, PI 77122): light purple, 1½". Possibly a form of *R. macrosepalum*.

'Venus' (Henson; 1971; PAF): pale pink, yellowish white blotch on upper lobe, rose bud-like, 4", waxy leaves; spreading vigorous growth; forcing plant holds well for Mother's Day.

Carlson Evergreen Azaleas

'In A Mist': white washed with pale purplish pink, fragrant.

'Star Pillow': effect of white stars with a few yellow speckles, fragrant.

'Star Scent' ('Mucronatum' hyb.): pale purplish pink, very fragrant.

'Take The Time': white tinged purplish pink, fragrant.

Kaempferi Hybrids

'Camisole Burgundy': dark reddish brown, hose-in-hose.

'Camisole Crimson': vivid red, hose-in-hose.

'Camisole Fuschia': vivid reddish purple, hose-in-hose.

'Camisole Rose': dark pink, hose-in-hose.

'Early On': yellowish pink, early blooming.

'Luminosity': vivid pink, mid-May.

'Pinkandescent': vivid purplish pink.

Czechoslovakian Hybrids

Information from the recent book *Czeckoslovenske slechteni rodu Rhododendron* L. (*Czechoslovak Breeding Efforts in the Genus rhododendron* L.) by Karel Hieke 1985. See also p. 261.

DECIDUOUS AZALEAS

'Dagmar' (B. Kavka 1939): deep pink, 2"; upright spreading habit.

'Vlasta' (B. Kavka 1939): vivid yellow, orange yellow blotch, 2¼", fragrant, 5–9 in truss; upright spreading habit.

'Zdena' (B. Kavka 1974): strong to light pink, throat white, dark yellow blotch, 2⅛", 4–8 in truss; upright spreading habit.

EVERGREEN HYBRIDS FOR OUTDOORS

Some damage occurs when winters are severe.

'Doubrava' (B. Kavka et al 1974): deep purplish pink, 1¼"; dense compact spreading habit, 18 × 38" wide.

'Ledikanense' (B. Kavka, M. Opatrna 1945): light reddish purple, dark brown purple spotting in blotch, 2⅜"; round spreading habit, 40 × 28" wide; very hardy.

'Orlice' (B. Kavka 1970): strong reddish purple, 1⅝", dense compact habit, 26 × 38" wide.

'Otava' (J. Jelinek 1969): strong purplish pink, 1¼"; compact spreading habit, 25 × 46" wide.

'Profesor Jersov' (B. Bavka 1970): strong red, 1¾"; dense upright rounded habit 56" high.

JAPANESE HYBRIDS FOR POT CULTURE

'Elektra' (J. Matous 1964): vivid pink, 1¾"; broadly spreading habit.

'Galathera' (J. Matous 1970): light pink with darker pink shading, 2¼", late, for March forcing; low compact, somewhat irregular.

'Kleopatra' (J. Matous 1964): strong purplish red, pronounced reddish brown blotch, 2⅛", late, for forcing in March; medium to strong habit, somewhat irregular.

'Minerva' (J. Matous 1979): white with yellow-green blotch, 2½" mid to late, for March forcing; compact dense habit.

'Ophelila' (J. Matous 1964): reddish purple, darker blotch, 2½", late, for forcing in March-April; medium to strong habit, somewhat irregular.

'Oslava' (J. Jelinck 1969): strong purlish pink, 1¼", compact spreading habit, 25 × 42 " wide.

'Vesna' (J. Matous 1964): yellowish pink, 2", early to mid early, for forcing about Christmas; strong, dense, compact habit.

INDIAN AZALEAS FOR POT CULTURE

'Alfa' (J. Sestak 1961): vivid red, 2¾"; vigorous habit.

'Antonin Dvorak' (B. Janouch 1967): 2⅜–3⅛"; compact habit, irregularly spreading.

'Ave' (M. Srpkova 1960): pink, somewhat marbled, regular compact habit.

'Bedrich Smetana' (B. Janouch 1967): light yellowish pink, single to double, 3"; compact spreading habit.

'Bohemia' (J. Sestak 1962): reddish orange, large double; vigorous compact habit; best propagated by grafting.

'Calypso' (B. Janouch 1961): yellowish pink, double; dense habit; grafts grow better.

'Hradecka' (M. Srpkova 1960): vivid red, 2⅜"; compact habit best propagated by grafting.

'Ivanka' (M. Srpkova 1977): white with yellow-green blotch, single, rarely semidouble; compact erect habit.

'Jaro' (J. Sestak 1968): light pink, semi- to double; low compact habit.

'Krajka' (J. Sestak 1968): vivid pink with pronounced green "eye", wavy and frimbriate, 2¼;; compact spreading habit; grafting recommended.

'Maj' (J. Sestak 1967): deep pink with purplish shading, red blotch, semidouble, remaining half open for a long time, 2¾"; compact irregular spreading habit.

'Melodie' (M. Srpkova 1968): deep yellowish pink, dark red blotch, 2½–3¾", single to semidouble; dense, compact, vigorous habit, somewhat erect.

'Mignon' (J. Sestak 1967): red, double, very wavy; compact habit, somewhat irregularly spreading.

'Perla' (M. Srpkova 1977): deep pink, dark red blotch, 3–3½"; vigorous habit, irregularly erect.

'Regina' (Z. Stiborek 1968): light yellowish pink, single to semidouble, 2½"; low medium dense habit.

'Sylvie' (Z. Stiborek 1974): deep pink with white margins, dark red blotch, double, sometimes single, 2¾–3¼"; medium dense habit, slightly irregular.

'Viktoria' (Z. Stiborek): deep pink, dark red blotch, semi- to double, 2¾"; compact, somewhat spreading habit.

Eden Linearifolium Hybrids

In the 1970s an odd seedling was saved of a cross 'David Haskell' × 'Mae Knapper' made by W. David Smith. The seedling was called 'Odd Ball', 'Pride of Paradise' and finally named 'Joy of Paradise' due to the unusual linear foliage and flower petals. In 1982–83 the cross 'David Haskell' × 'Mae Knapper' was repeated, and 6 linear foliage type seedlings were named. (*The Azalean* Vol. 7, #4, Dec. 1985.)

'Joy of Paradise' (syn. 'Odd Ball', 'Pride of Paradise' 1970s): light purplish pink, long, narrow, linear separate petals, 1½" long × ⅜" wide, leaves long and linear, 2 × ⅜" wide; upright compact habit; hardy in zone 6.

Due to Mr. Smith's poor health, descriptions on the following named plants are not available. For other Eden Hybrids see pages 262–264.

'Joy of David' — 'Joy of Eden'
'Joy of Jane' — 'Joy of Shangri-la'
'Joy of Verde Vista' — 'Joy of York'

Additional Greenwood Hybrids

The following Greenwood Hybrids are scheduled for release in 1986 and 1987. All are hardy to 0°F, and possibly hardier. For other Greenwood Hybrids see p. 266.

'Accent' ('Linda Jean' × 'Hahn's Red'): deep purplish pink 64D, hose-in-hose, 2", midseason; upright habit.

'Candy' ('Albert-Elizabeth' × 'Hino Crimson'): pale pink 56C, semidouble, 1¾–2", early; low compact habit.

'Greenwood Diablo' ('Albert-Elizabeth' × 'Hino Crimson'): strong purplish red 61B, semidouble, 2", early; low compact habit.

'Greenwood Lace' ('Linda Jean' × 'Satanta'): white, double, 2½", early midseason; upright habit.

'Lisa' ('Maria Elena' × 'Linda Jean'): strong purplish red 58D, double, 2¼", late; rounded habit.

'Nancy' ('Marie Elena' × 'Linda Jean'): strong purplish red 58D, double, 2¼", late; rounded habit.

'Nola' ('Linda Jean' × 'Springtime'): light purplish pink 62C, double 1½", midseason; upright habit.

'Pat' ('Maria Elena' × 'Linda Jean'): strong purplish pink 63C, semidouble, 2¼", very late; mounded habit.

'Pink Petals' ('Albert-Elizabeth' × 'Hino Crimson'): light purplish pink petals 56D, with white throat, semidouble, ruffled, 2"; low compact habit.

'Pink Tenino' (sport of 'Tenino'): very purplish red 61D, hose-in-hose, 3", late; semidwarf habit.

'White Splendor' ('Linda Jean' × 'Springtime'): white, double, 2½", early midseason; upright habit.

H. R. Schroeder Evergreen Azalea Hybrids

The late Dr. H. R. Schroeder of Evansville, Ind., U.S.A., began breeding evergreen azaleas in the early 1970s. His main goals were to develop cold hardy evergreen azaleas to withstand climatic conditions of the Midwest States of the U.S.A. and compact plants with colorful large single to double flowers.

About 4000 seedlings were lined out for evaluation in 1974. In 1984, 38 of the surviving plants were named. All plants listed are hardy to −15°F; flowering is mid to late May in the Midwest. Dr. Schroeder was active in the ARS and in the breeding of rhododendrons and azaleas and was a major contributor to the ARS seed exchange.

'Carrie Amanda' (3216; 'Elsie Lee' × 'Marion Lee'): white with deep purplish pink 55A border, 2½"; very compact habit, 24 × 24" in 10 yrs. Colored margin is unstable until plant matures.

'David Reynolds' (3209; 'Purple Splendor' × 'Vuyk's Scarlet'): deep pink 68A, with red spotting in upper petal, 2"; compact plant with distinct red stem coloration, 20 × 24" high in 10 yrs.

'Doctor Henry Schroeder' (3162; 'Mildred Mae' × 'Avalanche'): strong purplish pink 55B, 2½"; open spreading upright habit, 18 × 24" high in 10 yrs. Good evergreen foliage retention in winter.

'Doctor James Dippel' (3608; 'Purple Splendor' × 'Vuyk's Scarlet'): vivid reddish orange 33A, with dark reddish orange spotting in upper petal, ½"; compact spreading habit, 20 × 15" high in 10 yrs.

'Earl Webster' (3401; *R. kaempferi* selection): light purplish pink 55C, 1½"; open upright habit, 24 × 30" high in 10 yrs. Partially deciduous in winter.

'Eliza Hyatt' (3802; 'Elsie Lee' × 'Frosty'): varies from light pink 56C to light purplish pink 55D, faint green spotting deep in throat, double, 2"; compact habit, 24 × 24" in 10 yrs.

'Frosty Lee' (3805; 'Elsie Lee' × 'Frosty'): light purplish pink 55C, with reddish orange spotting in upper petal, 2"; compact habit, 24 × 24" in 10 yrs.

'George Hyatt' (3501; 'Purple Splendor' × 'Vuyk's Scarlet'): strong purplish red 64C, with large red spotting in upper petal, ruffled petals, 2½"; compact habit, 18 × 18" in 10 yrs.

'Henry Roland' (3852; syn. 'Roland'; 'Purple Splendor' × 'Vuyk's Scarlet'): deep pink 52C, with pale red spotting in upper petal, 2½"; compact habit, 24 × 18" high in 10 yrs.

'Holly's Late Pink' (3809; 'Elsie Lee' × 'Pink Gumpo'): strong purplish pink 55B, semidouble, hose-in-hose, 2½"; very compact dwarf habit, dark dense foliage, 18 × 10" high in 10 yrs.

'Hoosier Charm' (3302; 'Purple Splendor' × 'Vuyk's Scarlet'): deep purplish pink 55A, with dark red spotting in blotch, 2½"; compact habit, 15 × 10" high in 10 yrs.

'Hoosier Peach' (3300; 'Purple Splendor' × 'Vuyk's Scarlet'): strong pink 49A, dark red spotting in blotch, 2½"; compact habit, 18 × 18" in 10 yrs.

'Hoosier Rose' (3660; 'Purple Splendor' × 'Vuyk's Scarlet'): light purplish pink 55C, with dark pink spotting in blotch, 2"; compact, 24 × 15" high in 10 yrs.

'Hoosier Sunrise' (3807; 'Purple Splendor' × 'Vuyk's Scarlet'): strong purplish pink 55B, with faint red spotting in upper petal, semidouble, hose-in-hose, 2½"; compact habit, 18 × 15" high in 10 yrs.

'Margaret Hyatt' (3110; 'Elsie Lee' × 'Frosty'): strong purplish pink 73B, with red spotting in upper petal, semidouble, hose-in-hose, 2¾"; compact habit, 24 × 18" high in 10 yrs.

'Maryann Hyatt' (3016; 'Elsie Lee' × 'Frosty'): strong purplish pink 73B, semidouble, 2½"; somewhat upright and compact habit, 15 × 18" high in 10 yrs.

'Moby Dick' (3018; 'Mildred Mae' × 'Avalanche'): pale yellowish white with faint greenish yellow spotting in upper petal, 3"; dense compact habit, 30 × 18" high in 10 yrs.

'Mrs. Arthur Rogers' (3505; syn. 'Helen Rogers'; 'Elsie Lee' × 'Chanson'): light purplish pink 73C, brown spotting in upper petal, double, 2¾"; compact habit, 18 × 18"in 10 yrs.

'Mrs. Mildred Kinder' (3025; 'Elsie Lee' × 'Frosty'): deep purplish pink 73A, with faint red spotting in upper petal, double, ruffled petals, 2½"; 18 × 24" high in 10 yrs.

'Mrs. Henry Schroeder' (3026; 'Elsie Lee' × 'Frosty'): strong purplish pink 55B, very double, 2"; oval shaped foliage, compact habit, 24 × 18" high in 10 yrs.

'Mrs. Mary Schroeder' (3705; 'Elsie Lee' × 'Frosty'): light purplish pink 62C, with reddish brown spotting in upper petal, 2½"; compact, slightly upright, 24 × 30" high in 10 yrs.

'Mrs. Webster' (3028; 'Purple Splendor' × 'Vuyk's Scarlet'): strong purplish red 58C, with dark red spotting in upper petal, 3"; compact habit, 24 × 15" high in 10 yrs.

'Mrs. Nancy Dipple' (3835; 'Elsie Lee' × 'Frosty'): pale pink 56C, with distinctive pink stripe in one or two of its petals, double, 1½"; compact habit, 24 × 24" in 10 yrs.

'Purple Pride' (3840; 'Purple Splendor' × 'Vuyk's Scarlet'): vivid reddish purple 74B, with strong purplish red 67A blotch, ruffled petals, 2½"; compact habit, 24 × 18" high in 10 yrs.

'Red-Eyed Orchid Queen' (3841; 'Purple Splendor' × 'Vuyk's Scarlet'): light reddish purple 74C, with dark red spotting in upper petal, 2½"; compact habit, 24 × 18" high in 10 yrs.

'Robert Hyatt' (3849; 'Purple Splendor × 'Vuyk's Scarlet'): deep pink 52C, with dark pink spotting in blotch, 2¼"; compact habit, 18 × 15" high in 10 yrs.

'Rosemary Annette' (3860; syn. 'Rosemary'; 'Elsie Lee' × 'Frosty'): strong purplish pink 62B, with dark red spotting in upper petal, double, rosebud type, 2"; compact habit, 18 × 15" high in 10 yrs.

'Scarlet Frost' (3865; 'Purple Splendor' × 'Vuyk's Scarlet'): deep pink 52C, dark red spotting in blotch, 2½"; compact habit, 18 × 15" high in 10 yrs.

'Schroeder's Lavender Mist' (3870; 'Elsie Lee' × 'Frosty'): strong purplish pink 65A, with dark red spotting in blotch, 1 ¾"; compact habit, 18 × 18" in 10 yrs.

'Schroeder's Lavender Rose' (3872; 'Elsie Lee' × 'Frosty'): deep purplish pink 73A, with dark red spotting in throat, semidouble, 2¼"; compact habit, 24 × 24" in 10 yrs.

'Schroeder's Pink Perfection' (3874; 'Betty' × 'Elsie Lee'): deep purplish pink 55A, semidouble, hose-in-hose, petals in star shaped form, 2"; compact upright habit, 15 × 24" high in 10 yrs.

'Schroeder's Pink Splendor' (3660; 'Betty' × 'Elsie Lee'): deep purplish pink 55A, dark pink spotting in upper petal, 2½"; low compact habit, 24 × 18" tall in 10 yrs.

'Schroeder's Snowflake' (3876; 'Mildred Mae' × 'Avalanche'): white 155D, with faint yellow green spotting in upper petal, hose-in-hose, flowers unusually pendulous, 1½"; compact, somewhat upright habit, 24 × 30" high in 10 yrs.

'Schroeder's Sunray' (3880; 'Purple Splendor' × 'Vuyk''s Scarlet'): deep purplish pink 66C, with dark red spotting in upper petal, 1¾"; compact habit, 24 × 15" high in 10 yrs.

'Schroeder's White Glory' (3882; 'Elsie Lee' × 'Glory'): variegated white to pink, with purplish pink edging, hose-in-hose, 1½"; compact, 24 × 18" high in 10 yrs.

'Susan Camille' (3885; 'Elsie Lee' × 'Frosty): pale pink 56D, semidouble, hose-in-hose, 2½"; compact habit, 24 × 18" high in 10 yrs.

'Vonnie' (3886; 'Purple Splendor' × 'Vuyk's Scarlet'): strong purplish pink 55B, with dark red spotting in upper blotch, 2"; compact habit, 24 × 24" in 10 yrs.

'William Hyatt' (3887; 'Purple Splendor' × 'Vuyk's Scarlet'): deep purplish pink 66C, with dark red spotting in upper petal, 2½"; compact habit, 18 × 18" in 10 yrs.

Mauritsen Hybrids

The Mauritsen Hybrids introduced in 1986 by Steve Mauritsen of Kent, Washington, U.S.A., are crosses of 'Hahn's Red' × 'Ward's Ruby'. The plants are heavy bloomers and all flowers are single. Hardy to 0°F and possibly lower.

'Cherry Delight': strong red 52A, 1½"; plants compact, 24 × 30" tall in 5 years.

'Dragon Lady': deep reddish orange 42A, 1½"; plants compact spreading, 30 × 18" tall in 5 years.

'It's Magic': strong red 53C, 1½"; plants compact, 30 × 30" in 5 yrs.

'Last Tango': vivid red 46C, 2½"; plants compact spreading, 24 × 12" tall in 5 yrs.

'Morning Fire': deep red 46A, 1½"; plants compact, 30 × 36" tall in 5 yrs.

'Orange Daiquiri': deep reddish orange 42A, 2"; plants compact spreading, 30 × 12" tall in 5 yrs.

Additional McDonald Hybrids

Kurume—Kaempferi Hybrids

'Chessie's Pink' ('Elsie Lee' selfed): vivid pink, double, 1½ in., late midseason; 3 × 3 ft. in 9 yrs.; hardy to −3°F.

'Chessie's Purple' ('Elsie Lee' selfed): light purple, (darker than 'Elsie Lee'), double, 1½ in., late midseason; 36 × 40" wide in 9 yrs.; hardy to 0°F.

'New Generation Red' ('Girard's Hotshot' × 'Hershy Red Tetra'): strong red 52A, hose-in-hose, slightly ruffled, 2–2½ in., early midseason; broad upright habit, 31 × 26" tall; produces abundant pollen; hardy to 0°F.

'White Surprise' ('Dainty Rose' open pollinated): white with greenish yellow dots in throat, 1–1¼ in., early midseason; 24 × 33" tall in 10 yrs.; dark green glossy foliage; hardy to −3°F.

'Williamsburg Rose' ('Ripples' × 'Evening Glow'): strong purplish pink 55B-C, hose-in-hose, double, rosebud like midseason; broad spreading habit 40 × 25" tall in 9 yrs.; hardy to 10°F; further testing needed.

Satsuki Hybrids

'Negligee' ('Mai Hime' × 'Pink Gumpo', D. Wagner; grown and named by McDonald): very pale purplish pink with occasional dark pink sectors and dots, pink dots on upper petal, 2 in., late; low, 8 × 10" tall in 5 yrs.; hardy to 5°F.

'Williamsburg' ('Gumpo White' × 'Wakaebisi'): white, with deep yellowish pink 43C-D, occasional flowers are deep yellowish pink, hose-in-hose, 2½ in., late, broad mounding habit, 36 × 22" tall; glossy green leaves; hardy to 5°F.

Inter-Group Evergreen Hybrids

'Angelwing' (*indicum* × *nakahari;* D. Wagner; grown and named by McDonald): vivid purplish pink, single to semidouble, some strap-like petals, 1½–2 in., late; low tight growth habit, 33 × 22" tall in 10 yrs.; hardy to 0°F.

'Dreamsicle' ('Venus' (Henson) × 'Girard's Hotshot'): light yellowish pink 38C, attractive pale yellowish white blotch on upper petals and two side petals, petals tipped in white, anthers yellowish white, style dark pink, rare petaloid stamens, flat-faced, ruffled, 2–2¼ in.; broad spreading, 44 × 26" tall in 9 yrs.; hardy to 20°F; further testing needed.

Nuccio's Hybrids

The flowering seasons at Nuccio's Nursery are as follows:

Satsuki types	Belgians, Kurumes & hybrids
early March–April	Oct.–Jan.
midseason mid April–May	Feb.–March
late mid May–June	April–May

BELGIAN INDIAN AND SOUTHERN INDIAN HYBRIDS

'Nuccio's Brightside' ('Nuccio's Friendship' × 'Nuccio's Garden Party'): vivid reddish orange, semidouble, wavy margins, 3", midseason; vigorous upright habit. Release date 1990.

'Nuccio's Carnival Clown' ('Red Poppy' open pollinated): deep reddish purple, wavy margins, 3½", early midseason; vigorous upright habit.

'Nuccio's Carnival Music' ('Starlight' × 'Nuccio's Masterpiece'): pale pink, double, 2½–3", early to midseason; medium compact habit.

'Nuccio's Day Dream' ('Starlight' × 'Nuccio's Masterpiece'): pale pink, double, 2½–3", early to midseason; medium compact habit.

'Nuccio's Delightful' ('Starlight' × 'Nuccio's Masterpiece'): moderate pink, full double, 3", early to midseason; medium bushy habit. Release date 1989.

'Nuccio's Easter Delight' ('Nuccio's Friendship' × 'L. C. Bobbink'): shaded light violet, spaced pointed petals, 2½", mid to late; broad vigorous upright habit.

'Nuccio's Fashion Show' ('California Dawn' × 'Garden Party'): deep yellowish pink, semidouble, 3½", mid to late season; vigorous open habit. Release date 1987.

'Nuccio's Feathery Touch' ('Nuccio's California Dawn' × 'Nuccio's Garden Party'): white, hose-in-hose, base petals spidery type, 3", midseason; vigorous upright habit. Release date 1987.

'Nuccio's Fiesta' ('Mme. Alfred Sander' × 'Nuccio's Masterpiece'): deep pink, semidouble, 3½–4", early to midseason, long blooming season fall, spring; vigorous upright habit. Release date 1986.

'Nuccio's Garden Magic' (Nuccio's California Dawn' × 'Nuccio's Garden Party'): light pink, hose-in-hose, ruffled pointed petals, 2", midseason; vigorous upright habit.

'Nuccio's Grand Waltz' ('Nuccio's Orchid Robe' × 'Mercury'): white tinted pale purple, pink stamens, 4", midseason; vigorous compact growth. Release date 1990.

'Nuccio's High Society' ('Starlight' × 'Nuccio's Masterpiece'): strong yellowish pink, semidouble with fluted center petals, 3½", mid to late; vigorous open habit. Release date 1987.

'Nuccio's Ice Follies' ('Starlight' × 'Nuccio's Masterpiece'): white toned pale purple, double, 2½", midseason; upright habit. Release date 1987.

'Nuccio's Mamma Miq' ('Nuccio's California Dawn' × 'Mercury'): white, 3", mid to late season; vigorous compact habit. Release date 1986.

'Nuccio's Mexicali Rose' ('Mme. Alfred Sander' × 'Nuccio's Garden Party'): moderate pink, semidouble, 3", early to midseason vigorous upright habit.

'Nuccio's Punkin' ('Nuccio's California Dawn' × 'Nuccio's Garden Party'): deep yellowish pink with red spotted throat, hose-in-hose, 3", early to midseason; leaves large; vigorous broad habit. Release date 1986.

'Nuccio's Razzle Dazzle' ('Nuccio's Warm Heart' × 'Nuccio's California Dawn'): white, striped purplish pink with many sports, tubular, wavy petals, 3½", early to midseason; vigorous bushy habit. Release date 1988.

'Nuccio's Rise N' Shine' ('Mme. Alfred Sander' × 'Nuccio's Masterpiece'): deep yellowish pink, red spotted throat, wavy petals, semidouble, 3", early to midseason; medium compact habit. Release date 1986.

'Nuccio's Skyrocket' ('Nuccio's Ivory Tower' × 'Nuccio's Carnival Firecracker'): vivid reddish orange, 5–6 petals, 2", midseason; vigorous upright habit. Release date 1990.

'Nuccio's Snowbound' (sport of 'Spellbound'): white, semidouble, 3", midseason; vigorous upright habit.

'Nuccio's Snow Storm' ('Nuccio's Friendship' × 'L. J. Bobbink'): white, hose-in-hose, spider type petals, 2½", midseason; vigorous upright habit.

'Nuccio's South Pacific' ('Starlight' × 'Nuccio's Masterpiece'): light purplish pink, full semidouble, 3", midseason; vigorous upright habit. Release date 1990.

'Nuccio's Spring Festival' ('Nuccio's California Dawn' × 'Nuccio's Garden Party'): strong yellowish pink, semidouble, fluted petals, 3½", midseason; vigorous upright habit. Release date 1989.

'Nuccio's Spring Fling' ('Nuccio's California Dawn' × 'Nuccio's Garden Party'): deep yellowish pink with unusual light purple tones, semidouble, ruffled petals, 2½", midseason; vigorous spreading habit. Release date 1986.

'Nuccio's Spring Glory' ('Nuccio's California Dawn' × 'Nuccio's Pink Champagne'): light purplish pink, heavily spotted throat, pointed petals, 2½", midseason; vigorous spreading. Release date 1987.

'Nuccio's Spring Triumph' ('Duc de Rohan' × 'Nuccio's Pink Champagne'): pale pink, toned deeper pink, 2½", early to midseason; vigorous spreading habit. Release date 1986.

'Nuccio's Treasure Chest' ('Starlight' × 'Nuccio's Garden Party'): light yellowish pink with many variation of stripes, speckles, and tones of deep yellowish pink, semidouble to double, 3½", early to midseason; medium compact habit. Release date 1989.

'Nuccio's White Bubbles' (sport of 'Nuccio's Pink Bubbles'): white, double, 3", midseason; large foliage; vigorous compact upright habit. Release date 1988.

'Nuccio's Wishing Well' ('Starlight' × 'Nuccio's Masterpiece'): pale pink with deeper pink edges, semidouble, ruffled petals, 3½", mid to late season; vigorous loose habit.

'Nuccio's Wonderland' ('Starlight' × 'Nuccio's Masterpiece'): light yellowish pink, double, 3½", early to midseason; medium compact habit.

OTHER NUCCIO'S HYBRIDS

'Nuccio's Blaze' ('Pride of Dorking' × Exbury, dec.): deep reddish orange, 2", late; medium spreading habit. Release date 1986.

'Nuccio's Blue Diamond' ('Hino Crimson' × 'Laughing Waters'): light purple, 1½", midseason'; medium compact habit.

'Nuccio's Coral Seas' ('Mme. Alfred Sanders' × 'Gumpo'): light yellowish pink, wavy petals, 2", mid to late season; slow compact habit.

'Nuccio's Cream Puff' ('Hino Crimson' open pollinated): pale yellowish white, 1½", midseason; medium upright habit.

'Nuccio's Lady Finger' ('Hino Crimson' open pollinated): white, spaced 'spidery' petals, 1", midseason; medium compact habit.

'Nuccio's Mountain Smoke' ('Hino Crimson' open pollinated): pale reddish purple, 1½", midseason; very compact habit.

'Nuccio's Orchid Ruffles' ('Orchid Gem' × 'Nuccio's Blue Moon'): light purple, edges deep purple, heavily ruffled edges, 2½", mid to late season; vigorous compact upright habit. Release date 1988.

'Nuccio's Voodoo' ('White Lace' × 'Valo'): white, edged deep purple, semidouble, 2½", mid to late season; medium compact habit. Release date 1989.

Additional Wada Hybrids

Wada Hybrids [*tamurae (eriocarpum)* × *kaempferi*]: flowers smaller than *tamurae* but habit is like it. Blooms with Kurumes.

'Ariake': purplish red with brownish undertones.

'Asakanonari': deep yellowish pink, late.

'Bango Nishiki': reddish orange, semidouble.

'Chichibu': white, frilled, occasional light purple colors, 5–6 lobes; introduced as PI 127655 in 1938.

'Hana Chidori': purplish red.

'Higoromo': reddish orange; dwarf.

'Isochodori': pink.

'Matsuyi': pink.

'Yachiyo': light pink, hose-in-hose; blooms earlier than Kurumes.

Wada also had additional Kurumes and some azaleas falling into the Belgian Indian Hybrids group. He also named a hybrid of *R. y. poukhanense.*

'Forerunner': pink, 3", blooming soon after *R. mucronulatum* and earlier than any other evergreen azalea.

INDEX OF AZALEAS BY NAMES

The index lists (I) Azalea Sections and Subseries, (II) the Hybrid Groups, (III) Species, and (IV) Cultivars. Page numbers in bold type indicate the main entry for a plant. Page numbers for photographs are preceded by p. Synonyms for a plant are indicated as syn.

I. AZALEA SECTIONS AND SUBSERIES

II. HYBRID GROUPS

III. SPECIES

IV. CULTIVARS

SUBJECT INDEX

INDEX OF COLOR ILLUSTRATIONS

Indexed by color plate number.

General

Species

Cultivars and Common Names

Also published by Timber Press:

RHODODENDRON HYBRIDS
Homer Salley and Harold Greer

HYBRIDS AND HYBRIDIZERS
Edited by Philip Livingston and Franklin West

RHODODENDRON SPECIES, VOLUME 1: LEPIDOTES
H.H. Davidian

THE SMALLER RHODODENDRONS
Peter Cox

MANUAL OF CULTIVATED BROAD-LEAVED TREES AND SHRUBS VOLUMES I, II, III
Gerd Krüssmann
Translated by Michael Epp, Edited by Gilbert S. Daniels

ROCK GARDENING
H. Lincoln Foster and Laura Louise Foster

THE BERNARD E. HARKNESS SEEDLIST HANDBOOK
Mabel G. Harkness and Deborah D'Angelo

MANUAL OF ALPINE PLANTS
Will Ingwersen

For details of these and other books,
please write to:
Timber Press
9999 S.W. Wilshire
Portland, Oregon 97225